THE VIETNAM WAR
AND INTERNATIONAL LAW

Volume 2

The Vietnam War
and International Law

AMERICAN SOCIETY OF
INTERNATIONAL LAW

EDITED BY

RICHARD A. FALK

Volume 2

Princeton University Press

Princeton, New Jersey

1969

Note of Acknowledgments

ONCE AGAIN it is appropriate to thank the many people who have worked together to produce this volume. We thank, especially, the authors and publishers who have given us their permission to reprint material here and continue our efforts to facilitate the study of the legal aspects of the Vietnam War. Detailed permissions appear in the back of this volume.

Once again I would like to thank the members of the Civil War Panel for their continuing help and enthusiasm in carrying out our mandate to analyze the relevance of international law to contemporary experience with civil warfare. This continuing work has been made possible by a generous grant by the Carnegie Corporation to the American Society of International Law. Throughout the life of the Panel, Stephen M. Schwebel, Executive Vice President and Director of the Society, has given us indispensable guidance and encouragement; he has, in addition, been an active participant in the substance of the project by virtue of his membership on the Panel.

Princeton University Press has cooperated closely with the American Society of International Law to make possible the publication of this second volume of readings. We are most grateful to William McClung of the Press for sustaining his interest in the work of the Panel and to Marjorie Putney for once again editing our materials with such care and precision. Finally, I was greatly helped at either end of my editorial labors by two talented and energetic secretaries, by Priscilla Bryan at the Center of International Studies at Princeton University and by Irene Bickenbach at the Center for the Advanced Study in the Behavioral Sciences at Stanford, California. Their help and support enabled me to proceed through the seemingly interminable editorial process without succumbing altogether to the frustrations attendant thereupon.

RICHARD A. FALK

Contents

THE VIETNAM WAR
AND INTERNATIONAL LAW

Volume 2

Introduction
The Continuing and Evolving Legal
Inquiry into the Vietnam War*

THE PRESENT volume is a successor to *The Vietnam War and International Law* that appeared in 1968. It is also a product of the Civil War Panel of the American Society of International Law. There are two principal reasons for a second collection of readings on the legal aspects of the Vietnam War: first, a great deal of valuable writing on the main issues of law and fact has become available since the initial publication; and second, the scope of scholarly inquiry has expanded to include several central legal problems that were virtually ignored in the first collection.

The main objective of the Panel in putting out these collections is to encourage a deeper appreciation of the relevance of law to civil war. It is evident that such a task is heavily influenced by the interpretation given to the experience of the American involvement in the Vietnam War. Up to this point in time there is no sign of any scholarly consensus emerging that might lead to the endorsement of a single, generally accepted line of interpretation of the legal issues presented by the Vietnam War. Therefore, the Panel continues to believe that it can serve the public and itself best by making conveniently available those materials that might help a careful student of the subject either to form his own conclusions or to understand better the quality of scholarly disagreement. We have gathered together in this second collection of readings and materials those writings that we deem most worthy of serious attention. The volume as a whole has been planned as a balanced presentation of the controversial problems, although gaps in the available literature make it difficult to realize this goal in relation to some of the specific areas of concern.

A Note on Organization

This second volume includes a more specific and better focused literature than does its predecessor. It lends itself, accordingly, to a somewhat more systematic plan of organization.

In Section I we have included several general overviews of the law/policy questions at the center of the American role in the Vietnam

---

* This Introduction has been prepared for the Panel by its Chairman.

War. These presentations, some of which are obviously partisan in tone and content, are intended to update the policy setting. One notices that as the Vietnam War goes on there are definite shifts in the kinds of arguments advanced by advocates and opponents of the American position. It is important to notice these shifts and to identify, as well as possible, why they have taken place.[1]

Section II includes some of the more significant general scholarly writing that has been done on the legal issues since the first volume of readings appeared. Some of the selections are explicit responses to the legal analyses published in the earlier volume, whereas others are more or less fresh attempts to approach the overriding legal question as to whether the role of the United States in the Vietnam War constitutes a justifiable exercise of collective self-defense. Some of the articles in Section II also try to extend the boundaries of legal inquiry beyond this overriding question; and others, most particularly the piece by Jaro Mayda, raise doubts about whether the doctrines and procedures of international law can offer much meaningful insight into whether or not the United States involvement is "legal."

Sections III, IV, and V deal with significant segments of the legal context that were hardly dealt with in the earlier volume. Section III appraises what has been and what should have been the role of political organs of the United Nations in the Vietnam War and in Vietnam-type warfare of the future. Section IV deals with the very difficult problem of compliance and noncompliance with the laws of war by the various parties to the Vietnam conflict. Certainly one question of general concern is whether and to what extent the traditional laws of war can be applied to conditions of modern, protracted guerrilla warfare of the sort that has taken place in Vietnam. Section V

---

[1] The main character of these shifts in discussion has been away from the narrow justifications and refutations of the American role in Vietnam. It is as rare in the recent legal literature, as it was common in the literature two years ago, to find discussions of whether or not the United States' participation in the Vietnam War can be explained as an outgrowth of its participation in SEATO. Contributors to this new phase in the Vietnam debate defend and criticize the United States policies in Vietnam on the basis of the broader concerns of international law with the maintenance of world order. Thus, arguments are found in Section I, and also in Section II about the nature of national self-determination, about the character of wars of national liberation, and about the dynamics of revolutionary nationalism. At the same time that the more political commentary on the Vietnam War has been generalized in this fashion to deal with what might be called "the lessons of Vietnam," there has been a tendency on the part of professional international lawyers to place greater focus on some of the narrower legal issues generated by the war. Sections III, IV, and V will present some of the more interesting examples of these specific interests.

deals with the highly controversial questions arising from efforts by private litigants to raise questions about the legality of the American role in the Vietnam War in domestic courts of the United States. These selections also deal with the interrelations between constitutional and international law issues that arise from arguments about the application of the doctrine of the separation of powers to problems of war and peace and about the conditions under which the United States Constitution requires the President to obtain a Declaration of War as a legal basis for sending troops into foreign battle. The selections in III, IV, and V put the main issues in sharp focus, but there is very little agreement evident as to their appropriate resolution. The future of world order may be seriously influenced, however, by the ways in which principal governments decide to deal with these three groups of issues.

Section VI is the most historically conditioned portion of this volume as it presents some of the most prominent thinking on the settlement of the Vietnam War. It is characteristic of our time that major armed conflicts are "settled" rather than "won" or "lost." As a consequence, criteria as to what constitutes a reasonable settlement are needed to assess and guide the negotiating process. Reasonableness is partially a notion of a fair compromise, given the specific conditions prevailing. Reasonableness also involves finding a settlement that has a fairly solid prospect of keeping the peace in the future and that promises to have mostly beneficial effects on the country concerned. The selections in Section VI are thus concerned with interpreting the quality and status of the underlying conflict to which any settlement must be adjusted and with defining the sorts of conditions that the negotiating parties should be prepared to accept in their search for a mutually acceptable settlement. McGeorge Bundy's DePauw Address is also concerned with finding a strategy of de-Americanization in the event that a negotiated settlement proves impossible to achieve.

Section VII returns to the broad question of interactions between law and policy in civil war situations. The various selections offer different kinds of approaches to making and explaining how law and "lawyering" might influence the formation and execution of government policy. Two kinds of analyses are prominent among these authors. The first kind of analysis seeks to posit certain norms as authoritative guides for when it is proper to intervene and when improper; an author offers norms that both clarify and correctly draw the distinction between legal and illegal behavior. Policy arguments usually are advanced to support the proposal of specific norms of this kind. The other kind of analysis represented in Section VI is more concerned with the manner in which legal craftsmanship can turn a governmental decision into a constructive act. Thomas Ehrlich's paper is the most notable example of this approach. We have also included in this section several analyses of the proper orientation and goals of American foreign policy in light of the Vietnam experience.

The Documents in Section VIII are included to give close students of the Vietnam War convenient access to some primary materials of importance. With the exception of the "Working Paper of the United States State Department on the North Vietnamese Role in the War in South Vietnam," the documentary section is intended to complement the discussion of the settlement issues that is concentrated in Section VI.

A focus on the legal dimensions of the Vietnam War is a natural consequence of the continuation of this highly controversial war. However, a proper appreciation of the legal aspects of the Vietnam War has a significance that extends far beyond this particular conflict. In our view, general students of the relevance of international law to civil war will long benefit from giving attention to the legal argumentation produced by the Vietnam War, and for this reason we do not regard the materials assembled in this book as bearing only, or even primarily, on the debate generated by the Vietnam War. The future of American foreign policy and the character of world order will be considerably influenced in the years ahead by the final interpretation given to the main issues of law and policy lying at the crux of the Vietnam controversy.

A Note on the Work of the Panel

These two volumes of materials on the Vietnam War are one aspect of the work to date of the Civil War Panel. In addition, the Panel has commissioned a series of monographic studies that have been completed. These studies have been done by scholars who are not themselves members of the Panel, but who agreed to work within a common framework set up by the Panel. These studies are concerned with legal aspects of the American Civil War, the Spanish Civil War, the Algerian War of Independence, the Vietnam War, the Yemeni Civil War, the Congolese Civil War, and American relations to civil strife in Latin America. Each of these studies discloses some more general features of the relevance of international law to civil war and also accumulates hitherto unavailable empirical material. It is anticipated that this series of studies will be published in condensed form by The Johns Hopkins Press. There will be a general introduction explaining in detail the overall strategy of inquiry that has been adopted by the Panel and a concluding section that summarizes areas of agreement and disagreement that have emerged in relation to the various aspects of the international law of civil war.

The Panel also intends to produce a collective study of the subject. In this collective study a general statement of the actual and recommended role of law will be considered in relation to civil war. It has not yet been determined whether the Panel as a whole will be able to make a single, coherent statement or whether individual panelists will present studies clarifying the principal points of divergence. The general study will cover the following topics: the norms and procedures for classifying an instance of collective violence as "a civil war" for legal purposes, the processes of decision by which law and "lawyering" can be made relevant throughout a course of governmental action, the norms and procedures relevant to the conduct of a civil war, the procedures and regimes (such as neutralization or border monitoring) relevant to the settlement of a civil war, and the role of regional and global institutions in the initiation, moderation, and termination of civil wars. The Panel will attempt, also, to draw up a series of recommendations for the future and to state in clear terms the main areas of controversy among its panelists.

Richard J. Barnet	Myres S. McDougal
Thomas Ehrlich	John Norton Moore
Tom J. Farer	Stephen M. Schwebel
Wolfgang Friedmann	John R. Stevenson
G. W. Haight	Howard J. Taubenfeld
Eliot D. Hawkins	Burns H. Weston
Brunson MacChesney	Richard A. Falk, *Chairman*

I. SOME POLICY PERSPECTIVES

The Path to Viet-Nam: A Lesson in Involvement

WILLIAM P. BUNDY[1]

YOU HAVE asked me to speak this morning on the topic "The Path to Viet-Nam: A Lesson in Involvement." I welcome this opportunity to review the whole history of United States actions with respect to Viet-Nam—speaking personally as to the period up to 1961, during which I had no policy responsibility, and of course necessarily more officially for the period since January of 1961.

Quite apart from the enormous present importance of South Viet-Nam and our actions there, I have often reflected—as one who was tempted to become a professional historian—that the story of Viet-Nam, of Southeast Asia, and of American policy there forms an extraordinarily broad case history involving almost all the major problems that have affected the world as a whole in the past 25 years. For the strands of the Viet-Nam history include the characteristics of French colonial control compared to colonial control elsewhere; the end of the colonial period; the interrelation and competition of nationalism and communism; our relation to the Soviet Union and Communist China and their relationships with each other; our relation to the European colonial power, France; and—at least since 1954—the relation of Viet-Nam to the wider question of national independence and self-determination in Southeast Asia and indeed throughout Asia.

The Viet-Nam story is above all a product of Vietnamese aspirations and decisions. In the early period French decisions were critical. But I am sure you want me to focus on the American policy role, how and why we became involved, and how we reached the present position. This should not be a purely historical discussion, of course, and I know that you have natural and valid concerns that focus particularly on the decisions of the last 2 years and on the decisions that confront us now and in the future. So I shall touch briefly on these, fully expecting that your questions will be quite largely in this area.

For our mutual convenience in analysis, I have tried to isolate 10

[1] Address prepared for delivery by the Assistant Secretary for East Asian and Pacific Affairs before the 20th annual congress of the National Student Association at College Park, Md., on Aug. 15 (press release 177). Because of time limitations, Mr. Bundy read excerpts from the address, and the complete text was made available to the audience. For additional remarks made by Mr. Bundy on this occasion, see Department of State press release 177-A dated Aug. 15.

major American decisions going back to 1945. It is not for me to defend, or necessarily to justify, policy decisions taken before 1961, but it is essential to examine them if one is to understand the present position.

Decisions During French Colonial Era

Our first decisions affecting Viet-Nam were in 1945. President Roosevelt deeply believed that French colonial control in Indochina should not be restored, and this attitude led us in the closing months of the war against militarist Japan to adopt what the French have always considered an obstructive attitude toward their return. Separately, we briefly gave modest assistance to Ho Chi Minh as an asset against the Japanese. This story, like so much else in the whole record, is best told in Robert Shaplen's thoughtful "The Lost Revolution."

Second, when the French had returned, we stood aside. In the critical year 1946, and over the next 3 or 4 years, the French first made the Fontainebleau agreement and then broke it, so that major conflict started. It has often been argued, by Shaplen among others, that we could have exerted greater pressure, perhaps even effective pressure, on the French to go through with the Fontainebleau agreement and to set Viet-Nam on the path to early independence. The failure to exert such pressure may thus be construed as a negative policy decision on our part.

I myself am skeptical that we could conceivably have affected the unfortunate course that the French followed in this period. If it is argued that our overwhelming Marshall Plan aid to France should have given us leverage, then it must be pointed out at the same time that the Marshall Plan became operative only early in 1948 and that by then the die was largely cast. Moreover, I doubt very much if the proud and bruised French nation would have responded even if we had tried to act to end the colonial era, as we did to a major extent with the Dutch in Indonesia.

In a very real sense, the tragedy of Viet-Nam derives from the fall of France in 1940 and all the understandable emotions aroused by that event among French leaders, including notably De Gaulle himself. Restored control in Indochina was a badge, however mistaken, for a France that meant to be once again a world power. Although it may be argued that we should at least have tried, I doubt if this deep French attitude could have been shaken by anything we did or said and least of all by anything said or done in connection with the wise and right policy of helping France to get back on her feet.

The third period of American decision began in 1950, just before our involvement in the defense of Korea against Soviet-inspired aggression. The Communists had just taken control in China and entered into the 1950 alliance with the Soviet Union. Communism did then appear to our policymakers as something approaching a monolith, and we came to see the French stand in Indochina as part of a global attempt to repel Communist military adventures. In essence, we acted on two lines of policy between 1950 and 1954: on the one hand, economic and growing military assistance to the French; on the other hand, steady urging that the French proceed rapidly to grant real independence to Indochina, both for its own sake and as the best means of preventing Communist control.

Here it has been argued that we did too much assisting or at least too little urging. I find myself sympathetic to this point of view, as indeed it was expressed at the time by such wise men as Edmund Gullion, who served in Viet-Nam and much later became our distinguished Ambassador in the Congo from 1961 to 1963.

Yet, again I am not sure whether a different United States policy in this period could have brought about the desired result of a France first successfully waging a costly and bloody war to defend Viet-Nam and then granting it independence. Again, French attitudes and actions had deep roots in the still shaky situation of France and in the combination of a valid concern for the Communist threat and a desire to maintain a major French presence and hold in Indochina. Even if the French had acted wisely in every respect in this period, they might have been able to achieve nothing more than a division of the country into Communist and non-Communist areas. The vital difference might have been that valid non-Communist nationalism in Viet-Nam would have had a chance to stand on its feet and develop respected leaders before 1954; and if this had happened the whole later story might have unfolded in a very different way.

As it was, the spring of 1954 brought French defeat, in spirit if not in military terms, and left non-Communist nationalism in Viet-Nam almost bankrupt.

The Period of the Geneva Conference

The period of the Geneva Conference is the fourth period of American decision. That is a complex story, well told from a relatively detached viewpoint by Anthony Eden, now Lord Avon, in his memoirs.

We played a critical backstage role at Geneva. We maintained the possibility of military intervention, which, many observers at the time believe, played a crucial part in inducing the Soviets and the Communist Chinese alike to urge Hanoi to settle for a temporary division of Viet-Nam at the 17th parallel and for an independent Cambodia and Laos. And we began to lay the groundwork for SEATO, as part of the effort to show strength and to convince Communist China that it would not have a free hand in Southeast Asia.

Yet we were unwilling to participate fully in the framing of the Geneva accords,[2] apparently because our policymakers did not wish to associate themselves in any way with a loss of territory to Communist control. So the Geneva accords were framed largely between Hanoi, Communist China, and the Soviet Union on the one side and the French, who were under the urgent time pressure of their domestic politics, on the other. In the end we confined ourselves to saying two things:[3]

(a) That we would view any aggression in violation of the accords with grave concern and as seriously threatening international peace and security.

(b) That we took the same position on the reunification of Viet-Nam that we took in other "nations now divided against their will"—meaning, then and now, Germany and Korea—and that we would continue to seek unity through free elections supervised by the United Nations. In effect, we thus interpreted the election provision as providing for a free determination by the people of Viet-Nam as to whether they wished reunification and in that sense endorsed it consistent with the similar positions we had taken in Germany and Korea.

All sorts of things could be said about our decisions in that period. Some are of the view that we should have taken military action and tried to nail down at least a clear military division of Viet-Nam, or even to defeat Ho; I myself think that by the spring of 1954 that course would have been untenable.

It may also be argued—and I do not know the contemporary factors —that, involved as we already were by preceding decisions, we should have participated forthrightly in the making of the accords and lent our weight to them from the outset, declaring right then that we meant

2 For texts, see *American Foreign Policy, 1950–1955, Basic Documents*, vol. I, Department of State publication 6446, p. 750.

3 For background, see BULLETIN of Aug. 2, 1954, p. 162.

to stand—with the French if possible, but alone if necessary—in supporting non-Communist nationalism in South Viet-Nam. We would then have acted as we had done for non-Communist nationalism in Korea, although without its being necessary or desirable for us to put continuing forces on the ground as we had to do in the face of the conventional threat to Korea.

At any rate, in July 1954 a new national entity came into being in South Viet-Nam with what appeared at the time to be extraordinarily small chances of survival. At the very end, the French, with a degree of American pressure, installed the stanchly nationalist Diem as Prime Minister, hardly thinking that he would survive and looking rather to a short period in which the French could exit with some semblance of grace and let nature take its course.

Treaty Commitments in Southeast Asia

The fifth set of American decisions came in this setting and indeed overlapped the period of the Geneva Conference. The first aspect of these decisions was our leading role in the formation of the SEATO treaty,[4] signed at Manila in September of 1954 and ratified by our Senate in February 1955 by a vote of 82 to 1. In the SEATO treaty South Viet-Nam and its territory were specifically included as a "protocol state"; and the signatories specifically accepted the obligation, if asked by the Government of South Viet-Nam, to take action in response to armed attack against South Viet-Nam and to consult on appropriate measures if South Viet-Nam were subjected to subversive actions. The Geneva accords had, of course, already expressly forbidden aggressive acts from either half of Viet-Nam against the other half, but there had been no obligation for action by the Geneva participating nations. SEATO created a new and serious obligation extending to South Viet-Nam and aimed more widely at the security of the Southeast Asian signatories and the successor states of Indochina.

The second aspect of our decisions at this period was an evolving one. In late 1954 President Eisenhower committed us to furnish economic support for the new regime,[5] in which Diem was already showing himself tougher and more able than anyone had supposed possible. And in early 1955, without any formal statement, we began to take over the job of military assistance to South Viet-Nam, acting within

---

[4] For text of the Southeast Asia Collective Defense Treaty and protocol, see *ibid.*, Sept. 20, 1954, p. 393.

[5] For text of President Eisenhower's letter, see *ibid.*, Nov. 15, 1954, p. 735.

the numerical and equipment limitations stated in the Geneva accords for foreign military aid.

In short, in the 1954-55 period we moved into a major supporting role and undertook a major treaty commitment involving South Viet-Nam.

These decisions, I repeat, are not mine to defend. In the mood of the period, still deeply affected by a not unjustified view of monolithic communism, they were accepted with very wide support in the United States, as the vote and the debate in the Senate abundantly proved. And the Senate documents prove conclusively that there was full understanding of the grave implications of the SEATO obligations, particularly as they related to aggression by means of armed attack.

The important point about these decisions—and a point fervently debated within the administration at the time, according to many participants—is that they reflected a policy not merely toward Viet-Nam but toward the whole of Southeast Asia. In essence, the underlying basic issue was felt, and I think rightly, to be whether the United States should involve itself much more directly in the security of Southeast Asia and the preservation of the largely new nations that had come into being there since World War II.

There could not be the kind of clear-cut policy for Southeast Asia that had by then evolved in Northeast Asia, where we had entered into mutual security treaties individually with Japan, Korea, and the Republic of China. Some of the Southeast Asian countries wished no association with an outside power; others—Malaya, Singapore, and the northern areas of Borneo, which were not then independent—continued to rely on the British and the Commonwealth. So the directly affected area in which policy could operate comprised only Thailand, the Philippines, and the non-Communist successor states of Indochina —South Viet-Nam, Laos, and Cambodia.

Yet it was felt at the time that unless the United States participated in a major way in preserving the independence and security of these nations, they would be subject to progressive pressures by the parallel efforts of North Viet-Nam and Communist China.

The judgment that this threat of aggression was real and valid was the first basis of the policy adopted. Two other judgments that lay behind the policy were:

(a) That a successful takeover by North Viet-Nam or Communist China of any of the directly affected nations would not only be serious in itself but would drastically weaken and in a short time destroy the capacity of the other nations of Southeast Asia, whatever their international postures, to maintain their own independence.

(b) That while we ourselves had no wish for a special position in Southeast Asia, the transfer of the area, or large parts of it, to Communist control achieved by subversion and aggression would mean a major addition to the power status of hostile and aggressive Communist Chinese and North Vietnamese regimes. It was believed that such a situation would not only doom the peoples of the area to conditions of domination and virtual servitude over an indefinite period but would create the very kind of aggressive domination of much of Asia that we had already fought the militarist leaders of Japan to prevent. It was widely and deeply believed that such a situation was profoundly contrary to our national interests.

But there was still a third supporting judgment that, like the others, ran through the calculations of the period. This was that the largely new nations of Southeast Asia were in fact valid national entities and that while their progress might be halting and imperfect both politically and economically, this progress was worth backing. To put it another way, there was a constructive vision of the kind of Southeast Asia that could evolve and a sense that this constructive purpose was worth pursuing as a matter of our own ideals, as a matter of our national interest, and as a realistic hope of the possibilities of progress if external aggression and subversion could be held at bay.

These I believe to have been the bedrock reasons for the position we took in Viet-Nam and Southeast Asia at this time. They were overlaid by what may appear to have been emotional factors in our attitude toward communism in China and Asia. But the degree of support that this major policy undertaking received at the time went far beyond those who held these emotions. And this is why I for one believe that the bedrock reasons I have given were the true and decisive ones.

So the United States became deeply involved in the security of Southeast Asia and, wherever it was welcomed, in the effort to achieve economic progress as well. And the undertaking to support South Viet-Nam economically and militarily and through the protocol to the SEATO treaty must be seen as a part of the wide view that the choice was between fairly deep involvement in Southeast Asia or standing aside in the face of an estimate that to do so would cause Communist Chinese and North Vietnamese power and domination to flow throughout the area.

The Issue of Free Elections

The unfolding of this policy between 1954 and 1961 is a tangled and difficult story. Mistakes, even serious mistakes, were undoubtedly made then and later. Some of these, many believe, were in our economic and particularly in our military assistance policies in Viet-Nam; and it has been argued—to me persuasively—that we should have at least tried harder to counter the growing authoritarian trends of the Diem regime in the political sphere.

What was not a mistake, but the logical corollary of the basic policy, was the handling of the provision in the Geneva accords that called for free elections in 1956. It has been argued that this provision, which was certainly badly drafted, called for a single nationwide election, with reunification assumed. Our interpretation—that what was meant was in effect a plebiscite as to whether reunification was desired—has strong support in reason and the recollections of Geneva participants. What cannot be disputed is that the determination was to be free; the word appears three times in the article of the accords.

Much hindsight nonsense has been written about what took place in 1956 on this issue, and if any of you are planning a thesis subject, I commend to you the examination of the *contemporary* sources and discussion. You will, I think, find clear confirmation that by 1956 two propositions were accepted: first, that South Viet-Nam, contrary to most expectations in 1954, was standing on its own feet and had demonstrated that the makings of a valid non-Communist nationalism existed there; and, second, that North Viet-Nam—which had gone through a period of harsh repression in 1955 and 1956 in which Bernard Fall estimates that nearly 50,000 political opponents were killed outright—would not conceivably have permitted any supervision or any determination that could remotely have been called free.

In the face of these facts, Diem refused to go through with the elections, and we supported him in that refusal. Incidentally, I am told that we urged that he put the monkey on Hanoi's back and force them to refuse supervision or free conditions—as they would surely have done. Diem proudly rejected this advice, which did not change what would have happened but did leave the elements of a propaganda argument that still rages. It is, I repeat, hindsight nonsense, and I would only quote two contemporary statements—one by the then junior Senator from Massachusetts, John F. Kennedy, the other by Professor Hans Morgenthau.

Kennedy categorically rejected "an election obviously stacked and subverted in advance, urged upon us by those who have already broken their own pledges under the agreement they now seek to enforce."

And Morgenthau referred to the tremendous change between 1954 and 1956 and the "miracle" of what had been accomplished in South Viet-Nam. He went on to say that the conditions for free elections did not exist in either North or South Viet-Nam and concluded:

> Actually, the provision for free elections which would solve ultimately the problem of Viet-Nam was a device to hide the incompatibility of the Communist and Western positions, neither of which can admit the domination of all of Viet-Nam by the other side. It was a device to disguise the fact that the line of military demarcation was bound to be a line of political division as well.

Unfortunately, the promise of South Viet-Nam in 1956 was not realized in the next 5 years. In the face of Diem's policies, discontent grew—much as it grew in the same period in Korea under Rhee. As in Korea, that discontent might well have led to an internal revolution in a more or less traditional Asian manner. This is not what happened. Despite all that romantics like [Jean] Lacouture may say, what happened was that Hanoi moved in, from at least 1959 onward (Bernard Fall would say from 1957), and provided a cutting edge of direction, trained men from the North, and supplies that transformed internal discontent into a massive subversive effort guided and supported from the outside in crucial ways.

The realistic view, then and later, has been well summarized by Roger Hilsman in his recent book (with which, incidentally, I have serious factual differences on the period after 1963). Hilsman puts it thus (page 471 of his book):[6]

> Vietnam, in truth, was in the midst of two struggles, not one. The guerrilla warfare was not a spontaneous revolution, as Communist propaganda would have it, but a contrived, deliberate campaign directed and managed from Hanoi. But Vietnam was also in the throes of a true revolution, a social and nationalistic revolution very much akin to the "new nationalisms" that pervaded both the Congo crisis and Indonesia's confrontation with Malaysia. Even while the struggle went on against the Viet Cong, power was in the process of passing from the French-educated mandarin class to repre-

---

[6] *To Move a Nation* (Doubleday, Garden City, N.Y., 1967).

sentatives of the new nationalism, the Buddhists, the students, and the "young Turks" in the military.

Continued Engagement in Southeast Asia

This, then, was the situation as it confronted the Kennedy administration in January of 1961. All this is history. Reasonable men can and do differ about what was done. But those who believe that serious mistakes were made, or even that the basic policy was wrong, cannot escape the fact that by 1961 we were, as a practical matter, deeply engaged in Southeast Asia and specifically in the preservation of the independence of South Viet-Nam.

President Kennedy came to office with a subversive effort against South Viet-Nam well underway and with the situation in Laos deteriorating rapidly. And for a time the decisions on Laos overshadowed Viet-Nam, although of course the two were always intimately related.

In Laos, President Kennedy in the spring of 1961 rejected the idea of strong military action in favor of seeking a settlement that would install a neutralist government under Souvanna Phouma, a solution uniquely appropriate to Laos. Under Governor [W. Averell] Harriman's astute handling, the negotiations finally led to the Geneva accords of 1962 for Laos;[7] and the process—a point not adequately noticed—led the United States to a much more explicit and affirmative endorsement of the Geneva accords of 1954, a position we have since consistently maintained as the best basis for peace in Viet-Nam.

In Viet-Nam, the situation at first appeared less critical, and the initial actions of the Kennedy administration were confined to an increase in our military aid and a small increase of a few hundred men in our military training personnel, a breach—it may be argued—to this extent of the limits of the Geneva accords but fully justified in response to the scale of North Vietnamese violation of the basic non-interference provisions.

Although the details somewhat obscured the broad pattern, I think any fair historian of the future must conclude that as early as the spring of 1961 President Kennedy had in effect taken a seventh United States policy decision: that we would continue to be deeply engaged in Southeast Asia, in South Viet-Nam, and under new ground rules, in Laos as well.

This was *not*—despite the hindsight strawman recently erected by Professor [John Kenneth] Galbraith—because President Kennedy be-

---

[7] For texts, see BULLETIN of Aug. 13, 1962, p. 259.

lieved at all in a monolithic communism. Professor Galbraith forgets a good deal, and notably the Vienna meeting of June 1961 in which President Kennedy set out deliberately to work with the Soviet Union for the Laos settlement—even as at the very same time he dispatched Vice President Johnson to visit Viet-Nam and Thailand and in effect to reaffirm our courses of action there. The total pattern of United States policy toward Communist countries under both President Johnson and President Kennedy belies the Galbraith thesis.

No, neither President Kennedy nor any senior policymaker, then or later, believed the Soviet Union was still united with Communist China and North Viet-Nam in a single sweeping Communist threat to the world. But President Kennedy did believe two other things that had, and still have, a vital bearing on our policy.

First, he believed that a weakening in our basic resolve to help in Southeast Asia would tend to encourage separate Soviet pressures in other areas.

James Reston has stated, on the basis of contemporary conversations with the President, that this concern specifically related to Khrushchev's aggressive designs on Berlin, which were pushed hard all through 1961 and not laid to rest till after the Cuban missile crisis of 1962. At any rate, President Kennedy clearly did believe that failure to keep the high degree of commitment we had in Viet-Nam and Southeast Asia had a bearing on the validity of our commitments elsewhere. As Theodore Sorensen has summarized it (page 651 of *Kennedy*): ". . . this nation's commitment (in South Viet-Nam) in January, 1961 . . . was not one that President Kennedy felt he could abandon without undesirable consequences throughout Asia and the world."

Secondly, President Kennedy believed that the Communist Chinese *were* a major threat to dominate Southeast Asia and specifically that a United States "withdrawal in the case of Viet-Nam and in the case of Thailand might mean a collapse in the entire area."[8] Indeed, President Kennedy in one statement expressly supported the "domino theory."[9]

My own view, based on participation and subsequent discussion with others, is that the underlying view of the relation between Viet-Nam and the threat to Southeast Asia was clear and strongly believed

[8] A reply by President Kennedy during his press conference on June 14, 1962.

[9] For transcript of an NBC interview with President Kennedy on Sept. 9, 1963, see BULLETIN of Sept. 30, 1963, p. 499.

throughout the top levels of the Kennedy administration. We knew, as we have always known, that the action against South Viet-Nam reflected deeply held ambitions by Hanoi to unify Viet-Nam under Communist control and that Hanoi needed and wanted only Chinese aid to this end and wished to be its own master. And we knew, as again we always have, that North Viet-Nam would resist any Communist Chinese trespassing on areas it controlled. But these two propositions were not then, as they are not now, inconsistent with the belief that the aggressive ambitions of Communist China and North Viet-Nam—largely North Vietnamese in old Indochina, overlapping in Thailand, Chinese in the rest of Southeast Asia—would surely feed on each other. In the eyes of the rest of Southeast Asia, certainly, they were part of a common and parallel threat.

So, in effect, the policy of 1954-61 was reaffirmed in the early months of 1961 by the Kennedy administration. Let me say right here I do not mean to make this a personal analysis of President Kennedy nor to imply any view whatever as to what he might or might not have done had he lived beyond November of 1963. But some untrue things have been said about the 1961 period, and I believe the record totally supports the account of policy, and the reasons for it, that I have given.

Stemming the North Vietnamese Threat

We then come to the eighth period of decision—the fall of 1961. By then, the "guerrilla aggression" (Hilsman's phrase) had assumed truly serious proportions, and morale in South Viet-Nam had been shaken. It seemed highly doubtful that without major additional United States actions the North Vietnamese threat could be stemmed.

President Kennedy took the decision to raise the ante, through a system of advisers, pilots, and supporting military personnel that rose gradually to the level of 25,000 in the next 3 years.

I do not think it is appropriate for me to go into the detail of the discussions that accompanied this decision. Fairly full, but still incomplete, accounts have been given in various of the books on the period. What can be seen, without going into such detail, is that the course of action that was chosen considered and rejected, at least for the time being, the direct introduction of ground combat troops or the bombing of North Viet-Nam, although there was no doubt even then—as Hilsman again makes clear—that the bombing of North Viet-Nam could have been sustained under any reasonable legal view in the face of what North Viet-Nam was doing. Rather, the course of action which was adopted rightly stressed that the South Vietnamese role must remain crucial and primary.

In effect, it was decided that the United States would take those additional actions that appeared clearly required to meet the situation, not knowing for sure whether these actions would in fact prove to be adequate, trying—despite the obvious and always recognized effect of momentum and inertia—not to cross the bridge of still further action, and hoping strongly that what was being undertaken would prove sufficient.

Political Change in South Viet-Nam

This was the policy followed from early 1962 right up to February of 1965. Within this period, however, political deterioration in South Viet-Nam compelled, in the fall of 1963, decisions that I think must be counted as the ninth critical point of United States policy-making. It was decided at that time that while the United States would do everything necessary to support the war, it would no longer adhere to its posture of all-out support of the Diem regime unless that regime made sweeping changes in its method of operation. The record of this period has been described by Robert Shaplen and now by Hilsman. Undoubtedly, our new posture contributed to the overthrow of Diem in November 1963.

I do not myself think that we could in the end have done otherwise, but the important historical point is that our actions tended to deepen our involvement in South Viet-Nam and our commitment to the evolution of non-Communist nationalism, always foreseen to be difficult, that would follow the overthrow of Diem.

Unfortunately, the fall of Diem, while it had overwhelming popular support in South Viet-Nam, failed to produce an effective new government. For a year and a half South Viet-Nam wallowed in political confusion; and power finally passed, with the agreement of civilian political leaders, to the Thieu-Ky military-led government of June 1965.

This political confusion was disheartening, but it was not surprising. For South Viet-Nam had never been trained by the French to govern itself, and above all, it was faced with steadily rising North Vietnamese and Viet Cong terrorist and military action. Intensification of that action began almost at once after the overthrow of Diem and demonstrated—if it needed demonstrating—that the struggle was not over Diem, despite Communist claims and honest liberal qualms, but was an attempt to destroy non-Communist nationalism of any sort in South Viet-Nam.

In early 1964 President Johnson expressly reaffirmed all the essential elements of the Kennedy administration policies publicly through every action and through firm internal directives. It is simply not true to say that there was any change in policy in this period toward greater military emphasis, much less major new military actions. Further actions were not excluded—as they had not been in 1954 or 1961— but President Johnson's firm object right up to February 1965 was to make the policy adopted in late 1961 work if it could possibly be done, including the fullest possible emphasis on pacification and the whole political and civilian aspect.

The summer of 1964 did bring a new phase, though not a change in policy. The situation was continuing to decline, and North Viet-Nam may have been emboldened by the trend. Certainly, infiltration was rising steadily and, as we now know more clearly, began to include substantial numbers of native North Vietnamese. But, more dramatically, American naval ships on patrol in the Gulf of Tonkin were attacked, and there were two responding United States attacks on North Vietnamese naval bases.

This led President Johnson to seek, and the Congress to approve overwhelmingly on August 7, 1964, a resolution[10]—drafted in collaboration with congressional leaders—that not only approved such retalitory attacks but added that:

> The United States regards as vital to its national interest and to world peace the maintenance of international peace and security in southeast Asia. Consonant with the Constitution of the United States and the Charter of the United Nations and in accordance with its obligations under the Southeast Asia Collective Defense Treaty, the United States is, therefore, prepared, as the President determines, to take all necessary steps, including the use of armed force, to assist any member or protocol state of the Southeast Asia Collective Defense Treaty requesting assistance in defense of its freedom.

U.S. Decisions Based on Overall View

So things stood through the election period. But as 1964 drew to a close, the situation was moving steadily downward in every respect,

10 Public Law 88-408; for text, see BULLETIN of Aug. 24, 1964, p. 268.

both military and political. A review of policy was undertaken, analyzing three basic choices: to continue the existing policy with every improvement that could be devised within its limits; to take new and major military measures, while adhering to the same basic objectives that had been followed all along; or to move toward withdrawal.

From late November onward, these choices were intensively examined, even as the military threat grew, the political confusion in Saigon deepened, and all the indicators recorded increasingly shaky morale and confidence not only in South Viet-Nam but throughout the deeply concerned countries of Southeast Asia. By late January, it was the clear judgment of all those concerned with policy and familiar with the situation that the first choice was rapidly becoming no choice at all—and not, to use the phrase of one commentator, a "constructive alternative." To "muddle through" (that commentator's phrase) was almost certainly to muddle out and to accept that South Viet-Nam would be turned over to Communist control achieved through externally backed subversion and aggression.

This was a straight practical judgment. It ran against the grain of every desire of the President and his advisers. But I myself am sure it was a right judgment—accepted at the time by most sophisticated observers and, in the light of reflective examination, now accepted, I believe, by virtually everyone who knows the situation at all at first hand.

There were, in short, only two choices: to move toward withdrawal or to do a lot more, both for its military impact and, at the outset, to prevent a collapse of South Vietnamese morale and will to continue.

And as the deliberations continued within the administration, the matter was brought to a head by a series of sharp attacks on American installations in particular. These attacks were serious in themselves, but above all, they confirmed the overall analysis that North Viet-Nam was supremely confident and was moving for the kill. And as they thus moved, it seemed clear that they would in fact succeed and perhaps in a matter of months.

Let me pause here to clear up another current historical inaccuracy. The basis for the successive decisions—in February to start bombing; in March to introduce small numbers of combat forces; and in July to move to major United States combat forces—was as I have stated it. It depended on an overall view of the situation and on an overall view that what had been going on for years was for all practical purposes aggression—and indeed this term dates from late 1961 or early 1962 in the statements of senior administration spokesmen.

But there is a separate point whether, as has sometimes been asserted, it was the United States alone which unilaterally changed the character of the war in the direction of a conventional conflict. It is alleged that Hanoi was adhering to a tacit agreement that, so long as we did not bomb North Viet-Nam, Hanoi would not send in its regulars, at least in units.

Multiple and conclusive evidence which became available from the spring of 1965 onward seems to me to refute these contentions. As has been repeatedly made public over the past 2 years, we know that one North Vietnamese regiment entered South Viet-Nam by December 1964, and we know that several other regiments entered in the spring of 1965 on timetables of infiltration that can only have reflected command decisions taken in Hanoi prior to the beginning of the bombing.

From the standpoint of the basis for U.S. decisions, this evidence simply reinforces the February picture that Hanoi was moving for the kill. Native North Vietnamese, alone or in regular units, were in themselves no more and no less aggressive than the earlier native South Vietnamese who had gone north and become North Vietnamese nationals. The point is that Hanoi, as we suspected then and later proved, had taken major steps to raise the level of the war before the bombing began.

As to any tacit agreement, these facts alone seem to disprove that there ever was one. Moreover, students of North Vietnamese behavior, and especially of the recent major captured North Vietnamese documents, would in any event find such an allegation hard to credit. Is it not far more reasonable to conclude that Hanoi preferred to conceal its hand but was prepared at all times to put in whatever was necessary to bring about military victory—and that the regular units were simply a part of that policy, introduced after they had run out of native southerners and wanted to maintain and step up the pressure?

But this historical point is less important than the fundamental elements of the situation as it stood at the time. On the one hand, all of what I have earlier described as the bedrock elements still remained: a strong Chinese Communist and North Vietnamese threat to Southeast Asia, a crucial link between the defense of South Viet-Nam and the realization of that threat, and the validity of non-Communist nationalism, whatever its imperfections, in South Viet-Nam and in the other nations of Southeast Asia.

Moreover, the wider implications for our commitments elsewhere appeared on less valid than they had ever been. Viet-Nam still constituted a major, perhaps even a decisive, test case of whether the Communist strategy of "wars of national liberation" or "people's wars" could be met and countered even in the extraordinarily difficult circumstances of South Viet-Nam. Then as now, it has been, I think, rightly judged that a success for Hanoi in South Viet-Nam could only encourage the use of this technique by Hanoi, and over time by the Communist Chinese, and might well have the effect of drawing the Soviets into competition with Peking and Hanoi and away from the otherwise promising trends that have developed in Soviet policy in the past 10 years.

Finally, it was judged from the outset that stronger action by us in Viet-Nam would not operate to bring the Soviet Union and Communist China closer together and that the possibility of major Chinese Communist intervention could be kept to a minimum so long as we made it clear at all times, both by word and deed, that our objective was confined solely to freeing South Viet-Nam from external interference and that we did not threaten Communist China but rather looked to the ultimate hope of what the Manila Declaration,[11] of last fall, called "reconciliation and peace throughout Asia."

On the other hand, it was recognized from the outset that the taking of these new major military measures involved heavy costs and hazards. The South Vietnamese still had to play the crucial role in military security and, above all, in political and economic development and stability. A greater American role was bound to complicate South Vietnamese evolution. It was bound to increase the scale of the war and to cost significantly in lives and very heavily in resources. Even though the casualties and damage of the war remain far below what was suffered in Korea, war is never anything but ugly and brutal.

The balance was struck, after the most careful deliberation, in favor of the course that has since been followed. The key elements in the policy were stated in President Johnson's Baltimore speech of April 1965,[12] and the major combat-force commitment was explained in the President's statement of July 28, 1965.[13] These have been the cornerstones of policy, and they have been elaborated and explained repeatedly and at length by all senior administration spokesmen.

[11] For text, see *ibid.*, Nov. 14, 1966, p. 734.
[12] For text, see *ibid.*, Apr. 26, 1965, p. 606.
[13] For text, see *ibid.*, Aug. 16, 1965, p. 264.

Cornerstones of U.S. Policy

In essence:

(a) Our objective remained solely that of protecting the independence of South Viet-Nam from external interference and force. We declined, and still decline, to threaten the regime in North Viet-Nam itself or the territory and regime of Communist China.

(b) We indicated in April of 1965 that we were prepared for discussions or negotiations without condition, and we have relentlessly pursued our own efforts to enter into meaningful discussions as well as following up on a host of peace initiatives by others. Unfortunately, Hanoi has clung firmly to the objective of insuring a Communist takeover of South Viet-Nam and has refused to enter into any fruitful discussions. Indeed, Hanoi has rejected any discussions whatever—initially unless its basic objective was accepted in advance through the so-called "third point," more recently unless we agreed to a complete cessation of the bombing without any responsive action on their part. Hanoi's philosophy toward negotiation has now become authoritatively available, particularly in the section on "fighting while negotiating" in the captured remarks of one of the North Vietnamese leaders, Comrade Vinh.

(c) We continued to place every possible emphasis on the crucial nonmilitary aspects of the conflict, greatly strengthening our own contribution to the essentially South Vietnamese task of restoring stability and control in the countryside and working for the welfare of the people.

(d) Militarily, our actions were directed to proving to North Viet-Nam that its effort to take over the South by military force must fail and to extending and enlarging the areas in which the vital business of bringing real security and peace to the countryside could go forward with all the strength we could hope to give it. The total effort in the South remained primary, even as the bombing of military targets in the North was carried on—initially to demonstrate resolve but always and basically to make Hanoi's infiltration far more difficult and costly and to prevent levels of new men and equipment that could only, in the arithmetic of guerrilla warfare, multiply many times over, for each addition from North Viet-Nam, the requirement for forces in the South.

(e) We encouraged the South Vietnamese in their own resolve to move to a constitutional basis of government, a process set underway formally by Prime Minister Ky in January of 1966 and followed since that time in the face of all the difficulties and dangers of attempting to create such a basis in a country without political experience and ravaged by terrorism and by guerrilla and conventional military action.

(f) We encouraged the South Vietnamese at the same time to proceed on the track that has now become reconciliation, the holding out to members of the Viet Cong of the possibility of reentering the political life of their country under peaceful conditions. In essence, we seek and would accept a fair determination of the will of the people of South Viet-Nam along the lines well summarized by Ambassador Goldberg's Chicago speech of May 12, 1967.[14]

These were the South Vietnamese aspects of our policy. But then, as previously, the policy was seen in the wider context of the future of Southeast Asia. So it was that President Johnson lent our strong support in April of 1965 to the development of regional cooperation and of economic projects created through Asian initiative. By this vital element in our policy, we made clear again that our underlying objective was to do what we could to assist in the constructive task of bringing about a Southeast Asia of cooperative and independent nations, whatever their international postures might be.

We had a security job to do in Viet-Nam and were joined over time by five other area nations in supplying military forces to do that job. And we are assisting Thailand against a concerted Chinese Communist and North Vietnamese effort at external subversion, an effort begun—to keep the record straight—as early as 1962 and clearly and definitively by December 1964, before our major decisions in Viet-Nam. Our SEATO and ANZUS undertakings remain firm.

But we looked beyond these, and we must still look beyond these, to the whole question of the future of Southeast Asia and to the role that we can play in assisting the nations of the area to consolidate their national independence and to improve the welfare of their people.

This, then, is a barebones account of "The Path to Viet-Nam." Even within its own terms, it may omit what others would include. And, long as it may seem, it is still incomplete in two respects that it would take far too much time to cover.

First, it is plainly inadequate to focus solely on our policies toward Viet-Nam or even toward Southeast Asia as a whole. Those policies are intimately related to the rest of Asia; to the implications of Asian developments for other areas and, in the last analysis, for our own

[14] For text, see *ibid.*, June 5, 1967, p. 838.

national security; and to our central world purpose—the creation of an international order of independent states.

Secondly, I have tried to isolate what I consider to have been the major policy decisions. Obviously, policy is not just a matter of single decisions, however fully considered. A vast number of lesser policy decisions have accompanied these basic ones, and the way in which a basic policy is carried out in the end affects its substance. I have not tried to cover, for example, decisions on the balance of effort within South Viet-Nam, decisions on particular negotiating proposals, decisions on the pace and nature of the bombing of North Viet-Nam, or the subtle and difficult problem, over the years, of United States influence toward political progress in the South. I know full well that these are areas in which many of you undoubtedly hold strong views. I welcome discussion of them.

"The Lesson in Involvement"

What, then, is "the lesson in involvement"?

—Is it that we have been trapped into a difficult situation by a series of lesser decisions taken with no clear view of their implications?

—Is it that we should never have become engaged in Southeast Asia?

—Is it that we should never have attempted to support South Viet-Nam?

—Is it that, having supported South Viet-Nam in certain respects (including a treaty) and having become deeply engaged in Southeast Asia, we should nonetheless have decided—or should now decide—to limit the actions we take or even to withdraw entirely?

The first question seems to me both separate and difficult. At some point in the history, I have recited we became committed, deliberately and by formal constitutional process, to the support of the freedom of South Viet-Nam from external interference. That commitment included a strong treaty obligation, and that is a clear part of the story. But what is perhaps more to the point is that great powers must face two central points:

(a) As Irving Kristol has pointed out in his recent article in Foreign Affairs, the very definition of a great power is that not only its actions but the cases in which it declines to act have major consequences. At every stage in the Viet-Nam story, it has seemed clear to the leaders of this country that not to act would have the gravest effects. This is the way that successive choices have appeared to four successive Presidents.

(b) The second point that a great power cannot escape is that its actions in themselves affect the stakes. When great powers commit themselves, by treaty and by a total course of conduct extending over many years, an element of reliance comes into being, both within the area and within other areas in which commitments have also been undertaken.

Yet, all this being said, I do not think one can conclude that because we said or did *a*, we must necessarily say or do *b*—in an old phrase of Bismarck's. So I, for one, do not believe that the "lesson in involvement" is that we are the prisoners of history.

Rather, I think we should be focusing on the second, third, and fourth questions I have listed above.

These are big questions, and if I have tried to do anything today it is to stress that the matter has really been looked at for at least the last 13 years in this kind of larger framework. The policies followed today are, as they must be, the policies of this administration. No one can say whether another administration would have done the same. What can be said is that the underlying viewpoint and analysis of factors have been largely similar throughout the last 13 years, if not longer.

This does not prove, of course, that this analysis has been correct. The United States has no divine dispensation from error, and the most that your leaders at any time can do is to exert the best human judgment and moral sense of which they are capable. I, for one, am convinced that this has been done at all stages.

In essence, the question is not capable of geometric proof. Like all policy, it is a judgment. Our bet with history has been that Southeast Asia does matter, that the independence of South Viet-Nam crucially affects Southeast Asia, and that non-Communist nationalism in Southeast Asia and in Viet-Nam has in it the seeds of a peaceful, progressive, and stable area that can take its place in a world at peace.

Independence of Southeast Asia

Other factors enter in, as I have tried to summarize, and despite their variations from time to time remain of major general importance. But it is primarily from the standpoint of Southeast Asia that I would like to close my remarks today. How do the bets I have described look today?

Southeast Asia surely matters more than ever. A region which may have held as few as 30 million inhabitants in 1800—and which is carried under the heading of "peripheral areas" in some textbooks on

East Asia—now holds more than 250 million people, more than Latin America and almost as much as the population of Western Europe. The resources of this area are large, and its people, while not yet capable of the kind of dramatic progress we have seen in the northern parts of Asia, have great talent, intelligence, and industry. Its geographical location, while it should not be in the path of great-power collisions, is crucial for trade routes and in other respects.

From the standpoint of our own security and the kind of world in which we wish to live, I believe we must continue to be deeply concerned to do what we can to keep Southeast Asia from falling under external domination and aggression that would contribute to such domination. And I believe also that we have a wider concern in doing what we can, and as we are wanted, to assist sound programs on an individual country or regional basis and to improve the welfare of the peoples of the area. And I do not think that you can do the latter unless the former is achieved.

The second part of our bet is that the independence of South Viet-Nam critically affects Southeast Asia. South Viet-Nam and its 15 million people are important in themselves, but they assume an additional importance if the judgment is accepted that a success for aggression there would drastically weaken the situation in Southeast Asia and indeed beyond. That judgment cannot be defended solely by reference to the dynamics of major aggressive powers and their prospective victims in the past. I myself believe that those parallels have validity, but the question is always what Justice Holmes called "concrete cases." In this concrete case I think the underlying judgment has been valid and remains valid today.

None of us can say categorically that the Communist Chinese would in due course move—if opportunity offered—to dominate wide areas of Southeast Asia through pressure and subversion. But that is what the Chinese and their maps say, and their Communist doctrine appears to add vital additional emphasis. It is what they are doing in Thailand today and, through local Communist allies, in Burma, Cambodia, Malaysia, and Singapore. And it is what they would like to do in Indonesia again.

Surely Adlai Stevenson was right that the threat of Communist China is not so fanciful that it should not serve as a valid assumption of policy. And we can be more categorical that Hanoi intends to dominate at least the successor states of Indochina and would move rapidly to this end if it were to get practical control of South Viet-Nam.

Perhaps the hardest point for some to grasp is the psychological impact of a development such as the fall of South Viet-Nam in this setting. As to Hanoi and Peking, judgment and past experience point to the conclusion that it would greatly encourage them to push further. As to the threatened nations, the view of their leaders is a matter of record. All over Southeast Asia, whatever the posture of the individual nation, the great body of responsible opinion—and I invite you to check this against any firsthand account—accepts the judgment stated only the other day by the independent and nonalined Prime Minister of Singapore, Mr. Lee Kuan Yew: "I feel the fate of Asia—South and Southeast Asia—will be decided in the next few years by what happens out in Viet-Nam."

I could multiply that quotation 10 times over in public statements and 10 times more in private statements. As Drew Middleton of the New York Times reported last June after a trip in the area: "Despite some misgivings, non-Communist leaders from Tokyo to Tehran largely support United States policies in South and Southeast Asia."

This does not mean that every nation accepts our choice of military actions. Some would have us do more, some less. But it does lead to the clear conclusion that our own view accords with the deep sense in Southeast Asia, and indeed elsewhere in Asia, that the struggle in South Viet-Nam is crucial to the independence and continued ability to work for its people of each and every nation for a wide area.

Lastly, there is the question whether a new Southeast Asia is in fact being built and can be developed. On this point, surely the developments of the last 5 years, and particularly the last 2 years, have been vastly encouraging. Where Indonesia in 1965 was drifting rapidly to Communist control and practical alinement with Peking, it now stands on a stanchly nationalist basis, abandoning the threat to its neighbors and seeking to work out the chaotic economic problems left by Sukarno—with the multilateral help of ourselves and others. Regional cooperation within Southeast Asia, and among Asian nations as a whole, has taken great and historic strides. And it is the widely accepted view in the area—which I share—that these developments would have been far less likely if we had not acted as we did in 1965 and if Communist force had thus taken over in South Viet-Nam.

So all over Southeast Asia there is today a sense of confidence—to which Drew Middleton again testified from his trip. Time has been bought and used. But that confidence is not solid or secure for the future. It would surely be disrupted if we were, in President Johnson's words, to permit a Communist takeover in South Viet-Nam either through withdrawal or "under the cloak of a meaningless agreement."[15] If, on the contrary, we proceed on our present course—with measured military actions and with every possible nonmilitary measure and searching always for an avenue to peace—the prospects for a peaceful and secure Southeast Asia now appear brighter than they have been at any time since the nations of the area were established on an independent basis.

In short, I think the stakes are very grave indeed. The costs are large, and it is clear that we must steel our national capacity and resolve to continue in a tough struggle and still do those things that we must do to meet our problems at home. I find it impossible to believe that we do not have the national capacity and resolve to do both.

[15] *Ibid.*, Apr. 26, 1965, p. 606.

Questions about Viet Nam

ALASTAIR BUCHAN

THE VIET NAM WAR is the greatest tragedy that has befallen the United States since the Civil War. I looked at that sentence for a long time to make sure that I believed that it was true—knowing well the ability of ENCOUNTER readers to detect false quantities. And I emerged from this trauma convinced of it.

Look at the balance sheet. On the one side stand a small number of credit items. The Soviet Union and China know that the United States is very much opposed to the extension of Communism by any means, and that she is prepared to go to immense lengths to prevent it: for she is now spending on this one conflict in this small area of the world more than all her forty-four allies in four continents spend on defence and security—about $25,000 million a year. And her stand has considerably impressed the small countries of Southern Asia on whose territory the war is not being fought.

On the other side, the war has succeeded in obscuring the sharp image that the United States had created throughout the non-Communist world in the post-war decades, of a country that could use power with both purpose and restraint: of a super power, whose leaders might fumble from time to time, but whose motives were generally more trustworthy and disinterested than those of the old European great powers. It has turned the Asian country with the worst historic reputation in

Asia for cruelty and aggression into the brave little Belgium of international society. It has been accompanied by five years of falsified predictions about the outcome which have severely undermined the credibility of any governmental pronouncements from Washington. It has exerted very severe strains on the American political system and has revealed flaws in the Washington policy- and decision-making process which give serious grounds for doubt whether the United States can function as the centre of an international system covering a wide range of countries. It has helped turn the President who received the highest affirmative vote of any aspirant to that office in history and who had the best chance of modernising the social structure of the country into the most disliked of this century. Above all, Viet Nam has done for the United States what the Boer War did for the British: not only diminish its influence and give a superb diplomatic advantage to its adversaries, but destroy the confidence of its own people in their own vision of law and order and international justice.

A WRITER WHO has only flown over Viet Nam and never trodden its jungle paths, who has never fought in a guerrilla action, and whose principal experience is of Atlantis rather than Asia, must hesitate before further expanding the tonnage of analysis, description or polemic that now surrounds the Viet Nam war. I do so more for the purpose of setting out the kind of questions which the contemporary historian or the analyst of international conflict should be asking, than in the hope of providing clear—let alone final—answers to them.

Was it inevitable that the United States should get committed in Viet Nam to the extent of half a million soldiers and constant bombing of the North? If so, when was the irrevocable step taken? Does the frustration of American efforts carry a temptation to use larger weapons, or to use them against China, with the risk of major war? Can the United States defeat the Vietcong by a patient pursuit of its present policy? When and how will it be possible to get negotiations going: and what will they be about? Finally, has Viet Nam created or accelerated a new movement towards American isolationism?

IN A RECENT SPEECH before the National Student Association,[1] William Bundy, the Assistant Secretary of State for Far Eastern Affairs, has traced American concern with Viet Nam back to the end of the Roosevelt régime, and like other American officials has tried to place much of the blame for the course of events there on the post-war policy of France. In it he recalled the view of the Eisenhower Administration that "unless the United States participated in a major way in preserving the independence and security of these nations (of South-east Asia) they would be subject to progressive pressures by the parallel efforts of North Viet Nam and Communist China." In other words, the threat to South Viet Nam was an external one. This

corresponded with a considered view that had arisen out of much American academic and official debate in the later 1950s and early 1960s, namely that the most likely form of conflict throughout the world was neither nuclear nor guerrilla war but conventional war with limited means and objectives on the pattern of Korea or the Arab-Israeli wars. This led the Eisenhower régime to force South Viet Nam (and several other countries) to build large conventional armies which proved to be useless for purposes of internal control as well as absorbing the able people needed for the essentially political job of pacification and the construction of civil order. This was one of the major sources of disagreement between the American and the French military when they were still on speaking terms. For their post-war experience had convinced the French that *guerre révolutionnaire* was the real danger of an era that combined the existence of nuclear weapons with the rise of many new states. Undoubtedly the French do bear some responsibility for the current situation in Viet Nam, but official American attempts to throw most of the blame on them ignores the fact that in this basic argument of the 1950s the French were right and the Americans wrong.

President Kennedy inherited an unspecified commitment to an increasingly shaky country and (as Bundy says) he soon made a basic policy decision that "we would continue to be deeply engaged in South-east Asia, in South Viet Nam, and under new ground rules in Laos as well." Guerrilla warfare, in particular the murder of village officials in large numbers, had been going on for about four years. Although Roger Hilsman (Bundy's predecessor), Arthur Schlesinger, and others close to Kennedy attest to his conviction that insurgency, not external attack, was the real problem, this did not prevent Defence Secretary Robert McNamara from reorganising the United States Army for limited or conventional rather than guerrilla warfare.[2] The numbers of divisions were expanded, their mobility and their heavy equipment improved; for these were also the years of the Berlin crisis, and of an apparent danger of sub-nuclear conflict in Europe. In the process the kind of organisation and training required to help another country deal with an insurgent movement was largely neglected.[3] Worse still, the attitude of Dean Rusk, according to Hilsman and corroborated to me by others, was that Viet Nam was primarily a military and not a civil problem, thus neglecting British and French experience in Malaya and

---

[1] At the University of Maryland, 15 August 1967; reprinted in *Survival* (London), October 1967.

[2] See Roger Hilsman, *To Move a Nation* (Doubleday, 1967), p. 471. Arthur Schlesinger, *The Bitter Heritage* (Deutsch, 1967), p. 27.

[3] I would not wish to press this argument too far. By organising its main battle forces for limited war, the United States may have helped deter it in Asia and in Europe. Moreover I am not certain what alternative policies or organisation the American military establishment would have adopted, had *guerre révolutionnaire* been generally accepted as the most likely form of violence. Certainly the training of American *condottieri* was not the answer. Perhaps it should have taken the form of much greater emphasis on language training, on learning about foreign countries in general, and in teaching soldiers and small units to operate in difficult country with minimal logistic support.

Algeria (among other places), which showed that it could only be countered by a wide range of civil action, particularly in the fields of welfare, justice, and communications, and by efficient police rather than military force. Most senior American officers also supported the belief that the problem was a military one.

It is clear from Bundy's rationale of successive American decisions and from such accounts as Theodore Sorensen's White House record, that President Kennedy had quite conventional views about Viet Nam and Asia in general. He believed in the "domino theory": he believed that China was a major threat to South-east Asia; and that any weakening of the American position in Asia would encourage the Soviet Union in Europe. It is true that he saw the problem of maintaining stability in South Viet Nam as essentially a political one, but—perhaps because he refused to become besotted about Viet Nam at the expense of other problems—he seems to have done little to ensure the translation of his view into action. It was Kennedy's decision that the number of American military advisers and support units should be increased (from a few hundred to 25,000 men between 1961 and 1964), though only a handful could speak French or Vietnamese. They served only for a year out there and they had an impact on the ability of the South Vietnamese government to control terrorism far smaller than their quality deserved.

It was in the early part of 1963 that the real weakness of the American position in South Viet Nam became apparent. Having made the initial mistake of placing primary emphasis on the military aspects of counter-insurgency, the ability of Washington to modify this strategy was diminishing. The operations of the South Vietnamese army against the Vietcong were of dubious value. The "strategic hamlet" programme—based on Malayan experience and executed under the inspiration of R. G. K. (now Sir Robert) Thompson from Malaya—was losing its original effectiveness as it became more widely dispersed than resources permitted. There was now a two-way war between the Vietcong and the South Vietnamese government, and between Saigon and Washington, as Diem and the Nhu family became increasingly hostile to American pressure for social reform or to American press criticism of their handling of the Buddhists. And there were half-a-dozen inter-departmental wars in Washington which were reflected in Saigon and in the field.

Thus by now the two differences between the American position in Viet Nam and that of, say, the British in Malaya or the French in Algeria, had become clarified. The United States would not appoint a local proconsul to assume complete authority for all phases of counter-insurgency, a Templer, and it no longer trusted the indigenous consul, Diem, whom it had largely created. Even more important, it had no leverage either with Diem or with the South Vietnamese nationalists, for it had nothing positive to offer. There was the negative inducement of eventual freedom from terrorism, though at a cost which any intelligent Vietnamese knew must be high; there were also economic inducements which were really forms of bribery to influential Vietnamese, especially the military. But the United States lacked the trump card which the British had in Malaya and elsewhere or the French had in Algeria, namely the ability to offer the country political independence if the population would rally against the terrorists— for this had already been granted by the Geneva agreements of 1954. Having decided that nationalism was on the side of freedom, the United States became tied to whoever appeared to be the most effective nationalist.

Hence the agonising decision which confronted the Kennedy Administration in the autumn of 1963, whether to use the only leverage it possessed, namely to acquiesce in the slaughter of its erstwhile ewe lamb, President Diem, or to get out. Roger Hilsman—whose indiscretions, like those of other American ex-officials, make the task of the contemporary historian easier— describes a meeting of the National Security Council (on 6 September) at which only one man asked the right question, "What were we doing in South Viet Nam?"

> As he [Attorney-General Robert Kennedy] understood it we were there to help the people resisting a Communist take-over. The first question was whether a Communist take-over could be successfuly resisted with any government. If it could not, now was the time to get out of Viet Nam entirely, rather than waiting. If the answer was that it could, but not with the Diem-Nhu government as at present constituted, we owed it to the people resisting Communism in Viet Nam to give Lodge enough sanctions to bring changes that would permit successful resistance. . . .

But, in fact, the issue was never clarified. Yet another fact-finding mission was sent to Saigon —and as Hilsman points out, each one committed American prestige more and more closely to developments in Viet Nam—until Washington eventually acquiesced in Diem's murder two months later. As Theodore Draper has put it, "Kennedy's decision in 1963 not to block Diem's overthrow was the most deadly criticism of Kennedy's decision in 1961 to back Diem to the hilt."[4] There Kennedy's responsibility ends, for he was dead himself in a few weeks. But his Administration, which continued with hardly any changes until after the elections of a year later, never drew the proper lesson from the *débâcle* of Diem. If preventing a Vietcong take-over in the South was vital in terms of the broad objectives of American foreign policy—and few people in the Congress and the press questioned this in those days—and if there was no competent local leader, then the United States had no alternative but to create a pro-consular relationship with South Viet Nam. (Lodge and his successors had only limited powers over the American military and intelligence agencies in Viet Nam until this year, and never any real leverage over the Saigon government.) If it is argued that it was too late in history to establish such a relationship, that the "MacArthur syndrome" in any case makes Americans fearful of the domestic effects of creating such a powerful figure overseas, then the first half of Robert Kennedy's question of 6 September 1963, deserved a better analysis than it got. What is not fair is to blame the post-Diem confusion, as Bundy does, on France for not having trained the Vietnamese in self-government. The French never had much opportunity, and the people who caused the confusion after 1963 were the well-trained *protégés* of the Pentagon.

O NE QUESTION HAS ALWAYS puzzled me: how could the United States government, at any point after 1961, believe that victory over the Vietcong was attainable, except in terms of decades rather than years?

One of its admirable characteristics is to use a wide range of research institutes and universities to give greater depth and accuracy to its own operational and political analysis. By the early 1960s there were a number of American scholars at RAND, Harvard, and other places, who had made a very thorough study of guerrilla operations. Their conclusions did not greatly vary. Established authority, whether it be colonial or national, is inevitably on the defensive in a situation of insurgency and must remain so, for its task is to convince the insurgents and the neutral population for whose loyalty both are contending that continual terrorism carries diminishing returns. Taking the initiative against the insurgents is likely to be counter-productive: political action is as important as military operations. The nature of the terrain is also a crucial factor. In the Boer War the British could wire off open *veldt* and thus slowly isolate the Boer commandos, though even so it took them two years to bring guerrilla resistance to an end. Mountain bases were an invaluable asset to both the Algerians and the Cypriot insurgents. Kenyatta and his Kikuyus were virtually unassailable as long as they remained in the Kenyan jungle. How did anyone imagine that in a land, part jungle, part mountains, part swamp—with a hostile country on one side, two weak powers on the second, and an open coastline on the third—it would be possible to overcome the Vietcong in less than a generation? True, it had been done in Malaya over a fourteen-year period: but apart from the priceless assets of colonial government which I have already mentioned, a unified politico-military command and real political leverage, the Malayan insurgents were Chinese and physically distinct from the majority of the population. Probably technology (helicopters, new small arms, infra-red sensors, and all the rest) was the element that corrupted judgment, making it seem possible that the Americans could do what the natives or the old colonial powers could not.

Also, as Hilsman points out, except for 1962 when the South Vietnamese were getting the better of the Vietcong, hope was sustained largely by the circulation of statistics—about the ratio of weapons captured to those lost, about defections, about the "kill ratio"—which were either meaningless or inaccurate.[5]

Arthur Schlesinger has suggested that "in retrospect, Viet Nam is a triumph of the politics of inadvertence." Without engaging in too much hindsight, one cannot fail to be impressed by the slapdash manner in which decisions of profound importance were taken. (Which is not to say that other nations do not do the same.)

---

[4] Theodore Draper, *Abuse of Power* (Viking, 1967), p. 59.
[5] Hilsman himself compounds this difficulty by producing a table showing the steady increase in the number of Vietcong recruited in South Viet Nam each year, in which his own arithmetic is cock-eyed.

I HAVE ALREADY suggested that on the evidence of those involved, the real point of no return was reached in the autumn of 1963 when the United States had the option of leaving the fate of Viet Nam entirely in the hands of Diem to find that "Asian solution" which, four years later, is now so widely advocated. And, moreover, it was Kennedy's decision. To have exercised restraint thereafter would have involved curbing the immense national influence of the American military establishment. For the military Viet Nam was a war against Communism: and if it could not be won by the local inhabitants the United States must take over the job. Already in November 1962, General Earle Wheeler (who is now Chairman of the Joint Chiefs of Staff) was stating publicly,

> It is fashionable in some quarters to say that the problems in South-east Asia are primarily political and economic rather than military. I do not agree. The essence of the problem in Viet Nam is military.

But here one must distinguish between the decision to begin bombing North Viet Nam in February 1965, and to send in American troops in July. The roots of the bombing policy are only partly military: some of its strongest advocates were civilians who saw not the Vietcong but North Viet Nam as the real enemy. As far back as 1961 Walt Rostow (who succeeded McGeorge Bundy as Johnson's adviser on National Security) was arguing,

> The sending of men and arms across international boundaries and the direction of guerrilla war from outside a sovereign nation is aggression; and this is a fact which the whole international community must confront and whose consequent responsibilities it must accept. Without such international action those against whom aggression is mounted will be driven inevitably to seek out and engage the ultimate source of the aggression they confront.[6]

And, as the frustrating early '60s moved on, more and more people felt the force of this argument. Bundy says that "it is simply not true that there was any change in policy in this period [late 1963 to early 1965] toward greater military emphasis, much less major new military actions." But any visitor to either shore of

the Potomac in 1964 caught a strong whiff of this argument, and President Johnson's ludicrous over-reaction to an attack on two ships in the Gulf of Tonkin in August of that year (including a Congressional resolution that gave him greater powers than Kosygin possesses) seemed to me an index of the growing temptation to use airpower. Hilsman says that he, Ambassador Harriman and others, argued that to do this would simply raise the ante since Hanoi could respond by increasing the use of the infiltration routes to include northerners as well as southerners trained in the North. But Roger Hilsman had been fired by 1964 and Averell Harriman's influence had been restricted.

Viet Nam presented the Pentagon with special temptations to use airpower. First, there is practically no other country in the world, except Chile, which has the shape of the two Viet Nams, narrow and entirely accessible to carrier-borne aircraft. Consequently, the Navy for once had common cause with the Air Force. Second, the military were led to believe that the economy of North Viet Nam was more highly developed and vulnerable than in fact it is. Even the late Bernard Fall, well-informed and reasonably judicious, could write in January 1965 that "the temptation, assuredly, is great, for North Viet Nam is no guerrilla base but an organised State with conventional targets, such as cities, industries, and railroads."[7]

BUT AGAIN: Where was the analysis? Strategic theorists like Thomas Schelling were pointing out that if one state uses what he calls "compellence" as contrasted with deterrence, it makes compliance with its wishes that much more obvious and therefore difficult for the other state to undertake.[8] Perhaps American success in "compelling" the Soviet Union to withdraw its missiles from Cuba, an act of such compliance, had a corrupting effect on the judgment to use bombing against North Viet Nam. A small state may react very differently from a great one with much more at stake. But, there was also the *Strategic Bombing Survey* of World War II for all to read, with its clear message: bombing is not an effective instrument for changing national will unless it is used either to kill people in large quantities, or is concerted with a major ground force attack. Perhaps the trouble was that too few Americans have ever experienced bombing. Anyone over 35 brought up in southern England or industrial Germany could have told the Pentagon that even daily

---

[6] Address at the U.S. Army Special Warfare School, 28 June 1961.
[7] Bernard Fall, *Vietnam Witness 1953-1966* (Praeger, 1966), p. 291.
[8] Thomas Schelling, *Arms & Influence* (Yale University Press, 1966), p. 82.

bombing with high explosive bombs will not affect national morale if it merely destroys buildings. Bernard Fall, writing eight months after American air operations began, suggested that the use of bombers in South Viet Nam was having a far more demoralising effect on civil populations there than in the North.

WAS THE INTRODUCTION of American ground forces an inevitable corollary of the decision to bomb the North? Did the United States unilaterally escalate a guerrilla to a limited war? Here one can only report both sides of a bitter controversy on which too little solid evidence exists to form any final judgment. There was a tacit agreement, say the Administration's critics, that if the North were not attacked it would not contribute its regular units to the war in the South. They started coming in quantity only after the bombing began, thus presenting the United States with the alternatives of accepting *débâcle* in the South or intervening massively with its own army. There was no such tacit agreement, say the Administration's spokesmen: Hanoi was merely concealing its hand. There was one Northern regiment in the South by December 1964, and, according to Bundy,

> We know that several other regiments entered in the spring of 1965 on timetables of infiltration that can only have reflected command decisions taken in Hanoi prior to the beginning of the bombing. . . . The point is that Hanoi, as we suspected then and later proved, had taken major steps to raise the level of the war before the bombing began.

Again, did nobody in the counsels of the President point out the enormous damage that increasing commitment in Viet Nam would do to American influence in Europe and Japan, the ways in which it would fortify General de Gaulle, strengthen the Russian position in Europe, give Moscow an admirable reason for declining to co-operate on major arms control measures, or convince the Germans that the United States was losing interest in Europe? Washington is supposed to be the capital of a global power.

But the reasons why American ground forces went to Viet Nam in the first place are less important than the fact that they did go, and then were steadily augmented to the enormous figure

[9] David Bonavia's dispatch in *The Times*, 13 November 1967.

of half-a-million men by what Michael Howard has called the "Haig syndrome"—"Give me another hundred thousand men, Sir, and I can assure you we will have finished the job by Christmas. . . ." They have made it certain that the United States cannot be thrown out of Viet Nam. But they provide little or no assurance of a quick victory, for the Vietcong are unlikely ever to give them the opportunity to fight a major battle, a Dien Bien Phu in reverse. Occasionally there is a Vietcong attack in which American firepower scores a success, as with the battle of Loc Ninh in late October 1967, when it is reported to have lost 1,000 men. (I still remain sceptical of such figures: it takes a massive action to kill 1,000 men, and soldiers are as unreliable in estimating enemy casualties as fishermen are about their catch.)

General Westmoreland is now arguing that the operations of the past two years have been aimed only at establishing a secure basis from which to mount a more systematic campaign "to carry the war to the enemy and root him out completely."[9] Well, victory must be the aim of generals, but I do not believe that it is attainable within the next few years unless certain conditions are fulfilled.

First, the Americans must be prepared to accept the large casualties which would accompany any assumption of the initiative. At present they use firepower, artillery and strafing, to "soften up" Vietcong positions, with the consequence that the enemy more often than not has disappeared by the time they attack. A bold, even reckless, American strategy of using their tactical mobility to plummet units down in the midst of Vietcong strongholds without warning could, if skilfully directed, begin to demoralise and defeat their opponents. But it would probably mean trebling the annual American casualty rate of some 6 to 7,000 killed.

Second, since communication bombing of the North is a demonstrable failure as an exercise either in compulsion, or even in damming supplies to the South, "victory" requires the kind of bombing that deliberately kills people in order to dry up Northern manpower and break Hanoi's will: breaching the dykes to drown the paddy-field dwellers, and smashing Hanoi and Haiphong on the pattern of Rotterdam—deliberate genocide as contrasted with the marginal kind now practised with such revolting techniques as "pellet bombs."

Third, "victory" requires taking the pacification effort in the Delta out of the fumbling hands of the South Vietnamese, and either handing it over to some organisation of Asian "black and tans" like the South Koreans, or else to a ruthless centrally-directed American operation. (The Australians in their area seem to have been relatively successful in pacification by a combination of severity and centralisation of authority.)

NONE OF THESE CONDITIONS can be fulfilled, except perhaps the third, for the simple reason that the increasing commitment of American prestige to Viet Nam has had the effect of transferring the battlefield to the United States itself. With the political party conventions only eight months away, with Johnson's popularity at an all-time low, with American liberal and much conservative opinion—quite apart from world opinion—already alienated from the Administration, the President knows that any such measures might not only ensure his own defeat, but break the great coalition that Woodrow Wilson and Franklin Roosevelt forged, and send the Democratic Party into the wilderness for a generation.

Consequently, I cannot see L.B.J. authorising the kind of local escalation that might bring "victory" in Viet Nam in the foreseeable future. What about strategic escalation? I think one can rule this out as well, for it is hard to know what form it could take, or what it could be thought to accomplish. The bombardment of supply installations in China—quite apart from the colossal risk of Soviet intervention—would be marginally relevant, for the supplies that North Viet Nam receives from there could almost certainly be replaced from somewhere else in an Afro-Asian world that is becoming increasingly sympathetic to Hanoi. The same is true of the bombing or blockading of Soviet supply ships (whose difficulties have in any case been increased by the blocking of the Suez canal). Nuclear weapons? The United States Air Force has many experts within its ranks who point out that so-called tactical weapons, particularly the smaller air-delivered bombs which are deployed in large numbers in Europe, would be ideally suited to the task either of demolishing concentrations of Vietcong and North Vietnamese troops or of destroying Soviet ground-to-air missile sites, or of making infiltration routes dangerous to use by reason of

residual radio-active contamination. Any such idea resurrects all the arguments of the Korean war but in a much more delicate situation of global balance than existed in the early 1950s. Lyndon Johnson may be pig-headed, but he is not foolhardy.

THE THIRD ALTERNATIVE is to reconcile the American public to a long war stretching well into the 1970s. American troops would continue to fight with firepower rather than manpower in order to keep the casualty rate low. Bombing would be confined to interdiction targets, or even suspended indefinitely and used as a residual threat. Increased emphasis would be placed on the expansion of the South Vietnamese economy, the training of its civil as well as its military cadres, and an effective system of local administration gradually created, especially in the Delta, to make the task of pacification possible. In other words, if Viet Nam is as important as the Administration's spokesmen have been saying for years that it is, the United States can well afford an indefinite effort there, provided that the techniques employed can be reconciled with the American conscience. If the United States is really the centre of a great world system of power, it must expect to have troubled outposts, as the British had on the North West Frontier or the French in Morocco. The fact that the trouble is bigger may be no more than an index that their international system is bigger than its predecessors. This line of argument is well presented by one of the effective American pro-consuls, General Maxwell Taylor.[10]

THIS MAY BE the outcome. But there are several reasons why Americans may shy away from it as a deliberate policy.

1. In the first place, the longer the United States is fighting in Viet Nam, the harder it is to differentiate her position from that of the old colonial powers, something that not only provides ammunition for Peking and Moscow but still sticks in the gullets of Americans themselves. When a pillar of the Virginia Establishment, the Reverend Cotesworth Lewis, insisted to the captive President sitting below his pulpit in Bruton parish church on Sunday, 12 November, that "it is particularly regrettable that to most nations the struggle's purpose appears as neo-colonialism," he was speaking for a great many of his countrymen.

---

[10] *Responsibility and Response* (Harper & Row, 1967).

2. There is the cost of the war to be reckoned, in money, lives and the fabric of American society itself. The financial cost may be less than each year's increment in the American gross national product, but it must mean higher taxes, increased international pressure on the dollar, and serious inflation. Non-Americans are apt to think Americans rather sentimental about human life for a country bred in so much violence, but a death rate even of 5,000 a year is a large figure by any standards if projected over the indefinite future: its political impact is magnified by the incidence of selective service. And the effect of the war on the university generation could be disastrous. A Harvard friend of mine has pointed out that Viet Nam is already leading to a kind of class conflict between the not-so-bright who get called up, go to Viet Nam and support the war, and their brighter contemporaries who go to university and for the most part emerge as bitter critics.

3. The American people have got the Viet Nam war on their mind. This is not the colonial age where lonely colonels battled with Pathans or Berbers of whose existence the metropolitan populace was hardly aware. The spate of books, editorials, and TV programmes is growing in volume, and no politician can now ignore the issue, though he may, like Governor Romney, try and evade it. Except for the 1776 Revolution the United States has never been involved in a serious shooting conflict of over four years' duration: and Americans are not patient people.

4. Moreover, if Ho Chi Minh has read his 20th-century history (and the evidence suggests that he has), he will know that big powers generally lose small wars, not on the battlefield but at home. His interest in the liberal protest movement in the United States is not mistaken. Within nine months of dismissing the idea of Dominion Home Rule for Ireland and asserting that "he had murder by the throat" there, Lloyd George was negotiating unconditionally with the Irish leaders. Henry Hopkinson's "never" to independence for Cyprus preceded it only by a year or two. De Gaulle's decision to make peace with Algeria was preceded by the firmest of his firm statements about the indissoluble connection between France and Algeria. And so on. Ho accepts Johnson as an adversary whose determination is equal to his own, but even if Johnson is re-elected he has

respectable grounds for thinking that the United States will not last the course. Consequently, the most adamant declaratory position on the part of the United States government is unlikely, even if maintained beyond the 1968 election, to lead to much slackening of resolve in Hanoi: provided the war remains within its present boundaries, which for reasons I have tried to suggest, seems to me the only assumption that is realistic in terms both of domestic and international constraints.

5. An indefinite continuation of the war exposes the United States, as a universal power, to great risks. Anti-Americanism is making rapid strides in every European country, and, though the part that Viet Nam plays in this process varies, it plays some part in every country including Germany, by reason of the mixture of brutality and incompetence that it exhibits. It has provided the Soviet Union and even the distraught Chinese with diplomatic windfalls. It has led to an emasculation of the foreign-aid programme which is the basis of American influence in India and many African and Latin American countries. Five more years of this and the United States might be a country whose diplomatic influence was by no means proportional to its strength—or to its fundamental good intentions. Moreover, there are more than two parties to this conflict, for the United States has involved five of its Australasian and Asian allies, and at some point in a protracted conflict one or all of them might deliver the supreme rebuff of deciding to go home.

So there remains the alternative of negotiation. Here there have been almost as many proposals as there are heads of government in the world, and there would be no virtue in my trying to catalogue them. One group of them calls for a negotiation between all the combatants, with or without outside powers such as Britain and the Soviet Union, to re-establish the Geneva Agreement of 1954, to negotiate an end of hostilities and the withdrawal of all foreign troops, and to establish a neutral South Viet Nam. Theodore Sorensen recently suggested such an approach.[11] He implied that the United States would lose no face from such a negotiation, since it has been involved in Viet Nam merely to gain time for the establishment of a more broadly-based régime in Saigon: the recent elections and the new

---

[11] *Saturday Review* (New York), 21 October 1967, and *The Times* (London), 17 November.

government there have given a colourable excuse for saying that the job is done.

But there are two basic difficulties about such an approach. First, Hanoi has made it clear through every channel at its disposal that it is not interested in a formal negotiation at the moment since it believes that time is on its side. This appears to have Soviet backing. Second, there is no agreement on who should sit at the table. The United States has stated its readiness to talk both with the Vietcong and Hanoi, but the new régime in Saigon has not. It would be very difficult for the Soviet Union to participate in negotiations which involved any reciprocal concessions, though they might accept a *fait accompli*. Sorensen has suggested that they must be held in secret to prevent Chinese intervention, but it is very hard to see this happening in so leaky a place as South-east Asia.

The second approach is reciprocal de-escalation without any formal negotiation. The Johnson Administration's basic, though not fully declared, position is that if Hanoi would begin to pull back northern regiments, it would take more than equivalent action. (Though any question of withdrawing all American forces within six months, as promised by Johnson after the Manila Conference of a year ago, would be logistically impossible.) But Hanoi now has absolutely no intention of making the first move. They may think differently a year from now if Johnson has been re-elected with strong backing on a platform of maintaining an indefinite war of attrition. But surely Johnson cannot risk much on this, for if there is only a surmise and no certainty of a change in Hanoi's position he may not get re-elected (even though such signs as the San Francisco plebiscite suggest that there may be wider national support for his policy than affection for his person).

This leaves it to the United States to make the first move—something that was unthinkable a year ago when Mr. Rusk's attempt to smear any such suggestions with words like "Munich" and "appeasement," commanded more approbation than it does now. Washington is deeply interested in suggestions that have emerged through French sources from Hanoi that if the bombing policy were annulled the two capitals could be in negotiation on de-escalation within four weeks. Before this article appears Johnson may have tried the effect of a Christmas "bombing pause." But Hanoi will probably want more than this, namely a cancellation not

suspension of bombing, and to do this means confronting the solid opposition of American military opinion, as well as of the old Southern troglodytes at the head of the Congressional committees. Much depends then on who succeeds McNamara.

ONE OTHER UNILATERAL COURSE seems open to the President if Viet Nam is not to be a heavy political albatross in 1968. This would be to keep the bombing light through the early part of the year and then, some time in the early spring, to announce that ground operations in Viet Nam are going so well (or because of the completion of the projected electronic fence) that 50,000 American troops can be withdrawn. This would bring immediate political and diplomatic dividends, and since the battle statistics in Viet Nam can be made to prove anything, the basis of the statement might be hard to question.

FINALLY, there is the possibility of beginning an end to the war by negotiations at different levels. Robert Shaplen, the distinguished Asian correspondent of *The New Yorker*, who rejects the neo-isolationism of many American intellectuals, has outlined such a course in the October issue of *Foreign Affairs*. He points out that, adamant though Hanoi may be in public, captured documents show that many of the North Vietnamese leaders are saying that the time has come to combine fighting with negotiating. The first kind, he suggests, might consist of approaches, encouraged by the Saigon government, at the village level to representatives of the NLF (Vietcong) with the object of holding local elections, based on strictly local cease-fires, which both sides would contest. In other words, to turn a revolutionary struggle into something more like a two-party contest at the local level.

The second stage would be negotiations involving Washington, Saigon, Hanoi and the NLF, not about a sweeping settlement, but about what have hitherto been argued on both sides as the conditions of negotiation, namely, how to end the bombing and on what basis to withdraw troops. The third stage would involve the Soviet Union and perhaps Britain, and would be concerned with the creation of a buffer zone in Viet Nam, neutralisation of the widest possible area of South-east Asia (an idea originally rejected in the United States when it was proposed by de Gaullle and later by Anthony Eden), and perhaps an eventual plebiscite on the reunification of the two Viet Nams.

This range of ideas, which rests on the explicit hypothesis that the United States accepts the full policy implications of John Kennedy's views that it is up to the Vietnamese to find a solution to their own problems (a hypothesis on which President Kennedy himself did not act), cannot be reconciled with the Administration's public position of many years' standing that South Viet Nam is the victim of Northern aggression. But the difference can be glossed over and many people in Congress and in the American press seem prepared to participate in such a conspiracy. If in five years there is a government in Saigon in which the *NLF* is powerfully represented, I am inclined to doubt whether anyone will score significant political points for drawing attention to it.

T HE UNITED STATES is about to enter a period of introspection which would have occurred in any case because of the size of the problems involved in adapting a political, legal, and physical framework that is still largely geared to the assumptions of an agricultural state, to the needs of a rapidly expanding, primarily urban, technocratic society: the rebuilding of the cities, racial integration, the control of domestic violence, a more uniform system of local government, and a score of related problems. A politico-social revolution even more extensive than the New Deal has been fomenting for many years, and it has been delayed partly by the preoccupation of successive Administrations with the Cold War, and latterly by Lyndon B. Johnson's obsession with Viet Nam. Enormous resources, intellectual and economic, will be devoted to it, and as with many things (though not guerrilla warfare) to which Americans apply their best energies, the task will probably be successfully accomplished. In the process the United States will become an even richer and more self-contained state than it is today.

The danger of the Viet Nam war, preceding and delaying this inevitable era of American domestic preoccupation, and coming at a time when the continuous growth of American power tends to seal her off from normal relationships with the rest of the international community, is that many Americans will draw the wrong lesson from it. Instead of accepting the Viet Nam episode as the consequence of a series of official blunders, based on faulty assumptions and analysis, and therefore requiring the same drastic overhaul in the techniques of central government as are accepted as necessary at the state or city level, they may tend to assume that American power and resources are for some reason unusable to underwrite the stability and security of other areas of the world, that somehow they are unwanted in the world.

Lyndon Johnson himself displayed traces of such thinking when, having been sent by President Kennedy to Viet Nam in May 1961, he said:

The basic decision in South-east Asia is here. We must decide whether to help these countries to the best of our ability or throw in the towel and pull back our defences to San Francisco.

In fact these are not the true alternatives. There is every reason to think that the United States must and will remain involved in Asian politics; that there will be a range of threats to the security of these countries which they cannot handle themselves and which an off-shore American presence based on the Philippines and Australia can effectively deter; that she alone has the economic resources to provide a real incentive to regional co-operation among the smaller powers; that there is a great deal of basic nation-building, including the infrastructure of security and competent local government, to which she (with Britain) can contribute specialised technical assistance; and that she can help guarantee borders or neutrality arrangements where she cannot impose them. The fact that America could not successfully play midwife to a seething domestic revolution in one particular Asian country, with an especially turbulent history, and could only augment civil war rather than control it, is not an argument for drawing the interests of the country at a line east of Alcatraz.

The misfortune of Viet Nam is that whether from frustration or disgust, a significant majority of Americans may wash their hands of the world's largest continent—indeed of the world. But the true lesson of Viet Nam is that a power of universal interests cannot afford to become so deeply committed in one corner of the globe that it loses its ability to influence events elsewhere, a mistake which the other universal power, the Soviet Union, has never made.

The Growth of Awareness: Our Nation's Law and Law Among Nations

THURMAN ARNOLD

Each year American lawyers and American law schools join together on Law Day to celebrate the great ideal of Western civilization, that there are fundamental principles of law and justice that must be observed and also must be enforced against those who will not observe them, if free democratic society is to survive. On these occasions we think of law not as a set of rules but as a way of thinking about our society which, if followed, assures us of orderly progress in the face of industrial and social change. We do not celebrate real estate law, or administrative law, or the rules and regulations of the Securities and Exchange Commission. The kind of law we celebrate on Law Day is not a set of rules or specifically defined principles. At home it is a way of looking at society and the relations between individuals and their government. Abroad its most important aspect today is to restrain lawless international behavior and to prevent aggressive wars.

I. From Social Darwinism to the Warren Court—Growth of Awareness and Responsibility in Domestic Law

In the happy days of the 1920's, before the great Depression, everyone was certain what the fundamental principles of law which

Law Day Speech delivered at Valparaiso University, Valparaiso, Indiana, April 28, 1967.

we respected were. So far as international law was concerned, we assumed that we had made the world safe for democracy by winning the First World War—a war to end all wars. We had saved England and the British fleet. We could safely draw back into our shell and assume that international law would take care of itself. Later I will talk about the consequences of that decision.

At home we assumed that we had at last achieved a perfect society that operated automatically provided that our legislatures did not interfere with certain automatic rules by passing radical social legislation which violated our past traditions of the proper function of legislatures. We knew that if private property was protected the automatic rules of something referred to as "Capitalism" would assure us permanent prosperity and the elimination of poverty and social discontent. Private property meant in those days the freedom of great corporate empires to do as they pleased. If these great empires were not interfered with, individual human rights would take care of themselves. Darwin's law of the survival of the fittest would solve the problem of weak and underprivileged individuals by eliminating them. The Constitution of the United States was there to save us from the folly of legislatures in the event that they were seduced by demagogues into an undue interest in human rights as against property rights.

These were the attitudes and ideals which were implicitly read into the Constitution of the United States and molded the decisions of the Supreme Court of the United States before the great Depression.

But unfortunately, the great Depression did not respond to our old traditions of constitutional law. It soon became apparent that social legislation of a kind heretofore unknown in our traditional thinking about the Constitution of the United States was essential to meet the desperate economic situation which confronted us. A conservative and embittered majority on the Supreme Court saw in that legislation a threat to every freedom that Americans cherished. The American Bar Association denounced as unconstitutional all efforts to put human rights above property rights.

By 1937 there was such a cloud of unconstitutionality cast by a bitterly divided Court over every New Deal measure that the administration of the New Deal program became impossible. Principles which are taken for granted today were then denounced by all right thinking persons as socialistic. The fog of unconstitutionality which enveloped the whole New Deal was so thick that no regulatory law could be enforced until it had passed the scrutiny of the Supreme Court, a process which threatened to take years. Roosevelt was thus forced into a direct attack on the Supreme Court of the United States —the Court packing plan. I remember those days well. The fury of the educated citizens in the United States rose to incredible heights. Roosevelt was booed as an apostle of lawlessness by the students when he visited Harvard.

The Court packing bill came so near to passing that Chief Justice Hughes, who had been a constant dissenter from the decisions that had paralyzed the Government, was able to frighten the irreconcilable majority of the Court. Justice Van Devanter retired. Justice Roberts abandoned his extreme position and declared a new Agricultural Act constitutional.[1] It became no longer necessary to pack the Court. Out of the Court fight a new constitution emerged.

But its emergence was gradual. Over 30 years has passed, and the new constitution is not yet respected by a number of vociferous groups. For a period until the appointment of Chief Justice Warren a majority of the Court, under the influence of Justice Frankfurter, decided to play it safe. The Supreme Court stopped vetoing social and economic legislation. But the Court became a purely negative body concerned more with its own safety from public criticism than with the protection of the liberties of the individual citizen.

Under this protection Senator McCarthy rose to power. He frightened both the Truman and Eisenhower Administrations into establishing procedures by which citizens were tried and condemned as subversive on secret evidence without the American constitutional right of confrontation and cross-examination. Dorothy Bailey's conviction for disloyalty by a loyalty board on secret evidence was affirmed four-to-four by an equally divided Court.[2] From then on McCarthy had carte blanche. The Supreme Court had miserably failed in its duty. Every government official, indeed every teacher or writer, was made to realize that his career might be ruined and a badge of infamy pinned on him on secret evidence by faceless informers.

It was not until the appointment of Earl Warren as Chief Justice of the United States that our new Constitution began to be a positive force dedicated to the principle of human rights. I believe that Chief Justice Warren will go down in history with Marshall as one of the two greatest Chief Justices. As a result of the Court's

[1] Mulford v. Smith, 307 U.S. 38 (1939).
[2] Bailey v. Richardson, 341 U.S. 918 (1951).

decisions during his tenure, public servants can no longer be forced to take vague loyalty oaths which may later bring them into trouble because they hold unpopular opinions.[3] The government's vast "security" programs have been widely reformed and procedures substantially improved. The law has made us a more civilized nation.

We have also been made a more civilized nation as a result of the racial segregation cases.[4] Out of the bitter struggle which followed Chief Justice Warren's decision on school segregation the South is today beginning to accept the hitherto unpleasant fact that Negroes are citizens of the United States.

But perhaps the boldest and most successful principle ever to emerge through a Supreme Court decision is that voters in rapidly developing urban areas shall have an equal influence with voters in rural areas in determining state legislation.[5] Had the Supreme Court timidly refused to enforce the principle of One Man, One Vote— had it continued to declare this to be a political problem which could be solved only by an amendment to the Constitution—we would have been caught for the next twenty years in a rotten borough system where a minority could veto legislation adapted to the needs of the majority. State legislatures dominated by a reactionary minority of rural voters could never have solved the explosive problems of a growing urban society.

And with respect to the civil rights of individuals accused of crime the Warren Court has an equally great record, though often by five-to-four decisions. No longer can the police use a confession elicited from an indigent and mentally retarded person under arrest as a result of days of insistent questioning.[6] No longer can convictions be obtained where the accused is not represented by counsel.[7]

Thirty years have passed since Roosevelt introduced his Court packing plan. During that period the Supreme Court had first changed from a frustrating force hampering all government legislation to a purely negative institution which gave free rein to McCarthyism. Today a new Constitution has emerged protecting the civil liberties of citizens from the power of intolerant bigots, defending the right to a fair trial of indigent and ignorant persons accused of crime, and guaranteeing the right of a majority of our voters to prevail over

[3] Baggett v. Bullitt, 377 U.S. 360 (1963).
[4] Brown v. Board of Educ., 347 U.S. 483 (1954), 349 U.S. 294 (1955).
[5] Reynolds v. Sims, 377 U.S. 533 (1963).
[6] Davis v. North Carolina, 384 U.S. 737 (1966).
[7] Gideon v. Wainwright, 372 U.S. 335 (1962).

a minority in an election. The Constitution today resembles more closely the vision of the Constitutional fathers than it did before the Warren Court.

Nevertheless, this emerging Constitution has not yet been accepted by important minority groups who still want to impeach Earl Warren. Nor are the decisions of the Supreme Court universally respected by many of the intellectual elite who sit on law school faculties. Articles have been written by instructors at Harvard,[8] Yale [9] and the University of Chicago [10] complaining that the Supreme Court is not enunciating what they call neutral principles of constitutional law. On the other side we have the anguished cries of police chiefs and other citizens who want to suppress crime by denying certain procedural rights to criminal defendants.

Finally, we have the embattled minority of those who want to preserve the power of rural minorities to govern state legislatures through the rotten borough system. In 30 States resolutions have slipped past the legislatures to repeal the reapportionment decisions of the Supreme Court by calling a new constitutional convention—something that has not happened since the original Constitutional convention. If such a constitutional convention is called it will be an advertisement to the world that there is a struggle in America between those who believe in majority rule in a democracy and those who repudiate that principle under the doctrine of States' rights.

We need such a new constitutional convention about as much as we need more riots in our cities. And so I optimistically predict that even though enough States resolutions are passed to present the matter to Congress, Congress will refuse to take the ruinous step of calling a new convention in these troubled times. Certainly there are enough constitutional infirmities in these resolutions to justify Congress in ignoring them.

II. From Isolationism to Vietnam—Growth of Awareness and Responsibility in International Law

It is in the field of international law where the greatest danger lies. We are living in a lawless world, a world where small and relatively impotent nations can nevertheless start brush fires which may

[8] Hart, *Foreword: The Time Chart of the Justices, The Supreme Court, 1958 Term*, 73 Harv. L. Rev. 84 (1959).

[9] Bickel, *Foreword: The Passive Virtues*, 75 Harv. L. Rev. 40 (1961).

[10] Kurland, *Foreword: "Equal in Origin and Equal in Title to the Legislative and Executive Branches of the Government,"* 78 Harv. L. Rev. 143 (1964).

spread to our own shores. We have seen it happen twice—the First World War and again in the Second. But the world is even smaller today than it was in the Second World War. It has become so small that lawless aggressive action by any nation against another can threaten world peace. It is also a world where poverty and misery in the crowded nations which cannot feed themselves threaten revolutions which upset the balance of power. In such a world we need some sort of a world constitution ever more desperately than the Thirteen Colonies needed the Constitution of the United States after the Revolutionary War. And the keystone of that world constitution is the principle that no nation must be permitted to expand its borders and its power through an aggressive attack upon its neighbors. We are today attempting to enforce that principle in Vietnam.

It was our feeling of desperate need for a principle of international law against aggression which led us to abandon our distaste for the League of Nations and become a leader in the formation of the United Nations. But this action we felt was not enough. We wanted some judicial sanction for that fundamental principle on which all international law must rest—the outlawing of aggressive war. And so, after Hitler's defeat, the United States joined with the victorious nations, including the Soviet Union, in the first Nuremberg trial to prosecute the national leaders of Hitler's empire. The paramount purpose of that trial was to declare that an aggressive war was an international crime which justified imposing the death penalty on the leaders of the nation which started it. The trials for German atrocities represented no novel principle. The great principle of international law announced for the first time at Nuremberg was that aggressive war is in itself an international crime regardless of the way it is conducted.

At the time of the Nuremberg trials those who write the think columns in our press, such as Walter Lippmann, and independent organizations of intellectuals, such as Americans for Democratic Action, and liberal professors on our college campuses, acclaimed the principle of the outlawing of aggressive war as a great step forward in international law. Today they are bending every effort to prevent the enforcement of the principle that Nuremberg announced to the world. They are giving every aid and comfort to the enemy that they can in the light of their limited numbers. They are encouraging Hanoi to believe that if it will only hang on the United States will abandon its attempt to enforce the Nuremberg principle in Asia.

They proclaim that America cannot and must not be a world policeman.

One only has to go back to the First World War to show the cost of American blood and treasure which has resulted from that attitude.

In the 19th Century and until the First World War England was the world's policeman. At tremendous cost the British fleet was kept to a strength larger than all the other navies in the world combined. In those happy days sea power was equivalent to world power. From the time of the Monroe Doctrine on we have been protected by the British fleet. But in the First World War we discovered that sea power was not what it once was. America had to be sworn in as deputy world policeman and go to the rescue of the chief. In fact, the necessity of assuming the role of world policeman had descended on us, but we were completely unaware of it.

When the First World War was over we decided that our obligation to enforce some form of international law in the world was over and done with. One of the favorite songs of the 26th Division, in which I served, went as follows:

> We have paid our debt to Lafayette
> Who the hell do we owe now.
> We don't want any more trenches,
> Lordy, how we want to go home.

We reduced our army from nearly 5,000,000 men to 200,000. We left a garrison of a few thousand men in the Philippines. By winning the First World War we had made the world safe for democracy. Germany had been taught her lesson. Japan had been our ally. To provide an adequate force to protect the Philippines might seem an offensive move against Japan. It might even lead to war. The United States should never commit an army to Asia, for the mere purpose of stopping aggression in the Orient.

Even in the 1930's when it became apparent that Japan was boldly embarking upon a course of aggression in the Orient, we refused to put any military obstacle in her path by reinforcing the Philippines. After all, we were not the world's policemen with responsibility for enforcing international law. Once attacked, the Philippines fell in only a few months and Japan was free to go on. Think of the cost of American lives that resulted from our attitude.

Even after the defeat of France by Hitler, the intellectuals who now are condemning our efforts to enforce the international principle outlawing aggressive war failed to understand the role in international affairs which destiny had imposed on the United States.

A leader in that group was Walter Lippmann. His message today is that the United States has no responsibility in international affairs. It is not our duty, having announced the Nuremberg principle against aggressive war, to see that it is carried out. The President should admit before the world that our policy in Vietnam is morally wrong.

Mr. Lippmann believes in the futility of enforcing international law by American military force. His military advice is to use the army in Vietnam only for defensive purposes. He thought the same in 1940. I read from the Biography of General Marshall by Forrest Pogue:

> General Marshall was alarmed in late September when Walter Lippmann, in his widely read column, suggested that 'All popular doubts, political confusions, all ambiguity would be removed by a clear decision to shrink the Army and concentrate our major effort upon the Navy, the Air Force and lend-lease.' . . . . 'Today,' he argued, 'the effort to raise such a large army so quickly is not merely unnecessary but undesirable. . . .' He believed that the 'complex of circumstances' that centered on 'the great expansion of the Army' had become 'the cancer which obstructs national unity, causes discontent which subversive elements exploit, and weakens the primary measures of our defense, which are the lend-lease program and the naval policy. I think that a surgical operation is indicated—an operation to shrink the Army which will at the same time increase its efficiency.' [11]

This was after Hitler's successful invasion and conquest of France. Had Mr. Lippmann's advice been followed Hitler might have won the war. What he was saying in 1940 before Pearl Harbor, he is still saying today.

Mr. Galbraith, of the ADA, is quoted in the *New York Times* on April 3, 1967, as saying that the generals in Vietnam have not considered the political situation they are putting the Democratic Party in. He says: "But for the rest of us, there is no excuse for innocence. This disaster (i.e., a long war in Vietnam) could, indeed, mean the death and burial of the Democratic Party." In other words, the Democratic Party is more important than the enforcement of international law.

[11] Forrest Pogue, *George Marshall: Ordeal and Hope*, Viking Press, 1966, p. 76.

Professor Feuer, who left Berkeley for the University of Toronto, refers in the *New York Times* Magazine, of March 26, 1967, to the vociferous group of intellectuals who are now giving advice on military strategy and reaching for political power through the ADA as the "alienated intellectual elite." He says:

> Among other elites or professions—engineering, law or medicine—mistakes of high magnitude would undermine the practitioner's standing. Not so among the intellectuals. The Intellectual Elite is least answerable for its mistakes, which tends to corrupt it. The mistake is hidden in the bibliography, lost among the footnotes. [p. 76.]

Henry Steele Commager, another of our alienated intellectuals, testified at the Senate hearings before Senator Fulbright in support of Fulbright's position. Professor Commager said:

> It is my feeling that we do not have the resources, material, intellectual or moral, to be at once an American power, a European power, and an Asian power . . . It is not our duty to keep peace throughout the globe, to put down aggression wherever it starts up, to stop the advance of communism or other isms which we may not approve of. It is primarily the responsibility of the United Nations to keep the peace . . . If that organization is not strong enough to do the job we should perhaps bend our major energies to giving her the necessary authority and the tools.[12]

Does Professor Commager mean what he says that we should give the United Nations the necessary authority to keep the peace, that we should make U Thant our deputy Secretary of State and provide the United Nations with the tools to keep the peace? In the Council of the United Nations Russia has an absolute veto. In the Assembly over a third of the votes are cast by impotent and infinitesimal sovereignties whose knowledge of world affairs is in rough proportion to their size. Does Professor Commager want us to turn our armies over to that disorganized group?

Senator Fulbright, another alienated intellectual, has written a book accusing the United States of arrogance. Is it arrogance for the United States to enforce international law not for our own selfish interests but in the interest of world peace? We are the only nation in the world capable of that task. Must we allow aggressive power to build up until it thinks itself strong enough to attack us as Japan did at Pearl Harbor? Is it arrogance when we permit ourselves to be lectured

[12] *The Churchman*, April, 1967.

by a Burmese citizen named U Thant, and instead of resenting this criticism encourage and cooperate with him in all his plans for a settlement in the hope that they are not as futile and impractical as they seem to be? Our alienated intellectual elite have no realization that international law, like domestic law, can only exist if there is force behind it. For example, Reverend Eugene Carson Blake, General Secretary of the World Council of Churches, in attacking our attempts to enforce international law in the Orient, comes out with this gem:

"The more force we use the weaker become our best ideals." [13]

These people think we are engaged in a useless fight to establish a democracy in Vietnam. This is like saying that when the police put down a riot in Watts they are trying to establish democracy in that suburb. What we are fighting for is to preserve a principle of international law, without which there is no security for America in the lawless world.

Below the level of the more prominent group of alienated intellectuals we find those in academic circles who are not happy unless they are expressing their hatred of America. The following appeared in the *New York Times* Magazine of March 12, 1967. It was signed by seventeen members of the faculty of a respected institution, Western Reserve University:

> The appalling fact is that, by its actions in Vietnam, the American Government has forfeited any claim to moral superiority over the barbarism against which we are supposedly defending Western civilization. Messrs. Johnson, Rusk and McNamara—not to mention General Westmoreland—stand convicted, by their own words as well as their deeds, of crimes of war and crimes against humanity; and they do not even have the defense of the Nazi leaders at Nuremberg that the international laws against those crimes were ex post facto.

In a letter published in *The New Republic* on March 18, 1967, by a visiting professor at the respected Stanford University, where students apparently encouraged by faculty members did everything they could to insult the Vice President of the United States because he expressed his views before them, we find the following:

> I received calls from faculty members who, before the visit, had been unwilling to endorse the walkout, but who felt after that the only proper protest would have been for 1,700 of us to

[13] *Wall Street Journal,* April 27, 1967, p. 1.

have stood in the auditorium and chanted 'Shame!' for the full hour.

Here we find a new phase of disrespect for law among our alienated intellectuals, the abuse of the right to dissent and the abuse of the freedom of speech. Much as I abhor the days when Senator McCarthy was in power, we did not in those dark times have to hear such nonsense from college professors. Now that they can safely publish their dissenting views without retaliation they have advanced a new doctrine of dissent based on the premise that dissent deserves special consideration, immunity from criticism and the right to shout down persons who disagree with them. In a democratic society dissent is not sacred. Only the right to dissent is sacred. Yet this simple principle of law has not yet been learned by some of the alienated intellectuals on our college faculties.

There is no use arguing with such people. They have no feeling for the fundamental legal principle of freedom of speech; they have no sense of reality. I prefer to dismiss them with a verse from Kipling who was the poetic spokesman for British international policy:

> The poor little street bred people who vapor
> and fume and brag,
> They are lifting their heads in the stillness to
> yelp at the English flag.

I used this quotation before another college audience some time ago. At a small group meeting afterwards I was accused of interfering with freedom of speech of those who sincerely believe that the Vietnamese war was a moral atrocity and an international crime. I replied that I would defend their right to say it was but they ought to defend my right to say they were yelping at the flag. Did I get my point across? The answer is, No. Freedom of speech to them meant more than the right to speak, it meant freedom from harsh criticism; it also included the right to obstruct traffic.

Returning to the principle of international law that I am defending here tonight, i.e. the duty of the United States as the richest and most powerful country in the world to enforce the law against aggressive war, it is my belief that the majority of American citizens of both parties believe in that principle. I think they have learned the lesson that—in our present age—it is the function of a dominant world power to take the lead in establishing world order and enforcing international law, and that a disorderly consensus of bickering lesser powers such as the United Nations cannot now do the job. This role

56 THE GROWTH OF AWARENESS

imposes a costly burden in lives and money. But how much more costly we found it not to defend ourselves against the aggressive attempts of Japan to dominate the Orient until, encouraged by our lack of defenses in the Philippines, Japan felt confident enough of our weakness and irresolution to attack us at Pearl Harbor!

Gilbert and Sullivan were no doubt right when they composed the song "Taking One Consideration With Another, a Policeman's Lot is Not a Happy One."

But we have been forced as the result of the inevitable march of events to choose Vietnam as the place to demonstrate to the world our adamant policy in favor of peace against the uninhibited building up of empires by outside aggression.

I am one of those who believe that if we had not taken our stand in Vietnam, then Korea, which we have built up as one of the few strong economies in the Orient, would have become disillusioned and felt itself in danger. I believe we saved Malaya and Thailand. I believe that the present disorder in China and the growing weakness of the Chinese, heretofore aggressive, would not have taken place had China's onward march through Asia not been stopped in Vietnam.

But whether I am right or wrong, this much is clear: America cannot afford to adopt an irresolute and vacillating policy in international affairs. If we do, our enemies can never be convinced that we mean what we say. Harry Truman was forced to risk a war with Russia in order to convince the Russians that we meant what we said about Berlin. Kennedy had to risk an atomic war in order to convince Russia that we meant what we said about Russia maintaining atomic bases in the Western Hemisphere. The war in Vietnam, disheartening and bloody as it is, has far fewer risks. The greatest risk is to apologize and back down.

Our alienated intellectuals do not have the courage to say we should withdraw, a position I would respect however wrong it may be, Instead they think it is their function to stir up all the dissatisfaction and dissent they can and to do their best to portray the United States to the world as a stupid and brutal power unnecessarily killing thousands of people and burning villages. Their military advice is to stop shooting the enemy on the theory that if we did the gratitude of the enemy would be so great as not to take advantage of us.

It may be true that generals are not safe political advisers. But that does not mean that alienated intellectuals are safe military advisers.

Since the days of Secretary Dulles and the McCarthy era we have made one giant step toward the establishment of international law. In those days we felt it was our duty to oppose Communism with a big C. We were afraid of the infiltration of ideas. We encouraged wars of liberation in East Germany and in Hungary which were in essence revolts against the established sovereignty. Then when the citizens of a communist country did revolt, as they did in Hungary, we promptly let them down.

It is not the function of international law to reform independent sovereignties and to conduct war on Communism or any other ism. For the first time since the World War we have affirmatively recognized that principle. We are bending every effort to establish relations with communist powers. We conceive it today as our duty to get along with them. We are willing to recognize a communist government in Vietnam if it is not achieved by aggressive military force from the outside. We have stopped our policy of trying to inhibit the flow of radical ideas. This is a far cry from 1950 when the Government spent hundreds of thousands of dollars to convict Owen Lattimore because he had pointed out that the Chinese revolutionary government was a force to reckon with and to get along with. Neither an international policeman nor a local policeman should be concerned with arresting people because they had false ideas of government. If we succeed in outlawing aggressive war, then we need not be concerned with whether or not communism spreads by non-violent means.

The function of law, both domestic and international, is to suppress disorder and aggressive conduct which disrupt the processes of peaceful change and adjustment. If international law fails in this function there is no limit to the spread of disorder and violence and eventual war.

Our responsibility as guardian of the principle of international law will be a costly burden to us but it is nonsense to say that we do not have the resources to carry it. The burden on England in the 19th Century was infinitely more costly in terms of the economy of that time. To say that we do not have the resources to enforce international law against aggression and at the same time take care of poverty at home is nonsense. We not only had the resources to fight the Second World War, but we actually got rich in doing so. We went into the war in a period of depression; we came out of the war richer in terms of productive capacity than we had ever been before.

It is, after all, productive capacity that is the real wealth of a nation. Since World War II our economy has grown in terms of goods and services to produce $547 billion in 1960 and thence up to $750 billion in 1966. It is predicted that in 1970 our national product will amount to over a trillion. In terms of percentage of the gross national product our defense budget was costing us as of January of this year less than it did in 1960 when there was no Vietnamese war. The defense budget was 9.1 per cent of our gross national product in 1961. It had fallen to 8.9 per cent at the beginning of 1967. We have today, in spite of the war in Vietnam, more production—and a greater share of our production—to allocate to the war on poverty than we did five years ago.

There is no reason why we cannot carry our international burden and at the same time promote economic progress at home. We must do both. Today there is no safety at home in a lawless world. If we allocate the tremendous power of productive expansion with which the modern scientific revolution has endowed us to these two ends, the international law of the 20th century will be the gift of the United States to the world.

Law and Conflict: Some Current Dilemmas

HARDY C. DILLARD

Before launching into my subject, I would like to make an observation which I believe can be linked with the man in whose honor these lectures are named.

Recently I had the privilege of serving the government by acting as a member of the five-man committee charged with advising the Secretary of the Air Force concerning conditions at the Air Force Academy and the reasons for the widely publicized cheating episode of 1965. The Honor Code was presumably operative, why the breakdown?

Reflecting on my observations, I have come to see how stultifying a sense of tradition can be when uninformed by certain attributes and how significant it can be when these attributes are a felt part of the environment. This led me to reflect on the role of individuals in molding traditions and fashioning them to the higher ideals of a profession or a society.

Which brings me to John Randolph Tucker, grandson of St. George Tucker of William and Mary and son of Henry St. George Tucker who is credited with beginning the Honor System at the University of Virginia.

The Air Force Academy had no heroes. It did not even have a cemetery. It could not boast a Grant, a Lee, an Eisenhower, a MacArthur, a Nimitz or a Halsey. It could not even claim Arnold or Spaatz.

This is the John Randolph Tucker Lecture delivered at the School of Law, Washington and Lee University, on April 22, 1967. The word "dilemma" in the title is not used in its strict logical sense but only to suggest a perplexing problem.

It is not the abstraction but the living image that fires the imagination as every poet knows. In default of personified ideals you are reduced to merely quantitative symbols of excellence. And they are not enough. They are not enough because they speak only of the ends achieved and not the way of achieving them.

Think for a moment how much poorer our judiciary would be without its Marshalls, Holmeses, Cardozos, Brandeises and Learned Hands. Think how much poorer the whole bar would be without its John W. Davises, its Newton D. Bakers, its Ross Malones and its Lewis Powells to mention only some of your graduates.

When John Randolph Tucker took the side of the Chicago anarchists in the 1880's[1] and replied to his critics, "I do not defend anarchy. I defend the Constitution,"[2] he was speaking the kind of language and manifesting the kind of conduct which ennobles a profession by vivifying its ideals. Ideas which appeal to our reason are, of course, important; it is when ideas are wedded to ideals and identified with a vivid person that they become the stuff of a great tradition.

It is for me a distinct privilege to be on a lecture series which began with John W. Davis, in whose office I once worked, at a University which nourished my father, and in honor of one of those who helped to create your fine tradition.

So much by way of preface.

I turn now to my subject. It is a large one, and I fear it may appear to you to be overly abstract.[3]

I

Law as Value Oriented

Conflict involves both facts and attitudes about facts. Facts may be conveniently divided into "first-order" facts which are the raw

---

[1] Spies v. Illinois, 123 U.S. 131 (1887). The case involved a petition for a writ of error to the Supreme Court of Illinois. The writ was not allowed on the ground that the decision of the Federal question was clearly right. Mr. Tucker represented all three petitioners. The summary of his argument reproduced at 143-55 of 123 U.S. and especially his discussion of the scope of the fourteenth amendment and the argument of Benjamin F. Butler at 157-67, counsel for two of the petitioners, who were aliens, are particularly illuminating and interesting in light of contemporary problems.

[2] Quoted in Davis, *John Randolph Tucker, The Man and His Work*, in the JOHN RANDOLPH TUCKER LECTURES 1949-1952, 15 (1952).

[3] While I have modified the text to some extent for publication, I have not attempted to avoid the kind of informal diction that is appropriate in a lecture. Bearing in mind that the audience was not exclusively composed of law students and lawyers, I have included some matter that may seem elementary.

data pressing upon our five senses and "second-order" or "cultural" facts, which are the propositions believed in by men. It is hardly novel to suggest that first-order facts, filtered through the gateway of our senses, are to some extent (in a manner not clearly understood) conditioned by what goes on in our minds including the kinds of values to which we subscribe.[4] It is a first-order fact that I am speaking in Lee Chapel at noon today; it is a second-order fact that what I may say will doubtless appeal to some, disenchant others and weary many.

Arguments over events and first-order facts lend themselves to an answer keyed to truth. That is true which "corresponds" to reality as, for instance, that I have five fingers or that yesterday the Dodgers beat the Giants or that Robert Huntley will succeed Charles Light as Dean of the Washington and Lee Law School. We can say these things are true because we have a ready method of measuring the accuracy of the assertion by reference to a conventional standard.

When we shift our focus from events and facts to attitudes and motives which are subjective, to causes which are complex, and to consequences which are not always foreseeable, a simple analysis keyed to the "correspondence theory" of truth is inadequate. This is because there is no simple yardstick by which they may be measured.

Is euthanasia or birth control good or bad? Should we permit *Lady Chatterly's Lover* to be published or not? Is Martin Luther King saint or sinner? Is the open housing section of the Civil Rights Bill to be applauded or condemned? Is our involvement in South Viet Nam morally right or wrong?

Questions of this kind are not "truth" oriented but "value" oriented. The answer is not that they are true or false but that they are good or bad. And the criteria for judging what is good or bad differ markedly from the yardsticks which measure what is true or false.

I mention this because at the very outset of any understanding of law and conflict it is important to recognize that law is value oriented. In this respect it differs from both medicine and engineering. Except in extreme cases the doctor does not bother to ask whether health is good or bad; he simply assumes it is good. And the engineer

---

[4]Northrop, *Contemporary Jurisprudence and International Law*, 61 YALE L.J. 623 (1952) reprinted as *The Method and Neurophysiological Basis of Physical Anthropology* in NORTHROP, THE COMPLEXITY OF LEGAL AND ETHICAL EXPERIENCE 102 (1959). The thrust of Professor Northrop's analysis is to show that the relationship between perceived facts and overt behavior is not adequately accounted for by mere conditioned reflexes. See also, SIR JOHN ECCLES, THE BRAIN AND THE PERSON (Australia—THE BOYER LECTURES) esp. at 8, § 43-45 (1965). *Cf.* Boulding, THE IMAGE 47-63 (1961).

does not question whether traffic is good or bad; he simply assumes that if you want a bridge to span a river it should be a bridge that will sustain traffic.

This difference between a value oriented and non-value oriented discipline is critically important. Medicine is concerned with the application of principles of anatomy to the human body and its ailments; engineering is concerned with the application of the principles of physics and mechanics to physical nature. Each finds a concrete focus in the human body and the land, the sea and the air. It would be naive to assume that these foci are altogether tractable, but they are surely more tractable than the objects dealt with by law.

Law's focus is, in a sense, intangible. Concerned as it is with the relationships between human beings, its function is to so order these relationships as to maximize values that are worthwhile. Because its focus is intangible and value ridden, its complexities are many.

Conspicuous among the values which law seeks to promote is "Order" both in the domestic and international arenas. The antithesis of order is "caprice"—"arbitrary" action. A society which is not animated and sustained by a sense of order is not a society at all, but a rabble. But in a democracy, "Order" is not an exclusive value. You can compel order by fiat as Hitler and Mussolini did. What we seek in a democracy is not merely order but good order, that is, order directed to a purpose. What purpose?

Many answers have been given throughout history, each located in a theory of the good life which ethical scholars and leaders have supported with reason and proclaimed with fervor. Conspicuous among recent descriptions of democracy's purpose is simply "the realization of human dignity in a commonwealth of mutual deference."[5] Its supreme value is the promotion of the dignity and worth of the individual. Hence a democracy is a commonwealth of mutual deference where there is full opportunity to mature talent into socially creative skill free from artificially imposed and non-rational discrimination. This is the exact opposite of the ugly values symbolized by the Swastika of Nazi Germany. It is asserted to be the opposite of the values promoted by the symbol of the hammer and the sickle.[6]

---

[5]Lasswell and McDougal, *Legal Education and Public Policy: Professional Training in the Public Interest,* 52 YALE L.J. 203, 217 (1934) reprinted in McDougal and Associates, STUDIES IN WORLD PUBLIC ORDER 42, 59 (1960).

[6]WELDON, STATES AND MORALS—A STUDY IN POLITICAL CONFLICTS esp. at 165-75 (1947). While calling attention to the difficulties in terminology, Professor Weldon nevertheless discusses the different moral implications flowing from

If this is a valid democratic postulate, what is the function of law? The quick and easy answer is that its function is to promote these values. It is not an end in itself; it is not something to worship. Its function is to serve in such fashion as to justify its purposes.

Many people today fear that it is misfunctioning both domestically and internationally. They say its minimum function is to provide order yet look at what is happening. There were riots in Watts and surely more to come; there was open defiance by Wallace and Barnett; there is the preachment of civil disobedience by Martin Luther King. Has not respect for law diminished causing a loosening of the whole fiber of our society?

And if we turn from the domestic to the international arena, are we not beset by doubts and misgivings? Was "law" an operative factor in controlling State behavior in any of the crises of recent times?

In addressing myself to these large questions, I should, at the outset, impose a disclaimer. My purpose is not to analyze in depth the many disputes, at home and abroad, which now plague us. I propose only to lift out certain features which seem to me to be significant.

II

Civil Disobedience

Our domestic doubts and misgivings centering on "civil disobedience" are, of course, not new. Any competent historian would plead for a sense of perspective. He would remind us of the Stamp Act revolt, of Shay's Rebellion, of the Whiskey Rebellion, of the abortive revolution in New England at the time of the War of 1812; of the violent suffragette movement accompanied by many symbolic burnings of the Constitution and of numerous other instances in our brief history, including the unlamented days of Prohibition, when disobedience was deplored yet frequently vindicated by the march of subsequent events.

One way to analyze the question of civil disobedience dispassionately is to specify four basic attitudes we may have toward government and law.[7] Let me tick them off rapidly.

an "organic" (collectivist) type state and a "mechanical" one in light of "organic," "consent" and "force" theories. His restrained conclusion calls for the need to avoid dogmatic crusading attitudes, keyed to political and moral theories.

[7] I recall reading an analysis of this kind keyed to the problem of governments-in-exile in World War II written, I believe, by Arthur Goodhart. The reference eludes me.

(1) We may recognize the authority of government and obey the law. This is what most of us do, most of the time.

(2) We may recognize the authority of government but disobey the law. This is what most of us do some of the time. (As for instance when we double park.)

(3) We may refuse to recognize the authority of government yet obey the law. In this instance we obey sheerly from fear, as most Frenchmen and Belgians obeyed the Germans during the occupation. This is incipient rebellion.

(4) We may refuse to recognize the authority of government and disobey the law. This is open rebellion. This is the shot fired on Fort Sumter.

Despite the weird fulminations of some extremists and the utter lawlessness of the Watts' type rioting, it is yet clear that our civil disturbances have not reached the point of challenging the legitimate authority of government. Activist protests against social and economic conditions entailing the destruction of property are illegal by virtue of the destruction rather than the protest and thus fall short of insurrection or rebellion. This suggests that while lawlessness is to be deplored legislation directed against it which entails a repression of protests is likely to be misdirected. The patch must be commensurate with the hole.

Which brings us to our second point. Is it ever morally justifiable to break a law and to urge that it be broken?

This question is as old as Socrates, indeed, older, as the Antigone of Sophocles reveals. While I do not have time to develop it fully I will yet venture the opinion that the answer depends on two related factors. The first is directed to the purpose of disobeying and the second to its asserted need. If its purpose is to vindicate democratic values as opposed to those of the totalitarians, then it cannot be condemned out of hand. But this is only a necessary and not a sufficient condition. There must also be a need. This means that there must be no viable alternative to defiance—as through the ballot box or through the orderly processes of law—to achieve the purpose. The evaluation of the need is empirically oriented. If Negro voting rights are indeed frustrated and there is, in fact, as opposed to theory, no legal redress, then defiance may well be justified when it would not be justified otherwise.[8] To this last statement one qualification needs

---

[8] A sophisticated analysis would, of course, require a discussion of many other facets of the problem. The literature is extensive. For some recent discussions see,

to be added. The exercise of power whether in enforcing or defying law should always conform to the overriding principle of proportionality which, ever since Aristotle, has been considered a cardinal precept of justice.

Related but quite separate is the fundamental point that "protests" involving no defiance of law are a permissible form of persuasion in any society sincerely committed to democratic tenets. Although "freedom of speech" and "freedom of assembly" are neither ends in themselves nor absolutes, they are yet fundamental to the working of the democratic process, if for no other reason than that the alternative (*i.e.,* suppression) entails a denial of one of the basic values to which the society is committed. This assertion invites a corollary not always adequately appreciated. If the democratic process is rested on the assumption that freedom of expression contributes to the "rational" ordering of a good society, then protests impeding the "rational" exposition of a point of view (*i.e.,* speech) constitute a denial of one of the basic grounds for the exercise of freedom itself. Overzealous protestors either in defense or in opposition to our involvement in South Viet Nam would do well to bear this in mind. Surely "persuasion by protest" is purchased at too high a price when it obstructs or even impedes the right to speak and be heard. Such protests qualify for the wry comment that their advocates are all in favor of freedom of speech—they are only against its exercise.

III

The International Arena—Preliminary

So much for our domestic dilemmas. Permit me to turn to the international arena.

There can be little doubt that a conflict of values underlies the tensions between our Western heritage and those of our Communist adversaries. Its roots are deep. We have a dual inheritance—from Greece an instinct for freedom and from Rome an appreciation of order. We have attempted to weld the two in a democratic society, committed through flexibly designed institutions, to the principle of "ordered liberty." Our historic experience embraces the gradual

---

Burke Marshall, *The Protest Movement and the Law* 51 VA. L. REV. 785 (1965); Powell, *A Lawyer Looks at Civil Disobedience* 23 WASH. & LEE L. REV. 205 (1966); Frankel, *The Morality of Civil Disobedience* in THE LOVE OF ANXIETY AND OTHER ESSAYS 172 (1966); LAW AND PHILOSOPHY 3-105 (Hook, ed. 1964); *Walzer, The Obligation to Disobey,* 77 ETHICS 163 (1967); *Prosch, Toward an Ethics of Civil Disobedience,* 77 ETHICS 176 (1967). The indiscriminate lumping together of "revolutions," "protest movements," "ordinary criminality," and "civil disobedience" should, of course, be avoided.

erosion of feudalism, the rise of the Modern State System, the temp-
ering of the industrial revolution and the hoped-for elimination of
religious wars in inter-state relations.

The same experience has not been duplicated in Russia, Asia or
Africa where transitions have been abrupt and the break with tradition more violent. It follows that we share no international memories which might shape our concepts, condition our attitudes and
channel our rhetoric to common purposes.[9]

Thus the incidences of conflict are not over facts alone or even
"interests" as that word is usually meant. To a much greater extent
than in the domestic area, they are over attitudes about facts and
the values attributed to the assertion of interests.

Does this mean that "law" has only limited utility in the international arena or that when invoked it is merely an empty facade
masking the cruder play of power politics?

There are those who seem to think so and to say so. Or rather,
to be more accurate, there are those who concede a limited utility to
law in the world of foreign trade and commerce but believe it a useless
and possibly even an undesirable instrument where deeper values
are at stake. This, of course, is the attitude of the "real politik" school
and even of such perceptive scholars as George Kennan and Hans
Morgenthau.[10] It is implicit also in the general attitude of Dean
Acheson.[11]

Proponents of international law are usually quick to denounce this
view claiming it is shortsighted and inaccurate. Yet it reflects an attitude widely shared not only among the public but in some government circles. It is a demonstrable fact, for instance, that in the Senate
hearings on our involvement in South Viet Nam allusions to "law"

---

[9]*Cf.* Brogan, *Conflicts Arising Out of Differing Governmental and Political
Institutions,* in THE CHANGING ENVIRONMENT OF INTERNATIONAL RELATIONS 37-64
(Brookings Lectures, 1956).

[10]KENNAN, AMERICAN DIPLOMACY 1900-1950, at 95, 96 (1951); MORGENTHAU, IN
DEFENSE OF THE NATIONAL INTEREST 101 (1951) and MORGENTHAU, POLITICS AMONG
NATIONS 64 (1948). It should be stated that Kennan's views were somewhat modified
in his REALITIES OF AMERICAN FOREIGN POLICY (1954). Much of the dispute centers
on the ambiguities lurking in such elusive terms as "power" and "interest" to say
nothing of varying views as to the meaning of "law." The matter is discussed
generally in Dillard, *Some Aspects of Law and Diplomacy,* Hague Academy of
Int. Law RECUEIL DES COURS 449-534 (1957). Viewed as a protest against a sterile
manipulation of norms divorced from the realities of the international political
and social structure the writings of Kennan, Morgenthau and Acheson deserve a
degree of credit not sufficiently appreciated by some critics.

[11]Acheson, *The Lawyer's Path to Peace,* 42 VIRGINIA QUARTERLY REVIEW 337
(1966), and see *infra* note 17.

while not altogether absent were quite minimal and even misdirected.[12] The debate has now become a heated one among legal scholars, and the Legal Adviser has, of course, fortified the position of the government by two elaborate memoranda which are themselves the focus of much of the dispute.[13] Nevertheless, it is probably true to assert that "law" viewed either as a body of restraints or as a body of permissive doctrine appeared to be only tangentially significant.

In defense of the real politik view is the fact that while it narrows the scope of law it yet safeguards it against purely polemical uses. It thus blunts at the outset the accusation frequently made that legal arguments advanced in support of national policies are rationalizations cloaking the play of power politics. "Law" is not abused if it is irrelevant.

Nevertheless, this view is believed to be too restrictive, partly because it ignores the "order creating" or "constitutive" function of law and partly for other reasons to be suggested presently.

IV

A "Typology" of Conflict

A crude "typology" of conflict, borrowed from an analysis by Anatole Rapoport, might help to locate the role of law. Using this approach, we can detect three major types of conflict.

---

[12]Since the United States was already committed, it is perhaps understandable that the legal issue, viewed as a possible inhibition on the original commitment, was not a major subject of inquiry. Nevertheless, it is surprising to note that the Index to the Senate Hearings contains only one specific reference to International Law. Scattered references are, of course, made to the Geneva Accords, the Charter of the U.N. and the SEATO Treaty. Dean Rusk relied heavily on the latter treaty as an "obligation that has from the outset guided our actions in South Viet Nam." *Hearings on S.2793 Before the Senate Committee on Foreign Relations*, 89th Cong., 2nd Sess., pt. 1, at 567 (1966). The SEATO Treaty is significant, but it is not believed to be the basic legal justification for rendering military assistance to South Viet Nam.

[13]The second memorandum entitled *The Legality of U.S. Participation in the Defense of Viet Nam* (Mar. 4, 1966) is reprinted in 54 DEPT. OF STATE BULLETIN 474 (Mar. 28, 1966). The memorandum is vigorously criticized in a point by point analysis in FALK AND FRIED, VIET NAM AND INTERNATIONAL LAW, AN ANALYSIS OF THE LEGALITY OF THE U.S. MILITARY INVOLVEMENT (1967). This book by the Consultative Council of the Lawyers Committee on American Policy Towards Vietnam is the most thorough single treatment from the opponent's point of view. The most thorough and elaborately documented treatment in defense of the legality of U.S. involvement is McDougal, Moore and Underwood,, *The Lawfulness of United States Assistance to the Republic of Viet Nam*, 112 CONG. REG. 13232-33 (daily ed., June 22, 1966) and 112 CONG. REC. 14943 (daily ed., July 16, 1966) reprinted in 5 DUQUESNE UNIV. LAW REV. 235-352 (1967). See also, exchange between Professors Alford and Falk in *Legality of United States Participation in the Defense of Viet Nam: A Symposium*, 75 YALE L.J. 1109, 1122 (1966). The symposium also includes a reprint of the Memorandum of the Legal Adviser, Department of State, at 1085.

First, there is the "fight" type, although the term might be considered extreme. The "actors" are not operating within an accepted system of ordered relations; indeed, they are struggling either to sustain or overthrow the system. At best, the environment is characterized by a feeling of instability and, at worst, by one of hostility. Labor relations in the nineteenth century might represent a mild form of this type of conflict. Wars, revolutions and insurrections furnish more dramatic examples. The object of the fight is to weaken the enemy, even to harm him. Apparently, there are many, like the late Mr. John Foster Dulles, who consider our relations with the Soviet Union and the People's Republic of China as falling in this category.

Second is the "game" or "contest" type. In striking contrast to the fight type, the object is not to defend or overthrow a system but to operate within it. Indeed, without the system the "game" could not go on. The environment is relatively stable, and the object of the contest is not to weaken or harm an opponent although it might involve outmaneuvering him. Trade and commercial dealings fall in this category. Paraphrasing a remark of Boulding's the first type would have the actors saying, "If you do something nasty to me, I will do something nasty to you," whereas in the second type they would be inclined to say, in keeping with a spirit of reciprocity, "If you do something nice to me, I will do something nice to you."

Third there is the "debate" type. Here the object is not to overturn the system or to operate within it but to establish it by altering attitudes and beliefs. As Rapoport puts it:

> "The object of a debate is to change the opponent's image, not to prove his statements wrong. The opposing views in a genuine debate stem not from different notions of what the facts are, nor even from different inferences drawn from the facts. The opposing views stem largely from different criteria for *selecting what to see, what to be aware of.*"[14]

---

[14]RAPOPORT, FIGHTS, GAMES AND DEBATES 300 (1960). A cursory analysis of the role of law in this type of "conflict" has been eliminated from the printed version of the lecture. The matter is touched on in Dillard, *Conflict and Change: The Role of Law,* 1963 PROC., AM. SOC. INT'L L. 50, 61-67. Law in the developing nations is needed perhaps less as a device for settling specific disputes than as an ordering device to help bring about better conditions of political stability. It may be suggested that American conceptions of law are dominated too much by the "fuss fallacy"; by the image of third-party judgment and by the notion that "law" is merely the aggregate of specific "laws." An appreciation of the utility of legal "standards" as opposed to narrow "rules" is an antidote to these notions. I have attempted to deal with this aspect of the problem in Dillard, *supra* note 10 at 477-98.

Our relations with the developing nations fall under this type. There are, of course, many variants of each type and even other types, as, for instance, the kind of systems represented by a military alliance, a business partnership or a happy marriage where attitudes are based less on calculated reciprocity than on mutual cooperation toward desired ends.

Reverting to the three major types, it is too readily assumed that law plays no role in the first type which brute power is supposed to dominate; or even in the third type which is thought to be the exclusive prerogative of diplomacy. If this view is sound, the role of law in the international arena is reduced merely to regulating relations within a system. This is an important function, and there is little doubt that without law the system would not work. But is law so limited?

I think not. And it is my submission that the art of statesmanship and diplomacy can both be aided if the role of law is better understood. For clearly in our relations with our Communist adversaries it would be well if the first type of conflict were reduced to the second and if in our relations with the developing nations which, to repeat, is where the third type is located, the debate took a turn favorable to the values and institutional systems of the West.

The failure adequately to recognize the role of law in the first and third types is traceable, I believe, to intellectual confusion about the meaning of law itself.

V

Controlling vs. Affecting State Behavior

Let us take the recognition of the Communist government of China as an example.

Three views are visible. One is that the question is purely one of national discretion to be exercised as arbitrarily as the nation chooses. Under this view, law is said to be totally irrelevant. The second view is that law is relevant, and we have breached it. The third view is that law is relevant, and we have not breached it.[15]

---

[15] The argument that there is a "duty" to recognize the government of another state when it satisfies certain objective criteria is rested on the assumption that the failure to do so is a form of intervention, since it is an attempt to influence the form of government, economy, culture, or ideological presuppositions of another state. This is said to be contrary to the basic assumption of the International Legal Order which, ever since the Peace of Westphalia, has been rested on a concept of state sovereignty. According to this view, the role of international law is concerned exclusively with the external relations of states which by definition excludes internal matters, including in particular contending ideological or re-

The same stuttering dialogue is heard with respect to the Cuban missile crisis of 1962, the use of force in the Dominican Republic in 1965 and our current involvement in South Viet Nam.

One, though by no means the only, source of intellectual difficulty lies in the failure to distinguish between law as a body of restraints designed to constrain the bad man and law as a guide to action designed to assist the puzzled man. It is the confusion bred of failing to distinguish between a legal duty and a legal liberty or privilege.

Another source of difficulty lies in a concept which considers "law" as a mere body of autonomous rules abstracted from the institutional apparatus which not only gives it authority but meaning. I shall have more to say about this later.

Reverting to the recognition of the Communist Government of China, it is, I think, clear that although the decision to recognize or not is discretionary its exercise cannot be altogether arbitrary if, for no other reason, than that it is attended by serious legal consequences involving, among many others, title to property, the capacity to sue and the application of the Act of State Doctrine. These consequences are felt restraints on the government and affect its exercise of discretion.

Another way of putting the matter is to say that what the law fails to prohibit it permits. This is clearly seen in the domestic realm. Each of us may be free to enter a contract or not as we choose, or to vote or to strike or to play an electric guitar. This does not mean that the exercise of our freedom is unaffected by law or made in a legal vacuum.

VI

Recent International Disputes—Preliminary

Turning to Cuba, the Dominican Republic and South Viet Nam, the issue is likewise centered on whether the requirements of international law including in particular the express provisions of the Charter of the United Nations are absolute proscriptions on the choice of the military instrument or whether the language of the norms and

---

ligious movements. *Cuius regio eius religio.* One of the best brief statements of this position, echoes of which are heard in the Cuban, Dominican and South Vietnamese conflicts, will be found in Wright, *The Status of Communist China,* 11 JOURN. OF INT. AFF. 171 (1957). For a brief analysis of the varying criteria for recognition, see Dillard, *The United States and China: The Problem of Recognition* 44 YALE REV. 180-196 (1955). For a comprehensive bibliography including the problem of representation in the U.N., see Assn. of the Bar of the City of New York, *The International Position of Communist China,* HAMMARSKJOLD FORUM No. V, 73-113 (1965).

the expectations aroused permit an element of choice including the unilateral use of force. A subsidiary but by no means irrelevant factor is who is to say what the norms mean.

Time does not permit a detailed analysis of these disputes, each of which has unique features. Nevertheless, and at the risk of over-simplifying, I shall try to show why I believe the Charter and the requirements of international law have not been breached by our use of force, at least in the Cuban and South Vietnamese conflicts.

The critical norms are contained in Articles 2(4) and 51 of the Charter. The former states quite explicitly that members:

"...shall refrain in their international relations from the threat or use of force against the territorial integrity or political independence of any state, or in any other manner inconsistent with the Purposes of the United Nations."

Characterized as the "corner stone" of the Charter system, it is said to register the resolute will of the framers to "abolish the scourge of war." It is asserted to be a clear, definite proscription.[16]

Article 51 appears, however, to qualify the prohibition. It stipulates that:

"Nothing in the present Charter shall impair the inherent right of individual or collective self-defense if an armed attack occurs against a Member of the United Nations until the Security Council has taken the measures necessary to maintain international peace and security...."

In all three crises, a principal argument has centered on the term "armed attack." It is said that this alone can trigger the invocation of the "right" of self-defense.

Here again we have the hard-boiled view that law is irrelevant and a split view among those who say it is relevant. A representative of the first view is Dean Acheson who, speaking to the Cuban crisis declared:

"In my estimation, however, the quarantine is not a legal issue or an issue of international law as these terms should be understood. Much of what is called international law is a body of

[16]BRIERLY, THE LAW OF NATIONS 414 (6th ed. 1963). Henkin, *Force, Intervention and Neutrality in Contemporary International Law*, 1963 PROCEEDING, AM. SOC. INT'L LAW 147, 148, 167; Henkin, *International Law and the Behavior of Nations*, Hague Academy of Int'l Law, RECUEIL DES COURS 175, 204 (1965). The relative weight to be given Arts. 2(4) and 51 of the Charter has been vigorously disputed. For a view opposing that of Professor Henkin, see McDougal *Remarks*, 1963 PROCEEDINGS, AM. SOC. INT'L LAW, 163-65. The problem is discussed extensively in McDOUGAL and FELICIANO, LAW AND MINIMUM WORLD PUBLIC ORDER (1961); BOWETT, SELF-DEFENSE IN INTERNATIONAL LAW (1958); STONE, LEGAL CONTROLS OF INTERNATIONAL CONFLICT (1954) and in many other works.

ethical distillation, and one must take care not to confuse this distillation with law."

and again:

"I must conclude that the propriety of the Cuban quarantine is not a legal issue. The power, position and prestige of the United States had been challenged by another state; and law simply does not deal with such questions of ultimate power— power that comes close to the sources of sovereignty."[17]

I do not think it necessary to take this extreme position. As I indicated earlier, there is no need to assume that because law does not *control* state behavior it is therefore irrelevant. There is abundant evidence that our legal posture *affected* even if it did not control the decision-making process.[18]

VII

Cuba

The official U.S. position in the Cuban crisis was that our actions were legally justified under the resolutions of the OAS acting under the Rio Treaty. This resolution recommended members to take measures, including the use of armed force, to deny to Cuba the receipt of military materiel from the Sino-Soviet powers.

In light of this action, it was not thought necessary for the U.S. to rely on Article 51 of the U.N. Charter. Nevertheless, the issue has been hotly debated. Could Article 51 have been legitimately invoked?

I resist the temptation of spelling out all the technical arguments. Fundamentally, those who say "No" rely on a literalist reading of the Charter and a concept of the purposes of Article 2(4), which is almost absolute in its intended prohibition. And they narrowly limit the scope of Article 51. Self-defense, so they assert, does not embrace anticipatory self-defense nor should it. Furthermore, read the words "armed attack" as you will, they cannot be stretched to mean "arming for attack."[19]

I believe this restrictive interpretation, though ably and presuasive-

---

[17]Acheson, *The Cuban Quarantine—Remarks.* 1963 PROCEEDINGS, AM. SOC. INT'L LAW 13, 14.

[18]*Cf.* Chayes, *Law and the Quarantine of Cuba,* 41 FOR. AFF. 550 (1963). It is recognized that ambiguity lurks in the use of the term "legal issue." No doubt Mr. Acheson would concede that law is "relevant." However, it is important to note that "law" is involved even when the decision itself is not legally compelled.

[19]See references n.16 *supra.* See also, Windass, *The Cuban Crisis and World Order* 3 INT'L REL'S 1-15 (1966). For a comprehensive bibliography see, Ass'n of the Bar of the City of New York, *The Inter-American Security System and the Cuban Crisis,* HAMMARSKJOLD FORUM No. III, 73-87 (1964).

ly defended, is not compelled by the Charter and reflects a concept of law that is too narrowly focused on an *ex parte* reading of the norms themselves instead of considering the norms in conjunction with what Pound calls the "legal order," that is, the norms plus the institutional apparatus available for their interpretation and enforcement. The point is oriented jurisprudentially and is concerned in part at least with the delicate problem of determining when norms should be given a precise as opposed to a more flexible meaning.

VIII

The Dominican Republic

The nature of the Dominican dispute centers on whether our dispatch of 400 Marines in 1965, later augmented to 20,000, constituted an illegal act of "intervention" in a purely civil strife. Those who, like A. A. Berle, read the "first-order" facts one way are convinced that our acts were not only politically and strategically justified but also legally permitted. Others, of whom Wolfgang Friedmann is one, disagree both with respect to the facts and the meaning of the applicable norms.[20]

A partial inventory of the items in the conflicting interpretations of fact and law would reveal the following: On the side of justification is a reading of the facts which links the Dominican revolt with antecedent actions of both the USSR and Cuba at the time of the missile crisis in 1962; the announced policies of both governments to encourage if not prosecute "wars of liberation," including a policy by the USSR to support such wars in Latin America, including specifically the Dominican Republic; the guerrilla uprising in Venezuela in 1963; the dispatch of cadres of Dominicans for guerrilla training in both Cuba and Czechoslovakia, the existence of a plan to take over the government by these cadres and the dispatch of an appeal for help to the U.S. Government by a military junta which was the established government and which had been in substantial control of the country for two or three years.

The other side denies that the military junta was in fact the established government and considers the antecedent facts recited above to be irrelevant especially when contrasted with the acts of repression allegedly perpetrated by prior dictatorships. More specifically is the

---

[20]See discussion by Professors Thomas, Berle, Friedmann and Sandifer in Assn. of Bar of the City of New York, *The Dominican Republic Crisis*, HAMMARSKJOLD FORUM No. IX 1-141 (1967). As with other publications in this useful series, a comprehensive bibliography is appended to the working paper and the discussions.

denial that the revolt was either Communist inspired or dominated. According to this view, U.S. intervention, allegedly designed to prevent a Communist take-over, merely succeeded in throttling a legitimate social revolt.

Shifting to the legal side the critical issues do not focus on the original landing of Marines to protect the lives and property of U.S. citizens but on the later buildup and its justification as an act of "self-defense." The issue, already made familiar in the Cuban crisis, was again disputed. The argument that the invocation of self-defense was not justified proceeded on the "plain meaning" of the Charter provisions coupled with the assertion that a direct invasion from a third state was needed to constitute an "armed attack."

It is frequently asserted that international law does not and should not concern itself with civil strife, by which is meant revolts and insurrections inspired and manipulated exclusively within the state. This assertion does not, however, exhaust the inquiry when an appeal for help is registered by the recognized government, a point to be discussed later. In any event the legitimacy of the response is abetted if it can be shown (by no means a simple matter) that the incipient revolt was fomented from outside and that in responding to the request the responding government acted on a good faith interpretation of the facts.

Those who support the position of the United States invoke the legislative history of the Rio Treaty and also the provisions of Article 5 of the NATO Treaty. According to this view, "indirect wars" are sufficient to constitute an armed attack and thus to justify acts of intervention under the privilege of individual and collective self-defense. In contrast, Hungary is said to furnish an example of illegal intervention by the USSR because there was no evidence that the revolt was fomented or aided by any outside source.

The countervailing argument, as already noted, is keyed to an entirely different appreciation of the facts and a narrow concept of self-defense.

There were other legal issues involved including the relative roles of the U.N. and the O.A.S. and the meaning of "enforcement action" under Art. 53 of the U.N. Charter. These need not detain us.

IX

South Viet Nam

The grave concern manifested by the American people over our involvement in South Viet Nam centers principally on its moral, strategic and political aspects. To many thoughtful people the moral posture exhibited by a large and powerful nation bombing a small one appears at once cruel and obscene. And the mood of deep concern is heightened by public confusion over the strategic concepts animating the involvement and the political purposes to which it is directed. In this, as in other areas of dispute, the first-order facts, which include sobering statistical data, are colored by the second-order facts which, to repeat, are a product of the propositions believed in by proponents and critics of our policies.

Embraced in these propositions are certain notions about history and conflict which may be briefly noted.

According to the critics, our "globalistic" policies are stimulated by an exaggerated fear of a monolithic Communism; reveal a misguided reading of history especially the history of Southeast Asia; ignore the transcendent importance of the images believed in by men and assume an arrogance of power bordering on hubris. Basic to this view is the notion that the United States is resurrecting to its own and the world's detriment the ancient concept, with all its attendant evils, of religious wars which cut across national boundaries. It was precisely the function and purpose of the Peace of Westphalia to eliminate this kind of ideological dispute. Furthermore, international order and harmony are better promoted by allowing a free play to social revolutions—even if abetted from outside—since revolutionary movements tend to become less so once power and responsibility are achieved and once the apocalyptic fervor generated by the revolution has spent itself.

The contrary view takes more seriously the Communist threat and would allow more scope for the exercise of responsible power in arresting its spread. Basic to this view is a reading of international political history which sees that a balance of power system which maintained relative peace and security in the Nineteenth Century has now eroded. The United Nations Organization does not supply a collective security system, and there is thus a power vacuum which will be filled by aggressively minded Communist manipulators unless some form of countervailing power is provided. The requirements of a world public order based on a decent regard for human dignity make it politically and strategically imperative that this power be provided. In addition, our purposes are not geared to national aggrandizement, and our credibility is at stake in ways that transcend the issues in Viet Nam.

Putting these large matters aside and turning to "law," what is the nature of the dispute?

It is immediately apparent that some of the arguments advanced in the Cuban and Dominican cases are paralleled in South Viet Nam. The facts, many of which are disputed, center on the nature and extent of the assistance furnished to the Viet Cong by North Viet Nam; the extent to which the National Liberation Front represents the legitimate aspirations of the people and the significance to be attached to the many antecedent facts which gave rise to the Geneva Accords of 1954, the failure to hold elections in 1956 and the implications flowing from that failure. I shall relegate to an appendix references to these conflicting views.

One feature in the South Vietnamese situation which is absent from the others, although it also bears on the issue of recognition, has to do with the international status of South Viet Nam. Those who argue that there was an act of aggression from the North claim that it is sufficient to constitute such aggression that troops and materiel moved across the cease-fire line provided under the Geneva Accords. Their argument is, however, further fortified by the allegation that South Viet Nam is, in fact, an independent state, hence the nature of the conflict is mislabelled when characterized as civil strife. The argument supporting the assertion that South Viet Nam is an independent state finds a parallel in the status of Taiwan, which, in turn, bears on the representation of the Peoples Republic of China in the United Nations. Fundamentally, the argument is that history has overtaken whatever may have been intended at the time of the separation of one component from the other, and that customary criteria are available to demonstrate the existence of an independent South Viet Nam as evidenced by the recognition policies of other governments, participation in international bodies and the establishment of governmental controls over a designated territory.

Opponents of our involvement are not impressed with this argument, claiming that the separation of Viet Nam, which was intended to be provisional, should not strip the conflict of its essentially local character as a fight for control over a single state. Sophisticated arguments, along with many that are questionable, are advanced in support of this view.[21]

My own view inclines me to side rather with those who assert our actions are legally privileged than with those who contend they are legally prohibited. This seems to me so even if we take a "literalist" as opposed to a "liberalist" interpretation of the Geneva Accords, the

[21]See *supra* note 13. See also Appendix: BIBLIOGRAPHICAL NOTE ON SOUTH VIET NAM, compiled with the assistance of Professor John Moore and Mr. Jeffrey Howard (research assistant).

SEATO Treaty and the United Nations Charter. Furthermore, it seems to be so whether we characterize the tragic conflict as civil strife or not. The chief weakness in the opposing argument is rested in what might be called, somewhat sententiously, the "fallacy of the misplaced category."

The argument that our military involvement is "illegal" is rested on the assumption that it is contaminated by its purpose, which is said to be to arrest the spread of Communism. This is alleged to be not only contrary to customary international law but also a clear violation of Article 2(4). Under this view, the invocation of Art. 51 or the SEATO Treaty (which is surbordinate to the Charter) is alleged to be specious and the ungracious sequel is sometimes suggested that those who disagree are debasing "law" by allowing national bias to influence an "objective" analysis of law's clear meaning and intended reach.

Wherein lies the fallacy? It lies, I submit, in placing in the same category alleged breaches by South Vietnamese with the use of force by the North Vietnamese. Let me explain.

Let us assume *arguendo* that the National Liberation Front represents the aspirations of many people in South Viet Nam; that the Viet Cong is not merely a tool of Hanoi but the legitimate arm of the N.L.F. and that the genesis of the conflict antedates the Geneva Accords by many years. It still would not follow that our involvement was legally proscribed. Why?

The answer lies in the underlying purposes of both Article 2(4) of the U.N. Charter and the most critically important articles of the Geneva Accords which proscribed the use of force by either side.[22] Even the "literalists" concede that Article 2(4) applies to Viet Nam even though not a member of the U.N. And everyone concedes that the North has invoked the Geneva Accords in its dispute with the

---

[22]Article 1 established a "provisional military demarcation line"; article 11 provided for a "simultaneous cease-fire," and article 24 provided *inter alia* that "the armed forces of each party shall respect the demilitarized zone and the territory under the control of the other party." In fairness, it should be said that article 19 (much relied upon by critics of our involvement) provided that "no military base under the control of a foreign state may be established in the regrouping zone of either party; the two parties shall ensure that the zones assigned to them do not adhere to any military alliance and are not used for the resumption of hostilities or to further an aggressive policy." The provisions of the Geneva Accords are printed in the appendix to Falk and Fried, VIETNAM AND INTERNATIONAL LAW: AN ANALYSIS OF THE LEGALITY OF THE U.S. MILITARY INVOLVEMENT (1967) cited *supra* note 13 and in *Background Information Relating to South East Asia and Vietnam,* Committee on For. Rels., U.S. Senate 89th Cong. 1st Sess., 28-42 (Jan. 14, 1965).

South. The central purpose of both instruments was and remains the containment of the unilateral use of force.

Now the one big fact which emerges from the mass of other facts is that at no time did the government of Saigon mount an attack against the North or initiate any kind of aggression whether direct or indirect against the government of Hanoi. No one has contended that its use of force was other than in its own defense. Exactly the reverse is true of the use of subversion and force by the North. Despite some disagreement over the extent and timing of the infiltration, it is yet not denied that it occurred in substantial amounts prior to any substantial buildup of United States forces.[23]

Which brings us to the main point. Surely it is disingenuous to assert that the failure to consult about elections in 1954-55 or even the failure to hold them in 1956 or that some other alleged breach of some other provision of the Geneva Accords can serve as an excuse for the use of force in defiance of the flat prohibitions against its use. The acts are qualitatively in entirely different categories. Neither in the domestic jurisprudence of any state nor in international law has the strange contention been advanced that a breach of a provision of a contract or a treaty, even if deemed "material," furnishes a legitimate (*i.e.*, legal) excuse for the use of aggressive force.[24]

---

[23]Opponents have drawn conflicting inferences from the celebrated Mansfield Report entitled THE VIETNAM CONFLICT: THE SUBSTANCE AND THE SHADOW. Report to the Committee on For. Rels. U.S. Senate 89th Cong. 2d Sess. (Jan. 6, 1966). The report states that as of 1962 U.S. military advisers and service forces totalled approximately 10,000 which by May of 1965 had increased to about 34,000. The report states that at this time "the American force was still basically an advisory organization"(p. 2). By December 1965 American forces had increased to 170,000 troops augmented by 21,000 troops from the Republic of Korea, 1200 men from Australia and 150 from New Zealand.

In December 1965 Viet Cong strength in South Viet Nam was 230,000, approximately double that of 1962. Of this number 73,000 were main force soldiers including regular PAVN (Peoples Army of North Viet Nam). Infiltration of political cadres and soldiers from North Viet Nam through Laos is said to have been going on for many years with estimates placed at 1500 per month.

The best estimates seem to be that prior to 1961, the United States Military Assistance Advisory Group numbered approximately 800-900. In the period from 1959-1961, North Viet Nam infiltrated an estimated 10,000 men into the South. See, McDougal, Moore and Underwood, *The Lawfulness of United States Assistance to the Republic of Viet Nam*, 5 DUQUESNE UNIV. L. REV. 235, 272 (1967) cited *supra* n. 13; Dept. of State, Office of the Legal Adviser, *The Legality of United States Participation in the Defense of Viet Nam*, 75 YALE L.J. 1085, 1098 (1966). U. S. Dept. of of State, VIET-NAM INFORMATION NOTES 3 (Number 3, February 1967).

[24]Perhaps the strongest justification for the use of force would be the contention (as viewed from Hanoi) that the United States intended to prevent any future unification of Viet Nam by the establishment and long-range support of a permanent state hostile to North Viet Nam. While the declared purposes of the

The attempt to classify the struggle as "civil strife," while plausible, is also weak. This is so because the "civil strife" characterization assumes that there is a power struggle for the *whole* of Viet Nam and that it is legitimate for Hanoi to aid the N.L.F. since the N.L.F. is merely a contending faction in an internal thrust for power without reference to any division between North and South. This assumption would make Hanoi the only legitimate government and Saigon a rebellious government seeking to disrupt the unit of the area. Viewed legally, it is significant, however, that the Saigon government has been recognized as a legitimate government by sixty states, has participated in numerous international bodies and has been urged for membership in the U. N. as the representative of a new state. Even the U.S.S.R. has conceded, at least conditionally, the international status of the Saigon government.[25] In striking contrast to this kind of official benediction is the fact that while Hanoi has also been recognized by some governments, at no time has the N.L.F. been accorded any kind of diplomatic recognition.[26] This latter point is significant if we consider the civil strife to be located in South Viet Nam for the exclusive control of South Viet Nam.

Rightly or wrongly, international law, fortified by state practice, does not prohibit aid to a recognized government caught in a civil

---

United States deny this, Hanoi might consider the denial mere window dressing. Under this geopolitical approach the U.S. is the prime enemy, and the alleged breach by Saigon of article 19 would be subordinate and relatively immaterial. However the use of force by North Viet Nam antedated any substantial use of U.S. troops. From the point of view of "containing the use of force" Hanoi's acts, therefore, do not appear to be justified even if inspired by larger geopolitical considerations.

[25]In 1952 the General Assembly by a resolution recognized the Bao Dai government as representing a peace-loving state within the meaning of article 4 of the Charter. This resolution passed by a vote of 40 to 5 with 12 abstentions despite arguments by the Soviet Union that Ho Chi Minh's Democratic Republic of Viet Nam was the only government representing the state. 7 U.N. GAOR, Annexes, Agenda Item No. 19 at 10 (1952); 7 U.N. SCOR, 603rd meeting 9 (1952). Admission was blocked by the Soviet veto.

In 1957 when the issue was again raised the Soviet delegation did not oppose the admission on the ground that it was not a state but instead argued that *both* the Republic of Viet Nam and the Democratic Republic of Viet Nam should be admitted along with the divided States of Korea. See McDougal, Moore and Underwood *supra* note 23 at 9, 25 (1966).

[26]According to U.S. State Department records, North Viet Nam has full diplomatic relations with 24 countries of which 12 belong to what is sometimes referred to as the Communist bloc. *Legal Status of South Viet Nam,* Office of Public Services, Bureau of Public Affairs, U.S. Dept. of State (4/316 865BT). The N.L.F. was not formally created until December 1960. Its few representatives abroad do not claim diplomatic status. Fall, *Viet-Cong—The Unseen Enemy in Viet-Nam,* in Raskin and Fall, THE VIET NAM READER 252, 257, 260 (1965).

strife. It does prohibit aid to non-recognized factions whether labelled guerrilla forces or not.[27]

The civil strife argument for the North is rendered even more vulnerable if account is taken of the principle of "self-determination" also incorporated in the U.N. Charter [Art. 1(2)].

However vague the principle may be, it surely encompasses some notion of freedom to choose a representative government. If this purpose justifies civil strife, then it is difficult to see how the actions of Hanoi and the Viet Cong contribute to its fulfillment. Nor is it an answer to say that the Saigon government may itself be non-representative, or even repressive, unless the purpose of overthrowing it is to institute a regime vindicating the principle of self-determination.

A corollary of the "civil strife" argument also needs to be noted. If it is assumed (contrary to the weight of international law authority as previously shown) that third states may not assist either side *militarily*, then states committed to the principle of an open society are put at a distinct disadvantage over those in which state action is cloaked by secrecy. No doubt, all powerful governments have to some extent used clandestine means to influence weaker governments, but even after allowance is made for such behavior there is yet a difference in

---

[27]This is sometimes described as the classical view and may deserve to be re-examined. Nevertheless it has a long history and is generally conceded to represent the present weight of international authority. Thus Professor Henkin declares: "It is difficult surely to find today a norm forbidding support, even active military support, for the recognized government of a country.... More difficult to justify under traditional law has been military support for rebel causes against established governments." Henkin, *International Law and National Behavior, supra* n.16 at 232. In its Peace Through Deeds, G. A. Res. 380 (V), 5 U.N. GAOR Supp. 20, at 13 (1950) the General Assembly condemned "indirect aggression" and in 1965 by a vote of 109 to 0 with one abstention it declared:

> "direct intervention, subversion, as well as all forms of indirect intervention are contrary" to United Nations principles and are, "consequently, a violation of the Charter." The Assembly therefore declared that "no State shall organize, assist, foment, finance, incite or tolerate subversive, terrorist or armed activities directed to the violent overthrow of the regime of another State, or interfere in civil strife in another State...."

For additional treatment of the issue including both support and criticism of the classical view, see Moore, *The Lawfulness of Military Assistance to the Republic of Viet-Nam*, 61 AM. J. INT'L L. 1, 29 (1967); A. THOMAS and A. THOMAS, JR., NON-INTERVENTION 220, 221 (1956); Falk, *The International Regulation of Internal Violence in the Developing Countries*, 1966 PROCEEDINGS, AM. SOC. INT'L LAW 58, 59; P. HIGGINS, HALL'S INTERNATIONAL LAW 347 (8th ed., 1924); H. KELSEN, PRINCIPLES OF INTERNATIONAL LAW 28-29 (2nd ed., 1966); G. SCHWARZENBERGER, A MANUAL OF INTERNATIONAL LAW 70 (4th ed., 1960); Wright, *International Law and Civil Strife*, 1959 PROCEEDINGS, AM. SOC. OF INT'L. LAW 145-151; Q. WRIGHT, THE ROLE OF INTERNATIONAL LAW IN THE ELIMINATION OF WAR 61 (1961); W. FRIEDMANN, THE CHANGING STRUCTURE OF INTERNATIONAL LAW 265-267 (1964) and L. OPPENHEIM, INTERNATIONAL LAW 659-660 (7th ed., 1952).

kind between such acts and the kinds of subversion and acts of "liberation" represented by the Viet Cong. The difficult factual point would
be to determine when civil strife was indeed indigenous and when
fomented and even directed from a third state.

From this tedious dissection and my reading of the record, I come
to the conclusion that South Viet Nam is in fact an independent state
and that our assistance to the Saigon government was not contrary to
customary international law or the United Nations Charter.

X

Law and Language

It was suggested at the beginning that since "law" is value oriented,
the problem of arriving at a common understanding of our norms is
rendered much more difficult than is revealed in disciplines that are
truth oriented. The difficulty is intensified when the incidences which
the norms attempt to cover are so episodic and disparate. The difficulty
is captured in the wry remark that the algebraic formula $(a + b)^2 =
a^2 + 2ab + b^2$ is true only on condition that "a" is not stronger mind-
ed than "b." The great virtue of mathematical symbols is that they
ruthlessly eliminate, for purposes of their special discourse, all adven-
titious factors including the concrete and particular. Granted we
cannot attain such sterilized precision, how close can we approximate
it? And when is it desirable to do so?

The story of the three disputes which we have considered and the
literature of international law generally reveal varying answers to
the degree of precision which should attend the use of such terms as
"armed attack," "aggression," "threat or use of force," "self-defense"
and many others. Much of the dispute among scholars turns on the
extent to which they believe a high degree of precision is necessary
and good or unnecessary and bad.[28]

---

[28]In his scholarly and perceptive Hague Lectures of 1965 cited *supra* note 16
and in his much quoted address before the American Society of International Law,
Professor Henkin argues vigorously for a literal reading of "armed attack," together
with a heavy emphasis on Article 2(4) and a narrow construction of Art. 51 He does
not wish to weaken the virtues of certainty (deterring bad behavior) provided by
norms that are "clear, unambiguous, subject to proof and not easily open to misinterpretation or fabrication." Henkin (Hague Lectures) *supra* note 16, at 266. He
has the Korean image in mind and the dangers, in a Cuban type situation, of invoking Article 51. In speaking of "intervention," however, he concedes that for the
present

"... it may serve little purpose to insist that Article 2(4) goes farther than
many nations will tolerate. It may be better to leave its authority clear and

"A word," Holmes has reminded us, "is not a crystal, transparent and unchanged, it is the skin of a living thought and may vary greatly in color and content according to the circumstance and time in which is it used."[29] But if a word is not a crystal, neither is it an accordion. So the issue is not whether it is a crystal but when and under what circumstances it is permissible to treat it as one or as an accordion or, at the greatest extreme, like the "a" in the algebraic equasion. At what price precision? This may be called the "crystal problem."

Linked with it is the institutional problem of determining who shall say what the words mean. In the ordinary affairs of life we have numerous devices for determining "meaning" including the use of dictionaries. In the event of a simple contest or fuss, the inert authority of words in a book may suffice as in interpreting the rules of poker or bridge. When the contest is more complex and the words are less precise a "living" authority, i.e., an umpire or referee, is needed as in football or baseball. The institutional apparatus for determining the meaning of "legal" words rests ultimately in the organs of the state endowed by custom or agreement with the needed authority to decide specific issues in accordance with a developed technique for specifying issues. Despite periodic strains, this works well enough where confidence in the organs is by custom and tradition widely shared.

These seemingly obvious remarks point up the difference and the difficulty in fixing the meaning of terms in the international arena.

---

undisputed to cover at least cases of direct, overt aggression which is generally capable of objective and persuasive proof. The legitimate hope that it may yet become a rule against intervention by disguised force or threat of force threatening the independence of a nation may in fact be enhanced if Western Powers do not strongly insist on involving it in situations where, to many nations, independence is the inevitable victim between competing imperialisms, or, worse, where the West seems to be defending the interests which stand in the way of self-determination and independence. The battle of interventions, for the present, will have to be fought as political battles with little help from law."

Henkin, 1963 PROCEEDINGS, AM. SOC. INT'L LAW 147, 158. I do not believe it wise to give to the term "armed attack" too precise a meaning. It has not gone unnoticed that the equally official French text of Article 51 uses the term "agression armée," a much looser expression and one that eludes a precise definition. The French equivalent for "attack" is "attaque."

The term "attack" has the deceptive sound of a "terminal" word as opposed to a "process" word (to use a characterization employed by Gilbert Ryle). So construed it is like "launching" or "finding," i.e., a one-shot affair, as opposed, to say, "swimming" or "searching." The proclaimed virtues for this kind of construction are, in my opinion, outweighed by the difficulties it invites. This seems to me borne out by the present crisis in the Middle East. In the South Vietnamese war the issue is not properly framed in terms of an "armed attack" but rather an accelerating movement of troops over a period of time amounting to aggression.

[29]Towne v. Eisner, 245 U.S. 418, 425 (1917).

The authoritative bodies are the International Court of Justice and the organs of the United Nations together with regional organizations. The judgments and advisory opinions of the former and the flow of "resolutions" issuing from the latter carry an authoritative imprint that is by no means negligible.[30] The trouble lies in a condition, all too frequently absent, which in a developed municipal system is almost taken for granted. I refer to the recognition of legitimated authority and the joinder of authority, power and control. In the municipal arena a high level of predictability is possible, even in advance of an authoritative pronouncement, because everyone knows that the officially intoned words mean business. We can therefore speak with some assurance about the legal and the non-legal. On the other hand, when we speak of an act being "legal" or "illegal" in the international arena (e.g., the Cuban quarantine), we are in a sense betting that the action so described will carry the subsequent approval or invite the disapproval of an amorphous and even protean world opinion vocalized through the official organs of the international community.[31]

If the words of the Charter are clear and unambiguous (crystals), predictions with a high degree of probability may be entertained. When they are less so, doubts arise. The opinions of scholars and the pronouncements of official partisans are, of course, important. In a sense they are exercises in ultimate persuasion. When scholars disagree, the effort should be made to reach beyond the words in order to ferret out the criteria used by them in ascribing the term "legal" or "illegal" to the disputed actions. This effort is not exhausted by merely pointing to the words of the Charter, since this assumes too readily that the words bear a commonly shared meaning, irrespective of wide divergences in the first-order facts to which they are applied and the second-order facts believed in by those to whom they are applied. As with our Constitution, the meaning of the United Nations Charter must be sought by a process which uses "experience developed by reason and reason tested by experience."[32] It is not merely an

---

[30]For a thorough and perceptive analysis see, Schachter, *The Relation of Law, Politics and Action in the United Nations*, 109 Hague Academy RECUEIL DES COURS 171-200 (1963). *Cf.* HIGGINS, THE DEVELOPMENT OF INTERNATIONAL LAW THROUGH THE POLITICAL ORGANS OF THE UNITED NATIONS 1-10 (1963).

[31]*Cf.* H. L. A. HART, THE CONCEPT OF LAW, esp. at 229 (1961).

[32]Pound, *The Case for Law*, 1 VALPARAISO UNIV. L. REV. 201, 202 (1967) (Speech delivered in 1959.) The words of Holmes are again relevant:

"But the provisions of the Constitution are not mathematical formulas having their essence in their form; they are organic living institutions transplanted from English soil. Their significance is vital not formal; it is to be

aggregate of separate proscriptions, and the lenses through which it is read are distorted if they reflect the kind of image revealed by reading a municipal ordinance.

True in all three types of conflict to which allusion has been made, this is particularly true of the first type, where conditions of instability attended by threats and counter-threats prevail. The need is to discriminate more clearly among types of conflict with a view to determining in the context of present realities the degree of normative precision needed to help in their orderly management.[33]

Just as "civil disobedience" in the domestic area is not all of one piece, neither in the international arena are insurrections, revolutions and other forms of civil strife.[34] And perhaps there is an increased need to encourage greater reliance on regional organizations to give authoritative meaning to the norms.

Finally, one point needs to be reemphasized. We cannot expect to clarify a stuttering dialogue unless we dig beneath the surface manifestations of disputes in search of the underlying criteria which form the basis for our legal as well as our ethical and historical judgments. By airing these criteria and putting them in the public domain, we may not only narrow the area of disagreement but expose the kind of dogmatism that confuses fact with fancy and substitutes "stereotypes for sense and rage for reason."[35] This is why the dialogue on Viet Nam should continue unabated even if it makes uncomfortable the wielders of power. For democracy is rested on the premise that the wielders of power are not omniscient, and it is not the decisions alone that count but the way they are reached.

---

gathered not simply by taking the words and a dictionary, but by considering their origin and the line of their growth." Gompers v. United States, 233 U.S. 604, 610 (1914).

[33]This is only one of the many problems confronting the contemporary scholar. See, Falk, *New Approaches to the Study of International Law*, 61 AM. JOURN. INT'L LAW 477-95 (1967). Fortunately the American Society of International Law is currently sponsoring a number of studies in depth of significant subjects including both "peace keeping" and problems of "communication." For an interesting recent contribution to the problem of "intervention," see Farer, *Intervention in Civil Wars: A Modest Proposal*, 67 COLUM. L. REV. 266-279 (1967).

[34]Secretary McNamara is quoted as saying that of the 149 serious insurgencies in the past eight years, Communists have been involved in only 58 including 7 in which a Communist regime itself was the target of the uprising. SCHLESINGER, THE BITTER HERITAGE 73 (1967).

[35]*Id.* at 119.

APPENDIX

BIBLIOGRAPHICAL NOTE ON SOUTH VIET NAM

In the June 4, 1967 issue of the *New York Times* Book Review pp. 2, 26 John Mecklin, author of MISSION IN TORMENT: AN INTIMATE ACCOUNT OF THE U.S. ROLE IN VIETNAM, (1965), gives an overview of 25 recently published books dealing with various aspects of the war in Viet Nam. It is estimated that approximately 4,000 books and 5,000 articles have been written on Viet Nam. The bibliography which follows may provide a lead to some of the publications of special interest to the legal profession including a few mentioned by Mecklin.

I. *Historical*

Buttinger, VIETNAM: A DRAGON EMBATTLED, Volume I: *From Colonialism to the Vietminh*. Volume II: *Vietnam at War* (1967).

II. *Factual Background and Perspective*

Crozier, SOUTHEAST ASIA IN TURMOIL (1965).
Fall & Raskin (Eds.), THE VIETNAM READER (1965).
Fall, THE TWO VIET-NAMS: A POLITICAL AND MILITARY HISTORY (1965).
Fall, VIET-NAM WITNESS (1966).
Fulbright, THE ARROGANCE OF POWER (1967).
Gettleman (Ed.), VIETNAM (1965).
Goodwin, TRIUMPH OR TRAGEDY—REFLECTIONS ON VIETNAM (1966).
Honey, COMMUNISM IN NORTH VIETNAM (1963).
Lacouture, VIETNAM: BETWEEN TWO TRUCES (1966).
Pike, VIETCONG (1966).
Salisbury, BEHIND THE LINES—HANOI (1967).
Scheer, HOW THE UNITED STATES GOT INVOLVED IN VIETNAM (1965).
Schlesinger, Jr., THE BITTER HERITAGE—VIETNAM AND AMERICAN DEMOCRACY 1941-1966 (1967).
Taylor, RESPONSIBILITY AND RESPONSE (1967).
Thompson, DEFEATING COMMUNIST INSURGENCY: THE LESSONS OF MALAYA AND VIETNAM (1966).
Trager, WHY VIET NAM? (1966).
Warner, THE LAST CONFUCIAN—VIETNAM, SOUTHEAST ASIA, AND THE WEST (1964).
VIETNAM HEARINGS: (Intro. by Sen. Fulbright) (1966).
For sharply contrasting points of view compare: Aptheker, MISSION TO HANOI (1966) with: du Berrier, BACKGROUND TO BETRAYAL—THE TRAGEDY OF VIETNAM (1965).

III. *Recent Exchange*

Schlesinger, Jr., A MIDDLE WAY OUT OF VIETNAM, N. Y. Times Magazine 47 (Sept. 18, 1966).
Scalapino, WE CANNOT ACCEPT A COMMUNIST SEIZURE OF VIETNAM, N. Y. Times Magazine 46 (Dec. 11, 1966).

IV. *Background Documentation*

HEARINGS ON S. 2793 BEFORE THE SENATE COMMITTEE ON FOREIGN RELATIONS, 89th Cong. 2nd Sess., pt. 1 (1966).
Staff of Senate Comm. on Foreign Relations, 89th Cong., 1st Sess., BACKGROUND INFORMATION RELATING TO SOUTHEAST ASIA AND VIETNAM (Rev. ed. Comm. Print 1965).
The Reports of the International Commission for Supervision and Control in

Viet Nam deal with violations on both sides. They are published in Great Britain as Command Papers. The most frequently cited appear to be:

        1955: Nos. 9461, 9499, 9654
        1956: No. 9706
        1957: Nos. 31, 335
        1958: No. 509
        1959: No. 726
        1960: No. 1040
        1961: No. 1551
        1962: No. 1755
        1965: No. 2609

Reports from the SEATO Powers are embraced in the SEATO RECORD.

V. *Exchange of Briefs*

Memorandum of Law of Lawyers Committee on American Policy Toward Vietnam, reprinted in 112 CONG. REC. 2552, (daily ed. Feb. 9, 1966).

Meeker, Legal Adviser of the Dept. of State, *The Legality of U.S. Participation in The Defense of Viet-Nam* (March 4, 1966), reprinted in 54 DEP'T STATE BULL. 474 (March 28, 1966) and 75 YALE L.J. 1085 (1966).

VI. *Articles and Notes in Legal Periodicals*

Alford, *The Legality of American Military Involvement in Viet Nam: A Broader Perspective,* 75 YALE L.J. 1109 (1966).

Deutsch, *Legality of the United States Position in Vietnam,* 52 A.B.A.J. 436 (1966.)

Falk, *International Law and the United States Role In The Viet Nam War,* 85 YALE L.J. 1122 (1966).

Finman & Macauley, *Freedom to Dissent: The Vietnam Protests and the Words of Public Officials,* 1966 WIS. L. REV. 632.

Wright, *Legal Aspects of the Viet-Nam Situation,* 60 AM. J. INT'L LAW 750 (1966).

McDougal, Moore & Underwood, *The Lawfulness of United States Assistance to the Republic of Viet Nam,* 112 CONG. REC. 14943 (daily ed. July 14, 1966). Reprinted in 5 DUQUESNE UNIV. L. REV. 235-352 (1967).

Moore, *The Lawfulness of Military Assistance to the Republic of Viet Nam,* 61 AM. J. INT'L L. 1 (1967).

Partan, *Legal Aspects of the Vietnam Conflict,* 46 BOSTON UNIV. L. REV. 281 (1966).

Standard, *United States Intervention in Vietnam Is Not Legal,* 52 A.B.A.J. 627 (1966).

Note, *The Geneva Convention and the Treatment of Prisoners of War in Vietnam,* 80 HARV. L. REV. 851 (1967).

Note, *Canada's Role in the International Commission for Supervision and Control in Vietnam,* 4 CAN. Y.B. INT'L L. 161 (1966).

Note, *The Geneva Convention of 1949: Application in the Vietnamese Conflict,* 5 VA. J. INT'L L. 243 (1965).

Comment, *The United States in Vietnam: A Case Study in the Law of Intervention,* 50 CALIF. L. REV. 515 (1962).

II. THE LEGAL STATUS OF
UNITED STATES INVOLVEMENT

International Law and the Response of the United States to "Internal War"

EDWIN BROWN FIRMAGE

With the spectre of nuclear weapons acting as a restraint upon the nations in terms of the levels and types of violence they will employ to achieve national goals, warfare since 1945 has undergone radical change.[1] There has been no massive, overt aggression by one major power against another, although there have been half a dozen provocations which might well have led to international war in pre-nuclear times. NATO's central front, the major focus of attention in the late 1940's and early 1950's, is no longer considered a likely spot for open conflict between the communist and non-communist world. After the Soviet Union had taken full advantage of the position of its armies at the end of World War II by establishing Communist governments in the countries of Eastern Europe, some of the early prototypes for violence in our time emerged. The non-Communist Czechoslovakian government was toppled by a combination of intimidation from the Red Army and subversion by Czech Communists. A similar attempt by the Soviet Union to intimidate and subvert the government of Turkey failed largely because of the success of the Truman Doctrine and growing Western solidarity. A Soviet-sponsored civil war in Greece failed because of the same factors plus a coincidental break between Tito and Stalin which closed Yugoslavia as a conduit for supplies to Greek Communists. Western support also prevented the Government of Iran from being intimidated into collapse.

At the same time, a civil war was taking place in China which would have profound effect upon the form violence would take in the post-war world, due in part to the belief of its architect that under certain conditions his pattern could be successfully followed in many parts of the world as "wars of national liberation." An incredible end to at least one chapter of violence was written as Mao triumphed in his 20-year battle with Chiang Kai-shek over the mantle of Sun Yat-sen after suffering shattering early defeats. At first the Kuomintang, with their strategy of encirclement and annihilation, had severely defeated the Communists. But Mao broke through Chiang's blockade in Southern China and led 30,000 survivors 6,000 miles — the famous "Long March" to Northwest China and the caves at Yenan. There Mao developed a theory of warfare based upon the dogma outlined by Lenin at the Second Comintern Congress in 1920 and, more importantly, upon Mao's own experiences in the war with the Nationalists. Although forced to realize the vast military superiority of the Kuomintang, Mao came to discern the political weakness of the Nationalists, who held the major cities but who had little effective control or support in the countryside where the majority

---

[1] *See* H. ARENDT, ON REVOLUTION (1963), one of the pioneering studies on this transformation.

of the people lived. Although his position was militarily weak, Mao had growing political support because of his rural work among the peasants,[2] and from this situation emerged his classic pattern of guerrilla warfare: surrounding the cities from the countryside for a protracted war of attrition. His application of the formula "the enemy advances, we retreat; the enemy halts, we harass; the enemy tires, we attack; the enemy retreats, we pursue" eventually demonstrated the weakness of the Kuomintang military giant which had no political roots in the countryside. This lesson demonstrating the primacy of political strength in relation to ultimate military strength was not lost on Mao or upon those who would later emulate him. After some years of guerrilla warfare in this classic pattern, Mao's forces were strong enough to confront the Kuomintang in the more traditional patterns of encirclement and annihilation which the Nationalists had used with such initial success upon the Communists. But with Mao's support in the countryside, Chiang could not have in turn followed Mao's earlier strategy even if the Kuomintang had been sufficiently perceptive and responsive to attempt it.

The explosion of nationalism must also be recognized as adding to the controlling concepts which were shaping the nature of violence in the postwar world. As the forces of nationalism destroyed the remaining fabric of 19th century colonialism in a shockingly short 20 years, some colonial powers resisted the nationalist forces while others peacefully acquiesced to the inevitable. The most anguishing dilemmas were posed to framers of Western foreign policies on those occasions when the forces of nationalism and communism were merged to some indeterminate degree in opposition to "legitimate" Western-oriented governments.

A more traditional form of violence, having similarities to the factors of nuclear weapons, Maoist doctrine and example, and nationalism, still existed. Civil war, without communist or anti-colonialist overtones, also occurred as people with rising expectations and undiminished birth rates found that the progress they heard about on transistor radios and saw in the persons of foreign travelers could not be achieved in the form they wanted it or with the speed they demanded.

Can international law fashion a set of rules which could govern these several forms of violence? The traditional distinction between civil and international war and the different rules which follow the distinction are strained by the attempt to force such disparate types of violence into traditional molds. Tension is especially created by the interplay between two equally desirable goals. On the one hand, the interests of the United States and the future of international law and order would best be served if the United States avoided any "Metternich doctrine of legitimacy"[3] under which we opposed any revolutionary change in the fashion of a resurrected Council of Europe with 20th century America in the place of 19th century Austria. In so doing, it is essential that the United States distinguish a civil war between contend-

---

[2] *See* 4 MAO TSE-TUNG, SELECTED WORKS 190–95 (1963).
[3] *See* Friedmann, *Law and Politics in the Vietnamese War: A Comment*, 61 AM. J. INT'L L. 776, 782 (1967).

ing nationalist forces from an attempt by a Communist state to depose the non-Communist government of another state by some form of exported violence.[4]

On the other hand, it is equally essential to the interests of the United States, and I believe to the growth of meaningful international order, that we find appropriate means to oppose other forms of aggression. Democratic institutions which have had success in meeting blatant aggression must not now become immobilized, enervated, and separated from each other when faced with more subtle but no less dangerous types of aggression.

The primary problem, before deciding upon a course of action in response to violence, is to perceive accurately the nature of the violence and the identity of the participants. In analyzing these problems in regard to Viet-Nam, the Department of State and its critics have reached disparate results.

I. The Position of the Department of State

The Department of State has noted that the Geneva Accords of 1954 established a "demarcation line" between North Viet-Nam and South Viet-Nam and prohibited the use of either zone to "further an aggressive policy" against the other.[5] The Democratic Republic of Viet-Nam (D.R.V.N.) violated the Accords by engaging in an "armed attack" against the Republic of Viet-Nam (R.V.N.). The Department of State interpreted several courses of conduct of the D.R.V.N. as constituting, individually or collectively, "armed attack" within the meaning of Article 51 of the United Nations Charter. This conduct included the development of a "covert political-military organization" in South Viet-Nam composed of Viet-Minh cadres which had been left in the South after 1954, in violation of the Accords. Kidnaping, assassination of hamlet chiefs and officials of the R.V.N., and other acts of terrorism were instigated by the D.R.V.N. and constituted its major aggressive action against the South for approximately five years following the Geneva Conference.

From 1959 to 1961, the Department of State asserts, the D.R.V.N. infiltrated thousands of southerners who had gone to the North in 1954 back into the South to join the Viet Cong in guerrilla activity against the R.V.N. The Department of State estimates that by 1964 over 40,000 guerrillas had been infiltrated from the North into South Viet-Nam. The findings of the International Control Commission are cited as partial authority for this proposition.[6]

Beginning in 1964, the D.R.V.N. began infiltrating increasing numbers of native northerners into the South, because of an apparent exhaustion of its ranks of southerners. At this time also, according to the State Department, regular units of the PAVN (People's Army of Viet-Nam) began crossing into South Viet-Nam to aid the Viet Cong. The Department admits that it

[4] See Farer, *Intervention in Civil Wars: A Modest Proposal*, 67 Colum. L. Rev. 266 (1967).

[5] Office of the Legal Adviser, U.S. Dep't of State, *The Legality of United States Participation in the Defense of Vietnam*, 54 Dep't State Bull. 474 (1966), reprinted in 75 Yale L.J. 1085 (1966).

[6] *Id.* at 474–76.

is difficult to identify any one event or any fixed time when this mixture of clandestine and blatant aggression constituted an "armed attack," but it insists that the "infiltration of thousands of armed men clearly constitutes" such an attack, and that the infiltration had definitely reached such a status prior to February 1965.[7]

In response to this aggression, the Department of State has argued that the R.V.N. possesses the inherent right of individual and collective self-defense recognized by international law and reaffirmed in Article 51 of the United Nations Charter; that such right exists whether or not South Viet-Nam is considered to be a sovereign state or a temporarily divided zone; that such right, described by Article 51 as being "inherent," is not limited to members of the United Nations; and that collective self-defense is open to states acting unilaterally or within regional organizations. On these grounds, the State Department memorandum concludes that United States participation in the defense of South Viet-Nam at the latter's request was an act of collective self-defense permissible under customary international law and the United Nations Charter.

The memorandum maintains that United States actions prior to 1961 in supplying the R.V.N. with military equipment and advisors were within the provisions of the Geneva Accords which permitted replacement of existing personnel and equipment. With the withdrawal of French training and advisory personnel, the United States gradually enlarged its advisory and training forces in South Viet-Nam. Then, in response to "intensified" aggression, "increased infiltration," and terrorism in the South directed by the D.R.V.N., the United States found it necessary to "increase substantially" its military personnel and equipment. Such action was justified, according to the Department of State, by the international law principle that a material breach of an agreement (the Geneva Accords) by one party entitles the other "to withhold compliance with an equivalent, corresponding, or related provision."[8] The "systematic violation" of the Accords by the D.R.V.N. justified the R.V.N. in suspending its compliance with those portions of the Accords controlling the entry of foreign military personnel and equipment.

The refusal of the R.V.N. to implement the election provisions of the Accords is defended by the Department of State on the grounds that South Viet-Nam specifically objected to the election provisions at the time the Accords were signed by the participating states. Further, even if the R.V.N. were considered to be bound by the Accords generally, no breach occurred in the failure to implement the election provisions since the condition precedent to "free elections" had not been met — namely, the existence of conditions in North Viet-Nam such that fair, uncoerced elections could be held.[9]

II. The Critics

Various critics have taken opposition to every major point of the State Department memorandum. Both the origin of the hostilities in South Viet-Nam and the identity of the participants are disputed by these scholars.

---

[7] *Id.* at 475.
[8] *Id.* at 483.
[9] *Id.* at 483–84.

Professor Tom Farer[10] has presented a somewhat jaded analysis of modern United States foreign policy, which he views as being counterrevolutionary regardless of the participants:

[W]e now see each revolution as a potential or actual battle in an immense, world-wide struggle against Communism. Thus, the significance of every revolutionary civil war is grotesquely magnified, with the ultimate consequence that because we have decided that left-wing revolution is a threat to us, we guarantee that it will be a threat to the peace.[11]

Professor Farer's central question relates to the identification of norms which will restrict the participation of third parties in civil wars. He identifies four criteria by which to judge such norms: first, the chance that the norm would be accepted by the nations involved; second, the likelihood that it would reduce great power confrontation if accepted; third, the necessity that the norm be sufficiently unambiguous that serious violations are readily identifiable; and fourth, the capacity of the norms to facilitate geographic containment of violence.

Professor Farer maintains that the classical view (to which Washington "clings with rational rigidity") — that in a civil war's early stages outside powers can only aid the established government — has lost its force since the emergence of a host of relatively powerless governments has erased any real distinction between the ability of legitimate and insurgent forces to maintain domestic peace. No new norm to limit third power intervention in civil wars will develop, according to Farer, as long as the United States "insists on its right to intervene in any revolution with whatever scale of force is required to suppress it . . . ."[12] He rejects the most obvious norm, complete nonintervention in civil wars, on the plausible ground that it would be unenforceable and unacceptable because of resulting ambiguity in the interpretation of training programs, economic aid, military assistance prior to the outbreak of internal violence, and the definition of civil war in general.

In place of the traditional rule regarding third party participation in civil wars, Professor Farer proposes a norm which would prohibit tactical support by a third power to either side engaged in civil war. No third party could send forces — be they advisors, volunteers, transports, or whatever — into any zone of combat. Within the definition of "zone of combat" would be air defense installations, which could not be manned by foreign personnel.

Under the proposed norm, a country would be legally free to extend any type or quantity of aid other than forms of assistance which could involve its personnel in actual combat. There would be no justification for a state allied with the incumbent government to attack a state aiding the insurgents within the allowed limits; such aid would not

---

[10] Farer, *supra* note 4.

[11] *Id.* at 267.

[12] *Id.* at 273. Professor Friedmann has joined in the attack on the Administration position, criticizing the "Metternich doctrine of legitimacy" which permits assistance to the recognized government but not insurgents. Friedmann, *supra* note 3.

constitute an act of aggression against the country in which the civil war was being fought.[13]

The United States would have violated this norm in Viet-Nam at least by 1961 with its shuttling of R.V.N. forces to combat zones in helicopters.

Professor Quincy Wright has concluded that the D.R.V.N. committed no acts against the R.V.N. prior to the United States bombing north of the cease-fire line which would constitute "armed attack" upon the South.[14] Therefore, no justification for the United States bombings in the North could be made under color of "collective self-defense." Self-defense is permitted under international law and the United Nations Charter, according to Professor Wright, only if an "instant and overwhelming necessity permitting no moment for deliberation" exists.[15] He concluded that there was no evidence to support the assertion that organized contingents of the PAVN had crossed the cease-fire line prior to the bombings in February, 1965. Professor Wright termed "controversial" the question whether the infiltration by the D.R.V.N. of large numbers of irregular forces into the South prior to February, 1965, would constitute "armed attack" or merely "defense measures against the military activities of South Viet-Nam and the United States."[16] The activities of the D.R.V.N. prior to 1958, presumably including acts of planned assassination of village leaders and other acts of terrorism, "did not constitute aggression or armed attack in international relations but civil strife within the domestic jurisdiction of Viet-Nam, similar to the action of the North against the South in the American Civil War,"[17] since prior to that time Ho Chi Minh had been frustrated in achieving the elections provided for in the Geneva Accords. Professor Wright concluded that "the United States response by bombings in North Viet-Nam, which began in February, 1965, violated international law, the United Nations Charter, and the Geneva Agreement, if the latter were in effect."[18]

Richard Falk has proposed that "internal wars" in which third powers have intervened be treated as civil wars. Response would be limited to counter-intervention, and third countries would not be permitted to directly attack the homeland of the intervening power unless the intervention were on the massive scale of a Korean-type invasion.[19] "[A]n intervening nation whose own territory is not the scene of conflict may not attack the territory of a state intervening on the other side."[20] The alternative is to consider the

---

[13] Farer, *supra* note 4 at 276. "The possibility of combat is the crucial distinction. Any entry, whether by land, sea, or air, into war zones *i.e.* — any area in which organized units of both rebel and government forces are located . . . must be prohibited." *Id.* at 278.

[14] Wright, *Legal Aspects of the Viet-Nam Situation*, 60 Am. J. Int'l L. 750, 764 (1966).

[15] *Id.*

[16] *Id.* at 766.

[17] *Id.* at 767.

[18] *Id.*

[19] Falk, *International Law and the United States Role in the Viet Nam War*, 75 Yale L.J. 1122, 1123 (1966).

[20] *Id.*

act of foreign intervention of such importance that an internal war would thereby be turned into an international war, the intervention being considered as an "armed attack," thus permitting an act of collective self-defense directly against the aggressor nation by a third nation. The consequences of this geographic escalation in the nuclear age, however, are so dangerous, and the interest of international law in restricting the scope and intensity of the war consequently so great, that a severe if not impossible burden should be placed upon nations seeking to convert an internal war into an international war "by characterizing external participation as 'aggression' rather than as 'intervention.'"[21] Former Secretary of State John Foster Dulles is noted as suggesting that indirect aggression not be treated as an armed attack by one country upon another.[22] Professor Falk proposes, to build a stable international order, that internal wars be treated as civil wars, regardless of inter-

---

[21] *Id.*

[22] *Id.* at 1123–24. Professor Falk quotes a statement made by Secretary Dulles in 1957 in response to a question put him by Senator Fulbright during the Senate hearings on President Eisenhower's proposals regarding the Middle East. *Hearings on S.J. 14 and H.R.J. 117 Before the Senate Comms. on Foreign Relations & Armed Services,* 85th Cong., 1st Sess., pt. 1 at 28 (1957). Senator Fulbright was concerned about the wording of a proposed resolution which would authorize the President to "employ the Armed Forces of the United States as he deems necessary to secure and protect the territorial integrity and political independence of any such nation . . ." requesting such aid against *overt armed aggression* from any Communist nation. *Id.* at 27. Senator Fulbright feared that the statement pledging action only against overt armed aggression implied that we would not use force in any other circumstance even though our national interests might be threatened. The Senator proposed a hypothetical situation in which the Government of Mexico would be subverted by the U.S.S.R. without our taking action. Secretary Dulles assured the Senator that action would be taken, but that response to subversion could take other forms than military invasion of the subverting nation. It was at that point that the statement quoted by Professor Falk was uttered by Secretary Dulles. *Id.* at 28.

It is obvious from the context of this testimony that Secretary Dulles was talking of response to types of intervention far less violent than that committed by the D.R.V.N. upon the R.V.N. during late 1950's to the present. The response which the late Secretary would have made to clandestine subversion, propaganda, economic coercion and even acts of assassination would in all probability have been quite different from a response aimed at the infiltration of thousands of irregular and regular troops across a cease-fire line.

A year after the hearings quoted above, the crisis in Lebanon occurred. The level of foreign involvement was far less than what has occurred in Viet-Nam, and the United States response was therefore able to be contained within Lebanon. In commenting upon this situation, however, Secretary Dulles left little doubt as to his opinion regarding the necessity of opposing indirect aggression with sufficient force to deprive the aggressor of his intended goal:

Indirect aggression is nothing new. . . . Through use of inflamatory radio broadcasts; through infiltration of weapons, personnel and bribe money; through incitement to murder and assassination, and through threats of personal violence, it becomes possible for one nation to destroy the genuine independence of another.

It was in order to help to halt such practices that the United States responded to the urgent plea of the freely elected government of Lebanon and sent United States forces to Lebanon to assist that democratic country to retain its independence.

. . . .

The United States is convinced that if indirect aggression, in the form of fomenting civil strife or subverting foreign governments, is now tolerated as an instrument of international policy, events will indeed follow the tragic pattern which led to World War II . . . .

Text of Address by Secretary Dulles before the Veterans of Foreign Wars, N.Y. Times, Aug. 19, 1958, at 12, col. 2.

vention by third parties, permitting "a neutralizing response as a maximum counteraction."[23]

In his most recent writing,[24] Professor Falk has proposed that the "organized international community" (presumably the United Nations) give prior assent before a victim state be allowed to characterize indirect aggression in such a manner that "self-defense" would be justified as interpreted under Article 51 of the United Nations Charter. This would greatly reduce the unilateral discretion of the victim state,[25] the would-be ally of the victim state,[26] and the executive branch of that potential intervening third power.[27] World order would presumably be promoted by this restriction.[28]

In order to understand a criticism of these critics, it is essential first to understand the nature of the hostilities in Viet-Nam and to establish a chronology of events regarding certain critical stages in the escalation of third power intervention in 1961 and again in 1964–1965.

III. Subversion, Indirect Aggression, and Wars of National Liberation

Although Ho and Giap and others have made significant changes in Mao's doctrines on protracted war,[29] the war in South Viet-Nam has to date been a classic example of a so-called "war of national liberation," following Mao's model and preachments. After many years of French colonial domination, with French influence centered almost completely in the major cities, Viet-Nam clearly fit within Mao's doctrine of surrounding the cities from strong countryside bases supported by the peasants. Mao's rationale for this policy is equally applicable to Viet-Nam and French military policy there:

> Since powerful imperialism and its allies, the reactionary forces in China, have occupied China's key cities for a long time . . . [the revolutionary forces must] build the backward villages into advanced, consolidated base areas, into great military, political, economic and cultural revolutionary bastions, so that they can fight the fierce enemy who utilizes the cities to attack the rural districts, and, through a protracted struggle, gradually win an overall victory for the revolution.[30]

The long war fought by Ho against the French, along with the American bombing of the North, has aided Ho in turning nationalism into his tool as did Mao before him.[31]

---

[23] Falk, *supra* note 19, at 1125.

[24] Falk, *International Law and the United States Role in Viet Nam: A Response to Professor Moore*, 76 YALE L.J. 1095 (1967).

[25] *Id.* at 1142.

[26] *Id.* at 1149.

[27] *Id.* at 1150.

[28] *Id.* at 1140.

[29] *See* B. FALL, THE TWO VIET-NAMS 112–13 (2d rev. ed. 1967).

[30] 3 MAO TSE-TUNG, SELECTED WORKS 85 (1954). Those who propose an enclave theory based upon static defense positions around the coast of South Viet-Nam might pause to consider the Maoist doctrine of encircling the cities and fortified areas from the countryside, as developed by Mao and used with such success against the Kuomintang, and the record of Ho and Giap against the French policy of holding the cities and highways and fortified areas, leaving the countryside to the Viet Minh.

[31] *See* C. JOHNSON, PEASANT NATIONALISM AND COMMUNIST POWER (1962); H. SALISBURY, BEHIND THE LINES — HANOI (1967).

Mao's influence on Ho, Giap, Truong Chinh, and others later to play important roles in Viet-Nam is unquestioned.[32] Truong Chinh, then secretary general of the Indochinese Communist Party, wrote *The Resistance Will Win* in 1947. This was the first Vietnamese adaptation of Mao's *On Protracted War*, with its famous three stages of defensive strategy, equilibrium, and counteroffensive, which Mao developed against Chiang.[33] General Vo Nguyen Giap has followed Mao and Chinh in practice and principle.[34]

That both Mao and Ho would like to export this form of conflict to border countries can hardly be doubted. Past and present conflict in Laos, Cambodia and Thailand, supplemented by blatant statements of intent,[35] clearly

---

[32] FALL, *supra* note 29, at 98, 99, 112–14. *See also* SALISBURY, *supra* note 31, at 180, 181; F. TRAGER, WHY VIETNAM? 206 (1966); Hilsman, *American Response to the Guerrilla*, CHICAGO TODAY, Spring, 1967, at 34.

[33] B. FALL, *supra* note 29, at 112–13.

[34] V. GIAP, PEOPLE'S WAR PEOPLE'S ARMY (1962); Modelski, *The Viet Minh Complex*, in COMMUNISM AND REVOLUTION 185, 207–09 (C. Black & T. Thornton eds. 1964); Hilsman, *supra* note 32.

[35] See, for example, statement by Vice Premier and Defense Minister Lin Piao. Lin Piao, *Long Live the Victory of People's War!*, PEKING REV., Sept. 3, 1965, at 9–30.

On November 1, 1964, the "Thailand Independence Movement" was formally announced with backing from Peking and Hanoi. The purpose of this organization was to overthrow the Thai government and to sever all ties with the United States.

On January 1, 1965, the "Thailand Patriotic Front" was formed — again with the backing of Communist China and the D.R.V.N. — with the same objectives as the "Thailand Independence Movement." In March and April, 1965, Peking announced the arrival of representatives of both groups.

By late 1965 and early 1966, guerilla bands supplied and aided by Peking and Hanoi were increasingly active in the Phu Phan Mountains of Northeast Thailand. After several clashes with Thai security forces, documents were found linking the guerilla bands with the "Thailand Patriotic Front" and the "Thailand Independence Movement."

In May of 1965, the Foreign Minister of Thailand, Thanat Khoman, was on *Meet the Press*. The following exchange took place:

Question: Mr. Minister, the Chinese Foreign Minister tells us that Thailand is next on his list as a target for a Communist-supported war of national liberation. How do you evaluate this threat, and how vulnerable is Thailand to the kind of war that is being fought today in South Viet Nam?
Thanat: It amounts to a declaration of war. When a country says against another country that "we will start a war," be it a guerrilla war or an open war, it doesn't make much difference. It has been a declaration of war on the part of Communist China on Thailand. Now, of course, it is guerrilla war, and we are taking necessary measures and steps to meet the situation.
   We didn't take it lightly. We heeded the warning, the danger signal, and I assure you that both the government of Thailand and the people of Thailand are doing everything to preserve our freedom and our independence.
Question: What specific evidence is there of Communist China's intentions to infiltrate and to dominate Thailand?
Thanat: We start from a statement attributed to the Minister of Communist China, Che'n Yi, who said that the guerrilla warfare will begin in Thailand before the year is out. They have been trying to bring about the first phase of the subversive war. I'm referring to the process of sending agents, of recruiting sympathizers, of training cadres in Thailand, and of trying to build armed caches.

President Johnson has also emphasized the role of China:

Over this war, and all Asia, is another reality: the deepening shadow of Communist China. The rulers in Hanoi are urged on by Peking. This is a regime which has destroyed freedom in Tibet, attacked India, and been condemned by the United Nations for aggression in Korea. It is a nation which is helping the forces of violence in almost every continent. The contest in Vietnam is part of a wider pattern of aggressive purpose.

Address by President Lyndon B. Johnson, Johns Hopkins University, Baltimore, April 7, 1965, reprinted in VIET NAM: HISTORY, DOCUMENTS, AND OPINIONS ON A MAJOR WORLD CRISIS 324–25 (M. Gettleman ed. 1965).

support this view. Since the basic steps in domestic and world revolution are identical in Maoist theory,[36] what Mao did in China, according to Mao and his disciples, can be duplicated elsewhere under certain conditions.

For over 20 years, Mao has considered war between the United States and the Soviet Union to be unlikely. He believed that the major areas of conflict would be in colonial or former colonial areas outside the immediate spheres of interest of either super-power, and hence, in areas where the will of the United States to fight a protracted war would be very limited.[37] Ho found that the same thing was true regarding the French in Indo-China. Political support in France for the continuation of such a war gradually eroded, and the French Government found it politically impossible to send draftees to supplement the professional soldiers. Finally, Mendes-France was chosen Premier upon his promise to end hostilities in Indo-China within 30 days. It was within this context of bargaining power, eroded further by the defeat at Dien Bien Phu, that the French began the negotiations at Geneva in 1954.

There are, however, doctrinal and empirical indications that, when faced with firm opposition, those who would otherwise instigate wars of national liberation might refrain, or might terminate such a war on the basis of something considerably less than complete success. After discussing the concept of defensive war, Mao says:

> Secondly, the principle of victory. We do not fight unless we are sure of victory; we must on no account fight without preparation and without certainty of the outcome. . . . Thirdly, the principle of truce. After we have repulsed the attack of the die-hards and before they launch a new one, we should stop at the proper moment and bring that particular fight to a close. We must on no account fight on daily and hourly without stopping, nor become dizzy with success. Herein lies the temporary nature of every struggle.[38]

The Chinese Communists enjoyed geographical continuity with a friendly government, the Soviet Union — a factor which greatly aided their defeat of Chiang. The D.R.V.N. enjoys the same advantage with Communist China. But if tumult in China continues and increases, this advantage may look less reliable to the D.R.V.N. Ho displayed a propensity to settle for half a loaf by accepting the Geneva Accords in 1954, when his battlefield position entitled him to much more. It is hard to believe that this was motivated by any real hope that unsupervised elections would be held after the imposition of a Communist dictatorship and the elimination of all anti-Communist elements in the North.[39]

It is clear that Ho Chi Minh had intended to take over Cambodia and Laos as well as South Viet-Nam following the Geneva Accords of 1954. By February 1962, North Viet-Nam had 10,000 troops and advisors in Laos. *See* Address by Assistant Secretary of State William P. Bundy, *American Policy in South Viet-Nam and Southeast Asia*, 52 Dep't State Bull. 168–75 (1965). *See also* Bartelle, *Counterinsurgency and Civil War*, 40 N.D. L. Rev. 254 (1964).

[36] *See* Janos, *The Communist Theory of the State and Revolution*, in Communism and Revolution 32–42 (C. Black & T. Thornton, eds. 1964).

[37] *See* Mao Tse-tung, Selected Works 97–101 (1963). *See also* B. Fall, The Two Viet-Nams 117 (2d rev. ed. 1967).

[38] 3 Mao Tse-tung, Selected Works 199 (1963).

[39] *See* note 102 *infra* and accompanying text.

At this point the question may be asked whether a policy which limits response to indirect aggression and subversion to counter-intervention is a sufficient deterrent to those who would export their wars of national liberation. The challenge we face is finding a means of frustrating wars which are stimulated by third powers, while avoiding a counterrevolutionary policy which opposes any violent change even if it be of a completely internal nature. At the same time, the level of violence in any type of war must be kept below that level which could lead to a direct confrontation between the United States and the Soviet Union.

IV. Chronology of Escalation by Third Parties in Viet-Nam

Before evaluating the policies and pronouncements of the Administration and its critics, it is necessary to examine the record of escalation of third party activity in North and South Viet-Nam. Only from such a perspective can the policies of the Administration be meaningfully criticized.

The first major escalation of United States participation in hostilities in South Viet-Nam occurred in late 1961, when President Kennedy approved an increase in the number of military advisors in South Viet-Nam from 800 at the end of 1960 to 2,000 at the end of 1961 and 10,000 by late 1962. In addition, American pilots carried South Vietnamese units to combat zones in helicopters and air transports and provided essentially every service short of the introduction of American combat units into action.

Prior to this escalation — since the 1954 Geneva Convention — the D.R.V.N. had been making provisions for the destruction of the regime in the South. Although the Geneva Accords called for the regroupment of Communist forces north of the 17th parallel, thousands of former Viet Minh troops remained in the South. In addition, large arms caches were deposited in the South for future use. Bernard Fall reported that the pattern of assassination of village officials from 1954 to 1957 indicated "a *prima facie* case for the existence of close coordination between the Communist guerrillas in South Viet-Nam and the North Vietnamese intelligence apparatus."[40]

Roger Hilsman, a prominent critic of Administration policy in Viet-Nam, records the North Vietnamese actions which directly led to the decision by President Kennedy to drastically alter our participation in the defense of South Viet-Nam in 1961:

> After Mao's "East Wind prevails over West Wind" speech in November 1957, following the Soviet sputnik success, the North Vietnamese reactivated the Communist cadres who had remained in South Vietnam after the 1954 Geneva agreements, and began to use the old Ho Chi Minh trails through Laos to send down new cadres, selected from among the 90,000 southerners who had gone north in 1954. By mid-1961, the Viet Cong were estimated to have about 12,000 regular guerrilla troops, and they more or less controlled as much as a third of the

---

[40] *Id.* at 23.

countryside. Over 1,400 civilians, mainly village officials, had been assassinated in the previous twelve months, and over 2,000 kidnapped.[41]

It was only after the level of infiltration from the North and the number of D.R.V.N.-directed assassinations and other acts of terrorism had reached such a stage as to seriously threaten the R.V.N. government, that President Kennedy acted upon recommendations made by General Taylor and Walt Rostow, following their mission to South Viet-Nam, by increasing the number of American advisors and providing support units to the R.V.N.

Even with the high level of infiltration of men and supplies from the North during the 1959–1961 period, President Kennedy rejected the Taylor-Rostow recommendation that 10,000 American combat troops be committed to the defense of South Viet-Nam immediately. Instead, American support was extended only by increasing the number of advisors, the commitment of helicopters and other air transport groups, and the use of American pilots in air combat missions as instructors for South Vietnamese trainees[42] with instructions not to fire unless fired upon.[43]

In 1962 the International Control Commission reported that the D.R.V.N. had allowed its territory "to be used for inciting, encouraging, and supporting hostile activities in the zone in the South . . ." in violation of Articles 19, 24, and 27 of the Geneva Agreement. It also charged that the R.V.N. and the United States had violated Articles 16, 17, and 19.[44] The Chairman of the Commission, Gopalaswami Parthasarathy of India, stated, however, that in his opinion the United States and the R.V.N. had been forced to take action violative of the Agreements as a reaction to subversion by North Viet-Nam.[45]

From 1962 to 1964 the level of infiltration of men and supplies from the North increased. The Department of State has estimated that almost 13,000 men entered the R.V.N. from North Viet-Nam in 1962, and that by 1964 over 40,000 men had entered the South.[46]

During 1963 and 1964 a significant change in D.R.V.N. policy regarding the insurgency in the South occurred. First, D.R.V.N. control over the National Liberation Front became complete down to the village level. Douglas Pike reports that "in early 1963 well-known old-line Communist Cadres of the Viet Minh days, who had gone North, appeared for the first time at the provincial level and in August and September at the village level."[47] In August and September of 1963 "at least two generals from Hanoi

---

[41] Hilsman, *supra* note 32, at 36. For the Administration's account of the chronology and nature of escalation of D.R.V.N. and United States participation in hostilities in South Viet-Nam, see U.S. DEP'T OF STATE, PUB. NO. 7839, AGGRESSION FROM THE NORTH 404–25 (1965).

[42] Hilsman, *supra* note 32, at 37.

[43] N.Y. Times, March 16, 1962, at 1, col. 5.

[44] VIET NAM: HISTORY, DOCUMENTS, AND OPINIONS ON A MAJOR WORLD CRISIS 185–88 (M. Gettleman ed. 1965).

[45] N.Y. Times, May 26, 1962, at 1, col. 2.

[46] U.S. DEP'T OF STATE, CONCISE HISTORY OF ESCALATION IN VIET-NAM 2 (unpublished document).

[47] D. PIKE, VIET CONG: THE ORGANIZATION AND TECHNIQUES OF THE N.L.F. OF SOUTH VIETNAM 117 (1966).

arrived in the highland of the South to act as advisors, or possibly commanders, in the N.L.F.'s armed struggle movement."[48] Then, in late 1963 and 1964, thousands of North Vietnamese regular army (PAVN) soldiers were ordered to the South.[49] In 1964 at least a third of the 6,500 (the Department of State says 12,400) infiltrators were North Vietnamese, which indicated a change in the previous policy of infiltrating those forces which had been withdrawn to the North from the South following the Geneva Agreements in 1954. By 1965, almost all forces infiltrated into the South were native North Vietnamese.[50] The 325th Division of the PAVN was identified in action in South Viet-Nam by December, 1964.[51]

With this complete Northern control over the insurgency in the South, including leadership down to village levels and a dependence upon native Northerners for manpower, it is submitted that a state of "armed attack" by the D.R.V.N. upon the R.V.N. existed. Though many single events could be identified as constituting such an attack, including the infiltration of thousands of PAVN regular troops into the South along with native North Vietnamese irregular forces, this writer agrees with Professor Alford that "[u]nder conditions of modern military action, an 'armed attack' may be regarded as a process and not solely a single hostile offensive event."[52]

With the increased pressure from the North, it became obvious that the government in the South was in danger of collapse. It would appear that the Administration realized the necessity of increased American participation to avoid this collapse: by December, 1964, American military personnel totalled 23,000 men, although no regular combat units had yet been introduced.

After the Viet Cong attack upon American forces near Pleiku, the United States began "measured bombing attacks" upon military targets in the North. At the same time, Marine combat units were introduced for the first time to guard American installations previously defended by South Vietnamese forces.

While the real reason for American escalation at this point was not the isolated incident at Pleiku[53] — of which the Administration made too much in order to justify its action — the basic reasons for the escalation were impelling. As General Taylor testified before the Senate Foreign Relations Committee, "it became clear [by February, 1965] that we could no longer

---

[48] *Id.* at 102.

[49] *Id.* at 164.

[50] *Id.* at 324.

[51] U.S. DEP'T OF STATE, *supra* note 46.

[52] Alford, *The Legality of American Military Involvement in Viet Nam: A Broader Perspective*, 75 YALE L.J. 1109, 1113 (1966).

[53] See Charles Mahr's article in the N.Y. Times, Feb. 8, 1965, at 14, col. 6, where he reports that in terms of the size of the attacking Viet Cong force and the weapons they employed, the attack on Pleiku was of a different nature than attacks in the past. No evidence of Hanoi direction on this specific attack was found. That an American attack on North Viet-Nam had previously been planned is evidenced by the presence of all three attack carriers of the 7th Fleet in the South China Sea near the Vietnamese coast, while the usual procedure is for each carrier to form the nucleus of a separate attack force operating in different parts of East Asia.

tolerate this clandestine support from the immune sanctuary in North Vietnam which served as the external base for the Viet Cong insurgency."[54]

V. A CRITIQUE

The challenge to international law is to identify or create rules which would at once diminish the likelihood of violent conflict between nations and at the same time avoid proscriptions which would establish a Metternichian-type insurance for the eternal continuance of the status quo. From the United States' point of view the rules should discourage third party instigation of "wars of national liberation" or any other type of civil disorder fomented and supported by third powers dedicated to violent evangelism on behalf of communism.

Professor Farer proposed a norm which would prohibit tactical support by a third power to either side in a civil war.[55] Although a country could extend aid in the form of supplies and, presumably, arms of any type, no advisors, volunteers, or transports would be allowed in the tactical "zone of combat."

The difficulty in formulating one set of norms to govern many disparate situations is illustrated by Professor Farer's attempt. With the overwhelming presence of the war in Viet-Nam quite obviously serving as the nexus for Professor Farer's norm, other fact situations apparently were not considered. One initial weakness is that it is as necessary to define civil war under Professor Farer's norm as under the traditional one, even though Professor Farer rejected the simple rule of complete nonintervention in civil disputes in part to avoid having to attempt this definition.

In addition, the events concerning Cuba, the United States, and the Soviet Union from the Bay of Pigs to the missile crisis present especial difficulty for this norm. There was an internal conflict with significant third power inter-vention — the Soviet Union actively supported the Castro government and the United States extended erratic support to various insurgent groups. The transportation of Cuban exiles by the United States to the Bay of Pigs would represent a violation of Professor Farer's norm. Yet the potentially far more dangerous placement of offensive missiles in Cuba by the Soviet Union would not represent a violation since no tactical "zone of combat" existed there, and,

---

[54] THE VIETNAM HEARINGS 172 (Random House ed. 1966). For other statements defending and explaining the United States bombing of North Viet-Nam, see Statement of Secretary Rusk before the American Foreign Service Association, reprinted in U.S. DEP'T OF STATE, PUB. No. 7919 at 11 (Far Eastern Series 136, 1965); Statement of Secretary Rusk before the Senate Foreign Relations Committee, reprinted in THE VIETNAM HEARINGS, supra at 11. Secretary Rusk's first public comment on the 1965 escalation was before the American Society of International Law, April 23, 1965. He stated that the United States was providing assistance in the exercise of the right of collective self-defense under the U.N. Charter at the request of the Republic of Viet-Nam, and that "[o]ur assistance has been increased because the aggression from the North has been augmented. Our assistance now encompasses the bombing of North Vietnam. The bombing is designed to interdict, as far as possible, and to inhibit, as far as may be necessary, continued aggression against the Republic of Vietnam." He said that the insurgency "receives vital external support — in organization and direction, in training, in men, in weapons and other supplies," which violates general international law expressed in the U.N. Charter and the 1954 Geneva Accords. VIET NAM, supra note 44, at 333.

[55] See notes 12–13 supra and accompanying text.

according to the proposed norm, any type of supplies could be extended by third powers. That under Farer's norm, the Soviets could supply the Castro government with missiles but no Soviet troops would be permitted to man them, would further unstabilize the situation and make international war more probable. The suggested rule would in this case violate almost all of the criteria suggested by Farer as prerequisite tests for the norm. The likelihood of great power confrontation would be encouraged by the allowance of a supply of weapons which could be used against the territory of the United States; if the weapons were used, geographic containment would be virtually impossible; and the degree of ambiguity in the suggested norm which permits such a disparate treatment of two types of intervention in Cuba by the Soviet Union and the United States is obvious. Farer's focus upon a "war zone" as the critical area in which outside intervention would not be permitted is unrealistic in an age of intercontinental missiles.

Professor Falk proposed that internal wars be treated as civil wars, regardless of intervention by third parties, permitting a "neutralizing response as a maximum counteraction," with no action being taken beyond the initial territory within which the internal war was being waged.[56] For Falk, the maximum response in South Viet-Nam, if indeed any response would be justified, would be a neutralizing counter-intervention rather than a response to "armed attack."[57]

In an age when internationalized "civil" wars have become the predominant form of conflict, and when several nations have openly advocated the instigation of and support for such types of conflict, query whether the proposal of Professor Falk would possess significant deterrent capacity. Is there any real deterrent effect when the worst a potential aggressor would face, when contemplating indirect aggression, is the frustration of such efforts? Must our entire military strategy in the age of international civil wars and wars of national liberation be reactive? If all the international gambler has to lose would be the chips he chooses to place on the table, foreign adventurers would be free to intervene with relative impunity. They would know that the maximum response from third party nations friendly to the legitimate government would be an attempt to negate the intervention of the aggressor nation with counter-intervention.

Nations which choose to intervene in civil wars within other nations on the scale that North Viet-Nam has intervened in South Viet-Nam should recognize that force commensurate with their aggression might be employed against their homeland. Surely Richard Falk's proposal does not contain any sanction sufficient to meet Henry Kissinger's definition of deterrence: "Deterrence is the attempt to keep an opponent from adopting a certain course of action by posing risks which will seem to him out of proportion to any gains to be achieved."[58]

Further, it must be assumed as a prerequisite to Professor Falk's proposal that the "contending factions" within a country are in fact indigenous to the

---

[56] Falk, *supra* note 19, at 1123–25.
[57] *Id.* at 1125.
[58] H. KISSINGER, NUCLEAR WEAPONS AND FOREIGN POLICY 96 (1957).

country. From that point it may be argued, as Professor Falk does, that international law may permit (or at least does not proscribe) the intervention by an outside state on behalf of an indigenous insurgent group when such an insurgency reaches some degree of stability.[59] But it could hardly be argued that foreign support for a "contending faction" can be permissible under international law when that "contending faction" is *first created* and then directed, supplied, and maintained by another country. To permit one nation to first create an insurgent force within another country and then claim the right under international law to direct and support such a force since it has indisputable existence would turn the definition of civil war on its head. No more flagrant example of the bootstrap doctrine could be posed.

The most current information available to this writer would indicate that the National Liberation Front was created in the North and, though initially staffed to some extent by southerners who had gone North after 1954, has since 1963 been directed by northerners who in turn are controlled directly by Hanoi. Though the D.R.V.N. was able to exploit a revolutionary situation in the South, and though there are unquestionably many native nationalistic southerners in the N.L.F., it cannot legitimately be called an indigenous southern organization.[60]

Of course, if Viet-Nam is considered as one entity, this North-South distinction is meaningless. But to so do one must ignore the historical separateness of these regions,[61] the acts of recognition by over 60 states of the Republic of Viet-Nam, its membership in scores of international organizations, including specialized agencies of the United Nations, and most important of all, the de facto separate existence of North and South under separate governments for the last 13 years.[62]

Falk's thesis is sound at some lesser levels of intervention. "Subversive activities," or indirect aggression of the scope to which Secretary Dulles was

---

[59] Falk, *supra* note 19, at 1134–39.

[60] *See* D. PIKE, *supra* note 47; U.S. DEP'T OF STATE, DEALING WITH THE N.L.F. AS A PATH TO PEACE IN VIET-NAM 1 (unpublished document); Carver, *The Faceless Viet Cong*, 44 FOREIGN AFFAIRS 364 (1966); Chaffard, *Who Controls the Viet Cong?*, CHICAGO TODAY, vol. 4, Spring 1967, at 40; Fall, *Viet Cong — The Unseen Enemy in Viet-Nam*, in THE VIET-NAM READER (Raskin & Fall eds. 1965); *cf.* J. LACOUTURE, VIETNAM: BETWEEN TWO TRUCES 55 (1966); H. SALISBURY, BEHIND THE LINE — HANOI 159–74 (1967).

[61] Fall states:

> Viet-Nam, as a unified independent state, had again disappeared — if it can be said to have had time to bloom in the few chaotic months of the Tran Trong Kim regime under Japanese protection, and of the Ho Chi Minh regime under Chinese aegis. As in the sixteenth century, so again Viet-Nam was divided into two distinct states, but from 1946 until 1954, this was to be a new, strange, urban-rural division rather than a north-south division, with the Viet Minh holding much of the countryside, including the hill tribe areas; while the French and, later, the non-Communist Vietnamese administration were to hold the lowlands and, especially, the cities. In 1954, the "normal" north-south division of Viet-Nam was to appear again, only a few miles to the south of the ancient Wall of Dong-Hoi.
>
> And, once more, the two Viet-Nams began to build their own separate institutions.

B. FALL, *supra* note 29, at 77–78.

[62] *See* Moore & Underwood, *The Lawfulness of United States Assistance to the Republic of Viet Nam*, 5 DUQUESNE L. REV. 235, 239–70 (1967).

referring in his testimony quoted by Professor Falk,[63] could be met by the response of the legitimate government within that nation or perhaps by reciprocal subversive activities against the subverting nation. But third nation responses should be limited to countering such subversion within the territory of the state of the legitimate government. However, at some point in escalated intervention, surely by the time that cadres of troops and war supplies have been transported across borders or into a zone of a temporarily divided state, the aggressor nation must be faced with the possibility of a response directed at its homeland commensurate in strength with the original aggression.

Professor Falk has maintained that the classification of the actions of North Viet-Nam against South Viet-Nam as "armed attack" threatens to obliterate the distinction between international and civil war.[64] Is it really "civil war" when the entire leadership structure of the guerrilla forces, along with a significant portion of the manpower and essentially all of the arms and munitions are supplied by a third power? Granted that "the war in South Viet-Nam should be viewed as primarily between factions contending for control of the southern zone, whether or not the zone is considered a nation,"[65] when one of these factions is first created and then directed, partially manned, and supported by another state, it is submitted that this factor abolishes the distinction between international and civil war, and not a subsequent decision to classify a war as one or the other.

Professor Falk's most recent proposal[66] — that the discretion of the victim state, the potential intervening third state, and the executive branch of that third state be severely limited by prior "organized international community" assent to the characterization of covert aggression as "armed attack" — is based upon one gigantic assumption. That is that there exists an institution of the international community with sufficient integrity and responsibility to be the repository of such power. Though I would wish that the contrary were true, I do not believe that the United Nations possesses such qualifications at this time.

Even if it is agreed that international law should place no prohibitions upon the right of a third state to retaliate within the territory of another third power that is intervening in an internal war, when such intervention reaches the level of North Viet-Nam's intervention, however, it does not follow that such a response should be initiated. Factors of strategy and tactics, including the desire to limit the geographic escalation of violence emphasized by Professor Falk, should be carefully considered. But international law should place no absolute prohibition on retaliation by third powers because a potentially more unstabilizing effect would result from the elimination of a credible deterrent to foreign-sponsored wars of national liberation of the scope of the D.R.V.N. activities against the R.V.N.

---

[63] Falk, *supra* note 19 at 1123–24.
[64] *Id.* at 1133.
[65] *Id.*
[66] Falk, *supra* note 24, at 1142–50.

Two factors which are related to this problem have to do with the initial decision to resort to counter-intervention in an internal war. (It is at this point that a natural fire-break occurs. It may be easier and less costly in terms of lives, economics, credibility and prestige not to intervene in the first instance than to abide by certain rules limiting the scope of intervention once it has been initiated.) The first factor has been mentioned previously. That is the decision to categorize an internal war as primarily involving contending nationalistic elements vying for control of the government — in which case intervention is presumably not to our interest — or to categorize a war as primarily involving elements of foreign initiation and direction, leadership, manpower and supplies — in which case counterintervention is *possibly* within our interest.

One of the chief sources of frustration and dilemma for those attempting to analyze the struggle in Viet-Nam is that the factors of foreign Communist influence and genuine nationalism are so hopelessly intertwined. In Viet-Nam, communism and nationalism are present in almost equal amounts even within the major personality in the struggle, Ho Chi Minh. Ho has fought those who were imposing foreign control upon his country, from the French to the Japanese to the French once again. As a type of embodiment of the spirit of his people, he has also resisted a satellite status for North Viet-Nam in relation to Communist China. Those who would characterize him as a puppet of Peking do a great disservice to others who must bear the results of such characterization in the form of political and military strategy. Yet Ho is unquestionably a dedicated Communist who hopes to impose this ideology upon most if not all of Indo-China. This record does not support the suppositions of some that Ho would be an Asian Tito if left alone. Consequently, which element — that of dogmatic Communism with designs upon neighboring states, or legitimate expression of nationalism against those who would impose another form of foreign ideology — should the policy maker choose to characterize the nature of the violence in Viet-Nam? Either could be accepted — with substantial evidence to support it — as the chief characteristic of this violence. The choice has largely determined the nature of the American response.

Proponents of the American policy in Viet-Nam are fond of offering as precedents our reaction to guerrilla war in Greece, intimidation in Turkey, and subversion in Iran. Opponents are offended by this comparison and deny its applicability with equally broad statements. But while in this writer's opinion some similarities are present, the factors of internationally fostered communism and nationalism were not so hopelessly intertwined as they are in Viet-Nam. That crucial difference, it is submitted, goes a long way toward explaining why this nation is so dangerously divided over Viet-Nam and yet was able to meet the crises of 1947–1950 with considerably more unanimity. Today, either side may make its characterization with almost equal empirical validity.

The second factor which the United States must weigh before making the initial decision regarding counter-intervention is a purely pragmatic one.

What are the chances of success? This may be determined by factors which, according to Mao and Lin Piao, are the prime considerations of the Communist state that makes the initial intervention in support of a war of national liberation. Mao has said that "we do not fight unless we are sure of victory; we must on no account fight without preparation and without certainty of the outcome."[67] Lin Piao stated that "[r]evolution or people's war in any country is the business of the masses in that country and should be carried out primarily by their own efforts; there is no other way."[68] Translated into our own jargon, and viewed from the standpoint of counter-intervention, this would mean that there must be a sufficient national and non-Communist base to politically support a non-Communist government in dealing with truly internal dissent, and also offer a national base upon which a counter-intervening nation could build, in order to help frustrate intervention by an outside power.

Again, in South Viet-Nam this issue is so close that men of equally good will and similar liberal instincts have reached contrary conclusions. On the one hand, many factors indicate that there are a significant and probably dominant number of people in the South who prefer living under a non-Communist regime. These factors include the voluntary migration of almost one million people, mostly Roman Catholics, from North Viet-Nam to South Viet-Nam after the Geneva Agreements; the capacity of the South Vietnamese to bear appalling casualties for a protracted time and still continue as a political entity; and the absence of significant "Yankee go home" sentiment on the part of any major segment of the country, including Buddhist elements which are opposed to the government at Saigon.

On the other hand, no political figure or group has emerged who could serve as the nucleus of a government with which the people in the countryside could identify. No real political support in the countryside exists in favor of a man or a government, even though considerable opposition does exist toward the Communist North. This situation is dangerously close to that experienced by Chiang in pre-1949 China, when he had impressive military forces, some political support in the cities, but few political roots in the countryside. And as in China, the vast majority of the people of South Viet-Nam do not live in the cities. Diem was a legitimate nationalist and no one questioned the depth of his anti-Communism. Attempts to picture him as a French or an American puppet are completely erroneous. But his flaws eventually more than matched his impressive qualities. And no one since has had the stature or the background of fighting the nationalist fight against colonial powers. The southern equivalent of Ho is painfully absent. Without a man around whom the country can unite and with whom the people can identify, the chances of the formation of a stable government with true political power are slim. And without such a government the chances of successful American counter-intervention are equally slight. We would be faced with the choice of perpetual presence or the rapid evaporation of a politically rootless non-Communist government in the South.

---

[67] *See* 3 MAO TSE-TUNG, *supra* note 38.
[68] Lin Piao, *supra* note 35, at 19.

Again, the existence of such impelling factors on both sides of the question of the existence of a truly nationalistic yet non-communist society in the South make for excruciating political decisions for policy makers and critics alike.

This writer is in general agreement with Professors Moore and Underwood in categorizing the activities of the D.R.V.N. in South Viet-Nam as "armed attack."[69] To this extent, the General Assembly condemnation of Yugoslavia, Bulgaria, and Albania for aiding the Greek rebels is a relevant and appropriate citation of authority for the proposition that aiding rebellion in another country constitutes aggression under international law;[70] the high level of terrorism in the South which has been initiated, controlled, and directed by the D.R.V.N. constitutes aggression as well;[71] and Professor Kelsen's inclusion of supporting revolutionary movements in another country within the definition of "armed attack" under Article 51 of the United Nations Charter would seem to state correctly the better interpretation of this portion of the Charter.

> Since the Charter of the United Nations does not define the term "armed attack" used in article 51, the members of the United Nations in exercising their right of "individual or collective self-defense" may interpret "armed" attack to mean not only an action in which a state uses its armed force but also a revolutionary movement which takes place in one state but which is *initiated or supported by another state.* In this case the members could come to the assistance of the legitimate government against which the revolutionary movement is directed.[72]

Under this definition, the actions of the D.R.V.N. prior to their use of regular PAVN troops would have constituted aggression and an "armed attack." After the use of regular forces, and absent justification recognized under international law, there would be no question but that an "armed attack" had occurred.

Even if the actions of the United States in assisting the R.V.N. against the D.R.V.N. are technically lawful under customary international law and the United Nations Charter, there remains a larger and perhaps more important question regarding the use (or non-use) of the United Nations by the United States from 1954 to 1966. Granted that, as Lauterpacht and McNair maintain,[73] Article 51 only enlarges and restates an inherent right of self-defense; granted further that collective self-defense does not require prior Security Council approval;[74] and granted that the United States technically met its reporting obligations to the Security Council,[75] it was not until January 31,

---

[69] Moore & Underwood, *supra* note 62.

[70] *Id.* at 288–89.

[71] *Id.* at 290–91.

[72] KELSEN, COLLECTIVE SECURITY UNDER INTERNATIONAL LAW 88 (1954) (emphasis in original).

[73] Moore & Underwood, *supra* note 62, at 299–300.

[74] *Id.* at 301–04.

[75] *See* Statement by United States Ambassador to the U.N., Adlai Stevenson, in the U.N. Security Council, Aug. 5, 1964, reprinted in 51 DEP'T STATE BULL. 272–74 (State Dep't Pub. No. 7710, 1964); Letter from Ambassador Stevenson to President of the U.N. Security Council, Feb. 7, 1965, reprinted in 52 DEP'T STATE BULL. 240–41 (State Dep't Pub. No. 7817, 1965).

1966, that the United States through Ambassador Goldberg made a serious proposal in the form of a draft resolution to bring the question of the hostilities in Viet-Nam officially before the United Nations.[76] This writer does not doubt that sincere efforts are now being made to initiate negotiations, within and without the United Nations, through formal and informal means.[77] But it is difficult to avoid the conclusion that the United States has made serious use of the United Nations only when it became apparent that a favorable military solution to hostilities in South Viet-Nam would be either impossible or too costly, in terms of a prolonged and escalated presence in the face of an attrition of popular political support in the United States for such a war. In retrospect, one might wonder why the Soviet draft resolution proposing United Nations membership for both the D.R.V.N. and the R.V.N.[78] would not have provided the basis for a negotiated settlement in Viet-Nam many years ago.

It may be that the United States, not without precedent in other times and countries, has over-learned its lesson of the late 1940's that complete reliance upon the United Nations for purposes of collective security is not only foolish but potentially disastrous. Might it not be that at least within a certain limited area where the interests of the United States and the Soviet Union are not hopelessly opposite, the original suppositions of the founders of the United Nations regarding primary reliance upon the Security Council might be capable of fulfillment? With both the Soviet Union and the United States possessing nuclear weapons, with an increasing identity of interest between these countries to avoid the possibility of nuclear confrontation similar to that involving Cuba, and with a similar desire to check to some degree the aggressive tendencies of Communist China, it would seem that conditions for the fulfillment of big power unity are more nearly attainable now than they were in 1945.[79]

---

[76] Letter from United States Ambassador to the U.N., Arthur J. Goldberg, to the President of the Security Council, Jan. 31, 1966, reprinted in SENATE COMM. ON FOREIGN RELATIONS, 89th CONG., 2d SESS., BACKGROUND INFORMATION RELATING TO SOUTHEAST ASIA AND VIETNAM 271–73 (Comm. Print, 2d rev. ed. 1966) [hereinafter cited as BACKGROUND INFORMATION]; Letter from Ambassador Goldberg to Roger Seydoux, President of the U.N. Security Council, Jan. 31, 1966, reprinted in BACKGROUND INFORMATION, at 273; Statement by President Johnson, Jan. 31, 1966, reprinted in BACKGROUND INFORMATION, at 273–75.

[77] See Goldberg, An Ambassador on the War, NEWSWEEK, July 10, 1967, at 56.

[78] In early 1957, the Soviet Union introduced a draft resolution proposing the admission of the D.R.V.N., the R.V.N., the Democratic People's Republic of Korea, and the Republic of Korea. 11 U.N. GAOR, ANNEXES, AGENDA ITEM No. 25, at 5–7, U.N. Doc. A/SPC/L.9, A/3519 (1957). Debate on this resolution produced several speeches by the Soviet delegate recognizing the de facto existence of two separate states and two separate governments in Viet-Nam. United States-supported draft resolutions at this time called for the admission of Korea and Viet-Nam with the recognition of the Southern governments, respectively, in both countries as representing both the northern and southern portions.

Though the Soviet draft resolution was never accepted, it does show, some months after the Geneva Agreements deadline on national elections in Viet-Nam had passed, that the Soviet Union was willing to live with the reality of two states in Viet-Nam, and that they probably never really expected such elections to take place.

[79] See Firmage, A United Nations Peace Force, 11 WAYNE L. REV. 717, 727–37 (1965).

Though an accord would have to be reached with Peking and Hanoi, as well as with Moscow, the present tumult in China may make Hanoi increasingly dependent upon Moscow for supplies and increasingly less intimidated by Peking regarding any desired overtures toward serious negotiation. Consequently, opportunities missed in the past for a United Nations supervised truce might be capable of attainment in the future. The statement made by Moore and Underwood that the United Nations might have been utilized by other nations under Article 35 or the Secretary-General under Article 99 to bring the issue of Viet-Nam before the international body, even absent a United States draft resolution, misses the point.[80] It is obvious that international institutional gadgetry cannot accomplish what the major powers do not want accomplished. That fact applies in regard to the United States and its attitude toward a settlement in Viet-Nam as well as to the Soviet Union. If Hanoi is finally made dependent upon Moscow for its continued support of hostilities directed against the R.V.N., and if Moscow and Washington both desire a settlement in Viet-Nam, the United Nations offers an ideal forum for such a settlement and various possibilities for its implementation. It offers no more than this.

VI. The Election Provisions of the Geneva Accords

The Geneva Conference resulted in four separate documents and seven limiting declarations. These included three cease-fire agreements, one each for Cambodia, Laos and Viet-Nam,[81] and a Final Declaration of the Conference. The seven declarations were by Cambodia (2), Laos (2), France (2), and the United States (1). The cease-fire agreements were bilaterals between the Viet Minh and the Commander of the French Union Forces. The Final Declaration was not signed but was approved at the Final Plenary Session of the Conference, with the United States refusing to subscribe and issuing a unilateral declaration, and the State of Viet-Nam making an important reservation to its approval.

The Final Declaration of the Geneva Conference[82] provided for elections in Viet-Nam during "July 1956, under the supervision of an international commission composed of representatives of the member states of the International Supervisory Commission . . . ." These were to be "free general elections by secret ballot."[83] The failure of the R.V.N. to hold such elections has been cited by critics of the Administration position as a major reason for the resumption of hostilities by the D.R.V.N. and a justification recognized by international law for such action. Falk has attacked the memorandum of the Department of State for its defense of the refusal of the R.V.N. to enter into negotiations leading to elections. The memorandum's justification of Saigon's

---

[80] Moore & Underwood, *supra* note 62, at 323–24.

[81] Agreement Between the Commander-in-Chief of the French Union Forces in Indo-China and the Commander-in-Chief of the People's Army of Viet-Nam on the Cessation of Hostilities in Viet-Nam, Cmnd. No. 9239 (1954), reprinted in 60 Am. J. Int'l L. 629 (1966).

[82] Final Declaration of the Geneva Conference on the Problem of Restoring Peace in Indo-China, Cmnd. No. 9239 (1954), reprinted in 60 Am. J. Int'l L. 643 (1966).

[83] *Id.* at 644.

refusal on the basis that "free elections" were impossible in North Viet-Nam at that time are rejected by Falk on the ground that the "meaning of 'free elections' in Communist countries was well known to all"[84] and still such provisions were included in the settlement. The assumption made here, of course, is that such elections were actually expected by the parties and participants to be held.

Falk criticized the memorandum for its conclusion that under international law, North Viet-Nam was not justified in attempting to accomplish its political goals by force when the elections were not held. He stated that international law is ambiguous regarding the breakdown of a settlement of an internal war,[85] and that if the R.V.N. repudiated the Accords, the "principle of mutuality of obligation" would free North Viet-Nam from any proscriptions in the Accords.[86]

While the Final Declarations called for "free general elections by secret ballot,"[87] Quincy Wright agrees with Falk that the knowledge possessed by the participants at Geneva of conditions in Viet-Nam precludes belief that they considered conditions necessary for the holding of free and fair elections as a prerequisite to such elections.[88] Furthermore, the elections were such an integral part of the Cease-Fire Agreement, says Wright, that the failure to hold them justified the D.R.V.N. in resuming hostilities. Ho Chi Minh was entitled to regard the holding of elections in July 1956 as being obligatory upon France "and its successor in South Vietnam, Diem":[89]

> [The] provisions concerning elections in the final resolutions of the Geneva Conference were considered essential elements in the Cease-Fire Agreement. This agreement, therefore, became suspendable when the elections were frustrated by one of the parties and the other party, Ho Chi Minh, was free to consider his obligation to respect the cease-fire line suspended and to continue his long effort to unify Viet-Nam by force.[90]

Wright based this conclusion upon the assumption that Ho would not have signed the Cease-Fire Agreement in the first place unless he was sure that he could achieve his objective — the unification of Viet-Nam under his government — by means of the election.

Although Wright recognized that the R.V.N. was not a party to the Geneva Agreements, "France was, and the Diem government established in the Southern Zone as successor to France was bound by them."[91]

One major and two subsidiary questions result from this conflict between the memorandum and two of it critics. First and most important, was the

[84] Falk, *International Law and the United States Role in the Viet Nam War*, 75 YALE L.J. 1122, 1153 (1966).

[85] *Id.*

[86] *Id.*

[87] Final Declaration of the Geneva Conference, *supra* note 82, at 644.

[88] Wright, *Legal Aspects of the Viet-Nam Situation*, 60 AM. J. INT'L L. 750, 759 (1966).

[89] *Id.* at 759–60.

[90] *Id.* at 760.

[91] *Id.* at 762.

provision regarding elections really a significant factor in Ho's decision to sign the Accords? Was the provision such an integral part of the Cease-Fire Agreement in the intention of the parties, that failure to hold elections suspended the agreement? Second, was the R.V.N. a "successor to France" and thereby bound to honor the election provision of the Cease-Fire Agreement? This question is of lesser importance than the first, since if the provision for elections is not an integral part of the Cease-Fire Agreement, its breach would not provide grounds for suspension of the agreement in any event. Third, if the Republic of Viet-Nam is not a successor to France and is not bound by that or other conditions to the election provision of the Final Declaration, is North Viet-Nam thereby released from the cease-fire provisions under the principle of "mutuality of obligation?"

Bernard Fall has concluded that factors other than the belief that elections would be held motivated Ho Chi Minh to sign at Geneva.

> It is still not entirely clear why the DRVN accepted the compromise of a "temporary" division of Viet-Nam inasmuch as the prospects for the holding of a reunification election within two years, as provided by the Geneva agreements, seemed fairly slim from the outset. Soviet pressure on North Viet-Nam for the sake of improving Russian relations with France — more specifically, for the purpose of inducing Paris to block the creation of a European Defense Community including West Germany — may well have been the main factor behind Hanoi's agreement.[92]

The pragmatism Mao built into his doctrine of protracted war — that such wars should be temporarily concluded and consolidated rather than do serious injury to the country — has previously been mentioned.[93] Fall has concluded that this same pragmatism is shared by Ho:

> Another probable factor was the pragmatism of the North Vietnamese Communist leadership. Ho Chi Minh has characteristically settled for a safe half-loaf rather than fight to the finish merely to prove a point. Moreover, the consolidation of Communist power in North Viet-Nam after four years of Japanese depredation, one year of Chinese pilfering, and eight years of scorched-earth war with the French was a formidable enough problem to tackle.[94]

Intense Soviet pressure and North Viet pragmatism seem far more persuasive explanations for Ho's actions at Geneva than to think that one of the shrewdest revolutionaries of our century really believed that the government in the South would agree to hold elections the outcome of which would be fixed as much by Ho's complete destruction of opposition in the North as his unquestioned popularity throughout the country.

Although Wright believes that D.R.V.N. subversion of the government in the South began only after the failure to hold elections,[95] terrorism and planned subversion actually occurred from the time of the Geneva Agree-

---

[92] Fall, *North Viet-nam: A Profile,* in PROBLEMS OF COMMUNISM, vol. 14, July–Aug. 1965, at 18.

[93] *See* note 38 *supra* and accompanying text.

[94] Fall, *supra* note 92, at 18.

[95] *See* Wright, *supra* note 88, at 757–78.

ment, mounting in intensity as it became apparent that no elections would be held, and, more importantly, that the South would not collapse as a result of its own problems.[96]

Again, any reticence to begin immediate, massive infiltration of the South can be explained more credibly by the necessity of consolidation in the North than real hope for elections. Ho and Giap were finding it easier to "blow up a water main than to run a water-purification plant, and to sabotage the locomotive roundhouse of Hanoi than to run trains on time."[97] Ho was plagued with the problems of conducting constructive government rather than destructive guerrilla war; he was also following Mao's advice of consolidation and his own pragmatic bent of not going to war again if the desired result could be accomplished by other means. But it is submitted that the failure of Diem's government to fall apart under internal strain, rather than the failure of that government to hold elections, was the major factor in the timing of Ho's increased use of terror, assassination, and infiltration in the South. When it became increasingly clear that Diem had established a government which, with United States help, could last indefinitely, Ho had to use means familiar to him.[98]

That Ho needed a time of recovery seems to be unquestionable. The D.R.V.N. were unable to properly run the cement plants, textile factories, coal mines, and power plants.[99] The government was chaotic.[100] It must be remembered that while the 1946–1954 war with the French was a brilliant success for Ho and Giap, it was not the sort of victory that one could stand too frequently or endure forever. Their greatest victory, Dien Bien Phu, had cost them three men for every one lost by the French, and the overall Viet Minh casualties in the Indo-China war were three for each one of the 172,000 casualties suffered by the French Union Forces.[101]

Fall's description of events in North Viet-Nam immediately following the Geneva Agreement help explain Ho's temporary preoccupation with the North and Diem's reluctance to hold elections:

> Following the Geneva accords, the DRVN settled down to the task of transforming itself into a full-fledged "people's democracy." A "Population Classification Decree" issued in March 1953 had divided the population into distinct social categories, and the regime now proceeded to eliminate all landlords by methods of force and terror reminiscent of the Chinese Communists — and with similar results. Exact figures remain unavailable, but the number of peasants killed during the North Vietnamese "land reform" drives from 1954 to 1956 is variously estimated at between 50 and 100 thousand.
>
> This brutal policy led to the outbreak, in November 1956, of a veritable peasant rebellion in Nghe-An Province — the same region which had been the seat of the pro-Communist peasant uprising of 1930.[102]

[96] *See* F. Trager, Why Vietnam? 115–16 (1966).

[97] *See* Fall, *supra* note 92, at 138.

[98] *See* F. Trager, *supra* note 96, at 122–39.

[99] Fall, *supra* note 92, at 139.

[100] *Id.* at 139–41.

[101] *Id.* at 129.

[102] Fall, *supra* note 92, at 18.

Whether or not Diem would have acquiesced to "free" elections, there is no doubt that such elections could not have been accomplished in 1954, 1956, or any time thereafter. After the new D.R.V.N. constitution of 1960, elections were held in the North. They followed the familiar Communist pattern, with 99.8% of the voters casting ballots for 458 candidates who were competing for 404 seats. In Hanoi, two tiny minority parties were permitted to put up a few candidates as long as they continued to collaborate with the Communists.[103] Fall reported that the legislative elections held in 1964 "brought little apparent change . . . ."[104]

The participants in the Geneva Conference did not appear to be surprised at the failure to hold elections. The Soviet Union introduced a draft resolution calling for the admission of both the D.R.V.N. and the R.V.N. as members of the United Nations after the July 1956 deadline for elections.[105] The British had favored permanent partition in the first place.[106]

The assertion by Wright that the R.V.N. is a "successor" to France in its relationship to the Geneva Accords would seem to run afoul of the very definition of the term. Both France and the State of Viet-Nam[107] were represented at Geneva, France as a participant, the State of Viet-Nam as an associated state. As Professors Moore and Underwood have pointed out, the State of Viet-Nam had achieved independence and recognition from France prior to the Geneva Conferences;[108] Foreign Minister Bidault expressly so recognized at the Geneva Conference.[109] The State of Viet-Nam formally objected to the Final Declaration of the Conference and Dr. Tran Van Do, its representative at the Conference, refused to approve the Declaration as it stood and offered an amendment which expressed the intention of the State of Viet-Nam to abide only by the Cease-Fire Agreement.[110] Prior to this, on May 12, 1954, he had rejected the proposals for partition of the country and had called for national elections after international supervision of the terms of the cease-fire. He reserved for his government "complete freedom of action to guarantee the sacred right of the Vietnamese people to territorial unity, national independence and freedom."[111]

Mr. Bedell Smith, representing the United States, refused to approve the Final Declaration but instead offered a declaration which stated that the United States would "refrain from the threat or the use of force" to disturb the Cease-Fire Agreements and would "view any renewal of the aggression

---

[103] *Id.* at 21.

[104] *Id.*

[105] *See* note 78 *supra.*

[106] Moore & Underwood, *supra* note 62, at 260.

[107] The State of Viet-Nam was succeeded by the Republic of Viet-Nam in October, 1955, following a referendum vote. Ngo Dinh Diem became President of the R.V.N., succeeding Bao Dai as Chief of State.

[108] Moore & Underwood, *supra* note 62, at 245–47, 337–38.

[109] *Id.* at 337–38. No claim has been made that the State of Viet-Nam is a successor to treaties made by France since 1953. *See* 2 WHITEMAN, DIGEST OF INTERNATIONAL LAW 976–78 (1963).

[110] Moore & Underwood, *supra* note 62, at 334–36.

[111] DOCUMENTS ON AMERICAN FOREIGN RELATIONS 1954, at 315–16, 318 (Curl ed. 1955).

in violation of the aforesaid Agreements with grave concern and as seriously threatening international peace and security."[112] Then, with direct reference to the provision for elections which had been rejected by the State of Viet-Nam, the United States Declaration stated:

> In connection with the statement in the Declaration concerning free elections in Viet Nam, my Government wishes to make clear its position which it has expressed in a Declaration made in Washington on 29th June, 1954, as follows:
>
>> In the case of nations now divided against their will, we shall continue to seek to achieve unity through free elections, supervised by the United Nations to ensure that they are conducted fairly.
>
> With respect to the statement made by the Representative of the State of Viet Nam, the United States reiterates its traditional position that peoples are entitled to determine their own future and that it will not join in an arrangement which would hinder this. Nothing in its declaration just made is intended to or does indicate any departure from this traditional position.[113]

This was a direct endorsement of the position previously taken by the State of Viet-Nam — that it would respect the cease-fire, but reserve to itself complete freedom of action regarding the holding of elections. While the Republic of Viet-Nam has recognized the legitimacy of the Cease-Fire Agreement, it has from the beginning refused to consider itself bound to hold elections under the terms of the Final Declaration at Geneva.

The Democratic Republic of Viet-Nam approved the Final Declaration with full knowledge of the position of the State of Viet-Nam. The only portion of the Final Declaration which both the D.R.V.N. and the R.V.N. recognized was the cease-fire provision. The D.R.V.N. apparently did not rely upon the election provisions of the Geneva Agreement in deciding to negotiate a cease-fire, and the R.V.N. are clearly not successors to the French regarding provisions of an agreement which the R.V.N. expressly disavowed. Finally, it hardly follows that the refusal of a nonsignatory to abide by provisions which it had expressly disavowed at Geneva — those relating to elections — justifies a signatory in negating the one portion of the agreement — that relating to a cease-fire — recognized as binding by both.

VII. THE NATURE OF THE UNITED STATES COMMITMENT TO THE REPUBLIC OF VIET-NAM

Secretary Rusk has frequently cited the Southeast Asia Treaty as the source of our commitment to the Republic of Viet-Nam. Speaking before the American Foreign Service Association in 1965, he said that when President Johnson authorized combat missions for United States military units, he "recognized the obligations of this nation under the Southeast Asia

---

[112] *Further Documents Relating to the Discussion of Indo-China at the Geneva Conference* (Miscellaneous No. 20 [1954] Command Paper 9239). Great Britain Parliamentary Sessional Papers XXXI (1953–1954), at 5–7, quoted in 5 DUQUESNE L. REV. 328 (1967).

[113] *Id.*

Treaty . . . ." and "acted under the Joint Resolution of August 1964 . . . ."[114] The Secretary expanded on these views at his appearance before the Senate Foreign Relations Committee in 1966. He stated that under the Southeast Asia Treaty and its Protocol, a protocol state has the right to call on members for assistance and that "no doubt we are entitled to offer that assistance." In reply to Senator Fulbright's query as to whether we were obligated to do so, Secretary Rusk said that he did not want to get involved in the question of whether we had a legal way to avoid the commitments under the treaty. He stated that the United States is "entitled" to offer the assistance which was requested of us as a signatory by a protocol nation.[115] Later he stated that we had an obligation of policy rooted in the treaty[116] and that Article IV, paragraph 1 was the "fundamental . . . obligation that has from the outset guided our actions in South Vietnam."[117]

The reticence of Secretary Rusk to assert any legal commitment of the United States to unilaterally act under provisions of the SEATO Treaty[118] is well taken. Both its terms and its history indicate that while the United States may take unilateral action in the situation presented in South Viet-Nam, it is not legally obligated to do so.

Article IV, paragraph 1, states that:

> Each party recognizes that aggression by means of armed attack in the treaty area against any of the parties or against any state or territory which the parties by unanimous agreement may hereafter designate, would endanger its own peace and safety, and agrees that it will in that event act to meet the common danger *in accordance with its constitutional processes.*[119]

The Protocol designates "Cambodia, Laos, and the free territory under the jurisdiction of the State of Vietnam" as coming under Article IV. An understanding incorporated into the Treaty limits the United States commitment to act in response to "Communist aggression" only, with the further proviso that we would consult on other types of aggression. Paragraph 2 of Article IV requires consultation by the parties on measures for common defense, if the independence of any is threatened in any way other than by armed attack.

During the hearings held November 11, 1954,[120] Secretary Dulles made it quite clear that the Administration did not consider it essential under Article IV, paragraph 2, that consultation take place prior to United States action when an "armed attack" occurred.[121]

---

[114] Address by Dean Rusk, Washington, D.C., June 23, 1965, in U.S. DEP'T OF STATE, PUB. NO. 7919, VIET-NAM: FOUR STEPS TO PEACE 11 (Far East Series No. 136, 1965).

[115] THE VIETNAM HEARINGS 11–12 (Random House ed. 1966).

[116] *Id.* at 35–36.

[117] *Id.* at 234.

[118] 6 U.S.T. 81, T.I.A.S. No. 3170, reprinted in 60 AM. J. INT'L L. 646 (1966).

[119] *Id.* at 647 (emphasis added).

[120] *Hearings on the Southeast Asia Collective Defense Treaty and the Protocol Thereto Before the Senate Comm. on Foreign Relations,* 83d Cong., 2d Sess., pt. 1 (1954).

[121] See the dialogue between Senator Gilette and Secretary Dulles, *Id.* at 35–36.

The adoption in the SEATO Treaty of the "Monroe Doctrine formula" recognizing that an attack would "endanger its own peace and safety," and leaving each state to decide its own response "in accordance with its constitutional processes" seems to represent a deliberate rejection of the allegedly "automatic" response included in the NATO Treaty formula which provides that an attack on one is an attack on all. Individual discretion is allowed by the former formula.

Finally, Article IV, paragraph 1, provides for notification of the Security Council of any action taken. Secretary Dulles testified[122] that the SEATO Treaty was based upon Article 51 of the United Nations Charter, relating to self-defense, rather than Article 52, relating to regional arrangements, and, therefore, no approval by the Security Council was necessary before action could be taken. Thus, under the Charter, the Council must only be informed of actions taken.

VIII. CONCLUSION

Both by traditional criteria of international law and by de facto existence as a separate and sovereign state, the Republic of Viet-Nam is a State separate from that of the Democratic Republic of Viet-Nam, which fact has received de jure and de facto recognition from a host of states.

The National Liberation Front has been created, directed and maintained by the Democratic Republic of Viet-Nam, though a situation existed in the South which made that nation ripe for revolution. Southern influence within the N.L.F. has been increasingly muted and, since 1963, has become of relative insignificance in terms of leadership and control. Prior to the most significant American escalation of hostilities in Viet-Nam in February of 1965, the internal nature of that war had been internationalized by the commitment of native North Vietnamese regular and irregular forces in massive numbers. This drastic change in the nature of hostilities was sufficient to constitute an "armed attack" under Article 51 of the United Nations Charter.

The United States has made tardy use of the United Nations by delaying serious attempts to bring peace through that organization until January of 1966. The United Nations was not seriously utilized until it became clear that a favorable military solution might not be possible. This fact, however, does not excuse that organization from all blame since initiation need not come from the United States. However, in fairness it must be said that without receptivity upon the part of the United States and the Soviet Union, there would be no hope of any meaningful United Nations participation.

It may be that whatever chances existed for the use of the United Nations in settling hostilities in North and South Viet-Nam have passed. It would appear that the United States is now pursuing serious attempts to instigate negotiations through that organization as well as through other diplomatic sources, with little receptivity upon the part of the D.R.V.N. However, tumult in China, coupled with the possibility that the United States and the Soviet Union might be within negotiating distance of each other concerning

---

[122] *Id.* at 17.

a settlement in Southeast Asia, might make it possible to use the Security Council and the Secretary-General in ways which were anticipated in 1945 but not realizable until the present.

The enigma of events in Communist China may hold the answer to the possibilities of foreseeable negotiations. As the tumult within that country continues or increases, the likelihood that the Democratic Republic of Viet-Nam will desire a negotiated settlement also increases. To this time, however, the critical pressure points of the harvest, nuclear development, and supplies to North Viet-Nam have not been visibly affected by the violence in China.

Basically, our commitment in the Republic of South Viet-Nam is not one in law.[123] Rather, it derives from a combination of altruism and at the same time self-interest in preventing successful wars of national liberation, or Communist-inspired wars of aggression by any other name, from being exported successfully from one nation to another. Though elements of civil war exist in South Viet-Nam, it is not civil war which the United States opposes. It is, rather, the attempt of one country to force its will upon another by violence — assassination, subversion, and in South Viet-Nam, infiltration of regular and irregular troops on such a scale as to constitute "armed attack."

This commitment, however, is not irrelevant to law. For it is in the highest interest of all nations who truly love peace and order that one nation not be allowed to force its will upon another, whether by blatant and massive assault or by more devious and subtle, but no less fatal, means of indirect aggression.

---

[123] See an impressive list of communications between Presidents Eisenhower and Kennedy with Prime Minister Churchill and President Diem, and statements of commitment by President Johnson in WHY VIETNAM? (Gov't Printing Office, 1965).

Vietnam: A Study of Law and Politics

CORNELIUS F. MURPHY, JR.

IN a certain sense, the Vietnam conflict testifies to the viability of international law. Both those who defend the United States involvement and those who oppose the intervention have seen fit to cast their arguments in juridical molds.[1] This has several desirable consequences. A reference to legal rules either as the justification of national action, or as a measure of national policy, is, arguably, some evidence of an emerging world order. No matter how the rules are applied, their very presence demonstrates the desire of all concerned to move international affairs from its disordered condition to a more stable governmental foundation.

Yet, the prevalence of juridical formulae is not an unlimited value. The Vietnam war is a very complex affair, and many of its aspects are not readily susceptible to legal analysis. Southeast Asia is an arena of international politics—a meeting place of cold war ideologies—as much as it is the locus of legally cognizable rights and duties. An excessively lawyer-like evaluation of the problem fails to bring to light the extra-legal motivations of national policy which have influenced the decision to intervene at least as much as have purely legal considerations.[2] The failure to account for these political factors, no matter how persuasive the legal analysis, means an equivalent inadequacy of comprehensive analysis.

One contribution to the Vietnam question in which this apolitical juridicism is particularly prevalent, is in the critique of Professor Falk of Princeton University. His thesis is a brilliant one, and by far the most original contribution to the vast body of literature devoted to this issue. Because of the breadth and erudition involved in his analysis, its radically juridical and apolitical character is liable to be missed by all but its most careful readers. Yet it is a point of view which any serious student of the Vietnam situation should understand.

THE FALKIAN THESIS

Professor Falk's critique of United States involvement in Vietnam is guided by his more general ideas of the role of law in the present decen-

---

1. E.g., Deutsch, The Legality of the United States Position in Vietnam, 52 A.B.A.J. 436 (1966); Legality of United States Participation in the Viet Nam Conflict: A Symposium, 75 Yale L.J. 1084 (1966); Moore, International Law and the United States Role in Viet Nam: A Reply, 76 Yale L.J. 1051 (1967); Moore, Lawfulness of Military Assistance to the Republic of Viet-Nam, 61 Am. J. Int'l L. 1 (1967). See also Friedmann, Intervention, Civil War, and the Role of International Law, 59 Am. Soc. Int. Law Proc. 67 (1965).

2. See Alford, The Legality of American Military Involvement in Viet Nam: A Broader Perspective, 75 Yale L. J. 1109, 1117 (1966).

tralized international community. Keenly aware of the thermonuclear dangers posed by the cold war, Falk starts with a postulate of non-violence and builds upon it an elaborate structure of international rules whose purpose is to minimize the possibilities of armed conflict.[3] These ethico-juridical requirements of interstate peace are applied to the problem of international intervention in internal wars.[4]

Falk observes, very perceptibly, that national decision-makers contemplating intervention tend to characterize the conflict in a manner best calculated to justify their proposed course of action. For example, if foreign power A gives aid to insurgents engaged in conflict with incumbent government B; C, an adversary of A, and friendly towards incumbent B, feels free to characterize A's actions as "aggression"; which theoretically justifies a maximum response by C against the "aggressor" A. Through this unlimited discretion a civil war can become an international conflict. To restrain this unbridled power of characterization Falk constructs his juridical norms of non-violence.

The norms of interstate conduct are developed upon a three part model of internal wars. To each model there corresponds rules of conduct, required both by the ethic of non-violence and the necessity of mutual restraint in the present decentralized world.

The first type of strife refers to those instances where substantial and direct military force of one political entity is employed across the frontier of another. In such circumstances, of which the Korean war is illustrative, if prompt response is required, a defensive response, either individually or collectively is permissible.[5] The second model covers those cases of substantial military participation of a foreign power in a local revolution. Such a situation, as in the Spanish Civil War, carries great potentials of escalation; extensive intervention could very easily spill the conflict out beyond the borders of its origin. Here the restraints necessary to prevent expansion of the conflict necessitate a rule which would limit the participation of a second foreign state (after exhaustion of peaceful procedures) to a limited function—its use of an offsetting force, confined within the boundaries of the conflict.[6]

The final model covers those situations where there is an internal struggle for control of a national society with virtually no external par-

---

3. R. Falk, Law, Morality and War in the Contemporary World (1963) [hereinafter cited as Law, Morality and War].

4. Falk, International Law and the United States Role in the Viet Nam War, 75 Yale L.J. 1122 (1966) [hereinafter cited as Vietnam Critique].

5. Id. at 1126.

6. Id.

ticipation. In such circumstances, the discretionary power of states to intervene would be absolutely prohibited. Overall stability of world order would best be served by allowing the conflict to reach its own internal outcome.[7]

The official United States position is to characterize the Vietnam war as a Type I conflict: armed aggression by North Vietnamese military forces across the 17th parallel. By so characterizing the conflict, an optimum response, such as the bombing of the North, is officially justified.[8] Falk, on the contrary, believes that the war is really a Type III affair, a primarily local struggle for power which necessitates non-intervention. He will concede *arguendo* a Type II classification, thus restricting the national discretion to the use of force upon South Vietnamese territory.[9]

Falk's points are forcefully made, and their inexorable logic is extremely persuasive. It is a difficult thesis to criticize because of its symmetry, moral quality and obvious correspondence with the values which he deems critical: the minimization of violence and the development of rules of reciprocal restraint. Yet, in spite of its positive qualities, it fails to provide a satisfactory solution to the problem of intervention.

The primary weakness of the Falk theory is his determination to treat the problem exclusively at the plane of the external relations between states. The legality of intervention is evaluated strictly at the level of juridical abstraction;[10] political or ideological motivations of states are considered irrelevant to the functions of international law. But drawing a sharp dichotomy between law and politics gives the analysis an artificial character. Treating the problem in this manner necessarily excludes from consideration factors which are of substantial significance to the

---

7. Id.

8. Department of State, Office of the Legal Adviser, The Legality of United States Participation in the Defense of Viet Nam, 75 Yale L.J. 1085 (1966).

9. Vietnam Critique, supra note 4, at 1127.

10. Since the point of this article is to emphasize what the Falk thesis fails to consider, a direct evaluation of his juridical theory will not be undertaken. However, two observations are pertinent. First, legality of the use of force is more existentially grounded than Falk's thesis will allow. The test is one of reasonableness under all the circumstances, which might make licit a response across frontiers even if the strife does not fit strictly within the Type I model. Secondly, the theory, especially in Model III, assumes that international law has nothing to say about how changes in internal government shall occur. Exclusion of intervention leaves a vacuum to be filled by unbridled terror and subversion. Surely the world community has an interest in peaceful procedures of transition; the fact that the change occurs internally does not exclude the matter from international concern. Subsequent writings of Professor Falk on this topic reflect a greater appreciation of concrete factors. See Falk, International Law and the United States Role in Vietnam: A Response to Professor Moore, 76 Yale L.J. 1095 (1967).

states whose conduct he seeks to govern by rules. To consider the decision of the United States to intervene and support the Saigon Government as a simple exercise of national power grossly oversimplifies the
purposes which direct the course of state decision-making. States are not
merely integers in a power process; they seek to reflect in their international conduct the interests of the nations and people they represent.
In other words, the state is something more than a judicial abstraction
whose conduct can be meaningfully measured by purely external criteria.
It is an agent for a political society of which it is a part.[11] And it is precisely this connection between national decision-making and politics
that Falk strives to exclude from an evaluation of intervention by international legal norms. In doing so, he repeats an error of jurists for which
there is considerable historical precedent.[12]

INTERNATIONAL LAW AND POLITICS

An adequate legal evaluation of intervention involves consideration of
the political aspects of interstate relations as well as abstract juridical
analysis. Yet how can international politics be incorporated into the
legal order? The United States seeks to defend "freedom" in Vietnam;
the National Liberation Front (Viet Cong) and the Ho Chi Minh regime
seek to "liberate" the country. How can a system of law bring these
vagaries of politics and ideology within the scope of legitimate juristic
concern?

On the surface, the topic of international politics is a poor candidate
for juridical thought. The history of foreign relations reveals the unpleasant truth that the interaction of states has been largely a struggle
for power. This fact of interminable competition has been so prevalent
that the concept of international politics is often defined in precisely
those terms.[13] Its refractory character has made many believe that this
level of interstate action is incapable of resolution in the quasi-ethical or
normative discourse of legal science. The jurist shies away from this
dimension of international life and concentrates upon the purely legal
aspects of interstate relations. But before condemning the political realm

---

11. See J. Maritain, Man and the State 12 (1951).

12. De Visscher's comments about similar theories of international law are relevant. They
were erroneous, he wrote, because they "evaded direct confrontation of international law
with politics. At times [they] simply ignored the political, at others [they] attempted to
eliminate it by artificially bringing even its most elementary data under legal criteria. The
defects of such methods became increasingly marked as the profound upheavals in the life
of the peoples forced the man of law to grasp realities more firmly. Law has everything to
gain from dispelling by degrees 'the dangerous mystery surrounding the antithesis of the
political and the legal.'" C. De Visscher, Theory and Reality in Public International Law 70
(1957).

13. See H. Morgenthau, Politics Among Nations 13 (4th ed. 1967).

as juristically unredeemable, it is profitable to examine whether the facts of force and power exhaust the content of this complex reality.

At the level of history, it is inaccurate to characterize international politics purely in terms of a struggle for domination. The great periods of Imperialism, e.g., the Roman conquest of Europe, the Spanish explorations, the era of British colonization, were all, in an important sense, expansions of state power beyond national borders for a primary objective of domination. But to fix the adventures at the level of power ignores many important aspects of the total historical picture. When the Roman legions receded, there remained with the exploited territories a deposit of laws and language of immense cultural value.[14] The same observation is true of most similar ventures by other powers. The point is not to condone aggression, but to point to the positive aspects of the interactions between states, qualities which elude a definition of interstate politics which does not rise above the index of power. By emphasizing the cultural values that emerge, it is possible to infer that the state interaction is not totally foreign to the value processes which the legal order is commissioned to develop. These significant external factors bear some relationship to the internal motivations of the acting states.

To these cultural facts there corresponds the conviction of states that it is their mission to transmit moral values which have developed within the nation it represents. Expansion of national virtue is the residue of imperialism as seen from the perspective of the acting state. In our age, this missionary zeal has taken on new force. From specific values grounded in national spirit the state has become the herald of general theories of human existence which, while transcending national foundations, it nonetheless is the task of favored states to proclaim. This is the age of ideologies; the effort to transmit a universal view of life beyond national borders. The frictions which it generates are euphemistically termed the "cold war."[15]

Thus, in some measure, the history of international politics is not explicable solely in terms of an interminable struggle for domination. Beneath the violent facts of competitive strife there lies some effort or tendencies towards meaningful transmission of human values. Yet they are inherently unstable. Even where ideology has an arguably generic source, its expression and interpretation is too closely bound up with the particular interests and failings of the states which proclaim its message.[16] This is as true of American exportation of democracy as it is of North Vietnamese, Chinese or Russian thoughts on "national liberation."

14. See generally A. Toynbee, A Study of History (2d ed. 1962).
15. C. De Visscher, supra note 12, 71-87.
16. There is an incisive demonstration of these weaknesses in E. Carr, The Twenty Years' Crisis, 1919-1939 (2d ed. 1946).

Yet, given the decentralized structure of international society, the effort to introduce ideological interests into civil strife is bound to continue beyond the current Vietnam crisis. It is a prime political fact, one that cannot be wished away by purely juridical attempts at international stability. Juridical critique is indispensible, but it must be accompanied by an attempt to bring international politics within the measure of legal standards. The conviction of major states that they must defend or promote a way of life cannot be ignored, rather it must be elevated and judged by objective consideration of human purpose which essentially transcends the particular interests of the states. The sources of human purpose lie inchoate within the general objectives of the United Nations.

The purposes of the United Nations, as expressed in its Charter, reflect a conviction of the importance of human rights in the development of international law and the preservation of peace. It is an affirmation of faith in the value of human person.[17] More importantly, it seeks to impress the power of states into the service of these humanitarian objectives.[18] This is a factor of profound significance for international politics, since the inescapable inference is that for the existing competition for domination there should be substituted an accountability to international society for the use of that power in terms of genuinely human purposes.[19] This is of particular significance for the Vietnamese conflict.

A predominantly juridical evaluation of the violence should lead to a cessation of the armed conflict. Measured by a norm of proportionate use of force, continued violence bears a disproportionate relationship to justified objectives. But this is only a partial solution. What kind of settlement is compatible with the human values which the international community must respect?

Beneath the generalities of human dignity in the Charter, Declaration of Human Rights and Draft Covenants, there lies profound philosophical and ideological differences as to their scope and content. Because of these divergencies of ethical meaning, some jurists, including Professor Falk, prefer to ignore these dimensions in favor of a depersonalized juridical solution.[20] But the interested states are passionately concerned with

---

17. U.N. Charter, Preamble.

18. See McDougal and Leighton, The Rights of Man in the World Community: Constitutional Illusions Versus Rational Action, 59 Yale L.J. 60 (1949).

19. Although the nature of the binding force of the provisions is debatable, the overall commitment of the organization to the promotion of human rights necessarily entails some accountability of its members, especially in matters of peacekeeping since the Preamble expresses an interconnection between violation of human rights and the existence of warfare. Failure to maintain a connection between human rights and the activities of United Nations organs has been painfully demonstrated in the South West Africa Cases [1966] I.C.J. 4.

20. Law, Morality and War, supra note 3, at 12.

seeing their conceptions of human rights realized in South Vietnam. An attempt to deter them by superimposing upon their discretion the categorical imperatives of non-violence is futile. More importantly, the overall objective is to make the settlement of the Vietnam war a step towards the development of an international society. And by definition, a society is something more than the absence of violence; its very existence is dependent upon the positive sharing of a wide range of human values whose content exceeds mere physical security. The only creative way of measuring the conduct of states is to require them to justify their interpretations of human existence before the organs of the world community. International officials seeking to promote a settlement cannot avoid these humanistic considerations.

The point can be made forcefully by a specific example. Professor Falk makes much of the belief that if national elections were held in the fifties, Ho Chi Minh probably would have been victorious.[21] Yet if victorious, what would have been the status of human rights under a Ho regime? The widespread terror and executions in the North during 1955-1956 would very probably have been repeated throughout the country.[22] Could such actions pass muster before the conscience of mankind? Surely, at some point, the exigencies of Marxist history must come under some objective evaluation. Wherein lies the essential relationship between the person and the state? Does existence have meaning outside the demands of collective life? What judicial protection against the state does a commitment to human dignity require? These are not academic considerations, they bear directly upon the truly human dimensions of the Vietnam tragedy.

And what of our interest in the realization of democratic government in that suffering land? Is the constitutional assembly which we support truly representative of the people? Can there be genuine self-determination in South Vietnam where political power is held by wealthy Northern refugees? How can such a condition be truly conducive to the promotion of "social progress and better standards of life in larger freedom"?[23] Finally, do not the interests of all the people demand that all interested states moderate the absolutists demand of their ideologies?

In the modern world there can no longer be a purely democratic or socialistic government. All who are willing to accept peaceful procedures and fundamental human rights are entitled to participate in the political

---

21. Vietnam Critique, supra note 4, at 1129.

22. Department of State, Office of the Legal Adviser, The Legality of United States Participation in the Defense of Viet Nam, 75 L.J. 1083, 1099-1100 (1966).

23. U.N. Charter, Preamble.

processes. Through such coalition the abstractions of human dignity can take on greater particularizations.

We all desire the growth of a genuine international society, but insufficient attention is given to its attributes. World order is not just the absence of violence. Its vitality flows from a positive sharing of values. In spite of ideological differences, we must all strive to make these values more articulate. This is especially necessary in the civil war area because it is a focal point of conflicting ideologies. It requires an honest confrontation and dialogue between all those who hold contrary views as to the meaning of man and the nature of his destiny. Indispensable to this process is a confrontation of legal theory with the political motivations behind the actions of nation states. The international lawyer does both his nation and the world community a disservice if he abandons the political dimensions of foreign affairs in favor of a futile attempt to solve the question of intervention solely in terms of the imperatives of nonviolence.

A Critical Study of American
Intervention in Vietnam

CHARLES CHAUMONT

1. The most important international event of our time, by the actions to which it has given rise, its consequences, and its implications, is of such moment that it is difficult to grasp in its entirety. It can, of course, be discussed from various points of view, from its political, moral, or legal aspects, let alone the information it provides on different types of fighting and the efficacy of military weapons. None of these aspects can be isolated from the others. The war in Vietnam, moreover, cannot be considered dispassionately; the conscience of civilised man living in the second half of the twentieth century, despite, or perhaps because of the horrors of war this century has experienced, instinctively revolts against the military attempt of a Great Power to annihilate a poor people, whatever the strictly formal reasons which provide a cover for it may be. That is to say, it is impossible to remain completely neutral (1) before an event of this sort; too many basic values are involved, and among them one of the most fundamental, the image that man of the industrial age makes and gives of himself.

The fact that it is impossible to be completely impartial, (in the sense of an equal balance), does not imply either self-deception or dishonesty; there is a certain sanity of the heart which may well accompany the sciences of international relations and law; Machiavellian methods are not the only ones suitable in these fields, for a respect for nations and for international law, the condemnation of the use of force and aggression, despite the difficulties of enforcing it, are concepts as real to the

---

(1) So experienced and urbane a journalist as M. Lacouture, in his book *Ho Chi Minh*, (Paris, Seuil, 1967, p. 249) could not restrain himself from describing the U.S. Government and the General Staff in this struggle as « partners who dishonour their flag in one of the most unequal, cowardly and pointless wars in history ».

contemporary world as the hundred and one arguments used to justify the end by the means.

2. In point of fact we are not proposing to discuss all the different aspects of the war in Vietnam in this document. We are only concerned with American intervention, and again only with some of its aspects. The questions raised by the conduct of the war, and the types of weapons and armaments which have been employed, basic questions in a field of international law which is as essential to enforce as it is difficult, and one which most depends on the spiritual values of human progress, do not concern us here.

The question which does concern us here is the international validity of American intervention. Even that question will not be discussed from every angle, in all the variety of legal argument and counter-argument which tends to lose sight of the Vietnamese tragedy in the thickets of formal controversy.

The subject has been extensively covered in many excellent books and articles (2) which have dealt with a number of these diverse arguments, and we have no intention of simply repeating what has already been said and written. Other, non-legal, studies are extremely useful in so far as the legal problems spring from political or military situations (3).

Nor are we interested here in investigating methods of settling the conflict or conceivable or possible formulae for negotiation. These questions belong to politics and diplomacy. They are dominated by other factors than a plain observation of the facts and the predication of rules of law. They proceed beyond the facts and the law. And indeed, though everyone is at liberty to allow his fancy free play on these aspects, it is always a somewhat profitless amusement for those who do not hold the reins of power to imagine themselves in the place of negotiators and effective peacemakers. It is, on the contrary, both the right and the duty of every lawyer to know where the law stands and to make sure that it expresses the conscience of mankind. The task is then no longer Utopian, and is founded on the brighter and more beneficent aspects of human nature.

---

(2) For a presentation of the American point of view, see in particular the State Department Memorandum of March 8, 1966, to the Senate Committee on Foreign Relations, and the article by John Norton Moore, published in the American Journal of International Law, [A.J.I.L.] of January, 1967; for the presentation of the opposing point of view see the articles of Professor Friedmann in the A.J.I.L. of October 1965, Professor Wright in the A.J.I.L. of October 1966, and the collective work of the « Lawyers Committee on American Policy towards Vietnam », « Vietnam and International Law », published by O'Hare, Flanders, N.J., the United States, in 1967.

(3) See in particular : Chaffard, « Indochine, dix ans d'indépendance », Paris, Calmann-Lévy, 1964; Gigon, Les Américains face au Vietcong, Paris, Flammarion, 1965; Schlesinger, « The Bitter Heritage », André Deutsch, London, 1967. We have refrained from making use of the work of Communist writers, among them admirable works like those of Mme Riffaud, the correspondent of L'Humanité, and of the Australian journalist, Wilfred Burchett.

In short, this examination of the Vietnam dispute will concentrate on those points as we believe, the vital points, which certainly do not exhaust the subject, but which illuminate its significance and essential issues.

3. In the first place, in order to clarify the investigation, the position of substantive international law on intervention must be recalled, without entering upon the theoretical discussion of a question to which the United Nations in the course of recent years have devoted many important debates (4).

Article 2, para. 4 of the U.N. Charter forbids members of the United Nations to resort to « the threat or use of force against the territorial integrity or political independence of any State ». Article 15 of the Charter of the Organization of American States, to which the nations on the American continent have subscribed, forbids States to « intervene directly or indirectly, for any reason whatever, in the internal or external affairs of any other State ». The Resolution of the U.N. General Assembly of December 21, 1965, on non-intervention (5) adopted with one abstention, the « historic character » of which was stressed by certain speakers during the sessions, echoed and developed principles enunciated by the United Nations and by the Charter of the Organization of American States, condemned, in para. 3, « the use of force to deprive peoples of their national identity », and recognized that « every State has an inalienable right to choose its political, economic, social and cultural systems without interference in any form by another State ». The Resolution of the General Assembly of November 30, 1966, on the strict observance of the prohibition of the threat or use of force (6) considered that « any forcible action, direct or indirect, which deprives peoples under foreign dominion of their right to self-determination and freedom and independence, and of their right to determine freely their political status, constitutes a violation of the Charter of the United Nations », and condemned « the use of force to deprive peoples of their national identity ».

We have here a number of texts, to which it would be easy to add others, such as the various Resolutions on the right of peoples to self-determination, passed by the United Nations from 1952 onwards, implementing the concept enshrined in Article 1, para. 2 of the Charter, as well as the a fortiori extension of the principle of the non-intervention of the United Nations in matters which are essentially within the domestic jurisdiction of any State, (Art. 2, para. 7), to individual nations. These texts taken together form a corpus of rules sufficient to give a solid assurance to the principle of non-intervention in both external and internal affairs, as a part of substantive international law.

---

(4) See in particular the proceedings of the General Assembly and the « Mexico » Committee which it set up to study the principles of international law on friendly relations and co-operation between States; and the proceedings of the General Assembly on the prohibition of intervention in the internal affairs of States and the protection of their independence and sovereignty.

(5) Cf. U.N. Monthly Chronicle, January 1966, pp. 26 et seq.

(6) Cf. U.N. Monthly Chronicle, December 1966, pp. 61 et seq.

4. The essential purpose of these rules is to safeguard national identity against foreign interference; it consists, in the words of the Charter, of territorial integrity and political independence, and the right of peoples to self-determination and the choice of their own international and internal destiny. A rising current, sprung from the protest and revolt of the weak against the strong, has developed against that constant phenomenon of History, intervention, against the desire to dominate and the maintenance or extension of zones of influence, and this has given its meaning to the principle of non-intervention.

In so far as the actions of the United States are concerned, therefore, the essential question, in terms of these rules, can be resumed, we believe, in the three interdependent propositions which follow : a) American intervention, by consolidating the situation which had been created, has put, and continues increasingly to put the national unity of Vietnam in jeopardy; b) by the most extreme means, that is, a war expanding from day to day, American intervention has inhibited and compromised the right of the Vietnamese people to self-determination; c) in short, it is destroying the principle of the equal rights of peoples, an essential step in international law, displayed particularly in the choice of political regime, which has become a fundamental issue at stake in the war.

PART. I. — AMERICAN INTERVENTION AND VIETNAMESE NATIONAL UNITY

5. At the time the Geneva Agreements were signed in July 20, 1954, no doubt on the unity of Vietnam appeared possible. It had already been recognized in the Franco-Vietnamese Convention of March 6, 1946 (7) concluded between Ho Chi Minh and M. Sainteny, in which France « recognized the Vietnam Republic as a free State ... forming part of the Indochinese Federation and the French Union ». When, immediately after the Geneva Agreements, American diplomacy began to encourage Ngo Dinh Diem, who at that moment was himself against the dismemberment of Vietnam, the American Government made preparations not to give formal recognition to the legal validity of a partition (8).

In point of fact, the Geneva Agreements did not provide for partition in the strictly legal sense. Most writers on Vietnam have pointed out (9) that the demarcation line recognized by these accords was a provisional military line. The Final Declaration of the Geneva Conference laid especial stress on the fact that this line « should not in any way be interpreted as constituting a political or territorial boundary » (para. 6), and that one of the foundations of a political settlement in Vietnam was respect for unity and territorial integrity, as expressed in Paragraph 12. The

(7) On the history of this Convention, see Lacouture, *Ho Chi Minh*, Paris, Seuil, pp. 107 *et seq.*

(8) Cf. Chaffard, *op. cit.*, pp. 29-30.

(9) See in particular *Vietnam and International Law*, 1967, *op. cit.*, pp. 43-52.

demarcation line was drawn between the forces of the Vietnamese People's Army and the forces of the French Union. It dealt with a confrontation between France and Vietnam, excluding all foreign intervention; the Agreements and the Final Declaration of the Conference stressed the prohibition of the establishment of any foreign military bases (i.e., foreign to Vietnam and France) or the participation of the respective zones in any military alliance.

The fact that the Geneva Agreements took place within the framework of an international conference, and made use of a procedure of foreign control to supervise the implementation of some of the clauses, did not diminish their Franco-Vietnamese character, nor direct French responsibility in their implementation. Contrary to the attitude adopted by certain critics of American intervention, it is consequently unnecessary to regard the Americans as bound by these agreements. It is enough to remember that foreign nations were not entitled to intervene in their implementation, the rule *res inter alios acta* applying in both senses, that is, that if on the one hand foreign States, and especially the United States, were not obliged to implement these agreements, on the other they could not endanger them through their intervention (11). And what is more, in Paragraph 12 of the Final Declaration, the United States bound itself to respect the unity of Vietnam. In his statement on the Final Declaration, moreover, the U.S. representative at the Geneva Conference, Mr. Bedell Smith, explicitly declared that his government « will refrain from the threat or the use of force to disturb (the agreements) » having in addition « taken note » of the Agreements. The events which followed immediately on the signature of the Agreements are well known (12). France, responsible for the implementation of these agreements, withdrew from Vietnam and from the military standpoint this withdrawal was indeed essential after the Algerian revolt broke out on November 1. From that moment American intervention made its appearance and continued to develop; through opposition to Bao Daï, installed by the French and consequently treated with contempt; through the support given to Ngo Dinh Diem in the form of a flood of financial help, advisers, and pressure brought to bear on General Hinh, head of Bao Daï's army; and through the French abandonment of Bao Daï ratified in the Washington negotiations of September 1954. President Eisenhower negotiated directly with Diem, through the intermediary of the United States ambassador, on the best means by which a « judicious programme might help Vietnam », although at that time Vietnam was an associate member of the French Union. In December 1954 General Hinh was finally relieved of his command by Bao Daï, and the way was clear for Diem's final objective, the total eviction of the French army. This eviction was finally accomplished

(10) In particular, *Vietnam and International Law* (note 56 in that volume).

(11) This rule, *(ibid.)*, which seems to us of vital importance, was referred to in the following phrase (note 56). « It is an undisputed principle of international as well as domestic law, that C. cannot disturb an agreement between A, B, D and E on the pretext that he, C, is not party to their agreement. »

(12) An account of these events will be found in Chaffard, *op. cit.*, pp. 38 *et seq.*, and in the articles by Fontaine in *Le Monde* of 12, 13 and 14 February, 1967.

through a letter from Diem to General Collins, President Eisenhower's personal representative in Saigon, dated January 21, 1955, asking the United States to take over full responsibility for the organisation and training of the national army, and confirmed by an agreement between the successor of Hinh and the representative of the French Commander-in-Chief. Certainly a reversal of French policy was revealed in the note from the French Government to the State Department in April 1955 notifying them that the French Government refused to accept responsibility for future events in South Vietnam if the Americans persisted in their support of Diem. But the twin facts of French representations to Washington and such a repudiation of responsibility are themselves sufficient to show the extent of the French abandonment of a country for which she was still in theory responsible and whose future she had accepted at Geneva.

It was in fact simple to foresee that the real result of the French withdrawal would be the nullification of the whole Geneva settlement, since it would be only too easy for the Diem Government to invoke its non-participation in the Agreements as a reason for refusing to implement them. In appearance, however, the French Government still seemed to believe in elections in 1956. In a note circulated by the Agence France Presse on April 30, 1955 (13) French policy is presented as « subject to reservation » but desiring a stabilisation which would enable the elections of July 1956 to be prepared under favourable conditions. But a policy « subject to reservation » is itself incompatible with the Geneva Agreements : in Chapter II on the « principles and procedure governing implementation of the present agreements » Article 14 (a) lays down that « pending the general elections, which will bring about the unification of Vietnam, the conduct of civil administration in each regrouping zone shall be in the hands of the party whose forces are to be regrouped there in virtue of the present Agreement »; in Chapter 5 on « Miscellaneous provisions », Article 27 stipulates that « the signatories of the present Agreement and their successors in their functions shall be responsible for ensuring the observance and enforcement of the terms and provisions thereof »; in Chapter 6, on the commissions for supervision and control, Article 28 recalls again that « responsibility for the execution of the agreement on the cessation of hostilities shall rest with the parties. » Paragraph 2 of the Final Declaration of Geneva reaffirms French responsibility. The political reasons for the French abdication, apart from the Algerian insurrection, were the difficulty of maintaining a French diplomatic policy on a world scale, and the dependence of this diplomacy on the United States. This was all the greater since the failure of the C.E.D. project in the French Parliament had particularly antagonized the United States, greatly attached to this project, and there was also the especial consideration that the greater part of the costs of the French expeditionary forces in Vietnam had been borne by the United States.

Under Paragraph 7 of the Final Declaration of Geneva of July 21, 1954, « consultations will be held » ... (for the preparations for the 1956

---

(13) Quoted by Chaffard, op. cit., pp. 83-84.

elections) ..., between the competent representative authorities of the two zones from July 20, 1955 onwards. » In implementation of this clause the Hanoi Government officially asked Saigon on July 19, 1955 for the opening of negotiations (14). But on August 9, Ngo Dinh Diem, ignoring the fact that without the cease fire the southern regime would had been soundly beaten by the Vietnam People's Army (15), declared that his Government did not consider that it was bound in any way by the Geneva Agreements, to which it had not been a signatory (16), and the United States, through the voice of Mr. Foster Dulles, affirmed their agreement with the Diem Government (13). On the other hand the Ministry of Foreign Affairs of the State which was a party to the Agreements, and which was still theoretically responsible for the unity of Vietnam, i.e., France, considered at that period that the Geneva Agreements should be observed. The deposition of Bao Daï on October 20, 1955, and the dissolution of the French expeditionary corps on April 28, 1955, finally created the conditions which, by putting the finishing touches to the powers of the Diem dictature, made the adjournment of the elections of July 1956 inevitable.

It is clear from this historical sketch that two negative military and political situations directly contributed to the establishment and consolidation of the Diem Government, prime mover in the establishment of the State of South Vietnam and consequently in the breach of the Geneva Agreements and the fission in the unity of Vietnam; one was the withdrawal and abdication of France, a party to the Agreements and responsible for their implementation (17); the other the interference and intervention of the United States, not a party to the Agreements, and consequently incompetent to take any part in their implementation, and still less to take any steps towards their non-implementation. It is of small importance to distinguish which of the three principal actors can be held most responsible. The French withdrawal, American intervention and the manufacture of the Diem Government are three linked elements none of which could exist independently; a France which was capable of fulfilling its engagements would have been able to assure the elections of 1956, and the observance of agreements which were no concern of theirs by the United States would have made the establishment or maintenance of the Diem Government impossible.

6. In the light of later, well-known events, the artificial nature of the Diem Government, and generally speaking, all the governments of South Vietnam which followed it, is very clear.

Particularly significant were the deposition of the brothers Ngo

(14) For a detailed account of this crucial period in the history of Vietnam, see Chaffard, *op. cit.*, pp. 84-112.

(15) On this point see Lacouture, *Ho Chi Minh*, p. 231.

(16) Chaffard, *op. cit.*, pp. 97-98.

(17) On January 24, 1966, Ho Chi Minh, in a letter addressed to General de Gaulle discreetly recalled French responsibility by calling upon France to « carry out her obligations vis-a-vis the Geneva Agreements to the full. » (*Le Monde*, February 1, 1966).

(Diem and Nhu) by a military *coup d'Etat* and their assassination or suicide on November 1, 1963 after all American support had been withdrawn, a withdrawal which Nhu, on October 18, bitterly attacked, accusing the United States of having « started a process of the disintegration of Vietnam » (18); the establishment of the National Liberation Front in October 1960, and its development on a large scale, providing grounds for the assumption that the majority of the population of South Vietnam supports Vietnamese unity and independence; and the complete take-over of the war by the American forces from February 1965 onwards. The war in Vietnam is at the present time essentially a war between the United States on the one hand and the National Liberation Front and the Democratic Republic of Vietnam on the other, i.e., between the Americans and the Vietnamese. This war goes far beyond the aim of maintaining the south zone in face of the north. According to certain writers (19), the fire power of the American Seventh Fleet alone is thirty times greater than that of China. The military submergence of the Government of South Vietnam before the United States meant that on the one hand American intervention had deprived this Government of any military freedom of action and that, on the other, it was not sufficiently representative to be allowed it. In 1967 this freedom of action disappeared, and the South Vietnamese Army no longer played a direct and independent role. (20)

From that time on, behind the increasingly transparent screen of military aid given to South Vietnam against the NLF and North Vietnam, the reality of the war in Vietnam has become increasingly apparent : the confrontation of Americans and Vietnamese, in the south as in the north. The legal stabilization of the « State » of South Vietnam, based especially on the diplomatic relations established with sixty countries (21) and its membership of specialised agencies of the United Nations, assorts strangely with its political flaccidity. But it is only strange on first appearance; it is, on the contrary, completely logical, since it is due precisely to the fact that the « State » of South Vietnam has become an instrument for action in the hands of the greatest power in the world, thus acquiring an international position which the governments of Diem, Ky and Thieu could never have won for themselves. And in this connection it seems of little importance to argue about names, even that of the

---

(18) Quoted by Chaffard, *op. cit.*, p. 270.

(19) See in particular Gigon, *Les Américains face au Vietcong,* Flammarion, 1965, pp. 65 *et seq.* Gigon is of the opinion that « if a proper calculation is made of the unimaginable aggressive power of the Da Nang base, one is forced to the conclusion that this base has little to do with the war in Vietnam ». See also the detailed information in *L'Express* of January 10, 1966, pp. 18-21, in *Réalités* in January 1966, in the articles by R. Guillain in the *Monde,* particularly those of February 1966, and in vast numbers of articles published both in Western Europe and the United States.

(20) Cf. Gigon, *op. cit.*, p. 148. « What does South Vietnam represent ? Practically speaking the Government no longer exists ». And p. 156, « The N.L.F. alone is in real occupation of the terrain, dictates the law, imposes its tactics, and displays its determination to win. »

(21) According to the estimate given in the State Department Memorandum, Paragraph D, of March 4, 1966, cited above, note 2.

Government of South Vietnam (22). Even if it be true that, for instance, the SEATO Treaty (23), like the State Department (24), abstains from designating it by the name of « government », appearing thus to avoid confounding the shadow of words and the substance of things, none the less what is of real importance are things, not words. There is nothing against calling the indigenous authority of the South a « government », if it be borne in mind that this « government » is the instrument of a foreign Power. This fact alone is sufficient to define its nature, and especially, despite all electoral travesties, with the military and police representing the law (25), to deny its claim to represent a distinct State sprung from the destruction of Vietnamese unity.

Everything, consequently, that happened at the beginning, and everything that has happened since, suggests that the Government of South Vietnam was installed, organised and strengthened to prevent the one event which was both the reason for the cessation of hostilities and the evidence of Vietnamese unity, the elections of July 1956. The establishment of this government, the rejection of elections and the gradual substitution of American military action for the military action of the South are all elements of one single phenomenon, and must be taken in conjunction, if American intervention in Vietnam is to reveal its true significance. And in the light of its true significance, all the legal cavils over « infiltrations » from the North into the South are without any importance (26), even though it can be argued that American intervention long preceded these infiltrations (27), and that they cannot compare with the vast scope

---

(22) An interesting discussion on this point is to be found in *Vietnam and International Law,* pp. 37-39.

(23) The expression employed in the SEATO Treaty is « the free territory under the jurisdiction of the State of Vietnam ».

(24) The expression employed in the State Department Memorandum is « separate international entity ».

(25) With particular reference to the « elections » of September 1967. Another question is whether, once freedom has been won for the people of South Vietnam, a South « State » will not provisionally be maintained in being in the period before reunification. See in this connection the extremely flexible programme of the N.L.F. published at the beginning of September. (*Le Monde,* September 3-4, 1967, and the article by M. Devillers in *Le Monde,* 22-23 October, 1967).

(26) We do not of course underestimate the importance of legal arguments designed to refute the American thesis which bases the aid given by the United States on a legitimate defence of the South. The arguments on both sides have been presented in detail, on the one hand in the State Department Memorandum (in the first three sections), and on the other in the volume *Vietnam and International Law* (in which the first section is devoted to a refutation of the State Department arguments). There is no need, we believe, to resume this legal debate here in its purely formal aspects.

(27) Resistance in the South developed from 1957 onwards, owing to the persecution of former members of the Resistance by the Diem regime, and the agrarian counter-reform, in which land which had been distributed to the peasants was taken back from them. The N.L.F. consequently found support among the former members of the Resistance and the peasants, who together formed a substantial force, as subsequent events proved. In so far as the « infiltrations » from the North to the South are concerned, they only developed from the middle of 1964, when the United States had already more than 20,000 military advisers in the South. (See *Les Temps Modernes,* January 1966, pp. 1167-1171).

of this intervention (28). For the real question goes much further. There is a single Vietnamese people, there is a single Vietnamese nation; and the movements of the population and forces taking place from North to South and from South to North are movements within this people and this nation, whose profound unity cannot be abolished by a decision from without.

The whole Southern « State » is therefore based on a monumental misappropriation of power, the power which, with the tacit consent of the French Government, the United States arrogated to itself in the substitution of United States for French action, following the cease-fire in Indochina. For the basic condition of the cease-fire was the promise of elections for the unification of the country, and the People's Army of Vietnam would never have consented to end hostilities, in which they were victorious, without the assurance of these elections (29). In the speech delivered on July 15, 1954 before the Central Committee of the Lao Dong Party (30) explaining the decision for a cease-fire, Ho Chi Minh declared: « A demarcation of the zones for the regroupment of forces does not mean the division of the country, it is a provisional measure to achieve its reunification. » And in the pamphlet *Our Peace Policy* he wrote in 1955 : « Our compatriots of the South were the first to embark on the patriotic war. I am certain ... that hand in hand with the rest of our people they will devote all their strength to the struggle for peace, unity, independence and democracy throughout the whole of the country. » (31).

Considering the sacrifices made by the People's Army of Vietnam (32), the partial denial of the fruits of victory were, it is quite clear,

---

(28) See the figures provided by the Pentagon and reported by Claude Julien in *Le Monde,* July 11, 1967. The writer stressed in particular that the aid provided by Hanoi given the absence of aeroplanes, helicopters, tanks and heavy weapons, cannot possibly be compared to that provided by Washington. In the middle of 1967 a simple comparison of effectives revealed a proportion of 1 to 5 (100,000 North Vietnamese as opposed to half a million Americans), again according to Pentagon figures. See also the statement of September 16, 1967, made by U. Thant, Secretary-General of the United Nations, who said that there were some 50,000 North Vietnam regulars in South Vietnam, and some 500,000 American and allied forces in the South. « So the position » he said, « is that if Hanoi is asked to withdraw these 50,000 regulars from the South, I am afraid Hanoi will not comply with this ».

(29) This was a point particularly stressed by Professor Wright (A.J.I.L., October, 1966, p. 760) in the following comment : « This agreement, therefore, became suspendable when the elections were frustrated by one of the parties and the other party, Ho Chi Minh, was free to consider his obligation to respect the cease-fire line suspended and to continue his long effort to unify Vietnam by force ».
Professor Wright reached the conclusion (p. 767) that « ... in these circumstances Ho Chi Minh's action in support of the Vietcong did not constitute aggression » and that on the contrary, it was « the United States response by bombings in North Vietnam, which began in February, 1965, » which « violated international law, the United Nations Charter and the Geneva Agreement ».

(30) Taken from Lacouture, *Ho Chi Minh,* p. 160.

(31) *Ibid,* p. 230.

(32) According to Lacouture (*op. cit.,* p. 231), without the 1954 agreements the regime in the South « would not have survived the fall of Dien Bien Phu by more than a few weeks ».

accepted in order to achieve the peaceful reunification of Vietnam, founded on elections (33).

This partial frustration, on these grounds, was transformed to total frustration through American intervention, which took place with precisely such an object in view (34). Why ? Not so much to change the unity of Vietnam in the abstract, but because American policy does not and will not accept any sort of Vietnamese unity. For the political orientation of this unity is regarded as all-important by the United States (36); and here we find ourselves faced with the second essential question discussed in this study, as closely linked to the first as the container is to the content, which can be summed up in the following proposition : American intervention has inhibited and jeopardized the right of the Vietnamese people to self-determination.

PART II. — AMERICAN INTERVENTION AND THE RIGHT OF THE VIETNAMESE PEOPLE TO SELF-DETERMINATION

7. If we isolate the essential rules contained in the Declaration of the General Assembly of December 21, 1965 on non-intervention (37), it is clear that those dealing with the self-determination of peoples can be resumed in the following principles (set down in paras. 1 and 5); a ban on intervention in the external or internal affairs of another State; « the ' inalienable right ' of every nation to choose its own political, economic, social and cultural form of life without any interference on the part of any other State.

Both the external and the internal affairs of the Vietnamese people are involved in the Vietnam war.

1. The external affairs of the Vietnamese people

8. Article 2, para. 4, of the U.N. Charter safeguards the « political independence of any State » in international relations. The duty of

---

(33) See the following reflection of President Eisenhower in « Mandate for Change : The White House Years, 1953-1956 » (London, 1963) p. 372, who wrote that everyone who knows Indochina had always assured him that if the elections had taken place at the time of the fighting, they would have given 80 % of the votes to Ho Chi Minh.

(34) See the statement in the book by Herman and Du Boff, *America's Vietnam Policy, The Strategy of Deception*, Washington 1966, quoted by Julien in *Le Monde*, Juli 12, 1967 : declaring that the self-determination of South Vietnam « was incompatible with the basic objective of the United States for South Vietnam, that is, the preservation of a bastion which was allied to us ».

(35) See Lacouture's reference to the « great diplomatic change of direction » the United States does not know how to make, (*op cit.*, p. 249).

(36) For an account of the famous « domino » theory as put forward by President Eisenhower in his press conference at the beginning of 1954, see Schlesinger, *A bitter heritage*, p. 21. See also Julien on this theory in *Le Monde*, July 13, 1967.

(37) See above, para. 3.

respecting this independence is an obligation incumbent on all members of the United Nations, even in relation to non-member States, and this principle dominates both the United Nations and international society as a whole in its present legal structure.

One of the consequences that stem from this principle is that every State is entitled to follow the international policy which it considers suitable. The intervention of a foreign State in this policy can only be justified, according to the U.N. Charter, when the country which is the object of intervention has been subjected to armed attack (in conformity with Article 51 of the Charter).

Since 1954 no foreign country other than the United States has undertaken military operations in Vietnam. The end of the war with France was ratified in the Geneva Agreements, and since that date neither France nor any other Power, (as for instance China or the Soviet Union), have violated the cease-fire or attacked either of the zones. The consolidation of the Diem regime and the growing ascendancy of the United States was accomplished without encountering any foreign obstacles in Vietnam. And even if North Vietnam is to be considered a « foreign State », everyone is aware that the « infiltrations » from the North to the South only began several years (38) after the first financial, diplomatic, political and military manifestations of the American assumption of power in South Vietnam. The military and economic aid moreover given to the Democratic Republic of Vietnam by the Soviet Union and, to a lesser degree, by China followed and did not precede American intervention (39). In North Vietnam, faced by half a million Americans equipped with the most powerful land and air armaments in the world and supported by giant bases such as Ankhe, Bienoa, Camranh, Chulai and Da Nang, with the fire power of Okinawa, Cavite, Formosa and the Seventh Fleet behind them, there are no Russians, no Chinese, no military from any other region of the world; there are only Vietnamese, from the South and the North, re-united by the « hundreds of thousands of tons of steel, fire and iron » (40) which, from February 7, 1965, « has rained from heaven on the heads of the Tonkinese . »

II. — The Internal Affairs of the Vietnamese People

9. Even though it be true that the United Nations Charter is only completely explicit in forbidding the United Nations itself (Article 2, para. 7) « to intervene in matters which are essentially within the domestic jurisdiction of any state », it has always been accepted that what is forbidden to the Organisation is a fortiori forbidden to individual States

(38) See above, para. 6.

(39) It is important to note in this connection that the State Department Memorandum of March 4, 1966, previously referred to, only claims « armed attack » by North Vietnam against the South, and makes no allusion at all to any activities by the Soviet Union or China.

(40) Gigon, Les Américains face au Vietcong (p. 83).

themselves (41), and that in any case « respect for the principle of equal rights and self-determination of peoples » (Article 1, para. 2) implies non-interference in their internal affairs. This is the concept inspiring the Declaration of December 21, 1965 (42). These documents only formalize a principle which the contemporary world regards as fundamental, despite, or perhaps because of, the many interventions which have taken place in our time, i.e., that there are no peoples with unequal rights, and that each people has the right to choose its national structure, its regime, its own policies. There can be no compromise on this point. Only trust territories may, under the Charter, be legally subject to foreign « protection ».

This principle, a part of substantive law, gives rise to another, that no foreign state has the right to arbitrate on any internal dispute concerning the authority of the government or its loyalty to its international obligations, and still less to intervene, particularly when this intervention is designed to abstract a part of the national territory from the control of a government or to provoke a breach of an international engagement. Now no one will deny that the essential purpose of American intervention in Vietnam, from 1954 onwards, has been to prevent the ascendancy of the Government of Ho Chi Minh, the victor in the struggle with France, over the whole of Vietnamese territory. This objective completely explains the joint rejection of the elections of July 1956 by M. Diem and Mr. Dulles (43). We repeat, (44) the non-participation of the United States in the Geneva Agreements does not give them full freedom of action in relation to these Agreements.

The Geneva Agreements, strictly speaking, contain no essential stipulations concerning the elections, although they are anticipated in Article 14 (45). These provisions figure in Paragraph 7 of the Final Declaration of the Conference, which consists only of a common declaration ascribed to the Conference, the various countries (and consequently the United States) being referred to only as participants in the Conference. This procedure helps to distinguish the position of what are strictly speaking the Agreements (between France and the People's Army) from that of the Final Declaration. United States political and military intervention against the Agreements is one thing, their attitude towards the principles of the Final Declaration is another. The scope of the engagements undertaken by the foreign States about the elections in Vietnam can be gauged above all by the Final Declaration. This is rather a practical than a legal consideration, since legally the principle of elections is to be found in both the Agreements and the Declaration.

---

(41) See Report of the « Mexico » Committee of October 27, 1964 (Doc. A/5746), pp. 118-160.

(42) See above, para. 3.

(43) See the statement of Mr. Foster Dulles (quoted by Chaffard, op. cit., p. 98), declaring that the United States were in agreement with the Diem Government in finding that existing conditions in North Vietnam were not at that time conducive to free elections throughout the whole of Vietnam.

(44) See above, para. 5.

(45) Article 14, para A of the Geneva Agreement deals with civil administration in each zone « pending the general elections ».

Whatever the legal analysis of this Declaration, there seems to be little point here in adopting a position on the question of its binding powers. It only arises here if this Declaration in any way derogates from the right of the Vietnamese people to self-determination and from the rule of the non-interference of States. The contrary, however, is true. Together with the arrangements for the machinery of the elections in Paragraph 7, the Declaration mentions the position of third States considered individually, defining it as follows in para. 12 : « In their relations with Cambodia, Laos, and Vietnam, each member of the Geneva Conference undertakes to respect the sovereignty, the independence, the unity and the territorial integrity of the above-mentioned states, *and to refrain from any interference in their internal affairs* » (46).

The existence of such a provision renders pointless any detailed discussion on whether a third State is or is not empowered to give aid to a government *in matters of domestic concern*. Lawyers of great eminence have expressed great disquietude on this question (47). It is, however, indisputable that whether it assists an established or a *de facto* Government, foreign intervention is calculated by definition to deprive the people of their freedom of choice (48). This is more particularly the case when the elections in question will have the effect of re-organising the internal structure of the State. An established government can never be confronted by a major popular debate if each time such a contest appears or threatens to appear it can cut short by an appeal to a foreign power.

The elections of 1956 were an internal affair of Vietnam, internationally supervised and controlled under conditions restrictively defined in Article 7 of the Final Declaration, and completed by the detailed provisions of Chapter VI of the Geneva Agreements on « the International Commission for Supervision and Control in Vietnam on the cessation of hostilities employed for the elections ». Vietnam and France, the parties to the

---

(46) Our italics.

(47) See Friedmann (A.J.I.L.. October 1965, p. 886) : « Neither the United Nations nor any other country has been consistent in the application of the doctrine... The latter becomes an instrument to prevent social change, *which is a vital aspect of national sefl-determination* ». [The italics are ours]

(48) It is therefore impossible to concur in the declaration made to the Security Council of December 11, 1964, by M. Paul-Henri Spaak, at that time the Belgian Foreign Minister, on the Belgo-American intervention at Stanleyville, when he said there was no interference in the internal affairs of a country when the legal government of that country was given the assistance it required. There is interference, he declared, in the internal affairs of a country when support was given to rebellion or revolution against the legal government. When one remembers that a large number of these so-called legal governments troughout the world are in fact based on « an absence of legality », the real meaning of these rules can be appreciated. Domestic legality, moreover, is no concern of foreign States; they are only empowered to assess international legality, which ignores questions of a domestic order. Mr. Spaak added that if anyone had another explanation or definition of non-interference to propose, he wished he would make it, since for the well-being of the United Nations we should settle once and for all what non-interference meant. In any case, in so far as Vietnam is concerned, we consider that the Geneva Agreements and the Final Declaration, clarified after the event by the Resolution of the General Assembly of December 21, 1965, and in the tragic light of the war, provides a very clear explanation of non-intervention.

Geneva Agreements, dit not bind themselves to any other supplementary control procedure unprovided in the Final Declaration, and particularly not to any supervision and control exercised individually by a foreign State, even though it had participated in the Geneva Conference, a control which would undoubtedly be contrary to the duty of non-intervention incumbent on each of the participants. Unilateral declarations made by nations at Geneva have no legal power to alter the principle enunciated above, and consequently the statement made by Mr. Bedell Smith, the U.S. representative, at the final meeting of the Conference is only binding on the United States and without authority to bind others. The important passage in this statement is as follows : « In the case of nations now divided against their will, we shall continue to seek to achieve unity through free elections, supervised by the United Nations to ensure that they are conducted fairly ». The sort of predilection which the United States felt at that time for United Nations supervision is well-known. But that was not the system adopted at Geneva. The United States had no right to assist in the rejection of this system under the pretext that some other system, unmentioned in the documents, was preferable. In the same statement, moreover, Mr. Bedell Smith « took note » of the Geneva Agreements and of paragraphs 1 to 12 of the Final Declaration, and declared that the United States, with regard to the aforesaid Agreements and paragraphs, would « refrain from the threat or the use of force to disturb them ».

The arrangements set up at Geneva, therefore, should have been implemented (49). If in the event the elections might have seemed to have taken place in conditions open to criticism, or that circumstances at that time either materially prevented them or compromised the results, or if some of the results were contested, then, and only then, the countries which took part in the Geneva Conference, in conformity with Article 13 of the Final Declaration, could « consult one another ... on such measures as may prove necessary to ensure that the agreements ... are respected ».

Nothing in these documents, therefore, permits the United States to raise obstacles *in advance* to the process of elections as prescribed. It was only *after the event* that, together with the other Powers, they could study the situation if they believed it incompatible, not indeed with their own concept of elections, but with the Geneva Agreements.

The encouragement therefore given by American policy to the Diem Government to reject the elections constitutes not only a breach of the engagements undertaken by the United States, but equally interference in the internal affairs of Vietnam. The Geneva Conference, in restricting legitimate international intervention to supervision and control, implied that the principle of elections itself could not be re-examined from without. In point of fact the last sentence of Paragraph 7 of the Final Declaration

---

(49) It is on these grounds that we cannot accept the conclusions of M. Fontaine who wrote, in *Le Monde*, 12-13 February, 1967, that « it is clear that the validity of the engagement undertaken on the subject of elections can be contested, since it is an obviously political clause exceeding the competence of the French command ». The different engagements undertaken are legally binding.

only provides for consultation over the preparation of elections between
« the competent representative authorities of the two zones from 20 July
onwards ». It was this preparation which was proposed by North Vietnam and rejected by the South.

10. Even admitting that new circumstances arising in Vietnam between
1954 and 1956 had produced a new climate, they none the less gave no
authority to a foreign State to prevent the elections. The only new circumstances envisaged by the Agreements (Articles 39 et seq. in particular) were violations of the cessation of hostilities and the concomitant
arrangements. But « the conditions in North Vietnam during that period »
cannot be considered new circumstances on the pretext that they « were
such as to make impossible any free and meaningful expression of popular
will » (50). For neither Paragraph 7 of the Final Declaration nor any
other of the Geneva provisions subjected the elections to any appraisal
by the authorities of the South, let alone a foreign Government, of conditions in the North, that is, of conditions in the territory administered by
one of the parties to the agreements. Such an appraisal was very clearly
interference in the internal affairs of one of the parties.

In addition, as Professor Q. Wright has clearly indicated, (51) « the
conditions existing in Vietnam which might affect the freedom of elections
were well known to the members of the Geneva Conference when they
provided for the holding of elections in July 1956 » (52) (53).

In reality the genuinely new circumstances which had changed the provisional balance established in 1954 for the following two years were precisely the intervention of a foreign Power, the United States, in the settlement of a French colonial affair, a settlement reached at a time when the
United States had not even undertaken the responsibilities defined two
months later in the SEATO Treaty. The objectives of this treaty furthermore, specified in Article 2, was resistance to armed attack or to prevent
or counter « subversive activities directed from without » (54). At least
as expressed it cannot therefore provide a legal foundation for any interference in the internal affairs of Vietnam (55); even if the terms of the

(50) State Department Memorandum on the Legality of United States Participation
in the Defense of Vietnam, (Section 3, Paragraph D).

(51) A.I.J.L., October 1966, as above, p. 759.

(52) Vietnam and International Law, Chapter 4, Paragraph A.3, speculates why
the methods of government employed in South Vietnam should not have been equally
subject to examination.

(53) The event which made the deepest impression was the mass flight of
approximately a million Catholics from the North to the South. But this mass departure
was itself an implementation of Paragraph 8 of the Final Declaration of Geneva,
stipulating that « the provisions of the agreements on the cessation of hostilities intended
to ensure the protection of individuals and of property must be most strictly applied and
must, in particular, allow everyone in Vietnam to decide freely in which zone he
wishes to live. »

(54) Our italics.

(55) The United States Memorandum, in its Conclusion, declared that the United
States « undertook an international obligation in the SEATO Treaty to defend South
Vietnam against armed aggression » from the North. But even if the American standpoint

treaty had allowed it, it would have been without effect, since contrary to general international law and the Charter of the United Nations

An argument to this effect could indeed have been put forward on the grounds that the growing authority of foreign military advisers (56) and the diplomatic pressure of a great foreign Power were incompatible with free elections in the South, and the fact that the adherence of the southern zone to the SEATO Treaty constituted a « breach of Article 19 of the Geneva Agreements, by which the two parties accepted that they would not adhere to any military alliance ». North Vietnam could well have argued this foreign intervention, all the more because the task of the International Control Commission was literally sabotaged by the Government of South Vietnam (57). Neither the latter, on the other hand, nor the U.S. Government could, on the evidence, make use of such an argument : « nemo auditur propriam turpitudinem allegans ».

11. Since the elections envisaged by the Geneva Agreements did not take place, are we to conclude that the Vietnamese people were mute, and that the silence in Vietnam was only broken by the sound of artillery and bombs ? Not at all. People have other means of expressing the right to self-determination when the ballot boxes are closed. The behaviour and the activities of the masses are a form of expression no less valid, and probably more eloquent. This is a phenomenon fully recognized in international law in time of war, to maintain or establish the legitimacy of governments in countries occupied by the enemy.

South-Vietnamese resistance from 1957 onwards, the establishment of the National Liberation Front in 1960, the ever-diminishing authority of the governments of South Vietnam, replaced for all practical purposes of war by the American forces, and the inability of these forces to overcome the resisters despite their considerable military superiority, are all evidence of the support given by the majority of the Vietnamese population to the cause of the Resistance. As a result of the decision taken by the United States to bomb North Vietnam, the two struggles, on the one hand that in the South under the direction of the National Liberation Front, and in the North under the direction of the Democratic Republic of Vietnam, merged. The half million men of the South Vietnamese army are so unreliable that they are confined to the tasks of « pacification », i.e. policing duties, in which they are proving themselves more and more inadequate (58). In any event, collaborators who are willing to harry their com-

were accepted, no one has ever affirmed that there was Communist aggression from the North, or anywhere else, between 1954 and 1956. American interference in the elections cannot therefore be justified by reference to the SEATO treaty.

(56) The Military Assistance and Advisory Group, replacing the French Army, began to develop from February 1955.

(57) On the sacking and burning of the headquarters of the Commission in Saigon, and the boycott of the Commission, cf. Chaffard, op. cit., pp. 95-96, and Lacouture, op. cit., pp. 230-231.

(58) See the statement made at Saigon, July 23, 1967, by General Westmoreland, commander-in-chief of the American forces (*Le Soir,* July 25, 1967), recognising that improvement in pacification in the provinces of Binh Dinh and Phu Yen was largely due to the maintenance of American troops there, and that *had these troops been withdrawn the Vietcong would have re-established themselves there in force.* (Our italics).

patriots and fail to resent the settlement of their internal affairs by aliens can scarcely be regarded as expressing, even in elections organised by a military dictatorship (59), the will of a nation of thirty million inhabitants.

The resistance in the South, as we said, developed as a reaction to the persecution of former combatants by the Diem Government, and to the agrarian measures the latter adopted. In the beginning there were only local arms at their disposition, (60) help from the North arriving considerably later. But from that beginning, and increasing with time, the Resistance never failed to obtain aid from the population, without which, it is quite clear, they could never have succeeded in resisting an enemy increasingly equipped with a superiority of armaments and weapons. (61). The South Vietnamese authorities consequently found themselves in the position of occupation authorities in a territory where most of the inhabitants were hostile to them (62). The Resistance needs arms of course, and part of them are taken from the enemy. But arms are not enough for this type of war; the psychological adhesion of the masses is an essential weapon; had it been otherwise the Americans and the South Vietnamese authorities would have won this war (63).

In so far as North Vietnam is concerned, so much has already been written on it by numerous investigators (64), so much can be perceived from afar of the unconquerable energy of the population and its leaders under the intense bombing to which they have been subjected for the past two years (65), that the wholehearted adherence of the population

---

(59) We are referring in particular to the Presidential elections of September 1967.

(60) See Chaffard, *op. cit.,* p. 203 : « It appears that the greater part of the arms employed by the Resistance came on the one hand from caches of several thousand rifles, Lewis guns and a certain number of mortars, hidden away after the 1954 armistice, and on the other from primitive factories, as well as from arms taken in the fighting. »

(61) See the heading of a paragraph in *Les Americains face au Vietcong* by M. Gigon (p. 216) : « *Here, in their natural element !* » The experience of the Resistance in the 1939-45 War in territories occupied by the Germans provided ample evidence that no resistance movement can survive without the support of the local population.

(62) See Gigon (*op. cit.,* p. 228) : « The Vietcong has an assured advantage over its enemy; it regards them as traitors to the country »; (*ibid.,* p. 166) : « Only the N.L.F. really occupies the terrain, dictates its law, imposes its tactics, implants its doctrine, and displays its determination to win. » See also Guillain, *Le Monde,* February 18, 1966 : « Is not the entrenchment of the enemy (enemy of the Americans) so deep-rooted that Vietnam will have to be torn to pieces to get rid of the Vietcong ? »

(63) See Julien, *Le Monde,* July 12, 1967 : The governments of Saigon and their American allies have not been able to break this force (of the NLF) which, at the beginning of 1965, so shook the regime of the South that Mr. Johnson saw no other immediate solution than to bomb the North from the air ». M. Julien concludes that the answer cannot be found in supporting « dictatorial governments (in the South) which are uninterested in safeguarding what Mr. Goldberg and Mr. Rusk call the right of the South Vietnamese people to self-dertermination. »

(64) In particular Devillers, Gigon, Guillain, Lacouture. Mr. MacNamara, the former American Secretary of Defence, declared before the Senate on August 25, 1967 (*Le Monde,* August 27-28, 1967) « that there is little reason to believe that any level of conventional air or naval action... will deprive the North Vietnamese of their willingness to continue to support their Government's efforts. (our italics).

(65) According to *Le Monde,* June 16, 1967, « about 80,000 tons of American bombs fall each month on the two Vietnams ».

to their regime and their struggle cannot be doubted. Men, women and children are soldiers, and it is only extraordinary powers of improvisation allied to extraordinary courage which has enabled them to face a situation which for many other peoples would have proved untenable.

It is, therefore, because the Vietnamese in the North and in the South alike have displayed a tenacity reaching beyond questions of political opinions and attitudes, and where the essential question is the very existence of the nation, that, in the drastic words of M. Devillers (66) « the whole world is continuing to watch this escalation, a torture inflicted on an entire people » — « this colossal and unprecedented torture ».

PART III. — THE REAL QUESTION AND THE ISSUES AT STAKE

12. Beyond all the arguments and superficial reasons adduced, beyond the stalemate facing the military strength of a country which has never yet been defeated (67) and cannot accept the possible prospect (68), the heart of the question which justifies intervention in both the internal and external affairs of Vietnam in the eyes of the American leaders, and probably the greater part of American opinion, is the notion of « defending freedom ». An almost mystical notion, difficult to tie down, perplexing to define in the light of American society, still less easy to understand when one is well aware that, in terms of the U.S. responsibilities throughout the world, nearly everywhere the regimes it supports are based on either financial, military or police dictatorships (69).

And yet it is the cause of freedom which has been so consistently invoked not only in Vietnam, but also in Cuba and the Dominican Republic. It is the cause of freedom which was proclaimed in the first steps taken by the Americans (70). It constitutes the most important part

(66) *Le Monde,* September 15, 1966.

(67) For a psychological analysis of the « power complex », with which we are not here directly concerned, see *Les Temps Modernes* (No. 236, January 1966) p. 1192, and « The Arrogance of Power », by Senator Fulbright (especially pp. 3-32 and p. 199).

(68) See the statement of General Westmoreland, commander-in-chief of the American forces, made in New York, april 24, 1967 (quoted by Julien in *Le Monde,* July 13, 1967) « We ... are involved in a total undertaking ... in which ... the reputation and the very honour of our country are at stake. » See also the statement of Mr. Cabot Lodge, quoted in the same article, that the United States could not be driven out of Vietnam; and finally that of President Johnson at San Antonio, September 29, 1967, (*Le Monde,* October 1-2, 1967) dealing with the quest for military victory.

(69) See Schlesinger, *op. cit.* (p. 115) : « Marshall Ky, moreover, has become one of those Frankenstein monsters we delight in creating in our client countries. »

(70) See the statements of Mr. Foster Dulles above, made in the summer of 1956, paragraph 5.

of the official argument (71). In a declaration which forms part of the SEATO Treaty the United States Government limits « its recognition of the effect of aggression and armed attack... to communist aggression ». The famous « domino theory » referred to previously, according to which the fate of the countries of the Far East is indivisible, and the destiny of Formosa, Malasia, the Philippines and Thailand are linked to that of South Vietnam, has been continuously invoked from 1955 to 1967 (72).

The basic thinking implied by such an attitude is as follows. The United States is entitled to defend « freedom » against Communism, which is its enemy, and consequently to define and determine Communism. Communism is indivisible, as is freedom. The war in Vietnam, originally part of a policy, appears to have become an end in itself.

The American « mission »

13. The war in Vietnam, among other modern acts of intervention, has thrown a special and highly dramatic light on the basic political philosophy lying at the origin of the American thesis. It can be summed up in the three following propositions : The American conception of society harmonizes with the demands of national freedom; the Communist conception is incompatible with this freedom; it is the mission of the United States to promote the one and contain the other throughout the world wherever possible.

These propositions reveal the root argument common to most of the justifications put forward not only for intervention in Vietnam but for other interventions as well, such as in Cuba in 1962 and the Dominican Republic in 1965.

The axiom which postulates the objective value of American civilisation and denies the values of Marxist civilisation is most clearly revealed in the State Department Memoranda on these two affairs. In each of these cases the idea expressed at the Punta del Este meeting of the Foreign Ministers of the American Republics in January 1962, according to which the principles of communism were incompatible with the principles of the inter-American system, and the opinion that if a country fell under the authority of Communist conspirators, the right of the peoples of this country to decide its own destiny was meaningless (73) are strongly stressed. This attitude quite naturally gives rise to the

---

(71) See the State Department Memorandum, referred to previously, in particular Section 3, Paragraph D : « The Communist leaders were running a police state where executions, terror, and torture were commonplace. A nation-wide election in these circumstances would have been a parody... » and « with a substantial majority of the Vietnamese people living north of the 17th parallel ... would have meant turning the country over to the Communists. »

(72) See Schlesinger, op. cit., pp. 37 et seq., and Julien, Le Monde, July 13, 1967. Also President Johnson's speech at San Antonio on September 29, 1967 (Le Monde, October 1-2, 1967).

(73) State Department Memorandum on United States action in the Dominican Republic of May 7, 1967, Paragraph 4.

notion that the United States, which more than any of the others represents « the principles of the inter-American system », regarded as nothing more than the application of the universal principles of the right of people to self-determination, has the right, nay, more, the duty to intervene, even where the Government of the State concerned objects (74).

The original concept here, the identification of a certain type of civilisation (in this case Western capitalist civilisation) with the freedom of peoples, springs of course from a belief, and adherence to this belief, on the part of certain governing powers and circles, and, like every belief, is not susceptible of mathematical proof. In the world of to-day an equally large segment of humankind, in various stages of development, cherishes a contrary belief, to the effect that the type of civilisation in which the United States takes such pride is in fact an instrument for the oppression of peoples and alienation of the human person, especially where poverty-stricken countries or minorities are concerned (75). If the State Department could compare Cuba to a citizen suffering from smallpox, the partisans of Fidel Castro regard the great American companies which dominated Cuba before the advent of the new regime as basically contributing to the oppression and economic corruption, the arrogance of power and the tyranny of money. If in the eyes of the State Department the Democratic Republic of Vietnam has set up a regime which « has made free elections quite impossible », « the American protectors » (of Vietnam), in the eyes not only of the socialist countries, but also of many non-Communist sectors of world opinion, are in a country stripped of its national reality and without civic consciousness » (76) and where, despite electoral and other farces, the military distatorship of a Ky or a Thieu is much the same as that of a Diem (77).

In a world where there is no unity of philosophic thought, where theological authority and dogmatic infallibility no longer exist, mankind lives in a state of relativity, not only in Einstein's meaning of the word, Truth this side of the Pyrenees, error on the other (78).

---

(74) In so far as Cuba is concerned, for example, the fact that its government was no longer a member of the O.A.S. in 1962 appeared a matter of no importance since, (as the State Department Memorandum on Cuba of October 26, 1962, Paragraph 5) described it, a citizen suffering from smallpox, whether he liked it or not was a legitimate object of concern for the whole community, and would therefore have to be subjected to certain restrictions and certain measures of supervision and control.

(75) See the declarations made by the Negro leader Carmichael at the Conference of Solidarity of the Latin American Peoples at Havana on August 1, 1967 (*Le Monde*, August 3, 1967) « It is not the people of Vietnam who are oppressing us, who force us to live in ghettoes and exploit us... Vietnam shares our struggle ».

(76) Gigon, *op. cit.*, p. 149.

(77) Cf. Schlesinger, *op. cit.*, p. 115. « Marshall Ky, moreover, has become one of those Frankenstein monsters we delight in creating in our client countries. »

(78) Discussions on the superiority of one system to another are valueless from the standpoint of international law if it is to remain a universal code of law. Each government, and indeed each of us, may adhere to a system, and even regard it, from his point of view, as representing the truth; he may desire to develop it, he may not

Since there is no indisputable higher truth, and no undisputed high priest to establish it, there is no other criterion of a desirable civilisation than that which each nation accepts for itself. But if a State claims to impose its own on others as the only genuine criterion, it will be grotesque if it is a small country, and dangerous if it is a great country. The American claim cannot be dismissed as grotesque, on account of the military and economic power of the United States; it can only be dangerous (79). To do good to others by taking their place, or even in spite of them, has frequently proved a camouflage for projects of domination (80). Thus « the United States... reserves to itself the right : a) to determine whether an internal revolution involves a degree of participation by Communists regarded as dangerous by the United States and b) to intervene by force... This implies possible intervention in the internal affairs of any one of twenty Latin American States... The possibility of such intervention as greatly increased by the fact that a majority of these States have gross discrepancies between the great wealth of a small minority and the abject poverty of the masses, and that almost any revolution against any of the various incumbent right-wing governments will have strong left-wing elements, which can easily be described as « Communist » (81) (82). Intervention appears the necessary consequence of a superior long-established philosophy. Its present legal importance therefore goes far beyond the pragmatic significance of the Monroe Doctrine, for the maximum that can be envisaged as a contemporary prolongation of this doctrine is American action in Latin America. And finally there appears an old idea which for long inspired Europe in the era of its grandeur, and which has now been adopted by the United States, the idea of the privileged mission of one civilisation over the others, thus implying that it is the only true « civilisation ». That this notion should develop in the richest and most powerful country in the world is easily comprehensible. That it cannot be accepted as a philosophical truth and that it contradicts the « principle of equal rights of peoples » (Article 1, para. 2 of the U.N. Charter)

---

impose it. Humanity, finally renouncing wars of religions, must accustom itself to the idea that what appears garbed in the most seductive colours to one may be the object of the liveliest repugnance to the other. The average American sees the « Reds » as unnatural and dishonest persons; many people, not only the Communists, cannot on the other hand restrain their loathing for a civilisation founded on material goods, on the search for happiness through money and the selfish satisfactions it procures.

(79) See Senator Fulbright, *The Arrogance of Power* (especially pp. 197-241).

(80) See the lecture delivered at the American College in Paris, February 16, 1967, by Mr. Cleveland, permanent U.S. representative at the Atlantic Council (*Le Monde*, February 18, 1967), where the lecturer referred to the duties of a « Hercules-nation » like the United States, and justified by a theory of unlimited responsibility both the Truman doctrine and American intervention in Greece, the Philippines, Malaya, Burma, Korea, Cuba, the Congo, the Dominican Republic, Thailand, Laos and Vietnam.

(81) The State Department Memorandum on U.S. intervention in the Dominican Republic thought fit to assert (paragraph 3) that action (the revolt of the Constitutionalists) which began as a democratic revolution fell into the hands of a band of Communist conspirators. Everyone is aware that that is not so.

(82) Professor Friedmann. From an article in the A.J.I.L. October 1965, pp. 866-867.

which has taken on increasing importance in present-day international ideology, is more easily comprehensible still. It is the reason why each attempt by a great Power to coerce and dominate a country of the third world, whatever the political motives and legal justifications, is regarded as a colonial or neo-colonial enterprise. For what such a situation lacks is the essential element of reciprocity (83) which alone gives a dispute, however violent, the character of an explanation between sovereign and equal countries. As has sometimes been emphasised, Vietnam is not in an equal position vis-à-vis the United States; it is quite incapable of conducting a war against them corresponding to theirs, and only able to fight on its own soil (84). The war in Vietnam therefore, in the eyes of the Vietnamese people, appears less a war of rival blocs than an essential denial of their own rights, and Vietnamese resistance, despite its dominant ideological colour, is not basically different from the other forms of nationalism which contributed to the disintegration of the classic type of colonialism (85).

The first step towards stripping the mystique from this situation, in Vietnam as in so many other places, where a wealthy State arrogates powers to itself vis-à-vis a poor nation, is to understand that no political system has an *a priori* absolute and universal validity, that liberal capitalism just as authoritarian capitalism or socialism in all its different forms, may well be detested by some and preferred by others; that the right op peoples to self-determination is not linked to any predetermined system; that freedom has many meanings, and each people has the exclusive right to decide which meaning they will give it; that the fact that a people chooses suffering and the risk of annihilation, as in Vietnam, rather than the « freedom » brought by foreign soldiers and bombers means that the meaning they give to the word « freedom » equates better with their right to self-determination than the meaning forced on them from without and by that very fact is valid evidence (86); and that, in conclusion, the claim of the United States to have a mission of intervention is only one of the many versions of the « la raison du plus fort » immortalised by La Fontaine.

---

(83) See Schlesinger, *op. cit.*, p. 81. « How can the West continue to suppose it can assign itself a role in Asia which Asia cannot claim in Europe or America ? »

(84) See the pertinent comments of M. Julien in *Le Monde*, July 11, 1967, most appositely entitled « The principle of reciprocity ». « For North Vietnam reciprocity can only have a meaningless sound; the only equivalent to a halt in the bombing of its territory by the Americans would be a pause in the raids that the North Vietnamese air force is not in a position to make on the United States ».

(85) See the development of this idea in Fulbright (*op. cit.*, pp. 76 *et seq.*) and U. Thant's statement at Greensboro (United States, July 30, 1967) (*Le Monde*, August 1, 1967), when he declared that it was wrong to believe the war in Vietnam was a « kind of holy war against a particular ideology... *It is nationalism, and not communism*, that animates the resistance movement in Vietnam against all foreigners, and now particularly against Americans ». (Our italics.)

(86) In *Les Pensées*, Pascal, referring to the Apostles and the first Christians, declared his faith in the value of witnesses who allowed themselves to be massacred (rather than abstain from bearing witness).

II. — The indivisible and « foreign » nature of Communism

14. The « domino » theory, evolved in a period when the Cold War had a more simple significance than to-day, was based on the belief in a unified communism and the impossibility of dissociating international situations one from the other. American involvement in South Vietnam was generally regarded as a direct consequence of « the Dulles conception of the world as irrevocably split into two unified and hostile blocs » (87). Flagrant errors, later exploded by experience, were committed, such as the statement made by Mr. Rusk, then Assistant Secretary of State, on May 18, 1951, (88), according to which « The Peking regime may be a colonial Russian government » (89).

This picture of the world is out-of-date to-day, even in the United States. Yet the memory of the monolithic structure retains a nostalgic value, even in terms of Western solidarity, since the American leadership, for instance, is still strongly averse to admitting any independent policy on the part of their allies or friends.

What is undeniably true is that even if no one nowadays can maintain that there is a uniform « socialist camp » in existence, inspired by central directives, yet one very important concept has survived from the monolithic period, and one which is to be found at the very heart of American policy, particularly in Vietnam : the idea that Communist ideology is, by definition, a foreign ideology. Foreign to whom ? Going a little further, one discovers that it is always foreign to the people among whom it is spreading and achieving recognition. The arguments put forward by the legal advisers to the State Department in the cases of Cuba and the Dominican Republic are extremely revealing. « Quarantine » was pronounced by the State Department for Cuba in order to counter (90) what they described as the secret and dangerous installation of Soviet offensive weapons, and arms controlled by foreign authorities (91). For the Dominican Republic the Americans justified their actions (92) by the need to combat what they called conspiracy inspired from abroad, and the dangers of international communism and

---

(87) Schlesinger, *op. cit.,* p. 21.

(88) Schlesinger, *op. cit.,* p. 22.

(89) One of the conclusions of a report of the well-known Institute of Strategic Studies in London, which appeared in August 1967 (*Le Monde,* August 6-7, 1967) illustrates the distance we have since travelled. According to this report China, already a serious rival of Soviet Russia on the political and ideological level in the internal and external affairs of the Communist world, is quite certainly more dangerous for the Soviet Union than for the United States.

(90) *Op. cit.,* Paragraphs 3 and 5.

(91) Since 1962 the development of Cuban policy has made it very clear that the regime of Fidel Castro has no intention of becoming anyone's satellite. Among the many statements confirming this attitude, see that of M. Raoul Castro, Cuban Minister of Defence, to the Military Training College, July 24, 1967 (*Le Monde,* July 26, 1967); « The American Government seems unaware of the fact that relations between Cuba and the Soviet Union can only exist on the basis of the strictest mutual respect and absolute independence ».

(92) State Department Memorandum on the Dominican Republic, *op. cit.,* Paragraph 3.

the continued intervention of the Sino-Soviet bloc in the Western hemisphere, and in order to permit the Dominican people, as they said, the free choice of its government without external interference. For, the State Department declared, experience had shown that if a group directed by Communist conspirators and inspired by a foreign Power took control of a country by force, the right of the people of this country to self-determination was destroyed ».

Another form of « experience » has led many people, and many leaders, to consider that the « inspiration of a foreign Power » could also well take the form of the « continued intervention » of the American secret services in the affairs of a great number of countries throughout the world (93). In the polarized view of international life, political events thus take on the aspect of two underground and parallel conspiracies (94). This view of things has itself helped to crystallize situations (95) which, by nature and origin, are in reality much more complex. It must be understood that in the second half of the twentieth century the world is decidedly more polymorphic. The change goes back a number of years. In Europe the pacific Polish revolution of October 1956 marked the beginning of polycentrism in the People's Democracies; in Asia the Soviet denunciation of its military agreement with China on July 15, 1959 was one of the first symptoms of the great schism in international communism.

It is therefore a mistake to present any socialist regime in the world as necessarily and *a priori* inspired from without, and consequently it is difficult to see why « socialism » should be more « foreign » to Vietnam than the « capitalism » introduced in its modern form by foreign French colonisation and strenghthened by American neo-colonisation. The truth is that, in terms of — « my doxy is orthodoxy; your doxy is heterodoxy » — there is a natural tendency in men, and particularly in their leaders, to consider as monstrous and diabolical all forms of collective thought which do not correspond to their way of life, and which they make no attempt to understand. It is a fact that many of the developing countries, when they are in a position to choose their own regime (96), adopt a type of socialism suitable to their own economic and social conditions. And Marxist-Leninist thinking, in the Soviet Union, in China, and elsewhere since the death of Stalin, has frequently stressed that socialism can be reached by many roads.

---

(93) See Julien, *Le Monde*, July 13, 1967. He cites a number of notorious cases of the intervention of the C.I.A. (overthrow of the Mossadegh Government in Iran in 1953, overthrow of the Arbenz Government in Guatemala in 1954, the Bay of Pigs, etc.).

(94) For a criticism of this picture of two international conspiracies, international communism on the one hand, American imperialism on the other, see the article by M. Baechler, *Le Monde*, July 18, 1967 (Ubu in Vietnam) « It has become impossible to give communism a diplomatic and strategic content considering that each country which installs a « socialist » regime automatically strengthens the opposite camp. The Sino-Soviet quarrel has finally killed this myth ».

(95) Baechler *(ibid.)* pointed out that « there is no difficulty in showing that it is the myth (the unity of communism) and the behaviour which derived from it, which made it possible for a socialist camp to exist ».

(96) As for instance the U.A.R., Cuba and Algeria.

It is very interesting to observe that the theme of « foreign inspiration » has not been invoked in the official American thesis over South Vietnam (97). When the State Department refers to « communist aggression from the North » (98), the North referred to is North Vietnam, and not a Communist State in the North, such as the Soviet Union or China. To suggest that North Vietnam is « foreign » would really be too difficult, even were the political separation of the two zones accepted. As for North Vietnam itself, is is universally recognized that the Democratic Republic of Vietnam is maintaining a balance and a position of reserve between the Soviet Union and China (99), founded especially on the historical realities of Vietnam, the needs of the struggle and the demands which the task of maintaining itself as a nation make.

This relative relegation of the theme of « foreign inspiration » to the background, in the recent American formulations (100) of the U.S. war aims in Vietnam, is partly explained by a concern for Soviet susceptibilities. Despite the fact that the Soviet Union is the main supplier of armaments to the Democratic Republic of Vietnam (101), and thus makes a powerful contribution to the struggle, the U.S. Government has been taking great care in both word and deed to avoid steps which could directly implicate Soviet aid to Vietnam, and each time a Soviet ship is hit in the course of the U.S. bombing of North Vietnam, the American Government has presented its excuses. The war in Vietnam, it would seem, is becoming dependent on variations in global strategy.

III. — Is the war in Vietnam an end in itself ?

15. These observations lead one to the conclusion that the aims of the war in Vietnam and the fight against international communism have been dissociated, and that it is now no longer possible to present this war, as is often done in a simplified form, as an episode in the permanent combat waged between the United States and the Soviet Union, pursued through other countries.

---

(97) M. Julien, in his article in *Le Monde*, July 13, 1967, wrote : « No American leader has dared to come out bluntly with a claim that China provoked the launching of the Guerilla war in South Vietnam, when it was in bondage to Diem ».

(98) *U.S. State Memorandum on Vietnam*, chap. 2.

(99) See Lacouture. *op. cit.*, p. 205 : Ho Chi Minh, receiving a representative of French television in July 1964, who asked him whether North Vietnam would not inevitably become a satellite of China, replied, « Never ! » M. Lacouture added (p. 209) : « By avoiding the infernal dialectic of the Moscow-Peking conflict the Vietnamese leaders can best preserve and enrich their basic attachment to the « Vietnamese way ».

(100) See Julien (*Le Monde*, July 13, 1967), who quoted the statement of Mr. Goldberg, the U.S. permanent delegate to the United Nations on September 22, 1966, that they were not engaged in a holy war against Communism, and stressed the new weight given to the rather weak argument of the aggression of the North against the South.

(101) For an analysis of Soviet aid to the Democratic Republic of Vietnam, see the article by Mr. Isnard, *Le Monde*, July 13, 1967.

On the other hand it is sometimes admitted that what has occurred is that there has been a substitution in the choice of adversary, that the real purpose of the war in Vietnam is the creation of an anti-Chinese bastion (102), and that indeed the continuous attacks of the Chinese leaders against « Soviet-American collusion » only confirm this interpretation. It is not so much communism which is at stake in this struggle, but Communism in its Chinese form, which some Soviet circles believe can no longer be regarded as Marxism-Leninism. So many years after the October Revolution, during which Russian Communism was presented as a permanent conspiracy against Western civilisation, it seems that the Americans no longer impute the idea of « militant world revolution » to the Soviet Union. The heart of the conspiracy is now in Peking (103).

Nobody, we repeat, has seriously maintained that the Vietnamese Resistance has been inspired by China. Former combatants and peasants rose against the authorities of the South (104), and this had nothing to do with China. The assistance given at present by China to the Democratic Republic of Vietnam is less than Soviet aid (105), and since the Government in North Vietnam has scrupulously avoided taking sides in the Sino-Soviet dispute, it is difficult to claim that the Democratic Republic of Vietnam is a Chinese satellite. According to Ho Chi Minh « nothing is dearer to the Vietnamese than their independence and their dignity » (106).

It is the simple fact of Chinese proximity which makes Vietnam a special case. The United States, after all, tolerates the existence in the American continent of the Communist regime of Cuba, and the attempt on the Bay of Pigs has not been renewed. What, then, makes the North Vietnamese and N.L.F. regime more dangerously Communist than that of Fidel Castro, serving as an example and a flag for all the peoples subjected to Latin American dictatorships, at the very doors of the United States ? The one important difference is the geographical and strategic position of Vietnam. The people of Vietnam have the misfortune to be near neighbours of China (107) and have had to struggle

---

(102) For a development of this idea, see Schlesinger, *op. cit.,* pp. 70 *et seq.,* and particularly the following quotation from the Secretary of State, Mr. Rusk : « The object of our policy is to prevent Red China from establishing its hegemony over the East Asian land mass ».

(103 See the statement of Mr. Rusk on August 29, 1967 (*Le Monde,* August 31, 1967) declaring that China instigated the aggression in Vietnam.

(104) See above, paragraph 6 : see the leading article of *Le Monde,* July 21, 1967, « Vietnam, thirteen years after Geneva », declaring that « the Diem dictatorship quickly produced its antidote; the revolt of the peasants of the South, hungry for land reform, and that of the communists and liberals fleeing from oppression ».

(105) See *L'Express,* January 10-16, 1966, pp. 18-21.

(106) Quoted by Lacouture, *op. cit.,* p. 215, M. Lacouture gave an account of « the complicated helmsmanship of the leaders of North Vietnam between Soviet « revisionism » and Chinese « dogmatism » (pp. 201-215).

(107) See the letter sent to American scholars by South Vietnamese students, published in *Le Monde,* March 23, 1967. « We are convinced », they wrote, « ... that it is only to prepare for war against China that the United States wishes to dominate our country ».

against her to maintain their own individual existence throughout their history. There we have one of the unhappy curses on this people, with the result that their destiny was not and has not been in their own hands since the trusting but imprudent acceptance of the cease-fire in July 1954. No country enjoys a right to self-determination when a powerful foreign State, having assumed to itself a direct authority in its affairs, subordinates this right to considerations of zones of influence and strategy unconnected with the country itself. The exceptional size and importance of the military bases set up by the United States in South Vietnam have led many observers to believe that they represent « dispositions out of proportion with the Vietnamese war » (108) and that, in the light of these bases, this war « appears unreal and of secondary importance » (109).

Must one accept, on arguments of realism, that in the modern world the great Powers have a sort of right to maintain, or even extend their zone of influence — even in regions which, like Vietnam, are more than 6,000 miles from their shores — purely in defence of their political concepts, or, to put it bluntly, their interests (110), for which these political concepts for the most part serve simply as vehicles ? It must be understood that such a surrender would lead to the negation of international law and its complete replacement by brute law and the « arrogance of power ». For the most vital significance of the progress of international law, due to the principle « of sovereign equality » (Article 2, para. 1 of the U.N. Charter) consisted in freeing the fate of nations, and particularly small countries, from the hazards of their geographical situation, from the imposition of the protection of the great Powers, from the continual threat of foreign intervention. The progress of law is incompatible with the idea that thirty million human beings who are Vietnamese are pawns on an international checkerboard, manipulated by the politicians and business men, often the same, of a great foreign Power.

16. There are minds which find the terrible waste of lives and strength which characterises the war in Vietnam so unbelievable that the only explanation they can find of the *present* situation is an explanation à la Ubu, (111) taken from Père Ubu, a character invented by Alfred Jarry, who declared « I shall kill everyone, and then I'll be off »

---

(108) P. Darcourt, *L'Express*, January 10-16, 1966. For details on American bases, see *Réalités*, January 1966, and the articles by Guillain in several numbers of *Le Monde*, February 1966.

(109) Gigon, *op. cit.*, pp. 84-99, describing the American base of Da Nang, referred to its « unimaginable *agressive* power (our italics) and declared it possessed « the most sensitive and secret system of radar in the world ».

(110) President Johnson, in his speech at San Antonio on September 29, 1967, frankly declared, in connection with Vietnam, that the key to all their actions was their own security. (*Le Monde*, October 1-2, 1967).

(111) This is the explanation indirectly provided by Mr. Schlesinger, (*op. cit.*, p. 118), when he wrote that the American government, « disposed to the indiscriminate use of power, enmeshed in the grinding cogs of the escalation machine ... could not turn to de-escalation without considerable inner upheaval ».

(112). It is true that one of the most terrible features of the war is the vicious circle in which the United States are entrapped, a vicious circle only too clearly envisaged by the authors of the United Nations Charter when they based Chapters 6 and 7 on the belief that the first essential was to prevent an aggravation of the conflict (113) not only on account of the risk of creating an irrevocable situation, but also because it acquires its own validity and becomes an end in itself. In this respect the war in Vietnam demonstrates the dangers of all concepts which base peace on the existence of an international police selected among the Great Powers. Certain sections of public opinion, in the inter-war period and after 1945, loudly called for an end to the isolation of States and the extension of their international responsibilities. But it is the content of the international participation of States which is the vital question : and each State cannot be left its own judge in this matter. The system of security of the United Nations has to be both a system of participation and a system of limitation; the Great Powers must play a fundamental, but limited, role. Its failure has left the fate of peace, and of peoples at various danger points in the world, to the judgment of some politicians and military not necessarily noted for clear vision (114) or elevated sentiments. Even so exceptional a head of State as President Kennedy embarked on the affair of the Bay of Pigs and increased American involvement in Vietnam. The lesson that the war in Vietnam in fact teaches is that a great Power should never put itself into an international situation that it cannot, without an immense moral effort, radically change (115) (116).

17. To the question asked in the heading of the present section, is the war in Vietnam an end in itself, the answer is therefore both yes and no. It is not an end in itself in that the essential reasons for it go far beyond the fate of Vietnam itself, and form part of a global policy on the Far East, and that the scope of the war effort there seems to extend beyond the limited objective of a South Vietnamese State. It is an end in itself in that the magnitude of the American involvement is so great that it has taken on an independent significance, a symbolic value. For

(112) The comparison with Père Ubu originated with M. Baechler, in his article in *Le Monde,* July 18, 1967. « The later stakes have become so enormous that they have not only hidden the non-existence of the original stake, *but they have become the stake itself* (our italics); the desperate struggle is not to win, because there is nothing to win, but not to lose ».

(113) For the further development of this idea, see Chaumont, *La sécurité des Etats et la sécurité du monde* (Paris, Pichon et Durand Auzias, 1948).

(114) There is a body of opinion which believes that in view of the enormous military resources of the United States in the Far East, apart from Vietnam, they have no need of South Vietnam to confront China.

(115) Lacouture, (*op. cit.,* p. 249) fears that the United States will prove incapable of « a great diplomatic switch which would open the door to co-operation on a monumental scale ».

(116) See the statement of Senator Robert Kennedy of August 23, 1967, quoted in *Le Monde,* August 23, 1967, when he declared that America had built its foreign policy on fine anti-Communist words, and has found itself the prisoner of these fine words at the very time when the monolithic structure of Communism began to crumble.

the relegation of the South Vietnamese authorities to the background, and later their virtual inexistence, has only increased the concentration of the United States on their war (117) the lack of substance of the South keeping pace in a most contradictory fashion with the illusion of defending a real entity (118).

∴

18. It is not our intention, as we declared at the beginning of this study, to research into all the issues of American intervention, and in particular to examine if the character of this intervention leaves place for some sort of conciliation (119) by which, perhaps through the provisional retention of some of the American positions (120), the United States could abandon their sacred myths and accept the reunification of Vietnam and the choice of the Vietnamese people, *whatever it might prove to be.*

The preceding question will be answered one day, not too far away, one hopes, by statesmen, and not by the military. The problems discussed, in terms of an analysis of American intervention *as it exists,* are above all of value as testimony to the international reality and to the enforcement of law.

There is one piece of testimony which dominates all the others; the witness borne by the Vietnamese people in its flesh, its blood and its soul. Proof has been given that in our cruel century the unconquerable vigour of a people (122) fighting for its own soil, can hold in check the

---

(117) See Schlesinger, *op. cit.,* p. 72. « We have seized every opportunity to make clear to the world that this is an *American* war, and, in doing this, we have surely gone far to make the war unwinnable ».

(118) See Schlesinger (*ibid.,* p. 115). « One cannot blame Ky for pursuing his own policies; one can only blame the American Government for letting him try to decide American policy... I am sure that President Johnson did not intend to turn over American policy and honour in Vietnam to Marshal Ky's gimcrack, bullyboy, get-rich-quick regime ».

(119) Lacouture, at the end of his book on Ho Chi Minh, (p. 250) considers that the leader of the Democratic Republic of Vietnam « the day the Americans have shown that they really want to make peace in Vietnam », will know how to take the necessary steps to conciliation, as he knew (unfortunately without success) in 1946 and 1954.

(120) Up to the present Cuba has borne with the Guantanamo base. See also the position adopted in the United States by General Gavin, former U.S. Ambassador in Paris, appearing before the Senate Foreign Relations Committee, when he declared himself in favour of the progressive withdrawal of American forces and their regroupment in large bases (*Le Monde,* August 6-7, 1967).

(121) Senator Fulbright (op. cit., p. 179) writes : « I do not accept the view that criticism of the Vietnamese war is illegitimate in the absence of a foolproof plan for ending it; nor do I accept the view that because we are already deeply involved in Vietnam it is « academic » to debate the wisdom of that involvement... Far from being academic, the question... is of the greatest pertinence in deciding whether we should now sustain the war indefinitely ».

(122) According to Senator Fulbright (*ibid.,* p. 199) « There is something appropriate and admirable about a small country standing up defiantly to a big country ... the same behavior on the part of a big nation is grotesque ».

most perfected machinery of death (123). In this war, where the vast-ness of the suffering can only too easily lead to despair, it is the only gleam of light, illuminating the superiority of courage over unhappiness, the spirit of resistance over the spirit of surrender, right over napalm.

(123) According to U. Thant, Secretary-General of the United Nations, in his statement of May 11, 1967, quotes in the Monthly Chronicle of the United Nations, Vol. 4, no. 6 of June 1967, pp. 62-63, « the fact that the Democratic Republic of Viet-nam, a developing country, is continuing to withstand the pressure of an enormously superior power, has been and still is the essential factor which has prevented an enlargement of the conflict beyond the frontiers of Vietnam ». As a result Vietnamese resistance has reduced the risks of world war, avoiding the snare of the more direct involvement of Russia and China. This idea is confirmed by a statement attributed to Chou En Lai, President of the Chinese Council, by the Chicago Daily News (quoted by Le Monde, May 16, 1967) affirming that China would not allow America to approach too closely to her frontiers. As a consequence, this newspaper asserts, the American Government concluded that China would not intervene as long as the war was confined to certain geographical limits. Which is as much as to say that international escalation depends on the strength of the Vietnamese people. Is the international community prepared to accept the sacrifice of this people ?

Some Reflections on the Legal Controversies Concerning America's Involvement in Vietnam

F. B. SCHICK

> But the case of a people struggling against a foreign yoke, or against a native tyranny upheld by foreign arms, illustrates the reasons for non-intervention in an opposite way; for in this case the reasons themselves do not exist. A people the most attached to freedom, the most capable of defending and of making a good use of free institutions, may be unable to contend successfully for them against the military strength of another nation much more powerful. To assist a people thus kept down, is not to disturb the balance of forces on which the permanent maintenance of freedom in a country depends, but to redress that balance when it is already unfairly and violently disturbed. The doctrines of non-intervention, to be a legitimate principle of morality, must be accepted by all governments.
>
> JOHN STUART MILL

IT HAS BEEN the original purpose of this essay to scrutinize without undue delay some of the major contentions advanced by the United States government in a belated attempt to justify, with reference to principles and rules of international law, America's major military intervention in Vietnam.[1] It may be permissible, however, to reflect for a moment upon some general problems connected with the alleged right of covert and/or open military intervention of foreign powers in the affairs of smaller states, or areas, of which the tragic war in Vietnam represents only one out of many great-power experiences since the termination of World War II.[2] That such interventions have gained

[1] See, *The Legality of U.S. Participation in the Defense of Viet-Nam*, U.S. Department of State, Far Eastern Series 147 (March 1966), pp. 1-16 (hereinafter cited as *Government Brief*). It is alarming to note that no new, more comprehensive government document about the *legal* merits of its case has been published by the United States government after 1966. It is also noteworthy that the title of this document refers to Vietnam, thus rejecting at least by implication a division of Vietnam into two separate states. Similar announcements emphasizing the indivisibility of Vietnam have been made frequently by the governments of South Vietnam and of North Vietnam.

Since the author's reply to the *Government Brief* was written in 1966, a large amount of professional literature has been published. Some of these writings have been additionally mentioned in the text or added as references to the footnotes of this article within the compass of available space. However, no important textual changes have been considered necessary or feasible.

[2] For expositions of the classic views on intervention see e.g. Stowell, *Intervention in International Law* (1921); C. C. Hyde, *Intervention in Theory and Practice*; Mosler, *Die*

in frequency can hardly be doubted; and it may be assumed that they will occur, here and there, even after a settlement of the war in Vietnam. Regardless of whether these military interventions were carried out by some leading Western powers or by armed forces from among the Socialist bloc countries, and whether or not they occurred upon the "request" of a weak clientele government, it is characteristic of all of them that they were usually justified with references to extralegal concepts of a diametrically opposed sociopolitical and ideological nature. In spite of the frequently missionary zeal which predominates among these justifications,[3] the opposing intervening powers and their more or less willing protégé governments have tried in each of these cases to justify—or at least to supplement—the righteousness of their allegedly great ideological-political missions with references to general principles and specific rules of international law.

During past centuries it was frequently with the help of the undefined, and in an objective way undefinable *bellum justum* theory that states have invoked the use of military force on the territory of others. This practice of states has been given renewed respectability by the writings of international jurists whose community-type sociologic approach frequently rejects as "sterile" the application of positivist rules of international law as the determining factor in the ordering

---

Intervention im Völkerrecht (1937); and Oppenheim-Lauterpacht, 8th edn., par. 134-140aa. For more recent discussions see for example: Julius Stone, *Legal Controls of International Conflict, and Supplement, 1953-1958* (New York, 1959), pp. 60-63; Brierly, *The Law of Nations*, 6th edn., by Sir Humphrey Waldock (New York and Oxford, 1963), pp. 402ff., where the learned author quotes specifically the Draft Declaration of Rights and Duties of American States, approved on July 17, 1946 by the Governing Board of the Pan American Union, which reads "Intervention by any one or more states, directly or indirectly, and for whatever reasons in the internal or external affairs of another state is inadmissible." See further Rosenau, ed., *International Aspects of Civil Strife* (1964); Brownlie, *International Law and the Use of Force by States* (1963); and Wilhelm Wengler, *Völkerrecht* (Berlin-Göttingen, 1964), Vol. II, pp. 1038-1056, esp. p. 1038: "Das Interventionsverbot stellt eines der am wenigsten geklärten Kapitel des allgemeinen Völkerrechts dar." (The interdiction of intervention constitutes one of the least clarified chapters of general international law.)

Among some scholarly monographs closely connected with the question of intervention should also be mentioned: Bowett, *Self-Defense in International Law* (1958); Pinto, *Lès Règles du Droit International Concernant la Guerre Civile, Récueil dès Cours* (1965); and A. Thomas and A. Thomas, *Non-Intervention: The Law and Its Import in the Americas* (1956).

[3] The obsession of most Americans with the threat of Communism has been described in F. B. Schick, "Vietnam und das Image der USA," *Blätter für deutsche und internationale Politik* (Köln, Germany, November 1966), pp. 1021-1028.

of the relations between states.[4] Admittedly wide differences of interpretation exist also among legal positivists; but they usually agree on the omission from their *legal* analyses of considerations pertaining to national power policies and conflicting ideologies. This observation has an important bearing on legal analyses pertaining to intervention.

The term "intervention" is often used in a very broad sense, meaning any interference—direct or indirect, diplomatically, economically, or militarily—by one state or by one international entity in the affairs of another. Accordingly, intervention may be legally permissible, or it may constitute an illegal act depending upon the ascertained facts and the legal rules claimed to be applicable to each case.

In the absence of an internationally established fact-finding commission with unrestrained investigative powers and the willingness of most states to accept as legally binding the findings of fact-finding commissions, it is perfectly clear that the justification of any type of intervention, but especially any intervention involving great-power interests, will be based on highly divergent assertions of facts and legally incompatible approaches. The existing need for such a fact-finding organ, entitled to investigate, free of any restrictions, alleged facts and situations which are being used as the bases for claims and counterclaims, has more recently prompted members of the United Nations General Assembly to pass Resolution 1907 (XVIII). This resolution recommends further deliberations on the feasibility and desirability of "establishing a special international body for fact-finding or of entrusting to an existing organization fact-finding responsibilities complementary to arrangements already in being."[5] The interventions in Greece, in Lebanon, in Yemen, in Algeria, in the Congo, in Korea, in Hungary, in the Suez Canal crisis, in the Communist "war of liberation" against the Chiang-Kai-Shek regime on the Chinese mainland, in the Cuban missiles crisis, in Guatemala, in the Dominican Republic, and in Vietnam may here be cited as a few examples. In each of these cases, the conflicting interests of the parties concerned produced not only conflicting statements of facts but also conflicting legal analyses.[6] This applies particularly to cases where the "right" of inter-

[4] For some examples of this frequently self-serving type of sociological jurisprudence see McDougal and Feliciano, *Law and Minimum World Public Order* (1961), and John Norton Moore, especially in "The Lawfulness of Military Assistance to the Republic of Vietnam," *American Journal of International Law*, Vol. 61 (1967).

[5] *Yearbook of the United Nations*, 1964 (New York, 1965), p. 460.

[6] For analyses concerning some legal problems in connection with recent interventions see Roger Fisher, "Intervention: The Problem of Policy and Law," in Richard A. Falk,

vention and counterintervention by means of forceful interference into the affairs of another country is justified by outside powers with the asserted "right" of individual and/or collective self-defense against alleged aggression, subversion, rebellion, insurgency, or any other form of alleged "armed attack." Another characteristic feature of such military interventions may be seen in the legally and morally untenable attitude of opponents who claim certain rights for themselves while denying the very same rights to the other side.

It cannot be doubted that many rules of international law applicable to specific cases of intervention are vague, controversial, or ever so often nonexistent; and it is not surprising that attempts, therefore, have progressed to substitute the developing principles and norms of international organization for the unlimited right of intervention as frequently claimed in the past. Outstanding expressions of these attempts to curb the right of intervention by individual states may be seen in certain provisions of the Covenant of the League of Nations and the restrictive rules incorporated for this purpose in the Charter of the United Nations. In spite of such attempts, states continue to claim for themselves a wide measure of discretion, especially when justifying intervention in support of a "legitimate" government against alleged domestic rebellion on the basis of their inherent right of individual and collective self-defense. As so bluntly stated by an international jurist with specific reference to the conflict in Vietnam: "in the balance of international politics, the distinction between support for government as distinct from rebel movements, has become almost meaningless. The alternatives are either isolation of the conflict by neutrality, or intervention and counter-intervention with all the dangers illustrated by the gradual escalation of the Viet-Nam war. This points to the alternative of organized action by the international community."[7]

A legal approach aiming at a minimum of objectivity will find it even more difficult to accept legal justifications of interventions in civil wars or international conflicts if such interventions—and counterinter-

---

ed., *The Vietnam War and International Law* (Princeton, 1968), pp. 135-150, at p. 144 (This volume will hereinafter be cited as *Dialogue*).

[7] See e.g. Wolfgang Friedmann, "Intervention, Civil War, and the Role of International Law," in *Dialogue, op.cit.*, pp. 151-159, at 158. President Johnson and the U.S. Secretary of State Dean Rusk, have claimed this right of political intervention against Communism consistently and up to the time of the Paris meetings in June 1968. See also Tom Farer, "Intervention in Civil Wars . . ." in *Dialogue, op.cit.*, pp. 509-522, at 514ff.

ventions—are mainly caused, at least during their initial phases, by
ideological conflicts. It ought to be remembered that the United States
Government has relied for many years on its alleged moral commitments to implement the Truman Doctrine by giving aid, on a worldwide basis, to any government "fighting for freedom and democracy,"
while Communist governments have arrogated to themselves the right
to intervene, at least secretly and indirectly, in support of uprisings
or wars of "national liberation." Vietnam may be considered but another case resulting from an ideological conflict. Obviously, a legal
analysis of America's involvement in Vietnam, aiming at objectivity,
ought not to be colored by considerations of an ideological nature.

It is perfectly clear that a more comprehensive treatment of the
legal issues connected with the armed conflict in Vietnam lies far beyond the permissible scope of this essay. Accordingly consideration is
given only to some of the major legal arguments of the United States
Government advanced in support of its initial intervention in South
Vietnam and of its subsequent military escalation beyond the established demarcation line into North Vietnam.

The most elaborate case in support of the legality of United States
intervention has been stated in a document entitled *The Legality of
U. S. Participation in the Defense of Viet-Nam.* For purposes of
brevity, this analysis of the Department of State will be called the *Government Brief.* It is the only comprehensive legal document on Vietnam
issued by the United States since 1954. The *Government Brief* devotes
three major parts to the international aspects pertaining to conflict in
Vietnam:[8]

1. The United States and South Viet-Nam have the right under international law to participate in the collective defense of South
Viet-Nam against armed attack.

2. The United States has undertaken commitments to assist South
Viet-Nam in defending itself against communist aggression from the
north.

3. Actions by the United States and South Viet-Nam are justified
under the Geneva Accords of 1954.

[8] *Government Brief, op.cit.,* at 583, 591, 594. See also *Background Information Relating
to South East Asia and Vietnam,* 4th rev. edn., U.S. Senate, Committee on Foreign Relations, March 1968.

The spate of documentary literature, published in the United Kingdom, France, Germany, and Communist countries, has amassed much evidence which is apt to seriously
question the authenticity—if not the veracity—of many broad assertions introduced
in the *Government Brief* (See below, note 35).

The major contention on which the validity of the government's case rests, as stated in the very first section of the first part, is that "South Viet-Nam is Being Subjected to Armed Attack by Communist North Vietnam."

The *Government Brief* does not follow accepted legal standards and practice by defining clearly the legal meaning of "armed attack," or of "aggression," or by stating without ambiguity the evidence which, in accordance with generally accepted principles of international law, may permit a state to invoke the right of individual and collective self-defense. In order to prove the claims of the American government, which the North has steadfastly rejected, the *Government Brief* tries to substantiate its rather broad references to North Vietnam's violations of international law with the assertion that the "Hanoi regime," has, "during the 5 years following the Geneva conference of 1954 developed a covert political-military organization in South Viet-Nam based on Communist cadres it had ordered to stay in the South, contrary to the provisions of the *Geneva Accords*."[9] It should be noted that this general assertion covering the years 1954 to 1958 is neither substantiated in the *Government Brief* in any specific, legally meaningful way, nor has Secretary of State Dean Rusk, been able to produce documented evidence in this respect in spite of the fact that he has characterized this early development as constituting the initial violations of the Geneva Accords by North Vietnam, and, therefore, the legal basis upon which the case of the United States Government rests.[10]

According to seemingly unbiased expert reports and analyses, the civil uprisings in South Vietnam were not initially ordered by the authorities in Hanoi but were caused by the repressive measures of the Diem regime against any and all of his political, religious, and military opponents, the majority of whom were "neither Communist nor pro-Communist."[11] The State Department's version, according to which

[9] *Ibid.*, p. 1.

[10] See for example *Hearings* on S. 2793, U.S. Senate, Committee on Foreign Relations, 89th Cong., 2nd Sess., p. 569 (Hereinafter cited as *Hearings*).

[11] P. J. Haney, "The Problem of Democracy in Vietnam," in *The World Today* (February 1960), p. 73. See also Philippe Devillers, "The Struggle for the Unification of Vietnam," in *The China Quarterly* (January-March 1962), p. 12, where the well-known scholar writes: "This repression was in theory aimed at the Communists. In fact it affected all those, and they were many—democrats, socialists, liberals, adherents of the sects—who were bold enough to express their disagreement with the line of policy adopted by the ruling oligarchy."

It should be noted that even a popular American anti-Communist magazine, such as

the original violations of the Geneva Accords were committed by activities of a "covert organization" based on "Communist cadres" under the command of the "Hanoi regime," has also been refuted by *Foreign Affairs*, known to support, as a rule, the public policy of the United States.[12] The evidence produced in the writings of leading French experts on Vietnam is apt to question seriously the veracity of Dean Rusk's above-mentioned testimony.[13] Prominent American scholars have rejected as outright distortions many of the official statements made by the U.S. Department of State and other government officials.[14] It cannot be doubted that Washington has had abundant data at its disposal which clearly contradict its official testimonies presented in justification of the major American involvement in Vietnam. In fact "distortions of the record are not confined to public addresses of government officials but are also to be found in the published writings of officials in the employ of government, who disguise the fact that they have any governmental connections."[15]

The *Government Brief*, in the next paragraph, refers to the period from 1959 to 1961 in an attempt to prove that acts of aggression in the form of armed attacks have occurred. Hence the assertion is made that the American government was permitted to resort to counterforce in self-defense. However, the evidence cited in this section of the *Government Brief* rests on vague estimates only. Thus, it is stated that the "North Viet-Nam regime infiltrated [from 1959 to 1961] an *estimated* 10,000 men into the South" (emphasis supplied). The *estimate* for the year 1962 amounts to "13,000 additional personnel."[16] The *Government Brief*, finally, states in even more ambiguous terms that "by

---

Life (May 13, 1957) when referring to Diem's dictatorial "Ordinance No. 6 of January 1956, stated that "Only known or suspected Communists . . . are supposed to be arrested and 're-educated' under these decrees. But many non-Communists have also been detained. The whole machinery of security has been used to discourage active opposition of any kind from any source."

[12] William Henderson, "South Viet Nam Finds Itself," in *Foreign Affairs* (January 1957), p. 285, where the author states: "South Viet Nam is today a quasi-police state characterized by arbitrary arrests and imprisonment, strict censorship of the press and the absence of an effective political opposition."

[13] See, for example, Jean Lacouture, *Le Vietnam entre deux paix* (Paris, 1965); and George Chaffard, *Indochine: dix ans d'indépendance* (Paris, 1964).

[14] For one of the latest and best documented rejections of the basic claims made by the American government in justification of the United States military involvement in Vietnam see George McTurnan Kahin and John W. Lewis, *The United States in Vietnam* (New York, 1967).

[15] *Ibid.*, p. 120.   [16] *Government Brief, op.cit.*, p. 1.

the end of 1964, North Viet-Nam may well have moved over 40,000 armed and unarmed guerillas into South Vietnam."[17] The *Government Brief* remains silent on the military build-up of a large South Vietnamese army coupled with the import, from the United States, of huge quantities of military equipment; and it does not give the statistics, readily available to the American government, covering the American military personnel and equipment introduced into South Vietnam and Thailand during the same period under review. On the basis of all available evidence largely taken from official testimony produced by representatives of the U.S. Defense Department, by the midyear of 1964, the United States ground forces in Vietnam numbered 16,500, the regular and irregular forces of South Vietnam amounted to 356,000, the regular and irregular Vietcong forces were estimated at 114,000, and the number of regular forces of the Peoples' Army from the Democratic Republic of Vietnam operating with the South Vietnamese Vietcong was 4,500, or only three regiments.[18] The only evidence produced in the *Government Brief* for the period of 1959-1961 refers to a passage of a special report, dated June 2, 1962, which was addressed by the Indian-Canadian majority of the International Commission for Supervision and Control in Vietnam (ICC), created by the Geneva Agreement, to the Co-Chairmen of the Geneva Conference on Indo-China. It should be noted that the Polish Delegate dissented from the views expressed in this report only since it stated, in section 10, as quoted below, that the northern zone had violated the *Geneva Accords*.

According to Article 42 of the Geneva Agreement on Vietnam of July 20, 1954,[19] the majority report of the ICC is legally not cognizable since "the decisions of the International Commission must be unanimous." However, there is no reason to doubt the accuracy of the interim reports of the commission. In spite of the fact that this commission has endeavored to investigate claims and counterclaims of the parties concerned, the frequent lack of unanimity of its reports deprives the commission of the legal powers required of a fact-finding

17 *Ibid.* It is difficult to understand how "unarmed guerillas" can commit armed attacks.

18 Kahin and Lewis, *op.cit.*, p. 185, where a tabulation is given for the period covering the years 1954-1966.

19 For the official texts of the various Geneva armistice agreements of July 20, 1954, the Final Declaration, and the Unilateral Declaration on behalf of the United States made on July 21, 1954 at Geneva, see Geneva Conference, Doc. 1C/42/Rev. 2. The provisions creating the International Commission for Supervision and Control in Viet-Nam, commonly known as the International Control Commission (ICC), are contained in Arts. 34-46 of the Agreement on the Cessation of Hostilities in Vietnam, July 20, 1954.

organ as envisaged by the recent resolution of the General Assembly for purposes of facilitating the pacific settlement of disputes. However, the commission constitutes, at present, the only international organ established by the 1954 Geneva Agreements which is entitled to and charged with undertaking investigations similar to those of a fact-finding commission. It is understandable, therefore, that the opposing parties have frequently referred to the *Interim Reports* of the International Control Commission even in those instances where these reports lacked the agreement of all its members. In fact, the *Government Brief* relies heavily on the commission's special report of June 2, 1962, from which it quotes the following passage:

> . . . there is evidence to show that arms, armed and unarmed personnel, munitions and other supplies have been sent from the Zone in the North to the Zone in the South with the objective of supporting, organizing and carrying out hostile activities, including armed attacks, directed against the Armed Forces and Administration of the Zone in the South. . . . there is evidence that the PAVN (People's Army of Viet Nam) has alllowed the Zone in the North to be used for inciting, encouraging and supporting hostile activities in the Zone in the South, aimed at the overthrow of the Administration in the South.[10]

It would seem that a more balanced and less distorted presentation of the evidence as introduced by the United States would require at least the citation of some other passages contained in the very same *Interim Report*, and especially the conclusions reached in section 20 of this report which read as follows:

> Taking all the facts into consideration, and basing itself on its own observations and authorized statements made in the United States of America and the Republic of Viet-Nam, the Commission concludes that the Republic of Viet-Nam has violated Articles 16 and 17 of the Geneva Agreement in receiving the increased military aid from the United States of America in the absence of any established credit in its favor. The Commission is also of the view that, though there may not be any formal military alliance between the Governments of the United States of America and the Republic of Viet-Nam, the establishment of a U.S. Military Assistance Command in South Viet-Nam, as well as the introduction of a large number of

[20] *Government Brief, op.cit.,* pp. 1-2.

U.S. military personnel beyond the stated strength of the MAAG (Military Assistance Advisory Group), amounts to a factual military alliance, which is prohibited under Article 19 of the Geneva Agreement.[21]

The *Government Brief* admits that "there may be some question as to the exact date at which North Viet-Nam's aggression grew into an 'armed attack,'" but it concludes that "the infiltration of thousands of armed men clearly constitutes an 'armed attack' under any reasonable definition."[22] It is this type of alleged initial acts of aggression and armed attacks carried on almost since 1954 which, it would appear, is used by the American government as legal justification to invoke the right of individual and collective self-defense, and it is this allegedly existing right of self-defense to which President Johnson, Secretary of State Dean Rusk, and other government officials have referred, time and again. In fact, these assertions have been made so frequently so as to evoke the impression that they need no further legal proof.

The legal validity of this type of reasoning is not only rejected by Hanoi, its military and political supporters, and many informed individuals in areas sympathetic to the United States; it has also been submitted to serious scrutiny in the United States, including the U.S. Senate. Thus, during *Hearings* before its Committee on Foreign Relations, Secretary of State Dean Rusk was asked by Senator Gore to substantiate the official assertions of the American government according to which "an aggression by means of an armed attack" had been committed between November 1964 and January 1965. For it was during this time, as stated by Secretary Rusk, when the 325th Division of the North Vietnamese Army moved into South Vietnan. However, when asked by Senator Gore whether this happened "before or after we moved forces into South Vietnam," Secretary Rusk's reply was: "Well, the division moved after we had put, had reinforced our own forces there. Nevertheless, we did not have our combat personnel in South Vietnam for a period of years during which there was a steady infiltration of

21 "International Commission for Supervision and Control in Vietnam—Special Report to the Co-Chairmen of the Geneva Conference on Indo-China" (Saigon, June 2, 1962), reprinted in *Hearings, op.cit.*, pp. 736-741 at p. 740.

22 *Government Brief, op.cit.*, p. 2. The U.S. Department of State reference to an armed attack whose exact date is not known to the attacked state but was an act of aggression before it "grew into an armed attack," amounts to legal nonsense; it cannot be used with credibility or legal validity to invoke Art. 51 of the U.N. Charter, as has been done by the American government.

armed men and armed supplies from the north."[23] It is noteworthy in this connection that Mr. McNamara, the Secretary of Defense, in response to a question raised by the majority leader, Senator Mansfield, testified in 1966 that the total number of regular North Vietnamese Army personnel was estimated to have been "in the order of 12,000 for the year 1965," and "between 11,000 to 20,000 for the year 1966."[24] During the same period of time more than 340,000 members of America's armed forces in addition to approximately 614,000 combatants of South Vietnam and 39,000 allied troops have been involved in combat or combat-related duties in South Vietnam against 271,000 Vietcong, and 30,000 regular members of the People's Army of Vietnam.[25]

There is good evidence to show that some major events subsequent to the conclusion of the 1954 Geneva Agreements have been cited by the spokesmen of the American government out of the context of the established chronological sequence of these events. As will be demonstrated later, the seemingly deliberate introduction of this element of historical confusion has important bearings on an assessment of the legal nature and consequences attributed to these events, such as for example the progressive build-up of United States forces in Vietnam, or the dispatch of regular army units from North Vietnam to the South, or the steps leading to the establishment of the National Liberation Front of South Vietnam, or, in general, the alleged disregard of certain provisions of the 1954 Geneva Accords by the one or the other of the parties involved. It is perfectly clear that references made out of their historical context and sequence cannot produce a valid basis for legal scrutiny and conclusion.

The questions connected with the impartial establishment of pertinent facts and of a historically correct sequence of certain events necessary for a more objective legal analysis of the present conflict render it advisable to refer at the outset to the Geneva Accords of July 1954.[26]

[23] *Hearings, op.cit.,* p. 52.

[24] *Hearings* before the Committee on Armed Services and the Subcommittee on Department of Defense of the Committee on Appropriations, United States Senate, 89th Cong., 2nd Sess., January-February, 1966, p. 144.

[25] Kahin and Lewis, *op.cit.,* p. 185.

[26] See *Further Documents Relating to the Discussion of Indo-China at the Geneva Conference,* June 16-July 21, 1954, Command Paper 9239 (London, 1954); and *American Foreign Policy,* 1950-1955, *Basic Documents,* Vol. I (Washington, D.C., Department of State Publication 6446).

For the purpose of this paper it is convenient to distinguish between three different legal documents:

1. The Armistice Agreement, signed on the 20th day of July 1954 by the Commander-in-Chief of the French Union Forces in Indo-China, Brigadier-General Delteil, and the Vice-Minister of National Defense of the Democratic Republic of Viet-Nam, Ta-Quang-Bun.

2. The Final Declaration, dated the 21st July 1954, of the Geneva Conference on the problem of restoring peace in Indo-China, affirmed by the representatives of Cambodia, the Democratic Republic of Viet-Nam, France, Laos, the People's Republic of China, the State of Viet-Nam, the USSR, and the United Kingdom. It should be noted at this point that the United States representative, who had taken a leading part in the deliberations of the Geneva Conference during its early stages, refused on instructions from John Foster Dulles, the U.S. Secretary of State, to join the other parties in this legally binding declaration.[27] Apart from certain specific military provisions of the Armistice Agreement, the Final Declaration re-asserts in its operative articles most of the important stipulations contained in the former. Hence, these two documents will be considered together.

3. The Unilateral Declaration, issued at Geneva on July 21, 1954, by Under-Secretary Walter B. Smith on behalf of the United States at the concluding plenary session on Indo China.[28] This document will be discussed separately.

In order to lay the foundations for a more accurate legal analysis certain comments on some basic provisions of the Armistice Agreement and the Final Declaration are considered in the following:

Article 12 of the Final Declaration states that the parties to the Geneva Accords undertake "to respect the sovereignty, the independence, the unity and the territorial integrity of Cambodia, Laos and Vietnam." These terms express quite clearly one of the major objectives of the Geneva Conference. Moreover, as provided by Article 6 of the Final Declaration, the military demarcation line was to be solely "pro-

---

[27] The rather sudden refusal of the American government to affirm the Final Declaration is dealt with in Anthony Eden's *Full Circle* (Boston, 1960).

[28] The Unilateral Declaration was made on July 21, 1954 during the Eighth Plenary Session of the General Conference. For a useful collection of early documents see Allan B. Cole, ed., *Conflict in Indo-China and International Repercussions, A Documentary History 1945-1955* (Ithaca, N.Y., 1956). For another valuable collection of documents see Marvin E. Gettleman, ed., *Vietnam: History, Documents and Opinions on a Major World Crisis* (New York, 1965). See also below, note 32.

visional" and was not to be interpreted "in any way as constituting a political or territorial boundary." In view of the recent re-affirmation of the Geneva Accords as the basis for future "negotiations or discussions" by the Geneva Conference powers, references to some other provisions of the Geneva Accords may clarify further the intentions of the original parties.

It cannot be doubted that the Geneva Accords intended to continue and to maintain Vietnam as a unified state; and that the anticipated general elections of July 1956 were to be held *freely*, i.e., without discriminatory political restrictions, and *simultaneously* throughout the entire territory of Vietnam. In view of the military and political situation prevailing at the time the Geneva Accords were concluded, it is perfectly clear that no political party or group, however moderate or extreme, and however dominant or in the minority, was to be prevented from freely participating in these elections. In addition, the holding of these "general elections" was stipulated by Article 7 of the Final Declaration in the form of a mandatory clause. However, Article 7 provided that these elections were not to be held immediately, but were to take place in July of 1956 "in order to ensure that sufficient progress in the restoration of peace has been made, and that all the necessary conditions obtain for free expression of the national will." It was also the purpose of these elections, as stated in Article 7, "to permit the Viet-Namese people to enjoy the fundamental freedoms, guaranteed by democratic institutions established as a result of free general elections by secret ballot." Moreover, "as a result of free general elections by secret ballot"—and this is an important point in terms of a correct historical sequence—a "settlement of political problems [was to be] effected on the basis of respect for the principles of independence, unity and territorial integrity."

It is perfectly clear that the settlement of political problems, as they existed throughout Vietnam, was not to precede but was to follow these anticipated elections. The importance attached to the holding of these elections finds also clear expression in Article 14(a) of the Armistice Agreement which states that the anticipated elections "will bring about the unification of Viet-Nam" and it is obvious that the Geneva Accords did not permit or even envisage a permanent political partition of Vietnam as subsequently aspired to by Saigon and Washington.

An interpretation of Article 7 of the Final Declaration in accordance with the letter and the spirit of the Geneva Accords permits the assumption that the reference to "fundamental freedoms guaranteed by democratic institutions" was intended to include the right of the voters, residing anywhere within the Vietnamese territory, to vote in July 1956, for any political party or group of their choice. Since the American government has frequently justified the denial of all-Vietnamese elections by its Saigon protégé with reference to the large number of subversive infiltrators, allegedly all Communists, from the North, who were trying to overthrow the "democratic government" of the Republic of Vietnam, it should be pointed out that Article 8 of the Final Declaration states specifically that the Armistice Agreement "must be most strictly applied and must, in particular, allow everyone in Viet-Nam to decide freely in which zone he wishes to live." Hence, it would seem correct to conclude that if these "infiltrators" wanted to vote for a government other than that of Premier Diem, they would have been legally entitled to do so.

It appears, therefore, that the utterly repressive measures imposed by Premier Diem against the advocates of all-Vietnamese elections did not comply with the Geneva Accords. In fact, the refusal of the Diem government to implement Article 7 of the Final Declaration by consulting with representatives of the Hanoi regime on preparations for the required elections as requested by the North, may be regarded as the most serious initial violation of one of the most important clauses contained in the Geneva Agreements. It can hardly be doubted that this violation had the strong support of the United States Government.[29]

There is good reason to believe that the governmental and societal structure firmly established in North Vietnam after the withdrawal of France, under the leadership of Ho Chi Minh, was not expressive of the pluralistic political concepts as understood in some areas of the West, but especially by the former colonial master—France. However, Diem's rejection even of the discussion of the holding of free elections precluded the opponents of these elections from submitting, as a legally valid argument, that such elections would not have been conducted democratically in the Northern administration zone, hence could not have produced the results envisaged by Article 7 of the Final Declaration. In fact, it is difficult to believe that Saigon had a greater devotion to democratic political processes than was the case with Hanoi where at least 80 percent of the population supported Ho Chi Minh's regime. Moreover, Article 7 of the Final Declaration provided for the supervision of the elections, throughout the territory of Vietnam, by the

29 For an elaboration and further references see Kahin and Lewis, op.cit., pp. 66-98; for the origins of the insurrection in South Vietnam see ibid., pp. 99-146.

International Control Commission which is composed of representatives from Canada, India, and Poland. Since each of these countries is a member of the United Nations, and Canada as well as India subscribe to democratic governmental processes, it is even more difficult to accept, *a priori*, as a legally valid justification the assertions of Washington and Saigon that such supervision would not have guaranteed "free elections."

According to Article 17(a) of the Armistice Agreement, "the introduction into Viet-Nam of any reinforcements in the form of all types of arms, munitions and other war material such as combat aircraft, naval craft, pieces of ordnance, jet engines and jet weapons and armoured vehicles, is prohibited." Article 18, quite consistently, therefore, interdicted "the establishment of new military bases . . . throughout Viet-Nam territory." Article 19 extended this prohibition to any "military base under the control of a foreign State," and it imposed upon the signatories of the Armistice Agreement a strict obligation providing that the temporary zones "assigned to them do not adhere to any military alliance and are not used for the resumption of hostilities or to further an aggressive policy."[30]

Reference should finally be made to Article 13 of the *Final Declaration* since it expresses the agreement among the members of the Geneva Conference: "to consult one another on any question which may be referred to them by the International Supervisory Commission, in order to study such measures as may prove necessary to ensure that the agreements on the cessation of hostilities in Cambodia, Laos, and Viet-Nam are respected."

It should be noted that, *in theory*, the right and, perhaps, the legal obligation, to enforce the armistice provisions pertaining to Vietnam vis-à-vis the parties to the Armistice Agreement and their "successors in their functions" would have rested, in the first place, with the original signatories, i.e. France and the Democratic Republic of Vietnam, and in the second place, with the guarantor governments—especially the co-chairmen—which had joined affirmatively in the Final Declaration of the 21st of July, 1954. Such action would have required, as a preliminary, and after the withdrawal of the combatant forces to their assigned zones or country, a unanimous report from the International Control Commission about noncompliance with provisions of the Armistice Agreement on Vietnam. Assuming further that the states which affirmed the Final Declaration were legally entitled to "ensure"

[30] See supra, note 19.

compliance with its provisions and the stipulations of the Armistice Agreement, the refusal of South Vietnam to comply with the Geneva Accords, a categorical refusal which has persisted until recently, would have permitted a re-convening of the Geneva Conference only by means of a collective decision of the co-chairmen and probably a unanimous vote of the states that are parties to the Geneva Accords, and especially the Final Declaration.

It is not certain that the Geneva powers were collectively prepared to reconvene the Geneva Conference at the time when it became clear that the elections in Vietnam would not be held and that other, important provisions of the accords were being violated as was stated in the *Interim Reports* of the International Control Commission for Vietnam. This neglect is apt to assign to these Geneva powers the role of co-defendants should it be possible to prove their unwillingness to carry out their legal obligations under Article 13 of the Final Declaration. However, it is necessary to point out that at a much later date, in July 1964, the major powers, following an appeal by U.N. Secretary General U Thant, asked for the reconvening of the Geneva Conference. Hanoi, supported by the People's Republic of China, agreed without delay while the Johnson Administration gave "no hint of a willingness to explore even tentatively the possibilities that seemed to be opening up for a peaceful settlement of the conflict."[31]

It ought to be stated at this point that the Hanoi government has consistently demanded the observation of the Geneva Accords and has continuously requested that the parties to the Final Declaration ensure as against the zone in the South and the American government the strict observation of the Geneva Accords.[32] These demands have been

[31] Kahin and Lewis, *op.cit.*, p. 156 where President Johnson's statement rejecting the proposed negotiations is quoted as follows: "We do not believe in conferences called to satisfy terror."

[32] For further references see Bernard B. Fall, *The Two Viet-Nams*, Second Edition (New York, 1967), esp. chapters 15-17. See also Quincy Wright, "Legal Aspects of the Vietnam Situation," in *Dialogue, op.cit.*, pp. 271-291, esp. p. 288 stating: "There is no evidence of any action by North Viet-Nam which could be regarded as an armed attack upon the South prior to 1958, after Ho Chi Minh had engaged in four years of fruitless effort to carry out the resolutions of the Geneva Conference. In these circumstances Ho Chi Minh's action in support of the Viet-Cong did not constitute aggression or armed attack in international relations but civil strife within the domestic jurisdiction of Viet-Nam, similar to the action of the North against the South in the American Civil War. Whether called "intervention," "reprisals" or "collective defense," the United States response by bombings in North Viet-Nam, which began in February, 1965, violated international law, the United Nations Charter, and the Geneva Agreement, if the latter were in effect."

made since 1955, when the Government of Premier Diem, contrary to the stipulations of the Final Declaration, refused to consult with the authorities of North Vietnam on the preparation of general elections for July 1956. The recent testimony of the U.S. Secretary of State before the United States Senate, Committee on Foreign Relations, clarifies this point of historical sequence:

THE CHAIRMAN (Senator Fulbright):

I am informed that in 1955, in accordance with the treaty provisions, he [Diem] was requested by the north to consult about elections, and that he refused to do so. Is that correct?

SECRETARY RUSK:

Well, neither his government nor the government of the United States signed that agreement.

THE CHAIRMAN:

We will come to that as a separate point.—But it is correct that he refused to consult with the north on election procedure, is it not?

SECRETARY RUSK:

I think that is correct, sir.

THE CHAIRMAN:

Now we will come to your point of not signing. Why, in your opinion, didn't we sign the agreement? There were nine parties there, and seven signed it. We refused. Why didn't we sign it?

SECRETARY RUSK:

I have tried to find in the record a full discussion of that subject. Quite frankly, I have not been able to. I think, my general impression is, that the United States was at that time not persuaded that this was the best way to settle this affair, and did not want to be responsible for all of the elements of the agreement. . . .

THE CHAIRMAN:

Not having signed it, what business was it of ours for intervening and encouraging one of the participants not to follow it, specifically Diem?[33]

The third document of the Geneva Accords, namely the Unilateral Declaration of the United States, "takes note" of the various armistice agreements. In addition it refers, in an ambiguously worded statement, to paragraphs 1 to 12 of the Final Declaration by stating that the

[33] *Hearings, op.cit.*, pp. 48-49. For further references see also Allan B. Cole, *op.cit.*, p. 209, pp. 227-228.

government of the United States "will refrain from the use of force to disturb . . . the aforesaid agreements and paragraphs."

In spite of the apparent reluctance to give full support to the Geneva Accords, a reluctance which may be explained as a direct consequence of the public policy of the United States,[34] the American Unilateral Declaration, at the time when issued on July 21, 1954, accepted as legally binding the Geneva Accords; and it did support, *expressis verbis*, one major concept of the Geneva Accords, i.e., "free elections supervised by the United Nations." Moreover, it did not reject the other basic concept of these Accords, namely the territorial unity of Vietnam. However, the American obligation not to disturb these major concepts of the Geneva Accords was restricted by the ambiguous statement that "any renewal of the aggression" in violation of the Geneva Accords would be viewed "with grave concern and as seriously threatening international peace and security." It cannot be doubted that this statement referred only to the northern zone of Vietnam as borne out by subsequent assertions of the American government, assertions which try to justify the disregard of the Geneva Accords by the Saigon regime and its supporters.

The Initial Violations of the Geneva Accords

According to the best available Western sources, the major military provisions of the Armistice Agreement for Vietnam were faithfully observed by France and the Vietminh authorities in the northern assembly areas during the time immediately following the Armistice

[34] Although the American government did not expressly reject the observation of the Geneva Accords, it may be said that there existed a clear conflict between the then openly expressed policy of the American government and the obligation to respect the Geneva Agreements. In fact, the strong aversion of the United States Government to any adjustment of the Southeast Asian situation which would include pro-Communist political organizations of Vietnam and the basic policy decisions resulting therefrom were already expressed in 1950 by Secretary of State John Foster Dulles in his book entitled *War or Peace* (New York, 1950), as quoted here: "In Viet Nam the United States recognized the government of Bao Dai on February 7, 1950, after the Soviet Union on January 30th had recognized the rival regime of Ho Chi Minh. The stage is thus set for a test of influence. The chance for the success of a non-Communist government would have been improved if the French had moved more rapidly to grant real independence. As it is, there is a civil war in which we have, for better or worse, involved our prestige. Since that is so, we must help the government we back. Its defeat, coming after the reverses suffered by the National Government of China, would have further serious repercussions on the whole situation in Asia and the Pacific. It would make even more people in the East feel that friendship with the United States is a liability rather than an asset."

Agreement.[35] Moreover, the American government rejects these well-documented facts; and it justifies the support, from the very outset, of the Ngo Dinh Diem regime in its refusal to hold elections with the assertion that Ho Chi Minh's government had grossly violated the Armistice Agreement. Thus, Dean Rusk, the United States Secretary of State, when recently testifying before the Foreign Relations Committee of the United States Senate asserted that North Vietnam had, from the very beginning, committed "acts of aggression" when it violated the 1954 Armistice Agreement, which provided for the withdrawal of the opposing combatants to certain regrouping zones. He said: "At the time of the accords in 1954, many Communists fighting with the Vietminh had been directed by the Lao Dong Party in Hanoi to stay in the South, to hide their arms, and to devote their efforts to undermining the South Vietnamese Government."[36] Dean Rusk expanded on this statement in later testimony as follows: "Well, at the time of the split between North and South Vietnam, it was agreed that there would be a regroupment of the two sides. The Communist elements were supposed to go north and, as you know, one million northerners came south to get away from what was to come in the north.— Several thousands of those who were supposed to be regrouped to the north stayed behind."[37] The testimony assumes that those "several thousand" Vietnamese who did not move north but remained in the South committed covert "acts of aggression." It does not admit the possibility that the reluctance of these "several thousand" might have been prompted by the desire, similar to that of approximately one

---

[35] See, for example, Robert Scigliano, *South Vietnam: Nation Under Stress* (Boston, Mass., 1964); Jean Lacouture-Devillers, *La Fin d'une Guerre-Indochine*, 1954 (Paris, 1960); and the same author, "Vietnam: The Lessons of War," *New York Review* (March 3, 1966); Ellen J. Hammer, *The Struggle for Indo-China* (Stanford, 1954); Donald Lancaster, *The Emancipation of French Indo-China* (New York, 1961); Robert Scheer, *How the United States Got Involved in Vietnam* (Santa Barbara, 1965); Bernard B. Fall, *The Two Vietnams*, 2nd rev. edn. (New York, 1967); Jean Chauvel, "Coexistence in South East Asia: A French View," in Alastair Buchan, ed., *China and the Peace of Asia* (New York, 1965), esp. pp. 33-41; *Vietnam: Vital Issues in the Great Debate* (New York, 1966); American Friends Service Committee, *Peace in Vietnam . . .* (New York, 1966); and the extensive bibliographies given in both, Kahin and Lewis, *op.cit.*, and Bernard B. Fall, *op.cit.*; Marcus G. Raskin and Bernard B. Fall, *The Viet-Nam Reader: Articles and Documents . . .*, rev. edn. (New York, 1967); Schurman, Scott, and Zelnik, *The Politics of Escalation in Vietnam* (Boston, 1966); Victor Bator, *Vietnam: A Diplomatic Tragedy* (New York, 1965); Robert Shaplen, *The Last Revolution: The U.S. in Vietnam, 1946-1966* (New York, 1966), esp. chaps. I-VI; and J. William Fulbright, *The Arrogance of Power* (New York, 1967).

[36] *Hearings, op.cit.*, p. 569.   [37] *Ibid.*, p. 594.

million of their compatriots moving south, to escape the alleged or anticipated hardships of a Communist regime. However, the Secretary's testimony asserts that those "several thousand" who were supposed to have moved north had all been identified, apparently beyond any doubt, as members of the Vietminh, the Communists' regular armed forces—and would have had no persuasive reason for remaining where they were, namely in the South, even after they had relinquished their arms had it not been for the orders of Hanoi. Quite apart from this stunning exercise in political logic, it should be remembered that Article 14(d) of the Armistice Agreement permitted free movement between the temporary zones for "any civilians."[38]

It is only *after* the refusal of the Diem regime to honor the basic principles of the Geneva Accords, namely to permit free elections in July of 1956, in order to establish a government for a unified state of Vietnam, that civil war ensued within the area of South Vietnam. The historical fact appears well established that "at this time the resistance was composed of nothing more than southern groups organized in self-defense against Diem. Hanoi had made no connection with them.[39]

[38] Article 8 of the *Final Declaration* reaffirms that the armistice amendments "must, in particular, allow everyone in Viet-Nam to decide freely in which zone he wishes to live." No specific time limitation such as exists in Article 14 (d) of the Armistice Agreement, is incorporated into Article 8 of the Final Declaration.

[39] Jean Lacouture, in *Hearings, op.cit.*, p. 659, is quoted as follows: "A careful study of the history of South Vietnam over the last 10 years will show that from 1956 onward, strong resistance groups, the surviving members of political-religious sects crushed by Diem, were in active opposition to the regime in the South; they were in fact already called "vietcong" by the Diem regime at that time. Furthermore, this essentially nationalist dissident movement gained added support as a result of the rural discontent which led Diem to suppress the elected municipal councils in 1957; it spread further after the promulgation of the terrible law of 1959 which prescribed the death penalty for all "accomplices of Communists"—and communism comes cheap in South Vietnam. . . . The North Vietnamese did not begin to exploit this situation and infiltrate agents until 1959; and it was only after pressure from a southern congress of "former Vietminh resistants" in March of 1960 that they prepared to intervene. At the northern Communist Party congress in September of the same year, the Hanoi Government gave direct encouragement to the revolutionary activities in the south. Still, it was not until November 11, 1960, following an attempted military putsch against Diem, that the Vietcong—feeling the pressure of competition from military nationalists—gave itself formal identity and established a political headquarters by creating the National Liberation Front.

It should also be noted that leading experts on Vietnam agree that the guerilla forces in South Vietnam, which rose after Diem's refusal to hold elections, and after his suppression of most political factions were, at the beginning of the civil war, primarily composed of dissatisfied groups from the South. *See* e.g. John W. Holmes, "Techniques of Peacekeeping in Asia," in Alastair Buchanan, *op.cit.*, p. 246: "The Vietcong are not invaders from North Vietnam but largely South Vietnamese. They certainly get assistance from outside South Vietnam but most are native to the area and had, in many cases,

The correctness of this statement is confirmed by many other expert witnesses.[40] On the basis of such testimony, it is difficult to accept the official American version according to which the government of the northern administration zone initiated acts of aggression in the form of armed attacks within the territory of the southern administrative zone.

The statistical data submitted by the United States Secretary of State during the recent *Hearings* hardly support his contention that the United States military involvement in Vietnam, during the initial period of the insurrection in South Vietnam, was justified on the basis of the inherent right of self-defense against *acts of aggression* in the form of armed attacks from the northern zone. It should be noted at this point that the organ competent to make such a decision with legal validity is not the American government but the Security Council of the United Nations and, should the Security Council be unable to act, possibly the General Assembly in accordance with the Uniting for Peace Resolution. Although the American government has, on a few occasions, reported to the Security Council "on measures it has taken in countering the Communist aggression in Viet-Nam,"[41] it has never submitted to the Security Council a resolution requesting the latter to decide in accordance with Article 39 of the United Nations Charter that the Democratic Republic of Vietnam has committed an *act of aggression or other breach of the peace*. It is perfectly clear that

---

gone into hiding with their supplies in 1954 when regroupment took place." See also Richard A. Falk, "International Law and the United States Role in the Viet Nam War," in *Dialogue, op.cit.,* pp. 362-400, at p. 377, and the same, "International Law and the United States Role in Viet Nam: A Response to Professor Moore," *ibid.,* pp. 445-508. For opposing views see: Leonard Meeker, "Viet-Nam and the International Law of Self-Defense," U.S. Department of State, *Bulletin,* Vol. 46 (1967), pp. 54ff; John M. Moore, "The Lawfulness of Military Assistance to the Republic of Viet-Nam," in *Dialogue, op.cit.,* pp. 237-270 and the same, *ibid.,* pp. 401-444.

Although the *Dialogue* introduces the controversial question of the legal consequences attached to material breaches of the Geneva Accords, it appears that this question has little legal relevance in the context of the present essay since all Parties concerned have repeatedly affirmed their adherence to these Accords.

See also U.S. Senate, Committee on Foreign Relations, June 16, 1965, *Background Information Relative to Southeast Asia and Vietnam,* where tables of events, arranged in chronological order, give a vivid picture of how the guerilla uprising in the South began and spread.

See also Hans J. Morgenthau, *Vietnam and the United States* (Washington, D.C., 1965), especially the chapter entitled "Background to Civil War."

[40] See e.g., Kahin and Lewis, *op.cit.,* pp. 99-150; see also Schurman, Scott and Zelnik, *The Politics of Escalation* (Boston, 1966), pp. 23-25.

[41] *Government Brief, op.cit.,* p. 6.

the United States has not fulfilled its legal procedural obligation to the United Nations in this regard but has arrogated to itself the exclusive right to determine that North Vietnam has committed "acts of aggression." This fundamental question will subsequently be discussed in this essay. The statistics, as submitted by the United States government, indicate that by January 1961, when John F. Kennedy became President, the United States had already stationed in South Vietnam "about 800 United States military" *as part* of the United States "aid mission."[42] Using the same official testimony, by the end of 1961, the United States had 3,000 men in South Vietnam, and by the end of 1962 this number had risen to 11,000 regular members of the armed forces. These men, according to the United States Secretary of State were "advisers but they were also advising combat people in the field and were themselves engaged in combat during that period as advisers."[43] The "underlying legal basis" for United States assistance to South Vietnam, according to Secretary of State Dean Rusk, "is the right of individual and collective self-defense against an aggressor." And it has been the contention of the United States government that "there is clearly an aggression from the North here which has been persistent and since 1960 has been sharply increased."[44] In order to prove this "basic fact" of allegedly initial aggression, the United States Secretary of State, in his recent testimony, submitted that "in the 3-year period from 1959 to 1961, the North Vietnam regime infiltrated 10,000 men into the south."[45]

The facts as presented by the United States Government itself furnish clear evidence that the alleged infiltrations of guerillas from the North occurred to any meaningful extent only *after* the South had repudiated the two principal clauses of the Geneva Accords, and *after* an ever increasing number of American military personnel had been stationed in South Vietnam, and *after* United States military forces in large numbers had participated in military action against South Vietnamese guerilla forces, who had risen in opposition to the dictatorial rule of Premier Diem and his successors.

Even if the claims of American aggression made by the North Vietnamese authorities are rejected as "Communist falsifications," and even

42 *Hearings, op.cit.*, p. 606.

43 *Ibid.*, according to previous testimony of General Taylor (*Hearings*, p. 445), "shortly" after General Taylor's mission to South Vietnam, the number of American "advisors" went as high as 17,000!

44 Testimony of Dean Rusk in *Hearings, op.cit.*, p. 8.

45 *Ibid.*, p. 570.

if the frequent reports of the International Control Commission are disregarded as legally defective, it would seem perfectly clear that the testimony of United States Government officials alone destroys rather than supports the factual basis for the American claim of acts of military aggression originating in, and mainly directed by, North Vietnam. The conclusion, therefore, is at hand that this argument, advanced by the Secretary of State and others on behalf of the United States Government, cannot serve as a legally convincing proof to show that the validity of the Armistice Agreement and the Final Declaration had been voided or impaired *ab initio* only by North Vietnam.

It may here be in order to submit an additional observation in the context of alleged aggression by North Vietnam, an aggression which occurred *after* the repudiation by South Vietnam of the mandatory provisions for elections in 1956, as contained in Article 14 (a) of the Armistice Agreement signed between the military representatives of France and the People's Republic of North Vietnam, and *after* the Republic of Vietnam, in close cooperation with the United States, had grossly disregarded the provisions of Chapter III of the Armistice Agreement which interdicts the introduction of fresh troops, military personnel, arms, munitions, and the construction of military bases. Hanoi considered these acts as serious violations of the Armistice Agreement. As far as the Democratic Republic of Vietnam is concerned, the legal sanctions attached to serious violations of the Armistice Agreement could be applied. A customary rule of international law, codified in Article 40 of the Hague Regulations, is quite clear on this point. It provides that "any serious violation of an armistice by one of the parties gives the other the right to denounce it, and even, in case of urgency, to recommence hostilities at once." A similar view is expressed in Oppenheim's *International Law*: "Serious violations empower the other party to denounce the armistice, but not, as a rule, to recommence hostilities at once without notice; (3) only in case of urgency is a party justified in recommencing hostilities without notice. But since the terms 'serious violation' and 'urgency' lack precise definition, the course to be taken is in practice left to the discretion of the injured party." In connection with the alleged violations of the *Armistice Agreement* by Saigon and the United States, the contention seems legally irrelevant that the Diem regime had rejected the applicable clauses of the Geneva Accords on grounds that it did not sign them. After having demanded on many occasions a strict adherence to the armistice provisions and after having lodged numerous protests with the International Control Commission against their serious violations, the Hanoi regime was legally entitled to resume full-scale military actions across the temporary demarcation line. That Hanoi did not initiate any such organized military actions with its regular forces against South Vietnam during the early stages of the conflict is admitted by all parties concerned. But this restraint did not void Hanoi's legal right to resume massive military action. As quite correctly stated: "From and after July 21, 1956, the North Vietnamese have had every right under international law to march their armies in force across the 17th Parallel and to resume the full military occupation of the whole of Vietnam which they had yielded up in reliance upon the Geneva Covenant guaranteeing unifying elections at that time. To brand this or any lesser action calculated to achieve the same end as aggression is an arrant perversion of law."[46]

The Conflict in Vietnam and the Law of the United Nations

In view of the claims made by the American government based on "the right of individual and collective self-defense against an aggressor," it is necessary to examine in the following whether or to what extent the provisions of the Charter of the United Nations as invoked by the American government are applicable in this case.

The most important provisions of the Charter applicable to the armed conflict in Vietnam, as regards the parties directly involved at this time, will be considered on two levels: (1) the United States as a member of the United Nations, and (2) Vietnam as a nonmember.

As has been shown previously, the United States justifies its military actions in Vietnam with reference to Hanoi's violations of Article 2(4), and the permissive provision of Article 51, which, it is alleged, accords the American government the inherent right of individual self-defense against armed attack from the North. In addition, the United States, as will be discussed shortly, has also invoked its right of collective self-defense against acts of aggression from the North in connection with its regional commitments under the South East Asia Treaty Organization (SEATO), and its defense assurances with South Vietnam.

It should be noted that the United States Unilateral Declaration acknowledges specifically the obligation of the American government under Article 2(4) of the Charter. Section II of the operative part of the Unilateral Declaration, however, demonstrates clearly that the

[46] Malcolm Monroe, *The Means Is the End in Vietnam* (White Plains, N.Y., 1968), p. 47.

United States inserted in its Declaration the reference to Article 2(4) also in order to emphasize that this Article is binding on "any state" and not only on the United States or other members of the United Nations. The assumption may be justified that this specific emphasis in the United States Unilateral Declaration was directed particularly to the attention of the government of North Vietnam. It is also necessary to state in this connection that Article 2(4) only reaffirms a by now well-established principle of customary international law according to which the illegal use of force is interdicted in the relations between states. Hence, Article 2(4) is also binding on states that are not members of the United Nations. It should further be noted that the Charter of the United Nations, as originally signed and ratified, has conferred only upon the Security Council the right to make the final decision concerning the necessary measures to be taken if an armed attack has occurred against a member of the United Nations.

The Charter permits a member state under very special circumstances to initiate measures in self-defense. In exceptional cases such measures may also include the use of armed force. In order to legally justify its military involvement in South and North Vietnam, the American government, therefore, has mainly relied on Article 51, of the U.N. Charter. It is the thesis of this paper that the American case concerning the legality of its military actions in Vietnam stands or falls with an answer to the question as to whether or not the United States was legally entitled to invoke Article 51 of the U.N. Charter. For it cannot be doubted that general international law and the Charter of the United Nations do not permit any state to employ its national military forces against any other state without international authorization unless the right of self-defense can be invoked with legal validity. In fact, this analysis is acknowledged by the repeated assurances of United States officials who justify America's major military involvement in Vietnam on grounds of individual and collective self-defense against aggressive actions by "armed and unarmed" guerillas from the North, led and equipped by Hanoi, which, over the years, have grown into armed attacks. By organizing the Vietcong forces under the "subversive" political command of the National Liberation Front of South Vietnam (NLF), the United States, so runs the argument, was eventually compelled to resort to measures of individual and collective self-defense in accordance with Article 51 of the Charter. A clarification is here in order. Actions in "collective self-defense," by a third state which itself is not under armed attack are permitted only if the actions taken in self-defense by the attacked state can be legally justified. For it stands to reason that the illegal use of armed force under the pretext of individual self-defense cannot legalize the military support given to the violator of the law by a third state under the term of "collective" self-defense. Finally, a clarification is also in order with regard to the often repeated statements of American officials according to which the United States' use of military force in North and South Vietnam is legally justified as a response against continued "acts of aggression" from the North or, at least, "acts of aggression" directed by the Hanoi regime against the South. Since the American government relies primarily on Article 51 of the U.N. Charter, it should be stated that this Article does not contain any provisions pertaining to "acts of aggression." It cannot be doubted, however, that any illegal armed attack against an international person could be classified as an act of aggression by a competent organ of the United Nations in accordance with the stipulations of Article 39 of the Charter, or the applicable provisions of the Uniting for Peace Resolution.

As may be seen there exists an intimate connection between the right of self-defense and the response to an act of aggression in the form of an armed attack because Article 39 of the Charter contains the basic provisions with regard to acts of aggression while Article 51 specifies and restricts the initial right of self-defense conferred upon a member of the United Nations in case an act of aggression in the form of an armed attack has occurred against such a member.

It is a well-established principle that the *inherent* right of self-defense, as stipulated in Article 51 of the Charter, is only and solely an emergency right. However, if the theory is accepted that this right is an inherent, i.e., a natural right, its exercise is not only permitted in the case of an armed attack against a *member* of the United Nations but also if a state or "international entity" lacks membership in the United Nations. Accordingly, the Republic of Vietnam as well as the Democratic Republic of Vietnam are entitled to invoke this natural right. However, forcible measures taken with reference to this emergency right can be justified on legal grounds only and solely if, first, there exists a clear and present danger to the security or the very existence of the attacked state, and if, secondly, this danger is of such an overwhelming magnitude so as to leave to the attacked state no moment for deliberation and no choice to employ any means other than force in order to repel the armed attack.

Quite apart from this highly restrictive classic definition of self-defense which was given by the United States Secretary of State, Daniel Webster, in the famous case of the Caroline, leading contemporary scholars have agreed that the right of self-defense especially when viewed in connection with Article 2(4) of the Charter, must be strictly interpreted. Thus, Professor Brownlie shows that the discussions of the Dumbarton Oaks Proposals at the United Nations Conference on International Organization at San Francisco furnish no indication "that the right of self-defence in the Article was in contrast with any other right of self-defence permitted by the Charter or that the phrase 'if an armed attack occurs' was anything other than a characterization of the right of self-defence."[47] As further pointed out, the permissive right of self-defense under the Charter is a highly restricted right subject to the obligation of the attacked member of the United Nations to report such an attack *immediately* to the Security Council. Moreover, if the Uniting for Peace Resolution can be invoked without effective challenge to its constitutionality, the interpretation would be tenable that a subsidiary right to consider such a report, and to make recommendations, has been conferred upon the General Assembly.

Although the United States has, on occasion and quite belatedly, provided the Security Council with some "information" about "acts of aggression," allegedly committed by Hanoi, and the measures taken to counter these acts of aggression, no evidence exists that the United States has fulfilled its obligations to the Security Council in accordance with the spirit and letter of Article 51 of the Charter: namely to invoke Article 39 of the Charter by requesting formally that the Security Council, and if the Security Council cannot, the General Assembly, determine the existence of acts of aggression in the form of armed attacks by the Democratic Republic of Vietnam, and by demanding that the Security Council (or the General Assembly) decide upon the necessary measures to maintain or restore international peace and security. It is exactly this legal duty which Article 51 imposes as a matter of urgency upon any state invoking the right of self-defense since it is Article 51 which restricts this emergency right of self-defense "until the Security Council has taken the measures necessary to maintain international peace and security"; and it is obvious that the Security Council cannot act in cases of alleged aggression unless it has been asked to act. Any reasonable interpretation of Articles 39 and 51 of the Charter imposes the legal duty to request immediately such action of

[47] Ian Brownlie, *International Law and the Use of Force by States* (Oxford, 1963), p. 271.

the Security Council first and foremost upon the injured state or states which have invoked the inherent right of individual and collective self-defense against alleged acts of aggression. This is exactly the course which the United States took in the case of the Korean conflict in spite of the fact that the Democratic Republic of Korea and the Soviet Union did not participate in the discussions leading to the decision of the Security Council to use enforcement measures against North Korea; it is exactly the course which, in opposition to France, the United Kingdom, and Israel, was insisted upon by the United States during the Suez Canal crisis; and it is exactly the course followed by the United States in the Cuban missile crisis.

As previously indicated in this essay, American officials have also justified the intervention of the United States in Vietnam by pointing to the subversive activities of Communist groups aimed at overthrowing the government of the Republic of Vietnam, and permitting Hanoi to expand its Communist regime throughout the South of Vietnam. As in other instances, these activities have been classified by the American government as acts of "indirect aggression." The law of the United Nations does not contain any clause which would permit its members to resort to the use of armed force by invoking the so-called right of anticipatory self-defense for the avowed purpose of preventing expected armed attacks, acts of "indirect aggression," or "political subversion." This view is well exposed by Professor Brownlie. It is also shared by many other writers such as Professors Kelsen and Jessup.[48] Hence, it is hardly necessary to point out that the references of American officials to acts of anticipatory self-defense, or military measures against "indirect aggression," or "subversion" do not, by themselves, permit a state to invoke the right of self-defense.

It is an established fact that the widespread uprisings in South Vietnam, alleged to have been attacks of "armed and unarmed" Communist guerillas supported by a small number of regulars from the North were initiated by Diem's harsh police methods, by his rejection of elections, and by his refusal to carry out the promised land reforms.[49] It

[48] Brownlie, *ibid.*, pp. 275ff; see also Hans Kelsen, *The Law of the United Nations* (London, 1950), pp. 791ff; and Philip C. Jessup, *A Modern Law of Nations* (New York, 1948), pp. 165-166.

[49] Malcolm Monroe, *op.cit.*, p. 106 where the author, referring to the "McDougal Hedge," states: "the most significant, major breach of a covenant which if not the whole aim and purpose of the agreement, was certainly of the essence of the contract arose when the regime in the South, with the connivance and prodding of its American protagonists, refused to go forward with the promised elections, or even with the consultations which

is also an undisputed fact that the uprisings in the South were spread over a period of many years and it is obvious that this fact-situation lacks the legal criteria required for the application of Article 51. It does not seem plausible that such armed attacks as may have occurred on South Vietnamese territory, originally by uncoordinated groups of local dissidents, guerillas, and some infiltrators from the North, were of the magnitude and immediate danger to the United States and South Vietnam so as not to leave to their respective governments sufficient time for international steps as required by the universally accepted principles of international law, and by the Geneva Accords, and as rendered mandatory under Articles 33, 37, or 39 of the Charter of the United Nations. A review of the events leading to the present escalation of the Vietnamese conflict, when examined in their chronological sequence, therefore, renders it most difficult to justify the measures taken by the United States as actions commenced in self-defense against acts of aggression in the form of armed attacks as defined in international law and stipulated in the Charter of the United Nations. Hence, it is painful to admit that the United States lacks the legal basis under general international law and the applicable provisions of the U.N. Charter as a justification of its military actions in Vietnam, or the basis of the right of self-defense.

Reprisals and the Rule of Law

During the initial stages of military escalation, the President of the United States and other government officials have also claimed the right of reprisals in justification of America's major military involvement in Vietnam. This was done after the Gulf of Tonkin incident when, according to the U.S. version, North Vietnamese torpedo boats launched attacks on United States destroyers in international waters

---

the agreement provided for to precede them. . . . While it is not intended here to do more than point out the fallacies of the McDougal Hedge, it seems appropriate at least to show that the Government's most obvious answer to the line of argument here expounded is wholly devoid of merit. The Government's own Brief seeks to excuse the refusal to go forward with the elections upon the ground that police state repressions in the North would have made any such elections a "travesty." Such plea, under well established principles of American jurisprudence, is equitable in nature and, accordingly, comes squarely up against the "clean hands" doctrine—that a party who could plead in equity must come into court with clean hands." See also Richard N. Goodwin, *Triumph or Tragedy: Reflections on Vietnam* (New York, 1966) , p. 24, where the well-known author calls the refusal to hold elections in 1956 "the greatest political self-denial in history." See also Philippe Devillers, "The Struggle for Unification of Vietnam," *The China Quarterly* (January-March) , 1962, 2-23.

on August 2 and August 4, 1964.[50] According to Hanoi's version "the United States vessels had been on a provocative mission within the territorial waters of the Democratic Republic of Viet-Nam."[51] For the purpose of this analysis it is sufficient to note that, following the allegedly unprovoked attack by Hanoi, President Johnson announced, on August 4, 1964, thirteen hours after the alleged second attack, that an order of reprisals in the form of "Air action is now in execution against gunboats and certain supporting facilities in North Vietnam which have been used in these hostile operations."[52]

The United States Secretary of Defense, Mr. McNamara, reported in greater detail that heavy United States air attacks against three major North Vietnamese coastal bases had been carried out, and that these bases, together with 25 boats and local fuel depots, had either been damaged or totally destroyed.

Even if the American version of the Gulf of Tonkin incident should not be a distortion, the widespread destruction caused by the bombardment of North Vietnamese areas, as reported by Washington, was not commensurate with the offense—if this offense was at all committed on August 4, 1964. In fact, the destruction, justified as a measure of reprisals, was entirely out of proportion with the offense allegedly committed by Hanoi. These first "reprisals" on a large scale mark a new phase in America's military involvement. They may be considered as another significant stage in the escalation of the Vietnamese conflict. The second, far more intensive step in America's military involvement was carried out on February 7, 1965 in response to a Viet-

[50] For the official American version see U.S. Department of State, *Bulletin*, August 24, 1964. The accuracy of this version has come under serious questioning by the U.S. Senate during the *Hearings* on February 20, 1968, on the *Gulf of Tonkin Incidents of 1964*.

[51] *Yearbook of the United Nations*, 1964, p. 148. See also Kahin and Lewis, *op.cit.*, pp. 156-157, citing reports of the *New York Times*, July 23, 1964, and of *Le Monde*, August 7, 1964, concerning "South-Vietnamese sabotage missions inside North Vietnam 'by air, sea and land' "; and the complaint of Hanoi lodged with the International Control Commission for "intrusion by United States and South Vietnamese warships into its territorial waters as reported by the *New York Times*, August 10, 1964." For another well-documented analysis by the Chairman of the Center for Chinese Studies at the University of California at Berkeley and his associates pertaining to the situation preceding and immediately following the Gulf of Tonkin incident see "Tonkin Gulf Incident (July-August 1964) " in *The Politics of Escalation in Vietnam*, *op.cit.*, pp. 35-43.

[52] Cited in Kahin and Lewis, *op.cit.*, p. 158. See also Schurmann, Scott, and Zelnik, *op.cit.*, "Tonkin Gulf Incident (July-August 1964) ," pp. 35-43. It is common knowledge that Vietnam, like many other states, adheres to the 12-mile territorial water limit. During *Hearings* before the U.S. Congress, it was admitted that the *U.S.S. Maddox* went at least 11 miles from the coast line in order "to show that we do not recognize a 12-mile limit" (*Congressional Record*, August 6, 1964, p. 18407) .

cong attack near Pleiku in South Vietnam. During this attack 8 Americans were killed and 126 wounded.[53] The prompt retaliatory actions of the U.S. forces were also justified as "reprisals." According to a White House announcement, "these attacks were only made possible by the continuing infiltration of personnel and equipment from North Vietnam . . . To meet these attacks, the Government of South Vietnam and the U.S. Government agreed to appropriate *reprisal action* against North Vietnam. . . . As in the case of North Vietnam attacks in the Gulf of Tonkin last August, the response is appropriate and fitting" (emphasis supplied).[54] No evidence has been produced by the American government that these attacks were committed by North Vietnamese regulars, or with the knowledge and the approval of the government of North Vietnam. However, even if the Pleiku attack should have been ordered by the government of the Democratic Republic of Vietnam, the designation of the counterattacks as *reprisals* defies both general principles of international law and the Charter of the United Nations.

It cannot be doubted that reprisals in the form of military actions, unless justified as carried out in self-defense, have been outlawed since the end of World War I. The Covenant of the League of Nations, the Kellogg-Briand Pact of 1928, the Charter of the United Nations, and the writings of most highly qualified international jurists, all reject the legality of reprisals as sanctions permitted by a modern law of nations.[55] Numerous debates and resolutions of the U.N. Security Council support this fact.[56] As was consistently pointed out by the representative

[53] For a special report see Seymour Topping in the *New York Times*, February 9, 1965.

[54] U.S. Department of State *Bulletin*, February 22, 1965; see also Kahin and Lewis, *op.cit.*, pp. 168-175. See also Lawyers Committee on American Policy Towards Vietnam, *Vietnam and International Law* (Flanders, N.J., 1967), pp. 53-57 (hereinafter cited as *Lawyers Committee*).

[55] For quotations from leading writers see *Lawyers Committee, op.cit.*, pp. 54-57, and notes 84-94. See also Quincy Wright, *op.cit.*, p. 288; Richard A. Falk, *op.cit.*, p. 385. For an opposing view see John Norton Moore, *Dialogue, op.cit.*, pp. 254-256.

[56] See among others Adlai Stevenson, the U.S. Ambassador to the United Nations: "My Government has repeatedly expressed its emphatic disapproval of provocative acts and retaliatory raids, wherever they occur and by whomever they are committed" (U.N. Security Council, *Official Records*, January 12, 1956 and April 5, 1962); and see Security Council Resolution 188, passed on April 9, 1964, stating: "The Security Council Recalling Article 2, paragraphs 3 and 4 of the Charter of the United Nations,

1. *Condemns* reprisals as incompatible with the purposes and principles of the United Nations."

It is noteworthy that Ambassador Stevenson, representing the U.S. Government, abstained from voting since he preferred a more strongly worded text as follows: "*Condemns*

of the Soviet Union during the Security Council debate on the "complaint by the United States concerning the Democratic Republic of Vietnam," the retaliatory action of the United States during the Gulf of Tonkin incident is based on a "concept rejected in international law and renounced, *ipso facto*, in the recognition by Article 51 of the right of self-defense."[57]

In view of the foregoing analysis, it must be concluded that the military actions, ordered by the American government following the Gulf of Tonkin and Pleiku incidents, constitute serious violations of universally valid principles of international law, including the Charter of the United Nations.

Intervention and the Legal Status of Vietnam

It is the thesis of this paper that the events since the conclusion of the Geneva Accords have vitally changed the territorial status of the "State of Vietnam" as it existed in 1954. In view of these changes the two former temporary regrouping zones must, by now, be accorded the status of international entities or of *de facto* states. *Ex injuria jus oritur*, remains still the practice of powerful states in an international community unable to intervene effectively when a conflict has escalated beyond its initial stages. Hence, if it is correct to assume that the initial violations of the Geneva Accords by the regime of South Vietnam, rendered effective by means of American support, have changed the international legal status of South Vietnam from an administrative zone to an international entity or *de facto* state, the question still arises whether the government of the United States was legally permitted to make the commitments and to render the large-scale military assistance to the South which brought about the changes of its international legal status.

Apart from the disregard of the Geneva Accords, it appears that any military assistance to a legitimate government by a foreign power amounts to illegal intervention once there is clear factual proof that the government inviting such foreign aid "is threatened by an internal and potentially *successful* revolution."[58] It is precisely this legal position which was espoused by the United States and many other members of the United Nations during the Hungarian Revolution.

both attacks and reprisals as incompatible with the purposes and principles of the United Nations."

[57] *Yearbook of the United Nations*, 1964, p. 148.

[58] Roger Fisher, "Intervention: Three Problems of Policy and Law," *op.cit.*, p. 137.

Accordingly, the interpretation seems correct that "even if, as in Hungary, the existing government invites assistance from another nation, a popular revolution should be permitted to run its course without outside interference."[59] As the war in Vietnam, at least since the effective organization of the Vietcong in 1960, so tragically demonstrates, the disregard of this legal approach is bound to produce counterintervention and escalation of conflict since the right of intervention, assumed by one foreign power beyond the domestic stage of *de facto* belligerency and the assertion of effective control by the insurgents over certain areas and populations of the country involved in a civil war, will induce an opposing foreign power to claim the same right of intervention.[60] In spite of some lip-service given by the government of Saigon to the unalterable unity of Vietnam, it is fairly well established that Saigon as well as the United States intended the Republic of Vietnam to achieve and maintain an internationally independent legal status.

The independent legal status of North Vietnam can hardly be questioned when applying the traditional criteria attributable to a sovereign state. In terms of proven legal intent there exists, however, a fundamental difference between the South and the North. The very motivation for Hanoi's war against France and, after Saigon's serious violations of the Geneva Agreements, for Hanoi's major justification of its support offered the Vietcong against Saigon and the United States, was the unification of Vietnam as an independent state. It seems, however, that this intent alone only lends additional support to the established fact that the Democratic Republic of Vietnam is a *de facto* state or international entity.

There exists weighty opinion, also officially supported by the United States, that the Republic of Vietnam and the Democratic Republic of Vietnam, though temporarily divided, have remained parts of one and the same single state, namely the "State of Vietnam." Referring particularly to the Geneva Accords, leading international jurists maintain that North and South Vietnam continue to have the status assigned to them by these Accords.[61] If this interpretation is accepted, the con-

[59] *Ibid.*

[60] *Ibid.*, p. 138. See also Quincy Wright, *op.cit.*, stating: "The American intervention involving the use of armed force against the Viet-Cong in the south and the bombing of installations in the north was a violation of traditional international law forbidding intervention in the domestic affairs of another state and prohibited by the United Nations."

[61] For an excellent exposition of this point of view see "Memorandum of Law, Pre-

clusion would be at hand that the Vietnamese conflict has the character of a civil war with belligerency status[62] in which the military intervention of the United States and the subsequent indirect counter-intervention by the People's Republic of China, the U.S.S.R. and other Communist states were not authorized by any universally accepted rule of international law or by the Charter of the United Nations. On the basis of this opinion, the collective enforcement provisions of the Charter of the United Nations could have been applied by foreign states against the northern and/or southern administrative zones of the "State of Vietnam" only in accordance with Article 2(7), and in connection with a decision under Chapter VII of the United Nations Charter.

It is interesting to note that the American government, particularly in many of its earlier declarations, has insisted that there exists only one "State of Vietnam," i.e., the Republic of Vietnam, and that the various Saigon governments alone are entitled to represent this state. In view of this assertion, the theory was then advanced that Vietnam was seized by a civil war, that the legitimate government of Vietnam had requested American military and economic help and that such help, therefore, was not to be construed as foreign intervention. While it has been the more recent practice of the two super powers to give, upon "request," economic and military help to small states within the respective spheres of interest of these super powers—the crushing of the Hungarian Revolution by the Soviet Union, condemned as it was, as a flagrant act of aggression by the United States during the debate in the General Assembly, and the intervention of the United States in the Dominican Republic, may here be cited as but two examples—it should be recognized that the United States Government was bound not to "disturb" the provisions of the Geneva Accords. In the case of

---

pared by Lawyers Committee on American Policy Towards Vietnam," inserted in *Hearings, op.cit.*, pp. 627-713; see also *Lawyers Committee, op.cit.*, pp. 63-66, and Daniel G. Partan, "Legal Aspects of the Vietnam Conflict," *Boston University Law Review* (1966), 281-316; for an opposing opinion see John N. Moore, *op.cit.*, p. 239 where the author states that "The R.V.N. and the D.R.V. have at least been separate *de facto* international entities for the more than twelve-year period since the Geneva Accords of 1954 . . . In these circumstances the D.R.V. may not unilaterally resort to force against the R.V.N." It appears that, following Professor McDougal's dualistic approach to international law which ever so often seems to be subordinated to notions of American national interest, Professor Moore denies the legal right of unilateral resort to force to the Democratic Republic of Vietnam while according it to the Republic of Vietnam, America's puppet ally.

62 *Ibid.*, p. 692; see also *Lawyers Committee, op.cit.*, pp. 63-66.

"any renewal of the aggression in violation of the aforesaid agreements," the United States had the legal duty to implement the Geneva Accords by seeking, first of all, direct negotiations with Hanoi; secondly, by requesting all necessary action from the International Control Commission; in the third place, by asking for any appropriate action from the members of the Geneva Conference in accordance with Article 13 of the Final Declaration and by asking such action especially from its Co-Chairmen; and in the fourth place, after full "exhaustion of justice," by submitting a complaint to the jurisdiction of the competent United Nations organs demanding, in accordance with Article 2 section 7 of the Charter, that the Hanoi regime be estopped from interfering in the domestic affairs of the Republic of Vietnam by deciding that such interference constitutes an act of aggression (Article 39). None of these steps have been taken by the United States.

As previously stated the political situation which developed after the assumption of absolute power by the Diem regime and its successors leads to the conclusion that there have existed, and continue to exist, two separate *de facto* states in Vietnam with two separate governments, each claiming to exercise effective control over their respective areas and the populations living thereon, and each making the political assertion to be the sole spokesman for both the northern and southern zones of Vietnam. Although this claim made by the government of South Vietnam, even if restricted with regard to its effective territorial control of wide areas within the southern zone, is open to most serious challenge, it would, on the other hand, seem a denial of the effectivity principle, at least as far as North Vietnam is concerned, to reject the interpretation that two *de facto* governments have been established on the former territory of the state of Vietnam; and that diplomatic recognition has been granted to these two rival governments by certain states from whom these rival governments are receiving military, political, and economic assistance.[63] China, Germany, and Korea may here be cited as analogous situations.

Apart from the inherent right of self-defense, Article 2(4) of the Charter, and Article 7(2), which may be enforced collectively by members in connection with a decision under Chapter VII, the operative provisions of the United Nations Charter do not directly apply to the Republic of Vietnam in its relations with the Democratic Republic of Vietnam and vice versa since neither is a member of the United Na-

[63] See F. B. Schick, "Vietnam y la imagen de los Estados Unidos de America," CXLV *Cuadernos Americanos* (March-April 1966), 55-56.

tions. However, the Charter does not preclude the possibilities open to nonmembers under Articles 32 and 35(2). It is true that the Republic of Vietnam was prepared to submit in connection with the Tonkin Gulf incident the question of aggression from North Vietnam to the jurisdiction of the Security Council when the American government, at that time, requested the Security Council "to consider the serious situation created by deliberate attacks of the Hanoi regime on United States naval vessels in international waters." However, after lengthy discussions, the government of Czechoslovakia submitted to the members of the Security Council evidence provided by the government of the Democratic Republic of Vietnam, according to which the "United States vessels had been on a provocative mission in the territorial waters of the Democratic Republic of Viet-Nam," and that the "large-scale aggression against the territory of the Democratic Republic could only be regarded as an act of reprisal, such as the Council had previously condemned."[64] During the early debate in the Security Council, the delegate of the Soviet Union "in order to ensure an objective discussion of the conflict" submitted a draft resolution "inviting representatives of the government of the Democratic Republic of Viet-Nam to take part, without delay" in the meetings of the Security Council. In view of this draft resolution, the United States delegates requested that "if North-Vietnamese were invited, the Republic of Viet-Nam should also be invited to send representatives."[65] Although the parties directly involved submitted to the Security Council documents of a conflicting nature, Hanoi rejected the jurisdiction of the Security Council in the complaint against it on grounds "that the consideration of the problem did not lie with the Council but with the 1954 Geneva Conference," and that "only the two Co-Chairmen and participants in the 1954 Geneva Conference were competent to examine the problem and study measures to ensure that the agreements were respected.[66]

An additional argument advanced by the government of the Democratic Republic of Vietnam for its rejection of the submission to the Security Council—an argument which it has maintained consistently—has been made with reference to the principle of equal representation

[64] *Yearbook of the United Nations*, 1964 (New York, 1965), p. 148. It should be re-emphasized that the Charter of the United Nations does not permit reprisals. For further references concerning the illegality of reprisals see *Lawyers Committee, op.cit.*, pp. 53-57. See also Quincy Wright, *op.cit.*, pp. 288-289.

[65] *See Yearbook of the United Nations*, 1964, pp. 148-149.

[66] *Ibid.*, p. 149. The rejection of Hanoi is also based on the well-established principle of general international law known as "exhaustion of justice."

in view of the fact that both the Democratic Republic of Vietnam and the People's Republic of China would have no vote in the United Nations. According to this argument, the equal protection of Hanoi's interests would be in jeopardy. Many other states, including the Co-Chairmen of the Geneva Conference, France, the United Kingdom, and Soviet Russia, have supported this view. These states were even reluctant to put the question of Vietnam on the agenda of Security Council under Chapter VI of the Charter. Because of this reluctance and the refusal of the Democratic Republic of Vietnam to submit to the jurisdiction of the Security Council, it would be erroneous to deduce that the United States when relying on Article 51 of the Charter, had no legal duty to *immediately* report to the Security Council the military measures taken in self-defense and to demand, without any delay, the convening of an emergency meeting of the Security Council by invoking Article 39 of the Charter. It may be considered as certain that the Security Council cannot reject the holding of a meeting in cases where the injured state requests a decision that an act of aggression by means of an armed attack has occurred. In this connection it should be pointed out that the argument, frequently advanced in the United States, according to which such a meeting could not have produced a *decision* of the Security Council is probably correct but is legally meaningless. Regardless of whether or not the required resolution of the United States could have received the favorable votes as stipulated by Article 27 of the U.N. Charter, the United States had the legal duty to submit its military actions, which it justified on the basis of Article 51 of the Charter as measures against acts of aggression in the form of armed attacks, "immediately to the Security Council." Morever, the possible defeat of such a United States resolution would have permitted the submission of the question to the U.N. General Assembly for discussion and recommendations by means of a two thirds majority of the members present and voting. This is exactly the procedure upon which the United States insisted during the Suez Canal crisis, which prevented an escalation of that conflict, and which, finally, led to a pacific settlement of this dispute.

The South-East Asia Collective Defense Treaty (SEATO) and the Charter of the United Nations

Apart from its bilateral agreements with the Republic of Vietnam, the American government has also claimed the right of collective self-defense by means of military enforcement actions against North Vietnam on the basis of the United States commitment under the provisions of SEATO since the Republic of Vietnam is a protocol state within an allegedly existing "region" as envisaged by Chapter VIII of the Charter.[67] This claim proceeds from the legally unverified, hence erroneous, assumption that an act of aggression against South Vietnam has occurred *as determined by the Security Council* and that the latter has authorized the member states of SEATO to resort to military enforcement action against the aggressor. Moreover, Article 4(2) of the SEATO Treaty, as originally written, would have required the parties to this treaty to consult with each other prior to any military intervention in order to reach the stipulated common agreement before collective measures could have been taken "for the common defense." It ought to be added that the assertion of any American commitment under the provisions of SEATO is subject to Article 103 of the United Nations Charter, which must be considered as the *operational supremacy clause.*[68] In fact, the supremacy of this clause was expressly stipulated by Article 6 of the SEATO Treaty which proclaimed that this treaty:

> does not affect and shall not be interpreted as affecting in any way the rights and obligations of any of the Parties under the Charter of the United Nations or the responsibility of the United Nations for the maintenance of international peace and security. Each Party declares that none of the International engagements now in force between it and any other of the Parties or any third Party is in conflict with the provisions of this Treaty, and undertakes not to enter into any international engagement in conflict with this Treaty.

In view of the foregoing, the conclusion has to be drawn that the arguments of the American government with reference to its "Commitments under the SEATO Treaty"[69] have no validity in fact or in law.

The Mutual Defense Pact Between the United States and the Republic of Vietnam

As is the case with the SEATO Treaty, the mutual "defense alliance" between the United States and the Republic of Vietnam, which has

[67] For a more detailed analysis see George Modelski, ed., *Seato: Six Studies* (Melbourne, 1962) ; see also, *Lawyers Committee, op.cit.,* pp. 67-71; and Quincy Wright, *op.cit.,* pp. 289-299. For an opposing opinion see John Norton Moore, *op.cit.,* pp. 252-254.

[68] Article 103 states: "In the event of a conflict between the obligations of the Members of the United Nations under the present Charter and their obligations under any other international agreement, their obligations under the present Charter shall prevail."

[69] For an opposing view see *Government Brief, op.cit.,* p. 7.

been consumated as a military alliance in open violation of the Geneva Accords, must be interpreted as being legally subordinated to Article 103 of the United Nations Charter since this Article has the character of a supremacy clause. Accordingly, the enforcement provisions of this military alliance, even if it can be considered as a "regional arrangement" in compliance with Article 53 of the Charter, and even if it did not disregard the military provisions of the Geneva Accords, could have been executed only upon prior authorization by the Security Council, or, possibly, the General Assembly in accordance with the Uniting for Peace Resolution. On the basis of this interpretation, the attempt of the American government to justify its military involvement in Vietnam also with "additional assurances to the government of South Viet-Nam,"[70] lacks the necessary international legal basis. The conclusion is at hand, therefore, that it is not possible to support the American use of armed force in Vietnam with reference to SEATO or various direct assurances given South Vietnam by the United States.[71]

The Binding Force of the Geneva Accords on the United States and the Republic of Vietnam and the Successor Clause in the Armistice Agreement

Soon after the departure of all French union forces, Premier Diem rejected openly the Geneva obligations with the declaration that his government had neither signed the Agreement on the Cessation of Hostilities nor affirmed the Final Declaration.[72] At that time, Diem was "supported" by the United States Government which gave him "considerable aid."[73] The presumption certainly exists that Diem could not have rejected the legally binding force of the Geneva Accords without American political, economic, and military support; nor can it be denied that this strong political support on the part of the American government, coupled with an ever-increasing flow of military equipment and advisors under the terms of the United States Foreign Assistance Act, constitutes a serious "disturbance" of the Geneva Accords in disregard of the United States Unilateral Declaration of July 21, 1954. However, the question may still be raised whether a nonsigna-

---

[70] *Ibid.*, pp. 8-9.

[71] For references to direct U.S. commitments see *ibid.*, p. 9, and the corresponding notes 17, 18, 19, 20.

[72] For a summary see F. B. Schick, *op.cit.*, pp. 35-62. See also Lacouture, "Vietnam: The Lessons of War," as quoted in *Hearings, op.cit.*, pp. 655-661.

[73] U.S. Secretary of State, Testimony in *Hearings, op.cit.*, p. 47. See also Kahin and Lewis, "The United States in Vietnam," *Bulletin of the Atomic Scientists* (June 1965).

tory to the Agreement on the Cessation of Hostilities, i.e., the various military regimes of South Vietnam, could have been legally bound by an armistice treaty in which none had ever been a directly involved party and which, from the very beginning, they had clearly rejected.[74]

It may be observed that Article 27 of the Armistice Agreement states that "the signatories of the present Agreement *and their successors* (emphasis supplied) in their functions shall be responsible for ensuring the observance and enforcement of the terms and provisions thereof." In spite of this wording it is difficult to accept *a priori* the interpretation according to which this provision has a greater legal significance than any of the others as far as a nonsignatory to the Armistice Agreement is concerned.

It is commonly believed that states which are not parties to a treaty cannot incur obligations stipulated by such a treaty unless they accept the benefits bestowed upon them by such a treaty. As will be shown, this general rule does not apply in the case under discussion. The basis for this interpretation may be seen in an approximation—not an analogy—with the decision in the Aaland Islands Dispute. This decision was rendered on September 5, 1920, by the Committee of Jurists in its *Report* to the Council of the League of Nations. This *Report* considered the alleged violations by Russia of the Paris Treaty of 1856 as well as the change in sovereignty over the Aaland Islands from Russia to Finland. The *Report*, which took notice of the fact that Finland was not a party to the Treaty of Paris (1856), nevertheless concluded that the provisions of this treaty "concerning the demilitarization of the Aaland Islands are still in force."[75] Moreover, the *Report* recommended to the Council of the League of Nations that the aforementioned provisions of the Paris Treaty "should be replaced by a broader agreement, placed under the guarantee of all the powers concerned."[76] Such an agreement was finally concluded at Geneva on October 20, 1921, between Germany, Denmark, Esthonia, Finland, France, the United Kingdom, India, Italy, Latvia, Poland, and Sweden.[77] Finally, the demilitarization provisions of the Paris

[74] For a belated statement see, "Protest by the Vietnamese Delegation against the Geneva Conference Agreements, July 21, 1954, in *Basic Documents of the 1954 Geneva Conference* . . . (United States Information Service, Austria) , p. 40. For a reference to the laws of war concerning armistice see above.

[75] League of Nations, *Official Journal, Report, Committee of Jurists* (1920) , pp. 394-395.

[76] For the full text of the findings and a summary of preceding actions see Louis B. Sohn, ed., *Cases and Other Materials on World Law* (Brooklyn, N.Y., 1950) , pp. 117-118.

[77] The full text is contained in the *Convention Respecting the Non-Fortification and Neutralization of the Aaland Islands.*

Treaty of 1856, although this treaty had been signed only by Great Britain, Imperial Austria, France, Prussia, Russia, Sardinia, and Turkey, were again incorporated into the peace treaty concluded between Finland and Soviet Russia on February 10, 1947.[78]

The Aaland Islands Dispute is inducive to the thought that international servitudes may be created by treaty even if such servitudes do not solely create permissive or restrictive fights *in rem* in the sense that the burdened state incurs the obligation either to suffer a foreign activity on its territory or to desist from performing certain, specified activities. Indeed, it is difficult to accept the concept according to which a modern law of nations must adjust to the basic changes of our times but is not permitted to reject, for the same purpose, the shackles of certain orthodox schools of thought which insist that state servitude— if such a concept can, at all, be conceded a place in international law— must conform with the strictly formalistic pattern of Roman law. If one is prepared to accept the idea of a progressive development of principles and rules of international law one may, therefore, feel inclined to modify Professor Lauterpacht's opinion, followed as it is by many other writers, according to which "the object of State servitudes is the territory of a State,"[79] and that it is, therefore, "the territory as the object," which must be considered "the mark of distinction between State servitudes and other restrictions on the territorial supremacy,"[80] of a state.

It should be possible to broaden the restrictive definition of state servitudes by referring to more recent international practice, and by acknowledging the existence of two types of regimes which have been classified as state servitudes:

1. those created in the interest of one state only, and approximating to the servitude of private law,

and

2. certain regimes created in the interest of the community of nations, or at least of regional organization and security, and constituting an international restriction of sovereign competence.[81]

---

[78] For the text of the treaty see U.S. Department of State, *Treaties of Peace* (European Series 21, Part v), p. 3.

[79] Oppenheim, *International Law*, 8th edn., I, p. 538; see also F. A. Vali, *Servitudes of International Law* (London, 1958), pp. 330ff.

[80] *Ibid.*, pp. 538-539.

[81] D. P. O'Connell, *The Law of State Succession* (Cambridge, 1956), p. 51; see also the same author, in *International Law* (London, 1965), I, pp. 432-433. It should be noted

Although it should be stated clearly that the first part of the above-cited definition refers to rights *in rem* such as had been created in the case of the Aaland Islands or the servitude imposed upon the Zones of Upper Savoy and the District of Gex, there exists no persuasive reason why a modern law of nations could not apply the second part of the above-cited concept also to legal burdens *in personam*, i.e., in the form of certain political obligations and international restrictions of sovereign competence imposed with legal validity upon successors in governmental functions within a certain territory by an agreement of a predecessor government even though the one or the other of the successor governments should not have been a signatory or adherent to the original agreement or should have rejected it *ab initio*. In the case under discussion, this legal construction, therefore, applies not only to the territorial servitudes created by the Geneva Accords but also to other obligations such as the holding of elections at a certain date throughout the territory of Vietnam.

More recently, this modern concept has been supported and expanded by Professor McNair in his dissenting opinion, rendered in 1950, concerning the Status of South West Africa because it is in this opinion where the *general interest of nations* is considered a decisive legal element in justification of an international servitude binding also on states which have not been signatories of a treaty establishing such a servitude. As stated by Professor McNair with reference to the obligations imposed by the Covenant of the League of Nations on a Mandatory:

> From time to time, it happens that a group of great Powers, or a large number of States both great and small, assume a power to create by a multipartite treaty some new international regime or status, which soon acquires a degree of acceptance and durability extending beyond the limits of the actual contracting parties, and giving it an objective existence. This power is used when some public interest is involved, and its exercise often occurs in the course of the peace settlement at the end of a great war.[82]

that the obligation to hold all Vietnamese elections is such a restriction of sovereign competence.

[82] *International Status of South West Africa*, Advisory Opinion, *ICJ Reports*, 1950. See also the case concerning *Rights of Nationals of the United States of America in Morocco (France v. U.S.A.)*, 1952, *ICJ Reports*, pp. 176, 193, 217, where it was held in the *dictum* that newly established states are obligated by treaties concluded on their behalf before such states attained political independence.

It seems that the few cases under discussion may serve as guideposts for an interpretation of the Armistice Agreement on Vietnam and of the Final Declaration of the Geneva Conference. Accordingly, the conclusion may be in order that these agreements are expressive of a general public interest of a large number of states in the restoration and the maintenance of international peace and security in the region previously known as Indo-China. In view of this general public interest in the restoration and maintenance of international peace and security, any government succeeding in this area the original signatories of the Geneva Agreements, although not a signatory of them, must be considered as being legally bound by the provisions of these agreements.[83] For there cannot be any doubt that the Geneva Accords were approved by the regional states as well as by all leading powers in the interests of world peace and security.

It is not necessary to rely solely on the above approximation and the principles of a modern law of nations. For it was the government of the French Republic, within whose "framework" the "State of Vietnam" existed, which was constitutionally entitled to determine and conduct the military and foreign relations of the members of the French union.[84] The military defeat of the French union forces prompted the French government to conclude the various armistice agreements in 1954 on behalf of the states comprising the area formerly known as Indo-China; it was, therefore, the French government which was legally entitled to incur the obligations for the "State of Vietnam" as stipulated in the Armistice Agreement and the Final Declaration. The subsequent "objections" and "protests" of the Diem regime and its supporters are not sufficient to void those obligations of the Republic of Vietnam incurred as a partial successor state under international law.[85]

The Law of Treaties and the Violations of the Geneva Accords

Although the American government has tried to justify its military actions in Vietnam primarily with reference to the right of self-defense against acts of aggression, it advances also a secondary line of legal

[83] For an elaboration on this analysis see Daniel G. Partan, *Legal Aspects of the Vietnam Conflict* (Durham, N.C., 1966), pp. 291-292.

[84] Agreement between President Vincent Auriol (France) and Emperor Bao Dai (State of Vietnam), March 8, 1949 in *Documents on International Relations, 1949-50* (London, 1953), pp. 596-608.

[85] Partan, *op.cit.*, p. 291.

defense concerning noncompliance with the military provisions of the Geneva Accords. Officially admitting that "the United States found it necessary in late 1961 to increase substantially the numbers of our military personnel and the amounts and types of equipment intro- duced by this country [the USA] into South Viet-Nam," the United States justifies these increases with the assertion that "a material breach of an agreement by one party entitles the other at least to withhold com- pliance with an equivalent, corresponding, or related provision until the defaulting party is prepared to honor its obligations."[86] As far as the U.S. Department of State is concerned, the material breach of the Geneva Accords was committed "by North Vietnam."[87] It is regret- table that this part of the *Government Brief* neglects to submit addi- tional, and more specific evidence in support of this sweeping assertion. This would be especially needed in view of the fact that many *Interim Reports* of the International Control Commission for Vietnam not only reject the American assertion but show quite clearly that it was South Vietnam and the United States which, almost since the conclu- sion of the Geneva Accords, have disregarded them, time and again.

In view of the adverse reports of the International Control Commis- sion, legally meaningful evidence for the assertion of a material breach of the Geneva Accords would be necessary. Nor is the interpretation of multilateral treaties as simple as presented in the explanation of the *Government Brief*.[88] Moreover, the introduction of problems con- cerning the interpretation of certain treaty provisions in justification of their disregard, as admitted by the American government, must remain legally inadmissible as long as the alleged violations of the "other party" to the treaty in question, i.e., the Democratic Republic of Vietnam, have not been ascertained with legal validity by an inter- national organ entitled to make such a decision. It must, therefore, be concluded that the supporting legal basis submitted by the Ameri- can government in justification of its admitted noncompliance with the Geneva Accords is without legal validity.

It should further be noted that none of the parties directly involved has repudiated the Geneva Agreements with reference to a material breach of them. However, it seems to be clear that it is the Democratic

[86] *Government Brief, op.cit.*, p. 10.   [87] *Ibid.*

[88] For a well-documented repudiation of the official interpretation as published by the Department of State see *Lawyers Committee, op.cit.*, pp. 50-51; see also the scholarly treat- ment by Professor D. P. O'Connell, *International Law*, 2 vols. (London, 1965), pp. 271- 283, 298, 1102, and 1195.

Republic of Vietnam rather than the Saigon regime and the United States which—on the basis of overwhelming evidence—would have been entitled to invoke the right of partial or total treaty renunciation on account of a material breach of the Geneva Agreements.[89]

Conclusion

One of the most treasured values maintained in truly democratic social structures, as understood in the West, is to permit and to encourage the free expressions of thought even in the most controversial and politically sensitive situations. The possibility of voicing profound disagreement among international jurists about the legal merits concerning the use of force by the United States in Vietnam does not indicate a weakening of democracy as predicted by Marxist-Leninist doctrinaires. Quite to the contrary, it ought to be construed as an outstanding feature of strength, and of agreement on the fundamental philosophical values inherent in democratic societies. Considering the fact that municipal law operates within a national society as one of its ordering elements just as international law functions as the only common denominator of an international order which all members of the international community accept, at least in principle, as legally binding in their mutual relations, it is not surprising that differences in the approach and the analyses of legal questions should be voiced within and among the many democratically structured societies where law, as part of the social order, is permitted to play such an important role. Without such freedom of dissent, law would become the servile servant of politics.

This essay clearly demonstrates the differences in legal approaches and analyses as they exist in the West about Vietnam. No attempt has been made in this essay to evaluate in great detail the legal counter-arguments presented by scholars from Communist countries. As stated at the outset, Vietnam exemplifies but one from among many postwar interventions and counterinterventions by super powers in the affairs

[89] See e.g. Richard A. Falk, *op.cit.*, at p. 394, stating: "The self-serving argument . . . of the Memorandum (*Government Brief*) confers competence upon the United States and Saigon to find that a breach has taken place and to select a suitable remedy, but permits Hanoi only to *allege* a breach, and forbids it to take countervailing action until the breach has been impartially verified." And the same author, *ibid.*, at p. 462, states: "Ignoring the relevance of formal international engagements, Professor Moore also supports the double standard whereby North Viet-Nam's alleged export of coercion through the N.L.F. is viewed as a material breach of the Geneva Accords, whereas the United States' provision of military aid to Saigon, even though it admittedly preceded North Vietnamese coercion, is approved of as a 'permitted defensive response.' "

of a smaller state. The legality of the initial American intervention has been tested with reference to generally accepted principles and norms of international law, and especially the Charter of the United Nations; and the painful conclusion has been reached that the intervention of the United States in Vietnam cannot be defended on strictly legal grounds.

Aquinas, Grotius, and the Vietnam War

D. H. N. JOHNSON

THIS article will be in two parts. First, a review of the recently published work by Dr. Joan Tooke;[1] and, secondly, a brief consideration of some of the legal aspects of the Vietnam war.

I.

THE JUST WAR IN AQUINAS AND GROTIUS

In his short Foreword to Dr. Tooke's book Dr. E. L. Mascall makes some extremely sage remarks. He says that "to many contemporary readers, both Christian and non-Christian, a discussion of the thought of St. Thomas Aquinas and Grotius on the subject of the Just War will be dismissed as academic", but that nevertheless just such a study "is of very real value". He asserts too that "many people seem to be incapable of approaching the question of war from a rational and unemotional standpoint". Dr. Tooke's book, he says, has value because it shows how Christian thinkers in the past have addressed themselves to the problem of war and how "the traditional moral theology of war has been very closely involved with the notion of natural law". Here there is an acute problem because "there are at the present day many writers on Christian ethics who repudiate *in toto* the very idea of natural law, as either futile or sub-Christian, and try instead to base human conduct either upon the uninterpreted text of the Bible or upon existential decisions having no relation to any general principles". While agreeing that the notion of natural law is not simple or easy to apply, Dr. Mascall is "impressed by the fact that jurists and philosophers of law seem to be quite incapable of doing without it, or at any rate without some substitute for it which will play the part that it used to play".

Theology and Law

For her part Dr. Tooke begins by making some general remarks about the relation between theology and law, particularly international law. One can only applaud her view that "there should be considerable mutual appreciation and cooperation between theologians and lawyers". Equally one can agree with her when she says that "it may be because law is confessedly such a secular activity that many Christians have undervalued and made insufficient use of the contribution made by international lawyers." On the other hand, Dr. Tooke shows a tendency to exaggerate that contribution when she says that the international lawyers "by building up a tradition of faith in reasonable and just dealings between nations and a technique of dealing with dangerous situations and disputes, have already done much to prevent and assuage outbreaks of hostilities." (pp. xii-xiii). At least, in so far as this praise is deserved, it goes just as much to the often maligned profession of diplomacy as to the lawyers as such.

Dr. Tooke traces the development of the Christian attitude to war before Aquinas. This task has of course been performed many times before. It is well known that in the early centuries the attitude of Christians was basically pacifist, but there were exceptions to this. In any case, the reasons for this pacifism (e.g. that soldiers under the Roman Empire were required to take part in idolatrous ceremonies) are hardly relevant today. It was early apparent, however, that there was a possible contradiction between the view that a Christian should not avenge his own wrongs and the view that the State was an institution divinely ordained for the purpose of repressing crime and violence and one which the Christian must support. There is no doubt too that "gradually, the toleration of war increased" (p. 7), and that this tendency was accelerated after Christianity became the official religion of the Roman Empire.

Unresolved Ambiguity

Dr. Tooke emphasises that from early times two traditions have always existed in the Church. Thus there have been pacifist martyrs like Maximilian and St. Victrice as well as military saints like St. Maurice, St. Louis and St. Joan of Arc. Because of this ambiguity, and the uncertainty of the Scriptures, it is not surprising that orthodoxy found refuge in the pragmatic approach, based on natural law, of authorities like Cicero.

It was, however, St. Augustine who laid down the teaching that was to suffice for centuries. He took it for granted that a war of self-defence was justifiable, even obligatory. In order to be just, however, a war of aggression must be carried out by the authority of the prince, and have a just cause and a just intention. Nevertheless, despite the official doctrine on war, the Church between the sixth and the twelfth centuries regarded killing, even in a just war, as sinful and as requiring heavy penances. Thus, although William the Conqueror invaded England with a banner blessed by the Pope, those on the Norman side who took part in the Battle of Hastings had to do a year's penance for every man killed.[2]

It would be absurd, within the scope of this article, to attempt to summarise Dr. Tooke's treatment of the attitude to war of St. Thomas Aquinas and of Grotius. The reader is naturally directed to the work itself, which in these key chapters is of a high order. Despite the complexity of the matters dealt with, the author's style is nearly always clear and readable.

The Limitations of Thomism

Dr. Tooke makes the point that "the importance of the doctrine of the just war in Aquinas is due rather to his general eminence and that of the *Summa Theologica* in which it appears than to any original or outstanding treatment or exposition of the subject by him" (p. 25). Such has been the authority attributed at some (though not all) times in the Church to the teachings of St. Thomas that it is as well to realise some of the limitations of his approach to the problem of war. Among these may be mentioned:

(i) the failure to examine fully the implications of the requirement that war must be declared by a sovereign. In practice, St. Thomas, like other writers, accepted wars declared by the various feudal princes of the time despite the theory that such princes could not make war without imperial sanction;

(ii) the treatment of war as an individual subjective problem and the failure to draw a clear distinction between objective and social justice and subjective individual morality. This raises a very difficult problem, and Dr. Tooke is by no means convinced of the validity of this particular criticism;

(iii) the failure to investigate the possibilities of arbitration as an alternative to war, despite the Pope's efforts in that direction and other contemporary examples and theories in civil and canon law. This criticism is certainly justified in the light of hindsight, but Dr. Tooke is only being fair when she points out that "such a wide horizon was not visible from Aquinas's viewpoint." (p. 27).

Specifically Christian attitudes to War

A matter which interests Dr. Tooke very much is the effort to discover whether or not St. Thomas's treatment of war had anything about it that was specifically Christian. This leads her into an examination of the sources of Revelation which cannot be gone into here. For this controversy is largely a reflection of the deep theological problem of the relative weight to be accorded to Scripture and to Tradition. It is sufficient to say that Dr. Tooke finds great difficulty in reconciling natural law with Christian revelation and is therefore basically not impressed by the view that the Christian attitude to war should be stated in terms of the natural law tradition. For this reason she is not particularly sympathetic to either of the two subjects of her dissertation, both of whom looked to natural law for guidance in this matter. Of Aquinas she says that his direct teaching on war was "slight and unoriginal" (p. 170); of Grotius that he "did not sufficiently plead that the Christian virtues of forgiveness, repentance, tolerance, mercy, and love be expressed in international relations" and that "he did not apparently consider that Christian morality was appropriate to States". (p. 230).

As well as summarising the teaching on war of Aquinas and Grotius, Dr. Tooke surveys the development of doctrine on this subject between these two writers (e.g. Vitoria, Suarez, Belli, Gentili). She also attempts the briefest of summaries of the teaching between Grotius and the present day. These summaries, however, are extremely superficial, especially the latter one. Dr. Tooke is content to make the main point that after Grotius "the idea of just war became of little interest to the international lawyer" and that "war was simply war"; but that after the First, and more especially after the Second, World War there was a revival of the idea that a distinction should be drawn between legal and illegal war.

She also makes one or two interesting statements which however she does not sufficiently develop. The first is that "There is an increasing tendency to reject outright atomic weapons and the all-out war they bring about, but to retain and approve limited warfare. Conventional weapons are accepted as being sufficiently discriminative to be used as instruments of justice, whereas atomic weapons are condemned as too wholesale in their destructiveness" (p. 235). This position seems to lack logic and to confuse *jus ad bellum* with *jus in bello*. Moreover, it is not clear why a weapon's "discriminativeness" should be the sole criterion of the legality of the use of that weapon and even of the legality of the war in which it is used. The second position described is that of "situation pacifists" who consider that "although war in itself is not inevitably wrong, any war today is likely to spark off atomic conflagrations, and is therefore unjustifiable" (pp. 235-6). This position is distinguished from that of "christological pacifists" who feel that "the horror of atomic warfare is the logical development of man's acceptance of war in any form and that it only magnifies its intrinsic evil and stupidity." (p. 236).

In a brief concluding chapter Dr. Tooke reiterates her sceptical attitude towards natural law and consequently toward the "just war" doctrine associated with it, and puts forward the view that salvation may come through a curious amalgam of "international law, Christian pacifism, and non-violent resistance" (p. 244). These, she says, are all pioneer movements, but "progress has often come about through ideals which started in the apparently 'defeatist' position of being the possession of a minority". There is no disputing Dr. Tooke's sincerity, but it is difficult to know how to assess a writer who on almost the very last page of her work is content to describe international law as a "pioneer movement". International law is as old as the State system with which it has always been inextricably bound up, and it is somewhat muddling to confound international law, which until recently consisted largely of the laws of war, with modern pacifist movements whether of the "situation" or "christological" variety.

II.

LEGAL ASPECTS OF THE VIETNAM WAR

The Vietnam war has naturally led to a good deal of literature on its legal (or illegal) aspects. Four of the leading, and most accessible, statements on the subject are:

(i) "Vietnam and International Law" by the Lawyers Committee on American Policy towards Vietnam.[3] Prominent international lawyers on this Committee are Richard A. Falk, Professor of International Law at Princeton University (Chairman) and Quincy Wright, Professor Emeritus of International Law of the University of Chicago. Another well known member is Hans J. Morgenthau, Professor of Political Science and Modern History, University of Chicago.

(ii) "The Legality of United States Participation in the Defence of Vietnam". (State Department Memorandum of 4 March 1966, conveniently reproduced in *American Journal of International Law,* 60 (1966), p. 565).

(iii) "The Lawfulness of Military Assistance to the Republic of Vietnam". By J. N. Moore. (This is an article published in *A.J.I.L.,* 61 (1967), p. 1. It is based on a more comprehensive paper written by J. N. Moore and J. L. Underwood, in collaboration with Myres S. McDougal, Professor of International Law at Yale University, and distributed to Congress by the American Bar Association).[4]

(iv) "Legal Aspects of the Vietnam Situation." By Quincy Wright. (Article in *A.J.I.L.,* 60 (1966), p. 750).

It is naturally not proposed here to summarise all the legal arguments for and against the participation of the United States in the Vietnam war. The purpose is rather to set out the issues so that the reader — whether or not he is sympathetic to the doctrine of the "just war" — may have some idea of the difficulty of deciding whether, under contemporary conditions, a particular war is morally and/or legally justified. (No doubt the same difficulty would arise in relation to the Arab-Israeli war of June, 1967.)

Fortunately, although the contestants in this controversy may disagree violently as to the legality of the actions of the United States in Vietnam, there is a reasonable consensus as to what the principal issues are in both international law and American constitutional law. It is not proposed in this article to consider the question whether the President has been within his constitutional rights in committing American forces so extensively to the defence of South Vietnam, although of course that issue has been hotly debated in the United States. This article will concentrate on the international law issues.

The State Department Memorandum contends that South Vietnam is being subjected to armed attack by North Vietnam ; that international law (including the Charter of the United Nations) recognises the right of individual and collective self-defence against armed attack ; and that this right exists whether or not South Vietnam is a Member of the United Nations and even whether or not it is an independent sovereign State. The State Department further contends that the right of collective self-defence is not limited to "regional arrangements or agencies" within the meaning of Chapter VIII of the United Nations Charter (such as the Organisation of American States — OAS — almost certainly is and the Southeast Asia Treaty Organisation — SEATO — almost certainly is not). Still further, the Memorandum contends that the right of the United States to go to the assistance of South Vietnam is not limited by the Geneva Accords of 1954, and indeed that the United States was not merely entitled, but even bound, to render such assistance. The obligation to assist is said to arise from a statement made by the United States Government at the conclusion of the Geneva Conference to the effect that the United States "would view any renewal of the aggression in violation of the aforesaid agreements with grave concern and as seriously threatening international peace and security" ; from the Southeast Asia Collective Defence Treaty of 8 September 1954;[5] and from various assurances given by Presidents Eisenhower and Kennedy to the Government of South Vietnam as well as by President Johnson.

Conversely, the Lawyers Committee state that there is not and never has been a separate State of South Vietnam; that the Geneva Accords of 1954, while confirming the independence of a single, united Vietnam, made temporary provision only for two separate zones of North and South Vietnam, which zones were due to be reunited in 1956; and that the participation of the United States in the Vietnam war is an intervention in a civil war which violates general international law, the Geneva Accords of 1954 and also the Charter of the United Nations. The Lawyers Committee also allege that the methods used by the United States to prosecute the war (i.e. *jus in bello* as opposed to *jus ad bellum*) are illegal. That question will not be examined in this article.

Clerical Intuition?

It will readily be seen that, in order even to begin to resolve a controversy of these proportions, it would be necessary to examine a great many questions of both law and fact. It will not be possible within the limits of this article to do more than indicate how the problem might be approached by an international legal tribunal, in the unlikely event of it ever coming before one. The present writer has no idea how a moral theologian would approach the same problem in depth, although he has noticed a tendency on the part of some of these gentlemen to come to sweeping conclusions upon what, to a lawyer, would seem to have been the most cursory examination of both factual evidence and legal arguments. As Dr. Tooke said in her book, "there should be considerable mutual appreciation and cooperation between theologians and lawyers." But if lawyers are to be encouraged to rise above a merely positivist approach and to take moral considerations into their system, the least that can be expected in return is that the theologians should appreciate the importance of a critical examination of the factual evidence and should also make a serious attempt to understand the legal factors.

The Shackles of Past Events

A necessary starting-point, it seems, is to consider the political evolution of Vietnam from the time of the French ascendancy down to and including the present time. Quite apart from the question of the lawfulness of the participation of the United States in the present hostilities, a study of Vietnam's development should also throw light on the status both of the hostilities and of the participants in those hostilities. Is there, for instance, a war in Vietnam in the full international legal sense of the term "war"? If not, is there at least an international "armed conflict" in Vietnam, or is the armed conflict that is taking place there one "not of an international character"? The answer to these questions is vital in that each of the four Geneva Conventions of 1949[6] contains common articles to the effect that "the present Convention shall apply to all cases of declared war or of any other armed conflict which may arise between two or more of the High Contracting Parties, even if the state of war is not recognised by one of them"[7] (article 2), and that "in the case of armed conflict not of an international character occurring in the territory of one of the High Contracting Parties, each Party to the conflict shall be bound to apply, as a minimum, the following provisions" (article 3). The provisions that follow give a limited protection to the combatants, but falling far short of the full provisions of the Conventions.

An armed conflict "of an international character"?

It appears to be common ground that there is not at present in Vietnam a "war" in the full legal sense of that word. Consequently, the participants do not enjoy belligerent rights on the high seas and there is no question of other Powers having the duties and rights normally associated with "neutrality". Nevertheless, humanitarian considerations strongly point to holding that there is in Vietnam an armed conflict "of an international character" within the meaning of the Geneva Conventions. Fortunately legal considerations also point in the same direction. This does not, however, entirely dispose of the argument that the hostilities in Vietnam are basically a civil war within one State (Vietnam), with other States (the United States, South Korea, Australia, New Zealand etc.) intervening, rather than an armed conflict between two States or international entities (North Vietnam and South Vietnam) with the other States assisting South Vietnam by way of collective self-defence. In this situation, which is by no means unique (e.g. Germany, Korea), the parties most directly affected are apt to contend that the territory involved is a single unit which they alone are competent and authorised to govern. This lends some support to the view that the hostilities are basically of a civil rather than an international character, and this view is supported by those whose political and logistic situation is such that they can intervene effectively by supplying munitions and other supplies rather than by despatching combat forces and becoming directly involved themselves.

The evidence indicates that down at least to the Geneva Conference of 1954 Vietnam was regarded as a single State. In 1950, for instance, Vietnam, under Bao Dai, having been established as an Associated State of the French Union, was recognised as such by the United Kingdom and the United States, although much of the territory was in the hands of the Vietminh led by Ho Chi Minh. The so-called "Geneva Accords" of 1954 consisted of an "Agreement between the Commander-in-Chief of the French Union Forces and the Commander-in-Chief of the People's Army of Vietnam on the Cessation of Hostilities in Vietnam" and similar agreements relating to Cambodia and Laos ; and also of a "Final Declaration of the Geneva Conference on the Problem of Restoring Peace in Indo-China". The military agreement for Vietnam provided for a cease-fire and "a provisional military demarcation line" ; for a ban on the introduction of troop reinforcements, on the establishment of new military bases and on the adherence of the respective zones to military alliances ; and for an International Commission. In its Final Declaration the Conference asserted that "the military demarcation line is provisional and should not in any way be interpreted as constituting a political or territorial boundary." The Final Declaration also provided for general elections in Vietnam in July 1956 and for consultations on this subject "between the competent representative authorities of the two zones". The delegate of the United States made a separate statement to the effect that his Government was "not prepared to join in a declaration by the Conference such as is submitted". However, that Government did declare that it would refrain from the threat or the use of force to disturb the various agreements arrived at by the Geneva Conference. Similarly the Government of (South) Vietnam declared that it was not bound by the agreements, although it undertook not to disturb the cease-fire by force. Whether that Government is entitled to take up that position, or whether it must be deemed to be bound by the agreements as successor to France, is controversial.

In pari delicto . . . . . . ?

In any event elections were not held in Vietnam in 1956 and the situation steadily deteriorated. Although the responsibility is disputed, it is admitted that there have been serious violations of the Geneva Accords on all sides. In a Special Report in 1962 the International Control Commission endorsed the finding of its legal committee to the effect that "there is evidence to show that armed and unarmed personnel, arms, munitions and other supplies have been sent from the Zone in the North to the Zone in the South with the object of supporting, organising and carrying out hostile activities, including armed attacks, directed against the Armed Forces, and Administration of the Zone in the South". However, even the report to the Senate of Senator Mansfield does not contend that North Vietnamese regular troops entered South Vietnam on a large scale until towards the end of 1964. The United States began bombing targets in North Vietnam in February 1965, and began sending large contingents of combat forces to South Vietnam a little later. Previously only "military advisory personnel" had been despatched, although in January 1965 there were already over 20,000 of these. These facts are relevant to the question whether the United States is engaged in aggression or in collective self-defence in Vietnam.

Self-defence under the Charter

It is generally agreed that the Charter of the United Nations forbids a State to use force except under the authority of the United Nations or in self-defence, individual or collective. Leaving aside different interpretations of the facts, which may arise in any international dispute, there is much disagreement over the law regarding the right of self-defence, particularly so far as concerns the extent of that right.

Article 51 of the Charter provides:

"Nothing in the present Charter shall impair the inherent right of individual or collective self-defence if an armed attack occurs against a Member of the United Nations, until the Security Council has taken the measures necessary to maintain international peace and security . . . . ."

On an absolutely literal interpretation of this article, self-defence is justified if, but only if, "an armed attack occurs against a Member of the United Nations". On this view the actions of the United States in Vietnam would clearly be unlawful because, even if the activities of the North Vietnam units before February 1965 amounted to an "armed attack" — which is itself doubtful — South Vietnam was not then, and still is not, a Member of the United Nations. However, it is safe to say that no responsible commentator has ever taken such a restrictive view of Article 51. The general view is that Article 51 is not itself constitutive of the right of self-defence, but is rather declaratory of the "inherent right" to which it refers and that the right of collective self-defence applies whether or not the victim of the attack is a Member of the United Nations. The real difficulty consists, therefore, in defining the conditions under which the right of self-defence may be exercised by any State. Partly, but not wholly, this is a question of applying the term "armed attack" and often the problem arises in regard to what is called "anticipatory self-defence". More generally, there is the point that a State can be very seriously threatened even as to its basic existence without an "armed attack" having occurred or even being likely to occur.[8]

The paper and the cracks

It will now be convenient to return to the political status of Vietnam. It has already been said that down to 1954 it was more proper to regard Vietnam in law as a single State, although sadly divided in fact. The so-called "Geneva agreements" of that year really only reflected an acute disagreement. There is some evidence that the statesmen at Geneva envisaged a protracted partition of Vietnam. There is also some contrary evidence that they looked to the fairly early unification of the country. Whatever the intentions of the Geneva Conference may have been, there is no doubt that since then there has been a hardening of the division of Vietnam. Even so, it is apparently not contended by the United States that South Vietnam is a separate State. The State Department memorandum emphasises the fact that the 1954 Geneva demarcation line along the 17th parallel was "an internationally agreed line of demarcation" and that, even if not a State, "the Republic of Vietnam in the South has been recognised as a separate international entity by approximately 60 governments the world over".[9] The State Department's main point is that "there is nothing in the Charter to suggest that United Nations members are precluded from participating in the defence of a recognised international entity against armed attack merely because the entity may lack some of the attributes of an independent sovereign State". However, J. N. Moore argues that "the evidence indicates that the R.V.N. is a State under international law and that today there are substantial expectations that the D.R.V. and the R.V.N. are separate and independent States under international law."[10]

Difficulties of the civil war theory

Be that as it may, there is certainly strong evidence that the hostilities in Vietnam are truly of an international character and that it is unrealistic in fact and wrong in law to treat them as amounting to a civil war. Even if one were to accept the civil war theory, it would still be necessary to decide who the participants were. Would it be a civil war in South Vietnam only between the R.V.N. and the National Liberation Front (N.L.F.), with the R.V.N. supported from outside by the U.S.A. and the N.L.F. supported from outside by the D.R.V.? Or would it be a civil war in Vietnam as a whole between the R.V.N. on one side and the combined forces of the D.R.V. and the N.L.F. on the other?

Moreover, even if the civil war theory were to be accepted in either form, it would by no means follow that the United States intervention was illegal. Opinions naturally differ as to whether a movement such as the N.L.F. is in fact a national uprising or merely represents a dissident minority. That is a matter for political rather than legal appreciation. But there can be little doubt that the government of the R.V.N., recognised as it is by over 60 other governments, is a lawful government. Opinions differ too concerning the right of a lawful government to seek and obtain aid from outside for the purpose of suppressing an insurrection. Most would agree that, if the insurrection is assisted — and above all if it is largely sponsored — from outside, the lawful government is no less entitled to obtain help from other countries in order to put it down. If the rebellion is genuinely internal, the position is more controversial. In principle a lawful government is free to make such arrangements with other governments as it pleases, but some would say that this is subject to the right which the citizens of a country enjoy to self-determination. From that one may be led into stultifying enquiries as to whether the rebellion, even if genuinely internal, really represents the will of the majority or is rather a movement to seize power impelled by a powerful but unrepresentative clique.

Conclusion

These are just some of the problems of both law and fact that it would be necessary to clarify before a decision could be reached whether the participation of the United States in the Vietnam hostilities is or is not lawful under international law. It is assumed that an inquiry along similar lines would need to be made before the theologians could pronounce whether these hostilities amount to a "just war", and if so on which side. It was made clear that the purpose of this article was, if not to solve these problems, at least to ensure that the right questions were asked. It is hoped that it has been successful in doing at least that.

1. *The Just War in Aquinas and Grotius.* By Joan D. Tooke. [London: S.P.C.K. 1965. xiii and 337 pp. 63s. net.].

2. See the articles by Colonel G. I. A. D. Draper entitled "Penitential Discipline and Public Wars in the Middle Ages" and published in *The International Review of the Red Cross,* Geneva, April and May 1961.

3. Published by O'Hare Books, Flanders, New Jersey. 1967. This Committee has issued more than one Memorandum on the subject, as has also the State Department with which the Committee has been in regular disagreement.

4. 112 Cong. Rec. 14943 (14 July 1966). Professor McDougal is also co-author with Florentino P. Feliciano of "Law and Minimum World Public Order" (Yale University Press, 1961). This major work, the subtitle of which is "The Legal Regulation of International Coercion", is a massive authority in the field of the legal regulation of the use of force by States. Other principal authorities are D. W. Bowett, "Self-Defence in International Law" (Manchester University Press, 1958); I. Brownlie "International Law and the Use of Force by States," (Oxford at the Clarendon Press, 1963); and J. Stone, "Legal Controls of International Conflict" (Stevens and Sons Ltd., 1954).

5. The United Kingdom is also a party to this Treaty.

6. Convention for the Amelioration of the Condition of the Wounded and Sick in Armed Forces in the Field; Convention for the Amelioration of the Condition of Wounded, Sick and Shipwrecked Members of the Armed Forces at Sea; Convertion relative to the Treatment of Prisoners of War; and Convention relative to the Protection of Civilian Persons in Time of War.

7. The United States ratified the Geneva Conventions on 2 August 1955. South Vietnam acceded to them on 14 November 1953 and North Vietnam on 28 June 1957.

8. In May 1967 Israel certainly regarded its very existence as being at stake as the result of the closing by Egypt of the Straits of Tiran. McDougal and Feliciano put the right of self-defence on a broader but more realistic basis when they say that it extends to "all coercion, by whatever instrument or combination of instruments, military or other, which is directed with requisite intensity against such substantial bases of power as the territorial integrity and political independence of the target State". (*Op. cit.,* p. 259).

9. The Democratic Republic of Vietnam in the North has been similarly recognised by over 20 governments.

10. R.V.N. stands for Republic of Vietnam (i.e. South Vietnam). D.R.V. stands for Democratic Republic of Vietnam (i.e. North Vietnam).

Six Legal Dimensions of the United States Involvement in the Vietnam War

RICHARD A. FALK

THIS MONOGRAPH deals with the legal status of the United States involvement in the Vietnam war. It tries to move beyond the existing legal literature in two principal respects:

1. By developing arguments for bringing international law to bear more effectively on the foreign policy-making process in the future than has been evident through the course of the Vietnam war;

2. By expanding legal inquiry to include questions of war crimes, constitutional procedure, and war-related litigation; this second undertaking is carried out through the device of briefly considering the six major legal dimensions of the United States involvement in the Vietnam War.

It is important to make clear that I do not attempt a balanced, fully-documented argument on "the grand question" of aggression and self-defense in Vietnam. There is an abundant literature on this question that reflects a variety of normative perspectives.[1] My objective is to develop a coherent position that builds upon, rather than duplicates, my previous writing on the subject.[2] In this respect, the monograph proceeds from the presupposition that international law forbids both the underlying involvement and the battlefield practices being relied upon in Vietnam by the United States Government.[3]

At the same time, my purpose is not to engage in polemics; it is rather to argue for a constructive reconsideration of the governmental procedures and practice that enable an American president to involve the country in the internal affairs of a foreign society, especially

---

[1] Most of the more significant legal writing up through 1967 has been collected by the Civil War Panel of the American Society of International Law in Falk, ed., *The Vietnam War and International Law*, Princeton, Princeton University Press, 1968 [hereinafter cited as *The Vietnam War*].

[2] See especially *The Vietnam War*, pp. 362-400, 445-508.

[3] As such, I make no effort to consider and respond to the legal arguments that have been made on behalf of the position taken by the United States. My purpose is to delimit the contours of inquiry in as comprehensive a fashion as possible rather than to argue the merits of the various legal conclusions. The most effective presentation of the government position on the central legal questions is that of Professor John Norton Moore to be found in *The Vietnam War*, pp. 237-70, 303-17, 401-45; a rather comprehensive study generally supportive of the United States position is Roger H. Hull and John C. Novograd, *Law and Vietnam*, Dobbs Ferry, N.Y., Oceana, 1968.

through policies designed to influence the outcome of struggle for control of governmental machinery. The need for reconsideration extends far beyond the power that commits United States armed forces to battle without any prior legislative authorization. It extends to the discretionary use of CIA to effectuate desired political changes in foreign countries, if necessary, by means that violate the legal order of the target state. The need for reconsideration extends, as well, to the provision of military aid and advice to regimes that govern in a manner violating the liberal democratic creed that our government is pledged to uphold within the United States.

In my judgment, there has been a persistent failure by the United States throughout the Vietnam War to adhere to the specific rules of international law governing recourse to and conduct of war. This failure also characterizes the behavior of other principal sovereign states. Therefore, the criticism directed against the decision-process that operates in the United States Government is applicable to other states within international society, although the power of the United States and the severity of its apparent violations of international law make the focus on the American situation logical at this point.[4]

It may also be wondered why attention is not given to violations of international law that might be attributed to North Vietnam or the National Liberation Front in the Vietnam War. Would it not, it might be asked, be more persuasive to examine critically the legal status of each side's involvement in the Vietnam war?[5] Such an examination might be an appropriate supplemental task, but it is clearly supplemental, as the emphasis here is upon the role of international law in future foreign policy-making by principal sovereign states. It is the principal states that establish the patterns that dominate international society, and it is their acceptance or rejection of legal re-

[4] The prominent role of the United States throughout international society gives its conduct a particular influence in shaping patterns of diplomatic practice. There are other prominent states, of course, whose use of force may also exert a considerable influence, but it is the United States that has made the most frequent sustained uses of its military power in recent decades. Soviet military intervention in East European countries is also a great importance, both because of the formidable character of Soviet power and because it exerts so much influence upon the American image of conflict in international affairs. In this latter respect, it is impossible to overestimate the damage done to the cause of world order by the Soviet military interventions in Hungary in 1956 and in Czechoslovakia in 1968.

[5] Note that the arguments for and against the legality of the basic American claims to be defending South Vietnam against "aggression" are different from, although in some sense interconnected with, the arguments concerning the comparative legality of United States and North Vietnamese participation in the Vietnam War.

straint and of the entire habit of law that vitally shapes the system of order that prevails at any given time. North Vietnam is not such a principal state; its conformity to or violation of international law does little to influence the shape of the overall system.

Besides, the weight of evidence suggests a great disproportion between the violations of international law by North Vietnam and by the United States—the American violations involve the reliance upon hyper-modern modes of warfare to devastate on an indiscriminate basis a relatively undeveloped and undefended society. There is a David-and-Goliath category of international conflict in which it is a mockery to ask whether the weaker side is also guilty of illegal behavior. It is revealingly rhetorical to consider whether it is necessary to determine whether Ethiopia in 1935, Finland in 1939, or Czechoslovakia in 1968 violated international law in their effort to defend their national autonomy against encroachment by much more powerful states. It is absurd to suppose that the small state might have been the aggressor rather than the victim of aggression. The struggle in Vietnam is more complex in many ways than those mentioned two sentences ago, but the essential structure of conflict is the same—a powerful state, here the United States, is seeking by means of its superior military power to thwart the expression of the domestic balance of political forces in Vietnam. The many phases of the struggle for Vietnam since the late 1940's have all exhibited this characteristic of foreign intervention, first principally in the form of a French colonial intervention progressively displaced in the 1950's by the United States. This underlying political interpretation makes it casuistic to look seriously upon the contention that the Saigon regime is representative of South Vietnam or that this regime enjoys sufficient sociopolitical autonomy to be capable of "inviting" assistance from the United States.

The comparative merits of argument strike me as so unequal with respect to the underlying issue of justification in Vietnam that it does not appear worthwhile to examine the legal arguments against North Vietnam and the NLF in the same spirit as one examines the arguments against the United States. Of course, this assertion of disparity rests upon the earlier proposition that the American case on the grand issue of aggression and self-defense is unpersuasive. It also rests on the inequality in size between the United States and North Vietnam. The idea that the greatest military power in world history is the victim of the illegal conduct of a third-rank Asian country is hardly very persuasive, especially in circumstances where the United States homeland is completely free from military countermeasures by North Vietnam.

The Policy Framework

Insisting on the relevance of international law to the American role in the Vietnam War is significant for one overriding reason: to conduct foreign policy in conformity with international law tends to discourage those choices and acts most likely to produce or intensify political disorder and human suffering. This faith in law presupposes that patterns of adherence generally, but not always, are more compatible with human welfare than are patterns of violation. Otherwise, the anarchist's plea might well be heeded.

The case for law in international affairs is strengthened by the awesome fragility of the nuclear age. Despite such circumstance, the relevance of international law to the use of violence by national governments cannot be posited as a ground rule without considerable explication. The exercise of sovereign discretion to wage war remains deeply rooted in political consciousness and evident in the patterns of statecraft. As a consequence, it remains incumbent upon an analyst to persuade his audience of the importance of using law to erode the tradition of sovereign discretion as rapidly as is feasible, as part of the struggle to evolve a stronger system of world legal order.

Such an endorsement of the ideals of respect for law implies only that the rules, procedures, and institutions needed for an effective legal order should be established and sustained; there is no implication of such legal absolutism that it is never justifiable to act outside or against the law. The position being urged is only the more modest one that the burden of legal justification is upon the state that uses or escalates the use of force in international relations, and that every effort should be made to assure that decisions are reached in such a way as to reflect an appreciation of the legal status of proposed courses of action. In international law, the special precedent-setting role of principal sovereign states creates a distinctive responsibility for decision-makers not nearly so evident in nongovernmental settings.

It is this kind of jurisprudential basis that causes distress about the failure to heed the claims of law in relation to the initiation and prosecution of the Vietnam war. The United States Government has paid little attention to the legality of its involvement in Vietnam. This inattentiveness is evident whether principal concern is with the rules, procedures, and institutions applicable to the day-to-day conduct of the war or to the use of law to shape foreign policy through the incorporation into the decision-process of a set of authoritative world order goals (such as are embodied in the Charter of the United Nations). I am mindful, in making these assertions, of the difficulty that attaches to any effort to pass legal judgment in a situation of controversy about the facts and the content of many of the applicable rules; there exists a situation of considerable legal indeterminacy in relation to the international law of internal war. Nevertheless, judgment can be passed on the diligence and sincerity of the effort of officials in the United States Government to apply inherited legal doctrine or to evolve policy in such a way as to establish a body of precedent that might guide other governments confronted by future circumstances of a comparable character.

It is not correct, of course, to suggest that the United States Government has neglected international law altogether throughout the Vietnam War. Government officials have used legal arguments to vindicate the U.S. involvement, but these arguments have been advanced only after the commitment to defend the Saigon regime had been widely proclaimed. These legal arguments also appear to have been shaped to answer domestic critics of the war who first gave prominence to questions of legality.[6]

Coupled with the tardiness of their enlistment, the tenuousness at times apparent in their advocacy suggests that reliance on international law argumentation at a postcommitment stage is little more than a rationalization of conduct determined by nonlegal factors.[7] It is thus

[6] It was not until after the Lawyers Committee on American Policy Towards Vietnam had prepared a Memorandum of Law in 1965, questioning the legality of United States involvement in Vietnam (reproduced in Cong. Rec. of September 23, 1965), that the State Department issued an official legal justification of U.S. actions. On March 4, 1966, a second, more detailed State Department memorandum, entitled "The Legality of the United States Participation in the Defense of Vietnam" was issued, *U.S. State Department Bulletin*, Vol. 54, No. 1396, March 28, 1966. The Lawyers Committee challenged each of the State Department's conclusions and allegations in full in *Vietnam and International Law*, New York, O'Hare, 1967.

[7] In addition to the lateness of their invocation, the legal arguments supporting U.S. involvement in Vietnam have throughout the war been involved with uncertainty by administration officials. Until late 1965 the U.S. military involvement in Vietnam had been based largely on the moral basis of reputed promises or pledges of former presidents to Saigon. In the Senate Foreign Relations Committee Hearings of February, 1966, Secretary Rusk did make passing reference to communiqués from both Eisenhower and Kennedy to the Diem government, but the Secretary's main approach was to stress our "obligations" under SEATO. In his testimony, however, there was reason to believe that Rusk was willing to admit that the "obligations" under which we acted in Vietnam referred not neces-

important to distinguish between the relevance of law as a source of constraint and guidance, capable of establishing a framework for foreign policy, and legal argumentation that merely seeks to justify foreign policy positions by translating them into a rhetoric oriented toward law or world order.[8]

In assessing United States involvement in the Vietnam War it is useful to distinguish among considerations of prudence, morality, and law.[9] For instance, it is quite possible to conclude that the United States

---

sarily to our legal duties under the treaty, but to our moral duties or commitments that we believed implicit in the pact.

The Chairman. But in this case do you maintain that we had an obligation under the Southeast Asia Treaty to come to the assistance, an all-out assistance, of South Vietnam? Is that very clear?

Secretary Rusk. It seems clear to me, sir, that this was an obligation—

The Chairman. Unilateral.

Secretary Rusk. An obligation of policy. It is rooted in the policy of the treaty. I am not now saying if we had decided we would not lift a finger about Southeast Asia that we could be sued in a court and be convicted of breaking a treaty. This is not the point I want to talk about.—U.S. Congress, Senate, Committee on Foreign Relations, *Supplemental Foreign Assistance, Fiscal Year 1966-Vietnam*, 89th Cong., 2nd sess., 1966, S. Doc. 2793, Washington: G.P.O., 1966, p. 45.

Finding it difficult to obtain the basis of a clear-cut legal obligation for our actions in Vietnam from the SEATO Treaty, the terms of obligation in Vietnam have in the last year or two again relied more heavily on moral commitment and the jargon of credibility—in terms of both the credibility of the U.S. commitment to Vietnam and the credibility of U.S. power in general—to stop the expansion of Communist-led wars of liberation wherever they arise. See note 11, *infra.*

[8] The distinction drawn in this sentence is crucial to the basic line of argument and is subject to empirical investigation. It is the distinction between bringing law to bear on the shape and shaping of government policy and bringing legal language to bear so as to make as persuasive a case for government policy as possible. My argument rests on the proposition that we need to restructure both the bureaucracy and expectations about governmental behavior so that the role of law will be significant in the first sense as well as the second. It is well to appreciate that in more routine areas of governmental conduct the bureaucratic machinery does accord a significant guidance role to international law. The area of war and peace is one in which normal bureaucratic procedures are suspended and decisions reached and implemented by the direct participation of the top political officers in government. It is for political decision-making that the need exists for constitutional reform to assure a greater relevance for considerations of international law.

[9] It is of course obvious that there is considerable interplay among these three considerations. For instance, a deep moral feeling dictating certain minimal humanitarian standards of conduct is at the foundation of much of the law of war. And one can always argue that prudence is also a factor in obedience to this law, since disobedience may bring damaging reprisal from the enemy. But while such interplay is important to recognize, it seems necessary also to distinguish among these three categories as far as possible in order to understand more fully our actions in Vietnam in terms of justifications and results with varying connotations of gravity in both our international and domestic relations, such

role in the war has been imprudent in the sense that a disproportionate cost has been incurred given the end in view, as formulated over time by the administration. The future of Vietnam (or its relation to a South Asian balance of power) may very well not be of sufficient significance in the perspective of United States national interests to justify the expenditure of blood and money,[10] especially in view of the failure of even disproportionate means to realize or even to approximate the obscure and shifting ends of policy there.[11] Geopolitical considerations can also be invoked to suggest that the United States course in Vietnam is imprudent in terms of our national interest in upholding viable states, in promoting a regional balance of power, in containing the expansion of a Chinese sphere of influence, or in buying time for

---

results hinging in part on the conflict between the official line and the conclusions as to legality that one must draw from our conduct in Vietnam.

[10] The war in Vietnam became the longest war in U.S. history in June 1968. Among U.S. forces alone, over 26,000 soldiers had been killed in action and over a half million men were committed to the conflict, not including air and naval support forces located outside the territory of Vietnam. The cost of the war has been reflected in the observation that the U.S. was spending $300,000 to kill a single Viet Cong. (See "The War in Vietnam," prepared by the Staff of the Senate Republican Policy Committee, Washington, D.C., Public Affairs Press, 1967, p. 9.) These figures reflect none of the suffering of the "enemy" —the Viet Cong or "regular" North Vietnamese forces—or of the peasant caught in between the forces of war to face both the terror of the Viet Cong and the awesome firepower of the United States while living off land that has become pockmarked by bombs and defoliated by sprays. See note 39 *infra*.

[11] Just as the United States has based its "commitment" to defend South Vietnam on uncertain and shifting moral and legal grounds, so too have the reasons for our presence in Vietnam in terms of national interest undergone subtle changes, often in parallel with the changes in popular support of the war efforts. In the early years of the war, the apparently limited objectives of helping South Vietnam rid itself of the aggressive threat from North Vietnam and make the country safe for democracy, as it were, received wide public support in this country, a support that perhaps reached its high point after the Tonkin incidents of August, 1964. As the war shifted to the North after February, 1965, and more U.S. soldiers were injected into the struggle· without immediate and favorable results, the American public's patience with events in Southeast Asia seemed to diminish. The situation was not helped by continued reports of corruption in the Saigon government, alleged violations of the law of war, and persistent claims that the United States had repeatedly failed to take advantage of reported peace overtures from Hanoi. Increasing emphasis was placed on containing China and on regarding South Vietnam as the dike that kept the Communist flood from overrunning Southeast Asia. Perhaps to maintain at least a semblance of public support for the war in the United States, the reasons officially given for U.S. presence in Vietnam were slowly framed in new terms. Thus, the very security of the U.S. has been increasingly said to be at stake, a logical extension of the argument that if the United States does not fight Communism in Vietnam it may in the foreseeable future have to fight it in California. See also Franz Schurmann and others, *The Politics of Escalation in Vietnam*, Boston, Beacon Press, 1966.

the present states of South Asia to evolve more stable governments. Perhaps, despite the ghastly irony entailed by the great effort to produce a victory for the Saigon regime, these interests would be served better by a united and stable Vietnam under the leadership of a Hanoi regime or a regime including Communist elements indigenous to South Vietnam than by a divided Vietnam, each half of which is hostile to and afraid of the other. The point is that concern about the *prudence* of the United States involvement raises a different order of issues than does an assessment of its legal quality although there are notable areas of overlap.

Similarly, a moral assessment raises distinct issues. It is quite possible to conclude that the destruction of Vietnamese society, measured in terms of both devastation and human suffering, mainly inflicted by a great power whose own society is beyond the reach of its adversary, places an enormous moral burden of justification upon those who would defend the United States involvement. It should be noted, however, that these *moral* costs of involvement would not be necessarily reduced if the basis of United States involvement were found to be fully compatible with requirements of international law.

It is thus important to acknowledge that the prudential and moral status of the United States involvement is quite separable from its legal status. To be more concrete, the prudential and moral basis of the United States role in the Korean War is, and certainly was, subject to question, but few doubts were ever seriously expressed about the legality of the United States role in defending South Korea under the auspices of the United Nations in response to the massive (if somewhat provoked) attack by North Korea in June of 1950.[12]

12 The legality of U.S. action in Korea was enhanced by at least three conditions absent in the Vietnam situation. First, the North Korean attack, whatever the underlying reasons for it, was an open and large-scale attack across the border of South Korea, an act that with no difficulty could be labelled "aggression" even by nations which had no empathy with the South Korean Government. By contrast, North Vietnam's intervention into South Vietnam has been far less open and on a far smaller scale. Indeed there is considerable opinion that North Vietnamese intervention was not on the scale of an "armed attack" under international law, until large United States forces had been deployed in the South under the justification that they were assisting Saigon in meeting such an attack. See, for instance, *Vietnam and International Law*, 2nd edn., note 1 *supra*, at pp. 48-52.

Second, the aura of legality surrounding U.S. actions in Korea was greatly enhanced by the fact that they were undertaken within the international auspices of the United Nations. While the United States certainly played the major role by far in the Korean War, its participation under the cloak of the UN gave it a generally persuasive defense

It seems desirable to make explicit the various arguments that counsel a serious consideration of international law in a war/peace context such as is presented by the Vietnam war.[13]

First, it would appear that the welfare of domestic society would be better served at this historical time by strengthening the framework of legal restraint relevant to the formation and execution of foreign policy, thereby limiting the scope of executive discretion. The Vietnam War has made it clear to many Americans that the public requires protection from its own government just as surely in external arenas of action as it does in domestic affairs. We have reached a point at which public interest demands the structuring of certain legal constraints to regulate governments of democratic society whenever they propose long-term reliance on military forces to carry out their foreign policies. Some might say that a government cannot afford the luxury of adhering to a framework of constraint, that the imperatives of national security are so compelling as to require full trust in the wisdom of the

---

against any charges of unilateral action solely in the name of its own national interest. In Vietnam, on the other hand, such charges are far more difficult to meet. Not only has the UN not given its blessing to the U.S. effort, but its principal officer, U Thant, has been steady in his condemnation of that effort. In addition, while the United States enjoys token support in Vietnam from some of its Asian allies, it is significant that the two principal parties, other than the United States, to the SEATO Treaty—France and Pakistan—have openly disavowed U.S. actions in Vietnam. And South Korea, with the largest contingent of allied troops in Vietnam, is able and willing to offer that assistance only because the U.S. has made a similar number of its own troops available in South Korea and has agreed to equip most of the South Korean troops as a precondition to their presence in Vietnam, besides agreeing to rely to the extent possible on Korean sources of supplies for war-related need.

And third, South Korea possessed a reasonably stable government with a demonstrated capacity to govern its own society without external military support. In contrast, the South Vietnamese leaders have never appeared to enjoy a sufficiently wide base of public support to maintain governmental control unless the United States maintained a strong military presence in the country. Also Vietnam, unlike Korea, had experienced an anti-colonial war fought for control of the entire country and lost by those elements in South Vietnam that have been given support by the United States. Therefore, in Vietnam the military cause of the United States runs counter to the political drift of revolutionary nationalism, whereas in Korea the conflict was between two rather autonomous political entities each of which sought to subject the other to an alien ideology. North Korea was the aggressor mainly because it struck first across an international boundary. In South Vietnam the early phases of warfare were largely initiated and managed by southern opponents to the Saigon regime, and therefore, the charge of "aggression" against North Vietnam seems far too tenuous to sustain, even if these charges are approached on the basis of evidence gathered by employees of the U.S. Government. E.g., see Douglas Pike, *Viet Cong*, Cambridge, Mass., MIT Press, 1966.

[13] On the need for such explicitness critics and supporters of United States policy agree. See, in particular, Professor Moore's various presentations cited in note 3, esp. at pp. 430-44.

president. In earlier periods of history, especially in times of stress, such arguments in favor of unrestraint were often made with respect to the execution of domestic policy. The vitality of a law-ordered society has been often demonstrated by the non-erosion of legal procedures in periods of domestic stress. The overall balance and welfare of the society has seemed better served by endorsing the capacity of the Supreme Court to confine executive discretion than by allowing those pragmatic arguments advanced on behalf of unrestricted executive power to prevail. With regard to international policy, the necessity of quick action under threat of atomic war has also tended toward unrestraint on executive decision-making. Under conditions in which planned nuclear attack constitutes far less of a danger than does escalation from subnuclear to nuclear conflict over an extended period, the need for renewed restraints on executive action have become more obvious. Let the United States involvement in Vietnam serve as a learning experience to demonstrate that the welfare of the country would benefit from building a tradition whereby foreign policy is carried out with due regard for the restraints of law.

Second, to achieve this kind of framework of restraint, two kinds of structural reform appear necessary. The first is the creation of the post of the Attorney General for International Affairs, securing at cabinet level a person who would have a vested vocational interest in bringing to bear the legal dimension of proposed policy throughout the decision-making process.[14] The present structure of government is such that

[14] An individual trained principally in the law and somewhat independent of the internal political power struggles in decision-making circles in Washington could be expected to be persistent in his injection of legal consideration into any policy-forming process and, it is to be hoped, would be able to make his conclusions and recommendations felt at the highest level and at a pre-"commitment" stage. He might in addition, although this is by no means his principal intended role, be a rallying point for dissenters among top advisers, whose disagreement with imprudent or immoral policy could gain weight by its expression in legal as well as political terms.

A certain added importance could be given to the office by making its occupant a member of the highest official decision-making groups such as the National Security Council. At the same time it is to be hoped that Attorney General for International Affairs would, because he spoke—or would speak—for no interest group but that favoring world order, eventually become a trusted adviser outside official circles as well.

The methods by which an Attorney General for International Affairs should be selected or dismissed pose no special problem. As with other cabinet members the president would be expected to choose a competent individual to fill the office. In the case of the attorney general the president might, however, be expected to select a man of neutral convictions on legal issues, rather than one who sided with the chief executive on certain

no official expert on matters of international law has direct access to the policy-forming process except for the very diluted and generally belated access enjoyed by the Legal Adviser to the Secretary of State. This indirect access tends to exclude legal considerations until after policy has been shaped and a public commitment made. The role, then, of the Legal Adviser in critical cases often becomes one of rationalizing policy in such a way as to offset criticism of a legally controversial policy.[15] In contrast, an Attorney General for International Affairs might be expected and even encouraged to insist that the policy options considered by the government reflect the limits set by international law. Such expectations might appropriately accompany any effort to establish the office.

Leadership groups appear to be experiencing the infiltration of their political consciousness by world-order ideals. This process of infiltration takes place at an uneven rate and some leaders are more susceptible than others.[16] An important point seems to be, however, that this development has gradually made it more acceptable to appeal to legal restraint even in the setting of foreign policy-making. This appeal may be weak on occasion and it may be eventually overridden by other considerations of national interest: quite possibly legal consideration may be allowed to condition the execution of foreign policy to some extent, even after these considerations have been largely excluded from

---

important matters. Only in the event of such apolitical traditions of selection would the office fulfill its purposes.

One would also tend to minimize the possibility that the attorney general could be intimidated in any way by the threat of removal from office. Perhaps more than for any other officer in government, dismissal of the AGIA because of disagreement over basic issues in controversial situations like Vietnam would be an excellent indication that U.S. policy was not being formulated in consideration of the law of nations.

The entire proposal for an AGIA would be very much influenced by the context in which the office was created, the kind of considerations relied upon by its proponents, and the sorts of functions such an officer would be expected to perform. The initial selection of a candidate for the office would naturally have a considerable additional capacity to define the role. It seems essential to stress the responsibility of the AGIA to introduce legal considerations into foreign policy-making (and not to serve as a buffer against domestic criticism). Such a stress requires a professionalization of the proposed government post and a sense that its occupant would have the same kind of duty to abstain from partisan politics as does, say, a member of the Joint Chiefs of Staff.

15 This was so, for instance, with the March 4, 1966 memorandum on Vietnam. See note 1.

16 For some very suggestive discussion of these issues see Harold D. Lasswell, "The Social and Political Framework of War and Peace," UCLA Forum in Medical Science, No. 7, in Carmine D. Clemente and Donald B. Lindsley, eds., *Brain Function*, Vol. v, pp. 317-35, esp. 317-24.

the selection of the ends of foreign policy. The Bay of Pigs Expedition of 1961 offers an excellent example of a compromise between deference to world-order prohibitions on the use of force and the adoption of a course of action in foreign policy that flouted these prohibitions. The results, as we know, were disastrous, but perhaps not so irreversible as they would have been if no deference to world order expectations had been expressed, representing both a defeat for law-ordered foreign policy and a setback for a purely geopolitically determined foreign policy. Failures in action of this type are characteristic of periods of normative ambiguity and compromise, periods of transition from one belief-system to another. Blanket acceptance of the limits of international law decision-making in crises can not realistically be expected. However, the hope is that over time an exposure to the value of legal considerations in the planning and execution of short- and long-term policy formulation would lead the government toward becoming a government of laws, not men, in international affairs.

The second structural reform that the Vietnam War suggests as essential is a redefinition of the role of Congress in authorizing and sustaining policies that entail the use of military force. It seems clear that the present dichotomy between according Congress virtually no role and an insistence on a declaration of war is far too rigid to provide for meaningful legislative participation in the policy-forming process relevant to war-peace problems. In general, there exists a need to evolve a procedure of legislative participation that results in diluting the present degree of executive control over this subject matter. The practicalities of restraining recourses to military force appear to take precedence over the arguments for unrestrained executive discretion.

In searching for a new understanding of separation of powers between the principal branches of government, it is also important to consider carefully the role of domestic courts. Domestic courts have taken the position that a private litigant cannot question the legal status of the United States involvement in a war. The legality of the United States involvement is treated as a "political question" not susceptible to adjudication. If the general position urged here is correct—namely, that it is highly desirable to establish a framework of legal restraint relevant to foreign policy—then the protection of rights of individual redress through judicial action appears essential. If, as the Constitution and the Supreme Court have affirmed, the obligations of international law constitute part of the "supreme law of the land" then it seems inappropriate to hold that individuals are unable to rely upon this area of governmental restraint in resisting calls to perform government service, especially when these calls may entail risk to their lives, infringements of their consciences, or participation in internationally criminal behavior.

It is well to appreciate that the concentration of legal authority in the executive branch was accomplished at a time when international law made little pretense of regulating the discretion of a sovereign state to wage war. Only after the Kellogg-Briand Pact of 1928 was widely ratified by many states, including the United States, could it be persuasively argued that recourse to aggressive war was illegal.[17] This trend toward the legal prohibition of nondefensive uses of force in international affairs is carried strongly forward in the Charter of the United Nations. But prior to 1928 there was no occasion for judicial review, as there were no relevant legal criteria, by which to appraise a challenge directed at a given war policy. Similarly, the role of legislative participation was purely one of confirming a direction of national policy. There was no basis for a charge that the president was acting illegally by going to war, unless possibly in an unlikely circumstance in which the adversary state was joined to the United States by a treaty of alliance. The main conclusion on this issue is that international law has evolved so significantly in the area of war and peace as to make traditional notions about the separation of powers appropriate for this subject matter now seem dangerously obsolete.[18]

Third, it also now appears clear that the ideology of world order professed by the United States government in common with the governments of many other countries has influenced the attitudes of a significant portion of our domestic population. The class of the govern-

[17] For a convenient account of the legal steps taken to prohibit aggressive warfare see Quincy Wright, *The Role of Law in the Elimination of War*, Dobbs Ferry, N.Y., Oceana, 1961.

[18] This subject has been explored recently in preliminary hearings on the president's power of deployment and use of United States forces in Vietnam and related testimony on the Gulf of Tonkin Resolution. See United States Senate Foreign Relations Committee Hearings on S. Res. 151 relating to U.S. commitments to foreign powers. S. Res. 151, 90th Cong., 1st Sess.:

Whereas accurate definition of the term "national commitment" in recent years has become obscured: Now, therefore, be it *Resolved*, that it is the sense of the Senate that a national commitment by the United States to a foreign power necessarily and exclusively results from affirmative actions taken by the executive and legislative branches of the United States Government through means of a treaty, convention, or other legislative instrumentality specifically intended to give effect to such a commitment.

See also "Congressional Inquiry into Military Affairs," Senate Foreign Relations Committee, Memorandum of Legislative Reference Service of Library of Congress, March 1968.

ment's professed views with its actions in Vietnam has engendered a rising level of legal awareness among attentive members of the American public. This awareness has grown out of the atmosphere created by the controversy surrounding numerous legal points concerning United States intervention in Vietnam and, more recently, concerning the tactics of war there. In all probability, this trend toward awareness is not a temporary aberration of opinion provoked by an unpopular and unsuccessful war. The permanence of this growth of awareness is at least partly assured by the realization that major power confrontations of the future will, because of military technology, continue to be characterized by third-party intervention—initially carefully regulated, but almost inevitably tending to increase—in support of one or another faction within the borders of single, strife-torn states. This intervention will not often carry with it the aura of legality that would accompany a response to open aggression across state boundaries. Neither is it likely to involve methods of warfare that distinguish between the populace and the enemy.[19]

The American legal consciousness is sufficiently great at this time to suggest that a decision by the national government to carry out a foreign policy in apparent violation of the United Nations Charter and other standards of international law will predictably precipitate serious domestic opposition. A portion of the citizenry of democratic states now gives preference to the dictates of their sense of legal requirements even when these dictates contradict imperatives of national loyalty in the old sense of "my country right or wrong, my country." This

---

[19] One of the great tragedies of the Vietnam war is that the United States has employed as antipersonnel weapons napalm, phosphorus, cluster bomb units (CBUS), and gases that can cause horrible and unnecessary suffering. But this tragedy is enlarged by the fact that the traditional antiguerrilla concept of the necessity of separating the guerrilla from the population that may hide and support him has been applied in a most devastating way in Vietnam. The futility of attempts to separate the guerrilla from a population that gives him increasing assistance has led to tactics that apply massive firepower indiscriminately to "suspected" enemy areas in the form of blanket bombing or search-and-destroy operations. In addition, "Operation Ranch Hand" has sprayed millions of gallons of defoliants over South Vietnam to deprive the Viet Cong of both cover and food, particularly rice, in the area. The choice left to the "neutral" peasants in those areas bombed, burned, and sprayed is simple. Stay and be killed or move to "resettlement areas" under the control of the U.S. and allied forces. Separation of the fish from the water in which they swim has thus taken on a new and ugly meaning in Vietnam. For some documentation of these charges see the newspaper extracts collected in *In the Name of America*, Clergy and Laymen Concerned About Vietnam, Annandale, Virginia, Turnpike Press, 1968. For material on North Vietnam see John Gerassi, *North Vietnam: A Documentary*, New York, Bobbs-Merrill, 1968. See note 39, *infra*.

shift in public sentiment is a dramatic one and suggests the importance of taking seriously the restraining claims imposed on national discretion by international law. It is not now (nor has it ever been) accurate to presume that the population of a domestic society will blindly follow the flag into battle. As a consequence, a governmental decision to pursue a foreign policy regarded by a sizable segment of public opinion as illegal is likely to generate sizable domestic opposition.[20] The existence of this loyal opposition will imperil both the war effort and the maintenance of democratic traditions at home. The continuation of such a war for any length of time will place increasing pressure on a government to choose between upholding war commitments and maintaining domestic liberties.

Fourth, I think that it isn't possible to separate governmental attitudes toward international law from public adherence to ideals of respect for law in domestic society. It is very artificial to inculcate respect for law in our cities and practice lawlessness in Vietnam. As the more militant leaders of ghetto communities have made clear, the domestic order of our society is continuous with the sort of international order that prevails. In addition, it becomes more difficult to socialize citizens in the direction of respect for law in relation to the pursuit of personal goals if the government does not set an example of using comparable restraint in the pursuit of national goals.[21] Socializa-

---

[20] This opposition has persisted during the Vietnam War despite the warnings of administration spokesmen like Vice President Humphrey who told a group of business executives in late 1967: "I have not forgotten the lessons of the '30s when men cried 'peace' and failed a generation. . . . I, for one, would not want to be responsible for a policy which deferred today's manageable troubles until they became unmanageable . . . a policy of Armageddon on the installment plan." "Dissenting from the Dissenters," *Newsweek*, November 6, 1967. In August of 1968 it became evident that the president of the United States was deterred from attending the political convention of his own party because he was told of the unpopularity of his war policies.

[21] Disrespect for the law of nations by the U.S. can certainly be expected to promote an increasing disrespect for its domestic law among U.S. citizens, particularly minority groups that have for years been counseled to pursue their goals within the law and now see their country act on the international plane with very limited consideration of that law. This very real problem, when connected with the other domestic difficulties the Vietnam War represents, are well worth noting. Vietnam is a place where many Negroes find themselves fighting a war allegedly to protect democratic ideals that many of them have never fully enjoyed at home. It is for some a white man's war fought in disproportionate numbers by black men against yellow people with much of the same savagery of method that allowed the United States to decimate Hiroshima and Nagasaki during World War II. It is a war that has channelled billions of dollars away from long-promised domestic programs to improve the position of the black communities of America. And finally, and most important for the United States as a nation, it is a war in which many thousands of black men

tion is especially difficult in these circumstances for groups such as the blacks who are being urged to pursue their grievance against white America within the limits and through the procedures of law.

Fifth, the standards of law provide a yardstick that is relied upon by responsible groups in our society who seek to express their opposition to a line of policy. For instance, the Clergy Concerned About American Policy in Vietnam issued a strong moral condemnation of the American involvement in Vietnam documented by reference to instances of United States departure from the traditional standards of behavior embodied in the laws of war.[22] This was an instance in which legal norms provided an aura of objectivity that served to anchor moral judgment.

Sixth, principal sovereign states by their behavior establish global patterns that influence the behavior of all states in international society. Given a decentralized international system lacking a legislative organization, the most powerful sovereign states necessarily play a quasi-legislative role. Their acts set precedents upon which other states rely. At stake in the Vietnam War is the United States claim that substantial covert assistance to an insurgency is tantamount to an armed attack by one country upon another. Given the pervasiveness of insurgent behavior and given the allusiveness of the factual relations between insurgent groups and foreign governments, the United States has set an important precedent by its unilateral determination to engage on virtually unrestricted bombing of North Vietnam in response to North Vietnamese support of the NLF.[23] The experience of atmospheric nuclear testing illustrates how difficult it may be for even powerful states to repudiate the precedents they have created when these precedents are invoked by other states engaged in comparable activity. The United States and the Soviet Union are immobilized by their own

---

who have been badly disappointed by the lack of domestic progress return to the United States with a training in the tactics and strategy of guerrilla warfare that can very well be used by those seeking radical change in America.

[22] *In the Name of America*, pp. 1-15.

[23] The decision to bomb North Vietnam in February of 1965 was initially justified as a reprisal for the attacks on the large American air base at Pleiku, subsequently it was vindicated as an effort to interdict infiltration and, finally, as a means of "hurting" North Vietnam sufficiently to induce a settlement on terms acceptable to the United States government. Neither the claim of reprisal, nor the claim of interdiction, nor the claim of generalized belligerency rests, in my judgment, on firm legal foundation. The book by Gerassi, note 19, accumulates considerable material on the additional issue of whether, independent of the legal theory used to vindicate the bombing, the specific selection of targets disclose wilful violation of the most minimum humanitarian laws of war.

prior records of atmospheric testing in relation to positing objections to French and Chinese nuclear weapons tests. A kind of reciprocity operates in international relations, underscoring the importance of conditioning unilateral national action by a full awareness and acknowledgment of its legal consequences. One legal consequence of this common-law social process is to lend a presumption of legality to behavior by other states that falls within the province of national claims.

Seventh, reference to legal norms and procedures provides insight into the reasonableness or unreasonableness of a particular diplomatic posture. For instance, war-terminating proposals can be assessed for their reasonableness by reference to the degree to which they rest upon a mutual and symmetrical acceptance of the relevant restraints of law. This kind of insight into the character of reasonableness suggests a way of cutting through diplomatic impasses that result from each country's selectively perceiving and interpreting facts so as to conform to its preferences and failing to appreciate the contradictory perceptions and interpretations of its adversary.[24] Especially in a situation of the Vietnam type, potentialities for mutual misinterpretation are great. Each side sees facts that confirm only its claims and thereby feels vindicated in intensifying its response and its reliance on coercion. The only way to inhibit this process is to establish objective limitations, such as international boundary lines or third-party procedures, that assure reference to authoritative organs of conciliation and settlement.[25]

*The Six Categories of Legal Issues Relevant
to an Appraisal of the United States
Involvement in the Vietnam War*

Because of the incredible complexity of the legal issues generated by the Vietnam War, it seems useful to group these issues into a series of categories. These groupings are intended to assist understanding and should not be taken as rigid and mechanical separations.

1. *The Geneva Agreements*: There are a series of legal issues that

[24] See Ralph K. White, *Nobody Wanted War*, Garden City, N.Y., Doubleday and Co., Inc., 1968.

[25] Legal order evolves in a social setting that lacks a government in two principal ways: (1) substantive standards of limitation on behavior that are sufficiently self-defining to be self-enforcing; an international boundary line or a prohibition on nuclear weapons is such a clear standard; (2) procedural requirements of reference that allow either party to a dispute as to fact or law to solicit and obtain an impartial determination that will be accepted as binding by the losing side. Both of these ordering strategies can operate successfully in a society that exhibits little institutional centralization.

pertain to the origin of the Vietnam War. These issues concern primarily the interpretation of the Geneva Accords, a series of international agreements reached in 1954 at the end of the first Indo-China War that had been fought between the French and the Vietminh.[26] The Vietminh was the organization presided over by Ho Chi Minh and represented a coalition of anticolonial forces that prevailed against the French in the first Indo-China war. The basic diplomatic context at Geneva has remained very obscure. Many of the misunderstandings subsequent to 1954 appear to stem from doubt as to whether the Geneva Accords sought to ratify the battlefield victory of the Vietminh over the French or sought to reach a compromise whereby the country of Vietnam would be partitioned into a Communist North Vietnam and an anti-Communist South Vietnam. If the Geneva Accords are looked upon as ratifying the French defeat in much the manner that the Evian Accords of 1962 ratified the French defeat in the Algerian war, then the remainder of the issues tend to be resolved along the lines alleged by North Vietnam. If, on the other hand, the Geneva Accords are seen as producing a divided country of the Korean variety, then the interpretive issues are much more difficult to resolve. The Soviet Union acted as co-chairman with the United Kingdom at the Geneva Conference and yet urged in 1957, after the date for election on reunification had passed, that both North and South Vietnam be separately admitted to the United Nations. The Soviet effort was opposed by the United States although it now gives some support to the contention that Vietnam was converted into a divided country in 1954.[27]

Further dispute surrounding the Geneva Accords has dealt with the extent to which the Saigon regime was bound by the terms of the Geneva settlement, most specifically the extent to which it was bound to the obligation to hold elections in July of 1956. The Diem government never acknowledged its obligations to abide by the Geneva arrangements and persistently refused to enter pre-election consultations with North Vietnam despite the frequent requests that it do so by the Hanoi government.[28] It is also problematic as to what the full legal

[26] For convenient copies of the text of these Accords see *The Vietnam War*, pp. 543-64.

[27] The United States was pressing for the admission of the Republic of Vietnam, as the sole representative in the State of Vietnam, to be United Nations. For summary account see John Norton Moore and James L. Underwood, with the collaboration of Myres S. McDougal, "The Lawfulness of United States Assistance to the Republic of Viet Nam," privately published, May 1966, pp. 23-28.

[28] One of the fullest accounts of this period is to be found in Joseph Buttinger, *Vietnam: A Dragon Embattled*, New York, Praeger, 1967, pp. 845-1010. An able short analysis is

significance is of a failure to hold elections and how this failure relates to the responsibility of North Vietnam for instigating and supplying the NLF uprising in South Vietnam. In essence, then, the legal questions that center on the Geneva Accords concern the binding nature of those Accords and the apportionment of blame for their violation.[29] I think that we are forced to conclude that the Geneva settlement was extremely ambiguous on its face, that the Hanoi government was to some extent a victim of great-power diplomacy, and that the non-participation and non-assent of the Saigon regime prompted, if it did not altogether assure, a misunderstanding about the terms of settlement emerging subsequent to 1954. The North Vietnamese might have given tacit acquiescence to the existence of a divided Vietnam had the Saigon regime either collapsed on its own or displayed reasonable competence to govern South Vietnam in a tolerable fashion. However, the repressive policies of the Diem regime produced a revolutionary situation in South Vietnam such that a combination of indigenous insurgency and external support coalesced in the insurgency of the National Liberation Front.[30]

2. *The Charter Arguments*: Most of the legal debate about the United States involvement in Vietnam has raised the question of whether North Vietnam's assistance to the National Liberation Front has been equivalent to an "armed attack" against a sovereign state. The issue has been debated generally in terms of the United Nations Charter, and the question has been asked in terms of whether North Vietnam's support of the NLF constituted an "armed attack" of a sort that justified action in "self-defense" by South Vietnam and the United States, as these two legal terms are employed in Article 51 of the Charter. This issue raises the general questions as to whether assistance given to an insurgent faction is covered within Article 51 at all, and

---

contained in George McT. Kahin and John W. Lewis, *The United States in Vietnam*, Delta, 1967, pp. 66-126.

[29] One of the fullest studies of the Geneva Conference has been done as a Ph.D. thesis by an aide to Prince Bua Loc, who was the Prime Minister of the Saigon regime at the time of the Geneva Conference. Ngo Ton Dat, "The Geneva Partition of Vietnam and the Question of Reunification During the First Two Years (August 1954 to July 1956)," unpublished Ph.D. dissertation, Cornell University 1963. See also John S. Hannon, Jr., "A Political Settlement for Vietnam: The 1954 Geneva Conference and its Current Implications," 8 *Virginia Journal of International Law*, 4 (1968).

[30] See Jean Lacouture, *Vietnam: Between Two Truces*, New York, Random House, 1966, pp. 51-60 for a short analysis of the emergence of the Front. See also Bernard B. Fall, *The Two Viet-Nams*, New York, Praeger, rev. edn., 1964, pp. 203-384.

if so, what degree of assistance is equivalent to an armed attack on a foreign society. In Vietnam each side accuses the other of committing aggression and alleges its own use of only defensive force. The problem of aggression and armed attack under the Charter has several main elements: first, how do we evaluate legally North Vietnamese assistance to the NLF; second, how do we evaluate legally United States assistance to the Saigon regime; third, how do we assess the extension of the air war to North Vietnam after the Tonkin incidents in August of 1964 and then permanently after the Pleiku incident of February of 1965? In Charter terms, we are dealing with contentions that the principal belligerent states are violating Article 2, Paragraph 4, and are not acting within the scope of Article 51 defining self-defense.

There is a subsidiary argument made by the United States that its action on behalf of South Vietnam is a fulfillment of its obligations under the SEATO treaty. In my judgment, the SEATO treaty neither adds to nor detracts from the Charter Arguments, and if the United States possesses grounds for proceeding against North Vietnam, it possesses them on a Charter basis. There is, finally, the much-controverted question in this context as to whether the United States discharged its procedural duty, under Article 33 of the Charter, to submit the Vietnam conflict to the United Nations for peaceful settlement before having recourse to military force. The United States appears only to have sought a nominal involvement for the United Nations in the Vietnam conflict until after it had become evident that a military solution could not be achieved successfully at a tolerable cost.[31]

3. *The Westphalia-Budapest Arguments*: The basic structure of international society was constituted in 1648 at the Peace of Westphalia.[32] This structure rests on the coordinated principles of sovereign independence, territorial jurisdiction, the equality of states, sovereign immunity, and the doctrine of nonintervention. These Westphalia principles were formally evolved in the course of settling the bloody ideological conflict known to students of history as the Thirty Years' War. The basic idea at Westphalia was to rest international peace and

[31] For a fairly complete account up through October 1967 see "Submission of the Vietnam Conflict to the United Nations," Hearings, Senate Committee on Foreign Relations, 90th Cong., 1st sess., October 26, 27, and November 2, 1967.

[32] This Westphalia conception of the basis of international order is more fully discussed in Falk, "The Interplay of Westphalia and Charter Conceptions of International Legal Order: Past, Present, and Near Future," in Falk and Cyril E. Black, eds., *The Future of the International Legal Order*, Vol. 1, Chapter 2, Princeton, Princeton University Press, to be published 1969.

security upon the capacity and prerogative of national governments to maintain order within their national boundaries, and upon the endorsement of their exclusive authority to do so. The national government whose existence is internationally certified through the conception of diplomatic recognition, and more recently through access to international institutions, is the exclusive political authority able and entitled to act on behalf of a nation. The capacity of the constituted government includes its right to receive foreign aid, including military assistance, and in periods of emergency to request foreign military assistance to help repel external attack or to sustain internal order. In the Vietnam context, the Westphalia Argument has been strongly relied upon by the United States government. In essence, the argument of the United States government has been that the Saigon regime is the constituted government of South Vietnam, as legitimized by widespread diplomatic recognition.[33] This Saigon regime requested the United States government to provide military assistance to enable it to deal with an emergency created by the combined challenge of indigenous uprising and foreign aggression. The United States position, then, is that its military role in Vietnam is sanctioned by the view that it is coming to the rescue of a beleaguered incumbent government.

There are two fundamental difficulties with the application of the Westphalia Argument to the Vietnam situation. The first difficulty is that it is oriented toward the status quo. In certain circumstances, support of the constituted government may frustrate the realization of self-determination for the people and the society involved. In the event that a particular state is ruled by an oppressive government, then outside support of that government tends to reinforce regressive structures of domination. In effect, the Westphalia Argument needs to be correlated with certain internal considerations that bear on the capacity to govern and the degree to which fundamental human rights are protected by the government. To take extreme examples, it would be possible to contend that Germany under Hitler, like South Africa since 1946, lost its political legitimacy to such an extent that it was no longer entitled to receive external support of a military character. The Westphalia conception of world order, if taken too literally, appears to give no protection whatsoever to a right of revolution enjoyed by suppressed populations. When the ratio between the magnitude of external support and the contribution of the incumbent government

---

[33] See e.g., Moore and Underwood, note 27, pp. 28-29.

grows so great that the former overshadows the latter, then the external involvement appears incompatible with the values of self-determination.[34] These considerations support the conclusion that the Westphalia Argument provides only provisional justification for external military assistance in a situation of the Vietnam type. In essence, the consent of the incumbent regime is only one of several complementary considerations that enter into an appraisal of legality.

In the specific context created by the Vietnam War, a further set of difficulties is apparent. These difficulties are suggested by the argument made in support of the Soviet intervention in Hungary to suppress the uprising of 1956 (the Budapest Argument), or, even more flagrantly, the contention that the Soviet-led military intervention in Czech affairs was at the invitation of Prague leaders. It will be recalled that the Soviet government legitimized its military intervention in Hungary by according the symbols of political legitimacy to the Kadar elite. The Soviet intervention in Hungarian affairs could then subsequently be justified as the provision of support in response to an invitation by the constituted government. The Budapest Argument emphasizes the degree to which states can self-legitimize the conditions of their participation in foreign civil wars. This issue further suggest the need for some kind of centralized international procedure to identify which elite, if any, is entitled to act on behalf of a particular national society. In Vietnam it has now become common knowledge that the United States government, through the CIA and other official activities, participated in the selection, maintenance, and transformation of the various Saigon regimes that have been in existence since 1954. Therefore, the contention that the legitimacy of the United States role rests on the legitimacy of Saigon's request for assistance is a seriously circular argument. It is the United States prior intervention that itself provided successive Saigon regimes with the political orientation that would assure an invitation for United States assistance. Such a veil of legitimacy should be lifted in an inquiry into the legal basis for using military force in a foreign country.[35]

---

[34] There are some interesting implications to this effect in an essay by Karl W. Deutsch titled "External Involvement in Internal War," in Harry Eckstein, ed., *Internal War*, Glencoe, Ill., The Free Press, 1964, pp. 100-10.

[35] The point here is that an invitation from a constituted government is only one factor in the appraisal of legality that should be made when one state uses its military power within the territory of another. The legitimizing value of this invitation is diluted to the extent that the constituted government is subject to a serious internal challenge from a counterelite and it is rendered worthless if "the government" is constituted through the

These circumstances are accentuated in Vietnam by the evident incapacity of the Saigon regime to administer its national society in either an effective or reasonably consensual manner. The problem is further complicated by the plausibility of treating the Vietnam War as a secessionist struggle initiated by the southern zone of Vietnam.[36] In this connection, it is worth noting that even the South Vietnamese Constitution proclaims the unity of all of Vietnam as a single sovereign entity.[37] The removal of United States and North Vietnamese external assistance from South Vietnam would have led, it seems highly likely, to victory by the NLF at any relevant stage of the struggle for control of South Vietnam. Furthermore, the effective control exercised by the NLF over portions of South Vietnam suggests that there is a dual government prevailing in large sectors of the country. In a situation of dual government, outside states are entitled to treat either of the two contending elites as legitimate.[38] This set of circumstances existed during the Spanish civil war. In a situation of dual government, then, the United States might be entitled to aid the Saigon regime, but it could hardly contend that North Vietnamese assistance to the NLF amounted

---

prior intervention of the foreign state that is then the recipient of an invitation. The Soviet intervention in Czechoslovakia in August 1968 was a particularly crass example of invasion beneath a transparently false claim to be responding to an earlier invitation.

[36] That is, at minimum North Vietnam cannot be looked upon as an outsider in the setting of South Vietnamese development. There is considerable support for suggesting that the Geneva solution looked toward a unified Vietnam under Hanoi's control and that post 1954 efforts to prevent that expectation from being fulfilled were tantamount to secession by South Vietnam from the single country of Vietnam. In this light, the effort resembles the effort of Katanga to break away from the Congo with the United States playing the role supportive of secession in Vietnam that Belgium played in the Congo. In any event, North Vietnam's efforts to frustrate the division of its country in violation of a major international agreement gives its military participation in the struggle some legal and geopolitical foundation.

[37] Even the South Vietnamese Constitution of 1967 proclaims in Article 1 (1): "Vietnam is a territorially indivisible, unified and independent republic." And Article 107: "Article 1 of the Constitution and this Article may not be amended or deleted." "Background Information Relating to Southeast Asia and Vietnam," Senate Committee on Foreign Relations, 3rd rev. edn., 1967, pp. 287-304.

[38] For fuller consideration and some documentation of the dual-sovereignty argument see Falk in *The Vietnam War*, pp. 484-90. As of September 1968 the NLF has made no claim to be the legitimate government of South Vietnam, although its missions in over twenty countries are accorded diplomatic status normally reserved for foreign states. The failure to proclaim a government may reflect the continuing search for a political compromise such that a coalition of South Vietnamese interest, ethnic, and ideological groups might join in the governance of the country. The relevant point in the text is merely that the NLF exercises enough effective political control over enough of the country to allow third states to accord it governmental status equivalent to that enjoyed by the Saigon regime.

to aggression. All external participation would be placed on an equivalent legal level.

It is exceedingly difficult to resolve the legal issues that emerge in connection with the Westphalia Argument. These issues are extremely important, however, because so often the outcome of a civil war depends on which faction receives assistance at which stage and in what form. Given the frequency of civil warfare, it appears to be a most unfortunate precedent for the United States to assert not only that it was entitled to provide unlimited military support for a government elite it had helped to create, but that North Vietnamese military assistance to a counter-elite amounts to aggression of such a severe nature that it constituted an armed attack justifying action in self-defense.

4. *The Hague Arguments*: The legal issues presented under this heading are very diverse, but they may be grouped in two main categories. First of all, there are the various issues raised by the contention that the United States is conducting the war in multiple violation of minimal standards of legal restraint embodied in treaties of long standing. These treaties are principally the Hague Conventions of 1907 and the four Geneva Conventions of 1949. The rules of warfare contained in these treaties are made applicable to the armed forces by the field manuals issued to all servicemen, and have been accepted as binding upon the war policies of all countries. The range of apparent violative activity occurring in the course of the Vietnam war has now been rather fully documented in a series of persuasive publications.[39] The main kinds of violations involve the mistreatment of civilians, bombing of nonmilitary targets, the use of prohibited weapons, and the destruction of villages and other settlements of Vietnamese people. The legal consequence of the disparity between American battlefield practices and the laws of war suggests either that these laws are obsolete under conditions of modern guerrilla warfare, or that the United States is engaged in a massive and systematic violation of the most elementary humani-

[39] See books cited in note 20 and also Harrison Salisbury, *Hanoi—A View From the North*, New York, Harper and Row, 1967, and David Schoenbrun, *Vietnam: How We Got in It, How to Get Out*, New York, Atheneum, 1968, particularly pp. 3-78, for narrative accounts of the war, particularly in North Vietnam; see also Lawrence C. Petrowski, "Law and the Conduct of the Vietnam War," prepared for the Civil War Panel of the American Society of International Law, Part IV. See also Jean J. S. Salmon, "Violations du Droit de la Guerre par les Etats-Unis d'Amérique," a paper prepared for the Conference of the International Council of Jurists, Grenoble, 1968, and Henri Meyrowitz, "The Law of War in the Vietnamese Conflict," Part IV. See also *Crimes de guerre Américains au Vietnam*, Institut des Sciences Juridiques, Hanoi, n.d.

tarian rules evolved to restrain governments in periods of war. These rules were not formulated by idealistic reformers. The content of the laws of war, on the contrary, represent the hardcore, basic wisdom of practical men of affairs and statesmen trained to uphold the best interests of their particular countries. Therefore it seems to be a serious cause of concern that the United States Government has been led to conduct the war in Vietnam in such flagrant and comprehensive disregard of these rules of restraint. The role of international law in this area is very much connected with giving legal authority to fundamental principles of decency.

The second main category of issues arises directly from the conclusion that a counterguerrilla strategy rests on the sustained violation of the rules of warfare. It goes beyond the assertion that counterguerrilla tactics produce a series of specific violations of particular rules of war. The contention is that the only combat strategy available to the counterguerrilla faction, if the war is popularly based and has grown to a certain scale of magnitude, is to destroy large sections of the population of the society wherein the struggle is taking place. That is, the roots of insurgency sink so deeply into the society experiencing the struggle that they can be torn out of that society only through its substantial destruction. This view of the cumulative legal effect of the United States role in the Vietnam war, especially its role after 1965, suggests a conclusion of an entirely new legal magnitude. That is that the cumulative effect of counterguerrilla warfare is necessarily barbaric and inhumane to such an extent as to taint the entire effort with a genocidal quality.[40]

This line of argument does not ignore the fact that the NLF at early stages of the Vietnam War engaged in terrorist tactics often directed against civilian targets. I would suggest, however, that the insurgent faction in an underdeveloped country has, at the beginning of its struggle for power, no alternative other than terror to mobilize an effective operation. Wherever there is insurgency there is likely to be terror of this sort, whether it be South Africa or South Vietnam. An important element of differentiation is that insurgent terror tends to be discriminating in its application and to involve relatively small num-

[40] For a clarification of the conception of genocide in the Vietnam setting see note 52. The most complete accusation of genocide available is contained in the proceedings of the Russell Tribunal. See *Tribunal Russell*, Paris, Gallimard, 1968, Vol. II, pp. 312-39, 349-68; see also the separate declaration of Stokely Carmichael, pp. 370-71.

bers of victims. In contrast, the terroristic tactics of the regime and its supporters tend, as the conflict increases, to become increasingly indiscriminate and to affect larger and larger numbers of victims, most of whom must be presumed innocent of belligerent participation. A relatively isolated incumbent regime is gradually forced into the position of waging war against its own population, the weakness of the regime being disguised by the receipt of external military assistance. The foreign state becomes the critical adversary of the revolutionary faction, and the war takes on the character of a war of national defense, enlisting all patriotic energies against foreign domination. Such a sequence has been manifest in the Vietnam war, and has been most recently dramatized by the formation in April 1968 of the Alliance of National, Democratic, and Peace Forces whose leadership is drawn from conservative, upper-middle-class circles in the cities of Saigon and Hué.[41] The April Manifesto of the Alliance disclosed the agreement of this non-Communist coalition group with many of the objectives of the NLF, and most especially with the effort to secure the withdrawal of foreign armed forces from Vietnam.

We are faced, then, with the general question of the extent to which a major counterguerrilla effort can be generated in opposition to a well organized insurgency without violating the minimal rules of legal and moral restraint. The necessity of excluding these minimal rules is bound to have a brutalizing impact upon those who conduct such a war. It is also bound to result in domestic spillovers, especially to the extent that those who are conscripted into the counterguerrilla effort are themselves aggrieved members of a minority in their own society. It is worth recalling that the Algerian war of independence was initiated shortly after conscripts returned to Algeria from periods of service on behalf of the French in the first Indo-China war. It seems clear that learning how to fight against an insurgency also involves learning how to create and sustain a successful insurgency. Therefore, to send a conscripted army from the United States to fight in Vietnam poses something of a threat to our own domestic tranquility. It is no accident, I suppose, that various escalations of United States participation in the Vietnam war have been accompanied by parallel escalations of militancy on the part of ghetto leaders in the United States. The oppo-

---

[41] For some discussion of the Alliance see Falk. "A Vietnam Settlement: The View from Hanoi," Center of International Studies, Princeton University, Policy Memorandum No. 34, 1968.

nents of the established order in the United States, whether black militants or the New Left, have increasingly seen themselves as domestic homologues to the NLF; hence the symbolic act of carrying the NLF flag and the cult of admiration for the efforts of the NLF.

5. *The Tonkin Arguments*: There has been a growing debate about the degree to which the executive branch has complied with constitutional procedures in the course of making and increasing the commitment to use armed forces in Vietnam.[42] We are dealing here with a fundamental question about the separation of powers idea in the setting of war and peace. There has been a legislative tendency to defer to the executive branch whenever matters of foreign policy seemed to be involved. Courts, in particular, have used language suggesting that the making and conduct of foreign policy is a matter of executive discretion and therefore not susceptible to legal appreciation. The Congress, on the other hand, has tended to feel that the executive branch is in a better position to appreciate the national security requirements of the United States in periods of emergency and has deferred to the president as commander-in-chief of the armed forces, especially in time of war. We have grown accustomed to the idea that the president exercises extraordinary powers during a period of war.

The Vietnam War illustrates, I think, that we need to rethink very fundamentally the whole conception of separation of powers in the context of legislative and executive responsibilities for the waging and authorizing of force in foreign lands. It is one thing to give the president the authority to respond to emergency situations in which there is no time available for useful consultation with the legislative branch. In this respect, it might seem desirable to affirm the sort of executive authority, extreme though it was, exercised in the context of the Cuban missile crisis in 1962.[43] The Cuban missile crisis demanded an immediate response based on a very close appreciation of a mass of factual information, much of it secret and technical. However, in the

[42] The most complete analysis of these issues presently available is Lawrence R. Velvel, "The War in Vietnam: Unconstitutional, Justiciable, and Jurisdictionally Attackable," Part V; see also I. F. Stone, "International Law and the Tonkin Bay Incidents," in Marcus G. Raskin and Bernard B. Fall, eds., *The Viet-Nam Reader*, New York, Vintage, 1965, pp. 307-15; I. F. Stone, "McNamara and Tonkin Bay: The Unanswered Questions," *New York Review of Books*, March 28, 1968, pp. 5-12.

[43] See Elie Abel, *The Missile Crisis*, New York, J. B. Lippincott Co., 1966; Albert and Roberta Wohlstetter, "Controlling the Risks in Cuba," in Linda B. Miller, ed., *Dynamics of World Politics*, Englewood Cliffs, N.J., Prentice Hall, 1968, pp. 62-95. From a more juridical perspective see Neill H. Alford, Jr., "The Cuban Quarantine of 1962: An Inquiry into Paradox and Persuasion," 4 *Virginia Journal of International Law*, 35-72 (1964).

setting of the Vietnam War, the Senate has been effectively excluded from meaningful participation in the policy-forming process. The choice between a declaration of war and doing nothing appears too rigid in view of the policy consequences of either established alternative. There is, it seems clear, a need to find procedures that enable effective legislative participation in the evolution of executive policy that involves the waging of war in a foreign country. The present level of legislative participation involving mainly the power to disapprove budgetary recommendations and withhold appropriations from the executive is very inadequate. The typical congressional perception of this choice is one of withholding support from Americans on the battlefield confronted with threats directed at their lives. There is in this sense no real determination as to whether the waging of the war is itself in the interests of the United States. In addition, the role of Congress, especially the Senate, has been confined to debating with the executive branch through the device of widely publicized Senate Hearings, most particularly those conducted by Senator Fulbright as Chairman of the Senate Foreign Relations Committee.[44] Even this role, small as it is, has had a significant bearing on establishing a climate of opinion about the war in the United States: the depth and generality of opposition has become more and more pronounced and has solicited the participation of very responsible elements of the community. This kind of role for the Senate was largely a consequence of the fact that Senator Fulbright, with his enormous prestige, happened to be a strong opponent of the war. Such a fortuitous legislative circumstance does not seem adequately to preserve the possibility of establishing constructive legislative participation in the development of a war policy on behalf of the country. Therefore, it would seem that there does exist a need for a significant constitutional modification that aims to make the role of Congress, particularly the Senate, meaningful at early stages of a national commitment to use forces in foreign lands.

It would seem clear that a first step in this direction would be to establish some kind of presidential commission of the sort that has investigated other major unresolved problems of the society. This commission, perhaps modeled on the National Advisory Commission on Civil Disorders,[45] could study this question of legislative-executive rela-

44 "U.S. Commitments to Foreign Powers," Senate Foreign Relations Committee Hearings, 90th Cong., 1st sess. (1967); see also references cited in note 42.

45 See *Report of the National Advisory Commission on Civil Disorders*, New York, Bantam, 1968.

tions in a period of war and come forth with a set of recommendations as to how these relations might be reconstituted for the future.

There should also be parallel investigation of the relationships between the courts and the executive and the courts and legislature with respect to problems of war and peace. In this latter context, it would also be necessary to reappraise the political-question doctrine that has so far insulated from judicial appraisal most executive action in the area of foreign policy. Again, it is important to note that most of the thinking underlying the grant of broad discretion to the president in matters of foreign policy antedated serious efforts to outlaw nondefensive warfare.

This call for a reexamination of the conception of separation of powers in the war-peace area is prompted by the conviction that we need more effective procedures for regulating national policy. Such a need flows from the urgency of bringing law to bear on governmental behavior in the nuclear age when the margin of error tolerable by even a powerful country has grown very small.[46] There is also, it seems to me, a need demonstrated by the Vietnam War to make law a more significant strategy for the assertion of restraint within domestic structure whenever the government, or a part of it, has made commitments to use force abroad in a manner that arouses large-scale opposition, including moral and legal objection, in American society. The broad constitutional issue at stake involves the extent to which the United States can make democratic ideology meaningful for the real issues of the age by providing machinery and procedures whereby Americans can register legal objection in matters affecting their vital interests. It may not be possible or even desirable to determine foreign policy by the results of public-opinion polls, but it does seem desirable, except in situations of true emergency, to erode the tradition of executive discretion that has grown up over the years. There is, accordingly, a need to promote effective legislative and judicial review of executive policies involving the use of force in international society. The weight of per-

[46] The consequences of miscalculation in the area of war and peace have become so great that any additional source of restraint on governmental discretion seems constructive. Such a position runs contrary to the thought underlying deterrence theory, which seeks to discourage extreme provocation by credibly threatening unrestrained response. Given the terrible consequence of nuclear devastation it seems persuasive to me that the need to demonstrate a credible deterrence posture has been greatly exaggerated. In contrast, the dangers associated with unrestraint have been greatly understated. The effort to strengthen the world legal order by containing foreign policy within a legal framework is an effort to reduce somewhat these dangers of unrestraint.

suasion suggests that these executive policies should be subjected to far greater constitutional restraint in the future than they have been in the past.

The Vietnam War has itself, of course, given rise to extended arguments about the constitutionality of the American involvement and the legal basis upon which it rests. First, it has been contended that the United States is involved in an undeclared war and that the failure of the executive branch to secure a declaration of war is itself a violation of constitutional expectations. The argument here rests on the notion that the Gulf of Tonkin resolution does not amount either to a declaration of war or to a legislative authorization for a war of the magnitude waged after August 1964, when the resolution was initially adopted. The executive failure, in other words, to obtain a declaration of war is the allegedly unconstitutional act. In opposition to this claim, it can be contended with considerable persuasiveness that a declaration of war might have expanded the war without putting a brake on executive discretion. The presupposition of this argument is that if the executive had sought and received congressional authority to wage war against North Vietnam, then the theretofore limited character of objectives, and means used to obtain those objectives, would have been almost impossible to maintain. A domestic-war psychology would have taken hold in the country transforming dissent into treason or quasi-treason. The president might well have sought and received emergency powers. The war aims of the United States would probably have been expanded. A declaration of war probably would have ended the search for a negotiating settlement on reasonably favorable terms and replaced this search with a determination to win the war by obtaining the collapse or surrender of the National Liberation Front and North Vietnam. An official declaration of war against North Vietnam might also have activated whatever tacit or secret collective security arrangements exist between Communist countries, with the consequence of widening the war to include either or both the Soviet Union and China as active belligerents.[47] Therefore, it is plausible to argue that a declaration of war by the United States might have risked the initiation of World War III without even having established any legislative power of restraint over the exercise of presidential powers. The president did,

[47] In continuing compliance with the Geneva Accords of 1954, North Vietnam is not, so far as is known, a party to any formal arrangement of collective security with foreign states. See especially Article 19 of the Agreement on the Cessation of Hostilities in Vietnam, in *The Vietnam War*, p. 550.

it seems plain, have sufficient legislative backing for the Vietnam policies to obtain a declaration of war at virtually any stage of the Vietnam War, at least up to the presidential reversal of stance on March 31, 1968. The power of Congress to declare war would not, it is evident, provide the restraining check on the exercise of executive power that this monograph contends to be necessary.

It does not seem very prudent, in view of this analysis, to argue strongly that the war is unconstitutional simply because there has been a failure to declare war against North Vietnam. And the law has evolved a broad acquiescence in the power of the president to commit the country to the use of force in time of peace. This power, however, has never been tested in circumstances in which it has been alleged that the use of force violates international treaties to which the United States is a party. It is one thing to affirm the power of the president to order the use of force without a declaration of war; it is quite another thing to suggest that this power can be exercised in violation of international law. The former problem needs to be dealt with by the invention of procedures for legislative participation other than a declaration of war, whereas the latter is a more general issue of bringing international law to bear on the policies of government.

There is a second line of argument contending that the Gulf of Tonkin resolution was obtained by deception and that, at most, it indicated congressional authorization of the executive policy in Vietnam up through 1964. The Tonkin setting was a limited one created by the alleged attack by North Vietnamese patrol boats on two American destroyers that were officially described as operating in a peaceful and normal manner on the high seas. The reprisal raids directed against the ports in North Vietnam used by the torpedo boats seemed to be a limited, if disproportionate, act. The setting and language used in the Tonkin resolution does not vindicate the major war effort against North Vietnam that was initiated in February 1965, an effort that has eventually expanded to involve upward of 550,000 American soldiers in Vietnam and to include persistent, widespread bombing of North Vietnam. The Vietnam War since 1965 seems so different from the Tonkin context that there is no real ground for drawing the conclusion that legislative authorization was given in the Tonkin resolution for subsequent war policies of the executive in Vietnam.

The point here is that the Senate did not by the Tonkin resolution authorize subsequent executive policy. This point is rather important because of the effort of the executive to rely on the Tonkin resolution in response to critics in the Senate, especially those who alleged a failure to secure adequate legislative authorization for carrying the Vietnam War to its later stages. I would think that it would have been possible to draw up a presentment of impeachment against the president that relied upon the misuse of the Tonkin resolution, including the impropriety of using the resolution to satisfy the requirements for the balance of power between coordinate branches of government within the United States.

The third and final aspect of the Tonkin argument concerns deception that appears to have surrounded the reporting of the Tonkin incident itself and its presentation to the Senate. There is evidence, originally brought to public attention largely by the columnist I. F. Stone, and later confirmed in Senate hearings held during February 1968, that suggests that the executive branch distorted the Tonkin incident to secure from the Senate the authorization it received for a war build-up.[48] In particular, the aggressiveness of the North Vietnamese torpedo boats was exaggerated, the innocence of the American naval vessels was asserted in a manner that obscured their military role, and there was a failure to disclose the rising executive branch intention, independent of the Tonkin incident, to extend the war to North Vietnam. There was some indication that the executive branch sought an incident of this kind, maybe even to the extent of provoking it, to secure an adequate political pretext that might serve to justify an expansion of the war to North Vietnamese territory. In this context, then, the main argument bears on the misleading way the executive dealt with the Senate. The effect of this alleged deception was substantially to discredit whatever authorization was given the executive by the Tonkin resolution, as well as to establish some basis for charging the executive branch with a separate abuse of its relations with Congress. Here, too, in any strong indictment of the executive management of the war a heavy stress might be expected to be made upon the ways in which Congress was misled, either by an intentional desire to mislead or by a negligent failure to disclose. The emphasis on this level of insufficient communication between the executive and the legislature is justified to some degree by the failure of the executive to clarify the misunderstandings that appear to have emerged in the Tonkin context. It was only as a result of the probing criticism belabored over a period of years by certain Senate and other critics of the war that a reexamination of the facts and

[48] See reference cited in note 42, especially Velvel, at note 38, p. 454.

explanations underlying the Tonkin grant of legislative authorization took place.

The Tonkin arguments form part of the domestic legal context. These arguments are concerned with the extent to which the executive branch respected constitutional procedures in evolving national policies throughout the period of United States involvement in the Vietnam War. The deeper question raised at the outset of this section was whether the constitution itself needs to be reformed to provide for more constructive forms of legislative participation in American foreign policy-making than is presently possible in the area of war and peace. It does not appear desirable to confront the executive branch with the polar options of either declaring war or being completely at liberty to wage war at any level of violence without securing any direct legislative authorization. The policy issue is a broad and deep one and extends to the whole problem of defining legislative responsibility as well as legislative authority in the war-peace area. This kind of definition—or redefinition—would help strengthen domestic pressures growing in support of a more law-ordered foreign policy. Much of the concern with the legal dimension of the Vietnam War involves demonstrating the extent to which war policies affecting the security of the nation and its people are now evolved in a manner that did not assure much attention to counterbalancing forces implicit in the separation-of-powers doctrine that lies at the foundation of the American system of constitutional government.

There is also the question as to whether the president of the United States and, less directly, the coordinate branches of the government, are constitutionally empowered to pursue foreign policy in violation of international legal obligations. It should be remembered that the treaty rules to which the United States is subject form part of the supreme law of the land. It should also be remembered that domestic courts are normally expected to apply international law whenever it is relevant to domestic litigation, although if a federal statute is found in conflict with an international treaty, courts have held it to be their duty to apply the more recently incurred obligation. The broad constitutional point here is that it would seem that the president and his leaders are acting unconstitutionally to the extent that they are guilty of a foreign policy that violates the legal obligations to which the United States has given its formal assent. It may be quite reasonable to confer considerable discretion on the executive with respect to interpreting these legal obligations, especially in periods of emergency and urgency, but there seems very little justification in either policy or more formal terms for exempting the executive altogether from this framework of restraint. It is true that any framework of restraint may tend to hamper the discretion and flexibility of executive policy. But restraint is the purpose of all law, and it is certainly the cornerstone of any government that prides itself on being "a government of laws, not men." Legal order is a failure to the extent that it doesn't hamper flexibility. The underlying argument for establishing an effective system of world law is convincing precisely because unhampered national flexibility does not sufficiently assure the survival or welfare of the human race, nor does it give other societies the security they need. The argument that legal restraint is an encumbrance on the discharge of executive functions is always advanced in times of crisis and tension. During the Great Depression of the 1930's in the United States, the argument was often made on behalf of the New Deal administration that the Supreme Court was a serious inconvenience to the country in a period of dire emergency. It seems clear that the Supreme Court was an obstacle in the way of increasingly popular executive responses to the problems of national economic crisis. Efforts were made to undermine the authority of the Supreme Court so as to nullify legislative acts. The notorious court-packing plan of the 1930's was conceived to assure that a majority of New Deal judges would be appointed to the Court, and was narrowly defeated in Congress. In retrospect, it appears that the strength of the constitutional system was demonstrated by the very inconvenience the executive and the public endured as a consequence of judicial obstruction. This affirmation of an experience of constitutional restraint is particularly impressive because the New Deal experiment is looked back upon as very successful, whereas the Court's role is understood as largely reactionary and negative.

In the setting of the Vietnam War, by contrast, the executive is widely held responsible for fostering a regressive kind of policy orientation. In this setting the case is even more persuasive that action by legislative and judicial organs to inconvenience the executive might have worked out to national advantage. For the future, therefore, it seems clear that there is a need to establish a strong basis for implementing this international framework of restraint within the structure of national society; to reach this goal we need to bring the claims asserted on behalf of international law effectively to bear on executive action. This requires, as I have said, new modes of legislative participation that establish new conceptions of legislative authority and responsibility;

such a revision also demands a repudiation of the political-questions doctrine that has traditionally insulated executive policy in the war-peace area from judicial review. It now seems desirable to allow questions of executive policy to come before the courts as part of a wider effort to bring law effectively to bear on a government's action with regard to war-peace issues.[49]

6. *The Nuremberg Arguments*: These legal issues arise from the experience after World War II, at which time leaders of Germany and Japan were held individually accountable for inciting and waging an aggressive war and for specific war crimes. These determinations by duly constituted tribunals were significant because they clearly depended on an acceptance of the legal principle that an individual is not excused from complying with obligations under international law because he is acting in response to superior orders given him by his national government. The war-crimes tribunals, most notably the Nuremberg Tribunal, were exclusively concerned with defendants who occupied positions of leadership and responsibility in the state apparatus. However, the wider logic of Nuremberg extends to embrace all those who knowingly, at any rate, participate in a war effort they have reason to believe violates the restraints of international law. The degree of complicity with such an aggressive war effort needed to establish criminal responsibility has never been established authoritatively. On the other hand, there is no denial of the potential criminal responsibility of individuals other than leaders who participate in an aggressive war. This whole web of connection joining individual responsibility, national citizenship, and responsibility to impose the legal restraints on the use of force on nation-states enjoys a confused and indefinite status at the present time. It is for this reason essential that both scholars and tribunals attempt to clarify the effect of international law on individual responsibility with respect to participating in a war that is or is believed to be in violation of minimum constraints on the use of force.

Two central branches of the Nuremberg argument can be briefly mentioned. The first branch of the argument refers to the prosecution of governmental leaders for war crimes. By war crimes in this context, I have in mind three different categories of potential offenses that appear relevant to the Vietnam context. First, what are called "crimes

[49] The right of a citizen to obtain a judicial determination would be an important additional basis for securing governmental compliance with the rules and standards of international law. Such a right would complement other recommended steps to assure an increased role for international law in the foreign policy-making process.

against the peace"; namely, the contention that leaders in the United States and South Vietnam are responsible for the commission of aggression against North Vietnam subsequent to February 1965. This argument rests on the assumption that prior support given by the North Vietnamese to the National Liberation Front did not amount to an armed attack that might have legally justified recourse to action in self-defense against North Vietnam. As a consequence, the United States attack upon North Vietnam amounted to an armed attack on that territory of such magnitude that it should be viewed as aggressive war of the most serious variety. Second, what are called "war crimes," namely, the allegation that some of the battlefield tactics relied upon by the American, South Vietnamese, and other allied forces involve the systematic commission of specific war crimes. The very existence of a pattern of battlefield behavior incompatible with legal restraint establishes a kind of responsibility that could be imposed on either the military or civilian leadership of the country. Search-and-destroy missions, free bombing zones, forceable transfer of the civilian population, and mistreatment of prisoners would all appear to provide bases for criminal prosecution of the political and military leadership of counter-guerrilla forces and their allies.

The third sort of criminal charge that could be made against the leadership of the United States and South Vietnam would fall into the category called "crimes against humanity" and would involve the contention that the specific violations of the law of war have a cumulative impact that can fairly add up to genocide. That is, systematic counter-guerrilla tactics that must separate the enemy from population to achieve military victory requires the devastation of territory where the guerrilla faction exerts influence, as well as the removal of the population by transfer or death. The accounts of the Vietnam War increasingly suggest that where the guerrilla efforts of the National Liberation Front have taken hold the response of the Saigon-United States forces has been to create a kind of scorched-earth atmosphere to eliminate the guerrilla efforts. This kind of combat tactics has been partly responsible for producing over 4,000,000 South Vietnamese refugees by the beginning of 1968, in a country with a population of under 16,000,000. This drastic dislocation of the people of the country has not even led to military success. Therefore, whatever weight might be given the argument that these tactics are justified by considerations of military necessity has to be reduced by their failure to facilitate the attainment of military objectives, and by the overall failure of the

United States military effort in Vietnam. This argument that waging counterguerrilla warfare beyond a certain threshold of violence amounts to genocide[50] has been forcibly made by Jean-Paul Sartre.[51] Sartre argues that for the regime and its supporters there is no alternative to the destruction of the society and its population, where the guerrilla effort enjoys considerable popular support. Although the Russell Tribunal operated on the basis of one-sided adjudicative machinery and procedure, nevertheless it did turn up a good deal of evidence about the manner in which the war was conducted and developed persuasively some of the legal implications it seems reasonable to draw from that war.[52]

The second branch of the Nuremberg argument involves the defensive appeal to the principles of the Nuremberg judgment to avoid cooperating with the United States Government so far as participating in the war effort is concerned. There are many bases for this noncooperation that rest on rather unaugmented moral arguments that the war is wrong and therefore it is wrong to participate in the war. There are also, however, some legal arguments that seem to be increasingly seriously offered to domestic courts in the United States in various contexts. These arguments suggest various ways in which the Nurem-

[50] See *Tribunal Russell*, Vol. II, note 40, pp. 349-68.

[51] There is a common preconception that the crime of genocide occurs only when there is an effort to kill off an entire race or ethnic group in the manner of "the final solution" devised by the Nazis to eliminate the Jews. But the definition incorporated in the Genocide Convention, as approved by the United Nations General Assembly on December 9, 1948, in G.A. Res. 260 (III) is considerably broader, extending to the pursuit of policies that destroy *part* of that ethnic group. Article II of the Convention provides:

> In the present Convention genocide means any of the following acts committed with intent to destroy, in whole or in part, a national, ethnical, racial or religious group, as such:
>   a) Killing members of a group;
>   b) Causing serious bodily or mental harm to members of the group;
>   c) Deliberately inflicting on the group conditions of life calculated to bring about its physical destruction in whole or in part;
>   d) Imposing measures intended to prevent births within the group;
>   e) Forcibly transferring children of the group to another group.

For further elaboration of the Convention see Raphael Lemkin, "Genocide as a Crime Under International Law," 41 *American Journal of International Law*, 145-51 (1947).

In the Vietnam War the use of bombing tactics and cruel weapons against the civilian population appears to me to establish a *prima facie* case of genocide against the United States. By the Convention, genocide can be committed in a condition of either war or peace.

[52] The full record of proceedings is now available in a convenient French edition and warrants careful study. For citation see note 40.

berg judgment becomes relevant. First of all, the defendants may suggest that the legal standards governing the use of force with respect to both the recourse to war and the conduct of it provide an objective and externally verifiable correlative to their moral consciences. Such an attitude seems to accord with the whole tradition of just and unjust wars that has evolved over several centuries of western civilization. This tradition rests on the assumption that neither pacifism nor unqualified deference to the sovereign will follow from Christian morality. Some wars are just and other wars are unjust, and in cases of confusion it is up to the conscience of the individual to try to mediate between these two moral categories. The role of a domestic court should be to assess whether a particular assertion of individual conscience is in good faith, and whether, if it is, there exists some reasonably objective standard that can be verified by evidence external to the beliefs of the individual upon which to rest assertions of conscience. International law provides such a useful yardstick by which to measure claims of conscience. The Nuremberg conception reinforces this legal dimension of the problem by its stress on the need for individuals to find a way of determining which of two conflicting sources of obligation they are bound to uphold: obligations emanating from national governments, or obligations emanating from the perceived requirements of international law. The different ways in which the arguments about the individual's right to establish that the U.S. role in the Vietnam War is illegal have come up in domestic courts are illustrated in recent litigation: Eminente, Mitchell, Luftig, Mora, Berrigan, and Spock.[53] These cases all involve individuals who in one way or another regarded the United States involvement in the Vietnam War as unjust and felt that their individual obligations as human beings took precedence over their duty to obey the government or to respect its laws. Many of these cases arise when individuals refuse to be drafted. Cases may also arise when an individual, subsequent to induction, refuses to obey his military commander either by declining to train soldiers for activity or duty in Vietnam or by not following an order to report for duty in Vietnam. Analogous cases furthermore can arise if someone such as Dr. Spock or Rev. William Sloane Coffin counsels individuals not to co-

[53] Eminente v. Johnson, 361 F. 2d 73 (D.C. Cir. 1966), cert. den., 385 U.S. 929 (1966); Luftig v. McNamara, 373 F. 2d 664 (D.C. Cir. 1967), cert. den., sub. nom. Mora v. McNamara, 389 U.S. 934 (1967); Mitchell v. McNamara, 386 U.S. 972 (1967). See, in general, briefs submitted on behalf of Dr. Benjamin Spock and Michael Farber in U.S. v. Coffin and others, Criminal No. 68-1-F., U.S. District Court, Boston, Mass., 1968.

operate with the draft—when, in the language of the selective service statute, an individual aids and abets draft avoidance. The Spock prosecution was based on a conspiracy theory—cooperation among the defendants to counsel draft avoidance.

In these cases that have come before the domestic courts of the United States, there has been a consistent refusal to adjudicate the substantive issues posed by arguments of international law. The courts have held, with the partial exception of the Levy case, that the legality of the war and its conduct are matters beyond judicial appreciation, that these issues are embedded in foreign policy and must be taken up, if at all, within the executive branch. The Levy case, in the context of a court-martial, did permit the nominal presentation of evidence designed to show that *the conduct* of the war is illegal, although it did not consider the legality of the underlying involvement of the United States in the Vietnam War (see The Geneva and Charter arguments). The military court rejected Levy's contention of illegality and went on to find him guilty, and has sentenced him to three years in prison.

As I have observed earlier, the reassertion of an active judicial role in this area would appear to be a creative contribution to the doctrine of separation of powers in the war-peace context. It appears increasingly unfair and unfortunate to require individuals to participate in a war that by reason of conscience they object to. In addition, those who seek access to the courts in order to test the legality of the war—for instance, by refusing to pay all or part of their income taxes—are also, it would seem, entitled to a substantive determination of the issue. These citizens are, in effect, seeking to enforce the wider claims of the international community against their own government. It remains extremely important to try to reinforce this link between the individual and world society by allowing, and even requiring, domestic courts to assume an active role in the process of confining the scope of governmental action to those limits that are internationally permissible. Such a willingness to adjudicate these questions would not doom the domestic legal and political system. On the contrary, the availability of procedures to test the legality of governmental conduct is essential to the health of a system that claims to rest upon the exercise of political power within the limits set by law. The only convincing reason to refuse adjudication of such substantive issues is in order to insulate the exercise of power, however arbitrary, from serious legal challenge. To disrupt an "illegal" war, if that would be the consequence of judicial inquiry, would be to serve the national interest if adherence to law is

itself to be preferred over the arbitrary assertion of power. Such a result is unlikely to occur unless there were many other social, moral,
and political forces opposing the course of involvement in a war. Of
course, it is likely that there would be military and industrial leaders
and others who would bitterly oppose any judicial pronouncement that
might inhibit the continuation of an "illegal" war, but there would
always be groups unwilling to govern in accordance with a framework of legal restraint. This monograph is essentially a proposal that
the risks of law and order be taken in world affairs as surely as they
are taken for granted in domestic affairs.

Conclusion

The Vietnam War has demonstrated the vulnerability of the United
States political system to a prolonged involvement in a foreign conflict
perceived as illegal by a significant segment of the population. It
seems important to learn from this experience and to discourage its
repetition. The constitutional process needs reform and reorientation
in the area of war and peace. In the executive branch, it appears important, as we have suggested, to introduce the guidance of law earlier
in the policy-forming process and from a position higher in the bureaucratic structure.

The underlying integrity of the constitutional system of the United
States depends on the continuous implementation of the idea of a
separation of powers among the three principal branches of government. The Vietnam War has demonstrated persuasively that this balancing process of government, resting on the notion of separated and
divided powers, is no longer operating successfully in the area of war
and peace. For this reason it seems very important to reconsider ways in
which the legislative branch can participate more fully in the evolution and authorization of foreign policy involving the use of force. It
would not contribute to a solution of this problem to define more rigorously the conditions under which the use of force by the government
must be preceded by or accompanied by a declaration of war. There
may be a need for joint commissions of inquiry and periodic authorizations and review procedures that would raise questions about the
continuation of any particular use of force when the international
community had not itself provided the nation with either a prohibition or an authorization. Part of the position taken in this monograph is
that individuals need to be provided with legal procedures to uphold
dictates of conscience when these dictates collide with the will of the

government. For this reason there should exist some opportunity to challenge various obligations to participate in a war deemed unjust and illegal, through recourse to courts. Additionally, it is important that judges become persuaded of their competence and responsibility to restrain the execution of government policy by either executive or legislative institutions if such policy is found to exceed the boundaries set by international law.[54] The Vietnam War has given rise to an expression of widespread cosmopolitan attachments in the sense that many American citizens have felt it more important to uphold international obligations involving restraints on the use of force than to support their own national government in its pursuit of policy.[55] In effect, we may be witnessing a redefinition of the meaning of citizenship in the contemporary world, a redefinition in which the priorities of a citizen are reshaped in such a way as to ensure popular insistence upon the maintenance of a framework of restraint for his own government.[56] Such a development would be very encouraging. It would provide a way in which the sovereign state might be curbed, or at least inhibited, in the use of its military power by action taken within its own political structure. Such efforts, leading to restraint imposed from within, might create the sort of climate that would support transfers of sovereign authority from the national level to the regional and global levels and help the international community build more centralized structures of control over the affairs of state.

In moving toward the end of the Vietnam War, it seems important to reorient American foreign policy in a direction that avoids either the pseudo-globalism of neo-Wilsonism or the qualified isolationism of neo-Kennanism.[57] By neo-Wilsonism I intend to refer to the policies that have been associated especially with Dean Rusk and W. W. Rostow throughout the Vietnam War.[58] These policies suggest that the

[54] Such a view is endorsed by the most conservative elements of the legal community when the question in controversy is whether the foreign expropriation of alien property conforms with international law. See any of the extensive literature associated with the Sabbatino controversy. E.g., Eugene F. Mooney, *Foreign Seizures—Sabbatino and the Act of State Doctrine*, University of Kentucky Press, 1967; see esp. Bibliography, pp. 161-64.

[55] These attachments are "cosmopolitan" in the sense that they reflect the acceptance of universal standards and procedures impartially construed. At the same time such attachments are "nationalistic" in the sense of favoring a course of action that is in the best interest of the state given the belief that national adherence to law in foreign affairs promotes national security in the nuclear age.

[56] For fuller discussion see Chapter 23 in Falk, *The Status of Law in International Society*, to be published by Princeton University Press in 1969.

[57] Fuller discussion, *ibid.*, Chapter 22.

[58] For the specification of the Wilsonian ideas of national self-interest in world affairs

United States has a unilateral responsibility and prerogative to establish ideologically self-serving global rules of order as part of its mission to bring into being a peaceful world. It is the unilateral quality of the partisan political use of force that appears to be the most objectionable formal feature of neo-Wilsonism. It is also somewhat doubtful whether the United States is in any position to exercise moral leadership within an international setting so long as its own society is subject to such great discord and distress. Therefore, it does not seem appropriate for the United States to act against what it perceives to be aggression except in situations where there has been a direct military attack mounted across an international boundary of the Korean type or in situations where international institutions have genuinely authorized the use of defensive force.

Neo-Kennanism, in contrast, is a reaction against moralistic and legalistic rhetoric that one often finds associated with the neo-Wilsonian position. A neo-Kennanist argues that it is important to remove self-serving rationalizations of foreign policy and examine in each situation the real national interests of the United States in a more detached fashion. It would seem clear that when this neo-Kennanist perspective is allowed to operate, the United States has very few interests of the traditional sovereign sort that would warrant the use of military force outside the western hemisphere or in the defense of Europe. Therefore, neo-Kennanism leads to or implies a partial withdrawal from participation in world affairs. Senator Fulbright has been the most prominent advocate of a neo-Kennanist position, along with George Kennan himself.[59]

The inadequacy I find with the neo-Kennanist position—although I find much of it persuasive in its role as a criticism of the neo-Wilsonist pretensions—is that the quality of international society at present is such that it would be undesirable for the United States to withdraw to a position of defending only its immediate and generally perceivable interests. In fact, there is a need for American foreign policy to find a new normative foundation for the assertion of influence and military power throughout the world to replace the present combination of ideological resistance to Communism and geopolitical resistance to the expansion of the Soviet and Chinese spheres of influence. The Viet-

---

see Arno J. Mayer, *Wilson v. Lenin—Political Origins of the New Diplomacy 1917-1918*, New Haven, Yale University Press, 1959; N. Gordon Levin, Jr., *Woodrow Wilson and World Politics*, New York, Oxford University Press, 1968.

[59] E.g., J. William Fulbright, *The Arrogance of Power*, New York, Vintage, 1966.

nam War represents, it seems to me, the culmination and the termination of a tradition of foreign policy based on these considerations of ideology and geopolitics. This normative foundation should embody a world-order orientation—one that is sensitive to regional and world-community procedures for authorizing collective measures and that defines permissible recourse to international force by reference to treaty standards of prohibition directed at intervention in internal affairs and at nondefensive recourses to military action. I think that it is probably possible to conclude that direct military aggression of the type used in Korea is unlikely to be repeated in the context of east-west relations in the foreseeable future. However, it is equally plausible to anticipate considerable revolutionary violence throughout Asia and Africa that will bear on the relative degree of influence possessed by these competing centers of world power and guidance. The United States has played a largely counterrevolutionary role in world society since World War II, beginning in Greece and Turkey with the Truman Doctrine and culminating in its major involvement in the Vietnam War. The original basis for a counterrevolutionary posture was created by a very expansionist mood on the part of Stalinist Russia immediately after World War II, a mood that caused concern because of the weakness of the western European countries during that period. This weakness was made more serious both because of the apparent unity of the world Communist parties and because of large internal Communist parties in France and Italy. The Soviet Union's relation to eastern Europe is also counterrevolutionary, reaching a new high-water mark through its leadership of the anti-Dubcek intervention in Czechoslovakia in August of 1968.

The United States needs a new foreign policy to deal with revolutionary violence, a foreign policy that avoids unilateral military commitments to the constituted governments of other countries, especially when those governments are themselves imposed by external political forces on a society that is not susceptible to governance by such a regime. These sorts of conflicts should be left alone by the United States. The exception should involve occasions on which the host government appeals through an international institution for external military support and that appeal is endorsed by that institution. Even this kind of procedure is not secure against abuse. It is quite possible for the political vagaries of international organizations to produce legitimacy on behalf of a government that is oppressing its population by terroristic means. Despite this danger, however, it seems clearly preferable to risk the uncertainties of supranational consensus than to rest world order upon the claim of special imperial prerogatives by the United States or any other sovereign state.[60] It has become evident, in any event, that the domestic political system of the United States is not able to sustain support for such a foreign policy without forfeiting both order and liberty within its domestic setting.[61] It should also be clear that the United States military capability is not suited to waging successfully this kind of counterguerrilla struggle when the scale of the undertaking is substantial. International lawyers could have a major role to play by clarifying the consequences to the world of the choices that can be made with respect to foreign policy in the future. These choices can be highlighted by a careful analysis of the policy implications of the opposing sets of legal arguments that have been raised in the Vietnam War. These arguments suggest some of the problems that exist as a result of a legal superstructure's being designed for a world that had neither nuclear weapons nor large-scale and widespread revolutionary violence. It seems important in light of these developments in military technology and in the pursuit of domestic political objectives to re-think the legal basis for controlling violence in situations such as the Vietnam War. A central function of law is to help structure the expectations of national governments and their populations. This is a time when it is important to try to restructure expectations about what is permissible and impermissible in the context of a category of conflict of which the Vietnam War is the most prominent instance to date. Such a restructuring of legal expectations demands not only the assessment of the legal standards governing national behavior, but—even more importantly—a sense of how the procedures of national governments and international institutions may bring these standards to bear more effectively both throughout such a conflict and at pre-violent stages of conflict.

[60] For some consideration see George Liska, *Imperial America—The International Politics of Primacy*, Baltimore, Johns Hopkins Press, 1967; Ronald Steel, *Pax Americana*, New York, Viking Press, 1967.

[61] It is worth noting that Soviet citizens are reported to have demonstrated in Moscow against the Soviet military intervention in Czechoslovakia during August 1968. Although the demonstration is reported to have been quickly suppressed, the principal participants made defiant statements after their release. Domestic pressures against the excesses of one's own government appear to be growing throughout those national societies that have been modernized, although the right of opposition continues to be severely curtailed in many principal states of the world. For a brief account of the Soviet demonstration see *New York Times*, September 1, 1968, Sec. IV, p. 3.

The Vietnam Conflict and International Law

JARO MAYDA

I

AMONG the new dimensions which the strange and frustrating warfare in Vietnam has projected into various departments of contemporary government and society, not the least is the fierce public polemic about the legality or illegality of United States participation in the conflict.

There is, I believe, nothing comparable on record in the history of international law. Not even the discussion of the Nuremberg trials of war criminals after the Second World War comes anywhere close in scope and intensity. The polemic started in the United States in 1965. Since then it has developed in many other countries. Everybody who has felt the urge, seemed to know enough about international law to refer to it.

It would be understandable, though still distressing, if well-meaning persons with strong moral opinions but not enough information tried to strengthen their argument with rhetoric from international law. It is, after all, not uncomfortable to have such evidence of the continuing emotional appeal which international law exercises, even if law and legality are values too vital to all of us to be taken in vain.

The illustrious examples of this kind of argumentation range from the American historian Henry Steele Commager to the Finnish logician K. Von Wright, to the Soviet poet Yevzheny Yevtushenko.

On another level, a captured United States pilot in North Vietnam was quoted (and it does not necessarily sound like a fabrication) as saying that "[many] aspects of this war are illegal as specified by the *Geneva agreements* of 1954" (Associated Press, September 17, 1966). On the appeal of a draft evasion case in a federal court in New York City (November 8, 1966) Attorney Marc Lane (of Harvey Oswald fame) urged a retrial with jury so that it "be permitted to hear evidence regarding the *treaty* obligations of this country and the manner in which they are being violated in Vietnam." (Emphasis added)

The collective mood of this group was summarized as recently as in March 1968 when the magazine *Time* ended the review of a new book on *Law and Vietnam* (by Roger Hull and John Novgorod) with the words "the [conclusions] will surprise many people, including lawyers, who sincerely consider the war not only immoral but illegal as well."

But the polemic has to me two much more important and distressing aspects.

One is the deep split among *international* lawyers, including American professors such as Bishop (Michigan), McDougal (Yale), Baxter and Sohn (Harvard), and Goldstein (Texas), all in favor of legality; and on the opposite side Falk (Princeton), Morgenthau (Chicago), Quincy Wright, and others.

The other aspect is the general thrust and quality of the arguments on both sides, revealing the defects in the structure and methodology of contemporary international law as a viable instrument of policy and order.

On this occasion I'll limit myself to a general survey and critique of the United States debate (1965–67) as reflected in the major representative statements of both points of view.[1-6] I'll limit myself to the international legal aspects, leaving aside the parallel debate on the powers of the President under the United States Constitution, related to the Vietnam conflict. Except for a few personalized remarks at the end, I shall also leave out the general worldwide discussion. Although it has been frequently couched in international legal terms—and quite categorical at that—it really deals with political-military or ethical aspects of the conflict.

II

The opening salvo in the legal debate was a Memorandum of Law on "American Policy vis-à-vis Vietnam, in Light of Our Constitution, the United Nations Charter, the 1954 Geneva Accords and the South-East Asia Collective Defense Treaty." Prepared by the Lawyers' Committee on American Policy toward Vietnam, it was introduced into the Congressional Record by Senator Wayne Morse (Oregon) on September 23, 1965 with a speech in which he said among other "in Vietnam, we have totally flouted the rule of law, and . . . the United Nations Charter. This lip service given by the United States to . . . international law and procedures has done our country great injury among many international lawyers around the world."[1]

The Memorandum is on the order of 12,500 words of text and footnotes. The international legal criticism centers on three points:

[1-6] The notes refer to the numbered books listed in a Working Bibliography at the end of this chapter.

First, that the United States participation in the Vietnam conflict is an intervention in a civil strife.

Second, that it violates obligations the United States assumed under the 1954 Geneva truce agreements.

Third, that the alleged collective self-defense action under the SEATO violates Articles 51 and 53 of the U.N. Charter.

The principal counterarguments—that the U.S. participation in the Vietnam conflict is lawful—are contained in two documents: a memorandum by the Legal Adviser of the U.S. Department of State (March 4, 1966),[2] and a study produced at the Yale Law School (May 1966).[3]

The first is an artless brief the importance of which lies largely in its official standing. The second is a much more substantial document. It makes, I believe independently, several points that are parallel with my first reaction to the Memorandum of the Lawyers' Committee.[7] But it suffers somewhat from its polemic nature. This fact has imposed on it dialectic confines similar to the lawyers' memorandum.

To put these arguments and counterarguments into perspective, it is necessary to analyze them together with the relevant facts, some of them apparently forgotten or not generally known—although I will limit myself, partly on purpose, to information which can be obtained from such publicly accessible sources as the index of the *New York Times*.

III

The proposition that the United States presence in Vietnam is an intervention, since the conflict is not an international war but a civil strife is based on the conclusion that the 1954 Geneva Agreements established a unified Vietnam. Consequently, it is possible to analyze this point together with the argument that the United States has generally violated these agreements.

What are the 1954 Geneva Agreements, establishing "what might be called the Geneva order for Indochina of 1954"?[8] And what is the United States position with regard to them?

The 1954 Geneva Agreements consist of three truce agreements and six unilateral declarations signed or made by France, the Vietminh, Cambodia, and Laos; of a Final Declaration to which seven of the nine participants in the conference declared *orally* their approval or non-objection; and two separate unilateral declarations, by South Vietnam and by the United States.

The United States declaration, far from being a signature of anything—only the three truce agreements between France and the Vietminh were signed instruments—rather dissociated the United States from the product of the conference, except for some well-wishing and declarations that it will not use force to disturb the established status. It is typical of the U.S. position that it did not even note—and the intent is unmistakable—the oral agreement of the seven parties and guarantors to consult on measures which might be necessary to put in force the truce agreements.

Lest there be any doubt, President Eisenhower declared on July 22, 1954, the day after the Geneva conference ended, that the United States accepts the truce as the best of bad bargains and is not (legally) bound by its terms. (This position, reflecting mistrust as to the merits of the accord, differs sharply from the full backing and signature by the United States of the definite political and legal solutions at the 1962 conference on Laos, which partly amended the 1954 Accords.)

But is the United States not bound morally and paralegally by its unilateral declaration not to use force to disturb or alter the 1954 Geneva Agreements? To try to answer this question requires that one examine the status of these agreements since their signature and declaration.

IV

There is no question about the formal existence of the 1954 documents. If this is asserted, it would only seem fair to judge the American commitment in the same terms. In these formal terms it must be declared as nonexistent. But if one wants to insist on the question of *de facto* material obligations on the part of the United States, were there at the time when the United States committed its forces in Vietnam any 1954 Geneva Agreements materially speaking? In other words, did any situation exist based on them which United States could disturb by force.[2]

The State Department and the Yale memoranda call attention to the principle of customary international law that a treaty can be terminated or suspended when the other party has breached it. It is a fact that this principle was restated in the 1966 Draft Articles on the Law of Treaties, prepared for the 1968 diplomatic conference in Vienna.

To rely on this principle requires an analogy to be drawn between a treaty and the 1954 Geneva conglomerate. That is not impossible. But the problem really reaches beyond positive principles to the very infrastructure of international law.

It is axiomatic that international law, as any legal normative system, can be and is materially effective only as long as it formalizes and stabilizes a political agreement on an order which has some life expectancy.

The material base of the legal norms and paralegal commitments established by the 1954 Geneva Agreements disintegrated virtually within weeks. A series of events which neither the guarantors nor their agent, the International Control Commission (composed of Canada, India, and Poland) made any effective attempt to stop, turned the accords into an empty letter.

The southern and northern zones of Vietnam, set up only for the purpose of truce and demilitarization, were quickly converted into separate sovereignties. Already in the autumn of 1954, both applied for separate membership in the United Nations. A year later, the Soviet Union, a cochairman of the 1954 Geneva conference, was willing to have both the State of Vietnam (South) and the Democratic Republic of Vietnam (North) admitted to the U.N. under a so-called package deal. Both states were eventually widely recognized, the South having diplomatic relations with over fifty states, the North with over twenty.

The I.C.C. failed without any audible whimper on its obligation to consult on and work toward the national elections to reunify the country. In 1956, the Saigon government repudiated the Geneva Agreements, including the provision for national elections. Its right to do so was backed by the other cochairman of the 1954 conference, Great Britain, on the ground that the agreement was signed on behalf of the zone below the 17th parallel by France, not by South Vietnam. (In fact, the election agreement was in the unsigned Final Declaration, paragraph 7, stipulating elections "in order to ensure . . . free expression of national will"—and France barred before the 1954 conference any fixed date for the elections.)

In sum, instead of a progressive stabilization of order within the framework of the 1954 Agreements, Vietnam continued an area of disorder in the search for a new equilibrium on which to create a more adequate and viable legal-constitutional structure.

Changes and new developments in the power situation were reported by James Reston of the *New York Times* as early as November 1954; in addition, he reported three divisions and receipt of Chinese matériel

by North Vietnam, in violation of the Geneva truce and demilitarization obligations. In May 1957, Presidents Eisenhower and Diem issued
a joint statement in which they called attention to "the large build-
up of . . . military forces in North Vietnam."[2] By 1962, in one of its
rare signs of life, the I.C.C. reported (Poland objecting) that North
Vietnam was guilty of "subversion and covert aggression" in South
Vietnam. While the Indian chairman of the Commission charged the
United States with "violation of the 1954 accord by giving massive support to South Vietnam," he viewed it as a reaction to the subversion
from the North.

The second major argument centers around the right of collective
defense and application of the South-East Asia Treaty of 1954, in the
light of Articles 51 and 53 of the U.N. Charter.

The words referred to in the polemic are:

Nothing in the present Charter shall impair the inherent right of
individual or collective defense if an armed attack occurs against a
Member of the United Nations, until the Security Council has taken
the measures necessary.

Article 51— . . . no endorsement action shall be taken under regional arrangements . . . without the authorization of the Security
Council.

Article 53— . . . aggression by mean of armed attack in the Treaty
area against any of the parties or against any state or territory
which the parties may . . . [unanimously] designate, would endanger [each party's] own peace and safety, and [each party] agrees that
it will in that event act to meet the common danger in accordance
with its constitutional processes. (SEAT, Article IV, paragraph 1);
[the parties will consult if] integrity of territory . . . or political independence [of a member of the designated area] . . . is threatened
in any way other than by armed attack. (*Id.*, paragraph 2.)

The main issues which have been raised in this connection deal with
the definition and applicability of the term "armed attack" in the context of Article 51; with the principle of self-defense; and with the legi-
timity of the designation party by outside powers; of South-East Asia
as a collective defense area; and the action of the United States under
SEATO.

Unfortunately, much of the argument and counterargument moves on
the level of words rather than of substance.

The question of the "title" of some SEATO signatories has been raised. The argument is in function of the geographical distance. The question whether some states have or do not have defense interests in a given area is a political question, not a legal one. In an era when a whole mechanized army could be moved from one continent to another in a matter of two or three days—as the Texas to Berlin exercise some years ago demonstrated—the geographical distance argument looks specious.

But did the United States consult with its partners under Article IV, 2 of the SEAT? This is at least a wide open question, not one to answer categorically in the negative. Is it necessary to convoke a conference to consult? When the 1961 SEATO conference on Laos noted in paragraph 7 of its communiqué "which concern the efforts of an armed minority, supported from the outside in violation of the Geneva accords, to destroy the government of [South] Vietnam" and declared "its firm resolve not to acquiesce in any such take-over of the country," did this imply consultation or not? Was consultation with all members of the SEATO possible and, under a *clausula rebus sic stantibus,* obligatory when much of diplomatic confidence in the good faith of some signatories could have been lost since 1954? (In fact the climate can be gauged with regard to another field of sensitive common action —international monetary stabilization—where one of the prominent SEATO members had to be excluded recently from confidential negotiations after it has developed the habit of tolerating damaging leaks of classified information to its own press.)

V

If the preceding points involve at least some interpretation on merit, the other critical issues—armed attack and self-defense—appear in the argument and counterargument largely as question of semantics.

At best it seems possible to say of the issue of armed attack v. civil strife that it is like some common-law cases: there is enough fact and decisional law to make the *first* argument on both sides. But the balance of the equities does not decisively point to the civil strife interpretation. In fact, the better comments are in conditional terms.[5]

Even more illustrative of the quality of the arguments is the issue of individual or collective defense. The legalistic mode, admittedly based on the "literal language,"[1] has been answered on the same level. Naturally, to justify the resort to collective defense on basis of Article 51 of the Charter, the term "armed attack" had to be elaborately manipulated and the nonmembership of South Vietnam in the United Nations had to be argued away.[2] The ingenuity of this dialectic can be measured with reference to such arguments as the reason given for the nonmembership—the Soviet veto—leaving aside the much more relevant circumstance of the "package" admission deal which I have already mentioned.

If one wished to answer the illegality arguments based on Article 51 (and the related Article 53) in their literal terms, one would have to argue that Article 51 cannot apply at all since it speaks expressly of "a member of the United Nations" and South Vietnam is not a member. As to some more serious efforts at interpretation, it suffices to note the internal and mutual contradictions in and between Articles 51 and 53, already pointed out by Professor Kelsen in his *The Law of the United Nations* in 1950. One might also at least want to raise the question, which I shall not attempt to analyze here, to what an extent the identification by outside powers—members of the United Nations—of their defense interest with Vietnam made the conflict there a matter of their legitimate individual or collective defense.

Relevant to this point are other doubts about the contemporary meaning of Article 51. For instance, Professor Friedmann writes in *The Changing Structure of International Law* (1964): "The right of self-defense must possibly now be extended to the defense against a clearly imminent aggression, despite the apparently contrary language of Art. 51."

But is this only a question of more or less extensive interpretation? Or are we facing normative language which was poorly drafted in the first place, and which, more importantly, did not contemplate problems such as the present one. Article 51 was drafted in its present form in 1945. Article 6 of the Inter-American Treaty of Reciprocal Assistance (Rio de Janeiro, 1947) already speaks of "an aggression which is not an armed attack." Beginning with the coup d'etat in Czechoslovakia in 1948, the internal alternative to an armed attack was widely recognized. And the corresponding normative formulation—the antisubversion clauses—found their way in an increasingly explicit form into the Brussels Treaty of 1948, the North Atlantic Treaty of 1949 and the Southeast Asia Treaty of 1954. But the wording of Article 51 of the Charter has remained unchanged and, in the opinion of some, unaffected. Even the Holy Scriptures are not interpreted like that any more.

VI

What conclusions can be suggested?

1. The *fact* basis of the illegality arguments is impressionistic, that means selective, whether by design or by default. The *legal* interpretation is the most literal and narrow possible.[1,6] The *response* is on the same legalistic level.[2,4]

2. The better argument and response[3,5] illustrate the inadequacy of the general positive norms which are considered determinative; and a too diplomatic rhetoric of applicable particular treaty law.

3. The difficulty of applying positive international law is complicated by the *subsequent changes in concepts and circumstances.* A relevant statement was made by President Johnson in connection with the crisis in the Dominican Republic (May 1965): "In today's world . . . [of] wars of national liberation, the old distinction between the civil war and international war has already lost much of its meaning." To mention just another example: how to apply with any degree of precision the concept of aggression when the movement of men and matériel from North to South Vietnam has been in fact an infiltration around the demilitarized zone, through the territory of Laos, another sovereign state?[9]

4. It is impossible to reach on this basis any conclusions as categorical as those offered by the advocates of the illegality and legality theses. The best assumption, considering the factual and legal defects in the claim of illegality, seems to be that *there is nothing in positive international law to make the United States presence in the Vietnam conflict either mandatory or illegal.*

5. The polemic on the level of international law is merely an additional illustration of the dramatic need to apply and further develop modern jurisprudence in the field of international law. Much of the argument on both sides is in the worst tradition of mechanical jurisprudence discredited by Gény, Ehrlich, and others in Europe, and by Pound and Cardozo in the United States two generations ago. There is no wonder if politicians pay only lip service to such an art. Consider, as one example of retarded international jurisprudence, Article 51 of the Charter in the light of the preceding analysis. In established and conventional terms of general jurisprudence, it presents a gap. Any developed national legal system has an elaborate and legitimate technique to fill gaps in positive law. An influential and already classical thesis by Gény,[10] published almost 70 years ago, sustained the free-

dom of law-making (judicial in the national context of developed adjudicative organs) instead of excessive twisting of the normative text by means of interpretation. International jurisprudence has not arrived even at the level of realistic interpretation, which may under circumstances require some breadth and imagination.

6. In the popular polemic—that means by nonlawyers or by lawyers arguing as partisans—the "legal" arguments appear to be a stopgap when the information or general rhetoric did not seem to suffice.

VII

To conclude, let me address myself more to the last preceding point. Almost all of the polemic outside of the United States (and most of it accusatory, without any significant counterargument) took place on this level.

In a somewhat longer perspective than the majority of the critics chose to take, I believe that the United States involvement in Vietnam must be understood as an effort to create a material base for a legal order more durable than the Geneva improvisation of 1954. Until such a base is created—if it can be—the choice of policies and means remains debatable. These means are essentially military, political, and diplomatic, not legal. Informed and responsible criticism of strategic and tactical choices is possible and necessary. But to claim illegality is to exclude any such choices. That is quite something else.

At any rate, we are in a realm of opinion, not of law. One should not be overconcerned about the long-hair chorus. The particular forms of their outcry in re Vietnam are only symptoms of a more profound malaise in a world we have prepared for them. The judgment of adults is of a different order. There is no need to doubt that many of the outspoken critics are well meaning. But those who are in a position to influence public opinion at large have an inherent duty to be responsible and ethical. The minimum of responsibility requires that a definite opinion be based on sufficient information.

Those of us who were old enough during the Second World War to follow the crucial events as interested citizens, can now that many archives have been opened and the information published, compare what we knew then with the documented course of events.

This experience inspires caution as to categorical judgments about any contemporary events. It also raises a fundamental question of conscience. If in a situation in which the intellectual and moral duty is to doubt, one leans to one side or another, one is said to give the benefit of the doubt. The question of conscience, which can not be effaced by any amount of legal or other arguments, is this: does the record of efforts toward international peace, stability, and welfare since 1945 merit that the United States be given now such a benefit of doubt until the full evidence is before the judges?

WORKING BIBLIOGRAPHY

1. "Memorandum of Law of Lawyers' Committee on American Policy toward Vietnam," 112 Congressional Record, 89th Congr., 2d session, September 23, 1965.

2. U.S. Department of State, Office of the Legal Adviser, "The Legality of United States Participation in the Defense of Vietnam" (March 4, 1966) 52 pp. mimeographed. Reprinted in Department of State Bulletin (March 28, 1966).

3. John N. Moore and James L. Underwood (in collaboration with Myres S. McDougal), The Lawfulness of United States Assistance to the Republic of Vietnam (May 1966) 259 pp. mimeographed.

4. Eberhard P. Deutsch, "The Legality of the United States Position in Vietnam," 52 American Bar Association Journal, 436-442 (May 1966).

5. Richard A. Falk, "International Law and the United States Role in the Vietnam War," 75 Yale Law Journal, 1122-1160 (June 1966).

6. William L. Standard, "United States Intervention in Vietnam Is Not Legal," 52 American Bar Association Journal, 627-634 (July 1966).

7. Jaro Mayda, "The Legal Argument over Vietnam," The San Juan Star (March 11, 1966).

8. Lyman M. Tondel, Jr., ed., "The Southeast Asia Crisis" (The Eighth Hammarskjold Forum, by the Association of the Bar of the City of New York (October 18, 1965), ix, 226 pp.

9. "Aggression from the North" (State Department Report, February 27, 1965), in U.S. Senate, Committee on Foreign Relations, "Background Information Relating to Southeast Asia and Vietnam (rev. edn., June 16, 1965) pp. 163-190 (including transmittal by Ambassador Stevenson to the President of the U.N. Security Council).

10. François Gény, Method of Interpretation and Sources of Private Positive Law (American translation, 1963); Mayda, "Gény's Méthode after 60 Years: A Critical Introduction," in Id., pp. v-lxxvi, esp. pp. xliiff.

III. THE ROLE OF THE UNITED NATIONS

Intervention and the United Nations

OSCAR SCHACHTER

INTRODUCTION

BEFORE GETTING INTO the substance of my remarks, a few personal words are in order. Even though I am participating in the symposium in my private capacity, I must continue to observe certain restraints imposed by my status as an international official. For example, I will not pass judgment on the conduct of Member States of the United Nations, not even our own. At the same time, I am not without convictions or commitment. (United Nations officials may have to be politically celibate, but, as Dag Hammarskjöld once observed, they need not be political virgins.) My convictions as well as my position line me up on the side of the United Nations Charter and its established international institution and processes. Connected with this is a belief—a professional bias, you may call it—that the processes of law have a vital and creative role in achieving the Charter purposes.

ROLE OF THE UNITED NATIONS IN MAINTAINING WORLD ORDER

Scope of the Problem

Focusing on the potentiality rather than the history of the United Nations in relation to civil strife, several options are available. I am not going to suggest a menu of solutions, but my own experience in over two decades of participation in the United Nations has left me with a deep sense of the uncertainties, risks, and complexities of international action. The innumerable formulas and catch phrases that provided short-lived hope and eventual frustration remind us to guard against that illusory world where easy solutions, whether based on force or world law, are available.

Yet who can doubt the necessity, if not the inevitability, of a strengthened system of international authority exemplified by the United Nations? The tragedy of the United Nations, someone once observed, lies in the fact that it has become necessary before it has become effective. The pertinent but answerable question is whether it can be made more effective before it is too late.

No other subject seems more likely to put this question to the test than the topic of this symposium. "Foreign intervention in civil strife" has already imposed on the United Nations its greatest burdens, its most galling frustrations, and its most profound crises. No major continent has been immune to internal wars, which have become more frequent, more violent, and more protracted. The optimism of some years ago has long been dissolved. Initiatives are now less frequent, initiators have become scarce, great powers are apparently more impotent, and middle powers seem less venturesome. In effect, a large part of the world has been turning inward as domestic troubles have proven obdurate and dangerous.

A Legitimate and Necessary Approach

Before exploring how the United Nations can prevent or limit foreign intervention in civil strife, two basic assumptions should be made.

First, foreign intervention in civil strife is impermissible or, at least, undesirable. This, of course, raises the question of what is meant by intervention and recalls Tallyrand's quip about intervention being the same as nonintervention. The term "intervention" is used in a variety of senses. Sometimes it is employed in a factual sense alone to describe conduct; at other times it serves as a legal conclusion denoting illegality. Not infrequently both definitions are used interchangeably. It may also describe activities ranging from the use of military forces to more subtle pressures and influences, such as "tied" assistance. Obviously, if certain kinds of state conduct are to be proscribed, lines must be drawn with greater clarity and more specific criteria, but I will return to this topic later. It is sufficient here to recognize that certain types of involvement or interference by one state in the affairs of another are widely regarded as running counter to Charter obligations against the threat or use of force or, in a more general sense, against principles of sovereign equality, political independence, and territorial integrity.[1] This conclusion requires a second assumption, namely, that it is a legitimate purpose of the United Nations to seek the prevention of such conduct within appropriate limits and under appropriate conditions.

The array of measures that may be taken by the United Nations should be directed toward the various actors and not the intervening foreign state alone. These actors include:

[1] U.N. CHARTER art. 2.

1) the government of the state in which there is actual or potential internal strife,
2) the authorities or political groups contending for power in that state,
3) the intervening or potentially intervening states,
4) the regional organization of states,
5) the United Nations political bodies,
6) the major powers,
7) the Secretary General of the United Nations,
8) possible "conciliating" or mediating governments or persons, and
9) the specialized agencies and other intergovernmental organizations.

One might well add to this list certain nongovernmental organizations, such as trade unions or business organizations, and even individual enterprises, such as those in the fields of transportation, communications, or petroleum. There is, in fact, no a priori reason to exclude any actor that might play a useful role in obtaining the objectives delineated by the Charter.

This list of possible actors emphasizes the necessity of a many-sided approach to the problem of intervention. Each of the entities mentioned has its own needs and interests besides commanding its own measure of power and resources. The strategies and techniques suitable in one case may not be as effective in another. Viewed from the standpoint of the United Nations community, therefore, effective action will generally require an orchestration of effort rather than solo instrumentation.

ALTERNATIVES TO UNILATERAL INTERVENTION OFFERED BY THE UNITED NATIONS

The Development of Norms

Ideally, the catalysts for civil strife, such as poverty and social frustration, should be rendered impotent by progressive action. Realistically, civil strife, and hence foreign intervention, can be expected to plague international tranquillity for some time.

Normative evaluations by an impartial body can be of great value in preventing such interventions or minimizing the risks of escalation. From its inception, the United Nations has been involved in endeavors to build a body of rules defining and proscribing unlawful intervention. The rubrics have varied—"rights and duties of states" and "offenses against peace and security" were among the first—and the formulations continue to be made, varying in emphasis and import with new interventions contributing more specific data and fresh incentives. As the gap between what is preached and what is practiced has widened, the feeling of futility has naturally grown. Nonetheless, normative drafting continues in the form of political declarations by the General Assembly and special committee codification of international law relating to friendly relations. In spite of the obvious difficulties, the effort will go on, for there is a constant pressure to specify the acceptable limits of indirect aggression, subversive infiltration, support of guerrilla warfare, and other military and paramilitary assistance.

Alongside the effort to achieve more precise legal limits is the need for a broad, comprehensive framework for continued inquiry into patterns of conduct, attitudes, and objectives. Our normative stockpile is not, and should not be, limited to flat prohibitions. The more general concepts expressing major purposes and standards, such as self-determination and political independence, must be embraced along with more meaningful criteria for their application. There should be continued development toward standards of international consultation and recognition of the processes of international organization. Such norms should not be seen as self-enforcing ones but as expressions of purpose and legitimacy that enable the institutional processes of consultation and collective decision to become more firmly established. In this connection, attention should be given to evolving procedural rules, such as reporting measures taken under article 51 to the Security Council or providing for "good offices" missions.

A Preventive Measure: Furthering Restraint and Moderation

It is easy and seemingly tough-minded to concentrate on hard, clear-cut categories such as rules, troops, and economics. However, the less palpable influences of international mechanisms cannot realistically be ignored. Problems of civil strife and external intervention involve attitudes, perceptions, expectations, and will. True, we know rather little about factors that change basic attitudes of governments and people, but the transformations do occur. What seemed utterly impossible one day suddenly has become inevitable the next.

Obviously, the United Nations can play a major role in guiding the attitudes of Members toward restraint and moderation. The propaganda debates, the numerous informal conversations and contacts, and even the endless cocktail parties and receptions all facilitate the flow of communication and opinion which cannot be ignored. Part of this network is comprised of the international officialdom, particularly the Secretary General and his staff, whose positions in the structure and relative impartiality cast for them a salient role in furthering agreement on the basis of internationally accepted policy. Attitudes as to the legitimacy of an action or of governmental authority, whether embodied in formal resolutions or in unofficial, convergent views, affect the perception of policymakers in national governments. Moreover, experience shows that expressions of concern and of purpose in the international forums can provide support to domestic forces favoring moderation and restraint. Of course, the mechanism does not always achieve such moderation, nor is it always aimed at moderation. Nonetheless, its multinational and multipartisan character tend to have that effect, especially when the Members are split or when civil strife seems likely to escalate into external conflict.

Further, the United Nations mechanisms can be a decisive factor in situations involving rival powers when mistrust or outright hostility prevent such governments from reaching open agreements. When nations fear that moderation may be exploited by the enemy, often the question becomes, "Who will be the first to back down?" The United Nations provides a means to achieve coordination under the umbrella of the Charter and collective agreement. It may prove a decisive element in the agreement of rival states to refrain from intervention in internal strife.

United Nations Consensual Peacekeeping

Providing norms and influencing the attitudes of individual nations faced with an intervention option are important, if somewhat indirect, means of curtailing intervention. Promoting the objective of world order through consensual peacekeeping by a multinational organization presents a more direct alternative. The classic type of United Nations peacekeeping operation is based on the consent of the host government and undertaken by the Security Council to forestall or eliminate threatened foreign interference.

A continuing constitutional controversy exists as to whether such peacekeeping operations must be carried out in accordance with special agreements made with the Security Council under article 43 and the other provisions of chapter VII relating to military measures. The debate exhibits the concern of some countries that the "consensual" peacekeeping forces may be used against movements of national liberation unless such forces are under the strict control of the Security Council and the Military Staff Committee, on which all Permanent Members are represented.[2] Whether or not article 43 agreements can be worked out and effectively employed in civil strife situations still remains to be seen. In the meantime, Cyprus is a relevant example where the Security Council has, with unanimity, repeatedly extended the authorization for a policing type of operation under the direction of the Secretary General, although article 43 agreements were not employed.

[2] U.N. CHARTER art. 47.

Coercive Intervention by the United Nations

Some situations call for the containment or prevention of civil strife and the exclusion of unilateral foreign intervention. The formulation of norms to control foreign intervention, the development of attitudes of restraint and moderation in Members, and the consensual peacekeeping operations of the United Nations itself are all related to this topic. However, the international objectives are substantially different when the great bulk of Members believe that the United Nations should intervene on behalf of one party to the civil conflict. Rhodesia and South Africa are instances where the decision to oppose the authorities in control commanded a virtually unanimous consensus among the Members rather than a simple majority or two-thirds majority. The Members, of course, may disagree on the specific means to be used, especially as to the scope of military and other intensive coercive measures. However, the basic point is that the great majority of Members, including the major powers, have endorsed the United Nations role as guardian of fundamental rights, particularly human rights, in certain internal conflicts. One can see today how much of a change has occurred in the last two decades in this area.

Under the Charter, the legal condition for such coercive action must be a finding of a threat or breach of the peace or an act of aggression.[3] When this condition is fulfilled, the assumption that internal conflicts should be settled internally is discarded in favor of external action against the side flouting international standards. The Organization does not, and indeed cannot, take such action without an extremely wide consensus embracing all of the great powers and the overwhelming majority of the Members. Thus far, the instances are limited to the southern African area.[4] In Rhodesia, for example, the denial of minimum human rights evoked such strong opposition as to require a conclusion that the peace was threatened. As far as United Nations action is concerned, the critical questions concern the extent to which such action may command material and effective support rather than mere lip service. The experience in Rhodesian South Africa has been both discouraging and instructive. We now see that relatively minor forms of coercion do not work. In fact, they may harden resistance and foster greater cohesion and sense of sacrifice in the target group. It may, perhaps, be conceded that whether these outlaw minority regimes continue in power will depend far more on internal forces than on collective sanctions by the United Nations. Yet, I do not expect international pressures for such sanctions to abate. On the

---

[3] U.N. CHARTER art. 39.

[4] When "community policing action" is taken by a regional organization against a dissident member, issues different from coercive action in the United Nations are raised.

contrary, it probably will become increasingly difficult for the United Nations—and that includes the major powers—to drop the matter, for its decision inevitably will be viewed as a test of its genuine commitment.

A Preventive Measure: Peacemaking and Peace-Building

It is sometimes said that United Nations peacekeeping action, necessary as it may be, comes too late, for civil strife does not occur suddenly. It boils out of continuing crises, generally in poverty-stricken, newly independent countries. Long before the trouble and violence break out, there is evidence of grievance, tension, and imminent conflict. It has been suggested that an "early warning" system be employed, followed by a United Nations conciliation or assistance mission. United Nations technical assistance missions and information centers, present in almost all developing areas, could report internal strife that might lead to foreign intervention. Would not United Nations involvement in internal affairs be preferable to involvement of external powers with the attendant risks of counterintervention?

Objections quickly come to mind. First, governments facing domestic difficulties might use the international Organization to pressure internal opponents or even to involve them in counterinsurgency actions. Thus, the domestic strife could be escalated into an international conflict should the dissident forces seek external backers. Second, the international machinery might be manipulated to favor one political line, thus imposing external pressures on the troubled state. Some would probably worry about the possibilities of paternalism or neocolonialism that might result from the involvement of international officials in the political affairs of weak and recently independent states, with undue sympathy for the status quo and for the elite in power envisaged as a likely attitude.

These dangers cannot be lightly dismissed. Obviously, the consent or invitation of the de jure government alone may not be a sufficient safeguard. A United Nations mission attempting a conciliatory role with the requisite consent or acquiescence of all contending factions would be preferable. It was hoped that the United Nations mission sent to Aden would serve that function in an early stage of the crisis. Its failure underlines the difficulty of averting such a crisis but does not necessarily invalidate the concept.

Much safer grounds for United Nations "preventive action" may be found in the economic and social field where the principle of aid is widely accepted. Nearly all needy countries receive approximately 10 percent of their technical assistance and development aid from international organizations. However useful these forms of assistance have been, it is evident that they have been grossly inadequate. The tide of discontent has risen, and the endemic instability and widespread disorder in the under-developed areas have increased. Since 90 percent of present aid is given by individual nations, the case for increased United Nations assistance is a persuasive one. Better coordination of national aid programs may be furthered through greater "multilateralization," thereby reducing po-litical pressures from the donor states. The United Nations presence, visible in the form of hundreds of experts of all nationalities, races, and political beliefs, may be a strong counterweight to bilateral programs and thus may contribute to a greater sense of economic independence and self-determination in recipient countries. In the same vein, multilateral assistance may be able to cut more deeply into needed areas of reform since the general policy manifested in United Nations resolutions favors a wider sharing of power and more equitable distribution of economic resources. International teams guided by broad conceptions of social change probably would be less conservative than those sent from national states unwilling to upset tradition or established elites.

In addition, much of the international effort has been directed toward local self-help and community development in rural as well as urban areas. This "grass roots" approach has an obvious relation to building peace between different internal ethnic or linguistic communities by fostering joint community endeavors, building cooperatives, and extend-ing consultations among the leaders of mutually suspicious groups. Al-though the degree of success depends upon many variables, there is good reason to believe that international missions will be more acceptable than the missions of the great powers.

CONCLUSION

International order cannot be achieved without great effort, substan-tial cost, and painful mistakes. Obviously, slogans or incantations are not enough. Continuing commitment by governments, backed by more than mere words and accompanied by an effort of will and intelligence in sup-port of international authority, can foster the substructure of a lasting world order.

Since the "go it alone" policies can lead to disaster, the desirability of concerted multilateral action may become all the more evident. If so, we may yet respond affirmatively to the "unanswerable" question of whether the United Nations can be made more effective before it is too late.

The U.N. and Vietnam

LINCOLN P. BLOOMFIELD

Increasingly, as the Vietnam war drags on, responsible voices are heard urging that the United Nations somehow take hold of the problem. For several years, citizens' groups, editorial writers, and administration critics have called for UN action as a way to take the United States off the hook by internationalizing the problem. Pope Paul VI in January, 1966, suggested neutral arbitration of the conflict under United Nations auspices in order to end the war. Plans put forward by General James Gavin called for maintaining enclaves on the South Vietnam coastline, ceasing bombing attacks on the North, and seeking to "find a solution through the United Nations or a conference in Geneva."[1] A symposium of leaders of the world's religions meeting in New Delhi in January, 1968, called on the UN to take a major role in settling the conflict. Other appeals have similarly urged a UN route toward peace, although rarely specifying how or under what conditions this would happen.

But is is only in the past three or four years that the United States Government has acted with energy and apparent seriousness to involve the UN in one or another aspect of the Vietnam problem. The tempo of such efforts has been accelerating as the war drags on and criticism of United States military involvement mounts.

In the fall of 1967 a new American approach to the UN was linked to pressure from an increasingly concerned U.S. Senate. On October 25, Senate Majority Leader Mike S. Mansfield introduced a resolution sponsored by 54 Senators conveying to the President of the United States "the sense of the Senate" that he

consider taking the appropriate initiative through his representative at the United Nations to assure that the U.S. resolution of Jan. 31, 1966, or any other resolution of equivalent purpose be brought before the Security Council for consideration.[2]

---

[1] Testimony before the Senate Foreign Relations Committee, February 8, 1966.
[2] On introducing this resolution Senator Mansfield said "it is high time that we find out . . . where the members of the Security Council stand on this question." *New York Times,* October 26, 1967.

On November 30 the Senate passed the resolution without dissent, 82 to 0.

On .November 2, 1967, Ambassador Arthur J. Goldberg informed the Senate Foreign Relations Committee that in his considered view the adoption of Senator Mansfield's resolution would support the efforts he had been making at the UN "to enlist the Security Council in the search for peace in Vietnam." He reported that in September, 1967, the United States had circulated a draft Security Council resolution which, if passed, would affirm principles of cease-fire and mutual withdrawal, including a provision for "international supervision . . . through such machinery as may be agreed upon." It called for the convening of an international conference "for the purpose of establishing a permanent peace in Southeast Asia based upon the principles of the Geneva Agreements" of 1954 and 1962.

Ambassador Goldberg's efforts to "enlist the Security Council" had been faring badly: he told the Foreign Relations Committee that his recent canvass of the Council's membership showed a "general unwillingness for the Security Council either to [consider the U.S. resolution] or to take any other action on the matter."[3]

As had happened two years before, and indeed two months before, once again the effort failed. On December 20, Goldberg stated that "certain members," whom he characterized as "intransigent," had blocked his efforts to get the matter inscribed on the Council's agenda. There was little doubt that he meant the Soviet Union and France. He confessed that in two and a half years of service at the UN his greatest disappointment and frustration was his inability to "find a way to have the UN play a constructive role on making peace in Vietnam."[4]

During the same period an exceedingly curious episode took place involving the National Liberation Front (NLF), political arm of the Vietcong, and its relations with the UN. In September, the Front apparently wished to send a two-man team to New York for discussions with the delegates present at the General Assembly. According to Ambassador Goldberg, Washington was willing to issue visas. In any event, nothing happened. But in his testimony

---

[3]Statement to Senate Foreign Relations Committee, November 2, 1967. U.S. Department of State *Bulletin,* November 20, 1967, pp. 667, 671.
[4]*New York Times,* December 21, 1968.

of November 2, in response to questions, Ambassador Goldberg said that the U.S. would vote for participation by the Front in any Security Council discussion, and there were reports that the earlier U.S. plan had envisaged invitations to both the NLF and Hanoi after the draft U.S. resolution had been introduced in the Security Council.[5]

In the next episode, in mid-December, diplomats in New York were intrigued to see, in the form of a UN document circulated at the request of the Romanian delegation, what appeared to be a presentation by the NLF. As it turned out, there was nothing new in substance in the document, nor did it seem to alter the uncompromising line advanced by all Communist parties to the Vietnam war to the effect that the UN had no jurisdiction in the matter.

These recent inconclusive maneuvers followed an earlier series of requests and exhortations by Washington to the world Organization to involve itself in the Vietnam situation. In 1964 two peripheral matters were put before the UN. In May, Cambodia lodged a complaint over incidents on its Vietnamese border, and the U.S. suggested to the Security Council that a UN-sponsored peacekeeping or observation group might be established on the border to stabilize conditions upset by Vietcong operations there. With the Soviets abstaining, the Security Council voted for a fact-finding mission. It visited the area and reported that a UN observer group might well be useful. Cambodia, true to form, changed its mind and the border watch was not established.

In August, 1964, the United States supported the Security Council invitation to the Hanoi government to discuss the U.S. complaint of North Vietnamese torpedo-boat attacks against U.S. naval vessels in international waters as well as the American military response. The North Vietnamese Foreign Minister replied that the Vietnam problem was not within the competence of the Security Council and that his government would consider any decisions by the Council as "null and void."

In 1965, three months after the bombing of North Vietnam had begun and after the U.S. had begun a massive military buildup of its ground forces in South Vietnam, President Johnson, speaking at San Francisco in June on the twentieth anniversary of the

---

[5] *New York Times,* December 3, 1967.

signing of the UN Charter, appealed to members of the United Nations, "individually and collectively, to bring to the table those who seem determined to make war." The President reiterated this appeal on July 28 in a letter to UN Secretary-General Thant. At the same time, Ambassador Goldberg, in a letter to members of the Security Council, reminded them of their responsibility to persist in the search for an acceptable formula to restore peace and security in Southeast Asia, and of U.S. readiness to collaborate unconditionally in this quest.

On January 31, 1966, the United States formally requested that the United Nations consider the problem of achieving a peaceful solution in Vietnam. It proposed a draft resolution in the Security Council that called for immediate unconditional discussions to arrange a conference looking toward the application of the 1954 and 1962 Geneva accords and the establishment of a durable peace in Southeast Asia. The proposed resolution also recommended that the conference arrange a cease-fire under effective supervision, offered to provide arbitrators or mediators, and asked the Secretary-General to assist as appropriate in the implementation of the resolution. With a bare necessary majority of nine, the Security Council (France and three African states abstaining and the Soviet Union and Bulgaria opposing) voted on February 2, 1966, to inscribe the Vietnam problem on its agenda, and adjourned immediately after the vote for private consultations among members to determine whether and in what manner the Council might assist in moving the conflict to the conference table. The Council President, Ambassador Akira Matsui of Japan, after three weeks of intensive soundings reported on February 26 that the difference in views on the wisdom of Council consideration had "given rise to a general feeling that it would be inopportune for the Council to hold further debate at this time."

The United States in a letter dated December 19, 1966, appealed to Secretary-General Thant to "take whatever steps are necessary [to] bring about the necessary discussions" that would lead to a mutual cessation of hostilities.

On September 8, 1967, Secretary of State Dean Rusk reiterated to a news conference that "we believe that the United Nations has a responsibility under its Charter to deal with any situation affecting international peace and security, and we would welcome any contribution which the United Nations can make toward peace in Southeast Asia." On September 21, 1967, Ambassador Goldberg told the UN General Assembly that the UN has "the most explicit right and duty to concern itself with this question" and that the U.S. "continues to seek the active participation of the UN in the quest for peace in Viet Nam."

It is thus clearly on the record that the U.S. has made diplomatic efforts in recent months to involve the UN. But it is by no means as clear, as the State Department asserts, that "a UN presence in the area and formal debate in the United Nations have long been urged by the United States."[6] The fact is that anything resembling a serious focus on the UN for Vietnam diplomacy came late in the fourteen-year history of progressively expanding unilateral American commitments.

Before the French defeat at Dienbienphu, former U.S. Ambassador Ernest A. Gross reminds us, the U.S. Government, even while aiding the French, had fairly consistently spoken of the need for "united action" to meet threats "posed by aggression in Korea and Southeast Asia." On the possibility of direct U.S. intervention in the deteriorating situation in Indochina, Secretary of State John Foster Dulles said in May, 1954,

> We don't go in alone, we go in where the other nations which have an important stake in the area recognize the peril as we do. *We go in where the United Nations gives moral sanction to our action.*[7] [Emphasis added.]

When the French faced defeat at Dienbienphu, the inclination in some high and responsible quarters of the U.S. Government, far from neutralizing the area through the UN or other international auspices, was to intervene militarily on behalf of the French. When this was wisely vetoed by President Eisenhower, U.S. policy continued to defer to French preferences, chronically antipathetic to UN involvement in *any* colonial problems, even while developing a growing U.S. position in the area through unilateral diplomacy and, increasingly, through military assistance to the new indigenous Saigon government.

---

[6]"The Search for Peace in Viet Nam," *Vietnam Information Notes,* No. 2, February, 1967.

[7]Ernest A. Gross, "Vietnam — A Role for the UN," *Vista,* January-February, 1968.

As it became clear that Hanoi was not going to honor its commitments under the Geneva Agreement of 1954, there were some Americans, in and out of the State Department, who even then began to feel that some form of UN cognizance of the problem was desirable. The UN had successfully spotlighted infiltration into Greece by its northern Communist neighbors in the late 1940s; UN observation had monitored with fair success the Palestine armistice agreements; and UN observation had fixed, with extraordinary political value, the fact of North Korean invasion of the South on June 24, 1950.

The U.S. Government chose, however, not to use the UN in Vietnam through the entire development of mounting Vietcong terrorism, U.S. assistance, and finally open U.S.-Communist warfare. This was in part because of its policy at the time of frequently suppressing its own correct impulses and yielding to French insistence on UN non-interference in France's colonial problem areas. But the consistent rejection by U.S. decision-makers of any Vietnam role for the UN also represented a U.S. preference, unexceeded by that of France, for unhampered unilateral policy freedom in any situation believed to reflect what was then with some justice called the international Communist conspiracy.

In the same period some hitherto fixed things were changing. U.S. policy toward Laos had been reversed by President Kennedy and a neutral, coalition-type solution accepted. Earlier, President Eisenhower again had wisely vetoed unilateral U.S. military entanglement in the Congo, choosing a UN route instead. The Sino-Soviet split had become history, and the prevention of future major miscalculations came to involve differentiated policies toward potential Titos every bit as much as aid to beleaguered and weak local governments. But U.S. Vietnam policy benefited from none of these insights and remained on a single track, ever more steeply graded.

By the time the U.S. did turn to the UN, the problem had in many ways become quite inappropriate for UN handling. Despite American exhortations that the UN now face up to its responsibilities in Vietnam, the Organization has shown little collective interest in doing so under present conditions.

The reasons for this have become a topic of sharp debate.

Senator J. William Fulbright in a Senate speech on October 11, 1967, asserted that the UN was being deterred from action on Vietnam by the failure of the United States to encourage it to act. Secretary Rusk the next day said this was untrue, that the UN was not being permitted by Hanoi, Peking, and Moscow to find the key to unlock the problem, and that consequently the Organization was "hoping that other means and other procedures will find the key."[8] Both statements seem wide of the mark: the United States *has* tried to encourage the UN to act; at the same time it is in some measure responsible for the UN's failure to respond, for reasons analyzed below.

Under current conditions it is apparent that, except for such personal diplomacy as the Secretary-General is capable of venturing without perilously offending his superpower clients, the two main organs of the UN are unlikely to take effective action regarding Vietnam. The Security Council is potentially paralyzed by a Soviet veto from taking any action that seems, even by inference, to endorse U.S. policy, or that is not preceded by unilateral U.S. cessation of the bombing of the North. In the Assembly, a simple majority could probably be found today either to stop the bombing or perhaps to give general support to the U.S. 14-point peace program (see Appendix A); but neither alternative could secure the necessary two-thirds vote. The Assembly has in fact discussed Vietnam extensively—but only in individual speeches in the General Debate this year and last.

Arguments are advanced by responsible governments that UN action might have no real effect on the Vietnam situation, and that taking ineffective action might be damaging to the UN, as undoubtedly it would. But underneath one also senses a general unwillingness to be caught between quarrelling superpowers, *or* to appear to be endorsing the essentially unilateral actions that Washington has taken. Finally, of the principal signers of the 1954 Geneva Agreement on Vietnam two were not—and are not—members of the UN; two (Britain and France) for a long time did not want the UN involved; and the chief onlooker at Geneva—the United States — chose to take virtually the entire burden on itself.

It is thus in one sense too late for UN action; in another sense

---

[8]U.S. Department of State *Bulletin,* October 30, 1967.

it is too early. It nevertheless must be asked what the UN—or comparable international machinery—can realistically do, and under what conditions. For if the U.S. action in Vietnam has any meaning, it is as a unilateral form of collective security and peace-keeping which the world Organization, if *it* has any meaning, is itself in principle committed to undertake on a collective basis. Furthermore, as the chief international lobby with a powerful vested interest in non-violent resolution of international conflicts, the UN's help ought to be available to those who are genuinely prepared to compromise in order to be disengaged from unproductive and unpromising warfare. If there is *no* disposition to compromise, then of course there is little any diplomatic instrument can do.

II. THE LEGALITY OF U.S. — AND UN — ACTION IN VIETNAM

In seeking clarity on the perplexing question of a UN (or other multilateral) role in Vietnam, two points stand out sharply. One is legal, the other political. The first point is that most of the principal parties to the Vietnam conflict are not members of the UN—neither Communist China, South or North Vietnam, nor needless to say, the insurgent movement in South Vietnam. Thus, potential UN involvement raises the issue of its non-universality of membership. Indeed, whether any of the possibilities outlined below are real may well be determined by this issue.

The several legal-constitutional questions involved in U.S. action in Vietnam, and in the possibility of UN involvement, have been addressed at length by U.S. spokesmen and by the Communists.

Official American argumentation is chiefly concerned with the consistency of U.S. actions in the light of its UN Charter commitments and rights, notably the right under Article 51 of collective self-defense against violations of Article 2, paragraph 4, which in turn provides that

All Members shall refrain in their international relations from the threat or use of force against the territorial integrity or political independence of any state, or in any other manner inconsistent with the Purposes of the United Nations.

The State Department's Legal Adviser, Leonard C. Meeker, correctly points out that "the Charter nowhere contains any provision designed to deprive nonmembers of the right of self-defense against armed attack."[9] He disposes of the explicit reference in Article 51 to armed attack "against a Member of the United Nations" by arguing that it implies "no intention to preclude members from participating in the defense of nonmembers," and reinforces this with the reminder that South Vietnam "has been admitted to membership in a number of the United Nations

[9] This and subsequent references are found in a legal memorandum, "The Legality of United States Participation in the Defense of Viet-Nam," in U.S. Department of State *Bulletin,* March 28, 1966.

specialized agencies and has been excluded from the United Nations Organization only by the Soviet veto."

Intervention in a conflict having many characteristics of a civil war is addressed *en passant* by Mr. Meeker in pointing out that the 17th parallel line of demarcation "was intended to be temporary, it was established by international agreement, which specifically forbade aggression by one zone against the other.... In any event," he goes on,

> there is no warrant for the suggestion that one zone of a temporarily divided state — whether it be Germany, Korea, or Viet-Nam — can be legally overrun by armed forces from the other zone, crossing the internationally recognized line of demarcation between the two. Any such doctrine would subvert the international agreement establishing the line of demarcation, and would pose grave dangers to the international peace.
>
> The action of the United Nations in the Korean conflict of 1950 clearly established the principle that there is no greater license for one zone of a temporarily divided state to attack the other zone than there is for one state to attack another state. South Viet-Nam has the same right that South Korea had to defend itself and to organize collective defense against an armed attack from the North.

From a legal point of view, the jurisdictional question would appear not to be insurmountable. Above all, Article 2, paragraph 6 of the Charter charges the United Nations with responsibility for insuring that non-member states "act in accordance with [Charter] Principles so far as may be necessary for the maintenance of international peace and security." Article 32 provides that non-members can participate without vote in Security Council discussions:

> Any Member of the United Nations which is not a member of the Security Council or any state which is not a Member of the United Nations, if it is a party to a dispute under consideration by the Security Council, shall be invited to participate, without vote, in the discussion relating to the dispute. The Security Council shall lay down such conditions as it deems just for the participation of a state which is not a Member of the United Nations.

The conditions referred to have long been formulated in Rule 39 of the Council's Provisional Rules of Procedure providing that:

> The Security Council may invite members of the Secretariat or other persons, whom it considers competent for the purpose, to supply it with information or to give other assistance in examining matters within its competence.

Thus, as has happened often in the past, countries—even political groupings—not members of the UN can actually take part in Security Council deliberations (and this furnished the constitutional basis for Ambassador Goldberg's November 2 statements about NLF participation in Security Council discussions). But like many seemingly legal questions, this one is of course intensely political.

Secretary Rusk has placed UN jurisdiction on the basis that the Organization should act regardless of the participation or lack of participation of any recalcitrant parties to the conflict:

> Now, we believe this is a proper concern of the United Nations. The fact that one party, or one or two parties, refused to accept the jurisdiction of the United Nations has nothing to do with the world responsibilities of the U.N. under its own Charter.[10]

But this raises crucial questions: act for what? with whom? toward what end? and in what framework—coercion or cooperation? If UN action is to be coercive or punitive, then the absence of key parties is irrelevant, and the U.S. would be overjoyed to share with as many others as possible its self-assumed burden of collective security and peacekeeping. However, if to deal with the conflict means to negotiate a solution, it is not at all clear why it does not matter that some of the adversaries will have nothing to do with the effort.

What has in fact been the position of the non-member parties to the Vietnam war?

The *Republic of South Vietnam*—As indicated, the South Vietnamese Government has applied for UN membership, expressing its ability and willingness to abide by the Charter. Moreover, it maintains a Permanent Observer office at the New York Headquarters as well as at the European office of the UN in Geneva. Thus one might assume that it is disposed both to UN jurisdiction, and its own participation in UN debates. In December, 1967, Saigon strongly opposed any prospective Vietcong participation in UN peace talks, saying that "one should talk to the aggressors," that is, the North Vietnamese, not what it characterized as a "tool" of the North Vietnamese Army.[11]

---

[10]News Conference, September 8, 1967, U.S. Department of State *Bulletin,* September 25, 1967.

[11]*New York Times,* December 6, 1967.

Saigon's comments became even more pointed. On January 15, 1968, President Nguyen van Thieu openly criticized the United States for intensifying unilateral talk of negotiations. He regretted to say that "our allies sometimes have not avoided these pitfalls, by placing themselves at the center of peace efforts on Vietnam, for instance by asking the United Nations or other governments to help in solving the Vietnamese problem."[12] A week later Foreign Minister Tran van Do said South Vietnam would not recognize peace proposals from the United Nations or any other third party.[13]

North Vietnam—The Democratic Republic of Vietnam (DRVN) does pose a very major problem for possible UN efforts, although not the sole one. It has applied for UN membership and has never rescinded its application for admission. Yet during recent U.S. efforts to involve the UN, Hanoi has consistently rejected any role for the Organization. Just before the Security Council met on February 1, 1966, Hanoi, charging that "the United States is seeking again to use the United Nations to cover up expansion of the war of aggression in Vietnam and to force on the Vietnamese people a settlement," warned that any resolution the Council might adopt "intervening in the Vietnam question would be null and void."[14] A year later there had been no shift: "The Vietnam problem has no concern with the United Nations and the United Nations has absolutely no right to interfere in any way in the Vietnam question."[15] And in January, 1968, the Foreign Minister announced that

> the U.S. imperialists are scheming to bring the Vietnam question before the Security Council. . . . It is necessary to point out that the United Nations has no right to discuss the . . . question. Whatever resolution . . . is adopted . . . is null and void.[16]

Given these statements, it can be assumed that the DRVN will

---

[12]*Ibid.*, January 16, 1968.

[13]*Ibid.*, January 26, 1968.

[14]*Ibid.*, February 2, 1966. Hanoi said on that occasion that "consideration of the United States war acts in Vietnam falls within the competence of the 1954 Geneva Conference on Indochina, and not of the United Nations Security Council."

[15]Spokesman for DRVN Foreign Ministry, Hanoi VNA International Service in English, March 27, 1967.

[16]Foreign Minister Nguyen Duy Triah, on Hanoi radio. *New York Times*, January 3, 1968.

not be a part of any UN action unless it is sufficiently in Hanoi's interest to alter its position. Until such a change, the UN will be limited to actions that are not dependent on Hanoi's participation. As discussed later, however, the prospects of UN involvement in bringing peace may well be dependent on a reconsideration of the basic problem of UN membership, not only with regard to North Vietnam, but the other Asian party to the Geneva agreements as well—Communist China.

National Liberation Front—The U.S. position toward NLF participation in negotiations matured further in Ambassador Goldberg's November 2 response to Senatorial questions in which he stated that the U.S. would favor NLF participation in any Security Council discussion of Vietnam. But if the Front itself is to be believed, its rejection of UN involvement has been identical with that of Hanoi:

> The NFLSV is determined to expose before the public the United States imperialists' perfidious plot to hide behind the United Nations flag to accelerate the aggressive war in South Vietnam and the war of destruction against North Vietnam. The NFLSV solemnly declares: the United Nations has no right to make decisions concerning the affairs of the South Vietnamese people.[17]

It is unclear what degree of relative independence from Hanoi the NLF might have in the unlikely event either one decided to liquidate the war on terms the other did not favor. From the evidence of the NLF's intimate relationship with Hanoi,[18] it seems premature, if not fruitless, to speculate on a diplomatic scenario in which the NLF participated in international negotiations on any basis but the consent of Hanoi.

For *China*, Peking's unchanging rejection of UN jurisdiction is part of its over-all hostility toward the Organization that continues to bar it from membership:

> The Vietnam question has nothing to do with the United Nations. The 1954 Geneva agreements were reached outside the United Nations and the latter has no right whatsoever to interfere in the affairs

---

[17] Statement by NLF Central Committee February 2, 1966, cited by Ambassador Goldberg in his testimony of November 2, 1967, *supra*.

[18] See, for example, Douglas Pike, *Vietcong: The Organization and Techniques of the National Liberation Front of South Vietnam* (Cambridge: MIT Press, 1966).

of Vietnam and Indochina. It is the duty of the countries participating in the Geneva conference to safeguard the Geneva agreements and no meddling by the United Nations is called for, nor will it be tolerated. This is the case today as it was in the past, and so will it remain in the future.[19]

It is . . . clear to everyone that the United Nations has no right whatever to meddle in the Vietnam question, nor can it solve the issue. The Vietnam question has nothing to do with the United Nations.[20]

One can speculate on the likely solidarity of the Hanoi-Peking front in the face of hypothetical circumstances inclining one but not the other to serious negotiations. Based on the evidence, the one so inclined would be Hanoi, with China the reluctant dragon. Peking would be likely to disfavor any action in which North Vietnam seemed to give up on its basic aims on the South, or in general diminished its militancy. Since Chinese policy undoubtedly plays a highly influential role in North Vietnamese perceptions and calculations, we can surely assume that Chinese hostility toward the UN would probably be an additional factor constraining Hanoi from taking the UN route even if tempted to do so. Indeed, if Hanoi wants to disengage, Peking's anti-UN posture might be an additional reason for Hanoi to avoid a UN role. If we stand the question on its head and ask whether Hanoi would be influenced to use the UN channel if Peking were invited to take a seat at the UN, the answer would still probably depend on the strength of Chinese convictions about the correctness of a policy of militancy on the part of Hanoi.

---

[19]*Peoples Daily,* April 10, 1965.
[20]*Ibid.,* August 7, 1965.

III. UN POSSIBILITIES VIS-A-VIS THE WILL
TO COMPROMISE

The distinction I have been urging about what kind of use of the UN one has in mind leads directly to the second broad point, basically political. It may be formulated roughly thus: *the possibilities of UN involvement in Vietnam vary in direct proportion to the willingness of both sides to move toward a genuine compromise settlement.* By any logic, this has to mean, in concrete terms: moderating Hanoi's basic aim of control of South Vietnam, and/or Washington's basic aim of destroying the Vietcong operations in South Vietnam, plus turning back North Vietnam. These aims are of course totally incompatible. A subordinate proposition would hold that *UN possibilities also vary significantly according to the anxiety of one or both sides to terminate hostilities.*

So far, diplomatic efforts have taken place in a setting in which neither side will compromise its aims, and only one—the U.S.—displays even moderate interest in terminating hostilities. This is the background for the basically negative reaction the U.S. has encountered so far in trying to mobilize the UN behind its side in the war (as well as for its efforts to bring Hanoi to negotiate). The crucial and central questions are and remain: *whether the party that wants to stop the fighting is also willing to compromise its basic aims;* and *whether the fighting can be stopped without at least one side moderating its aims.*

To sharpen this ratio between UN possibilities and the disposition of one or both sides to terminate the fighting or moderate their aims, a range of possible situations can be set forth, each representing a different prospect for constructive UN action.

1. *Neither side is anxious enough to terminate hostilities to show any disposition to compromise aims.*

This has appeared to many to be the prevailing situation, although it may be in process of changing. The most probable role of the UN, if the situation continues, would be the least desirable from the American standpoint. A growing majority will tend to lump both sides together indiscriminately and regardless of merit, and to pressure the most readily available party—the U.S.— to back down. This tendency has characterized international diplomacy, in and out of the UN, since the 1965 U.S. decisions on bombing and buildup.

The frustrations and mounting sense of urgency and even despair on the part of others can take a variety of forms. Typical was the "Appeal of the Heads of State and Government of Seventeen Non-aligned Countries Concerning the Crisis in Vietnam," calling for "negotiations without preconditions," and handed to the U.S. Government on April 1, 1965, by seventeen UN neutrals. More specific was the proposal made to the General Assembly by Canada on September 27, 1967, of a four-step plan for a return to the cease-fire arrangements worked out at the Geneva Conference of 1954 (see Appendix C).

The organ most likely to act in the circumstances would be the General Assembly. Not having to act as a "third-party" to the dispute, as the Security Council does, in one view the Assembly "despite objections from both sides, would reactivate diplomacy and alert a wide audience that there were uncharted dangers ahead."[21] As suggested earlier, the United States would probably look like the least resistant target. If continued warfare led to UN action, it would probably take the form of pressure on the United States to stop the bombing and otehwise moderate its political goals in Vietnam. This is, of course, not necessarily all bad. If the author may be forgiven the sin of quoting himself, it has long been axiomatic that "if political war aims were defined by a UN majority rather than by any single nation, including our own, hostilities might be brought to an end more promptly than otherwise and a chance bought to try again with weapons of diplomacy."[22]

---

[21]Abraham Bargman, "Can the UN Act on Vietnam?" *War/Peace Report,* October 1967, pp. 12-13.

[22]Lincoln P. Bloomfield, *The United Nations and U.S. Foreign Policy* (Rev. ed.; Boston: Little Brown, 1967), Chapter 5.

The Vietnam matter is technically still on the Security Council's agenda. But the role of the Security Council under present conditions is nil, short of major U.S. policy shifts, because of the virtual certainty of a Soviet veto, and perhaps also a French one. U Thant has pointed to the unlikelihood that the Council could contribute toward finding a settlement in the face of opposition of one permanent member.[23]

The role of the Secretary-General is not as circumscribed as either of the two major political organs. U Thant has already sought to act as interlocutor, source of formulas, and potential mediator, negotiator, or arbiter. For three years he has submitted ideas and proposals to the parties with a view "to creating conditions congenial for negotiations," proposals which they have not accepted. On March 14, 1967, reviewing this record, U Thant in an *aide-mémoire* to the parties proposed three steps: a general stand-still truce, preliminary talks, and reconvening of the Geneva Conference. He emphasized that cessation of the bombing of North Vietnam was the essential preliminary step. In the same paper he pressed for the participation in any talks of the NLF—a condition in general accepted by Washington. U Thant wanted it clearly understood that "he is acting within the limits of his good offices purely in his private capacity,"[24] a circumlocution worthy of his predecessor. He has incurred the wrath of both sides at times. The U.S. has not enjoyed U Thant's criticism of the bombing, and in its reply Washington accepted the three steps but made no mention of the essential precondition involving the bombing.[25]

Earlier the Secretary-General had proposed three points, the first and foremost of which was cessation of the bombing, but the second of which was the "scaling down of all military activities by all sides in South Vietnam"—a proposal that apparently degraded his stock in Hanoi. (The third point called for "willingness to enter into discussions with those who are actually fighting.")[26] The first point remains at the heart of U Thant's position, and the third seems to have been accepted by the U.S. The second seems

---

[23]Secretary-General's Press Conference, September 16, 1967, *UN Monthly Chronicle,* October, 1967, p.24.

[24]UN Press Release SG/SM/683, March 28, 1967.

[25]U.S. Mission to the UN Press Release 31, March 18, 1967.

[26]For the Secretary-General's proposals, see Appendix B.

to have been subsequently dropped—another example of the tendency of prolonged stalemate to focus criticism and exhortation on the most susceptible side rather than remaining even-handed.

U Thant has recently made the prediction that if only the bombing of the North were ceased, "meaningful talks would take place in a matter of three to four weeks."[27] Many delegations appear to share his general attitude toward the Vietnam conflict. A majority of delegations at the 1966 General Assembly session endorsed his earlier 3-point program in the course of debate. His later 3-point program received wide approbation at the 1967 session.

There is no reason in UN constitutional theory why the Secretary-General could not take an initiative under Article 99 of the Charter to stimulate and even shape a formal deliberation by the Security Council over Vietnam. But U Thant seems inhibited by the same factors that have given a large number of UN delegations a feeling of, at worst, impotence, at best, grave uncertainty as to how and with what effect the UN can act under present circumstances.

2. *Both sides want to stop the fighting.*

In this case various international organization actions might be realistically contemplated, differing according to the degree to which both Hanoi and the Vietcong will compromise their aim of gaining control of South Vietnam, and the degree to which the United States will accept a coalition government in Saigon.

(a) *Hanoi is unwilling to abandon its takeover attempt.* The will to stop fighting could create the modalities for negotiation, whether under UN auspices or not. But as in Korea in 1952-53, international action would be limited at most to cease-fire diplomacy and the housekeeping of negotiations. UN or other international peace observation or peacekeeping would in this case be rejected by Hanoi. It could of course function on one side only, as in Korea. (This possibility is elaborated in the next section.) But UN willingness to operate the cease-fire on the South Vietnamese side only, with South but not North Vietnamese consent, is highly dubious: Moscow would undoubtedly oppose it,

---

[27]See, for example, Secretary-General's Press Conference, September 16, 1967, *UN Monthly Chronicle,* October, 1967, p. 24.

and without NLF concurrence the majority of members would be most unlikely to agree to such an arrangement.

(b) *The U.S.—and Saigon—accept NLF participation in a coalition government.* UN involvement in post-armistice arrangements would probably emphasize face-saving political devices such as a diplomatic "presence" and perhaps observation of new elections in South Vietnam. In addition, UN agencies would be in a position to furnish or administer economic aid and technical assistance programs of reconstruction. "Peacekeeping" would obviously not be the problem.

(c) *The DRVN is willing to abandon its takeover attempt.* This is of course the easiest case of all. The objectives of international diplomatic actions would be to save face for the parties, facilitate negotiations, assist in execution of agreements that may be reached, enable the departure of U.S. and allied forces, provide reassurances against resumption of hostilities, facilitate chosen solutions such as elections, neutralization of Indochina, and sealing off or opening up the 17th parallel, assist in political development, and help to restore the Vietnamese economy and otherwise bind wounds. All organs and agencies of the UN are usable. The moment would have come that was forecast by Secretary Rusk on January 31, 1966: "Now, there would come a time, if the other side is willing, when the United Nations might play an extremely useful role in observing, safeguarding, watching, patroling, insuring that agreements are, in fact, carried out."[28] All the same functions could be performed by a revived Geneva Conference and ad hoc control machinery, or by the latter in combination with UN operations for certain specified tasks.

3. One side wants to stop the fighting.

This may reflect increasingly the real situation, with the U.S. the party most interested in termination of hostilities. The conditions suggest in turn two subordinate cases:

(a) *The U.S. is anxious enough for an end to the war to compromise its aim of decisively liquidating the Communist takeover effort in South Vietnam.* This would clearly represent a basic change of position for the United States. It would presumably lead Washington unilaterally to end the bombing of North Viet-

---

[28]News Conference, U.S. Department of State *Bulletin*, February 14, 1966.

nam unconditionally, and to accept ambiguous or coalition-type political arrangements under which it could gracefully withdraw even with the risk of later NLF takeover. Under these conditions it seems certain that a strong UN majority could be found to support an active UN diplomatic role toward that end — including pressures on Hanoi. It is then not out of the question to contemplate an active UN peace observation role in South Vietnam, ranging from border observers to technical assistance to the Government akin to that given to the Congo during the UN operation. On the other hand, this solution does not really call for the type of international observation and peacekeeping tasks that would be effective in protecting South Vietnam from further depredations.

The Security Council might become a possible focus of diplomacy, since Moscow might well be able to support action there, on the assumption that for Hanoi there would be nothing but benefit from such a multilateral U.S. de-escalation and acceptance of a significant NLF role in the South. In view of the fact that the UN continues to refuse a seat to Communist China, the latter, it can be assumed, would object to use of the UN. The relative strength of Hanoi's greater dependence economically as well as ideologically on Peking or Moscow might determine whether Hanoi would defy China's anti-UN prejudices and participate (as China itself participated in UN debates on Korea in early 1951) despite the war between China and the United Nations.

(b) *The U.S. wishes to end the fighting but is not willing to moderate the requirement that Hanoi relinquish its goals in South Vietnam.* This would represent a modification of the present situation that at this writing seems more likely. UN involvement might be possible, even with no abandonment of fundamental U.S. aims of defending the political independence and territorial integrity of South Vietnam, if the U.S. showed itself willing to de-escalate the shooting war in order to confine it to South Vietnam. (Former U.S. Deputy Representative Charles Yost made a comparable prediction to the Senate Foreign Relations Committee on October 26, 1967, saying that the UN might be willing to act if the United States took "concrete, unambiguous, and unconditional measures of de-escalation" and Hanoi did not respond.) [29]

---

[29] *New York Times,* October 27, 1967.

If the U.S. stopped the bombing, it would then be possible —
though not certain — that substantial majorities could be found
in the General Assembly for some forms of international involvement even over Hanoi's — and therefore Moscow's — objections.
Given a cessation of the bombing, it is possible that a two-thirds
Assembly majority would support active UN involvement in efforts
to bring about a negotiated settlement. If the U.S. were to cease
the bombing *and* also make specific proposals envisaging a compromise political solution for Vietnam, it is possible — though not
certain — that a two-thirds majority would support steps that
would be consistent with the remaining minimal U.S. aim of defending South Vietnam against externally directed terrorism and
subversion. Former U.S. Representative Ernest A. Gross has recommended that the cessation of bombing be followed by a special
session of the General Assembly, which we would strongly urge
to adopt without delay a call for a cease-fire and a negotiated
settlement.[30]

Given unconditional cessation of the bombing, there would be
a fair—but only fair—possibility of securing enough political support to enable a modest UN peace observation operation to be
mounted on the South Vietnamese side of the 17th parallel, and
possibly in Laos, to monitor further North Vietnamese infiltration
into the South—either to discourage it, or to give greater international credence to what is now purely U.S. evidence.

Such a neutral UN observation and reporting operation could
be in the highest interests of both the U.S. and South Vietnam.
At best it could act as a politically influential deterrent to significant North Vietnamese infiltration; it could attract new support
to Saigon's own efforts; and it could contribute to politicizing
an operation that many feel is seen by Washington in excessively
military terms. At worst, if the war went on indefinitely, the U.S.
would not suffer under the stigma, as it now is, of acting virtually
alone.

There is one related action the United Nations could take that
would be dependent only on the United States' willingness to consider stopping the bombing, and irrespective of Hanoi's views.

The U.S. has said that it might stop the bombing in North

---

[30]In *Vista, op. cit.,* p. 68.

Vietnam on the "assumption," contained in the President's San Antonio speech of September 29, 1967, that the other side would not exploit the pause to seize a new tactical advantage. Secretary of Defense Clark Clifford has interpreted this to mean that North Vietnam would not be required to halt its "normal" supply of men and material into South Vietnam.[31] Even if Hanoi intended to negotiate, the situation would in all probability be highly ambiguous, given the Asian tendency to continue hostilities during peace negotiations. Particularly given this inherent ambiguity, the United States can expect great international pressure to ignore even a significant escalatory buildup by Hanoi after the bombing stops. Even apart from Hanoi's disappointing response to the original San Antonio formula, I suppose that this is one major reason why the United States has hesitated to take this step.

I am attracted by the notion of the United States inviting a representative international team to go to Saigon *prior* to any such suspension of the bombing, there to be fully briefed on order of battle, deployments, and resupply rates and routes. The purpose would be to provide neutral and objective observation of what happens when the bombing stops. Perhaps this team could have its own neutral photo-reconnaissance experts to preclude ambiguities about alleged major escalation preparations, by being able to compare "before" with "after" without having to rely on the word of the United States—or of Hanoi.

Among other things, this would give the UN a constructive role to play. The action suggested would make the best use of the UN, i.e., in placing credible neutrals on the ground, in advance, as witnesses to an international action in order to prevent it from forever being blurred by ambiguity. This was the great value of the UN Commission, chaired by an Indian, which sat on the 38th parallel in Korea on the night of June 24, 1950, and it could usefully be duplicated in Vietnam. Finally, the least the stop-the-bombing advocates among neutral nations could do is facilitate U.S. moves in this direction by making personnel available to ensure that minimum conditions would be observed. Serious consideration should, in my opinion, be given to making this a part

---

[31]*New York Times,* January 26, 1968.

of a bargain between Washington and the UN before any cessation of the bombing.

Let me sum up the political equations that emerge from this analysis. While hostilities continue without redefinition of either side's war aims, the UN's role in promoting the end of hostilities is marginal at best. The more unyielding the two sides are in their aims, the less constructive the role for any diplomatic instrumentality. So long as the United States is carrying the war to North Vietnam—an ally of the Soviet Union, among other things—even UN action to encourage negotiations seems unlikely. Since it is unthinkable politically for the UN either to substitute for U.S. power in containing the Communist attack on South Vietnam or to endorse unilateral American efforts to do so, the UN under present conditions will remain essentially irrelevant to Vietnam except to the extent it can persuade the parties to moderate their hitherto inflexible objectives. Despite the rhetoric, there has never really been any doubt on this score in Washington. As Secretary Rusk told a news conference in early 1966, "I think it is rather unlikely that the United Nations would provide troops or forces until there has been some sort of understanding about peace and a cease-fire.... I think it is unlikely that the Security Council would provide forces for the purpose of fighting in the present struggle."[32]

On the positive side of the ledger, the more willing one side is to disengage, the more likely it is to receive UN political support, despite the fact that the UN is severely handicapped by the nonmembership of most of the parties. The more willing one or both sides are to move the war from the battlefield to the conference table, the greater the number of means whereby international diplomacy can be helpful in promoting an end to the hostilities and assisting in the negotiations. And the more willing both sides are to compromise their political ends, the greater the role the UN or other international organizations can play in guaranteeing the peace, restoring order, and promoting economic development.

[32]January 31, 1966, U.S. Department of State *Bulletin,* February 14, 1966.

IV. AFTER THE FIGHTING STOPS

Once diplomacy has moved the situation from the battlefield to negotiation and cease-fire, one can then envisage a substantial role for the UN or ad hoc international machinery, always keeping in mind the alternative possibility of gradual de-escalation and fade-out without any formal negotiations, as happened in the Greek insurgency of the late 1940s and the Malayan emergency of 1948-60.

Once fighting has stopped, if an observation and peacekeeping role for third parties is accepted by South Vietnam alone, and hopefully by both sides, it will not matter particularly whether the UN or some other international machinery is engaged in the effort. Under the most optimistic of our scenarios the effort would be focused on reconstruction and even reunification of the two Vietnams. Under the more plausible circumstance, the prime object will be to create conditions enabling the U.S. to withdraw substantial armed forces, while at the same time affording the South Vietnamese reassurance in the form of guarantees against renewed North Vietnamese-led terrorism and attempted takeover, and assistance in building a nation capable of withstanding pressures that may well be permanent, as they are in Korea and Germany.

Without prejudice to whether this role is played by the UN, a renewed Geneva Conference, or a new ad hoc arrangement, several essential tasks are involved. The first broad category might be called peace observation—essentially the supervision of a truce. The functions involved would include:

(1) *Observing that an agreed cease-fire is maintained.* This is a task of inspection and public reporting that can be performed in three ways: directly by the adversaries; by partisans of each state, e.g., the United States and the Soviet Union or China; or by third-party observers neutral to the fight, e.g., Asians, Scandinavians, and other UN neutrals. The latter is clearly the best type, assuming competent and unbiased individuals, if recriminations are to be avoided. Its disadvantage is to run the theoretical danger

of temptation to overlook Communist violations in order to preserve the cease-fire. This possibility is usually dealt with by ensuring a balanced composition, along with maximum openness of reporting channels.

(2) *Observing the agreed withdrawal of non-South Vietnamese forces.* The North Vietnamese may simply melt back into the North (and the Vietcong into the woodwork in the South); but the United States cannot do the same. The latter's withdrawal is promised in point 8 of the U.S. 14 points to take place "not later than six months after" fulfillment of the conditions that "the other side withdraws its forces to the North, ceases infiltration, and the level of violence thus subsides." The contemplated timing of the first point is unclear, i.e. how U.S. forces will be withdrawn "as the other side withdraws its," but only *after* this condition has been fulfilled. Presumably it means after assurances are in hand with regard to the latter.

(3) *Controlling the possible routes of infiltration into South Vietnam* (or, it must be added, from the latter into the North, if Vietnam ever entered the stage sometimes seen in Korea when a jingoist Seoul regime actively sought the "liberation" of the North). The Canadian proposal referred to earlier envisages as a "first step" alongside the bombing cessation the restoration of the "intended status" of the demilitarized buffer zone along the 17th parallel. This would be internationally supervised, either by the UN or by an ad hoc arrangement.[33]

The latter raises fundamental questions of the sort that have bedevilled the Vietnamese situation. A barrier between the two Vietnams presupposes that reunification is at the very least deferred, if not ruled out as a solution. It is also uncommonly hard to implement.

The entire recent history of Vietnam underscores how phenomenally difficult it is even today, with virtually unlimited manpower and technological resources, to monitor the flow of men and material across the passes and through the Ho Chi Minh trails in Laos. Even to control infiltration across the 17th parallel in Vietnam proper requires a billion-dollar electronic barrier.[34]

[33]See UN Document A/PV.1569, September 27, 1967.

[34]Announced by Secretary of Defense Robert S. McNamara, September 17, 1967.

In the most unpromising case, with the cease-fire purely and simply a Communist trick to gain time while preparing for another war, effective border control is no more possible in Vietnam as a preventive than it was in 1950 in Korea (or even today in that unhappy land). If it were undertaken, nevertheless, the observation force required would be large, and its costs would be far beyond anything the UN had done previously.

But if fighting ceases, several things also change. For one thing, if Hanoi has reason to believe it can benefiit more from observing the agreement and working through the political process in Saigon, inspection would be minimal, and in that sense virtually purely symbolic. If Hanoi intended to call off the war while continuing to infiltrate a modest level of support and personnel to reinforce Vietcong cadres and units in the South, such a supply operation would pose a real problem of control but, given the quantities, might not be as important to choke off as during a war. And finally, given a cease-fire, the inspection process can take place in ways that are infeasible under combat conditions, e.g., unhampered low-level aerial reconnaissance, fixed control posts along the border, and more open assistance to Laos and even Cambodia to curtail infiltration through their territories.

It is in the latter connection that the planned electronic barrier between North and South along the inaptly-named Demilitarized Zone (DMZ) might facilitate the task of controlling possible infiltration after a cease-fire. In effect, the task would be to monitor an electronic minefield with a view to detecting and possibly apprehending significant infiltration. As indicated above, "significant" is a function of the durability of the cease-fire. In the Middle East, occasionally Bedouin families, goats, and even sometimes terrorists and saboteurs for a decade crossed the line of demarcation patrolled by the UN along the Gaza Strip, but did not upset the truce so long as the parties were not anxious to resume open hostilities. The same thing occasionally happens along the patrolled truce line in Kashmir.

If there is a genuine cease-fire or truce, political conditions might then alter sufficiently to make possible extension of the DMZ through Laos to the Mekong River, thus establishing a modest but effective international barrier—and deterrence—to substantial cheating. This would require substantial personnel, and this raises serious questions of feasibility.

If the electronic barrier were actually manned by international observers, the numbers and types of personnel needed would be of an unprecedented order of technical skills adequate to operate sophisticated anti-infiltration devices such as radar, acoustical, and infrared detectors. It seems evident that UN operation of such a barrier is improbable, given both the expense and skills involved in maintenance, and the fact that the deterioration rate of the barrier contemplated now is relatively rapid, i.e., one year or so, unless substantially renewed. Perhaps more to the point, such a barrier would run directly counter to one not improbable political scenario that would involve opening up rather than sealing off the two Vietnams.

Short of that, but still assuming a cease-fire regarded as a genuine truce, however vigorous the efforts to gain political power and even to reinforce the cadres in the South, border control could be planned and staffed as an essentially symbolic assurance, with a minimum level of infiltration actually tolerated. The level of manning required under these circumstances, on the UNEF model (1 post every 1/2 km) with aerial, helicopter, and mobile inspection teams, could be as small as UNEF (5,000 to 6,000) and in all events probably not more than 10,000.

(4) *An international "presence" in South Vietnam.* One possible form is the classic UN "presence," which performs assigned operational or diplomatic functions, and also implies symbolically the concern of the international community. One man appointed by the UN Secretary-General sufficed to convey such an impression in Amman following the troubled summer of 1958. Eight UN observers observed the situation in Sarawak and North Borneo in 1963 and confirmed the desire of the inhabitants to form a union with Malaysia. There is no reason why UN neutrals cannot actually observe the fairness of a new all-Vietnamese election (as the United States implied might be done after the 1954 Geneva accords).

Other kinds of observation operations discussed earlier would require a fairly substantial force of UN-armbanded soldiers or police, even to undertake essentially symbolic observation of possible avenues of infiltration, to observe elections, or to create a country-wide presence. In this connection, it might be very desirable to work out alternative calculations now of those needs, and to use the results in a formula for withdrawal of U.S. forces under specified conditions. For example, under one of our postulated scenarios approximately 10,000 uniformed international neutrals would be required. Assuming 500,000 U.S. military personnel in Vietnam at that time, the ratio would be 1 to 50. The U.S. position on phased withdrawal could specify that every UN observer installed along the 17th parallel, or elsewhere, would be matched, *pari passu,* by the departure of fifty Americans. Under the most favorable conditions for UN intervention—i.e., U.S. stand-down, Soviet cooperation, and a formula for eventual neutralization and reunification of Vietnam—presumably the ratio might rise to one neutral UN soldier for every 100 Americans who departed.

The semantic line between "peace observation" and "peace-keeping" is rather nebulous. Nonetheless, to sharpen the issue of UN involvement, the category of *peacekeeping* is useful. At the most—and least likely diplomatically—would be an international force actively engaged in dealing with breaches of the truce and prepared, as in the Congo, to defend itself. At the least, the armistice apparatus would have the task of investigating and eventually mediating and arbitrating breaches of the truce, in the process arranging cease-fires, as has been the case virtually wherever this type of operation has been entered upon, such as Palestine, Kashmir, or Cyprus. As a UN field operation, at a minimum it would report back to the Security Council, or the Secretary-General, and thus to the membership of the UN and the news media of the world. This would seem a signal advantage of the UN over virtually any other kind of monitoring arrangement.

The matter of expenses for anything resembling UN peace-keeping can be resolved only on the basis of the strength of interest on the part of countries such as the United States in using the facilities and symbols of the Organization. The cost of maintaining UNEF, with 5,000 or so men, was approximately $20 million per year. The UN Congo force, with almost 20,000 men, cost close to $140 million per year. The UN Cyprus force, financed by voluntary contributions, costs approximately $20 million a year for about 5,000 men.

The obvious answer is that if such devices will enable the United

States honorably to disengage from Vietnam, it should be delighted to pay the relatively minor costs of UN peacekeeping. Politically, however, the likelihood of such operations is minimal without Soviet cooperation or at least acquiescence. The chronic question would therefore be posed as to whether only the Security Council is to authorize the expenses involved—a position Moscow has clung to with rigidity throughout the peacekeeping-financing crisis of the last half-decade. Washington has been equally insistent that the Assembly may apportion such expenses.

In order that *this* peace observation and/or peacekeeping not have to carry the additional freight of finding definitive new formulas for UN financing, it may be that voluntary contributions similar to those for Cyprus would be the politically most expedient method, despite U Thant's plaintive and obviously deeply held conviction that it represents just about the worst possible method from the standpoint of predictable administration.

It must be repeated that all the above presupposes changed circumstances. U Thant has stated that UN truce supervision is not feasible under present conditions. Even assuming a stand-still truce along the lines of his three points, he said on April 1, 1967, that "supervision of the truce, under present circumstances, is impractical." Presumably he meant supervision on both sides of the border. Perhaps he was also minimizing for tactical diplomatic reasons any premature implication of deep UN involvement.

In a similarly cautious vein, U.S. planning ought to assume that North Vietnam would probably not welcome UN peace observation, and further that any inspection regime, if it were accepted, would be subject to the disabilities attending all international efforts to monitor agreements behind Communist lines, e.g., Berlin, Vienna, North Korea—*and* the International Control Commission (ICC) in Laos and North Vietnam.

It can however be argued that under the most likely, if not the most desirable, circumstances the important task will lie in South Vietnam. Assuming the latter's willingness, there is no inherent obstacle to such UN presences or operations. There is no fixed form that such a UN role would necesarily take.

Past UN practices and presences show that a role may take many different forms. It may be limited or extensive; minimal at the outset and remaining so, or developing into larger dimensions; strictly UN in character or undertaken in collaboration with non-UN entities; and limited either to political or military or economic spheres, or comprising a combination thereof. Further, such a role may be originated by the Security Council, the General Assembly, or the Secretary-General. It may involve either the "decision-making" stage or the "implementation" stage, or both. Finally, a UN role may emerge before, during, or after cease-fire negotiations, or at all three stages.

Some recent peace observation and peacekeeping efforts have operated outside the UN framework. The obvious one is the International Commission set up in the Geneva Agreement of 1954 "for the control and supervision over the application of the provisions of the agreement on the cessation of hostilities in Viet-Nam." Consisting of Canada, Poland, and India, with the latter as chairman, it was required to fulfill tasks of "control, observation, inspection and investigation." These involved the movements of armed forces, controlling the demarcation lines, and watching for possible violations at ports, airfields, and frontiers in order to regulate "the introduction into the country of armed forces, military personnel and of all kinds of arms, munitions and war material." Recommendations were by majority vote, the chairman's vote to be decisive; but when dealing with alleged violations, the vote had to be unanimous. Unlike the Korean armistice supervisory organization, the ICC had the distinction of operating within the northern, Communist half of a divided Asian state. However, it has been hopelessly divided on the rights and wrongs of the violations that have taken place on both sides virtually from the start.

Another example might be the four-nations Joint Military Committee set up independently of the UN, although carrying out a UN resolution, to obtain the evacuation of Chinese Nationalist troops from the northern provinces of Burma in 1953-54.

Perhaps the closest relevant analogy would be the Neutral Nations Supervisory Commission (NNSC), established under Swedish chairmanship after the Korean armistice, and endowed with functions roughly comparable to those given the ICC in Vietnam. It had even less success in penetrating the Communist half of the areas.

The essential point is that, given a cease-fire, a number of important functions can be performed by observers, mediators, policemen, and reporters. These functions can be performed by the sides themselves in an adversary operation. They can be performed by an ad hoc organization constituted, like the ICC, for the purpose and subsequently disbanded. They can be performed by a regional international organization — of which there is none in the Asian region. They can be — and have been — performed by the United Nations.

It needs to be said finally that these functions can be dispensed with completely, relying instead on the basic self-interest of the parties in living up to the agreement. Some close observers discount entirely the need or desirability of any policing plan whatever. Robert Shaplen, for example, argues that "if the South is to rediscover its own revolutionary traditions, and to preserve and modify them in the relation to the communist North, it must be as unmolested and even as unsupervised as possible . . . not under the gaze of an ineffective international police element."[35] He was referring to the ICC, and even suggested that the UN be used to underwrite a Geneva-type agreement. But it is at least arguable that Shaplen's point applies to *any* attempt to structure a supervisory function in post-hostilities Vietnam.

So far I have been discussing a supervisory function. Surely it is far less ambiguous that help will be needed on a substantial scale in South Vietnam in rebuilding, binding up the wounds of the latest war, and assisting in moving the country toward the level of social, economic, and political development that alone might fortify it against successful subversion. Many of the same problems will also exist in North Vietnam — or in a united country.

I assume that the United States would under any circumstances be the largest contributor to an aid program and, whatever international programs were brought in, would also contribute aid unilaterally. It would be logical to mobilize all available resources for the job, and the UN family of agencies has an obvious role to play. Existing organizations such as ECAFE, the Asian Development Bank, the World Bank, the Mekong River program, UN social and economic assistance and advisory programs in rural and community development, housing, building, planning, and public ad-

---

[35]Robert Shaplen, "Viet-Nam: Crisis of Indecision," *Foreign Affairs,* October, 1967, p. 108.

ministration, and UNICEF — all these can and should be brought to bear. The UN High Commissioner for Refugees could operate under an expanded mandate in assisting with the frightful human problem of millions of displaced and uprooted persons.

It is not always remembered that during the UN operation in the Congo a substantial and useful civil program, in fact the largest technical assistance program ever undertaken by the UN involving most if not all of the vital sectors of Congolese governmental operations, operated alongside the UN force in the Congo. In Vietnam, if the UN were not involved in the peacekeeping aspect of the operation, perhaps there would not be the same impetus of support for a comparable effort. But U.S. planning might well consider now the ways in which humanitarian and developmental programs under international auspices could be included as part of the negotiating package of which cease-fire and phased U.S. military withdrawal would also be parts.

Perhaps the most analogous recent post-hostilities international operation was the UN Korean Reconstruction Agency (UNKRA), established by the General Assembly after the Korean fighting ended, and following delegation to the U.S. by the Security Council of the responsibility for emergency relief. UNKRA over the next five years or so furnished help on a broad spectrum ranging from fisheries and textile production through transport, power facilities, mines, irrigation, and flood control, to classrooms and paper for textbooks. Administered by an Agent-General (who was an American), UNKRA operated under a five member Advisory Committee (consisting of the U.S., U.K., Canada, India, and Uruguay). Forty states contributed to the program, which was coordinated with American assistance. When it ceased active operations on June 30, 1958, UNKRA had supplied about $150 million of aid of which the U.S. contributed 66.4 per cent.

There is no inherent reason why this kind of operation could not be conducted in South Vietnam, and, as President Johnson has several times implied, in North Vietnam as well. It may well be that the only way in which a majority of UN members could be enlisted to support such an enterprise would be if the offer were made to both Vietnams. The U.S. negotiating posture and the possibilities of sharing some of the continuing burdens might be improved if the U.S. agreed in advance to place the substantial economic aid already pledged at the disposal of the UN and related agencies.

V. SOME CONCLUSIONS

In the end, we go back to the beginning. Apart from the rhetoric of propaganda, the UN has no operationally useful role to play in the Vietnam war until such time as both sides have a disposition to negotiate seriously — meaning something short of total achievement of political objectives, combined with a genuine desire to stop fighting. Then and only then can the UN play a major part — and it could be an important one in terms of peace observation and peacekeeping. Prior to that time, it seems to me only a disservice both to the Organization and the cause of common sense to pretend otherwise.

In the foregoing sections I have suggested some intermediate steps in which the UN might be helpful, for example in facilitating the stopping of the bombing by furnishing a responsible "before" and "after" presence on the ground, and the possible tactical diplomatic value of making such a presence a precondition to cessation of bombing. I have suggested that UN diplomacy can be marginally useful in influencing one and perhaps both sides to redefine their objectives in order to pave the way to negotiations, and perhaps more than marginally useful if the Secretary-General can play skillfully his role of intermediary and diplomatic innovator. I have suggested a rising scale of possible UN contributions to a cease-fire and follow-up, with proportionate substitution for a given number of U.S. soldiers of one UN observer, and again, the possible desirability of including this now in the U.S. negotiating package in order to make our promised withdrawal more credible, while leaving some international capacity behind for assurances and warning of gross violations. I have tried to sketch out some specific observations and patrol operation ranging from symbolic to effective, from a small political "presence" in the South Vietnamese capital to the manning of a continuing electronic barrier along the border. I have suggested a range of potential international organization contributions to help repair the ravages of the war, based on well-proven models from prior comparable situations, which in many past cases have involved varying mixes.

But the political backdrop behind all of these inescapably includes two hard facts: the high likelihood of continued subversive warfare by Hanoi upon its neighbors; and the present fact of non-universality of the United Nations (or any other international organization).

The first fact is a limiting condition to any serious prospect for reconciliation, unification of Vietnam, and peaceful coexistence in Southeast Asia. But the universality issue is, in the first instance, only as intractable as the United States of America continues to make it.

The non-membership in the UN of several key parties to the Vietnam war is neither a prime cause of the war nor the principal reason the war continues. But neither is it totally unrelated to the impotence and irrelevance of the UN during a most savage and costly war. A case can be made that increased international interaction and pressures over the last decade might have resulted in a different course of events in Vietnam. Among other possible outcomes, South Vietnam might today be under Communist rule. But it is not wholly improbable that broadening the diplomatic focus for Vietnam a decade ago would have finally produced a Laotian-type solution. However unsatisfactory the latter in absolute terms, it might look considerably better today than either Vietcong takeover or the present war. That is all water over the rice paddy. The problem now is the period ahead and the prospects for an honorable solution enabling the United States to terminate hostilities.

As one casts about for handles on the diplomatic problem of disengagement with honor, the issue of UN membership seems to be one of the few variables open to manipulation. Any change in U.S. policy toward China in the UN of course has to be balanced against disadvantages. But there seem few advantages left in continuing to appear to take the lead in keeping Peking — and Hanoi — out of the United Nations.

I have indicated in several places in this analysis the commonly held belief that the utility of the UN in helping to facilitate a stand-down in Vietnam may be fatally impaired by the non-membership of North Vietnam, particularly since Hanoi would presumably have already displeased Peking by deciding to stop the fighting. The availability of a UN seat to Peking, under conditions that suitably protect Taiwan's continued independent UN participation, would thus seem an essential prerequisite to U.S. policy objectives of honorable disengagement.

More than that, however, attempts to achieve a settlement of Vietnam that might endure, while also minimizing the chances for the U.S. to become isolated in future similar unilateral operations, should surely seek to include in a package an attempted diplomatic stabilization of relations with China. That China so far has avoided open conflict with the United States would seem reason enough to accept a *prima facie* case of non-aggressiveness, whatever the bluster, to justify altering U.S. policy toward Peking representation in the UN and, if enough advantages can be found, diplomatic recognition as well. The criterion for U.S. policy — the only criterion — must be self-interest.

Nothing about this suggestion implies any belief that China is not pathologically hostile to the United States, or that UN membership would necessarily have a softening effect. It is based exclusively on a calculus of benefit and gain concerning the Vietnam war and the general historic period ahead. *The Vietnam war in fact makes universality more rather than less desirable, necessary, or feasible.* It is extraordinarily difficult to see that we would be worse off if there were an obvious and automatic diplomatic nexus including all parties to the Vietnam war (or any other war for that matter) along with a potentially available range of good offices, peace observation, and peacekeeping mechanisms. The cost would be a marginal increase in frustrations and incivilities along the East River; but this would hardly seem to outweigh the potenial benefits.

A serious case can probably be made that in the long run American interests would be better served if *all* nations were represented in the UN by their effective governments, regardless of whether we approve of those regimes or not. It seems at least arguable that this country would benefit from the ability to confront and deal, publicly and within the UN, with the representatives of all states including those with which it has no direct diplomatic relations (for instance North Korea after the *U.S.S. Pueblo* incident of late January, 1968). Many values inhere in requiring them, as the United States is required, to account for and justify themselves in public confrontation before the rest of the international community. *In the world of the late 1960s membership in the UN should be regarded not as a right, but rather as an obligation that none should be permitted to escape.*

If this were the American philosophic view of the UN, the details of individual membership would be likely to fall into place, rather than resting on the myth we have embraced for two decades that the UN is a club of like-minded, peace-loving nations (it is not) ; that membership cannot be "a reward for aggressive behavior" (it sometimes is) ; or that Congress will impeach the President if he ceases to object to a seat for Communist China (few still think so). If these were ever meaningful or profitable policies, they are not now.

As for Vietnam, the broader issue is the three divided states — Germany, Korea, and Vietnam. The United States has generally opposed the admission of both halves of these countries as members because this would appear to confirm the legitimacy of the Communist regimes and the permanence of the divisions. West Germany, Monaco, South Korea, South Vietnam, the Vatican, and Switzerland are now represented by observers. U Thant suggested that the time has come to accept observers from other non-member nations (though for a time he carefully excluded East Germany), to maintain contact with the world which "would surely lead to a better understanding of the problems of the world and a more realistic approach to their solution."[36] East Germany itself created a minor stir by proposing that it become a member, and in the autumn of 1966 Soviet Foreign Minister Andrei Gromyko proposed that both Germanys be admitted.[37] U Thant has several times stated that the greatest impediment to the serious involvement in the Vietnam question of the UN is the fact that of all the parties heavily engaged in the conflict, only one — the United States — is a member of the Organization.

It would clearly be politically undesirable for the divided countries to be admitted to the UN on grounds that they are all *de jure* successors to earlier single states. But in all three cases, at war or at peace, successor governments are exercising *de facto* control over

---

[36]"Introduction to the Annual Report of the Secretary-General on the Work of the Organization," *UN Monthly Chronicle,* October, 1966, p. 121.

[37]Address to the General Assembly's 1413th Plenary Meeting, September 23, 1966, *New York Times,* September 24, 1966.

halves of the territories, and are so recognized by numbers of their peers. Admission to the UN of both halves of the three countries would not have to imply acceptance of any change in status for states that do not recognize them. The device of successor states was in fact used when the United Arab Republic broke up (but was not employed to bring in Pakistan after the partition of India). Perhaps a special form of "provisional membership" would ensure that the future disposition of all three was clearly acknowledged to be *sub judice,* and without prejudice.[38]

The history of our times is full of episodes in which, after carrying a unilateral policy to the point of no return, the UN is at last resorted to. Among other things this use of the UN as a *pis aller* helps to explain the modesty of its successes in the face of virtually hopeless and intractable problems. Some examples make the point — Britain in Palestine in 1947; the Netherlands in Indonesia in 1947-48; the U.S. in Korea in 1950; the U.S. and Britain in Lebanon and Jordan in 1958; Belgium in the Congo in the early 1960s; Britain and France in Suez in 1956; NATO in Cyprus in 1963-64; and Britain in Rhodesia in the past two years.

In each such case the country in question was initially determined to handle the problem its way, without outside "interference" or "meddling," and certainly without the participation of either the Communists or the neutrals. In each case, unilateral policy reached the end of the road and the UN became, in effect, a receiver in bankruptcy. Its record as such is not bad at all.

Without predicting that this will happen in Vietnam, it does occur to me to wonder what would happen if a great power, while it is still in control of events, had the foresight to take in advance the needful thought and action.

---

[38]Lincoln P. Bloomfield, "China, The United States, and the United Nations," *International Organization,* Autumn, 1966.

APPENDIX A
United States 14-point Peace Program
January 1966

1. The Geneva Agreements of 1954 and 1962 are an adequate basis for peace in Southeast Asia;

2. We would welcome a conference on Southeast Asia or on any part thereof;

3. We would welcome "negotiations without preconditions" as the 17 nations put it;

4. We would welcome unconditional discussions as President Johnson put it;

5. A cessation of hostilities could be the first order of business at a conference or could be the subject of preliminary discussions;

6. Hanoi's four points could be discussed along with other points which others might wish to propose;

7. We want no U.S. bases in Southeast Asia;

8. We do not desire to retain U.S. troops in South Vietnam after peace is assured;

9. We support free elections in South Vietnam to give the South Vietnamese a government of their own choice;

10. The question of reunification of Vietnam should be determined by the Vietnamese through their own free decision;

11. The countries of Southeast Asia can be non-aligned or neutral if that be their option;

12. We would much prefer to use our resources for the economic reconstruction of Southeast Asia than in war. If there is peace, North Vietnam could participate in a regional effort to which we would be prepared to contribute at least one billion dollars;

13. The President has said: "The Viet Cong would not have difficulty being represented and having their views represented if for a moment Hanoi decided she wanted to cease aggression. I don't think that would be an insurmountable problem."

14. We have said publicly and privately that we could stop the bombing of North Vietnam as a step toward peace although there has not been the slightest hint or suggestion from the other side as to what they would do if the bombing stopped.

APPENDIX B
Secretary-General's Proposals
May 1966

1. The cessation of the bombing of Vietnam.

2. The scaling down of all military activities by all sides in South Vietnam.

3. The willingness to enter into discussions with those who were actually fighting.

March 1967

1. A general stand-still truce.

2. Preliminary talks.

3. Reconvening of the Geneva Conference.

APPENDIX C
Canada's 4-step plan proposed September 1967

1. The bombing of the North might be terminated and the demilitarized zone restored to its intended status, subject to effective international supervision.

2. A freezing of the course of military events and capabilities in Vietnam at existing levels.

3. The cessation of all hostilities between the parties, that is, a cease-fire.

4. Following the cease-fire, withdrawal of all outside forces whose presence in the area of conflict was not provided for at Geneva, and the dismantling of military bases.

Vietnam, the United States, and
the United Nations

MAX GORDON

THE ATLANTIC CHARTER, Robert E. Sherwood has said, contained the "first planted seed" of the United Nations.[1] Almost simultaneously there was also planted the seed of the "Vietnam Situation," which in varying form has plagued and frustrated the UN ever since.

The Charter was proclaimed by Roosevelt and Churchill on August 12, 1941. Three weeks earlier Washington, reacting to the Vichy Government's capitulation to Japanese demands for bases in Indochina, had "bluntly" informed Vichy that either Japan or "we" would "take over" Indochina, depending on the outcome of the developing worldwide conflict. Our ambassador to Vichy, Admiral Leahy, later recalled that the "whole affair had but one meaning in my mind—the end of the French colonies in Asia."[2] On August 21, nine days after the proclamation of the Atlantic Charter, Secretary of State Hull again threatened French possession of Indochina by announcing American acceptance of the postwar restoration of allied empires—the *status quo ante* principle—except that, with respect to France, this would be contingent upon the defense of her colonial territories.[3]

The British and French recognized no exceptions to colonial restoration, and during the UN's four-year gestation period culminating in the blessed event at San Francisco, the tug of war between Roosevelt and his imperial allies over the postwar fate of Indochina dogged the prenatal preparations. In its first 23 years of life, the UN has been unable to surmount this fatal heritage. The conflict in Indochina, or Vietnam, and the UN have uniquely coexisted from the onset of both; and the world body has found itself impotent to deal with the conflict. An examination of the content of the relationship between the two may tell us something of both.

I

Despite Hull's August 21 statement Roosevelt interpreted the Atlantic Charter's promise of self-determination as applying universally,

---

[1] Robert E. Sherwood, *Roosevelt and Hopkins*, (New York, 1950), I, 36.

[2] William D. Leahy, *I Was There* (New York 1950), 44-45.

[3] Department of State, *Foreign Relations of the United States*, 1944, Vol. 3 (Washington, 1965), 770.

whereas Churchill conceived it as referring solely to European areas overrun by the Nazis.[4] At a White House Conference with Soviet Foreign Minister Molotov in June 1942, FDR projected the concept of international trusteeship for colonial possessions in the Far East, specifically mentioning Indochina and the islands held by Japan under League of Nations Mandate, as well as a couple of British and Dutch colonies. The aim would be to prepare these possessions for "self-government," which in most cases might take "20 years." Molotov responded that the proposal deserved serious allied attention and would certainly receive it in Moscow.[5]

In March of 1943, during preliminary discussions on the UN with British Foreign Minister Eden, Roosevelt again broached the idea of trusteeship for Indochina and the Japanese mandated islands. This "troubled" the British, who feared the effect upon their own imperial system.[6] From then until his death in 1945, the President continually pressed for his UN Trusteeship plan, charging that the French had "milked" the Indochinese for 100 years. At Cairo and Teheran he obtained the acquiescence of Chiang Kai Shek and Stalin. But at Yalta, Churchill had exploded at discussion of colonial trusteeships. He was mollified when told that they would apply only to territories taken from the enemy or voluntarily liberated.[7] In the case of Indochina, which would have to be wrested from Japanese control, the formula was sufficiently ambiguous to permit straddling. Because of Churchill's reaction, Roosevelt agreed to couch UN arrangements on colonies in general language, with the territories involved to be specified after the birth of the UN.[8]

Less than a month before his death Roosevelt told Charles Taussig, adviser to the U.S. delegation to the forthcoming UN Conference, that he had not changed his mind about a UN trusteeship for Indochina, but would agree to France as trustee provided she pledged independ-

---

[4] *New York Times*, October 28, 1942, cited by Foster R. Dulles and G. E. Ridinger, "The Anti-Colonial Policies of Franklin D. Roosevelt," *Political Science Quarterly*, LXX (1955), 8; Sherwood, op.cit., I, 440-41.

[5] Sherwood, op.cit., II, 157-58.

[6] Cordell Hull, *Memoirs* (New York, 1948), II, 1596; Ruth B. Russell, *A History of the United Nations Charter* (Brookings Institution, 1958), 90-91.

[7] *Foreign Relations*, 1944, Vol. 3, 773; ibid., 1943. *The Conferences at Cairo and Teheran* (Washington, 1961), 485; ibid., 1945, *The Conferences at Malta and Yalta* (Washington, 1955), 844.

[8] *Public Papers and Addresses of Franklin D. Roosevelt*, compiled by Samuel I. Rosenman, 1944-45 volume (New York, 1950), 562.

ence, not dominion status, as the goal. That, FDR said, is the policy "and you can quote me in the State Department."[9]

Roosevelt's position had both military and political repercussions. He instructed the State Department that no French troops were to be allowed to take part in Indochinese operations. Countering this, the British Foreign Office instructed its secret operations group in Indochina to collaborate only with French elements, avoiding native groups. The British also requested the U.S. Office of War Information in New Delhi to discontinue appeals to the native population in Thailand and Indochina, and tried to supplant the American Office of Strategic Services teams in Indochina. An OSS operative reported on an agreement between the British and the Dutch, into which the French were being brought, "to win back and control Southeast Asia, making the fullest use of possible American resources but foreclosing the Americans from any voice in policy matters." Lord Mountbatten, Chief of the Southeast Asia Command, was pressing for some control over Indochina, which was in Chiang Kai Shek's war theater. Without American agreement, he was gathering a French expeditionary force for participation in the liberation of Indochina.[10]

In March of 1945 the Japanese ousted the collaborating French administration in Indochina, killing or jailing French officials and troops. American Generals Wedemeyer and Chennault in China turned down pleas for aid on the grounds that their orders from Roosevelt barred support for the French in Indochina.[11]

General de Gaulle, who viewed Roosevelt's anticolonial policy and his championship of the UN as designs to assure for the United States "an enormous political and economic clientele," considered French military participation in the liberation an essential deterrent to FDR's trusteeship plan.[12] He also felt impelled to counter the trusteeship proposal by gestures toward autonomy for Indochina. If the great powers were "going to pretend that they conquered empires with motives of Christian charity . . . then France will give them a run for their money along that line," veteran *New York Times* correspondent Harold Callendar wrote from Paris describing de Gaulle's attitude. The

[9] *Foreign Relations,* 1945, Vol. 1 (Washington, 1967), 124.

[10] *Ibid.,* 1944, Vol. 3, 778-83.

[11] Bernard Fall, *The Two Vietnams* (New York, 1964), 55-57; Charles de Gaulle, *War Memoirs* (New York, 1960), III, 190.

[12] De Gaulle, op.cit., 227, 187-88; *New York Times,* March 22 and 29, 1945.

French leader announced a limited form of self-government for an Indochinese Federation presided over by a French Governor-General, as part of a French Union. Ministers of the Federation would be responsible to the Governor-General. Power would thus remain with Paris.[13]

With FDR's death, American policy with respect to Indochina underwent rapid change. On May 12, a month after Truman's accession to the presidency, Navy Secretary Forrestal's diary recorded this query posed by Ambassador Harriman at a State Department meeting that day: "Indochina. Do we want any military rights in Indochina? Do we want to let the French have a free hand and drop the proposals for trusteeship?" By the end of August, Truman informed de Gaulle that the United States would not oppose the return of French authority in Indochina.[14]

Removal of Roosevelt's pressure for trusteeship influenced military operations in the Pacific. At Potsdam in July, the U.S. military command declared it no longer had operational interest in Southeast Asia and responsibility was given to the British, Dutch, Portuguese and "perhaps eventually the French." A British proposal to extend its theater to the southern half of Indochina was accepted. As *quid pro quo* the British agreed not to resist U.S. retention of the Admiralty Islands.[15] The military decisions were interpreted by an American commentator as signifying Washington's acquiescence in restoration of allied colonialism in the Pacific area in opposition to the spirit, if not the letter, of the newly adopted UN Charter.[16]

Potsdam conferred upon the British the responsibility for postwar disarming of the Japanese south of the 16th parallel in Indochina, and upon the Chinese north of that line. Two French divisions composed of "white men" were to be assigned to the country, relieving Mountbatten of a "problem which could be satisfactorily handled by Frenchmen."[17] The British and Chinese were supposed to keep hands off domestic developments. But the British under General Gracey threw out a newly established Vietnamese revolutionary authority in

[13] *New York Times*, March 26, 1945.

[14] De Gaulle, op.cit., 242; *New York Times*, March 25, 1945.

[15] *Foreign Relations*, 1945, *The Potsdam Conference* (Washington, 1960), 1313-15.

[16] Harold Vinacke, "United States' Far Eastern Policy," *Pacific Affairs*, XIX (1946), 351-52.

[17] *Foreign Relations*, 1945, *Potsdam Conference*, 337, 1465.

Saigon and, in Foreign Minister Eden's words, "occupied the southern half of the country until the French were able to resume control."[18]

Would the trusteeship issue, and thus the future of Vietnam, have been decided differently if FDR had lived? There is no way to determine this, of course. The forces which shaped the direction of American policy after the war may have influenced him in fundamentally the same ways as they did Truman. On the record, Roosevelt and Truman differed sharply on one major question which determined American policy in the Pacific. American military leaders, and the War and Navy Departments, strongly insisted upon postwar retention of control of the Japanese mandated islands as bases to secure the nation's future in the Far East. Secretary of State Stettinius protested that this undercut our anticolonial position in the United Nations.[19] Truman sided with the War and Navy Departments, thereby precluding a vigorous anticolonial stance.[20] At Yalta, Roosevelt had opposed annexation of the mandated islands and had insisted that they be placed under trusteeship. Any other course, he said, would be contrary to the provisions of the Atlantic Charter and was unnecessary.[21] And at his last press conference, a week before his death, FDR reiterated his insistence that the mandated islands should be placed under UN control.[22]

Though Truman agreed to the repossession—actually reconquest—of Indochina by France before the cold war is generally assumed to have begun, the attitudes which shaped the decision are not irrelevant to current discussions concerning the responsibility for that war. At Teheran in 1943, Admiral Leahy reports, he took vigorous issue with Roosevelt on the proposal to turn the mandated islands over to the UN. "For our own future security," Leahy insisted, "the United States should maintain exclusive sovereignty." Prior to the UN preparatory conferences of the Big Four at Dumbarton Oaks in the fall of 1944, the Joint Chiefs of Staff pressed FDR for exclusive sovereignty of the islands "in the interests of national defense" and succeeded in blocking discussions on trusteeships and dependent peoples at these conferences.[23] As a result, this was the one area for which no joint preparatory

---

[18] Anthony Eden, *Full Circle* (Boston, 1960), 88.

[19] Hull, op.cit., II, 1599; Walter Millis, ed., *The Forrestal Diaries* (New York, 1951), 37-38.

[20] Harry S Truman, *Memoirs* (Garden City, L.I., 1956), I, 274; Vinacke, op.cit., 353.

[21] *Conferences at Malta and Yalta*, 57.

[22] Dulles and Ridinger, op.cit., 17; Russell, op.cit., 586n.

[23] Leahy, op.cit., 210, 258; Russell, op.cit., 346-48.

work had been done when the San Francisco conference opened. In opposition to the Joint Chiefs, Secretary Hull insisted that there be no exceptions to placing all territories taken from the Axis under UN control since any such exceptions would make it difficult for the U.S. to object to Soviet territorial acquisitions in the name of security.[24]

Whereas the military leaders stressed *national* security and *national* defense, War Secretary Stimson—a veteran diplomat—argued that Washington had to retain "absolute power to reform and fortify" these islands in behalf of Pacific security "for the future world." So long as the United States remained "the principal safeguard against aggression in that area," its strength ought "not to be hamstrung by unconsidered idealism. The policeman must be armed." Stimson also argued that Washington must insist that its purpose was to ensure peace and freedom in the area. Since everyone knew this to be our goal, no one would object to our keeping the bases.[25]

The concept of a *Pax Americana*, of a world unilaterally ordered by American military might, is plainly suggested, as is the thesis that the United States is uniquely objective in its international relations. Both would appear to be in conflict with the guiding UN principle of the sovereign equality of all nations and the *collective* responsibility for the maintenance of world peace. Though the vast power preponderance of the United States, particularly in the Pacific, at the end of the war was necessarily temporary—a war-born phenomenon—the military leaders intended to keep it, and at that point they had the support of the congressional leadership. They soon had the executive with them, as well.

Under pressure from the military and from his imperial allies, FDR retreated from his initial anticolonial position of firm UN control of all dependent peoples. He accepted revisions in the trusteeship formula, permitting the United States to retain operative control of "strategic areas." But at the time of his death he still insisted on placing all mandated Pacific islands under a system of UN trusteeship as a step toward the eventual abolition of colonies through the UN. After his death, the executive retreat "looked more like a rout."[26]

In the end, the trusteeship plan which emerged from San Francisco

[24] Russell, op.cit., 346.

[25] Henry L. Stimson and McGeorge Bundy, *On Active Service in Peace and War* (New York, 1947), 599-602.

[26] Robert C. Good, "The U.S. and the Colonial Debate," in Arnold Wolfers, ed., *Alliance Policy in the Cold War* (Baltimore, 1959) 227-28.

was limited to League of Nations mandates, areas taken from the enemy and those voluntarily "liberated." "Strategic" trust areas were so defined as to include all the United States-held Pacific islands, and the provisions for them were so drawn as to ensure Washington a free hand as administering authority.[27] San Francisco thus failed to provide effectively for the advance of independence through the UN, and American public opinion was disturbed at subsequent British and French efforts to reestablish their colonial empires.[28]

At least two prominent figures associated with the foreign service were sharply critical of American responsibility for this. Sumner Welles, former Under Secretary of State and an intimate of Roosevelt, condemned in 1946 the "timid and vacillating attitude" of the United States toward colonial independence and maintained that the "tragedy and ruin" which were sweeping Indochina and Indonesia could have been averted by proper Washington leadership within the UN. He warned that "the United Nations can and must assume the ultimate responsibility for the great transformation of the Orient now under way if the peace of the world is to be assured." And he left no doubt of his belief that Roosevelt's death had changed the direction of American policy. As a result of FDR's loss, the view had gained ascendancy that "American superior military power could provide security, and that a frankly imperialistic policy involving the acquisition of far-flung strategic bases throughout the world would be essential if our military might were to become predominant."[29] A decade later, in 1956, Secretary of State Dulles strikingly confirmed the gloomy prophecy. He told Eisenhower's speech-writer Emmett Hughes: "We have a clean base there [in Vietnam] now, without a taint of colonialism. Dienbienphu was a blessing in disguise."[30]

In November of 1945 Patrick Hurley, Ambassador to China, resigned in vehement protest against American colonial policy. "Instead of putting our weight behind the Charter of the United Nations," he wrote President Truman, "We have been definitely supporting the imperialist bloc."[31] His critique pointed to the tortuous path which led to Vietnam's tragedy and America's agony.

[27] Russell, op.cit., 589.
[28] Council on Foreign Relations, *The United States in World Affairs* (New York, 1947), 301.
[29] Sumner Welles, *Where Are We Heading?* (New York, 1946), 288, 332, 341, 365.
[30] Emmett J. Hughes, *The Ordeal of Power* (New York, 1962), 182.
[31] *The China White Paper, August 1949* (Palo Alto, 1967), II, 582-83.

II

While the UN's sponsors debated the issue of trusteeship or reassertion of French control, Indochinese revolutionaries rejected both. Undeterred by Stalin's participation at Teheran, the Indochinese Communist Party, which in 1943 led a national liberation coalition, reacted with hostility to the discussions there. "The allied powers who devoted themselves as 'liberators' at Teheran do not have the right to impose any kind of yoke on other people," it declared. The party also rebuffed suggestions of imperial reform by de Gaulle. It insisted on independence, and its leaders did not hesitate later to invoke the UN's professed goals and rhetoric of freedom as aids in their struggle.[32]

A common national front, organized in 1941, harassed the Japanese with some effect during the war. By early 1945 guerrilla groups under Ho Chi Minh's leadership controlled several northern provinces. They had established contact with the OSS, and had received some American arms and supplies in exchange for information and aid in rescuing allied pilots downed by the Japanese. In the latter stages of the Pacific War, five OSS teams were operating with Ho's Vietminh.

In mid-April of 1945, two weeks before the onset of the UN's labor pains at San Francisco, a revolutionary military conference in the jungles of Indochina took note that the "question of the Pacific region was placed upon the [UN] agenda, and with it the question of the . . . future of the oppressed nations of the Far East." The conference cited construction of "a new world of democracy" as "one of the conditions that will ensure the victory of the national liberation revolution of our people."[33]

In July the Vietminh requested U.S. authorities to press for French "guarantees" to Indochina of "all the liberties proclaimed by the United Nations." And soon after the defeat of Japan, Ho Chi Minh requested Washington to transmit a plea to the UN to realize its "solemn promises that all nationalities will be given democracy and independence." If the UN failed to grant Indochina full independence, Ho's message said, "we will keep fighting until we get it."[34] There is no evidence that Washington acted upon these appeals and no rec-

---

[32] Charles B. McLane, *Soviet Strategies in Southeast Asia* (Princeton, 1966), 262-65.

[33] *Breaking Our Chains*, Documents on the Vietnamese Revolution of August, 1945, (Hanoi, Foreign Language Publishing House, 1960), 23-26.

[34] Allan B. Cole, ed., *Conflict in Indochina and International Repercussions; A Documentary History, 1945-55*, 17; Robert Shaplen, *The Lost Revolution* (New York, 1965), 30.

ord of a UN response. Since Ho was as good as his word, the omissions have been costly.

With their surrender, the Japanese abruptly ceased to govern Indochina and their puppet "nationalist" regime under Emperor Bao Dai quickly disintegrated. The allied forces assigned at Potsdam to disarm the Japanese had not yet arrived. The Vietminh took power throughout the country. In the towns and villages peoples' committees were immediately organized, or had already been organized by the guerrilla forces, and took over the job of governing. A southern regional committee was set úp in Saigon and a central regional committee in Hue, while the Ho regime exercised national power from Hanoi. At Cairo and Teheran, Roosevelt had advocated a trusteeship of "20 or 30 years" to prepare the Indochinese for self-government. His miscalculation concerning the capacities of the Indochinese revolutionaries was to suffer repeated emulation by his successors.

The new regime's Declaration of Independence, read by President Ho before "500,000 people gathered at Ba Dinh Square," said: "We are convinced that the allied nations which at Teheran and San Francisco have acknowledged the principles of self-determination and equality of all nations will not refuse to acknowledge the independence of Vietnam."[35]

Some weeks later the British under General Gracey arrived at Saigon, bringing with them a couple of French divisions. Though Gracey's instructions emphasized that he was not to get involved in keeping order, he has himself described his actions: "I was welcomed on arrival by Viet Minh who said 'welcome' and all that sort of thing. It was a very unpleasant situation and I promptly kicked them out."[36] Gracey restored French administration in Saigon but the allied forces were too thin to prevent the Vietminh from maintaining control of the Cochin-China countryside. In the north, the Chinese offered no serious obstacles to Vietminh rule.

During the takeover, relations between Ho and the Americans on the scene remained friendly. American troops, OSS men, and journalists in Hanoi formed a Vietnam-American Friendship Association. As a mid-August Communist Party conference indicated, the Ho government was aware that the "contradictions" between the United States, Britain and France on one side and the USSR on the other, might lead

---

[35] *Breaking Our Chains*, 66-67.
[36] Cited by B.S.N. Murti, *Vietnam Divided* (New York, 1964), 3n.

to American concessions to France, allowing them to retake their empire. Anxious to avoid isolation, however, the Ho regime decided to try to "win over" the Soviet Union and the United States.[37]

Late in August, Truman had his meeting with de Gaulle, and State Department officials in Hanoi informed Ho that he could not expect political support from Washington. Ho also learned that France would be permitted to buy $160,000,000 worth of surplus American war equipment.[38]

With the United States avenue closed, Moscow remote and occupied elsewhere, and the Chinese Communists still some years away from power, Ho opened negotiations for an arrangement with France. Among his demands was a guarantee of the liberties proclaimed in the UN Charter. A treaty negotiated in March of 1946 granted Ho's regime a measure of independence within a French Union, but not enough to satisfy either Ho or his nationalist allies. In Cochin-China, which had separate status as a French colony, a referendum was to be held on unification with the north. While Ho was in Paris conferring on disputed aspects of the treaty, the French Governor-General in Saigon broke it by installing a puppet Cochin-China regime. Elsewhere in the country the French military, the bureaucracy, and the *colons*, resisting independence, provoked fighting incidents. Militant nationalists in Ho's camp, dissatisfied with the treaty's limitations, did not exert themselves to maintain peace. The outbreaks culminated in a French massacre of thousands of Vietnamese in Haiphong, and a retaliatory massacre of French troops in Hanoi. With this the Indochinese War began.

Washington's cold war position as developed by Walt Rostow, an influential State Department and White House advisor, is that the Indochinese War originated in 1946 as part of a Stalinist Asian offensive.[39] And for President Truman the struggle was part of the worldwide Soviet conspiracy to weaken Europe and to divert American attention from it so that the USSR could gain a free hand there.[40] There is no evidence, however, that the Russians played any role in postwar developments in Indochina. A detailed study of Soviet policy in Southeast Asia concluded that it took scant notice of events there

---

[37] *Breaking Our Chains*, 66-67.

[38] Donald Lancaster, *The Emancipation of French Indochina* (Oxford, England, 1961), 143; Shaplen, op.cit., 6.

[39] Cited by Theodore Draper, *Abuse of Power*, (New York, 1967), 23.

[40] Truman, op.cit., I, 331, 378, 380.

until 1948 or 1949. Its international concern was with Europe, and its primary interest was in the power struggle in France where Communists were members of a coalition government. Until this was resolved, support for an anti-French war in Indochina was precluded. Ho had acted entirely on his own initiative and in the face of advice from French Communists to pursue a "moderate" policy. He did in fact initially attempt such a policy. At the outset he undertook negotiations with France secretly, fearing resistance from some of his non-Communist allies.[41] Moderation failed because French interests in Indochina were determined to maintain their imperial position. Ironically Ho's revolutionary effectiveness, unique among Communists of the smaller lands of Asia, appears to have been a result not of Stalinist influence but of relative freedom from that influence.[42]

Developments in the UN appear to confirm this. On September 12, 1947, the Ho regime addressed a letter to UN Secretary-General Trygve Lie requesting the Security Council to sponsor negotiations between it and France "on the basis of independence and territorial integrity." There was no reply from Lie and no evidence of Soviet support for this plea.[43]

In November of 1948, Ho's Democratic Republic of Vietnam applied for UN membership. The USSR did sponsor this application, defeated in the Council by a vote of 10 to 1, but it took no other action. Four years later the Soviet delegate complained that the 1948 application had not been accorded routine issuance as a UN document, an "oversight" hastily corrected after the Soviet protest.[44]

Recognizing that the Ho regime, which controlled most of the countryside, could not be defeated militarily, the French again turned to Emperor Bao Dai in the hope of splitting non-Communist nationalists from Ho through a French-sponsored "nationalist" regime. After lengthy dickering over "independence" terms, Bao Dai was installed as head of an Indochinese government in December of 1949.

At that time, according to a remarkably prescient 1950 article in *UN World*. Ho's prestige was overwhelming among nationalists of all persuasions and he had the backing of more than 80 percent of the Vietnamese (the precise figure later used by Eisenhower in describing

[41] McLane, op.cit., 266-73; see also Shaplen, op.cit., 31, and Joseph Buttinger, *A Dragon Embattled* (New York, 1967), II, 700.

[42] McLane, op.cit., 480.   [43] Buttinger, op.cit., II, 658-59.

[44] Cole, op.cit., 70; UN Department of Political and Security Council Affairs, *Repertoire of the Practice of the Security Council*, Suppl. 1952-55, 91; United Nations Official Reports (UNOR), Doc. S 2780.

the extent of Ho's support during the Indochinese War). According to author Roger Pinto, a lawyer with several years experience both in Saigon and Hanoi, half a million troops would be required to defeat Ho. Native troops were unreliable, and many Frenchmen believed the troops would have to be American. Pinto noted that Ho's government represented a wide united front of nationalist elements with 11 non-Communists in a cabinet of 16, and support for it extending even into Bao Dai's cabinet. Reporting a widespread opinion that the regime's "extreme nationalist tendencies" made it "Titoist," Pinto predicted that it would some day find itself "caught between Russia and China."[45] Other respected experts on Indochina have written that the Bao Dai government's authority extended little beyond the area occupied by the French Army, and that popular organizations comprising the united front behind Ho embraced millions of members.[46]

Until the Bao Dai "experiment" Washington cautiously tried to avoid too deep an involvement in Pacific colonial struggles. Though aligned politically and economically with the colonial powers, it was anxious to preserve its anticolonial image among underdeveloped peoples, particularly in the light of the emerging cold war. By mid-1949, however, its attitude toward Indochina underwent change. It recognized the Bao Dai regime early in 1950, and began to extend direct economic and military aid in May of that year. Though it wanted to channel all assistance through Bao Dai to avoid the taint of helping a colonial power, steady desertions of Bao Dai's forces to the Vietminh made this impracticable. Hence military aid went to the French armed forces and economic aid to the Bao Dai government.

In a detailed 1950 review of American policy in Southeast Asia, Laurence S. Finkelstein, who had served with the State Department, the UN Secretariat, and the Council on Foreign Relations, attributed the policy shift to the need for ready access to strategic raw materials and control over the rice districts upon which vast Asian populations depended, and the need to deny both to a potential enemy; the strategic military position of Southeast Asia in the Pacific area; the fear of a "bandwagon" psychology in case of a Communist victory (the "domino theory"); the importance to European allies of retaining

[45] Roger Pinto, "Duel for Indochina," *UN World* (April, 1950) 15-18.
[46] Ellen J. Hammer, "The Bao Dai Experiment," *Pacific Affairs,* XXIII (1950), 58; Fall, op.cit., 214; J. R. Clementin, "The Nationalist Dilemna in Vietnam," *Pacific Affairs,* XXIII (1950), 303.

their hold on their raw materials resources and markets in Southeast Asia; and the link between the allied military load in Southeast Asia and the capacity to contribute to the European Defense Community.[47] None of these reasons, plainly, could justify interference with Indochinese self-determination under the terms of the UN Charter, but neither then nor later was this a consideration in shaping policy.

Finkelstein maintained that Washington had lost control over its policy in Southeast Asia. The Bao Dai experiment was a failure but the U.S. was committed to support any anti-Communist government, no matter what its complexion. He also observed, interestingly, that Washington had cautiously backed Indonesian independence in the UN, but had played no such role with respect to Indochina. Ellen Hammer has argued that the explanation lies in extensive investments by American and British business in Indonesia and lack of them in Indochina, the political nature of the respective revolutionary movements and the greater importance of France than the Netherlands as a European ally.[48]

With expanding American aid (which swelled to $2,000,000,000 by the time of the Geneva Conference) and the Communist takeover in China, the war escalated. Opposition developed in France. Former Premier Eduard Daladier, Radical Socialist leader, moved in the Chamber of Deputies in late 1951 that the UN be asked to resolve the conflict while French troops pulled back to coastal areas. His motion was defeated.[49] French leaders feared that this would bring their actions in Indochina under continuous UN survey and would hand the United States another lever of control there.

In 1952 the UN acted upon the membership applications of the Bao Dai regime and the Democratic Republic of Vietnam. Though the Bao Dai government was isolated and had been imposed by France, and the DRV plainly had the support of the large majority of Indochinese, the Security Council voted 10 to 1 in favor of admission of the Bao Dai government (Soviet veto) and 10 to 1 against admission of the DRV.[50] The pattern was to be repeated several times, suggesting the accuracy of the observation made by Professor Inis L. Claude, leading American academic authority on the UN, that the United

[47] Laurence Finkelstein, "U.S. at Impasse in Southeast Asia," *Far Eastern Survey* (September 27, 1950), 65-72.

[48] Ellen J. Hammer, *The Struggle for Indochina, 1940-1955* (Palo Alto, 1966), 202.

[49] Cole, op.cit., 92.

[50] *International Organization*, World Peace Foundation, VII (Boston, 1953), 120-21; *UNOR* S/2446 and S/2466.

States leads and directs the apparatus of the UN, "making it primarily an element of the anti-Communist program, and secondarily a device for alleviating the tensions of the struggle over colonialism."[51]

In the 1953 General Assembly session the point was made directly by the delegate of a recently liberated Asian nation. Secretary Dulles had excoriated the Soviet bloc for instigating the Indochinese War in order to "expand by violence the Soviet camp." He was joined in the attack by the British delegate. While the six Soviet-bloc delegates who spoke in the general debate were curiously silent on Indochina, the Burmese delegate counterattacked. If people under colonial rule seek to gain the freedom promised by the UN Charter, he argued, "the reaction of the paramount power is violent." If they fight back, the world is informed their struggle is Communist-inspired. If they seek peaceful redress in the UN Assembly, they are told the matter is one of domestic jurisdiction. Despite the "high-sounding affirmation and the pious hopes expressed in the Charter," he said, "the Assembly itself may become the means of perpetuating colonial and imperial rule."[52] Soviet-bloc silence may have marked the Soviet drive for détente, which affected the Geneva settlement the following year.

By early 1954, the French public was insistent on an end to the war. A four-power Foreign Ministers' Conference in February decided to include Indochina in a forthcoming Geneva conference on Korea. The two Indochinese regimes, as well as China, were to be invited to participate. A forum outside of the UN was necessary not only because Peking was not represented in the UN, but because Washington rejected the idea of inviting her to participate in a UN debate for fear that this would open the door to membership.[53]

The decision to hold the conference, compelled by the pressure of French public opinion, was followed by efforts of Secretary Dulles to thwart it either through direct military intervention in the war or through prior organization of a Southeast Asia anti-Communist regional pact under Article 51 of the UN Charter. But President Eisenhower would not agree to military intervention unless Congress supported it, and this was unlikely unless the intervention were undertaken jointly with other countries. In March, the administration initiated an intensive campaign to win Congress and the British to joint military air support of the French. Dulles delivered a major policy

[51] Inis L. Claude, Jr., *Swords into Plowshares* (New York, 3rd edn., 1964), 363.
[52] *UNOR* A/p.v. 434-449, General Assembly, 8th session, September, 1953.
[53] Murti, op.cit., 13-14.

address at the Overseas Press Club, Eisenhower wrote to Churchill on April 4 and held a press conference on April 7. In all three moves a Communist takeover in Indochina was described as intolerable "by whatever means" it occurred;[54] that is, whether by war, negotiations, or elections likely to result from negotiations. Since Eisenhower has confessed that according to all reports received by him, "possibly 80 percent" of Indochinese then supported Ho Chi Minh,[55] Administration policy appeared to be aimed at blocking self-determination, which could scarcely be avoided if the conference were to take place.

Administration reasons advanced for this need to prevent a Communist victory in Indochina followed essentially those outlined by Finkelstein in 1950, and are briefly summarized in Eisenhower's memoirs: the rich natural resources of Southeast Asia, its strategic military importance and the effect on other nations in the area.[56] More than nine years later, on August 3, 1965, Secretary Rusk repeated them with startling fidelity while telling the House Foreign Affairs Committee why American combat troops had formally entered the war.[57]

Efforts by Dulles to scuttle the Geneva Conference persisted after it convened. Late in June Churchill and Eden flew to Washington to dissuade him and Eisenhower from proclaiming an anti-Communist alliance for Southeast Asia since this would break up the conference. Apparently as *quid pro quo*, the British leaders agreed to a seven-point program to present to the Conference. This included partition of Vietnam, no political arrangement in the southern part which would permit the Communists to gain power, and no restriction on importation of arms and military advisors to ensure "internal security" in the south.[58] Again, this would appear to be an explicit demand for denial of self-determination in the south and for the right of the Western powers to enforce this denial by military means.

III

The Geneva Conference rejected the joint U.S.-British demands. As is now well known, there was no partition of Vietnam. Two "pro-

---

[54] Dwight D. Eisenhower, *Mandate for Change* (Garden City, L.I., 1963) 343, 346; Arthur Lall, *Modern Industrial Negotiations: Principles and Practice* (New York, 1966), 174; Department of State *Bulletin*, April 12, 1954, 539-42.

[55] Eisenhower, op.cit., 372.   [56] *Ibid.*, 333.

[57] United States Government, Executive Department, *Why Vietnam* (Washington, August, 1965), 9.

[58] Eden, op.cit., 143-49; Eisenhower, op.cit., 368.

visional" truce zones were established to permit regrouping of the intermingled armies for armistice purposes, with elections for a single all-Vietnam government to take place within two years. The demarcation line was finally set in negotiations between the Vietminh and French military commands weeks after the close of the Conference. The famous Point 6 of the Final Declaration said flatly that "the military demarcation line is provisional and should not in any way be interpreted as constituting a political or territorial boundary." Article 14 of the Agreement on the Cessation of Hostilities read: "Pending the general elections *which will bring about the unification of Vietnam*, the conduct of civil administration in each regrouping zone shall be in the hands of the party whose forces are to be regrouped there." (Emphasis added) Unification was unconditional and there was no hint of two states, before or after the scheduled elections, in the Agreements.

Though refusing to sign the accords, the United States formally pledged to "refrain from the threat or use of force to disturb them, in accordance with Article 2 (4) of the Charter of the United Nations." Article 2, Section 4, of the UN Charter obliges members not to interfere forcibly with the independence or territorial integrity of any nation. The American statement also called for elections sponsored by the UN rather than by an International Control Commission, as provided in the accords. Washington, at the time, dominated the UN but would not be able to control the Commission, composed of India, Poland, and Canada.

The status of Vietnam as a single nation was emphasized in post-conference statements by the participating powers. Eden in Parliament, the French and Soviet Governments, Senator Mike Mansfield in a "study" report to the Senate following a trip to Vietnam,[59] all spoke of the undertaking by all conferees to respect the "unity and territorial integrity" of the three nations emerging from the conference. Eisenhower has written that the settlement in Vietnam "was recognized as a military—not a political or territorial one." General elections were to be held "in Vietnam, Laos, and Cambodia." French troops were to be withdrawn when the *three* Governments requested it.[60]

[59] Cole, op.cit., 139, 188, 191; Senate Committee on Foreign Relations, 83rd Cong., 2nd Sess., *Report of Senator Mike Mansfield on a Study Mission to Vietnam, Cambodia and Laos*, October 15, 1954 (Washington, 1954), 6-7.
[60] Eisenhower, op.cit., 371.

But on July 23, two days after the accords were signed and the U.S. pledge delivered, Dulles told newsmen: "One of the good aspects of the Geneva Conference is that it advances the truly independent status of Cambodia, Laos, and southern Vietnam."[61] It would thus appear unarguable that from the outset the Eisenhower administration did not take seriously the agreement at Geneva for a unified Vietnam, and its pledge not to disturb it—a conclusion drawn by B.S.N. Murti, Indian member of the International Control Commission for three years.[62] General Maxwell Taylor has testified that the U.S. military mission was established "almost at once after Geneva,"[63] violating also the provisions in the Agreements against importation of military advisors. The timing suggests that later explanations of State Department spokesmen concerning prior violations by Hanoi cannot be taken seriously.

Six weeks after Geneva, the Southeast Asia Treaty Organization was formed—with Laos, Cambodia, and "the free territory under the jurisdiction of the State of Vietnam" designated as protocol states under its protection. There was no hint that the status of Vietnam was temporary. Laos and Cambodia rejected the unsought protection in line with their Geneva Conference obligation to remain unaligned. Saigon did not. In October, Eisenhower despatched his famed letter to Premier Ngo Dinh Diem pledging assistance in developing and maintaining "an independent Vietnam endowed with a strong government." This letter has been cited by both the Kennedy and Johnson administrations as the source of their commitment to successive Saigon regimes.

In October and November of 1954, the UN General Assembly and its Ad Hoc Political Committee debated the admission *en masse* of "qualified states" whose applications had been rejected by the West or vetoed in retaliation by the USSR. In August, Australia had transmitted a proposal to admit Laos and Cambodia. A transmittal message explained that Vietnam was not included because the Geneva accords provided for a "final political settlement" in 1956. "At this stage," the message continued, "there is no government in Vietnam which could accept the obligations contained in the Charter of the

[61] Department of State *Bulletin*, August 2, 1954, 163-64.
[62] Murti, op.cit., 179.
[63] *Public Hearings Before the Committee on Foreign Relations, U.S. Senate, 89th Cong., on S. 2793*, Jan. 28-Feb. 18, 1966 (Washington, 1966), 446.

United Nations *on behalf of the whole territory and population of Vietnam.*"[64] (Emphasis added)

The Australian resolution had the additional sponsorship of two other Asian members of SEATO—Pakistan and Thailand—when it reached the floor of the Ad Hoc Political Committee in late October, some weeks after the SEATO Conference. During the debate Australia repeated its reason for not including Vietnam in its resolution. Thailand, Pakistan, and New Zealand—all Asian members of SEATO —specifically associated themselves with Australia's stand, which plainly assumed the reunification of Vietnam. The delegate of France, also a SEATO member, explained that while his government favored the admission of Vietnam, it "considered that the existence of the two zones in no way affected the unity of Vietnam or its international status." During the debate the United States introduced an amendment to the Australian resolution to add "The Republic of Korea and the Republic of Vietnam" to the nations to be admitted to the UN.[65]

The Ad Hoc Political Committee was unable to resolve the issue of "package" admission of new members and it went to the Security Council in December of 1955. Here a 28-member resolution was introduced calling for the admission *en masse* of 18 nations, including Laos and Cambodia but excluding Vietnam and Korea. A Chinese amendment provided for adding the latter two. Nine members voted for this amendment, France and Britain explaining that they did so without prejudice to the unification of Vietnam. The British delegate declared that the United Kingdom "was closely concerned with efforts to achieve" unification, and the French delegate said that unification "is one of the objectives of French policy." The only Pacific member of SEATO on the Council that year, New Zealand, abstained from the vote on admission of Vietnam, which was defeated by Soviet veto. Four of the five Asian members of SEATO were among the 28 nations sponsoring the motion to admit the 18 members. The United States abstained in the vote on this motion.[66]

Thus, in December of 1955, all SEATO members except the United States and the Philippines had taken formal positions in the UN for unification of Vietnam as decreed at Geneva. During the debates al-

[64] *UNOR*, A/2709; Resolution A/AC.76/L.4, General Assembly, 9th Sess., 1954.

[65] The debate in the Ad Hoc Political Committee took place at the 17th through 27th meetings, October 29 through November 15, 1954, *UNOR* A/AC/SR 17-27.

[66] *UNOR* Security Council, 10th year, 701st to 706th meetings, December 10-15, 1955.

most every UN delegate who spoke on the Vietnam issue hailed the Conference decisions. Ambassador Lodge and the Chinese delegate were exceptions. Lodge, in arguing for admission of South Vietnam and South Korea, declared that "countries which are divided only because of the aggressive actions taken against them by others should not be barred by virtue of that illegal decision." By thus placing responsibility on the Communists for the division, he avoided both a commitment to unification and isolation in the face of the virtuously unanimous expressions of support for it.

Yet at the time that the Security Council debate took place, the world knew that Saigon's Premier Diem and his American sponsors had no intention of permitting the country to be reunified. The Geneva accords specified that discussions on the terms of the elections were to begin in July 1955, and Hanoi's repeated requests to Diem for these discussions had been ignored. Even earlier, major Western newspapers flatly declared that the elections never would take place. In January 1955, the London *Economist* editorialized that the aid given to Diem by Washington "presumed that the only intelligible aim of American policy was to give the Southern Government the best possible chance of survival on as permanent a basis as that of South Korea." C. L. Sulzburger declared in the *Times* of March 12 that the elections "really will never be held. . . . The non-Communist south cannot afford the slightest risk of defeat." Robert Gullion of *Le Monde* wrote from Saigon on March 21 that the United States "does not want an election because it does not want the reunification of North and South Vietnam despite the Geneva Agreement."[67]

The accuracy of these journalistic evaluations of Washington's intentions at the time was strikingly confirmed a few months ago by Lt. General James Gavin (ret.) who was then Army Chief of Plans. He is quoted in the *Times* of February 13, 1968, as saying: "We decided to support what Eisenhower hoped would be a stable, representative, independent government in South Vietnam. The fact that this was contrary to the Geneva accords seemed somehow irrelevant."

The difference in attitude toward Vietnamese unification between Washington and other SEATO powers suggested in the UN debates was systematic at the time, according to Sherman Adams, Eisenhower's presidential assistant. Whereas Eisenhower and Dulles conceived of SEATO as a shield against Communist encroachment, most of the

---

[67] Newspaper statements are quoted by Murti, op.cit., 180.

other members were concerned with defense of their borders, not with any general threat of Communist advance.[68] Dulles, according to Adams, complained of the allied attitude at a cabinet meeting in June of 1954, during a critical period in the Geneva negotiations. "It is not difficult to marshal world opinion against aggression," Dulles is quoted as saying, "but it is quite another matter to fight against internal changes in one country. If we take a position against a Communist faction within a foreign country, we have to act alone. We are confronted by an unfortunate fact—most of the countries of the world do not share our view that Communist control of any government anywhere is in itself a danger and a threat."[69] This scarcely leaves room for honoring a commitment to a world organization whose principles specifically exclude interference in the internal affairs of other nations, Communist or non-Communist, and specifically dictate collective, not individual, action where aggression is alleged.

The SEATO pact was formulated with an eye toward enabling the United States to play the unilateral role implied by Dulles under cover of an international arrangement formally appearing to comply with the UN Charter. Secretary Rusk told the Senate Foreign Relations Committee at the 1966 televised public hearings that the language of SEATO imposes an individual obligation, which does not require collective decision, to repel aggression. "If the United States determines that an armed attack has occurred against any nation to whom the protection of the treaty applies, then it is obligated to act . . . without regard to the views or actions of any other treaty member," Rusk testified.[70] In April of 1968, Eisenhower was still enunciating this go-it-alone theme. In a *Reader's Digest* article, he listed a series of cold war measures taken against the "Communist conspiracy," and added: "These things we must continue to do, even when we stand alone . . . even when so-called friendly nations criticize our action."[71]

This unilateral policy in Vietnam was recently subjected to a rather impassioned critique by John W. Holmes, who was Canada's observer at the Geneva Conference and later Canadian member of the International Control Commission. Writing in the publication of the Canadian Institute of International Affairs last summer, Holmes charged that Dulles "walked out on Geneva, walked out on his part-

[68] Sherman Adams, *First Hand Report* (New York, 1961), 126.

[69] *Ibid.*, 124.   [70] *Public Hearings, U.S. Senate*, 1966, op.cit., 567.

[71] Dwight D. Eisenhower, "Let's Close Ranks on the Home Front," *Reader's Digest* (April, 1968), 53.

ners, and started in his own direction, a direction which has led to the present impasse." America's Vietnam policy since 1954 has been essentially unilateral, according to Holmes. He maintained that it was not flatly opposed by America's closest friends in the 1950s because they hoped "to bend and mitigate" a policy which they considered unwise. Because of the enormous disproportion of American power, he wrote, it was doubtful whether "a strong alliance system or a UN security system" could be developed "in which more than one voice was decisive." But, he complained, Dulles never even tried "because he was obsessed with the view that the United States, untainted by imperialism, was alone morally qualified for the job and he set the United States on the way to imperial responsibilities more oppressive than those of any empire."[72]

Whatever their actual differences with United States policy, the show of independence of SEATO members at the UN in the fall of 1954 was momentary. In February 1955, a SEATO conference "reaffirmed the determination" of its members to support the "freedom and independence of Laos, Cambodia, and the free territory under the jurisdiction of Vietnam." The Soviet press immediately charged that SEATO's purpose was to block Vietnamese reunification. "America's representatives in South Vietnam are frankly stating that the USA will not permit general elections in 1956 since they fear that the popular forces . . . may achieve victory at the polls," *Izvestia* maintained on March 2. Professor Philippe Devillers, leading French authority on Indochina, put the matter slightly differently; SEATO, he said, "Was a pointer that the United States would not sit by quietly if faced with the prospect that South Vietnam might go Communist, even perhaps as a result of free elections." A Sino-Hanoi communiqué of July 7, 1955, claimed that under the protection of the SEATO pact the United States was coverting South Vietnam into a colony and war base. The "war base" charge received confirmation from none other than Secretary Dulles when he told Eisenhower's speech writer, as mentioned earlier, that the United States has "a clean base in South Vietnam now, without a taint of colonialism."[73]

IV

In the aftermath of Geneva, as Ellen Hammer has written, it was the Americans, not the Vietnamese, who decided to retain the French ap-

[72] John W. Holmes, "Geneva, 1954," *International Journal*, XXII (1966-67), 482-83.
[73] See page 327.

pointee Ngo Dinh Diem as head of an independent South Vietnamese government. If his regime was marked by widespread corruption, repression, gross inefficiency, and little public support, United States policy was hardly blameless. Faced with the alternative of building a popular base by seeking reconciliation of former pro-French and pro-Vietminh forces or of making South Vietnam "a spearhead of militant anti-Communism in Asia," the U.S. chose the latter course. Diem was pressed "to discard and treat with suspicion both the liberal elements among the educated classes and the non-Communist fighters of the resistance." This, plus his pervasive Catholicism, led him to depend upon Catholic refugees from the north as his base of support. The political dominance of this group has persisted in Saigon. Yet in 1955, according to a veteran American correspondent, Americans in Saigon estimated that 50 to 70 percent of South Vietnamese villages were under Vietminh influence or control. French experts set the figure at 60 to 90 percent.[74]

The evidence is impressive that the anti-Diem insurrection developed locally in South Vietnam in 1957, following failure to hold the mandated unification elections; that it was sparked by Diem's efforts, in violation of the Geneva Agreements, to root out the Vietminh administrations in the towns and hamlets throughout the south; that it was initially opposed by Hanoi and South Vietnamese Communists because of Sino-Soviet détente policies toward the West; and that it was not until 1959—as repeatedly affirmed by Washington's spokesmen—that Hanoi began to give the insurrection active support.

B.S.N. Murti, Indian member of the International Control Commission, has written that the Diem regime launched a drive against Vietminh elements in the villages in mid-1957, compelling them to become guerrillas. Some 2,000,000 southern Vietnamese had fought with the Vietminh, many of them for nine years against both Japanese and French, and the peasantry was considerably closer to them than to Diem's apparatus. Hence the insurrection continued to expand. Jean Lacouture, veteran correspondent in Indochina for *Le Monde* and a leading historian of the Indochinese War, maintains that the insurrection was initiated by non-Communist independence fighters, with the Communists hanging back because of lack of reaction in Hanoi, Peking, or Moscow to the cancellation of the elections. Only after pressure on Ho Chi Minh from the insurrectionists, who charged him with

---

[74] Hammer, *The Struggle for Indochina*, op.cit., 356; Joseph Alsop, *The Herald Tribune*, March 1, 1955 (cited by Hammer, p. 230); Murti, op.cit., 196-97.

betrayal, did Hanoi extend aid in 1959. According to Devillers, in 1959 the insurrection had spread through the entire Mekong delta where there was not the slightest trace of northern infiltration. "All serious reports were in agreement; several rural regions were in rebellion against the corrupt administration and the methods of the police," Devillers has written. He adds that in April of 1960, a number of Saigon politicians joined the insurrection on the grounds that "armed resistance was henceforth unavoidable."[75]

According to Secretary Rusk, Hanoi began to interfere in South Vietnam in 1959. All accounts agree, however, that the insurrection began in 1957. The discrepancy underscores the comment by Bernard Fall that the claim of North Vietnamese infiltration as the cause of the war "omits the embarrassing fact that anti-Diem guerrillas were active long before infiltrated North Vietnamese elements entered the fray." In fact, both administration spokesmen and opponents of the war are in agreement that at least until the end of 1964 all "infiltrators" from the north were southerners who had gone north as a result of the regrouping agreement at Geneva, presumably until the nation was reunified in 1956. The Defense Department estimated early in 1965 that of a total of 330,000 Vietcong dead and alive, only 63,000 had infiltrated from the north. More than a quarter million, or some 80 percent, had been recruited from among people who lived in the south.[76]

From the outset, the striking fact about the war in the south has been the capacity of the Vietcong, before and after the entry of northern troops, to inflict defeat upon a foe vastly superior both numerically and in equipment. In the early stages the Diem regime "could not by itself control a rebellion by a few thousand poorly armed peasants," according to John Mecklin, Director of U.S. Information Services in Saigon from 1962 to 1964. The reason, both American and Saigon officials have abundantly confessed, is that the popular allegiance has been commanded by the National Liberation Front, and not by Saigon. Mecklin, an ardent "war hawk," has written that the Saigon regime "was a sorry match for the Vietcong in a struggle where the decision would go to the side that could win the people." Major General Edward Lansdale, counterinsurgency specialist who was Diem's inti-

[75] Murti, op.cit., 196-99; Lacouture, *Vietnam Between Two truces* (New York, 1966), 52-54, and the introduction by Joseph Kraft, xii-xiii; Devillers, "French Policy and the Second Vietnam War," *The World Today*, Vol. 23 (June, 1967), 255.

[76] Fall, *op.cit.*, 344; Defense Department estimate of Vietcong forces cited by Richard Goodman, *Vietnam, Triumph or Tragedy* (New York, 1966), 27.

mate adviser from 1954 to 1956 and later returned to Saigon as special assistant to the ambassador, declared in a 1964 *Foreign Affairs* article that in this "peoples' war" the Vietcong "is embedded within the population" and draws its support from the people. This, he indicated, was not true of the Saigon regime, which depends on the bureaucracy and the army.[77]

On September 1, 1965, the *New York Times* carried two reports of interviews with the then Premier, now Vice-President, Nguyen Cao Ky. In one he confessed his regime was not ready to compete politically with the Vietcong because of the economic and political injustices Saigon had visited upon the people. In the other, by columnist James Reston, he said that "the Communists were closer to the people's yearnings for social justice and an independent national life than his own government." Late in February, 1966, *Times* correspondent Charles Mohr quoted Ky as saying in another interview: "For us to go in a weakened condition to the peace table would be committing suicide." Mohr wrote that even if the Vietcong guerrilla units were to be disbanded, Saigon's leaders believed they could not survive a peaceful settlement. Hence the aim of "pacification" was "the creation of an ironlike system of political control over the population." Nine months later, at Manila, a top Saigon official was still saying: "Frankly we are not strong enough yet to compete with the Communists on a purely political basis."[78]

The judgment was confirmed by General Wallace Greene, Marine Commandant, early in 1966. "There can be no victory in Vietnam until the villagers are rehabilitated and politically reorganized," he said. "You can kill every Vietcong and North Vietnamese in Vietnam and still lose the war until you make a success of the pacification program." The thesis that the United States has the right to "rehabilitate" and "politically reorganize" a foreign people is itself a curious one. But the failure of "pacification" has been almost a daily journalistic item throughout the war.[79]

To bring the story up to date, *Times* correspondent Jack Langguth reported in April of 1968 that the present Saigon regime fears negotiations because, as its leaders admit, they could not match the NLF in open elections. Langguth maintained that some six to seven million

[77] Mecklin, *Mission in Torment* (Garden City, N.Y., 1965) 19, 36; Lansdale, "Revolution in Vietnam," *Foreign Affairs*, 43 (October, 1964), 81-82.

[78] *New York Times*, February 11 and October 24, 1966.

[79] *Ibid.*, January 18, 1966.

South Vietnamese "either sympathize with the Vietcong or live at least partly under its control," and have for years constituted the *de facto* government over four-fifths of South Vietnam's territory. Official estimates last December by Robert W. Komer, civilian chief of pacification, suggest that Langguth's figure is low. Komer reported that some 4,000,000 live in areas governed exclusively by the Vietcong; 2,000,000 are in areas largely under Vietcong control; and another 4,000,000 are "clearly" under government control but the "Vietcong may continue to collect taxes and have perhaps half of the hamlet guerrilla force [than previously] still on duty." These figures were cited before the 1968 Tet offensive which shifted the balance drastically in favor of the Vietcong, and they do not include the large numbers of NLF sympathizers among the 3,000,000 in the Saigon metropolitan area. Thus, with more than half of the 17,000,000 South Vietnamese living in areas governed exclusively or partly or the NLF, the official explanation that we are fighting a war against external aggression leaves a rather wide credibility gap even if the unified character of Vietnam is overlooked.[80]

American military intervention and escalation, of course, is directly related to the popular strength of the National Liberation Front and the absence of popular support for the Saigon regime. Each major military step taken by Washington was in response to the imminent collapse of the Saigon government. In 1961 and 1962, President Kennedy sent some 10,000 troops as "military advisers" to prevent the collapse of the Saigon government and a takeover by the NLF.[81] Since the Geneva agreements barred increases of foreign personnel above the level existing at that time—685, in the case of the U.S.—this decision "amounted to outright abrogation" of the agreements.[82] Administration spokesmen have repeatedly affirmed that the bombing of the north initiated in early 1965 and the subsequent direct involvement of American combat troops stemmed from the need to bolster collapsing Saigon regimes. Since the Defense Department estimated at the time that there were no more than 400 North Vietnamese soldiers in the south, the threat to these regimes obviously did not come from northern aggression.[83] This tends to underscore both the nature of

[80] Langguth, *New York Times Magazine*, April 7, 1968, 29, 114, 117; Komer, *New York Times*, December 2, 1967.

[81] Arthur Schlesinger, Jr., *A Thousand Days* (Cambridge, Mass., 1965) 544-48.

[82] Mecklin, op.cit., 106.

[83] Defense Department estimate of North Vietnamese soldiers cited by Theodore Draper, *Abuse of Power* (New York, 1967) 78-79.

Washington's intervention as an effort to impose by force unpopular regimes upon an unwilling people, and the unreality of its long resistance to the independent participation of the NLF in peace negotiations or in a government in the south.

V

During the post-Geneva period, the only substantive Vietnam issue before the UN concerned membership. Early in 1957 a 13-power resolution requested Security Council approval of the applications of "the Republic of Korea and the Republic of Vietnam." The Soviet Union countered by requesting admission of North and South Vietnam, as well as North and South Korea, on the basis of the "principle of universality." A Special Political Committee of the Assembly approved the 13-power resolution 44 to 8, with 23 abstentions, and turned down the Soviet resolution 35 to 1, with 35 abstentions. The General Assembly subsequently approved the 13-power resolution, which was then vetoed by the USSR in the Security Council. Saigon's admission was again proposed the following year by the United States, and again supported in the Assembly. The Security Council vote was 8 for, 1 against (Soviet veto) and two abstentions (Canada and Iraq).

Until mid-1964 both the UN and its Secretary-General were largely divorced from the expanding war in Vietnam. There were some peripheral skirmishes, such as the Laos complaint in 1959 against violations of its border by the DRV, and a similar complaint by Cambodia against the Americans and South Vietnamese. Neither resulted in action. The Russians and Cambodians insisted that investigation or settlement of such complaints was the province of the International Control Commission, not the UN. A UN fact-finding mission on persecution of Buddhists by the Diem regime got to Saigon a week before the coup which overthrew the regime. This deflated its purpose and it wound up with a noncommittal report.

But in July of 1964, Secretary-General U Thant initiated a persistent, continuous effort to bring the war to the negotiating table. And in August the Security Council for the first time debated the substantive issues of the war on the basis of a specific resolution—a complaint brought by the United States against Hanoi for attacking U.S. warships in the Tonkin Gulf.

U Thant often explained thereafter why the UN was inactive. In mid-1966 he said typically that its impotence was inevitable with only one party to the fighting a member. Moreover two major powers, the USSR and France, were opposed to any peace-keeping role for the UN on the grounds that this was the province of the Geneva agreements machinery, and the United Kingdom was likewise reluctant on that score. Asked at a press conference whether UN membership for the Peking Government would have facilitated settlement, he replied: "I have no doubt of that." On another occasion he cited Hanoi's refusal to sanction any UN intervention because of fear that this would dilute the Geneva agreements. Since the first requisite for Security Council action was to hear both sides, U Thant argued, Hanoi and Peking would have to participate in any discussion and both would refuse to do so.[84] It might be added that still another reason for UN inaction was that Washington saw little possibility of obtaining UN support for its position on Vietnam.

On August 5, 1964, however, Washington did notify the Security Council that DRV torpedo boats had attacked its naval vessels in the Tonkin Gulf on August 2 and 4, and that it had retaliated by bombing "torpedo boats and support facilities" within North Vietnamese territory. It called for immediate convening of the Council in accordance with the requirements of the UN Charter. At the meeting, Soviet and Czech delegates charged the United States with having invaded North Vietnamese waters and with participation in the shelling of North Vietnamese islands on July 30 and 31, which Ambassador Stevenson promptly denied. French and Soviet delegates called for Hanoi's participation in the Council's discussion of the U.S. complaint, and Stevenson insisted that in such a case Saigon should also be invited. At the following session, Council President Nielsen of Norway reported that Hanoi had rejected the invitation to participate on the grounds that the dispute came within the purview of the Geneva Conference machinery.[85]

This ended the matter for the Council. The facts of the Tonkin Gulf dispute have been widely aired and debated, but Council discussions have their own special flavor. At the outset, the Soviet delegate requested a day's delay in order to communicate with his government. The Czech delegate—Jiri Hajek, Foreign Minister in the new Czech regime—joined the request on the grounds that Council members had had no opportunity to acquaint themselves with the facts of the dispute; the alleged DRV attack on American destroyers had taken

[84] *UN Monthly Chronicle*, June, 1966, 31-32; *ibid.*, May, 1966, 33.
[85] *UNOR*, Security Council, 1140 and 1141 meetings, August 5 and 7, 1964, Document S/5849.

place only a day before and U.S. retaliation only a few hours before the meeting. Stevenson opposed the pleas for delay on the grounds that Article 51 of the Charter required "immediate" reporting to the Council of an act of self-defense. Since he had already "reported" the act in his letter to the Council, Stevenson obviously interpreted the Charter provision to mean an immediate meeting of the Council. When Washington notified the Secretary-General of the extension of the war to North Vietnam in February of 1965 and again of the entry of American combat troops in July of 1965, however, it did not ask for a Security Council meeting though both actions were formally taken in defense of South Vietnam under cover of Article 51.

In the debate, the Czech delegate charged that acts of reprisal had been specifically condemned by the Council just four months earlier (April 9, S/5650) and he quoted Stevenson as having said at the time: "My Government has repeatedly expressed its emphatic disapproval of provocative acts and of retaliatory raids whenever they occur and by whomever committed." Stevenson's response was that the American aerial attacks were not retaliatory; they had been undertaken in self-defense since they were directed at torpedo boat installations, and the DRV attack had been made with torpedo boats. The Soviet delegate promptly quoted Defense Secretary McNamara as saying: "In retaliation of this unprovoked attack on the high seas, our forces have struck the bases used by the North Vietnamese patrol craft." The Soviet delegate also argued that Article 51, which protects the right of self-defense, precludes retaliation as does international law generally. The American ambassador did not respond further. None of the nonpermanent members of the Council, with the exception of the Czech delegate, took part in the debate. The two Latin American members—Brazil and Bolivia—and the two African members—Ivory Coast and Morocco— were silent, as was the Council President.

The Tonkin Gulf incident protected President Johnson against charges of "softness on Communism" levelled against him by supporters of his presidential rival, while his taking the issue to the UN preserved his image as a man of peace. More important, the incident provided him with the opportunity to get a special congressional resolution giving him uninhibited authority to use the armed forces in Southeast Asia. But the Security Council debate, though it dealt with issues involving international law as defined by the Council itself, was plainly irrelevant to the actual developments in this historic, war-expanding incident.

The Council was again called into session on the Vietnam issue by a United States letter of January 31, 1966, requesting an urgent meeting to consider an American peace resolution which would charge the Council with the task of arranging a conference looking to application of the Geneva agreements.[86] Two events appear to explain the American action. First, just a couple of days earlier, amid a storm of international and domestic protest, the United States had resumed the bombing of North Vietnam after a 37-day pause. Second, the Senate Foreign Relations Committee—dominated by "doves"—had just opened televised public hearings on the war under conditions of intense public interest. Since Washington well knew that its resolution was unacceptable to the French and the Russians, it was patently using the UN as an instrument for blunting the effects of both developments.

The Council debate centered on placing the U.S. resolution on the agenda. The delegates of France, USSR, Mali, Nigeria, Uganda, and Bulgaria, in their discussion, opposed UN action on the usual ground of absence of several parties involved in the war. Jordan asked for postponement of debate, The Netherlands proposed inviting the non-member war participants. China opposed an invitation to Peking. Several delegates—notably those of Mali, Nigeria, and The Netherlands—observed that in the light of the bombing resumption this was a poor time for the United States to present a peace resolution to the Council. In the end nine nations voted for placing the question on the agenda, two against (USSR and Bulgaria), and four abstained (France, Mali, Nigeria, and Uganda). Typically, the four abstainers had made strong speeches against the motion. The discussion went no further when it was learned that Hanoi, as expected, had again rejected UN intervention.[87] "If the UN wants to act in favor of peace," Hanoi said, "it must compel its member country, the United States, to stop the aggressive war in Vietnam."[88]

During the last quarter of 1967, following demands from 27 Senate "doves," the administration canvassed the possibility of submitting the dispute once more to the Council. A resolution was drafted which Ambassador Goldberg incorporated into his opening Assembly address that fall. The resolution called for immediate cease-fire and disengagement of warring armies; elimination of all military forces and

[86] *UNOR*, Security Council, January 31, 1966, Documents S/7105, 7106.
[87] *UNOR*, S/p.v. 1271-73, Feb. 1 and 2, 1966; *UN Monthly Chronicle*, March, 1966, 3.
[88] George Kahin and John Lewis, *The United States in Vietnam* (New York, 1967), 224-25.

bases in the south and north except those under the control of the respective governments; respect for the borders between South and North Vietnam; settlement of the reunification question by the people of Vietnam without foreign interference; and supervision of the settlement by international machinery. Much of this paralleled Hanoi's program, but point 2—elimination of all military forces except those under government control—was obviously a demand for NLF surrender. The administration did not expect the Council to act, but wanted to demonstrate to its Senate critics that nothing could be anticipated from the UN. After a canvass of friendly members on the Council, the administration decided not to introduce its resolution. One reason was fear that the Soviet, Bulgarian, or a neutral Council delegate might call for unilateral cessation of the bombing of the north, that the Assembly might be provoked into condemning U.S. actions in Vietnam, or that it might call for participation of the NLF as a significant element in Vietnamese affairs.[89] Reportedly the British, Danes and Canadians had told the Americans that because of public opinion, they could not guarantee not to vote for a cessation of the bombing if such a resolution were introduced.[90]

There was also the sticky question of an invitation to the NLF to participate in any UN discussion. In November, Ambassador Goldberg told the Senate Foreign Relations Committee that the United States would not object to an invitation to the Front, which had indicated a desire to come to the UN. He also departed from the previous intransigeant position over NLF participation in negotiations by saying that an international conference could determine for itself who the conferees should be. An immediate outcry from Saigon caused the State Department to retreat hastily. Its position regarding the Front, it said, referred only to discussions before the Security Council; imposition of any form of coalition involving the Front was "still against U.S. principles."[91] That Washington should have operative, and overriding, "principles" concerning the political identity of participants in a government in Saigon is an interesting commentary on the tension between American involvement in Vietnam and its commitment to the UN Charter. In any case Washington decided that the risk of a boomerang was too great, and it abandoned the idea of putting the Council to the test by introduction of its resolution.

[89] *New York Times*, September 7, 8, 22 and December 13, 1967.
[90] Murray Kempton in the *New York Post*, December 15, 1967.
[91] *New York Times*, November 3 and December 9, 1967.

Some Observations

The UN grew out of the determination of the anti-Axis powers, during World War II, to prevent a third world holocaust and a realization that this required, in Secretary of State Hull's words, "the creation of a system of international relations based on rules of morality, law, and justice, as distinguished from the anarchy of "unbridled and discordant nationalism."[92] Nuclear weaponry added further urgency to the necessity of readjusting relations among nations to the material realities of the modern world, and in the immediate postwar period much was written and said about this need to transform the conduct of nations from the Machiavellian "reasons of state," or "vital national interests," to the rule of international law. The UN was born in the hope and expectation that it would be the instrument of this transformation.

This is not seriously entertained today. Appeals to international law as determinant of national action are dismissed somewhat contemptuously as "legalism," and those who make them are viewed as naive. It is assumed that the conduct of nations is still determined by unbridled nationalism, deterred by power but undeterred by provisions of the UN Charter.

The history of Washington's intervention in Vietnam suggests that this Machiavellian assumption is valid for the conduct of American foreign relations. As I have indicated explicitly and implicitly, this history from the outset has disregarded Charter commitments and has violated the Charter's basic principles. In his interior memoir of the Kennedy administration, Arthur Schlesinger, Jr., implies indirectly that this disregard is general. Washington, he observes, "had an ineradicable tendency to think of foreign policy as a matter between the United States and another nation or, at most, as between the United States and an alliance. The idea of policy as lying between the United States and the mess of a hundred nations in New York was alien and uncongenial."[93]

The violations in Vietnam embrace, broadly, two major principles of the Charter. One is denial of self-determination and forcible interference with territorial integrity and sovereignty; the other is unilateral definition of aggression and unilateral intervention against it. From the Truman Administration's first proffer of aid to the Bao Dai regime

[92] Radio address, September 12, 1943, Department of State *Bulletin*, September 18, 1943, 178.
[93] Schlesinger, op.cit., 464.

in May of 1950, Washington's aim has been to prevent the Vietnamese from choosing their own rulers. The reason is not obscure. In the early cold-war years, American policy-makers were often asked how they would resolve the conflict between containment and self-determination should a people voluntarily choose a Communist leadership. They evaded by responding that no people would ever do so. In Vietnam, Washington knew, the people would make this choice. Hence it supported French efforts to set up a puppet regime in the hope of defeating Ho Chi Minh by siphoning off some of his massive support from nationalists. When that failed, the United States attempted to salvage at least the south under conditions which would permit imposition of an anti-Communist regime despite popular opposition. In pursuing this course Washington forcibly disrupted Vietnam's territorial integrity and interfered with her sovereignty in violation of Article 2, Section 4 of the Charter. At Geneva, the United States had explicitly invoked this section of the Charter as basis for her pledge not to obstruct the settlement establishing Vietnam as a single independent nation.

Washington's efforts to obscure the violation by maintaining that she intervened at the request of a legitimate government to aid in defence against a foreign aggressor illustrates the irrationality and incoherence to which the tension between her actions and Charter requirements have reduced her. The rationalization compels definition of the U.S. goal as securing the independence of South Vietnam, and Johnson administration spokesmen have proclaimed this as their purpose in every statement on the war. But the preamble of the new Saigon constitution, adopted in March of 1967, declares it to be the aim of the government to "unite the nation, unite the territory." Article 1 states that "Vietnam is a territorially indivisible, unified, and independent republic." And the final Article 107 declares that Article 1 "may not be amended or deleted." There is, then, no foreign aggressor attacking Saigon, and the United States is fighting for goals which the regime inviting its defense rejects.

Violations of the Charter were specifically charged to the United States by UN Secretary-General U Thant in an address to the World Conference of Friends on July 30, 1967. He cited the intervention in Vietnam as an example of the failure of UN members to observe the "fundamental injunction to refrain in their international relations from the threat or use of force against the territorial integrity or political independence of any state." Vietnamese are fighting, he maintained, out of a "desire to win their national independence and establish their national identity." The war will not be ended "until the United States and her allies recognize that it is being fought by the Vietnamese not as a war of Communist aggression, but as a war of national independence."[94]

The unilateral nature of American intervention in Vietnam has been described earlier. This, too, ignores the fundamental UN principle that enforcement of international peace and security is the collective responsibility of the UN, not of any one nation. Arthur Lall, former Indian ambassador to the UN and an authority on its operations, has written that no UN member "may arrogate to itself the powers of enforcement which are to be set in motion by decision of the United Nations under the relevant provisions of the Charter."[95]

The violation is not surmounted by resort to SEATO since the UN Charter (Article 52) specifies that actions of regional agencies must be consistent with the principles of the Charter. The use of SEATO to cover disruption of Vietnam's territorial integrity or unilateral enforcement actions under its provisions are plainly inconsistent with UN principles.

As indicated, diverse explanations have been offered for Washington's intervention, including defense of her own "vital interests" and defense of the right of South Vietnam to be "let alone by her neighbors." During the Indochinese War and for years after the Geneva Conference, however, Washington policy-makers frankly gave as their aim the blocking of Communist expansion in Asia. Dulles, as noted above,[96] was explicit about the need for the United States to intervene in the internal affairs of any nation to prevent this expansion. He thus anticipated by many years the recently projected "Brezhnev Doctrine" whereby Moscow proclaimed the right to intervene in the internal affairs of any Communist-led nation to prevent restoration of Capitalism. Neither position is compatible with the UN Charter, which assumes that all nations, Communist and non-Communist, are equally sovereign and inviolate in their internal affairs.

Ideology has a powerful impact of its own on the action of nations as of individuals. But it generally receives at least an initial impetus from more material factors. The United States emerged out of World War II with a vast concentration of power extending around the globe.

---

[94] "The United Nations and the Human Factor," UN Press Release SG/SM/782 (UN Office of Public Information, July 28, 1967).

[95] Lall, op.cit., 124.   [96] See page 340.

The relative extent of this power was bound to shrink as other nations recovered from the effects of the war, as Soviet power expanded, and as colonies of America's allies broke away from the control of the American-dominated European imperial system to become at least partially independent of it.

But the United States, in the fashion probably of any dominant nation, has not willingly accepted this diminution of its relative power even if some of its own measures have contributed to the diminution. The greatest threat to the retention of its power position has been the expansion of Communist power. For wherever Communism has taken over, American influence—economic and political—has been eliminated or barred. Elsewhere, it could utilize its immense economic and political power to retain or gain influence. Hence, as spur to the ideology of anti-Communism has been the drive to maintain America's world-dominant power position at as close to the relative postwar level as possible.

Vietnam is a specific application of this process. Following the war, the United States had virtually a power monopoly in the Pacific. Almost immediately it was confronted with the necessity of defining its attitude toward colonial liberation movements. Support for them would win their friendship, and liberation would permit American power to penetrate them economically and politically more freely than could be done under colonial status. But liberation would also intensify the economic plight of its allies and might weaken the relative world political power of the Western alliance if the liberated nations should move away from it. In the end Washington backed non-Communist movements for independence. In Indochina, however, it pursued the dual and contradictory policy of giving massive aid to the French to suppress the independence movement led by the Communist, Ho Chi Minh, while simultaneously pressing the French to grant greater freedom of motion to the puppet Bao Dai regime. Under this policy the Vietminh became, in the eyes of the Truman and Eisenhower administrations, the "aggressor" in their own land against the French, who were defending "freedom"—while simultaneously Washington criticized the French for refusing to grant the very "freedom" they were defending.

The explanation given by President Eisenhower and Secretary Dulles, later repeated by Secretary Rusk, for pressing the fight against the Vietminh, and later the Vietcong, suggest the American will to retain its economic, political and military power in the Pacific. They stressed the need to prevent "loss" of the "rich natural resources" of Southeast Asia; the strategic position of Indochina, or South Vietnam, militarily; and the political effects of a Communist-led government in the rest of Southeast Asia. The irrelevance of these considerations to the right of the Vietnamese to determine their own destiny is, of course, beside the point.

But the relative power positions of nations are in constant flux, and the expanded power of Peking China and Soviet Russia has challenged that of the United States through the material aid given to the Vietnamese. Chinese and Soviet power has not been great enough to permit them to compel the United States to call off its intervention, but it is great enough to deter the U.S. from uninhibitedly employing its vast military strength to wipe out the resisting Vietnamese, north and south, as it surely would have done but for the fear of engaging at least the Chinese directly. What might otherwise have been a brief encounter has been transformed into a major war, the longest in American history.

This factor of constantly shifting power relations among nations is generally overlooked by the "realist" theoreticians of international relations, who tend to transform a description of power as the arbiter of these relations into a defence of the system. With changes of relative material power come pressures for commensurate readjustments of political power. And since the declining power will not readily give up its political position, the result is conflict leading to war. This has been the history of the last two world wars. The world could afford the luxury of such wars in the prenuclear age. It cannot afford them in the nuclear age.

Collisions arising out of changing power relations present themselves to each side, naturally, as defense of "vital national interests" and "national security." The theme recurs *ad nauseam* in the statements of the Johnson administration. Thus the President told the nation at San Antonio that "the key to all we have done [in Vietnam] is really our own security."[97] If this is valid for our presence in the south, how much more valid is it for the North Vietnamese? Or, in the light of geography, for the Russians—in Vietnam or in Czechoslovakia? Or for the Chinese—in Vietnam or even India? As Arthur Lall has also written, the UN Charter "does not allow a country to plead that im-

[97] *New York Times*, September 30, 1967.

pelled by vital interests, it has to have recourse to force or threats of force for furthering or protecting those interests."[98]

The record thus suggests strongly that from the outset the United States was not concerned with the manner in which its actions conformed to the UN Charter, a fact which can scarcely have failed to have its influence on the viability of the organization, especially in the light of the American power position in the postwar world. It may be, as a former member of the UN Secretariat, Conor Cruise O'Brien has suggested, that the UN has not fulfilled its expectations because mankind is not ready for the revolutionary change in relations among nations required by it. But if it cannot abolish war, O'Brien argues it can exercise other valuable peace-keeping functions. Its efficacy, however, depends upon its moral authority. In escalating the conflict in Vietnam while the UN watched helplessly, the United States has weakened that moral authority and inspired considerable speculation concerning the world body's further usefulness.

It also appears clear from the Vietnam experience that Washington has weakened the UN by employing it so blatantly as an instrument in its power struggle in Asia. From 1950 the persistent refrain in the UN has been the inability to act effectively to resolve the Vietnam conflict in the absence of Peking. This absence, and Secretary Dulles' hostility to any invitation to Peking to participate in Council debate, compelled a settlement of the Indochinese War outside of the UN and thereby deprived the world organization of the possibility of exercising later significant influence. After 1954 the absence of Hanoi also proved paralyzing. It is possible that even without Peking's presence the membership of Hanoi and Saigon, as proposed by the Russians in 1957 on the basis of the "principle of universality," would have enhanced the UN's capacity to deal with the conflict, possibly even settling it before it erupted into a major war.

Perhaps, as Canadian diplomat John Holmes said in a passage cited earlier, it is inevitable in today's world that the United States should exercise its "enormous disproportion" of power in what it deems to be its vital interests. If so, that preponderance of power stands in the way of effective world organization for peace and suggests another reason why membership of Peking China could prove to be beneficial to the organization. It would reduce America's proportionate power within it and hence permit it to function, even if minimally, in areas

98 Lall, op.cit., 154.

of American interest. For, as O'Brien has observed, when the United States is involved in war and perseveres in waging it, "the principal organs of the United Nations . . . are at present not even able to formulate any opinions about the matter . . . neither the Council nor the Assembly can reach any coherent decisions or recommendations on this subject."[99]

If the actions of the United States in Vietnam, and of other great powers elsewhere, are still determined principally by Machiavellian assumptions of the primacy of unbridled "vital interests," it does not follow that it must always be this way. The shape of international relations have been influenced since World War II by nuclear developments. But there has not been the transformation in these relations called for by the developments. Since cultural changes generally lag considerably behind material developments, however, the impact of nuclear weaponry may yet compel actual realization of UN Charter principles as the primary "vital interest" of all nations. Evolution of this has unquestionably been set back by the Vietnamese War. Perhaps the widespread opposition to the war among America's youth foreshadows gradual recognition of the need to transform international politics in line with the realities of the nuclear world. In any case the present reliance upon power and "national interest" as arbiter of international relations, while perhaps tolerable from Machiavelli's day to World War II, has become outmoded and too perilous to be tolerable today.

[99] "How the UN Can End the War," *New York Review*, March 28, 1968, p. 22.

IV. THE LAWS OF WAR

Maltreatment of Prisoners of War
in Vietnam

HOWARD S. LEVIE

After the adoption of the Southeast Asia (Gulf of Tonkin) Resolution by the Congress of the United States in August, 1964,[1] there was a substantial increase in the American military presence in South Vietnam and consequent and parallel increases in the range and extent of belligerent activities. In accordance with its customary practice, the International Committee of the Red Cross[2] (hereinafter referred to as the ICRC) thereupon addressed a letter to the several parties to the conflict,[3] pointing out that they had all ratified or adhered to, and were bound by, the 1949 Geneva Conventions for the Protection of Victims of War.[4] The ICRC reminded the parties of their specific obligations under the Conventions,[5] and requested information as to the measures being taken by each of them to conform to the duties devolving upon them.

---

[1] P.L. 88-408, 79 Stat. 384, approved August 10, 1964.

[2] The International Committee of the Red Cross is a century-old humanitarian organization composed entirely of Swiss citizens which maintains a strictly neutral status in all armed conflicts, offering its services equally to both sides. Since 1864 it has been the motivating force behind the series of humanitarian "Geneva" Conventions. Its status and activities in wartime are officially recognized and formalized in the 1949 Geneva Conventions, note 4 infra.

[3] This letter, dated June 11, 1965, was sent to the governments of the United States, the Republic of Vietnam (hereinafter referred to as South Vietnam), and the Democratic Republic of Vietnam (hereinafter referred to as North Vietnam). The ICRC stated therein that it would "endeavor to deliver it also to the National Liberation Front." 60 Am. J. Int'l L. 92 (1966), 4 Int'l Legal Mat. 1171 (1965).

[4] There are four of these Conventions. Our concern here will be solely with the 1949 Geneva Convention Relative to the Treatment of Prisoners of War, 6 U.S.T. 3316, T.I.A.S. No. 3364, 75 U.N.T.S. 135 [hereinafter referred to as the Convention]. The United States ratified this Convention on August 2, 1955. 6 U.S.T. 3316, T.I.A.S. No. 3364, 213 U.N.T.S. 383. South Vietnam adhered to it (as the State of Vietnam) on Nov. 14, 1953 (181 U.N.T.S. 351). North Vietnam adhered to it on June 28, 1957 (274 U.N.T.S. 339). Ratifications and adherences by other States involved in Vietnam, either directly or indirectly, are as follows: Republic of the Philippines, Oct. 6, 1952 (141 U.N.T.S. 384); USSR, May 10, 1954 (191 U.N.T.S. 367); Thailand, Dec. 29, 1954 (202 U.N.T.S. 332); People's Republic of China, Dec. 28, 1956 (260 U.N.T.S. 442); Australia, Oct. 14, 1958 (314 U.N.T.S. 332); New Zealand, May 2, 1959 (330 U.N.T.S. 356); and the Republic of Korea, Aug. 16, 1966 (55 Dep't State Bull. 694 (1966)).

[5] Concerning the Prisoner-of-War Convention, the ICRC letter, supra note 3, said: "In particular the life of any combatant taken prisoner, wearing uniform or bearing an emblem clearly indicating his membership in the armed forces, shall be spared, he shall be treated humanely as a prisoner of war, lists of combatants taken prisoner shall be communicated without delay to the International Committee of the Red Cross (Central Information Agency), and the delegates of the ICRC shall be authorized to visit prison camps." The items so specified clearly indicate that the ICRC considered the armed conflict in Vietnam to be of an international character. Indeed, the tenor of the letter leaves no doubt on this score.

Replies were received from all of the parties concerned. The United States advised that it "has always abided by the humanitarian principles enunciated in the Geneva conventions and will continue to do so." Specifically, it affirmed that it was "applying the provisions of the Geneva Conventions [in Vietnam] and we expect the other parties to the conflict to do likewise."[6] The Republic of Vietnam (hereinafter referred to as South Vietnam) assured the ICRC that it was "fully prepared to respect the provisions of the Geneva Conventions and to contribute actively to the efforts of the International Committee of the Red Cross to ensure their application."[7]

The reply received from the Democratic Republic of Vietnam (hereinafter referred to as North Vietnam) was the usual propaganda tirade which appears to be endemic in Communist documents, thus making it rather difficult to isolate any truly responsive portions. However, the letter did state that North Vietnam would "regard the pilots who have carried out pirate-raids, destroying the property and massacring the population of the Democratic Republic of Vietnam, as major [war] criminals caught in flagrante delicto and liable for judgment in accordance with the laws of the Democratic Republic of Vietnam, *although captured pilots are well treated.*"[8] The National Liberation Front (hereinafter referred to as the NLF), the political arm of the Vietcong, flatly refused to apply the Conventions, stating that it "was not bound by the international treaties to which others beside itself subscribed . . . . [T]he NLF, however, affirmed that the prisoners it held were humanely treated and that, above all, enemy wounded were collected and cared for."[9]

This article has well-defined limitations in scope. It will be concerned solely with some of the instances of maltreatment of prisoners of war which constitute violations of several of the more important humanitarian provisions of the 1949 Geneva Prisoner-of-War Convention, or of customary international law, which appear to have occurred during the course of the fighting in Vietnam.[10] Unfortunately, the positions taken by North Vietnam and the NLF necessitate at least some discussion of the problems created by their attitude toward compliance with the humani-

---

[6] 53 Dep't State Bull. 447 (1965), 4 Int'l Legal Mat. 1173 (1965), 5 Int'l Rev. of the Red Cross 477 (1965).

[7] 4 Int'l Legal Mat. 1174 (1965), 5 Int'l Rev. of the Red Cross 478 (1965). As we shall see, these promises have not been fully carried out.

[8] 5 Int'l Legal Mat. 124 (1966), 5 Int'l Rev. of the Red Cross 527 (1965) (emphasis added).

[9] 5 Int'l Rev. of the Red Cross 636 (1965). The final assertion was undoubtedly included because of the charge frequently advanced by American combat troops that the Vietcong made a practice of shooting enemy wounded found on the battlefield. N.Y. Times, Dec. 1, 1965, at 1, col. 8.

[10] We will not be concerned with violations of the technical provisions of the Convention; nor will we be concerned with the violations of a number of the more important humanitarian provisions of the Convention which have undoubtedly occurred, but as to which there is a paucity of acceptable facts presently available.

tarian aspects of the law of war and by the question of the applicability of the Convention under the circumstances which exist in Vietnam.

I. PAST COMMUNIST PRACTICE WITH RESPECT TO THE TREATMENT OF PRISONERS OF WAR

Inasmuch as the long list of States which have ratified or adhered to the 1949 Geneva Conventions[11] contains all of the Communist countries, including the major sponsors of North Vietnam and the NLF, *viz* the USSR and the People's Republic of China, it is obvious that the refusal of North Vietnam and the NLF to consider themselves bound by even the limited humanitarian provisions enumerated in Article 3 of the Convention[12] cannot be because these provisions are in any manner contrary to the Communist concept of the law of war.[13] The only alternative is to assume that they consider that it is in their own self-interest not to be under any of the constraints imposed by a requirement to comply with these purely humanitarian aspects of the law of war. However, one engaged in armed hostilities, even as a rebel in a civil war, cannot thus divest himself of the requirement to comply with those portions of the law of war which constitute a part of the customary rules of international law recognized by all civilized nations—and, as we shall shortly see in more detail, the provisions of Article 3 of the Convention, for the most part, fall within this category.[14]

A. *The USSR during World War II*

During World War II, the USSR acknowledged that it was bound by the 1907 Hague Regulations[15] and the 1929 Geneva Wounded-and-Sick Convention,[16] and took the position that the provisions of these two agreements covered "all the main questions of captivity."[17] Based upon this statement the ICRC assumed that there would be, among other things, exchanges of lists of prisoners of war and of mail and relief pack-

---

[11] The Republic of Malawi adhered to the four 1949 Geneva Conventions on Jan. 5, 1968, becoming the 117th Party to those Conventions. Letter to the author from the Swiss Federal Political Department, Jan. 31, 1968.

[12] See note 34 infra.

[13] For arguments supporting this position, see the remarks of General Nikolai Slavin, chief of the Soviet delegation at the 1949 Diplomatic Conference which drafted the Conventions. Final Record of the Diplomatic Conference of Geneva of 1949, Vol. IIB, at 13-14 [hereinafter referred to as Final Record].

[14] See text in connection with notes 65-67 infra.

[15] Regulations attached to Hague Conventions No. IV of 1907, Concerning the Laws and Customs of War on Land, 36 Stat. 2277, T.S. No. 539, 100 Brit. For. & State Papers 338.

[16] 1929 Geneva Convention for the Amelioration of the Condition of Wounded and Sick of Armies in the Field, 47 Stat. 2074, T.S. No. 847, 118 L.N.T.S. 303.

[17] 1 Report of the International Committee of the Red Cross on its Activities during the Second World War 412 (1948) [hereinafter referred to as ICRC Report]. To the same effect see Trainin, Hitlerite Responsibility under Criminal Law 40 (1945).

ages, and that its delegates would be permitted and enabled to enter Russia and to inspect prisoner-of-war camps located in that country. This was also the assumption of the enemies of the USSR. Despite continuous efforts on the part of the ICRC, however, none of these things ever eventuated.[18] One author ascribed this negative policy adopted by the USSR to the alleged "official Soviet position, that any soldier who fell into enemy hands was *ipso facto* a traitor and deserved no protection from his government."[19]

B. *North Korea*

During the Korean hostilities the North Korean Government announced that its forces were "strictly abiding by principles of Geneva Conventions in respect to Prisoners of War";[20] and in the lengthy dispute during the armistice negotiations regarding "forced repatriation" of prisoners of war, the North Korean and Chinese Communists relied very heavily on certain articles of the 1949 Convention.[21] Despite this, only two lists of American prisoners of war, totalling just 110 names, were ever sent to the Central Tracing Agency of the ICRC in Geneva (in August and September 1950, shortly after hostilities began), death marches occurred, prisoners of war were inadequately fed, and mail was allowed only on an irregular basis (usually to serve some propaganda purpose). Repeated efforts, which continued even during the course of the armistice negotiations, were unsuccessful in obtaining permission for the ICRC to send a delegate into North Korea to inspect the prisoner-of-war camps located there.[22]

C. *North Vietnam*

Now, in Vietnam, we have a third instance of a Communist regime (North Vietnam) which has agreed to be bound by a humanitarian war convention but which, when the conditions arise under which the convention is to be applied, declines to comply with its provisions. North

---

[18] ICRC Report 404-436.

[19] Dallin, German Rule in Russia 420 (1957). A rumor to this general effect caused the German Embassy in Ankara, where the negotiations were being carried on, to raise the question with the ICRC delegate. ICRC Report 415. Many persons continue to believe that most of the Soviet soldiers who were repatriated to Russia from prisoner-of-war camps at the end of World War II were either executed or were sent to Siberia and that the knowledge of the fate which awaited them was the cause of the wave of suicides which occurred in the camps after the fall of Germany. Some sought and obtained asylum in Switzerland. Castrén, The Present Law of War and Neutrality 165 (1954).

[20] Le Comité International de la Croix-Rouge et le Conflit de Corée: Recueil de Documents 16 (1952).

[21] Hermes, Truce Tent and Fighting Front 141, 145 (1966); Vatcher, Panmunjom 116 (1958).

[22] British Ministry of Defence, Treatment of British Prisoners of War in Korea 33-34 (1955); Vatcher, Panmunjom, photograph opposite 114 (1958); Joyce, Red Cross International 200-201 (1959).

Vietnam persists in refusing to provide the names of persons held as prisoners of war, refusing to permit correspondence between the prisoners of war and their families, and refusing to permit the neutral ICRC delegates to inspect the prisoner-of-war camps so as to be able to determine whether the prisoners of war are, in fact, receiving the humane treatment to which they are entitled and which that regime long ago committed itself to provide. Similarly, the NLF refuses to consider itself bound in any way, even by the limited provisions of Article 3 of the Convention.[23]

It would seem, at this point, to be fairly well established that the Communist countries, while ready to become parties to humanitarian war conventions, are not ready to comply with their provisions, for they are either not concerned about obtaining reciprocal treatment for their captured personnel, or, possibly, they may assume that by their present method they will still obtain humane treatment for Communist personnel without any need to reciprocate—which is what has actually occurred in both Korea and Vietnam. Unfortunately, the result of this procedure can only be that eventually the other side in international armed conflicts, and the established government in civil armed conflicts, will refuse to apply the Convention until confirmation of the fact that it is being applied by the Communist side.[24] Although this procedure certainly would leave much to be desired from the immediate humanitarian point of view, it might, in the long run, prove to be more humanitarian to the greater number of persons. Of course, the argument would undoubtedly be made, in opposition to such a procedure, that the obligation to comply with the Convention does not depend upon reciprocity, but upon the undertaking made to all the other parties thereto, and also that the Convention creates individual rights which may not be withdrawn because of the failure of one side to comply.[25] While this may well be true, it is unquestionably going to be increasingly difficult to persuade a coun-

---

[23] See text in connection with notes 8 and 9 supra.

[24] Although not engaged in armed conflict with a Communist opponent, the French indirectly followed this course of action during the civil war in Algeria, with the result that the Provisional Government of the Algerian Republic, the political arm of the rebellion, not only committed itself to apply the 1949 Geneva Conventions, but considered it appropriate to actively seek French compliance. Algerian Office, White Paper on the Application of the Geneva Conventions of 1949 in the Franco-Algerian Conflict (1960). The White Paper cites (at 13) a newspaper article by Professor Roger Pinto, of the Faculty of Law of the University of Paris, giving as one reason for the French reluctance to apply the Conventions "the absence of reciprocity in respect to the humanitarian rules."

[25] This argument is particularly applicable to Article 3 dealing with armed conflict not of an international character, note 34 infra, inasmuch as a proposed provision requiring reciprocity, which had been included in the working draft, was intentionally deleted by the 1949 Diplomatic Conference. Castrén, Civil War 86 (1966); Coursier, L'Evolution du Droit International Humain, 99 Hague Recueil des Cours 357, 395 (1960); Pinto, Les Règles du Droit International Concernant la Guerre Civile, 114 Hague Recueil des Cours 451, 530 (1965).

try engaged in armed conflict with a Communist country, or an established government engaged in civil strife with a Communist uprising, that it must give Communist prisoners of war the benefits of the Convention while its own captured personnel do not even receive the minimum benefits of customary international law. They will undoubtedly tend to take the position that there must be a point at which the refusal of the Communist side to comply with the provisions of the Convention releases the other side from its obligations thereunder.[26]

II. Does Article 2 of the 1949 Convention Apply in Vietnam?

Whether the fighting which is taking place in Vietnam constitutes an international armed conflict or a civil war has been the subject of considerable dispute. It is the official position of the United States that what is taking place in Vietnam is an international armed conflict.[27] This position has received support from unofficial sources.[28] Opponents of United

---

[26] Under the third paragraph of Article 2, parties to the Convention are not bound with respect to another party to the conflict which is not a party to the Convention unless "the latter accepts and applies the provisions thereof." Under these circumstances it is somewhat difficult to accept the contention that a party to the Convention is absolutely bound when the other party to the conflict is a party to the Convention, even though the other party patently flaunts it and does not even purport to apply its provisions. Such a construction merely encourages adherences by states which have no intention of ever complying with the Convention. Is this, perhaps, what has occurred?
At the Hearings held to determine whether the Senate should give its advice and consent to the ratification of the 1949 Conventions by the President, the then General Counsel of the Department of Defense, Wilbur M. Brucker, testified: "Should war come and our enemy should not comply with the conventions, once we both had ratified—what then would be our course of conduct? The answer to this is that to a considerable extent the United States would probably go on acting as it had before, for, as I pointed out earlier, the treaties are very largely a restatement of how we act in war anyway.
If our enemy showed by the most flagrant and general disregard for the treaties, that it had in fact thrown off their restraints altogether, it would then rest with us to reconsider what our position might be." Hearings on the Geneva Conventions for the Protection of War Victims Before the Senate Comm. on Foreign Relations, 84th Cong., 1st Sess., at 11 (1955).
[27] Meeker, The Legality of U.S. Participation in the Defense of Viet-Nam, 54 Dep't State Bull. 474, 477 (1966). In a speech delivered to the Foreign Policy Association on Nov. 14, 1967, Secretary of State Rusk ridiculed those who take the position that the fighting in Vietnam is "just a civil war." 57 Dep't State Bull. 735, 740 (1967). Of course, his argument was based largely upon the ground that North Vietnamese Army units had been committed to the fighting in South Vietnam; while those who argue that it is a civil war draw the opposite conclusion from this same fact! Secretary Rusk does strengthen his argument by pointing to the post-World War II problem of the bifurcated States which appear in each instance to have become two separate sovereignties: Germany, Korea, and Vietnam.
[28] Moore, Underwood & McDougal, The Lawfulness of United States Assistance to the Republic of Vietnam 32 (unpublished ms., Yale Law School, May 1966); Moore, The Lawfulness of Military Assistance to the Republic of Vietnam, 61 Am. J. Int'l L. 1, 2 (1967); Johnson, Aquinas, Grotius and the Vietnam War, 16 Quis Custodiet? 69, 67, 70 (1967); Kutner, "International" Due Process for Prisoners of War, 21 U. Miami L. Rev. 721, 730 (1967). Many of those who support the official position do not find it necessary to reach the question of the nature of the conflict. Deutsch, The Legality of the United States Position in Vietnam, 52

States participation in the Vietnamese hostilities assert that it is a civil war.[29] Before proceeding to a discussion of specific instances of the improper treatment of prisoners of war, let us examine the law applicable under the various possibilities.

The first paragraph of Article 2 of the 1949 Convention provides that:

[T]he present Convention shall apply to all cases of declared war *or of any other armed conflict* which may arise between two or more of the High Contracting Parties, *even if the state of war is not recognized by one of them.* (Emphasis added).

The meaning of the quoted provisions is clear; and at no time since the drafting of the Convention in 1949 has any state indicated the existence of any question with respect to that meaning. In fact, it is among those provisions of the Convention which have been given both uniform interpretation and general approval.[30]

A.B.A.J. 436 (1966). In Partan, Legal Aspects of the Vietnam Conflict, 46 B.U.L. Rev. 281, 299 (1966), the author discusses the problem but reaches no conclusion. See also, the ICRC letter, notes 3 and 5 supra.

[29] Fried (ed.), Vietnam and International Law 63 (1967); Falk, International Law and the United States Role in the Viet Nam War, 75 Yale L.J. 1122, 1127 and passim (1966); Standard, United States Intervention in Vietnam is not Legal, 52 A.B.A.J. 627, 630 (1966); Wright, Legal Aspects of the Viet-Nam Situation, 60 Am. J. Int'l L. 750, 756 (1966). Standard appears to argue from a conclusion already reached when, after pointing out the State Department position, he says: "It is hardly open to dispute that the present conflict in South Vietnam is essentially a civil war." Certainly, Messrs. Rusk and Meeker (the latter the Legal Adviser of the Department of State) would dispute it! And Kutner, supra note 28, just as easily reaches the opposite conclusion, stating: "Considering Communism's commitment to the success of all wars of 'national liberation' and the participation of United States military on a large, escalating scale, it would be unrealistic to consider the conflict as purely domestic." The dispute on this question clearly indicates the correctness of the statements that "the dividing line between international and internal war is often exceedingly tenuous" (Greenspan, International Law and its Protection for Participants in Unconventional Warfare, 341 Annals 30, 31 (1962)) and that "all international war is, to some extent, civil war, and all civil war, international war." Pinto, supra note 25, at 455 (translation mine).

[30] See Stone, Legal Controls of International Conflict 313 n.85 (Rev. ed. 1959), where the following appears: ". . . Art. 2, para. 1, of the revised Prisoners of War Convention, 1949, declaring its provisions applicable not only to declared war but also to 'any armed conflict . . . even if a state of war is not recognized' by a belligerent Contracting Party, is a welcome recognition of the need to place the point beyond doubt." And in Pictet, Commentary on the Geneva Convention Relative to the Treatment of Prisoners of War 22-23 (1960) [hereinafter referred to as Commentary], it is stated: "By its general character, this paragraph deprives belligerents, in advance, of the pretexts they might in theory put forward for evading their obligations. There is no need for a formal declaration of war, or for the recognition of the existence of a state of war, as preliminaries to the application of the Convention. The occurrence of de facto hostilities is sufficient.

. . . Any difference arising between two States and leading to the intervention of members of the armed forces is an armed conflict within the meaning of Article 2, even if one of the Parties denies the existence of a state of war." And, finally, in Institute of Law, Academy of Sciences of the USSR, International Law 420 (ca. 1960) [hereinafter referred to as Soviet International Law], this statement is made: "The absence of a formal declaration of war does not deprive hostilities, which have in fact begun, of the character of war from the point of view of the need to observe its laws and customs. The Geneva Conventions of 1949 require that their signatories apply these Conventions, which are a component part of the

The only specific legal excuse ever advanced by North Vietnam for its insistence that the Convention is not applicable, and that persons captured by it are not entitled to the humanitarian protections afforded by the Convention, has been that there is no "declared war."[31] It is surely beyond dispute that there is an "armed conflict" in Vietnam between two or more of the parties to the Convention. Under these circumstances, the fact that there has been no declaration of war, or that a state of war is not recognized as existing, is completely irrelevant to the requirement to apply the Convention. There is, then, no validity whatsoever to the sole legal reason put forward by North Vietnam to justify its refusal to apply the Convention by which it voluntarily elected to be bound a number of years before the armed conflict in Vietnam reached its present status.[32] The wording used in drafting the first paragraph of Article 2 leaves no doubt that it was the intent of the Diplomatic Conference which approved it that the Convention be applicable in every instance of the use of armed force in international relations—and, beyond any shadow of doubt, this intent was attained. It appears equally clear that the refusal of North Vietnam to apply the Convention under the circumstances which exist in Vietnam—whether or not the United States is "waging a war of aggression"[33]—constitutes a blatant disregard of an international obligation, freely accepted.

---

laws and customs of war, in the event of a declaration of war or in any armed conflict, even if one of the parties to the conflict does not recognize the existence of a state of war."

[31] A news article from Cairo which appeared in the N.Y. Times, Feb. 12, 1966, at 12, col. 3, stated: "The sources quoted the [North Vietnamese] Ambassador as having rejected the American contention that United States airmen captured in attacks on North Vietnam should be treated as prisoners of war under the terms of the Geneva conventions.

He was reported to have told influential Egyptians that this was impossible 'because this is a case where no war has been declared' by either country."

[32] It will have been noted that the Convention provision quoted in the text states that the Convention is applicable in an armed conflict between two or more High Contracting Parties even if a state of war is not recognized by one of them. In Vietnam a state of war, in the legal sense, is not recognized by *any* of the parties involved. 52 Dep't State Bull. 403 (1965). Does this remove the armed conflict in Vietnam from the reach of Article 2? To answer this question in the affirmative would seem to be directly contrary to the intent of the Article and to the object and purpose of the Convention. The ICRC states that it does not avoid Article 2. Pictet, supra note 30, at 23. Lauterpacht believed that it was the intention of the draftsmen to make the Convention applicable even if a state of war was not recognized by "one or both of them." 2 Lauterpacht's Oppenheim, International Law 369 n.6 (7th ed. 1952).

[33] One of the major purposes of the provision was to preclude a State from indulging in the excuses put forward by Japan during the China Incident and by Nazi Germany during World War II as a basis for not applying earlier humanitarian conventions: that there had been no declaration of war, that legally a state of war did not exist, that the existence of a state of war was not recognized, that the armed conflict was only a "police action," etc. See the Judgment of the International Military Tribunal for the Far East 1008-09 (mimeo. 1949) [hereinafter referred to as IMTFE Judgment]; Latyshev, The 1949 Geneva Conventions Concerning the Protection of Victims of War, 7 The Soviet State and Law 121 (1954) (original in Russian).

III. Does Article 3 of the Convention Apply in Vietnam?

Article 3 of the Convention[34] is sometimes referred to as a "convention in miniature,"[35] or as a "mini-convention."[36] The draftsmen attempted to include in a single article those basic humanitarian provisions which render prisoner-of-war status somewhat less horrendous than it inherently is—thus, in a relatively simple manner, calling to the attention of the participants in a non-international armed conflict the specific humanitarian rules which control their actions from the very outset.[37] Unfortunately, even this minimum approach has frequently proven unsuccessful.[38]

The idea of including in an international convention a provision regulating civil wars was extremely novel.[39] While the ICRC had been aim-

---

[34] Article 3 states:
In the case of armed conflict not of an international character occurring in the territory of one of the High Contracting Parties, each Party to the conflict shall be bound to apply, as a minimum, the following provisions:
(1) Persons taking no active part in the hostilities, including members of armed forces who have laid down their arms and those placed hors de combat by sickness, wounds, detention, or any other cause, shall in all circumstances be treated humanely, without any adverse distinction founded on race, colour, religion or faith, sex, birth or wealth, or any other similar criteria.
To this end the following acts are and shall remain prohibited at any time and in any place whatsoever with respect to the above-mentioned persons:
  (a) violence to life and person, in particular murder of all kinds, mutilation, cruel treatment and torture;
  (b) taking of hostages;
  (c) outrages upon personal dignity, in particular, humiliating and degrading treatment;
  (d) the passing of sentences and the carrying out of executions without previous judgment pronounced by a regularly constituted court affording all the judicial guarantees which are recognized as indispensable by civilized peoples.
(2) The wounded and sick shall be collected and cared for.
An impartial humanitarian body, such as the International Committee of the Red Cross, may offer its services to the Parties to the conflict.
The Parties to the conflict should further endeavor to bring into force, by means of special agreements, all or part of the other provisions of the present Convention.
The application of the preceding provisions shall not affect the legal status of the Parties to the conflict.
[35] Statement of Mr. Morosov (USSR), Final Record, supra note 13, Vol. IIB, at 325-26; Pictet, Commentary, supra note 30, at 34.
[36] Pictet, The XXth International Conference of the Red Cross: Results in the Legal Field, 7 J. Int'l Comm'n Jurists 3, 15 (1966).
[37] "[F]uture generations may consider it a sad commentary on our times that the nations of the world thought it necessary in these conventions to provide that in case of an internal conflict, murder, mutilation, torture and other cruel treatment should not be practiced on prisoners and other noncombatants. . . ." Yingling & Ginnane, The Geneva Conventions of 1949 in 46 Am. J. Int'l L. 393, 396 (1952).
[38] Greenspan, supra note 29, at 40; Note, The Geneva Conventions of 1949: Application in the Vietnamese Conflict, 5 Va. J. Int'l L. 243, 249 (1965).
[39] Pictet, supra note 36; de la Pradelle, Le Contrôle de l'Application des Conventions Humanitaires en cas de Conflit Armé, 2 Annuaire Français de Droit International 343, 364 (1956).

ing for such as extension of the Geneva-type Conventions for many years, it was not successful in this respect until the 1949 Diplomatic Conference.[40] The main objection voiced during the discussions in committee and in the plenary sessions of the Diplomatic Conference was that under a number of the proposals the established government would seemingly be required to apply the Convention even in cases of brigandage.[41] The other problem that had to be solved was the determination as to which provisions of the Convention should in an appropriate case be applied.[42] The compromise ultimately adopted left the term "armed conflict not of an international character" undefined—which, in effect, was a determination to make the term as broad and all-encompassing as possible. On the other hand, the minimum provisions which the parties to the armed conflict are obligated to apply are enumerated at length, rather than providing for the application of the entire Convention (as the working draft had done) or of all provisions falling within certain broad categories (as the USSR had proposed).[43]

What is the effect of Article 3 of the Convention on the parties to an "armed conflict not of an international character?" As far as the established government is concerned, if it is a party to the Convention it is bound by the provisions of Article 3 just as much as it would be bound by all of the provisions of the Convention in an armed conflict of an international character.[44] And the same is true of third states which intervene to support either side in a civil war.[45]

---

[40] Pictet, Commentary, supra note 30, at 28-34.

[41] Id. at 32. During the debate General Slavin (USSR) made the following statement: "[T]he United Kingdom Delegation had alluded to the fact that colonial and civil wars were not regulated by international law, and therefore that decisions in this respect would be out of place in the text of the Conventions. This theory was not convincing, since though the jurists themselves were divided in opinion on this point, some were of the view that civil war was regulated by international law. Since the creation of the Organization of the United Nations, this question seemed settled. Article 2 of the Charter provided that Member States must ensure peace and world security. . . . Colonial and civil wars therefore come within the purview of international law." Final Record, supra note 13, Vol. IIB, at 14.

[42] The Stockholm (working) draft would have made the entire Convention applicable. Id., Vol. I, at 73. The provisions of the draft article proposed by the USSR would have obligated each party to an armed conflict not of an international character to implement all of the provisions of the Convention which guarantee "humane treatment of prisoners of war" and "the application of all established rules for the treatment of prisoners of war." Id., Vol. III, Annex 15, at 28.

[43] In construing the provision which was adopted, Pictet, Commentary, supra note 30, at 42, states: "In the case of armed conflict not of an international character . . . the Parties to the conflict are legally only bound to observe Article 3, and may ignore all the other Articles. . . ."

[44] Id. at 37; Note, The Geneva Conventions of 1949: Application in the Vietnamese Conflict, 5 Va. J. Int'l L. 243, 248 (1965).

[45] Pinto, supra note 25, at 529. Pinto says: "When the parties to the civil war receive foreign assistance, the assisting States have a strict obligation to comply with and to require compliance with Article 3. . . . Thus the United States and the Democratic Republic of Vietnam are equally responsible for the application of Article 3 in the civil war on the territory of South Vietnam." (Translation mine).

The foregoing has caused comparatively few legal problems.[46] Where problems arise, however, is with respect to the obligation of the insurgents. How, it will be asked, can the action of the established government in becoming a party to the Convention, an action perhaps taken many years before the rebellion was even contemplated, now be held to bind the insurgents?[47] This is the position taken by the NLF.[48] While it may have some minimum legal basis—this is the most that can be said for it—there are a number of valid legal theories under which a finding that the insurgents are bound by the provisions of Article 3 can be fully justified.[49]

While Soviet legal writers do not specifically state that insurgents[50] are bound by the provisions of Article 3, that is certainly the only logical conclusion which can be drawn from their writings. Thus, their widely distributed textbook states:

> [T]he Soviet delegation secured the [1949 Diplomatic] Conference's recognition of a number of important humane clauses which were included in the new Conventions. For example, the obligatory character of the application during armed conflicts which are not of an international character of such principles as the humane treatment of persons not taking a direct part in military operations or who have ceased to take part in these operations as a result of sickness, illness or captivity, was recognized . . . .[51]

It has been said that the established government cannot be prejudiced by applying Article 3, "for no Government can possibly claim that it is *entitled* to make use of torture and other inhuman acts prohibited by the

---

[46] Of course, established governments have not infrequently failed to comply with their obligations under Article 3—but this was not necessarily because they considered Article 3 invalid per se. See note 24 supra. As a matter of fact, when the French finally agreed to permit the ICRC to function in Algeria, it was specifically stated that this action was taken "in accordance with Article 3 of the Geneva Conventions." LeClercq, L'Application du Statut du Prisonnier de Guerre depuis la Convention de Genève de 1949, in 43 Revue de Droit International et de Droit Comparé 35, 45 (1966).

[47] In Yingling & Ginnane, supra note 37, at 396, the authors, both lawyer-members of the United States delegation to the 1949 Diplomatic Conventions, said: "Insofar as Article 3 purports to bind the insurgent party to the conflict to apply its provisions, its legal efficacy may be doubted."

[48] See text in connection with note 9 supra.

[49] For a discussion of the several theories which have been advanced for holding a rebel organization bound by the provisions of Article 3, even though it had never itself agreed to be bound, see Note, The Geneva Convention and the Treatment of Prisoners of War in Vietnam, 80 Harv. L. Rev. 851, 856-58 (1967). See also Lauterpacht, The Limits of the Operation of the Law of War, 30 Brit. Y.B. Int'l L. 206, 213 (1953), where that noted authority said: "The effect of these provisions [relating to armed conflict not of an international character] is to subject the parties to a civil war—including the party which is not a recognised belligerent —to important restraints of the law of war. . . ."

[50] The correct jargon, of course, would be "national liberation movements."

[51] Soviet International Law, supra note 30, at 410; and see the further quotation from this textbook in note 69 infra.

Convention as a means of combating its enemies."[52] It would certainly seem that this argument is equally applicable to the insurgent party, for how can armed conflict be conducted with different rules controlling the actions of the two contending sides?[53]

Finally, there is much merit in a further statement made in the official ICRC interpretation of Article 3 of the Convention to the effect that:

> If an insurgent party applies Article 3, so much the better for the victims of the conflict. No one will complain. If it does not apply it, it will prove that those who regard its actions as mere acts of anarchy or brigandage are right . . . .[54]

Certainly, any insurgent force or alleged "national liberation movement" which does not comply with the provisions of Article 3 requiring humane treatment, and prohibiting violence, murder, torture and maltreatment of prisoners of war falls within the category of brigands and terrorists.

What if, despite the foregoing, insurgents take the position that they are not bound by the provisions of Article 3, and this position gains acceptance? Except for the rare case such as Algeria, where the insurgents themselves sought application of the Convention,[55] Article 3 will become a dead letter. Unusual, indeed, would be the government willing to grant captured insurgents the benefits flowing from Article 3 while knowing that its own personnel, when captured, are tortured, otherwise maltreated and slaughtered. Although the requirement for granting these benefits to captured insurgents is stated to be absolute, and not to be dependent upon reciprocity,[56] once again it will be extremely difficult to convince any government and its people that such a unilateral compliance should be expected of them.

---

[52] Pictet, Commentary, supra note 30, at 38 (emphasis in original). He also states: "What Government would dare to claim before the world . . . that, Article 3 not being applicable, it was entitled to leave the wounded uncared for, to torture and mutilate prisoners and take hostages? No Government can object to observing, in its dealings with enemies, whatever the nature of the conflict between it and them, a few essential rules which it in fact observes daily, under its own laws, when dealing with common criminals." Id. at 36-37. Unfortunately, experience shows that some governments do just what is described, but without any such bald admission.

[53] Several years ago the suggestion was made that in any armed conflict in which United Nations forces were involved, they should not be bound by the law of war, but their opponent should be. The reaction to this proposal was violent and caustic, and properly so. See Bothe, Le Droit de la Guerre et les Nations Unies (1967).

[54] Pictet, Commentary, supra note 30, at 37-38. Of course, if they are mere brigands, they are not entitled to the protection of the Convention.

[55] It is essential to bear in mind that the last paragraph of Article 3 specifies that the fact that a party complies with the provisions of the Article "shall not affect the legal status of the Parties to the conflict." This provision was obviously included in order to permit the established government to comply with Article 3 without recognizing the existence of a state of belligerency with the insurgents. Paradoxically, in Algeria it was the insurgents themselves who called attention to this provision of the Article. Algerian Office White Paper, supra note 24, at 17-18.

[56] See note 25 supra; Pictet, Commentary, supra note 30, at 35; Draper, The Geneva Conventions of 1949 at 114 Hague Recueil des Cours 59, 96 (1965).

We may then be in a position in which there is no applicable international legislation governing the actions of the insurgents and we would, therefore, have need to resort to the customary law of war. What are the customary rules accepted by the civilized nations of the world? Are they binding upon insurgents?

IV. THE PERTINENT CUSTOMARY LAW OF WAR

In the opinion rendered by the Nuremberg International Military Tribunal (hereinafter referred to as IMT), which all Communist nations seemingly regard as a revelation second only to those of Marx, Engels and Lenin (and, it is to be assumed, of Mao in China), it is stated that by 1939 the 1907 Hague Regulations[57] were "declaratory of the laws and customs of war."[58] It is also there confirmed that an individual is not held as a prisoner of war for purposes of revenge or punishment, but merely to prevent him from further participation in the conflict and that he is, therefore, a helpless person whom it is contrary to military tradition to kill or injure.[59] One of the subsequent Nuremberg Military Tribunals, in deciding *The High Command Case*,[60] correctly construed the IMT opinion as holding that by 1939 both the 1907 Hague Regulations and the 1929 Geneva Prisoner-of-War Convention[61] "were binding insofar as they were in substance an expression of international law as accepted by the civilized nations of the world."[62] Every military force engaged in armed conflict, whether or not international in character, and whether representing an old or a new state, an established government or an insurgent party, is bound to comply with these established rules of the civilized nations of the world.[63] Failure to do so places that military force, and the political organization which it represents and from which it takes its orders and policies, in direct violation of the foregoing principles enunciated at Nuremberg.

The Tribunal in *The High Command Case* did not limit itself to the general statement that the 1907 Hague Regulations and the 1929 Geneva

---

[57] See note 15 supra.

[58] Nazi Conspiracy and Aggression: Opinion and Judgment 83 (1947).

[59] Id. at 61-62. In speaking of Nazi violations of the law of war, the IMT said (at 57): "Prisoners of war were ill-treated and tortured and murdered, not only in defiance of the well-established rules of international law, but in complete disregard of the elementary dictates of humanity. . . ."

[60] United States v. von Leeb et al., 10 Trials of War Criminals Before the Nuernberg Military Tribunals 1 (1948) [hereinafter cited as Trials]. This opinion carries over into Vol. 11 of the series).

[61] 1929 Geneva Convention Relative to the Treatment of Prisoners of War, 47 Stat. 2021, T.S. No. 846, 118 L.N.T.S. 343.

[62] United States v. von Leeb et al., 10 Trials 1 at 11 Trials 532-34 (1948).

[63] Note, The Geneva Convention and the Treatment of Prisoners of War in Vietnam, 80 Harv. L. Rev. 851, 858 (1967). A well known French expert in this field has said: "These obligations [enumerated in Article 3] correspond to those which the domestic public law of civilized States recognizes, even in cases of insurrection, riot or civil war. . . . The summary execution of prisoners is prohibited." Pinto, supra note 25, at 532 (translation mine).

374 MALTREATMENT OF P.O.W.'S IN VIETNAM

Prisoner-of-War Convention now represented customary law. Inasmuch as there were obviously provision in those two Conventions dealing with details which could not be construed as customary law, the Tribunal assumed the task of designating exactly which provisions of the two agreements did fall within that category. It proceeded to review the specific provisions of each of the two Conventions and found that those provisions requiring humane treatment of prisoners of war, and those protecting them from acts of violence, insults, public curiosity, corporal punishment and acts of cruelty, were "an expression of the accepted views of civilized nations."[64]

Of course, the Tribunal in *The High Command Case* was concerned only with those aspects of the law accepted by civilized nations of the world under which violations had been proven in the case before it. Its list is not, therefore, all-inclusive. Some writers have extended it to include the four groupings listed in Article 3 of the Convention,[65] probably on the extremely plausible theory that in rejecting both the ICRC and USSR proposals[66] the Diplomatic Conference had selected for inclusion in Article 3 (to be binding on both sides in a *civil* war) only those humanitarian principles which already had received demonstrable acceptance by the civilized nations of the world.[67] It also appears that both the Tribunals and the writers have definite ideas with respect to the imposition upon prisoners of war of vicarious punishment in the form of reprisals.[68]

Do these customary rules of warfare apply to insurgents? There seems little doubt that they do, even though the rules have so frequently been honored only in the breach. The Soviet textbook states that "the laws and customs of war apply not only to armies in the strict sense of the word, but also to levies, voluntary detachments, organised resistance movements and partisans."[69] Under existing circumstances, where every insurgent movement other than one which is avowedly anti-Communist immediately becomes a "national liberation movement" enjoying full Communist support, further citation of authority would appear to be redundant.

---

[64] United States v. von Leeb et al., 10 Trials 1 at 11 Trials 535-38. But see Draper, supra note 56, at 90, where he states: "Undoubtedly, the prohibition of murder, mutilation or torture is absorbed in the customary prohibitions of the law of war. On the other hand the taking of hostages, outrages upon personal dignity, the passing of sentences by irregular tribunals, unfairly conducted, are not yet prohibited by the customary law of war. . . ."

[65] See note 34 supra.

[66] See text in connection with notes 42 and 43 supra.

[67] Pictet, Commentary, supra note 30, at 39 and 141; Smith, The Geneva Prisoner of War Convention: An Appraisal, 42 N.Y.U.L. Rev. 880, 889 (1967); Pinto, supra note 63.

[68] See text in connection with notes 156-163 infra.

[69] Soviet International Law, supra note 30, at 423. Elsewhere (at 407) the statement is made that "the laws and customs of war must be observed in any armed conflict."

From the foregoing, it may be properly concluded that apart from any international legislation represented by the Hague or Geneva or other Conventions, minimum customary law requires that prisoners of war be treated humanely; forbids the use against them of all forms of violence including corporal punishment, torture, cruelty and killing; and protects them from insults and public curiosity. With this in mind, we may now proceed to an examination of the incidents reported to have occurred or to have been threatened in Vietnam, applying the provisions of the Convention generally, those of Article 3, or customary international law where appropriate.[70]

V. Charges Made Against the United States

It has already been pointed out that the United States responded promptly to the ICRC letter concerning the application of the Geneva Conventions in Vietnam and committed itself to apply the 1949 Convention.[71] This commitment was thereafter adopted by the various nations which have furnished military forces to support South Vietnam and it has been reiterated on several appropriate occasions.[72] Although, strangely enough, no report has been found of a Vietcong or North Vietnamese charge of improper treatment of their captured personnel by United States military forces in Vietnam,[73] there has been one charge of improper action in this respect made in the United States.

---

[70] It is not unusual to find, after hostilities have ended, that many incidents (or at least many of the more gory details thereof) which have been reported during the course of hostilities, were basically figments of the imagination: perhaps a minor incident which has been built up out of all proportion to the actual facts by the addition of horrendous details, perhaps an entirely imaginary incident conceived by a public relations officer or a reporter when headline news was lacking. However, the major violations to be discussed herein are in the nature of admissions against interest: actions constituting, or allegedly constituting, violations by the United States and the South Vietnamese, reported by the American news media; and actions constituting, or allegedly constituting, violations by the North Vietnamese and the Vietcong, reported by Radio Hanoi and the Liberation Radio, or by other sources in Hanoi. (As the alleged violation mentioned in note 9 supra does not meet this criterion, it will not be discussed. It is, however, one of the most heinous violations not only of the Convention, but also of the customary law of war).

[71] See text in connection with note 6 supra.

[72] Joint Communique of the Honolulu Conference, Feb. 8, 1966, at 54 Dep't State Bull. 304, 305 (1966); Joint Communique of the Manila Summit Conference, Oct. 25, 1966, at 55 Dep't State Bull. 730, 731 (1966); Text of Communique of the Washington Meeting, April 21, 1967, at 56 Dep't State Bull. 747, 749 (1967). The nations involved in the latter two meetings were Australia, New Zealand, the Philippines, South Korea, South Vietnam, Thailand, and the United States.

[73] That incidents of maltreatment of prisoners of war by American personnel have occurred is beyond dispute. There will never be a war fought in which there are not, at the very least, isolated instances of maltreatment of prisoners of war on both sides. The general moral environment in which the individual soldiers have been raised may be judged, and the training which they have received while in military service may be measured, by the frequency with which such incidents occur. While Clergy and Laymen Concerned About Vietnam in their book, In the Name of America (issued in February, 1968 after this article had been substantially completed), allocates a chapter of 45 pages to the reprinting of published items about the maltreatment of prisoners of war, there is only an occasional,

As early as 1964, when American personnel were serving in Vietnam solely as advisers to South Vietnamese military units, reports began to reach the United States of the maltreatment of Vietcong prisoners of war by members of the South Vietnamese combat forces.[74] American photographers and newsmen were present during these episodes and, presumably, American military personnel were also present. Photographs of this nature continued to appear in the American press from time to time during 1965 and occasionally, although much more rarely, during subsequent years.[75] In a few instances American personnel were pictured standing by while the maltreatment of the prisoners of war occurred.[76] These incidents apparently took place either at the scene of the fighting or during evacuation from it.

Humanitarian reaction to these clear indications of violations of the Convention quickly appeared in the United States.[77] The legal problem presented by these incidents, in view of the nature of the United States position in Vietnam, is whether the United States had a duty or was in a position to do more than remonstrate with the South Vietnamese authorities.[78]

and frequently misleading, indication (usually based on hearsay) of such misconduct by American troops. The weakness of the "evidence" quoted to support the organization's thesis of misconduct is, in itself, extremely persuasive of the inaccuracy of the conclusion reached by one of the commentators (at 23) that "these combat practices are so widespread in their occurrence as to suggest that their systematic commission is a direct result of decisions reached at the highest levels of civilian and military command." When Ambassador Harriman sent the ICRC a Department of Defense report on the methods used by the several military services of the United States to disseminate information concerning the requirements of the Conventions, the ICRC President replied: "We are convinced that in the context of the war in Vietnam the U.S. Forces are devoting a major effort to the spread of knowledge on the Geneva Conventions." Letter from Samuel A. Gonard to W. Averell Harriman, January 5, 1968, on file in the Department of State.

[74] A series of photographs and extracts from news stories recording maltreatment of prisoners of war by the South Vietnamese which had appeared in a number of respected American publications were collected and published in a brochure entitled What are we tied to in Vietnam? by Massachusetts Political Action for Peace, Cambridge, Mass. (1964).

[75] St. Louis Post-Dispatch, Oct. 22, 1965, at 3B; id. Nov. 3, 1965, at 2A; id. April 27, 1966, at 2A; id. Feb. 9, 1968, at 1B.

[76] Id. Dec. 30, 1965, at 1A. Photographs indicating kind and generous treatment by American personnel have also appeared (id. Mar. 5, 1966, at 2A; Mar. 6, 1966, at 12A), but these are suspect as they are self-serving and could easily have been posed for an enterprising photographer.

[77] The brochure referred to in note 74 supra is a good example of this reaction.

[78] A letter to the editor of the N.Y. Times from the Chairman of the University Committee on Problems of War and Peace at the University of Pennsylvania said: "Responsible American journalists have frequently reported the torture of Vietcong prisoners by their South Vietnamese captors. Because of these reports W. W. Rostow, chairman of the foreign policy research division of our State Department, was asked . . . 'why does the United States not abide by the Red Cross Convention in the treatment of Vietcong prisoners?' His reply was that the United States does not take prisoners in Vietnam, and that we were merely advisers to the South Vietnamese Government, which bore the responsibility for dealing with prisoners.

Because of this immoral apathy, and narrow legalistic position taken by our

There is no provision in the Convention making a contracting party responsible for violations committed by one of its allies against prisoners of war captured and held by that ally. A search of the Final Record of the 1949 Diplomatic Conference which drafted the Convention has failed to bring to light even a suggestion to this effect made by any delegation.[79] The reasons for this lacuna are obvious. To have included such a provision would have created vicarious responsibility for a situation which, in the great majority of cases, could not be remedied by the state so held responsible. Moreover, no state would willingly accept a responsibility which could well bring it into sharp conflict with one or several of its allies during the course of a life-or-death struggle.

There was, then, no legal duty imposed upon the United States by the 1949 Convention to ensure that South Vietnamese troops did not maltreat personnel captured by them. Of course, it is equally clear that the United States (and every other contracting party) is under a moral obligation to exert all its influence to bring about full compliance with the relevant provisions of the Convention by any other party engaged in armed conflict.[80]

When units of the United States armed forces were committed to combat a new situation arose, because, unlike the earlier period just mentioned, the United States itself then began to take prisoners of war. These prisoners were turned over to the South Vietnamese for detention in prisoner-of-war camps. At first, the transfer of custody was made in the field immediately upon capture. But apparently because most of the incidents of maltreatment occurred at this time and in this area, in mid-

---

State Department, neither the United States nor the South Vietnamese, nor the Vietcong, nor the North Vietnamese are committed to adhere to any of the 'sanctions established by international law for the protection of war prisoners.'" N.Y. Times, June 30, 1965, at 36, col. 5. The writer of the letter erred in both his assumptions and his conclusions, but he certainly raised the moral issue.

[79] This problem did arise in one context at the Diplomatic Conference—in connection with Article 12, which concerns custody of prisoners of war transferred from one ally to another. Under Article 12 the transferring state retains some residual power with respect to prisoners of war it transfers, because it can request return of the prisoners to its custody where the transferee state is guilty of violating the Convention in their regard. Article 12 requires that this procedure be followed where the Protecting Power finds violations of the Convention and the Detaining Power does not correct them. The Communist countries have all reserved as to this Article, insisting that the capturing power remain fully responsible for any maltreatment suffered by prisoners of war at the hands of the transferee detaining power. See, for example, the USSR reservation made at the time of signing (75 U.N.T.S. 135, 460) and maintained at the time of ratification (191 U.N.T.S. 367).

[80] "The major United States effort, besides setting up its own procedures, has been to persuade the South Vietnamese to go along. [South Vietnamese] Governmen officials, once openly hostile to the convention, now grudgingly accept the American position. Much remains to be done, however, to persuade the average South Vietnamese soldier to stop using torture. Each soldier will soon be shown a training film prepared with American help. Most have already received booklets outlining the proper treatment of prisoners. N.Y. Times, July 1, 1966, at 6, col. 3. See also Pinto supra note 45.

1966 the United States changed its procedure. Thereafter, prisoners of war captured by United States units were evacuated to divisional headquarters and from there directly to the rear-area prisoner-of-war camps maintained by the South Vietnamese.[81] The United States Commander-in-Chief in Vietnam has stated categorically that "these prisoners are not being mistreated. They are handled in accordance with the provisions of the Geneva Conventions."[82] There is no evidence to indicate that his statement is not correct, nor have any claims been made which contradict it.[83] Of course, even after prisoners of war captured by United States forces reach the camps and are turned over to the custody of the South Vietnamese, the United States remains under a contingent responsibility for their humane treatment in accordance with the provisions of the Convention.[84]

VI. CHARGES MADE AGAINST SOUTH VIETNAM

There appears to be little doubt that at least well into 1966 South Vietnamese combat troops regularly maltreated captured enemy personnel by using threats, torture, and other acts of violence in order to obtain intelligence information.[85] These acts were and remain direct

---

[81] "United States officials are quietly putting into effect an important change in their handling of prisoners of war. Vietcong and North Vietnamese fighters captured on the battlefield will no longer be turned over to the South Vietnamese Army immediately after the fighting has died down. Instead, they will be sent to American divisional headquarters and kept in American hand [sic] until they can be transferred to new Vietnamese prisoner-of-war compounds. . . . The system has been adopted to enable the United States to meet its responsibilities under Article 12 of the Geneva Convention of 1949 governing the treatment of prisoners of war. The article requires the country turning prisoners over to another country to guarantee their well-being." N.Y. Times, July 1, 1966, at 6, col. 3. The current official directive establishing this procedure is United States Military Assistance Command, Directive No. 190-3, April 6, 1967.

[82] 55 Dep't State Bull. 336, 338 (1966).

[83] As stated in note 73 supra, there have without doubt been some acts of maltreatment of prisoners of war by American personnel. Thus, it was reported that in the trial by court-martial of Captain Howard B. Levy there was defense testimony that American Special Forces ("Green Beret") personnel maintained a "permissive policy toward the torture of Vietcong prisoners by the South Vietnamese" and that a bounty of $10 was paid to the Montagnards for every right ear brought in. N.Y. Times, May 25, 1967, at 2, col. 3. In view of the hearsay nature of the testimony, and the partisan context in which it was given, it does not fall within the criterion adopted for this article. For another incident of alleged maltreatment see St. Louis Post-Dispatch, Feb. 9, 1968, at 1B, col. 1.

[84] See note 79 supra. The United States has officially acknowledged its contingent responsibility. Dep't State Vietnam Information Note, No. 9, Prisoners of War, Aug. 1967, at 3. It maintains small detachments of American military police at each South Vietnamese prisoner-of-war camp, apparently to ensure that its responsibility is being met.

[85] See text in connection with note 74-76 supra. When the ICRC considered that there was sufficient evidence to warrant raising the issue with the South Vietnamese authorities, the latter responded by conveying to the ICRC "a file on atrocities attributed to NLF forces. It also invited the Committee to investigate the plight of Vietnam prisoners held by he Democratic Republic of Vietnam." ICRC, The International Committee and the Vietnam Conflict, 6 Int'l Rev. of the Red Cross 399, 405 (1966) [hereinafter referred to as ICRC, Vietnam]. It does

violations of the law of war, whether considered from the point of view of the entire Convention, Article 3, or customary international law. The combined pressure of the ICRC and the United States (and, perhaps, of other allied countries) has apparently gradually made itself felt, at least at the official level. The Government of South Vietnam has complied with the Convention by a liberal interpretation of the provisions of Article 4 defining the categories of persons entitled to prisoner-of-war status,[86] by supplying lists of persons detained as prisoners of war to the Central Tracing Agency of the ICRC,[87] by disseminating to its troops information concerning the duties imposed upon captors by the Convention and by other methods of instruction of its troops,[88] and by permitting unlimited inspection visits to the prisoner-of-war camps by delegates of the ICRC.[89] The fact that reports of further instances of maltreatment of prisoners of war by South Vietnamese combat troops have become more sporadic probably indicates that the campaign of education has had some degree of success. However, it may also mean that South Vietnamese combat commanders have been able to conceal most of such incidents from those who might report them.

To summarize: while the South Vietnamese Government has now substantially complied with the obligations which the Convention imposes upon it, during the course of a period extending over several years there was apparently an officially countenanced practice of the use of torture on newly-captured prisoners of war by South Vietnamese combat troops for the purpose of extracting information from them. The South Vietnamese Government appears now to accept the fact that such conduct constituted a direct and major violation of the Convention and, therefore, in 1966 instituted a campaign of education which seems to have been at least partially successful in putting an end to this grossly illegal practice. However, instances of maltreatment of newly-captured prisoners of war by South Vietnamese combat troops continue to be re-

---

not appear that there was a denial of maltreatment by the South Vietnamese; rather there was a defense of tu quoque aimed at the Vietcong and the North Vietnamese. Whatever the merit of the cross-complaint, it is no excuse for violating the Convention.

[86] Id. at 404-05; 7 id. 188. For the categories of persons being given prisoner-of-war status, see para. 4, United States Military Assistance Command, Directive No. 20-5, Sept. 21, 1966.

[87] E.g., 7 Int'l Rev. of the Red Cross 189 (1966).

[88] 6 id. 141 (1966); 7 id. 188 (1967). See also note 80 supra.

[89] 5 id. 300, 470, and 481 (1965); 6 id. 98, 405, 542, and 597 (1966); 7 id. 125, 126, 188, 189, and 246 (1967). For a report of an unofficial and unauthorized visit by an American newsman to Pleiku, one of the largest prisoner-of-war camps maintained by the South Vietnamese, see Gershen, A Close-Up Look at Enemy Prisoners, Parade, Dec. 10, 1967, at 10. These ICRC inspection visits to the camps, which have uniformly included private and unsupervised consultations with selected prisoners of war designated by the ICRC delegate, do not appear to have brought to light any instances of major violations of the Convention once that captured personnel had reached the camps.

ported.[90] The individuals responsible for such incidents, both soldiers who commit the actual violence and commanders who permit and even encourage these acts, are guilty of violations of the Convention and of the customary law of war.

VII. CHARGES MADE AGAINST NORTH VIETNAM

A. *Parading Prisoners of War*

With respect to the North Vietnamese treatment of American prisoners of war we have only the information which they have seen fit to disclose.[91] However, even this limited source of information has revealed one major violation of the Convention and the threat of what was asserted to be another. While this latter was apparently prevented by an unprecedented mobilization of world opinion by the United States, it will be discussed below in section VII B.

On July 6, 1966, presumably to whip up local support for the trial of captured American pilots as "war criminals,"[92] the North Vietnamese authorities caused these men, handcuffed in pairs, to be paraded through the crowd-lined streets of Hanoi. Word of the incident was broadcast by Radio Hanoi[93] and press releases[94] and photographs[95] were issued by the official North Vietnamese press agency.

The United States Government immediately charged that this constituted a violation of the Convention.[96] The ICRC clearly was of the same opinion, for on July 14, 1966, it drew the attention of the North Vietnamese Government to the fact that the Convention specifically prohibited the subjection of prisoners of war to public curiosity.[97] The North Vietnamese did not deny the occurrence of the incident; they merely

---

[90] Wyant, Barbarity in Vietnam Shocks U.S., St. Louis Post-Dispatch, Feb. 9, 1968, at 1B, col. 1. The televised shooting of a just-captured Vietnamese by the head of the South Vietnamese National Police during the attack on Saigon early in 1968 served to highlight this problem.

[91] The sources of this information have included broadcasts over Radio Hanoi, information released by the official North Vietnamese press agency, and an occasional dispatch from foreign reporters based in Hanoi. Information in depth, complete accuracy of which is questionable, has been disseminated through the medium of newsmen from other Communist countries. East German journalists and photographers were the source of the material used in the article, U.S. Prisoners of War in North Vietnam, Life, Oct. 20, 1967, at 21-33. These East German sources likewise provided the motion picture material purchased and televised by NBC late in 1967. Information concerning the treatment of South Vietnamese prisoners of war by the North Vietnamese is of insufficient reliability for discussion.

[92] See text in connection with notes 109-115 infra.

[93] N.Y. Times, July 8, 1966, at 3, col. 1.

[94] Id. July 13, 1966, at 1, col. 7, and 5, col. 1.

[95] Id. July 8, 1966, at 3.

[96] Id. at 3, col. 1.

[97] ICRC, Vietnam, supra note 85, at 404. Art. 13 of the Convention requires the protection of prisoners of war "against insults and public curiosity." Para. 1(c) of Art. 3, quoted at note 34 supra, prohibits "outrages against personal dignity, in particular, humiliating and degrading treatment."

called attention to their previous communications concerning the non-applicability of the Convention.[98]

In May, 1967, Agence France Presse (the French news agency) reported from Hanoi that three captured American pilots, one of whom was apparently suffering from an injury, "were paraded through angry, shouting crowds" on the streets of Hanoi and were later "put on display" at the International Press Club in Hanoi.[99] Once again the United States Government immediately charged that this constituted a "flagrant violation" of the Convention and stated that it was sending a protest to North Vietnam through the ICRC.[100]

Over a century ago Francis Lieber's first codification of the customary law of war included a statement to the effect that prisoners of war were not to be subjected to any "indignity."[101] The 1929 Geneva Prisoner-of-War Convention,[102] the predecessor of the Convention with which we are here concerned, had (in its Article 2) a prohibition against subjecting prisoners of war to "insults and public curiosity." In interpreting this provision in the course of World War II, the Judge Advocate General of the Army said: "The 'public curiosity' against which Article 2 . . . protects them is the curious and perhaps scornful gaze of the crowd . . . ."[103] During World War II a group of American prisoners of war was marched through the streets of Rome by the Nazis as a propaganda measure. After the war the Nazi commander responsible for the march was tried and convicted of the war crime of failing to protect prisoners of war in his custody from insults and public curiosity.[104] The International Military Tribunal for the Far East, the Pacific counterpart of the International Military Tribunal of Nuremberg fame, included in its opinion a heading entitled "Prisoners of War Humiliated" and listed thereunder various episodes in which prisoners of war had been marched down city streets and exhibited to jeering crowds, specifically labeling such treatment as a violation of the law of war.[105] It has already been noted that the Military Tribunal which heard *The High Command Case*

---

[98] For the first of these communications, see text in connection with note 8 supra. The new reply also stated that "the policy of the Government of the DRVN [Democratic Republic of Vietnam] *as regards enemy captured in time of war is a humane policy.*" (Emphasis added.) The ambiguous italicized words could be interpreted as meaning "we have a policy of being humane to prisoners of war captured during a war, but this is not a war and, therefore, there is no obligation on our part to be humane!"

[99] N.Y. Times, May 9, 1967, at 15, col. 1.

[100] 56 Dep't State Bull. 825 (1967).

[101] Instructions for the Government of the Armies of the United States in the Field, General Orders No. 100, Apr. 23, 1863, Art. 75.

[102] See note 61 supra.

[103] 2 Bull. JAG 299 (1943).

[104] Trial of Lt. Gen. Kurt Maelzer, 11 Law Reports of Trials of War Criminals 53 (1946) [hereinafter cited War Crimes Rep.].

[105] IMTFE Judgment, supra note 33, at 1092-95 and 1030-31.

at Nuremberg found that the protection of prisoners of war from insults and public curiosity was a part of the customary law of war recognized by civilized nations.[106]

Both Articles 3 and 13 of the Convention contain provisions which prohibit the exhibiting of prisoners of war by parading them through city streets; and it would appear that this rule has most probably attained the status of being part of the customary law of war.[107] It follows that the actions of North Vietnamese authorities on the two occasions mentioned (and on other less well publicized occasions) were violations of the Convention and of the customary law of war.[108]

B. *War Crimes Trials*

It will be recalled that in answering the letter from the ICRC in August, 1965, North Vietnam referred to captured American pilots as "major [war] criminals caught in flagrante delicto and liable for judgment in accordance with the laws of the Democratic Republic of Vietnam."[109] Many statements of similar import were subsequently made by the North Vietnamese.[110] By mid-July, 1966, press dispatches from Communist newsmen in Hanoi were mentioning that trials were definitely planned[111] and tension began to build in the United States.[112] It

---

[106] See text in connection with note 64 supra.

[107] As we have seen, in so far as North Vietnam is concerned there are strong arguments for the position that the entire Convention is applicable and, that at a minimum, Article 3 of the Convention (note 34 supra) is certainly applicable, despite the untenable position to the contrary taken by North Vietnam. It is, therefore, not even necessary to find that this paricular humanitarian rule has attained the status of being a part of the customary law of war in order to find that it is binding on North Vietnam.

[108] It has been mentioned that in the parade conducted on July 6, 1966, the prisoners were handcuffed in pairs. During the World War II commando raid on Dieppe the manacling of German prisoners of war by Canadian troops was itself challenged by the German Government as a violation of the law of war and resulted in a series of reprisals and counter-reprisals. For differing versions of this affair see British War Office, The Law of War on Land (Part III of the Manual of Military Law) 53 n.2(*a*) (1958); Castrén, The Present Law of War and Neutrality 159 (1954); and ICRC Report, supra note 17, at 368-70.

[109] See text in connection with note 8 supra.

[110] N.Y. Times, Sept. 30, 1965, at 1, col. 6 and at 3, col. 3; id. Feb. 12, 1966, at 12, col. 3; id. July 13, 1966, at 1, col. 7 and at 5, col. 1. An ICRC report stated: "The [North Vietnamese] Red Cross and the authorities of the DRVN have made known to the ICRC that the captured American pilots are treated humanely, but that they cannot, however, be considered as prisoners of war. The DRVN Government is in fact of the opinion that the bombing attacks constitute crimes for which these prisoners will have to answer before the courts and that the Third Geneva Convention (prisoners of war) is consequently not applicable to them. . . ." ICRC, Vietnam, supra note 85, at 403.

[111] N.Y. Times, July 15, 1966, at 1, col. 3 and at 3, col. 1; id. July 19, 1966, at 3, col. 1; id. July 20, 1966, at 1, col. 8. The bombing of Hanoi and Haiphong had begun in June, 1966.

[112] Between July 15 and July 25, 1966, the newspapers in the United States carried several stories on this subject every day. Questions were asked of the President and statements were made which indicated that any trials, convictions,

was then that the United States mounted a diplomatic offensive which resulted in the intervention of personages from around the world, including those who sided with the United States position in Vietnam, those who opposed it, and those who were neutral.[113] On July 23, 1966, the North Vietnamese Government announced the appointment of a committee "to investigate United States 'war crimes' "[114] and then, on that same day, North Vietnam President Ho Chi Minh took advantage of a cabled inquiry from the Columbia Broadcasting System to state that there was "no trial in view" for the American pilots.[115] A few days later Ho was quoted as saying that the "main criminals" were not captured pilots, "but the persons who sent them there—Johnson, Rusk, McNamara—these are the ones who should be brought to trial."[116] For ten days in July, 1966, there was excitement and debate on this subject throughout the world, with claims, counterclaims, and citation of legal authorities and purported legal authorities for and against the trial.

Actually, the statement and allegations made by the North Vietnamese in their August 31, 1965, letter to the ICRC and frequently thereafter pose two interwoven questions concerning the captured American pilots: (1) are they entitled to the status of prisoners of war? and (2) do the North Vietnamese have the right to try them for alleged war crimes? It will be appropriate to discuss these two questions in the order stated.

The captured pilots are all members of the United States Navy and Air Force. They were captured when forced to eject from their planes while flying combat missions over North Vietnam. They were wearing American flight uniforms when captured and made no attempt to hide their identity. (Of course, this series of statements includes a number of assumptions—but they all appear to be reasonable ones and there is no indication that any one of them is really disputed.) These facts being accepted, the American pilots are entitled prima facie to prisoner-of-war status under the 1907 Hague Regulations,[117] the 1929 Geneva Prisoner-

---

and executions would be followed in short order by severe retaliatory action by the United States. Id. July 19, 1966, at 3, col. 3; id. July 21, at 14, col. 2.

[113] Neutrals who sought to dissuade the North Vietnamese from their proposed course of action included U Thant, the Secretary General of the United Nations (id. July 17, 1966, at 8, col. 3), the Pope (id. July 21, 1966, at 1, col. 5), and the ICRC (id. July 23, 1966, at 2, col. 6). Americans opposed to the war in Vietnam who interceded with the North Vietnamese included Norman Thomas, The National Committee for a Sane Nuclear Policy (id. July 20, 1966, at 1, col. 8) and the so-called Senate "doves," spearheaded by Senator Frank Church of Idaho (id. July 16, 1966, at 1, col. 1 and at 3, col. 2). Many competent observers of the international scene consider that this latter appeal was probably the most effective on Communist pragmatism.

[114] Id. July 24, 1966, at 1, col. 1.
[115] Id. July 25, 1966, at 1, col. 8.
[116] Id. July 26, 1966, at 3, col. 2.
[117] Supra note 15, Art. 1.

of-War Convention,[118] and the 1949 Geneva Prisoner-of-War Convention.[119] In fact, it would be difficult to imagine a more clear-cut case of entitlement to such status.

The North Vietnamese apparently do not contest the facts stated and assumed above, but they attempt to avoid the conclusion which necessarily flows from these facts by asserting that the Convention does not apply to "war criminals."[120] The syllogism would be: war criminals are not entitled to the protection of the Convention; American pilots are war criminals; therefore, American pilots are not entitled to the protection of the Convention. Both the major and the minor premises of that syllogism are incorrect. The North Vietnamese position therefore necessitates a brief review of the events preceding and following the approval of Article 85 of the Convention by the 1949 Diplomatic Conference.[121]

When the war in the Pacific ended in 1945, General Yamashita, who had commanded the unsuccessful Japanese defense of the Phillipine Islands, was charged with a number of war crimes and was brought to trial before an American Military Commission in Manila. His counsel contended that he was entitled to all of the trial protections contained in the 1929 Prisoner-of-War Convention. These protections were denied to him and on appeal to the United States Supreme Court (after his conviction and death sentence) the denial was affirmed on the ground that the trial protections contained in that Convention applied only to trials for post-capture—not pre-capture—offenses.[122]

In the preparatory work which preceded the 1949 Diplomatic Conference, the ICRC convened a group of "Government Experts" who recommended, as one variation from the 1929 Convention, a provision that prisoners of war prosecuted for pre-capture offenses should enjoy the benefits of the Convention *until* convicted after a regular trial. When this was submitted to the XVIIth International Red Cross Conference at Stockholm in 1948, where the final draft which was to be the working draft for the 1949 Diplomatic Conference was prepared, it was decided to change the provision drafted by the Government Experts so that pris-

---

[118] Supra note 61, Art. 1.

[119] Supra note 4, Art. 4.

[120] N.Y. Times, May 9, 1967, at 15, col. 1. This is also the only logical interpretation which can be placed on the letter of Aug. 31, 1965, from the North Vietnamese Government to the ICRC, note 8 supra. See also the ICRC report quoted in note 110 supra.

[121] Article 85 of the Convention reads as follows: "Prisoners of war prosecuted under the laws of the Detaining Power for acts committed prior to capture shall retain, even if convicted, the benefits of the present Convention."

[122] Matter of Yamashita, 327 U.S. 1, 21, 22, 24 (1946). This position was adopted generally by war crimes tribunals and national courts after World War II. 4 War Crimes Rep. 78 (1948). At least one noted Soviet legal writer took the same position, stating: "On account of these inhuman crimes committed by him, Ritz ceased to be a soldier even before he was seized by units of the Red Army, and consequently did not become a war prisoner when he was seized. . . ." Trainin, Hitlerite Responsibility under Criminal Law 88 (1945).

oners of war would continue to benefit by the provisions of the Convention even *after* conviction of a pre-capture offense.[123]

At the Diplomatic Conference, the USSR proposed an amendment to the draft provision under which once a prisoner of war had been convicted of a war crime (apparently this meant a conventional war crime) or a crime against humanity, he could be treated as an ordinary criminal.[124] This was, in effect, a return to the recommendation made by the Government Experts. General Slavin, chief delegate of the USSR, stated to the committee charged with the preparation of the Prisoner-of-War Convention, that the USSR proposal applied only to prisoners of war who had been convicted.[125] The committee's report to the Plenary Meeting called attention to the difference of approach represented by the Stockholm draft and the USSR proposal, and stated that the great majority of the committee considered that even after a prisoner of war had been convicted of a pre-capture violation of the laws and customs of war, he should continue to enjoy the protection of the Convention.[126] The Diplomatic Conference rejected the Soviet proposal and approved the Stockholm draft provision.[127]

The effect of Article 85 of the Convention was, then, to change the rule expounded in *Yamashita* and other similar cases.[128] Now a prisoner of war retains the benefits of the Convention from the moment of capture to the moment of release and repatriation. If, while in captivity, he is tried and convicted of a pre-capture violation of the law of war he is entitled to all the judicial safeguards of the Convention.[129]

---

[123] Statement of R. J. Wilhelm representing the ICRC. Final Record, supra note 13, Vol. IIA, at 318-19.

[124] The proposed amendment stated: "Prisoners of war convicted of war crimes and crimes against humanity under the legislation of the Detaining Power, and in conformity with the principles of the Nuremberg Trial, shall be treated in the same way as persons serving a sentence for a criminal offence in the territory of the Detaining Power." Id. at 319.

[125] Id. at 321. In a statement made to the Plenary Meeting, General Skylarov, another Soviet delegate, said that under the Soviet proposal prisoners of war guilty of war crimes or crimes against humanity, *"once their guilt has been established and they have been sentenced by a regular court,"* should no longer enjoy the benefits of the Convention. Id. Vol. IIB, at 303 (emphasis added).

[126] Id. Vol. IIA, at 570-71. In supporting the Soviet proposal in the discussion at the Plenary Meeting, the delegate from Czechoslovakia pointed out that "it concerns those prisoners of war who have been convicted" (id. Vol. IIB, at 305) and the Bulgarian delegate stated that "it is assumed that sentence has already been pronounced" and that "we are dealing with war criminals convicted as such." (id. at 307).

[127] Id. at 311. The Soviet proposal was rejected by a vote of 8-23-7. The only change made by the Diplomatic Conference in the Stockholm (working) draft was the substitution of the word "retain" for the word "enjoy" in the English version.

[128] Yingling & Ginnane, supra note 37, at 410; Public Prosecutor v. Oie Hee Koi et al., [1968] 2 W.L.R. 715, 727.

[129] Pictet, Commentary, supra note 30, at 425. Those safeguards are found in Arts. 84-88 and 99-108, inclusive, of the Convention. After World War II several Japanese commanders were tried and convicted of being responsible for unfair

The USSR and all of the other Communist countries, both those present at the Diplomatic Conference in Geneva and those which subsequently adhered to the Convention, have made reservations to Article 85.[130] This fact caused some concern to the United States Senate when it was asked to give its advice and consent to the ratification of the Convention by the President. In its report to the Senate the Committee on Foreign Relations said:

> [I]n the light of the practice adopted by Communist forces in Korea of calling prisoners of war "war criminals," there is the possibility that the Soviet bloc might adopt the general attitude of regarding a significant number of the forces opposing them as ipso facto war criminals, not entitled to the usual guaranties provided for prisoners of war. As indicated above, however, the Soviet reservation expressly deprives prisoners of war of the protection of the convention only after conviction in accordance with the convention.[131]

When North Vietnam advised the Swiss Government of its adherence to the four 1949 Geneva Conventions in June 1957, the communication included a reservation to Article 85 reading as follows:

> The Democratic Republic of Vietnam declares that prisoners of war prosecuted for and convicted of war crimes or crimes against humanity, in accordance with the principles laid down by the Nu-

---

trials of captured American airmen. Trial of Lt. Gen. Shigeru Sawada, 5 War Crimes Rep. 1 (1948); Trial of Lt. Gen. Harukei Isayama, id. at 60; Trial of Gen. Tanaka Hisakasu, id. at 66. The IMTFE reviewed and condemned, by implication, the Japanese trials and executions of American airmen. IMTFE Judgment, supra note 33, at 1024-31. In its "Notes on the Case" dealing with United States v. Alstotter et al. (The Justice Case), 6 War Crimes Rep. 1, 103 (1948), the United Nations War Crimes Commission enumerated the requirements for a fair trial, its conclusions being drawn from a number of sources and representing customary international law.

[130] The reservation to Article 85 made by the USSR at the time of signature (75 U.N.T.S. 135, 460) and maintained at the time of ratification (191 U.N.T.S. 367) states: "The Union of Soviet Socialist Republics does not consider itself bound by the obligation, which follows from Article 85, to extend the application of the Convention to prisoners of war who have been convicted under the law of the Detaining Power, in accordance with the principles of the Nuremberg trial, for war crimes and crimes against humanity, it being understood that persons convicted of such crimes must be subject to the conditions obtaining in the country in question for those who undergo their punishment." In response to an inquiry concerning the meaning of the foregoing reservation, the Soviet Foreign Ministry said, in a note dated May 26, 1955, to the Swiss Federal Council, that: "[T]he reservation . . . signifies that prisoners of war who, under the laws of the USSR, have been convicted of war crimes or crimes against humanity must be subject to the conditions obtaining in the USSR for all other persons undergoing punishment in execution of judgments by the courts. *Once the sentence has become legally enforceable*, persons in this category consequently do not enjoy the protection which the Convention affords." Pictet, Commentary, supra note 30, at 424 (emphasis added).

[131] Senate Comm. on Foreign Relations, Geneva Conventions for the Protection of War Victims, S. Exec. Rep. No. 9, 84th Cong., 1st Sess. 28-29 (1955). For some of the factors which caused Senate perturbation, see Levie, Penal Sanctions for Maltreatment of Prisoners of War, 56 Am. J. Int'l L. 433, 443 n.37 (1962).

remberg Court of Justice shall not benefit from the present Convention, as specified in Article 85.[132]

Having made this reservation, it must be assumed that the North Vietnamese authorities fully understood its meaning—and it is difficult to find any real ambiguity in it so far as the present problem is concerned.[133] The American pilots have not been "prosecuted and convicted." Under Article 85 of the Convention and the North Vietnamese reservation to it, they are entitled to the benefits of the Convention until prosecution *and* conviction for war crimes or crimes against humanity have occurred. The North Vietnamese contention that the American pilots are "war criminals" and not entitled to the protection of the Convention is, therefore, without merit.[134] It is, in and of itself, a major violation of the Convention to arbitrarily deny prisoner-of-war status to individuals entitled to that status. If the North Vietnamese desire to comply with the international commitment which they have made by voluntarily adhering to the Convention, they are under an obligation to recognize that American pilots captured while flying combat missions over North Vietnam are entitled to the status of prisoners of war and to the protections provided by the Convention which flow from that status.

The first question posed above, are American pilots entitled to the status of prisoners of war, must be answered in the affirmative. This leads us to the second question, do the North Vietnamese have the right to try them for alleged war crimes?

In the discussions which took place in connection with the drafting of

---

[132] The original adherence, including the reservations, was in the Vietnamese language. It was accompanied by a French translation. Letter to the author from the Swiss Federal Political Department, Jan. 31, 1968. The French translation includes the words "poursuivis *et* condamnés"—"prosecuted *and* convicted." 274 U.N.T.S. 340 (emphasis added).

[133] It has been suggested, for example, that the "and" in the words "prosecuted for and convicted of" might have been intended to be read disjunctively. Note, The Geneva Convention and the Treatment of Prisoners of War in Vietnam, supra note 63, at 862. Under this interpretation it is said that a prisoner of war could be deprived of the benefits of the Convention by the mere filing of a charge against him alleging a war crime or a crime against humanity. But "et" is not given a disjunctive intendment in French, and if "et" or "and" were to be construed disjunctively this would mean that a prisoner of war *prosecuted but not convicted* (prosecuted and acquitted) could still be denied the benefits of the Convention because one of the two alternatives possible under the disjunctive construction would have been met—he would have been prosecuted. This obviously does not make sense!

[134] The argument might be made that absent the Convention we are relegated to customary international law—and that this is what the courts applied in Matter of Yamashita, 327 U.S. 1, and other similar cases. But as we have already seen, in so far as North Vietnam is concerned, it is undeniable that the Convention is applicable (see text in connection with notes 27-33 supra) and, that in any event, at a minimum, Article 3 is applicable (see text in connection with notes 34-45 supra). Para. 1(d) of Art. 3 (note 34 supra) specifies the protections to be accorded persons charged with offenses.

Article 85, it was at no time suggested by any delegation that prisoner-of-war status should protect an individual from prosecution for an alleged *pre-capture* offense which constituted a violation of the law of war. In fact, all of the parties who engaged in the discussion apparently assumed that this was the rule. As we have just seen, the only dispute on this subject concerned the regime under which the detaining power would be entitled to place the individual *after* his trial and conviction for a pre-capture offense. Under the circumstances, there seems to be little doubt that the second question posed, do the North Vietnamese have the right to try the American pilots for war crimes alleged to have been committed prior to capture, should also be answered in the affirmative.

However, this answer requires amplification, because standing alone it is subject to misconstruction. In the first place, the right to try a prisoner of war for an offense which he is alleged to have committed prior to capture does not mean that there is a right to treat him *prior* to trial and conviction in the manner in which he might be treated *after* trial and conviction. (This, of course, is inherent in the discussion and resolution of the first question on this subject discussed immediately above.) In other words, a prisoner of war retains the status of prisoner of war, and all the protections incident thereto, *at least until he has been finally convicted.*

In the second place, while it appears that the North Vietnamese charge against the American pilots is that they have been guilty of bombing non-military targets, such as civilian residential areas,[135] at this stage in the development of the law of war, there may be considerable doubt expressed as to whether even "target-area" bombing, a much more indiscriminate and inhumane act than that apparently charged against the American airmen, is a violation of international law. During World War II both sides engaged in this type of warfare. No one who lived through that period or has read its history could have forgotten the German bombing of such targets as Warsaw, London, Coventry and Rotterdam, and the Allied bombing of Berlin, Essen, Cologne and Tokyo. No political leader, no military commander, and no airman was ever convicted of any alleged war crime arising out of these activities.[136] One will look in

---

[135] See Dep't State Memorandum to the International Committee of the Red Cross, Entitlement of American Military Personnel Held by North Viet Nam to Treatment as Prisoners of War, etc., July 13, 1966. Charges that the use of napalm bombs is a violation of the law of war have also been heard with some frequency. An Indian scholar has said, in this regard: "[D]uring the Second World War and during the hostilities in Korea the use of flame-throwers and of napalm and incendiary bombs appear to have been regarded as legal." Singh, Nuclear Weapons and International Law 151 (1959). While the question may not be free from doubt, it is certainly sufficiently controversial to preclude unilateral decision by the North Vietnamese with respect thereto.

[136] During the course of the July, 1966, excitement Senator Thomas J. Dodd of Connecticut, who had been a member of the prosecution at Nuremberg, issued a statement in which he pointed out: "No Luftwaffe pilot, or Luftwaffe commander

vain in the opinions of the IMT or of the IMTFE for any reference to such activities as constituting a war crime. For more than ten years the ICRC has been endeavoring, so far with not even a modicum of success, to evolve a convention which would protect the civilian populations in time of war and which would be acceptable to the governments.[137] This proposed Convention, in its Article 10, specifically forbids target-area bombing.[138] The fact that it is considered necessary to include such a prohibition in a new draft international convention on the law of war would seem to indicate rather conclusively that no such prohibition is presently included therein.[139] And, as has been stated, if target-area bombing is not definitely outlawed, then certainly the lesser charge which appears to have been levelled against the American pilots does not come within a prohibited category.

In the third place, we have moved far along the road from the era of vicarious punishment to a point where individuals are punished only for their own acts. While evidence, such as "confessions," might be available to the North Vietnamese with respect to some of the airmen, what of the others? Why is the charge of being a war criminal levelled against *every* captured American airman held by the North Vietnamese?[140] Certainly,

for example, was brought to trial because of his participation in the bombing of London despite the fact that London bombings were directed primarily at the civilian population. . . ." 112 Cong. Rec. 16, 224 (daily ed., July 25, 1966).

[137] After several years of preparatory drafting by the ICRC, the Draft Rules for the Limitation of the Dangers Incurred by the Civilian Population in Time of War were published and distributed in 1956 so that they could be discussed and acted upon at the XIXth International Red Cross Conference in New Delhi in 1957. They were discussed at New Delhi, and they have been the subject of much discussion since then, but their status as an unofficial proposal has not changed.

[138] The commentary to Art. 10 states, in part: "It was . . . to prevent target area bombing from being accepted as a regular practice, or even condoned, that the ICRC felt it desirable to insert the relevant rule in Article 10 and thus to lay emphasis on the prohibition of indiscriminate bombing." Id. at 91.

[139] One expert in this field takes the rather paradoxical position that target-area bombing was legal during World War II, and so remains, but that indiscriminate bombing is a violation of the law of air warfare. Spaight, Air Power and War Rights 271, 272, and 277 (3d ed. 1947).

[140] It has been intimated that the North Vietnamese take the position that as the United States is guilty of making "aggressive war," the airmen are all guilty of crimes against peace. This is the category of war crime specified in Article 6(a) of the London Charter of the International Military Tribunal, which reads: "Crimes against peace: Namely, planning, preparation, initiation, or waging a war of aggression, or a war in violation of international treaties, agreements, or assurances, or participation in a common plan or conspiracy for the accomplishment of any of the foregoing." Nazi Conspiracy and Aggression: Opinion and Judgment 3 (1947). Article 5(a) of the IMTFE differs only in minor respects. IMTFE Judgment, supra note 33, Annex 5-A, at 21. Apart from the trials of the major Nazi leaders by the IMT and by some of the Nuremberg Military Tribunals and of the major Japanese leaders by the IMTFE, no one has ever been tried for this war crime which, obviously, can only be committed by those who have the *power* to make war, and not by those who do the *fighting*. In United States v. von Leeb et al., 10 Trials 1, at 11 Trials 489 (1948), the Military Tribunal said: "If and as long as a member of the armed forces does not participate in the preparation, planning, initiating or waging of aggressive war on a policy level, his war activities do not fall under the definition of Crimes against Peace. It is not a person's

there is no evidence available to them that *every* captured American air-man participated in bombing or other attacks on purely civilian targets. Some of the airmen were probably shot down on their first missions before they could drop a bomb. Some were probably flying in unarmed reconnaissance planes, perhaps as photographers. Some were probably flying fighter protection armed only with air-to-air weapons. These, and probably many others, are within categories against whom no legitimate war-crimes charge can be laid, even assuming that it can against the others.[141]

Finally, there arises the problem of whether prisoners of war accused of pre-capture war crimes can be or should be tried during the course of hostilities. On this subject the author has previously said:

> While there was never any concrete proposal made at the Diplomatic Conference that trials of prisoners of war for pre-capture offenses should be postponed until the cessation of hostilities, the matter was the subject of inconclusive discussion during the debate on Article 85, two delegates (Lamarle of France and Slavin of the U.S.S.R.) expressing the opinion that such trials should not be put off until the close of hostilities, and one delegate (Gardner of the United Kingdom) expressing the opposite view. The International Committee of the Red Cross has long taken the position that, if such a trial is conducted during the course of hostilities, an accused does not have a fair opportunity to produce all of the evidence which might be available to disprove or lessen his responsibility.
>
> As we have already seen, a number of prisoners of war were tried for alleged pre-capture offenses during the course of World War II. The patent unfairness of these trials glaringly reveals the danger of trials for pre-capture offenses conducted during the course of the war.[142]

To summarize: captured American airmen are entitled to the status of prisoners of war until such time as they have been prosecuted *and* convicted of pre-capture violations of the law of war; while they may legally be tried during the course of hostilities, there are serious practical objections to such a procedure; and, if they are tried, they must be afforded all of the judicial safeguards contained in the Convention.

---

rank or status, but his power to shape or influence the policy of his State, which is the relevant issue for determining his criminality under the charge of Crimes against Peace." This is the real meaning of the announcement by Ho Chi Minh that no trials of American airmen were then contemplated, but that Rusk, McNamara and Johnson were in a different category. See text in connection with note 116 supra.

[141] One American sailor, Apprentice Seaman Douglas Hegdahl, who fell overboard from his ship and some hours later was rescued by North Vietnamese fishermen and made a prisoner of war, is apparently receiving exactly the same treatment as the alleged war criminals—no mail, no relief packages, no visits by the ICRC, etc.

[142] Levie, supra note 131, at 461-62. A footnote to the last sentence quoted points out that when trials are postponed until after the cessation of hostilities the deterrent effect of widespread publicity is lost. Id. at 462 n.115.

VIII. Charges Made Against the Vietcong

Very little information is available as to how many prisoners of war, American or South Vietnamese, are held by the Vietcong; even less is known as to how they are being treated. However, there is reason to know that they do hold some American prisoners of war—and that there have been at least two identical instances of major violations of the law of war in the treatment of prisoners by the Vietcong.

As we have seen, despite Vietcong insistence to the contrary, the generally accepted position appears to be that insurgents such as the Vietcong are bound by the provisions of Article 3 of the Convention;[143] and that, in any event, they are at a minimum bound by the customary law of war.[144] Specifically, it appears to be well established that customary international law prohibits the use of violence and acts of cruelty against prisoners of war and, in all probability, also prohibits making them the objects of reprisals.[145]

On April 9, 1965, a Vietcong terrorist was tried, convicted and sentenced to death by a South Vietnamese court. At that time the Vietcong announced that if the sentence of execution was carried out, Gustav C. Hertz, a kidnapped civilian American aid officer, would be shot.[146] The terrorist was apparently not executed. Whether or not the threat against Hertz was the reason for the clemency shown the terrorist has not been disclosed.

On June 22, 1965, another Vietcong terrorist was executed by a South Vietnamese firing squad in Saigon after he had been tried, convicted and sentenced for acts of terrorism by a South Vietnamese special military court.[147] Three days later both Radio Hanoi and the Liberation Radio announced that an American soldier held as a prisoner of war by the Vietcong (Sergeant Harold G. Bennett) had been executed in reprisal for the execution of the Vietcong terrorist.[148] The United States labeled the act as "murder"; and a statement released by the Department of State said that "people around the world cannot help but be appalled and revolted by this show of wanton inhumanity."[149]

---

143 See text in connection with notes 47-56 supra. Certainly, the 59 nations which drafted and signed the Convention and the 117 which have ratified or adhered to it had no qualms about the validity of Article 3. Only Portugal made a reservation to that Article at the time of signing, but its reservation did not question the validity of Article 3 and was not maintained on ratification.

144 See text in connection with notes 57-70 supra.

145 See text in connection with notes 64-68 supra, and 156-163 infra.

146 N.Y. Times, June 22, 1965, at 6, col. 1.

147 Id. at 1, col. 7. He had been apprehended in Saigon while attaching a fuse to a bomb which was to have exploded five minutes later.

148 Id. June 25, 1965, at 1, col. 6; id. June 26, 1965, at 1, col. 8 and at 2, col. 7.

149 53 Dep't State Bull. 55 (1965). The statement also said that "these Communist threats to intimidate, of course, will not succeed." Subsequent events have revealed that this portion of the statement was incorrect!

On September 22, 1965, three more Vietcong terrorists were executed in Da Nang after a trial, conviction and death sentence by a South Vietnamese court. Four days later, on September 26, the Liberation Radio announced that the Vietcong had retaliated by the executions of two American prisoners of war, Captain Humbert R. Versage [Versace] and Sergeant Kenneth M. Roraback.[150] Once again the United States labeled these reprisal executions as "murder" and as violations of the Convention.[151] It filed a protest with the ICRC which was transmitted to and rejected by the NLF.[152]

A "reprisal" is defined as an otherwise illegal act committed by one side in an armed conflict in order to put pressure on the other side to compel it to abandon a course of illegal acts which it has been committing and to comply with the law of war.[153] For a reprisal (a normally illegal act) to be legal there are three requirements: the act of the state against which it is directed must have been illegal; it must not be directed against an individual who, by the law of war, is specifically protected against reprisals or against acts of the nature that the contemplated reprisal will take; and it must be directed against the state which first violated the law of war.

Were the alleged acts of reprisal of the Vietcong mentioned above valid applications of the rules governing reprisals? The first requirement for a valid reprisal is that the act or acts against which it is directed have been illegal. The acts against which these reprisals were directed were the June 22 and September 22, 1965, executions of the Vietcong terrorists. Were those executions illegal? According to the newspaper accounts, in each instance the individuals had been tried, convicted and sentenced by a South Vietnamese court in accordance with the law of South Vietnam.[154] While the National Liberation Front called the June 22 execution "[a] crime of bloodthirsty men"[155]

---

[150] N.Y. Times, Sept. 28, 1965, at 1, col. 1.

[151] 53 Dep't State Bull. 635 (1965).

[152] ICRC, Vietnam, supra note 85, at 411. Despite the American statement concerning no intimidation, supra note 149, no Vietcong terrorist has been executed since September, 1965, and when three Vietcong terrorists were convicted and sentenced to be executed on November 17, 1967, they were given a last minute reprieve by South Vietnamese Premier Nguyen Can Loc. N.Y. Times, Nov. 17, 1967, at 16, col. 6.

[153] 2 Lauterpacht's Oppenheim, International Law 561 (7th ed. 1952). An example of a legitimate act of reprisal is given in United States Army Field Manual 27-10, The Law of Land Warfare 177 (1956), where it is stated: "For example, the employment by a belligerent of a weapon the use of which is normally precluded by the law of war would constitute a lawful reprisal for intentional mistreatment of prisoners of war held by the enemy."

[154] N.Y. Times, June 22, 1965, at 6, col. 1; and id., Sept. 28, 1965, at 1, col. 1. It should be borne in mind that at no time have the Vietcong or the NLF ever contended that the executed Americans had committed any act warranting execution or that their executions were pursuant to the sentence of a court.

[155] N.Y. Times, June 26, 1965, at 2, col. 7.

and presumably feels the same about the September 22 execution, it has never indicated in what way the executions constituted a crime—other than the implication that it is a crime to try, convict and execute a Vietcong apprehended in the course of committing what was probably a Vietcong approved and ordered act of terrorism.

The reprisals, then, failed to meet the first requirement for a valid reprisal, that it be called forth by an illegal act by the other side. Now let us examine the second requirement for a reprisal to be valid under the law of war—that it not be directed against a specifically protected person. Shortly after the Second Hague Peace Conference of 1907, the German War Office issued a *War Book* which escaped general attention until some years later. During the course of World War I, it became well known and widely condemned because of its emphasis on the the principle of military necessity and its disregard for the customary and conventional law of war. Concerning reprisals against prisoners of war the *War Book* said:

> As regards the admissibility of reprisals, it is to be remarked that these are objected to by numerous teachers of international law on grounds of humanity. To make this a matter of principle, and apply it to every case, exhibits however, "a misconception due to intelligible but exaggerated and unjustifiable feelings of humanity, of the significance, the seriousness and the right of war. It must not be overlooked that here also the necessity of war, and the safety of the State are the first consideration, and not regard for the unconditional freedom of prisoners from molestation."
>
> That prisoners should only be killed in the event of extreme necessity, and that only the duty of self-preservation and the security of one's own State can justify a proceeding of this kind is today universally admitted.[156]

Thus, even a directive which was subjected to almost universal condemnation limited reprisals against prisoners of war to cases of "extreme necessity," self-preservation, and the security of the State.

World War I so vividly demonstrated the inhumanity of reprisals against helpless prisoners of war that restrictions on the use of this procedure were incorporated into a number of agreements reached by the belligerents for the protection of prisoners of war during the course of those hostilities.[157] A specific provision completely prohibiting reprisals against prisoners of war was thereafter included in the 1929 Convention.[158]

---

[156] Morgan, The German War Book 74 (1915).

[157] See, e.g., para. 20 of the Anglo-German Agreement of July 2, 1917 (111 Brit. & For. State Papers 257, 263); Art. XXI of the Anglo-Turkish Agreement of Dec. 28, 1917 (id. at 557, 566); and para. 42 of the Franco-German Agreement of Apr. 26, 1918 (id. at 713, 721).

[158] Supra note 61, Article 2. It is repeated in Article 13 of the 1949 Convention.

Writing in 1942, an American scholar stated that "it seems reasonable to assume that reprisals, with prisoners of war as the objects, are permissible within limits in customary international law."[159] A few years later the legality of reprisals against civilian hostages was considered at great length in *The Hostage Case*, a decision by one of the Nuremberg Military Tribunals. The Tribunal said:

> It is a fundamental rule of justice that the lives of persons may not be arbitrarily taken. A fair trial before a judicial body affords the surest protection against arbitrary, vindictive, or whimsical application of the right to shoot human beings in reprisal. It is a rule of international law, based on these fundamental concepts of justice and the rights of individuals, that the lives of persons may not be taken in reprisal in the absence of a judicial finding that the necessary conditions exist and the essential steps have been taken to give validity to such action. . . . We have no hesitancy in holding that the killing of members of the population in reprisal without judicial sanction is itself unlawful.[160]

Inasmuch as members of the general public had not then been recognized as specially protected persons, it would appear that, a fortiori, everything the Tribunal said about the protections to which civilians were entitled would apply to prisoners of war.

In considering the opinion quoted above, another Nuremberg Military Tribunal, which would probably not have permitted reprisal executions under any circumstances, stated in its opinion in *The High Command Case*:

> In the Southeast Case [Hostage Case], United States v. Wilhelm List, et al., (Case No. 7), the Tribunal had occasion to consider at considerable length the law relating to hostages and reprisals. It was therein held that under certain very restrictive conditions and subject to certain rather extensive safeguards, hostages may be taken, and after a judicial finding of strict compliance with all preconditions and as a last desperate remedy hostages may even be sentenced to death. It was held further that similar drastic safeguards, restrictions, and judicial preconditions apply to so-called "reprisal prisoners." *If so inhumane a measure as the killing of innocent persons for offenses of others, even when drastically safeguarded and limited, is ever permissible under any theory of international law, killing without full compliance with all requirements would be murder. If killing is not permissible under any circumstances, then a killing with full compliance with all the mentioned prerequisites still would be murder.*
> . . . In the instance of so-called hostage taking and killing, and the so-called reprisal killings with which we have to deal in this case, the safeguards and preconditions required to be ob-

---

[159] Flory, Prisoners of War 44 (1942).
[160] United States v. List et al., 11 Trials 757, 1252-53 (1948). This case is sometimes referred to as The Southeast Case.

served by the Southeast judgment were not even attempted to be met or even suggested as necessary. Killings without compliance with such preconditions are merely terror murders. If the law is in fact that hostage and reprisal killings are never permissible at all, then also the so-called hostage and reprisal killings in this case are merely terror murders.[161]

And in reviewing the overall war crimes program which followed World War II and the law which evolved from it, the United Nations War Crimes Commission, in publications issued in 1947 and in 1949, stated without equivocation that the killing of prisoners of war without due cause violated both customary and conventional international law.[162]

Undeniably, then, there are compelling arguments to support the position that reprisals against prisoners of war are prohibited by customary international law. But even if one is unwilling to accept these arguments, certainly customary international law does specifically prohibit all acts of cruelty and violence against prisoners of war,[163]— who are, therefore, protected persons in so far as this type of treatment is concerned. And with equal certainty it can be stated that in all civilized countries killing is an act both of cruelty and of violence. Hence, killing a prisoner of war as a reprisal constitutes cruelty and violence against a person who is protected from such treatment by customary international law. The reprisals, then, also failed to meet the second requirement for a valid reprisal, that they not be directed against a protected person.

The third requirement for a legal reprisal under international law is that it be directed against the state which had first violated the law of war.[164] The "crime" charged by the NLF as the basis for the reprisal was, beyond dispute, an act of the South Vietnamese authorities, and not of the American authorities. The alleged acts of terrorism were committed within the territorial jurisdiction of South Vietnam, the culprits were tried by South Vietnamese courts which reached the decisions finding guilt and ordered the death sentence imposed, and the

---

[161] United States v. von Leeb et al., 11 Trials 528 (1948) (emphasis added).

[162] Notes on The Dreierwalde Case, 1 War Crimes Rep. 86 (1947); Digest of Laws and Cases, 15 War Crimes Rep. 99 (1949). In the former the statement is made that "the killing of prisoners of war constituted a war crime under the customary International Law even before the promulgation and ratification of the Conventions of 1907 [Hague] and 1929 [Geneva]." (Emphasis added).

[163] See text in connection with note 64 supra.

[164] "According to the existing international law, reprisals against an ally of an enemy-state for acts of the enemy-state are not permissible as they are not directed against the state responsible for the act. Reprisals, therefore, may, according to the existing rules of the laws of war, only be employed against the responsible state." Moritz, The Common Application of the Laws of War Within the NATO-Forces, 13 Mil. L. Rev. 1 (July 1961). To the same general effect, see United States v. List et al. (The Hostage Case), 11 Trials 1270 (1948).

executions were carried out by the South Vietnamese authorities. If reprisals were justified, and no ground for them has so far come to light, under the law of war they should have been directed against the state which had by its alleged illegal conduct created the need for and the right to take reprisals. This was obviously not done—and the reason why it was not done is equally obvious.

To summarize: to be authorized by international law, reprisals, which are otherwise illegal acts, must meet certain specific conditions. The undisputed facts clearly disclose that the Vietcong had no legal justification for taking reprisals and, moreover, that the reprisals were taken against prisoners of war who were protected persons under customary international law and against whom reprisals, especially of a cruel or violent character, were specifically prohibited both by international legislation binding upon the Vietcong and by customary international law. Under these circumstances, the reprisals taken against the American prisoners of war were nothing less than murder and constituted war crimes for which, pursuant to the Nuremberg principles upon which the Communists so heavily rely, those who ordered the executions and those who carried them out are all subject to penal sanctions.

IX. Conclusion

A number of conclusions have been reached in the course of this discussion. To recapitulate:

1. There is no legal justification for the position taken by the North Vietnamese that they are not bound by the 1949 Geneva Prisoner-of-War Convention. At the very least, they are bound by the provisions of Article 3 thereof.

2. While there is some legal basis for the position taken by the NLF that it is not even bound by the provisions of Article 3 of the Convention, on balance the decision probably should be that it is so bound. In any event, it is bound by the customary law of war.

3. A state which is a party to hostilities is not legally responsible when an ally violates the provisions of the Convention, but it is morally bound to attempt to persuade its ally to conform to the obligations accepted by adhering to the Convention. It does have a contingent responsibility for the proper treatment of prisoners of war captured by its armed forces and turned over to the custody of an ally for detention.

4. Torture or other maltreatment of prisoners of war in order to obtain intelligence information from them, or for any other reason, or for no reason, constitutes a serious violation of the Convention.

5. Parading prisoners of war before a hostile populace constitutes a violation of the prohibition, contained in conventional and customary

international law, against subjecting them to insults, public curiosity and humiliating and degrading conduct.

6. Even under a reservation to Article 85 of the Convention, such as that made by North Vietnam, it is a serious violation of the Convention to deny captured enemy personnel prisoner-of-war status on the ground that they are war criminals *prior* to their prosecution *and* conviction of a pre-capture war crime by a trial court in which they have been accorded all of the required judicial safeguards.

7. There is no legal impediment to the trial of a prisoner of war for an alleged pre-capture war crime while hostilities are still being conducted. However, as noted immediately above, such a prisoner of war continues to be entitled to all of the protection of the Convention, including the judicial safeguards therein contained.

8. Reprisals against prisoners of war are prohibited by the Convention and, probably, by customary international law. In any event, a reprisal which includes a corporal act, such as killing, against a prisoner of war is prohibited by Article 3 of the Convention and by customary international law, both of which prohibit cruelty and acts of violence against prisoners of war.

And finally, although the application of the Convention is presumably not dependent upon reciprocity, persistent and regular refusal by the Communist nations to be bound by it during actual cases of armed conflict in which they are involved may compel other countries to give second thoughts to the doctrine which requires compliance without reciprocal compliance.

The Geneva Convention and the Treatment of Prisoners of War in Vietnam

Note from *Harvard Law Review*

As early as the spring of 1965[1] the International Committee of the Red Cross took the position that: "The hostilities raging at the present time in Vietnam both North and South of the 17th parallel have assumed such proportions recently that there can be no doubt they constitute an armed conflict to which the regulations of humanitarian law as a whole should be applied."[2] The Committee was referring to the four Geneva Conventions of 1949,[3] which not only set out provisions for the benefit of war victims, both civilian and military, in case of armed conflict between two or more of the signatory States but also establish in Article 3, common to all four Conventions, minimum standards to be respected even in the case of civil war.

The actual participants in the Vietnam conflict have disputed among themselves the applicability of the Conventions, even though all are signatories except the Viet Cong's political arm — the National Liberation Front of South Vietnam (NLF).[4] The United States,[5] the Republic of Vietnam (South Vietnam),[6] and New Zealand[7] support the Red Cross opinion, but the Democratic Republic of Vietnam (North

---

[1] As of June 7, 1965, American military personnel in South Vietnam numbered only slightly over 50,000. N.Y. Times, June 17, 1965, at 4, col. 3.

[2] Letter of June 11, 1965, addressed to the governments of the Democratic Republic of Vietnam, the Republic of Vietnam, and the United States and to the National Liberation Front of South Vietnam, 5 INT'L REV. OF THE RED CROSS 417 (1965).

[3] Geneva Convention for the Amelioration of the Condition of the Wounded and Sick in Armed Forces in the Field, Aug. 12, 1949, [1955] 3 U.S.T. 3114, T.I.A.S. No. 3362, 75 U.N.T.S. 31; Geneva Convention for the Amelioration of the Condition of Wounded, Sick and Shipwrecked Members of Armed Forces at Sea, Aug. 12, 1949, [1955] 3 U.S.T. 3217, T.I.A.S. No. 3363, 75 U.N.T.S. 85; Geneva Convention Relative to the Treatment of Prisoners of War, Aug. 12, 1949, [1955] 3 U.S.T. 3316, T.I.A.S. No. 3364, 75 U.N.T.S. 135 [hereinafter cited as *Convention*]; Geneva Convention Relative to the Protection of Civilian Persons in Time of War, Aug. 12, 1949, [1955] 3 U.S.T. 3516, T.I.A.S. No. 3365, 75 U.N.T.S. 287.

[4] Prior to partition, Vietnam acceded to the Prisoners of War Convention, 181 U.N.T.S. 351 (1953), and North Vietnam acceded separately in 1957, 274 U.N.T.S. 339. The Soviet Union — which has military advisers serving in North Vietnam, N.Y. Times, Oct. 3, 1966, at 1, col. 1 — ratified in 1954, 191 U.N.T.S. 365, and Communist China acceded in 1956, 260 U.N.T.S. 442. The United States ratified in 1955, 213 U.N.T.S. 383; the Philippines in 1952, 141 U.N.T.S. 384; Australia in 1958, 314 U.N.T.S. 332; and New Zealand in 1959, 330 U.N.T.S. 356. Thailand acceded in 1954, 202 U.N.T.S. 332, and South Korea has recently acceded as well, 6 INT'L REV. OF THE RED CROSS 547 (1966). The last five countries are allies of the United States with forces fighting in Vietnam. *See* N.Y. Times, Sept. 28, 1966, at 1, col. 1.

[5] Letter from Secretary of State Dean Rusk to the International Committee of the Red Cross [hereinafter identified as the Red Cross], Aug. 10, 1965, 5 INT'L REV. OF THE RED CROSS 477 (1965).

[6] Letter from Minister of Foreign Affairs Dr. Tran-Van-Do to the Red Cross, Aug. 11, 1965, *id.* at 478. Thus, South Vietnam considers itself bound by the accession of Vietnam in 1953.

[7] Letter from Prime Minister Keith Holyoake to the Red Cross, 6 *id.* at 142 (1966).

Vietnam) [8] and the NLF [9] consider the Conventions inapplicable, though both avow that the prisoners they hold are accorded humane treatment. This Note will evaluate the claims of the NLF and North Vietnam in relation to the Geneva Convention Relative to the Treatment of Prisoners of War. [10]

The 143 articles of this Convention regulate, among other things, the internment, the labor, the medical care, the discipline, and the trial of captives. They provide for the safeguarding of prisoners' rights by the supervision of protecting powers [11] and by the punishment of "grave breaches" of the Convention according to national legislation which each party agrees to enact. [12] The prerequisites for application of the Convention are set out in Article 2, which states that it "shall apply to all cases of declared war or of any other armed conflict which may arise between two or more of the High Contracting Parties . . . ," and in Article 4, which defines prisoners of war as persons "who have fallen into the power of the enemy" and belong to one of certain designated categories, including: "[m]embers of the armed forces of a Party to the conflict," participants in "organized resistance movements" who meet certain qualifications, "[m]embers of regular armed forces who profess allegiance to a government or authority not recognized by the Detaining Power," and even "[i]nhabitants of a non-occupied territory" who spontaneously take up arms to repel an invasion of enemy troops.

Article 3 is the only provision of the Convention which applies

---

[8] North Vietnam refuses to apply the Convention to American pilots captured during bombing runs on the theory that they are war criminals rather than prisoners of war, N.Y. Times, July 13, 1966, at 1, col. 7, but the pilots have been promised humanitarian treatment, *id.*, July 24, 1966, § 1, at 8, col. 1. *See* Letter from Acting Head of the Cabinet Mr. Bui Tan Linh to the Red Cross, 5 INT'L REV. OF THE RED CROSS 527 (1965).

[9] 5 INT'L REV. OF THE RED CROSS 636 (1965).

[10] The United States maintains that the entire Convention is applicable, but there is a serious question whether the United States is violating its obligations by turning prisoners over to South Vietnam. *See* Cohen, *The Law and the Viet War*, Boston Globe, Aug. 7, 1966, § A, at 6, col. 1. Article 12 provides: "Prisoners of war may only be transferred by the Detaining Power to a Power which is a party to the Convention and after the Detaining Power has satisfied itself of the willingness and ability of such transferee Power to apply the Convention."

[11] "A Protecting Power is, of course, a State instructed by another State (known as the Power of Origin) to safeguard its interests and those of its nationals in relation to a third power (known as the Detaining Power)." 3 GENEVA CONVENTIONS OF 12 AUGUST 1949, COMMENTARY 93 (J. Pictet ed. 1960) [hereinafter cited as COMMENTARY]. The Convention declares: "Representatives . . . of the Protecting Powers shall have permission to go to all places where prisoners of war may be," and: "They shall be able to interview the prisoners . . . without witnesses . . . ." Art. 126. Moreover, prisoners "shall . . . have the unrestricted right to apply to the representatives of the Protecting Powers . . . in order to draw their attention to any points on which they may have complaints to make regarding their conditions of captivity." Art. 78. North Vietnam has rejected offers from various countries to serve as the protecting power of the United States. *See, e.g.,* N.Y. Times, Jan. 16, 1966, at 2, cols. 5–6 (United Arab Republic). Article 10 provides:
When prisoners of war do not benefit . . . , no matter for what reason, by the activities of a Protecting Power . . . , the Detaining Power shall request a neutral State [or an organization comparable to the International Committee of the Red Cross] . . . to undertake the functions performed under the present Convention by a Protecting Power . . . .
It appears that North Vietnam has not complied with this article.

[12] *Convention*, arts. 129, 130.

"[i]n the case of armed conflict *not of an international character* occurring in the territory of one of the High Contracting Parties."[13] It declares that "[p]ersons taking no active part in the hostilities, including members of armed forces who have laid down their arms and those placed *hors de combat . . .* shall in all circumstances be treated humanely . . . ." It also expressly prohibits with respect to these individuals:

(a) violence to life and person . . . ;
(b) taking of hostages;
(c) outrages upon personal dignity . . . ;
(d) the passing of sentences and the carrying out of executions without previous judgment pronounced by a regularly constituted court affording all the judicial guarantees which are recognized as indispensable by civilized peoples.

Finally, it places an affirmative duty on the parties to the conflict to gather and tend to the wounded and sick.

The Convention is distinctive in establishing standards from which derogation is impermissible, at least for the duration of conflict. Traditionally suspension of treaty obligations has been regarded as a legitimate response to material breaches,[14] but Article 13 of the Convention expressly prohibits "[m]easures of reprisal against prisoners." And Article 142, which sets out a procedure for the denunciation of the treaty, renders suspension ineffective until termination of the conflict.[15] Thus, a party involved in hostilities cannot avoid responsibilities under the Convention once it has agreed to undertake them. The NLF, however, never expressly consented to the Convention, and it denies that a rebel party is bound by the accession of the state it seeks to control. North Vietnam did accede to the Convention, but it made an important reservation in regard to the rights of war criminals.[16] The Vietnam conflict, therefore, offers an opportunity to test in an especially significant context the impact of insurgency and unilateral reservations on the effectiveness of a multilateral treaty.

I. A Standard for Interpretation

When disputes as to the interpretation of the Geneva Convention arise, the International Committee of the Red Cross may take a position, and its opinion should carry considerable weight. The Convention itself expressly recognizes the Committee's "special position" as a humanitarian organization assisting prisoners of war. Composed only of Swiss nationals, it is a neutral body and is specifically charged

---

[13] *Convention*, art. 3 (emphasis added).
[14] *Cf.* 2 L. Oppenheim, International Law 140 (7th ed. Lauterpacht 1952) [hereinafter cited as Oppenheim]; International Law Comm'n, Draft Articles on the Law of Treaties, 21 U.N. GAOR, Supp. 9, at 17, U.N. Doc. A/6309/Rev. 1 (1966) [hereinafter cited as *Draft Articles*].
[15] *Convention*, art. 142: "[A] denunciation of which notification has been made at a time when the denouncing Power is involved in a conflict shall not take effect until peace has been concluded . . . ."
[16] *See* pp. 863–64 *infra*.

with supervising, along with the Protecting Powers, the administration of the treaty by detaining States.[17]

The Convention does not, however, establish any organization to provide a binding interpretation of ambiguous terms. Only the member States as a group can determine the meaning of the treaty.[18] As a practical matter, of course, the large number of signatories [19] makes it difficult for the parties to reach authoritative decisions in this manner. The drafting of the Convention in 1949 was a response to the inadequacies of an earlier treaty [20] as brought to light by experience in the Second World War.[21] Without a comparable showing that the 1949 Convention is unsatisfactory, it seems doubtful that the member States would expend the effort to convene and consider questions of interpretation.

Thus, if the Convention is to survive and be effective, it must be treated as having a potential for growth similar to that which has characterized the customary rules of warfare.[22] The object of interpreting the treaty, therefore, must be to determine how its purposes may be best achieved in the light of changing conditions. In particular, the specific purposes of the Geneva Convention demand that ambiguities be resolved in favor of the widest possible coverage. The goals of mitigating the excesses of war and providing humane treatment for war victims require a broad and flexible construction of the treaty. To some extent, of course, provisions for implementing these ideals reflect a compromise between humanitarian goals and a desire to preserve national sovereignty; the balance should not be upset by a one-sided view of the treaty's purposes. But in many significant disputes such a conflict between legitimate interests is not presented. The Convention was "drawn up first and foremost to protect individuals, and not to serve State interests," [23] and the remarks of the International Court of Justice with regard to the Genocide Convention of 1948 apply with equal force here: [24]

> In such a convention the contracting States do not have any interests of their own; they merely have, one and all, a common interest, namely, the accomplishment of those high purposes which are the *raison d'être* of the convention. Consequently, in a convention of this type one cannot speak of individual advantages or disadvantages to States, or of the maintenance of a perfect contractual balance between rights and duties. The high ideals which inspired the Convention provide, by

---

[17] *Convention*, arts. 125, 126. Its delegates, like those of the Protecting Powers, are subject to approval by the Detaining Power.

[18] *See* COMMENTARY 1.

[19] There were 111 parties to the Convention as of September 1966. 6 INT'L REV. OF THE RED CROSS 481 (1966).

[20] Geneva Convention Relative to the Treatment of Prisoners of War, July 27, 1929, T.S. 846, 118 L.N.T.S. 343.

[21] COMMENTARY 5–6.

[22] "This law is not static, but by continual adaptation follows the needs of a changing world." The Nurnberg Trial, 6 F.R.D. 69, 109 (Int'l Mil. Trib. 1946).

[23] COMMENTARY 23.

[24] Advisory Opinion on Reservations to the Convention on the Prevention and Punishment of the Crime of Genocide, [1951] I.C.J. 15, 23 [hereinafter cited as *Genocide Reservations Opinion*].

virtue of the common will of the parties, the foundation and measure
of all its provisions.

Thus, the Geneva Convention must be interpreted creatively in light
of its special purposes in order that it may be both useful and enduring.

II. THE POSITION OF THE NATIONAL LIBERATION FRONT

In some civil wars, literal application of particular provisions of the
Geneva Convention will be obviously inappropriate. Article 19, for
example, declares that prisoners "shall be evacuated, as soon as possible after their capture, to camps situated in an area far enough from
the combat zone for them to be out of danger." An insurgent force which
is not in control of a part of the national territory cannot comply with
this requirement unless, as seems true in Vietnam, it has access to sanctuaries over the border. On the other hand, in many African and
Asian nations even the established government does not exercise effective
territorial control in rural areas, and this may be the case even
in peacetime. Provisions such as Article 19 were drafted with conventional European conflicts in mind, but fulfillment of their basic
purposes is no less important in the context of guerrilla warfare in
tropical jungles. Hence, it seems parochial to read such provisions
literally and to reject them when the language seems inapplicable. Instead, the Convention should be construed to require compliance to
the extent feasible, recognizing that inconveniences are similarly entailed in compliance during a conventional war. Under such a standard,
it would not be necessary to confine the responsibilities of insurgents
and the established government to those set forth in Article 3.[25]

It may seem, in fact, that the entire Convention applies to insurgent
forces, because Article 4A(2) includes in the definition of prisoners of
war "[m]embers of . . . organized resistance movements, belonging
to a Party to the conflict . . . ."[26] But the drafters of the Convention
were referring here to the resistance groups of World War II, and
clearly intended insurgents to be bound under Article 3 alone,[27] and
the phrase "Party to the conflict" must be read as referring to a signatory State in the sense of Article 2, not to a rebel party that has not

---

[25] For an analysis of the factors which should determine when the entire Convention should be invoked in a civil war see Note, *The Geneva Convention of 1949:
Application in the Vietnamese Conflict*, 5 VA. J. INT'L L. 243, 254–62 (1965).

[26] *Cf.* ALGERIAN OFFICE, WHITE PAPER ON THE APPLICATION OF THE GENEVA
CONVENTIONS OF 1949 TO THE FRENCH-ALGERIAN CONFLICT 23–25 (1960), *cited
in* Note, *supra* note 25, at 259 n.97; 2 OPPENHEIM 370 n.1 (recognition of rebels as
belligerents brings entire Convention into play).

[27] G. DRAPER, THE RED CROSS CONVENTIONS 16 (1958); Note, *supra* note 25, at
259 & n.99; Yingling & Ginnane, *The Geneva Conventions of 1949*, 46 AM. J.
INT'L L. 393, 395–96 (1952). In place of Article 3, several countries proposed
alternatives that would have applied the entire Convention to insurgent communities fulfilling conditions similar to those of Article 4(A)(2), but all these
solutions were rejected. Siordet, *The Geneva Conventions and Civil War*, 3
SUPPLEMENT, REVUE INTERNATIONALE DE LA CROIX-ROUGE 201–10 (1950). And the
text of Article 3 itself implies this intention: "The Parties to the conflict should
further endeavour to bring into force, by means of special agreements, all or part of
the other provisions of the present Convention." (Emphasis added.)

adhered to the Convention.[28] Unless the NLF is considered an arm of North Vietnam, therefore,[29] it would not be bound under the entire Convention. For the purpose of determining obligations under Article 3, it will be assumed in this Note that the NLF is an independent rebel group and that its obligations, if any, do not stem from those of North Vietnam.

Curiously, the delegates to the 1949 Conference did not pay much attention to the question whether any convention could bind insurgent parties that are not signatories.[30] Three theories have been advanced to establish the binding force of Article 3, but each seems inadequate under traditional concepts of international law. According to the first, Article 3 "is regarded as setting forth established law independently of contractual obligation."[31] The article may be treated, in other words, as declarative of previously formed customary rules of warfare. "Support for [this] . . . contention will be found in the very content of the article, as well as the fact that the weight of world opinion subscribes to these provisions."[32] But if the humanitarian content of Article 3 is a restatement of principles developed from the customs of States, its invocation against insurgents would be novel; the rules of warfare traditionally govern only hostilities between States or civil wars in which the rebel party has been recognized as a belligerent.[33]

This theory might be more persuasive if modified to suggest that, to the extent Article 3 constitutes an innovation, it has itself become customary law since 1949. The NLF might be required to comply with Article 3 if other insurgent forces have customarily acted as if the provision were legally binding.[34] But the pattern of actual practice

---

[28] COMMENTARY 57.

[29] The United States holds that the conflict in South Vietnam is due to "armed attack from the Communist North. . . . [taking] the forms of externally supported subversion, clandestine supply of arms, infiltration of armed personnel and most recently the sending of regular units of the North Vietnamese army into the South." Dep't of State, Office of the Legal Adviser, *The Legality of United States Participation in the Defense of Viet Nam*, 75 YALE L.J. 1085 (1966). North Vietnam, on the other hand, maintains "that the war in Viet Nam is a civil war being waged to determine control of South Viet Nam rather than a civil or international war to determine control of the whole of Viet Nam." Falk, *International Law and the United States Role in the Viet Nam War*, 75 YALE L.J. 1122, 1133 n.43 (1966).

[30] Siordet, *supra* note 27, at 212.

[31] M. GREENSPAN, THE MODERN LAW OF LAND WARFARE 624 (1959) [hereinafter cited as GREENSPAN].

[32] *Id.*

[33] Insurgents are said to achieve formal status as belligerents when the following conditions are met:

[F]irst, there must exist within the State an armed conflict of a general (as distinguished from a purely local) character; secondly, the insurgents must occupy and administer a substantial portion of national territory; thirdly, they must conduct the hostilities in accordance with the rules of war and through organized armed forces acting under a responsible authority; fourthly, there must exist circumstances which make it necessary for outside States to define their attitude by means of recognition of belligerency.

H. LAUTERPACHT, RECOGNITION IN INTERNATIONAL LAW 176 (1947). This Note assumes that the NLF has not satisfied these conditions; as yet, in fact, no state has formally recognized it as a belligerent.

[34] *Cf.* Verdoodt, *The Significance of the Universal Declaration of Human Rights*, 6 INT'L REV. OF THE RED CROSS 287, 291 (1966). *See generally* C. PARRY,

since 1949 probably does not warrant such a conclusion: [35]

> Those situations since the drafting of the Convention which have had
> characteristics of "armed conflicts" envisioned by Article 3 include:
> the British operations in Malaya, the Hungarian Revolt of 1956, the
> Mau-Mau movement in Kenya, the Katanga Rebellion, the Algerian
> Revolt, and the 1964 Rebellion in the Congo. There have been viola-
> tions of Article 3 by both sides in many cases.

The Algerian conflict, in fact, is the only instance found where the insurgents endeavored to comply with Article 3 in the belief that they
were legally obliged to do so.[36] Thus, even on this narrower basis the
first explanation seems untenable.

The second theory asserts that "the rebels are bound because the
original adherence of the legitimate government to a convention containing the article binds all its subjects even though some of them later
may rebel against that government . . . ." [37] This is the basis on which
the International Committee of the Red Cross seems to consider the
NLF bound.[38] But this theory too is inconsistent with the traditional
view that rebels are not subject to international law until they are
accorded belligerent status.[39]

The third theory maintains that the insurgent community "is bound
by the very fact that it claims to represent the country, or part of the
country." [40] A treaty is usually viewed as binding the state and not
merely the particular government which negotiated it; [41] this characterization serves to stabilize international relations by insulating treaty
obligations from the effect of internal political changes. Any force
which claims to be the government of the State is said, then, to be
bound by the treaty, too. This approach may escape the conceptual
problem of obligating insurgents in an international legal system whose
rules apply only to States, because their responsibilities are made to
stem from their own contentions: consent to be treated as a government
is found in the claim to be one. But insurgents who merely claim to
represent the people do not necessarily assent to the obligations of a
government; the finding of consent may well be fictional.

The failure of all three theories is due to the difficulty of finding
obligations under a legal system whose concepts originally developed
solely to regulate the affairs of nation-states. But these doctrines
should not be permitted to impede the solution of new problems. Since

---

THE SOURCES AND EVIDENCES OF INTERNATIONAL LAW ch. 3 (1965); MacGibbon,
Customary International Law and Acquiescence, 33 BRIT. Y.B. INT'L L. 115 (1958).

[35] Note, *supra* note 25, at 249 (footnotes omitted).

[36] *See* ALGERIAN OFFICE, *supra* note 26. Various parties to the Korean war
apparently considered the entire Convention as binding customary law, GREEN-
SPAN 96 n.4, but since they treated the conflict as an international one for purposes
of the Geneva Conventions, no question arose as to the legal force of Article 3 in
cases of insurgency.

[37] GREENSPAN 623–24.

[38] Letter, *supra* note 2.

[39] *Cf.* A. McNAIR, THE LAW OF TREATIES 676 (1961).

[40] COMMENTARY 37; *accord*, Kelly, *Legal Aspects of Military Operations in
Counterinsurgency*, 21 MIL. L. REV. 95, 102 n.23 (1963).

[41] *E.g.*, RESEARCH IN INTERNATIONAL LAW, PART III, LAW OF TREATIES, art.
24, at 662 (J. Garner reporter 1935): "Unless otherwise provided in the treaty
itself, the obligations of a State under a treaty are not affected by any change in
its governmental organization or its constitutional system."

1945, civil war has been the principal form of armed conflict,[42] and Article 3 of the Convention represents an effort to mitigate its excesses. Moreover, the legitimate interests of insurgent groups were not overlooked in this effort; countries of all ideologies participated in drafting the Convention, and the 111 States that are now signatories include many that advocate national "wars of liberation." Probably, no greater protection can be given to the interests of insurgents, short of requiring their consent. By definition, insurgents cannot adhere to a treaty prior to the commencement of hostilities, and if the applicability of Article 3 were made to turn on accession afterwards, there would be too great a risk of nonadherence merely as a short-sighted response to the pressures of the moment. For this reason the parties to the Convention themselves agreed that denunciation of the treaty during wartime would not take effect until the termination of that war.[43] Accordingly, it does not seem unfair to bind insurgent groups without their consent.

In fact, no practical reason exists for holding the NLF free from the provisions of Article 3. The obligations imposed do not depend in any way upon the special purposes of their revolution or on the existence of any one political ideology. Of course, the requirements of rebellion — the necessities for quick movement and secrecy, in particular — may make it difficult for them to comply, but the drafters of the Convention took this into account by the separate treatment of civil war and the imposition of more limited duties; military necessity cannot justify disregard of prohibitions themselves embodying a consensus as to what is necessary.[44]

Finally, application of Article 3 to the NLF is not as great a doctrinal innovation as might appear. Belligerents and new states have always been obliged to respect the customary rules of warfare,[45] which are no more extensive than those set out in Article 3, even though such parties neither participated in the development of these rules prior to 1949 nor acceded to the Convention afterwards. Thus, a formalistic application of the doctrines of international law might seem consistent with the contention of the NLF. But if international law is to have any capacity for responding to new problems, its doctrines must have at least enough flexibility to take into account the similarities between civil and international wars and to uphold the validity of Article 3, as applied to the NLF.

III. The Position of North Vietnam

North Vietnam maintains that it need not treat American captives as prisoners of war under the Convention. One reason given is that

---

[42] Note, *supra* note 25, at 244.

[43] *Convention*, art. 142.

[44] The plea of necessity in the trial of German war criminals was disallowed on the ground that in the evolution of the laws of war the demands of military necessity had been taken into account. GREENSPAN 279, 314.

[45] The binding force of customary law on new states may be explained on the ground that application for recognition as a state necessarily implies consent to be bound under international law. MacGibbon, *supra* note 34, at 137 n.5.

406   THE GENEVA CONVENTION AND P.O.W.'S

neither country has formally declared war.[46] Article 2 states that "the present Convention shall apply to all cases of declared war or of any other armed conflict which may arise between two or more of the High Contracting Parties, even if the state of war is not recognized by one of them"; the argument seems to be that a formal recognition by at least one country is necessary, based on the negative implication of the last phrase and aided by the fact that preliminary drafts of the Article provided for application even when no participant recognizes a state of war.[47] But the language of the article as a whole can also be read plausibly to suggest that the Convention was intended to apply to *all* armed conflicts between signatories. Moreover in light of the purposes of the Convention, no legitimate interest could be served by the narrower reading. A declaration of war is not an empty formality, and it should have important legal consequences as to some issues,[48] but lack of a declaration in no way makes less necessary the humanitarian safeguards established by the Convention.

North Vietnam also seeks to justify its position by alleging that American pilots who have bombed its territory are war criminals under the Nuremberg Charter.[49] This Charter was annexed to the 1945 agreement among the United Kingdom, the United States, France, and the Soviet Union, providing for the organization of an International Military Tribunal. The Charter defined the following classes of crime over which the Tribunal would have jurisdiction: [50]

> (a) Crimes Against Peace: namely, planning, preparation, initiation or waging of a war of aggression, or a war in violation of international treaties . . . or participation in a common plan or conspiracy for the accomplishment of any of the foregoing:
>
> (b) War Crimes: namely, violations of the laws or customs of war. Such violations shall include, but not be limited to, murder . . . murder or ill-treatment of prisoners of war . . . killing of hostages . . . wanton destruction of cities, towns or villages, or devastation not justified by military necessity:
>
> (c) Crimes Against Humanity: namely, murder, extermination, enslavement, deportation, and other inhumane acts committed against any civilian population, before or during the war, or persecutions on political, racial or religious grounds in execution of or in connection with

---

[46] N.Y. Times, Feb. 12, 1966, at 12, col. 3 (North Vietnamese Ambassador to Egypt).

[47] *See* COMMENTARY 20.

[48] Perhaps the most important is to enhance the domestic powers of the government declaring war.

[49] N.Y. Times, July 19, 1966, at 3, cols. 1, 4. Whether the charge of the crime of aggressive war can be sustained is a hotly debated issue. *See, e.g., Legality of United States Participation in the Viet Nam Conflict: A Symposium,* 75 YALE L.J. 1084 (1966). It has been held that a State aiding a government in counterinsurgency operations may not legally attack the territory of a State intervening on the other side. *See* Falk, *supra* note 29, at 1123. Thus, to legitimate its raids on North Vietnam, the United States contends that "[i]n the guerrilla war in Viet Nam, the external aggression from the North is the critical military element of the insurgency . . . ." Dep't of State, *supra* note 29, at 1086.

[50] The Nurnberg Trial, 6 F.R.D. 69, 77–78 (1946). Only one trial was conducted under the Nuremberg Charter, but the principles it expressed were implemented by other military tribunals, such as the American courts which heard the twelve trials at Nuremberg between 1946 and 1949. GREENSPAN 425–27.

any crime within the jurisdiction of the Tribunal, whether or not in violation of the domestic law of the country where perpetrated. . . .

In attempting to bring the conduct of American pilots within these categories, North Vietnam has explicitly stressed crimes against peace. One North Vietnamese lawyer, for instance, alleged: [51]

By betraying the 1954 Geneva agreements [on the status of Vietnam] solemnly recognized by their own government and by conducting an aggressive war in South Vietnam and expanding the air war of destruction in North Vietnam, the U.S. imperialists have been committing crime after crime against peace.

But North Vietnam has also alleged perpetration of traditional war crimes and crimes against humanity — the second and third categories. The attorney referred to above was careful to include an allegation of "concrete war crimes" in the catalogue of United States evils; indeed, he also alluded to breach of the Genocide Convention by action taken in South Vietnam.[52]

Even if North Vietnam can assert colorable charges of war crimes within one of the Nuremberg categories, American pilots would still be entitled to substantial protection under the Geneva Convention. Article 85 declares: "Prisoners of war prosecuted under the laws of the Detaining Power for acts committed prior to capture shall retain, even if convicted, the benefits of the present Convention." This provision was adopted in response to a line of decisions following the Second World War which held that prisoners of war charged with the commission of war crimes before capture were not guaranteed certain safeguards of the 1929 Geneva Convention (the immediate predecessor to the current treaty). The leading case was *In re Yamashita*,[53] in which a Japanese general, sentenced to death for failure to restrain his troops from committing atrocities against Americans and their allies, sought a writ of habeas corpus in the United States Supreme Court on the ground that the procedure at his trial violated Article 63 of the 1929 Convention. That article required the detaining power to try prisoners of war by the same procedure used in trials of its own soldiers, and hearsay and opinion evidence had been admitted at Yamashita's trial, even though the American Articles of War proscribed the use of such evidence in trials of American soldiers. The Court held that "examination of Article 63 in its setting in the Convention plainly shows that it refers to sentence 'pronounced against a prisoner of war' for an offense committed while a prisoner of war, and not for a violation of the law of war committed while a combatant." [54]

One case after *Yamashita* arrived at the same conclusion by relying not only on the "setting" of Article 63 in the 1929 Convention but

---

[51] Do Xuan Sang, quoted in Nhan Dan [official newspaper of North Vietnamese government], July 10, 1966, translated in FOREIGN BROADCAST INFORMATION SERVICE, July 11, 1966, at JJJ7 (No. 132).

[52] *Id.*

[53] 327 U.S. 1 (1946), followed by the Netherlands and Italy, but ultimately rejected by France, COMMENTARY 413–14. The cases are collected in GREENSPAN at 132 n.117.

[54] 327 U.S. at 21.

also on a rule of customary law that those who have abused the laws of war are not entitled to the protection they offer.[55] But the tendency of these decisions was to prejudge the guilt of the accused by denying him the guarantees of a prisoner of war before he was proved to be a war criminal.[56] Article 85 not only cures this defect but accomplishes a major change in the rule of customary law by continuing the guarantees even after conviction.[57] This does not mean, however, that prisoners of war may no longer be tried, convicted, and executed for war crimes. It does mean that the determination of guilt must be made according to the same procedures used by the detaining power for trial of its own military personnel and in conformity with certain minimal standards established in the Convention.[58] For example: [59]

> The prisoner of war shall be entitled to assistance by one of his prisoner comrades, to defence by a qualified advocate or counsel of his own choice, to the calling of witnesses and, if he deems necessary, to the services of a competent interpreter.

The Soviet-bloc countries, however, have made reservations to Article 85; the Soviet Union's statement is generally representative: [60]

> The Union of Soviet Socialist Republics does not consider itself bound by the obligation, which follows from Article 85, to extend the application of the Convention to prisoners of war who have been *convicted* under the law of the Detaining Power, in accordance with the principles of the Nuremberg trial, for war crimes and crimes against humanity, it being understood that persons convicted of such crimes must be subject to the conditions obtaining in the country in question for those who undergo their punishment.

The Soviet Union has given its assurance that this reservation does not alter the effect of Article 85 until "the sentence has become legally enforceable." [61] If so, the result of the reservation is to maintain the

---

[55] Trial of Hans Albin Rauter, 14 L. Rep. Trials of War Crim. 89, 115–17 (No. 88) (Special Ct. of Cassation, Neth. 1949).
[56] *See* COMMENTARY 414–15.
[57] *Contra*, Case of Kappler, 36 RIVISTA DI DIRITTO INTERNAZIONALE 193 (Sup. Mil. Trib., Italy 1952), *abstracted in* 49 AM. J. INT'L L. 96 (1955). This is the only known case interpreting Article 85 but is clearly wrong. The defendant was a German soldier who had been captured by the British and handed over to Italy to be tried for the mass slaughter of civilians. He challenged the legitimacy of the transfer of jurisdiction by invoking Article 85. Without deciding whether the 1949 Convention applied retroactively, the court held that the Article did not apply to those who violated the laws of war before capture, thus restoring the *Yamashita* doctrine. The court interpreted the phrase "under the laws of the Detaining Power" in the Article not to include crimes against international law. But if "[s]uch an interpretation of Article 85 . . . were correct, the reservations entered by the USSR and other States [including North Vietnam] would be incomprehensible." COMMENTARY 426. North Vietnam, therefore, could not persuasively avail itself of the *Kappler* holding.
[58] *Convention*, art. 102.
[59] *Id.*, art. 105.
[60] 75 U.N.T.S. 460 (1950) (reservation made on signature) (emphasis added), confirmed in instrument of ratification, 191 U.N.T.S. 367 (1954).
[61] Letter from the Ministry of Foreign Affairs to the Swiss Federal Council, May 26, 1955, COMMENTARY 424. The U.S.S.R. added that "the protection afforded by the Convention becomes applicable again only after the sentence has been served . . . ."

rule that war criminals do not enjoy the privileges of a prisoner of war, but to reject *Yamashita*'s deprivation of such privileges before conviction.

The North Vietnamese reservation varies only slightly from the Soviet Union's, and the difference may well have been accidental. Potentially, however, this difference may be of considerable significance: [62]

> The Democratic Republic of Viet-Nam declares that prisoners of war *prosecuted for and convicted of* war crimes or crimes against humanity, in accordance with the principles established by the Nuremberg Tribunal, will not enjoy the benefits of the provisions of the present Convention as provided in article 85.

There are two possible constructions of this language. If the "and" is read conjunctively ("prisoners of war prosecuted for *and also* convicted of"), then the reservation is equivalent to that of the Soviet Union. But if the "and" is read disjunctively ("prisoners of war prosecuted for and prisoners of war convicted of"), all the obligations of the Convention may be circumvented simply by indicting a prisoner for war crimes.[63] The latter construction has been advanced by a North Vietnamese lawyer,[64] and if it is accepted, the reservation would restore the pre-1949 doctrines which Article 85 was supposed to cure.

The second version may seem to be less reasonable than the first because it would render the "and convicted of" phrase superfluous. But under the first reading the "prosecuted for" phrase would be equally unnecessary: under the Convention conviction necessarily entails prosecution.[65] On grammatical grounds, at least, the first reading seems the more plausible, since the disjunctive meaning is ordinarily achieved by the use of the word "or," while "and" is normally a conjunctive particle; this analysis, however, is hardly compelling. More important is the need to construe narrowly all limitations on the Convention's coverage, because its role is not merely to create obligations to States as such but rather to insure minimum humanitarian safeguards for individuals.[66] In this light, it seems clear that the North Vietnamese reservation should be read in the conjunctive sense, requiring both prosecu-

---

[62] 274 U.N.T.S. 340 (1957) (emphasis added). The ambiguity of the "prosecuted for and convicted of" phrase also exists in the French text.

[63] *Cf.* MINISTRY OF DEFENCE, TREATMENT OF BRITISH PRISONERS OF WAR IN KOREA 32 (1955), *quoted in* Levie, *Penal Sanctions for Maltreatment of Prisoners of War*, 56 AM. J. INT'L L. 433, 443 n.37 (1962): "[T]he Chinese in Korea, by simply maintaining that all soldiers fighting for their '*bourgeois*' or 'imperialist' opponents were, *ipso facto* 'war criminals,' succeeded to their own satisfaction in justifying their complete disregard of the convention."

[64] Do Xuan Sang, *supra* note 51, at JJJ8 (emphasis added):

> In its note of 5 June 1957 announcing its adherence to the said convention, the Government of the DRV deliberately and clearsightedly ruled out those *prosecuted and accused of* war crimes and crimes against mankind in keeping with the principles set by the Nuremberg international military tribunal, and held that these persons are not allowed to enjoy the protection of the 12 August 1949 Geneva convention.

[65] *See Convention*, arts. 3(1)(d), 102, 105. Article 3(1)(d) must apply along with the rest of Article 3 (the civil war provision) in cases of international conflict as well, since Article 3 represents only minimum obligations for the protection of prisoners of war. COMMENTARY 38.

[66] *See* pp. 854-55 *supra*.

tion and conviction before a prisoner of war can be denied the protection of Article 85.

Another argument against North Vietnamese reliance on its reservation involves the language referring to "war crimes or crimes against humanity." If these terms are used in the sense of the Nuremberg definitions, the reservation would seem inapplicable when the conduct charged falls only within the third category of Nuremberg crimes — crimes against peace. It might be contended that the North Vietnamese allegation of crimes against peace, based on the claim that the United States is waging an aggressive war, necessarily implies an allegation of "war crimes"; under a charter patterned after that of the Nuremberg Tribunal,[67] the International Military Tribunal for the Far East held, for example, that "[i]f . . . the war . . . is . . . unlawful, then this involves unlawful killings . . . at all places in the theatre of war and at all times throughout the period of the war." [68] But most authorities insist upon "the necessity of maintaining the operation of rules of war regardless of the illegality of the war." [69] The risk inherent in granting one party immunity on the basis of an assessment made by himself of the actions of another [70] seems to outweigh any deterrent effect the contrary rule might have on the potential aggressor. Even if the war is considered illegal, therefore, combatants should not automatically be guilty of war crimes or crimes against humanity, and the charge of crimes against peace should not suffice to bring the North Vietnamese reservation into play.

Hence, North Vietnam must rely on the other allegations to invoke its disclaimer to Article 85. These allegations [71] may also be untenable as a matter of law; even if the reservation is read in the disjunctive sense, North Vietnam may be unable to establish that it can in fact prosecute American pilots for war crimes or crimes against humanty. The claim that the United States is committing crimes against humanity in South Vietnam cannot justify prosecution of pilots who have taken no part in this activity but have been involved only in action against North Vietnam. Furthermore, the alleged bombing of civilian targets in the North does not seem to constitute a war crime under customary law in the light of the often indiscriminate aerial bombardment on both sides during the Second World War.[72] On the other hand, Article 18 of the Geneva Convention Relative to the Protection of Civilian Persons in Time of War [73] declares that civilian hospitals "may in no circumstances be the object of attack," and North Vietnam has specifically charged the bombing of such targets.[74] Thus, only this allega-

---

[67] GREENSPAN 424–25. The charter was proclaimed in 1946 by the Supreme Commander for the Allied Powers in the Pacific.

[68] *In re* Hirota and Others, [1948] Ann. Dig. 356, 365 (No. 118) (Int'l Mil. Trib. for the Far East).

[69] 2 OPPENHEIM 218; *accord,* GREENSPAN 9.

[70] *Cf.* GREENSPAN 411: "[E]xperience has shown that instead of compelling adherence to the laws of war, reprisals have often formed the pretext for their wholesale abandonment."

[71] *See* p. 860 *supra.*

[72] *See* J. STONE, LEGAL CONTROLS OF INTERNATIONAL CONFLICT 625–27 (1954).

[73] *See* note 3 *supra.*

[74] Letter, *supra* note 8.

tion seems sufficient to justify invocation of the reservation to Article 85. Indeed, the fact that, to date, no American prisoners have actually been prosecuted may reflect North Vietnamese respect for these principles.

The North Vietnamese position may, however, be strengthened by doctrines governing the legality of reservations to multilateral treaties. As a corollary to the doctrine that a State could not be bound without its consent, the accepted view used to be that "no reservation was valid unless it was accepted by all the contracting parties without exception . . . ." [75] The effect of this was to eliminate the reserving party completely from the convention, even as to terms it was willing to ratify. But at least where multilateral conventions were concerned, some relaxation of the customary rule seemed necessary in order that States might adhere to the treaty with respect to obligations on which agreement could be obtained. [76] The breakthrough occurred in 1951 when the International Court of Justice delivered an advisory opinion on the validity of reservations to the Genocide Convention of 1948. Objections had been made to certain of the reservations tendered, and many views had been expressed in the United Nations General Assembly as to the consequence, the Convention itself being silent on the subject. Accordingly, the Assembly referred the question to the court. [77] Among the issues presented were whether the Convention allowed any reservations to be made and, if so, of what kind. The court first found that the parties had intended to leave some scope for reservations. [78] And in answer to the second question the court held: [79]

> [A] State which has made and maintained a reservation which has been objected to by one or more of the parties to the Convention but not by others, can be regarded as being a party to the Convention if the reservation is compatible with the object and purpose of the Convention; otherwise, that State cannot be regarded as being a party to the Convention.

Even though the decision was expressly limited to reservations made to the Genocide Convention, [80] the International Law Commission has found the compatibility test "suitable for adoption as a general criterion of the legitimacy of reservations to multilateral treaties and of objection to them." [81] The Commission justified its view on the ground that multilateral agreements have two goals — to establish certain

---

[75] *Genocide Reservations Opinion* 21.

[76] This development may be compared to the loosening of the common law rules of offer and acceptance accomplished in commercial law. *See* UNIFORM COMMERCIAL CODE § 2–207.

[77] For discussion of the advisory jurisdiction of the court see J. STONE, *supra* note 72, at 119–22.

[78] *Genocide Reservations Opinion* 22 (7 votes to 5).

[79] *Id.* at 29 (7 votes to 5).

[80] *Id.* at 20.

[81] International Law Comm'n, Report, 17 U.N. GAOR, Supp. 9, at 21, U.N. Doc. A/5209 (1962) [hereinafter cited as I.L.C. Report]. The test was inserted in *Draft Articles*, art. 16(c), to be applied "[i]n cases where the treaty contains no provisions regarding reservations." This was a change in position for the International Law Commission due in part to the de facto observance on the part of the Secretary General of the *Genocide Reservations Opinion* for over a decade. *See* I.L.C. Report, arts. 18–20 commentary, at 19–24.

standards and to win for them universal acceptance.[82] Allowing reservations may lessen the respect particular treaty provisions will command. But it will also tend to expand the number of signatory States and thus enhance the prestige of the treaty as a whole; partial implementation of such agreements may well be better than nothing at all.[83] Critics of the *Genocide Reservations Opinion* point out that these arguments assume some States will not become signatories unless they can make particular reservations; the universal endorsement of humanitarian ideals in the case of certain conventions is said to belie the assumption.[84] Approval of humanitarian principles, however, does not necessarily imply acceptance of detailed provisions for securing those principles; indeed, the NLF and North Vietnam profess to accord captives decent treatment at the same time that they reject the applicability of the Geneva Convention.

Of course, universal agreement to a convention emasculated by reservations would be meaningless; the function of the compatability test is to achieve a balance between the competing goals of integrity and universal acceptance. While this test has been criticized for lack of certainty,[85] greater precision may be impossible as long as some recognition is to be given to each of these purposes.

The analysis in the *Genocide Reservations Opinion* does not provide an unequivocal solution for the case of the Geneva Convention and the North Vietnamese disclaimer to Article 85. The Convention is silent on the question whether any power to make reservations exists. North Vietnam and the Soviet Union would argue that such a right is to be implied, especially since the Soviet Union's reservation to Article 85 was made on signature.[86] The United States would probably agree in view of its apparent policy of tolerating reservations in order to extend the Convention's coverage; on ratifying the Convention, the United States announced that, though it rejected the reservations other States had made, it accepted "treaty relations with all parties to that Convention, except as to the changes proposed by such reservations." [87]

---

[82] *See* I.L.C. Report 22; *cf. Genocide Reservations Opinion* 24:
The complete exclusion from the Convention of one or more States would not only restrict the scope of its application, but would detract from the authority of the moral and humanitarian principles which are its basis. It is inconceivable that the contracting parties readily contemplated that an objection to a minor reservation should produce such a result. But even less could the contracting parties have intended to sacrifice the very object of the Convention in favour of a vain desire to secure as many participants as possible.

[83] *See* I.L.C. Report 22; *cf.* Fitzmaurice, *Reservations to Multilateral Conventions*, 1953 INT'L & COMP. L.Q. 1, 15–16 [hereinafter cited as Fitzmaurice (1953)].

[84] *E.g.*, Fitzmaurice (1953), at 18–19.

[85] *Genocide Reservations Opinion* 44 (dissenting opinion); *accord*, J. BRIERLY, THE LAW OF NATIONS 323–24 (6th ed. Waldock 1963).

[86] These countries also made statements in regard to other articles, but there is some question whether they actually are reservations. Although they alter the legal effect of the provisions to which they are attached, they do not seem to lessen the obligations of the reserving States. Thus, it has been said that "the only genuine reservation" is the one made to Article 85. Pilloud, *Reservations to the 1949 Geneva Conventions*, 5 INT'L REV. OF THE RED CROSS 343, 349 (1965). *But see Draft Articles*, art. 2(d).

[87] 213 U.N.T.S. 383 (1955). Furthermore, the United States itself entered two reservations, one to the Geneva Convention for the Amelioration of the Condition

New Zealand and Australia, however, might wish to dispute the validity of the contention that a power to make reservations was contemplated. Upon ratification New Zealand declared: "Whilst Her Majesty's Government . . . regard those States [referring to several that had made reservations] as parties to the Conventions in question, they will regard any application of such a reservation as constituting a breach of the Convention to which the reservation relates." [88] Australia made a similar declaration upon ratification,[89] and its statement specifically refers to North Vietnam, whereas New Zealand named other states, omitting North Vietnam. It may be inferred from both declarations that the two countries regard all reservations as impermissible. On the other hand, both countries do find the reserving States to be parties to the Convention, and assuredly they cannot be made members on terms they reject.[90] Both statements, therefore, are self-contradictory and perhaps for that reason should be read against the declarants. On balance, the power to make reservations seems as justified under the objects of the Geneva as under the Genocide Convention.

If so, then is the North Vietnamese reservation valid? While the Soviet Union's reservation retains the customary rule of law for the treatment of war criminals, it at least does not invoke that rule upon the mere prosecution for war crimes. Therefore, it seems "compatible with the object and purpose of the Convention." The North Vietnamese disclaimer, if read in the disjunctive sense, would seem incompatible since it would permit the evasion of treaty responsibilities by simply alleging violations of the laws of war and initiating prosecutions. But if the reservation is incompatible, it would follow under the rule of the *Genocide Reservations Opinion* that North Vietnam is not a member of the Convention at all. This prospect creates an additional reason for construing the North Vietnamese reservation narrowly; just as ambiguities should be resolved in favor of the greatest protection for individuals in particular situations, so it is even more essential that reservations be construed, if at all possible, to avoid the case of incompatibility, which would leave the reserving State bound only by the limited restrictions of customary law in all situations. Accordingly, the reservation should be read in the conjunctive sense, and it is compatible.

of the Wounded and Sick in Armed Forces in the Field, *id.* at 378, 380, and the other to the Geneva Convention Relative to the Protection of Civilian Persons in Time of War, *id.* at 384. The statement the United States made upon ratification was perhaps suggested by a dictum in the *Genocide Reservations Opinion*:

[I]t may be that a State, whilst not claiming that a reservation is incompatible with the object and purpose of the Convention, will nevertheless object to it, but that an understanding between that State and the reserving State will have the effect that the Convention will enter into force between them, except for the clauses affected by the reservation.

Genocide Reservations Opinion 27 (dictum); *cf. Draft Articles*, arts. 17, 19; Pilloud, *supra* note 86.

[88] 330 U.N.T.S. 356, 359 (1959).
[89] 314 U.N.T.S. 330, 335–36 (1958).
[90] *Cf.* Roto-Lith, Ltd. v. F.P. Bartlett & Co., 297 F.2d 497, 500 (1st Cir. 1962) ("a reply to an offer stating additional conditions unilaterally burdensome upon the offeror is [not] a binding acceptance of the original offer plus simply a proposal for the additional conditions").

The United States, however, made a statement rejecting reservations two years before North Vietnam's accession, and this statement seems to have been intended to apply prospectively. The United States, therefore, rejected the North Vietnamese reservation, yet accepted treaty relations with that country except for Article 85.[91] But this leaves unanswered the crucial question of the effect of the United States statement on the obligations of both countries with respect to issues dealt with in Article 85, and there is wide disagreement among international lawyers as to the obligations of reserving and rejecting States in such a situation. If the situation is viewed as analogous to rejection of a counter-offer in a contract negotiation, there would be no agreement between the parties on questions to which the reservation relates;[92] under this view only customary law would apply to both countries on questions covered by Article 85,[93] and under the rule approved by the United States Supreme Court itself, captives prosecuted for war crimes would not be entitled to many important procedural safeguards. In the case of a humanitarian treaty such as the Geneva Convention, however, this approach seems unnecessarily harsh to the individuals involved. Each State considers itself a party to the Convention, and each is willing to provide somewhat greater safeguards than those required by customary law; there seems to be no practical objection, therefore, to requiring prisoners to be provided with at least the benefits that are acceptable to the reserving State.

At the other extreme, if it is stressed that on adherence to the Convention each State accepts certain humanitarian obligations as not excessively onerous, each party would be required to provide the safeguards accepted to captives of *all* nationalities in order to provide, in accord with the Convention's general purpose, the maximum protection for individuals. Under this view the United States would be bound by Article 85 and North Vietnam by the terms of its reservation. But the lack of reciprocity implicit in this scheme makes it difficult to accept; each State would be left free to limit its own obligations — subject to the compatibility requirement — without fear that the protections due its own nationals would be thereby diminished.

Another possibility is that both the United States and North Vietnam would be bound to provide the safeguards required by Article 85, as qualified by the North Vietnamese reservation. This seems a strange consequence of the United States rejection, since it is precisely the situation that would have resulted had the reservation been *accepted*.[94] But this interpretation is not implausible in the case of a

---

[91] North Vietnam also made other statements upon accession which may or may not be reservations, *see* note 86 *supra*; consequently, the articles to which these are attached may also not be in force between North Vietnam and the United States.

[92] *See* J. BRIERLY, *supra* note 85, at 322–23.

[93] If North Vietnam considered agreement to abide by its reservation a prerequisite to its undertaking mutual obligations with any country, it would be impossible for the United States to reject the reservation and yet accept treaty relations apart from Article 85; the United States statement would necessarily have the effect of barring agreement with North Vietnam on all aspects of the treaty. It seems more likely, however, that North Vietnam did not consider its acceptance of other obligations under the Convention conditional on agreement to its reservation.

[94] *See Draft Articles*, art. 19(1).

reservation that limits the application of a particular provision without proposing additional obligations. Both countries have, in fact, accepted treaty relations except with respect to the changes proposed by the reservation, and a reservation that merely limits a treaty provision does not propose any changes in that provision with respect to obligations within the suggested limits. Such obligations were, therefore, actually accepted by both countries, and both should be bound to this extent.[95] The only satisfactory solution, therefore, is to regard both the United States and North Vietnam as bound by Article 85, subject to the limits proposed in the North Vietnamese reservation.

IV. Conclusion

Some of the NLF and North Vietnamese claims that have been considered are not frivolous or unreasonable. The fact that there is legitimate disagreement over the applicability of the Geneva Convention suggests that the virtually universal adherence to the Convention is misleading. But resolution of the issues presented is impeded primarily by the failure of international law to adapt its traditional doctrines to new problems. The effect of reservations is difficult to determine when the concepts of treaty negotiation are divorced from the realities of the process by which States adhere to large-scale multilateral conventions. Similarly, the obligations of insurgent groups are difficult to articulate if analysis must be confined to traditional concepts and if consideration of practical problems is deemed illegitimate. Only if these doctrines are able to grow and respond to changing conditions can international law continue to have relevance for the solution of important problems in the modern world.

---

[95] *See Draft Articles*, art. 19(3). The rules formulated in the *Draft Articles* clearly contemplate that acceptance and rejection will have identical effects in this situation. *Compare* art. 19(1) *with* art. 19(3).

The Geneva Convention of 1949: Application in the Vietnamese Conflict

Note from *Virginia Journal of International Law*

I. INTRODUCTION

The Communist theory of "wars of national liberation"[1] adds a new force to the conduct of war itself and gives cause for a re-examination of the regulation of warfare in the mid-twentieth century. The Geneva Conventions of 1949[2] have been considered a significant though limited aspect of the attempt to gain adherence to certain rules of conduct.

Traditionally there were thought to be two kinds of warfare: civil

---

1. Address by N.S. Krushchev to the Higher Party School, the Academy of Social Sciences, and the Institute of Marxism-Leninism attached to the CPSU, Jan. 6, 1961, in *Hearing before the Subcommittee to Investigate the Administration of the Internal Security Act and Internal Security Laws of the Senate Committee on the Judiciary*, 87th Cong., 1st Sess. 64-65 (1961).

2. Geneva Convention for the Amelioration of the Condition of the Wounded and Sick in Armed Forces in the Field, Aug. 12, 1949, [1956] 3 U.S.T. & O.I.A. 3114, T.I.A.S. No. 3362; Geneva Convention for the Amelioration of the Condition of the Wounded, Sick and Shipwrecked Members of the Armed Forces at Sea, Aug. 12, 1949, [1956] 3 U.S.T. & O.I.A. 3217, T.I.A.S. No. 3363; Geneva Convention Relative to the Treatment of Prisoners of War, Aug. 12, 1949, [1956] 3 U.S.T. & O.I.A. 3316, T.I.A.S. No. 3364 [hereinafter cited as Convention]; Geneva Convention Relative to the Protection of Civilian Persons in Time of War, Aug. 12, 1949, [1956] 3 U.S.T. & O.I.A. 3516, T.I.A.S. No. 3365.

wars,[3] in which two factions within a state are vying to represent the state as its government, and wars between states,[4] in which one makes a declaration of war or commences hostilities against the other. The first anticipation that there may be an intermediate category of warfare occurred in commentaries on the Spanish Civil War.[5] Since these "international civil wars" [6] are the principal means by which warfare since 1945 has been carried on, it is particularly appropriate to study the application of the Convention to a current and very important example of this type of a conflict, South Vietnam today.

In addition we will look briefly at how the Vietnamese conflict has affected other aspects of the law of war in both South Vietnam and the United States.

II. STATUS OF PARTICIPANTS UNDER MUNICIPAL LAW

A. South Vietnamese Laws

Extremely liberal treaty provisions with the government of South Vietnam have given American servicemen rights comparable to some higher members of the diplomatic mission, viz., immunity from both civil and criminal jurisdiction.[7] Technically, the more than 23,000 American advisers [8] are attached to the diplomatic mission itself with the duty of training the South Vietnamese in the use of the weapons supplied under the U.S. military aid program.

Given a right of entry by treaty and by invitation of the South Vietnamese government, the traditional rules of international law concerning the protection of aliens are applicable. Responsibility will fall upon the South Vietnamese government when its officers have not been reasonably diligent in protecting American advisers from injury at the hands of the Viet Cong "criminals".[9] Recent events in South Vietnam have emphasized the possibility of an American claim on behalf of its advisers, for harm above that which may have been anticipated by the United States.[10] Such a claim however, in

---

3. See 3 HYDE, INTERNATIONAL LAW 1698 (2d rev. ed. 1945).
4. 2 OPPENHEIM, INTERNATIONAL LAW 271 (7th ed. Lauterpacht ed. 1952).
5. MODELSKI, THE INTERNATIONAL RELATIONS OF INTERNAL WAR (1961); Garner, *Questions of International Law in the Spanish Civil War*, 31 AM. J. INT'L L. 66 (1931).
6. Bartelle, *Counterinsurgency and Civil War*, 40 N.D.L. REV. 254 (1964).
7. Agreement for Mutual Defense Assistance in Indo-China with Cambodia, France, Laos, and Vietnam, Dec. 23, 1950, [1952] 2 U.S.T. & O.I.A. 2756, T.I.A.S. No. 2447.
8. The decision to give large scale American assistance in a military adviser capacity occurred on July 18, 1961. See N.Y. Times, July 19, 1961, p. 3, col. 2. Six months later there were reportedly 2,000 U. S. military advisers in South Vietnam. *Id.*, Dec. 20, 1961, p. 1, col. 1. The most recent figure of 23,000 was given early in 1965. *Id.*, Feb. 12, 1965, p. 1, col. 8, at 13, col. 3 (city ed.). An additional 3,500 American marines have now been stationed in Vietnam. N. Y. Times, March 8, 1965, p. 1, col. 2 (city ed.).
9. BRIERLY, THE LAW OF NATIONS 289 (6th ed. 1963).
10. In the recent bombing of American barracks at Pleitku, there were widespread claims that South Vietnamese security officers had negligently failed

view of the present situation is not likely to be raised by the United States government.[11] Evidence indicates that the South Vietnamese government has been diligent in its duty [12] to pursue the Viet Cong and bring them to justice for injury or capture of American nationals.[13]

To meet the increasing encroachment of the Viet Cong on the normal functioning of the South Vietnamese government, new laws have been formulated to restrain rebel activity. A 1959 law on national security subjected private persons who have committed any of the enumerated offenses against national security to the jurisdiction of special military tribunals.[14] This Act, and the ones following it, make it a crime to join or associate with an organization endangering national security.[15]

With respect to an extra-judicial detention by the Viet Cong, the American adviser is not accorded any greater legal importance [16] than a captured South Vietnamese soldier, so long as the South Vietnamese law enforcers meet minimal international standards of due care.

B. United States Laws

1. Application to military discipline and foreign sovereignty.

Laws about discipline within the armed forces or those respecting foreign territorial sovereignty are not likely to be the subject of much legislative activity. Military discipline is covered by the Uniform Code of Military Justice, enacted in 1950.[17] Since this Act is a great aid to military commanders in attaining an ultimately political goal of destroying a designated armed group, the term "enemy" used in the

---

to detect Viet Cong terrorists. N.Y. Times, Feb. 8, 1965, p. 1, col. 6 (city ed.).

11. It is one of the ironies of the present situation in Vietnam that while upholding the sovereignty of the South Vietnamese state with respect to the encroachments of the North Vietnamese, the United States finds itself unable to make claims on behalf of its injured nationals.

12. BRIERLY, op. cit. supra note 9, at 290.

13. See, e.g., N.Y. Times, Oct. 26, 1964, p. 7, col. 1; id., April 12, 1962, p. 11, col. 1.

14. South Vietnam Law No. 10/59 (May 6, 1959) (For the Punishment of Sabotage and Offenses Against National Security or Against the Lives and Property of the People, and for the Establishment of Special Military Tribunals), reprinted in The Judge Advocate General's School (U.S. Dep't of the Army), Law and Population Control in Counterinsurgency, Jan. 1965, p. 119.

15. South Vietnam Law No. 10/59, art. 3 (May 6, 1959); State of Emergency, South Vietnam Decree Law No. 18/64, art. 5 (Aug. 7, 1964) (prescribing death for "terrorists, people who indulge in sabotage, speculators on the national economy"), reprinted in The Judge Advocate General's School, op. cit. supra note 14, at 141.

16. Kelly, Legal Aspects of Military Operations in Counterinsurgency, 21 MIL. L. REV. 95, 118 (Dep't of the Army Pam. 27-100-21, 1963).

17. Uniform Code of Military Justice, 10 U.S.C. §§ 801-940 (1958), as amended, 10 U.S.C. §§ 802-936 (Supp. V, 1963).

definitions of "misbehavior" and "aiding the enemy" undoubtedly encompasses the Viet Cong forces.[18]

Similarly, the U.S. Neutrality Act has for a long time prohibited U.S. nationals from conspiring to conduct military expeditions or enterprises against the territory of a people with whom the United States is at peace.[19] This Act appears to be motivated by the principle that United States involvement in foreign military activities should be left to the discretion of the executive. Thus any activities of American nationals which form a "natural, if not inevitable, part" of the military operations of the Viet Cong will result in criminal liability,[20] regardless of the status which may be accorded the Viet Cong under international law.

2. Necessity of amending present laws.

In other areas more closely associated with the rights of private individuals, the nature of modern-day warfare has forced the United States to fashion new standards. For example, certain activities not of a military nature which do not approach those prohibited by the Neutrality Act may come under Treasury Department regulations against the sending of goods to the "Communist-controlled area of Vietnam." [21] Foreseeing other problems brought to light by the unprecedented American commitment in Southeast Asia, Congress has amended the War Hazards Compensation Act [22] to allow compensation for employees of government contractors captured by a "hostile force or person," as opposed to the former term "enemy",[23] and to define the new phrase to accord with the language of the Geneva Conventions.[24] Still more recently, the 1964 amendments to the

18. 10 U.S.C. §§ 899, 904 (1958). There may be some doubt whether "misconduct as a prisoner," 10 U.S.C. § 905 (1958), applies with such force to those captured by the Viet Cong, but it seems that it was applied in one case where a U.S. adviser was held by the Viet Cong. N.Y. Times, June 26, 1962, p. 9, col. 1.

19. The Neutrality Act of 1917, 18 U.S.C. § 960 (1958); *cf.* An Act in addition to the Act for the Punishment of Certain Crimes against the United States, § 5, 1 Stat. 381 (1794).

20. United States v. Sander, 241 Fed. 417, 420 (S.D.N.Y. 1917); United States v. Chakraberty, 244 Fed. 287 (S.D.N.Y. 1917).

21. See 15 C.F.R. §§ 370.2, 371.8(a)(1)(i), 371.10 n.1, 371.13(a)(1)-(2), 371.21(a) (1963). The term "Communist-controlled area" would seem to be required by the fact that the Geneva Pact used the term "regrouping area" in reference to North Vietnam. See note 84 *infra.* Apparently such a broad term has prompted its extension to Viet Cong-held areas of South Vietnam as well. Most likely these are the regulations alluded to recently in prohibiting a group of Haverford College students from sending medical aid "to either North Vietnam or the Vietcong." N.Y. Times, Dec. 4, 1964, p. 18, col. 1. See specifically 15 C.F.R. § 371.10 n.1 (1963).

22. 42 U.S.C. §§ 1701-17 (1958).

23. 42 U.S.C. § 1701(b) (1958).

24. 42 U.S.C. § 1711(c) (1958). The new term pertains to situations of "armed conflict" against a U.S. ally, or an "armed conflict between hostile forces of any origin." See also 42 U.S.C. § 1701(d)(3) (1958) (specific mention of the Geneva Convention of 1949).

Missing Persons Act [25] explicitly state that the benefits afforded by the Act are not limited only to those military personnel "besieged" by a "hostile force" in the traditional sense, but also to those "detained in a foreign country against their will." [26]

The problem of allowing compensation for the vicissitudes of "warfare", but avoiding public indemnity for the acts of common criminals, is merely a prelude to the problems still confronting the drafters at the international level.

III. APPLICATION OF THE GENEVA CONVENTION

The Geneva Conventions [27] were established in 1949 to restate and reinforce certain basic humanitarian rights that belong to every individual involved in an armed conflict.[28] These four Conventions have been cited as a lesser alternative to the promulgation of a more rigorous definition of the law of war.[29] Using the conflict in Vietnam as a focal point we shall examine the suitability, under modern warfare conditions, of the third Convention, dealing with prisoners of war [hereinafter cited as Convention].

Under its present design there are two fundamental bases upon which the Convention is expected to operate. First, the parties to the Convention are bound to respect its provisions under all circumstances, and therefore may not suspend any of them as a reprisal for actions by another party.[30] Secondly, where violations have occurred, the only recourse against the individual violator is to bring him before a properly constituted municipal court having jurisdiction over his person.[31] Therefore the guarantees of the Convention to both captured insurgents and captives of the insurgents seem small when compared with the criminal sanctions legally available to the established government [32] and the techniques normally used by insurgent forces against prisoners.[33] Nevertheless, insurgents like the Viet Cong who are nationals of a state whose government has ratified the Convention are legally obligated to observe its provisions.[34]

25. 50 U.S.C. App. §§ 1001-18 (1958), as amended, Pub. L. No. 88-428, 78 Stat. 437 (1964).
26. 78 Stat. at 437 (1964).
27. See note 2 *supra*.
28. PICTET, COMMENTARY ON THE GENEVA CONVENTION RELATIVE TO THE TREATMENT OF PRISONERS OF WAR 1-16 (1960).
29. Lauterpacht, *The Problem of the Revision of the Law of War*, 29 BRIT. YB. INT'L L. 360 (1952).
30. See Convention art. 1; PICTET, *op. cit. supra* note 28, at 17.
31. Convention art. 3, para. 1(1) (d) ; art. 129, para. 4.
32. PICTET, *op. cit. supra* note 28, at 28; Vietnam Ordinance 47 (Aug. 21, 1956) (Prescribing the Punishment of Crimes Against the External Security of the State), reprinted in The Judge Advocate General's School, *op. cit. supra* note 14, at 105.
33. An extreme example of insurgent atrocities is to be seen in the recent uprisings in the Congo. See N.Y. Times, Nov. 18, 1964, p. 1, col. 4; *id.*, Nov. 25, 1964, p. 1, col. 7.
34. Bartelle, *supra* note 6, at 274; GREENSPAN, THE MODERN LAW OF LAND WARFARE 623-24 (1959).

A. Article 3—detention during a "conflict not of an international character"

Article 3, pertaining to armed conflicts which are not of an international character, has been called the most important of the Convention.[35] In it is found the principal way in which the Convention applies to the bulk of contemporary warfare—by prohibiting an established government from inhumanely treating captured insurgents who, according to the criminal law of the established state, are mere criminals.[36] Article 3 captives are not to be tortured, humiliated or summarily executed, and unless certain procedures are complied with they cannot be executed without violating the Article.[37]

By not specifically mentioning or attempting to characterize the new phenomenon of an international civil war, the Convention has avoided some serious drafting problems,[38] but has a fortiori depended

---

35. Kelly, *supra* note 16, at 101.
36. See, *e.g.*, statutes cited notes 14-15, 32 *supra*.
37. The full text of Article 3 reads as follows:

   In the case of armed conflict not of an international character occurring in the territory of one of the High Contracting Parties, each Party to the conflict shall be bound to apply, as a minimum, the following provisions:

   (1) Persons taking no active part in the hostilities, including members of armed forces who have laid down their arms and those placed *hors de combat* by sickness, wounds, detention or any other cause, shall in all circumstances be treated humanely, without any adverse distinction founded on race, colour, religion or faith, sex, birth or wealth, or any other similar criteria.

   To this end the following acts are and shall remain prohibited at any time and in any place whatsoever with respect to the above-mentioned persons.

   (a) violence to life and person, in particular murder of all kinds, mutilation, cruel treatment and torture;

   (b) taking of hostages;

   (c) outrages upon personal dignity, in particular humiliating and degrading treatment;

   (d) the passing of sentences and the carrying out of executions without previous judgment pronounced by a regularly constituted court affording all the judicial guarantees which are recognized as indispensable by civilized peoples.

   (2) The wounded and sick shall be collected and cared for. An impartial humanitarian body, such as the International Committee of the Red Cross, may offer its services to the Parties to the conflict.

   The Parties to the conflict should further endeavor to bring into force, by means of special agreements, all or part of the other provisions of the present Convention.

   The application of the preceding provisions shall not affect the legal status of the Parties to the conflict.

38. It is feared that enlarging the scope of an international agreement regarding essentially the rights and duties of individuals may necessitate the definition of certain very general concepts. *Cf.* Bridges, *The Case for an International Court of Criminal Justice and the Formulation of International Criminal Law*, 13 INT'L & COMP. L.Q. 1255, 1269 (1964). This must not be a prerequisite to effecting the Convention, since there appears no hope of clearly delimiting such broad terms as aggression. See 2 [1951] YB. INT'L L. COMM'N 69 (A/CN.4/Ser.A/1951).

upon voluntary application of its provisions. How well its humanitarian goals are adapted to current circumstances, as reflected in Vietnam, is the main question to be discussed herein.

1. Application of Article 3.

Article 3 is generally held to come into effect "when a State can no longer maintain order through the normal application of its internal common law and is thus obliged to adopt a special code beyond its common laws." [39] Although some authors have suggested that recognition of an insurgency by the established government is a necessary prerequisite to the operation of Article 3, the better view is that no formal declaration is needed.[40] The evidence is sufficient to place the situation in Vietnam under this Article.

But it is fairly clear that under present circumstances the full benefits of the Convention do not apply in all cases in which participants in the Vietnamese conflict are captured by another participant.

2. Efficacy of the Article.

International law recognizes a right of revolution against the government of the rebel's state.[41] There is, conversely, a right in the established government to use its police power against dissident factions who seek to overthrow it.[42] It is the basic purpose of Article 3 that in any such "armed conflict" all persons, whether participants or not, should be free from any treatment which is inhumane and unnecessary for the conduct of military operations.[43] Whether such a limited objective can hope to succeed will be discussed later.

Those situations since the drafting of the Convention which have had characteristics of "armed conflicts" envisioned by Article 3 include: the British operations in Malaya,[44] the Hungarian Revolt of 1956,[45] the Mau-Mau movement in Kenya,[46] the Katanga Rebellion,[47] the Algerian Revolt,[48] and the 1964 Rebellion in the Congo.[49] There have been violations of Article 3 by both sides in many cases.[50] Furthermore, each side appears to relish the publication of atrocities which are supposed to have been committed by the other party to the

---

39. ALGERIAN OFFICE, WHITE PAPER ON THE APPLICATION OF THE GENEVA CONVENTIONS OF 1949 TO THE FRENCH-ALGERIAN CONFLICT 19 (1960). This is an adumbrated version of the characteristics of an Article 3 situation discussed by other commentators. See PICTET, *op. cit. supra* note 28, at 35-36; Kelly, *supra* note 16, at 99-100.
40. PICTET, *op. cit. supra* note 28, at 36.
41. Wright, *Subversive Intervention*, 54 AM. J. INT'L L. 521, 529 (1960).
42. *Cf.* Bartelle, *supra* note 6, at 272.
43. Article 3 is common to all four Geneva Conventions. See note 2 *supra*.
44. Kelly, *supra* note 16, at 100.
45. JOYCE, THE RED CROSS INTERNATIONAL 169-70 (1959).
46. *Id.* at 187-89.
47. See Kelly, *supra* note 16, at 110.
48. ALGERIAN OFFICE, *op. cit. supra* note 39, at 19.
49. See N.Y. Times, Nov. 25, 1964, p. 1, col. 6; *id.*, Nov. 29, 1964, p. 1, col. 4.
50. See, *e.g.*, N.Y. Times, Nov. 26, 1964, p. 18, col. 1 (Congo situation). *Cf.* JOYCE, *op. cit. supra* note 45, at 225.

military struggle.[51] Such action is hardly conducive to an undertaking to put the Convention into effect unilaterally regardless of the diligence with which the other party performs its Convention obligations.

In South Vietnam today the struggle is between the present Saigon government and the Viet Cong group known as the "National Liberation Front." [52] Whether the latter is in fact a facade "directed" by North Vietnam,[53] or a grass-roots movement,[54] there can be no doubt that the conflict is of international import, especially in view of the Communists' commitment to the success of all wars of national liberation [55] and the necessity for the West not to abandon the uncommitted nations.[56] These broader political motives are probably the principal reason why the Viet Cong have in fact treated the U. S. advisers captured by them with unexpected care. Nevertheless, although exhorted by their theorists to treat *all* their prisoners humanely,[57] the Viet Cong have not done so in the case of captured South Vietnamese troops.[58]

One immediate explanation for a lack of fair treatment by the rebels is the practical necessity for swift movement [59] to avoid capture by the government's troops. On the other hand, it is only reasonable that if the Viet Cong claim the status of a "government", they should attempt to assume the responsibilities of protecting persons of any origin who may come within their control.

3. Agreements to bring in more of the Convention.

Article 3 recommends that the parties "bring into force by means of special agreements, all or part" of the rest of the Convention.[60]

---

51. See JOYCE, *op. cit. supra* note 45, at 185-86. *Cf. id.* at 206-07 & n.*. Compare N.Y. Times, Nov. 25, 1964, p. 1, col. 7, *with* N.Y. Times, Nov. 28, 1964, p. 2, col. 3.

52. This group was established on March 30, 1961, under the auspices of North Vietnam. N.Y. Times, March 31, 1961, p. 1, col. 8.

53. U.S. DEP'T OF STATE, WHITE PAPER ON AGGRESSION FROM THE NORTH— THE RECORD OF NORTH VIETNAM'S CAMPAIGN TO CONQUER SOUTH VIETNAM, in N.Y. Times, Feb. 28, 1965, p. 30, col. 1 (city ed.) [hereinafter cited as WHITE PAPER].

54. Letter from Dr. R. W. Wolfson, M.D., in Vietnam, Dec. 30, 1964, N.Y. Times, Jan. 23, 1965, p. 24, col. 6; *cf.* Letter from Q. Wright, Jan. 25, 1965, *id.*, Jan. 31, 1965, § 4, p. 8, col. 5 (comparing the right of "self-determination" in Vietnam to the doctrines enunciated by this country in 1776 and 1823, and suggesting an end to "outside involvement").

55. See note 1 *supra*.

56. Hilsman, *A Report on South Viet-Nam*, 47 DEP'T STATE BULL. 526 (1962).

57. GIAP, PEOPLE'S WAR, PEOPLE'S ARMY, THE VIET CONG INSURRECTION MANUAL FOR UNDERDEVELOPED COUNTRIES (1962).

58. Many South Vietnamese soldiers have been "captured" but thus far there is no evidence that they are still under detention or that they have been released. See, *e.g.*, N.Y. Times, May 8, 1962, p. 6, col. 6 (25 soldiers captured).

59. Greenspan, *International Law and Its Protection for Participants in Unconventional Warfare*, 341 Annals 30, 34 (1962).

60. Convention art. 3, para. 2.

Thus far there have been no conflicts falling into the Article 3 classification in which the parties have agreed between themselves to bring into effect more of the Convention's provisions.[61]

Although there have been an increasing number of agreements between governments where mutual recognition does not exist,[62] there are still grave problems in any accord of this kind. The conclusion of any agreement between parties engaged in hostilities is particularly difficult in a civil insurgency, where one party's whole basis for existence is grounded upon the overthrow of the other party.

These circumstances lead to a situation where the humanitarian aims of the Convention are frustrated by political effects resulting from, or thought to result from, a bargain entered into by the established government with a rebellious group of its own citizens in order to secure better treatment for its own captured soldiers.

However, agreements of the type contemplated are not altogether beyond the realm of possibility. The last line of Article 3 provides that the application of the preceding provisions shall not affect the legal status of the parties.[63] It is reasonable to assume that the same absence of legal effect would apply to further portions of the full Convention brought in by agreement.[64] There is no reason why this type of agreement cannot operate completely apart from any legal implications beyond the adoption of practices to conform with the provisions agreed to.

Agreements between hostile parties are not unknown in the present day, and their existence in situations resembling the struggle in Vietnam, is encouraging. Agreements dealing with passes,[65]

---

61. The only recorded use of this expansion provision was in the Yemen conflict, where the overthrown government has been fighting to regain control. The situation is distinguished both by the magnitude of the foreign involvement and by the more conventional type of warfare conducted under desert conditions. Use of such an agreement may also have been prompted by the presence of the United Nations. See N.Y. Times, Nov. 10, 1963, p. 27, col. 4 (the International Red Cross builds a hospital in the demilitarized U.N.-controlled zone for patients from rebel-held territory).

62. See, e.g., note 65 infra.

63. This clause is considered to be of such importance that without it the Convention would never have been adopted. It is viewed as assurance that a de jure government's right and means of repressing a civil rebellion will not be interfered with by applying the Convention. PICTET, op. cit. supra note 28, at 43.

64. One authority states that the final clause of Article 3 governs the provision for special agreements, and this could hardly mean less than that the content of those agreements themselves would not alter the legal status of the parties. PICTET, op. cit. supra note 28, at 43.

65. Agreements providing for limited traffic across fortified boundaries have been concluded between the government of East Germany and the city of West Berlin without official recognition of the former by the municipal authorities. N.Y. Times, Dec. 18, 1963, p. 1, col. 5; 2 WHITEMAN, DIGEST OF INTERNATIONAL LAW 592 (1963).

arrangements for release of prisoners,[66] and legislative reference to insurgents [67] have recently occurred without involving recognition or acceptance of legal standing. It appears that an agreement as contemplated in Article 3 is conceivable in Vietnam, if a negotiator for the Viet Cong can be found.[68]

But it must not be overlooked that this approach to the problem is burdened by the serious weakness of placing the attainment of a full and effective humanitarian regulation of armed conflicts at the initiative of the very parties to the conflict. There is nothing voluntary about the application of Article 3, and on this basis alone it would not be unreasonable to make obligatory at least some additional Convention benefits.

4. Violations of the Convention.

Some authorities [69] have suggested that progress towards international jurisdiction over crimes against humanity has been impeded by the adoption of the Geneva Convention. But on the other hand, the operation of the articles dealing with "grave breaches" of the Convention [70] may aid this development by familiarizing municipal law with its humanitarian aims, thus leading nations to realize the importance of effectively guaranteeing some recognized minimal standard of treatment. Article 129 in fact requires a signing party "to enact any legislation necessary to provide effective penal sanctions for persons committing, or ordering to be committed" any of the enumerated grave breaches. Pursuant to this Article, some signatories have enacted laws giving universal jurisdiction in the event of such violations.[71] The United States has not as yet undertaken such a broad solution to the problem, but prefers to leave enforcement to its military tribunals,[72] which for all practical purposes in South Vietnam will be the only judicial bodies dealing with such offenses.

---

66. The United States obtained from the Castro revolutionaries in Cuba in 1958 the release of captive American nationals without recognizing his government. 2 *id.* at 583.
67. It is said that even a reference to an insurgent force by name in the legislation of the established government does not indicate a legal recognition of the insurgents by the ruling government. 2 *id.* at 602-04.
68. The International Red Cross has found it extremely difficult to locate, anywhere in the world, an agent of the Viet Cong. N.Y. Times, Oct. 20, 1964, p. 15, col. 1.
69. Baxter, *Constitutional Forms and Some Legal Problems of International Military Command*, 29 BRIT. YB. INT'L L. 325, 354 (1952).
70. Convention arts. 129-31. A "grave breach" includes "wilful killing, torture or inhumane treatment, including biological experiments." Art. 130.
71. "Any person whatever his nationality, who, whether inside or outside the United Kingdom, commits or aids, abets or procures the commission by any other person of, any such grave breach of any of the scheduled conventions . . . shall be guilty of felony. . . ." Geneva Conventions Act, 1957, 5 & 6 Eliz. 2, c. 52, § 1; see Geneva Conventions Act, Act No. 6 of 1960, § 3 (India).
72. Yingling and Ginnane, *The Geneva Conventions of 1949*, 46 AM. J. INT'L L. 393, 425-26 (1952).

Though the liability of a member of the South Vietnamese Army who has committed, or ordered to be committed, a grave breach is clear, the duties of an American adviser who is not so closely tied to the chain of command is presently unclarified. The United States requires in situations like the South Vietnamese conflict that its forces "encourage" their local allies to apply the provisions of Article 3.[73] So long as American advisers follow this directive, they will be free from the criminal sanctions now in effect. If, however, a U. S. adviser suggested mistreatment of a Viet Cong prisoner, or perhaps if he were silent at a time when his government and the South Vietnamese expected some opinion, he might well be found guilty of violating the Geneva Conventions Acts passed by some countries.[74]

Should the Viet Cong wish to try any captive who falls into its hands, it would be met by the serious obstacle that it has no competent tribunal for this purpose, since there is no territory over which it is recognized as the valid government.[75] It might still attempt either of two possible routes. First, by an accession to the Convention, the Viet Cong National Liberation Front would at least be identifiable before this international body.[76] Arguably this would allow the Viet Cong to establish a court for the purposes of Convention violations only. On the other hand, it is likely that without a more explicit statement, the Convention did not intend to *confer* jurisdiction in any signing group. It is doubtful furthermore whether such an international body has the authority to confer such power over the nationals of a particular state.[77]

The second possibility is that the Viet Cong might take its prisoners across the border to a competent municipal tribunal in Cambodia or North Vietnam. At international law prisoners of war who are brought under detention into a neutral country are ipso facto considered free.[78] This principle would surely be applicable where the "prisoners" are Article 3 detainees. Moreover, since the captives can no longer be detained by the insurgent group but are now in the charge of an independent nation, they are guaranteed the

---

73. U.S. DEP'T OF THE ARMY, FM 100-20, FIELD SERVICE REGULATIONS: COUNTERINSURGENCY (U) para. 61(b)(1) (1964).
74. See British statute in note 71 *supra*.
75. An insurgent force has no authority to convene courts and there appears no way by which it can try either captives or convention violators according to the standards of a duly and regularly constituted court of justice. Kelly, *Legal Aspects of Military Operations in Counterinsurgency*, 21 MIL. L. REV. 95, 117 (Dep't of the Army Pam. 27-100-21, 1963).
76. Such an accession was made by the Algerian forces fighting against the French in 1960. By this act they sought the protection and privileges of Article 3 of the Convention. BEDJAOUI, LAW AND THE ALGERIAN REVOLUTION 217-20 (1961).
77. In *In re Piracy Jure Gentium*, [1934] A.C. 586, at 589 (P.C.), Lord Sankey said, "With regard to crimes defined by international law, that law has no means of trying or punishing them."
78. 2 OPPENHEIM, INTERNATIONAL LAW 718 (7th ed. Lauterpacht ed. 1952).

treatment traditionally accorded to prisoners of war. The rights of South Vietnamese and U. S. soldiers would then be separable, in the sense that the United States itself could sue the detaining power for a denial of justice to its accused advisers and for their return if acquitted.[79]

B. Article 4—capture of "prisoners of war"

Though the struggle in Vietnam today is, in many respects, not carried on according to the conventional methods of traditional warfare, it is an armed conflict, and it is not infrequent that captives are taken by both sides. When this occurs there arises the type of situation for which the Convention was designed.

The 143 articles of the Convention provide for a high degree of comfort and the maximum of humane and civilized treatment that can be conceived in war conditions. Within these articles are found specific and detailed descriptions of the treatment to which each captive is entitled.[80]

1. The conservative approach.

According to the conservative interpretation of the Convention, without a confrontation between members of armed forces of two or more "national entities" there are no prisoners of war, and captives will not be accorded the benefits of the full Convention.[81] In Vietnam there are three persons to whom Article 4 treatment will be extended: a soldier of the North Vietnamese government who is captured by South Vietnamese troops, and members of the South Vietnamese or United States armed forces who are captured and held by North Vietnamese troops.[82]

---

79. BRIERLY, THE LAW OF NATIONS 276-77 (6th ed. 1963).
80. See generally PICTET, COMMENTARY ON THE GENEVA CONVENTION RELATIVE TO THE TREATMENT OF PRISONERS OF WAR (1960).
81. The Convention uses the terms "armed forces of a Party" and "regular armed forces" of an unrecognized "government" or "authority" in the enumeration of persons to whom Article 4 treatment should be accorded. Convention art. 4A(1), (3). However, since the Convention was intended to operate without changing the legal status of the parties, it will not be applied without some recourse to the traditional notion of a state or nation. By avoiding reference to these terms the Convention may in the end emphasize the difficulty of using these terms in the area of prisoner of war treatment, but for now with the exception of Article 3 the status of a captive depends upon the legitimacy of the authority directing him.
82. According to Pictet, the drafters of the Convention meant that it should make "no difference how long the conflict lasts, how much slaughter takes place, or how numerous are the participating forces; it suffices for the armed forces of one Power to have captured adversaries falling within the scope of Article 4." PICTET, op. cit. supra note 80, at 23. There is some authority that in the context of an insurgency, foreign troops fighting against the established government should not be accorded Article 4 treatment. See Kelly, supra note 75, at 112. However the intention of the drafters seems to support the application of Article 4 on the basis of the character of the captive and the position of the detaining power. Cf. id. at 112-13.
    In addition to this lack of a legitimate "national identity," the Viet Cong

There are two problems in applying the Convention to a situation such as the Vietnam conflict. The first difficulty is that even though both North and South Vietnam have signed the Convention,[83] each claims to represent the whole of Vietnam.[84] Therefore each might refuse to accord Article 4 treatment to the other's forces on the ground that the other party is not the legitimate authority over the area under its control. But the Convention has clearly rejected this very conservative approach to the treatment of prisoners of war, which would require mutual recognition between the parties involved.[85] Since the application of Article 4 was meant to depend upon facts outside of formal recognition, it is not unreasonable, and it will be assumed for purposes of discussion, that the full Convention should apply where North Vietnam and South Vietnam are concerned.

The other difficulty is that the sending of United States advisers even at the invitation of the South Vietnamese government may be a violation of present international law.[86] Even assuming that a par-

---

have generally avoided all confrontations with the established government which might be considered conventional armed conflicts. For this reason it is thought that the Viet Cong would not be considered "regular armed forces" within the terms of the Convention. See ROSENAU, INTERNATIONAL ASPECTS OF CIVIL STRIFE 205 (1964).

83. See PICTET, *op. cit. supra* note 80, at 9.

84. North and South Vietnam were established under the Geneva Pact not as separate states but as "regrouping areas" for the troops of both sides after the French forces departed in 1954. See Agreement on the Cessation of Hostilities in Vietnam, July 20, 1954, art. 14, GENEVA CONF. DOC. No. IC/42/Rev. 2, in 1 AMERICAN FOREIGN POLICY: 1950-1955 BASIC DOCUMENTS 750, 755. The established governments of each of the areas has thus been free to claim that in a legal sense it is the government which represents the whole territory of Vietnam.

In a more practical sense, the recognized facts of separate governments and armies, a well-delineated border and vast political differences provide a sound basis for the two-nation approach. As one commentator has said, "if such [armistice] lines have been long continued and widely recognized, as have those in Germany, Palestine, Kashmir, Korea, Vietnam and the Straits of Formosa, they assume the character of international boundaries." Wright, *International Law and Civil Strife*, [1959] AM. SOC'Y INT'L L. PROC. 145, 151. Professor Lauterpacht apparently also considers North Vietnam and South Vietnam as separate states. 1 OPPENHEIM, *op. cit. supra* note 78, at 258. The United States has implied that North Vietnam is a separate national entity, capable of committing aggression upon South Vietnam in recent official publications of the United States. See WHITE PAPER, *supra* note 53.

85. Convention art. 4A(3). This provision was meant to reverse the strict approach adopted by the Germans and Vichy French under which the Free French Forces of General DeGaulle were not to be accorded prisoner of war status when captured. See PICTET, *op. cit. supra* note 80, at 62.

86. The most suspect activity undertaken by the United States under its aid program to South Vietnam, and that most likely to bring Americans into the hands of North Vietnamese soldiers, is the recent bombing of North Vietnamese bases. See N.Y. Times, Feb. 8, 1965, p. 1, col. 8 (city ed.). Although the infiltration of Viet Cong forces by the North Vietnamese is thought to justify the presence of American advisers, N.Y. Times, May

ticular national action violates international law [87] or that a soldier himself contravenes the laws of war, the Convention prohibition of taking reprisal measures against captives [88] demands that other means must be found to redress these violations. Whether the United States has in fact committed aggression in Southeast Asia is an issue outside the scope of this note.[89]

2. Problems in the conservative approach.

The presence of North Vietnamese soldiers in South Vietnam, advising and fighting with the Viet Cong, is a fact not now conclusively established but assumed for purposes of discussion.[90] Even silence by the North Vietnamese government concerning their presence should not affect the Article 4 status of these soldiers, since that is an issue between the two governments and not between a government and an individual.[91] The conception of the North Vietnamese soldier as legally subject to his own state even while fighting side-by-side with the Viet Cong, leads to an interesting and revealing hypothetical, or perhaps actual, problem in applying the Convention to such a situation.

Consider the plight of two uniformed [92] combatants, one a North

---

26, 1962, p. 1, col. 2 (opinion of the International Control Commission), this factor has been criticized as too tenuous to justify bombing the North under either the United Nations Charter or the Geneva Pact, N.Y. Times, March 4, 1965, p. 10, col. 1 (city ed.) (Times news comment); id., March 9, 1965, p. 3, col. 6 (city ed.) (opinion of the International Control Commission).

87. There has been some discussion indicating that the outlawing of aggression should necessarily imply that all persons engaged in furthering the struggle who know that this is an aggressive war should be criminally liable. In re Hirota, [1948] Ann. Dig. 356, 373 (No. 118) (separate opinion by the President). But this view has been criticized, and is certainly not a realistic proposal under the present strong pressures of nationalism. See Dunbar, Act of State in the Law of War, 8 JURID. REV. (n.s.) 246, 261 & n.48 (1963).

88. Convention art. 13. See also art. 1.

89. For discussion of the implications of United States policies in Southeast Asia, see authorities cited in note 86 supra; Comment, The United States in Vietnam: a Case Study in the Law of Intervention, 50 CALIF. L. REV. 515, 528-29 (1962).

90. See WHITE PAPER, supra note 53, at 30, col. 4.

91. Aggression has traditionally been the subject of claims between states only, even where one state has refused to enter into negotiations or assume responsibility. Because South Vietnam is under a duty to apply the Convention to members of armed forces as defined in Article 4, even in the absence of a declared war, these North Vietnamese prisoners are immune from reprisals for belligerent acts they performed for their country. See HINGORANI, PRISONERS OF WAR 14, 76-77 (1963).

92. It might be argued that where a foreign soldier is caught without his uniform he will not be accorded the rights under Article 4 which he would have received were he wearing his uniform. It should not matter, however, whether it is his own country's or a rebel uniform. Where, as in South Vietnam, the conflict has developed to the point where the Viet Cong markings are well known and fairly standard, of what difference during a battle is the fact that a North Vietnamese soldier has his own uniform or

Vietnamese soldier and the other a native of South Vietnam, acting in concert on a terrorist mission in South Vietnam, who are captured by government forces. According to the Convention the North Vietnamese soldier, because he was engaged in an "international conflict" and because of his recognizable military posture, would be entitled to the full benefits of the entire Convention under Article 4. However, the Viet Cong rebel would receive at most the minimal protections of Article 3. By the terms of the Convention he occupies an inferior status to his compatriot and accomplice. But it is neither reasonable nor just to say that the same offense committed by both men is in one case an act of hostility by a foreign country and in the other merely part of a "conflict not of an international character."

There are three arguments which may be put forth to justify disparities in the treatment of persons who are outwardly indistinguishable. First, it may be said that the North Vietnamese captive is the citizen of a foreign state whereas the Viet Cong is rebelling against the established government. The former because of his international posture as a military representative of another state, is entitled to a higher degree of treatment. The Viet Cong captive on the other hand does not deserve more than the minimum of humane treatment, for he is merely violating the criminal laws of his own country. Persuasive as these conceptions may be, such a disparity of treatment for two men who have engaged in the same belligerent act is contrary to the humanitarian aims of the Convention, especially where both men may have been acting under the same directive and for the same reasons.

The second argument presents the idea that whereas the North Vietnamese soldier has been compelled by military discipline and training to participate in the conflict that has resulted in his capture, the South Vietnamese insurgent has taken up arms against his government by his own volition.[93] However it seems certain that the

---

a Viet Cong one? After capture, if the North Vietnamese can be identified as foreign military personnel, there seems little reason for according less than Article 4 status. An analogous situation developed in the Korean conflict, where soldiers of various nationalities, wearing their own uniforms, were acting under the authority of the U.N. but were still accorded Article 4 treatment. See Dulles, *Statement on the Geneva Conventions of 1949*, 33 DEP'T STATE BULL. 72, 76 (1953). Note also that the United States, as a matter of national law, does not prohibit its soldiers from using the enemy's uniform "as a ruse". U.S. DEP'T OF THE ARMY, FM 27-10, THE LAW OF LAND WARFARE para. 54 (1956). It is unlikely that international law or the Convention will protect a soldier in that event. See HINGORANI, *op. cit. supra* note 91, at 29.

93. Evidence shows that this is not an accurate representation of the facts in South Vietnam. The Viet Cong rebels have been supported by a "hard core" of former South Vietnamese residents who have been thoroughly indoctrinated by the North Vietnamese in Communist doctrines of revolutionary warfare, and who have used coercive means to recruit native South Vietnamese into their clandestine activities. WHITE PAPER, *supra* note 53, at 30, cols. 3, 7-8.

drafters of the Convention, concerned as they were with only the principles of humane treatment,[94] did not intend to have the great difference between Article 3 and Article 4 treatment turn upon a distinction between military discipline and the indoctrination into, or choice of, a particular political viewpoint.

The third line of reasoning which would seek to sustain the difference in treatment between the two captives is perhaps the most persuasive. It deals with the practical difficulties involved in providing the same treatment to both. In a small country beseiged with political instability and entangled in a serious civil conflict with the practical problem of lack of means to support the necessary camps and special facilities weighs heavily against affording full Convention treatment to captured rebels as well as to foreign soldiers who are taken prisoner. Even more important to the established government is the deterrent effect of the South Vietnamese criminal laws on Viet Cong activities. Of prime importance in this sphere is the reduction and prevention of further voluntary enlistment by its own subjects into the rebel forces. However, in a situation like the one in South Vietnam, which has grown to such proportions and which is a matter of considerable concern to the major powers of the world, these practical and local difficulties should not be used to defend what would otherwise be an unjust result.

One way in which the situation in Southeast Asia could be ameliorated would be to establish a regional judicial body. Such a tribunal would afford the would-be, or actual, insurgent an alternative to insurgency, if his complaint before this body indicated that he was motivated by sincere and reasonable political beliefs for which he could find no legitimate means of expression in his own country.[95] Of course, it would have no power to reprove the established government in any direct sense, but it could suggest remedies to the political authorities and if necessary, provide for the complainant's transportation to a country more inclined to allow the expression of his particular beliefs.

Another approach to the problem is to eliminate the disparity of treatment by providing for the compulsory invocation of additional Convention provisions when the insurrection has reached a certain

---

94. For a variety of internal reasons the drafters of the Convention did not express at any one point the motives which brought them together. It can be assumed that these motives were not unlike those behind the 1929 Geneva Convention which endeavored to ameliorate the hardships of war and alleviate the fate of prisoners of war. See PICTET, op. cit. supra note 80, at 12-16.

95. A U.N. team acted in a capacity similar to that proposed here a short time before the revolt against the Diem Regime. Pursuant to charges by some countries of "violations of human rights," N.Y. Times, Sept. 13, 1963, p. 1, col. 8, and with initial approval from the Saigon government, the U.N. team in fact held open hearings before which any citizen of South Vietnam was invited to come and make his complaint against his government, id., Oct. 27, 1963, p. 24, col. 1.

clearly defined level. To meet the challenge of the international civil war it is important to amend the Convention so as to encompass unequivocally the kind of situation discussed above.

But in amending the Convention to automatically bring in more of its articles, care must be exercised to see that none of the additional provisions encroach upon certain prerogatives traditionally and exclusively thought to be associated with sovereign states. The right of repatriation and some aspect of communications privileges [96] could conceivably imply the existence of sovereignty or nationality to an insurgent force or a rebel authority.

3. The liberal application.

There is some authority for applying, even without amendment, the full benefits of the Convention to an insurgent group when its army has satisfied the four conditions of Article 4 A (2) and its "government" has been substantially recognized throughout the world as the representative of the people.[97] The basis for this interpretation of the Convention comes mainly from the implication that the major part of the Convention deals with conflicts of an international character, and the view that this does not require that every such conflict be an international war in the traditional sense before the full Convention becomes applicable.[98] This is generally recognized not to have been the intention of the drafters of the Convention,[99] but Pictet suggests that the application of provisions outside Article 3 only by voluntary

---

96. The term repatriation is bound up in the concept of two *nations* trading or exchanging their captives. As such it in most cases would be unsatisfactory in the eyes of the established government, which could not impart even this relatively small recognition of nationhood to the insurgent authority. Unfortunately the Convention uses only the term repatriation, but this should not prevent an agreement outside the Convention for an exchange of captives. The privilege of a prisoner to communicate with the outside world has been and could be further achieved, under the auspices of the Red Cross, without the implication that a rebel authority has the authority to receive and dispatch postal or other communications as would inhere in a sovereign state.

97. See ALGERIAN OFFICE, WHITE PAPER ON THE APPLICATION OF THE GENEVA CONVENTIONS OF 1949 TO THE FRENCH-ALGERIAN CONFLICT 23-25 (1960).

98. Article 4 is construed to include "organized resistance movements operating in or outside their own territory, even if this territory is occupied," provided they meet the following four conditions: a responsible commander, fixed sign, the carrying of open arms, and operations in accordance with the laws of war. *Id.* at 24.

99. The United States was in fact the sponsor of an alternate to Article 3 which would have applied the entire Convention when the insurgents have a state-like organization, exercise de facto control over the persons within a determinate territory, direct their forces in accordance with the laws of war, and agree to be bound by the provisions. Yingling and Ginnane, *supra* note 72, at 395, citing 2B FINAL RECORD OF THE DIPLOMATIC CONFERENCE OF GENEVA OF 1949 at 128. The debates clearly show that the compromise finally adopted was intended to reject this application of the full Convention. Yingling and Ginnane, *supra* note 72, at 396.

agreements is unrealistic in view of the humanitarian purposes of the Convention as a whole.[100]

In both the American Civil War,[101] and the French conflict in Indo-China,[102] both sides recognized the traditional rules for treatment of regular prisoners of war, even where there was no formal recognition of belligerency. In Algeria, although there is evidence that the French did not grant the A.L.N. (Army of National Liberation) even Article 3 treatment,[103] the rebels applied the Convention liberally to suggest that they should be accorded not only Article 3 but also Article 4 status.[104]

Without the weight of an opinion by some competent international body, there are few factors which would be satisfactory to indicate that an insurrection has acquired an "international character." The mere joining of foreign soldiers with the insurgents is of precarious value, by itself, as a test of the character of the conflict.[105] Neither should it matter that the South Vietnamese government has deemed it expedient to adopt an "open arms" policy,[106] under which Viet Cong who have been drafted involuntarily may now surrender their arms without punishment. This is certainly an indication of the gravity of the insurrection, but if this legislation is going to be used as a criterion for applying the full Convention, it could conceivably prevent the established government from enacting the ameliorating legislation at all.

Nor do the more external aspects of the situation appear to be acceptable to most nations for determining the character of the conflict. The fact that a nation has recognized the insurgents does not of itself give the insurgents any greater rights against the established government.[107] However, recognition as a state by many countries, is important evidence that the insurgent group is responsible enough to be accorded Article 4 status.[108] Similarly, when the established government invites foreign assistance, either in an advisory

---

100. PICTET, *op. cit. supra* note 80, at 42.
101. See FOOKS, PRISONERS OF WAR 280 (1934).
102. See N.Y. Times, April 14, 1954, p. 2, col. 3.
103. See ALGERIAN OFFICE, *op. cit. supra* note 97, at 26-55; BEDJAOUI, *op. cit. supra* note 76, at 214.
104. See ALGERIAN OFFICE, *op. cit. supra* note 97, at 23-25.
105. The presence of foreign troops should not be the only criterion for applying the full Convention to the insurrectionists. Were that the only criterion, a neighboring country might appear benevolent before the world by sending its own troops to fight with the insurrectionists in order to gain them Article 4 status. This moral escalation would be of doubtful value, and in direct conflict with well-recognized legal principles against intervention.
106. See The Judge Advocate General's School (U.S. Dep't of the Army), Law and Population Control in Counterinsurgency, Jan. 1965, pp. 150-57; Richmond Times-Dispatch, April 17, 1963, p. 15, col. 2.
107. In fact, it is generally recognized that a premature recognition by one nation of the belligerent status of insurgents in another nation would be a tort at international law. Yingling and Ginnane, *supra* note 72, at 395.
108. See ALGERIAN OFFICE, *op. cit. supra* note 97, at 24.

capacity [109] or for purposes of bombing rebel-held territory,[110] the conflict begins to assume an international character. Such a closely guarded political prerogative, however, can be only one of several relevant factors.

It has been suggested that the nature and comparative establishment of the insurgent authority, along with the response it receives from the people in the areas it controls, should be decisive factors in determining the status accorded members of its armed forces who are captured by the established government.[111] Particularly where the structure and tactics of the rebel establishment are "directed" by sources outside the country, there are good reasons for according greater rights to the unfortunate captives of military conflicts with the established government.[112]

Even though there may be a sufficient criterion among the factors above to decide when a conflict has acquired an "international character," there is still the question of what kind of body would be capable of determining the facts and their legal effect. Because of their

---

109. See note 21 *supra*.

110. See, *e.g.*, N.Y. Times, March 12, 1965, p. 1, col. 2 (city ed.).

111. See note 39 *supra* and accompanying text; Powers, *Insurgency and the Law of Nations*, 16 JAG J. 55, 57 (Office of the Judge Advocate General of the Navy, 1962). *Cf.* Green, *The Status of Rebel Armies*, 3 U. MALAYA L. REV. 25, 33 (1961) (the restored government is liable for postal orders issued by a rebel authority in effective control of a part of the state), citing *The Tinoco Concessions*, 1 U.N. Rep. Int'l Arb. Awards 369 (1923). But note that the requirement of organization should not be applied too strictly where the guerillas are vying initially for status under Article 3. Greenspan, *supra* note 59, at 34.

112. The presence of North Vietnamese troops in South Vietnam and the propaganda, infiltration and probable direction by the Hanoi government indicate at the least a foreign agitation of local instability. As a part of a plan of international aggression and domination it can hardly be denied that in reality the Viet Cong in South Vietnam are involved in a struggle of international consequences approaching an armed conflict of an "international character." *Cf.* note 21 *supra;* Kelly, *supra* note 75, at 116 & n.81.

It is possible that there is yet another possibility intermediate between an "international civil war" as defined here and the traditional category of a civil insurrection against an established government. Inherent in the proposal for a judicial body open to complaints against the government (see text accompanying note 95 *supra*) is an understanding that there may be factions within a state which have political beliefs in common with some of the operating governments of the world, but whose only means of expressing them is by a resort to force. From the position of *ad hoc* international justice it would seem that the participants of such an intermediate type struggle ought to be accorded better treatment than either a traditional insurrectionist who may have no constructive suggestion for the operation of the government of his state, or a rebel who is merely following the directives of a foreign power attempting to impose its own form of government. International law, being dependent on national status, does not presently seem to recognize such a situation. Only at rare and distant moments in history does such an initial basis for revolt gain a means of expression. *Cf.* U.S. DECLARATION OF INDEPENDENCE (1776).

political implications, determinations at the national level would not be entirely free from doubt.[113] On the international level, we may ask whether there is as yet an appropriate authority.

4. Present international machinery.

At present there is no international body which has been entrusted by the nations of the world with sufficient power to deal with any violations of the right to fair treatment. The International Red Cross has, of course, done a splendid job whenever it has been given a chance by the parties involved to perform its humanitarian tasks.[114] In Vietnam, however, it has been hampered by inability to find a responsible Viet Cong representative.[115] Moreover, the impartiality [116] necessary for performing its functions precludes the Red Cross from being employed as a fact-finding body.[117] Other bodies more intimately connected with the legal relationships between states have been hampered by lack of authority and the general vagueness so often surrounding the policies and positions of the parties concerned in situations like Vietnam. Neither the services of a Protecting Power envisioned by the Convention,[118] the International Control Commission [119] nor the United Nations [120] have proved effective in clarifying the situation.

In addition to this lack of appropriate remedial machinery, there is a definite incompleteness in attempting to apply humanitarian principles without defining the legal effect of other acts which necessarily accompany such conflicts. One of the cornerstones of the Convention is that there shall be no reprisals against prisoners or de-

---

113. *But see* PICTET, *op. cit. supra* note 80, at 43. Pictet, citing no examples in which the Convention has been applied, seems to be underestimating the force of national opinion when he refers to "an existing situation which neither of the parties can deny." *Ibid.*

114. A brief discussion of the activities of the International Committee of the Red Cross in recent world conflicts ranging from the Mau-Mau rebellion to the Hungarian revolt is found in JOYCE, RED CROSS INTERNATIONAL 167-90, 197-205 (1959). The Convention specifically provides for the agency of the Red Cross and gives it special standing in Articles 3, 125, and 126.

115. See note 68 *supra*.

116. PICTET, *op. cit. supra* note 80, at 601.

117. The great respect the Red Cross commands and much of its effectiveness is due to its rigid observance of neutrality and impartiality in performing its exclusively humanitarian services. Were it to become embroiled in disputes as a fact-finding tribunal it would inevitably risk the loss of some if not most of its effectiveness.

118. Convention art. 8. "The Protecting Power is a neutral State who has received a mandate from the captee State to look after the welfare of the latter's captured personnel." HINGORANI, *op. cit. supra* note 91, at 179.

119. See WHITE PAPER *supra* note 53, at 30, col. 2; N.Y. Times, May 23, 1964, p. 3, col. 1.

120. The Secretary-General has said that "there are many difficulties in the way of attempting a United Nations solution to the problem in view of its past history and the fact that some of the principal parties are not represented in the United Nations." N.Y. Times, Feb. 13, 1965, p. 6, col. 1 (city ed.).

tainees.[121] The strains on this principle are evident in cases in which there have been bombings of rebel-held civilian areas, a subject outside the purview of the Convention, by the forces of the established government or its allies. Another important provision, the presumption that if a captive's status under Article 4 is in doubt he receives the full benefits of the Convention,[122] does not seem to have been voluntarily applied to cover possible Article 3 situations.[123] In a similar fashion the unreasonable difference in treatment accorded the two men in the hypothetical situation discussed above can be explained only by the serious dependence of the Convention on municipal laws, like the "open arms" policy, to redress any such unfairness.

Lastly, the Convention has been attacked for not having recognized and coordinated its efforts with other machinery and international pacts already in existence.[124] The fact that the Convention has been tacitly recognized to apply universally to signatories and non-signatories alike [125] gives rise to the hope that eventually a coordinated effort will result in an effective guarantee of freedom for everyone from unfair treatment by governing authorities of every character.

5. Proposal for an international criminal court.

That crimes against international law are committed by men, and not abstract entities, is now recognized by international law.[126] This is in accord with the spirit of the Convention, which in providing for the possibility of universal jurisdiction over certain grave offenses has emphasized that the suppression of crime is an interest common to all states and all mankind.[127] It seems likely that the ideal of ridding the world of aggression could be greatly enhanced by establishing better means of impressing all people with the standards under which armed hostilities of any kind may be carried out, and by enforcing these standards at the supra-national level.

The Convention itself requires the signatories "to include the study [of the text of the Convention] in their programmes of military and, *if possible,* civil instruction." [128] (Emphasis added.) The United

---

121. Article 13 provides that "measures of reprisal against prisoners of war are prohibited." See also PICTET, *op. cit. supra* note 80, at 141-42.
122. Article 5 states that the captive shall enjoy the protection of the full Convention until his status has been determined by a competent tribunal.
123. *Cf.* JOYCE, THE RED CROSS INTERNATIONAL 170 (1959) (on the Hungarian revolt).
124. Jenks, *The Conflict of Law-Making Treaties,* 30 BRIT. YB. INT'L L. 401, 416 (1953); *cf.* Lauterpacht, *The Problem of Revision of the Law of War,* 29 BRIT. YB. INT'L L. 360, 380 (1952).
125. The North Koreans, Communist China, the United States, and the Soviet Union by applying the Convention in the Korean conflict all tacitly assumed the Convention was "binding law irrespective of treaty obligations." GREENSPAN, THE MODERN LAW OF LAND WARFARE 96 n.4 (1959).
126. 1 TRIALS OF THE MAJOR WAR CRIMINALS BEFORE INT'L MILITARY TRIBUNAL, NUREMBERG, 223 (1947).
127. Jennings, *Extraterritorial Jurisdiction and the United States Antitrust Laws,* 33 BRIT. YB. INT'L L. 146, 156 (1957).
128. Convention art. 127.

States has been criticized for not adequately preparing its own troops in the use of the Convention,[129] and it appears that there are no countries which have trained their own civilians.[130] One suggestion is that the International Red Cross be allowed to assure that there is proper instruction of persons who might some day be required to apply the Convention, as a deterrent to individual violation of its provisions. Moreover, a universal dissemination of the Convention may aid in the understanding among all peoples that certain acts may not be done even if sanctioned and carried out under the authority of a nation. The power of informed public opinion could be a serious deterrent to the mobilization of popular support for the use of inhumane methods of warfare by national leaders bent on destroying any threat to their power.

Authorities have suggested that the Convention as it stands is an invitation to the establishment of the legal machinery necessary to guarantee the operation of its humanitarian principles.[131] The inevitable bias, or at least suspicion of bias, by a court at the national level makes it imperative to establish criminal jurisdiction at an international level.[132] If such a court were established, there would be no reason to limit its application strictly to the crimes enumerated by the Convention. Especially in the context of an armed conflict as in South Vietnam of such international import, it would be natural for it to assume jurisdiction over other acts of "officials" on both sides which contravene the laws of warfare, thus bringing within the purview of one authority all acts tending to promote reprisals against captives. Though the insurgents have traditionally not been accorded recognition at international law, this does not seem an insuperable obstacle to trying its leaders for violations of the Convention or other principles of warfare. The Convention itself has given some significant recognition to insurgents by referring to these groups as "parties" for the purposes of Article 3.[133] Even stronger acknowledgement is seen in the United States declaration that the Congolese rebels would be held "responsible" for mistreatment of the hostages, including American nationals, held by them.[134] The common principle behind these statements is that just as the heads of estab-

---

129. Baxter, *Forces for Compliance with the Law of War*, [1964] AM. SOC'Y INT'L L. PROC. 82, 86.
130. *Cf. ibid.*
131. HINGORANI, *op. cit. supra* note 91, at 229; McDOUGAL & FELICIANO, LAW AND MINIMUM WORLD PUBLIC ORDER 731 (1961).
132. Bridges, *The Case for an International Court of Criminal Justice and the Formulation of International Criminal Law*, 13 INT'L & COMP. L.Q. 1255, 1269 (1964).
133. Convention art. 3, para. 1. See PICTET, *op. cit. supra* note 80, at 37-38.
134. N.Y. Times, Nov. 18, 1964, p. 1, col. 4; see also Green, *supra* note 111, at 25 (citing *Ex parte* Choeldi, 26 Malaya L.J. 184 (1960) referring to "members of a Revolutionary Indonesian Organization bearing arms against the established Government of that country").

lished governments are held responsible for orders to their troops which violate international law, so also it would not be unreasonable to hold the leaders of an insurgency of sufficient size responsible for illegal orders which may so easily affect persons beyond the bounds of their own state. Whether on a regional level, or throughout the world, the establishment of an international criminal court would be indispensible to implement the high principles of the Geneva Convention.

Thus both in the publication of principles of humane treatment, and in the enforcement of these rights, the Convention has pointed the way toward an international guarantee of standards of conduct recognized by all peoples. Where as in Vietnam, an armed conflict has not only international repercussions but also a basic international orientation, the individuals most involved should not be placed at the mercy of the vicissitudes of modern military forces. The aspirations of the Convention hopefully will prompt nations to realize that for the sake of their own independence and for the protection of all people strict sovereignty must give way to the implementation necessary to promote international order.[135]

WADE S. HOOKER, JR.
DAVID H. SAVASTEN

---

135. "States today are not in the position to invoke their sovereignty in order to restrict or avoid the operation of international law. . . . In reality the concept of sovereignty has been replaced by independence under international law." Bridges, *supra* note 132, at 1272.

Law and the Conduct of the Vietnam War*

LAWRENCE C. PETROWSKI

I. Objectives of the Study

ASIDE from inhibiting recourse to war, a basic goal of international law is to confine the conduct of war within civilized bounds. The present conflict in Vietnam is a focal example of the failure of international law to fulfill this task—a failure resulting from its inability to keep pace with rapidly changing methods and technology of warfare, particularly the peculiar hybrid of guerrilla-conventional warfare common to international-civil wars** in our era. The principal objective of this study is to illustrate and accent that shortcoming, with the perhaps unrealistic hope that such an undertaking will contribute in some meaningful way to the greater effectiveness of the international law of war in future conflict situations.

Some understanding of the development and content of the law of war seems an essential part of the examination of the failure of the law of war in any single war. The international lawyer who wishes to promote the effectiveness of the law of war must undertake to clarify the law and the difficulties inherent in its application before making any attempt to recommend reforms that would be of benefit to all nations, weak as well as strong, primitive as well as advanced.

The initial step in the study of the role of the law of war in international-civil war is an examination of the role of such law in the more familiar category of international war, war between nations. The law of war arose to meet the conditions of international war; rules applicable to civil wars are mainly derivative from rules developed to regulate war between sovereign states.

II. The Development of the Law of War

Following the Thirty Years' War, an elaborate set of customary rules governing the conduct of states during war began to be developed. The

* This study is a revised version of a position paper, "Law and the Conduct of Internal War," prepared for the Civil War Panel of the American Society of International Law, mimeo., Washington, D.C., December 1967.
** The term international-civil war will be defined here to include those conflict situations characterized initially by civil war, and eventually including significant third-state intervention—particularly of materiel and armed forces—on the side of the incumbent and insurgent factions. Intervention is "significant" if it substantially prolongs the conflict.

necessity for that development was stressed by Hugo Grotius in a famous passage in the Prolegomena to his great treatise that appeared in 1625:

> Fully convinced by the considerations which I have advanced, that there is a common law among nations, which is valid alike for war and in war, I have had many weighty reasons for undertaking to write upon this subject. Throughout the Christian world I observed a lack of restraint in relation to war, such as even barbarous races should be ashamed of; I observed that men rush to arms for slight causes, or no cause at all, and that when arms have once been taken up there is no longer any respect for law, divine or human; it is as if, in accordance with a general decree, frenzy had openly been left loose for committing of all crimes.[1]

Avoidance of needless suffering and the unnecessary destruction of property were the principal justifications for the development of many of the rules regulating warfare. Reinforced by action in the form of reprisal, these rules generally were upheld by both sides in a conflict. In the planning of war strategy and in combat itself, the law was sometimes usurped when the dictates of military policy demanded. But nations took pains to legitimize their disobedience in terms of the very same system of law they had violated. Thus a violation was often justified under the label of reprisal. And, independent of the effectiveness of the law during war itself, nations were to find that that law was useful in determining which of the enemy were to suffer additional punishment as war criminals and how reparations were to be assessed at the end of war.

It is important to note that the law of war applied to the conflict regardless of who was the "aggressor," or who had "justice" on his side in going to war. It was apparent that making the availability of rights under the law depend on a state's "justness" in going to war, or duties under the law of war depend on a state's lack of justness in going to war would present insurmountable problems of interpretation. The most obvious of these problems arises from the absence of an acceptable method to determine the relative justness of the cause underlying the belligerency of each state participating in a given war. This difficulty underlies the limited role that has been played by the "just war" concept.

[1] Hugo Grotius, *De Jure Belli ac Pacis*, 1625, Prolegomena.

III. The "Just War" Concept

The idea of distinguishing between "right" and "wrong" wars can be traced back to the writings of ancient Greece.[2] But it was the Romans, careful to make their wars legally correct, so as to legitimize them before the deity, who made the major contributions to the early development of the theory of *justum bellum*.[3] Although the Romans considered violence to be part of the natural order of man, recourse to arms was permitted only after an injury had been suffered and after the guilty party had refused to atone for the injury.[4] Building on this foundation, Roman contributions to the doctrine of *justum bellum* were largely procedural. Hall notes that Gentili cited Roman usage in support of the belief that "the voice of God and Nature" ordered men to openly declare war before commencing hostilities.[5] Grotius referred to the Roman roots of a demand for reparation in case of injury and notice of war if reparation was not given.[6]

Christianity added much to the substantive core of the just war concept passed on from the Romans. At first the Church challenged war as a consequence of original sin and allowed no Christians to become soldiers.[7] Eventually, however, the conversion of Constantine and the end of Christian persecution by the Roman army led to a relaxation of the pacific attitude of the Church, and war began to be looked upon as a necessity. Through the writings of St. Augustine the Christian purpose of a just war becomes not victory, but peace—maintenance of justice for the common good and restoration of ordered society.[8] The three fundamental characteristics of just war according to Augustine are: (1) that it be waged under the authority of a responsible leader of a nation, not by a private individual enjoying the support of only

[2] Joachim von Elbe notes: "Thucydides calls it a 'most awful act when men take vengeance upon an enemy and an aggressor.' Aristotle speaks of the 'art of war' which ought to be practiced 'against men who, though intended by nature to be governed, will not submit; for war of such kind is naturally just.' The object of war must be the establishment of peace. As to the causes of war, Plato finds 'at the roots of all wars' the necessity to enlarge our borders. 'The original healthy state is no longer sufficient. . . . The country which was enough to support the original inhabitants will be too small now.'" (footnotes omitted) Joachim von Elbe, "The Evolution of the Concept of the Just War in International Law," *A.J.I.L.*, 33 (1939), 665-66.

[3] *Ibid.*, p. 666.

[4] Morton A. Kaplan and Nicholas deB. Katzenbach, *The Political Foundations of International Law* (New York: John Wiley & Sons, Inc., 1961), p. 201.

[5] A. Pearce Higgins (ed.), *Hall's International Law* (8th edn., Oxford: Clarendon Press, 1924), p. 446.

[6] *Ibid.*   [7] von Elbe, note 2 *supra*, p. 667.

[8] *Ibid.*

part of that nation; (2) that it have a just cause to provoke it, i.e., that it be preceded by an unredressed injury; and (3) that in righting the wrong the belligerents use force proportional to the injury suffered.[9] St. Thomas Aquinas adds to the requirement of just cause the subjective test that the belligerents be animated by the right intention in going to war; that they advance the good and avoid the evil.[10] As a just cause for war, Aquinas requires not only injury suffered, but culpability which demands punishment on the part of the wrongdoer.[11]

With the breakup of the power of the Church and the coming of the Restoration, the concept of *justum bellum* undergoes subtle changes. The Spaniard Vittoria follows Augustine's teachings in evolving the medieval doctrine of the just war. He agrees that the only just cause for commencing war is an injury received, and adds the idea that war is an essential element of sovereignty.[12] Vittoria further contends that the case in which *both* parties are justified in going to war cannot occur, "for if the right and justice of each side be certain, it is unlawful to fight against it, either in offense or in defense."[13] "Invincible ignorance" on the part of those who wage objectively unjust war is, however, a "complete excuse."[14] Ayala agrees that in an objective sense only one side in any war is just, though subjectively a war might be just on both sides. Gentili believes it possible for both sides to be just, since the weakness of human nature does not allow acquaintance with the purest and truest form of justice and does not permit one side to question the contention of the other side that its cause is just.[15]

[9] *Ibid.*, and Kaplan and Katzenbach, note 4 *supra*, p. 202.

[10] von Elbe, note 2 *supra*, p. 669.   [11] *Ibid.*

[12] Kaplan and Katzenbach, note 4 *supra*, p. 202.

[13] Francisco de Vittoria, *De Jure Belli*, p. 177, and William B. Ballis, *The Legal Position of War: Changes in Its Practice and Theory from Plato to Vattel* (The Hague, 1937), p. 86. Cited in von Elbe, note 2 *supra*, p. 675, note 83. In the same note von Elbe points out: "Suarez, the other great founder of the Spanish school of international law, calls 'entirely absurd' the assumption that war may be just on both sides; for 'two rights contrary to each other cannot both be just.'"

[14] Vittoria, note 13 *supra*, p. 177: ". . . it may be that on the side where true justice is the war is just of itself while on the other side the war is just in the sense of being excused from sin by reason of good faith, because invincible ignorance is a complete excuse"; p. 186: ". . . princes . . . who in reality have no just cause of war, may nevertheless be waging war in good faith, with such good faith, I say, as to free them from fault; as, for instance, if the war is made after a careful examination and in accordance with the opinion of learned and upright men." Cited in von Elbe, note 2 *supra*, p. 675, note 84.

[15] von Elbe, note 2 *supra*, pp. 676-77.

Attempting to restore the idea that justice lies on only one side in war, Grotius lists the just causes of war as he perceives them: defense, recovery of property, and punishment for wrongs inflicted. His unjust causes include the wish to rule others against their will on the pretext that it is for their own good, and the desire of one state to attain political independence of another.[16] In addition to this enumeration, Grotius conceives a role for the states not party to the controversy: they are expected to refrain from acting against the just state or for the unjust state.

The concept of the just war is thus given new life by Grotius. Yet, as he formulates it, the *justum bellum* theory contains many inherent faults. Grotius' belief that the "judgment" of neutral states would tend to support just causes and deter unjust wars assumed agreement on what the just cause was. But who was to determine when the cause was just, when defense was not preemptive attack or open "aggression," or when recovery of property was not simply expansionism? Machiavellian considerations showed the weakness of Grotius' thought as neutrals turned into participants espousing just causes on both sides of the conflict.[17]

Grotius' ideas on the role of neutrals are refined into a more useful doctrine by Pufendorf and Bynkershoek. Both consider the principle of just cause important as between the initial belligerents, but they maintain that it should not concern the neutrals, who were to do nothing to involve themselves in the war.[18] Vattel carries the concept of the just war even further out of the realm of law and into the realm of ethics and morality. While sovereigns should not go to war without just cause, according to Vattel, the presence or absence of this cause does not affect the legality of the war.[19]

Most writers of the nineteenth century continue to look upon war as a legitimate instrument of the sovereign, and the concept of the just war as a legal theory is abandoned until it reemerges in slightly differ-

---

[16] Grotius, note 1 *supra*, Bk. II, Chap. I, Sec. II.

[17] von Elbe, note 2, *supra*, pp. 679-80.

[18] *Ibid.*, pp. 680-81, and Kaplan and Katzenbach, note 4 *supra*, p. 204.

[19] Emmerick de Vattel, *The Law of Nations*, trans. of 1758, Fenwick (ed.), (Washington: Carnegie Institution, 1916), pp. 382, 386: ". . . the rights founded in the state of war, the lawfulness of its effects, the validity of the acquisitions made by arms, do not, externally and between mankind, depend on the justice of the cause, but on the legality of the means in themselves. . . . There would be no stability in the affairs of mankind, no safety in trading with nations engaged in war, if we were allowed to draw a distinction between a just and an unjust war, so as to attribute lawful effects to one which we denied to the other." Cited in von Elbe, note 2 *supra*, p. 683, note 142.

ent form in the Nuremberg era.[20] These writers contend that since sovereign states are equal, no state can judge the others when it comes to the justness of their causes for war. War becomes an instrument of self-help in the hands of the sovereign. War becomes a fact question, not a law question, and the concept of justness is no longer useful in such a setting. When war exists, the law of war and neutrality comes into force regardless of the justice or injustice involved on competing sides. States thus shifted their concentration from the "right" to go to war to the range of actions allowed once that state of war is established, from the legality or justness of commencing war to the conduct of war itself.[21]

IV. The Current Law of War

The law of war is composed principally of customary rules, treaty rules, particularly multipartite agreements, national codes of warfare formulated by the principal powers and generally incorporating the aforementioned elements, and draft rules not adopted by states but having certain persuasive authority. Publication of recognized international law institutions such as the Institut de Droit International, the International Law Association, and the American Society of International Law also carry persuasive weight, as do the writings of noted international jurists.[22]

From its early history, the law of war is grounded in three balancing principles. First, the belligerent was believed justified in using any

[20] The concept of the just war was reincarnated in the London Agreement and its appended Charter of 1945 organizing the International Military Tribunal and setting forth certain categories of crimes for the Nuremberg trials. Among these crimes were the controversial "crimes against peace" which included the preparation, initiation, or waging of war of aggression; or a war in violation of international treaties, agreements, or assurances; or participation in a common plan or conspiracy for their accomplishment. Whether such crimes existed prior to the time of commission of the acts for which the defendants at Nuremberg were prosecuted is central to the criticism that Nuremberg applied *ex post facto* law on this point. The trials are discussed in more detail in Sections VII and VIII, *infra*.

[21] von Elbe, note 2 *supra*, pp. 684ff. Fenwick notes: "Where Grotius had appealed to broad principles of moral conduct, jurists now began to appeal to legal obligations binding upon nations by reason of established custom or the provisions of treaties." One must always "distinguish sharply between the legality of a resort to war and the legality of the ways and means by which war might be prosecuted once it had begun." Charles G. Fenwick, *International Law* (4th edn., New York: Appleton-Century Crofts, 1965), p. 650.

[22] For a general account of the history of the law of war, see Joseph L. Kunz, "The Chaotic Status of the Laws of War and the Urgent Necessity for Their Revision," *A.J.I.L.*, 45 (1951), 37-61, and Kunz, "The Laws of War," *A.J.I.L.*, 50 (1956), 313-37.

amount or kind of force to overcome the opposition. Second, a principle of humanity, developed out of the horrors of war in the Middle Ages, acted to restrain that first principle by demanding that the degree of force *necessary* to overcome the enemy not be exceeded. Third, the principle of chivalry was to be observed in order to introduce an element of "fairness" into warfare.[23]

A. TREATY RULES

Codification of the law of war into treaties incorporating these three principles to varying degrees took place for the most part after 1850. They cover instruments and methods of warfare, occupation of enemy territory, treatment of prisoners, intercourse between belligerents, and sanctions imposed for nonobservance of the rules of war. Among these codifications are:

1. The Declaration of Paris of 1856 on warfare at sea. It abolishes privateering, holds that a neutral flag protects noncontraband enemy goods and that noncontraband neutral goods under an enemy flag cannot be seized, and formulates the rule that a blockade must be effective to be binding.[24]

2. The Geneva Convention of 1864 on the amelioration of the condition of wounded soldiers in the field. A new Geneva Convention on the same subject was formulated in 1906. The principles of the Convention were adapted to maritime warfare by Conventions of the First and Second Hague Peace Conferences.[25]

3. The Declaration of St. Petersburg of 1868. It prohibits the use of projectiles under 400 grams (14 ounces) that are either explosive or charged with inflammable substances.[26]

4. The Hague Convention of 1899 on the law of land warfare enacted at the First Hague Peace Conference.[27]

[23] For discussion and references relating to the concept of military necessity and the conduct of war see Myres S. McDougal and Florentino P. Feliciano, *Law and Minimum World Public Order* (New Haven: Yale University Press, 1961), pp. 72ff., and William G. Downey, Jr., "The Law of War and Military Necessity," *A.J.I.L.*, 47 (1953), 251-62.

[24] For the text of the Declaration see Higgins and C. J. Colombos, *The International Law of the Seas* (4th edn., New York: Longmans, Green and Co., 1959), p. 1.

[25] For the text of the Convention see Higgins, *The Hague Peace Conferences* (Cambridge: Cambridge University Press, 1909), p. 8. Hereafter referred to as *Conferences*.

[26] For the text of the Declaration see *Conferences*, p. 5.

[27] For the text of the Convention see *Conferences*, p. 100, and William M. Molloy, *Treaties, Conventions, International Acts, Protocols and Agreements Between the United*

5. The Hague Declarations of 1899 and 1907 on expanding bullets, projectiles and explosives launched from balloons, and projectiles containing asphyxiating or deleterious gases.[28]

6. The Hague Conventions of 1907 enacted at the Second Hague Peace Conference. The "rules of war" codified in Convention IV of the Second Conference is a revision of the 1899 Convention and is understood to be supplemented by customary rules and usages.[29]

7. The Hague Conventions of 1907 on the laying of automatic submarine contact mines and the bombardment by naval forces in time of war.[30]

8. The Geneva Protocol of 1925 on the use of asphyxiating, poisonous, and other gases, and bacteriological warfare.[31]

9. The Geneva Conventions of 1929 on the treatment of sick and wounded prisoners of war.[32]

10. The London Protocol of 1936 on the use of submarines against merchant vessels.[33]

11. The London Agreement (with its appended Charter) of 1945, between the United States, Britain, France, and Russia, organizing the International Military Tribunal and setting forth categories of international crimes for the Nuremberg trials.[34]

12. The four Geneva Conventions of 1949 on (1) treatment of prisoners of war, (2) the amelioration of the condition of the wounded

---

States of America and Other Powers, 1776-1937 (Washington: 1910-1938), Vol. II, p. 2269. Hereafter referred to as Treaties.

[28] For the text of the Declarations see Conferences, pp. 484ff., and Robert L. Scott (ed.), Hague Conventions and Declarations of 1899 and 1907 (New York, 1915), p. 220. Hereafter referred to as Scott. Fenwick notes that none of the three declarations was at the time signed by a sufficient number of states to give them "general validity." Fenwick, note 21 supra, pp. 668-69 and notes.

[29] For the text of the Conventions see Scott.

[30] For the text of the Conventions see Conferences, p. 328, and Scott, p. 576.

[31] For the text of the Protocol see Manley O. Hudson (ed.), International Legislation (Washington, 1931-1950), Vol. III, p. 1670, and League of Nations Treaty Series (Geneva, 1920-1944), Vol. XC, p. 65. Hereafter referred to as League.

[32] For the text of the Conventions see Hudson, note 31 supra, Vol. V, p. 20.

[33] For the text of the Protocol see A.J.I.L., 31 (1937), Suppl., 137. For the relationship between the Protocol, the Treaty of Washington of 1922, and the London Naval Treaty of 1930, see Hersh Lauterpacht (ed.), Oppenheim's International Law (7th edn., London: Longmans, Green and Co., 1952), Vol. II, pp. 490-91.

[34] See note 81 infra.

and sick of armed forces in the field, (3) the amelioration of the condition of wounded and sick and shipwrecked members of the armed forces at sea, and (4) the protection of civilians during war.[35]

B. DRAFT RULES

Some draft rules, while not adopted as binding treaties among nations, nevertheless may contain formulations of generally recognized principles of international law expected to guide nations' conduct even if not adopted by them in the textual form of multipartite conventions. One such draft is the Hague Rules of Aerial Warfare completed in 1923 by a commission of international jurists.[36] The draft covers many of the special problems raised by air warfare, but its most important clauses, particularly Articles 22 and 24, regulate bombardment:

Article 22: Aerial bombardment for the purpose of terrorizing the civilian population, of destroying or damaging private property not of a military character, or of injuring non-combatants is prohibited.

Article 24: 1) Aerial bombardment is legitimate only when directed at a military objective—that is to say, an object of which the destruction or injury would constitute a distinct military advantage to the belligerent.

2) Such bombardment is legitimate only when directed exclusively at the following objectives: military forces; military works; military establishments or depots; factories constituting important and well-known centres engaged in the manufacture of arms, ammunition, or distinctively military supplies; lines of communication or transportation used for military purposes.

3) The bombardment of cities, towns, villages, dwellings or buildings not in the immediate neighborhood of the operations of land forces is prohibited. In cases where the objectives specified in paragraph (2) are so situated that they cannot be bombarded without the indiscriminate bombardment of the civilian population, the aircraft must abstain from bombardment.

[35] For the text of the Conventions see: *T.I.A.S.* 3362 (convention on wounded and sick members of the armed forces in the field) ; *T.I.A.S.* 3363 (convention on wounded, sick, and shipwrecked members of the armed forces at sea) ; *T.I.A.S.* 3364 (convention on prisoners of war) ; *T.I.A.S.* 3365 (convention on civilian prisoners in time of war).

[36] See J. M. Spaight, *Air Power and War Rights* (3rd edn., New York: Longmans, Green and Co., 1947), pp. 212-38, where the bombardment clauses are examined.

4) In the immediate neighborhood of the operations of land forces, the bombardment of cities, towns, villages, dwellings, or buildings is legitimate provided that the military concentration is sufficiently important to justify such bombardment, having regard to the danger thus caused to the civilian population.[37]

The draft is given added weight by the argument put forth in Article 62 that aerial warfare is only a particular means of conducting hostilities and as such is subject to the general rules of land warfare:

Except in so far as special rules are here laid down, and except also so far as the provisions of Chapter VII of these Rules or international conventions indicate that maritime law and procedure are applicable, aircraft personnel engaged in hostilities come under the laws of war and neutrality applicable to land troops in virtue of the customs and practice of international law and of various declarations and conventions to which the states concerned are parties.[38]

The same principle was applied earlier when the participants in the Hague Conference of 1907 failed to adopt a general convention governing the conduct of maritime warfare. Instead of formulating a code regulating sea warfare modeled after the Hague rules of land warfare, the powers agreed that the principles of land warfare should be applied to sea warfare.[39]

C. NATIONAL CODES

The Hague rules of land warfare first written in 1899 were not intended to be exhaustive, but were the basis upon which signatory nations were to frame supplementary instructions for the conduct of their armies. Article 1 of the Hague Convention declares: "The High Contracting parties shall issue instructions to their armed land forces, which shall be in conformity with the Regulations respecting the Laws and Customs of War on Land annexed to the present convention."[40] The model for the formulation of such national codes was the manual on "Instructions for the Government of the Armies of the United States in the Field," drafted by Dr. Francis Lieber during the American Civil War.[41] The purpose of the code, written for a largely

---

[37] *Ibid.*   [38] *Ibid.*   [39] See note 25 *supra.*
[40] For a citation to the text of the Convention see note 27 *supra.*
[41] James W. Garner, *International Law and World Order* (London: Longmans, Green and Co., 1920), Vol. I, pp. 2-3. (See also Section VI, the treatment of "War Crimes Trials," *infra.*

nonprofessional army, was to clarify existing rules of war and to set down regulations to meet particular exigencies presented by the conflict.

Other governments followed the example of the United States, as the Netherlands in 1871, France in 1877, Serbia in 1879, Spain in 1882, Portugal in 1890 and Italy in 1896 issued similar manuals.[42] After the Hague Conference of 1899 the major powers revised their codes. In 1902 the German general staff prepared the *Kriegsbrauch im Landkriege*, patterned on the somewhat harsh views—especially with regard to rights of belligerents—of the von Clausewitz school.[43] An additional feature of the German manual was its vague and often derisive references to the Hague Convention. This was in direct contrast to the French manual, *Les Loirs de la Guerre Continentale* (4th edn.) published in 1913, and the 1908 edition of "Laws and Customs of War on Land," issued by the government of Britain. Along with the revised American manual on the "Rules of Land Warfare," which appeared in 1914, the French and English codes embodied the provisions of the Hague Conventions of 1899 and 1907, which in turn drew heavily on Lieber's code of 1863.[44] A number of states also issued rules for the governance of their naval forces, although no such obligation was imposed by the Hague Conventions.[45]

These national codes as such are of course binding only upon the forces of the governments which issue them. They do, however, incorporate much of the law of war governing all nations and they have, in addition, as a body become important formulations of international law, filling the interstices left by multipartite agreements. Their publication by the major powers has led to their adoption in revised form by many other states seeking to codify clear and humane regulations governing the conduct of war.

D. CUSTOM

All other major sources of the international law of war incorporate to varying degrees the customary rules of war developed through usage over time. Some customary rules, according to Grotius, develop from the law of nature, "a dictate of right reason, which points out that an act, according as it is or is not in conformity with rational nature, has in it a quality of moral baseness or moral necessity, and that in conse-

---

[42] *Ibid.*, p. 3 and notes.   [43] *Ibid.*, p. 4.
[44] *Ibid.*, pp. 6-8.   [45] *Ibid.*, pp. 8-9.

quence, such an act is either forbidden or enjoined by the author of nature, God."[46]

That universally recognized rules underlying social conduct are meant to supplement codified laws governing the conduct of war is clearly stated in the preamble to the Hague Convention of 1899:

> Until a more complete code of the laws of war can be drawn up, the High Contracting Parties deem it expedient to declare that in cases not covered by the Rules adopted by them, the inhabitants and belligerents remain under the protection and governance of the principles of the law of nations, derived from the usages established among civilized peoples, from the laws of humanity, and from the dictates of public conscience.[47]

Following the same line of reasoning to hold that nations were bound to apply the principles of international conventions to which they had not acceded, the Nuremberg International Military Tribunal said in 1946:

> The rules of land warfare expressed in the Convention undoubtedly represented an advance over existing International Law at the time of their adoption. But the Convention expressly stated that it was an attempt "to revise the general laws and customs of war," which it thus recognized to be then existing, but by 1939 these rules laid down in the Convention were recognized by all civilized nations and were regarded as being declaratory of the laws and customs of war. . .[48]

A more recent reference to the importance of the unwritten law of war was made in 1963 in the case of *Shimoda and Others v. Japan.*[49] The District Court of Tokyo allowed the claimants, injured by the atomic bombing of Japan, no remedy when it upheld the custom of international law that individual citizens cannot sue governments, especially their own governments, unless such stipulations have been made

---

[46] Grotius, note 1 *supra*, Bk. I, Chap. I, Sec. 10.

[47] For a citation to the text of the Convention see note 27 *supra*.

[48] Judgment of the Tribunal, *Opinion and Judgment* (Washington, 1947), pp. 64, 125. The entire Judgment of 283 mimeographed pages is reproduced in *A.J.I.L.*, 41 (1947), 172-331.

[49] For a discussion of *Shimoda* and the opinion of the court see Richard A. Falk and Saul H. Mendlovitz (eds.), *The Strategy of World Order: Toward a Theory of War Prevention* (New York: World Law Fund, 1966), Vol. I, pp. 307ff., and Falk, *Legal Order in a Violent World* (Princeton: Princeton University Press, 1968), pp. 374-413.

in treaties. The court also said that it was neither possible nor necessary to conclude that international law forbids all uses of atomic weapons. However, it did intimate that the use of such weapons against cities would be illegal by noting that the attacks upon Hiroshima and Nagasaki caused such severe and indiscriminate injury to persons and property that they violated the most basic rules of the conduct of war:[50] ". . . it is not too much to say that the pain brought by the atomic bomb is severer than that from poison and poison-gas, and we can say that the act of dropping such a cruel bomb is contrary to the fundamental principle of the laws of war that unnecessary pain must not be given."[51] The court also gave added persuasiveness to the general principles embodied in the draft of the Hague Rules of Aerial Warfare when it added that: ". . . it is a long-standing, generally recognized principle in international law respecting air raids, that indiscriminate aerial bombardment is not permitted on an undefended city and that only aerial bombardments on military objective [sic] is permitted."[52]

V. The Conflict Among the Principles of War: Military Necessity v. Humanity and Chivalry

The three principles of warfare mentioned earlier—military necessity, humanity, and chivalry—set limits on each other's exercise and generally guide the use of force within civilized bounds when they are properly observed. Understanding the ease with which the doctrine of military necessity has often overbalanced the principles of humanity and chivalry is, however, not difficult.

First, a duality in military necessity should perhaps be recognized. McDougal argues that the concept of "necessary violence" embraces two related requirements: that of relevancy and that of proportionality:

Destruction is characterized as irrelevant when it is not directed toward the achievement of the legitimate objective specified. Clearly, such destruction is unnecessary in respect of such objective. Put a little differently, the relevancy of destruction refers to "the degree to which there was a definite and foreseeable connection between the act committed and the alleged military necessity." . . . Proportionality is commonly taken to refer to the relation between the amount of destruction effected and the military value of the objective sought in the operation being appraised. Disproportionate de-

[50] *Ibid.*
[51] Falk and Mendlovitz, note 49 *supra*, pp. 343-44.
[52] *Ibid.*, p. 340.

struction is thus, almost by definition, unnecessary destruction. Just as disproportion includes in its reference a whole continuum of degrees, so relevancy is a relative thing. (footnote omitted)[53]

McDougal further emphasizes that while the brutality of war cannot be eliminated, it can be limited: "All that can be derived from past formulations and experience is that the disproportion should be minimal and not gross, and that the connection between the destruction actually imposed and the objective postulated by the destroyer should be reasonably proximate and not remote."[54]

The concepts of proportionality and relevancy as checking devices built into the concept of military necessity would seem in turn to be aspects of the principles of humanity and chivalry that were earlier looked upon as external checks limiting the use of force to that quality and quantity necessary to overcome the enemy. The interaction of these principles guiding the use of force is noted in the preamble to the Hague Convention IV of 1907:

. . . being animated also by the desire to serve . . . *the interests of humanity* and ever-progressive needs of civilization; and thinking it important, with this object, to revise the general laws and customs of war, with the view on the one hand of defining them with greater precision, and on the other hand, of confining them within the limits intended to mitigate their severity as far as possible . . . these provisions, the drafting of which has been inspired by the desire to diminish the evils of war, *so far as military requirements permit,* are intended to serve as a general rule of conduct for the belligerents in their mutual relations and in their relations with the inhabitants. (emphasis added) [55]

The phrase "so far as military requirements permit" does not allow contracting parties to justify all their actions under the doctrine of military necessity. Article 22 of the Hague rules of land warfare provides that the right of belligerents to adopt means of injuring the enemy is not unlimited. Other articles of the agreement, such as Article 23 on poison and poisoned weapons, prohibit certain actions absolutely.[56] Where such positive rules apply, no plea of military necessity is legally permissible.[57]

---

[53] McDougal and Feliciano, note 23 *supra*, p. 524.   [54] *Ibid.*, p. 525.

[55] For a citation to the text of the Conventions see note 27 *supra*.

[56] For a discussion of these prohibitions see Morris L. Greenspan, *The Modern Law of Land Warfare* (Berkeley: University of California Press, 1959) , p. 314.

[57] For example, regarding the use of poison, the United States code of land warfare

Limits imposed by principles of international law on the doctrine of military necessity have in the past been challenged by a theory following the German proverb *Kriegsraison geht vor Kriegsmanier* (necessity in war overrules the manner of warfare) .[58] This formulation of military necessity claims that if the situation demands, the law of war can be usurped by the commander in the field.[59] This theory has been rejected by international commentators "because to accept it would withdraw the character of law from the laws of war."[60] As was noted in *United States v. List et al.*, the "Hostages Case":

They [the German Generals] invoke the plea of military necessity, a term which they confuse with convenience and strategic interests. Where legality and expediency have coincided, no fault can be found insofar as international law is concerned. But where legality of action is absent, the shooting of innocent members of the population as a measure of reprisal is not only criminal but it has the effect of destroying the basic relationship between the occupant and the population. Such a condition can progressively degenerate into a reign of terror. It is apparent from the evidence of these defendants that they considered military necessity, a matter to be determined by them, a justification of their acts. We do not concur in the view that the rules of warfare are anything less than they purport to be. Military necessity or expediency does not justify a violation of positive rules. International law is prohibitive law. . .[61]

VI. Problems in Applying the Law of War to War in General

The domestic or municipal law of nations is effective in its operation for a variety of reasons. First, most of the law governing the day-to-day relations of individuals within society is familiar to those individuals and is continually revised to meet the needs of that society. Second, any dispute arising over interpretation of the law or its application can readily be decided by a system of courts acting on facts brought be-

---

provides: "This prohibition extends to the use of means calculated to spread contagious diseases; but it does not prohibit measures being taken to dry up springs, to divert rivers and aqueducts from their course, or to contaminate sources of water by placing dead animals therein or otherwise, *provided such contamination is evident or the enemy is informed thereof.*" (emphasis added) United States Department of the Army, *The Law of Land Warfare* (FM 27-10) , (Washington: U.S. Government Printing Office, 1956) , par. 28.

[58] Lauterpacht, note 33 *supra*, pp. 231-33.   [59] *Ibid.*

[60] *Ibid.*, Fenwick, note 21 *supra*, p. 655, and Greenspan, note 56 *supra*, p. 314.

[61] XI Trials of War Criminals, pp. 1252-57. Cited by Downey, note 23 *supra*, p. 253.

fore it by both sides to such disputes. And third, while the majority of individuals submits voluntarily to law in the interest of an ordered society, those who would not or do not submit voluntarily are deterred from or punished for unlawful action by the threat or use of sanctions applied under that law. On each of these points the international law of war faces many difficulties in its operation.

A. LEGISLATING THE LAW OF WAR

Perhaps with the exception of the Geneva Conventions of 1949, the codified law of war remains decades behind the warfare it is designed to regulate. In writing of the period between the First and Second World Wars, Kunz notes that the neglect of the law of war was due to the influence of two opposing tendencies: ". . . the ideology of the extreme pacifists, well intentioned, good, but utterly utopian and the thinking of hard and shrewd people, who did not, like the first group, believe that war has been 'abolished,' but who wanted to keep their hands free as to the conduct of the next war."[62]

Widespread violation of the law of war in the Second World War did not deter the arguments of those opposed to its revision. In 1949 the International Law Commission reviewed the law of war but took note of the suggestion that: ". . . war having been outlawed, the regulation of its conduct had ceased to be relevant. The majority of the Commission declared itself opposed to the study of the problem at the present state. . . . It was considered that . . . public opinion might interpret its action as showing lack of confidence in the efficiency of the means at the disposal of the U.N. for maintaining peace."[63] Despite the provision of Article 13(1) (a) of its Charter, making it the task of the General Assembly to initiate studies and make recommendations for progressive revision of international law, the United Nations found itself following the course of the League of Nations in avoiding revision of the law of war.

Since the 1907 Hague Conventions applicable to land warfare in general, the few advances in the law of war have thus dealt with limited areas.[64] They include the Geneva Protocol of 1925 on gas, chemical and bacteriological warfare;[65] the Geneva Convention of 1929 for

---

[62] Kunz, "The Chaotic Status of the Laws of War," note 22 *supra*, p. 39.

[63] *Ibid.*

[64] For a description of the progress made in the development of the law of war from 1951 to 1956 see Kunz, "The Laws of War," note 22 *supra*, pp. 313-15.

[65] For a citation to the text of the Protocol see note 31.

the amelioration of the condition of the wounded and sick of the armies in the field;[66] and the London Protocol of 1936 on submarine warfare against merchant vessels.[67] (The London Agreement instituting the International Tribunal for the Nuremberg trials is discussed in detail below.) Even the 1949 Geneva Conventions—the only major international agreements on the law of war since the Second World War—deal only with noncombat aspects of war. While these conventions represented a great step forward in the development of the law of war at their formulation, they have always contained certain weaknesses, not the least of which are their reservations of military necessity.

B. JUDGING THE CONDUCT OF NATIONS UNDER THE LAW OF WAR

A second major difficulty with the law of war is that there exists no permanent, central fact-finding and fact-interpreting body to determine when the law has been violated and to make that conclusion known to the world community. The determination of whether a particular nation has usurped the law of war depends on the ability to gather enough relevant facts to both fully describe that nation's action and to determine whether such action is justifiable under the particular circumstances described by those facts. Unbiased fact-gathering and interpretation are not easy tasks in warfare, when access to prison camps, occupied towns and villages, or actual combat zones—areas in which most violations of the law of war occur—is often controlled by belligerent forces not eager to allow such violations to be uncovered. Unsuccessful pleas by the United States that the Viet Cong allow representatives of the International Red Cross to inspect VC prison camps and insure humane treatment of American prisoners are illustrative of this problem.

Thus, such organizations as the International Committee of the Red Cross (ICRC), special U.N. observer teams, the International Control Commission in Vietnam, or even the world press, are fully dependent on permission of the warring factions for access to areas controlled by them. Even if such access is given, it may be only to a particular area or under such stringent conditions that the fact-finding process is limited and hence the fact-interpretation is incomplete or distorted.[68]

[66] For a citation to the text of the Conventions, see note 32 *supra.*

[67] For a citation to the text of the Protocol, see note 33 *supra.*

[68] The ability of neutral organizations groups, or individuals to carry out fact-finding and fact-interpreting processes in relation to violations of the law of war *in territory controlled by the complaining power* may become a significant factor in future conflict situations. The recent finding of the ICRC of evidence of the use of poison gas by

C. SANCTIONING VIOLATORS OF THE LAW OF WAR

Even if the law of war was clarified and updated, and violators could be more easily brought to light, application of sanctions against these violators would remain a major problem. Because international law is a law among nations, its operation depends to a large extent on the subordination of the national interests of individual nations to the uni-

---

Egyptian forces in Yemen was sufficiently publicized to create at least a moderately strong sanction in the form of world public opinion against repeated use of the gas. But the fact that the report was never officially made public by the Committee but had to be obtained by the *New York Times* illustrates the precarious position of the ICRC in such situations. The Committee cannot hope to retain the confidence of warring parties necessary for carrying out its humanitarian goals, while at the same time making public the inhumanitarian actions of such parties. The text of the report of the ICRC as recorded in the *New York Times* of July 28, 1967, is as follows:

Washington, July 27—following is the text of a report by André Rochat, head of the International Committee of the Red Cross delegation to Yemen:

On May 11, 1967, the I.C.R.C. delegation to Jidda received appeals for assistance from the two villages of Gadafa and Gahar in the Wadi Herran, in the southwestern Jauf. According to these appeals a proportion of the inhabitants of these villages had been poisoned by gas dropped from raiding airplanes.

Some hours later this news was confirmed by representatives of the Yemeni Royalists and by the Saudi Arabian authorities, who requested the I.C.R.C. delegation to go immediately to the assistance of the victims.

The head of the delegation decided to proceed immediately to the scene, accompanied by another delegate, two doctors and a male nurse; members of the I.C.R.C. medical team, and a Yemeni escort. The two-lorry convoy, loaded with food and medical supplies, left Amara on May 13, after having given due notice of its line of march and timetable to the Egyptian authorities.

Unfortunately, following an air attack on the I.C.R.C. convoy, it was not until the night of May 15-16 that the mission reached Gahar. This village is situated atop a hill some 500 feet in height. All the houses are clustered closely together, giving the appearance of a small fortress.

Account of Survivors

According to the inhabitants, 75 people were gassed during a raid in the early hours of May 10, 1967.

The account given by the survivors is as follows:

The bombers circled the village for some time, then dropped three bombs on the hillside, east of and below the village, two or three hundred yards away to windward (wind direction from east to west).

No houses were damaged. The explosions were relatively mild. The bomb craters were about eight feet in diameter and 20 inches deep, smaller than the usual craters.

Twenty minutes after dropping the three gas bombs, the planes dropped four or five high-explosive bombs on the village and the western flank of the hill. Only one of these bombs caused any damage: this was sustained by a house in the center of the village.

Many animals, including almost 200 cattle, sheep, goats, donkeys and numerous birds, were also killed. The villagers, who were not contaminated, burned the dead

versal interest of an ordered international community. This applies especially to the law of war. War, when undertaken to advance national objectives placed above international order on a nation's hierarchy of interests, is the clearest example of action not in the interest of the international community. The regulation of the conduct of such war by international standards may prove difficult if one or more of the belligerents involved feels that attainment of any war objectives may be threatened by adherence to these standards. On the other hand, the pressure brought to bear by the threat or actual use of various sanctions against violations of the law of war may for the belligerent outweigh in importance any interference with national objectives that adherence to the rules of war involves. When the threat or use of such sanctions is an instrument in the hands of a large segment of the community of nations rather than individual states, its force, and consequently the tendency to adhere, will *usually* be increased.[69]

---

animals in a large pit west of the village, while the 75 humans killed were buried in four large communal graves.

Report of Observations

The I.C.R.C. delegates, for their part, observed the following.

They inspected the village for several hours, checking, whenever possible, the accuracy of the information mentioned above.

The doctors examined the four surviving gas casualties. Their medical report is attached hereto.

The head of the mission had one of the four communal graves opened. There were 15 corpses in it. An immediate autopsy by Dr. Brutschin and Dr. Janin left no doubt that death was due to pulmonary edema (see attached medical report and photograph).

The 75 gas casualties were either within range of the gas when it was released or were in its path as it was blown by the wind. Some of the victims were found dead in their homes, as if they had died in their sleep.

Other inhabitants, working in the field or watching over the livestock, were eastward of the area where the gas bombs fell, some of them were near to the spot, and none of them were affected.

The four survivors who were in the contaminated area are all in pain from their eyes and almost blind. All have pains in the chest and none has any wound.

The doctors cannot testify to an air raid with gas bombs of which they were not personally witness. On the other hand, they stress that all the evidence leads to the conclusion that edema was caused by the breathing of poison gas.

The delegates were later informed that on May 17 and 18 the villages of Gabas, Nofal, Gadr and, for the second time, Gadafa were raided with gas bombs and that as a result 243 persons were killed.

[69] All other things being equal, the greater the number of countries collectively willing to apply such sanctions, the greater the force behind them. However, that force will be increased or diminished in direct ratio to the number of so-called Great Powers that loan their support to the effort to sanction.

1. INTERNATIONAL ENFORCEMENT

The only international organization which might now supply collective action for sanctioning violations of the law of war is the United Nations. Judging by its inherent inability to institute effective action to stop many "illegal" wars themselves, however, the U.N. must necessarily be considered less than an ideal institution for applying sanctions against violators of the law as well. Under the organization's Charter, the U.N. cannot exercise punitive action if any of the permanent members—the United States, Russia, Britain, France, or Nationalist China—uses its veto.[70]

Although the General Assembly effectively usurped some of the Council's powers during the "police action" in Korea, the U.N. has since then acted to meet situations like that in the Congo in 1960 and the Suez in 1956 on an *ad hoc* basis. For example, the recommendations of the General Assembly to the Security Council leading to the establishment of a U.N. Emergency Force to "secure and supervise the cessation of hostilities" in the Middle East in 1956 subsequently led to the withdrawal of British, French, and Israeli forces from the area. But the collective power of the U.N. or its Emergency Force did not force these troops out; they left voluntarily. It is also questionable whether any of the three invading countries would have been in further violation of international law had they not accepted *the Assembly's* efforts to restore peace. In this respect, Whitaker notes:

> The three states withdrew their forces because of the adverse distribution of power of which both UNEF and the Assembly resolutions were only reflections and symbols. We cannot be sure precisely which factors influenced the decisions to comply but we do know that only the Americans or the Russians, both of them part of the majority, could provide the oil to keep France and Britain warm and to keep their transportation systems operative during the winter season. We do know, too, that a substantial portion of Israel's national income originates in the United States. And we may recall that the Soviet Union not only advertised the possibility that Russian troops might come to Egypt's assistance, but also took the occasion to remind the world that Tel Aviv, Paris, and London are only minutes by missile from Moscow.[71]

[70] See, for instance, Urban G. Whitaker, Jr., *Politics and Power* (New York: Harper and Row, 1964), pp. 222ff.
[71] *Ibid.*, p. 225.

A threat of sanctions, not by the U.N. but by two of the Great Powers which happened to be members of the organization, thus led not to collective enforcement of the General Assembly's resolution on the Suez, but to *self-enforcement* by the aggressive states involved. Had Russia and the United States been on opposite sides of the dispute—as was the case in Hungary in 1956 and the Dominican Republic in 1965—it is doubtful that any Suez-type action would have been taken by the U.N. Effective action by the United Nations in preventing or halting open hostilities between nations continues to depend upon a degree of cooperation by the greatest of the Great Powers, Russia and the United States. Clear evidence of this can today be found in the situation existing in Southeast Asia.

2. SELF-ENFORCEMENT

Because the ability of the U.N. to apply effective sanctions against nations participating in "illegal" warfare appears clearly related to its ability to apply similar sanctions against nations violating the law of war during that warfare, it would seem that effective operation of this law must depend on self-enforcement by the belligerent nations or factions in conflict. Self-enforcement depends on self-interest, and self-interest depends in turn upon the sanctions that individual nations may impose on the violators of the law of war. Lauterpacht thus divides the means of securing legitimate warfare into three classes. The first class includes measures of self-help or reprisals, the punishment of war crimes committed by enemy soldiers and other enemy subjects, and the taking of hostages. The second class comprises complaints lodged with the enemy and with neutral states, and good offices, mediation, and intervention on the part of neutral states. The third class includes the rights of compensation.[72]

A brief discussion of two of Lauterpacht's most extreme sanctions—reprisals and punishment of war crimes—serves to point out their limited value as deterrents when their invocation is dependent on the judgment of a single state.

a. Reprisals—They are in effect generally unlawful but constitute an authorized reaction to prior acts of the opposition for the purpose of deterring repetition of such antecedent unlawful acts. As McDougal points out, the use of reprisals is justified only to deter improper conduct of the enemy *during* war, not as a device of self-defense against

[72] Lauterpacht, note 33 *supra*, pp. 557-58.

the initiation of aggressive war itself: "Securing the minimum destruction principles requires that the reprisals doctrine become available to the defender only when the aggressor, subsequent to the violation against *resort* to violence, breaches the requirements of the law on the *conduct* of violence."[73]

The major obstacle to the effective operation of reprisals as sanctions against violations of the law of war is the fact that the belligerents are allowed to determine for themselves not only when an act of the enemy violates law and makes reprisal legitimate, but also if the manner of conducting such reprisal is lawful. Such a freedom in judgment may lead to reprisals disproportionate to the original unlawful conduct or action against persons and areas normally protected under the law of war. This in turn may give rise to counterreprisals and eventually to complete abandonment of the law of war in certain dimensions of warfare.[74] In addition to these difficulties, reprisals may not serve their legitimate purpose—cessation of unlawful acts by the enemy—if they are not conducted according to certain criteria. Reprisals instituted without both prior exhaustion of alternative remedies and some form of communication to the enemy may be viewed not as retaliatory measures taken to prevent reoccurrence of unlawful acts but as part of the ordinary course of warfare. This misconception may in turn lead to counterreprisals viewed by their initiator as reprisals. Many factors may also make resort to reprisals illogical in the first place. The actor's vulnerability to counterreprisal may minimize his threat of reprisal use. Reprisal may not be used if it might adversely affect world opinion or the outlook of neutral nations toward the conflict. Reprisal might make the enemy less likely to defect for fear that some form of reprisal might be taken against him once captured and reprisals directed against or involving the civilian population may strengthen the enemy's will to fight. Reprisals can thus be expected to play only a limited role as a sanction against violations of the law of war.

b. War Crimes Trials—Lauterpacht also cites war crimes trials as sanctions against violations of the law of war. Nuremberg does not, of course, mark the beginning of such trials. As early as 1474 Sir Peter Hagenback was tried in Germany for crimes which on their surface were analogous to the "crimes against humanity" enumerated at Nuremberg.[75] General recognition of the necessity to conduct war operations according to certain minimal humanitarian standards has for

---

[73] McDougal and Feliciano, note 23 *supra*, p. 681.

[74] *Ibid.*, pp. 679-90.

[75] Greenspan, note 56 *supra*, p. 4.

many years led states to make provisions in their municipal and military law for the trial of war criminals, whether members of the enemy or their own forces. For instance, U.S. Army Field Manual 27-10 lists acts "representative of the violations of the laws of war" in addition to "grave breaches" of the Geneva Conventions of 1949.[76] These acts include making use of poisoned or otherwise forbidden arms or ammunition, maltreatment of dead bodies, firing on localities which are undefended and without military significance, poisoning of wells or streams, and pillage or purposeless destruction.[77] The manual also notes that those accused of war crimes, including grave breaches of the Geneva Conventions of 1949, will be accorded at least the minimal benefits of the appropriate articles of the Conventions. War crimes are put within the jurisdiction of general courts-martial, military commissions, provost courts, military government courts, and other military tribunals of the United States, "as well as of international tribunals."[78]

The law to be applied in such trials, as well as those subject to these laws, are also clearly defined. Recognizing the "obligations of belligerents under customary international law to take measures for the punishment of war crimes by all persons, including members of the belligerent's own armed forces,"[79] the manual notes that: "As the international law of war is part of the law of the land in the United States, enemy personnel charged with war crimes are tried directly under international law without recourse to the statutes of the United States. However, directives declaratory of international law may be promulgated to assist such tribunals in the performance of their function."[80] Whether applying generally accepted law of war or specific provisions of U.S. military law based on this law, the United States manual is a clear illustration of the provisions made by nations to prosecute war criminals during or after war.

There is no doubt that under such provisions states will do all possible to bring enemy war criminals to trial. The difficulty in relying upon the enforcement of the law of war by individual states arises when a nation must try war criminals from the ranks of its own armed forces. Military necessity will be more apt to overshadow humanitarian standards both in a nation's conduct of war and in the trial of its own forces for war crimes if the absence of such trials does not provoke effective

---

[76] *The Law of Land Warfare*, note 57 *supra*, par. 504.
[77] *Ibid.*
[78] *Ibid.*, par. 505.
[79] *Ibid.*, par. 506.
[80] *Ibid.*

countermeasures on the part of the enemy, or the widespread institution of such trials is evidence of, or gives rise to, a curb on military policy that may appear to threaten seriously the nation's major war objectives. Token trials of its own war criminals can often be combined with a military strategy which employs methods and weapons of warfare of questionable humanitarian character, particularly if the nation exercises a distinct military advantage over its opponent, thus making effective reprisal unlikely. No nation can realistically be expected to enforce strictly all provisions of the law of war against its own forces under such circumstances, unless it can be made answerable to a third, greater force. That force must, however, be capable of applying sanctions which constitute a threat of such significance as to call for a reappraisal of the value of principal war objectives that might be interfered with by strict adherence to the law of war.

VII. The Nuremberg Trials

Consideration of the possibility of such a sanctioning force leads one to examine the effect on international law of the International Military Tribunal at Nuremberg, unique as a modern example of the cooperative sanctioning of violators of the law of war.

The four major Allied powers signed the London Agreement on August 8, 1945, providing for the postwar trial of war criminals whose crimes "have no particular geographical location whether they be accused individually or in their capacity as members of organizations or groups or in both capacities." The Charter appended to the Agreement was in effect a constitution of the International Military Tribunal which was given jurisdiction under Article 6 to try "crimes against peace," "war crimes," and "crimes against humanity," along with the crime of conspiracy to commit these crimes.[81]

The most serious criticisms, both substantive and procedural, leveled at the Nuremberg trials centered on "crimes against peace," listed in Article 6(a) of the Charter: "(a) Crimes against Peace: Namely, plan-

[81] "Agreement by the Government of the United States of America, the Provisional Government of the French Republic, the Government of the United Kingdom of Great Britain and Northern Ireland and the Government of the Union of Soviet Socialist Republics for the Prosecution and Punishment of the Major War Criminals of the European Axis" (1945) *U.S. Department of State Bulletin* XIII, p. 222; *Trial of War Criminals* (Washington: Department of State Publication 2420, 1945), p. 13. Nineteen other states adhered to the Agreement without being represented on the Tribunal. For the text of the Charter, January 19, 1946, as amended April 26, 1946, see *U.S. Department of State Bulletin*, XIV, pp. 361, 890.

ning, preparation, initiation or waging of a war of aggression, or a war in violation of international treaties, agreements or assurances, or participation in a common plan or conspiracy for the accomplishment of any of the foregoing." For the purposes of this study, however, these criticisms will not be examined, since these "crimes" were related more to the ultimate objectives of the war than to its conduct. The categories of "war crimes" and "crimes against humanity" were, however, related to that conduct, and the criticisms relating to the formulation of these categories and prosecution under them will be examined in determining the role of Nuremberg as it affected the international law of war.

A. PROCEDURAL CRITICISMS

While some studies have concluded that the makeup of the Tribunal, with its absence of at least neutral representatives, stacked the cards against the Germans regarding prosecution of "crimes against peace,"[82] it is unlikely that this was a major factor in undermining the legality of the prosecution of defendants for traditional "war crimes" and "crimes against humanity." For as von Glahn notes, the offenses of the accused under these headings

> were so horrifying, so lacking in the minimum of decency and of the aspects commonly associated with the Judaeo-Christian civilization, that neutral judges, listening to the evidence, could not have remained neutral. Furthermore, they would inevitably have had to consider that their own state might be the victim of similar events if the offenders of the Second World War had not been punished, so that they may easily have been influenced in favor of punishment as a deterrent.[83]

To those who would suggest German representation on the Tribunal, one must agree that the post-World War I failure of the German government adequately to prosecute war criminals after it had been given permission to do so by the Allies was a lesson to be heeded.[84]

A major procedural criticism leveled at Nuremberg was that it was a

---

[82] Supporting this view of the Tribunal are F. B. Schick, "Crimes Against Peace," *Journal of Criminal Law and Criminology*, xxxviii (1948), 445, and George A. Finch, "The Nuremberg Trial and International Law," *A.J.I.L.*, xxxi (1947), p. 20. A generally critical study of the Nuremberg undertaking is found in Lord Maurice Hankey's *Politics, Trials and Errors* (Chicago: Henry Regnery Co., 1950).

[83] Gerhard von Glahn, *Law Among Nations* (New York: Macmillan Co., 1965), p. 707.

[84] *Ibid.*, p. 704.

trial of only the offenses of the losers. In keeping with the terms of the Charter, the Tribunal made no effort to go into the war crimes attributed to members of Allied forces. One must contend, however, that this specific factor did not weaken the effect of the Nuremberg undertaking. If we agree that the defendants were prosecuted for criminal offenses (an issue discussed below), it does not make sense to argue that they were any less criminally responsible because the circumstances at the moment did not allow them to prosecute their adversaries who may have been guilty of the same crimes. The argument for prosecuting Allied defendants might be persuasive if there was reason to believe that Nuremberg's purpose was to set a precedent dictating that individuals of a particular religion, nationality, or political persuasion would always find themselves the object of retribution following a war. But, in fact, Nuremberg served as a warning that individuals of *any nation*, who during war committed any of the acts enumerated in the Charter, might in the future be punished for such acts following that war.

B. SUBSTANTIVE CRITICISMS

Individuals were held liable for their acts in all three categories of "crimes" under the Charter: "*Article 8*: The fact that the Defendant acted pursuant to order of his Government or of a superior shall not free him from responsibility, but may be considered in mitigation of punishment if the Tribunal determines that justice so requires." Thus the defense of "superior orders" no longer constituted an absolute defense for individuals accused of any of the crimes prosecuted at Nuremberg. Neither was the "act of state" doctrine permitted to stand in the way of prosecution of such individuals. The Tribunal said in its judgment:

> It was submitted that international law is concerned with actions of sovereign States, and provides no punishment for individuals; and further, that where the act in question is an act of state, those who carry it out are not personally responsible, but are protected by the doctrine of the sovereignty of the state. In the opinion of the Tribunal, both these submissions must be rejected. That international law imposes duties and liabilities upon individuals as well as states has long been recognized. . . . Crimes against international law are committed by men, not by abstract entities, and only by punishing

individuals who commit such crimes can the provisions of international law be enforced.[85]

As traditionally formulated, the act of state doctrine prevented the courts of one state from sitting in judgment on the public acts of another state done within the latter's territory. Few nations today would deny their duty to prevent their nationals from acting in contravention of international law. This duty is clearest with regard to official acts of government, acts of state. The more generally recognized the violation, the more obvious the duty. If nations are unwilling or incapable of so regulating their nationals, those individuals who commit such violations as agents of their governments should not be permitted to use the act of state doctrine to shield themselves against prosecution under international law by international authority.

In determining the degree of guilt at Nuremberg the plea of superior orders was approached through familiar criminal law principles related to *mens rea*. If the individual did not know the illegal nature of the order he was carrying out he was held not responsible. In the "Hostages Case" the Tribunal noted: "If the illegality of the order was not known to the inferior and he could not reasonably have been expected to know of the illegality, no wrongful intent necessary to the commission of the crime exists and the inferior will be protected."[86] However, if the character of the order made it manifestly illegal to anyone, who, although lacking extensive knowledge of the law of war, was "of a common humanity," knowledge of the illegality of the order was imputed to the individual.[87] Illustrations of such obviously unlawful orders were cited in later national war crimes tribunals as orders for the killing or ill-treatment of prisoners of war, the massacre of survivors of sunken ships, and the mass extermination, torture, and mutilation of the civil population in occupied countries.[88]

The defense that the individual may be compelled in wartime under threat of punishment to obey military orders was carefully limited by the "High Command Case":

The defendants in this case who received obviously criminal orders were placed in a different position but servile compliance with orders clearly criminal for fear of some disadvantage or punishment

---

[85] Judgment of the Tribunal, note 48 *supra*, p. 411, and *A.J.I.L.*, note 48 *supra*, 220-21.
[86] War Crimes Reports, Vol. VIII (1948), p. 50, cited in McDougal and Feliciano, note 23 *supra*, p. 691.
[87] McDougal and Feliciano, note 23 *supra*, p. 691.   [88] *Ibid.*

not immediately threatened cannot be recognized as a defence. . . . [T]here must be a showing of circumstances that such a reasonable man would apprehend that he was in such imminent physical peril as to deprive him of freedom to choose the right and refrain from the wrong.[89]

Myres McDougal points out that two further requirements for exempting duress as a defense to superior orders were that the accused show that the harm inflicted by compliance with the unlawful order was not disproportionately greater than the punishment he could expect to receive by noncompliance, and that the accused must not have been "in accord with the principle and intent of the superior" who issued the order.[90]

To support their contention that the concept of individual responsibility was held applicable at Nuremberg only to those high echelon officials directly concerned with the planning and execution of the war, commentators have noted the failure of the Tribunal to prosecute individuals from the ranks.[91] This would not, however, seem to be a decisive factor determining the responsibility of these individuals under international law. The sheer magnitude of such an undertaking would have made it prohibitive. Prosecution of individuals most closely associated with decision-making in the course of events covered by the indictment certainly could not be said to rule out the right of the Tribunal to prosecute members of lower echelons for various categories of "crimes" if the other substantive arguments could be met successfully.

C. WAR CRIMES

The crimes set forth in Article 6(b) of the Charter under "war crimes" appeared in keeping with generally accepted standards of international law:

(b) War Crimes: namely, violations of the laws or customs of war. Such violations shall include, but not be limited to, murder, ill-treatment or deportation to slave labor or for any other purpose of civilian population of or in occupied territory, murder or ill-

[89] War Crimes Reports, Vol. XXII (1948), p. 72. See also "The Einsatzgruppen Case," Trials of War Criminals, Vol. IV (1947), p. 471, cited in McDougal and Feliciano, note 23 supra, p. 693.

[90] "The Einsatzgruppen Case," ibid.

[91] See Gerald J. Adler, "Resistance to Law: National vs. International Standards," Houston Law Review, V (1968), 634ff.

treatment of prisoners of war or persons on the high seas, killing of hostages, plunder of public or private property, wanton destruction of cities, towns or villages, or devastation not justified by military necessity.

These war crimes were in essence a crystallization of those principles embodied for many years in both codified and customary law of war as recognized by all nations, violations of which were commonly punished by national courts and military tribunals in traditional "war crimes" trials.[92]

D. "CRIMES AGAINST HUMANITY"

As with "crimes against peace," criticism was directed against the category of "crimes against humanity," which, some charged, included offenses never before punished under international law. Two different sets of offenses come to light in Article 6(c) of the Charter. The first set includes ". . . murder, extermination, enslavement, deportation, and other inhumane acts committed against any civilian population." These could be labeled "ordinary" war crimes similar to those listed in Article 6(b). Article 6(c) stated that these acts were considered criminal when done "before," as well as during war. Among the second set of crimes under the "crimes against humanity" listed in Article 6(c) were "prosecution on political, racial, or religious grounds in execution of or in connection with any crime within the jurisdiction of the Tribunal, whether or not in violation of the domestic law of the country where perpetrated."

Several commentators have held that the first part of the text when referring to acts "before" war and the last part of the Article together constitute a "reiteration of the existence of fundamental human rights superior to the law of any state and protected by international sanctions."[93] However, the Tribunal avoided this "human rights" issue separate from the war itself when it decided that it could deal only with acts under Article 6(c) committed after the war had broken out:

> To constitute Crimes against Humanity, the acts relied on before the outbreak of war must have been in execution of, or in connection with, any crime within the jurisdiction of the Tribunal. The Tribunal is of the opinion that revolting and horrifying as many of

[92] See Section VI, the treatment of "War Crimes Trials," *supra.*

[93] Gerhard von Glahn, note 83 *supra*, p. 711, cited in Lauterpacht, note 33 *supra*, p. 579, note 5, and E. Schwelb, "Crimes against Humanity," *B.Y.I.L.*, Vol. XXIII (1946), pp. 178-226.

these crimes were, it has not been satisfactorily proved that they were done in execution of, or in connection with, any such crime. The Tribunal therefore cannot make a general declaration that the acts before 1939 were Crimes against Humanity within the meaning of the Charter. . .[94]

As von Glahn has noted, "crimes against humanity," at least those beyond traditional war crimes, were alleged offenses against civilians, not as individuals, but as the population of a country *per se*. The most controversial aspect of this expansion of the coverage of international law was the fact that these crimes were not limited to offenses against alien populations only, nor was the law of the states where such acts were committed accepted as authority for those acts: "Even acts by Germans against their fellow citizens were deemed to fall within the purview of the authority of the Allies, despite the fact that German law would have sanctioned a number of the acts involved."[95] This "unprecedented innovation in the law of nations" prompts von Glahn to question the prosecution of Germans for "crimes against humanity," despite the fact that "the enormities committed by the Axis Powers . . . called for the strictest punishment." He concludes that: "With due respect to any humanitarian motives implied in the concept of crimes against humanity beyond traditional war crimes, it is still rather doubtful that international law recognized then or now a body of fundamental human rights superior to national law and protected somehow by the community of nations as a collective entity."[96] Contrary to this conclusion, I believe that international law both then and now does recognize such a body of fundamental human rights. While the specific list of human rights under the Charter of the Tribunal was not *formally* recognized in multilateral agreements prior to 1939, it is difficult to doubt that the very same elements of humanity and conscience underlying a large segment of the law of war before that date also supported the outlawing of specific crimes against humanity as they were spelled out at Nuremberg. One should again look at the most controversial of these crimes as listed: ". . . or prosecution on political, racial or religious grounds *in execution of or in connection with* any crime within the jurisdiction of the Tribunal, whether or not in violation of the domestic law of the country where perpetrated." (emphasis added)

[94] *A.J.I.L.*, note 48 *supra*, p. 249, cited in von Glahn, *loc.cit.*
[95] *Ibid.*, p. 712.   [96] *Ibid.*

Initially one must consider that in a very clear sense the "prosecutions on political, racial or religious grounds"—notably the internment and killing of millions of Jews—were both "in execution of" a war of aggression ("crimes against peace") and "in connection with" war crimes (whether listed under war crimes proper or crimes against humanity). Each of the crimes in the indictment was in fact related to the other. Commission of a war crime such as mass deportation of civilians was necessary before the extermination based on religion—one of the controversial crimes against humanity—could be undertaken. And this extermination was in turn a necessary element in the expansion of Germany, the "aggressive" war or "crimes against peace." Even if we are not willing to admit that in 1939 aggressive war was a crime against peace punishable by international sanction, there is no doubt that mass deportation of civilians and "other inhumane acts committed against any civilian population" were international crimes under the law of war if these civilians in question were enemy civilians. If a nation committed such acts against her own citizens should this have been considered less of a crime? In fact, the result was the same whether the citizens were enemy or not: suffering by noncombatants outside the scope of any reasonably formulated definition of military necessity as understood by the international community. It was this needless suffering that the law of war was designed to prevent. The suffering itself, not the nationality of the objects of that suffering, was the crucial factor.

Against the international community's right and indeed need to prevent such suffering inflicted by a nation on its own citizens is of course the traditional notion that nations never intervene in or interfere with the sovereign powers of other states as exercised upon their own citizens in their own territory. Article 2, paragraph 7 of the U.N. Charter, drafted before the Nuremberg trials took place, provided that intervention was prohibited "in matters that are essentially within the domestic jurisdiction of any state." One must immediately ask if the extermination of a whole racial-religious group within its population as a step in a plan to wipe out members of that group in all countries which it overran was "essentially" a German "domestic matter." Was it not rather a matter directly affecting all civilized nations, an added threat to international peace and security, and an open challenge to the fundamental human rights that it was the purpose of the United Nations to reaffirm and protect? Neither can one believe that the concept of "human rights," the protection of which was a basic objective of the organization, was divorced from crimes against humanity enumerated at Nuremberg as a logical outgrowth of the principles underlying the law of war. In this respect there could certainly be no valid charge that the prosecution of German defendants for crimes against humanity contained the same legal drawbacks as did those prosecutions under "crimes against peace." The conclusion is that as regards both conventional war crimes and the related crimes against humanity the International Tribunal at Nuremberg correctly applied international law.

VIII. The Law of Nuremberg Today

Having examined the relation of international law to the prosecution of defendants for war crimes and crimes against humanity, a more important question must now be answered: What effect did the London Agreement and the Charter and Judgment at Nuremberg have on the international law of war as it exists today? One can begin to answer this question by looking at the work of the United Nations in the post-Nuremberg period.

In December 1946, the General Assembly of the United Nations unanimously passed Resolution 95(I) affirming "the principles of international law recognized by the Charter of the Nuremberg Tribunal and the judgment of the Tribunal," and directing that: "the committee on the codification of international law established by resolution of the General Assembly of 11 December 1946 . . . treat as a matter of primary importance plans for the formulation, in the context of a general codification of offenses against the peace and security of mankind, or of an International Code, of principles recognized in the Charter of the Nuremberg Tribunal and in the Judgment of the Tribunal."[97]

The Committee on Codification did not formulate the plans for codification of offenses mentioned in Resolution 95(I), but recommended that the International Law Commission prepare such a code. The recommendation was accepted in Assembly Resolution 177(II), directing the ILC to: "(a) Formulate the principles of international law recognized in the Charter of the Nurnberg Tribunal and in the judgment of the Tribunal, and (b) Prepare a draft code of offenses against the peace and security of mankind, indicating clearly the place to be accorded to the principles mentioned in sub-paragraph (a) above."[98]

[97] U.N. G.A. Res. 95 (I) , December 11, 1946. U.N. G.A.O.R. 1st Sess., 2d Part, Plenary Mtg. 55, p. 1144, U.N. Doc. A/236 (1946) ; see also U.N. A/CN. 4/22 (1952) *Ybk. Int. L. Comm.* (II) , p. 181.

[98] U.N. G.A. Res. 177 (II) , November 21, 1947.

The Commission's report to the Assembly's fifth session contained the formulation of Nuremberg principles:

Principle I. Any person who commits or is an accomplice in the commission of an act which constitutes a crime under international law is responsible therefor and liable for punishment.

Principle II. The fact that domestic law does not punish an act which is an international crime does not free the perpetrator of such crime from responsibility under international law.

Principle III. The fact that a person who committed an international crime acted as Head of State or public official does not free him from responsibility under international law or mitigate punishment.

Principle IV. The fact that a person acted pursuant to order of his government or of a superior does not free him from responsibility under international law. It may, however, be considered in mitigation of punishment, if justice so requires.

Principle V. Any person charged with a crime under international law has a right to a fair trial on the facts and law.

Principle VI. The crimes hereafter set out are punishable as crimes under international law:
a. Crimes against Peace:
(1) Planning, preparation, initiation or waging of a war of aggression, or a war in violation of international treaties, agreements or assurances;
(2) Participation in a common plan or conspiracy for the accomplishment of any of the acts mentioned under (1).
b. War Crimes: namely, violations of the laws or customs of war. Such violations shall include, but not be limited to, murder, ill-treatment or deportation to slave labour or for any other purpose of civilian population of or in occupied territory, murder or ill-treatment of prisoners of war or persons on the seas, killing of hostages, plunder of public or private property, wanton destruction of cities, towns or villages, or devastation not justified by military necessity.
c. Crimes against Humanity: namely, murder, extermination, enslavement, deportation and other inhuman acts done against a civilian population, or persecutions on political, racial or re-

ligious grounds, when such acts are done or such persecutions are carried on in execution of or in connection with any crime against peace or any war crime.

Principle VII. Complicity in the commission of a crime against peace, a war crime or a crime against humanity, as set forth in Principle VI, is a crime under international law.[99]

In 1954 the International Law Commission submitted to the General Assembly a Draft Code of Offenses against the Peace and Security of Mankind containing many of the crimes listed in the Nuremberg Charter and Judgment. The most important provisions of the Code for the purposes of this study are:

Article 1

Offenses against the peace and security of mankind, as defined in this Code, are crimes under international law, for which the responsible individuals shall be punished.

Article 2

The following acts are offenses against the peace and security of mankind:

(1) Any act of aggression, including the employment by the authorities of a state of armed force against another state for any purpose other than national or collective self-defense or in pursuance of a decision or recommendation by a competent organ of the United Nations.

(2) Any threat by the authorities of a state to resort to an act of aggression against another state.

(3) The preparation by the authorities of a state for the employment of armed force against another state for any purpose other than national or collective self-defense or in pursuance of a decision or recommendation by a competent organ of the United Nations.

. . .

(9) Acts by the authorities of a state or by private individuals, committed with intent to destroy, in whole or in part, a national, ethical, racial or religious group as such, including:

(i) killing members of the group;

(ii) causing serious bodily or mental harm to members of the group;

---

[99] 5 U.N. G.A.O.R. Suppl. 12, pp. 11-14, par. 99, U.N. Doc. A/1316 (1950).

(iii) deliberately inflicting on the group conditions of life calculated to bring about its physical destruction in whole or in part;

(iv) forcibly transferring children of the group to another group.

(10) Inhuman acts by the authorities of a state or by individuals against any civilian population, such as murder, or extermination, or enslavement, or deportation, or persecutions on political, social, religious or cultural grounds, when such acts are committed in execution of or in connection with other offenses defined in this article.

(11) Acts in violation of the laws or customs of war.

. . .

Article 3

The fact that a person acted as Head of State or as responsible government official does not relieve him from responsibility for committing any of the offenses defined in this Code.

Article 4

The fact that a person charged with an offense defined in this Code acted pursuant to order of his government or of a superior does not relieve him from responsibility, provided a moral choice was, in fact, possible to him.

Article 5

The penalty for any offense defined in this Code shall be determined by the Tribunal exercising jurisdiction over the individual accused, taking into account the gravity of the offense.[100]

It is noted that while the Draft Code listed several acts as crimes which were not specifically punishable at Nuremberg, it nevertheless serves as an additional restatement of the principles of the Tribunal and follows the same general divisions of crimes into categories of crimes against peace, war crimes, and crimes against humanity.

Despite the deliberations of the ILC on the Code and the possible establishment of a related International Criminal Court, neither proposal has been formally adopted by the international community.[101] The reasons for this lack of positive action by the United Nations centers essentially on Article 2(1) of the Code, and can be explained by an understanding of the desire of most states to retain the right to decide when the use of force is aggression in violation of international

---

[100] 9 U.N. G.A.O.R., Suppl. 9, pp. 11-12, U.N. Doc. A/2693 (1954).
[101] See von Glahn, note 83 *supra*, pp. 714ff.

law and when it is justified as self-defense under Article 2(4) and Article 51 of the U.N. Charter. National interest in this area has not yet been checked to the degree that all nations can agree on set definitions of aggression embodied in a draft convention.[102]

General Assembly Resolutions 95(I) and 177(II) and the formulation of the Nuremberg Principles and the Draft Code by the International Law Commission, are, however, important in considering the effect of Nuremberg on present international law, particularly the law of war. At the least, the resolutions should be taken as evidence of world community support for the Nuremberg undertaking. While such resolutions *per se* are not law-creating instruments, they do represent a general international consensus that the principles applied at Nuremberg should be considered part of international law. In fact, it might be contended that the Nuremberg proceedings, *together with* international approval embodied in these resolutions and the Code, do in fact make the Nuremberg principles part of international law.

In any case, states should be bound to adhere to the principles embodied in the Charter of the Tribunal from the moment they became signatories. Lauterpacht has pointed out that: "In so far as the instruments referred to above give expression to the views of the states concerned as to the *applicable principles* of International Law—applicable generally and not only as against the defeated enemies—they may be fairly treated as evidence of International Law and as binding on them."[103] There can be little doubt in this respect that it was the clear intention of the United States to bind itself to the principles of Nuremberg. As Justice Jackson stated: "If certain acts in violation of treaties are crimes, they are crimes whether the United States does them or whether Germany does them, and we are not prepared to lay down a rule of criminal conduct against others which we would not be willing to have invoked against us."[104] The inclusion in U.S. Army Field Manual 27-10 of the three categories of offenses enumerated at Nuremberg as crimes against international law is further proof that the United States considers mandatory its adherence to the Nuremberg principles.

The failure of the international community to approve the Draft Code because of the inability to agree on a definition of aggression does

[102] For a discussion of United Nations efforts to define aggression see John H. Hazard, "Why Try Again to Define Aggression?," *A.J.I.L.*, LXII (1968), 701-10.

[103] Lauterpacht, note 33 *supra*, p. 582.

[104] *International Conference on Military Trials* (Washington: Department of State Publication 3880), p. 330.

not detract from these arguments. Such a definition may at present not be possible. But it is possible to assume that in time of war endangering the peace and security of the international community, a nation's reasons for using force or its methods of employing such force may be so obviously contrary to accepted standards of law and humanity as to ultimately subject its citizens as individuals to international sanction in the form of prosecution for crimes against peace as well as war crimes and crimes against humanity.

Apart from Nuremberg and U.N. resolutions supporting the undertaking, two further enactments—the Genocide Convention[105] and the Universal Declaration on Human Rights,[106] both of 1948—carry the protection of human rights of indigenous populations, in peace as well as war, into the realm of customary international law. Genocide is defined in Article 2 of the Convention:

> In the present Convention, genocide means any of the following acts committed with intent to destroy, in whole or in part, a national, ethical, racial, or religious group as such:
> (a) Killing members of the group;
> (b) Causing serious bodily or mental harm to members of the group;
> (c) Deliberately inflicting on the group conditions of life calculated to bring about its physical destruction in whole or in part;
> (d) Imposing measures intended to prevent births within the group;
> (e) Forcibly transferring children of the group to another group.

The Convention came into effect in 1951 and over forty states have now signed the instrument. The United States' failure to ratify the Convention is based not upon disagreement with the principles of the Convention but on domestic constitutional questions, particularly the allegation that in preventing and punishing acts of genocide under Article 1 the federal government would be usurping rights constitutionally reserved to the individual states.[107]

---

[105] 78 U.N.T.S. 277 (1948).

[106] U.N. G.A.O.R. 3rd Sess., 1st Part, Resolutions, p. 71, U.N. Doc. A/810 (1948).

[107] See Oriel L. Phillips, "The Genocide Convention: Its Effect on Our Legal System," *American Bar Association Journal*, XXXV (1949), 623-25, and George A. Finch, "The Genocide Convention," *A.J.I.L.*, XLIII (1949), 732-36.

The concept of human rights protection under international law has been introduced into the war setting by the Geneva Conventions of 1949.[108] More than including humanitarian considerations, the Conventions address themselves to the plight of the individual—soldier or civilian—whose interests in the past have been only minimally protected in the face of the doctrine of military necessity. The purpose of the Conventions is not to show nations how best to conduct war, but how best to avoid needless suffering by innocent members of society. They underline the value of human life as such. In this most important respect the 1949 Geneva Conventions have become the first step in a most necessary restructuring of the law of war proper, allowing it to reflect the standards of humanitarian conduct emphasized by the work of the United Nations in the post-Nuremberg era.[109] But the formulation of rules of conduct more in keeping with modern technology and methods of warfare does not necessarily insure their successful application in combat situations.

IX. The Belligerency Question in Applying the Law of War to Civil Wars and International-Civil Wars

Many of the same problems of legislation, fact-finding and interpretation, and sanctioning of violations that plague the operation of the law of war affect the process of determining when the protection of this law is to be afforded to parties in conflict, particularly civil conflict. Central to this determination is the recognition of a status of belligerency of the rebelling faction, particularly by the *de jure* government in civil war, and additionally by the third-party state assisting that government in international-civil war.

The extension of a status of belligerency to a rebellious faction, such as the Viet Cong, in civil conflict or international-civil conflict operates on a kind of fiction. To be war the contention must be *between states*.[110] Hence, war between the *de jure* government, assisted by a third-party state, and a body of armed individuals is not technically war in the language of international law. How then are the rules of war to relate to rebel factions? The United States and Britain faced this problem in the early 1800's when they were forced in the interests of humanity and self-protection to develop a legal atti-

---

108 See note 35 *supra*.

109 For a discussion of this development see F. Siordet, "The Red Cross and Human Rights," *International Review of the Red Cross*, No. 84 (1968), pp. 118-34.

110 Lauterpacht, note 33 *supra*, p. 202.

tude toward revolting colonies in the Americas.[111] It became practice that where a *de facto* political organization had been set up by the rebellious faction and such organization evidenced ability to maintain itself and conduct its operations in accordance with the law of war, and at the same time the parent state exercised belligerent rights of blockade and search and seizure, the situation was recognized as "public war."[112]

This recognition by third states in effect gave the rebellious faction as a belligerent community the status of a state at war in its relations with them. Foreign states could extend such recognition whether or not the lawful government of the state had extended the status of belligerency to the rebels.

But behind these rules of international law the fact still remains that nation-states can almost at will grant or withhold the status of belligerency according to their judgment of whether the insurgent faction has satisfied the criteria for such recognition. (States can then grant or withhold aid to such factions according to their chosen thesis from divergent writings of international lawyers on the subject.) [113]

The facts which would have to be proven before recognition of belligerent status *should be* lawfully extended would include, according to von Glahn:

> . . . the existence of a civil war *beyond the scope of mere local revolt* (existence of a "state of *general hostilities*"); *occupation* of a *substantial part* of the national territory by the rebels, together with the existence of *a degree of orderly and effective administration* by that group in the areas *under its control*; *observance* of the rules of war

---

[111] Fenwick, note 21 *supra*, p. 165.   [112] *Ibid.*, p. 166.

[113] As to the duties under international law of foreign states toward the warring factions there is much disagreement. Hall maintains that there can be no legal basis upon which foreign states can interfere in civil strife. (Higgins, *Hall's International Law*, note 5 *supra*, p. 347.) Hyde and Lawrence hold similar views. (Ian Brownlie, *International Law and the Use of Force by States* [Oxford: Clarendon Press, 1963], p. 323.) Garner, on the other hand, follows the position that a foreign state has the right to assist only the incumbent government, with its consent. (James W. Garner, "Questions of International Law in the Spanish Civil War," *A.J.I.L.*, 31 [1937], 66.) Vattel has commonly been cited as the leading exponent of the third view that a state may intervene to assist the faction that has "justice" on its side (note 19 *supra*, Bk. II, p. 131) . A variation on these views is put forth by von Glahn: "If the rebel group has been recognized by a foreign state as the *de facto* government of the entire state in which the civil war is going on, then the foreign state must abstain from all assistance to the lawful (*de jure*) government of the state at war, being free, at the same time, to give or deny such aid to the belligerent community." (von Glahn, note 83 *supra*, p. 84.)

by rebel forces, acting under the command of some *responsible and ascertainable* authority; and, finally, the existence of a need on the part of other states to take a *stand* on the existence of the civil war and to define and classify their attitudes and policies toward it (emphasis added).[114]

Interpretation of the underlined words and phrases in the above quotation naturally leaves great leeway in the hands of the state extending or withholding belligerent status. What sort of occupation is necessary by the rebels? Full control, partial control, control by day or by night? And how much is a substantial part of the national territory? More than half, a third? On the basis of interpreting the criteria set out above, third states and the *de jure* government may extend or withhold belligerent status from the rebellious faction in many cases just as their national interests suit them. The protection of many of the rules of war must under international law be extended to the rebellious faction by the lawful government only after the former has attained this belligerent status. When it is considered that the *de jure* government will consider any gain in status on the part of the rebels as a partial victory in the struggle for support, particularly in the international community, it is easy to see why that government would do all in its power to prevent the status of belligerency and hence protection of many of the laws of war from being extended to the rebels.

X. *The Special Problem of Identity in Guerrilla Warfare in Relation to the Application of the Law of War*

In addition to the problems surrounding extension of belligerent status to rebellious factions in civil or international-civil war, the nature of war itself—particularly when such war includes guerrilla activities—adds many difficulties to the operation of the law of war.

Some of the most obvious differences between international war, war between states to which the law of war automatically applies, and civil or international-civil war characterized by guerrilla operations center on the issue of the identity of combatants, an issue affecting both the status of captured forces as prisoners of war and the annihilation of such forces in actual combat.

Deciding who is included in the armed forces of a state is a matter of domestic jurisdiction and not a question of international law. The bulk of a country's armed forces are combatants, but these are sup-

---

[114] von Glahn, note 83 *supra*, p. 552.

ported by noncombat units and individuals, such as medical units including doctors, nurses, and medical corpsmen. Generally speaking, noncombatants as well as combatants of regular armed forces are to be treated as prisoners of war if captured. The sex of members of the armed forces is irrelevant as far as legal status is concerned.[115]

Any war may also include the employment of irregular forces, either authorized by a belligerent power or operating independently. Formerly only authorized irregular or guerrilla forces were granted the privileges normally extended to armed forces of belligerents. Other irregulars could be shot as war criminals if captured.[116] Thus the Hague Conference in 1899 branded as illegal the activities of guerrilla troops in occupied territories, since "the continuation of the struggle after the national territory had been totally occupied by the enemy without there remaining any hope of restoring the position is a senseless act of defiance which merits reprobation."[117] The Hague rules of land warfare of 1907 carried forth this theory and allowed guerrilla activities only outside occupied territories. The Geneva Conventions of 1949, however, permit such operations in occupied territories as well, and allow captured guerrillas the status of prisoners of war provided they satisfy the four criteria previously set down in the Hague Conventions of 1907. Thus the Geneva Convention of 1949 on prisoners of war states in Articles 3 and 4 that members of militias and volunteer corps which do not form part of the regular armed forces, as well as members of "organized resistance movements, belonging to a Party of the conflict and operating in or outside their own territory, even if this territory is occupied," are entitled to be treated as prisoners of war provided they (1) are commanded by a person responsible for his subordinates, (2) have a distinctive sign recognizable at a distance, (3) carry arms openly, and (4) conduct military operations in accordance with the laws and customs of warfare.[118]

While the criteria for extending to guerrillas prisoner of war status are harsh, Lauterpacht contends that they are fair:

> The fulfillment on the part of the occupant of his obligation to respect the life and liberty of the civilian population may be put under a considerable strain if the safety of his troops and administration are menaced by forces which attack with an effectiveness en-

---

[115] *Ibid.*, p. 553.   [116] Lauterpacht, note 33 *supra*, p. 256.
[117] *Ibid.*, p. 213.
[118] For a citation to the text of the Convention see note 35 *supra*.

hanced by secrecy and which at the same time claim to be protected by the rules of war designed for ordinary combatants.[119]

Others contend that since successful guerrilla warfare depends on stealth, hit-and-run attacks, and clandestine operation, obeying the specified conditions, especially those relating to wearing of signs and carrying of arms, would be tantamount to suicide. At any rate, it would appear that guerrillas cannot operate effectively if they adhere fully to the Geneva Conventions.

While prisoner of war status may be held out to such forces as an inducement to surrender, guerrillas operating "illegally" by not satisfying the conditions of Articles 3 and 4 will continue to be subject to execution as war criminals under the laws of the state in which they operate. War crimes tribunals have held that civilians not exhibiting the characteristics of lawful irregular forces as set forth in Article 1 of the 1907 Hague Regulations were not entitled to prisoner of war status, and their execution did not constitute a war crime.[120] The 1949 Geneva Convention on treatment of civilians now requires judicial determination of the fact of participation in "illegal" guerrilla activities before execution.[121]

Individuals operating as partisans or "part-time" guerrillas can still be shot as war criminals under the 1949 Geneva Conventions. In this respect, Baxter notes:

> Article 5 of the same Convention, in addition to limiting the extent to which the Convention is applicable to persons guilty of hostile acts in occupied territory, states with respect to the "territory" of a Party to the conflict" that "an individual protected person (i.e. any person in enemy hands not otherwise protected) who is engaged in or suspected of hostile activities is not entitled to claim such rights and privileges under the Convention as would imperil the security of the detaining state.[122]

Baxter further contends, that the failure of Article 5 to refer to areas outside occupied areas or the territory of the detaining state suggests that: ". . . both Articles 4 and 5 were directed to the protection of in-

---

119 Lauterpacht, note 33 *supra*, p. 215.

120 McDougal and Feliciano, note 23 *supra*, p. 84, note 211.

121 In addition, Articles 65-77 provide the occupant with a readily applicable code of criminal law and procedure.

122 Richard R. Baxter, "So-Called 'Underprivileged Belligerency': Spies, Guerrillas, and Saboteurs," *B.Y.I.L.*, Vol. XXVIII (1951), p. 328.

habitants of occupied areas and of the mass of enemy aliens on enemy territory and that unlawful belligerents in the zone of operations were not taken into account in connexion with the two articles."[123] He concludes that no provision of the Convention precludes the death penalty for unlawful belligerents in contested areas and that "a fortiori, lesser penalties may be imposed."[124]

The conflict in the law of war between the demands of patriotism which in many instances instigate guerrilla warfare, and the legitimate military necessity of protecting regular belligerent forces is thus evident in the formulation of rules governing the status of guerrilla forces.

XI. The War in Vietnam

A. EFFORTS OF THE ICRC TO INSURE MINIMUM STANDARDS OF RESTRAINT

The International Committee of the Red Cross has sought to promote full compliance by all parties in the Vietnam conflict with at least the minimal provisions of the 1949 Geneva Conventions. On June 11, 1965, the Committee addressed the following letter to the governments of the Democratic Republic of Vietnam (North Vietnam), the Republic of Vietnam (South Vietnam), the United States, and the National Liberation Front of South Vietnam:

> The hostilities raging at the present time in Viet-Nam—both North and South of the 17th parallel—have assumed such proportions recently that there can be no doubt they constitute an armed conflict to which the regulations of humanitarian law as a whole should be applied.
>
> All parties to the conflict, the Republic of Viet-Nam, the Democratic Republic and the United States of America are bound by the four Geneva Conventions of August 12, 1949, for the protection of the victims of war, having ratified them and having adhered thereto. The National Liberation Front is bound by the undertakings signed by Viet-Nam.
>
> Pursuant to the common Article 1 of the four Geneva Conventions, "The High Contracting Parties undertake to respect and to ensure respect for the present Convention in all circumstances." It is likewise said in Article 2 that "The present Convention shall apply to

[123] *Ibid.*   [124] *Ibid.*

all cases of declared war or of any other armed conflict which may arise between two or more of the Contracting Parties, even if the state of war is not recognized by one of them."

In keeping with its humanitarian tradition, the International Committee of the Red Cross in Geneva reminds the governments of the aforesaid countries and the National Liberation Front of their obligations pursuant to the Geneva Conventions.

It is incumbent on them to implement the provisions thereof and to permit the ICRC to carry out its mission as a neutral intermediary, as laid down in these Conventions.

In particular the life of any combatant taken prisoner, wearing uniform or bearing an emblem clearly indicating his membership of the armed forces, shall be spared, he shall be treated humanely as a prisoner of war, lists of combatants taken prisoner shall be communicated without delay to the International Committee of the Red Cross (Central Information Agency), and the delegates of the ICRC shall be authorized to visit prison camps.

In addition, parties to the conflict shall respect and protect civilians taking no part in hostilities, they shall abstain from attack against such persons and subject them to no form of violence.

The ICRC is prepared to co-operate with the authorities concerned as far as it is able in the loyal and strict application of the Geneva Conventions drawn up by the community of nations to alleviate the hardships engendered by war.

The ICRC conveys the present communication to the governments of the three aforesaid countries and will endeavor to deliver it also to the National Liberation Front. It would be pleased to know what measures are taken by the governments in conformity with the duties devolving upon them pursuant to the Geneva Conventions.[125]

Despite the position of the ICRC, the major participants in the Vietnam War are not in agreement on the applicability of the Geneva Conventions. While all except the National Liberation Front have either ratified or adhered to the Conventions,[126] only the United States, South

---

[125] *International Legal Materials*, Vol. 4 (1965), p. 1171.

[126] Prior to partition, Vietnam acceded to the Conventions, 181 U.N.T.S. 351 (1953), North Vietnam acceded separately, 274 U.N.T.S. 339 (1957), and the United States ratified in 1955, 213 U.N.T.S. 383.

Vietnam, and New Zealand officially support the ICRC opinion, while North Vietnam and the Front consider the Conventions *per se* inapplicable. Secretary of State Rusk replied to the ICRC letter on August 10, 1965:

> . . . The United States has always abided by the humanitarian principles enunciated in the Geneva Conventions and will continue to do so. In regard to the hostilities in Vietnam, the United States Government is applying the provisions of the Geneva Conventions and we expect the other parties to the conflict to do likewise.
>
> Among the particular measures being taken to implement the Conventions at the present time, the United States Government is developing plans to assist the Government of the Republic of Vietnam to expand and improve facilities and procedures to process and care for an increased number of captives taken in combat. The two governments are also increasing programs of instruction for personnel in the details of the provisions of the Conventions.
>
> As you are aware, those involved in aggression against the Republic of Viet Nam rely heavily on disguise and disregard generally accepted principles of warfare. From the outset it has therefore been difficult to develop programs and procedures to resolve fully all the problems arising in the application of the provisions of the Conventions. Continued refinement of these programs and procedures in the light of experience will thus undoubtedly be necessary.[127]

A similar reply was made on August 11, 1965, by Dr. Tran Van Do, Minister of Foreign Affairs of the Republic of Vietnam. It stated that:

> . . . the Government of the Republic of Vietnam is fully prepared to respect the provisions of the Geneva Conventions and to contribute actively to the efforts of the International Committee of the Red Cross to ensure their application. It is to be hoped that for their part the Viet Cong will show the same humanitarian concern. Appropriate measures have already been considered by our Government to accelerate the promulgation and dissemination of these conventions.
>
> I should like further to inform you that the Geneva Conventions although not yet promulgated in Viet Nam have, in fact, always

[127] *International Review of the Red Cross*, Vol. v (1965), p. 477.

been applied. Viet Cong prisoners have always received the most humane treatment from our civilian and military authorities.[128]

A letter of August 31, 1965 from the North Vietnamese Minister of Foreign Affairs did not reply directly to the ICRC request, but constituted instead an attack on the "United States and its agents in Saigon" who "are engaged in committing crimes in their war of aggression in Viet Nam, undermining peace, violating the laws and customs of war and perpetrating acts against humanity." It added:

> In order to compensate for its defeats in the undeclared war of aggression in South Viet Nam, the United States Government has, without any justification, given orders to its air and naval forces to make surprise attacks on the Democratic Republic of Vietnam, in flagrant violation of the Geneva Agreements of 1954 on Viet Nam and of the rules of international law. It has employed napalm and phosphorus bombs, poisonous chemical products, and its aircraft and warships have indiscriminately bombed hospitals, schools, road transport stations, markets, villages, fishing vessels, churches, pagodas, etc., massacring large numbers of innocent civilians and violating the Geneva Conventions of August 12, 1949, for the protection of the victims of war, as well as other rules of war.[129]

The NLF did not reply formally to the ICRC letter, but like the DRV gave assurances that, while it considered the Conventions inapplicable, any prisoners it captured in the course of the conflict were assured of humane treatment.[130]

Yet, despite the ICRC request and the apparent respect shown by all parties involved to the principles of international law governing the conduct of war, the Committee was forced to issue the following press release on February 9, 1968, almost three years after its initial plea:

> The International Committee of the Red Cross in Geneva is constantly being questioned about press news describing inhuman acts committed during the fighting now taking place in Vietnam.
>
> The ICRC reminds belligerents that in all circumstances they are bound to observe the elementary and universally recognized rules of humanity. These rules demand that the lives of combatants who have

---

[128] *Ibid.*, p. 478.   [129] *Ibid.*, p. 527.   [130] *Ibid.*, p. 636.

been captured be spared, that the wounded, the sick and those giving them medical care shall be respected, that the civilian population shall not be subject to attack from the air and lastly, that summary executions, maltreatment or reprisals shall be prohibited.

The ICRC has often made known to those taking part in the hostilities the obligations they must fulfil. It ardently hopes that they will shortly put an end to this blood-stained conflict and meanwhile urgently calls upon them to observe the basic rules of humanity.[131]

The last sections of this study focus on incidents of warfare in Vietnam, both North and South of the 17th parallel, which have given rise to these pleadings and reminders by the ICRC. I have chosen to concentrate on only those incidents for which the United States and its principal ally, South Vietnam, appear responsible. Admittedly, all parties have in fact been guilty of actions which in their frequency and pattern imply a conscious disregard for the international law of war. It would seem, however, that the United States, as the leader of "Western civilization" and the most "advanced" nation of the world, should feel a special commitment to hold itself and its allies to the highest standards of conduct in war. Actions of the NLF and the North Vietnamese in derogation of the law of war detract in no way from this responsibility. As Richard Falk has noted:

The violations by the other side do not vindicate our own unless committed in specific reprisal. Our basic combat tactics appear unrelated to the degree to which the other side conforms or not to governing rules of international law. Besides, the violations on the other side are mainly those entailed by pursuing a guerrilla strategy against an opponent that enjoys a great superiority in military and material resources. If the war was allowed to reach an outcome on the basis of an internal play of Vietnamese, or even South Vietnamese forces, there is little doubt that North Vietnam and the National Liberation Front would have long since succeeded. It is the massive American military presence, including its great weapons superiority, that accentuates recourse to illegal practices by both sides. Such illegality is an almost inevitable consequence of guerrilla warfare on the scale taking place in Vietnam.[132]

[131] *Ibid.*, Vol. VIII (1968), p. 138.
[132] Clergy and Laymen Concerned About Vietnam, *In the Name of America* (Annandale, Virginia: Turnpike Press, Inc., 1968), p. 25.

A most important additional point justifying concentration on the actions of the United States and South Vietnam is of course the fact that both have given their official assurances that they will apply all provisions of the 1949 Geneva Conventions in the war.

B. THE NATURE OF THE CONFLICT

By mid-1968 the war in Vietnam was being fought by 540,000 American and 758,000 South Vietnamese and Allied troops opposed by 378,000 Viet Cong and North Vietmamese regulars. Supporting the forces of the Free World Military Assistance Command were approximately 5,500 aircraft, including over 2,500 helicopters, and 95 ships, 840 tanks, and 400 cannon. By late 1967 over 1,000 Americans were being killed in action every month; over 25,000 had died by late June of 1968. Three months later total American casualties surpassed 200,000, or almost 60,000 more than were killed, wounded, and missing in Korea. South Vietnamese and Allied casualties totaled about 500 monthly, while North Vietnamese and Viet Cong killed in action rose from about 3,500 to 7,000 a month between late 1965 and the end of 1967. Total Viet Cong and North Vietnamese dead by September, 1968, were estimated at between 390,000 and 780,000, with an undetermined number wounded.[133]

Perhaps more than in any major war in history these figures give a very incomplete picture of the conflict's devastating effects on the country in which it is being fought. The war in South Vietnam is not between armies in open battle over precious territory, but between armies and peasants in jungles, in thick forests, on hills and plains, rivers and lowlands, and very often in and around population centers which are themselves the objectives of the opposing forces. The people of the South are involved in the war not only as members of the local militia, the ARVN, or the Viet Cong. They are involved, whatever their profession or location, as civilians whose support is sought by both sides in a peculiar mixture of guerrilla and conventional warfare. Their involvement has increased not only as the prize of the conflict but as its target—a population whose security and existence is constantly endangered by the tactics of war. In North Vietnam aerial and naval bombardment, whether designed to interdict men and supplies, "punish" North Vietnam for its intervention in the South, or pressure Hanoi into a settlement, has often included destruction of installations which enjoy few of the traditional characteristics of military objectives.

[133] *U.S. News & World Report*, September 16, 1968.

On one side of the war is the devastating firepower of American military technology, a technology which has dropped more TNT over Vietnam than was delivered on Europe and Africa during all of World War II. On the other side is the guerrilla hit-and-run, terrorist strategy of the Viet Cong, coupled with the more conventional methods of the regular North Vietnamese army. In this type of warfare the law of war has until now exercised only minimal restraint. As the late Bernard Fall has commented:

> Another aspect of the progressive irrelevance of the human aspect of the Vietnam war is the universally callous attitude taken by almost everybody toward the crass and constant violations of the rules of war that have been taking place.

> As personal questions to both American and Vietnamese unit commanders have shown (and I have made a point of touching on the subject with most of them), there is only the vaguest idea among them as to what exactly is covered by the 1949 Convention; in the few cases where the terms "rules of war" meant anything at all, the officer concerned very often confused the rules of land warfare of the Hague and the Geneva Conventions on Prisoners of War of 1929, the 1949 Convention, the Red Cross Convention and the American Code of the Fighting Man.[134]

Even those who know the rules of war do not necessarily apply them. An American official in Saigon attempts to justify this conduct: "People on the outside just have no idea of what this war is all about or how it is fought. It's a rough and brutal war. The Viet Cong has never heard of the Marquis of Queensbury or Geneva Conventions, and we can't afford to lose just because we have heard of them."[135] That comment brings to mind the now infamous declaration of a U.S. Army major after the obliteration of Ben Tre with the loss of 500 to 1000 civilian lives: "It became necessary to destroy the town to save it," he said.[136] One wonders how large a role that same philosophy plays in American and Allied strategy with regard to the entire conflict in Vietnam.

C. THE AMERICAN-ALLIED STRATEGY

It is unfortunate and ironic that the nature of the conflict in Vietnam has led to an American and Allied policy which at once evidences

---

[134] Bernard B. Fall, "Vietnam Blitz," *New Republic*, October 9, 1965.
[135] Malcolm W. Browne, AP, March 25, 1965.
[136] *New York Post*, February 7, 1968.

careful restraint against traditional military targets and widespread lack of restraint against targets of more questionable military value. For instance, in the early stages of the air war, American air power made the immediate destruction of the bulk of North Vietnam's war-making capability both possible and illogical. It was illogical first because of the advisability of keeping up a steady pounding to promote negotiations while at the same time sparing certain targets as a bargaining point in such negotiations. Another point in favor of limiting bombing of the North was perhaps a fear of Chinese intervention. And one can believe that a certain air of humanity among top policy makers also prevailed to keep U.S. airpower within definite bounds.

An additional, more subtle reason for sparing selected North Vietnamese military targets throughout the air war may have been to enable North Vietnam to retain the capability of engaging in conventional war, rather than forcing it to revert to the slower tactics of the Viet Cong, tactics which might result in a steady depletion of enemy forces but lack the potential of spectacular morale-raising battles which are often deemed necessary in the face of a vastly superior foe.

In any case, there is good reason to believe that the United States Air Force was avoiding many vital targets in North Vietnam as late as August 1967, two and a half years after the air war over the North began. For instance, a report issued by the Senate Preparedness Investigation Subcommittee stated on September 1, 1967:

> Recently the J.C.S. and Cincpac target lists have been combined into the operating target list. This now contains a total of 427 targets and as of Aug. 25, 1967, 359 of these had been recommended for strike and strikes had been authorized against 302. Thus, there were 57 targets recommended by the Joint Chiefs of Staff against which strikes have not been authorized.

> This addresses itself to only part of the picture. Many long-recommended targets were authorized for the first time in August, 1967. As a matter of fact, Admiral Sharp had recommended 129 targets to Secretary McNamara when he briefed him in Saigon in July, 1967. General Wheeler stated that as of Aug. 9, 1967, there were 111 unauthorized targets and that the J.C.S. recommended that 70 of them be authorized for strike. The remaining 41, while retained on the target list, were not recommended at that time.

. . .

On Aug. 25, 1967, there were 57 targets recommended by the Joint Chiefs of Staff against which strikes have not been authorized. Another 68 targets on the operating list are not currently recommended by the Joint Chiefs. The Secretary of Defense in his appearance before the subcommittee took great pains to minimize and deprecate the significance of the 57 recommended targets which have not been approved. He said: "The present importance of such targets as these has not been shown to warrant risking the loss of American lives." Yet in the past many American lives have been lost by striking approved targets which were clearly of much less significance than many of those recommended but not approved.

It was clearly implied by the Secretary of Defense that few, if any, important military targets remained unstruck. The great weight of the military testimony was to the contrary: General McConnell states: "There are many valuable targets remaining unstruck." General Wheeler stated that the 57 targets under discussion were worthwhile targets and said: "There are many lucrative targets that have not yet been struck," and "that we consider important." As late as Aug. 28, General Greene said: "The key targets have not even yet been hit."[137]

The United States strategy under these circumstances, whatever the reasoning behind it, has kept enough pressure on North Vietnam to force it to continue to look to conventional military battles for occasional face-saving victories, but at the same time that pressure was not so excessive as to completely destroy that conventional war-making ability and turn North Vietnam to unconventional guerrilla warfare that in the long run would have had a more taxing effect on U.S.-Allied forces, at least in terms of a lengthier, nonconclusive war.

The sparing of authentic, fixed military targets in North Vietnam, coupled with the fact that the air raids above the 17th parallel continued unabated prompts one to ask what was the nature of those targets being hit. This question takes on added significance in view of Secretary McNamara's testimony before the same Senate Preparedness Investigation Subcommittee on October 11, 1967. Admitting that he did not believe that the bombing had "in any significant way affected" the "war-making capability" of North Vietnam, the Secretary also cast doubt on the interdiction effectiveness of the raids: "All of the evidence

[137] *New York Times*, September 1, 1967.

so far is that we have not been able to destroy a sufficient quantity of war material in North Vietnam to limit the activity in the South below the present level and I do not know that we can in the future."[138] Yet, despite his doubts, McNamara still found some justification for the raids: they were "increasing the price" of North Vietnam's "aggression" in South Vietnam.[139]

Specific instances of how that "price" is being paid by North Vietnam will be discussed later. But a conclusion drawn naturally from the above statements is that air power was being directed against targets of decreasingly little or no military value. Under such conditions civilian suffering has appeared to increase as the war has dragged on. There is evidence that such increase in civilian suffering held true even when bombing raids were limited to the narrow southern panhandle of North Vietnam from April to July 1968. This conclusion is supported by figures showing that while the bombing had in fact been "limited" geographically, it had been stepped up quantitatively. Mission totals for 1968 since the bombing "curb" began, with 1967 mission totals in parentheses were: April—3,412 (2,925); May—3,593 (3,237); June—3,792 (3,607); and the first three weeks of July—2,723 (3,819).[140] A second factor indicating the likelihood of increased civilian casualties in the heavily populated area was the fact that 30 U.S. planes were shot down from March 31 to mid-July, 1968, while over the same period in 1967, 133 aircraft had been lost.[141] One might conclude initially from such figures that targets being hit were simply less than well defended and of only minimal military importance. This conclusion might be buttressed by Department of Defense assurances that the raids during that period were directed principally against infiltration routes. But such a conclusion becomes questionable since in the same breath it was admitted that infiltration had *increased* during the period.[142] In fact, reports from civilian visitors to the heavily populated panhandle region indicated that scores of raids were being directed against farmlands and villages.[143]

As in North Vietnam, use of U.S. airpower and artillery in South Vietnam raises serious legal and moral questions about the conduct of the war. Numerous accounts of correspondents, visiting scholars,

---

[138] *New York Times,* October 11, 1967.
[139] *Ibid.*
[141] *Ibid.*
[140] *New York Post,* July 23, 1968.
[142] *Ibid.*
[143] See Richard A. Falk, "A Vietnam Settlement: The View From Hanoi," Policy Memorandum No. 34, Center of International Studies, Princeton University (1968), p. 8.

and others indicate that targets of secondary, tertiary, and in many cases no conceivable military importance have come under air and artillery bombardment. These occurrences are perhaps partly the result of having such vast firepower and so few stationary targets of a conventional military character.[144] In addition, two of the principal reasons for limiting bombing of the North—the negotiation and Chinese intervention factors—are absent in South Vietnam. A freer reign on air and artillery operations in the South could also serve to diminish divisiveness in overall United States war policy by keeping American military commanders from turning completely sour on a war run by politicians in Washington whose first concern appeared to many to be over-restraint of military force.[145]

D. METHODS OF WARFARE: CIVILIAN PROPERTY, AND NON-MILITARY TARGETS—APPLICABLE PROVISIONS OF THE LAW OF WAR

Relevant provisions of the Hague Convention IV Annex, Regulations Respecting the Laws and Customs of War on Land (October 18, 1907) are:[146]

Article 22: The right of belligerents to adopt means of injuring the enemy is not unlimited.

Article 23(g): In addition to the prohibitions provided by special Conventions, it is especially forbidden—To destroy or seize the enemy's property, unless such destruction or seizure be imperatively demanded by the necessities of war.

Article 25: The attack or bombardment, by whatever means, of towns, villages, dwellings, or buildings which are undefended is prohibited.

Article 26: The officer in command of an attacking force must, before

---

[144] The use of airpower and artillery to hit questionable targets was recently explained by a retired Air Force captain familiar with operations in Vietnam. Normal procedure was to allow low echelon personnel, often an airman first class or below, to assign targets to airborne squadrons which were unable to hit primary objectives or had ordnance left over from their first strike. Often, all area targets, even the most questionable targets like fishing villages, rice paddies, or clusters of huts with seemingly normal activity around them, had been hit several, even scores of times. The result was to assign strikes to targets of decreasing military significance.

[145] The Senate Preparedness Investigation Subcommittee sided with the military in urging President Johnson to expand the air war and abandon "carefully controlled" bombing. *New York Times*, September 2, 1967.

[146] For a citation to the text of the Convention see note 28 *supra*.

commencing a bombardment, except in cases of assault, do all in his power to warn the authorities.

Article 46: Family honour and rights, the lives of persons, and private property, as well as religious convictions and practice must be respected. Private property cannot be confiscated.

Article 50: No general penalty, pecuniary or otherwise, shall be inflicted upon the population on account of the acts of individuals for which they cannot be regarded as jointly and severally responsible.

Relevant provisions of the Geneva Convention Relative to the Protection of Civilian Persons in Time of War (August 12, 1949) are:[147]

Article 29: The Party to the conflict in whose hands protected persons may be, is responsible for the treatment accorded to them by its agents, irrespective of any individual responsibility which may be incurred.

Article 31: No physical or moral coercion shall be exercised against protected persons, in particular to obtain information from them or from their parties.

Article 32: The High Contracting Parties specifically agree that each of them is prohibited from taking any measure of such a character as to cause the physical suffering or extermination of protected persons in their hands. This prohibition applies not only to murder, torture, corporal punishment, mutilation and medical or scientific experiments not necessitated by the medical treatment of a protected person, but also to any other measures of brutality whether applied by civilian or military agents.

Article 33: No protected persons may be punished for an offence he or she has not personally committed.

Collective penalties and likewise all measures of intimidation or of terrorism are prohibited.

Pillage is prohibited.

Reprisals against protected persons and their property are prohibited.

Article 53: Any destruction by the Occupying Power of real or personal property belonging individually or collectively to private persons, or to the State, or to other public authorities, or to social or cooperative organizations, is prohibited, except where such destruction is rendered absolutely necessary by military operations.

[147] For a citation to the text of the Convention see note 35 *supra.*

Article 146: The High Contracting Parties undertake to enact any legislation necessary to provide effective penal sanctions for persons committing, or ordering to be committed, any of the grave breaches of the present convention defined in the following article.

Each High Contracting Party shall be under the obligation to search for persons alleged to have committed, or to have ordered to be committed, such grave breaches, and shall bring such persons, regardless of their nationality, before its own courts. It may also, if it prefers, and in accordance with the provisions of its own legislation, hand such persons over for trial to another High Contracting Party concerned, provided such High Contracting Party has made out a *prima facie* case.

Each High Contracting Party shall take measures necessary for the suppression of all acts contrary to the provisions of the present Convention other than the grave breaches defined in the following Article.

In all circumstances, the accused persons shall benefit by safeguards of proper trial and defence, which shall not be less favorable than those provided by Article 105 and those following of the Geneva Convention relative to the Treatment of Prisoners of War of August 12, 1949.

Article 147: Grave breaches to which the preceding Article relates shall be those involving any of the following acts, if committed against persons or property protected by the present Convention: wilful killing, torture or inhuman treatment, including biological experiments, wilfully causing great suffering or serious injury to body or health, unlawful deportation or transfer or unlawful confinement of a protected person, compelling a protected person to serve in the forces of a hostile Power, or wilfully depriving a protected person of the rights of fair and regular trial prescribed in the present Convention, taking of hostages and extensive destruction and appropriation of property, not justified by military necessity and carried out unlawfully and wantonly.

Article 148: No High Contracting Party shall be allowed to absolve itself or any other High Contracting Party of any liability incurred by itself or by another High Contracting Party in respect of breaches referred to in the preceding Article.

In Vietnam, as in all hostilities involving guerrilla warfare, the enemy works among and seeks the support of the civilian population.

To destroy the effectiveness of such an enemy he must be killed or captured in battle or separated from his supply lines and the support of the civilian population. In Mao Tse-tung's terminology, the fish must be taken out of the water in which they swim.[148] But these methods of destroying the guerrillas' effectiveness often work against each other. If the Allied forces wish to avoid alienation of the population and support for the Viet Cong, the VC must be ferreted out from among the noncombatants before firepower is brought to bear. This has been the major problem in Vietnam, where firepower is so incredibly potent. Along with the use of air and artillery bombardment to hit targets of questionable military significance, the American strategy has apparently included the realization that sifting the guerrillas out from the population which often supports and shields them is a far more difficult task than moving the peasants themselves to areas in which they can safely be insulated from guerrilla forces. Saturation bombing, the use of area coverage antipersonnel weapons like cluster bomb units (CBU's), scorched earth campaigns, and the widespread use of defoliants have prompted civilians to move out of contested areas or suffer the consequences of being labeled enemy sympathizers. Over two million refugees have been created by this policy in a country of sixteen million people.[149] While the transfer of peasants to government-controlled protected areas or camps has given the Allied forces a speedy method of gaining control over increased numbers of the population, it has at the same time resulted in widespread alienation of those segments of the population forced away from their homes and land to live with minimum freedom in restricted areas with little of the already limited appeal of their native areas under war.

In the process of prompting civilians into controlled areas, noncombatant deaths have become one of the most shocking elements in the Vietnam conflict. The war-injured ratio has been estimated to be as high as ten civilians to one soldier. Other estimates claim at least 25,000 civilians were killed in the war in 1966 and that by early 1967 over a quarter of a million children had been killed and a million

[148] Methods of guerrilla and counterguerrilla warfare are discussed in Mao Tse-tung, *On Guerrilla Warfare* (New York: Frederick A. Praeger, Inc. 1961), Franklin Mark Osanka (ed.), *Modern Guerrilla Warfare* (New York: Free Press of Glencoe, 1962), T. N. Greene (ed.), *The Guerrilla—And How to Fight Him* (New York: Frederick A. Praeger, Inc., 1962), and Charles W. Thayer (ed.), *Guerrilla* (New York: Harper & Row, Inc., 1963).

[149] Speech by Sen. Robert F. Kennedy, *New York Times*, February 9, 1968.

wounded.[150] The majority of such civilian casualties are the result of air raids and artillery fire, prime instances of which are described by Desmond Smith and Bernard Fall:

> . . . The First Cav love their war. Basically it is Indians and Cavalry spread over an OA (area of operations) of some 3,000 square kilometers. . . .

> . . . From a briefing on how the First Cav "softened up" the Bong-Son plain preparatory to moving in:
> "Three hundred and sixty-five air strikes."
> "Yes."
> "More than thirty ARCLIGHTS—that's code for B-52 strikes."
> "Yes."
> "And that was the start. Then we lobbed in better than a million shells."
> "In between the air strikes, we dumped more than a million psywar leaflets on the plain."
> "Yes."
> "Well, do you correspondents have any questions?"
> "Well, only one. According to your handout, all you have captured so far in OPERATION PERSHING is thirty hand grenades, four rounds of large calibre ammunition, three tons of rice, and three tons of salt."
> "Sir?"
> "It appears that you've levelled virtually every village and hamlet, killed or driven more than 50,000 peasants off the land with your firepower. My question is, how do you intend to go about winning the hearts and minds of these people?"
> "I'm afraid you'll have to take that up with the S.5, sir, but jeeze, it's a real good question."[151]

In describing a raid on a fishing village, Fall gives further evidence that American methods of warfare do not allow civilians to remain neutral in the war against the guerrilla:

> . . . Our "Skyraider" was loaded with 750-pound napalm bombs and 500-pound napalm bombs, plus our four 20-millimeter cannon. Our wing plane carried 7,500 pounds of high explosive antipersonnel

[150] See stories by Chandler Brossard, *Look* (April 18, 1967), Jesse W. Lewis, Jr., *Washington Post*, February 5, 1967, and George W. Cornell, AP, October 24, 1966.

[151] Desmond Smith, "There Must Have Been Easier Wars," *The Nation*, June 12, 1967.

bombs, plus our four cannon. . . . As we flew over our target it looked to me very much as any normal village would look: on the edge of a river sampans and fish nets in the water. It was a peaceful scene. . . . The napalm was expected to force the people—fearing the heat and burning—out into the open. Then the second plane was to move in with heavy fragmentation bombs to hit whatever—or whomever—had rushed out into the open. Then we came in a third time and raked over the village with our cannon. . . . There were probably between 1,000 and 1,500 people living in the fishing village we attacked. It is difficult to estimate how many were killed. It is equally difficult to estimate if there were actually any Viet Cong in the village, and if so, if any were killed. . . . I read an official report later which described the village as a Communist rest center, and said it had been successfully destroyed.[152]

Blanket bombing and attacks on "rest centers" constitute only a part of the cause of civilian casualties and destruction of civilian property in Vietnam, where military commanders have had to ask themselves many questions in conducting military operations. For example, if a Viet Cong sniper shoots at your troops from a nearby village, do you go around the village, go after the sniper and further endanger your own troops, or simply burn down the village? In some officers' eyes, it would be considered a matter of "military necessity" to burn down an entire village to kill one sniper. Similar problems arise when observation planes are shot at from villages, and air strikes—often indiscriminate in their accuracy—are called up to put the enemy out of action. Related to these problems is the question of the aerial bombardment of oil or other military supplies or bunkers in proximity to populated areas. Not uncommon, too, are "scorched earth" actions:

The 25th Division's Wolfhounds trudged through the vast swamplands thirty miles west of Saigon, destroying homes, food, gardens, livestock and even pets—everything that could be of use to the Communists.

. . . The operation . . . covered more than 100 square miles in the northern end of the Plain of Reeds, an area of swamp and marsh long dominated by the Viet Cong and a major route for Communist units moving between the Mekong Delta and Cambodia into War Zones Z and D.

[152] Fall, "This Isn't Munich, It's Spain," *Ramparts*, December 1965.

Scores of civilians who had slipped back into the area after an earlier operation to evacuate them were taken to government controlled areas. Hundreds of fires dotted the countryside as U.S. infantrymen destroyed homes, farm wagons and even piles of rice straw.

. . . Colonel Marvin Fuller, Commander of the 25th's Second Brigade, said anyone living in his operation area was presumed to be Viet Cong. He said the systematic slaughter of water buffalo, ducks, chickens, and pigs was to deny fresh meat to the enemy battalions.[153]

Add to these episodes the use of chemical warfare to destroy crops which *might* be used by the enemy and you have at least a partial picture of the plight of the civilian in Vietnam. Neil Sheehan wrote of the result in late 1966:

The flow of refugees from the countryside is the most eloquent evidence available of the gradual destruction of rural society under the impact of the war. The number of refugees has now passed the million mark. It takes a great deal to make a Vietnamese peasant forsake his land and the graves of his ancestors.

Most refugees I have questioned told me that the Viet Cong taxed them and made them work harder than usual, but that they could live with the Communists. They left their homes, they said, because they could no longer bear American and South Vietnamese bombs and shells.

Deserted hamlets and barren rice fields, now a common sight, are other evidence of what the war is doing to rural South Vietnam. In several provinces on the northern central coast as much as one-third of the rice land has been forsaken. The American policy of killing crops in Communist held areas by spraying them with chemical defoliants from aircraft is hastening this process. During the first six months of this year 59,000 acres were destroyed.[154]

Chemicals are also being used in increasing amounts to destroy vegetation concealing enemy infiltration routes in forests and along waterways. The Department of Defense has noted that between 1965 and 1968 annual expenditures on these chemicals rose from $10 million to $70 million.[155] The "chemical war" has prompted many sci-

153 John T. Wheeler, AP, March 13, 1967.
154 Neil Sheehan, "Not a Dove, But No Longer a Hawk," *New York Times Magazine*, October 9, 1966.
155 *New York Times*, July 20, 1968.

entists to express concern about the harmful effects of defoliants on both the environment and inhabitants in South Vietnam. In July 1968, the board of directors of the American Association for the Advancement of Science, largest scientific organization in the nation, urged that the United Nations undertake a long-term study of these effects. The recommendation was spurred by the Association's conclusion that it could not agree with the Department of Defense "that seriously adverse consequences will not occur as a result of the use of herbicidal chemicals in Vietnam."[156]

The civilians of South Vietnam are not alone in their suffering. Many North Vietnamese have also found themselves directly involved in the conflict, particularly those living in and around the cities of Hanoi and Haiphong, where transportation facilities, power plants, and the stores of war have gained little protection from their proximity to populated areas. In the winter of 1966 the dispatches of Harrison Salisbury of the *New York Times* first described the air raids on the North to the American people. One of the places Salisbury visited was Namdinh:

> We came into Namdinh from the north, and almost all the streets we drove through bore signs of bomb damage. . . . The principal industries, in addition to the big cotton textile works, were a silk mill, a fruit canning factory, a farm tool plant, a rice mill and a cooperative which made thread.
>
> Namdinh may be North Vietnam's third largest city, but if this was all it produced, it heardly sounded like a prime target. . . .
>
>   . . .
>
> After my dispatches began appearing in *The Times*, Arthur Sylvester, then the chief spokesman for the Pentagon, urged that I walk down the main street of Namdinh, where, he said, I would find a large antiaircraft installation. I only wished I could have taken him with me on the stroll. My car had passed down the main street and turned at an intersection. No antiaircraft installation was in sight that day. Nor was one in sight on New Year's Day when some other visitors were in Namdinh. The nearest thing to a military installation which I saw on Namdinh's main street was a rather pretty militia woman, or traffic officer. She had a small revolver on her hip,

156 *Ibid.*

but I doubted that it would have been effective against a super-sonic attack bomber.[157]

More recent stories from the area leave reason to believe that civilian suffering is often far too prevalent to be incidental to the destruction of military objectives. Richard Falk wrote of his visit to North Vietnam in June, 1968:

> American air power is virtually unchallenged in North Vietnam ex-cept around the major cities. We spent a day in the town of Phat Diem, reported to us to have been bombed 406 times, and defended only by defense militia armed with single-bolt rifles. It is a difficult experience for an American to walk through the rubble of churches and convents at Phat Diem. . . . One must go through the village countryside to experience the brutal impact of the war on North Viet-nam, and of course the devastation of South Vietnam is far worse. How does one explain bombing patterns directed against village communities? How are we to comprehend the use of antipersonnel bombs, napalm, and delayed-action bombs against rural areas that are far from supply lines and remote from battlefields? Who gave the orders to bomb Phat Diem? And what was the rationale? Americans will need to confront these questions sooner or later. It will not long assuage our moral conscience to purport ignorance or impotence.[158]

The story told by Salisbury and Falk is repeated scores of times in John Gerassi's *North Vietnam: A Documentary*.[159] Together, these reports provide a damaging indictment of American conduct of the war north of the 17th parallel.

It should perhaps be repeated that the "one-sided" description of events in Vietnam to this point is not meant to imply that only Amer-ican forces are violating or stretching many of the rules of war beyond their central humanitarian principles in the name of military necessity. Viet Cong terrorist attacks, which do not differentiate between civilian and enemy in many cases, are not uncommon. Reports of the use of civilian hostages by the Viet Cong in combat have also been made, and it can be assumed that reprisals against villages friendly to Allied forces are widespread. But again it would seem that the United States, in con-

157 Harrison E. Salisbury, *Behind the Lines—Hanoi* (New York: Bantam Books, Inc., 1967), pp. 85-88.
158 Falk, note 143 *supra*, p. 4.
159 John Gerassi, *North Vietnam: A Documentary* (New York: Bobbs-Merrill Co., Inc., 1968).

trol of such massive firepower and virtually unbeatable militarily speaking, would be bound to do much more than it has in preventing civilian casualties and destruction of civilian property in Vietnam, no matter what the actions of the enemy.

E. WEAPONS OF WARFARE—APPLICABLE PROVISIONS OF THE LAW OF WAR

Relevant provisions of the Hague Convention IV Annex, Regulations Respecting the Laws and Customs of War on Land (October 18, 1907) are:[160]

> *Article 22:* Aerial bombardment for the purposes of terrorising the civilian population, of destroying or damaging private property not of a military character, or of injuring non-combatants is prohibited.
>
> *Article 23(a):* In addition to the prohibitions provided by special Conventions, it is especially forbidden—
> To employ poison or poisoned weapons.
>
> *Article 23(b):* In addition to the prohibitions provided by special Conventions, it is especially forbidden—
> To kill or wound treacherously individuals belonging to the hostile nation or army.
>
> *Article 23(e):* In addition to the prohibitions provided by special Conventions, it is especially forbidden—
> To employ arms, projectiles, or material calculated to cause unnecessary suffering.
>
> *Article 24: 1)* Aerial bombardment is legitimate only when directed at a military objective—that is to say, an object of which the destruction or injury would constitute a distinct military advantage to the belligerent.
>
> 2) Such bombardment is legitimate only when directed exclusively at the following objectives: military forces; military works; military establishments or depots; factories constituting important and well-known centres engaged in the manufacture of arms, ammunition, or distinctively military supplies; lines of communication or transportation used for military purposes.
>
> 3) The bombardment of cities, towns, villages, dwellings or buildings not in the immediate neighborhood of the operations of land

---

160 For a citation to the text of the Convention see note 28 *supra*.

forces is prohibited. In cases where the objectives specified in paragraph (2) are so situated that they cannot be bombarded without the indiscriminate bombardment of the civilian population, the aircraft must abstain from bombardment.

4) In the immediate neighborhood of the operations of land forces, the bombardment of cities, towns, villages, dwellings, or buildings is legitimate provided that there exists a reasonable presumption that the military concentration is sufficiently important to justify such bombardment, having regard to the danger thus caused to the civilian population.

Also relevant to a discussion of the weapons used in the war are:

The Second Declaration of the Hague Peace Conference of 1907, the signatories of which agreed "to abstain from the use of projectiles the sole object of which is the diffusion of asphyxiating and deleterious gases." (This is a reformulation of a similar declaration at the 1899 Conference.)[161]

The Third Declaration of the Hague Peace Conference of 1907, the signatories of which agreed to abstain from the use of "bullets which expand or flatten easily in the human body, such as bullets with a hard envelope which does not entirely cover the core, or is pierced with incisions." (This is a reformulation of a similar declaration at the 1899 Conference.)[162]

The Geneva Gas Protocol of 1925, prohibiting the use of asphyxiating, poisonous, or other gases, of bacteriological methods of warfare, and of all analogous liquids, materials, or devices.[163]

The Draft Rules for the Protection of the Civilian Population from the Dangers of Indiscriminate Warfare (submitted to the New Delhi Conference in October 1957, by the International Red Cross) prohibiting the use of weapons "whose harmful effects—resulting in particular from the dissemination of incendiary, chemical, bacteriological, radioactive or other agents—could spread to an unforeseen degree of escape, either in space or in time, from the control of those who employ them, thus endangering the civilian population."[164]

[161] *Ibid.*   [162] *Ibid.*
[163] For a citation to the text of the Protocol see note 31 *supra*.
[164] For a discussion of the draft convention see Kunz, "The Laws of War," note 22 *supra*, pp. 323-25, and *New York Times*, October 27, 1957.

Just as the methods of guerrilla warfare tend to involve the civilian population in actual combat to a greater degree than does conventional warfare, so the weapons of antiguerrilla warfare tend to be indiscriminate when applied in a war designed to destroy not only the enemy's armed forces and materials of war, but his will to fight. In Vietnam, destroying the enemy, either by the sheer weight of firepower brought to bear, as in blanket bombing by B-52s or by tactical fighter-bomber attacks, involves a degree of arbitrariness apparent in all phases of the military effort. It is an arbitrariness involving two developments which the law of war must control. First is the employment of weapons of high killing power and area devastation effect regardless of the danger to noncombatants. Second is the employment of weapons which cause unnecessary suffering and pain no matter who is the target.

Extensive firepower arbitrarily used presents a definite problem in Vietnam. B-52s are employed in pattern bombing to devastate wide swaths of countryside, not to strike at specific military targets. The effect may be to lower the Viet Cong morale, but as has been noted, such strikes on areas considered to be "controlled" by Viet Cong take their toll in civilians. Other weapons often appear to be employed by U.S. forces in an equally arbitrary manner. One example is the AC-47, sometimes known as "Puff, the Magic Dragon." Fitted with a trio of .30-calibre or 7.62 mm. gatling guns, the AC-47 is capable of firing 18,000 rounds per minute while circling slowly above the suspected enemy.[165] Another widely used weapon is the armed helicopter. Stocked with a combination of rockets, grenade launchers, and machine guns, the Huey helicopter is often used in "reconnaissance by fire" tactics: if the aircraft are not shot at, they turn their weapons on a suspicious-looking area, hoping for a response.[166] Use of both of these weapons, it would seem, often does not allow one to distinguish between VC supply or "rest" areas and Vietnamese villages built beneath the thick green treetops that cover much of the country. Nor do they appear to permit one to distinguish between the Viet Cong and the innocent civilian, often similarly clad:

> . . . Now, as we skimmed across the paddies, our gunner suddenly opened up with a burst and a farmer fell down. Later the pilot asked him what he had seen, and the young man, who was very inexperi-

165 C. M. Plattner, "Limited-War Concepts Weighed in Battle," *Aviation Week* (January 31, 1966).
166 *New York Times*, April 19, 1967.

enced, claimed that he had seen the farmer go for a gun. But the pilot and I had been watching too, and we were sure that the farmer had done nothing, that the youngster was just nervous.[167]

A variety of weapons used in Vietnam might also be questioned as causing unnecessary pain and suffering, therefore challenging the basic humanitarian principles underlying the law of war. One such weapon is the cluster bomb unit (CBU), a metal container dropped from aircraft and opening in mid-air to release many small bombs, grenades, or other munitions over a wide area. CBU's can also carry the so-called Lazy Dog, a drum of steel pellets dropped from a plane and exploding at about 6,000 feet to spray men and equipment below with a deadly buckshot effect.[168] A variation on Lazy Dog includes a weapon consisting of several hundred baseball-size explosives which detonate on impact and spray hundreds of pellets in all directions. In some cases, the pellets may be coated with napalm-like material, causing them to stick to whatever they hit.[169]

Also employed as an antipersonnel, area-coverage weapon in Vietnam is napalm, the jellied gasoline first used in World War II and a center of controversy in the Korean action. The case against napalm as an antipersonnel weapon is put forth by Greenspan:

> To burn a man to death or disable him by burning must in *all* circumstances cause the victim agonizing pain and suffering. Burning can never offer an instantaneous and comparatively painless death such as may be afforded by a bullet or shell fragment. It is true that the latter too may inflict wounds which result in a horrible and lingering death. But such a consequence is not inevitable, while it is inevitable when fatal wounds are inflicted by burning.[170]

The use of napalm and fire bombs in general is permitted, with conditions, by U.S. Army Field Manual 27-10:

> The use of weapons which employ fire, such as tracer ammunition, flame throwers, napalm and other incendiary agents, against targets requiring their use is not violative of international law. *They*

---

167 David Halberstam, *The Making of a Quagmire* (New York: Random House, 1964), p. 85.
168 *New York Times*, May 3, 1965.
169 Lee Lockwood, "Recollections of Four Weeks with the Enemy," *Life* (April 7, 1967).
170 Greenspan, note 56 *supra*, p. 361.

*should not, however, be employed in such a way as to cause unneces-
sary suffering to individuals.* (emphasis added) [171]

As one army officer in Vietnam confirmed, today's napalm burns hotter, longer, and covers more area than the variety used in Korea and
makes the World War II type "seem like a pocket lighter by comparison."[172] Only when it is not expressly used *against personnel* of the
enemy could such a weapon not be considered to cause "unnecessary
suffering to individuals," a suffering described in an AP dispatch by
Robert Tuckman:

> A company of U.S. infantrymen suffered heavy losses today when
> American jets mistakenly dropped two canisters of flaming napalm
> into its position during a close-quarter battle with the Viet Cong.

> . . . Two Columbia Broadcasting System men, Correspondents Mor-
> ley Safer and Cameraman Jerry Adams, were with the troops pre-
> paring to film the napalm strike when the canisters fell.

> Safer said in a dispatch to his headquarters in New York, it dropped
> no more than fifty yards from where the two men were standing.

> "We hit the dirt," he said. "I put my head up and the jungle in
> front of us was on fire. Running out of it were dozens of men, their
> clothes ablaze, some of them screaming, some rolling in the mud.
> In a moment it was all over."[173]

While not specifically violating international law, the use of napalm,
flame-throwers, and even white phosphorus bombs against personnel, could be considered a violation by analogy. Napalm and phosphorus weapons physically affect their victims with at least the same
degree of suffering caused by the gases and liquids condemned by the
1925 Geneva Protocol. The corrosive spray banned by the same protocol would be similar in its effects on the human body to those caused by
fire sprayed by a flame-thrower.

Another controversial weapon used by both U.S. and Vietnamese
forces in Vietnam is the .223-calibre AR-15 or M-16 rifle. With a
tremendous velocity the bullet tumbles end over end on striking its
target, and a huge jagged wound is the effect. According to the *Medical
World News*, "You have to open the patient up enough to evaluate the

171 *Ibid.*   172 Wheeler, AP, April 6, 1966.
173 Robert Tuckman, AP, August 26, 1966.

muscle and other tissues around the wound, and extensive debridgment is necessary."[174] The M-16's "effectiveness" is not publicized:

> . . . Tests of lethality by firing at goats or even at large blocks of gelatin (courtesy of the anti-vivisectionists) are never published. And a report on the effectiveness of the AR15 in Vietnam was suppressed mainly because of gruesome photographs it contained.
>
> The AR15 bullet is deadly because it imparts tremendous shock when it hits, and on striking flesh it yaws and tumbles end over end, literally tearing its way out. This aspect of the AR15 lethality has not been publicly emphasized by the Army, perhaps because it has been suggested that it could be considered a technical violation of the Hague Convention against the uses of expanding (or dumdum) bullets.[175]

The similarity of the effect of the projectile fired by the M-16 to that caused by the dumdum bullet, which was declared contrary to international law in 1899 and 1907 declarations at the Hague,[176] would seem more than a technical violation of the law of war.

Controversy also surrounds the use of chemical and gas warfare, which is sometimes used both arbitrarily and inhumanely, and has been blamed for deaths and lesser casualties in Vietnam. Defoliants and crop-killing chemicals used to deprive the Viet Cong of cover and food in many parts of the South have already been discussed. The use of gas in Vietnam, even of nonlethal gas, may be considered a technical violation of the 1925 Geneva Protocol. The Protocol in fact bans the use of "asphyxiating, poisonous, or other gases and all analogous liquids, materials or devices."[177] Lauterpacht cites a 1930 British memorandum on chemical warfare that considers this prohibition to cover lachrymatory gases.[178] On the dangers of discriminating between various types of gases, he adds: "It is true that some gases are not so deadly or so cruel as others, but the dangers of recognizing any categories of permitted gases and thus sanctioning the manufacture of the necessary equipment for using them are obvious and great, so that, it is submitted, the society of States has adopted the right policy in endeavoring to extirpate this mode of warfare *in toto*."[179]

---

174 "Medicine Battles the Odds in Vietnam," *Medical World News* (November 18, 1966).

175 John S. Tompkins, *The Weapons of World War III* (New York: Doubleday & Co., Inc., 1966), p. 127.

176 For a citation to the text of the Declaration see note 28 *supra*.

177 For a citation to the text of the Protocol see note 31 *supra*.

178 Lauterpacht, note 33 *supra*, p. 343, note 2.   179 *Ibid*.

Some would contend that the Protocol as such did not become effective as international law because it was not ratified by all of the signatories of the 1922 Washington Treaty, including the United States. However, the Protocol has been ratified or adhered to by some forty states. Citing war crimes trials conducted by the U.S.S.R. for alleged violations of the Protocol, von Glahn contends that: ". . . most writers today are in agreement that the Geneva Protocol is binding in practically all states, through the development of a general rule of customary law springing from the provisions of the Protocol."[180]

This same prohibition of dumdum bullets by a general rule of customary law would seem to be applicable to the United States in its use of the M-16 rifle, despite the fact that this country did not sign either the 1899 or 1907 Hague declarations prohibiting such bullets.[181] And again analogizing, it would appear, particularly if the harmful effects on civilians of defoliants and other chemicals used in Vietnam could be established conclusively, that such weapons might also be considered as contrary to the spirit, if not the letter, of international law.

This cursory look at the arsenal being employed against the Viet Cong and North Vietnamese in Vietnam is, of course, not meant to be exhaustive. Neither is concentration on the questionable humanitarian nature and arbitrary application of American and allied weapons meant to intimate that the Viet Cong and perhaps North Vietnamese have not made use of weapons equally arbitrary in their firepower and equally inhumane in the suffering they cause, despite the fact that they are often more primitive. Bamboo stakes at the bottom of a grass-covered pit, or steel spikes driven through a piece of wood and concealed point up in a rice paddy are not weapons that necessarily seek out the enemy, nor do they wound or kill with a minimum of suffering.[182] It is more reasonable to expect, however, that a nation capable

---

[180] von Glahn, note 83 supra, p. 588, citing Lauterpacht, note 33 supra, p. 343, note 2.

[181] Great Britain and the United States both refused to sign the Declaration in 1899. In 1907 Great Britain adhered to the Declaration with the U.S. still in opposition. The U.S. Army today recognizes that the use of dumdum bullets has become illegal through custom. The Law of Land Warfare, note 57 supra, p. 18.

[182] One of the most horrible weapons is described by Salisbury: "In another room was a ghastly device—a kind of bird cage with movable cross-wires to which were fitted a set of jagged fishhooks. The bird cage was buried on a trail and covered with a light scattering of leaves. When a man came down the trail his leg would thrust down into the cage and the fishhooks would dig in. If he tried to lift his limb or struggle out, each pull would drive them deeper, more cruelly into the flesh. The barbs could not be removed except by a surgeon's knife. This was not a weapon of the past. This was a

of developing such exotic weaponry as we have dispersed in Vietnam would be equally capable of using that weaponry within the guidelines, both written and unwritten, of international law.

F. TREATMENT OF PRISONERS—APPLICABLE PROVISIONS OF
THE LAW OF WAR

Relevant provisions of the Geneva Convention Relative to the Treatment of Prisoners of War (August 12, 1949) are:[183]

Article 3: In the case of armed conflict not of an international character occurring in the territory of one of the High Contracting parties, each Party to the conflict shall be bound to apply, as a minimum, the following provisions:

(1) Persons taking no active part in the hostilities, including members of armed forces who have laid down their arms and those placed *hors de combat* by sickness, wounds, detention, or any other cause, shall in all circumstances be treated humanely, without any adverse distinction founded on race, colour, religion or faith, sex, birth or wealth, or any other similar criteria. To this end the following acts are and shall remain prohibited at any time and in any place whatsoever with respect to the above-mentioned persons:

(a) violence to life and person, in particular murder of all kinds, mutilation, cruel treatment and torture;

(b) taking of hostages;

(c) outrages upon personal dignity; in particular, humiliating and degrading treatment;

(d) the passing of sentences and the carrying out of executions without previous judgment pronounced by a regularly constituted court affording all the judicial guarantees which are recognized as indispensable by civilized peoples.

(2) The wounded and sick shall be collected and cared for. An impartial humanitarian body, such as the International Committee of the Red Cross, may offer its services to the Parties to the conflict.

The Parties to the conflict should further endeavor to bring into

---

deadly device being set out that very day and every day in the jungle trails of the South where the Americans were seeking to flush out the Vietcong strongholds." Salisbury, note 56 *supra*, pp. 44-45.

[183] For the citation to the text of the Convention see note 35 *supra*.

force, by means of special agreements, all or part of the provisions of the present Convention.

The application of the preceding provisions shall not affect the legal status of the Parties to the conflict.

Article 4: A. Prisoners of war, in the sense of the present Convention, are persons belonging to one of the following categories, who have fallen into the power of the enemy:

(1) Members of the armed forces of a Party to the conflict, as well as members of militias or volunteer corps forming part of such armed forces.

(2) Members of other militias and members of other volunteer corps, including those of organized resistance movements, belonging to a Party to the conflict and operating in or outside their own territory, even if this territory is occupied, provided that such militias or volunteer corps, including such organized resistance movements, fulfill the following conditions:

(a) that of being commanded by a person responsible for his subordinates;

(b) that of having a distinctive sign recognizable at a distance;

(c) that of carrying arms openly;

(d) that of conducting their operations in accordance with the laws and customs of war.

(3) Members of regular armed forces who profess allegiance to a government or an authority not recognized by the Detaining Power.

Article 5: The present Convention shall apply to the persons referred to in Article 4 from the time they fall into the power of the enemy and until their final release and repatriation. Should any doubt arise as to whether persons, having committed a belligerent act and having fallen into the hands of the enemy belong to any of the categories enumerated in Article 4, such persons shall enjoy the protection of the present Convention until such time as their status has been determined by a competent tribunal.

Article 12: Prisoners of war are in the hands of the enemy power, but not of the individuals or military units who have captured them. Irrespective of the individual responsibilities that may exist, the Detaining Power is responsible for the treatment given them.

. . . Prisoners of war may only be transferred by the Detaining

Power to a Power which is a party to the Convention and after the Detaining Power has satisfied itself of the willingness and ability of such transferee Power to apply the Convention. When prisoners of war are transferred under such circumstances, responsibility for the application of the Convention rests on the Power accepting them while they are in its custody. Nevertheless, if that Power fails to carry out the provisions of the Convention in any important respect, the Power by whom the prisoners of war were transferred shall, upon being notified by the Protecting Power, take effective measures to correct the situation or shall request the return of the prisoners of war. Such requests must be complied with.

Article 13: Prisoners of war must at all times be humanely treated. Any unlawful act or omission by the Detaining Power causing death or seriously endangering the health of a prisoner of war in its custody is prohibited, and will be regarded as a serious breach of the present Convention. In particular, no prisoner of war may be subjected to physical mutilation or to medical or scientific experiments of any kind which are not justified by the medical, dental or hospital treatment of the prisoner concerned and carried out in his interest. Likewise, prisoners of war must at all times be protected, particularly against acts of violence or intimidation and against insults and public curiosity. Measures of reprisal against prisoners of war are prohibited.

Article 17: Every prisoner of war, when questioned on the subject, is bound to give only his surname, first names and rank, date of birth, and army, regimental, personal or serial number, or failing this, equivalent information. If he wilfully infringes this rule, he may render himself liable to a restriction of the privileges accorded to his rank or status.

Article 82: A prisoner of war shall be subject to the laws, regulations and orders in force in the armed forces of the Detaining Power; the Detaining Power shall be justified in taking judicial or disciplinary measures in respect of any offense of orders. However, no proceedings or punishments contrary to the provisions of the Chapter shall be allowed. If any law, regulation or order of the Detaining Power shall declare acts committed by a prisoner of war to be punishable, whereas the same acts would not be punishable if committed by a member of the forces of the Detaining Power, such acts shall entail disciplinary punishments only.

Article 129: The High Contracting Parties undertake to enact any legislation necessary to provide effective penal sanctions for persons committing, or ordering to be committed, any of the grave breaches of the present Convention defined in the following Article.

Each High Contracting party shall be under the obligation to search for persons alleged to have committed, or to have ordered to be committed, such grave breaches, and shall bring such persons, regardless of their nationality, before its own courts. It may also, if it prefers, and in accordance with the provisions of its own legislation, hand such persons over for trial to another High Contracting Party concerned, provided such High Contracting Party has made out a *prima facie* case.

Each High Contracting Party shall take measures necessary for the suppression of all acts contrary to the provisions of the present Convention other than the grave breaches defined in the following Article.

In all circumstances, the accused persons shall benefit by safeguards of proper trial and defense, which shall not be less favourable than those provided in Article 105 and those following of the present Convention.

Article 130: Grave breaches to which the preceding Article relates shall be those involving any of the following acts, if committed against persons or property protected by the Convention: wilful killing, torture or inhuman treatment, causing great suffering or serious injury to body or health, compelling a prisoner of war to serve in the forces of the hostile Power, or wilfully depriving a prisoner of war of the rights of fair and regular trial prescribed in this Convention.

Article 131: No High Contracting Party shall be allowed to absolve itself or any other High Contracting Party of any liability incurred by itself or by another High Contracting Party in respect of breaches referred to in the preceding Article.

As mentioned earlier, the United States and South Vietnam have agreed to apply the 1949 Geneva Conventions to the conflict. Although it is also a signatory of the Conventions, North Vietnam, like the NLF, has not been willing to give the same assurances, though both parties have said that prisoners would be afforded humane treatment. Both the NLF and North Vietnam would seem bound by the Conventions, as contended by the ICRC. The Front would appear responsible for upholding the Conventions whether we look upon it as an arm of Hanoi or as a faction indigenous to South Vietnam.[184] The fact that the NLF is not a party to the Conventions would not, in any case, seem to diminish U.S. and South Vietnamese liability for conduct in violation of them. This is especially true of the Convention on prisoners of war, as Greenspan notes:

> [This convention] applies to all armed conflicts between parties to the Convention, whether war has been declared or not, and even if one of the parties refuses to recognize a state of war. It also applies to all partial or total occupations of the territory of a party, even if the occupation is not resisted. The parties undertake to respect and ensure respect for the convention in all circumstances, including those conflicts in which one or more of the participants are not parties to the conventions. In the latter case, parties are bound by the conventions in their mutual relations, and also as regards the nonparties, provided the latter in fact accept and apply its provisions.[185]

It might be contended that nonobservance of the rules by one side would absolve the other side from its own responsibility under them. The Nuremberg Tribunal, it will be recalled, affirmed that observance of the rules of war even against a nonsignatory was binding as "being declaratory of the laws and customs of war."[186]

In fact, however, the United States officially has gone even further than declaring the war to be an international conflict to which all provisions of the 1949 Geneva Conventions apply.[187] The United States Military Assistance Command in Vietnam (USMACV) has issued several directives on the treatment of prisoners of war setting forth standards even beyond those in the 1949 Conventions.[188] United States mili-

---

[184] Insurgent factions are obligated to uphold international standards in the sphere of activity subject to their control. The insurgent faction is even deemed bound by the obligations of the *de jure* government to the extent that these obligations have been embodied in international agreements. The theory of insurgent obligation rests on the assumption that the constituted government can contract with foreign states on behalf of its entire society and that from the viewpoint of international law the insurgent faction is treated as a component of the national population.

[185] Greenspan, note 56 *supra*, pp. 96-97.   [186] See note 48 *supra*.

[187] See Section XI, Rusk's letter of August 10, 1965, *supra*.

[188] These include Directive 20-5 (change 1) of December 16, 1966 and Directive 190-3 of April 6, 1967.

tary personnel also receive regular instruction on the law of war, particularly the 1949 Conventions and the provisions of the 1907 Hague Convention IV respecting the laws and customs of war on land and the regulations annexed thereto. U.S. Army Field Manual 27-10, governing the conduct of United States forces in the field, devotes its longest chapter to the treatment of prisoners of war.[189] All personnel in Vietnam are also issued an instruction card for the treatment of prisoners.[190] It forbids mistreatment and humiliation of prisoners or confiscation of personnel effects which do not have significant military value. It requires that medical aid not be refused. In addition it instructs the detaining soldier to handle the prisoner "firmly, promptly, but humanely," and take him to security quickly. It points out that "mistreatment of any captive is a criminal offense," and "every soldier is personally responsible for the enemy in his hands." All prisoners, "whether suspects, civilians, or combat captives," are to be protected against "violence, insults, curiosity, and reprisals of any kind."[191]

The United States has officially held itself to such high standards partly in the hope that it will encourage reciprocal action on the part of the North Vietnamese and the Viet Cong. A total of 300 to 1,200 American prisoners are believed held by both groups,[192] and little is known of their treatment, since both the North Vietnamese and Viet Cong have refused to allow ICRC representatives to inspect the conditions of their internment.[193] The situation is further complicated by the American policy of transferring almost all its prisoners to the South Vietnamese forces. As Neil Sheehan has noted, this puts the United States in a poor bargaining position: "The United States is in the unhappy position of asking humane treatment for American prisoners of Communists while it has declined to guarantee similar treatment to Viet Cong taken prisoner by American ground combat units."[194] From the many news stories, books, and articles written about the war it would appear that many provisions of the Geneva Convention on prisoners of war covering transfer and treatment of prisoners (particularly Article 12) are being widely violated by the Allied forces. Pete Hamill's report is not uncommon: ". . . An American unit will move into a

---

189 *The Law of Land Warfare*, note 57 *supra*, pp. 25-82.

190 The directives in note 188 *supra* and a copy of the instruction card were obtained from the Office of the Secretary of Defense.

191 *Ibid.*   192 *New York Post*, July 29, 1968.

193 *New York Times*, May 12, July 18, 1967.

194 *New York Times*, September 30, 1965.

village, or an area, and round up every male. A South Vietnamese liaison officer will then interrogate each man, and if he believes that the man is a Viet Cong guerrilla or even a sympathizer, the man will be taken off to a detainment camp. After detailed interrogation, he is usually executed."[195] Others have noted the common use of torture used by the South Vietnamese in interrogating prisoners:

The favorite methods of torture used by Government troops are to slowly beat a captive, drag him behind a moving vehicle, apply electrodes to sensitive parts of his body or block his mouth while water spiced with hot pepper is poured down his nostrils. . . .[196]

In one known case two Viet Cong prisoners were interrogated on an airplane flying toward Saigon. The first refused to answer questions and was thrown out of the airplane at 3,000 feet. The second immediately answered all questions. But he, too, was thrown out.

. . . Other techniques, usually designed to force onlooking prisoners to talk, involve cutting off fingers, ears, fingernails or sexual organs of another prisoner. Sometimes a string of ears decorates the wall of a government military installation. One American installation has a Viet Cong ear preserved in alcohol.[197]

And Bernard Fall has described the often passive role of American soldiers who witness violations of the law of war on the part of their allies:

. . . In this war, there is no respect for the wounded. The Communist prisoner in the photograph had been shot in the back. He was bleeding when I found him lying on the floor. . . . I told an American officer who was with the unit that the man was wounded and should get some attention. His answer: "Yes, I know he needs help, but there isn't anything I can do about it. He's in Vietnamese hands. That is why I walked away, don't you see?" I saw. I also walked away and said nothing.[198]

THIS STUDY has examined selected characteristics of the war in Vietnam and, on this basis, reports one principal conclusion: United States and Allied actions, particularly under the headings of methods of warfare, weapons employed, and treatment of prisoners, disclose what seems to

195 *New York Post*, July 25, 1966.   196 *New York Times*, September 30, 1965.
197 *New York Herald Tribune*, April 25, 1965.
198 Fall, note 152, *supra*.

be a persistent, even if not planned, disregard of the basic rules, principles, and standards governing the conduct of war.[199]

Search and destroy missions, scorched earth campaigns, blanket strategic bombing, artillery and tactical aerial bombardment, defoliation, and crop destruction are methods of warfare that strike only secondarily at the enemy. Their primary impact is upon the persons and property of civilians. Such battlefield behavior cannot be defended by an appeal to the idea of "military necessity." Military necessity is a legally satisfactory excuse only when the tactics employed can be shown to be relevant to specific military objectives and when the damage to civilian and nonmilitary targets is incidental to the pursuit of those objectives.

Even the claim that the controversial behavior took place in the heat of battle or that it could be explained by the necessity of the kind of war taking place in Vietnam is absent when we consider the treatment of prisoners and suspected enemy detainees. Despite the obvious care which the United States has taken in the treatment of prisoners in its own custody, its failure to adhere strictly to the provisions of the 1949 Geneva Conventions governing the transfer of prisoners of war is a serious matter. Past treatment of prisoners of war transferred to the South Vietnamese authorities has in many instances been so obviously contrary to the provisions of the Convention that the United States has a clear duty to discontinue such transfers unless adherence on the part of its principal ally is guaranteed.

These several aspects of conduct in war are governed by the traditional law of war as it has developed over the centuries. The Nuremberg Judgment, particularly as it defined crimes against humanity should also be considered in judging the war actions of the United States and South Vietnam. Perhaps the most tragic story of the war in Vietnam involves the plight of civilians in the South, especially the problems created by the massive forced transfers of civilians into refugee camps. The intentional use of defoliants, crop killers, and blanket bombing to drive large sectors of the civilian population into these refugee centers and camps so that they can be more easily "controlled" is the practice followed in this war that is most lacking in legal or moral justification. The effect on the people who survive the experience and on the overall character of Vietnamese society will long remain uncertain. We must hope that no other people and no other

---

[199] See *In the Name of America*, note 132 *supra*, for a compilation of hundreds of such accounts.

country will be subjected to such horrors administered either purposely or accidentally in the name of peace and freedom. Both as a citizen and as a member of his profession, the international lawyer has a duty to do all in his power to prevent future Vietnams and ensure that when such conflicts do occur they will be effectively restrained by a law of war relevant to modern technology and methods of warfare.

The Law of War in the Vietnamese Conflict*

HENRI MEYROWITZ

INTRODUCTION

THE STUDY and evaluation of the war in Vietnam in the light of international law is an arduous task. It plunges the analyst directly into a mass of controverted legal ideas and political and legal concepts charged with ideology: armed aggression, legitimate self-defense, and collective defense; intervention and nonintervention; just war; reprisals; legitimacy; divided states; recognition of governments; recognition of states; recognition of belligerents; wars of national liberation; revolutions; international civil wars, etc. One has to deal with confused political and military data, often of an odd and peculiar nature, and legal analysis of this material is not simple. The difficulties of certain questions which a legal evaluation must meet are so great, however, that jurists cannot avoid this task. What is at issue is nothing less than the creation or the transformation, by means of precedent, of rules of international law in the domains touched by this conflict.[1] For this reason, governments and public opinion in countries not immediately involved in this war have a direct interest—and at the same time both a right and a duty—to judge the actions of the parties to the conflict: by their silence as much as by their express approval, they help to confer a legality upon the practice of the belligerents; by their disapproval, they prevent this practice from becoming law. Thus it is because he is conscious of his responsibility to the international law at issue—and not because he arrogates to himself the role of judge—that the impartial jurist of a noninvolved state is led to make a considered judgment on the claims and the conduct of the parties.

The problems of international law raised by the Vietnamese conflict

---

* Translated from the French by Allan J. Graf.

[1] Cf. Major J. B. Kelly, "Legal Aspects of Military Operations in Counter-Insurgency," *Military Law Review* (July 1963), 95ff. "In this field [of counterinsurgency], the American army, whether it wants to or not, will fashion the law, because it is what the United States Army does today that determines, in a large measure, the law for the next thirty or forty years." This claim has received official approval: a publication edited by the Judge Advocate General's School of the United States Army and destined for the instruction of officers has accepted the cited passage as official opinion (*Legal Aspects of Counter-Insurgency*, July 1964, p. 24).

are of two orders: the ones relating to *jus ad bellum* and the ones relating to *jus in bello*.[2] While the first set of problems has been the object of an extensive literature, especially in the United States,[3] the second set has been little studied. This article is limited to the examination of *jus in bello* applicable to and applied in the Vietnamese conflict. If, in so delimiting our subject, we set aside the question of the legality of the examined actions with regard to *jus ad bellum*, this reservation does not affect the validity of the answers in which our research results. Because, according to constant practice and incontestable principle, the status of belligerents with regard to *jus ad bellum* is without effect on their situation with regard to *jus in bello*.[4]

In order to become acquainted with the rules of *jus in bello* applicable to the Vietnam War, it is first necessary to study the categories in

[2] The same act can be subjected to both *jus ad bellum* and *jus in bello*. Thus the decision by the American Government to bomb North Vietnam raises norms of *jus in bello* and *jus ad bellum*. What one terms escalation is an act which, by definition, occurs in the middle of a war; it may be that this act should not be judged only according to *jus in bello*, but should also be understood with regard to *jus ad bellum*, even if it does not have as its object or as its effect the extension of the war to a country up to then uninvolved in the hostilities.

[3] The Vietnamese drama has provoked a grave schism in American public opinion, and particularly in university circles. A grave schism which could not help but equally affect the legal sciences. Note especially, affirming the legality of the action of the government: the declaration of 31 professors of international law, Nov. 1965, reproduced in the *Congressional Record*, Jan. 27, 1966, p. A410; E. P. Deutsch, "The Legality of the United States Position in Vietnam," *Am. Bar Ass. Journal* (1966), 436ff.; J. N. Moore and J. L. Underwood, in collaboration with M. S. McDougal, "The Lawfulness of U.S. Assistance to the Republic of Vietnam," *Cong. Rec.*, July 14, 1966, pp. 14943ff.; N. H. Alford, "The Legality of American Involvement in Viet Nam," *Yale Law Journal*, 75 (1966), 1109ff.; J. N. Moore, "The Lawfulness of Military Assistance to the Republic of Vietnam," *Am. Journal of Int. Law* (1967), 1ff.; *id.*, "International Law and the United States Role in Vietnam: A Reply," *Yale Law Journal*, 76 (1967), 1051ff.

Criticizing the action of the government and the justifications invoked by the above: Lawyers Committee on American Policy towards Vietnam, *American Policy vis-à-vis Vietnam in Light of Our Constitution, the UN Charter, the 1954 Geneva Accords, and the Southeast Asia Collective Defense Treaty*, reproduced in the *Cong. Rec.*, Sept. 23, 1965, pp. 24010ff.; W. L. Standard, "U.S. Intervention in Vietnam is not Legal," *Am. Bar Ass. Journal* (1966), 627ff. R. A. Falk, "International Law and the United States Role in the Viet Nam War," *Yale Law Journal*, 75 (1966), 1122ff.; *id.*, "International Law and the United States Role in Viet Nam: A Response to Professor Moore," *ibid.*, 76 (1967), 1095ff.; Q. Wright, "Legal Aspects of the Viet-Nam Situation," *Am. Journal of Int. Law* (1966), 750ff.; W. Friedmann, "Law and Politics in the Vietnamese War: A Comment," *ibid.* (1967), 776ff.; Consultative Council of the Lawyers Committee on American Policy towards Vietnam, *Vietnam and International Law*, 1967.

[4] At least it is so for direct relations between the belligerents *durante bello*, see H. Meyrowitz, "Le principe de l'égalité des belligérants devant le droit de la guerre" (forthcoming).

which these hostilities may be placed. The law of conventional war distinguishes two kinds of conflict which it regulates differently: interstate armed conflicts and armed conflicts "not presenting an international character," according to the formulation of Article 3 common to the four Geneva Conventions of 1949. The first type of conflict is subject to all of the customary and conventional rules of the law of war—the applicable conventional rules depending upon the content of the contractual obligations of the parties to the conflict. In the second type of conflict, whose most typical form is civil war, the use of force is subjected to a restricted set of rules, including, besides Article 3 of the Geneva Convention,[5] only a part of the customary rules of the law of war.[6]

Between these two categories of armed conflicts, the only ones foreseen by the law of conventional warfare, there are to be found conflicts which do not engage *states*, but of which it is, nevertheless, impos-

[5] This article provides:

"In the case of armed conflict not of an international character occurring in the territory of one of the High Contracting Parties, each Party to the conflict shall be bound to apply, as a minimum, the following provisions:

"1) Persons taking no active part in the hostilities, including members of the armed forces who have laid down their arms and those placed *hors de combat* by sickness, wounds, detention, or any other cause, shall in all circumstances be treated humanely, without any adverse distinction founded on race, color, religion or faith, sex, birth or wealth, or any other similar criteria.

"To this end the following acts are and shall remain prohibited at any time and in any place whatsoever with respect to the above mentioned persons:

a) violence to life and person, in particular murder of all kinds, mutilation, cruel treatment and torture;

b) taking of hostages;

c) outrages upon personal dignity, in particular, humiliating and degrading treatment;

d) the passing of sentences and the carrying out of executions without previous judgment pronounced by a regularly constituted court affording all the judicial guarantees which are recognized as indispensable by civilized peoples.

"2) The wounded and sick shall be collected and cared for.

"An impartial humanitarian body, such as the International Committee of the Red Cross, may offer its services to the Parties to the conflict.

"The Parties to the conflict should further endeavor to bring into force, by means of special agreements, all or part of the other provisions of the present Convention.

"The application of the proceeding provisions shall not affect the legal status of the Parties to the conflict."

[6] The *jus in bello* which is applicable in conflicts of a noninternational character thus includes two parts: Article 3 of the Geneva Conventions and a fund of rules constituted by the essential norms of the customary law of war. These fundamental rules are obligatory in conflicts of a noninternational character, not as "the laws and customs of war," but as the minimum norms of human rights.

sible to say that they "do not present an international character." In the present international situation, conflicts are to be foreseen which will be ascribable, in whole or in part, to this *third category of armed conflicts*. To this unnamed category, the obligatory rules in the conflicts referred to by Article 3 are, at least, applicable. There is thus no war which eludes international law. But there can be divergent interpretations and controverted claims concerning the characterization of a given conflict. This is particularly the case when it is a question of a *complex phenomenon* such as "international civil war." Theoretically, the question of the characterization of this phenomenon is capable of four different answers: intrastate conflict; interstate conflict; conflict of an international nature but non interstate; mixed conflict, combining elements of the three categories of conflicts. We do not pretend to bring universal and definitive answers to this problem of the characterization of international civil wars with regard to *jus in bello*. Our purpose is limited to the study of a particular case. We shall see how this problem is posed in Vietnam, what its theoretical and practical importance is, what the attitude adopted in this regard by the parties to the conflict is, and what the lessons which one can draw from this experience are.

Our study will be divided into two parts: I. Determination of the rules of the law of war applicable in the Vietnamese conflict; II. The application of the law of war by the parties to the conflict.

PART ONE

DETERMINATION OF THE RULES OF THE LAW OF WAR APPLICABLE IN THE VIETNAMESE CONFLICT

The problem of knowing which rules of the law of war[7] are applicable in the Vietnamese conflict depends in the first place, in the absence of unequivocal and concordant declarations by all the parties engaged,[8] on the characterization of the conflict with regard to the law of war. Then, it is a question of determining the composition of the applicable rules either in the relations between all the belligerent parties, or

---

[7] The term law of war is used henceforth to mean *jus in bello*.

[8] Beyond the norms of human rights obligatory in conflicts of a noninternational character, the rules of the law of interstate war can be made applicable to these conflicts by two procedures: by *special agreements*, formal or tacit (foreseen in the penultimate paragraph of Article 3) or by the recognition of belligerency by the legal government. As this article was being written and edited, none of these procedures has been utilized in South Vietnam.

the relations between any particular group of belligerents, depending on, on the one hand, the legal nature of the conflict, and, on the other hand, the particular individual and mutual obligations of and between the parties. Hence, the two sections of this first part: I. Characterization of the Vietnamese Conflict with Regard to the Law of War; II. Specification of the Rules of the Law of War Applicable in the Vietnamese Conflict.

*I. Characterization of the Vietnamese Conflict with Regard
to the Law of War*

1. INTEREST IN THE CHARACTERIZATION

The *interest* and the *stake* in the characterization of the Vietnamese conflict with regard to the law of war lies in the difference separating the laws of interstate war from the limited obligatory rules governing noninternational conflicts. This difference is not only a difference of degree—which is called to attention if one compares Article 3 with the body of the four Geneva Conventions which are veritable codes— it is a difference in nature. It is contrary to the law of interstate war, Article 3, and other rules of human rights applicable in noninternational conflicts which protect persons belonging to one or another side in their *capacity as men*, not in their capacity as *members of a political collectivity*; all the more reason they do not protect the political personality of the adversary state. Even if the object of the war is the total destruction of the political independence of the adversary, the law of interstate war obliges the belligerents to respect, *durante bello*, the political personality of the enemy state. Examples of this obligation of states at war to respect each other's political personality abound in the Geneva Conventions of 1949 in which several of the most important provisions protect both the *person* of the individual finding himself in the enemy's hands and his quality as an *agent* or *citizen* of the state to which he belongs. Thus Article 17 of the Third Convention relating to the treatment of prisoners of war, after having indicated that the prisoner, at the time of his interrogation, is obliged only to declare his name, rank, birth date, and serial number, prohibits any coercion, physical or mental "inflicted on prisoners of war to secure from them information of any kind whatever." Article 50 forbids compelling prisoners of war to work on projects of a military nature or projects destined for military use, while Article 130 condemns as a "grave breach" the act of "compelling a prisoner of war to serve in the forces of the hostile Power." Likewise, the Fourth Convention relating to the protection of civilians in time of war, forbids any physical or mental coercion of the persons protected "in particular to obtain information from them or from third parties" (Article 31) and prohibits not only forced enlistment in the armed forces and auxiliary units of the occupying power, but also all "pressure and propaganda which aims at securing voluntary enlistment" (Article 51), and the act of "compelling a protected person to serve in the forces of a hostile Power" is considered a "grave breach" (Article 147).

The above provisions protect the enemy *state*. The mutual protection of the political personality of belligerent collectivities is absent from the law of internal conflicts. It is contrary to the essence of civil war. This is a struggle which develops within the domain of the exclusive and full territorial competence of *a state*, whose government exercises the legal monopoly of supreme power, a monopoly which cannot be shared with a rival and whose possession constitutes the very object of the struggle. International law is indifferent to civil war when it concerns *jus ad bellum*. (Allow me to bring up an idea at this point relating to international war): it does not prohibit the use of force against a legal government. However, it is nonetheless true of the law that it gives to governments in power a very strong protection, establishing for their benefit a discrimination whose most striking expression consists of the fact that the law of civil wars *ignores the status of prisoners of war.* Whether, in their armed action against the established authority, the insurgents observe or do not observe the laws of war, international law permits the government to treat them as rebels; in other words, to punish the sole fact of taking up arms against the legal government.

2. THEATER OF WAR

If one ignores some minor engagements which occurred on the high seas, the conflict has been fought on the territory of Vietnam.[9] Concerning the characterization of this territory with regard to international law, two questions have been debated. Does Vietnam constitute

---

[9] This geographical limitation of the conflict simply results from the relationship of the armed forces present. A large part of the American bombers used against North Vietnam are based in Guam and Thailand. The Democratic Republic of Vietnam would have the right to attack military air fields in Guam, an American possession, or in Thailand, as well as, of course, American warships on the high seas—not to mention the armament plants and military bases in the United States.

THE LAW OF WAR IN VIETNAM

a single state? If not, do the two parts of Vietnam, to the north and the south of the seventeenth parallel, constitute *states?*

The unification of Vietnam was the objective envisaged by the Geneva Accords of 1954. It is one of the principal goals of the Government of the Democratic Republic of Vietnam; it is also one of the political goals of the National Liberation Front of South Vietnam; finally, it is a propaganda theme of the Government of Saigon.[10] Unity of the two parts of Vietnam is presently neither a political nor a legal reality. In addition, none of the parties seriously supports, with the political and legal consequences which this thesis entails, the idea that a single Vietnamese state presently exists or has existed at any particular moment after the agreements of 1954.

The second question—which is different from the first because the absence of a single Vietnamese state does not necessarily mean that the two halves of Vietnam constitute *states*—has especially been discussed from the angle of *jus ad bellum* with the purpose of supporting or combatting the official American position according to which the action of the United States in Vietnam is justified as legitimate collective defense against aggression committed across an international frontier by North Vietnam against South Vietnam, an independent state. The characterization is also important for the characterization of the conflict with regard to *jus in bello* because the customary and conventional law of war is only wholly applicable between entities possessing the capacity of *states*. In fact, this debate is purely academic: every participant in the conflict not only affirms the statehood of the part of Vietnam that it represents, but also has recognized explicitly or implicitly the independent legal statehood of the other part.[11] Each one

10 At the time of the presidential election of Sept. 4, 1967, Generals Thieu and Ky had adopted as the emblem of their ticket's ballot an image representing, under the flag of South Vietnam, the silhouette of a united Vietnam.

11 The Hanoi Government does not recognize the Saigon regime. But it does acknowledge a separate personality for South Vietnam and the organization—at least temporarily—of this zone as an independent state (declaration of the Government of the DRV, Sept. 2, 1967, *Courrier du Vietnam*, Sept. 11, 1967). This has also been the consistent position of the NLF. Cf. P. Isoart, "Les conflits du Vietnam: positions juridiques des Etats-Unis," *A.F.D.I.*, 1966, pp. 50ff. (p. 71). The Soviet Union acknowledged, in January 1957, the existence of two separate states of Vietnam, since it then proposed—while awaiting their reunification—the simultaneous admission to the United Nations of the two Republics of Vietnam (see the proposed resolution A/SPC/L.9; cf. Gen. Ass. 663rd. plenary session, Feb. 28, 1957).

On February 21, 1964, the Department of State declared again that the United States "does not recognize the northern zone of Vietnam as a state, nor the self-proclaimed

of the two states of Vietnam is, in addition, recognized by a certain number of states which are not involved in the hostilities. Moreover, it is advisable to remember the application of the rules of the law of war is independent of the recognition of the government, or even of the recognition of an enemy belligerent state.[12] Whatever the legal situation created by the texts of the Geneva Accords of 1954 was, it must be admitted that, as far as the international status of the two zones is concerned, things have evolved and that the two Republics of Vietnam constitute today, at least in regard to international law, *two states*.[13]

3. FORCES PRESENT

The conflict has engaged, on the one side, the Government of the Republic of Vietnam and expeditionary corps from six countries: United States, South Korea, Australia, New Zealand, Philippines, Thailand; on the other side, the Democratic Republic of Vietnam (DRV)

Democratic Republic of Vietnam as a government" (*Am. Journal of Int. Law* [1964], 1005). Since then, President Johnson has addressed Ho Chi Minh in his capacity as President of the DRV, and the American Government has continuously proclaimed that it does not have as its objective threats to the political independence or territorial integrity of the DRV nor the instigation of a change of regime in the DRV. This is not just a simple promise of nonaggression toward the Northern "Zone"; it is a *de facto* recognition of the DRV. It must be observed that the official American position does not require that the DRV, accused of armed aggression, be considered a *state* and its central authority as a government. During the entire Korean conflict, the United States and the United Nations took great care, while designating North Korea as an aggressor, of avoiding the use of a term which could be interpreted as implying recognition, or even simply noting the Popular Democratic Republic of Korea's character as a *state*.

[12] *States not recognized* by other states presently constitute the hot points of the globe. Their number and their importance is so great that the law of war would risk becoming a dead letter if it was subordinated to recognition of a belligerent enemy state. The fact that the law of war is independent of the recognition of an enemy state has a corollary that the application of the rules of war to an unrecognized state does not imply the recognition of that state. A government will not be contradicting itself if, after the war, it persists in refusing to recognize a state although it recognized its obligations under the law of war.

[13] The legal situation, in this case, is analogous to Germany. Ho Chi Minh and his Prime Minister Pham Van Dong—who is originally from the South, just as former prime minister and current vice president, General Ky, is originally from the North—can speak of the fatherland (*patrie*) or the Vietnamese nation and of their compatriots in the South without violating historical or natural truth. Likewise, the West Germans call their brothers in the East compatriots. The frontier between the Federal Republic of Germany and the German Democratic Republic is designated officially, in the words of Bonn, as a "line of demarcation." But would one qualify this situation as a "civil war" in law or a "conflict not of an international character"—an armed struggle which was raging between the two Germanies?

and the forces of the National Liberation Front of South Vietnam (NLF), generally called the Vietcong in non-Communist states.

The number of forces effectively present in the South Vietnamese war theater was established in December 1967 as approximately:

Government of Saigon
   Regular forces, 300,000
   Police and militia, 450,000

Allied contingents

United States, 478,000[14]	Thailand, 2,800
South Korea, 47,000	Philippines, 2,000
Australia, 7,500	New Zealand, 400

Regular forces of the DRV infiltrated into South Vietnam
   American estimate, 54,000

Forces of the NLF
   American estimate, 170,000 to 194,000 (According to the Pentagon, these forces are divided as follows: regular troops, 64,000; guerrillas, 70,000 to 90,000; administrative services, 35,000 to 40,000. According to other American estimates, to these figures must be added between 120,000 and 150,000 part-time guerrillas and members of rural self-defense units and about 80,000 political agents of the NLF.)

In equipment, the proportion of forces between the states fighting on the side of the Saigon Government is such that all the land, air, and naval operations are undertaken almost exclusively with materials furnished by the United States.

4. ANALYSIS OF THE CONFLICT

As much by its theater of operations as by its active participants, the war in Vietnam forms a complex issue whose diverse elements should be analyzed separately with the aim of achieving a legal characterization of the struggle. Let us observe here that if this analysis of the conflict should lead to a differentiation of the legal regime, that would not be in itself anything extraordinary.

14 This figure was raised to 525,000 in the first half of 1968 (this figure is greater, by 53,000, than the number of American forces actively engaged in the Korean War). It is advisable to add here that about 85,000 American servicemen participate in the military operations from the air fields in Thailand and Guam or from aboard the ships along the coasts of Vietnam.

It is commonly known that in a war fought by a coalition, the belligerents are not all tied to the same rules of the law of war. It is true that the diversity, in this case, only concerns the rules established by conventions; this diversity does not, in effect, derive from the differentiation of the legal nature of the conflict, but simply from the individuality of the conventional bonds and obligations between the belligerent states. The result, nevertheless, is similar. It would be wrong to depart from the logical or practical necessity of having a unified legal regime in a given conflict in order to impose in advance on our analysis the conclusion that the war in Vietnam should not be able to entail a compromise characterization, and that it should be treated as being either entirely a civil war or entirely an interstate war or entirely an international conflict without being an interstate conflict.

Four separate confrontations can be distinguished in the conflict:

1. Government of Saigon v. NLF
2. United States[15] v. NLF
3. Government of Saigon v. North Vietnam
4. United States v. North Vietnam

This enumeration corresponds to the chronological development of the hostilities, but it does not mean that it furnishes an adequate plan for legal analysis. It seems to us more appropriate to begin by studying the two confrontations in which the international element is most evident, being concretized by the existence of an international frontier, and then by analyzing successively the confrontation between Saigon and the NLF and the confrontation between the United States and the NLF.

HOSTILITIES AGAINST NORTH VIETNAM

1. *The Confrontation between the United States and North Vietnam.* Obviously, this confrontation constitutes an interstate conflict. This characterization is applied to the hostile acts directed against the territory of the DRV or against North Vietnamese ships by the forces of the United States, as well as in the struggle against the regular armed forces of the North infiltrated into South Vietnam. The beginning of this international war between the United States and the DRV should probably be placed—at least not in any case before—at Au-

---

[15] The legal situation is identical for the United States and for its non-Vietnamese allies.

gust 7, 1964, the date of the Tonkin Gulf Resolution[16] in which the Congress gave to the President of the United States a blank check authorizing him to undertake any armed action against North Vietnam.[17] The confrontations with the regular forces from the North in South Vietnam began several months later. The first infiltrations of North Vietnamese units occurred, in effect, only toward the end of 1964. The systematic bombing of North Vietnam by American forces began in February 1965.[18]

[16] On the 2nd and 4th of August, 1964, two incidents occurred between two American destroyers and some North Vietnamese torpedo boats, incidents which Senator Fulbright said later were "very vague" and that the "aggression" which, according to the official version, the North Vietnamese boats committed—and which furnishes the pretext for the resolution of August 7—had been caused by a "single hole" (*Look* [May 3, 1966], cited by Kahn and Lewis, *The United States in Vietnam*, 1967, p. 158). During the night of August 4, American air and naval units bombed the bases being used by the North Vietnamese naval units. This action was presented by the American Government as an isolated and limited measure of reprisal, which it was in effect. On the other hand, the Resolution of August 7 is of a general character. Although it avoids the terms "war" and "state of war," it reveals the *animus belligerendi* of the American Government and it prevents the actions undertaken from this date on by the forces of the United States against the territory and forces of the DRV from being considered as incidents of reprisal.

[17] In February 1962, Robert Kennedy, then Attorney General, characterized the American commitment to Vietnam as a "struggle short of war" (cited by J. N. Moore, *loc.cit.*, p. 14961); this characterization, which corresponds, from the point of international law, to non-war remained valid up to August 7, 1964.

[18] Before August 1964, commando operations had been made against North Vietnam by detachments of the Special Forces. The problem of the characterization of these actions and the determination of the international status of the Special Forces prior to the state of war between the United States and the DRV is interesting only in retrospect. Created in 1952 and strongly reinforced during the Kennedy Administration, the Special Forces—"green berets"—are a corps of volunteers within the American Army specially recruited (the percentage of refugees from Communist countries is particularly high) and trained for the purpose of commando missions, guerrilla and counterguerrilla warfare, and *counterinsurgency*. The situations in which they are called upon to function include not only interstate war and civil war but also the Cold War and "sublimited wars," situations hotter than the Cold War but which are not quite wars. International law ignores these gradations. It only knows two situations—war and peace, which is non-war. Commando actions undertaken against North Vietnam by special American groups before August 7, 1964, took place outside of a situation of war. The secret character and the specific nature of these operations excluded the American Government's possible intention of considering these acts as constituting a war situation. The necessary conclusion is that these actions, which no longer had the character of reprisals, were beyond the scope of the law of war. Even then, forces participating in these operations could not, in case of capture, benefit from the status of prisoner of war. The fact that they executed an official mission or that, in their activities, they wore a uniform is as inoperative as is the question of determining whether these acts of violence which have been committed would have been legal or illegal according to the law of war if they had been committed during the war. (On this last point, one can observe that these special units, trained and

The fact that the American Government has not issued a declaration of war[19] and that it refuses to admit the existence of a state of war[20] is without influence on the applicability of the rules of the law of war as is the issue of determining whether the action taken by President Johnson conforms with the Constitution of the United States.[21]

2. *The Confrontation between Saigon and the DRV*. This is equally an interstate conflict, since, we have seen, the two Republics of Vietnam form, with respect to international law, two states, and that the Government of Saigon is, internationally, the representative of the state of South Vietnam. It is not easy to determine the date at which the conflict began because we do not possess here an act comparable to the Resolution of Congress of August 7, 1964. Practically, one can place this date at the point when the first encounters between South Vietnamese forces and the regular units of the North which were being infiltrated in took place—toward the end of 1964 or in the beginning of 1965.[22]

---

equipped for the methods of marginal wars, characterized officially as *unconventional war*, do not have, *a priori*, in the conception and execution of their clandestine and unorthodox military operations the same concern about international legality that a traditional army has. On the activities of the Special Forces in Vietnam, see the book by Robin Moore, *The Green Berets* [1965, also translated into French in 1965; despite its childish romanticization, all the experts were in agreement on its authentic character]) . These acts constituted violations of the municipal law of the DRV. To have avoided the application of municipal law, they needed a state of international war. The international protection of members of the Special Forces captured before August 7, 1964, was thus limited to the rules formulated in Article 3 of the Geneva Conventions, which was not applicable as such, but as the minimum standard of human rights.

[19] The reasons—debatable ones—for this refusal have been set forth in a report drawn up by the Department of State at the request of the Senate Foreign Relations Committee. The Department of State emphasizes that, despite the absence of a declaration of war, the customary and conventional rules of the law of war are applicable to the conflict between the United States and North Vietnam because it may be characterized as an international conflict.

[20] Declaration of the Department of State, *Dept. of State Bulletin*, March 22, 1965, p. 403.

[21] We agree with the majority of American opinion, including the criticisms of President Johnson's action, that he has not overstepped his powers. Under Secretary of State Katzenbach is probably right in affirming that even without the Resolution passed by the Congress on August 7, 1964, the President would have had, by virtue of the Constitution, the authority to act in Vietnam as he did (*Int. Herald Tribune*, Aug. 22, 1967) .

[22] Since 1961, the air force and Special Forces of South Vietnam, set up and instructed by the American Special Forces, have made commando raids against North Vietnam. The observations which we made above (note 18) about Special Forces also applies

THE HOSTILITIES AGAINST THE NLF

1. *Confrontation between Saigon and the NLF*. In order to characterize this struggle, the term *civil war* comes immediately to mind. However, all the parties engaged reject this characterization. Perhaps the
positions of the parties in conflict are above all *justifications* of a
certain policy in whose choice international law has not had a determining role or skillful exercises in legal argumentation. But the conclusions of an official position dictated solely by self-interest cannot
help being less than exact—in other words, they cannot correctly
translate the legal situation as it presents itself to an objective analysis. However, true or false, these official positions cannot be cast aside
lightly in the analysis of the situation: often, in fact, they form an element of the situation. The manner in which a government unilaterally
characterizes its action in a conflict, the claims which it invokes, whether
they are right or wrong, can be important elements in the legal nature
of a conflict. Finally, an official position about a particular fact can
have a legal consequence as well as being evidence of the intention of
the government in question, in the case in which this intention is
important for analysis of the legal situation.

The interest which the American Government has in contesting the
characterization of the Vietnam conflict between Saigon and the NLF
as a civil war is obvious. This characterization would make American
action in Vietnam an *intervention,* under debatable authority, while
the American Government thinks it has found an indisputable international authority in its position of maintaining that the subversion
in South Vietnam is only a form of "armed aggression" (within the
meaning of Article 51 of the United Nations Charter) committed by
North Vietnam—an aggression justifying, indeed requiring, the action of legitimate collective defense by the United States.[23] For the
same reasons, the Saigon Government believes that its interests forbid
it from characterizing the struggle which places it in conflict with the
NLF as a civil war. According to Saigon, it has to deal with *external
aggression*—the NLF being nothing more than an instrument of Hanoi.

---

to these operations and to the international status of these Southern military forces
which have participated in such activities (before the end of 1964) .

[23] This thesis, set forth in innumerable declarations of the American Government,
has been presented as a legal memorandum by the Department of State (March 4, 1966) ,
edited by Mr. Meeker, the Legal Adviser to the Department (reproduced in the *Am.
Journal of Int. Law* [1966], 565ff.) . Cf. also "Vietnam and the International Law of
Self-Defense," *Dept. of State Bulletin,* Jan. 9, 1967, pp. 54ff.

The interest of the NLF and the Hanoi Government in rejecting the qualification of the war as a civil war is less easily explicable,[24] all the more so because the official explanations are very rare and hardly explicit. In several arguments put forth by the spokesmen of the NLF or Hanoi, the idea appears which establishes the conflict as a *war of national liberation*,[25] which, in Communist doctrine, is contrary to civil war.[26] For the NLF, the war of national liberation in Vietnam for the South did not end in 1954: in place of French colonial power, American imperialist power has been substituted. More often, however, the declarations of the NLF and of Hanoi make reference to "American aggression" against Vietnam, aggression in which the Saigon Government is only an auxiliary.

Despite their agreement, the positions of the parties are not evidently sufficient to imprint objectively the character of an international conflict on the struggle between Saigon and the NLF. The authors who

[24] In an article which appeared in the newspaper *Nhan Dan* in Hanoi, two North Vietnamese jurists considered the position, notably defended by the Lawyers Committee on American Policy towards Vietnam, as erroneous in which it is argued that the conflict in South Vietnam constitutes a civil war (see the extracts in the *Courrier du Vietnam*, April 24, 1967).

[25] This is also, in substance, the opinion of the Secretary General of the United Nations: ". . . this is not a question of Communist aggression but of a war of national independence" (speech of June 30, 1967, United Nations, *Monthly Chronicle*, Aug.-Sept., 1967, p. 88).

[26] According to Communist legal theory, wars of national liberation assume *ab initio* the status of *international conflict*. See especially G. I. Tunkin, *Droit International Public: Problèmes Théoriques*, 1965, p. 50 (the following passage is an English translation of a French text): "This is why a nation struggling for its independence and the creation of its own state should be considered by contemporary international law as a subject of international law, although because of the opposition of the colonialists it [the nation] could not yet form an independent state and its creation is still to come."

Cf. G. Ginsburg, "Wars of National Liberation and the Modern Law of Nations— The Soviet Thesis," *Law and Contemporary Problems*, Vol. 29, 1964, pp. 910ff.

The war of national liberation can double as a political and social revolution. The importance of this element is variable. It had already played a considerable role in the First Indochinese War. See on this subject, General Giap, *Guerre du peuple, armée du peuple*, Paris, 1967, p. 40 (the following passage is an English translation of a French text): "Our resistance was a war of the people, since its political objectives were to break the imperialist yoke in order to reconquer the national independence, and to destroy the class of feudal proprietors in order to give the land to the peasants." When this revolution actually takes the form of a civil war, the problem of the characterization of this element with regard to international law is a particular kind of question. The possibility of a division of global war into an international war led against a colonial power, and a civil war, opposing the revolutionary party to the local legal government, should not be *a priori* dismissed. Thus the struggle against the Saigon Government by the NLF has completely merged with the struggle against the "American aggressor."

support the characterization of the conflict as a *civil war* principally emphasize that the object of the struggle in South Vietnam is the typical object of the civil war: "to establish a new political regime which it has not been possible to realize by constitutional procedures."[27] This object is, in effect, evident. But one must wonder whether this internal element can be isolated from the international context in which it has, from the beginning, found itself inserted, and whether it is the truly determining characteristic of the conflict which places the conflict in the legal category of civil wars. It also seems to us that this object presents itself in Vietnam under an atypical aspect. What constitutes the originality of the Saigon-NLF conflict is that the struggle has burst forth *not within a preexisting state* but within a state *in statu nascendi.* Can one really say that there has ever been a legal government in the Southern zone that has exercised its power *effectively* throughout the zone? At the time of the Geneva Accords, the Government of the DRV maintained that two million South Vietnamese living in the regions controlled by the Viet Minh had never once been under colonial domination since the proclamation of independence in 1945.[28] This figure is unreliable; but the fact does remain that a large number of Vietcong and inhabitants of the regions in the hands of the NLF have never been subjects of the South Vietnamese state or effectively controlled by an authority other than the Vietcong. Because of its peculiarities, the struggle in South Vietnam seems less like a struggle between a legal government and insurgents than like a conflict between two pretenders to the same territory.[29]

27 R. Pinto, "Les regles du droit international concernant la guerre civile," *Recueil des Cours,* I (1965), 453ff. (p. 460).

28 B.S.N. Murti, *Vietnam Divided,* 1964, p. 96.

29 Before becoming a state, South Vietnam had been a *zone.* The statehood of this zone has been affirmed in the measure in which the Saigon Government has succeeded—thanks uniquely to American aid—in establishing its effective control. One can, from a material point of view, consider the struggle between two pretenders in a zone as a civil war; but one must observe that this is not an ordinary civil war. Civil war is characterized by a rebellion against an *established state order.* The existence of such a state order before the rebellion was absent in South Vietnam.

One should wonder whether, in a similar case, the central government has the same status as the one which the legal government in an ordinary civil war possesses. It has, surely, the right to defend itself against an adversary seeking to extend its control over the whole of the territory. But the question remains whether it can assume this privileged status which is enjoyed by the legal government in a civil war: the status of *inequality* which constitutes the essence of the legal regime of the civil war. It is sufficient just to raise this question here. It is not necessary that it be resolved in the case of Vietnam because, for reasons put forth above which are independent of the intrinsic

Finally and above all, assuming that at its origin, the confrontation between Saigon and the NLF could have been considered a civil war, it is again advisable to examine whether this characteristic has remained unchanged. But everything indicates that there has been a transformation of the conflict between the NLF and Saigon. The war in Vietnam has ended by being entirely internationalized. The center for political and military decision-making concerning the war is not found in Saigon but in Washington (this is true for the NLF—its decisions are made by the DRV). Not only are the strategic direction and the conduct of all operations in South Vietnam in the hands of the United States, but the political fate of the entire conflict depends, since 1965, exclusively on the will of the government in Washington. In September 1963, President Kennedy could still say: "In the final analysis, it is their war. They have to win it or lose it. We can help them, equip them; we can send them our men as advisers, but it is they who must win this war."[30] One year later, President Johnson was speaking of the struggle led by Saigon against the Vietcong under American military *leadership* and direction,[31] but American military personnel in South Vietnam still served only as advisers and their number did not surpass 20,000. Since 1965, the conflict has become, militarily and politically, an *American war*. The Government of the United States is the absolute master of this war, and it acts openly as such. In these conditions, the characterization of civil war applied to the confrontation between Saigon and the NLF seems like a legal construction without any relation to political and military reality.[32]

The problem of the effect of foreign intervention on the nature of

---

structure of the confrontation between Saigon and the NLF, the Vietnamese conflict should, according to us, be qualified as a conflict of an international character.

[30] *New York Times*, Sept. 3, 1963.

[31] Campaign speech, Sept. 28, 1964, cited in the *New York Herald Tribune*, March 20, 1966.

[32] Would one say that if the United States should decide to withdraw, the legal nature of the civil war in the Saigon-NLF conflict would reappear which would prove that it had never "disappeared" but only that it was concealed by the massive nature of the American intervention? Recalling the reservation we made on the subject of the characterization of the conflict, it is evidently possible that, once American intervention had ceased, the conflict would undergo a new transformation and resume the original character which it had before the Americanization of the war. But this new transformation would not prove that during the period of internationalization, the conflict had preserved its original character. Moreover, it is not a question of denying that the struggle between Saigon and the NLF presents, even in its international phase, an aspect or an element of civil war. It is a question of knowing what its determining characteristic is— the one which decides its legal characterization.

an internal conflict does not lead to any general and theoretical answer. The solution depends on the forms and the degree of intervention, the goals pursued by the intervening power or powers, as well as the relationship between the intervening state and the assisted state in political and military strategy. According to Professor Falk, "significant multinational participation transforms an internal war into a species of international war."[33] If by the adjective *multinational* the author means that, in order to transform an internal conflict into an international war, the participation of at least two foreign states is necessary, we cannot accept the analysis. In the case of Vietnam, the intervention of the United States has such weight that it would suffice, even without the intervention of the DRV, to imprint the conflict in South Vietnam with the character of an international war. Professor Rousseau had emphasized as early as 1938, on the subject of the war in Spain— in which, however, foreign military intervention was insignificant compared to the American intervention in Vietnam—the artificial character of the term civil war in case of "active participation in the conflict by foreign military forces."[34] Opposing this view, Professor Pinto believes that "foreign assistance in internal armed conflicts does not modify the legal nature of the territorial state under the impetus of a civil war."[35] Besides, the Vietnamese conflict has not remained circumscribed to the State of South Vietnam; it seems to us that the "territorial framework of the state" is not the only criterion for a civil war. Article 3 of the Geneva Conventions clearly indicates that only conflicts *occurring within the territory of a contracting state* and *not presenting an international character* can be excluded from the text. The territoriality of a conflict does not exclude its international character.

2. *Confrontation between the United States and the NLF.* For stronger reasons, the confrontation between the United States and the NLF should be characterized as an international conflict.[36] It has certainly

33 "Janus Tormented: The International Law of Internal War," in Rosenau (ed.), *International Aspects of Civil Strife*, 1964, pp. 185ff. (p. 218).

34 "La non-intervention en Espagne," *Revue de droit int. et de lég. comp.* (1938), 473ff. (p. 474).

35 *Loc.cit.*, p. 464.

36 Kelsen states that if a foreign state gives military assistance to a legal government in its struggle against insurgents not recognized as belligerents, the action of this state would have the same legal character as that of the assisted government: the action would constitute "in the final analysis, an action of the assisted state since it is authorized by the [assisted state]" (*Principles of International Law*, 2nd edn., 1967, pp. 28-29). The first fault in this reasoning is its abstraction; whereas, it concerns a matter in which legal

had this character since 1965; in other words, since American forces in South Vietnam became *combatants* and were no longer *military advisers*.[37] Does one object to the use of the term international conflict for this particular confrontation because of the absence of a state-to-state relationship? But *international conflict* is not synonymous with *interstate conflict*. In addition, the law of war does not presuppose, for all its rules, that the belligerent collectivities must be *states*.[38] The characteristic or the absence of the characteristic of statehood of belligerents does play, however, a decisive role in the specification of the rules of the law of war applicable in a conflict.

II. *Specification of the Rules of the Law of War Applicable in the Vietnamese Conflict*

1. THE RULES APPLICABLE BETWEEN THE STATES PARTY TO THE CONFLICT

In the relations between states participating in the struggle for Vietnam, the customary rules of the law of war are applicable as well

---

analysis should be based on the political and military facts of a concrete situation. In this regard, the *authorization* of the legal government, on which Kelsen rests his argument, is one of the most doubtful criteria. If the "authorizing" government is dependent upon the "authorized" state, it is, "in the last analysis," the intervening state which will have authorized its own intervention. On the other hand, from a theoretical point of view, it seems very questionable to view the *requested intervention* as a kind of *representation*. Kelsen has, moreover, recognized that "it is more than paradoxical not to consider such an action . . . as a war within the meaning of international law" (*The Law of the United Nations*, 1951, pp. 934-35).

[37] Before this date, the characterization, with regard to international law, of the relations between the United States and the forces of the NLF—and, consequently, the determination of the international status of the American *military advisers* in South Vietnam—was problematical. Here again, the nature and the size of foreign assistance is a decisive element in the characterization.

Cf., in the same vein, D. Schindler "Die Anwendung der Genfer Rotkreuzabkommen seit 1949" *Annuaire suisse du droit int.*, 1965, pp. 75ff. (pp. 95-96), and J. A. Frowein, "Volkerrechtliche Aspekte des Vietnam-Konfliktes," *Zeitschr. f. ausl. öff. Recht und Volkerrecht*, Vol. 27, 1967, pp. 1ff., who believes that the participation of foreign forces on the side of a legal government does not transform the legal nature of the civil war. Frowein does admit, however, that it is doubtful that his position can be applied to the case of a military participation as massive as that of the United States in Vietnam (p. 18).

[38] Several provisions of the Geneva Conventions of 1949 envisage situations in which a belligerent state confronts an entity which is not a state. See notably, Article 4, A, 2 of Convention III, paragraph 3 of the same article recognizing the status of prisoners of war of "members of regular armed forces who profess allegiance to a government or an authority not recognized by the Detaining Power." The expression "authority" indicates that the entity from which these forces may originate is not necessarily a state.

as those rules of conventions to which the states are parties.[39] Uncontestable and uncontested, this solution does not present any difficulties, neither in principle nor in this particular case. The customary and conventional rules are applied to the relations between, on the one hand, the Saigon Government and its allies, and, on the other hand, the DRV and its regular forces in South Vietnam. The rules are also applicable to any authority which might be invoked by one side or the other in order to justify its action with regard to *jus ad bellum*.

2. THE RULES APPLICABLE TO RELATIONS WITH THE NLF

THE POSITIONS OF THE PARTIES

The struggle between Saigon and the NLF, like that between the United States and the NLF, should be characterized, as we have seen, as a conflict of an international nature. But they are not interstate conflicts.[40] Also the relations between these belligerents are not,

[39] All the states involved in the conflict are parties to the four Geneva Conventions of 1949. The assent of the Republic of Korea dates only from Aug. 16, 1966. The "State of Vietnam" (South) had assented to the Conventions on Nov. 9, 1953; however, it was only by the decree of March 31, 1967, issued by the Saigon Government, that the four Conventions were "adopted." (See *Revue Int. de la Croix-Rouge* [1967], 336-37.)

[40] The status of the NLF, being in a constant state of evolution, is not easy to characterize. While refusing to constitute itself as a provisional government (interview of Mr. Nguyen Van Tien, a member of the Central Committee of the NLF, *Le Monde*, Dec. 23, 1967), it seems that in certain of its declarations, it claims the capacity of a *de facto* government without, however, insisting on it. It has established permanent delegations in eleven countries. Its delegations to Cuba, North Korea, Cambodia, and Communist China have diplomatic status. The Havana Government has named an ambassador *extraordinaire* to the NLF, a gesture which is generally interpreted as being equivalent to recognition of a government.

In the regions of South Vietnam controlled by it, the NLF does in fact exercise quasi-governmental functions. These regions, according to official American intelligence estimates, represented, in December 1967, a total of about 40% of the surface territory of South Vietnam, including some 40% of the rural population: 3,989 villages with about 2.8 million inhabitants, or about 20% of the total population of the country (*Int. Herald Tribune*, Dec. 1, 1967). There is, however, a need to note one particular item. Among the conditions which an insurgent group must fulfill in order to be recognized by third states as a rival government to the legal government, is one that requires that the group should generally show effective control of a "continuous territory"—a territorial expanse constituting an important part of the territory of the contested state. The regions in the hands of the NLF, considerable in their total extent, form neither a continuous nor a stable territorial expanse. The inherent mobility of guerrilla operations makes the map of South Vietnam resemble the skin of a leopard—a skin on which the "red spots" are often changing positions. Mao-tse-Tung had already noted a similar characteristic regarding the civil war in China: "in a revolutionary civil war, the front lines cannot be stable. . . . The instability of the front lines entails the instability of the territory of our support bases. They [the front lines] are expanded or contracted

from the formal point of view of law, subjected to the rules governing the hostilities between states. The specification of the norms of the law of war applicable to these relations poses some delicate problems which the declarations of the engaged governments do not hint at; namely, is the conflict in South Vietnam governed by the Geneva Convention?[41] In June 1965, the International Committee of the Red Cross addressed an appeal to the belligerent governments in which it expressed the opinion that, by reason of the extension of the hostilities, the struggle in Vietnam had taken on the nature of a struggle to which the Geneva Conventions of 1949 should be completely applied (*Revue Int. de la Croix-Rouge* [1965], 385-86). The United States, Australia, and New Zealand have responded affirmatively to this appeal (*ibid.* [1965], 441-42; [1966], 130, 360).[42] The Saigon Government declared that it was "fully ready to respect the provisions of the Geneva Accords" (*sic*) and that the "Geneva Accords (*sic*) have, in fact, always been applied" (*ibid.*, pp. 165, 442), a response which denoted a re-

---

constantly and it often happens that isolated bases are born or disappear. Such a changeability of the territory is due entirely to the mobility of military operations." (Passage translated from the French: "Problèmes stratégiques de la guerre révolution- naire en Chine," 1936, reproduced in *Ecrits militaires*, Peking, pp. 153-54.) In order to know whether this peculiarity involves consequences affecting the international status of the NLF, it would first be necessary to have more complete information on the *de facto* situation than we now possess.

41 These governments do not believe that the struggle against the NLF releases them from Article 3. The assent of the Seoul Government to the 1949 Conventions (note 39) is, in this regard, significant. Until August 1966—and thus during the Korean War— South Korea was only bound by the Geneva Convention of 1864 and by Article 3 of the 1949 Conventions which the President of the Republic of Korea had signed on July 4, 1950 (an unusual procedure). Although, according to the strategic plans determined by the American commander, the South Korean units in South Vietnam are employed principally against the Vietcong, the United States urged the South Korean Govern- ment, in view of this struggle, to adhere to the entire body of the Geneva Conventions of 1949.

42 It is true that the declarations are not absolutely unequivocal. They do not reveal whether the *application*, affirmed by the governments, results from their conviction that these treaties are not *obligatorily applicable* to the conflict with the NLF or whether it constitutes a spontaneous and gratuitous gesture which is, hence, revocable. But it is necessary to emphasize that nothing in the public declarations or the behavior of these governments indicates that this second interpretation is correct.

That the above-mentioned declarations took only the Geneva Conventions into ac- count is explained by the fact that they were destined for the ICRC. Although the gov- ernments in question remained silent on this point up to then, one may also suppose that they also considered the customary rules of the law of war as applicable to the conflict with the NLF.

markable ignorance of the fundamental treaties on the part of the foreign minister who had signed the letter.

As for the NLF, the appeal of the International Committee of the Red Cross (ICRC) of June 1965 declared that the Front was "equally bound by the commitments signed in the name of Vietnam." In its response, the NLF "made known to the ICRC in October 1965 that, not having participated in the Geneva Conventions, it was not bound by them, and that these Conventions contained some provisions which do not correspond either to its action or to the organization of its armed forces. It announced, nevertheless, that it would follow a humane and charitable policy toward prisoners finding themselves within their hands" (*ibid.*, 1966, p. 360; cf. 1965, p. 585). Here is the heart of the problem. Is the position of the ICRC, laudable in its human concern, defendable in law? Is the position of the NLF, so discouraging, justified?

THE STATUS OF THE NLF FORCES WITH REGARD TO THE LAW OF WAR

The answer of the NLF is based on two arguments, an argument of form: the nonparticipation of the NLF at the Geneva Conventions, and an argument of substance: the inadaptability of certain provisions of the Conventions to the specific conditions of its action and the organization of its armed forces.

Concerning the first argument, it is necessary to point out that the NLF is certainly bound by the provisions of Article 3 of the Conventions, not because this text would be applicable to the struggle in South Vietnam,[43] but because it constitutes a résumé of the minimum norms of human rights whose observance is imperatively imposed in every armed struggle between political collectivities. On the other hand, the position of the ICRC is debatable concerning the Conventions as a whole.

[43] If one believes that the confrontation between Saigon and the NLF should be considered, in its origin, a civil war, Article 3 is obligatorily applicable to it, as such, up to the point of the transformation of the struggle into an international conflict, a transformation which happened toward the end of 1965 or in the beginning of 1966.

Before this date, the American *military advisers*, who fell into the hands of the NLF, were only protected by Article 3. The American authorities accepted at this time that these soldiers (all professional) could not assume the status of prisoners of war: see Kelly, *Military Law Review* (July 1963), 111; cf. Judge Advocate General's School, *Legal Aspects of Counter-Insurgency*, July 1964, p. 6.

Likewise, the infiltrated North Vietnamese units, fighting in the ranks of or on the side of the NLF formations, whether or not they belonged to the North Vietnamese army, could, in case of capture, claim only the protection of Article 3.

In the system of Conventions, there are only two hypotheses. Either one considers the NLF as a party to the conflict within the jurisdiction of Article 3—which is not the opinion of the ICRC—or one considers it as a party to an international conflict. It is in this context that the problem of the NLF's participation in the Conventions is posed, in effect. The indefiniteness of the Conventions does not permit us to postulate that the adhesion of the "state of Vietnam" can produce an effect with regard to a rival authority of the Saigon Government and to confer on the latter the prerogatives that the Conventions reserve only to the contracting states. Probably the possession of statehood or of a government is not required by all the provisions of the Conventions; but if the special rules which do not presuppose the possession of statehood or of a government are applicable to the NLF, it is not by virtue of the signature of the "state of Vietnam." It is equally possible that, despite the indefinite status of the NLF, the totality of the Conventions becomes applicable to relations with the NLF, but this result will then be caused by the NLF's own intention. The assent of the state of South Vietnam to the Conventions is only capable of having an effect with regard to the governments succeeding the signatory government of the act of consent, and only in what concerns the relations between the South Vietnamese state and *every other* belligerent *state* which is party to the Conventions.

It is, therefore, up to us to ascertain whether the NLF is bound by the Geneva Conventions. The response addressed to the ICRC seems to indicate, in addition, that at this present stage, the Front does not desire to be so bound. The possibility of fully participating in the Conventions is open to the NLF under paragraph 3 of Article 2 which makes provision for the belligerent parties to the Conventions to be obligated to a "power" (*"puissance"*) which is not a party "if the latter accepts and applies the provisions thereof." This text does not exclude the interpretation, which the objective of the Conventions recommends, according to which this procedure, stripped of its diplomatic formalism, constitutes the appropriate means for allowing a non-state collectivity, which is a party to an international conflict, to accede to the Conventions.

The fact that the NLF is not bound by the Geneva Conventions does not prevent its armed forces from being, under certain conditions, protected by these treaties. Article 4, A, 2 of the Third Convention extends the status of prisoners of war to members of the militia and voluntary corps not in the regular armed forces,

... including those of organized resistance movements, belonging to a Party to the conflict and operating in or outside their own territory, even if this territory is occupied, provided that such militias, or volunteer corps, including such organized resistance movements, fulfill the following conditions:

  a) that of being commanded by a person responsible for his subordinates.

  b) that of having a fixed distinctive sign recognizable at a distance.

  c) that of carrying arms openly.

  d) that of conducting their operations in accordance with the laws and customs of war.

In this text, the expression "Party to the conflict" designates a power which is party to the Conventions; it is thus now inapplicable to the NLF. On the other hand, the interpretation does not seem to be rejected according to which the armed forces of the NLF can be regarded as a military organization falling within the definition of "organized resistance movements, belonging to a Party to the conflict."[44] The word "belonging" does not allude to the bond of dependence or allegiance in the sense of public or private international law but rather a *de facto* connection relating to military strategy. Consequently, to consider the NLF as an organized resistance movement[45] "belonging" to the DRV would not contradict the NLF's affirmation of independence with regard to North Vietnam.

The cited text subordinates the protection to some *conditions* which must be fulfilled by the above-mentioned military organizations. These conditions are also understood to be the minimum requirements in the provision Article 4, A, 3, according the same protection to "members of regular armed forces who profess allegiance to a government or an authority not recognized by the Detaining Power," a provision which does not seem possible to be applied to the NLF, so long as it concerns the regular troops[46] of the former.[47] Thus, the status

[44] Article 13, 2 of Convention I (wounded and sick) and Convention II (wounded, sick, and shipwrecked on the high seas) contains the same provision.

[45] In the text cited, the term "movements of resistance" does not imply that the country in whose territory these movements are formed, is the object of an *occupatio bellica* in a technical sense.

[46] Nothing prevents, it seems to us, the consideration of paragraphs 2 and 3 of Article 4 A from being cumulatively applicable to the NLF; the first to its irregular units and the second to its regular troops.

[47] Doubtless, in the mind of the authors, the provision cited as well as the one related to the "movements of resistance," conceived because of the experiences of World

of the NLF forces with regard to the Geneva Conventions depends, definitively, on the *behavior* of these forces. Here the problem of observance is posed—observance by the Vietcong forces of the laws and customs of war—a problem which leads us to the second argument invoked by the NLF: the affirmation according to which certain provisions of the Geneva Conventions *correspond neither to its actions nor to the organization of its armed forces.*

It is a fact that many of the provisions of the Geneva Conventions suppose, for their effective operation, a material or legal infrastructure of which only states can dispose. But the impossibility of applying all their provisions is not an obstacle to formal participation in the Conventions and to the application of those rules which can be effectively observed. However, it is probably not that impossibility which the NLF had in mind in its response to the ICRC. What it wanted to express is, very probably, something more serious: it is the thesis that the law of war in general, the customary and conventional law, is not applicable to its struggle because it is not adapted to its action (guerrilla warfare) and to the organization of its forces.

One cannot ignore the fact that one is confronted with a real problem here, a problem which is not limited to the Vietnamese conflict but one which will appear in every future struggle having the character of a "war of national liberation." Speaking of the first war in Vietnam, General Giap described some of its characteristics which can also be applied to the present war:

> The protracted popular war in Vietnam demanded equally from the appropriate forms of combat: appropriate for the revolutionary nature of the war in relation to the balance of forces then showing a clear enemy superiority, and appropriate to the material and technical base, still very weak, of the Popular Army. *The form of combat adopted was guerrilla warfare.* One can say that the war of national liberation of the Vietnamese people was a long and vast guerrilla operation. . . . Guerrilla war is the war of the masses of an

---

War II, referred to marginal situations, occurring in a vast war of coalition. It is probable that they had not envisaged the hypothesis of an armed conflict in which a contracting state confronts a belligerent collectivity *solely* within the definition of paragraph 3, or a belligerent collectivity *principally* within the scope of the definition of organized resistance movements. It is not any less true that the text does not exclude the application of the two provisions to such a hypothesis, and that this application, whatever the provisions of the authors are, cannot be considered as contrary to the spirit of the Conventions.

underdeveloped country standing up against an aggressive army, powerfully equipped and well-trained.[48]

This form of struggle does not find its place in the traditional law of war. Is this to say that it is forbidden? It would be presumptuous— and besides ridiculously futile—to maintain that guerrilla war is forbidden. All that one can show is that neither historically nor materially, the law of war has been used to regulate this form of war. This fact answers, at the same time, the question of knowing whether the NLF is obligated by the *customary law of war*. At first glance, an affirmative response seems correct. It seems to be the counterpart of the Communist theory of legal wars of national liberation. In effect, if one attributes to the nation or the people struggling for their independence the quality of a participant in international law, is it not logical to subject this person to customary international law from the time of the first act by which he participates in international life, even if this act is an act of war? But the customary law of war is built on, in some cases, practice and conditions fundamentally different from the material, military, and political conditions of revolutionary wars of national emancipation. Also the conclusion seems inevitable that this customary law is not, *as such*, completely applicable to these wars.

Let one consider, from a formal point of view, Article 4, A, 2 as applicable or not applicable to the forces of the NLF. The four conditions set forth in this article are those to which the positive law of war grants the benefit of the status of prisoner of war. Can the NLF maintain that these conditions[49] correspond to conflict situations entirely different from "wars of national liberation" and that, for this reason, they are not, in law, applicable to those of its forces which are not regular troops? Let us remember that the Vietcong forces are organized into three categories, and each one is adapted to a form of specific military action (and political action): the *guerrillas*, the *regional forces*, made up of peasants who are part-time soldiers, and the *regular troops*. The guerrilla war is principally the activity of the

[48] *Op.cit.*, p. 44; italics are Giap's. In a study published (August 1967) in the Hanoi press and a résumé of which appeared in the *Courrier du Vietnam* of Oct. 2, 1967, the Minister of National Defense of the DRV and the Commander in Chief of the People's Army of Vietnam used the same terms in talking about the second war in Vietnam: "total resistance," "resistance of all the people," "protracted resistance," and "war of the people."

[49] In fact, the discussion concerns the second, third, and fourth conditions since the forces of the NLF evidently and obviously respond to the first condition—that of hierarchic organization.

guerrillas, but such action is also assigned to the regional forces. As for the regular forces, the question discussed here does not pose itself: it is not alleged that these units do not fulfill the conditions formulated in Article 4, A, 2. It is to the action and the organization of its guerrilla formations and its regional forces that the NLF probably referred to in its answer to the ICRC.

Probably, the most remarkable characteristic of the war in South Vietnam is the enormous disproportion of the forces at hand. On the one side, the most powerful and most industrialized nation in the world, on the other side, a small underdeveloped country. This material inequality reaches, in the case of South Vietnam, to the extreme; but it must be understood clearly that it constitutes a necessary feature in the "wars of national liberation." It creates a situation so novel that one cannot avoid questioning whether it does not necessarily affect the law. One of the essential characteristics of the law of war is its practicality; and one of the conditions of this practicality—a condition which concerns the fundamentals: the *equality* of belligerents—is that the observance of these rules neither benefits nor harms either one of the two camps. But, would it not be precisely the same case if, in the struggle against a power enjoying a crushing military, material, and technical superiority and profiting to the maximum from this inequality, the weak power would be obliged by law to adopt rules which would not only make its action ineffectual but which would also cause it to sacrifice itself? In an unequal war situation, the temptation of the weak power has always been to maintain that all means are allowed it and to look for ways to compensate for its inferiority by means which are forbidden under the law of war. In the case discussed here, we are concerned not only with this subjective desire, which the law of war must reject absolutely, but with an objective situation of intrinsic inequality. Is it possible to reconcile this irremediable organic inequality with the fundamental supposition of the law of war—a supposition historically and universally true: the equality of states in war? Here is one of the most serious issues posed to the theoretician concerned with the law of war—the phenomenon of the "wars of national liberation."

Again, is it proper not to exaggerate the dimensions of the problem. Practically, it reduces itself to the conditions put forth under the letters "b" and "c" of Article 4, A, 2: the requirement of a "fixed distinctive sign" and the obligation of "carrying arms openly." It is probably accurate that these conditions are fulfilled only rarely by the Vietcong guerrillas. From what we have shown, is it too much to conclude that the observance of these two conditions is perhaps not an obligatory rule for the guerrilla[50] in a "war of national liberation." On what basis can one conclude that the members of these forces should be accorded the status of prisoners of war, even if they have not respected the two conditions. One must wonder, however, if in the final analysis, the NLF really gains an advantage from the nonobservance of these two prescriptions. Because it inevitably involves this consequence—the adversary forces are led to see a clandestine combatant in every peasant able to carry arms. The confusion is facilitated by a particular circumstance in Vietnam. The black pajama, the traditional garb of the peasants, is also the uniform of the guerrillas. That is in itself perfectly legal; Article 4, A, 2 does not require any particular uniform—only a "fixed distinctive sign recognizable at a distance." However, Government and American forces have come to consider the traditional black pajama as a sort of uniform which connotes Vietcong sympathy. But is this not precisely the result which is sought by the NLF?

Concerning the last and principal condition: we have discussed earlier the obligation of the irregular corps "of conducting their operations in accordance with the laws and customs of war" and the issue of whether the NLF is obligated by the rules of the customary law of war. We reached the conclusion that the customary law does not bind the NLF, as such. However, in the last part of Article 4, A, 2, we are not concerned with the entire customary law of war, but only the observance by irregular formations, in their operations, of the *laws and customs of war*. These "laws and customs of war" are far from having a well-defined content, and it is neither unreasonable nor unjust to conceive of them in a less extensive and a less detailed manner when their observance is imposed on irregular combatants than when obligations fall upon the regular army. It is important, in defining them, to be neither too demanding nor too lax. What is important is to prevent this particular form of warfare from degenerating into barbarity or from degrading the law of war in general. The "laws and customs of war" to which irregular combatants are obligated to conform include, besides the elementary norms formulated in Article 3 of the Geneva Conventions, the fundamental rules relating to the status of prisoners of war, to the means used to injure the enemy, and to the

---

50 The situation is different, in this regard, when it concerns guerrilla operations in the countryside or guerrilla operations in urban centers. In the cities, the observation of these two conditions are not absolute, and they can be renounced.

conventions between the belligerents. The rules concerning the means of injury consist of a catalogue of prohibitions that one can enumerate, following the order of Section II of the Hague Convention: prohibition against the use of poison or poisoned weapons; the killing or wounding of individuals after betraying promises or guarantees of safety; the killing or wounding of individuals who, having laid down their arms, voluntarily surrender; declarations of no quarter; using weapons, projectiles, or materials which cause unnecessary damage or injury; undue use of the national emblem or the military insignia of the enemy as well as that of the Red Cross; causing destruction not justified by the necessities of war; directing attacks against the civilian population; and looting and pillage. It is also necessary to add the prohibition against the use of toxic chemical weapons, asphyxiants, and biological warfare.[51]

The treatment which, by virtue of the "laws and customs of war," the irregular combatants should apply to their prisoners of war is not the same as those rules prescribed in the Third Geneva Convention. It is simpler, approaching more the status foreseen in the Hague Conventions of 1899 and 1907. In this regard, Article 4, A, 2, implies an imperfect reciprocity since the legal regime which the enemy belligerent state is obliged to accord to the captured irregular combatants is properly the complete statute of the Third Convention. One should wonder whether, in this domain, there is room to consider, first, the fact that the confrontation with the NLF is not an interstate conflict, and second, the fact that this struggle is, at the same time, a revolutionary war. It seems, in effect, unreasonable and unrealistic to ask the legal government as well as the NLF itself to apply to its prisoners of war those provisions of the Geneva Convention which are designed less to protect the person of the prisoner than his quality as a *national* or *agent of an enemy state.*

3. THE RULES APPLICABLE TO THE RELATIONS WITH THE CIVILIAN POPULATION IN SOUTH VIETNAM

THE FOURTH GENEVA CONVENTION OF 1949

In their responses to the ICRC, mentioned above, the American, Australian, and New Zealand Governments allowed the ICRC to understand that they considered the four conventions to be applicable to

---

[51] There is no need to recall that the most employed methods of injuring the enemy in guerrilla warfare—ambush, mines, and sabotage—are legal.

the Vietnamese conflict.[52] What should one think about this position concerning the Fourth Convention which relates to the protection of civilians in time of war? We have seen that none of the Conventions is in effect in matters concerning the relations *between the NLF and its adversaries.* However, as for Convention IV, it is necessary to wonder—this question can seem so ridiculous at first glance—whether this instrument does not govern the relations *between the United States and the nationals of South Vietnam.* This Convention is not only applied in ordinary circumstances of belligerent occupation, but, as Article 2, paragraph 3, specifies: "to all cases of . . . occupation," even beyond a situation of "declared war or of any other armed conflict." The fact that the presence and the action of the United States on South Vietnamese territory has been *requested* by the Saigon Government excludes the applicability of the provisions of the Convention to the relations between the United States and *this government.* But what are the relations between the United States and the South Vietnamese nationals? If one holds that Article 2, paragraph 2 does not exclude a certain sort of applicability of the Convention to the relations between an intervening power and an assisted state,[53] it is again necessary to examine whether the nationals of this state really answer to the *definition of protected persons* put forth in Article 4, paragraph 1: "Persons protected by the Convention are those who, at a given moment and in

[52] This view is shared by the Government of the Federal Republic of Germany. By putting at the disposition of the German Red Cross the hospital ship *Helgoland* (sent to a South Vietnamese port where it serves as a hospital for civilians), the Bonn Government, after conversations with the ICRC, has decided to give the status of "civilian hospital," in the sense of the Fourth Geneva Convention, to this ship (see *Die Welt,* Aug. 10, 1966).

[53] The issue is controversial. According to P. Urner, *Die Menschenrechte der Zivilpersonen im Krieg gemäss der Genfer Zivilkonvention von 1949,* 1956, pp. 45-46, the Convention is not applied in the case of a requested occupation. But this author admits that, practically, it is often difficult to determine whether it is a belligerent or peaceful occupation. He cites especially the case in which the government of a satellite requests the intervention of its protector in order to maintain itself in power.

Before 1949, the doctrine acknowledged that the rules of *occupatio bellica* was also imposed, if need be, in different kinds of peaceful occupations or quasi-occupations. The term "occupation" no longer has in international law a technical, fixed definition. One thing is certain: the authors of 1949 intended to exclude from the field of application of the Fourth Convention the relations between a government and its own nationals. Concerning the relations between an intervening state and the subjects of the assisted state, this situation was not specifically considered, it seems, by the authors of the Convention. However, this is not sufficient evidence to decide that the diplomatic conference intended to leave this situation—which is an *international* relationship—beyond the scope of the Convention.

any manner whatsoever, find themselves, in case of a conflict or occupation, in the hands of a Party to the conflict or Occupying Power of which they are not nationals."[54]

This text makes the Convention inapplicable to the relations *between the legal government and the South Vietnamese nationals*. According to the definition of the general law of war—and nothing indicates that the authors of the Convention wanted to set aside this definition —the term "Occupying Power" is applied to a state which undertakes against persons or property on the territory of another state and under some particular title of authority acts which are primarily acts of war and which, by their nature, come under the jurisdiction of the rules relating to "occupation." The rules are characterized by the fact that they involve a *physical contact*[55] between the forces of the occupying state and the civilian subjects of the other state, a contact which must be analyzed as *de facto* dominance based on military force. This is the dominance which is designated in Article 4 by the words: "find themselves . . . in the hands of a Party to the conflict or Occupying Power." This formula is applicable to the existing relations, in the pacification zones, between the South Vietnamese civilians and the American forces. That this relationship is only transient matters little. Whether—conforming to the agreements between the United States and the Saigon Government, which reserves to the latter the exercise of executive and judicial powers with regard to South Vietnamese nationals—the American control over these people is only *de facto* and not legal is equally unimportant. The United States exercises military power in South Vietnam. It is actual physical control which allows the United States to exercise these military powers with regard to the South Vietnamese civilians; the exercise of these powers places the American forces in the situation of and under the obligation of observing the applicable provisions of the Fourth Convention. The United States cannot exon-

[54] Persons protected by Conventions I, II, III should be excluded from this definition.

[55] According to *Article 4, paragraph 2*, "nationals of a co-belligerent State, shall not be regarded as protected persons while the State of which they are nationals has normal diplomatic representation in the State in whose hands they are." As the condition of "normal diplomatic representation" indicates, the nationals of a co-belligerent state are excluded from the Convention's protection because it is assumed that normal diplomatic protection is sufficient to prevent or to stop violations on the part of the power under whose authority they find themselves. This *ratio-legis* is inapplicable in the case of South Vietnam. South Vietnamese in the contested regions are not protected by the Saigon Government against possible excesses by American forces in the pursuit of *pacification* activities.

erate itself from this obligation and from the responsibility which flows from it—by an agreement with the Saigon Government.[56]

The major part of the provisions of the Fourth Convention is destined to be put into effect only in the case of real *occupatio bellica*. The ones which, in the case of an intervention requested by the legal government of a state which is a party to the Conventions, are applied to the action of pacification by the intervening power are not any less important. These are notably: Article 5, protection of persons apprehended as spies or saboteurs or because they are "definitely suspected of or engaged in activities hostile to the security of the state"; Article 27, treatment of protected persons; Article 29, responsibility of the occupying power and its agents; Articles 31 and 32, prohibition of coercion, corporal punishment, and torture; Article 33, prohibition of collective punishments and reprisals; Article 47, protection of rights guaranteed in the Convention from changes in local institutions; Article 53, prohibition of destruction without absolute military necessity; Article 78, protection in the case of internment; Articles 146 to 148, preventive measures and sanctions against violations of the Convention.[57]

THE CUSTOMARY LAW OF WAR

According to customary international law,[58] the relations between the American forces[59] and the civilian population of South Vietnam

---

[56] There is a *duality of legal regimes* concerning the relations with the South Vietnamese civilians: Convention IV and the international law of war in general bind the United States while Saigon is internationally obligated only to observe the laws protecting human rights. This duality, as we have said, is nothing exceptional. It is by no means impractical, although it does raise some difficulties. In no instance can the United States "resolve" these difficulties by unloading its international obligations on the Saigon Government.

[57] The provisions cited take into account military necessity; they cannot be ignored, however, under the pretext of these necessities. Their observance is equally imposed in the zone of operations.

[58] The customary rules of *jus in bello* are applicable in all cases in which an army undertakes acts of force against persons or property in the territory of another state. The fact that one acts by virtue of the authority conferred by the government of the assisted state only matters for relations between the intervening power and that *state*. This authority does not influence the relations which exist, with regard to *jus in bello*, between the intervening forces and the subjects of the assisted state. No agreement between Saigon and the United States could make the latter a police agent of the former.

[59] The relations between *Saigon* and the *civilian population of South Vietnam* is subject to the obligatory rules of conflicts of a noninternational character: Article 3, to which it is necessary to add the prohibition of persecutions for political, religious, or racial motives (see Article 6, c of the Statute of the International Military Tribunal

are governed, on the one hand, by those rules of the general law of occupation which are applicable to these relations, and, on the other hand, by the norms of the law of war relating to the protection of civilian populations against attacks. The first include the following provisions of the Hague Convention:[60] Article 46, prescribing respect for the honor and rights of the family, life of individuals, private property as well as religious convictions and the exercise of religious observances; Article 47, prohibiting pillage; Article 50, prohibiting collective punishments; Article 56, forbidding the intentional destruction or desecration of religious establishments, charitable institutions, schools, institutions of arts and sciences, historical monuments, and works of arts. As for the norms protecting civilians against attacks, they are the ones which are derived from the principle of the immunity of civilian populations.

THE LAW OF OCCUPATION AND GUERRILLA WARFARE

General Giap has characterized the guerrilla warfare of the First Indochinese War in these terms: "each inhabitant was a soldier; each village a fortress. . . . The entire population participated in the armed struggle, fighting, according to the principles of guerrilla warfare, in small units. . . ."[61] When the hostilities extended throughout the country, our Party launched the order: *lead a total war of popular resistance.* This is the fundamental content of the war of the people."[62]

We have considered, due to another quote from Giap, the guerrilla from the aspect of "partisan"; in other words, from the angle of the rules relating to legitimate combatants. The passage from General Giap that we have just cited—and which was also valuable despite its exaggeration in understanding the conflict occurring in South Viet-

---

of Nuremberg) and this fundamental principle of the law of war—the prohibition of attacks directed against the civilian population.

Against the enemy—or against the occupier, even if he is not an "enemy" in a technical sense—the law of war offers to the civilian population a broader and stronger protection than the one which the law of human rights can provide. This difference concerns, in particular, imprisonment, deportations to the interior regions of the country, and the fact that Article 3 does not prohibit attacks against property.

[60] It is generally admitted today—this opinion has been sanctioned by the International Military Tribunal of Nuremberg—that the provisions of the Hague Convention have comparable value to the rules of customary law. They thus apply to the Vietnamese conflict, notwithstanding the fact that the two states of Vietnam, Australia, and New Zealand are not parties to the Convention.

[61] *Op.cit.*, p. 45.

[62] *Ibid.*, p. 90. Italics are Giap's.

nam—is related to the other aspect of the phenomenon of guerrilla warfare, the *"civilian aspect."* At first glance, the people's guerrilla seems to collide with one of the foundations of the law of war: the distinction between combatants and the civilian population. Every institution of occupation rests on this distinction, as vital for the occupier as for the occupied. However, if it is true that the guerrilla causes difficult and serious problems for the law of war, it is not necessary to overestimate them and still less to exaggerate them. One cannot appreciate the phenomenon of guerrilla warfare in South Vietnam by separating it from the concrete conditions of the struggle. It is important not to forget this verity—the American occupation (or quasi-occupation), like the authority of the Saigon Government, is not effective through the entire extent of South Vietnam, whose political and military map presents a spotted and fluctuating configuration. Historically and institutionally, however, the law of occupation presupposes a territorial base, certainly not immutable, but constant and relatively stable, in which the occupier can exercise *effective* control. There is more. To the lack of territorial stability must be added the mercurial mobility of the operations. In this theater of war, the airplane, especially the helicopter, have not only destroyed the notion of the front but they also have shaken the distinction between the zone of operations and the zone of occupation.

It has been maintained that guerrilla war is contrary to the law of war for two reasons: first, because it implies that civilians will *occasionally* become *combatants*; second, because it implies that the civilian population forms, in a permanent way, the most important part of the *logistical and information network* of the guerrilla forces. With regard to the first of these elements, the particular circumstances that we have just mentioned are without effect. According to what we have said above, the Vietcong partisans are either legal combatants or illegal combatants. The conditions that irregular combatants must fulfill are, in effect, the same in occupied territories as in the zone of operations. But these circumstances have an effect on the second element—in which some have tried to see a violation of the law of war. Because outside the regions which are not subjected to the effective occupation of the enemy, civilians can legitimately execute works of a possible military nature: in transport, construction, etc. These activities are not contrary to the law of war. But, during the times when they execute these works, the inhabitants cannot evidently avail themselves of the civilian immunity against attacks. When the frontiers between occupied regions, contested regions, front lines, and rear zones change continually, it becomes difficult to fix the status of the inhabitants of the affected regions in regard to international law. In any case, it is not possible to consider the full extent of the territory of South Vietnam, even theoretically, as occupied and to claim that, in principle, the inhabitants throughout the country have an obligation to remain passive since international law requires such from the population of occupied countries. In the regions controlled by the NLF, the participation of the inhabitants in its war effort, a participation which cannot always be voluntary, is a part of the actual administration of the territories. In spite of what has been maintained by the two sides, for various propaganda reasons, there does not exist in South Vietnam a generalized "people's war." The manner in which the guerrilla is dressed is not illegal and cannot, in any manner, serve as a pretext to American authorities to suspend the application of the rules of the law of war. In addition, the Fourth Geneva Convention furnishes sufficient means of defense to American forces against South Vietnamese civilians whatever the serious motives for judging them dangerous to American security. These means are—besides legal sanctions for individual crimes:[63] Article 49, paragraph 2, which permits the occupying power to "undertake total or partial evacuation of a given area if the security of the population or imperative reasons so demand"; Article 53, which permits the destruction of real or personal property in cases where "such destruction is rendered absolutely necessary by military operations"; Article 78, which permits forced residence and house arrest and internment if "imperative reasons of security" make these measures necessary.

[63] By virtue of agreements with Saigon, American authorities, not having penal authority with regard to South Vietnamese nationals, turn over to the Saigon authorities all persons apprehended in the course of operations. The United States must maintain its obligations and responsibility to assure that these persons are treated in conformity with the prescriptions of the Geneva Conventions. This holds true for Vietcong combatants and for civilians suspected of having participated or intending to participate in military action against the Government.

PART TWO

THE APPLICATION OF THE LAW OF WAR BY THE
PARTIES TO THE CONFLICT

I. The Means of Injuring the Enemy

1. THE BOMBING

THE BOMBING OF NORTH VIETNAM

Let us remember that the bombing undertaken by American air and naval forces against North Vietnam interest us here only from the angle of *jus in bello*. What distinguishes these bombardments above all is their *excessiveness*[64] and their unilateral character.[65] Despite these two characteristics, the American Government has claimed that the war has been "limited." Would one use this term if North Vietnam responded identically against South Vietnam, Thailand, South Korea, and the United States? The bombing is limited if one measures it against the enormous power of the United States,[66] but not if one con-

[64] The total tonnage of bombs dropped by American planes on Vietnam (North and South), whose area is scarcely that of Italy's, surpassed, as of November 15, 1967, the tonnage of bombs dropped during World War II on all of Europe: 1,630,500 tons (by comparison: 635,000 tons during the Korean War; 502,180 tons in the Pacific Theater of World War II); 53% of this tonnage has been delivered against North Vietnam, the object of the greatest concentration of bombing ever known (*Int. Herald Tribune*, Dec. 4, 1967). These figures—which do not include land artillery and naval bombardments—support President Johnson's statement that the bombings tend to impose on North Vietnam a burden nearly equal to the one which the Communists are inflicting in the South (*Dept. of State Bulletin*, March 27, 1967, p. 515). The burden is almost mathematically exact—if one includes the ravages caused in South Vietnam by American bombing. Did the President want to allude to the victims of Vietcong terrorism? Terrorism, a permanent feature of every internal struggle, is composed of two elements: acts of sabotage, which are legal according to the *law of war* if they are directed against military targets, and terrorism properly said to be either selective or blind. The jurisdiction over these acts belongs to the Saigon Government. These acts of terrorism do not authorize the United States to take reprisals against North Vietnam: there is no distinction between active or passive subjects. In addition, it is impossible, as repugnant as the idea is, not to leave room for a terrible compensation: the atrocities committed by the South Vietnamese Government. As for the "balance," there is no even comparison with the terror of American bombings.

[65] The ground-to-air missiles, the fighters, and the radar systems furnished by the Soviet Union and which North Vietnam uses does not modify this characteristic. The disproportion remains immense between the unlimited attack potential and the limited defense capability. But, more especially, the attack does not give rise to an identical retaliation.

[66] Dean Rusk has described without exaggeration the weight of this power when he said that the American people came out of World War II with incredible military and economic power, which has since multiplied many times. See *Dept. of State Bulletin*, June 12, 1967, p. 878.

siders the country which is being bombed. Among the reasons invoked by the American Government in order to justify the bombing are some which concern *jus ad bellum* and others which concern *jus in bello*. It is evident that these unilateral justifications which are ascribed to *jus ad bellum* cannot confer upon the United States rights more extensive than *jus in bello* allows. Thus, when President Johnson declares that the American bombing has as one of its goals the imposition of a penalty on North Vietnam for the violation of the Geneva Accords,[67] this reason—a type of unilateral pretension—does not authorize the United States to ignore the rules of the law of war relating to bombing. It being understood that the decision of the United States to carry the war to North Vietnam is subject to *jus ad bellum*, the United States has, according to *jus in bello*, the right to attack *military objectives* in that country.[68]

Included as military targets are barracks, camps, supply depots, ports, airfields, arms factories, military convoys, etc. There are some "mixed targets": installations and buildings which serve primarily the needs of the civilian population but are also utilized or can be utilized for military purposes such as railroad stations, railways, roads, bridges, power plants, fuel storage dumps, etc. These targets can be attacked only if their destruction is imperatively demanded by reasonably understood military necessity. In addition, casualties and material destruction caused by the bombing of these targets should not be out of proportion to their military advantage.[69] The *reasonable proportionality* which must exist between the damage caused and the military gain anticipated constitutes the essential criterion of the legality of bombing directed against targets not having a purely military character.[70]

[67] *Ibid.*, March 27, 1967, p. 515.

[68] *All* military objectives, including those which do not have a direct relationship with the infiltration of men and supplies into South Vietnam by the North, or whose destruction would be out of proportion to the nature and volume of these infiltrations? Without wanting to make a general rule, *let us suppose* here that the United States has such a right. But it should be noted that this interpretation is not the one which is put forth in the Army Manual on International Law, for the manual states that the law of war requires that belligerents "abstain from using all manner and all degree of violence which is not really necessary for the attainment of military objectives" (FM-27-10, *The Law of Land Warfare*, 1956, Section 3). According to this text, the bombing should be limited, as to nature and degree, to military objectives whose destruction would be effectively required by the real dimensions of the infiltrations.

[69] Cf. FM 27-10, Section 41.

[70] The school of Professor McDougal wants to substitute the *minimum destruction principle* for the principle of proportionality. McDougal and Moore have argued (once in 1966, *loc.cit.*, see note 2, and once in the spring of 1967) that the bombing of North

THE LAW OF WAR IN VIETNAM

In a small agricultural country like North Vietnam, authentic military targets are not numerous and are relatively quickly eliminated, considering the means of destruction used. By the effect of a simple operation of subtraction, the bombing will then take mixed objectives as its targets; and, then, more and more, the targets will be objectives used primarily by civilians and which serve the vital daily needs of the population.[71] As these bombardments seriously attack the resources and the foundations of economic life, indeed, of physical life (the inhabitants), it becomes a question of an attack on the civilian population, an attack which it will no longer be possible to characterize as being *accessory* or *indirect*. This attack directed against the civilian population is no less illegal than deliberate attacks on purely civilian objectives—homes, schools, hospitals, churches; attacks which are rare in North Vietnam and which are certainly contrary to the directives of the American Government.[72] When the losses[73] and destruction suffered

Vietnam conforms both to the principle of proportionality and to the principle of minimum destruction. Do they maintain this position while the level of the bombing has reached megaton proportions? Probably, yes. In the McDougal doctrine, in effect, the *minimum destruction principle* is related to the scale of political, material, and intellectual values of the Free World, conceived as a projection of the United States. The application which is made of it in understanding the Vietnam conflict shows that the *minimum destruction principle* is a subjective and relative concept, charged with ideology. Furthermore, by reason of its antinormative character, it is incapable of furnishing objective rules for the conduct of states at war. What kind of authority can one accord to a doctrine which leads its defenders to affirm literally the thesis developed by Professor Moore (*Am. Journal of Int. Law*, pp. 21, 29) that the use of force by the DRV against South Vietnam constitutes a serious disruption of "minimum public world order" that justifies the level of bombing delivered against the North by men who are respectful of the "preservation of values"? Thus, the *minimum destruction principle* allows a unilateral accusation of aggression to be sanctioned unilaterally by the unilateral deployment of such devastating power, whose gigantic dimensions are declared unilaterally to be proportional to the so-called offense. As for the affirmation that the bombing conserves values of public order, one should recall the statement of the Secretary General of the United Nations who said "what is really at stake in Vietnam is the independence, identity, and survival of the country itself." (Dec. 30, 1966: United Nations, *Monthly Chronicle*, 1967, p. 5.)

[71] The port of Haiphong is the kind of mixed military objective upon which an attack is legal because of its predominantly military utility. It has long been spared by the American Air Force for fear of the international complications arising from the presence of ships belonging to countries, namely the Soviet Union, which supply military equipment to the DRV or trade with her.

[72] Given the excessive and disproportionate volume of the bombing, the attacks on purely civilian targets being attributable to error or resulting from a culpable imprudence are evidently frequent.

[73] The American Government is happy to emphasize the relatively low number of civilian victims from the bombing. But this has been due to the fact that the in-

by the North Vietnamese civilians result from the fact that the persons and property affected are found in the vicinity of these mixed objectives which are bombed, these damages are only justified according to the law of war if the target objectively has a certain military value and if the damages are not out of proportion with the military advantage gained by neutralizing the objective. But for the reasons that we have just indicated—the progressive elimination of military objectives and mixed objectives of a preponderantly military nature—there exist few targets which now fill these two conditions.[74]

Numerous neutral observers have established that, in the raids against the DRV, the American Air Force uses *antipersonnel* bombs[75] (bombs which fragment on impact). This new weapon at first raises the question of whether, by reason of its characteristics, it does not fall within the prohibition of weapons, missiles, or materials which cause unnecessary wounds or damage ("des armes, des projectiles ou des matières propres à causer des maux superflus"), formulated in Article 23 (e) of the Hague Convention, and whether, in particular, these weapons should not be likened to the dum-dum bullets which are forbidden by the Third Declaration of the Hague (1899).[76] The presumptions concerning the illegality of these weapons seem to us very strong; but since neutral military experts have failed to speak out on the issue, we shall abstain ourselves from making a pronouncement.[77] To suppose that these bombs should be considered legal raises

habitants of the urban centers have been largely evacuated. Low casualties have also been due to an ingenious, effective, local organization of civil defense. See the interview of the North Vietnamese Minister of Health on this subject in *Le Monde*, Nov. 25, 1967.

[74] The method, inevitably blind, of bombing small boats whose principal use is exclusively for vital civilian needs (fishing, transport of consumer goods) can hardly be justified as military necessity.

[75] The bombs consist of a "mother-bomb" containing, depending on the type, some 20 (the type called Pineapple) or 600 (the type called Guava) smaller bombs ("daughter-bombs") which are released at the time of the explosion. Each "daughter-bomb" encloses some 300 balls of steel—each ball approximately 6mm in diameter. The "daughter-bombs" are elliptically shaped—about 500mm long and 250mm wide. See the technical description of these weapons by J. P. Vigier, chief of research at *C.N.R.S.*, in *Tribunal Russell: Le jugement de Stockholm*, 1967, pp. 157ff.

[76] The United States is not a Party to this declaration. However, Manual FM 27-10 contains in its paragraph 34, interpreting Article 23 (e) of the Hague Convention, a definition which, for practical purposes, covers the dum-dum bullet. The Judge Advocate General of the United States Army, in an opinion given in 1942, stated that the prohibition set forth in the said declaration was a part of the laws of war obligating the United States (*Bulletin of the Judge Advocate General of the Army*, 1942, p. 207).

[77] The same question is also raised for other experimental weapons used by the American forces in Vietnam. Thus, in the Battle of Dak To, in November, 1967, American

the question of a weapon which, by its nature, is exclusively directed against persons. All testimony and observation attest to the fact that these bombs, useless against buildings, are employed on nonmilitary objectives. They are thus a form of attack on civilians—an attack which is certainly illegal.

The use of napalm against military objectives is not prohibited. During the Korean War, the Security Council and the General Assembly tolerated the use of these munitions by the United Nations forces. Because of their intense incendiary power and the terrible burns which they cause, the use of these weapons should be limited strictly to military objectives. This restriction is not always observed in the raids against North Vietnam.[78]

THE BOMBING IN SOUTH VIETNAM

The bombing in South Vietnam, effectuated by the American Air Force, Navy, and artillery, is subject to different rules as it affects the regions *controlled by the NFL* or the *contested zones*. Probably, the extreme mobility of the front, or fronts, which characterizes the war in South Vietnam, diminishes the practicality of distinguishing between bombing *behind the lines* and bombing in the *zone of operations*; but the principle of this distinction remains. The first type of bombing is subject to the same restrictions as the bombing of North Vietnam: only military objectives can be attacked. In the zone of operations, the rights are more extensive. All "defended" localities can be bombed to the extent necessary to prepare for, to facilitate, and to effect the taking of these localities. Against a position which is being

---

artillery used a new type of mortar shell called the "Bee-Hive" which, upon exploding, throws off a hail of tiny sharp pieces of lead which, literally, chop up everything that they encounter (*Newsweek* [Nov. 27, 1967]).

Certain primitive weapons used by Vietcong self-defense groups are clearly prohibited by Article 23 of the Hague Convention: traps whose pits are filled with pointed bamboo or iron spikes; poisoned arrows; tubes of iron, like mines, which are stuffed with dirt, scrap iron, pieces of broken glass, old nails, and which are discharged when the enemy is less than ten meters away.

[78] This restriction is even less respected in the bombing of South Vietnam. Manual FM 27-10 declares that the use of napalm bombs "against targets requiring their use" is not illegal (Section 36). This formulation does seem to exclude a direct attack with napalm on human targets, whether military or civilian. However, it is not infrequent that American planes bomb Vietcong troops with napalm. These bombs offer the assailant the advantage of being able to be dropped with great precision while flying at a low altitude. For this reason, is it sufficient to consider these enemy troops, finding themselves in direct contact with American units, to be targets requiring the use of these weapons?

effectively defended, the distinction between military and nonmilitary targets does not have to be observed. However, the presence—real or assumed—of certain Vietcong forces in an area or the presence of arms hidden in homes by the NLF is not sufficient to qualify these areas as "defended" localities or to qualify each home as a military target. It is unjustified to subject these areas to concentrated bombing (*bombardement de destruction*).

But, in South Vietnam, American forces openly practice a *strategy of devastation* by means of massive aerial bombardments and artillery pounding, a job which is completed, if need be, by fires set by the infantrymen and which the bulldozers finally come to finish up. This strategy ignores the distinction between bombing behind the lines and bombing in the zone of operations because it makes a joke out of the notion of a military target. The desired result is not to take an area held by the NLF in order to *occupy* it, but to prevent this area from again falling into the hands of the NLF. Is not the most assured way to obtain this result then to raze the area? If an army cannot or does not want to take possession of an area which is being contested by the enemy, it does not have the option, according to international law, to destroy it. This strategy of devastation[79] cannot be justified either by military necessity[80] or by arguments based on the particular character of guerrilla warfare.[81, 82]

[79] The rules of the law of war relating to bombardments and to occupation also concern the property of the enemy. The fact is that the Saigon Government is not obligated with regard to property belonging, individually or collectively, to South Vietnamese nationals; by the same restrictive rules, it is without influence on the powers and authority of the United States—these powers being determined by the international law of war.

[80] Article 23 (g) of the Hague Convention forbids destruction "except in cases in which (it) would be imperatively required by the necessities of war" (translated from the French). All writers emphasize that this provision should be interpreted restrictively, the accent being put on the adverb "imperatively."

Cf. FM 27-10, Section 56; it states that the limits of allowable destruction and devastation are the "strict" necessities of war. Destruction as an end in itself or as an independent means of war is not authorized by the law of war. There must be a tight relationship between the destruction of property and the defeat which must necessarily be inflicted on the enemy. This relationship is absent in the action of the American forces in South Vietnam, where devastation is not an exceptional measure, limited in time and space, but is practiced in conformity with a general strategy—a strategy which hopes to prevent the necessity for occupation.

The trial against General Jodl by the International Military Tribunal of Nuremberg has established the act of having ordered the "evacuation of all the inhabitants of northern Norway and the destruction of their houses to prevent them from aiding the Russians" as a war crime (*Procès des grands criminels de guerre devant le Tribunal militaire international*, I, p. 348). The American judges at Nuremberg have admitted the

2. CHEMICAL WARFARE

American forces use, in South Vietnam, chemical agents against *men* and against *vegetation*.

GASES

These concern incapacitating agents or irritants—gases which produce nausea and vomiting and especially tear gas—employed on a relatively moderate scale[83] against Vietcong and North Vietnamese units.[84]

---

excuse of "military necessities" in some exceptional circumstances. In the trial of von Leeb and others, the Tribunal stated: "The accused often found themselves, during the retreat, in some difficult situations where their troops were seriously threatened with being cut off and isolated. In such circumstances, a commander must necessarily make rapid decisions in dealing with the particular situation. Because of this, a substantial liberty of action should be accorded to him. The question of knowing what, in such situations, constitutes destruction surpassing military necessity demands a detailed examination of the facts relating to operations and tactics. We do not believe that, in the present case, the proof furnished to the Tribunal permits establishing the guilt of the accused on this point of accusation" (translated from the French, *ibid.*, XI, p. 541) . Likewise, in the trial of von List and others, the American judge declared "the destruction, by troops fighting in retreat, of public or private property capable of being useful to the enemy can constitute a situation included within the exceptions set forth in Article 23 (g) " (translated from the French, *ibid.*, p. 1296) . The exceptional circumstances to which these two passages are related are in no way comparable to the situation as it exists in South Vietnam.

[81] Oppenheim and Lauterpacht consider devastation to be legal in the case in which the enemy, after the defeat of its forces and the occupation of its territory, disperses the remainder of its army into little groups in order to pursue guerrilla warfare, with the guerrillas receiving supplies and information in such a way that one cannot expect the end of the war, except for having recourse to general devastation which deprives the guerrilla of any possibility of supply (*Oppenheim's International Law*, 7th edn., 1952, p. 416) . The authors, however, insist on the fact that general devastation can only be justified by an imperative military necessity, and only if the occupier does not have the possibility of employing less rigorous means. These observations apply to Vietnam only superficially. Devastation is not a measure used against a guerrilla resisting the occupier; it is a strategic principle of offensive warfare, designed to do away with the necessity for occupation. In spite of the term "general devastation" used by Oppenheim and Lauterpacht, these authors had not imagined ravages as generalized as those which South Vietnam has suffered.

[82] Neither does the nature of *total war* that the resistance to American forces takes on for the Vietcong as well as the DRV, and, which can be invoked by one side or the other, allow them to set aside the prescriptions of the law of war. The means of defense derived from total war has been rejected by the tribunals which judged the German and Japanese war criminals. The argument of total war has equally been refuted, *precisely on the subject of rules relating to aerial bombardments*, by the civil tribunal of Tokyo in the Shimoda Case (Dec. 7, 1963; see the English translation in Falk and Mendlowitz, *The Strategy of World Order*, 1966, I, pp. 314ff.) .

[83] One will not get too far believing that this relative moderation is due to the very clearly hostile reaction that had been provoked in world public opinion, in March

The Geneva Protocol of 1925 concerning the prohibition of the use in war of asphyxiant gases, toxic gases, and other bacteriological means of war is not formally applicable in the Vietnamese conflict—the United States and the two Vietnams not being parties to this convention.[85] Moreover, the interpretation formerly shared by numerous states party to the convention, according to which the definition of chemical weapons prohibited by the Protocol included incapacitating agents and irritants which are not normally fatal or injurious to health, is expressly rejected today by certain governments.[86] In the current state of positive law, it is thus impossible to affirm with certainty that, in a general fashion, the use by the United States of incapacitating chemical agents or irritants is illegal. That does not mean that all the chemical weapons used by the American forces in Vietnam escape the prohibition of international law. The problem of knowing whether this or that chemical agent falls or does not fall within the scope of this interdiction is an individual question. A new gas of weak toxicity, classed provisionally as an irritant or incapacitant, may, under certain combat situations (besides the case of accidents) cause grave lesions or even death.

1965, when the first news concerning the use of nausea-inducing gas and tear gas became known. But at the same time, the fact that, despite this universal protestation, the American army continues to use these arms, proves that the United States, if they are sensitive to the reaction of public opinion, uses them rather to manifest its will to safeguard its freedom of action in this matter. In legal terms, this behavior signifies the refusal of the American Government to contribute, by its conduct, to the formation or the consolidation of a customary rule relating to the non-use of incapacitating or irritating chemical weapons.

[84] According to American information sources, the NLF employs tear gas on rare occasions.

[85] Can one maintain that the two Vietnams are bound by the Protocol as successor states to France? The object and the goal of this multilateral convention suggested such a solution; but it has not been practically adopted.

[86] The existence of a rule of international law concerning the use of chemical weapons, a rule which binds all states which are not parties to the Geneva Protocol, is indisputable, at least since the General Assembly vote on the resolution of December 5, 1966, inviting, "all states to conform strictly to the principles and objectives" of the Protocol of 1925 and to adhere to this treaty. This resolution was adopted by 91 votes (including that of the United States) without opposition and with four abstentions. As for the definition of prohibited chemical weapons, it appears from the discussion in the First Committee that the controversy on the scope of this definition still persists, the United States as well as several Western countries vigorously raising objections against an interpretation according to which prohibition should be extended to all chemical agents which incapacitate and to irritants.

CHEMICAL AGENTS USED AGAINST VEGETATION

Chemical agents are massively used in South Vietnam against vegetation in two kinds of operations: *defoliation* of the jungle or of plantations which serve or supposedly serve as cover for Vietcong forces and the *destruction of rice paddies* which serve or supposedly serve to supply and to feed the Vietcong. Considering these methods as *weapons,* the interpretation according to which these methods are included within the definition of agents whose use is forbidden by the Geneva Protocol or by customary international law is not generally acknowledged, as long as it concerns products which are not injurious to the health of men. However, when herbicides are used against the rice harvests in the regions controlled by the NLF, it is not the aspect of "weapon" but the *aspect of "target"* which is decisive for the examination of the legality of this method.

The destruction of harvests capable of feeding enemy troops had been practiced during the American Civil War by Union troops and during the Boer War by the English army. Certain Anglo-Saxon writers have shown themselves to be tolerant with regard to this method, justifying it by military necessity or exceptional circumstances.[87] The manual on the law of war of the American army cautiously declares that it is not forbidden to destroy, by chemical or bacteriological agents which are not injurious to men, harvests destined solely to feed enemy troops, adding, between parentheses: "if this fact can be established."[88] This formula condemns the use of herbicides against rice paddies in regions in the hands of the NLF. It is, in effect, completely impossible to maintain that the rice harvests are solely destined, or even, for that matter, mostly destined, to feed NLF combatants. It is because it affects the civilian population to an important degree, not accidentally but in a deliberate fashion, that this method cannot be considered legal.[89]

[87] See especially J. M. Spaight, *War Rights on Land*, 1911, pp. 133-38, which seeks to excuse the devastations and destructions of the Transvaal harvests because of the method of guerrilla war adopted by the Boers.

[88] FM 27-10, Section 36.

[89] The destruction of rice paddies in South Vietnam can no more be justified by assimilating this means to two situations in which the law of war allows measures which tend to starve the enemy without making a distinction between the combatants and the civilian population: *siege* and *blockade*. The blockade constitutes a special legal regime, fashioned historically by the conditions of maritime war, and which the law of war does not permit to be extended to hostilities on land. In a siege, the besieging

II. The Treatment of Prisoners of War

1. PRISONERS OF WAR IN THE HANDS OF THE
UNITED STATES AND THE GOVERNMENT OF SOUTH VIETNAM

The American, South Vietnamese, Australian, and New Zealand Governments have affirmed that they apply the Third Geneva Convention to their prisoners of war. We have seen that, theoretically, the complete applicability of this Convention is indisputable concerning members of the regular armed forces of North Vietnam captured in South Vietnam, but that, with regard to Vietcong prisoners, various complications become evident because the conflict which opposes the United States and the Saigon Government to the NLF is an international conflict but not an interstate conflict. Certain provisions of the Convention, we have concluded, cannot be applied in the relations between the Saigon Government and the NLF because they imply the protection of the political personality of the adversary. To formulate the principle of this choice is easier than to define exactly what constitutes protection of political personality. We have cited three provisions in which the respect for political personality seems particularly marked: Articles 17, 50, and 130. When it is a question of Article 17, paragraph 4, forbidding all physical and mental torture in order to obtain information, we do not hesitate to consider this prohibition as binding without any restriction,[90] knowing full well that its observation protects, through the person of the prisoner, the political collectivity to which that prisoner belongs.[91] On the other hand, it seems to us that Article 50, prohibiting the coercion of prisoners of war to work

---

army has the right to prevent the entry of supplies into the besieged area to starve out the inhabitants in order to cause their prompt surrender. It is by an abused analogy that an American author draws from these two special circumstances the conclusion that the systematic destruction of harvests destined principally for the feeding of the civilian population can be considered permissible (Colonel Brungs, "The Status of Biological Warfare in International Law," *Military Law Review*, [April 1964], 47ff.). Neither militarily nor legally is the destruction of harvests in the enemy's territory comparable to a siege or a blockade.

[90] To limit the prohibition to physical torture, in other words, to tolerate mental torture or "coercion" would be a deception. In fact, no torture exists, especially with modern police methods, which is clearly physical or mental. For the sake of morality as well as law, there is only one possible attitude with regard to torture: to outlaw it absolutely.

[91] The prohibition of torture, and this is its most profound sense, is as important for possible victims as well as for possible torturers. It is important to protect both against barbarousness and human degradation. Also the true legal good protected by this rule (and this is true for the rules of war in general) is *humanity*.

on military projects, has not been observed by the Saigon Government with regard to its Vietcong prisoners. The provision of Article 130 making it a "serious breach" to force a prisoner of war to serve in the armed forces of an enemy power raises a more serious question—does it obligate the Saigon Government with regard to members of the NLF who are captured? Hesitation is possible on this point, however detestable such a procedure may be.

The principal obligation of a belligerent with regard to individual enemy soldiers within its power is to treat as prisoners of war all those who have such a right by virtue of the Third Geneva Convention. According to American sources of information, the United States and the Saigon Government have divided persons captured in the course of military operations into four categories: civilians recognized as innocent; deserters from the South Vietnamese army; civilians who commit acts of sabotage and terrorism and who are subject to South Vietnamese justice; prisoners of war. The status of prisoner of war is accorded to Vietcong combatants or North Vietnamese captured in the course of military operations.[92] But the status is accorded only to men who are captured with weapons in their hands. This definition of persons who benefit from the status of prisoners of war is, with regard to Article 4 of the Third Convention, incorrect. Concerning members of the North Vietnamese army infiltrated into the South as well as soldiers of the regular NLF units, the criterion is not the weapon in hand but the uniform. When members of other combat formations of the NLF wear, for lack of a uniform, a distinctive emblem or sign establishing their membership in one of these formations, they should be accorded the status of prisoners of war. Sometimes, the fact that irregulars do not openly carry their arms can constitute a breach; but the punishment of this infraction is subject to the protective rules set forth in the Third Convention.[93]

[92] See *Revue Int. de la Croix-Rouge* (1966), 365.

[93] Article 5, paragraph 2, imposes on American forces and the Saigon Government the obligation of provisionally according the protection of the Third Convention to any captured individual who has committed or is suspected of having committed a hostile act, but whose membership in the North Vietnamese army or the regular or irregular forces of the NLF is subject to question. The definitive determination of the status of the person in question is to be left to a "competent tribunal." Even if this term does not designate a judicial body, it does, however, emphasize the seriousness of a decision to refuse the status of prisoner of war and marks the obligation of the capturing state to make this decision with a minimum of guarantees of dispassion and objectivity. With regard to the Vietnamese captured by American forces, this function and this responsibility belong to the United States.

According to numerous American witnesses (as well as others), we know that, at the beginning of their captivity, many Vietcong prisoners were subjected to a treatment which flagrantly violated the essential prescriptions of the Third Convention.[94] In particular, the most reprehensible acts are committed at the time of the interrogation of prisoners: torture and inhuman treatment that Article 130 classifies among "serious breaches." Constituting crimes which can be characterized as war crimes,[95] these acts involve, besides the international responsibility of the capturing state,[96] the criminal responsibility of the individual who committed them, who ordered them to be committed, or who made themselves accomplices.[97] Concerning Vietcong combatants or suspects captured by American forces, the material authors of these acts seem, in the large majority of these cases, to be agents of the state of South Vietnam. But there is no doubt that, according to the general rules of common penal law, the American military which observes these acts without trying to prevent them while they have the power to do so, must be considered as accomplices, if not actual collaborators.

In conformity with the accords made with the Saigon Government, the Americans transfer their Vietcong and North Vietnamese prisoners to the Saigon Government after a brief period in classification centers[98] where interrogation takes place.[99] Article 12 allows a belligerent to transfer its prisoners of war to another power which is party to the Convention only after being assured that this power has the "willingness and the ability" to apply the Convention to the transferred pris-

[94] Inhuman treatment constitutes a "serious breach" whatever the status of the person who is its object. No one is released from either Convention III or Convention IV in this regard. Torture and punishment and cruel, humiliating, and degrading treatment would be forbidden even if the Saigon Government believed that the struggle against the NLF was governed solely by Article 3.

[95] See the definition of war crimes in Article 6 (b) of the Statute of the International Military Tribunal of Nuremberg.

[96] This responsibility will be speculated upon only at the end of hostilities. The injured party cannot argue breach of responsibility in order to indulge himself in reprisals against prisoners of war belonging to the guilty state (see Article 13, paragraph 3).

[97] It is necessary to remember that legal proceedings against war crimes are themselves subject by the Convention to strict rules which guarantee due process.

[98] There exist also in South Vietnam, South Korean and Australian temporary detention centers.

[99] Nineteen North Vietnamese sailors have constituted an exception to this rule. Captured in July 1966, in the Gulf of Tonkin, they continue to remain under American guard.

oners. The responsibility for the application of the Convention then passes to the receiving state during the time that it detains the prisoners. However, the capturing state is not definitely released from its responsibility toward the transferred prisoners. But if the new detaining power "fails to carry out the Provisions of the Convention in any important respect" Article 12, paragraph 3 stipulates that "the Power by whom the prisoners of war were transferred shall, upon being notified by the Protecting Power, take effective measures to correct the situation or shall request the return of prisoners of war. Such requests must be complied with." In the absence of a "Protecting Power," a notification from the International Committee of the Red Cross[100] should have the same result. It is not, in reality, the "notification" which sets in motion the obligation to act to regain its initial responsibility on the part of the transferring state, but the fact of having had knowledge of important defects on the part of the new Detaining Power.[101] Besides the grave excesses, committed immediately after capture and during interrogation, which are amply attested to, it is also not known whether the general treatment of war prisoners by the Saigon authorities gives rise to more criticism.

[100] The ICRC has interceded with South Vietnamese and American authorities to demand that certain types of treatment used against prisoners be stopped (*Revue Int. de la Croix-Rouge* [1966], 366). It should be noted that, contrary to the DRV, the Saigon Government has authorized the Red Cross to make visits to the prison camps, as well as to prisons and to "reeducation centers" (where people are detained to whom the status of prisoner of war has not been accorded). Likewise, this government provides the ICRC with lists of the names of the prisoners of war. These lists included, by the end of October 1967, close to 7,000 names (*Revue Int. de la Croix-Rouge* [1967], 512).

[101] Like other Communist bloc countries adhering to the Geneva Conventions, North Vietnam has put a *reservation* on Article 12. The reservation states that the transfer of prisoners of war by the detaining power to another power, party to the Conventions, does not release the initial detaining power from its responsibility concerning the application of the Convention. This reservation, like all other reservations made by the Communist states, has been rejected by the United States as well as by Australia and New Zealand. Independently of the general problem of reservations against which an objection can be raised by other parties, the scope of the reservation to Article 12 is limited. As we have seen, the transfer of prisoners does not terminate the responsibility of the transferring state. If the reservation were to be accepted, its effect would be to add to the obligation of remedying (the transferring power must remedy the deficiencies of the new detaining power), an *obligation of surveillance* (the transferring power must check up on the new detaining power to see that it does apply the Conventions). This surveillance does seem to occur in a certain measure: according to the *New York Times* of Jan. 26, 1967, a detachment of five American advisers is attached to each prison camp which is under South Vietnamese control in order to assure that the prescriptions of the Geneva Conventions are observed.

2. PRISONERS OF WAR IN THE HANDS OF
THE DRV AND THE NLF

We do not possess information on the treatment of combatants made prisoners in the South by the North Vietnamese army.[102] Thus in speaking of prisoners of war in the hands of the DRV, we are principally referring to American, South Vietnamese, and allied soldiers[103] captured in the Demilitarized Zone north of the 17th parallel, in North Vietnamese territorial waters, or on the high seas, as well as American aviators who are made prisoner on North Vietnamese territory. It is especially the treatment given to the aviators which preoccupies public opinion in the West because their fate has been the object of a particular kind of publicity on the part of the Hanoi Government. At different times, North Vietnamese authorities have produced the aviators in public in disputable[104] condition, if not manifestly illegal.[105] But what has above all enraged American opinion and provoked protests on the part of Washington has been the intention announced by Hanoi, in July 1966, to try the American aviators held by the DRV for war crimes. Although this project has been abandoned, it is not useless to return briefly to the discussion which it raised. It is necessary to distinguish, on this subject, questions of substance from questions of form.

As for the *substance*, the North Vietnamese Government affirms that the attacks against civilian targets constitutes a war crime. The absence of a clear precedent has been raised against this position. It is true that in the trial of the Japanese and German war criminals at the end of World War II, the proper methods of conducting war had scarcely been evoked.[106] One of the reasons for this discretion lies in the fact

---

[102] Are these prisoners transferred to the territory of the DRV? This is probably the exception. Are they transferred to the NLF? This would be contrary to Article 12 which authorizes transfer only to a Power which is party to the Convention.

[103] According to the Pentagon, the number of American soldiers captured by the DRV was 212 in October 1967. In addition, 570 men are missing in action, several of whom probably fell into the hands of the enemy. The number of South Vietnamese and Allied prisoners is not known.

[104] American pilots were presented in press conferences in Hanoi and were photographed in humiliating ways which causes doubt that the declarations of good treatment written or dictated by the prisoners were always spontaneous.

[105] In July 1966, the authorities in Hanoi made some fifty American pilots march in the streets of the capital where they were subjected to the insults of the population. This treatment, which constitutes a flagrant violation of Article 13, paragraph 2, does not seem to have been repeated.

[106] The definition—nonlimiting—of war crimes in Article 6 (b) of the Statute of the International Military Tribunal of Nuremberg mentions: "the destruction, without pur-

that the intensification of the war had led the Allies themselves to use means and methods of war against Germany and Japan which would have ended by excluding every accusation made against the Germans and the Japanese. Probably this practice has not occurred without effecting the contents of the rules of the law of war; but it cannot be said that the effect of the practice has been to abolish totally these rules. There is a so-called precedent found in the Japanese Law of August 13, 1942, which prescribed the death penalty or imprisonment for a minimum of ten years for any allied aviator who participated in the bombing of illegal targets.[107] This law was applied in several trials, and many American and allied aviators were condemned to death and executed. After the War, certain Japanese military officers who were being tried before the International Military Tribunal of Tokyo were accused of having participated in the execution of allied aviators in the application of this law. However, in no trial was this law declared to be contrary to international law.[108] The accused were condemned, not for having applied the law in question, but for having ordered or tolerated the sentencing of the pilots *without a regular trial* or having taken part in *irregular condemnations*.[109] In no way can these legal proceedings be invoked as a precedent against the idea that the directing of attacks against prohibited targets is a violation of the laws and customs of war and constitutes a war crime. Also, although the difficulties raised by the projected war crime trials do not

---

pose, of cities and villages or devastation which is not justified by military necessity" (translated from the French). Let us also remember on this point that in the report presented in 1919 to the peace conference, the Committee on Sanctions drew up a list of violations of the laws and customs of war made by Germany and its allies. The list classified the violations into 32 categories, among them were the following: intentional bombing of defenseless areas; destruction of fishing boats; intentional bombing of hospitals. At the end of World War II, certain allied countries believed that this list corresponded to positive law and should be incorporated into their laws suppressing war crimes. This was the case for Australia (the Law of Oct. 25, 1945), for the Dutch East Indies (decree No. 44 of 1946), and for China (the Law of Oct. 24, 1946). One cannot thus truly speak of the absence of legislative precedents.

[107] See the text of this law in: *International Military Tribunal for the Far East. Dissenting Judgment by Justice R. P. Pal*, Calcutta, 1953, pp. 676ff.

[108] In an *obiter dictum*, the judgment of the International Military Tribunal has criticized the law, not for having condemned acts which were not prohibited, but for having treated as crimes practices that Japan had itself instituted (*ibid.*, p. 1026). But the International Tribunal has not drawn from this argument that the law was internationally illegal.

[109] See especially the U.S. Military Commission, Shanghai, Sept. 3, 1946 (case of Hisaku and others), *Law Reports of Trials of War Criminals*, v, pp. 66ff.

concern *the legal element* of the infraction, but its *moral element:* the accused—supposing the illegal bombings to have been intentional —*could they have known the illegality* of their acts? Also, the problem raises serious questions about the *rules of form* to be followed.

Concerning the punishment of war crimes, the form takes on such importance that it becomes itself a rule of substantive importance: Article 130 of the Third Convention ranks among "serious breaches"— in other words, war crimes—the fact of depriving a prisoner of war "of the rights of fair and regular trial prescribed in this Convention." However, according to the Hanoi Government, these prescriptions would not apply to American aviators that it accuses of being war criminals. While affirming that these prisoners enjoy humane treatment, it has made known to the ICRC that it refuses to consider them as prisoners of war.[110] In support of this position, Hanoi has invoked the reservation it formulated on the subject of Article 85 of the Third Convention. This Article stipulates: "Prisoners of war prosecuted under the laws of the Detaining Power for acts committed prior to capture shall retain, even if convicted, the benefits of the present Convention." All the countries of the Communist bloc have expressed reservations concerning this article, reservations which are expressed in more or less identical terms. Here is the reservation formulated by the DRV: "The Democratic Republic of Vietnam declares that prisoners of war prosecuted and condemned for war crimes or for crimes against humanity, in conformity with the principles enunciated by the Court of Justice [read International Military Tribunal of Nuremberg] will not benefit from the provisions of the present Convention as well as the specified Article 85."[111] This reservation differs from those of other Communist states by an ambiguity: the other reservations speak of "prisoners of war condemned"; Hanoi says "prisoners of war prosecuted and condemned." The formula is obviously strange —the condemnation supposes that there will be a trial. An anonymous commentator in the *Harvard Law Review* has drawn attention to this difference in language, suggesting that it might well be due to an inadvertence.[112] This is our opinion; because we do not share the opinion of this commentator according to which the formula would be capable of two interpretations, accordingly as one attributes to the word "and" a copulative or disjunctive meaning. In order to have the suggested meaning, that of "prisoners of war prosecuted and *those*

---

[110] See the *Revue Int. de la Croix-Rouge* (1966), 363-65.
[111] See N.U. *Recueil des traites,* 274 (1967), 340.   [112] 80 (1967), 862.

condemned" it would be necessary to add a term to the text in order
to modify it, while the formula "prosecuted and condemned" is superfluous. Two other arguments militate against the disjunctive interpretation of the formula employed by the DRV. (1) The meaning of
the Soviet reservation, which has served as a model for the other Communist states has been precise in a note of the Ministry of Foreign
Affairs in Moscow dating from May 26, 1955 and addressed to the Swiss
Government and communicated to all the other Parties of the
Conventions.[113] The result of the note was to point out that the application of the reservation occurs only from the time that the sentence is
pronounced against the prisoner of war and his status as a war criminal
has become definite. Up to this time, that is during the duration of
the trial, the prisoner remains under the protection of the Third Convention. (2) Giving a disjunctive sense to the reservation of Hanoi
would result in a holding seriously contrary to the purpose of Article
85[114] that one must consider to be *incompatible with the object and
the goal of the Convention*—in other words, according to the dominant
opinion, confirmed by the Committee on International Law[115] as forbidden. Since the Hanoi Government has not followed its plan to bring
the American aviators to court as war criminals, nothing permits us
to believe that Hanoi interprets its reservation to Article 85 in such an
exorbitant manner, contrary to the text as it should be correctly understood.[116] But, independently of Article 85, the fact remains that the
DRV has not, up to now, granted the status of prisoner of war to these
Americans. This refusal can be based neither on the Third Convention
nor on the general rules relating to the punishment of war crimes.[117]

[113] See the text of the note: *Commentaire de la III⁰ Convention*, published under the
direction of J. Pictet (1958) , pp. 449-50.

[114] Contrary also to the holding of Article 130, a provision to which the DRV has attached no reservation.

[115] Cf. Projet d'articles sur le droit des traites, 1966, Article 16 (c) .

[116] The United States has rejected the reservations made by other states party to the
Conventions (except for those concerning Article 68, paragraph 2) while agreeing to
enter into conventional relations with the reserving states, except for the modifications
proposed by these reservations. Cf. C. Pilloud, "Les reserves aux Conventions de Geneve
de 1949," *Revue Int. de la Croix-Rouge* (1957) , 409ff., and (1965) , 315ff. In cases in
which Hanoi would make use of its reservation to Article 85 (in the sense that its
first declarations would lead one to believe) , the United States would be able to consider this conduct as a violation of Article 85, a violation not covered by a legal reservation.

[117] Neutral and American testimony seems to indicate that, apart from the facts
mentioned above, American prisoners do receive suitable treatment. One should regret,
however, the fact that up to now the ICRC has been refused permission to visit prison
camps in North Vietnam.

No provision of the Third Convention forbids a Detaining Power to judge *before the end of hostilities* prisoners of war for violations of the laws and customs of war committed before their capture. But it is essential that the accused prisoners have, as required by Article 99, paragraph 3, the *possibility of defending themselves*. This possibility, which includes the right to call witnesses (Article 105, paragraph 1), can only be assured *durante bello* in cases of flagrant violations, but not normally in a matter as complex as the bombing since it concerns the examination of government directives and the orders of commanders[118]—in other words, to interrogate witnesses from the enemy side. These are the rules of form, guarantees of due process and of a free trial—guarantees not only of justice but also of the soundness of judgment, which prevent, in the great majority of cases, the organization of trials against prisoners of war before the end of hostilities.

A small number of soldiers and American civilians are in the hands of the NLF. By dint of such circumstances, the treatment of these prisoners of war will never be able to be that which was foreseen in the provisions of the Third Convention. Moreover, as we have seen, the NLF is not bound by this Convention, but only by the "laws and customs of war."[119] In October 1965, two American prisoners were executed by the NLF, as a measure of reprisal for the execution of two Vietcong accused of acts of terrorism by the Saigon authorities. Do the "laws and customs of war" forbid reprisals against prisoners of war? Is this interdiction, which does not figure in Article 3 of the Third Convention, as absolute as that put forth in Article 13 of the Third Convention? An affirmative response seems to be the only correct one.[120]

[118] It is thus, not in spite of, but because of the "principle of Nuremberg" which states that "the fact of having acted under the order of one's government or of a superior does not release the author of the act from his responsibility in international law" (translated from the French: Commission du droit international, "Formulation des principes de Nuremberg," principle IV. *Rapport sur les travaux de la 2ᵉ session*, 1950, p. 13).

[119] That the NLF refuses the ICRC the permission to visit the prisoners of war which it detains is understood by the precarious position of their bases. But nothing prevents them from communicating to the ICRC the names of the prisoners.

[120] It is, however, necessary to understand that the solution is doubtful. The law of war does not, in general, forbid reprisals; it forbids them only against persons and property protected by the four Conventions. If a belligerent victim of a violation of the law of war (or a so-called violation; the entire law of reprisals is based on a unilateral claim of sanction) finds himself in a situation where he cannot exercise reprisals and can only exercise them against the prisoners of war in his hands, to forbid him recourse to this means that amounts to the sole remedy which he has to redress an illegality, is to deny his right to take reprisals. It must be agreed that there is an absolute prohibition imposed against reprisals in such situations since the public conscience is so deeply involved. Experience has shown that putting prisoners of war to death is not profitable.

III. The Treatment of the Civilian Population of South Vietnam

The civilian population of South Vietnam pays twice as much in the war: in the first place, it pays through the *losses* and *destruction* which it suffers because of the military action and terrorism of the belligerents;[121] and, in the second place, it suffers from the *treatment* which the American, South Vietnamese, and allied forces apply to it. We have already spoken of the bombings and the strategy of devastation practiced by the American forces in South Vietnam. It remains for us to consider the treatment given to the South Vietnamese civilians in the regions where the American and allied armies operate. This treatment, as we have seen, is subject to the Fourth Geneva Convention. The United States, in effect, acts in South Vietnam not as an agent of the Saigon Government, but by virtue of its proper international status, a status which makes the relations between the United States and South Vietnamese civilians the same as those between *occupier and occupied*. The principal criticisms addressed to the United States, in this regard, concern, on the one hand, the treatment of civilians arrested as suspects, and, on the other hand, the practice of displacing and uprooting the population.

It is true that guerrilla warfare, the ideal model of military action for the NLF, involves a profound and permanent complicity between the guerrillas and the population. It is also normal that the Government and allied forces which fight the guerrillas do not consider the inhabitants of contested zones or regions controlled by the NLF to be, *a priori*, peaceful and not dangerous. However, this situation—which is not so different from the one in which the German army found itself in Russia and Yugoslavia during the Second World War—does not justify the scorn and neglect shown for the fundamental rules of the Fourth Convention. Forced residence and internment, decided according to regular procedures, are legal measures of preventive security, if they are imposed by "imperative reasons of security" (Article 78).

---

121 The losses inflicted on the South Vietnamese civilians surpass those suffered by American and South Vietnamese forces: for the year 1967, there were about 24,000 killed and 76,000 wounded, according to statistics from Saigon. These figures deal only with the losses recorded in the regions controlled by the Saigon Government (for comparison: for the period of January 1-November 30, 1967, 8,001 American soldiers killed, 24,521 wounded; 9,566 South Vietnamese soldiers killed). About 55% of the civilians hospitalized have been women and girls (of more than 13 years of age); about 20% are children under 13 years of age. These figures include the victims of Vietcong terrorism: to December 2, 1967, according to Saigon, there have been 3,487 killed and 6,861 wounded; in addition, one may include 4,487 people kidnapped (*Int. Herald Tribune*, Dec. 13, 1967).

But under no circumstances nor for any purpose are reprisals, collective punishments, and measures of intimidation and terrorism permitted—even if these methods are named "counterterrorism" (Article 33). Numerous American and neutral witnesses have attested to the fact that civilians apprehended in the course of "sweeps" (*ratissage*) have been exposed to bad treatment, in particular during their interrogations—acts which are formally prohibited by Articles 31 and 32. A delicate problem is posed on this subject. The Fourth Convention contains no provision analogous to Article 12 of the Third Convention, discussed above, permitting an occupying power to transfer protected persons to another contracting party. Article 29 stipulates the principle of the responsibility of the state under whose power the protected civilians find themselves. On this principle, the Convention has only one modification concerning one category of protected persons: enemy nationals on the territory of a belligerent state. Article 35 permits the transfer of these persons under the same conditions as Article 12 of the Third Convention authorizes the transfer of prisoners of war. From the combination of the two articles, the conclusion seems to be imposed that the transfer of persons protected by an occupying power (or a quasi-occupying power) is not permitted. How can this prohibition be reconciled with the obligation of the United States to respect the sovereignty and authority of the Saigon Government? Here is a conflict of international obligations which we cannot give detailed analysis here. The principle, set forth in Article 29, of the absolute responsibility of the occupying power and the principle, set forth in Article 47, of the inalienability of the rights of the persons protected in an occupied territory[122] prevents the United States from unloading its responsibilities so that if they hand over to the Saigon Gov-

---

[122] Article 47 commands that "Protected persons who are in occupied territory shall not be deprived, in any case or in any manner whatsoever, of the benefits of the present Convention . . . by any agreement concluded between the authorities of the occupied power and the Occupying Power. . . ." By this provision, the authors of 1949 wanted to prevent the rights of the inhabitants of an occupied territory from being diminished in the occupier's interest. This situation is, thus, politically the opposite of the situation in South Vietnam. Here it is the South Vietnamese Government which made an agreement with the United States in order to diminish its responsibilities under the Fourth Convention to its own citizens for its own interests. However, it is nonetheless true that such an agreement is embraced by the definition of illegal agreements in Article 47. It should also be remembered that Article 148 provides that no contracting state "shall be allowed to absolve itself or any other High Contracting Party of any liability incurred by itself or by another High Contracting Party in respect of breaches referred to in the preceding Article."

ernment civilians under its authority, it must consider the Saigon Government as its agent. At the very least, the obligation of the United States with regard to South Vietnamese civilians is equal to the obligation which it has with regard to prisoners of war turned over to the Saigon authorities.

The law of war specifically prohibits deportation *out of the occupied territory*.[123] Concerning displacements of protected persons within the country, Article 49, paragraph 2 of the Fourth Convention allows an occupying power to "undertake total or partial evacuation of a given area if the security of the population or imperative military reasons so demand." It is certain that *"imperative military reasons"* are more than simple military convenience. It is also evident that this notion involves an element of subjective evaluation which makes the appreciation of concrete decisions difficult. However, in the face of the enormous dimensions of the population transfers in South Vietnam, one should wonder if these systematic evacuations, instead of being justified by one or another of the reasons indicated in paragraph 2, are not instead dictated by the strategy of scorched earth and devastation which we have dealt with above. What heightens the gravity of these population transfers is the fact that they are often accompanied by the destruction of the villages concerned, a destruction which makes it impossible to follow the final prescription of this paragraph: "Persons thus evacuated shall be transferred back to their homes as soon as the hostilities in the area in question have ceased." Probably, the United States does conform to the prescriptions of paragraph 3 of Article 49 which commands that the transfers and evacuations be effected in the most convenient and suitable manner for the people concerned. But the fact of assuring the installation of displaced persons in camps, villages, or centers cannot erase the illegality of evacuations not justified by Article 49, paragraph 2. Some legal complications result from the

123 See Convention IV, Article 49, paragraph 1 and Article 6 (b) of the Statute of the International Military Tribunal of Nuremberg. Let us remember, however, that in the passage cited above (note 80), the I.M.T. upheld the charge against the accused Jodl for having ordered the transfer of the inhabitants of a region of northern Norway in order to prevent them from assisting the Russian army and for burning their houses down. The passage is, nevertheless, equivocal. The passage does not permit us to conclude that the Tribunal made displacement of population a special crime, independently of the destructions which followed this measure. But precisely these two elements—forced transfer of inhabitants and destruction of their homes—have been found in combination in numerous cases in South Vietnam. The I.M.T. has thus considered the motive invoked by the German commander (to prevent inhabitants from aiding the enemy army) as not justifying his action.

fact that the Saigon Government is not obligated by the same prohibitive rules as is the occupying or the quasi-occupying foreigner.
This dualistic legal regime, which is derived from the status of the
United States and the Saigon Government with regard to the South
Vietnamese population, cannot be *corrected* by an agreement between
the two states. In all situations in which there is a conflict between
the obligations of the United States by virtue of imperative international law and its contractual commitments with the Saigon Government, the first must prevail. The fact that American military action
in South Vietnam is, politically, an intervention in favor of a government exposed to an insurrection does not modify in any way either the
nature or the force of American obligations according to the law of
war.

December 1967

International Law and Military Operations against Insurgents in Neutral Territory

Note from *Columbia Law Review*

INTRODUCTION

Public interest in international law probably is greatest during periods of world crisis. Thus, the debate between the United States and Cambodia concerning the right to pursue the Viet Cong into Cambodian territory has been followed quite widely. The press has styled the right claimed by the United States the right of "hot pursuit." The use of the phrase "hot pursuit" is enough to give a purist pause because the term has a definite meaning in international law. Briefly, it refers to the right of a coastal state to pursue and apprehend the vessels of another state on the high seas when those ships have violated a law of the coastal state in its territorial waters.

Obviously, actions which may be tolerated on the high seas may not necessarily be permitted in the course of land warfare. However, the ideological strife prevalent in modern international relations, as manifested in "wars of national liberation," makes it impossible to confine "hot pursuit" to the maritime problem.[1] At a time when nations are willing to look to international law for guidance, as appears to be the case with the United States and Cambodia, an effort should be made to articulate the relevant principles.

It is well established that an infringement upon the territory of a sovereign state is an illegal violation of its territorial integrity[2] unless justified by some principle of international law. The belligerent bears the burden of showing justification if it wishes to avoid the sanctions[3] which the international

---

1. The doctrine of hot pursuit in maritime law cannot be extended directly to hot pursuit on land. *See, e.g.,* Le Monde, Sept. 4, 1957, at 1, col. 3; *see also* D. BOWETT, SELF-DEFENCE IN INTERNATIONAL LAW 40 (1958). In maritime law, the coastal state's interest in enforcing its laws outweighs the interest of the outlaw ship or the state whose flag it flies in maintaining the freedom of the seas. *See* 1 J. WESTLAKE, INTERNATIONAL LAW 177 (2d ed. 1910). This priority of interests does not necessarily hold true for neutrals and belligerents in regard to land warfare. Furthermore, the maritime doctrine is applicable in times of peace and does not involve violating the territorial integrity of any state; the right ends when the ship enters the territorial waters of its home state or of a third state. *See* Convention on the High Seas, art. 23, [1962] 2 U.S.T. 2318-19, T.I.A.S. No. 5200; Schwarzenberger, *The Fundamental Principles of International Law,* 87 RECUEIL DES COURS DE L'ACADÉMIE DE DROIT INTERNATIONAL 191, 333 (1955). A better analogy would be the right of a belligerent vessel to pursue ships of its enemy into neutral territorial waters. Here, however, it has been conceded that without a valid claim of self-defense or refusal of the neutral to remove the offending vessel from its waters, such action would constitute a violation of neutral rights. *See* J. STONE, LEGAL CONTROLS OF INTERNATIONAL CONFLICT 400-01 (1954); 2 H. WHEATON, INTERNATIONAL LAW 398-403 (7th Eng. ed. 1944); *see generally* Borchard, *Was Norway Delinquent in the Case of the Altmark?,* 34 AM. J. INT'L L. 289 (1940); *cf.* The Vrow Anna Catharina, 165 Eng. Rep. 681 (High Ct. of Admiralty 1803).

2. *See* U.N. CHARTER art. 2, para. 4.

3. Sanctions which may be imposed by the Security Council as punishment for breaching the peace and committing acts of aggression may be found in Chapter VII of the United Nations Charter. Among them are the severance of diplomatic relations, "complete or partial interruption of economic relations and rail, sea, air, postal, telegraphic, radio and other means of communication" (Article 41), and collective military or quasi-military action by members of the United Nations (Article 42). Furthermore,

community imposes upon such wrongful conduct. Belligerents have sought to satisfy this burden either by claiming that hot pursuit is a matter of self-defense or by asserting that even though a particular incursion is not self-defensive, it is justifiable because the neutral state[4] has violated one of its duties by allowing its territory to be used as a refuge. It is the purpose of this Note to analyze each of these arguments in depth, to determine their status under current international law, and to test their utility for the maintenance of orderly relations between states during the course of modern limited wars.

I. SELF-DEFENSE

Belligerents tend to think of the hot pursuit of insurgents into neutral territories as an exercise of "self-defense." In international law, self-defense, when properly invoked, may be employed to justify action which

---

if the belligerent can be brought before the International Court of Justice or an arbitration tribunal, it may be required to indemnify the aggrieved state.

Another sanction which may possess considerable deterrent value as the international community becomes more sophisticated is the sanction of non-participation, through which a delinquent state is deprived of the benefits of taking part in the activities of functional international organizations, such as the International Monetary Fund, International Labor Organization, and International Bank for Reconstruction and Development. For a thorough discussion of this sanction, see W. FRIEDMANN, THE CHANGING STRUCTURE OF INTERNATIONAL LAW 88-95 (1964).

4. At this point it is appropriate to question whether the laws of neutrality can logically be said to apply in the context of a civil war. Strictly speaking, neutrality is a concept which applies only to international warfare, and its status in a civil war in which the rebels have not been recognized as belligerents is highly doubtful. *See* Castrén, *Civil War*, 142-2 SUOMALAISEN TIEDEAKATEMIAN TOIMITUKSIA 120-23 (Ser. B 1966). This follows from the premise that a civil war is solely an internal matter, to be conducted by the military and police forces of the established government as they deem fit. *See* Castrén, *supra*, at 97; Kunz, *Die Anerkennung von Staaten und Regierungen im Völkerrecht*, 2 HANDBUCH DES VÖLKERRECHTS, Part 3, at 173 (1928). On the other hand, some writers have maintained that at least some of the laws of international war should be observed by the parties to a civil war, generally those relating to humanitarianism. *See, e.g.*, Garner, *Questions of International Law in the Spanish Civil War*, 31 AM. J. INT'L L. 66 (1937). If this latter proposition is accepted, it still does not follow that third states are bound to follow the laws of neutrality.

Nevertheless, this does not affect the analysis of the problem significantly because the duties which a neutral state would be called upon to observe in an international war, in terms of permitting rebel troops asylum on their territory or a base of operations, are hardly different from the duties of non-intervention in domestic affairs. *See generally* E. STOWELL, INTERVENTION IN INTERNATIONAL LAW 345-55 (1921). Furthermore, the problem is less important in major "civil wars," such as those in Spain and Vietnam. In both cases, the political arm of the rebels was recognized by third countries as the legitimate government of the country which was the theater of military operations, and in both the rebels controlled substantial portions of the national territory. This may well go beyond recognition of belligerency, and it gives the war an international character which for all practical purposes should bring the laws of neutrality into effect. Realistically, it is difficult to characterize the wars in Spain, Algeria, and Vietnam solely as domestic uprisings. Even if the belligerency of the rebels is not formally recognized either by the established government or by third states, conditions may exist to afford the rebels a *de facto* belligerent status. For examples, see Castrén, *supra*, at 74-75, 100. A similar situation may occur when the rebels have been recognized by third powers as insurgents. For a full discussion of the legal effects of the recognition of insurgency, *see id.* at 207-23. For the purposes of this Note, it will be assumed that the conflict has reached sufficient proportions to make the recognition of belligerency justifiable. But see the discussion of the recognition of the Franco insurgents as the *de jure* government of Spain by Germany and Italy as not conferring the status of belligerent on the Nationalists, in N. PADELFORD, INTERNATIONAL LAW AND DIPLOMACY IN THE SPANISH CIVIL STRIFE 17 (1939).

otherwise would be illegal and may supersede the right of territorial integrity guaranteed by the United Nations Charter.[5] However, there is no simple rule which determines what action is self-defensive and therefore permissible; proper analysis involves examining the problem in each of its several factual contexts and comparing them with the principles of law now in existence.

The claim of self-defense may be advanced in three quite distinct situations. Once warfare has broken out, a belligerent may feel that the threat posed by the presence of hostile forces in a neighboring neutral state warrants anticipatory defensive action. Such measures are anticipatory because they are motivated merely by the possibility of an attack. Of course, the belligerent may also claim self-defense in response to an actual attack. When the attack occurs from within neutral territory, he may assert the right to take necessary[6] protective measures even though to do so involves operations on neutral soil. Several operations by France against Algerian rebels firing upon them from Tunisian territory[7] provide a convenient example. Finally, defensive measures may be necessary where neutral territory is used as a sanctuary for tactical retreat and a base of operations for repeated raids. This is the basis on which the United States has sought the right to pursue the Viet Cong into Cambodia. This Note will examine in turn these three categories—action

---

5. See D. BOWETT, supra note 1, at 31; 2 L. OPPENHEIM, INTERNATIONAL LAW § 326, at 698 (7th ed. H. Lauterpacht 1952). Bowett distinguishes territorial integrity from territorial inviolability. The former is a right subject to the rights of other states; the latter is an absolute right imposing strict international liability upon a state which permitted its military forces to enter upon the territory of the aggrieved state. Oppenheim finds the terms synonymous and would subject them to the right of other states to self-defense. 2 L. OPPENHEIM, supra, §§ 52a, 52aa, at 154-55.

6. The word "necessary" is used here in a strict sense and should not be confused with "military necessity," self-preservation and Kriegsraison. The phrase "military necessity" is generally used to justify the expedient. It means that a nation engaged in war can take any steps it feels are warranted by the "necessity of war" or "self-preservation," the latter term creating a subjective test for determining the danger into which the state or its armed forces is placed. See discussion at notes 85-88, infra, and accompanying text.

7. The French, in asserting this right, referred to it as the "droit de riposte." See, e.g., Le Monde, April 27, 1960, at 5, col. 2. In exercising this right, France often bombed insurgent gun emplacements inside Tunisia which allegedly were engaged in firing upon French units close to the border. The French attempted to justify the aerial attack on Sakiet-Sidi-Youssef on February 8, 1958 as an exercise of self-defense on the ground that Algerian rebels in Tunisia had been shooting at the French planes involved while they were over Algeria. See id., Feb. 11, 1958, at 3, col. 3; 38 U.S. DEP'T OF STATE BULL. 333 (1958) (news conference of Secretary of State Dulles). However, the State Department did not regard this operation as an exercise of hot pursuit. The American definition of hot pursuit at that time was explained by Secretary Dulles as follows:

Hot pursuit is a situation where there has been an attack over domestic or international territory and the attacker is followed with continuity back to his base, which may be in other territory. The element of continuity is essential to any concept of hot pursuit. . . . actually following physically an attacker. . . . But there was no element of hot pursuit in this case, or in most of these Tunisian cases, as far as I am aware.

Id.

If the plane responded to enemy fire emanating from neutral territory, however, this might well have been a justifiable measure of self-defense. The "continuous chase" doctrine is not a prerequisite to the exercise of self-defense by a belligerent in a neutral state as discussed in this Note.

against anticipated attack, action against tactical retreat, and action against actual attack.

A. *Action Against Anticipated Attack*

International law is most clearly settled with regard to action against anticipatory attack.[8] This is because the *Caroline* case has established a strict definition of the necessity which will warrant defensive action. The belligerent must show a "necessity for self-defense, instant, overwhelming, and leaving no choice of means, and no moment for deliberation."[9] Under the *Caroline* test, a virtual emergency is required before anticipatory action is lawful. Senator Calhoun spoke of the requirement

> laid down by all writers . . . that nothing short of *extreme necessity* can justify a belligerent in entering, with an armed force, on the territory of a neutral power . . . . (Emphasis in the original.)[10]

Likewise, Lord Campbell, in defending the destruction of the *Caroline*, argued that a similar threat would be posed by the erection of guns on the American shore by Canadian insurgents in order to fire at British troops on the other side.[11] Although the analogy refers to action against actual attack, it does reflect the imminent danger which is required to make anticipatory action permissible. The *Caroline* doctrine received support from Vattel, the progenitor of the law of neutrality, whose treatise, written almost one hundred years earlier, was the foremost authority on the law of war during the *Caroline* period.[12] Furthermore, the Nuremberg War Crimes Tribunal explicitly relied on the *Caroline* doctrine as authority to reject the claim that the invasion of Norway was a justifiable measure of self-defense.[13]

As its use at Nuremberg suggests, the *Caroline* doctrine remains a sensible balancing of the interests of belligerent and neutral states. Although some have said that its scope is unduly restrictive in an era of nuclear weapons,[14] this objection does not apply to a war in which the use of even "tactical" nuclear weapons is highly unlikely. Furthermore, its strict approach to the use of anticipatory action is in accord with Professor McDougal's useful notion of "minimum world public order"[15] as a basis for international law. At

---

8. The use of this term in the context in which it is employed in this Note can be found in Green, *Armed Conflict, War, and Self-Defence*, 6 ARCHIV DES VÖLKERRECHTS 387, 433 (1957).

9. *See* 2 J. MOORE, DIGEST OF INTERNATIONAL LAW 412 (1906).

10. CONG. GLOBE, 27th Cong., 1st Sess., App., at 82 (1841).

11. *See* 2 LIFE OF JOHN, LORD CAMPBELL 119 (2d ed. M. Hardcastle 1881). For a contemporary application of this argument, see note 7 *supra*.

12. *See* 2 E. DE VATTEL, LE DROIT DES GENS, § 119, at 149 (Fenwick transl. 1916); *cf. id.* §§ 120-30, at 149-52.

13. *See International Military Tribunal (Nuremberg), Judgment and Sentences*, reprinted at 41 AM. J. INT'L L. 172, 205-07 (1947).

14. *See* McDougal, *The Soviet-Cuban Quarantine and Self-Defense*, 57 AM. J. INT'L L. 597, 598 (1963).

15. *See generally* M. MCDOUGAL & F. FELICIANO, LAW AND MINIMUM WORLD PUBLIC ORDER (1961).

the same time that the *Caroline* doctrine realistically permits action by a belligerent to protect itself from virtually immediate danger, it fosters restraint upon the belligerent's otherwise less inhibited resort to force. If a neutral's border may be ignored only in extreme situations, the need for the breach can be more easily comprehended and tolerated. Therefore, tensions between states at peace are minimized; and, more importantly, the conflict is apt to remain locally confined.

The major difficulty in applying the established principles is in determining when the danger to the established forces has become so imminent that the "necessity for self-defense" is "instant" and "overwhelming." Contrary to the views of some members of Congress,[16] this need does not occur when the insurgents are merely preparing for an attack at some future time, even if within a matter of days. To suppose otherwise would condone action which the United States condemned in the *Caroline* case itself. Although such preparations might serve as a basis for preventive action against a hostile state under Article 51 of the Charter,[17] it is more reasonable to impose a stricter requirement on preventive measures which infringe the sovereignty of a neutral state. In particular, there should be very substantial and convincing evidence that the hostile forces are poised to strike from neutral territory and that it would be impossible to defend the positions held within the belligerent state.

B. *Action Against Tactical Retreat*

Action against tactical retreat is in a sense action against anticipated attack. The action is motivated by the expectation that the enemy will return to the theater of war. But unlike anticipatory action, such measures do entail the pursuit of an enemy after his initial attack. Typically, the enemy retreats into neutral territory in order to achieve temporary sanctuary. This retreat may be due to defeat in battle or to a tactical decision to break off the engagement. Although this situation probably represents the large majority of instances in which hot pursuit is a militarily desirable tactic, international law has not explicitly treated the problem. There are, however, good reasons to apply a more flexible rule than the one applied to ordinary anticipatory action.

It has been said, sometimes by scholars of eminent prestige, that the pursuit of retreating forces into neutral states is categorically forbidden.[18]

---

16. A special subcommittee of the House Armed Services committee recommended that American forces take unspecified "search and surveillance measures" to prevent the use of Cambodian territory for supply routes and staging areas. *See* N.Y. Times, Dec. 14, 1967, at 4, col. 4.

17. *See* Green, *supra* note 7, at 430-35. *Contra*, Henkin, *Force, Intervention, and Neutrality in Contemporary International Law*, 57 Am. Soc. of Int'l L. Proc. 147, 151 (1963); Kunz, *Individual and Collective Self-Defense in Article 51 of the Charter of the United Nations*, 41 Am. J. Int'l L. 872, 878 (1947); *cf.* 2 L. Oppenheim, *supra* note 5, § 52a, at 154 (based upon violation of Article 2(4)).

18. *See, e.g.,* 2 L. Oppenheim, *supra* note 5, § 320, at 684-85; T. Benton, Thirty Years' View 290 (1856); *cf.* Brownlie, *International Law and the Activities of Armed Bands*, 7 Int'l & Comp. L.Q. 712, 734 (1958).

However, the examples cited to support this position involve the retreat into neutral territory of defeated forces which never returned during the duration of the insurrection.[19] It was the finality of the insurgents' retreat into Austria-Hungary during the Polish Insurrection of 1830 which would have made pursuit by the victorious Russians a violation of international law.[20] The same is true of the crossing of thousands of Hungarian insurgents into neutral Austria during the abortive 1956 revolt.

History, however, provides numerous examples of hot pursuit undertaken against forces using neutral territory as a base for recurring raids. General Jackson, for example, pursued into Florida, then owned by the Spanish, Seminole Indians who had frequently attacked American positions in Georgia.[21] In the course of pursuit and battle in Florida, several Spanish forts were seized. After the Indians were subdued, possession of the forts was restored to Spain, and reparations were made for injuries to Spanish property and citizens. There was evidence that despite treaty obligations to keep the Indians in Florida at "peace" with the United States,[22] the Spanish authorities had neither the strength nor the inclination to implement their pledges. Interestingly enough, there is no evidence that the Spanish government contended that American action was not in accordance with international law, perhaps because the Spanish had failed to fulfill their treaty obligations.

Similarly, the United States engaged in hot pursuit against Mexican bandits who regularly pillaged and terrorized communities in Texas from 1870 to 1877. Not only was it apparent that the Mexican central government had taken no action to prevent such incidents, but it also was clear that friends of the bandits were in military and political control of the Mexican states adjacent to the Texas border.[23] After many years of indecision, the United States gave the commanding general in Texas authority

> in the use of his own discretion, when in pursuit of a band of the marauders, and when his troops are either in sight of them or upon

---

19. There is precedent for holding that the pursuit of decisively defeated insurgents into neutral territory is not an exercise of self-defense and therefore constitutes an unjustifiable breach of the neutral's territorial integrity. During the Mexican revolution of 1877, in which General Diaz overthrew the Lerdo government, a battle occurred in Mexico in which forces of the former defeated and dispersed troops of the latter. Upon doing so, the Diaz troops pushed their adversaries into Texas. The Secretary of State instructed the United States minister to Mexico to call attention of the new government to the breach of international law, demand reparations from the state, and punishment of the offenders. H.R. REP. No. 701, 45th Cong., 2d Sess., App. B, at 254 (1878). The Mexican government agreed with the Secretary's characterization of the incursion, describing it as "an unjustifiable invasion, that is condemned by international law," and ordered an investigation so that "the parties who prove to be guilty may be punished . . . [and if any] officer of Mexico has ordered an invasion of the territory of the United States . . . that . . . the reparation . . . be made for this act which is in justice due." *Id.* at 256.

20. *See* Castrén, *supra* note 4, at 43.

21. *See, e.g.,* 2 J. MOORE, *supra* note 9, at 402-06.

22. *See* Treaty of Friendship, Limits and Navigation Between the United States of America and the King of Spain, Oct. 27, 1795, art. V, 8 Stat. 138, 140-42 (1846).

23. *See* H.R. REP. No. 701, *supra* note 19, at ix-x and App. B; H.R. REP. No. 343, 44th Cong., 1st Sess. vii-viii, 33, 57-58 (1876).

a fresh trail, to follow them across the Rio Grande, and to overtake
and punish them, as well as retake stolen property . . . found in their
hands on the Mexican side of the line.[24]

The Americans were not alone in thinking such action necessary and proper.
The British authorities in Honduras responded in the same way when faced
with acts of terrorism by Mexican bandits along their border.[25]

The legitimacy of hot pursuit under such circumstances is indicated by
the acquiesence of Mexico in the violation of its border during the "Cortina
War." Juan de Cortina was a Mexican bandit who waged a six-month insurrection against the United States and the State of Texas, vowing, at one time,
to push the Mexican border back to the Nueces River. He and his men made
use of sanctuary in Mexico to avoid capture by American troops and Texas
Rangers. Finally, on February 4, 1860, the Americans crossed the Mexican
border and dispersed the Cortina band. Although the local military commander asked for the withdrawal of American troops, no complaint was made
by the Mexican central government. In fact, its military commander in the
region agreed that American troops should be empowered to pursue and arrest Cortina and his men wherever found.[26]

Such tolerance toward action against raiders who use neutral territory
for sanctuary is not surprising. The first duty of any government is to protect
its citizens and territory. The danger to both is apparent when bands of insurgents or bandits regularly cross the border into neutral territory in order
to evade government forces, rearm, and regroup. The danger is exacerbated
if either the central government of the neutral state or its political and military
representatives at border areas, whether through sympathy with the cause of
the rebels or inability properly to police its territory adjacent to the border,
permit the insurgents to use its territory with impunity.[27]

The self-defensive character of pursuit in these instances normally arises
from the recurring nature of the insurgents' activities. It hardly accords with
human nature to ignore a long-standing course of conduct by insurgents and
to say that pursuit is not self-defensive when it is manifest that inevitably

---

24. H.R. Rep. No. 701, *supra* note 19, at 241. For the favorable editorial reaction of
the American press, *see, e.g.,* N.Y. Herald, June 1, 1877, at 4, col. 5; *id.,* June 2, 1877,
at 4, col. 3.
25. *See* N.Y. World, June 6, 1877, at 4, col. 4.
26. *See* H.R. Exec. Doc. No. 81, 36th Cong., 1st Sess. 102-04 (1860).
27. The right of a belligerent to enter neutral territory to destroy forces of its enemy
whom it suspects are regaining strength to renew their attacks is supported by Vattel:
> On the other hand, it is certain that, if my neighbour offers a retreat to my
> enemies, when they have been defeated and are too weak to escape me, *and allows
> them time to recover and to watch for an opportunity of making a fresh attack
> upon my territory* . . . [this is] inconsistent with neutrality . . . [H]e should
> . . . not allow them to lie in wait to make a fresh attack upon me; *otherwise he
> warrants me in pursuing them into his territory.* This is what happens when
> Nations are not in a position to make their territory respected. It soon becomes
> the seat of the war; armies march, camp, and fight in it, as in a country open to
> all comers.
3 E. de Vattel, *supra* note 12, § 133, at 277 (emphasis added).

they will resume the attack in the near future. Thus, self-defense under the circumstances of modern guerrilla warfare should be given an expanded meaning to permit the pursuit of retreating forces where there is reason to believe that they are using neutral territory as a base of operations for future attacks.

C. *Action Against Actual Attack*

The claim of self-defense is strongest where forces are under actual attack from within neutral territory. Before the advent of long range weapons, instances of such attack were perhaps rare; modern technology has made it a significant danger. There are, moreover, other more subtle ways in which attacking forces can exploit the sanctity of a neutral border to the detriment of their opponent. They may, for example, occupy positions just outside the neutral state, secure in the knowledge that they cannot be challenged from the rear. Or they may pin their opponent against the border and force him to choose between retreat, defense of an untenable position, or advance into neutral territory.

Despite the obvious need to violate neutral territory in such situations, justification under international law is not clear. Such measures, however, are comparable to the doctrine of self-defense encountered in municipal legal systems throughout the world. Reliance on this doctrine would in general mean that forces, if attacked, could take necessary defensive measures without regard for the existence of a neutral border.

In view of the similarity of this type of self-defense to self-defense as it is understood in criminal law, it is surprising that most international legal scholars have ignored the domestic law on this subject. It cannot be said that better sources are available because there exist neither conventions nor recorded customs which indicate the appropriate rules. Fortunately, it is permissible to resort to "general principles of law recognized by civilized nations" as a source of international law.[28]

It is generally accepted that when a person's life is in danger because of the unlawful actions of an assailant, that person may use deadly force, if necessary, to protect himself. The right of self-defense is recognized by the common and civil law systems, and many, if not most, of the newly independent states have retained the penal laws of their former colonial masters. The right of self-defense, moreover, is recognized in the Penal Code of the Russian Soviet Federated Socialist Republic.[29]

The almost universal recognition in municipal law of a right to self-defense against attack suggests that as a general principle, the defensive protection of military forces should justify an otherwise unlawful incursion

---

28. *See* I.C.J. STAT., art. 38, para. 1(c).
29. *See* note 36 *infra.*

into the territory of a neutral state. That the exercise of self-defense occurs in a state of war is not relevant; the principle can be extended rationally to safeguard the right of combat troops to protect themselves as organized units when they are engaged in battle.

Self-defense, of course, presupposes that the actor is the victim of aggression. Aggression, however, is not meant in the broad sense frequently used in international politics. To assert that because the insurgents were responsible for initiating the state of war they are the "aggressors" for all purposes is to say too much. Although this is one of the bases for exercising the right to engage in activities recognized under Article 51 of the Charter, it is not helpful in determining permissible conduct in actual combat situations. To rely on a general characterization of aggression would provide the forces of the established government with an unrestricted license to cross into neutral territory whenever it was convenient to do so.

Generally speaking, the side that provoked the specific attack should not be entitled to invoke self-defense. Thus, if the troops of the established government or its allies have spotted the insurgents and have attacked them, for example, on a "search-and-destroy" operation, they are the aggressors for the purpose of that encounter. When the going gets excessively difficult, they may not claim self-defense to justify action within neutral territory. However, if they are ambushed or attacked by the insurgents, the opposite result should follow in most cases. Furthermore, the right to enter neutral territory in self-defense should not be unavailable to troops who have resorted to actions which are provocative but do not constitute initiation of battle. If a conflict such as the Spanish Civil War or Vietnamese War has reached the stage in which it is difficult to assert that either party holds the territory it controls under claim of right or sovereignty, then the entry of troops of one side into territory held by the other may be a provocative act, but it is not aggression; and if the latter troops attack, they have engaged in aggression from which the provocateurs may protect themselves.[30]

The problems of identifying the aggressor are not the only difficulties encountered in applying the municipal law of self-defense to combat situations. In general the right of self-defense is not created merely by the actor's subjective belief that his situation warrants defensive action. For example, the Model Penal Code, the most progressive formulation of American criminal law to date, denies justification for the use of deadly force if the actor is reckless or negligent in believing that the use of such force is necessary.[31] This

---

30. An exception to the general rule that the right to engage in "protective measures" should be unavailable to the initial aggressor may arguably occur when the enemy, engaging in defense, employs an unlawful method of warfare and thus increases the intensity of battle beyond its lawful limits.

31. MODEL PENAL CODE § 3.09(2) (Proposed Official Draft 1962):
When the actor believes that the use of force upon or toward the person of another is necessary for any of the purposes for which such belief would establish

reasonable-belief test is found in the common law of all the states[32] and in other common-law jurisdictions.[33]

Under the Continental penal codes, however, the plea of self-defense is not conditioned on the reasonableness of the actor's belief but is based on the stricter test of cause in fact—that is, that regardless of the actor's belief, there was an actual danger which justified the use of force.[34] Typical is the provision of the Italian Penal Code which provides "[a] person who has committed an act having been compelled by necessity to defend his own or another person's right against the actual danger of an unjust injury is not punishable . . . ."[35] The Penal Code of the Russian Soviet Federated Socialist Republic is to the same effect:

> Measures of social defence shall not be applied at all to persons who
> have committed acts within the scope of the penal law if the court
> recognizes that the acts were committed by them in necessary defence

---

a justification under Sections 3.03 to 3.08 [including the Use of Force in Self-Protection, § 3.04] but the actor is *reckless* [defined in § 2.02(2)(c) as a conscious disregarding of "a substantial and unjustifiable risk . . . [which] disregard involves a gross deviation from the standard of conduct that a law-abiding person would observe in the actor's situation."] or *negligent* [defined in § 2.02(2)(d) as the "failure to perceive [a substantial and unjustifiable risk which] . . . involves a gross deviation from the standard of care that a reasonable person would observe in the actor's situation."] in having such belief or in acquiring or failing to acquire any knowledge or belief which is material to the justifiability of his use of force, the justification afforded by those Sections is unavailable in a prosecution for an offense for which recklessness or negligence, as the case may be, suffices to establish culpability.

32. *See, e.g.*, ILL. ANN. STAT. tit. 38, § 7-1 (Smith-Hurd 1964); People v. Miller, 403 Ill. 561, 87 N.E.2d 649 (1949); N.Y. PEN. CODE § 35.15 (McKinney 1967); Shorter v. People, 2 N.Y. 193 (1849); Harris v. State, 96 Ala. 24, 11 So. 255 (1892); Morgan v. Sate, 35 Tenn. 475 (1856); R. PERKINS, CRIMINAL LAW 883-85 (1957); *cf.* Etter v. State, 185 Tenn. 218, 205 S.W.2d 1 (1947) (reasonableness of use of deadly force); People v. Syed Shah, 91 Cal. App. 2d 722, 205 P.2d 1077 (1st Dist. 1949) (reasonable-belief standard for assault). Louisiana, the only civil-law jurisdiction in the United States, likewise adheres to the reasonable-belief test. LA. CODE ANN. tit. 14, art. 20 (1951).

33. *England*: Regina v. Symondson, 60 J.P. 645 (1896); Regina v. Smith, 8 Car. & P. 160, 162, 173 Eng. Rep. 441, 443 (N.P. 1837); *cf.* Regina v. Chisam, 47 Crim. App. 130 (1963); Regina v. Rose, 15 Cox Crim. Cas. 540 (Oxford Assizes 1884) (defense of another). *Australia*: Gotti v. The Crown, 22 W. Austl. L.R. 11 (1919); Regina v. Griffin, 10 S. Ct. R. (N.S.W.) 91 (1871); Regina v. Haley, 76 W.N. (N.S.W.) 550, 552 (Ct. Crim. App. 1959); CRIMINAL CODE OF 1899, 63 Vict., No. 9, Sched. 1, § 271 (Queensl.); Rex v. Keith, 27 Queensl. J.P. Rep. 109, 129-32 (Ct. Crim. App. 1933); Regina v. Tikos (No. 1), [1963] Vict. 285, 297-98 (dictum); *cf.* The Queen v. McKay, [1957]Vict. 560, 64 Austl. Argus L.R. 648 (1957), *application for leave to appeal denied*, 98 Commw. L.R. 673 (1957). *Canada*: CRIMINAL CODE OF 1954, 2 & 3 Eliz. 2, c. 51, § 34(2) (Can.). *India*: INDIAN PEN. CODE §§ 97, 99-100, 102 (8th ed. H. Gour 1966). *New Zealand*: CRIMES ACT OF 1961, 10 Eliz. 2, No. 43, § 48(2). For common law jurisdictions generally, see J. ARCHBOLD, PLEADING, EVIDENCE & PRACTICE IN CRIMINAL CASES §§ 2496-97 (35th ed. T. Butler & M. Garsia 1962); J. STEPHEN, DIGEST OF THE CRIMINAL LAW art. 305, at 251-52 (9th ed. L. Sturge 1950).

The reasonable-belief test is of comparatively recent vintage; earlier English legal scholars adhered to the stricter cause-in-fact test. *See, e.g.*, 1 M. HALE, PLEAS OF THE CROWN *478-92; E. COKE, THIRD PART OF THE INSTITUTES OF THE LAWS OF ENGLAND *55-56. The cause-in-fact test is prevalent in the Continental penal codes, discussed in notes 34-36 *infra* and accompanying text.

34. *See, e.g., France*: C. PÉN. art. 328 (59th ed. Petits Codes Dalloz 1962); *Germany*: StGB § 53 (28th ed. C. H. Beck 1966).

35. C. PEN. art. 52 (Hoepli 1963) (transl. British Foreign Office 1931).

against . . . any attempt on the person or the rights of the individuals thus defending themselves or of any other person. . . .[36]

It is clear then that the reasonable-belief standard is not established as a fundamental principle common to all municipal legal systems. It may also be argued that it is inapplicable to an international system which lacks effective machinery for judging adherence to minimum standards of behavior and punishing deviations from the established norms. This conclusion is buttressed by the fact that during a state of war, the law which applies is most notable for its ambiguity, the lack of an independent forum to which complaints can be made, and its indulgence of the broadest "right" of self-preservation.[37] Cause in fact may well be the only justification which a neutral state can be expected to accept.

On the other hand, there is good reason not to punish an officer for doing what he reasonably believed necessary. Among a field commander's primary objectives is to protect the lives of his troops. Although military training emphasizes the importance of cool thinking under stress, there are situations which call for the quickest possible decision-making: delay itself may create an unreasonable risk of life.[38] Thus, a field commander in actual combat conditions must promptly make the decision which seems most reasonable *to him* under the circumstances. When the neutral state complains of his decision to cross its border either to push the enemy back or to engage and destroy it, the "reasonableness" of his decision will be subject to review by his superiors, and his provision for the safety of his troops in the field must necessarily be accorded great weight—his conduct should, at minimum, be considered presumptively correct.

This dilemma may be resolved by imposing different standards of conduct on the state and on the commander in the field. In view of the international interest in confining war, the state should not be permitted to violate a neutral border without assuming the risk that its action will later be proved unnecessary. The absence of cause in fact would, for example, justify condemnation by the Security Council and appropriate action under the United Nations Charter. The military officer, however, should be free of liability if in view of the extreme circumstances under which he had to act, those actions were reasonable.

Another problem with the use of self-defense as a doctrine of justification in international law is that of assessing the amount of force which may be used.[39] A point is reached in which self-defense becomes aggression under any

36. R.S.F.S.R. 1960 UGOL. KOD. (Criminal Code) art. 13 (1966) (transl. British Foreign Office 1934).
37. *See* J. STONE, *supra* note 1 at 349.
38. Compare Schwarzenberger, *supra* note 1, at 333.
39. *Compare* D. BOWETT, *supra* note 1, at 54, *with* H. KELSEN, PRINCIPLES OF INTERNATIONAL LAW 75 n.68 (2d ed. R. Tucker 1966) and the principle common to all municipal legal systems that the force used in self-defense be only that necessary to protect the

well developed system of law. Secretary Webster recognized this when he said in connection with the *Caroline* case that the means taken in exercise of the right must not be "unreasonable or excessive, since the act, justified by the necessity of self-defense, must be limited by that necessity, and kept clearly within it."[40] However, the exercise of hot pursuit often leads to excesses which cause death of citizens and destruction of property in the neutral state into which the battle is carried. Illustrations of this pattern may be found in the French bombing and invasion of Tunisian territory during the Algerian war. In one notable incident, when French soldiers encountered rifle fire from a hillcrest approximately 200 yards inside Tunisia, five French planes crossed into Tunisia from Algeria and bombed in the region of the village of Bourma, killing one Tunisian civilian, wounding two others, and destroying eight houses.[41]

Such mistakes, however, are not particularly surprising. Often in the heat of fighting, it may be difficult to exercise the reasoned judgment necessary to prevent a minor incident from becoming a matter for consideration by the United Nations. But the effort must be made. As in the case of testing the need for defensive measures, it is appropriate to hold the state and the military commander to different standards. The state should be liable if the force was in fact excessive, and the officer if he did not reasonably believe it was absolutely necessary to accomplish his immediate military objective.

In summary, defensive actions which infringe the sovereignty of a neutral state should be justifiable under international law if they are responses to an anticipated attack which cannot be met by any other means, if they are necessary to end repeated raids from a neutral sanctuary, or if they are required to protect the safety of troops under actual attack. Unless such reasonable measures are permitted by a system of international law, it can be expected that international law will be dismissed as an idealistic conception unresponsive to the realities of war and therefore ignored. On the other hand, if these are the standards for justification, it is more likely that actions which fall outside their scope will be condemned on a legal basis by an international polity able to impose punitive sanctions. If this is to happen, the preconditions of an effective system of international law will be fulfilled.

II. Violation of Neutral Duties

In all of the instances of self-defense discussed above, defensive measures were necessary in part because the neutral state had failed to prevent the use

---

actor in the circumstances. Whether the standard is "reasonable necessity" or "necessity in fact" depends upon the particular legal system; however, the standards used generally follow the geographical pattern discussed in notes 31-36 *supra* and accompanying text.

40. Letter from Secretary of State Webster to Mr. Fox, April 24, 1841, [1843] 61 Accounts and Papers, *Papers Relative to the Special Mission of Lord Ashburton to the United States in 1842*, at 49.

41. *See* N.Y. Times, Sept. 15, 1957, at 1, col. 2; *id.*, Sept. 16, 1957, at 3, col. 4; Le Monde, Sept. 18, 1957, at 2, col. 4.

of its territory by a belligerent force. Under some conceptions of the law of neutrality, this failure is a violation of the neutral's duty of strict impartiality and terminates the right to territorial integrity. This theory, however, has come under attack, and the view has been advanced that the neutral may aid the side which it considers the victim of aggression without losing its neutral status. It might appear that this doctrinal debate is of no concern to those who believe that the right of hot pursuit is founded primarily on the necessity for defensive measures against a particular attack. But the difficulty is that these measures of self-defense are more likely to be accepted by the international community if they can be associated with some culpability on the part of the neutral.

The idea that a state claiming neutral status must remain aloof and completely impartial became popular after the end of the Napoleonic Wars.[42] Building on this foundation, the traditional law of neutrality established an elaborate system of proto-Hohfeldian rights and duties, many of which were codified in Hague Convention V of 1907.[43] Among them was the duty of insuring that neutral territory would not be used by one belligerent as a base of operations from which to attack the other. Another was the duty to take measures which would insure that forces retreating into neutral territory were rendered inoperative and preferably permanently cut off from the theater of war.[44] A neutral state was thought to be partisan if it permitted the use of its territory for unrestricted asylum or recoupment. *A fortiori*, it violated its duties if it permitted forces engaged in hit-and-run tactics to remain in its

---

42. Hall made what is the most familiar statement of the positivist theory of neutrality. He declared that a neutral state is one whose

amity must be colourless in the eyes of both [belligerents]; in its corporate capacity as a state it must abstain altogether from mixing itself up in their quarrel.

W. HALL, INTERNATIONAL LAW 73 (7th ed. 1917).

43. 36 Stat. 2310 (1907).

44. Thus, Article 11 of Hague Convention V required the neutral state to intern forces of a belligerent which crossed into its territory, preferably as far from the theater of warfare as possible. 36 Stat. 2310, 2324 (1907). Writers affirm the duty of neighboring states to intern rebel forces when their belligerency has not been recognized. Otherwise it would be possible for the rebels to return to occupied territory and thereby cause the neighboring country indirectly to interfere with the prosecution of the war effort of the established government through an illegal omission. *See* Castrén, *supra* note 4, at 120-22; Wehberg, *La Guerre Civile et le Droit International*, 63 RECUEIL DES COURS DE L'ACADÉ-MIE DE DROIT INTERNATIONAL 1, 58 (1938); *cf.* Balladore Pallieri, *Quelques Aspects Juridiques de la Non-Intervention en Espagne*, 18 REVUE DE DROIT INTERNATIONAL ET DE LÉGISLATION COMPARÉE 285, 290 (1937) (interning rebel men-of-war upon entry into the ports of third countries); *see* Kunz, *supra* note 4, at 202-03.

However, the view that a state not directly involved in a civil war is under a duty to intern forces entering its territory from the theater of war is not unanimous. In response to a question in the House of Commons, Edward Heath, then Lord Privy Seal, stated:

There is nothing in the rules of international law to oblige the Thai Government to intern [Royal] Laotian forces which have crossed into Thai territory, unless Thailand recognised the contending forces in Laos as belligerents. This she has not done. . . . Thailand is not bound by the Geneva Convention to intern these forces unless she has recognized them as belligerents in Laos. . . .

661 PARL. DEB., H.C. (5th ser.) 21 (1962).

territory without official interference.[45] When sentiment in the neutral country was unfavorable to the claims of the victim of these tactics[46] and the government of the neutral state unresponsive to previous demands for redress, self-help proportional to the exigencies of the situation was considered appropriate.[47]

The traditional law, moreover, does not exonerate a neutral simply because it has used its best efforts. It may be wondered why a violation occurs when the neutral, through no fault of its own, is unable to effect proper protective measures. The conceptual answer is that states possess exclusive jurisdiction over their national territory and are faced with the responsibility for insuring that the effective authority of the government is maintained throughout. Thus the claim to territorial integrity under the Charter or under Article I of Hague Convention V is based upon the proposition that adequate police measures will be taken by neutral states. But on more practical grounds it appears that the need for hot pursuit may be just as great when the neutral is unable to fulfill its obligations as when it is unwilling to do so. For the belligerent there is no difference between, for example, Cambodia's physical incapability to repel the infringing insurgents because of its long, undefined, unmarked border, domestic instability, and inadequate armed forces and Tunisia's refusal to repel them.

The claim by a belligerent that hot pursuit is appropriate when other demands for recompense go unrequitted has fairly strong support, not only among the majority of commentators but in historical precedent. Historical examples are not confined to the American practice. For example, in 1870 the Prussians feared that a large number of French troops would escape to neutral Belgium, which might be reluctant or unable to disarm and intern them.[48] As

---

45. *See* 3 E. DE VATTEL, *supra* note 12, § 133, at 277.

46. The neutral's traditional duty of impartiality does not forbid official expression of sentiment in favor of one belligerent. *See* 2 L. OPPENHEIM, *supra* note 5, § 294, at 655.

47. Kelsen considers self-defense as a part of the larger concept of self-help. The former is considered a means of enforcing the law; the latter includes within its purview the imposition of reprisals. *See* H. KELSEN, *supra* note 39, at 74 n.67 (equating Bowett's concept of self-defense with self-help, which he considers the totality of measures by which a state can protect its legally protected interests) and 80 n.71. Other writers define self-defense more broadly, virtually equating it with protection of "vital national interests." *See* D. BOWETT, *supra* note 1, at 20-24, 270-71; 1 J. WESTLAKE, *supra* note 1, at 312-13.

The distinction which Kelsen draws is more important today than in the period during which traditional neutrality was in its heyday. The older concept of neutrality did not distinguish between mere violation of neutral duties and loss of neutral status. It maintained that the neutral state which showed any degree of preference to one belligerent by violating one of its neutral duties was an accomplice of the favored side. *See* Curtis, *The Law of Hostile Military Expeditions as Applied by the United States*, 8 AM. J. INT'L L. 1, 5 (1914). Accordingly, the belligerent adversely affected was entitled to exact reprisals against the "neutral" state as punishment for its complicity. Today the exaction of reprisals against neutral states which had violated a duty of neutrality would probably be unlawful, particularly if the reprisals were disproportional to the violation they were designed to punish.

48. *See* J. SPAIGHT, WAR RIGHTS ON LAND 480 (1911), *quoting from* 2 DER DEUTSCH-FRANZÖSISCHE KRIEG 1870-71 Part 1, App., at 286* (1875).

a result, General von Moltke issued an order in which he stated, "should the enemy pass over into Belgium without being at once disarmed, he is to be pursued thither without delay."[49] Bismarck justified this proposed hot pursuit into Belgium on the ground that Prussia's respect for Belgian neutrality was contingent upon reciprocal respect by France.[50] Another example occurred during the Boer War when British forces threatened to cross the border into neutral Swaziland to attack retreating Boer commandos.[51]

Furthermore, history does not support the proposition that hot pursuit is used exclusively by Western powers in their internecine wars or imperialistic adventures. The Soviet government responded to White Guard activity by crossing the Mongolian border in 1921 in pursuit of the insurgents and the Manchurian border as late as 1929.[52] The Soviet position on the use of hot pursuit to redress violations of neutral duties is shown in its note to the Foreign Minister of Rumania on August 13, 1921:

> In its desire to assist the Rumanian authorities to disperse the bands organized in Bessarabia and Rumania for the purpose of carrying out acts of aggression against the Soviet Republics, the allied Soviet Governments consider it necessary that if such bands, when pursued by Soviet troops, should cross into territory occupied by the Rumanian authorities, they should be followed into the latter territory, the Rumanian authorities being informed in time so that the operations . . . shall not be interpreted as acts directed . . . against the Rumanian Government and people.[53]

The Soviet government also demanded that Rumania end moral and material support to the White Guards, expel the leaders of these groups from Rumanian territory, disband their counter-revolutionary detachments, and sever diplomatic relations with the "Ukranian People's Republic."[54] The Soviet note did not mention self-defense and apparently regarded hot pursuit as permissible if "neutral" Rumania persisted in its previous violations.

The most important problem confronting those who maintain that hot pursuit is appropriate under the traditional view of neutrality is the absence of either supporting convention or custom. In international law custom means not only usage but also that the usage is regarded as binding by the parties involved. Virtually every state into whose territory hot pursuit has been undertaken or threatened has protested the action as being contrary to principles of international law and a violation of its territorial integrity. Indeed, the United States took this position in the *Caroline* case.[55] When Cambodia

---

49. *See* J. Spaight, *supra* note 48.
50. *Id.*
51. *Id.*
52. *See* Brownlie, *supra* note 18, at 732-33. Note, however, that the Soviet Union justified its action on the basis of self-defense against die-hard White Guard units. *See* 2 J. Degras, Soviet Documents on Foreign Policy 407, 413 (1952).
53. *See* 1 J. Degras, *supra* note 52, at 254.
54. *Id.* at 253.
55. *See* Letter of Secretary Webster to Lord Ashburton, July 27, 1842, in 30 Brit. and Foreign State Papers 193-95 (1842).

indicated that it would not oppose American forces militarily, it recognized only that the United States had the power to engage in this policy and did not admit its right to do so.[56]

But a more significant challenge to the traditional rules of neutral duties is that the ideal of strict impartiality on which they were founded is no longer accepted. Many distinguished writers have returned to a derivative of Grotius's *bellum-justum* principle.[57] This view is reflected in Article 12 of the Draft Convention on Rights and Duties of States in Case of Aggression[58] which provides that a state which does not cooperate in the conduct of hostilities does not owe the "aggressor" any neutral duties but may assert against the latter all the rights to which neutrals are entitled.[59] Writers such as Wright and Brierly go further and assert that a neutral state has the *duty* to discriminate against the offending state and assist the state acting in "self-defense."[60] It is said that the neutral is entitled to violate the traditional requirement of impartiality because its rights under the Kellogg-Briand Pact have been violated by the "aggressor" in starting the war and "continue to be infringed

---

56. The statement of the Royal Cambodian government, reproduced in N.Y. Times, Dec. 28, 1967, at 17, col. 2, does not discuss the right of the United States to engage in the more traditional means of redress such as diplomatic protest and demands for reparation. Moreover, the Cambodian government admitted the existence of a policy on its part to keep its territory free of armed Viet Cong troops, though denying the United States a right to call Cambodia to account for violations of this policy.

57. *See, e.g.,* Brierly, *Some Implications of the Pact of Paris,* 10 Brit. Y.B. Int'l L. 208, 210 (1929) ; Lauterpacht, *Rules of Warfare in an Unlawful War,* Law and Politics in the World Community 89, 110-13 (G. Lipsky ed. 1953) ; Wright, *The Meaning of the Pact of Paris,* 27 Am. J. Int'l L. 39 (1933) ; *cf.* 2 L. Oppenheim, *supra* note 5, § 320, at 684-85; *but see* J. Stone, *supra* note 1, at 407.
This view was not confined merely to Anglo-American scholars. For a Continental exposition reaching the same conclusion, *see* N. Politis, Neutrality and Peace 44-99 (F. Macken tran. 1935). However, Politis detected that state practice would tend to undermine the logical implications arising from the existence of the League and the Pact, particularly in regard to the introduction of non-aggression pacts in the 1930's. *See id.* at 73-78.
Nor has the experience of World War II and its aftermath dimmed the faith of the adherents of the "new neutrality." In another context, Professor Wright maintained his belief that the positivist approach to international law has been displaced by the decidedly anti-war position of the Charter. *See* Wright, *Legal Positivism and the Nuremburg Judgment,* 42 Am. J. Int'l L. 405, 413 (1948).
Professor Hans Kelsen, a legal positivist, questions the utility of the *bellum-justum* theory. He concludes that the principle "reflects political wishes rather than scientific thinking." H. Kelsen, General Theory of Law and State 341 (1945). An analysis of the jurisprudence of war in light of the United Nations Charter can be found in Kelsen, *Sanctions in International Law under the Charter of the United Nations,* 31 Iowa L. Rev. 499 (1946). One comment which bears repetition in light of the reliance upon the Charter for the adoption of the "new neutrality" is "[i]f the enforcement actions provided for by the Charter are true sanctions, the Charter is a perfect realization of the *bellum-justum* principle." *Id.* at 501-02. *Quaere* whether the post-war experience has indicated that the enforcement actions are "true sanctions."

58. 33 Am. J. Int'l L. Supp. 844, 902-04 (1939).

59. *Id.*

60. *See* Brierly, *supra* note 57; Wright, *The Future of Neutrality,* [1928] 242 Int'l Concil. 352, 362. Other authors imply that the neutral has a right to discriminate in favor of the belligerent acting in self-defense. *See, e.g.,* Boce, *Shall a State which Goes to War in Violation of the Kellogg-Briand Pact Have a Belligerent's Rights in Respect of Neutrals?,* 24 Am. J. Int'l L. 766, 769-70 (1930) ; Lauterpacht, *supra* note 57, at 110-13.

every minute the war continues. . . . [U]nder the Pact . . . the primary belligerent had ceased to enjoy its benefits."[61]

This alternative to the traditional theory of neutrality is almost certainly unworkable. Even if it is true that the pact gives a neutral the right to discriminate against the aggressor, it does not follow that each state is free to determine for itself where the blame lies.[62] Professor Wright recognizes the need to identify the aggressor for the reason that otherwise the neutral might be subject to heavy reparation payments should an arbitration tribunal decide that he had aided the aggressor and not the victim.[63] But this is only a small part of the problem; the same need exists in the usual case where no centralized body with recognized judicial power passes upon the aggressiveness of either party to the hostilities. There are also situations in which neither side will be innocent under the law of the Pact and the Charter.[64] Furthermore, in the event of a civil war within the confines of a single state intervention would be permitted only on the side of the established government if it requests aid, regardless of any question of aggression.[65] Therefore, there will be little incentive to identify the aggressor.

To make each state the sole judge of culpability is to add to the ambiguity which already characterizes international law concerning war[66] and to

---

61. Wright, *supra* note 57, at 59-60.

62. Recently Professor Henkin reaffirmed what essentially was the position of Professors Wright and Brierly in the 1930's, except that he placed primary reliance for determining the source of aggression upon the organs of the United Nations. Henkin, *supra* note 17, at 159-62. But it does not appear that the United Nations is able effectively to undertake this task. The military provisions of the Charter (Articles 43-50) have never been implemented. Permanent collective security has given way to ad hoc peacekeeping forces and a reliance upon mutual-security agreements outside of the United Nations framework. Furthermore, even if the collective-security arrangements of the United Nations were institutionalized, the presence of the veto vitiates the effectiveness of the Security Council, and the General Assembly is without competence to implement them. For a discussion of the inherent deficiencies of a collective-security system, see I. CLAUDE, SWORDS INTO PLOWSHARES, ch. 12 (3d ed. 1964).

A determination by the General Assembly is, at best, merely evidence of what the law is (*see* Johnson, *The Effect of Resolutions of the General Assembly of the United Nations*, 32 BRIT. Y.B. INT'L L. 97, 118 (1955-56) (interpreting I.C.J. STAT. art. 38, para. 1(d))); more realistically, it is an expression by the majority of what it thinks the law should be. As the Security Council has the sole authority under the Charter to deal decisively with the breach or threatened breach of international security, its determinations are the only ones entitled to binding effect upon the membership of the United Nations. Even under the Uniting for Peace Resolution, the General Assembly is legally little more than a forum for the expression of world opinion as to the merits of both sides to an international dispute. The resolution of the General Assembly may have large persuasive value if it represents a large majority, perhaps at least two-thirds, of the membership of the United Nations. Nevertheless, it does not have the power under the Charter to render a determination legally binding upon the parties to an international dispute. *Compare* Sloan, *The Binding Force of a 'Recommendation' of the General Assembly of the United Nations*, 25 BRIT. Y.B. INT'L L. 1, 31-33 (1948) *and* Lande, *The Changing Effectiveness of General Assembly Resolutions*, 58 AM. SOC'Y OF INT'L L. PROC. 162 (1964) *with* Skubiszewski, *The General Assembly of the United Nations and Its Power to Influence National Action, id.* at 153-61.

63. *See* Wright, *supra* note 57, at 60-61.

64. *See* Kunz, *supra* note 17, at 879.

65. *Cf.* Borchard, *"Neutrality" and Civil Wars*, 31 AM. J. INT'L L. 304, 305-06 (1937).

66. P. JESSUP, A MODERN LAW OF NATIONS 205 (1948).

legitimate the anarchy which prevails in international politics.[67] The thesis that under the Pact and Charter the neutral state has a duty to assist the victim of aggression is tenable only if there exists a set of standards which members of an international tribunal can apply impartially, regardless of their ideological inclinations, to determine which side has in fact struck the first blow. At the present time and for the forseeable future, such standards are at best an idealist's dream; all attempts to formulate even a definition of aggression have resulted in failure.[68] Even if acceptable standards can be found, the propaganda efforts of both sides to an international dispute make the process of evidentiary fact-finding an arduous, if not an impossible, task. Furthermore, the ideological bent of the observer has a profound influence upon the way in which the evidence is interpreted. Thus, a Communist assessing the relevant facts in a "war of national liberation" will be influenced, perhaps unconsciously, by Marxist notions of capitalistic imperialism. It is probably too much to expect the necessary impartiality, even from lawyers, when national and doctrinal differences are as strong as they are today.

Most importantly, however, state practice during the forty years since the signing of the Kellogg-Briand Pact has been inconsistent with the interpretation which Wright and others place on that document. For example, the Pact of Friendship, Non-Aggression and Neutrality Between Italy and the U.S.S.R. of 1933 provides, "Should either High Contracting Party be the object of aggression on the part of one or more third Powers, the other High Contracting Party undertakes to maintain neutrality throughout the duration of the conflict."[69] As Bowett points out, this provision is hardly in keeping with the "just war" theory of neutrality which the Pact supposedly espoused.[70] Neutrality was declared during the Chaco War by Argentina, Brazil, and Uruguay.[71] Perhaps the greatest blow to the notion that a neutral might aid the victim of aggression was the Pittman Resolution,[72] which resulted in the strict neutrality of the United States during the Italian conquest of Ethiopia. During the Spanish Civil War, an amendment to the Pittman Resolution required an American arms embargo[73] which, in light of the extensive military assistance which the insurgents were receiving from Germany and Italy, was detrimental to the Republican cause. This was done on the grounds that the United States, as a neutral, had to manifest its "impartiality" by refusing aid to either side.[74]

---

67. See Jessup, The Birth, Death and Reincarnation of Neutrality, 26 AM. J. INT'L L. 789, 793 (1932).

68. See R. FALK, LEGAL ORDER IN A VIOLENT WORLD 63-64 (1968); W. FRIEDMANN, supra note 3, at 254-55.

69. Article 2, 148 L.N.T.S. 327 (1933).

70. D. BOWETT, supra note 1, at 163.

71. See Wilson, War and Neutrality, 27 AM. J. INT'L L. 724 (1933).

72. Pub. Res. of Aug. 31, 1935, ch. 837, 49 Stat. 1081.

73. Pub. Res. of Jan. 8, 1937, ch. 1, 50 Stat. 3. See Borchard, supra note 65, at 306.

74. For Congressional discussion of the purposes of the resolutions, see 79 CONG. REC. 13955, 14366-69 (1935); 81 CONG. REC. 74, 77-79, 90, 93 (1937).

Nor does conduct subsequent to the outbreak of World War II in Europe support the case for Wright's view of neutrality. Rather it supports Bowett's assertion that favoritism was undertaken to protect vital security interests of the neutral states, not to defend a principle of "just war."[75] Although American action in support of the British during 1940-41 may be rationalized on the ground that Germany had forfeited its rights under the Kellogg-Briand Pact,[76] it is clear that during that period aid to Great Britain was a matter of American security. Even during this period the United States admitted that its actions were based on self-defense, although it adhered to its position that neutrality did not require strict impartiality between the belligerents.[77] The same is probably true of the positions of neutrals such as Tunisia and Cambodia. The authority of the newly established Bourguiba government would have been badly shaken, if not destroyed, if it had maintained a position of impartiality toward the war in which its brethren in Algeria were engaged.[78] It may well have been far safer to risk hot pursuit by the French than a possible uprising. Similarly, it has been suggested by a student of Cambodian foreign policy that Prince Sihanouk believed that the continued independence of his state depended upon entering into a *modus vivendi* with the Chinese People's Republic and the Democratic Republic of Vietnam.[79] At present, Cambodia is threatened by a Communist inspired insurgency;[80] the consequences probably would have been far worse for the Cambodian government had impartiality been maintained throughout the war in Vietnam.

However, some modification of the traditional view of neutrality is probably desirable. For example, it is not now maintained that the violation of the duty of strict impartiality gives cause to treat the neutral as a belligerent.[81] Thus the right of hot pursuit when a neutral has permitted a belligerent to use its territory is generally justified not as a punishment or reprisal, but as self-help necessitated by the neutral's inaction. This approach, moreover, presents the best hope for confining war because the belligerent is allowed to take necessary measures without bringing another state into the conflict.

But even this modified form of the rules of neutrality established by Hague Convention V was rejected by the Soviet Union and the Arab delega-

---

75. *See* D. Bowett, *supra* note 1, at 164-67.

76. This rationale was offered by the then Attorney General of the United States. *See* Address of Robert H. Jackson, Attorney General of the United States, Interamerican Bar Association, Habana, Cuba, March 27, 1941, in 35 Am. J. Int'l L. 348, 353-54 (1941). The inadequacy of the explanation is pointed out in J. Stone, *supra* note 1, at 405 n.18.

77. *See* 3 C. Hyde, International Law, Chiefly as Interpreted and Applied by United States 2236 (2d rev. ed. 1945). *See also* 4 U.S. Dep't of State Bull. 89-90 (1941).

78. *Cf.* El Moudjahid, Sept. 5, 1957, at 1, col. 1, asserting that the Tunisian people would throw themselves into the Algerian war to eliminate French imperialism from northern Africa if the conflict were to persist.

79. *See* M. Leifer, Cambodia: The Search for Security 7-19, 138-42 *passim* (1967).

80. *See* N.Y. Times, March 14, 1968, at 7, col. 1.

81. For a presentation of the former view, see Curtis, *supra* note 41.

tions during the United Nations debate on French actions against Tunisia.[82] It may be argued by the Socialist and newly independent states that they have no obligation to recognize this "western imperialist" concept because it is adverse to their interests, and they had no part in its formulation.[83] But although the principle may have been formulated by a minority of states, if the uncommitted nations do not like it, they have the numerical superiority with which to change it by convention or otherwise.[84] Moreover, it is not clear that they would desire such a change. The traditional principle, although not immutable or ideal, does have the advantages of ease of application, compatibility with the common-sense notion of what neutral behavior should be, and maintenance of some semblance of order in an international system. Furthermore, as "wars of national liberation" and even purely domestic revolts become more frequent in newly independent states, the established governments, many of which dislike the principle today, may appreciate the protection it provides against those states which would aid their opponents. The development of a posture toward international law, like the conduct of foreign policy, cannot be undertaken solely on an *ad hoc* or short-run basis.

It seems then that the neutral's failure to prevent the use of its territory by any belligerent provides an additional basis in international law for the necessary defensive measures outlined earlier. Should a violation of a neutral duty also justify action which did not meet the rather strict requirements for justification by self-defense? The question is one for which modern international law provides no ready answer. If an answer can be ventured, it must involve a balancing of diplomatic considerations and the respect for territorial integrity inherent in the theory of sovereignty with a realistic appraisal of the needs of the military in conducting modern limited warfare. Thus, hot pursuit, when not a matter of self-defense, should not be undertaken unless other avenues of redress, such as diplomatic protest, invocation of the facilities of

---

82. For the view of the Soviet Union, see 15 U.N. GAOR, 1st Comm. 239 (1960); for the reaction of the Algerians, see M. BEDJAOUI, LAW AND THE ALGERIAN REVOLUTION 151 (1961). The Tunisians reacted to the French exercise of hot pursuit by declaring a state of emergency at its border areas. *See* Brownlie, *supra* note 18, at 712 & 712 n.2.

83. *Cf.* Castañeda, *The Underdeveloped Nations and the Development of International Law*, 15 INT'L ORGANIZATION 38, 39, 43 (1961). Professor Wright has indicated the ways in which Afro-Asian states have contributed to changes in international law. *See* Wright, *The Influence of the New Nations of Asia and Africa upon International Law*, 7 FOREIGN AFFAIRS REPS. (India) 33, 37-39 (1958).

84. All too often, however, Western commentators maintain the attitude that it is the practice of their countries which establish the norms of international law. Note the following statement by Robert Gauthier, expressing one French response to the Tunisian position that hot pursuit was unlawful:

We can continue to extend sympathy to a country . . . only if it remembers always that the rules of international law—*those to which western nations submit themselves*—carry obligations and limit actions which they might wish to undertake—even in favor of men with whom they sympathize and whom they refuse to regard as rebels. [Emphasis added.]

Le Monde, Sept. 4, 1957, at 1, col. 3 (transl. A. Fraleigh, *The Algerian Revolution and the International Community* 184-85 (unpublished study)).

the United Nations, demands for reparations, proposals to strengthen international border commissions, and requests for judicial or arbitral settlement
have been futile. Negotiations with the neutral state should always be undertaken. It may then be possible to distinguish between those states who refuse
to fulfill their obligations and those who merely cannot. A settlement may be
arranged with the latter by which the borders of these states can be policed
sufficiently to make hot pursuit unnecessary.

Conclusion

Military action within neutral territory may be justified as a measure of
self-defense or as an appropriate response to the failure of a neutral state to
prevent the use of its territory by belligerent forces. In international law, the
second justification has been more clearly articulated through the concept of
neutral duties. It is suggested, however, that international law should permit
and encourage primary reliance on self-defense as a justification. The presence
of belligerent forces within neutral territory will always be a violation of the
neutral's duty of strict impartiality; the doctrine of self-defense, however,
imposes additional and probably acceptable restraints on the use of force
against this violation.

Many writers on international politics have indicated that the conduct of
war is in practice governed by an unwritten set of rules that all parties adhere
to out of their own self-interest. These rules may be summarized in the notion
that one belligerent will not jeopardize the vital interest of another state unless
its own vital interests are at stake. International law can best influence the
conduct of war if it gives moral support and legal authority to these unwritten
rules. The doctrine of neutral duties alone does not serve this purpose because
strict impartiality may often be inconsistent with a neutral's vital interests and
at the same time unnecessary to the vital interests of a belligerent. Primary
reliance on the justification of self-defense, on the other hand, will tend to
assure that at least a significant interest of the belligerent state is involved.

Further development of the justification of self-defense will make it
possible to dispense with the broad, non-legal notion of "military necessity"
or "self-preservation" which generally is a rationalization for aggression,
such as the invasion of neutral Belgium in 1914,[85] or the employment of excessive or unlawful force,[86] such as the bombardment of neutral villages and the
use of poison gas. Before the First World War, some writing on international
law, particularly by the Germans,[87] tended to support this sweeping idea of

---

85. *See* 2 J. GARNER, INTERNATIONAL LAW AND THE WORLD WAR 191-93, 198-201
(1920).

86. *See, e.g.,* J. STONE, *supra* note 1, at 351-53; O'Brien, *The Meaning of 'Military
Necessity' in International Law,* 1 WORLD POLITY 109, 169, 171, 173-76 (1957); Schwarzenberger, *supra* note 1, at 343.

87. *See* J. STONE, *supra* note 1, at 351-53 and authorities cited therein. However, the
Germans were not alone in their advocacy of the doctrine. *See* W. HALL, *supra* note 42

raison de guerre. However, it is recognized today by virtually all writers that this doctrine tends to destroy the international legal order, rather than preserve it. According to Brierly, the concept makes all obligation to adhere to law merely conditional, and "there is hardly an act of international lawlessness which it might not be called upon to excuse."[88] If proper self-defense is clearly defined in international law, such excuses will no longer be available.

---

at 322; 1 A. RIVIER, PRINCIPES DU DROIT DES GENS 277-79 (1896); *cf.* 2 E. DE VATTEL, *supra* note 12, § 119, at 149.

88. J. BRIERLY, THE LAW OF NATIONS 404 (6th ed. H. Waldock 1963). The Germans recognized this themselves. *Cf.* Strupp, *Das Völkerrechtliche Delikt*, 3 HANDBUCH DES VÖLKERRECHTS, Part 3 at 174 (1920).

V. THE VIETNAM WAR AND THE CONSTITUTION

Vietnam and Civil Disobedience

GIDON GOTTLIEB

THE TWO great crises of American life in 1967, Vietnam and the race riots, have revived ancient disputes between the citizen and the state. Opposition to United States actions in the war and to racial domination by the white majority has led, in many cases, to acts of civil disobedience and resistance. These in turn have prompted a debate on the limits of civil disobedience and on the duty to obey the law.

Objections to civil disobedience rest on three related juridical premises: that there is a legal duty to obey the law and that the boundary between legitimate and illegitimate orders, practices, and enactments can be clearly drawn; that the duty to obey the law entails a duty to obey the lawfully constituted authorities; and that in democracies the avenues for peaceful change provide an alternative to unlawful modes of protest and civil disobedience.

Insofar as the Vietnam War is concerned, however, none of these assumptions is warranted. Complex questions arise when Government actions are of questionable legality and when doubts about their legality cannot be dispelled by adjudication; these difficulties are compounded when none of the three branches of the Government appears to abide by governing principles of law.

In this essay, I propose to outline some constitutional and jurisprudential aspects of the troubling issues that have been raised about the legality and the constitutional propriety of resistance to the Government's war policy, touching briefly on their most striking features.

I

Vietnam: The Claims for Disobedience and Resistance—Expert professional opinion has charged the President with unlawful action in Vietnam.[1] It has accused him of violating the Constitution, the law of nations, and the treaties which are the supreme law of the land.[2]

[1] Lawyers' Committee on American Policy Towards Viet Nam, Consultative Council, *Viet Nam and International Law: An Analysis of the Legality of the U.S. Military Involvement* (1967). Cf. Hull & Novogrod, *Law and Vietnam* (1968). For an excellent collection of materials and essays, see R. Falk, *The Vietnam War and International Law* (1968); Clergy and Laymen Concerned About Viet Nam, *In the Name of America* (1968).

[2] See, e.g., the current case involving Messrs. Coffin, Ferber, Goodman, Raskin, and Spock. See also Mora v. McNamara, 389 U.S. 934 (1967); Mitchell v. United States, 386 U.S. 972 (1967).

The executive branch has thus itself been accused of disobedience, of disregarding the requirements of the rule of law.

The Vietnam War has led an important body of citizens into direct conflict with the Government. Attempts to alter American policy in Vietnam were confined at one time largely to the exercise of first amendment rights of speech, assembly, and petition. A number of attempts, however, have recently been made to have the courts determine the legality of the war itself. This they have thus far declined to do. Opponents of the war accordingly claim to have exhausted the avenues for peaceful change provided in the Constitution. They claim that the magnitude of the wrong which forms the basis of their complaint is truly enormous, requiring an urgent and effective remedy.[3] These opponents do not seek to impose their political will on an unwilling majority. Their claims are *not* political but juridical. They advance primarily legal and moral claims involving the legal authority of the Administration, though admittedly the *motives* for their opposition are not legal or constitutional. On the other hand, the Government's case against draft card burners, deserters, and other opponents is based on the principle of the rule of law.[4] It is in *response* to attempts to enforce the law that opponents of the war are led to challenge the legitimacy of the state's own actions. They claim, in reply to charges that they are violating the law, that they are merely resisting the lawless behavior of the state itself.[5]

Thus, while it is perfectly true that the opposition to the war is not primarily motivated by constitutional considerations, criticism of that opposition is dominated by a concern for law and order. This *sequence* is important. It situates the legal issues in the web of justifications, claims, and counterclaims. Ultimately, however, opposition to the war on *moral* grounds requires that, *even* should there be no doubts about the constitutionality of the State action, the demands of morality prevail. But the conflict between the demands of law and morality arises *only* when the legitimacy of government action is itself beyond doubt. The strategy of arguments involves, therefore, a *sequence* of claims and responses which can be summarized as follows:

1. Opponents of the war, guided by moral or pragmatic considera-

---

[3] On the principle of proportionality, see Williams v. Wallace, 240 F. Supp. 100, 106 (M.D. Ala. 1965): "The extent of the right to assemble, demonstrate and march peaceably along the highways and streets in an orderly manner should be commensurate with the enormity of the wrongs that are being protested and petitioned against."

[4] See the Coffin case.   [5] See the Coffin case.

tions, urge civil disobedience and resistance involving violation of the draft laws and other laws.

2. The Administration, guided by legal and political considerations of its own, seeks to punish alleged violations of the law.

3. Opponents respond that under the Constitution the authority of the President is limited by domestic and international law and that in his conduct of the war he is usurping powers not granted to him. They justify their violations as an attempt to resist illegitimate authority after having failed to do so by persuasion and by adjudication.

4. Critics of the opposition respond that there has been no court determination that the conduct of the war is unlawful in any way and that in the absence of such determination the claims of the opposition are unfounded. There is, moreover, a presumption that the acts of a legitimate government are lawful.

5. Opponents respond that in light of the courts' refusal to hear their arguments about the legality of the war, under the "political question" doctrine, they are fully entitled to determine for themselves in good faith the issue of legality; in such circumstances, they claim, the presumption of legality can be rebutted.

6. Critics of the opposition argue that the law is what the courts say it is and that judicial rejection of the opponents' claims, even in the form of a refusal to hear their case, amounts to a legitimation of government action.

7. Opponents respond that under the Constitution the courts do not have the exclusive right to determine what is constitutional and what is not, and that the courts have clearly chosen not to decide the issue.

In this succession of claims and counterclaims, hard questions are raised as to the role of the courts in our system of government. They are again invited to rule upon one of the great conflicts tearing American society apart and threatening the integrity of its institutions.

II

Civil Disobedience: Constitutional Values at Stake—The call to resist illegitimate authority poses delicate legal problems. Significantly, international law and treaty obligations are now resorted to as a basis for challenging the legitimacy, rather than the morality, of government action. International law provides a juridical basis for objecting to state actions that may otherwise satisfy the demands of the domestic legal order. It provides a legal standard for assessing the behavior of states just as natural law once provided its own standards. It is not always clear when authority is legitimate, when laws are constitutional, and when actions are lawful. When uncertainty prevails, protesters take their chance. They may challenge a law, they may challenge the authority of a government official, and the final outcome of adjudication will often be uncertain.

The gravest legal and moral problems arise, however, where opposition and resistance is contemplated against plainly valid laws and clearly legitimate government orders on the grounds that a superior moral law or the dictates of conscience so require. In such circumstances, the constitutional values involved are weighty and fundamental. Resistance to laws of unquestionable legal validity compels the state to resort to coercion. Such resort necessarily weakens voluntary compliance and acceptance by the people of government authority. Government by consent—the rule of law—and the modes of peaceful change are then correspondingly weakened. Historical memories also turn to the proven danger of mobs initially animated by a burning passion for justice that are later swept by a desire for plunder and revenge. This threat was in Mr. Justice Black's mind when he said that:

> Experience demonstrates that it is not a far step from what to many seems the earnest, honest, patriotic, kind-spirited multitude of today, to the fanatical, threatening, lawless mob of tomorrow. And the crowds that press in the streets for noble goals today can be supplanted tomorrow by street mobs pressuring the courts for precisely opposite ends.[6]

The rule of law is not designed only to secure order and protect established interests. It is the only substitute for force and power yet devised in political societies. As the guarantor of liberty and peaceful change, it far transcends its traditional role as the defender of the status quo. Civil resistance unquestionably weakens the hold of the rule of law and its acceptance by the governed. In this weakening, the whole equilibrium of a force-free society is upset. The constitutional values at stake are not merely the demands of order as against the claims of conscience and justice. What is involved is government by consent of the governed and the pursuit of life, liberty, and happiness. Some have suggested that what is at stake is the survival of society itself. For, as Mr. Justice Whittaker has recently reasserted, disorderly society cannot

---

[6] Cox v. Louisiana, 379 U.S. 559, 584 (1965) (dissenting opinion), see also Cox.

survive.[7] We must never forget, however, that even whole societies can be criminal, committed to horror, tyranny, and domination; that it is not always possible to put respect for the body politic above the claims of conscience and justice.

In the final analysis, the denial of fundamental human rights is itself subversive of the fundamental design of the rule of law. Pervasive injustice militates against government by consent. The denial of equal protection of the laws on the basis of race or income threatens the avenues of peaceful change. Injustice rots the pillars of popular acceptance of authority. Inasmuch as the rule of law is designed to substitute the assent of the governed for the force of the ruler, it is irrevocably wedded to the pursuit of social justice. The necessary connection between the rule of law and the pursuit of a just social order has long been obscured by dominant theories of legal positivism. Cataclysmic events both at home and abroad have now made this link manifest.

III

The War Power and Congress—The Founding Fathers could not have foreseen that foreign affairs and war powers would one day become the Presidency's most potent attribute. Their intent was to vest the power to commit the United States to war in the Congress. It was conferred upon Congress *alone* while the President was left with the authority to repel sudden attacks only. The growth of presidential power over foreign affairs was accompanied by a corresponding growth of treaty limitations on the international use of force and the conduct of warfare. Despite the supremacy clause in Article VI of the Constitution, the full force of these treaties has never been brought to bear upon the Presidency. The reluctance of the Supreme Court to become involved in foreign relations questions has in practice allowed the executive to interpret *public* rights under treaties politically, without fear of judicial pronouncement.[8] More recently, however, the President has grown so dominant that the checks of congressional participation in foreign relations are becoming increasingly inadequate. The rela-

[7] C. Whittaker & W. Coffin, *Law, Order and Civil Disobedience* (1967).

[8] Where public rights are involved in a treaty, the courts accept the interpretation of the political departments. "So far as treaties are regarded as international compacts the national rights and obligations accruing thereunder are determined by the political departments of the government." I. Willoughby, *Constitutional Law of the United States* 578 (2d edn. 1929). C. Post, *The Supreme Court and Political Questions* 81 (1936).

tions between the President and Congress have been reviewed by the United States Senate Foreign Relations Committee.[9] The Committee pointed out that:

> Our country has come far toward the concentration in its national executive of unchecked power over foreign relations, particularly over the disposition and use of the armed forces. So far has this process advanced that, in the committee's view, it is no longer accurate to characterize our government, in matters of foreign relations, as one of separated powers checked and balanced against each other.[10]

It cited with approval the language of the Supreme Court in *Myers v. United States*:

> The doctrine of the separation of powers was adopted by the Convention of 1787, not to promote efficiency but to preclude the exercise of arbitrary power. The purpose was, not to avoid friction, but, by means of the inevitable friction incident to the distribution of the governmental powers among three departments, to save the people from autocracy.[11]

The Committee concluded as follows:

> Claims to unlimited executive authority over the use of armed force are made on grounds of both legitimacy and necessity. The committee finds both sets of contentions unsound.
>
> The argument for legitimacy is based on a misreading of both the Constitution and the experience of American history. A careful study of the Constitution and of the intent of the Framers as set forth in the extensive documentation which they bequeathed to us leaves not the slightest doubt that, except for repelling sudden attacks on the United States, the founders of our country intended decisions to initiate either general or limited hostilities against foreign countries to be made by the Congress, not by the executive.[12]

It is indeed salutory to recall that our major wars were the outcome of presidential policies in the making of which Congress played a distinctly secondary role.[13]

---

[9] Hearings on S. 151 Before the Senate Comm. on Foreign Relations, 90th Cong., 1st Sess. (1967). See also S. Rep. No. 797, 90th Cong., 1st Sess. (1967).

[10] S. Rep. No. 797, 90th Cong., 1st Sess. (1967).

[11] 272 U.S. 52, 293 (1926).

[12] S. Rep. No. 797, 90th Cong., 1st Sess. 23 (1967).

[13] E. Corwin, *The President: Office and Powers* 249 (3d edn. rev. 1948).

The adjustment of the relationship between the legislative and the executive branches in making decisions about war and peace which is recommended by the Senate Committee, requires the fencing in of presidential powers by *political* action. These powers have already been formally checked by treaties, restricting the freedom of the United States to wage war and regulating the conduct of hostilities—treaties such as the Kellogg Briand Pact, the United Nations Charter, and the 1949 Geneva Conventions. The powers of the Presidency are not left intact by these treaties. In a well-known opinion, Mr. Justice Miller discussed the President's duty to take care that the laws be faithfully executed:

Is this duty limited to the enforcement of acts of Congress or of treaties of the United States according to their express terms, or does it include the rights, duties and obligations growing out of the Constitution itself, our international relations, and all the protection implied by the nature of the government under the Constitution?"[14]

As Corwin reminds us, Attorney General William Wirt had argued that the "laws" to which the "faithfully executed" clause referred comprised not only the Constitution, statutes, and treaties, but also "those general laws of nations which govern the intercourse between the United States and foreign nations."[15] The United States, having become a member of this society of nations, was obliged to respect the rights of other nations under that code of laws and the President, as the chief executive officer of the laws, and as the agent charged with superintendence of the nation's foreign intercourse, was bound to rectify injury and preserve peace. When Theodore Roosevelt "took Panama," Senator Morgan (a precursor of Senators Morse and Fulbright) said in the Senate:

The President has paused in his usurpation of the war power, but not until he had gone to so great a length that he believed Congress would be compelled to follow the flag to save appearances and adopt a war that he was actually waging against Colombia under guise of treaty obligations to protect the transit across the Isthmus of Panama. . . . To obtain ratification of his excessive adventure he comes to the Senate and appeals to its special treaty-making power to join him in giving sanction to the war he had begun and is conducting with a display of war power at sea that is far greater than was mustered

[14] In re Neagle, 135 U.S. 1, 64 (1890).   [15] 1 Op. Att'y Gen. 566, 570 (1822).

in the war with Spain, all under the pretext of protecting the isthmian transit. He asks the Senate to usurp the power of Congress to declare war, instead of making his appeal to Congress.[16]

The Senate, rather than the courts, was the effective arena for charging that the President's conduct in Panama had violated the treaty obligations of the United States. The courts' noninvolvement was complete. This passivity ended in *Youngstown Sheet & Tool Co. v. Sawyer*[17] in which the Supreme Court reviewed the President's authority to seize the nation's steel mills, distinguishing *Mississippi v. Johnson*,[18] in which it had confessed its inability to enjoin the President from exceeding his constitutional powers. Mr. Justice Brennan, speaking for the Court in *Baker v. Carr*,[19] indicated that the question whether the courts would adjudicate is itself a constitutional question:

> Deciding whether a matter has in any measure been committed by the Constitution to another branch of government, or whether the action of that branch exceeds whatever authority has been committed, is itself a delicate exercise in constitutional interpretation, and is a responsibility of this Court as ultimate interpreter of the Constitution.[20]

IV

The Supreme Court and the Vietnam War—The attempts to challenge the legality of the United States action in Vietnam have failed so far even to evince a consideration of plaintiffs' claims on their merits. The Supreme Court has had the opportunity to hear the issue. In *Mitchell v. United States*,[21] the Court denied certiorari over the dissent of Mr. Justice Douglas. In that case, petitioner did not report for induction as ordered, was indicted, and sentenced to 5 years imprisonment. The issue of the legality of the war was raised as a defense in the criminal prosecution. His case raised a number of questions:

1. Whether the Treaty of London is a treaty within the meaning of article VI, cl. 2?
2. Whether the question as to the waging of an aggressive "war" is in the context of this criminal prosecution a justiciable question?
3. Whether the Vietnam episode is a "war" in the sense of the Treaty?

16 Cited in Corwin, supra note 13, at 475-76.
17 343 U.S. 593 (1952).
18 71 U.S. (4 Wall) 475 (1867).
19 369 U.S. 186 (1962).
20 Id. at 210-11.
21 386 U.S. 972 (1967).

4. Whether petitioner has standing to raise the question?

5. Whether, if he has, the Treaty may be tendered as a defense in this criminal case or in amelioration of the punishment.[22]

Mr. Justice Douglas was of the opinion that certiorari should have been granted. He referred to "a considerable body of opinion that our actions in Vietnam constitute the waging of an aggressive 'war,' " and indicated that the question raised was a recurring one in Selective Service cases. The dissent of Justices Douglas and Stewart in the per curiam decision to deny certiorari in *Mora v. McNamara*[23] has now raised the remote possibility that the courts may be willing at some future time to review the legitimacy of government actions in the light of governing treaty obligations. In *Mora,* the three accused had already been inducted and convicted of willful disobedience of an order in violation of article 90 of the Uniform Code of Military Justice.[24] In one instance, the order directed the individual concerned to board a sedan which would take him to an air force base for further transportation to Vietnam. On other occasions, the individuals had been ordered to board an aircraft for transportation to Vietnam. The main contention of the three soldiers was that each of the orders was unlawful because American participation in the Vietnam conflict is illegal. The United States Court of Military Appeals held that under domestic law the presence of American troops in Vietnam is unassailable and that the legality of such presence under international law is not a justiciable issue. The Supreme Court proceedings arose out of a suit brought by petitioners to prevent the Secretary of Defense and the Secretary of the Army from carrying out orders for their transportation to Vietnam; petitioners requested a declaratory judgment that United States military activity in Vietnam is "illegal." The suit did not involve an appeal from the conviction for disobedience. The suit was dismissed by the District Court and the Court of Appeals affirmed. The Supreme Court denied certiorari, over the dissent of Justices Stewart and Douglas.[25] Mr. Justice Stewart indicated that the following questions were raised by that case, which had not been raised in the *Mitchell* case:

I. Is the present United States military activity in Vietnam a "war" within the meaning of Article I, Section 8, Clause 11, of the Constitution?

---

[22] Id. at 973.   [23] 389 U.S. 934 (1967).

[24] United States v. Johnson, 18 U.S.C.M.A. 246 (1967).

[25] Luftig v. McNamara, 373 F.2d 664 (D.C. Cir.), cert. denied, 389 U.S. 934 (1967).

II. If so, may the Executive constitutionally order the petitioners to participate in that military activity, when no war has been declared by the Congress?

III. Of what relevance to Question II are the present treaty obligations of the United States?

IV. Of what relevance to Question II is the Joint Congressional ("Tonkin Gulf") Resolution of August 10, 1964?

   (a) Do present United States military operations fall within the terms of the Joint Resolution?

   (b) If the Joint Resolution purports to give the Chief Executive authority to commit United States forces to armed conflict limited in scope only by his own absolute discretion, is the Resolution a constitutionally impermissible delegation of all or part of Congress' power to declare war?

These are large and deeply troubling questions. Whether the Court would ultimately reach them depends, of course, upon the resolution of serious preliminary issues of justiciability. We cannot make these problems go away simply by refusing to hear the case of three obscure Army privates. I intimate not even a tentative answer upon any of these matters, but I think the Court should squarely face them by granting certiorari and setting this case for oral argument.[26]

In a more elaborate dissent, Mr. Justice Douglas outlined the governing provisions of domestic and international law and repeated his view that the petitioners should be told whether "their case is beyond judicial cognizance. If it is not, we should then reach the merits of their claims, on which I intimate no views whatsoever."[27]

Both in *Mitchell* and in *Mora*, the Supreme Court denied certiorari. In both cases, the dissents turned on the question whether the Supreme Court ought to hear plaintiffs' arguments on the serious preliminary issues of justiciability. In these cases, the Supreme Court refused even to hear arguments on the justiciability of plaintiffs' contentions, let alone on the merits of their claims.

V

The Political Question Doctrine—The political question doctrine ferries in its shallow wake webs of connected rationales. This doctrine is of primordial importance in any analysis of the concept of state lawlessness—and of the consistency of state action with the Constitu-

[26] 389 U.S. at 934-35.   [27] Id. at 939.

tion. Professor Bickel in his influential book, *The Least Dangerous Branch*, wrote that the doctrine of political question is the culmination of a progression of devices for withholding the ultimate constitutional judgment of the Supreme Court.[28] The Supreme Court, in his view, has a considerable area of choice in deciding whether, when, and how much to adjudicate. This choice, however, is not regulated by principle—it is not that of principled adjudication. The essential fact in his view is that the Court wields a three-fold power:

> It may strike down legislation as inconsistent with principle. It may validate or, in Charles L. Black's better word, "legitimate" legislation as consistent with principle. Or *it may do neither*. It may do neither, and therein lies the secret of its ability to maintain itself in the tension between principle and expediency. . . .
>
> When the Court, however, stays its hand, and makes clear that it is staying its hand and not legitimating, then the political processes are given relatively free play. Such a decision needs relatively little justification in terms of consistency with democratic theory. It needs more to be justified as compatible with the court's role as defender of the faith, proclaimer and protector of the goals.[29]

Set against this view is the theory that the Court must be deemed to legitimate whatever it is not justified in striking down and that the "practical" result of not striking down action or legislation is the same as if there had been a decision to legitimate. The corollary of this theory is that the courts are the only possible tribunal to make a determination of constitutionality; if the courts declare, when a particular action is challenged, that they have no jurisdiction to decide the question, this is a declaration that no power exists to make a finding of unconstitutionality. The "judicial monopoly" theory thus reserves to the Supreme Court the exclusive right to pass on the consistency of state action and legislation with the Constitution: since only the courts can "invalidate" state action, whatever they fail to invalidate is thereby made legitimate.[30]

---

[28] A. Bickel, *The Least Dangerous Branch* (1962). See also McCloskey, Foreword: The Reapportionment Case (pts. I-III), 76 *Harv. L. Rev.* 54, 59, 64 (1962); Scharpf, Judicial Review and the Political Question—A Functional Analysis, 75 *Yale L. J.* 517 (1966).

[29] A Bickel, *The Least Dangerous Branch* 69, 70 (1966).

[30] D. Morgan, *Congress and the Constitution* (1966); Hughes, The Political Question Doctrine and Civil Disobedience, 43 *N.Y.U.L. Rev.* (1968) comments on the relationship between civil disobedience and the political question doctrine raised by this author in a public debate.

Another theory regarding the doctrine has been advanced by Professor Wechsler:

> All the doctrine can defensibly imply is that the courts are called upon to judge whether the Constitution has committed to another agency of government the autonomous determination of the issue raised, a finding that itself requires an interpretation.
>
> I submit that in cases of the kind that I have mentioned [political question cases], as in others that I do not pause to state, the only proper judgment that may lead to an abstention from decision is that the Constitution has committed the determination of the issue to another agency of government than the Courts. Difficult as it may be to make that judgment wisely, whatever factors may be rightly weighed in situations where the answer is not clear, what is involved is in itself an act of constitutional interpretation, to be made and judged by standards that should govern the interpretive process generally. That, I submit, is *toto caelo* different from a broad discretion to abstain or intervene.
>
> The Supreme Court does have a discretion, to be sure, to grant or to deny review of judgments of the lower courts in situations in which the jurisdictional statute permits certiorari but does not provide for an appeal. I need not say that this is an entirely different matter.[31]

In *Baker v. Carr*,[32] the Supreme Court carefully considered the various aspects of the political question doctrine. Mr. Justice Brennan's opinion for the Court, despite some comments to the contrary, did not wholly equate the political question doctrine with the separation of powers problem. It identified six distinct considerations involved in the doctrine:

> Prominent on the surface of any case held to involve a political question is found a textually demonstrable constitutional commitment of the issue to a coordinate political department; or a lack of judicially discoverable and manageable standards for resolving it; or the impossibility of deciding without an initial policy determination of a kind clearly for nonjudicial discretion; or the impossibility of a court's undertaking independent resolution without expressing lack of respect due coordinate branches of government; or

[31] H. Wechsler, *Principles, Politics and Fundamental Law* 11, 12-13 (1961).
[32] 369 U.S. 186 (1962).

an unusual need for unquestioning adherence to a political decision already made; or the potentiality of embarrassment from multifarious pronouncements by various departments on one question.[33]

Indeed, although the political question doctrine is "primarily" a function of the separation of powers, the other itemized factors are also considered by the Court:

The question here is the consistency of state action with the Federal Constitution. We have no question decided, or to be decided, by a political branch of government coequal with this court. Nor do we risk embarrassment of our government abroad, or grave disturbance at home if we take issue with Tennessee as to the constitutionality of her action here challenged. Nor need the appellants, in order to succeed in this action, ask the Court to enter upon policy determinations for which judicially manageable standards are lacking. Judicial standards under the Equal Protection Clause are well developed and familiar, and it has been open to courts since the enactment of the Fourteenth Amendment to determine, if on the particular facts they must, that a discrimination reflects *no* policy, but simply arbitrary and capricious action.[34]

In a noteworthy dissent, Mr. Justice Frankfurter urged the consideration of factors other than those involved in the separation of powers doctrine:

It may well impair the Court's position as the ultimate organ of "the supreme Law of the Land" in that vast range of legal problems, often strongly entangled in popular feeling, on which this Court must pronounce. The Court's authority—possessed of neither the purse nor the sword—ultimately rests on sustained public confidence in its moral sanction. Such feeling must be nourished by the Court's complete detachment, in fact and in *appearance,* from political entanglements and by abstention from injecting itself into the clash of political forces in political settlements.[35]

Without resorting to more detailed analysis of the Court's decisions involving the doctrine of political question, it is possible to conclude that in its *Baker v. Carr* formulation the doctrine features, at the very least, an amalgam of prudential and legal considerations dominated by

[33] Id. at 217.
[34] Id. at 226 (footnote omitted).   [35] Id. at 267 (emphasis added).

the separation of powers theory. This amalgam contains express reference to the respect due to coordinate branches of the government, to the possibility of an unusual need for unquestioning adherence to a political decision already made, and to the risk of embarrassing the Government abroad as well as that of grave disturbances at home. These references suggest that the Court might well be guided by considerations other than principle, despite Professor Wechsler's appeal. Politics, foreign relations, and prudential calculations are all expressly recognized as proper considerations for determinations whether to adjudicate a case or not. The Court's decision in *Baker v. Carr* appears to bear out Professor Bickel's theory about the Court's triad of functions. Under Professor Bickel's theory, under Professor Wechsler's plea, as well as under the Court's decision in *Baker v. Carr*, it can be stated that the constitutional validity of state action remains undetermined whenever the Court invokes or fails to review lower-court decisions in reliance upon the political question doctrine. In other words, the Court's dismissal of a case impeaching the validity of state action, when it relies on the political question doctrine, *does not amount to a legitimation* of the challenged action. (This, of course, must be distinguished from denial of certiorari by the Supreme Court.) The constitutionality or validity of state action then remains to be determined by means other than judicial proceedings. Despite the presumption in favor of the legality of government acts, one *cannot*, under the American legal system, claim that government orders must always be presumed to be valid unless and until invalidated by the courts.

It has also been argued that when a citizen in good faith believes in the illegality of the Government's conduct, public expressions of such belief cannot be the basis of an indictment or crime. In the Supreme Court's decision in *Keegan v. United States*, Mr. Justice Roberts said: "One with innocent motives, who honestly believes a law is unconstitutional and, therefore, not obligatory, may well counsel that the law shall not be obeyed; that its command shall be resisted until a court shall have held it valid."[36]

In considering the political question doctrine it is instructive to note that legal experts, judges, and lawyers from 75 countries, meeting under the auspices of the International Commission of Jurists agreed that the existence of effective safeguards against the possible abuse of power by the executive is an all important aspect of the rule of law. Judicial con-

[36] 325 U.S. 478, 493-94 (1945).

trol over the acts of the executive should insure, in the opinion of these experts, that "The executive acts within the powers conferred upon it by the constitution and such powers as are not unconstitutional"; and also:

(b) Whenever the rights, interests or status of any person are infringed or threatened by executive action, such person shall have an inviolable right of access to the Courts and *unless the Court be satisfied that such action was legal*, free from bias and not unreasonable, be entitled to appropriate protection;

(c) Where executive action is taken under a discretionary power, the Courts shall be entitled to examine the basis on which the discretion has been exercised and if it has been exercised in a proper and reasonable way and in accordance with the principles of natural justice;

(d) The powers validly granted to the executive are not used for a collateral or improper purpose.[37]

To assert that government actions are necessarily valid unless and until disallowed by the courts runs counter to this concept of the rule of law. This contradicts, moreover, the premises of the Declaration of Independence and of the Universal Declaration of Human Rights.

VI

Resistance to Illegitimate Authority—American constitutional law is revolutionary in origin. This historical fact is not without significance for theories of civil disobedience. The *ius resistendi*, that is, the right of the ruled to resist the ruler, if need be by use of violence in case of unlawful usurpation of power, played a decisive role in the formation of modern constitutional law. Some early American bills of rights recognized it. Article 3 of the Virginia Bill of Rights of 1776 provided that:

When any government shall be found inadequate or contrary to these purposes, a majority of the community have an indubitable, unalienable, and indefeasible right to refrm, alter or and abolish it, in such manner as shall be judged most conducive to the public weal.

[37] Int'l Commission of Jurists, *The Rule of Law and Human Rights* 15 (1966) (emphasis added).

In the Maryland Bill of Rights of 1776, it was provided that: "The doctrine of non-resistance against arbitrary power and oppression is absurd, slavish, and destructive of the good and happiness of mankind."

The French Declaration of the Rights of Man of 1789 provided that: "The end of all political association is the conservation of the natural and inalienable rights of man. These rights are liberty, security, property and resistance to tyranny."

In the French Declaration, therefore, the right to resist tyranny was elevated to one of the four natural and fundamental rights of man. These historical documents reflect political doctrines similar to those which inspired the Founders of the American Constitution and the drafters of the Declaration of Independence.

Emphasis on the right to resistance was characteristic of eighteenth century constitutional theory. In the nineteenth century, however, the duty of obedience to the state was again emphasized. Under the much criticized Austinian model, obedience was due to commands of the sovereign who was defined, in empirical terms, as a determinate (group of) human superior(s) not in the habit of obedience to a like superior, but in receipt of habitual obedience from the bulk of a given society. The Austinian sovereign, a political superior who can compel others to obey, *is incapable of legal limitation.*[38] In the still influential Austinian model, obedience to the law is equated with obedience to the commands of the sovereign—obedience to law and obedience to constituted authorities are then one and the same.

This identification of the sovereign with legality has been challenged in twentieth century legal theory. Under the theories of Salmond, Kelsen, and Hart, the legal sovereign cannot be accounted for in empirical terms. Rather, legal sovereignty is a juridically defined concept which has little meaning outside normative contexts.[39] Obedience to law is one thing; it must not be confused with obedience to a determinate human superior or superiors.

These rival theories—obedience to the commands of a determinate person or persons and deference to rules identified as legal—are reflected in attitudes to civil disobedience and resistance. Government lawlessness is a concept difficult to reconcile with the Austinian command theory. It is more accessible under the theories of Hart and Kelsen. Under the command theory, the crucial problem is to identify

[38] J. Austin, *The Province of Jurisprudence Determined* 254 (Hart ed. 1954).
[39] Id., Introduction by H. Hart.

the sovereign and the lawfully constituted authorities. Once this is done, doubts about the legality of commands can be resolved with ease. Under the other theories mentioned, the crucial problem is to identify the juridical limits of state authority under the rules of the system. The command theory calls for an empirical test of political supremacy, while the other theories call for a decision as to legal validity.

The difficulties caused by the courts' failure to adjudicate key issues involving government actions are compounded when authoritative legal provisions are on the statute books and govern the very issues which the courts refuse to hear. This involves the ingredients that make up what Lon Fuller calls the "internal morality" of the law: congruence between official action and the rules as announced:

> We arrive finally at the most complex of all the desiderata that make up the internal morality of the law—congruence between official action and the law. This congruence may be destroyed or impaired in a great variety of ways. . . . Even the question of "standing" to raise constitutional issues is relevant in this connection; haphazard and fluctuating principles concerning this matter can produce a broken and arbitrary pattern of correspondence between the constitution and its realization in practice.[40]

Repeated failure by the courts to apply the Constitution and the supreme law of the land raises concern about the absence of a discernible link between the orders of the President and the Constitution which he is sworn to execute. Thus the Constitution and treaties might just as well not have been there at all if they were not reflected in presidential actions in the Vietnam War.

A total failure by the courts and the executive to apply governing constitutional and treaty law would result, according to Fuller, in something that is not properly called "law" at all:

> Certainly there can be no rational ground for asserting that a man can have a moral obligation to obey a legal rule that does not exist, or is kept secret from him, or that came into existence only after he had acted, or was unintelligible, or was contradicted by another rule of the same system, or commanded the impossible, or changed every minute. It may not be impossible for a man to obey a rule that is disregarded by those charged with its administration, but at

---

[40] L. Fuller, *The Morality of Law* 81 (1964).

some point obedience becomes futile,—as futile, in fact, as casting a vote that will never be counted.[41]

His conclusion is that in situations in which the inner morality of law is impaired:

> there can be no simple principle by which to test the citizen's obligation of fidelity of law, anymore than there can be such a principle for testing his rights to engage in a general revolution. One thing is, however, clear. *A mere respect for constituted authority must not be confused with fidelity to law.*[42]

In a similar vein, Hart suggests that unless a legal system is capable of protecting what he calls "the minimum content of natural law," there is then no point in having a legal system at all. Significantly the link between minimum natural law, human rights and the right to rebel against illegitimate authority has been reaffirmed in the 1948 Universal Declaration of Human Rights, which confirms in its preamble that:

> Recognition of the inherent dignity and of the equal and of the inalienable rights of all members of the human family is the foundation of freedom, justice, and peace in the world. . . . Disregard and contempt for human rights have resulted in barbarous acts which have outraged the conscience of mankind, and the event of the world in which human beings shall enjoy freedom of speech and belief and freedom from fear and want has been proclaimed the highest aspiration of the common people. . . . It is essential, if man is not to be compelled to have recourse, as a last resort, to rebellion against tyranny and oppression, that human rights should be protected by the rule of law.

The principles of the 1948 Declaration are now generally recognized to be obligatory for the member states of the United Nations, and to constitute a highly authoritative interpretation of the United Nations' Charter, which is itself incorporated in United States law under the supremacy clause.[43]

---

[41] Id. at 39.

[42] Id. at 41 (emphasis added).

[43] Commission to Study the Organization of Peace, The United Nations and Human Rights, 18th Report 5 (1968): "While the Declaration is not directly binding on United Nations members, it strengthens the obligations under the Charter by making them more precise. . . . Moreover, the Declaration can be considered as an authoritative interpretation of the Charter of the highest order."

VII

In conclusion, theories of resistance to illegitimate authority have been founded on a number of alternative propositions:

1. On the right of the ruled to resist the ruler, if need be by means of violence, in case of any unlawful usurpation of power (under national or international law);
2. On the right of the ruled to resist the ruler when the laws of God or the dictates of morality so require;
3. On the right of the ruled to resist the ruler when fundamental human rights are not protected by the rule of law;
4. On the right of the ruled to resist the ruler when there is a general and drastic deterioration of legality or pervasive uncertainty about the legality of the ruler's own actions;
5. On the right of the ruled to resist the ruler in the absence of procedures for achieving peaceful change.

The heightening of domestic tensions in the United States and in other countries is accompanied by the refinement of juridical theories reaffirming the right of resistance to illegitimate authority. This marks a return to eighteenth century theories which molded the institutions of this nation.[44]

[44] On the subject of this essay in general, see Allen, Civil Disobedience and the Legal Order (2 pts.) , 36 *U. Cinn. L. Rev.* 1, 175 (1967) .

Congress, the President, and the Power to Commit Forces to Combat

Note from *Harvard Law Review*

Over a very long period in our history, practice and precedent have confirmed the constitutional authority to engage United States forces in hostilities without a declaration of war.

—Department of State, *Memorandum*.[1]

It is . . . imperative that Congress guard zealously against any executive usurpation of its exclusive power to declare, or to decline to declare war.

—Lawyers Committee on American Policy
Toward Vietnam, *Memorandum*.[2]

The question of the legality of the Vietnam conflict has two distinct aspects: the justifiability of United States intervention under international law, and the constitutionality of such action under domestic law. The first has been the subject of considerable debate; [3] the second has received less attention. Where it has not been dismissed as academic [4] the issue has usually been approached polemically. One side vigorously asserts the constitutional authority of the President to act as Commander in Chief of the armed forces, while the other side with equal vigor brandishes that provision of the Constitution which gives Congress the power to declare war. The two sides assert claims which have support in constitutional history and are not incompatible but which bypass the real issue: how is the President's authority as Chief Executive and Commander in Chief to be reconciled with Congress' power to declare war? Thus phrased, the question calls for an analysis of the proper constitutional allocation between the President and Congress of the power to control the use of force in foreign affairs.[5]

---

[1] U.S. Dep't of State, *The Legality of United States Participation in the Defense of Viet-Nam*, 54 DEP'T STATE BULL. 474, 488 (1966), reprinted in *Symposium — Legality of United States Participation in the Viet Nam Conflict*, 75 YALE L.J. 1084, 1085 (1966) [hereinafter cited as *Memorandum*].

[2] Lawyers Comm. on American Policy Toward Vietnam, *American Policy Vis-à-Vis Vietnam, Memorandum of Law*, in 112 CONG. REC. 2666, 2672 (1966).

[3] *See, e.g., Symposium — Legality of United States Participation in the Viet Nam Conflict*, 75 YALE L.J. 1084 (1966); Partan, *Legal Aspects of the Vietnam Conflict*, 46 B.U.L. REV. 281 (1966); Comment, *The United States in Vietnam: A Case Study in the Law of Intervention*, 50 CALIF. L. REV. 515 (1962).

[4] *See* Wright, *Legal Aspects of the Viet-Nam Situation*, 60 AM. J. INT'L L. 750, 768 (1966) ("[t]he issue seems unimportant in view of the broad Constitutional powers of the President to use armed force without Congressional support or declaration of war"). *Compare* Moore, *International Law and the United States Role in Viet Nam: A Reply*, 76 YALE L.J. 1051, 1091–93 (1967), *with* Falk, *International Law and the United States Role in the Viet Nam War*, 75 YALE L.J. 1122, 1154 (1966).

[5] The recent hearings before the Senate Foreign Relations Committee constitute the most thorough attempt to date to approach the issue in these terms. *See Hearings on S. Res. 151 Before the Senate Comm. on Foreign Relations,*

I. Sources of the Power: The Textual Authority

A. The Power of Congress to Declare War

1. The Original Understanding. — Article I, section 8 confers on Congress a number of specific powers relating to the regulation and control of the armed forces; among these is the power "to declare War." [6] Construed literally, the clause would give Congress no more than the purely formal power to issue a document called "a declaration of war." The function of such a document, it might be argued, would be to distinguish "war" in the constitutional sense from all other hostilities. Its issuance would effectuate certain legal results with potentially profound consequences. Treaties would be canceled; trading, contracts, and debts with the enemy would be suspended; vast emergency powers would be authorized domestically; and legal relations between neutral states and the belligerents would be altered. [7] But though there may have been a time when these changes in legal status were uniquely the result of the issuance of a formal declaration, this is clearly no longer true today. [8] Countries have long engaged in undeclared hostilities which in terms of the effort involved, the impact on citizens, and the effect on domestic and international legal relations are often indistinguishable from a formally declared war. [9] Both in American courts [10] and in international contexts [11] rules of law which become effective on a finding that "war" exists do not depend critically on ascertaining that certain formal steps have been taken. [12] The only function which uniquely remains for the formal declaration of war is largely that of a solemn act of state which serves as a means of arousing popular support at home and abroad and which is usually reserved for extreme cases. In fact, the formal declaration of war in the modern context is often deliberately avoided precisely because of the apparent commitment to total victory

---

90th Cong., 1st Sess. (1967) [hereinafter cited as *Hearings on National Commitments*]; Senate Comm. on Foreign Relations, National Commitments, S. Rep. No. 797, 90th Cong., 1st Sess. (1967) [hereinafter cited as National Commitments Report]. The result of the hearings — Senate Resolution 187 — is set out at note 140 *infra*. A recent and comprehensive survey of the presidential and congressional precedents in this area may be found in R. Russell, The United States Congress and the Power To Use Military Force Abroad, Apr. 15, 1967 (unpublished thesis in Fletcher School of Law and Diplomacy Library).

[6] U.S. Const. art. I, § 8:

The Congress shall have Power . . . [t]o define and punish Piracies and Felonies committed on the high Seas, and Offences against the Law of Nations; [t]o declare War, grant Letters of Marque and Reprisal, and make Rules concerning Captures on Land and Water; [t]o raise and support Armies, but no Appropriation of Money to that Use shall be for a longer Term than two Years; [t]o provide and maintain a Navy; [t]o make Rules for the Government and Regulation of the land and naval Forces . . . .

[7] *See* Prize Cases, 67 U.S. (2 Black) 635, 687–88 (1862) (dissenting opinion); J. Rogers, World Policing and the Constitution 27, 34–35 (1945).

[8] *See* Eagleton, *The Form and Function of the Declaration of War*, 32 Am. J. Int'l L. 19, 20, 32–35 (1938).

[9] *See* F. Grob, The Relativity of War and Peace 283–89 (1949).

[10] *See* note 23 *infra*.

[11] F. Grob, *supra* note 9, *passim*.

[12] *See* U.S. Dep't of State, *The Question of a Formal Declaration of War in Vietnam*, in Senate Comm. on Foreign Relations, 90th Cong., 1st. Sess., Background Information Relating to Southeast Asia and Vietnam 175–77 (Comm. Print 3d rev. ed. 1967).

and the general hardening of attitudes likely to result.[13] Hence, a literal interpretation of the clause would give Congress a minimal role under modern conditions: the President would be able to "make" what in virtually all respects amounts to "war"; he just could not "declare" it.

That the war-declaring clause is not confined to such a narrow interpretation is made clear from the history of the clause in the Constitutional Convention. An earlier draft by the Committee of Detail gave Congress power to "make" rather than "declare" war. In direct contrast to the power of the British sovereign to initiate war on his own prerogative, the clause was the result of a deliberate decision by the framers to vest the power to embark on war in the body most broadly representative of the people.[14] The clause remained in its original form in the committee drafts several weeks after other foreign relations powers had been transferred from the whole Congress to the Senate and then to the President.[15] When the proposal to substitute "declare" for "make" was introduced, the debates over the issue indicate that the new wording was not intended to shift from the legislature to the Executive this general power to engage the country in war. At most, the sole reason for the substitution was to confirm the Executive's power "to repel sudden attacks." [16] In all other cases the commitment of the country to a trial of force with another nation was to remain the prerogative of Congress.[17] Both the purpose and

---

[13] *See id.* at 175; Falk, *supra* note 4, at 1154.

[14] C. BERDAHL, WAR POWERS OF THE EXECUTIVE IN THE UNITED STATES 79 (1921); THE FEDERALIST No. 69 (A. Hamilton). Later comments by Hamilton indicate that in his view the power to embark on war was ordinarily an executive function which in the case of the United States was deliberately given to the legislature. *See* 7 WORKS OF ALEXANDER HAMILTON 81 (J. Hamilton ed. 1851). There is considerable evidence from the history of the colonial period and experience under the Articles of Confederation, however, that this power, in America at least, was generally considered an inherently legislative function. *See* R. Russell, *supra* note 5, at 22, 27; *cf.* J. ROGERS, *supra* note 7, at 29–31.

[15] *See* J. ROGERS, *supra* note 7, at 28.

[16] This is the reason advanced by Madison during the debate over the proposed change. An earlier vote had resulted in a defeat of the motion to change the language from "make" to "declare." At least one delegate, Mr. Ellsworth, changed his vote when it was pointed out that "make war" might be construed to give Congress power to "conduct war" after it had begun — a function clearly meant to be given to the Executive. *See* 2 M. FARRAND, THE RECORDS OF THE FEDERAL CONVENTION OF 1787, at 313, 318–19 (rev. ed. 1937). Since it is impossible to tell what reasons actually motivated those who voted for the change, it is not completely accurate to conclude that the Executive was to have even the power to "repel sudden attacks." At any rate Mr. Ellsworth's remarks make untenable any suggestion that the change in wording was designed to alter to any substantial degree Congress' power to "make" war. Other views expressed during the debates are recorded by Madison as follows. Mr. Pinckney objected to the original version, arguing that the House of Representatives was too numerous and, hence, too slow to be vested with the sole power to make war. He agreed with Hamilton that the Senate would be a better repository for this power. Mr. Butler felt the same objections were applicable to the Senate and the power should be given to the President, who would not make war except when the nation would support it. To this Mr. Sherman objected that the Executive "should be able to repel and not commence war," and Mr. Gerry expressed the view that he "never expected to hear in a republic a motion to empower the Executive alone to declare war." He supported Madison's motion to insert "declare," striking out "make" and leaving to the Executive "the power to repel sudden attacks." *Id.* at 318–19.

[17] What little is added to the Convention debates by the debates over ratification indicates that the most that was left to the President was the power to

intent of article I, section 8 are thus more accurately conveyed by construing that clause to give Congress not simply the power formally to "declare," but also the power generally to "initiate" war.[18]

2. *The Meaning of "War."* — If article I, section 8 is interpreted to mean that there shall be no war — declared or otherwise — unless Congress takes the initiative, the problem of defining "war" and "initiation" of war must be faced. From the beginning it has been recognized that not every involvement of the armed forces can be a "war" requiring congressional action.[19] In the modern context where international conflict has so many forms, the problem is even more difficult. Despite occasional judicial attempts to discover a unique, general legal definition applicable in all contexts,[20] it seems clear that no verbal formula can identify one class of armed hostilities as properly subject to rules and considerations wholly different from those applicable to other classes.[21] At best "war" will assume different meanings depending on the context which prompts the investigation,[22] whether it be the interpretation of a contract, a life insurance policy, a statute, or a constitution.[23] Accordingly, the meaning of "war" in the context of the constitutional allocation of power to use force in foreign relations must be determined with reference to the purpose of the war-declaring

---

defend against imminent invasion when Congress was not in session. *See* R. Russell, *supra* note 5, at 63.

[18] *See Hearings on National Commitments* 9–10; *cf.* Corwin, *The President's Power,* NEW REPUBLIC, Jan. 29, 1951, at 15.

[19] *Cf.* J. ROGERS, *supra* note 7, at 21.

[20] *Compare* Prize Cases, 67 U.S. (2 Black) 635, 666 (1863) ("[w]ar has been well defined to be, 'That state in which a nation prosecutes its right by force'"), *with* Bas v. Tingy, 4 U.S. (4 Dall.) 37, 40 (1800) (separate opinion) ("[i]t may . . . be safely laid down, that every contention by force between two nations, in external matters, under the authority of their respective governments, is . . . war").

[21] *See* Osgood, *War and Policy,* in AMERICAN DEFENSE POLICY 109, 114 (1965).

[22] *Compare* Bas v. Tingy, 4 U.S. (4 Dall.) 37 (1800) (hostilities with France from 1798 to 1800 constituted war within the meaning of a statute granting recovery of salvage value for private vessels recaptured from "the enemy"), *with* Gray v. United States, 21 Ct. Cl. 340 (1886) (same conflict was not a war for purposes of a 1778 treaty with France whose terms were to remain in force only while France was "at peace" with the United States).

[23] The United States Court of Military Appeals in determining that the Korean conflict constituted a war within the meaning of that term as used in the Uniform Code of Military Justice gave the following reasons for its decision:

> We believe a finding that this is a time of war, within the meaning of the language of the Code, is compelled by the very nature of the present conflict; the manner in which it is carried on; the movement to, and the presence of large numbers of American men and women on, the battlefields of Korea; the casualties involved; the sacrifices required; the drafting of recruits to maintain the large number of persons in the military service; the national emergency legislation enacted and being enacted; the executive orders promulgated; and the tremendous sums being expended for the express purpose of keeping our Army, Navy and Air Force in the Korean theatre of operations.

United States v. Bancroft, 3 U.S.C.M.A. 3, 5, 11 C.M.R. 3, 5 (1953).

For a review of this and similar cases attempting to determine whether the Korean conflict was a war see Pye, *The Legal Status of the Koeran Hostilities,* 45 GEO. L.J. 45 (1956). For an illustration of the difficulties of defining "war" even in the context of a life insurance policy compare the majority with the dissenting opinion in New York Life Ins. Co. v. Bennion, 158 F.2d 260 (10th Cir. 1946).

clause: to safeguard the United States against unchecked executive decisions to commit the country to a trial of force.

There are two possible reasons for requiring such a safeguard from the body most directly representative of popular sentiment. The first is that such a decision involves a risk of great economic and physical sacrifice not to be incurred without such approval. The second is that even in cases where no significant physical effort is likely to be required — as, for example, in a conflict with a weak nation unsupported by allies — the very act of using force against a foreign sovereign entails moral and legal consequences sufficiently significant to require an expression of popular approval.[24] These two rationales provide at least a starting point for formulating a definition of "war" which will give operational content to article I, section 8. The first argues for a definition phrased in quantitative terms, which would require congressional action prior to engaging in "major" hostilities above a certain level of intensity. The second would result in a more comprehensive, qualitative definition which would forbid any use of force against a foreign sovereign without prior congressional approval. Much of the early struggle between the President and Congress in this area can be read as an attempt to translate these admittedly vague conceptions into workable guidelines for determining the proper procedures for employing the military in foreign contexts.

B. The President as Commander in Chief and Chief Executive

Discussions of the President's power to control the armed forces invariably focus on the provision in article II that "[t]he President shall be Commander in Chief of the Army and Navy of the United States." As a source of power, however, this provision ought to play a rather meager role. From the first it has been interpreted as simply placing the President at the top of the pyramid of military command, making him, in Hamilton's words, "first general and admiral of the confederacy."[25] Since the clause contains nothing to indicate the purposes for which the President may exercise the power thus granted to command the troops, these purposes must ultimately be found in other provisions of article II. Sections 1 and 3, which vest the "executive power" in the President and require him to "take Care that the Laws be faithfully executed," have long been construed to give the President the power to enforce the laws and "the peace of the United States" by any means he finds necessary.[26] While there has been some dispute over the extent to which inherent or implied powers of his office allow the President to use force without prior statutory authorization in other areas — notably to aid civil authorities or to protect states from domestic violence [27] — the authority of the Presi-

---

[24] Cf. J. ROGERS, supra note 7, at 34–35.

[25] THE FEDERALIST No. 69, at 515–16 (J. Hamilton ed. 1864) (A. Hamilton). This view was endorsed a half century later in a Supreme Court opinion by Chief Justice Taney. See Fleming v. Page, 50 U.S. (9 How.) 603, 615 (1850).

[26] See In re Neagle, 135 U.S. 1, 63–64, 67, 69 (1890); Ex parte Siebold, 100 U.S. 371, 394–95 (1880) (dictum).

[27] See E. CORWIN, THE PRESIDENT: OFFICE AND POWERS 130–39 (4th rev. ed.

dent to use the armed forces, at least in the absence of restrictive legislation, in order to enforce within the United States substantial federal interests evidenced by the nation's laws is now generally accepted.[28]

If the President's power to employ troops extended only to situations involving the maintenance of internal law and order, there would be little room for conflict between presidential power to commit troops to combat and congressional power to initiate war. Except where he was repelling "sudden attacks" the proper exercise of the President's powers should not result in direct conflict with a foreign nation.

While there is some evidence that, absent an attack, the framers never intended troops to be used outside the country without congressional consent,[29] a rapid expansion of presidential power to use force abroad soon took place. The expansion began with the advance of the view that the duties of the Chief Executive included the power to protect American property and lives abroad — a view which received judicial support in the mid-nineteenth century in an opinion by Mr. Justice Nelson.[30] The authority for the exercise of such power seems to have been traced at times to the inherent powers of the Chief Executive [31] and at other times to the explicit duty to "take Care that the Laws be faithfully executed." [32] Although occasional efforts were made to limit this presidential power to the protection of "rights" of person and property as distinguished from the enforcement of broader national "interests," [33] the validity of such a distinction soon became questionable. Since international law as well as statutes and treaties had long been considered part of the "laws" to which the "faithfully executed" clause refers [34] any interests evidenced by those laws became a potential subject for presidential protection by force. Further, even

1957); Note, *Riot Control and the Use of Federal Troops*, 81 HARV. L. REV. 638, 647-52 (1968).

[28] *See In re* Debs, 158 U.S. 564, 582 (1895) ("the entire strength of the nation may be used to enforce in any part of the land the full and free exercise of all national powers and the security of all rights entrusted by the Constitution to its care"); E. CORWIN, *supra* note 27, at 134.

[29] Since neither a standing army nor a navy was originally thought necessary, any military venture abroad would inevitably have required congressional participation in authorizing the expedition by raising troops or calling up the militia. Even where troops were available, resort to Congress was sought prior to their use abroad during the nation's first twenty-five years under the Constitution. *See* R. Russell, *supra* note 5, at 59-60, 146; *cf.* NATIONAL COMMITMENTS REPORT 9.

[30] Durand v. Hollins, 8 F. Cas. 111 (No. 4186) (C.C.S.D.N.Y. 1860). The case arose out of the bombardment of a Nicaraguan town because of the refusal of local authorities to pay reparations for an attack by a mob on the United States consul. (For a detailed account of the incident see 7 J. MOORE, A DIGEST OF INTERNATIONAL LAW 346-54 (1906).) Suit was brought by a private person against the naval officer for the value of property destroyed. Mr. Justice Nelson, then on circuit from the Supreme Court, upheld the defense that the officer was following legitimate orders of the President of the United States, declaring that citizens abroad, no less than citizens at home, are entitled to look to the Executive as head of the nation for the protection of person and property.

[31] *Id.*

[32] *See* M. OFFUTT, THE PROTECTION OF CITIZENS ABROAD BY THE ARMED FORCES OF THE UNITED STATES 5 (1928).

[33] *See* E. CORWIN, *supra* note 27, at 198-201.

[34] *See In re* Neagle, 135 U.S. 1, 63 (1890); 1 OP. ATT'Y GEN. 566, 570-71 (1822).

where there was no formal legal basis for such action, the President often undertook to protect broad foreign policy interests of the United States under inherent powers of the Chief Executive over foreign affairs. By the end of the nineteenth century the capacity of the Executive to protect apparently without distinction the great variety of such interests, whether evidenced by statutes, treaties, international law, or broad foreign policy aims, was well documented.[35]

C. The Area of Conflict

If all of these interests are proper subjects for presidential protection, it is apparent that the exercise of presidential powers over the military may well lead to interference with the rights or interests of other nations and thus launch the United States into war without congressional assent. At this point the constitutional issue arises of the extent to which Congress' power to declare war limits this power of the President to employ the armed forces abroad. To some extent the problem is not peculiar to the question of the power to control the military. The conflict between the grants of power in articles I and II is but a specific example of the more general problem of determining where the Constitution lodges the power to determine United States foreign relations.[36] As early as 1793, the problem arose in connection with President Washington's issuance of a neutrality proclamation on the outbreak of war between France and Great Britain. In the ensuing debate carried on in the "Pacificus-Helvidius" exchange between Hamilton and Madison, the latter argued that since the power over foreign affairs could effectively become the power to commit the country to a course which would lead to war, that power belongs to Congress by virtue of the war-declaring clause. Hamilton, on the other hand, argued that the power to determine foreign policy is essentially an implied or inherent function of the "executive power" although the implementation of such policies may depend on the subsequent exercise of concurrent or independent congressional powers.[37] By and large it is Hamilton's view which has prevailed. The President is recognized as possessing a wide variety of powers, the exercise of which does not constitute an infringement on congressional power to initiate war despite the possibility that his acts may provoke another country to resort to war.[38] But though the initiative in shaping foreign policy rests with the President, the power to implement that policy through the actual employment of the military theoretically still remains with Congress, wherever such employment would amount to making "war."

---

[35] *See* J. ROGERS, *supra* note 7, at 79–80.

[36] The powers conferred on the executive and legislative branches which bear on relations with other nations have been characterized as "an invitation to struggle for the privilege of directing American foreign policy." E. CORWIN, *supra* note 27, at 171.

[37] *See id.* at 177–81.

[38] Examples include the power to dismiss foreign ambassadors, to break off diplomatic relations with other countries, and to extend recognition to political factions claiming to constitute the legitimate government of a foreign nation. *See* C. BERDAHL, *supra* note 14, at 26–37; Q. WRIGHT, THE CONTROL OF AMERICAN FOREIGN RELATIONS 285 (1922).

As indicated by the debates, only in certain defensive situations where the President is responding to an attack is his power to use force without restriction — even to the point of waging war if necessary — compatible with the intent of article I, section 8. Hence, the struggle in this area with respect to the specific question of the power to control the use of the military can be viewed as centering on two major issues. The first is the problem of determining those "defensive" cases in which the President may wage war without congressional authorization. The second is essentially the problem discussed above of defining "war" in the sense of article I, section 8 as a limit on the President's power to use force to protect or advance American interests in all other situations.

The resolution of these problems has largely been left to historical practice. The courts have from the beginning shown a reluctance to enter this classic separation-of-powers debate [39] and, on the particular issue of the proper allocation of the power to embark on war, have been virtually silent.[40] What answer there is to the constitutional issue must come from the interpretations provided through history by the two concerned parties themselves — the President and Congress.

II. PRESIDENTIAL POWER TO ENGAGE IN WAR: THE THEORY OF SELF-DEFENSE

Though the war-declaring clause was intended to give Congress the power to initiate war in most cases, the debates suggest that at least in the case of a "sudden attack" the President was to be able to respond without prior congressional sanction, even though such response would amount to "making war." The rationale for conceding the existence of this power in the President no doubt lies in the recognition that where the defense of the country itself is at stake, there is simply no room for procedural restrictions which might hamper the republic's ability to survive intact. Thus viewed, the power need not rest on any specific provision of the Constitution; as a necessary concomitant of sovereignty itself, the inherent right of national self-defense gives the President full power to defend the country against sudden attack with whatever means are at his disposal as Commander in Chief.[41]

Left unresolved, however, are such questions as what constitutes a "sudden attack," whether the attack must be directed against the United States, who is to determine when such an attack has occurred, and to what extent the President in repelling the attack must limit his actions solely to acts of defense.

---

[39] *Cf.* Foster v. Neilson, 27 U.S. (2 Pet.) 253, 309 (1829) (Marshall, C.J.) ("[a] question like this . . . is . . . more a political than a legal question").

[40] *See* J. ROGERS, *supra* note 7, at 38. In recent attempts to bring precisely this issue — the constitutionality of the President's action in Vietnam — before the courts, the cases have been dismissed as involving political questions in an unconsented suit against the government. *See* Luftig v. McNamara, 373 F.2d 664 (D.C. Cir.), *cert. denied*, 387 U.S. 945 (1967); Mitchell v. United States, 369 F.2d 323 (2d Cir. 1966), *cert. denied*, 386 U.S. 972 (1967).

[41] *See* C. BERDAHL, *supra* note 14, at 58–62; *cf.* United States v. Curtiss-Wright Export Corp., 299 U.S. 309, 316–18 (1936).

A. The Historical Development

Precedents for the President's defensive powers were established under the country's first administration. In the course of American campaigns against the Indians in 1794 the Indians elected at one point to take a stand at a British fort located twenty miles within American territory. While technically an act of invasion, it was not clear that establishment of the fort by the British was in any way intended as an act of aggression against American territory. Though anxious to avoid a new conflict with the English which might arise if they supported the Indians against an American attack, President Washington nevertheless dispatched instructions to the American commander which left no doubt of his confidence that he possessed the power to begin such a conflict if necessary.[42] Fortunately, collision with the garrison proved unnecessary.[43]

The question of the scope of the President's power to respond to a foreign declaration of war arose early in Jefferson's first administration. When the Bey of Tripoli threatened to declare war on the United States Jefferson dispatched a squadron of frigates to the Mediterranean to protect American commerce there against attack in the event the threat were carried out. Before the squadron could arrive, war was declared "by the established custom of chopping down the flagpole of the consulate."[44] Doubtful of the extent of his power to act without congressional approval, Jefferson instructed his commander to release any prisoners taken and to release any vessels captured after having disarmed them. In the President's view his authority to act in defense of the country did not extend to taking further aggressive action, even against a declared adversary, in the absence of congressional authorization.[45] This conservative interpretation of the scope of the President's defensive powers was bitterly attacked by Hamilton. In his view once the country is attacked or war is declared by a foreign nation, the President has full power to respond with whatever force he deems fit. As long as the United States is not the initial aggressor, the President's actions will remain "defensive" requiring no further congressional

---

[42] The instructions, issued without consulting Congress, read: "If, . . . in the course of your operations against the Indian enemy, it should become necessary to dislodge the party at the rapids of the Miami, you are hereby authorized, in the name of the President of the United States, to do it." Instructions from General Knox, Sec'y of War, to General Wayne, in C. FISH, AMERICAN DIPLOMACY 83–84 (1915).

[43] The account is from C. BERDAHL, *supra* note 14, at 62–63.

[44] S. BEMIS, A DIPLOMATIC HISTORY OF THE UNITED STATES 176 (4th ed. 1955).

[45] In a message to Congress on December 4, 1801, Jefferson explained his actions:

Unauthorized by the Constitution, without the sanction of Congress, to go beyond the line of defence, the vessel, being disabled from committing further hostilities, was liberated with its crew. The Legislature will doubtless consider whether, by authorizing measures of offence also, they will place our force on an equal footing with that of its adversaries. I communicate all material information on this subject, that, in the exercise of this important function confided by the Constitution to the Legislature exclusively, their judgment may form itself on a knowledge and consideration of every circumstance of weight.

11 ANNALS OF CONG. 12 (1801).

action to enable him to continue to wage the war thrust on the country.[46]

Hamilton's view received support in the Mexican War a half century later. President Polk instructed General Taylor to occupy disputed territory and to treat any crossing of the Rio Grande [47] as an invasion authorizing him to attack first in defense and even enter Mexican territory in pursuit of the invaders.[48] The instructions were carried out, two skirmishes were fought, and hostilities finally erupted in April, 1846. Although he immediately asked for congressional approval of his actions, the President sought to justify his recourse to arms without first securing such approval by the claim that he was defending the United States against attack. At the conclusion of a bitter debate over the factual basis for Polk's assertions that "war exists by act of Mexico," and that his response was a "defensive" one,[49] Congress finally accepted the President's claims and authorized further hostilities.[50]

The final stamp of approval on this expanding power of the President to make war without prior authorization under the theory of defense was given during the Civil War. In the *Prize Cases* [51] the Supreme Court upheld the validity of Lincoln's proclamation of a blockade of the Southern ports. The President was recognized as possessing unlimited power to wage war in defending against a war begun through invasion or rebellion; in addition, he was to be the sole judge of when such invasion or rebellion amounted to "war," thereby authorizing assumption of his full defensive powers.[52] Although four

---

[46] 7 WORKS OF ALEXANDER HAMILTON 746–47 (J. Hamilton ed. 1851) (emphasis in original):

[I]t is the peculiar and exclusive province of Congress, *when the nation is at peace* to change that state into a state of war; whether from calculations of policy, or from provocations, or injuries received: in other words, it belongs to Congress only, *to go to War.* But when a foreign nation declares, or openly and avowedly makes war upon the United States, they are then by the very fact *already at war,* and any declaration on the part of Congress is nugatory; it is at least unnecessary.

[47] The Rio Grande was the boundary claimed by the independent Republic of Texas since 1836 and subsequently by the United States on the annexation of Texas in 1845. *See generally* S. BEMIS, *supra* note 44, at 232–38.

[48] *See id.* at 239; C. BERDAHL, *supra* note 14, at 70–71.

[49] Message to Congress, May 11, 1846, in CONG. GLOBE, 29th Cong., 1st Sess. 783 (1846).

[50] Act of May 13, 1846, ch. 16, 9 Stat. 9. Two years later, in passing a resolution of thanks to General Taylor the House tacked on an amendment reading "that the war was unnecessarily and unconstitutionally begun by the President of the United States." A subsequent motion to expunge this amendment from the journal was tabled. *See* CONG. GLOBE, 30th Cong., 1st Sess. 95, 343–44 (1848).

[51] 67 U.S. (2 Black) 635 (1863).

[52] The Court stated:

If a war be made by invasion of a foreign nation, the President is not only authorized but bound to resist force by force. He does not initiate the war, but is bound to accept the challenge without waiting for any special legislative authority. . . .

. . . .

. . . The President was bound to meet it in the shape it presented itself, without waiting for Congress to baptize it with a name . . . .

. . . .

Whether the President . . . has met with such armed hostile resistance

Justices, including Chief Justice Taney, vigorously opposed this result [53] the decision remains uncontroverted today.[54]

This expanding power of the President to engage in "defensive wars" is, however, not without inherent limits. The basis of the theory in the *Prize Cases* is essentially Hamilton's: when another nation has "openly or avowedly" made war upon the United States [55] the President in responding is not himself "initiating" war but is merely accepting the challenge thrust on the country by the foreign attack.[56] Hence, in each case the determination must be made whether the hostile acts committed against the United States constitute "war," enabling assumption of his defensive war-making powers. In making this determination, definitional problems similar to those discussed above with respect to "initiating" war [57] must be faced. Hamilton's views notwithstanding, a declaration of war against the United States need not automatically place the country at war. Thus, when Bulgaria, Hungary, and Rumania declared war on the United States on December 13, 1941, President Roosevelt ignored the declarations. Only later, as a gesture of friendship to the Soviet Union, did he ask Congress to recognize that the United States was at war with those countries.[58] Such empty declarations still leave open the decision whether to turn the "paper war" into an actual war [59] and, hence, theoretically remain candidates for congressional, rather than presidential war making.

Similarly, not every use of force against the United States is an act which places the country at war, justifying presidential defensive war making. Almost any attack on or invasion of the United States proper would probably qualify as such an act, as would a similar act aimed at United States territorial possessions.[60] Polk's actions set a precedent for also viewing as "war" the invasion of disputed territory claimed under a treaty of annexation. Less likely candidates are cases of attacks on United States ships or personnel stationed abroad. The response to an attack on the *Pueblo,* for example, could hardly be characterized as "defending the country" in a war thrust on the United States by act of North Korea; rather, the response in such a situation is more

---

. . . as will compel him to accord to them the character of belligerents, is a question to be decided *by him* . . . .
Id. at 668–70 (emphasis in original).
Technically, the Court's statements constitute an alternative holding since the blockade was also recognized as retroactively sanctioned by Congress. *See id.* at 670–71.
[53] While recognizing the President's authority to use force to meet the rebellion under existing laws, the dissent would have denied effect, absent a formal declaration of war by Congress, to rules of law on blockade in time of war.
[54] *See* Mora v. McNamara, 389 U.S. 934, 937 (1967) (Douglas, J., dissenting), *denying cert.* to No. 20,420 (D.C. Cir., Feb. 20, 1967).
[55] *See* note 46 *supra.*
[56] *See* note 52 *supra.*
[57] *See* pp. 1774–75 *supra.*
[58] Message to Congress, June 2, 1942, in 88 CONG. REC. 4787 (1942); *see* F. GROB, *supra* note 9, at 290.
[59] *See generally* F. GROB, *supra* note 9, at 289–302.
[60] Though also accompanied by a declaration of war, the bombing of Pearl Harbor was recognized by Congress the following day in its declaration of war as having "thrust" war on the United States. Act of Dec. 8, 1941, ch. 561, 55 Stat. 795.

accurately a case of protecting American rights and interests abroad.[61]

It is the lesson of the *Prize Cases* that in all of these situations this determination — whether an attack against the United States has occurred which "thrusts war" on the country for purposes of presidential, defensive war making — is exclusively the President's. The rationale of the decision, however, does not extend to anything short of such an attack.

B. *The Modern Context: Collective Self-Defense*

The historical development of the self-defense rationale would limit independent presidential power to engage in war to certain cases involving direct attacks against the United States. The recent State Department memorandum suggests, however, that a "direct attack" is no longer a realistic prerequisite for exercise of the President's power to act unilaterally in national self-defense: in view of the delicate balance of power among nations as well as the frightening technology of modern warfare, an attack on a foreign country may just as surely threaten our security as a direct attack on United States territory.[62]

The notion that the United States possesses extraterritorial security interests is hardly novel. As early as 1811, in a resolution declaring that the Government would not view with indifference the transfer of Florida to any other power, the idea of "defining a security zone" of the United States was introduced into American foreign policy.[63] By the end of the nineteenth century, with the development of the Monroe Doctrine, the entire Caribbean area had come to be regarded as just such a zone.[64]

It was left, however, to the twentieth century and the experience of two world wars to give full birth to the idea of linking American defense with extraterritorial security interests. National security became world security, and there emerged the thesis of collective self-defense: war was an evil which the peaceful nations of the world must guard against by developing common means of halting an outbreak of aggression. The United Nations Charter explicitly recognized "the inherent right of individual or collective self-defense," [65] and the United States proceeded accordingly in the years following World War II to conclude a number of regional and bilateral security agreements. By these the United States generally agreed to regard an attack on a member nation as threatening its own safety and to assist in defensive measures.[66]

---

[61] See generally pp. 1787–94 *infra*.

[62] See *Memorandum, supra* note 1, at 484.

[63] See D. PERKINS, THE AMERICAN APPROACH TO FOREIGN POLICY 108 (rev. ed. 1962).

[64] See *id.* at 108–09. For a brief history of the development of this "security thesis" see *id.* at 107–15.

[65] U.N. CHARTER art. 51.

[66] See, e.g., Southeast Asia Collective Defense Treaty, Sept. 8, 1954, art. IV, para. 1, [1955] 1 U.S.T. 81, T.I.A.S. No. 3170 ("[e]ach Party recognizes that aggression by means of armed attack . . . against any of the Parties . . . would endanger its own peace and safety"); North Atlantic Treaty, Apr. 4, 1949, art. 5, 63 Stat. 2242 (1949), T.I.A.S. No. 1964 ("an armed attack against one or more of [the Parties] shall be considered an attack against them all"); Charter of the Organization of American States, Apr. 30, 1948, ch.

There are a number of difficulties with the theory that, for purposes of presidential war-making power, an attack on another country — even if under circumstances specified by a mutual defense treaty — is equivalent to an attack on the United States. Presumably, any resort to war — even where authorized by Congress — is justified only because in some sense United States security is thought to be at stake. Hence, the fact that "security interests" are involved does not in itself alter the normal processes for deciding whether such interests are worth defending at the price of war. That decision, where a foreign state is attacked, will depend on a variety of factors — proximity to the United States; the value of the country as an ally; other United States interests involved, such as military bases and military sites; and the nature of the aggression and the aggressor.[67] In each case difficult political and military decisions must be made which may well lead reasonable men to different conclusions in determining whether the interest involved is necessary to the defense of the United States. Where, on the other hand, the attack is against the United States itself, there can be no question presumably that the "security interest" involved warrants defending at the cost of war if necessary; to require the President to await what amounts to an obvious, foregone conclusion on the part of Congress is at best a needless formality, and at worst may occasion dangerous delay.

Yet, even if it be granted that not every eruption of violence abroad poses a threat so inimical to our own security that the defense of the United States itself is immediately involved, still, there may be *some* cases where such a threat *is* posed. For example, an invasion of Canada by communist forces — even if clearly aimed solely at that country — may be thought to represent a threat to our continued existence which is indistinguishable from that posed by a similar invasion of Alaska. Again, though, Hamilton's arguments point to a fundamental, albeit somewhat conceptual, difference between the two cases which suggests that in the case of Canada, though not in the case of Alaska, the President must seek congressional authorization to defend against the attack where time permits. The debates suggest that one of the prerequisites for unilateral presidential response even in defense of the country is that the attack be so "sudden" that resort to Congress is militarily precluded.[68] Although this requirement was apparently dispensed with in

---

V, art. 24, [1951] 2 U.S.T. 2394, T.I.A.S. No. 2361 ("[e]very act of aggression by a State against . . . an American State shall be considered an act of aggression against the other American States"); Inter-American Treaty of Reciprocal Assistance, Sept. 2, 1947, art. 3, para. 1, 62 Stat. 1681 (1948), T.I.A.S. No. 1838 ("an armed attack by any State against an American State shall be considered as an attack against all the American States").

For an exhaustive listing of similar American commitments evidenced by treaty, by less formal arrangements, and by official unilateral declaration see U.S. Dep't of State, *United States Defense Commitments and Assurances, August, 1967*, in *Hearings on National Commitments* 52–71.

[67] *Cf.* Wolfers, *"National Security" as an Ambiguous Symbol*, in AMERICAN DEFENSE POLICY 1, 4, 6 (1965). The State Department in fact insists on interpreting current defense commitments so that after an attack on another nation has occurred, it still remains to the United States to determine "in light of future facts" exactly "what is necessary." Statement by N. Katzenbach, Under Sec'y of State, in *Hearings on National Commitments* 71, 97.

[68] *See* p. 1773 & notes 16, 17 *supra*.

the case of a direct attack,[69] the reasons which justify dropping the requirement do not extend to the case of an attack on a foreign state. In the event of an armed attack on United States territory itself, Congress' decision whether or not to go to war is not simply bypassed as obvious; it is recognized as being completely superfluous: the President is simply assuming his wartime role as Commander in Chief in a situation in which the decision to resort to war has been taken out of the country's hands by the unilateral action of another state.[70] In the case of an attack aimed solely at Canada, on the other hand, the decision whether the United States will become involved in the conflict is still open. As long as this is the case, steps taken to repel the attack would amount, from the United States point of view, to "commencing" rather than "repelling" war: the type of decision the convention debates indicate was to be made by Congress.

To say that the President must seek congressional approval before going to war where "security interests" are threatened does not mean that the President's ability to defend the country will be unreasonably restricted. Especially in the context of nuclear warfare, the understanding of what constitutes an attack has been vastly altered; retaliatory action need not lose its defensive character merely because no physical blow has actually reached the nation's shores. But the fear of nuclear war which haunted the fifties helped give rise to a sense of need for prompt executive action which is often exaggerated in the context of current crises and the reemergence of more conventional warfare.[71] In these cases the constitutional interest in allowing Congress to decide what is worth the price of war should be accommodated as much as possible. While the President must still be left with the power to judge in the first instance whether a given event constitutes an imminent threat to our survival and demands a response which leaves no time to seek Congress' asquiescence in that judgment, such limited discretion falls far short of authorizing assumption of his defensive war-making powers whenever the interest jeopardized is labeled a "vital security interest." None of the recent examples of overseas conflict presents a convincing case for the President's use of force under the theory of self-defense. Neither the invasion of South Korea during President Truman's administration, the Arab threat to Lebanon during Eisenhower's, the sending of missiles to Cuba during Kennedy's, nor the disorder in the Dominican Republic during the current administration constituted a threat requiring an immediate response in order to defend the territorial sovereignty of the United States. With the

---

[69] In the examples discussed above, Jefferson, Polk and Lincoln each had time to seek congressional approval before the action taken. Though action was taken unilaterally, each sought and received congressional authorization concurrently with or immediately after the steps taken. *See* Act of August 6, 1861, ch. 63, § 3, 12 Stat. 326 (confirming all acts, proclamations, and orders of the President, after the 4th of March, 1861); Act of July 13, 1861, ch. 3, 12 Stat. 255 (authorizing a variety of emergency measures, including in § 4 the capture and condemnation of vessels attempting to enter certain ports); Act of May 13, 1846, ch. 16, 9 Stat. 9 (authorizing Polk's actions against Mexico); Act of Feb. 6, 1802, ch. 4, 2 Stat. 129 (authorizing Jefferson to carry on hostilities against the Barbary Powers).

[70] *See* p. 1781 & note 46 *supra*.

[71] *See* NATIONAL COMMITMENTS REPORT 6.

possible exception, discussed in the following section, of the attacks on United States destroyers in the area this is also true of the current conflict in Vietnam.

C. Preparing for Defense: Some Unexamined Assumptions About The Power of the Commander in Chief

Although the commander-in-chief clause places the President at the head of the armed forces, it says nothing about the purposes for which or circumstances under which the military may be used.[72] Even the President's power to defend against attack stems primarily from the power inherent in the sovereign status of the United States under the Constitution to defend itself with its armed forces without first completing formal authorizing procedures; only in a derivative sense does this power devolve on the Commander in Chief as head of those forces. Accordingly, although a long line of precedent beginning with Lincoln's actions in the Civil War transformed the clause into "a vast reservoir of indeterminate powers in time of emergency," [73] such emergency powers were generally confined to the necessities of dealing with domestic problems in time of actual war.[74] However, a widespread practice has developed of citing the commander-in-chief clause as independent authority for doing apparently "anything, anywhere that can be done with an army or navy." [75] Such claims are clearly too broad. Yet even if the power to command and deploy the troops is restricted to actions which are necessary steps in preparing to defend the country,[76] considerable room is left for conflict with Congress' power to declare war. It will be possible to deploy troops in situations where, though combat is technically not involved, either the danger of provoking conflict is evident, or the deployment of troops itself is difficult to distinguish from a commitment of forces offensively against a foreign country.

Examples are provided by presidential actions prior to American entry into World War I and World War II. After the defeat through a Senate filibuster of a bill which would have given congressional approval to President Wilson's proposal for arming United States merchant ships in 1917, Wilson proceeded under "the plain implication of my constitutional duties and powers" [77] to order the arming of such vessels with instructions to fire on sight at submarines. The action was justified as a necessary measure of defense against the dangers to neutral United States shipping inherent in submarine warfare; yet, as Wilson himself later acknowledged, the action was "practically certain" to draw us into the war.[78] Nearly a quarter of a century

---

[72] See p. 1775 supra.

[73] E. CORWIN, supra note 27, at 261.

[74] See id. at 228-34

[75] Youngstown Sheet & Tube Co. v. Sawyer, 343 U.S. 579, 641-42 (1952) (Jackson, J., concurring) (referring, apparently with disapproval, to government claims of the scope of power conferred by commander-in-chief clause).

[76] See Mathews, The Constitutional Power of the President to Conclude International Agreements, 64 YALE L.J. 345, 383 (1955).

[77] Address before Congress, Feb. 26, 1917, in 54 CONG. REC. 4273 (1917).

[78] Message to Congress, April 2, 1917, in 55 CONG. REC. 103 (1917).

later similar actions were taken by President Roosevelt. On September 3, 1940, in the famous "Fifty Destroyer Deal," the President announced to Congress that he had exchanged fifty over-aged destroyers for British bases in the Western Atlantic, which were later occupied by American ships and troops.[79] In April, 1941, troops were sent to occupy Greenland, a Danish possession since 1814, under an arrangement with the Danish Minister in Washington — Denmark itself having been invaded by Germany on April 9, 1940. Two months later a similar occupation of Iceland, an independent nation, took place at that country's request, relieving the British troops which until then had occupied the strategic island. All of the troop movements involved were taken under Presidential authority as Commander in Chief for strategic reasons in insuring the defense of the Americas. All of the actions were easily subject to the interpretation that military force was being used to aid an enemy of Germany and might easily have led to immediate American involvement in the war.[80]

It might be argued that the fact that a foreign country may look on the deployment of military force in certain situations as a threat requiring retaliation does not mean the President has exceeded his authority. The fact that by shaping and directing American foreign policy he can provoke a country into an attack does not mean he has unconstitutionally "initiated" war.[81] At most, the argument continues, it is only the actual commitment of troops to combat, not their deployment in noncombat situations, which is subject to congressional control.

Where, however, military force is involved, there are strong arguments for recognizing limits on the employment of such force — by virtue of the war-declaring clause — regardless of whether such employment involves actual commitment to combat or mere deployment in friendly countries abroad in preparation for defense. The difficulty of distinguishing "mere troop deployment" from actual offensive employment against another nation is illustrated by the Greenland and Iceland examples. Secondly, even where forces are "peacefully" deployed abroad, a difficult problem arises if hostilities do in fact erupt, involving American troops in combat. An illustration is provided by one aspect of the current conflict in Vietnam. The incident which

---

[79] A short account of the incident and the debate which it touched off is given in T. Bailey, A Diplomatic History of the American People 718-20 (6th ed. 1958).

[80] See J. Rogers, supra note 7, at 68-71; E. Corwin, supra note 27, at 202-04.

[81] See p. 1777 & note 38 supra. Presidential control of foreign relations has in fact been the dominant factor in American entry into most of the major conflicts in our history. Of the nine conflicts through World War II which historians recognize as "wars," only five were "declared." The remaining four (the Naval War with France of 1798-1800, the Barbary War of 1801-05, the Second Barbary War of 1815 and the Mexican Hostilities of 1914-17 either were justified under the theory of self-defense or, arguably, were authorized by congressional resolution in some form. See J. Rogers, supra note 7, at 45-56. Even the "declared" wars, however, with the exception of the War of 1812, involved little more than mechanical congressional "recognition" of an existing state of war begun by the foreign country in response to American policies formulated largely by executive initiative. See E. Corwin, supra note 27, at 204; J. Rogers, supra note 7, at 54-55. Such broad executive power over foreign relations argues for even closer scrutiny of whatever powers do remain to Congress to control the use of the military.

gave rise to the Gulf of Tonkin Resolution involved two alleged attacks by communist torpedo boats on a United States ship. It might be argued that this attack authorizes the war in which we are involved under the President's powers of self defense. If this argument were valid, the theoretical limits on the President's power to wage war would disappear in practice. Merely by sending troops to "hot spots" in the world, the President could insure that an attack on a foreign country would also be an attack on the United States troops stationed there. Although undoubtedly United States ships and troops abroad may defend themselves against attack without authorization, there must surely be a point when the attack has been repelled, and the enemy has indicated its hostilities are no longer directed at the United States, so that to continue the conflict or even to remain in the area would amount to aggressive war by the United States. Unlike an attack on United States territory proper, an attack on troops stationed abroad will generally still leave a decision to be made in determining whether the interest involved is worth the risk of war inherent in further military action. Since this is the type of decision which properly belongs to Congress, there are good reasons for requiring congressional approval before rather than after the conflict has started [82] and, hence, at least where the likelihood of conflict is apparent, for requiring approval of the dispatch of troops in the first place.

III. PRESIDENTIAL POWER TO PROTECT AMERICAN RIGHTS AND INTERESTS ABROAD: MILITARY MEASURES "SHORT OF WAR"

For the most part the United States has escaped the type of attack which would justify presidential use of defensive war-making powers. By far the most difficult struggle between the President and Congress over the power to control the use of the military has occurred in attempting to decide what limits are to be placed on the President's power to use force in all other situations — situations where, though the country itself has not been attacked, its interests and national aims abroad are threatened and require force for their protection or advancement. Although the President early assumed the power to enforce all sorts of national aims [83] Congress' power to declare war, if it is not to be purely formal, must include the power to decide when the country will go to war to protect such aims. Formally, then, the problem is one of definition: under what circumstances does the use of force abroad — for whatever purpose — involve a commitment of the country to a trial of force of the sort which prompted the requirement for prior congressional consent?

A. The Historical Development

The reasons for assigning to Congress the power to decide whether to initiate war — namely, to insure broadly based approval of a step likely to entail serious economic, physical, or moral consequences [84] —

---

[82] *See* p. 1796 *infra.*
[83] *See* pp. 1776–77 *supra.*
[84] *See* p. 1775 *supra.*

led to development of the notion that certain limited forms of military action, because they lacked such far-reaching consequences, are not "wars" and do not require prior congressional approval. The form which this theory assumed in the nineteenth century resulted in what might be called a "qualitative" definition of war. The basic theory was that force could constitutionally be used without congressional approval when employed "neutrally" with respect to foreign political entities.[85] The theory was spelled out in 1912 in an attempt to justify President Taft's employment of the armed forces in Nicaragua. In a carefully documented survey of nineteenth-century practice, the State Department drew a distinction between "intervention," which included interference with the political concerns of another state or political faction, and "interposition," which was confined solely to the protection of the persons or interests of the interposing country. Acts of the latter sort, it was argued, were justified under international law, and under the Constitution did not require ancillary legislation from Congress.[86] Most of the instances of presidential use of force during the nineteenth century can with varying degrees of success be reconciled with this theory.

The vast majority of the incidents involved landings to protect American property or lives abroad.[87] Generally undertaken during periods of disorder or civil unrest when local authorities could no longer provide protection against ordinary outlawry, these landings were, at least superficially, intended to maintain strict neutrality between contesting political factions.[88] The few landings to protect American treaty and other broad policy interests occurred primarily in the Canal Zone and, with the opening of Japan, occasionally also in the Far East. Again a similar pattern was supposedly followed: troops were stationed to protect the interests involved without direct interference in local political struggles.[89] A number of incidents involved the use of force to suppress piracy and the slave trade.[90] Such action was said to be aimed not at any sovereign nation, but at scattered gangs of "criminals" unanimously branded as such by both domestic and international law.[91] A similar theory was used to justify incidents involving punitive raids or reprisals against native islands and villages in so-called "uncivilized" areas of the world. These were generally undertaken in retaliation for crimes against citizens of the United States where normal diplomatic redress from the local natives was thought impossible. The practice was quick to fall into disuse as nearly

[85] See R. Russell, *supra* note 5, at 242–43, *quoted in* NATIONAL COMMITMENTS REPORT 11–12.

[86] U.S. DEP'T OF STATE, RIGHT TO PROTECT CITIZENS IN FOREIGN COUNTRIES BY LANDING FORCES 24–34, 40, 44, 48 (3d rev. ed. 1934) (Memorandum of the Solicitor).

[87] See LEGISLATIVE REFERENCE SERVICE, THE CONSTITUTION OF THE UNITED STATES OF AMERICA — ANALYSIS AND INTERPRETATION, S. DOC. No. 39, 88th Cong., 1st Sess. 541 n.9 (6th ed. 1964).

[88] *Compare* U.S. DEP'T OF STATE, *supra* note 86, at 33, *with id.* at 36.

[89] See *id.* at 34–38; R. VAN ALSTYNE, AMERICAN DIPLOMACY IN ACTION 642 (rev. ed. 1947).

[90] See NATIONAL COMMITMENTS REPORT 11.

[91] R. Russell, *supra* note 5, at 165–66.

all such "primitive areas" came under the protection of one or another European power.[92] Finally, there were incidents where, in defending against attack or in suppressing outlaws, the President ordered "hot pursuit" of the attackers across the boundaries of another nation. Examples extend from President Monroe's orders to General Jackson in 1818 to pursue Indians in the South into Spanish territory of Florida to President Wilson's dispatch of troops in 1916 to pursue the Pancho Villa bandits across the Mexican border.[93]

The complications with Mexican authorities which resulted from the latter expedition [94] illustrate how easily this "neutrality" theory is abused. Indeed, landings to protect American interests abroad must almost invariably affect internal political struggles. The very presence of American force, which can potentially aid a favorable government if a rebellion threatens to succeed and which at the very least relieves local troops from guard duty, will tend to result in support for the status quo [95] and is easily viewed as an intervention in a civil struggle. A prime example is furnished by President McKinley's action in the Boxer Rebellion in 1900. Without express authorization from Congress a naval force had been sent to China and was subsequently employed, not merely for the purpose of rescuing and protecting American lives and property, but also to aid in avenging and punishing the rebels. Yet the President continued to maintain that our aims were directed solely at the legitimate purpose of rescuing imperiled citizens and that no "war" was involved.[96]

Finally, with President Roosevelt's intervention in Panama in 1903 the "neutrality" theory was apparently completely abandoned as a limit on the President's power to advance American interests through use of the armed forces. Invoking an 1846 treaty with Columbia which bound the United States to maintain the "perfect neutrality" of the Isthmus, Roosevelt ordered gunboats in the area to prevent Colombian troops from engaging the rebellious Panamanian "army." [97] The orders sent [98] and the actions taken strongly support the conclusion that military force was deliberately being used against the state of Colombia to establish a government more favorable to American canal interests.[99] The action set a precedent for later interventions and temporary occupations of countries in Central America and the Caribbean under Presidents Roosevelt, Taft and Wilson.[100] Although fre-

---

[92] *Id.* at 180–82.

[93] *See* C. BERDAHL, *supra* note 14, at 65–67.

[94] *See* S. BEMIS, *supra* note 44, at 552–53.

[95] *See* R. Russell, *supra* note 5, at 186.

[96] Message to Congress, Dec. 3, 1900, in 34 CONG. REC. 4 (1900).

[97] The "army" consisted largely of 500 "bought" Colombian troops and members of the local fire department — a force which probably would have proved inadequate but for the use of American naval vessels to prevent Colombian troops from landing at Colon. *See* T. BAILEY, A DIPLOMATIC HISTORY OF THE AMERICAN PEOPLE 492 (6th ed. 1958).

[98] A collection of the correspondence including the orders sent to American ships in the area is contained in UNITED STATES SENATE, DIPLOMATIC HISTORY OF THE PANAMA CANAL, S. DOC. NO. 474, 63d Cong., 2d Sess. 345–76 (1914).

[99] *See generally* T. BAILEY, *supra* note 79, at 491–94; S. BEMIS, *supra* note 44, at 513–15.

[100] *See generally* S. BEMIS, *supra* note 44, at 519–38.

quent attempts were made to justify the interventions on previous theories of neutrality [101] many of the actions taken were simply incapable of being accurately described as "neutral" with respect to the interests of foreign political entities.[102]

Yet despite the apparent abandonment of the "neutrality" theory as a limit on presidential power to use force abroad, the "Panama Policy" of Roosevelt, Taft and Wilson was not necessarily inconsistent with the primacy of congressional war-making power. The states of the Caribbean were in no position to respond to American intervention with sufficient force to occasion a major conflict. So predominant was American might in this area of the world that Government publications were able to claim that a threatened revolution could usually be quieted by the mere arrival of an American cruiser.[103] From a purely military point of view the operations involved, even in the extended occupations of Haiti and the Dominican Republic, were for the most part minor affairs.[104] Hence, it is possible to conclude that "war" in the sense of article I, section 8, requiring congressional sanction, does not include interventions to maintain order in weak countries where a severe contest at arms with another nation is not likely to result.[105] Under such a "quantitative" definition of war, there was no infringement on Congress' power to initiate *major* conflicts.

B. The Modern Context: Diminishing Limits on the President's Power

1. The Changed Setting. — Though the history sketched above indicates a gradually shrinking interpretation of what is left to Congress by virtue of its power to declare "war," it is only during this century and particularly the last twenty years that the President has asserted powers over the military which, if taken at face value, all but reverse the original distribution between the Executive and Congress of the power to embark on war. The transformation has taken place against the background of a drastically changed factual setting which raises issues not easily answered by reference to history alone. The emergence of the United States at the turn of the century as a world power and the final, if somewhat reluctant, exchange after World War

---

[101] *See* p. 1788 *supra.*

[102] *Compare* the strict observance of neutrality in an incident mentioned in T. ROOSEVELT, AN AUTOBIOGRAPHY 549 (1913) (to protect American property both sides were instructed to do their fighting outside the town, which was then given to the victor), *with* the clearly nonneutral incident described in S. BEMIS, *supra* note 44, at 532 & n.1 (unhappy with Nicaraguan dictatorship, the United States employed American troops to help establish a new regime: bombardment of revolutionists was prevented on the grounds that it might injure American lives and property). Two methods of "interpreting the facts" to fit the neutrality theory developed. Actions were either described as intended to protect American lives and property without interference in local struggles, or, where American troops did take sides in the fighting, the opposing forces were labeled "bandits" or "outlaws," rather than members of a political entity. *See* F. GROB, *supra* note 9, at 231; SELECT COMMITTEE ON HAITI AND SANTO DOMINGO, INQUIRY INTO OCCUPATION AND ADMINISTRATION OF HAITI AND THE DOMINICAN REPUBLIC, S. REP. NO. 794, 67th Cong., 2d Sess. 10, 12–14 (1922).

[103] *See* C. BEARD, THE IDEA OF NATIONAL INTEREST 477 n.135 (1934).

[104] *See* F. GROB, *supra* note 9, at 231; *cf.* C. BEARD, *supra* note 103, at 483–84. *But cf.* J. ROGERS, *supra* note 7, at 74–78.

[105] *See* F. GROB, *supra* note 9, at 231–35.

II of isolationist policies for "foreign entanglements" far beyond anything envisioned by the framers, make the question of the President's
power to protect "broad American interests" far more relevant to the
issue of Congress' power to initiate war than at any time in the nineteenth century. For the first time in its history America possesses a
standing army, sufficiently large, sufficiently well-equipped, and sufficiently mobile to make possible, through presidential action alone and
on very short notice, conflicts of unforeseeable dimensions anywhere
in the world.[106] Distinctions between "the power to initiate war," "the
power to direct American foreign policy," and "the power to use military force" begin to vanish as the military weapon is integrated into
foreign policy as simply another tool of diplomacy. To ask when and
by whom war was "initiated" in Vietnam is to illustrate the difficulty
of attempting to determine which of the steps in a gradually increasing commitment should have been taken by the President and which
by Congress.

The same changed circumstances, however, also lend increased significance to the constitutional concern, embodied in the war-declaring
clause, that Congress express the country's willingness to undergo the
internal repercussions which military conflicts are likely to entail.
The difficulty lies in attempting to accommodate this constitutional concern with the need, in at least some situations, for speed, secrecy, and
efficiency — the inherent advantages of the Executive.[107]

2. Recent Precedents. — The most striking illustration of the shift
in the power to commit forces to combat is the Korean episode. Faced
with the invasion of South Korea, President Truman after brief consultation with advisors, committed the nation's troops to repel the invaders.[108] At no time was congressional authorization sought for the
full-scale conflict which resulted. Although there is considerable evidence that without immediate action Korea would have been overrun,[109] there is also evidence that the sequence of events [110] left time
to seek congressional approval and that failure to do so reflected a
deliberate assertion of presidential prerogative.[111] Attempts were made
to justify the decision on the grounds, *inter alia,* that the action was
taken under the United Nations Charter, a part of both the treaty and

---

[106] In 1789, when the Department of War (now the Department of the Army)
was established, the number of military personnel on active duty totaled 718.
By 1812 the number had reached over 12,000. In the nineteenth century, with the
exception of the years during and immediately following the Civil War, the
total never significantly exceeded 50,000 until the Spanish-American War in
1898. It then increased to 200,000. For twenty years following World War I
the average remained between 250,000 and 300,000. After reaching a World War
II peak of 12.1 million in 1945, the total dropped to approximately 1.5 million
(1947 to 1950) and, since 1950, has remained at approximately three million. *See*
BUREAU OF THE CENSUS, U.S. DEP'T OF COMMERCE, HISTORICAL STATISTICS OF THE
UNITED STATES, COLONIAL TIMES TO 1957, at 736–37 (1960).

[107] *See* E. CORWIN, *supra* note 27, at 171.

[108] For the background to Truman's decision to enter the war see Hoyt, *The
United States Reaction to the Korean Attack: A Study of the Principles of the
United Nations Charter as a Factor in American Policy-Making,* 55 AM. J. INT.
L. 45 (1961).

[109] *See* P. SEABURY, POWER, FREEDOM, AND DIPLOMACY 216 (1963).

[110] *See generally* R. LECKIE, THE WARS OF AMERICA 850–58 (1968).

[111] *Id.* at 858.

international law which the President is constitutionally empowered to execute, and that the President was protecting "the broad interests of American foreign policy." [112] Significantly, though, constant attempts were made by the administration to describe the conflict, not as a "war," but as a mere "police action," [113] suggesting that, indeed, the President's power to use force to protect such interests was somehow limited to military measures short of war. The action, however, was clearly not "neutral" with respect to foreign political entities; equally clearly, the conflict was not a "minor" one. The nature and size of this country's commitment, however measured — number of troops, number of casualties, extent of emergency legislation, dollar cost [114] — warrant the conclusion that however the line between "major" and "minor" is drawn this, at least, was the type of involvement which the war-declaring clause was meant to preserve for legislative approval.[115]

Largely as a consequence of the dissatisfaction which subsequently developed over "Truman's War," President Eisenhower, when confronted during his administration with the necessity for military intervention in Formosa (1955) and the Middle East (1957), hastened to seek congressional authorization for his action.[116] Yet when troops finally were sent to Lebanon in the midst of its crisis with the United Arab Republic, Eisenhower claimed to be acting, not under the authority of the resolution, but under his inherent constitutional power to protect American lives and property abroad and to protect a nation whose independence was vital to United States interests and world peace.[117]

A joint resolution from Congress was also involved in the Cuban Missile Crisis in 1962. Passed one month before the quarantine proclamation, the resolution, as well as a resolution of the Organization of American States, was recited in the proclamation as authority for the action taken.[118] Though the evidence is ambiguous, President Kennedy apparently also claimed the inherent power to take whatever military action was necessary for the protection of American security interests.[119] President Johnson's landing of marines in the Dominican

---

[112] See U.S. Dep't of State, *Authority of the President to Repel the Attack in Korea*, 23 DEP'T STATE BULL. 173 *passim* (1950).

[113] See R. LECKIE, *supra* note 110, at 858.

[114] Cf. note 23 *supra*.

[115] Cf. R. LECKIE, *supra* note 110, at 858; P. SEABURY, *supra* note 109, at 208.

[116] See T. BAILEY, *supra* note 79, at 834–35, 844–45.

[117] See Statement by the President, July 15, 1958, in 104 CONG. REC. 13,903–04 (1958). The Middle East Resolution by its terms was limited to situations involving armed aggression by any country controlled by international communism. See Middle East Resolution, Pub. L. No. 85-7, § 2, 71 Stat. 5 (1957). There was, however, some suggestion by Secretary of State Dulles that the action was within the Eisenhower Doctrine, first, because the resolution did not require that the aggression be communist controlled, and second, because in any event this particular incident was communist inspired. See Krock, *Law and Intervention*, N.Y. Times, July 16, 1958, at 8, col. 4; *id.* at 3, col. 5.

[118] See Presidential Proclamation No. 3504, 27 Fed. Reg. 10,401 (1962).

[119] Cf. *id*; Statement by President Kennedy, News Conference, Sept. 13, 1962, in N.Y. Times, Sept. 14, 1962, at 12, col. 1; *Hearings on National Commitments* 19. The Cuban incident is an example — undoubtedly one of many — where the

Republic in 1965 without congressional authorization was rationalized initially as necessary to protect the safety of American citizens,[120] and subsequently as an exercise of the President's power to preserve the security of the hemisphere in accordance with principles announced in the OAS Treaty.[121] In the current conflict in Vietnam, although additional reliance is placed on the Gulf of Tonkin Resolution, the State Department also argues that even without the resolution current actions are fully within the constitutional authority of the President as Chief Executive and Commander in Chief.[122]

All of these assertions share a single feature: following the precedent set during Korea, the theories which history has established with respect to the purposes for which the President may employ force abroad are heavily stressed, while the historical limitations which developed concurrently with those theories — if they did not in fact precede them — apparently are ignored. This shift in the manner used to justify presidential action is emphasized in the findings of the Senate Foreign Relations Committee in its recent report on national commitments [123] and is well supported by a comparison of recent and traditional presidential rhetoric. Assertions recognizing a limit on the President's powers to use force abroad by virtue of Congress' war power are on record from Presidents Jefferson, Madison, Jackson, Buchanan, Lincoln, Grant, McKinley, Wilson and Franklin D. Roosevelt.[124] Although some of these statements may well be merely "gestures of obeisance to Congress' power to declare war," [125] they nevertheless express recognition of a definite separation of powers in this area which, though incapable of precise definition and subject to easy abuse, at least requires some attempt to accommodate congressional interest in deciding what is worth the price of war with presidential determination to enforce and protect American interests. Any theory which purports to find a constitutional norm for such an allocation of power on the basis of an analysis of historical precedents will, by its very generality, be open to counterexamples. Yet the recognition that there are limits on executive military powers will at least direct efforts toward either constructing a more adequate theory or admitting that exceptional instances are departures from proper constitutional practice. To abandon recognition of such limits — even if only in the rhetoric [126] — and to rely on an asserted inherent power to use force, apparently without restriction, to protect American "interests" makes such efforts pointless and should cause

---

more warlike branch was not the executive but the legislative. Many members of Congress were calling for far more drastic action than the President, including the invasion of Cuba. *See* N.Y. Times, Oct. 14, 1962, at 1, col. 6.

[120] *See* N.Y. Times, Apr. 29, 1965, at 1, col. 8; *id.*, Apr. 30, at 1, col. 8.

[121] *See* Statement by the President, May 2, 1965, in N.Y. Times, May 3, 1965, at 10, col. 1.

[122] *See Memorandum, supra* note 1, at 484–85.

[123] *See* NATIONAL COMMITMENTS REPORT 13, 23.

[124] The statements are collected in Putney, *Executive Assumption of the War Making Power*, 7 NAT'L UNIV. L. REV. 1, 6–30 (May 1927).

[125] E. CORWIN, *supra* note 27, at 201.

[126] Since, with the exception of Korea and the Dominican Republic, congressional resolutions were involved in recent crises, presidential *practice* at least is not necessarily inconsistent with traditional recognition of congressional power to control use of the military.

particular concern in an area where, as here, the only precedents on which future actions can be based are those set by the executive branch itself.

IV. The Proper Allocation of the Power: Restoring the Constitutional Balance

A. The Relevance of the Constitutional Analysis

Theoretically the federal courts could assume the role of answering questions about the constitutionality of specific military actions. The obvious occasion would be a suit by a draftee resisting service or a particular assignment on the ground that the conflict was illegal.[127] But in recognition of the likelihood of direct conflict with the Executive and the appropriateness of such questions for political resolution, the courts so far have refused to consider these questions.[128]

In the absence of any final authority to whom appeal can be made or from whom enforcement can be sought, any attempt to brand particular conflicts as constitutional or unconstitutional is likely to be of little consequence. The constitutional analysis is better viewed as yielding a working directive to the executive and legislative branches that the commitment of the country to war be accomplished only through the closest collaboration possible, rather than an automatic formula for condemning or approving particular presidential action. The question should be: what concrete steps should the two branches take to assure that the policies behind the constitutional scheme are served?

B. Results of the Constitutional Analysis: Requiring Congressional Authorization for the Use of Force Abroad

1. When Should Authorization Be Sought? — (a) *Presidential Discretion.* — One position which might be taken in attempting to comply with this constitutional directive is that the respective roles of the Executive and the Congress in controlling the use of the armed forces should continue unaltered, following the general trend suggested, if not made completely explicit, by recent practice. Under an extreme form of this theory the President could continue to send troops abroad and even commit them to combat according to his interpretation of the needs of the broad policy and security interests of the country. While the President would still seek congressional approval when he determined that such a course was feasible, under the official policy these resolutions would neither be necessary for the action nor would they limit his ability to commit troops beyond the terms of the resolution.

In view of the constitutional policy favoring congressional authorization of war, this position must rest on the argument that it is im-

---

[127] *See* Luftig v. McNamara, 373 F.2d 664 (D.C. Cir.), *cert. denied*, 387 U.S. 945 (1967); United States v. Mitchell, 369 F.2d 323 (2d Cir. 1966), *cert. denied*, 386 U.S. 972 (1967).

[128] *See* note 40 *supra*. For a review of some of the potential issues in such a suit see the dissenting opinions by Justices Stewart and Douglas in Mora v. McNamara, 389 U.S. 934, 934-39 (1967), *denying cert. to* No. 20,420 (D.C. Cir., Feb. 20, 1967).

possible in the contemporary context to require anything less than ultimate executive control. The contention would be that in order to make the Constitution workable, the war-declaring clause must be interpreted to place minimum limits on the President's power to respond with speed and flexibility to meet military crises.[129]

Even without traversing for the moment the basic premise of such a theory, the most that it could legitimately authorize would be presidential use of force in emergency situations where vital American interests would be jeopardized by the delay involved in any attempt to secure prior congressional action. But to equate all instances requiring the use of force with such emergencies seems clearly untenable. The position approaches acceptability only where there is no alternative which would allow greater participation by Congress while substantially preserving American interests.

(b) *"Major" Conflicts.* — An alternative is to require congressional authorization whenever the President's use of force, outside of the strict defense of the United States, is likely to result in a "major" conflict. Under this approach the purposes of the war-declaring clause would be satisfied by leaving for congressional action only the upper extremity of a whole scale of international conflicts of ascending intensity and scope.[130] Although there are obvious difficulties in attempting to draw a line on such a scale between "major" and "minor" conflicts, the theory assumes that at least there will be clear instances at both ends. The President would still be left with virtual discretionary power to decide when force must be used to protect American rights and interests, but he would be bound to seek congressional authorization where such action would be tantamount to initiating "war." Although the theory has considerable support in American history, in the present international context practical difficulties prevent the theoretical limitation from ever being employed as a guide for satisfying the constitutional norm for allocating control of the military.[131]

(i) *Problems of Prediction.* — One of the major problems inherent in any theory which depends on a determination of whether a sequence of events will result in a sizable conflict is the impossibility of predicting which particular events are most likely to result in war.[132] This is especially true in light of modern conceptions of the role of force in international politics. The use of the armed forces in a potentially explosive situation may, under the deterrence theory, actually lessen rather than increase the likelihood of war; but to pretend to be able to tell in advance whether war or peace will be the result of such action is to lay claim to a degree of prescience which few would find credible

---

[129] It is questionable whether this argument can ever achieve constitutional respectability once it is admitted that control over the decision to go to war belongs to Congress in ordinary circumstances. *Cf.* A.L.A. Schechter Poultry Corp. v. United States, 295 U.S. 495, 528 (1935) ("[e]xtraordinary conditions do not create or enlarge constitutional power"; Congress held to have exceeded its powers to regulate interstate commerce).

[130] *See* p. 1790 *supra; cf.* Osgood, *War and Policy,* in AMERICAN DEFENCE POLICY 109, 114 (1965).

[131] *See* Jones, *The President, Congress, and Foreign Relations,* 29 CALIF. L. REV. 565, 578-80 & nn.43-44 (1941); *cf.* Mathews, *supra* note 76, at 385.

[132] Mathews, *supra* note 76, at 385.

today.[133] These difficulties of prediction illustrate the crucial factual distinction between the context in which this quantitative limitation on the President's powers developed in the late nineteenth and early twentieth centuries and the context in which it is invoked today. At the time when the theory developed it was rare for such interventions to reach the stature of war.[134] The world had not yet achieved the uneasy stalemate of today in which every country is classified as friend, foe, or neutral and even the most minor skirmish which threatens to upset the balance raises the spectre of war of unknown dimensions. The unpredictability of the result of rushing troops to Lebanon,[135] the constantly revised predictions about the nature and extent of our involvement in Vietnam indicate that it can no longer be said with any degree of assurance that the commitment of troops to combat under *any* conditions is unlikely to result in major conflict.

(*ii*) *The Fait Accompli Problem.* — Lack of predictability would not be a serious problem if Congress could meaningfully decide whether to continue hostilities which have already commenced; but once our military forces are engaged, Congress often has little choice but to acquiesce. The de facto power of the President to present Congress with the *fait accompli* of a state of war has been demonstrated repeatedly in the past [136] and is reflected again today in aspects of the current Vietnam conflict.[137] This problem, too, has been aggravated by changed circumstances. With the assumption of worldwide commitments, the United States has come to occupy the center of a stage where indecision, a clash of wills between Congress and the President over the course to pursue in foreign affairs, or sudden "about-faces" in tactics is felt to discourage the confidence of our allies and encourage the actions of our enemies. The result is to make presidential action in the modern context largely irreversible.[138]

(*c*) *Returning to the "Neutrality" Theory.* — The conclusion suggested by the above considerations is not that there can be no limits on the President's power to employ the armed forces,[139] but that a quantitative limitation can no longer serve as a satisfactory guideline for the proper allocation between the President and Congress of the power to commit troops to combat. If Congress' war power is not to become purely symbolic, there must be as much room as possible for congressional expression of its will prior to the use of force abroad for whatever purpose, at least where such use is not "neutral" with respect to foreign political entities. Yet there are very few occasions today in which a truly "neutral" use of force is possible. Only the protection of American lives and property during civil disorder appears to remain

---

[133] Eisenhower's intervention in Lebanon, for example, was felt to have averted rather than precipitated a conflict, though at the time not even the President attempted to predict such a result. *Compare* N.Y. Times, July 24, 1958, at 5, col. 1, *with id.*, July 16, 1958, at 1, col. 8.

[134] J. ROGERS, *supra* note 7, at 80; *see* M. OFFUTT, *supra* note 32, at 4.

[135] *See* note 133 *supra*.

[136] *See* note 81 *supra*.

[137] *See* p. 1804 *infra*.

[138] *See* E. CORWIN, *supra* note 27, at 222.

[139] This is apparently the conclusion which critics of the "major conflict" theory reach. *See* Mathews, *supra* note 76, at 385.

as a possible candidate for such neutrality and even here the employment of the armed forces will generally be highly suspect. Intervention at the request of a local government to suppress a revolutionary guerilla band usually is tantamount to taking sides in a political contest which, as Vietnam illustrates, may grow to unforeseeable dimensions when the rebels have external support or sympathizers. Consequently, every decision to commit troops to combat becomes a potential subject for congressional deliberation.[140] At the same time, however, it must be recognized that there will be cases where in the Executive's judgment there simply is no time to secure congressional authorization before acting. In such cases, where he believes that Congress would agree with his judgment that the interest at stake is worth defending at the risk of war,[141] the President should be able to take action while *simultaneously* seeking congressional authorization. These cases should be few. None of the recent military actions appears to have involved such genuine urgency as to preclude congressional participation in the decision to employ the military.[142] Even fewer should be the cases where the demands of secrecy preclude resort to Congress.[143] There will also be difficulties in determining the extent of the control over the armed forces which is to remain with the President as Commander

---

[140] The resolution which emerged from the recent hearings in the Senate Foreign Relations Committee expresses a similar sentiment:

Resolved, That a commitment for purposes of this resolution means the use of, or promise to a foreign state or people to use, the Armed Forces of the United States either immediately or upon the happening of certain events, and

That it is the sense of the Senate that, under any circumstances which may arise in the future pertaining to situations in which the United States is not already involved, the commitment of the Armed Forces of the United States to hostilities on foreign territory for any purpose other than to repel an attack on the United States or to protect United States citizens or property properly will result from a decision made in accordance with constitutional processes, which, in addition to appropriate executive action, require affirmative action by Congress specifically intended to give rise to such commitment.

S. Res. 187, 90th Cong., 1st Sess. (1967). Although the resolution is ambiguous in crucial phases (Where is the United States "not already involved"? How does the "definition" of "commitment" in the first paragraph affect the meaning of "commitment" in the second paragraph? What is "specifically intended affirmative action by Congress"?), if interpreted to reflect the sentiment that presidential use of force must be restricted to cases where employed neutrally in order to preserve Congress' power to initiate war, the resolution seems an accurate description of the constitutional responsibilities of the President and Congress and a commendable attempt to restore the proper constitutional balance.

[141] The effort to review and define the "national commitments" of the United States — the original focus of the hearings in the Senate Foreign Relations Committee, *see Hearings on National Commitments* 51 — seems most relevant as a possible guide in making such a judgment.

[142] *Id.* at 3.

[143] It has been suggested that the Bay of Pigs episode is an illustration of such a case. *See* R. Russell, *supra* note 5, at 425. A precedent for secret legislative proceedings to authorize the use of force against a foreign nation was established in 1811 in a series of acts authorizing the President to occupy and hold Florida against Spain. Apparently four such "secret laws" were passed, one of which, though referred to by Adams, has yet to be found. *See* C. Berdahl, *supra* note 14, at 46 n.12. *See also* Parry, *Legislatures and Secrecy,* 67 Harv. L. Rev. 737 (1954) (examining the success of the British Parliament in handling security matters through secret session during World War II).

in Chief.[144] To require congressional approval for every decision to deploy American troops is hardly either desirable or constitutionally required. Yet there will be some situations, such as the rushing of troops to Lebanon at that government's request which, although not involving immediate commitment to combat, so clearly entail the possibility of conflict that prior approval should be sought. Other cases, such as the Greenland and Iceland examples where the movement of troops is hard to distinguish from a hostile employment of force against another nation, are also candidates for prior congressional authorization. But although the difficulty of drawing a line cannot be avoided and must ultimately be left to the discretion of the President, at least the general presumption in accordance with which that discretion is exercised would be reversed: instead of assuming that the President may deploy American forces as he sees fit and only in the exceptional case need he seek congressional approval, the presumption should be that congressional collaboration is the general rule wherever the use of the military is involved, with presidential initiative being reserved for the exceptional case.

2. *What Constitutes Authorization?* — The problem of what constitutes adequate congressional authorization where it is needed is intimately connected with the problem of whether Congress is capable at all of meaningfully participating in decisions involving the use of the armed forces. An excessively wooden concept of what constitutes congressional exercise of its power to declare war would have the effect, not of preserving congressional authority, but of transferring more and more decisions to the more flexible executive branch. At the other extreme, when the President can count on securing a blank check from Congress whenever he envisions the need to employ force abroad, congressional participation, whatever form it takes, is largely meaningless. Between these extremes, a balance must be sought which secures genuine participation by Congress in controlling the use of the armed forces, while still permitting sufficient executive flexibility to meet constantly changing developments.

(a) *Treaties as Authorization.* — A claim often heard today is that mutual defense treaties which commit the United States to come to the aid of an attacked ally serve as authorizations to the President to use force if he deems it necessary in particular contexts for United States "aid" to take that form. The argument raises the question whether the congressional power to initate war may be exercised by the Senate alone through the treaty power, rather than by both houses of Congress acting together. Further, even if the treaty power is a legitimate mode of authorizing use of the military instrument, the problem remains whether existing treaties can properly be interpreted to constitute such authorization.

(i) *Constitutional Limitations.* — The treaty-making power has been held not to extend "so far as to authorize what the Constitution forbids" [145] — a limitation which has been construed to prevent the Senate

---

[144] *See* pp. 1785–87 *supra*.
[145] Geofroy v. Riggs, 133 U.S. 258, 267 (1890).

and President from exercising by treaty a power exclusively vested elsewhere by the Constitution. Two such powers, cited in the past, are contained in article I, section 9 ("no money shall be drawn from the Treasury but in Consequence of Appropriations made by Law") and article I, section 7 ("all Bills for raising Revenue shall originate in the House of Representatives"). Although it has been argued that "appropriation by law" includes appropriation by treaty as part of the law of the land,[146] the provision has generally been construed otherwise: in order to implement treaties which require appropriations, a statute and, hence, independent legislative action by both houses is needed.[147] The debate whether article I, section 7 similarly forbids revenue-affecting provisions in treaties [148] has become largely academic through the use of congressional-executive agreements and statutes.[149]

The question remains whether the war-declaring power, like the power to control appropriations and, arguably, revenue laws, also requires participation by the House of Representatives. The language of the Constitution itself offers nothing to distinguish this provision from any of the other enumerated powers in article I, section 8, most of which have been the subject of treaties.[150] Indeed the same clause which gives Congress the power to declare war also confers the power "to Make rules concerning Captures" which has long been shared with the treaty power.[151] Yet despite these considerations, there remains serious doubt that action by the Senate alone meets the general intention of the framers respecting congressional involvement in war decisions. The possibility of giving the Senate alone the power to declare war was specifically considered and rejected. According to Madison's notes, Mr. Butler pointed out that objections based on the slow proceedings of the House were equally true of the Senate. Mr. Mason opposed giving the power of war to the Senate "because [it was] not so constructed as to be entitled to it." Both he and Mr. Ellsworth felt that it should be easier to get out of war than into it and hence, that while it would be sufficient to give the Senate alone power to ratify peace treaties, the entire "legislature" had the power of war.[152] These notes seem to

---

[146] See Feidler & Dwan, *The Extent of the Treaty-Making Power*, 28 GEO. L.J. 184, 192 (1939); McDougal & Lans, *Treaties and Congressional-Executive or Presidential Agreements: Interchangeable Instruments of National Policy*, 54 YALE L.J. 181, 306 (1945).

[147] See 1 W. WILLOUGHBY, THE CONSTITUTIONAL LAW OF THE UNITED STATES 549–52 (2d ed. 1929); LEGISLATIVE REFERENCE SERVICE, *supra* note 87, at 469–70; McLaughlin, *The Scope of the Treaty Power in the United States*, 42 MINN. L. REV. 709, 756–57 (1958).

[148] Arguably, a treaty is not a "bill" to raise revenues and, hence, is free from article I, section 7's requirement that such bills originate in the House of Representatives. *See* 1 W. WILLOUGHBY, *supra* note 147, at 558. *See generally* H.R. REP. No. 2680, 48th Cong., 2d Sess. (1884).

[149] See 1 W. WILLOUGHBY, *supra* note 147, at 559; LEGISLATIVE REFERENCE SERVICE, *supra* note 87, at 470.

[150] See E. CORWIN, THE PRESIDENT'S CONTROL OF FOREIGN RELATIONS 2 (1917); McDougal & Lans, *supra* note 146, at 217–18.

[151] See Q. WRIGHT, THE CONTROL OF AMERICAN FOREIGN RELATIONS 299, 355 n.45 (1922). An example is the Hague Convention of 1907 limiting the rights of belligerency. *See* E. CORWIN, *supra* note 27, at 425 n.23.

[152] See 2 M. FARRAND, THE RECORDS OF THE FEDERAL CONVENTION OF 1787, at 318–19 (rev. ed. 1937).

indicate a deliberate intent to include the House of Representatives, with its popular representation, in the war-making decision.

(*ii*) *Treaty Interpretation.* — Regardless of the outcome of the constitutional issue, there is considerable support for the conclusion that none of the existing collective security and treaty agreements to which the United States is a party is by its terms designed to alter the distribution of the war-making power. A typical example of the guaranty provisions contained in such agreements is article five of the North Atlantic Treaty: [153]

> The Parties agree that an armed attack against one or more of them in Europe or North America shall be considered an attack against them all; and consequently they agree that, if such an armed attack occurs, each of them . . . will assist the Party or Parties so attacked by taking . . . *such action as it deems necessary*, including the use of armed force . . . .

When the treaty was submitted for ratification the contention that the United States was automatically committed to go to war in the event that one of the other members was attacked was specifically rejected in the Senate Committee Report and by the Secretary of State. The signatories, it was explained, were to be left free to decide for themselves in each instance what action was necessary.[154]

Partly to avoid the debates provoked by the NATO treaty over this issue, subsequent treaties have adopted language from the United Nations Charter [155] which even more clearly illustrates the neutrality of their obligations with respect to the internal distribution of the war-making power. Thus, article IV of the SEATO treaty provides that in the event of armed attack on any member each signatory will "act to meet the common danger in accordance with its constitutional processes"; article IX requires that "the Treaty shall be ratified and its provisions carried out by the Parties in accordance with their respective constitutional processes." [156] Similar langauge in each of the forty-two

---

[153] North Atlantic Treaty, Apr. 4, 1949, art. 5, 63 Stat. 2244 (1949), T.I.A.S. No. 1964 (emphasis added).

[154] *See* D. CHEEVER & H. HAVILAND, AMERICAN FOREIGN POLICY AND THE SEPARATION OF POWERS 128 (1952); McLaughlin, *supra* note 147, at 676.

[155] Article 43 of the Charter describes the special agreements to be made by member nations in fulfilling their obligations to make armed forces available to the Security Council on certain conditions. It concludes with the provision that such agreements "shall be subject to ratification by the signatory states *in accordance with their respective constitutional processes.*" U.N. CHARTER art. 43, para. 3 (emphasis added).

The question which governmental department had the power to determine for the United States the number of troops to be placed at the disposal of the Security Council was settled by Congress in the United Nations Participation Act, 22 U.S.C. § 287d (1964). The Act provides that any special agreement negotiated by the President respecting the number and type of armed forces to be made available must be submitted to Congress for its approval. "[T]he controlling theory of the act is that American participation in United Nations shall rest on the principle of departmental collaboration, and not on an exclusive presidential prerogative in the diplomatic field." E. CORWIN, *supra* note 27, at 221 (emphasis deleted).

[156] Southeast Asia Collective Defense Treaty, Sept. 8, 1954, art. IV, para. 1, art. IX, para. 2, [1955] 1 U.S.T. 81, T.I.A.S. No. 3170.

mutual defense pacts to which the United States is a party [157] has led
to general agreement that current postwar security treaties have not
changed the relative powers of Congress and the President with respect
to the use of the armed forces.[158]

   (b) *Implied Authorization: Appropriations and Congressional Inaction.* — In addition to legislative instruments specifically authorizing
use of the military it has been urged that where Congress under its
power to raise and support armies [159] makes appropriations to support
military operations abroad, such action constitutes at least implied approval of the President's war making and serves as authorization to
continue the campaign. The difficulty with the argument is that since
such appropriations must generally come after the hostilities have already begun, the effective choice remaining to Congress is likely
to be severely limited. The "approval" which is expressed by the fact
of such appropriations (in order not to "desert our fighting boys") is
not unlike the "approval" of President Theodore Roosevelt's action
expressed by Congress' appropriating the money to bring back the
fleet he sent halfway around the world.[160] The more blatant the *fait
accompli* which forces Congress' hand, the less should exercise of its
power of appropriation be taken as "consent" to the action. Even
where there is no *fait accompli*, if the power over appropriations had
been thought a sufficient safeguard against presidential war making,
it becomes difficult to understand why the framers were so concerned
about withholding the war power from the Executive in the first place.
Although it may be admitted that an appropriations bill could be introduced under circumstances which leave room for no interpretation
other than "a vote for the bill is a vote for the war," it is hard to see
why, even in such cases, resort to implied rather than express authorization is necessary. If the issue at stake in voting for the appropriation
really is so clear, a separate resolution to that effect, expressly authorizing the use of the appropriation for a specific military endeavor abroad
will avoid later problems of "proving" congressional intent not evident
on the face of the bill.

   A variation of this argument is that failure of Congress to reduce
appropriations or limit the size of the armed forces to a level which
would make impossible continued prosecution of a war indicates consent to continuing the action. In addition to the objections raised
above, arguments which rely on congressional inaction to show congressional approval completely shift the responsibility for initiating
the war from Congress to the Executive. Further, the burden of securing a majority is shifted from those favoring to those disapproving
authorization — a not insignificant factor in the political arena.

   (c) *Resolutions as Authorization.* — The claim has been made that
where authorization is needed nothing short of a formal declaration
of war will satisfy the Constitution's demand for congressional control of

---

[157] *See Hearings on National Commitments* 96–97.
[158] *See id*; NATIONAL COMMITMENTS REPORT 15; note 67 *supra*.
[159] *See* note 6 *supra*.
[160] *See* J. ROGERS, *supra* note 7, at 83–84.

the war power.[161] It is difficult, though, to find any rationale for such a claim. In addition to the obsolescence and general undesirability of a formal declaration today,[162] the claim finds support neither in the language of the Constitution, the intent of the framers, the available historical and judicial precedents nor the purposes behind the clause. The framers' desire to vest the war power in Congress is in no way defeated by allowing Congress through joint or concurrent resolutions or acts of congress to deliberate and decide whether or not to authorize specific military undertakings. As early as President Adams' administration similar procedures short of a formal declaration were followed to authorize the "undeclared war" with France [163] and were apparently accepted as entirely appropriate by courts considering claims which arose out of the conflict.[164] Since that time the use of the resolution, especially in recent years, has become the predominant means by which congressional participation in the decision to commit troops to combat has been sought.

But though potentially the resolution could serve as a vehicle for congressional participation in the decision to commit troops to combat, it is easily turned into nothing more than a device for rubber-stamping executive decisions. A resolution authorizing the President to use armed forces without restriction for whatever purposes he saw fit would seem an improper delegation of Congress' power because of its lack of sufficiently articulated standards. Two Supreme Court opinions, however, indicate that at least with respect to matters connected with foreign relations a wide latitude will be given to executive and congressional judgment of what constitutes sufficient standards, and hence, a proper delegation of authority by Congress to the President.[165] Yet considerations similar to those involved in the delegation doctrine are involved in determining the propriety of the resolution as a means of congressional authorization. The dangers are illustrated by recent practice. The resolutions on Formosa, the Middle East, Cuba and Vietnam are all ambiguous at best with respect to the function they are supposed to serve. At times specific words of authorization are employed, at other times only general words of encouragement and approval.[166] Usually presented in the context of an immediate crisis

---

[161] *See* Lawyers Committee, *supra* note 2, at 2672–73.

[162] *See* pp. 1772–73 *supra*.

[163] Act of July 9, 1798, ch. 68, 1 Stat. 578; Act of May 28, 1798, ch. 48, 1 Stat. 561; *see* C. BERDAHL, *supra* note 14, at 83–84.

[164] *See* Bas v. Tingy, 4 U.S. (4 Dall.) 37 (1800); Talbot v. Seeman, 5 U.S. (1 Cr.) 1, 28 (1801) (Marshall, C.J.) ("[i]t is not denied, nor in the course of the argument, has it been denied, that congress may authorize general hostilities").

[165] *See* Youngstown Sheet & Tube Co. v. Sawyer, 343 U.S. 579, 635–37 (1952) (concurring opinion); United States v. Curtiss-Wright Export Corp., 299 U.S. 304, 324 (1936). The latter case has been interpreted as withdrawing "virtually all constitutional limitation upon the scope of congressional delegation of power to the President to act in the area of international relations." Jones, *The President, Congress and Foreign Relations*, 29 CALIF. L. REV. 565, 575 (1941).

[166] *Compare* Formosa Resolution, Pub. L. No. 4, ch. 4, 69 Stat. 7 (1955) ("the President . . . hereby is authorized to employ the Armed Forces of the United States"), *with* Middle East Resolution, Pub. L. No. 85–7, § 2, 71 Stat.

they are unable to suggest a specific plan of action, but are confined to offering vague measures of support for the President in carrying out a still undefined policy. Conscientious congressmen express concern that a blank check is being given to the President, and subsequent State Department interpretations of the scope of the authority granted do little to allay such fears.

Not all of these difficulties can be avoided; many of them are the inevitable result of the inability to foresee crises and predict their outcome. Others can be remedied in part by recognizing the significance of the resolution: that it *does* confer authority, potentially, to embark on war and that, therefore, the scope of authority should be clearly and unambiguously expressed. Where problems of predictability seem insurmountable, limited authority should be granted by providing for expiration and renewal after a specified time and by confining the authorization to specific areas and specific purposes.

Much of the burden of making such resolutions meaningful devices for securing congressional consent must fall on Congress itself. The temptation to shift to other shoulders the responsibility for a decision as distasteful as that of entering into war or authorizing the use of force has no doubt been partly responsibile for congressional lack of concern in the past over presidential intrusion into this area. In situations where real emergencies are involved and unilateral executive action may be required, the burden falls on Congress either to voice its disapproval or give its consent without needless delay. To claim well after the fact of intervention that the country is now so involved that Congress has no real choice will invoke little sympathy if Congress' own delay in expressing its opinion has helped accomplish the fact. Finally, prophylactic measures such as a current review of the extent and nature of United States commitments may prove desirable.[167] With the lessons of the Vietnam War as a guide both to the sacrifices those commitments may entail and the difficulties in interpreting authorizing resolutions, a careful review of the language of those commitments may avoid later difficulties.

V. CONCLUSION: VIETNAM

Under the analysis in this note the validity of the President's actions in Vietnam depends on whether or not specific congressional approval has been secured for the war which has developed. The action is not a response to an attack on or a declaration of war against the United States. In terms of troop commitment and casualties — which now exceed those of the Korean War [168] — the conflict, excluding the Civil War, has become the third largest in American history: it is "war" within the meaning of article I, section 8. Current treaty agreements, in particular the SEATO Treaty, do not purport to serve as authorization for such a war. Such authorization, if it has

---

5 (1957) ("if the President determines the necessity thereof, the United States is prepared to use armed forces").

[167] *See* p. 1797 & note 141 *supra*.

[168] *See* N.Y. Times, March 15, 1967, at 1, col. 5.

been secured, must be found in the Gulf of Tonkin Resolution, which provides a clear example of both the difficulties and potentialities inherent in the resolution as a device for securing congressional consent.

The first clause of that resolution states that "the Congress approves and supports the determination of the President, as Commander in Chief, to take all necessary measures to repel any armed attack against the forces of the United States and to prevent further aggression." [169] The clause alone hardly represents more than a congressional rallying around the flag in response to the attack on a United States ship, and merely approves what could obviously be done without such approval: the repelling of an attack on American armed forces. Were this the entirety of the resolution, present operations would be justified only under the implausible construction that they were a continuing and necessary defensive response to the Gulf of Tonkin incident.[170] The second section, however, proclaims that "the United States is . . . prepared, as the President determines, to take all necessary steps, including the use of armed force, to assist any member or protocol state of the Southeast Asia Collective Defense Treaty requesting assistance in defense of its freedom." [171] This rather comprehensive language certainly supports the interpretation given it by the administration: that it is a functional equivalent of a declaration of war [172] and as such the President may conduct the war as he sees fit. He has the power to bomb North Vietnam [173] and presumably even China if that is deemed necessary to defend South Vietnam's freedom.

Despite apparent statements to the contrary when the bill was being debated,[174] Senator Fullbright claims, however, that there was no understanding that the resolution extended to the authorization of war.[175] In his defense it must be admitted that the circumstances surrounding the passage of the resolution hardly lent themselves to minimizing misunderstandings. The resolution was presented in an atmosphere of great urgency immediately after the attack. This factor, coupled with the allusions to that attack and the request for approval of a response to it, creates a strong suspicion that the implications of the second section were overlooked. Although such a result is surely as much the fault of Congress as of the administration, under the circumstances, compliance with the principle that Congress be given the closest possible participation in such decisions would have demanded at the least that prior to the decision the following year vastly to increase the commitment of troops to the area, congressional reassertion of its approval be sought. Arguments have been for the view that this is what was done in the May, 1965 appropriations request: the administration expressly stated that the

---

[169] Vietnam Resolution, Pub. L. No. 88–408, § 1, 78 Stat. 384 (1964).

[170] See p. 1787 supra.

[171] Vietnam Resolution, Pub. L. No. 88–408, § 2, 78 Stat. 384 (1964).

[172] See Hearings on National Commitments 82 (testimony of N. Katzenbach, Under Sec'y of State); 110 CONG. REC. 18,403, 18,409-10 (1964).

[173] See 110 CONG. REC. 18,409 (1964).

[174] See id. at 18,403-04, 18,409-10 (1964).

[175] See NATIONAL COMMITMENTS REPORT 21.

request was not for a routine appropriation, but was being made as a means of presenting the Vietnam issue.[176] At the same time, however, the President made clear that the additional funds were needed to "protect our men and supplies" [177] and to provide them with modern equipment, thus illustrating the difficulty in attempting to construe such appropriations as equivalent to explicit authorization for the war. At best, the Gulf of Tonkin Resolution, even coupled with subsequent appropriations, leaves unclear the extent to which congressional authorization of the war has been expressed.

With respect to the future, the problem can be avoided by placing a strict time limit on the resolution, giving Congress adequate time to deliberate and review the resolution and encouraging the Executive to seek further specific support later. With respect to the present, although the *fait accompli* problem can no longer be avoided, the ambiguity is best resolved, not by relying on Congress' failure to repeal the resolution as provided for in the third clause,[178] but by resubmitting for congressional approval a resolution specifically phrased to give consent to the war.

---

[176] Message to Congress, May 4, 1965, in SENATE COMM. ON FOREIGN RELATIONS, 90TH CONG., 1ST SESS., BACKGROUND INFORMATION RELATING TO SOUTHEAST ASIA AND VIETNAM 160–63 (Comm. Print 3d rev. ed. 1967); *see* Moore & Underwood, *The Lawfulness of United States Assistance to the Republic of Viet Nam,* in 112 CONG, REC. 15,519, 15,557–58 (1966).

[177] Message to Congress, May 4, 1965, *supra* note 176, at 160.

[178] "This resolution . . . may be terminated . . . by concurrent resolution of the Congress." Vietnam Resolution, Pub. L. No. 88–408, § 3, 78 Stat. 384 (1964).

The War in Viet Nam:
Unconstitutional, Justiciable, and
Jurisdictionally Attackable

LAWRENCE R. VELVEL

I. INTRODUCTION

Of late, some members of the academic community have begun to rebel vigorously against their profession's "traditional emphasis on morally neutral research and on the withdrawal of the scholar from active participation in public issues."[1] The rebels believe that one embarks on a fruitless voyage when one seeks ultimate neutrality in social science, and that the academic would therefore do better to use his talents in "defense of civilized values."[2] A product of the rebel camp, this article is an attempt to propound the author's conception of certain constitutional values.

The article is dedicated to the proposition that the Vietnamese war is patently unconstitutional because the executive has exceeded its constitutional power and has in effect usurped Congress' power to declare war. An article dedicated to this proposition is a logical outgrowth of the fact that the author is involved in litigation which challenges the legality of the war. The article also represents an attempt to provide a blueprint which, with the many necessary modifications, could be converted into a brief by any others who may wish to challenge the war.

To those traditionalists who may consider it unscholarly to write an article for the reasons envisioned here, the answers are simple and direct. First, as indicated before, in today's highly troubled world the academic can make as great a contribution by using his professional capabilities to openly advance conceptions of fundamental values as by attempting to maintain a mask of neutrality which, in the ultimate sense, will necessarily turn out to be illusory when one deals with issues as divisive as are those stemming from the current war.[3] Furthermore, in propounding his values, the academic will be forced to the effort necessary to justify them, and human knowledge will thereby be advanced. Second, there is no good reason why the academic lawyer need be

---

[1] Duberman, *Double Indictment*, N.Y. Times, March 17, 1968 (Book Review), at 3. (The book review is of *The Dissenting Academy*, which is edited by Theodore Roszak.)

[2] T. ROSZAK, THE DISSENTING ACADEMY, quoted in Duberman, *supra* note 1.

[3] The author does not say that *all* neutrality is impossible in social science. For example, both proponents and opponents of a war can agree that 50 men were killed in a particular skirmish. He says, rather, that neutrality is not possible in regard to the ultimate issues of social science, such as whether a war is wise, just, or constitutional. One's values inevitably color his appraisal of such ultimate issues. *See* Miller & Howell, *The Myth of Neutrality In Constitutional Adjudication*, 27 U. CHI. L. REV. 661, 661-83 (1960); *compare with* R. DAHL, MODERN POLITICAL ANALYSIS, 101-07 (1963).

forever confined to the rather narrow view of his craft which has so dominated the art of legal writing. Other professions continually experiment with new assumptions and techniques, and there seems no reason why professors of law should not do likewise.

Finally, it should be mentioned that this article was written mainly before the President's speech of Sunday, March 31, 1968, in which he announced a bombing pause which would hopefully lead to peace negotiations.[4] What the war situation will be when this piece appears in print is impossible to forecast: peace negotiations could be progressing well or slowly or not at all; the pace of fighting may be slackened or increased. If there have been any major changes in the war situation when this piece appears, in a few minor respects it may be necessary for the reader to bear in mind that it was written before such changes occurred. Similarly, the Supreme Court's decision in *Flast v. Gardner*,[5] a pending case which is relevant to a later section of this article,[6] may come down before the article is in print; and, if it does not, it will presumably be handed down shortly thereafter. Hopefully the reader will bear with this circumstance as well. In regard to the possibility that peace negotiations should be in the offing or underway when this article appears, it remains true that the Vietnamese war has raised constitutional issues which far transcend this war alone, issues which have occurred in the past and which, regrettably, may occur again in the future. Thus, the author's opinion is that neither peace negotiations nor the ending of the war will cause this work to lose whatever analytical value it may have.

II. THE MERITS

Article I, section 8, clause 11 of the United States Constitution states, in clear and unequivocal language, that the *Congress* shall have the power to declare war.[7] It is the author's contention that, by conducting continuous large-scale military operations in Viet Nam, the executive branch is acting beyond its constitutional powers and has in effect usurped Congress' power to declare war. For this reason, the judiciary should require that the executive either obtain a congressional declaration of war, be it a declaration of general or limited war, or discontinue fighting in Viet Nam, such discontinuance to be carried out with all deliberate speed. Alternatively, if peace negotiations are in the offing or are underway when a judicial decision is made or if the war is over at that time, a court, in order to avoid jeopardizing hopes for obtaining and maintaining peace, should merely issue a declaratory judgment that the war is unconstitutional because the executive has exceeded its authority and has in effect usurped Congress' power to declare war.

---

[4] The text of the President's speech can be found in the N.Y. Times, April 1, 1968, at 26, cols. 1-6.

[5] Probable jurisdiction noted, 88 S. Ct. 218 (1967). Oral argument was heard in this case on March 12, 1968. Graham, *Ervin Asks High Court to Allow Church-State Taxpayer Suits*, N.Y. Times, March 10, 1968, at 23, col. 1.

[6] It is relevant to the question of standing, discussed at text accompanying notes 152-89 *infra*.

[7] Art. I, § 8 states: "The Congress shall have Power . . . (11) To declare War . . . ."

The framers of the United States Constitution deliberately placed the power to declare war in the Congress rather than in the President. Being familiar with the British system, under which the King had the power to declare war, the framers ardently wished to avoid giving the executive a similar power. They feared that the power of the executive might involve the nation in the "calamities of foreign wars";[8] they distrusted the executive's belief in its superior wisdom about the necessity of engaging in war;[9] they were fearful that the desire for prestige might cause the executive to overstep constitutional bounds;[10] and they recognized the danger of military supremacy over civilian government.[11] Two great Americans, Abraham Lincoln and Justice Story, have summarized the reasons which impelled the framers to lodge the power to declare war in Congress. Lincoln said:

> The provision of the Constitution giving the war-making power to Congress was dictated, as I understand it, by the following reasons: Kings had always been involving and impoverishing their people in wars, pretending generally, if not always, that the good of the people was the object. This our convention understood to be the most oppressive of all kingly oppressions, and they resolved to so frame the Constitution that no one man should hold the power of bringing this oppression upon us.[12]

Justice Story concluded:

> [t]he power of declaring war is not only the highest sovereign prerogative; but it is in its own nature and effects so critical and calamitous, that it requires the utmost deliberation, and the successive review of all the councils of the nation. War, in its best estate, never fails to impose upon the people the most burthensome taxes, and personal sufferings. It is always injurious, and sometimes subversive of the great commercial, manufacturing, and agricultural interests. Nay, it always involves the prosperity, and not unfrequently the existence, of a nation. It is sometimes fatal to public liberty itself, by introducing a spirit of military glory, which is ready to follow, wherever a successful commander will lead; and in a republic, whose institutions are essentially founded on the basis of peace, there is infinite danger that war will find it both imbecile in defense, and eager for contest. Indeed, the history of republics has but too fatally proved, that they are too ambitious of military fame and conquest, and too easily devoted to the views of demagogues, who flatter their pride, and betray their interests. It should therefore be difficult in a republic to declare war; but not to make peace. The representatives of the people are to lay the taxes to support a war, and therefore have a right to be consulted, as to its propriety and necessity. The executive is to carry it on, and therefore should be consulted, as to its time, and the ways and means of making it effective. The cooperation of all the branches of the legislative power ought, upon principle, to be

[8] 1 M. FARRAND, THE RECORDS OF THE FEDERAL CONVENTION 316 (1911).

[9] Statement of Professor Ruhl V. Bartlett of the Fletcher School of Law and Diplomacy, *U.S. Commitments to Foreign Powers, Hearings Before The Committee On Foreign Relations Of The United States Senate*, 90th Cong., 1st Sess. 9 (1967) [hereinafter cited as *National Commitments Hearings*].

[10] *Id.* The framers were even afraid that the executive, if able to declare war, might assert the prerogatives of the British crown. *Id.*; 3 M. FARRAND, *supra* note 8, at 250; Statement of George Montross, *National Commitments Hearings* 305. *See* Statement of James Madison, quoted in E. CORWIN, THE PRESIDENT: OFFICE AND POWERS 180 (4th ed. 1964).

[11] Statement of Professor Bartlett, *supra* note 9.

[12] E. CORWIN, *supra* note 10, at 451, n.7; S. REP. No. 797, 90th Cong., 1st Sess. 11 (1967) [hereinafter cited as *National Commitments Report*].

required in this the highest act of legislation, as it is in all others. Indeed, there might be a propriety even in enforcing still greater restrictions, as by requiring a concurrence of two thirds of both houses . . . . This reasoning appears to have had great weight with the convention, and to have decided its choice. Its judgment has hitherto obtained the unqualified approbation of the country.[13]

As the present war unequivocally demonstrates, the reasons which impelled the framers to place the power to declare war in Congress are as valid today as when the Constitution was written. Modern wars bring about burdensome taxes; the present war, for example, has led to excise taxes and to a request for a significant income tax surcharge. Modern wars are injurious to economic interests; the present war, for example, has materially contributed to a rather serious inflation, to a balance of payments crisis and a crisis in gold, and to a cutback in programs designed to help the poor. Modern wars bring about great personal suffering; in the present war, for example, over 25,000 Americans have been killed, and more than 100,000 have been wounded. Modern wars may involve the very existence of nations; the present war, for example, has led some people to fear that a third world war, or war with China, could be the ultimate result of the conflict in Viet Nam. Modern wars involve sweeping assertions of executive power and lead the executive to disregard constitutional restraints;[14] for example, while the executive does claim that the Tonkin Gulf Resolution authorizes the current war effort[15]—a claim which will later be shown to be patently in error[16]—it also makes the sweeping claim that it could fight the current war if Congress had never passed the Gulf of Tonkin Resolution,[17] and it further makes the incredibly unlimited claim that it could fight the current war even if Congress were to repeal the resolution and thereby express its disapproval of the war.[18] Finally, modern wars are justified as being for the good of the people and are sometimes fought because the executive thinks it necessary to fight and to maintain prestige; the present war, for example, is justified by its executive proponents as being in the self-interest of Americans and as being necessary to maintain American prestige.

Since the reasons which impelled the framers to lodge the power to declare war in Congress are still true today, it remains equally true that no one man and no small group of men in the executive branch should have the power to carry on long-sustained and large-scale warfare without a congressional declaration of limited or general war. As were the framers, the present generation should be leery of believing that any one man or small group of men have such superior

---

[13] 2 J. Story, Commentaries on the Constitution of the United States 89-90 (2d ed. 1851).
[14] For a description of the ways in which past wars have led the executive to disregard normal restraints, see E. Corwin, The President: Office and Powers 227-62 (4th ed. 1964).
[15] Statement of Under Secretary of State Katzenbach, National Commitments Hearings 82, 84, 89, 137, 140; Department of State, Office of the Legal Adviser, The Legality of United States Participation In the Defense of Viet Nam, 75 Yale L.J. 1085, 1102-06 (1966) [hereinafter cited as Legal Adviser].
[16] See text accompanying notes 123-35.
[17] Katzenbach, supra note 15, at 99, 143, 145, 169; Statement of President Johnson, quoted at id. 221; Legal Adviser 1100-02; National Commitments Report 21-22. See the discussion of statements by Secretary Rusk at National Commitments Hearings 177, 180.
[18] Katzenbach, supra note 15, at 147.

wisdom that they should be permitted to plunge America into the "calamities of foreign wars." Rather, the constitutional mandate which gives Congress the power to declare war should be upheld. This mandate insures that the power to make the most critical decision a nation can make—whether to go to war—will belong not to a tiny handful of men in the executive, but will be dispersed among the 535 federal legislators.[19]

Judged by the constitutional standard that Congress has the power to declare war, the present conflict is hopelessly unconstitutional. There has been no congressional authorization to fight a long-sustained and large-scale war on the Asian continent. It is the executive alone which has authorized this, even though it has no constitutional power to do so. The executive, of course, believes that the war is wise and just while others disagree with this assessment. However, these are issues which are irrelevant to the war's constitutional status and therefore to this article. The only claims made here are that the war is unconstitutional and that it provides an apt modern illustration of the framers' idea that, if America is to fight, it must do so pursuant to a *congressional* declaration of war.[20]

III. The Government's Arguments

In speeches, briefs, congressional testimony, and articles, the executive branch has asserted various reasons for claiming that it has the power to fight the current war. Commentators have enumerated a few other reasons for permitting the executive to fight at its own behest. The vast majority of such arguments are utterly without merit, the rest of them have but small merit, and all of them are nothing more than rationalizations for permitting the executive to evade the Constitution by effectively arrogating unto itself the power to declare war.

A. *The Power to Repel Attack*

The executive branch points out, quite correctly, that the framers of the Constitution recognized that the executive might sometimes have to repel

---

[19] Perhaps an even wider dispersal of the power to declare war would be ideal; *e.g.*, perhaps the President and Congress should both have to declare war. Of course, this is in effect what happens when the executive seeks and obtains a declaration of war from Congress. It is probably not practicable to require the populace to vote on a declaration of war. In any event, the present constitutional mandate that Congress shall declare war is the best that we now have, and if it is not respected, it may well be only a question of time until this nation "will be threatened with tyranny or disaster." *National Commitments Report* 27.

[20] The following quotation is both pithy and apt:

Already possessing vast powers over our country's foreign relations, the executive, by acquiring the authority to commit the country to war, now exercises something approaching absolute power over the life or death of every living American—to say nothing of millions of other people all over the world. There is no human being or group of human beings alive wise and competent enough to be entrusted with such vast power. Plenary powers in the hands of any man or group threaten all other men with tyranny or disaster. Recognizing the impossibility of assuring the wise exercise of power by any one man or institution, the American Constitution divided that power among many men and several institutions and, in so doing, limited the ability of any one to impose tyranny or disaster on the country. The concentration in the hands of the President of virtually unlimited authority over matters of war and peace has all but removed the limits to executive power in the most important single area of our national life. Until they are restored the American people will be threatened with tyranny or disaster.

National Commitments Report 26-27.

armed attacks against the nation before there would be time to assemble Congress and obtain a declaration of war.[21] In other words, sometimes the executive would of necessity have to *make* war before Congress could be assembled to *declare* war. Because the President has to make war in order to repel sudden attacks, the framers used the phrase "the Congress shall have the power to declare war," instead of the phrase "the Congress shall have the power to make war."[22]

From the indisputable fact that the executive may sometimes have to make war in order to repel sudden attacks, the executive branch now deduces that the President may, in his total discretion, carry on any degree of warfare, for any length of time, anywhere on the globe, regardless of whether or not there is time for Congress to act.[23] For example, this country has conducted large-scale military operations in Viet Nam for over three years. During that long period, there has been ample time for the Congress to declare a limited or general war. Yet, according to the executive branch, congressional action, though eminently feasible, is entirely unnecessary.[24] Rather, the President, in his sole discretion, had the power to escalate efforts from the mere repelling of an attack on two destroyers in the Gulf of Tonkin to a point where over 500,000 men are engaged in both offensive and defensive operations and where more bomb tonnage has been dropped than was dropped on America's European enemies in World War II. It is eminently clear that this particular executive branch theory is nothing more than a prescription for entirely nullifying the congressional power to declare war.[25] As Abraham Lincoln said in rejecting the theory that the President can take unlimited action under the guise of repelling invasions:[26]

> Allow the President to invade a neighboring nation, whenever *he* shall deem it necessary to repel an invasion and you allow him to do so, *whenever he may choose to say* he deems it necessary for such purpose—and you allow him to make war at pleasure. Study to see if you can fix *any limit* to his power in this respect, after you have given him so much as you propose.

In order to save the congressional power to declare war, the following clear guideline, one which accords with the constitutional scheme envisioned by the

---

[21] *Legal Adviser* 1101; *National Commitments Report* 8-9; 2 M. FARRAND, *supra* note 8, at 318, 320; see *National Commitments Hearings* 10.

[22] *Id.*

[23] This is clearly apparent in the statements cited in *supra* notes 17, 18, and in many of the government's arguments discussed *infra*.

[24] *Id.*

[25] The executive's argument is certainly not aided by the fact that serious questions have recently been raised as to whether the destroyers were acting provocatively and whether they were attacked twice, as the government claimed, or only once. *The Gulf of Tonkin, The 1964 Incidents, Hearings Before The Committee on Foreign Relations,* United States Senate, 90th Cong., 2d Sess., with The Honorable Robert S. McNamara, Secretary of Defense; Excerpts from Senator Morse's speech on Tonkin Incidents, N.Y. Times, Feb. 22, 1968, at 15, cols. 2-8; Finney, *Fulbright Says McNamara Deceives Public on Tonkin,* N.Y. Times, Feb. 14, 1968, at 1, cols. 6-7, at 15, col. 1; Grose, *Fulbright Urges Congressional Inquiry Into War Policy,* N.Y. Times, Feb. 26, 1968, at 1, col. 6, at 3, col. 1; Finney, *McNamara Tells of Secret Data on Tonkin Attack,* N.Y. Times, Feb. 24, 1968, at 1, col. 4; *Captain Confirms Attack in Tonkin,* N.Y. Times, Feb. 24, 1968, at 1, col. 7, at 4, col. 3; Finney, *McNamara Says Destroyers In '64 Warned of Enemy,* N.Y. Times, Feb. 5, 1968, at 1, col. 3, at 29, col. 1; Kenworthy, *Nine Senators Feel U.S. Overreacted on Tonkin,* N.Y. Times, Feb. 24, 1968, at 29, col. 1.

[26] E. CORWIN, *supra* note 10, at 451; *National Commitments Report* 11.

framers,[27] should be adopted: the President has the power to use all necessary force to repel sudden attacks; however, as soon as possible, he must go before Congress to obtain a limited or general declaration of war.[28]

Quite obviously, in case of an atomic missile attack there would be no time to come to Congress; and the President himself could order full-scale retaliation in order to provide, to the extent possible, for the safety of the nation. But the situation is vastly different where, as in conventional wars, the President can consult Congress. Here he must obtain a declaration of war as soon as possible. This guideline was followed by President Roosevelt in World War II; and, if it is not followed today, the nation will be in a position where a President may, in his sole discretion, commence an enormous war on the basis of a minor attack.

B. *The President's Power Under Treaties*

The executive branch claims that, because the United States has entered defensive treaties with many nations, the President may commit the nation to war in order to carry out its treaty obligations.[29] In particular, the SEATO treaty provides that an armed attack against one of the parties poses a danger to all the parties, and that each party will act to meet the danger in accordance with its "constitutional processes."[30] The executive branch interprets "constitutional processes" to mean that the President, in his sole discretion, shall decide whether to fight.[31]

This executive branch argument is also spurious. A treaty cannot override the Constitution,[32] and under the Constitution it is the Congress, not the President, which is to declare war. Thus, the Congress must decide whether particular treaty obligations require entry into war. The words "constitutional process" in the SEATO treaty therefore must mean that the Congress shall make this decision. If they mean the President shall make it, then in this respect the SEATO treaty is void under the United States Constitution because it in effect gives the President the power to declare war. Neither can it be argued that, because the Senate approves treaties, the Senate has delegated the power to declare war to the President. As will be later pointed out, the power to declare war cannot be delegated to the President even by the full Congress. Still less can it be delegated by the Senate, since it does not belong to the Senate alone, but to the Senate and House together.[33]

---

[27] See materials cited *supra* notes 9, 12, 21.

[28] Whether, in repelling an attack, the President can take so-called offensive actions or must limit himself to so-called defensive actions is a theoretical point having little practical significance. See the text immediately following this footnote, and see note 216 *infra*.

[29] *Legal Adviser* 1101-02; Statements of Under Secretary Katzenbach at *National Commitments Hearings* 81-82, 146, 164-65, 182; Statement of Prof. Bartlett, *id.* at 39; Statements of Secretary Rusk, quoted at Falk, *International Law and The United States Role in the Vietnam War*, 75 YALE L.J. 1122, 1148-49 (1966).

[30] *National Commitments Hearings* 58; *Legal Adviser* 1101.

[31] *Legal Adviser* 1101-02; Statements of Under Secretary Katzenbach, *National Commitments Hearings* 165.

[32] Reid v. Covert, 354 U.S. 1, 15-19 (1957); Geofroy v. Riggs, 133 U.S. 258, 267 (1890).

[33] The framers specifically rejected a proposal to permit the Senate alone to declare war. 2 J. STORY, *supra* note 13, at 91-93.

In sum, like its other arguments, this executive branch argument is a pre-scription for nullifying the Constitution by removing the power to declare war from the Congress and giving it to the President. This nation has treaties or agreements with 42 nations.[34] Under the executive branch argument, the President, in his sole discretion, could theoretically commit it to 42 different wars. A plainer constitutional usurpation is difficult to imagine.

C. *AID*

The executive branch apparently claims that it has the power to carry on the current war because, under AID programs, Congress has authorized economic and military assistance to Viet Nam.[35] Merely to put this argument is to answer it. Congress' purpose in sponsoring economic AID programs is not to authorize war and destruction, but to promote peace and development. Similarly, Congress' purpose in providing military equipment and military advisors for foreign nations is not to authorize America to fight large-scale and sustained wars, but to enable the foreign nations to protect themselves.

D. *The President's Duty to Take Care That the Laws be Faithfully Executed*

It may be argued that the President can fight the current war because he has the duty to take care that the laws be faithfully executed.[36] Thus, it is said, he has the right to determine whether and to what extent force shall be used to implement AID programs and treaties. Quite obviously, this argument is nothing more than a restatement of the aforementioned arguments based on the presidential power under treaties and AID programs. As has been pointed out, the President does not have the power to execute treaties and AID programs by in effect declaring war. Only Congress can declare war. The idea that the President can violate the Constitution under the guise of carrying out his duty to faithfully execute the law was specifically rejected in *Youngstown Sheet & Tube Co. v. Sawyer*.[37] The Supreme Court there said that, in seizing the nation's steel mills, the President was not executing the laws of Congress, but was exercising Congress' power to make the laws.[38] The same is true here. In fighting the Vietnamese war, the President is not executing the laws of Congress; he is usurping Congress' power to declare war.

E. *The President as Chief Executive*

The executive branch argues that the President has the power to fight the

---

[34] *National Commitments Hearings* 50, 52-60.

[35] *See* Statement of Secretary Rusk, *Southeast Asia Resolution, Joint Hearing Before The Committee On Foreign Relations and the Committee on Armed Services of the United States Senate*, 88th Cong., 2d Sess. 20-23, on a joint resolution to promote the maintenance of international peace and security in Southeast Asia [hereinafter cited as *Tonkin Gulf Hearings*] (quoted in *National Commitments Hearings* 173).

[36] *See* E. CORWIN, *supra* note 10, at 194, 229; *Legal Adviser* 1100. *Cf.* Youngstown Sheet & Tube Co. v. Sawyer, 343 U.S. 579, 587-89 (1952). *See also* Statements of Secretary Rusk, *Tonkin Gulf Hearings* 22-23.

[37] 343 U.S. 579 (1952).

[38] *Id.* at 587-89.

current war because he is the Chief Executive.[39] However, as emphasized in *Youngstown Sheet & Tube,* the constitutional clause which states that "the Executive Powers shall be vested in a President"[40] means that the President shall execute the laws passed by Congress, not that he shall usurp the law-making or war-declaring functions of Congress.[41] The grant of executive power to the President is not a grant of unlimited power to do as he pleases despite constitutional restrictions. As Justice Jackson said in his concurring opinion in *Youngstown,*[42] if the above-noted executive power clause did grant the President unlimited executive powers,

> [i]t is difficult to see why the forefathers bothered to add several specific items [of executive power], including some trifling ones.[43]
>
> The example of such unlimited executive power that must have most impressed the forefathers was the prerogative exercised by George III, and the description of its evils in the Declaration of Independence leads me to doubt that they were creating their new Executive in his image. Continental European examples were no more appealing. And if we seek instruction from our own times, we can match it only from the executive powers in those governments we disparagingly describe as totalitarian. I cannot accept the view that this clause is a grant in bulk of all conceivable executive power but regard it as an allocation to the presidential office of the generic powers thereafter stated.

F. *The Commander-in-Chief Clause*

The executive claims that the President can carry on the current war because he is Commander-in-Chief of the armed forces.[44] It is said that he can therefore commit United States forces to combat, apparently for any length of time and in any strength he desires. This argument is a perversion of the Constitution. Nothing is more firmly established in our tradition than civilian supremacy over the military. To permit the President to carry on indefinitely long and large-scale warfare because he is Commander-in-Chief is to make the military supreme over the civilian authority which has the power to declare war, that is, over the Congress. The President was not made Commander-in-Chief in order to exalt military authority over civilian authority, but to insure civilian supremacy.[45] Furthermore, the President's power as Commander-in-Chief is no more than the power of any top-ranking military officer.[46] Under our

---

[39] *Legal Adviser* 1100, 1108. *See* E. CORWIN, *supra* note 10, at 179, 181, 426 n.31; Statements of Under Secretary Katzenbach, *National Commitments Hearings* 143-47. *Cf.* Youngstown Sheet & Tube Co. v. Sawyer, 343 U.S. 579, 587-89 (1952).

[40] U.S. CONST. art. II, § I, cl. 1.

[41] 343 U.S. 579, 587-88 (1952).

[42] *Id.* at 640-41.

[43] "'. . . he may require the Opinion, in writing, of the principal Officer in each of the executive Departments, upon any Subject relating to the Duties of their respective Offices . . . ,' U.S. Const. art. II § 2. He '. . . shall Commission all of the Officers of the United States.' U.S. Const. art. II, § 3. Matters such as those would seem to be inherent in the Executive if anything is." *Id.* at 641, n.9.

[44] *Legal Adviser* 1100, 1108; Brief for Appellee at 10, Luftig v. McNamara, 373 F.2d 664 (D.C. Cir.), *cert. denied,* Mora v. McNamara, 88 S. Ct. 282 (1967). *See* Statements of Under Secretary Katzenbach, *National Commitments Hearings* 169-170; and Secretary Rusk, *Tonkin Gulf Hearings* 23. *See also* E. CORWIN, *supra* note 10, at 197. *Cf.* Youngstown Sheet & Tube Co. v. Sawyer, 343 U.S. 579, 587 (1952).

[45] Youngstown Sheet & Tube Co. v. Sawyer, 343 U.S. 579, 587 (1952) (Justice Jackson concurring).

[46] E. CORWIN, *supra* note 10, at 228; THE FEDERALIST No. 69 (Hamilton), *quoted in* E. CORWIN, *id.*; *National Commitments Hearings* 311.

Constitution no top-ranking military officer can declare war—no five-star general or admiral can declare war. Neither, then, can the supreme commander declare war. Only the Congress can declare war. As pointed out in *Youngstown Sheet & Tube Co. v. Sawyer,*[47] the steel-seizure case which occurred during the grave emergency presented by the Korean war, the President's position as Commander-in-Chief does not give him the power to usurp the functions of Congress.

G. *The President's Foreign Policy Power*

The executive branch maintains that the President has the power to fight the current war because he is supreme in the area of foreign policy.[48] Thus, goes the argument, if he thinks a war necessary to the nation's foreign policy, he can proceed to fight it. Because of this specious argument, it must be reiterated that, regardless of whether the Constitution makes the executive supreme in the field of foreign affairs, it specifically makes Congress supreme in the matter of declaring war. Moreover, the executive branch's argument greatly overstates the case for executive supremacy in foreign affairs. Congress has many constitutional powers which enable it to play a significant role in foreign affairs. It must pass the statutes upon which many important foreign policies depend, for example, laws providing assistance to foreign nations. It must appropriate the money without which executive policies cannot be carried out. It has passed laws, and the Senate has approved treaties, which provide for the stationing of troops abroad. It has the power to pass laws, such as tariffs and various taxes, which vitally affect various foreign policies. It declares war, raises armies, and provides navies. A full listing of the many congressional powers which give Congress a vital voice in the conduct of foreign relations would have to include the powers to tax and spend, to establish duties, to provide for the common defense and general welfare, to borrow money, to regulate foreign commerce, to regulate the value of money, to define and punish piracies and offenses against international law, to declare war, to raise armies and navies, to establish rules for the armed forces, to regulate immigration, and to make laws necessary and proper to carry the foregoing into execution. There is further the Senate's power to give advice and consent to the making of treaties and to the appointment of ambassadors and other public officials, such as the Secretaries of State and Defense.[49] In sum, not only is it untrue that executive dominance in foreign affairs gives the executive the power to override the Consitution and declare war, but it is also untrue that the Congress does not have an important role to play in foreign affairs.

H. *Urgency, Expertise and Secret Information*

It is often argued that the President must have the power to declare war be-

[47] 343 U.S. 579, 587 (1952).

[48] *Legal Adviser* 1100. *See* Statement of Under Secretary Katzenbach, *National Commitments Hearings* 76-77; E. CORWIN, *supra* note 10, at 185.

[49] All of the powers mentioned in the text are in the U.S. CONST. art. I, § 8; art. I, § 9, cl. 1; and art. II, § 2, cl. 2.

cause such decisions are urgent, because they require expert knowledge, and because the President has access to secret information.[50] Insofar as urgency is concerned, the need for immediate action is often vastly exaggerated, as it was in the Bay of Pigs, Dominican Republic, and Vietnamese situations.[51] Indeed, even Under Secretary Katzenbach has agreed that the nation might have benefitted from some delay in regard to Viet Nam.[52] Further, the Congress has shown itself capable of acting with dispatch when this has seemed necessary, as when it declared two World Wars and when it passed the Gulf of Tonkin Resolution.[53] The President, as pointed out above, has the power to take the urgent action necessary to repel attacks. What the President may not do is to fight a large-scale war for over three years on the claim that for this entire period urgency precluded a congressional declaration of war. Rather, he must come to Congress for a declaration of war as soon as possible.

Insofar as secret knowledge is concerned, the executive can make such knowledge available to Congress in closed hearings. Professor Bartlett has aptly commented on the notion that the executive may declare war because it has access to knowledge which it can keep from the Congress:[54]

> It is true that diplomatic negotiations in many instances may require secrecy, but the results of negotiations and factors that influence them should be open to all. Nothing is more destructive of democratic institutions than the concealment of information essential to them. The idea that the President should be allowed to determine foreign policy because he has access to better or more complete information than the Congress is an idea that Congress can accept only at its peril.

In regard to the executive's expertise, it can be made available to Congress, and the Congress too has expert committees and expert staffs in the area of foreign affairs and defense. Neither the executive nor Congress has a monopoly of expertise in these areas, and, as one Senate report has remarked, neither has a monopoly of mistakes in these areas.[55] Professor Bartlett has also commented on the idea that the executive should be permitted to declare war because of its alleged expertise in the field of foreign relations:[56]

---

[50] Statement of Prof. Bartlett, *National Commitments Hearings* 20. *See* THE FEDERALIST No. 64 (Jay), *discussed in* E. CORWIN, *supra* note 10, at 171. The thrust of Jay's statements is that the President has great advantages in foreign policy matters because his office possesses "unity," a "capacity for secrecy and dispatch," and "superior sources of information." *See also* Statements of Under Secretary Katzenbach, *National Commitments Hearings* 72, 182; and United States v. Curtiss-Wright Export Corp., 299 U.S. 304 (1936). That the need for urgency is often vastly exaggerated has also been pointed out by Prof. Bartlett at *National Commitments Hearings* 20, by Senator Fulbright, *id.* at 3, 181, 182, 252, and by the *National Commitments Report* 24-25. The *Report* says that the need for haste was overplayed in cases involving Formosa, the Middle East, Cuba, and the Gulf of Tonkin.

[51] *See* the Statements of Senator Fulbright, *National Commitments Hearings* 47, 181, 182, 251; *National Commitments Report* 14. The *National Commitments Report* also says that the United States could have profited by delay in regard to the passage of the joint resolutions pertaining to Formosa and the Middle East. *Id.* at 24.

[52] *National Commitments Hearings* 181.

[53] The Tonkin Resolution was introduced on August 5, 1964, and passed on August 7, 1964. 112 CONG. REC. 18132, 18470-71, 18555.

[54] *National Commitments Hearings* 20.

[55] "Congress, it seems clear, was deficient in vision during the 1920's and 1930's, but so were Presidents Harding, Coolidge, Hoover and—prior to 1938— Roosevelt. Just as no one has a monopoly on vision, no one has a monopoly on myopia either." *National Commitments Reports* 14.

[56] *National Commitments Hearings* 20.

The third argument is the theory of expertness. It is the idea that foreign relations in their economic, political, and military aspects are so intricate and complex as to be largely beyond the understanding of Congressmen and far beyond the comprehension of the ordinary citizen. Such matters must be left, therefore, to experts in the Executive branch of the Government. In addition to being insulting, this argument is utterly fallacious. Experts are needed in the mechanics of many things whether they are called professions or something else, but there are no experts in wisdom concerning human affairs or in determining the national interest, and there is nothing in the realm of foreign policy that cannot be understood by the average American citizen.

In sum, the argument for the executive branch based on urgency, secret knowledge, and expertise is, like other arguments, a fallacious prescription for putting the lives and fortunes of 200 million citizens in the hands of a few alleged experts, instead of in the hands of the Congress, where America's charter of representative government places them.

I. *The President as Representative of All The People*

Closely allied to the aforementioned expertise argument is the argument that the President should be permitted to declare war because he represents all the people and will therefore take an overall view of foreign affairs, whereas Congressmen and Senators represent smaller segments of the people and will therefore take a parochial view of foreign affairs.[57] Furthermore, might run the argument, executive decisions to declare war are not really made by a handful of men, but result from a broad, informed view developed in the deliberations of large and expert foreign affairs and military bureaucracies. Such arguments are meritless. Regardless of whether or not the President represents all the people, the Constitution vests the power to declare war in Congress. It does so for reasons which are still valid, and it ought to be respected. The argument that Congressmen and Senators will necessarily take a parochial view of foreign affairs does not even merit rebuttal. The positions of Senators who have spoken out on both sides of the current debate over the war illustrate the speciousness of such an argument. Finally, if the executive is permitted to declare war, the ultimate decision lies not with the bureaucracy, but with a tiny handful of men who stand at the pinnacle of executive power. Indeed, the situation would be no better if the decision did rest with the bureaucracy, for then the most critical decision this nation can make would rest with a non-elected group of minor officials—with a bureaucracy whose inadequacies have been exposed to view since the death of John F. Kennedy.[58]

J. *The Allegation That a Declaration of War is Outmoded*

The executive branch claims that it has the power to initiate war because formal declarations of war are outmoded.[59] Such declarations were all right in

---

[57] *See* Stratton, *Presidential Power—Too Much or Too Little?*, N.Y. Times, January 30, 1957, § 6, at 11.

[58] *See* the text of, and the material cited in, Velvel, *Geographical Restrictions on Travel: The Real World and the First Amendment*, 15 KAN. L. REV. 35, 43-46 (1966). *See generally* G. KENNAN, MEMOIRS: 1925-1950 (1967).

[59] Statements of Under Secretary Katzenbach, *National Commitments Hearings* 80-81, 161, 174.

earlier days, it is said, because in those days total wars were fought.[60] Today, when it is necessary to fight limited wars for limited objectives, a declaration of war is outmoded because it would mislead other nations as to United States objectives and would therefore have undesirable consequences.[61] Thus, the President can initiate war without a congressional declaration; indeed, the only purpose served by congressional actions in this regard is to show that the Congress supports the President.[62]

This particular executive branch argument is bad history, bad logic, and bad law. The idea that declarations of war have become outmoded is not a new one, but is one which has been bandied about since the very beginning of the Republic. In *The Federalist,* published just after the Constitutional Convention, Alexander Hamilton said that declarations of war had fallen into disuse.[63] Justice Story, in his famous constitutional commentaries, also noted that nations often fight wars without formal declarations.[64] It has been expertly estimated that of 117 wars which took place between 1700 and 1870, only ten were declared wars.[65] Thus, it is entirely misleading to claim, as the executive in effect does, that declarations of war were all the vogue when the Constitution was written but today are a relic of a more antique age. They were not all the vogue when the Constitution was written, but the framers nevertheless wisely chose to hem in Presidential power by allocating to Congress the power to declare war.

It is no more accurate to claim that declarations of war are outmoded because today limited wars for limited objectives are fought. The concept of limited war is not a new one; it is as old as this country, and it was, as George Kennan has pointed out, particularly prevalent in the eighteenth century[66] when the Constitution was written. Before this nation was ten years old, the Congress authorized the President to fight a limited naval war for limited objectives against France.[67] In a case arising out of that French naval war, John Marshall, speaking for the entire Supreme Court, said that the Congress has the power to declare either a general or a limited war.[68] This same point was made by the Justices of the Supreme Court in *seriatim* opinions in another case arising out of the war.[69] In the latter case, the opinion of Justice Chase specifically spoke of Congress' power to declare a war which is "limited in place, in objects and in time,"[70] while Justice Washington spoke of wars "limited as to places,

---

[60] *Id.*

[61] *Id.*

[62] *Id.* at 145, 185-86. *See* Statement of Senator Gore, *id.* at 187; *National Commitments Report* 7, 22.

[63] *Cited in* Corwin, *Who has the Power to Make War?,* in J. MacLean, President & Congress—The Conflict of Powers 155, 156 (1955).

[64] 2 J. Story, *supra* note 13, at 96.

[65] J. F. Maurice, Hostilities Without a Declaration of War. From 1700 to 1870, at 4 (1883), cited in Eagleton, *The Form And Function of the Declaration of War,* 32 Am. J. Int'l Law 19, 20 (1938).

[66] G. Kennan, Memoirs: 1925-1950, 310 (1967).

[67] The President was authorized to use the navy for the purpose of protecting American shipping. Statement of Prof. Bartlett, *National Commitments Hearings* 10. Talbot v. Seeman, 5 U.S. (1 Cranch) 1, 28-30 (1801).

[68] Talbot v. Seeman, 5 U.S. (1 Cranch) 1, 28 (1801).

[69] Bas v. Tingey, 4 U.S. (4 Dall.) 35, 38-39 (opinion of Washington, J.) 41, 42 (opinion of Chase, J.), 43 (opinion of Paterson, J.) (1800).

[70] *Id.* at 41.

persons and things."[71] Thus, if a declaration of general war is undesirable to-day, the Congress has the power to declare a limited war, stating what the limited objectives are, setting limits on the amount of force that can be used to achieve those objectives and, if Congress wishes, putting time limits on the period during which force can be used.[72] This congressional power stems, as indicated before, from Congress' power to declare war. It can also be traced to Congress' power to raise armies and provide navies[73] and to its power to make rules regulating the armed forces.[74] A Congress which has the power to raise armies and navies in order to provide for the national defense has the power to say when and to what extent these instruments shall be used in the national defense. A Congress which can make rules to govern the armed forces can make rules governing when and to what extent these forces shall be used in warfare.

K. *The Triggering of Treaties*

Related to the argument that declarations of war are outmoded is the potential argument that such a declaration is undesirable because it might trigger treaty obligations of those who oppose United States policy.[75] This argument has little merit. It would seem that in today's world, where even small wars could lead to atomic holocausts, nations aid their allies or refuse to aid them primarily on the basis of national self-interest and not on the basis of whether the proper authorities have formally declared a limited war.[76] For example, North Viet Nam has not formally declared war on South Viet Nam; yet, because of an executive belief that it is in America's self-interest to do so, this nation is massively engaged in the Vietnamese war. Correlatively, this country has not formally declared war either on the Viet Cong or on North Viet Nam; yet Russia and China have provided massive material support to those combatants, obviously because the Russians and Chinese feel such actions are in their self-interest. Similarly, there appears no reason to doubt that, even

---

[71] *Id.* at 39.

[72] If Congress should later wish to increase United States objectives or the amount of force to be used, it could of course do so.

[73] U.S. Const. art. 1, § 8, cls. 12, 13.

[74] *Id.* at cl. 14.

[75] Falk, *International Law and the United States Role in the Viet Nam War,* 75 Yale L.J. 1122, 1154 (1966); Statement of Senator Russell, 112 Cong. Rec. 4371-72.

[76] Consider the following statement by G. Kennan, Memoirs: 1925-1950 at 408 (1967):

Secondly, I had little confidence in the value of written treaties of alliance generally. I had seen too many instances in which they had been forgotten, or disregarded, or found to be irrelevant, or distorted for ulterior purposes when the chips were down. I had no confidence in the ability of men to define hypothetically in any useful way, by means of general and legal phraseology, future situations which no one could really imagine or envisage. What was needed, it seemed to me, was a realistic consciousness of where one's vital interests really lay. Given that, military policy would flow correctly of its own accord—it needed no legal obligations or prescriptions. The suggestion, constantly heard from the European side, that an alliance was needed to assure the participation of the United States in the cause of Western Europe's defense, in the event of an attack against it, only filled me with impatience. What in the world did they think we had been doing in Europe these last four or five years? Did they suppose we had labored to free Europe from the clutches of Hitler merely in order to abandon it to those of Stalin? What did they suppose the Marshall Plan was all about? Could they not see that we were well aware of the real dangers with which Western Europe was faced, and that we were acting, as generously and effectively as we could, to combat them?

though the Congress does not formally declare war, the Chinese or Russians would enter the fighting in a more direct way if they felt that such action would be in their best interests. The Chinese in fact did enter the undeclared Korean war when they felt that their security was threatened. In sum, it is at best doubtful that a congressional declaration of war, especially of limited war for limited objectives and authorizing only limited force, would have more effect on possible enemies' actions than the *de facto* large-scale war which is presently being fought.

The foregoing arguments also imply another reason why the so-called "treaty-trigger" argument has little merit. Throughout the course of the present war, the executive has made decisions as to what the nation's objectives should be and as to the amounts and kinds of force to be used. In making such decisions, the executive presumably considered possible response which its actions might elicit from the Russians and the Chinese, including responses which might be triggered by treaties. But that is precisely what the Congress would have to do if it, rather than the executive, were to decide whether to fight, what the objectives should be, and what amounts and kinds of force should be used. If the executive can weigh possible enemy responses, including treaty responses, when making an unconstitutional *de facto* decision to declare limited war, there seems no valid reason to argue that the Congress should be deprived of its power to constitutionally declare war because it, instead of the executive, would have to evaluate possible enemy responses, including treaty responses.

L. *The Non-Recognition Argument*

Another argument related to the theory that a declaration of war is outmoded is that both international law and American foreign policy bar a declaration of war against the Viet Cong or North Viet Nam.[77] The answers to this argument are plain. International law does not necessarily prevent the nation from declaring war against a highly-organized and long-existing belligerent group such as the Viet Cong.[78] And, if any doctrine of international law does bar declaring war against the Viet Cong, then the choice would be to either sacrifice the international law doctrine or to sacrifice the constitutional provision giving Congress the power to declare war. There is only one answer to such a choice. The Constitution, America's supreme law, cannot be sacrificed in favor of a mere doctrine of international law.

A similar answer must be given to those who argue that a declaration of war against the Viet Cong is undesirable because it would confer international status upon that group, and that the United States should not declare war against North Viet Nam because to do so would constitute implicit recognition of a regime which America does not presently recognize. If a declaration of war would confer international status upon the Viet Cong or would constitute recognition of North Viet Nam, then so be it. For if the choice is between

---

[77] Colleagues and students have suggested these arguments to the author.

[78] *Cf.* Eagleton, *supra* note 65, at 25-27.

sacrificing the constitutional clause giving Congress the power to declare war, on the one hand, or sacrificing the foreign policy of not recognizing North Viet Nam and not conferring status on the Viet Cong, on the other hand, then there can be only one legitimate answer: the paramount law of the land must prevail over mere doctrines of foreign policy. Additionally, it may be noted that many other countries already recognize the North Vietnamese government,[79] that some have already conferred international status on the Viet Cong,[80] and that to declare war on North Viet Nam need not necessarily mean *de jure* recognition of Ho Chi Minh's regime. Thus, a declaration of war would not confer any benefits upon the United States' enemies that have not already been conferred upon them by some other nations.

M. *The Fait Accompli Argument*

It has been claimed that the President has the power to fight the current war because, as a practical matter, most wars in which the United States has participated have been commenced before Congress formally declared war and have occurred because of Presidential foreign policies.[81] It may be true that sometimes, as in the Second World War, hostilities commenced before a congressional declaration of war. Nevertheless, this circumstance does not mean that the President can carry on large-scale hostilities for an indefinite period of time without a declaration of war. The President, as did President Roosevelt, can enter hostilities before a declaration of war in order to repel a sudden attack. But as soon as possible he must, as did President Roosevelt, obtain a congressional declaration of war.

It may also be true that most declared wars have occurred because of presidential foreign policies. For example, the actions of President Polk prior to the Mexican War and of President Roosevelt prior to World War II are commonly cited as having led to war.[82] Nevertheless, that Presidents have created situations in which Congress deemed it necessary to declare war does not mean that today the President can dispense with the constitutional necessity of a declaration of war. As stated before, the purpose of the clause giving Congress the power to declare war was to insure that no one man or small group of men shall have the power to plunge this country into the calamities of warfare. This

---

[79] Moore, *International Law and the United States Role in the Viet Nam War: A Reply*, 76 YALE L.J. 1051, 1056 (1967).

[80] A colleague in international law informs me that various Communist nations have conferred international status on the Viet Cong by receiving diplomatic representatives of the National Liberation Front. The assertion that Front representatives have been received by Communist nations comports with the author's personal recollections, which stem from a daily reading of the *New York Times*. For further confirmation, see A. Casella, *The Stubborn Smile*, 58 FAR EASTERN ECONOMIC REV., Dec. 7, 1967.

It is also noteworthy that the fact that both sides to the Vietnamese war have received outside assistance from foreign nations suffices to confer international status on the parties to the war. In regard to recognition of belligerency, see W. BISHOP, INTERNATIONAL LAW CASES AND MATERIALS 338-39 (2d ed. 1962).

[81] United States v. Mitchell, 246 F. Supp. 874, 898 (D. Conn. 1963), *aff'd*, Mitchell v. United States, 369 F.2d 323 (2d Cir. 1966), *cert. denied* 386 U.S. 972 (1967); Statements of Under Secretary Katzenbach, *National Commitments Hearing* 79, 99.

[82] For a description of Roosevelt's actions, see E. CORWIN, THE PRESIDENT: OFFICE AND POWERS 202-03 (4th ed. 1964). The stationing of troops abroad by a President is a contemporary example which is often pointed to as a presidential policy which could involve us in war. See *infra*, text material in subsection III Q, *The Stationing of Troops Abroad*.

purpose is particularly relevant today, especially in light of the executive branch's assertion of the need to fight limited wars for limited objectives. It is no secret that many members of Congress do not agree with the extent of American military operations in Viet Nam. Thus, if the Congress had declared a limited war in Viet Nam, it might have set different limits than has the executive as to the amounts and kinds of force to be used and the period of time during which such force was to be used. Similarly, it is no secret that congressional objections had a restricting influence on the executive's potential use of force in the recent uprisings in the Congo. If it is necessary to fight limited wars in the future, the Congress may, in a declaration of war, place greater or lesser limits than would the executive on the amount of force to be used, or may, indeed, refuse to permit the nation to fight though the executive would fight if left to its own devices. Not only is it true that Congress might not authorize the use of as much force as might be authorized by the executive, but this possibility in itself might cause the executive to be more hesitant to follow policies which increase the likelihood of having to resort to force. Thus, to require that Congress declare war is not a mere formality which can be dispensed with merely because past Presidents have followed policies which led to war. Rather, that Congress declare war is a vital cog in the constitutional machinery designed to insure that no small group of men can plunge this country into disaster, constitutional machinery which is itself of particular importance in these days when even a small war could conceivably lead to atomic destruction.

N. *Ratification by Appropriating Money*

The executive branch suggests that, by appropriating money to support the military in Viet Nam, the Congress has ratified the President's actions and has, in effect, made the necessary declaration of war.[83] It is, however, erroneous to assert that a vote in favor of Vietnamese appropriations is a vote which ratifies the current war. Regardless of whether a Congressman agrees or disagrees with the executive's policy, as a matter of common morality, as well as political survival, he cannot vote to deny bullets and food to American soldiers who are facing savage enemy attacks. As long as American soldiers are fighting in Viet Nam, and even if they are fighting there as a direct result of the executive's usurpation of Congress' power to declare war, Congressmen are forced to provide the money which is necessary for their survival. This fact has been recognized by experts in foreign affairs, by Senators who support the President's policy and by Senators who oppose it. For example, Senator Richard Russell,[84] Senator Sam Ervin,[85] Senator Joseph Clark,[86] Senator Peter Dominick,[87] Sena-

---

[83] *Legal Adviser* 1106, 1108; Brief for Appellees at 11, Luftig v. McNamara, 373 F.2d 664 (D.C. Cir. 1967); *National Commitments Report* 7. *See* Statements of Under Secretary Katzenbach at *National Commitments Hearings* 75, 166; Statement of Professor Bartlett, *id.* at 17, 43.

[84] 112 CONG. REC. 4372.

[85] *National Commitments Hearings* 219, 220.

[86] 112 CONG. REC. 4382.

[87] *National Commitments Hearings* 246.

tor Bourke Hickenlooper,[88] Representative Paul Findley,[89] Professor Ruhl J. Bartlett[90] and Professor W. Stull Holt[91] have all pointed this out on the floor of Congress or in congressional hearings. Moreover, before passing a Vietnamese appropriations bill in March, 1966, many Congressmen and Senators indicated that their votes for the bill were *not* to be interpreted as authorizing large-scale military escalation,[92] of which there has since been a great deal.

It is therefore clear that it is the worst sort of bootstrap argument to say that a vote to appropriate money is a vote which gives congressional ratification to the President's action. Such a theory, like other executive branch arguments, gives the President unlimited power to declare war. Under such a view he can commit men to action and then, when Congressmen vote for appropriations because they do not wish to see American forces harmed for lack of ammunition and food, claim that these Congressmen have ratified the executive action. Furthermore, the ratification by appropriation argument is constitutionally impermissible for another reason as well. The Supreme Court has made clear that, where executive action is of dubious constitutionality—let alone clearly unconstitutional, as here—it is not sufficient to argue that Congress has impliedly ratified the action by appropriating money.[93] Rather, explicit ratification is necessary in order to insure "careful and purposeful consideration by those responsible for enacting and implementing our laws. Without explicit action by lawmakers, decisions of great constitutional import and effect would be relegated by default to administrators who, under our system of government, are not endowed with authority to decide them."[94] As is shown by the above-mentioned comments of Senators and Congressmen, appropriating money to keep American men alive does not constitute the necessary explicit ratification of the executive's unlawful action.

O. *Lack of Formal Congressional Disapproval*

It has been suggested that the President has the power to fight the current war because Congress, if it disapproves of what is being done, could pass a resolution of disapproval or could announce that in the future it will not appropriate money to carry on the war. This argument is wrong on four counts. First, it puts the cart before the horse. Under the Constitution, the executive does not have power to fight a large and sustained war merely because the Congress fails to tell him *not* to fight it. Rather, he has the power to engage in a sustained war only if Congress formally authorizes him *to* fight it. To argue otherwise is like arguing that the executive has the power to pass tax laws or to pass laws regulating interstate commerce unless the Congress tells him not to, or that the executive has the power to try criminal cases unless the courts

---

[88] *Id.* at 219, 248.
[89] *Id.* at 235.
[90] *Id.* at 38, 43. *See id.* at 23.
[91] *Id.* at 247, 248.
[92] Kenworthy, *Senate To Avoid Viet Nam Clash,* N.Y. Times, March 1, 1966, at 1, col. 7.
[93] Greene v. McElroy, 360 U.S. 474 (1959).
[94] *Id.* at 507.

tell him not to. The latter arguments are absurd, and the former one is no less so. Under the Constitution each branch has only the powers expressly or impliedly given to it, and not the powers expressly or impliedly given to it plus all others it can get away with.

Second, as pointed out above, *Greene v. McElroy* held that the appropriation of money does not constitute the explicit congressional ratification necessary to legitimize dubious executive action. Still less, then, can congressional silence, in the form of a failure to bring up or enact a resolution which in some manner shows disapproval of the war, constitute the explicit ratification necessary to legalize the executive's actions in Viet Nam.

Third, the argument under discussion here is wrong not only as a constitutional matter, but as a practical matter as well. The *Senate Report on National Commitments* unequivocally points out that, in the last twenty-five years, the Congress has all too willingly acquiesced in the transfer of the power to declare war from itself to the executive.[95] The *Report* goes on to point out, quite correctly, that this trend must be reversed if we are to maintain the idea that no small group should have the power to make so critical a decision.[96] However, to argue that the President can fight a war unless the Congress tells him not to is simply to encourage Congressmen to shirk a duty which the Constitution places upon them, which they have already shirked far too often, as the Senate *Report* points out,[97] and which, perhaps for understandable reasons, they are only too willing to shirk, as the *Report* also indicates.[98] Thus, in order to insure that the critical decision of whether to go to war remains in the hands of Congress, it is necessary, as a practical matter, to bring Congressmen face to face with that decision by maintaining the view that the executive has no authority to fight a long-sustained and large-scale war without congressional authorization.

Fourth, neither is it feasible for Congress, as evidence of its disapproval, to announce that it will refuse to appropriate money at some future date. For if the President, after Congress' announcement, should not withdraw American forces, but instead continue to carry on the war, Congress would be in unenviable circumstances. As discussed above, it would eventually be forced to appropriate money to insure the well-being of American men in Viet Nam. Such a dilemma is well illustrated by the conflict between President Theodore Roosevelt and the Congress. When Roosevelt wanted to send the fleet around the world, a great deal of public opposition developed,[99] and the chairman of the Senate Committee on Naval Affairs announced that the fleet could not go because Congress would not appropriate the money.[100] Roosevelt replied that he already had enough money to send the fleet to the Pacific coast, and there it

---

[95] *National Commitments Report* 6, 14, 26.

[96] *Id.* at 23, 25, 26-27.

[97] *Id.* at 6, 14-15, 21.

[98] *Id.* at 14-15, 26.

[99] T. ROOSEVELT, AN AUTOBIOGRAPHY 552 (1929); H. PRINGLE, THEODORE ROOSEVELT 410 (1931); J. BISHOP, THEODORE ROOSEVELT AND HIS TIMES 66 (1920).

[100] T. ROOSEVELT, *supra* note 99, at 552-53; H. PRINGLE, *supra* note 99, at 410; J. BISHOP, *supra* note 99, at 66.

would stay unless Congress appropriated the money to bring it back.[101] Faced with this situation, the Congress was forced to appropriate the money to send the fleet around the world.[102] Moreover, Roosevelt's action is only one of several examples in which Presidents have taken military or other actions for which the Congress, faced with the executive's *fait accompli,* was later forced to appropriate money.[103]

P. *History*

The executive branch claims that the President has the power to fight the current war because, on some 125 occasions, the President, without a congressional declaration of war, has ordered the armed forces to take some action or to maintain some position abroad.[104] However, with the exception of the Korean war, these instances do not provide precedents for stating that, without a congressional declaration of war, the President has the power to fight a large-scale land, sea, and air war of long duration on foreign shores.[105] As Under Secretary of State Katzenbach has said, "most of these [precedents] were relatively minor uses of force."[106] Indeed, in many cases troops were landed, but little or no fighting actually occurred. In other cases, any fighting that occurred was over rather quickly. Minor and short-lived uses of force provide no precedent for the current large-scale and long-sustained war in Viet Nam. Some of the uses of force involved cases in which the President acted to preserve American lives and property during unstable situations or to punish the depredations of pirates, bandits, or cattle rustlers. Such action is justified under the President's power to repel attacks on American citizens and property, does not amount to an act of war,[107] and thus provides no precedent for the current war, where executive actions have gone far beyond the protection of American lives and property and do amount to acts of war.[108] Some of the uses of force were undertaken by Presidents who simultaneously admitted that their constitutional range of action was limited to repelling attacks and that they

---

[101] T. ROOSEVELT, *supra* note 99, at 553; H. PRINGLE, *supra* note 99, at 410; J. BISHOP, *supra* note 99, at 66.
[102] T. ROOSEVELT, *supra* note 99, at 553; H. PRINGLE, *supra* note 99, at 410; J. BISHOP, *supra* note 99, at 66.
[103] These are listed in L. WILMERDING, THE SPENDING POWER 9-18 (1943); E. CORWIN, THE PRESIDENT: OFFICE AND POWERS 399, n.58 (4th ed. 1964).
[104] *Legal Adviser* 1106-07; Brief for Appellees at 10, Luftig v. McNamara, 373 F.2d 664 (D.C. Cir.), *cert. denied,* 88 S. Ct. 282 (1967). *Cf.* Statement of Secretary Rusk, *Tonkin Gulf Hearings* 3.
[105] Descriptions of past presidential uses of force without a declaration of war, and of past presidential statements in this connection, can be found in the following sources: Statement of Professor Bartlett, *National Commitments Hearings* 10-20; *National Commitments Report* 9-23; E. CORWIN, THE PRESIDENT: OFFICE AND POWERS 194-204 (4th ed. 1964); J. ROGERS, WORLD POLICING AND THE CONSTITUTION 57-84, 93-123 (1945); Putney, *Executive Assumption of the War Making Power,* 7 NAT'L U.L. REV., May 1927, at 1, 11; Comment, *The President, The Congress, and the Power to Declare War,* 16 KAN. L. REV. 82, 83-85 (1967).
[106] *National Commitments Hearings* 81.
[107] E. CORWIN, THE PRESIDENT: OFFICE AND POWERS 198 (4th ed. 1964). *See* Putney, *Executive Assumption of the War Making Power,* 7 NAT'L U.L. REV., May 1927, at 1, 7-8. *See* Corwin, *The President's Power* in THE PRESIDENT: ROLES & POWERS 360, 361 (D. Haight & L. Johnston eds. 1965).
[108] Edward S. Corwin has given us the following summation of presidential uses of force abroad: As to the cases in which "American Presidents have repeatedly committed armed forces abroad without Congressional consultation or approval," the vast majority involved fights with pirates, landings of small naval contingents on barbarous or semi-barbarous coasts, the dispatch of small bodies

could not take offensive action without congressional authorization. Such defensive uses of force provide no precedent for the large-scale offensive operations that have taken place in Viet Nam.

Just as no support for the current war is provided by the Presidential uses of force abroad which have been discussed above, so the current war similarly receives no support from the actions of President Lincoln in the Civil War. It is true that Lincoln, without a declaration of war, took the large-scale military actions necessary to save the Union,[109] and that one such action, a blockade, was approved in the *Prize Cases*.[110] However, both Lincoln's actions in general and the *Prize Cases* in particular are clearly and easily distinguishable from the Vietnamese war. (1) Lincoln's military actions were necessary to save the Union from imminent and certain destruction in an American civil war. The current war is not an American civil war, but a foreign war;[111] and it does not involve the imminent and certain destruction of the Union. (2) In the Civil War in general and the *Prize Cases* in particular, the President's military actions were clearly authorized by preexisting statutes which provided for the suppression of insurrection.[112] There is no preexisting statutory authority for the current war. (3) In the Civil War in general and the *Prize Cases* in particular, a ground for upholding the President's actions was that they had been clearly and explicitly ratified by Congress.[113] No such ratification exists for the current war. (4) In the Civil War in general and the *Prize Cases* in particular, a ground for upholding the President's actions, taken without a formal declaration of war, was that no nation formally declares war against insurgents who are rebelling against its authority.[114] In the present case, there is no rebellion against the *de jure* authority of the United States. Indeed, the American government claims that the Vietnamese war is not a rebellion at all, but is foreign aggression from the North. If it is a rebellion, it is a rebellion not against the American government, but against the South Vietnamese government. (5) In the Civil War in general and the *Prize Cases* in particular, a ground for up-

---

of troops to chase bandits or cattle rustlers across the Mexican border, and the like. Except for Polk's deliberate precipitation of war with Mexico in 1846 and a few cases occurring in the Carribean area since 1902, they exhibit a uniform pattern of measures undertaken for the protection of American lives and property against impending or actual violence or for punishment of such violence. Such episodes are small compared with Truman's claim of power to put an indefinite number of troops in Europe for an indefinite time in anticipation of war, without consulting Congress. Corwin, *The President's Power* in THE PRESIDENTS ROLE AND POWERS 361 (D. Haight & L. Johnston eds. 1965).

[109] These actions are described in E. CORWIN, THE PRESIDENT: OFFICE AND POWERS 229-31 (4th ed. 1964).

[110] 67 U.S. (2 Black) 635 (1862).

[111] "At no time did President Lincoln ever indicate that he believed that the President had the power to employ force abroad without the consent of Congress." Putney, *supra* note 105, at 17.

[112] 67 U.S. (2 Black) 635, 668, 691-92 (1862).

[113] For example, in the *Prize Cases* it was pointed out that in 1861, the first year of the war, the Congress passed an act "approving, legalizing and making valid all the acts, proclamations, and orders of the president, & c., as if they had been *issued and done under the previous express authority* and direction of the Congress of the United States." (Emphasis in original.) *Prize Cases*, 67 U.S. (2 Black) 635, 670 (1862). And, in 1863 the Congress ratified Lincoln's suspension of the writ of habeas corpus by passing a statute which said that "the President is authorized" to suspend the writ. E. CORWIN, THE PRESIDENT: OFFICE AND POWERS 229-30 (4th ed. 1964).

[114] 67 U.S. (2 Black) 635, 666, 667 (1862).

672 LEGAL WEAKNESSES OF THE WAR

holding Lincoln's actions, taken without a formal declaration of war, was that Congress cannot declare war against a state of the United States.[115] As said before, however, Congress can declare war against North Viet Nam, and it can also, if it wishes, declare war against a highly-organized and long-existing belligerent group such as the Viet Cong. (6) In the *Prize Cases,* four dissenting Justices stated that, while the President had the statutory power to repel an invasion or suppress an insurrection, in the constitutional sense he did not have the power to declare war, and therefore the legal rights and obligations accruing from war did not arise until Congress acted.[116] Thus, the opinion of the five majority Justices approving Lincoln's action does not support the constitutionality of the current war, and the opinion of the four dissenting Justices provides even less support.

As said before, the one use of force upon which the current war might be supported is the Korean war, which was a long-sustained and large-scale foreign military operation fought without a congressional declaration of war.[117] The existence of one precedent, however, does not serve to validate the current war. Rather it is more likely that, as many public figures claimed, that precedent also involved an unconstitutional usurpation of the power to declare war. Indeed, one can say that, even if there were many precedents for the current war, all of them combined could not, for two reasons, validate the executive's current usurpation of the power to declare war. First, in *Youngstown Sheet & Tube*[118] the government argued that President Truman had the power to seize the steel mills because on several occasions other Presidents had seized private businesses in emergency situations.[119] The Supreme Court replied, however, that even if other Presidents had seized private industries, Congress had not thereby lost its exclusive power to make the laws, and the seizure of the mills was a legislative act.[120] So it is in this case. Even if Presidents have used force without a declaration of war, Congress has not thereby lost its exclusive power to declare war.

Second, today it is more important than ever that Congress' power to declare war be respected. Presently five nations have atomic capabilities; Russia's has long been highly developed and China's has apparently made rapid strides. It is also possible that, if the nuclear proliferation treaty fails, many other nations will acquire atomic capabilities. Thus, in the world of today and tomorrow, even small wars can cause a chain of events which could bring mass destruction to the human race. In such circumstances, it is more necessary than ever that

---

[115] *Id.* at 668.

[116] 67 U.S. (2 Black) 635, 682 (1862) (dissenting opinion).

[117] Some would distinguish the Korean war from the present one on the basis that, a few days after American troops first went into action in Korea, the United Nations Security Council passed a resolution authorizing the use of force in defense of South Korea. U.N. Doc. No. s/1511, set forth in W. BISHOP, INTERNATIONAL LAW CASES & MATERIALS, 762-63 (1962). While this may be a plausible distinction, the author doubts it, since the Constitution no more gives the United Nations the power to declare war on behalf of the United States than it gives the executive the power to do so.

[118] 343 U.S. 579 (1952).

[119] *Id.* at 588-89.

[120] *Id.* at 588.

no small group of men in the executive be given the power to carry on long-sustained and large-scale warfare without a congressional declaration of war. Such wars have a way of escalating, as has the struggle in Viet Nam. They thus carry with them the ultimate risk of nuclear war. If the nation is to run this risk, the decision to do so should be as widely dispersed as the Constitution permits—the decision should be made by 535 federal legislators rather than a tiny handful of executive officials.[121]

Q. *The Stationing of Troops Abroad*

Another argument, inseparable from such preceding ones as the Commander-in-Chief argument, the foreign policy argument, the history argument, and the *fait accompli* argument, is that the war is constitutional because the President has the power to station troops abroad without the consent of Congress.[122] If the executive can order troops to Santo Domingo or Viet Nam, runs the argument, he can order them to engage in war once they are there. This argument is vastly oversimplified. Assuming that the executive does have the power to station troops abroad without the consent of Congress—an assumption which can be debated—it does not follow that he can order them to engage in large and sustained warfare once they are there. If such a thing did follow, then once again the Congress' power to declare war would be nullified.

A proper analysis of the meaning of the President's assumed power to station troops abroad would be as follows. On the one extreme, it is clear that the executive has the power to repel sudden attacks on American forces or property, wherever they may be, without a declaration of war. On the other extreme, it is equally clear that the executive has no power to carry on a large and sustained war without a congressional declaration of war. In the middle of the continuum of power lies a gray area consisting of various actions, such as stationing troops abroad without Congress' consent, as to which the executive's power is not clear. But that there is a gray area in the middle of the continuum does not mean that the situations are not clear at either end or that courts should not rule on the latter, polar situations. On the contrary, the existence of a gray area makes it even more imperative for courts to rule that the executive cannot carry on a large and sustained war without a congressional declaration. For, as pointed out above in regard to the *fait accompli* argument, such a ruling might make future executives more reluctant to take "gray-area" actions without congressional approval when such "gray-area" actions might eventually lead to the executive having to come to Congress for a declaration of war which the Congress might refuse altogether or might give on a more limited basis than the executive desires. By thus limiting the executive's freedom of action, a judicial decision that the executive cannot fight a large and sustained war with-

---

[121] It is perhaps worth noting that, in comparison with America's nuclear abilities at the time and in comparison with her own later nuclear capabilities, Russia did not have a highly developed atomic capability when the Korean war started in June of 1950.

[122] *Legal Adviser* 1100, 1101. *See* the statement of the problem as raised by Senator Hickenlooper, *National Commitments Hearings* 171-73.

out a congressional declaration would have the effect of placing an institutional restraint upon the executive. Such an institutional restraint is desirable because of: (1) the executive's ever increasing power, (2) the fact that the American system of government is in effect a system of institutional restraints upon the exercise of power, (3) the necessity of maintaining the idea that no small group of men in the executive shall make the most critical decision this country can face—whether to go to war, and (4) the danger that, if courts do not place such an institutional restraint upon the executive, the future situation will be even worse, since future executives will be able to point to not one but two wars—Korea and Viet Nam—as precedents supporting the President's power to fight substantial wars without a congressional declaration of limited or general war.

R. *The Gulf of Tonkin Resolution*

The Gulf of Tonkin Resolution, the full text of which is set forth in the accompanying footnote,[123] was passed at a time when America was not yet heavily engaged in large-scale land, sea, and air action in Viet Nam. The Resolution was a response to North Vietnamese attacks upon two American destroyers. The attacks had been repulsed, and the executive had mounted an air strike against the bases which were the source of the attack.

While the executive branch has repeatedly said that it could fight this war if the Tonkin Resolution had never been passed or even if the Resolution were repealed, it also claims that the Resolution constitutes congressional authorization for the current long-sustained and large-scale offensive and defensive actions in Viet Nam.[124] In other words, the executive claims that, under the Constitution, the Resolution is, in Under Secretary Katzenbach's phrase, the

---

[123] Whereas naval units of the Communist regime in Vietnam, in violation of the principles of the Charter of the United Nations and of international law, have deliberately and repeatedly attacked United States naval vessels lawfully present in international waters, and have thereby created a serious threat to international peace; and

Whereas these attacks are part of a deliberate and systematic campaign of aggression that the Communist regime in North Vietnam has been waging against its neighbors and the nations joined with them in the collective defense of their freedom; and

Whereas the United States is assisting the peoples of southeast Asia to protect their freedom and has no territorial, military or political ambitions in that area, but desires only that these peoples should be left in peace to work out their own destinies in their own way: Now, therefore, be it

Resolved by the Senate and House of Representatives of the United States of America in Congress assembled, That the Congress approves and supports the determination of the President, as Commander in Chief, to take all necessary measures to repel any armed attack against the forces of the United States and to prevent further aggression.

Sec. 2. The United States regards as vital to its national interest and to world peace the maintenance of international peace and security in southeast Asia. Consonant with the Constitution of the United States and the Charter of the United Nations and in accordance with its obligations under the Southeast Asia Collective Defense Treaty, the United States is, therefore, prepared as the President determines, to take all necessary steps, including the use of armed force, to assist any member or protocol state of the Southeast Asia Collective Defense Treaty requesting assistance in defense of its freedom.

Sec. 3. This resolution shall expire when the President shall determine that the peace and security of the area is reasonably assured by international conditions created by action of the United Nations or otherwise, except that it may be terminated earlier by concurrent resolution of the Congress.

112 Cong. Rec. 1841.

[124] *Legal Adviser* 1102-06; Statements of Under Secretary Katzenbach, *National Commitments Hearings* 82, 84, 89, 137, 140.

"functional equivalent" of a congressional declaration of war.[125] The Resolution, however, is certainly not a declaration of war and was not intended to authorize a sustained and large-scale offensive and defensive war in Viet Nam.

As the text of the Resolution illustrates, any reasonable man must concede that, if one considers only the language of the Resolution and totally ignores the congressional intent expressed in its ample legislative history, its language is broad enough to authorize the President, in his sole discretion, to fight a large-scale land, sea, and air war on the continent of Asia. Indeed, if one considers only the language of the Resolution and ignores the intent expressed in its legislative history, its language is broad enough to authorize the President, in his sole discretion, to initiate the atomic holocaust of World War III should he alone believe that World War III must be commenced in order to stop Communist aggression in Southeast Asia. This fact graphically demonstrates that, as is true with any legislation, the language of the Resolution cannot be considered in isolation from the congressional intent displayed in the legislative history. That history shows that Congress did not intend to authorize the executive, in its sole discretion, to fight the present long-sustained and large-scale land, sea, and air war on the continent of Asia.

At 112 Congressional Record 18132 is a message from the President in support of the Resolution. That message contains a clause which, as the debates show, played an instrumental role in Congress' thinking when it approved the Resolution. "As I have repeatedly made clear," said the President, "the United States intends no rashness *and seeks no wider war.*" (Emphasis added.) At 112 Congressional Record 18402 and 18403 is a colloquy between Senator McGovern and Senator Fulbright, who was instrumental in managing and sponsoring the Resolution in the Senate. Senator McGovern said American policy was to confine the war to South Viet Nam and not expand it to North Viet Nam. He then asked Senator Fulbright if there was any danger under the Resolution that this policy would change. Senator Fulbright replied that there was no such danger under the Resolution, and that the war was to be confined to South Viet Nam. At 112 Congressional Record 18403 Senator McGovern again stated his concern that the nation not engage in "some kind of strike in the north." At 112 Congressional Record 18403 Senator Brewster said that he "would look with great dismay on the landing of large land armies on the continent of Asia." He therefore asked Senator Fulbright if the Resolution would approve "the landing of large American armies in Viet Nam or China." Senator Fulbright replied, "There is nothing in the resolution, as I read it, that contemplates it. I agree with the Senator that that is the last thing we would want to do." Senator Fulbright, speaking for the Foreign Relations Committee, continued by stating that everyone he had heard agreed that the United States must not become involved in an Asian land war and that the purpose of

[125] *Id.* at 82. In using the phrase "functional equivalent" at page 82, the Under Secretary apparently meant that the combination of the SEATO treaty and the Tonkin Gulf Resolution was the functional equivalent of a declaration of war. Nevertheless, his phrase aptly describes the executive's repeated assertions as to the powers it received from the Tonkin Resolution standing alone.

the Resolution was to deter the North Vietnamese from spreading the war. Senator Fulbright admitted that the *language* of the Resolution would not prevent the President from escalating the war, but he clearly indicated that this was not the congressional *intent*. The intent did not contemplate vast escalation, but deterrence of it.

At 112 Congressional Record 18404 Senator Morton said that he too shared the apprehension that the United States might land vast armies on the Asian continent. The purpose of the Resolution, he said, was to prevent this. Senator Fulbright agreed fully, further stating that the nation ought not to bomb Hanoi and other places. At 112 Congressional Record 18405 Senator Fulbright again stressed that Congress did not want to expand the war and the Resolution was in fact to prevent expansion. At 112 Congressional Record 18406 Senator Nelson asked if the Resolution expressed the sense of Congress that the President might, if he deemed it necessary, land as many divisions as he wishes in Asia. Senator Fulbright said that, as long as he had been in the Senate, it was an article of faith not to land a large army on the Asian continent. He said the Resolution was not determinative of whether the President could do such a thing, and he indicated that a decision on such action should await the possible necessity of taking the action. At 112 Congressional Record 18407 Senator Nelson said that the Resolution did not authorize a radical change in the American objective in Viet Nam, and he said that it had been repeatedly stated that the nation's purpose was not to authorize a direct land confrontation by the American army or a substantial reinforcement of American army units in Viet Nam. Senator Fulbright told Senator Nelson that he (Fulbright) did not interpret the Resolution as authorizing a complete change in the United States' mission. At 112 Congressional Record 18410 Senator Cooper asserted that the nation ought to avoid a war in Southeast Asia, and that there is a distinction between defending the armed forces from attack and taking offensive actions in South Viet Nam. At 112 Congressional Record 18411 Senator Russell said the Resolution approves the retaliatory action taken in defense of United States ships, that the President's response was commensurate to the attack, and that, *if there were further attacks upon our forces,* response under the Resolution would be tailored so as to be commensurate to such attacks.

At 112 Congressional Record 18415 Senator Stennis said that the Resolution was intended to avoid full-scale war. At 112 Congressional Record 18415, Senator Church said that, as emphasized by the President, the retaliation for the attacks upon American ships in the Gulf of Tonkin did not mean the United States had changed its purpose, and the policy was not to expand the war. At 112 Congressional Record 18417 Senator Pell said that the nation should act with prudence and calmness. At 112 Congressional Record 18418 Senator Cooper said that America should find a solution in Asia without fighting a war, and that it should not expand the war except for its own defense. At 112 Congressional Record 18419 Senator Randolph said that the course of action did not involve the danger of unlimited hostile activity. At 112 Congressional

Record 18423 Senator Humphrey, now Vice President, said that the government does not desire to extend or expand the war in Southeast Asia. At 112 Congressional Record 18456 Senator Keating said that the Resolution was not a blank check authorizing policies that might be carried on in the future without congressional consultation. At 112 Congressional Record 18457 Senator Aiken said he hoped the President's action would save more lives than it would cost.

At 112 Congressional Record 18459 Senator Nelson offered an amendment to the Resolution, the purpose of the amendment being to make even more clear that the mission in Southeast Asia was not to be changed, that it was to remain confined to providing aid, assistance, and advice to the South Vietnamese, and that there was to be no expansion of the military commitment in Viet Nam. Senator Fulbright said that Senator Nelson's amendment accurately reflected what the President said would be the policy, what Senator Fulbright thought to be the policy, what other Senators had stated to be the policy, and what every member of the Senate Foreign Relations Committee, with one or two exceptions, thought to be the policy. The only reason Senator Fulbright felt compelled to reject the amendment was that, if accepted, the amendment would create delay in adopting a final resolution at a time when speed was thought to be essential.[126] The House was then voting on the Resolution, and Nelson's amendment, if accepted, would cause delay in a House-Senate Conference. At 112 Congressional Record 18462 Senator Fulbright said that the Resolution was calculated "to prevent the spread of war, rather than to spread it."

At 112 Congressional Record 18539 Congressman Morgan said the resolution "is definitely not an advance declaration of war. The committee has been assured by the Secretary of State that the constitutional power of Congress in this respect will continue to be scrupulously observed." At 112 Congressional Record 18543 Congressman Adair stated that Congress was not abdicating its power to declare war, that Congress was not abdicating its foreign affairs powers, and that it was the attitude of the executive that the Resolution was not an advance approval of any action the executive might see fit to take in the future. The Resolution, he said, only meant that the American flag could not be fired on and was intended only to meet a specific situation. At 112 Congressional Record 18576 Congressman Gross said that the Resolution was not a declaration of war. It was only an after-the-fact endorsement of action taken by the President (*i.e.* in repulsing the attacks upon American ships and bombing the sources of the attacks). At 112 Congressional Record 18549 Congressman Fascell said that the Resolution was not a declaration of war, that it did not impinge on Congress' power to declare war and that no member of the House advocated a declaration of war. At 112 Congressional Record 18552 Congress-

---

[126] It was thought necessary to adopt the resolution as quickly as possible in order to have a speedy demonstration of national unity. *National Commitments Report* 20; Statement of Secretary Rusk, *Tonkin Gulf Hearings* 4.

man Edmondson indicated that the United States should use every available channel to stave off conflict.

The congressional intent behind the Gulf of Tonkin Resolution was not only manifested in the debates which took place while the Resolution was under consideration; it has also been expounded upon by various Senators in the recent National Commitments Hearings. At pages 82 and 83 of *National Commitments Hearings* Senator Fulbright, the instrumental figure in obtaining Senate passage of the Resolution, said that the Resolution was not a declaration of war, that it did not represent a congressional decision to wage a full-fledged war against a foreign government, and that it was, rather, a response to an attack on our forces in a situation which had been presented as an emergency. At page 85 of *National Commitments Hearings* Senator Fulbright said that the Resolution illustrates the distinction which must be made between repelling an attack and waging war in the broad sense. At page 86 of the *Hearings* Senator Fulbright indicated that the Resolution had been passed quickly in order to support the President *in his immediate response to the attacks on our ships.* At page 87 of the *Hearings* Senator Fulbright said that the Resolution was an emergency response to an attack. He further said that it was passed and must be interpreted against a background of repeated statements by Presidents Johnson and Kennedy that America's policy was not to fight in Asia, that its armed forces would not be used there, and "that American boys would not do the fighting that Asian boys should do for themselves."

At page 88 of the *Hearings* Senator Gore said, "I did not vote for the Resolution with any understanding that it was tantamount to a declaration of war." On pages 93 and 94 of the *Hearings* Senator Gore said that, when the Resolution was passed, no Congressman could foresee the bombing of North Viet Nam or the commitment of American troops, "particularly in view of the repeated statements of President Johnson in contravention of such a policy." At page 109 of the *Hearings* Senator Gore said that he knew of no one who, when passing the Resolution, interpreted it in the light "of a commitment of combat troops against which the Executive had declared."

At page 114 of *National Commitments Hearings* Senator Percy said that a survey showed that 40 Senators publicly disagreed with the President's position, and that he did not know if the Resolution would have been approved if it had been expressed that over 500,000 Americans would eventually be committed in Viet Nam. At page 118 Senator Hickenlooper said that few if any Congressmen who voted for the Resolution thought they were "authorizing an all-out war all over Viet Nam." He further said that the Resolution has been "used as a lever to open the door to a much wider operation than anybody really thought about." At page 138 Senator Fulbright approvingly paraphrased statements which said that the Resolution was not a declaration of war, but merely an approval of the President's response to attacks on American forces and to any further attacks on them. At page 148 Senator Fulbright approvingly quoted his response, in 1964, to Senator Nelson's aforementioned amendment, to wit, that the Nelson amendment stated American policy in regard to its mission in Viet Nam, and that any military response by the United States should be limited and appropriate to the provocation.

At page 145 of *National Commitments Hearings* Senator Gore said that the Resolution was presented in the light of an attack on American ships and of the President's pledge of a fitting and limited response. He further said the executive was usurping authority because it was committing acts far beyond the contemplation of Congress when the Resolution was passed. At page 146 Senator Gore said the President's decision to land troops was not approved by the Congress when it passed the Resolution. At page 205 Senator Fulbright said that, in passing the Resolution, Congress did not intend "to have things develop as they have." At page 207 Senator Fulbright pointed out that the congressional intent must be judged against the circumstance that in campaigning for reelection against Senator Goldwater, who "took . . . the hawkish position," President Johnson said that the nation must avoid "the risk of a wider war and must not commit American boys to fight wars which Asian youths should fight for themselves." At page 205 Senator Gore pointed out that the congressional intent must be judged not only against the President's campaign statements, but against the President's message to Congress promising a limited and fitting response and asserting that "we seek no wider war." Senator Gore again said that Congress had not intended to authorize the use of combat forces in Viet Nam.

The *Senate Report* on the above hearings on National Commitments[127] points out that, in approving the language of the Resolution, the Congress was not intending to authorize the President to take any action he desired, but was only recognizing that the delays concomitant to a change of language were undesirable at a time when a speedy affirmance of national unity was thought to be necessary.[128] The *Report* further points out that, while the language of the Resolution can be read to authorize full scale war in Asia, in point of fact Congress believed that it was preventing such a war.[129]

Finally, the intent of Congress in passing the Resolution must be judged against the following statement of Secretary Rusk, made to a joint hearing of the Senate Foreign Relations and Armed Services Committees when the Resolution was pending before Congress. "Therefore, if the Southeast Asia situation develops, and if it develops in ways which we cannot now anticipate, there will continue to be close and continuous consultation between the President and the Congress."[130]

The foregoing demonstrates that, in passing the Tonkin Gulf Resolution, Congress did not intend to declare war or to authorize the sustained large-scale hostilities which the executive branch has carried on in Viet Nam. It thus demonstrates that the executive branch is not justified in basing its actions on

---

[127] *National Commitments Report.*
[128] *Id.* at 20. *See* Statement of Secretary Rusk, *Tonkin Gulf Hearings* 4.
[129] *National Commitments Report* 21.
[130] *Tonkin Gulf Hearings* 3.

the Resolution. However, if it is assumed, contrary to fact but in accordance with executive branch arguments, that the Resolution does authorize the President, in his total discretion, to fight a large and sustained land, sea, and air war on the continent of Asia, then the Gulf of Tonkin Resolution is violently unconstitutional. For under this assumption, the Resolution represents a total delegation to the President of the Congress' power to decide when, where, against whom, and to what extent the United States is to declare war. Congress cannot in this manner totally delegate away its power to declare war. If it could, then the clause giving Congress the power to declare war would be a nullity; and contrary to the purposes of the Constitution, the lives and fortunes of 200 million Americans would rest not in the hands of the entire Congress, but in the hands of one man or a small group of men.

It has been shown that the legislative history of the Tonkin Gulf Resolution amply demonstrates that Congress did not intend to authorize the current hostilities.[131] In the past, however, the executive has pointed to certain statements, made on the floor of Congress when the Resolution was passed, as indicating that Congress did intend to authorize the current hostilities.[132] These statements are of no effect for three reasons. (1) The sum of such statements is greatly outweighed by the numerous contrary statements set forth above. Furthermore, to the extent that the statements cited by the Government were made by opponents of the Resolution,[133] they are even further outweighed because they are not the views of the proponents of the Resolution—who prevailed. (2) A resolution delegating Congress' power to declare war to the President would be unconstitutional even if every single Congressman and Senator intended to make such a delegation. Obviously, then, such a delegation is not less unconstitutional when only a *few* Congressmen and Senators intended to delegate away Congress' power to declare war. (3) In actuality, the most that the statements pointed to by the executive can show is that some Congressmen and Senators may have been somewhat confused as to the extent of the power they were granting the executive. However, that some legislators were confused is no constitutional basis for claiming that Congress has in effect declared war. If it were such a basis, then Congress' power to declare war would be a nullity and would in effect have passed to the executive. In that case the executive could submit to Congress a broadly-worded resolution authorizing

---

[131] It is not necessary to rely on the fact that the executive, when obtaining the Tonkin Gulf Resolution, may have deceived Congress as to the nature and existence of the attacks upon the destroyers in the Tonkin Gulf, as has lately been charged by several Senators after hearings on the Tonkin Gulf events. *See* the material cited in note 25 *supra*. But while it is unnecessary to rely on the possibility of such deception, it must be admitted that the alleged deception does not aid the executive's case that the Tonkin Resolution authorizes it to conduct the current war. For it can be argued that, somewhat like the restitution doctrine of mistake of fact, even if Congress had intended to authorize the current war, its authorization would be void if based on an improper understanding of the facts of the Tonkin Gulf attack, let alone a deliberate deception as to the facts of the attack.

[132] *Legal Adviser* 1103-05.

[133] *E.g.,* the Statements of Senator Morse quoted at *Legal Adviser* 1105, n. 13. To this category may be added the many other statements made during the Tonkin Resolution debate by Senators Morse and Gruening—the two Senators who voted against the Resolution (112 Cong. Rec. 18471)—to the effect that the Resolution gave the executive the power to fight a war. *See* 112 Cong. Rec. 18426-27; 18443-48, 18469.

military action; it could obtain passage of such a resolution by insisting that there is no time to change the wording and by assuring the Congress that its policy is to take strictly limited military action rather than to seek a wider war; many Congressmen, who would not vote for a declaration of war, would vote for the resolution under the impression that they are not authorizing large-scale warfare; and the executive could later renege on its former statements and undertake large-scale war on the claim that there were some statements in the legislative history which could be read to indicate that Congress did intend to authorize such warfare. To verify this possibility, one need only examine the actual legislative history of the Tonkin Resolution, which was submitted to the Congress by the executive.[134] Since that history shows that the overwhelming legislative intent was not to authorize large-scale and sustained warfare, but to prevent it, it is clear that, had the executive asked Congress for a declaration of war, it could not have obtained one. Yet today, the executive, which could not have obtained a declaration of war at the time of the Tonkin Resolution, claims that its large and sustained war can be justified on the basis of the Resolution. Clearly, then, in order to have a valid declaration of war, the Congress must be made aware of what it is doing, as has been the case when it has declared war in the past.[135]

S. *Conclusion of the Merits*

There is no valid constitutional basis for the current hostilities. Rather, the current war represents a flagrant executive usurpation of Congress' power to declare war. Indeed, it is not too much to say that, if the executive has the power to fight the war in Viet Nam without a congressional declaration of war, then the clause giving Congress the power to declare war is as much as gone from the Constitution. Thus, a court should require the executive either (1) to obtain a congressional declaration of limited or general war, or (2) to discontinue fighting in Viet Nam, such discontinuance to be carried out with all deliberate speed. Alternatively, if there are any hopes for peace when a court makes its decision, the court should merely issue a declaratory judgment that the war is unconstitutional.

IV. The Question of Justiciability

In assessing the justiciability of the question involved, it is crucial to keep in mind exactly what that question is. It is *not* whether or not the United States

---

[134] *See* Grose, *Fulbright Urges Congress Inquiry Into War Policy*, N.Y. Times, Feb. 26, 1968, at 1, col. 6.

[135] There may be some debate as to whether a declaration of limited or general war need actually contain the words "declare war," or whether it is enough if the declaration merely says that it "authorizes" certain actions. *Cf. National Commitments Report* 18, 25-26. It seems much better to include the phrase "declare war," because the phrase will insure that Congressmen cannot avoid knowing the full seriousness of the step they are contemplating. When the word "authorizes" is used without the phrase "declaration of war," as in the Tonkin Resolution, Congressmen are not always aware of the extremely serious consequences which may flow from the executive's interpretation of their action. It may be sufficient to merely use the word "authorize," however, when Congress is contemplating actions which clearly do not amount to a declaration of limited or general war.

is to fight a large-scale war in Viet Nam. Rather, the question is which branch of government has the power to declare war. In other words, the question is not *whether* the nation is to fight a large war, but which branch of government has the *power to decide* if it is to fight such a war. The author would be the first to agree that *whether* this country is to fight is a political question; but which branch has the *power to decide* whether to fight is a judicial question.

There is a clear distinction between the question whether a court can decide which branch of government is entrusted with responsibility for a particular political decision such as whether to fight a war, and the question whether courts are to participate in making the political decision itself. Since the first of these questions involves nothing more than constitutional interpretation of the most familiar type, no problem of justiciability should arise: in the present instance, for example, the first question poses only the problem of the power of the President vis-á-vis Congress. Justiciability should become a consideration only when a court is asked to pass upon the second question, *i.e.,* to pass upon the correctness of a political decision made by a coordinate branch of government to which the decision has been committed by the Constitution. In the present instance, for example, problems of justiciability should arise only if courts were asked to hold that America should not fight a war even if Congress were to declare war.

The proposition that a court may not rule on the issue whether the President must seek a congressional declaration as a prerequisite to prosecuting the Vietnamese war—whether for the reason that the question is "political" or for any other reason—is at best very dubious, since it denies the court the power to delineate the authority of the various branches of government. Since *Marbury v. Madison,*[136] it has been clear that this power is a major part of the courts' role in the constitutional scheme. The continued vitality of this simple principle is evidenced by the decision in *Youngstown Sheet & Tube Co. v. Sawyer.*[137] In that case, the extent of the President's warmaking power was at issue; more specifically, the question was whether the President had the power to take over the steel mills in order to more effectively wage the Korean war. In deciding that question in the negative, the Court did not feel constrained to so much as mention the problem of justiciability. Similarly, the question here is whether the President has the power to prosecute the hostilities in Viet Nam without a congressional declaration of war. That question is no more political than the one decided in *Youngstown.*

That the issue involved here is justiciable is graphically demonstrated by past cases. Courts have pronounced upon it on more than twenty occasions, ranging from the earliest days of the Republic to the mid-nineteen sixties.[138]

---

[136] 5 U.S. (1 Cranch) 137 (1803).
[137] 343 U.S. 579 (1952).
[138] United States v. Macintosh, 283 U.S. 605, 622 (1930); The Pedro, 175 U.S. 354, 363 (1899); Tyler v. Defrees, 78 U.S. (11 Wall.) 331, 345 (1870); The Prize Cases, 67 U.S. (2 Black) 635 (1862); Fleming v. Page, 50 U.S. (9 How.) 603, 614, 615, 618 (1850); Talbot v. Seeman, 5 U.S. (1 Cranch) 1 (1801); Bas v. Tingey, 4 U.S. (4 Dall.) 37, 40 (opinion of Washington, J.), 43 (opinion of Chase, J.), 45 (opinion of Paterson, J.) (1800); National Savings & Trust Co. v. Brownell, 222 F.2d 395, 397 (D.C. Cir. 1955);

Some of these cases are United States Supreme Court decisions, some are lower federal court cases, and some are state supreme court cases. Some involve the legality of military acts committed by the United States or its citizens, some involve the power to draft men, and some involve insurance recoveries dependent upon which branch has the power to declare war. When so many courts, over so long a period and in so many causes of action, have ruled on the question of which branch has the power to declare war, then it is clear that this question cannot be a political one, but must be a judicial one.[139]

Moreover, even if the constitutionality of the war is thought to present a question of justiciability, none of the indicia of nonjusticiability set forth in *Baker v. Carr*[140] is present, and the question therefore is clearly a justiciable one. In *Baker*, the Court suggested that the presence of a "political question" might occur frequently in the separation of power context and, emphasizing the need for case-by-case analysis, enumerated several factors which might indicate that the issue under consideration is inappropriate for judicial determination.

One such factor is whether there are judicially discoverable and manageable standards for resolving the question. When the present case is properly viewed as involving not the question whether America is to fight in Viet Nam, but the question of which branch of government has the power to decide whether America is to fight, it becomes plain that there are judicial standards which are eminently clear, manageable, and constitutionally ordained. These standards are that, under the unequivocal language of the American Constitution, the Congress and not the executive has the power to declare war. The President may repel sudden attacks without a declaration of war, but he cannot in his sole discretion continue to fight for as long as he pleases, wherever he pleases, and with as much force as he pleases. Rather, as soon after the sudden attack as possible, the executive must go to the Congress for a declaration of limited or general war. These standards are more clear, more manageable, and more

---

Hamilton v. McClaughry, 136 F. 445, 449-51 (C.C.D. Kan. 1905); Durand v. Hollins, 8 F. Cas. 111 (C.C.S.D.N.Y. 1860); U.S. v. Smith, 27 F. Cas. 1192, 1230 (C.C.D.N.Y. 1806); United States v. Mitchell, 246 F. Supp. 874 (D. Conn. 1963), aff'd, 369 F.2d 323 (2d Cir. 1966), cert. denied, 386 U.S. 972 (1967); Savage v. Sun Life Assur. Co., 57 F. Supp. 620 (W.D. La. 1944); Beley v. Pennsylvania Mut. Life Ins. Co., 373 Pa. 231, 95 A.2d 202, 205 (1953); Pang v. Sun Life Assur. Co., 37 Hawaii 208 (1945); Rosenau v. Idaho Mut. Ben. Ass'n, 145 P.2d 227 (Idaho 1944); West v. Palmetto State Life Ins. Co., 25 S.E.2d 475 (S. Car. 1943); Stankus v. New York Life Ins. Co., 44 N.E.2d 687 (Mass. 1942); Perkins v. Rogers, 35 Ind. 124 (1871); Sutton v. Tiller, 46 Tenn. (6 Cold.) 487 (1869); Western Reserve Life Ins. Co. v. Meadows, 256 S.W.2d 674, 679-81 (Tex. Civ. App. 1953).

[139] Especially is this so when one considers the fact that, to the best of the author's knowledge, in the entire history of this country there has been only one case which can truly be said to have held, at least by implication, that the question of which branch of government has the power to declare war is a political question rather than a justiciable one. Luftig v. McNamara, 252 F. Supp. 819 (1966), aff'd 373 F.2d 664 (1967), cert. denied, Mora v. McNamara, 88 S. Ct. 282 (1967). Another case, cited by the government, only arguably held this, Eminente v. Johnson, 361 F.2d 73, cert. denied, 385 U.S. 929 (1966), and the author believes that the current war *may* have given rise to a third, but still unreported, case which held similarly. Thus, most of the cases which the government's briefs cite in regard to the justiciability of the war have nothing to do with the questions involved here. They involve questions such as: whether aliens can be tried and imprisoned by our military or can obtain access to the federal courts, Johnson v. Eisentrager, 339 U.S. 763 (1950); whether CAB orders approved by the President are subject to judicial review, Chicago and Southern Airlines v. Waterman S. S. Corp., 333 U.S. 103 (1948); and whether the President need grant a commission to a doctor. Orloff v. Willoughby, 345 U.S. 83 (1953).

[140] 369 U.S. 186 (1962).

explicit in the Constitution than were the standards which *Baker* relied on to hold reapportionment a justiciable question instead of a political one. *Baker* said the equal protection clause provided sufficient standards for reapportionment.[141] Under this clause, government action cannot be arbitrary or capricious; it must be rational.[142] But as the history and literature of reapportionment show, there are many possible plans of apportionment which could be considered rational and non-arbitrary, plans ranging from one man—one vote to schemes encompassing elements of representation by geography, economic interests, political boundaries, ethnic groupings, racial groupings, political party affiliations, etc. Thus, if the equal protection clause provided sufficient standards to make apportionment a justiciable question instead of a political one, then *a fortiori* the clear and simple standards emanating from the declaration of war clause mean that the question of which branch has the power to declare war is a justiciable one rather than a political one. To reiterate these standards, the President can repel a sudden attack, but, as soon as possible, he must come to Congress for a declaration of limited or general war.

Another factor suggested in *Baker* for determining if a question is non-justiciable is whether the question is one which the Constitution textually and demonstrably commits to another branch of government.[143] The question of *whether* a war is to be fought *is* committed to another branch. Under the Constitution it is textually and demonstrably committed to the legislature, not the executive. But the question of *which branch is to decide* whether to fight a war is not committed to another branch. It is a traditional judicial question. It has been a function of courts in this nation to maintain the separation of powers by saying where the divisions of power lie in the United States. In other words, courts have traditionally pronounced against the unconstitutional usurpations of power which, if unchecked, would destroy our fundamental plan of government.

Furthermore, if reapportionment did not involve questions which under the Constitution were textually and demonstrably committed to another branch, then, *a fortiori*, neither does the present situation. Article I, section 2 of the Constitution indicates that the *states* shall determine the qualifications of voters. Article I, section 4 says that the *states* shall regulate the holding of elections and the *Congress* can alter such state regulations. The second section of the fourteenth amendment prescribes a non-judicial remedy for malapportionment, and Article I, section 5 says that each house of Congress shall judge the qualifications of its members. Despite these textual constitutional phrases which arguably commit apportionment to the Congress and the states, and despite the fact that the federal courts had traditionally refused to interfere in matters of apportion-

---

[141] *Id.* at 226.

[142] *Id.*; Justice Stewart dissenting in Lucas v. Forty-Fourth General Assembly, 377 U.S. 713, 751, 753 (1964).

[143] 369 U.S. 186, 217, 226 (1962).

ment,[144] the Supreme Court found that apportionment is a justiciable question, not a political one. Even more clearly, then, the present question is a justiciable one. The text of the Constitution does not commit to a non-judicial branch the question of which branch has the power to decide if the nation is to fight a war.

In *Baker v. Carr* the Court said that another factor in judging a question's non-justiciability is whether it would be impossible for a court to decide the question without expressing disrespect for a coordinate branch of government.[145] A judicial decision that Congress has the power to declare war expresses no disrespect for another branch. On the contrary, it expresses respect for the power of Congress. It cannot be argued that such a decision would express disrespect for the executive. If that were true, then disrespect for the executive has been expressed by every court which has ever said that the Congress has the power to declare war, by every decision which has ever struck down executive usurpation of power, including *Youngstown Sheet & Tube Co. v. Sawyer,* and by the very clause of the Constitution which gives Congress the power to declare war. Such conclusions are absurd. Again, to hold that the executive does not have the power to decide whether to fight a war is not to express disrespect for the executive, but to respect the functions of Congress under the United States Constitution.

In *Baker* the Court said that another factor in judging a question's non-justiciability is whether there is a need to recognize another branch's determination as final, and whether embarrassments would be caused if the other branch's determination is not permitted to be final.[146] In the present case, the executive branch has made the decision that it, and not the Congress, has the power to decide that this nation shall engage in conflict in Viet Nam. There is, however, no need to give finality to an executive decision of this nature. On the contrary, there is every need *not* to give finality to it. For if such a usurpation of the power to declare war is allowed to stand, then the Constitution is nullified. Directly contrary to the Constitution, the most important decision which a nation can make, whether to initiate war, will be in the hands not of the Congress, but of a small group of men. And, if the executive can usurp the most important decision which a nation can make, it could presumably usurp lesser decisions as well, and the integrity of many Constitutional provisions might be threatened. Moreover, it is only speculative that embarrassments and difficulties would be caused by a judicial decision holding that Congress has the power to declare war. Such a view rests on the impermissible and unstated assumption that the Congress is not to be trusted to make an intelligent decision. This assumption simply cannot be made under a Constitution which vests the power to make the laws and the power to declare war in the Congress. Rather than embarrassments, a judicial order requiring a declaration of war by Congress

---

[144] Many of the cases in which the federal courts had refused to act in apportionment matters are collected in Velvel, *Suggested Approaches To Constitutional Adjudication and Apportionment,* 12 U.C.L.A.L. REV. 1381, 1397-98, n. 76-80 (1965).

[145] 369 U.S. 186, 217 (1952).

[146] *Id.* at 217, 226.

might bring beneficial consequences. For instance, the Congress might declare war, and thus quell opposition to the war based on the premise that it is unconstitutional, unite a country which is deeply divided, and rally allies who are fearful of a lack of American will and purpose. Or, the Congress might refuse to declare war and thus avoid much further destruction and loss of life, hearten those allies who fear that the present war is a bad mistake, and make possible a peaceful rapprochement between opposing great powers. If there are hopes for peace when a judicial decision is made and the court were therefore to merely issue a declaratory judgment that the war is unconstitutional, it is also very difficult to envision difficulties. A declaratory judgment would give little comfort to the other side in the negotiations since the executive can always go to the Congress for a declaration of war if the negotiations break down.[147] In sum, to say that a judicial decision on the war's constitutionality should be avoided because it would cause foreign or domestic difficulties is to claim powers of omniscience that belong only to God. Indeed, if the probabilities are at all assessable, it seems likely that a ruling would have only the desirable effect of increasing the likelihood that future Americans will not go to war merely because a small group of executive officials think they should.

Finally, if the alleged need for finality and avoidance of embarrassment did not turn *Youngstown* and *Baker* into political questions, then the present question is not a political one either. In *Youngstown,* the executive made a decision that it had the power to seize the mills, and it alleged that a contrary judicial decision would heap disaster upon America's war effort and its allies.[148] Yet the Court did not regard the executive's usurpation of authority as a non-justiciable question. Neither, then, is the present usurpation a non-justiciable question. In the reapportionment example as well, it was constantly argued that legislative decisions to malapportion need to be given finality lest judicial decisions paralyze the political process and thereby cause the nation to descend into wrack and ruin.[149] However, such arguments did not make apportionment a non-justiciable issue, and analogous arguments do not make the present question non-justiciable.

Baker said that another criterion for judging the non-justiciability of a question is whether the decision of the question involves an initial policy determination which is not suitable for judical discretion.[150] But, as has been shown above, the policy determination of *which branch decides* if war is to be fought is entirely appropriate for a judicial decision. To reiterate, courts have many times pronounced on this question, there are clear criteria, the question is not com-

---

[147] Some might fear that a declaratory judgment could harm negotiations because the enemy might believe that Congress would not declare any sort of war whatever subsequent to a breakdown in the negotiations. Not only does this fear probably misjudge both Congress and the fundamental bases of enemy actions, but the slim possibility that such a fear is warranted can be obviated if a court were to withhold its decision until the conclusion or breakdown of negotiations.

[148] 343 U.S. at 582-84 (1952).

[149] *See, e.g.,* Reynolds v. Sims, 377 U.S. 533, 620, 624 (1964) (dissenting opinion); Wesberry v. Sanders, 376 U.S. 1, 20-24, 48 (1964) (dissenting opinion); Baker v. Carr, 369 U.S. 186, 327 (1962) (dissenting opinion).

[150] 369 U.S. 186, 217 (1962).

mitted to another branch, no disrespect would be shown another branch, and there is every need not to accord finality to the executive's decision that it can usurp the power to declare war. Finally, if *Youngstown* did not involve a decision which should be left to other branches even though it involved an executive action which was allegedly necessary to ward off a wartime national disaster, then neither does the present case involve a decision which must be left to other branches.

In concluding the section on justiciability, one other point may be noted. As shown by cases involving reapportionment, voting rights, and free speech, it is the function of courts not only to maintain the separation of powers by striking down usurpations of power, but to safeguard and insure a free political process and representative government.[151] Courts should perform this function in regard to the power to declare war: they should insure that this power remains in the people's legislative representatives to be exercised through the political processes of Congress. The judicial branch must function to guarantee that no man or small group of men can circumvent constitutional government by arrogating unto themselves the power to declare war.

V. Standing to Sue

In cases where citizens or taxpayers of the United States challenge unlawful government action, the government ritually asserts that, under the rule of *Frothingham v. Mellon*,[152] the citizens lack standing to sue. With respect to the constitutionality of the Vietnamese war, however, it can be argued: (1) that citizens have standing to sue under the presently existing rules laid down by the Supreme Court in *Frothingham* and subsequent cases; (2) that if they do not have standing to sue under presently existing rules, then the rules should be changed, at least to the extent of permitting citizen's suits in cases involving fundamental questions about our constitutional structure; (3) that it would be improper to dismiss a case for lack of standing so long as the Supreme Court, in *Flast v. Gardner*,[153] is engaged in reconsidering the rule laid down in *Frothingham v. Mellon*.

A. *Citizens Have Standing to Sue Under Existing Doctrines*

The Supreme Court has laid down many different verbal formulations for determining when citizens or taxpayers have standing to challenge the constitutionality of government action. In *Frothingham,* the Court said that plaintiffs must suffer a direct injury and must not merely suffer in some indefinite way in common with people generally.[154] The later case of *Doremus v. Board of Education* defined this criterion to mean that a taxpayer could meet the direct injury test if his action is a good faith pocketbook action.[155] An examina-

---

[151] The Court's statements in *Reynolds v. Sims* exemplify this. *See* 377 U.S. 533, 554-55, 565-66 (1964).
[152] 262 U.S. 447 (1923).
[153] *Prob. juris. noted*, 88 S. Ct. 218 (1967).
[154] 262 U.S. 447, 488 (1923).
[155] 342 U.S. 429, 434-35 (1952).

tion of the past and future injuries suffered by the average citizen shows that, particularly if a case were brought as a class action,[156] the tests of *Doremus* and *Frothingham* could be met under the circumstances generally prevailing as a result of the Vietnamese war.

Since the beginning of 1965, the present war has cost an average of roughly 20 to 25 billion dollars a year.[157] This expense means that the war has cost each citizen an average of 100 to 125 dollars a year, or 375 dollars since 1965, and it has therefore cost each family about 200 to 250 dollars a year, or a total of 600 to 750 dollars since 1965. It has cost even more for citizens who pay higher tax rates, and it will continue to cost citizens heavily in the future. The war expenditures, in the virtually unanimous opinion of every economist, politician, and knowledgeable private citizen, have contributed to a severe inflation. The rate of inflation was about three and one-half percent in the last year. Thus, in that year alone, a man making 10,000 dollars a year lost approximately 350 dollars of purchasing power. A man making 25,000 dollars lost about 875 dollars of purchasing power. This inflation, which is in large part attributable to the Vietnamese war, is proceeding apace, and will thus cause further financial injury in the future. As a result of inflation the government has maintained excise taxes, and the President is asking for a heavy income tax surcharge. Again, direct financial injury has been suffered and will continue to be suffered. Because of a balance of payments problem which is greatly accentuated by heavy wartime expenditures, this nation is undergoing a gold crisis which could result in severe economic dislocations and perhaps even devaluation of the dollar. These results could work great hardships on United States citizens. Heavy wartime expenditures have forced cutbacks in spending for research and

---

[156] A suit challenging the constitutionality of the war would be a proper one for a class action. Rule 23 of the Federal Rules of Civil Procedure states:

    (a) *Prerequisites to a Class Action.* One or more members of a class may sue or be sued as representative parties on behalf of all only if (1) the class is so numerous that joinder of all members is impracticable, (2) there are questions of law or fact common to the class, (3) the claims or defenses of the representative parties are typical of the claims or defenses of the class, and (4) the representative parties will fairly and adequately protect the interests of the class.

    (b) *Class Actions Maintainable.* An action may be maintained as a class action if the prerequisites of subdivision (a) are satisfied, and in addition:

    (1) the prosecution of separate actions by or against individual members of the class would create a risk of . . . (B) adjudications with respect to individual members of the class which would as a practical matter be dispositive of the interests of the other members not parties to the adjudications or substantially impair or impede their ability to protect their interests; or

    (2) the party opposing the class has acted or refused to act on grounds generally applicable to the class, thereby making appropriate final injunctive relief or corresponding declaratory relief with respect to the class as a whole; or

    (3) the court finds that the questions of law or fact common to the members of the class predominate over any questions affecting only individual members, and that a class action is superior to other available methods for the fair and efficient adjudication of the controversy.

Rule 23 is plainly met in this case. As for 23(a), the class is so numerous that joinder of all members is impracticable, there are questions of law and fact common to the class—whether the executive can declare war or has been authorized by Congress to fight the current war, the claims of plaintiffs are typical of the class, and proper plaintiffs would fairly and adequately protect the interests of the class. As for 23(b), separate actions by members of the class would create a risk that adjudications with respect to individual members of the class would be dispositive of the interests of the other members, the parties opposing the class have acted on grounds generally applicable to the class, the questions of law and fact common to the class predominate over any questions affecting only individual members, and a class action would be a superior method of litigating the question involved.

[157] The cost of the war is currently running at about 30 billion dollars a year.

social welfare projects. The people who depend on such spending have suffered a direct injury. Many American citizens will be drafted and will be wounded or killed in the current war. There can be no more direct injury than that. In sum, then, the average citizen has suffered and will continue to suffer direct injuries, both financial and physical.

In addition to suffering direct injuries in common with others, some citizens will suffer very specific repercussions, repercussions which are neither indefinite nor shared by the population generally. For example, a man who will be wounded or killed in the current war will suffer not an indefinite injury, but a definite one; he and his family will have a very personal suffering, not one in common with people generally. A citizen on a small fixed pension suffers a definite injury from inflation, an injury whose degree is not shared generally by more fortunate citizens. A man of low income suffers a serious injury from income taxes, excise taxes, and income tax surcharges; the extent of his suffering is not shared generally by people of high income. An unskilled worker who lives in the ghetto is more likely than other people to lose his job if the gold crisis leads to severe economic dislocations; his suffering is a definite injury not shared by people generally. A man who depends on government spending for research projects or for social welfare suffers a definite injury not shared by people generally.

In sum, the tests of *Frothingham* and *Doremus* are met here not only because of the situation regarding taxes and appropriations, but because of other economic and physical factors as well, such as inflation, economic dislocations, wounds, deaths, etc.[158] And with regard only to taxes and appropriations, unlike the situation in *Frothingham,* taxpayers' interest in the money spent on the war is not speculative, remote, and indeterminable.[159] It is very real; it is a good faith pocketbook interest. Not only is this interest demonstrated by logic, it is demonstrated by precedent as well. In *Doremus,* the Court explained that a taxpayer had had standing to sue in *Everson v. Board of Education,*[160] where the taxpayer was challenging a New Jersey statute which provided for the reimbursing of parents who transported their children to parochial schools. The reason there had been standing in *Everson,* said the Court, was that *Everson* involved a measurable appropriation or disbursement of public funds.[161] In the present case, there is a measurable disbursement of public funds; thirty billion dollars a year is currently being spent on the war.[162] In *Adler v. Board of Edu-*

---

[158] If the rules of *Frothingham* and *Doremus* preclude a citizen's suit challenging the war, this preclusion is tantamount to admitting that under those rules it will almost never be possible to bring a citizen's suit challenging governmental action. However, see note 189 *infra.*

[159] 262 U.S. 447, 487 (1923).

[160] 330 U.S. 1 (1947).

[161] 342 U.S. 429, 434 (1952).

[162] It has been suggested to the author that the standing of state or local taxpayers can be differentiated from the standing of federal taxpayers and therefore that *Everson,* which involved a township appropriation and a local taxpayer, does not provide a precedent for asserting that a citizen, because he pays federal taxes, has standing to challenge the war. The basis of this argument is that municipal and state taxpayers have a larger and more determinate financial stake in municipal and state taxes and appropriations than federal taxpayers do in federal taxes and appropriations. Even if this argument were correct, citizens would still have standing to challenge the war because of the many non-tax, non-appropriation injuries they are

cation[163] the Court did not question the standing of taxpayers and parents who challenged a state anti-subversive statute even though the statute caused no new expenditures of meaningful proportions and even though Justice Frankfurter vigorously dissented on the standing point.[164] In *Wieman v. Updegraff,*[165] citizens and taxpayers sued to enjoin salary payments to professors who had refused to take a loyalty oath. Since the compensation of state employees presumably remained the same regardless of whether they took the oath, and since the employees would presumably be replaced if fired,[166] the case had no impact on public expenditures. Yet the Court did not question the taxpayers' standing. Clearly, then, if the Court did not question the taxpayers' standing in *Adler* and *Wieman,* cases where little if any money was involved, there is even less reason to challenge a citizen's standing in the present situation, where billions of dollars are involved.[167]

A citizen also has standing to sue under the doctrine of *Baker v. Carr.*[168] There the Court said that "the gist of the question of standing" is whether complainants have "alleged such a personal stake in the outcome of the controversy as to assure that concrete adverseness which sharpens the presentation of issues upon which the court so largely depends for illumination of difficult constitutional questions."[169] Complainants do not have standing, said the Court, if they

---

suffering, *e.g.*, inflation, economic dislocations, and wounds. Moreover, the argument is not sound. (1) When the Supreme Court, in *Doremus,* explained why the plaintiff had had standing in *Everson,* the Court did not rely on the fact that the plaintiff had been a local taxpayer, but only on the fact that there had been a measurable appropriation. The appropriations for the current war are quite measurable. (2) In today's world, there are distinct limits to the distinction between the size and determinability of the financial stake of state and local taxpayers in state and local taxes and appropriations and the size and determinability of the financial stake of federal taxpayers in federal taxes and appropriations. For example, a federal taxpayer who is in the thirty-percent income tax bracket would have as much of an interest in the thirty billion dollars now being spent yearly on the war as a state taxpayer who pays a 3% state income tax would have in one of the medium-sized appropriations of a state government which spends billions of dollars a year. *See generally,* 3 K. DAVIS, ADMINISTRATIVE LAW TREATISE § 22.09, at 244 (1958), quoted in W. LOCKHART, Y. KAMISAR, and J. CHOPER, CONSTITUTIONAL LAW, CASES-COMMENTS-QUESTIONS 59-60 (1964 ed.).

[163] 342 U.S. 485 (1952).
[164] 342 U.S. 497, 501-03 (1952).
[165] 344 U.S. 183 (1952).
[166] Comment, *Taxpayers' Suits: A Survey and Summary,* 69 YALE L.J. 895, 922 (1960).
[167] Even if, as is unlikely, the state employees would not have been replaced in *Wieman,* the impact on public expenditures could not compare with the present case.

A comment in the *Yale Law Journal* has argued that the *Adler* & *Wieman* "cases may be distinguished by the arguments that the standing of the taxpayers in *Adler* was deemed irrelevant because of the presence in court of other plaintiffs with different kinds of interests and, perhaps more persuasively, that *Wieman,* by the time it reached the Court, was no longer a taxpayer's suit, but an appeal by professors about to be dismissed. Nonetheless, *Adler* & *Wieman* have been regarded in the literature as taxpayers' suits . . . ." *Taxpayers' Suits: A Survey and Summary,* 69 YALE L.J. 895, 923 (1960). I would add that not only have *Adler* & *Wieman* both been considered taxpayers' suits, but *Adler* cannot be satisfactorily distinguished in the way the *Yale Law Journal* has tried to do. The fact that non-taxpayers were present in *Adler* proves nothing at all. In the analogous area of ripeness, the Supreme Court, in United Public Workers v. Mitchell, 330 U.S. 75 (1947), refused to decide the issues raised by federal employees whose cases were not ripe, although it went ahead and decided the very same issues raised by an employee whose case was ripe. (In a broad sense, the relevant issue was whether Congress can constitutionally prevent federal employees from taking an active part in political campaigns; in a narrow sense, the issue was whether federal employees can be prevented from working at the polls on election day.) In short, the mere fact that one eligible complainant was in the case did not stop the Court from dismissing the ineligible ones. Thus, the mere fact that non-taxpaying interests were present in *Adler* does not mean that the Court would have permitted the taxpaying interests to remain in the case even if they had lacked standing.

[168] 369 U.S. 186 (1962).
[169] *Id.* at 204.

assert "merely a claim of 'the right, possessed by every citizen, to require that the government be administered according to law.' "[170] In *Baker* the Court ruled that there was standing because the plaintiffs were alleging that malapportionment impaired the votes of citizens living in malapportioned counties.[171] In the present situation, individuals have such a personal stake in the outcome of the case as to assure that adverseness which sharpens the presentation of issues; and in the present case, there is much more at stake than "merely" the right to have the government run in accordance with the Constitution. American citizens are suffering and will continue to suffer from inflation due to the war, from taxes due to the war, from lack of research funds and social welfare programs that have been curtailed because of the war, from a gold crisis due to the war, and from being drafted, wounded and killed because of the war. Surely citizens' interests in such matters are as important as was the right to an unimpaired vote in *Baker*. Indeed, the value of the right to vote is also seriously impaired if, without any constitutional authority, the executive branch can fight a large and sustained war which has imposed dire consequences upon innumerable citizens. In circumstances such as the present, there can be no doubt about the existence of a high degree of adverseness. Neither can there be any doubt that many Americans have received financial and physical injuries that go beyond the "mere" right to have the government administered according to law.

Finally, private citizens have standing to sue within the doctrines of cases that have permitted citizens to raise challenges to government action which denies rights to third parties. For example, in *Pierce v. Society of Sisters*,[172] a state statute required parents to send their children to public schools. Because this statute threatened the property rights of a private school, that school was allowed to challenge the statute on the ground that the state was violating the parents' right to send their children to the school of their choice.[173] The situation in the present case is similar. Citizens are being financially injured because of an unconstitutional war, and they can therefore raise the rights of other citizens not to be taxed, drafted, wounded, killed, etc. in an unconstitutional manner. In *NAACP v. Alabama*[174] and *Barrows v. Jackson*,[175] the Supreme Court ruled that plaintiffs had standing to assert the rights of others when a denial of the others' rights would result in harm to the plaintiffs and when plaintiffs' suits were the only practicable way in which the other people's rights could be vindicated. So it is in this case. The denial of the rights of others outlined above is occurring because of an unconstitutional war effort which is also harming the potential plaintiffs. And, the rights of the "others" can in many cases be vindicated only by a citizens' suit brought by the potential plaintiffs. For example, an elderly man living on a small fixed pension suffers greatly

---

[170] *Id.* at 208.
[171] *Id.* at 207-08.
[172] 268 U.S. 510 (1925).
[173] This is made plain in Barrows v. Jackson, 346 U.S. 249, 257 (1953).
[174] 357 U.S. 449, 458-60 (1958).
[175] 346 U.S. 249, 255-59 (1953).

from inflation and taxes caused by the war. He has a right not to suffer in this way unless the war is a constitutional one. Yet, as a practical matter, such a person cannot financially afford to bring a case challenging the war. Similarly, people who depend on social welfare programs which have been curtailed because of the war have a right not to suffer because of the executive's usurpation of power. But they, too, cannot afford to vindicate this right in court. Men who are already in the armed forces and who may be wounded and killed have a right not to receive such injuries in an unconstitutional war. But, as a practical matter, these men too cannot afford to bring a case asserting their rights. The bringing of a case is liable to cause them to be harrassed or imprisoned, to be denied promotion, and, if they are professional military men, to ruin their careers. Suit by a citizen is necessary to vindicate the rights of such men.[176]

Finally, in *Griswold v. Connecticut*,[177] the Supreme Court ruled that a party can assert the rights of others when there is a case or controversy[178] and when others' rights "are likely to be diluted or adversely affected"[179] if not raised by the party in court.[180] Thus, in the present situation, a citizen entitled to sue in his own right should also be able to assert the rights of elderly people living on fixed pensions, of those who depend on social welfare programs, and of men in the military. Otherwise, the right of such people not to suffer because of an unconstitutional war is obviously "likely to be diluted or adversely affected." In summary, then, citizens have standing to sue within the doctrines of past cases such as *Frothingham, Doremus, Everson, Adler, Wieman, Baker, Pierce, Barrows, NAACP v. Alabama*, and *Griswold*.

B. *If Necessary, the Rules of Standing Should be Altered in Cases Involving the Fundamental Structure of Constitutional Government*

If individual citizens do not have standing under traditional rules, then those rules should be altered to the extent of enabling citizens to raise questions which concern the fundamental structure of constitutional government. The requirement of standing basically stems from the constitutional phrases providing that the judicial power shall extend to cases and controversies.[181] From its inception, the doctrine of standing has been a method for insuring that a real case or controversy exists. In other words, standing is a way of insuring that the parties are truly adverse, that the issues are not feigned or collusive, that there is a real

---

[176] This is illustrated by the case of Captain Dale Noyd, an Air Force officer with a good service record who was nonetheless court martialed, dismissed from the service, and sentenced to prison because, pursuant to his belief that the current war is unjust, he refused to train pilots for duty in Vietnam. Kneeland, *Capt. Noyd is Sentenced to a Year at Hard Labor*, N.Y. Times, March 10, 1968, at 3, col. 1; Kneeland, *Captain is Convicted for Refusal to Train Pilot for Vietnam War*, N.Y. Times, March 9, 1968, at 1, col. 6, at 2, cols. 3-5. *See also* Robinson, *Two at Fort Jackson Face Court Martial Over War Doubts*, N.Y. Times, Feb. 22, 1968, at 10, col. 5.

[177] 381 U.S. 479 (1965).

[178] *Id.* at 481.

[179] *Id.*

[180] In *Griswold* the parties in Court had a confidential relationship with those whose rights they were asserting. 381 U.S. at 481. The confidential relationship, however, was hardly the crucial point. The crucial point was that the third parties' rights would be diluted if not raised by the parties in court.

[181] Frothingham v. Mellon, 262 U.S. 447 (1923); Doremus v. Board of Education, 342 U.S. 429, 435-36 (1952) (dissenting opinion).

clash of interests, and that the court is not being asked to render an advisory opinion.[182] These requirements are met when there is a clash over governmental action which is fundamental to the constitutional structure. In regard to the Vietnamese conflict, many citizens are completely adverse to the executive branch's view that it has the power to decide whether this nation is to fight a war. Certainly, the issue of whether the executive or the Congress has the power to decide whether America is to fight is not feigned or collusive, but is of vital importance. As can be judged by the severe financial and physical injuries being suffered by citizens, there is a severe clash of interests. Indeed, when one considers that many people allege that the current unconstitutional war could lead to war with China or Russia, it becomes clear that the clash of interests is immense. Finally, a court would not be asked to render an advisory opinion. On the contrary, what is needed is an order or judgment which could vitally affect both the current war and future ones.

Many commentators have criticized the notion that citizens and taxpayers do not have standing to challenge governmental action which is critical to the constitutional structure. For example, in an article in the *New York University Law Review,* Justice Douglas suggests that citizens should have standing to challenge action which invades precious first amendment commands such as the separation of church and state.[183] As the Justice pointed out, if citizens cannot challenge governmental action which destroys the constitutional structure, massive public injuries will go unredressed.[184] The decision to enter warfare is the most critical decision a nation can make. It is a decision which the Constitution deliberately vests in the legislature rather than in one man or small group of men. If citizens lack standing to challenge an executive usurpation of the power to make this decision, then the lives and fortunes of 200 million people will rest in the hands of a small group of men. To permit this is to permit the Constitution to be undermined and is therefore to permit a massive public injury. Citizens should be able to protect themselves against such injury by challenging the executive's usurpation of power. By permitting such a challenge, federal courts would not be embarking on a novel course, since approximately thirty-four states permit citizens to challenge governmental action regardless of the effect of such governmental action on public expenditures.[185] Rather than embarking on a novel course, federal courts would be preventing an incredible inversion of values exemplified as follows: when government action is of a relatively minor nature and affects relatively few citizens, the affected citizens can sue; but when government action is a gross constitutional violation which affects the great majority of the citizenry, affected citizens cannot sue.

---

[182] Frothingham v. Mellon, 262 U.S. 447, 485 (1923); Doremus v. Board of Education, 342 U.S. 429 (1952) (dissenting opinion).
[183] Douglas, *The Bill of Rights Is Not Enough,* 38 N.Y.U.L. Rev. 207, 224-27 (1963).
[184] *Id.* at 226.
[185] Comment, *Taxpayers' Suits: A Survey and Summary,* 69 Yale L.J. 895 (1960); Jaffe, *Standing To Secure Judicial Review: Public Actions,* 74 Harv. L. Rev. 1265, 1280-81 (1961).

As previously mentioned, the requirement of standing basically stems from the need for a case or controversy. However, some claim that it is also a rule of self-governance which the Court has developed for cases "confessedly within its jurisdiction."[186] To the extent that this claim is valid, it is nevertheless irrelevant in the present situation. The doctrine of standing should no more bar a suit challenging the constitutionality of the war because it may stem from a rule of self-governance than because it stems from the case or controversy requirement. If necessary it should be altered to permit a challenge to the war. It would be a perversion of the judicial role, which is to protect individuals against unconstitutional injuries and to maintain the separation of powers, if courts were to use a mere rule of self-governance to avoid a case where there is a deep clash of interests, where more than an advisory opinion is sought, where there is reliance on the fundamental constitutional division of powers respecting the momentous decision of whether to go to war, and where massive injuries are being visited upon the entire public.

As a matter of fact, in cases involving the Court's rule on standing to raise the rights of third parties, the Court has recognized that its rule, being only one of practice, should yield in the proper circumstances. In *Barrows v. Jackson,*[187] the Court said:

> Under the peculiar circumstances of this case, we believe the reasons which underlie our rule denying standing to raise another's rights, which is only a rule of practice, are outweighed by the need to protect the fundamental rights which would be denied. . . .
> In other unique situations which have arisen in the past, broad constitutional policy has led the Court to proceed without regard to its usual rule. [Discussing *Pierce v. Society of Sisters.*]

The present circumstances would certainly seem appropriate for disregarding the standing rule.

C. *A Court Should Decide the Other Issues Even if it Believes That Citizens Lack Standing*

The Supreme Court, in *Flast v. Gardner,* is presently reconsidering the rule of *Frothingham v. Mellon,* the keystone in the government's ritual argument that citizens have no standing to sue. In these circumstances, it would be improper for a court to dismiss a citizen's suit for lack of standing.

One cannot, of course, forecast whether the Supreme Court will decide for or against the taxpayers in *Flast,* and neither can one foresee the exact grounds of the Court's decision. However, it seems likely that a decision for the *Flast* taxpayers would have a favorable impact on the standing of a citizen to litigate the war's constitutionality. On the other hand, it is perhaps equally likely that a decision against the *Flast* taxpayers would *not* necessarily have an *un*favorable

---

[186] Ashwander v. TVA, 297 U.S. 288, 346 (concurring opinion); Rescue Army v. Municipal Court, 331 U.S. 549, 568-75 (1947); Flast v. Gardner, 271 F. Supp. 1 (S.D.N.Y. 1967), *prob. juris. noted,* 389 U.S. 895 (1967); Davis, *Standing to Challenge Governmental Action,* 39 Minn. L. Rev. 353, 424 (1955).
[187] 346 U.S. 249, 257 (1953).

impact on the standing of individual citizens who challenge the war, since the threatened injuries to the taxpayers in *Flast* are not nearly as severe as the actual and threatened injuries to the American people caused by the war. In *Flast*, the taxpayers are challenging the use of federal funds in support of religious schools. Thus the injuries to the taxpayers are the money spent to support the schools and the results of a possible breach in the doctrine of separation of church and state, including an alleged injury to spiritual and intellectual freedom.[188] While these are serious potential injuries, they do not compare with the injuries suffered because of the Vietnamese war. Like a diminution in the separation of church and state, war causes a diminution in spiritual and intellectual freedom. But war also diminishes physical freedom, which aid to parochial schools does not. Furthermore, the government is now spending thirty billion dollars a year of the taxpayers' money on the war, thus causing citizens a larger financial injury than is caused by the amount of taxpayers' money being spent on religious schools. The present war has caused citizens to suffer because of severe inflation and a cutback in research and social welfare projects; these things are not caused by support for religious schools. The present war threatens to bring severe economic dislocations, which are not threatened by support for religious schools. The present war is causing numerous persons to be wounded and killed; these injuries are not caused by support given to religious schools. Finally, the present war involves the question of who has the constitutional power to make decisions which in this day and age can conceivably lead to atomic destruction; atomic destruction is not threatened by aid to parochial schools. In sum, even if the taxpayers in *Flast* should lose, a citizen challenging the executive's war actions might nevertheless have standing because the currently unconstitutional war is causing larger and more direct injuries than are involved in *Flast*.[189]

Since a decision favorable to the *Flast* taxpayers would probably help those citizens who challenge the war's constitutionality, while a contrary decision

---

[188] Flast v. Gardner, 267 F. Supp. 351, 354-55 (S.D.N.Y. 1967), granting a motion for a three judge court, whose decision appears at 271 F. Supp. 1 (S.D.N.Y. 1967), *prob. juris. noted,* 389 U.S. 895 (1967).

[189] It might be thought that, in regard to standing, the *Flast* taxpayers have one advantage over citizens who bring a suit challenging the war. Where aid is given to religious schools, the beneficiaries of the aid are not likely to bring suit challenging their benefaction. Thus, if taxpayers cannot challenge the constitutionality of the aid, there may be no one to do so. The constitutionality of the war, however, might be challenged even if citizens do not have standing to bring a suit raising the question. For example, a soldier who is prosecuted for refusing to go to Viet Nam might challenge the constitutionality of the war. The author does not believe, however, that the circumstance under discussion gives any significant advantage to the *Flast* taxpayers. (1) In so many other ways, described in the text, citizens challenging the war have a better case in regard to standing than do the *Flast* taxpayers. (2) Courts have been extremely reluctant to permit soldiers who disobey orders or civilians who refuse induction to raise the constitutionality of the war as a defense to prosecution. I know of but one case which allowed such a defense to be raised—unsuccessfully. (3) As is shown by *Griswold v. Connecticut, supra* note 177 and accompanying text, when it is necessary to prevent a third party's rights from being diluted or adversely affected, a party in court can raise the third party's rights even though the third party could himself vindicate his rights if brought into court. This principle applies here, since the rights of soldiers and draftees will be adversely affected if those persons must risk criminal prosecution or other severe harassment in order to assert their rights. *Cf.* Dombrowski v. Pfister, 380 U.S. 479 (1965), where the Court stressed that "'the threat of sanctions may deter . . . almost as potently as the actual application of sanctions,'" *id.* at 486, and that a test of the validity of government action should not have to depend upon the courage of "those hardy enough to risk criminal prosecution to determine the proper scope of regulation." *Id.* at 487.

would not necessarily hurt them, a court should not dismiss a challenge to the war for lack of standing even if it disagrees with the contention that the standing requirements are satisfied. Rather, because of the vast public importance attaching to a suit against the war, a court should proceed to a decision on the other issues involved, and postpone its ruling on standing until after the Supreme Court's decision in *Flast v. Gardner*. At that time, a decision on standing to challenge the war could more accurately be arrived at. The purpose of proceeding to a decision on the merits, while postponing a decision on standing, is to save time; that is to say, the merits could be decided or close to decision when *Flast* comes down. And, in any litigation on the war, maximum possible speed is desirable if not essential: here time is not only money, measured in two to three billions per month, but it is life as well, measured in the unknown thousands of men who may yet die in a war presently unconstitutional.

VI. The Courts' Statutory Jurisdiction

Like any other suit brought in a federal court, a case challenging the constitutionality of the Vietnamese war must meet the requirements for federal jurisdiction. Here the judicial branch has such jurisdiction over the question by virtue of 28 U.S.C. section 1361, and 28 U.S.C. section 1331(a).

A. *Jurisdiction Under 28 U.S.C. Section 1361*

28 U.S.C. section 1361 states that "The District Court shall have original jurisdiction of any action in the nature of mandamus to compel an officer or employee of the United States or any agency thereof to perform a duty owed to the plaintiff." This statute would cover litigation of the present question with precision. (1) Officers of the United States, such as the President, the Secretary of Defense and the Secretary of State, could be made defendants. (2) An action would be in the nature of mandamus. Since *Marbury v. Madison*[190] it has been recognized that an action is in the nature of mandamus when a complainant seeks to have a court order an official to perform duties which he is lawfully bound to perform and which he cannot in his discretion refuse to perform. That is what would be involved here. Since the Constitution explicitly vests the power to declare war in Congress, it is clear that the executive has a duty to obtain a suitable declaration of war from Congress before it proceeds to fight a large, sustained war.[191] (3) The executive owes this duty to every American citizen. The power to declare war was given to Congress for

---

[190] 5 U.S. (1 Cranch) 137, 166-72 (1803).

[191] As said earlier, the author is involved in litigation challenging the war. In this litigation, the U.S. Marshal served the complaint upon the Secretaries of State and Defense, but refused to serve the President. The government, in support of the Marshal's refusal, asserts that the doctrine of separation of powers bars the President from being "personally and formally subject to the jurisdiction of the courts for the exercise of his duties as Chief Executive. State of Mississippi v. Johnson, 71 U.S. (4 Wall.) 475 (1867); *see also,* Trimble v. Johnson, 173 F. Supp. 651." Defendants' Motion to Dismiss, Civil Action No. T-4417, United States District Court for the District of Kansas, p. 4, n.1.

As a practical matter, of course, service upon the President is unnecessary, since the two Secretaries have been served. However, without getting into an analysis of the cases cited by the government, suffice it to say that the author believes that, at least in an action in the nature of mandamus, the President should also be serveable. As said in the text, *Marbury v. Madison* established that mandamus can be

the specific purpose of protecting American citizens from the possibility that the executive could, in its own discretion, bring down upon citizens the taxes, deaths, wounds, impoverishments, and economic injuries which accompany war.[192] Indeed, the entire United States Constitution was established in order to safeguard the citizens of the United States.[193] Thus, if the President's duty to obtain a declaration of war before engaging in large-scale and sustained hostilities is not owed to the citizens of the United States,[194] then it is impossible to know to whom it is owed.[195]

B. *Jurisdiction Under 28 U.S.C. Section 1331(a)*

28 U.S.C. section 1331(a) provides that "the District Courts shall have jurisdiction of all civil actions wherein the matter in controversy exceeds the sum or value of $10,000 . . . and arises under the Constitution, laws, or treaties of the United States." This statute also covers the present situation. Any suit would be a civil action. It would be based on the Constitution, more specifically on article I, section 8, clause 11 of the Constitution. And the matter in controversy would exceed the sum or value of 10,000 dollars. In the latter connection, in an injunction or declaratory judgment suit such as one challenging the war, the amount or value of the matter in controversy depends upon the amount or value of the right which will be protected by the decision.[196] The injunction or de-

---

issued to executive officials who must perform a given duty and who have no discretion not to perform it. See note 190 *supra* and accompanying text. The government's argument to the contrary notwithstanding, the doctrine of separation of powers does not demand or imply that, even "formally," the President be above the law. Unless the President *is* above the law, a court, under the doctrine of *Marbury v. Madison,* should be able to issue a mandamus to him when he has a duty which he must perform. Thus, the President should be serveable with a complaint requesting that a mandamus be issued to him.

[192] See text accompanying notes 12 and 13 *supra.*

[193] U.S. Const. Preamble.

[194] As said above, the author's claim is that the President has a duty to obtain a declaration of war before fighting a large and sustained war. Some might view the matter from the other end, *i.e.,* the President has a duty not to fight a long and large-scale war unless he first obtains a declaration of war. But the two ways of looking at it are, in practical effect, a distinction without a difference. Moreover, it is certainly a distinction which is legally irrelevant. (1) Mandamus lies both to compel an official to do a duty which he must perform, and to prevent him from doing something which he is dutybound not to perform. Adams v. Nagle, 303 U.S. 532, 542 (1938); La Buy v. Howes Leather Co., 352 U.S. 249, 256-57 (1957). (2) The Senate Report on § 1361 pointed out that the purpose of the statute is to compel government officials to perform duties owed to plaintiffs. Even if the matter is viewed as one in which the executive has a duty not to fight before obtaining a declaration of war, that duty is owed to all citizens. (3) The Senate Report also indicated that the statute is designed to permit suits when officials have acted without legal authority, which is exactly what the executive has done here.

[195] As the text shows, jurisdiction would clearly exist under 28 U.S.C. § 1361 insofar as a citizen may seek an order that the executive either obtain a declaration of war or else discontinue fighting. Moreover, jurisdiction also exists under § 1361 insofar as a citizen may alternatively seek a declaratory judgment. The Declaratory Judgment Act, 28 U.S.C. §§ 2201-02, does not affect jurisdiction, but merely adds another remedy where a court would otherwise have jurisdiction to grant affirmative relief. Longview Tugboat Co. v. Jameson, 218 F.2d 547 (9th Cir. 1955); Van Buskirk v. Wilkinson, 216 F.2d 735, 737 (9th Cir. 1954); West Publ. Co. v. McColgan, 138 F.2d 320, 324 (9th Cir. 1943); Southern Pacific Co. v. McAdoo, 82 F.2d 121, 122 (9th Cir. 1936); 1 W. Barron & A. Holtzoff, Federal Practice & Procedure § 39, at 208 (1960); 3 *id.* § 1268, at 312; C. Wright, Federal Courts § 100, at 392 (1963). Thus, since courts would have jurisdiction under § 1361 to grant affirmative relief in a suit challenging the constitutionality of the war, they also have jurisdiction under § 1361 to grant a declaratory judgment in such a suit.

[196] Mississippi & Mo. R.R. Co. v. Ward, 67 U.S. (2 Black) 485 (1862); Pennsylvania R.R. Co. v. City of Girard, 210 F.2d 437 (6th Cir. 1954); Landers Frary & Clark v. Vischer Prods. Co., 291 F.2d 319 (7th Cir. 1953); Davis v. American Foundry Equip. Co., 94 F.2d 441 (7th Cir. 1938); Delaware, L. & W.R. Co. v. Frank, 110 F. 689 (C.C.W.D. N.Y. 1901); 1 W. Barron & A. Holtzoff, Federal Practice & Procedure § 24, at 111 (1960); 3 *id.* § 1264, at 312-14 (1960); C. Wright, Federal Courts § 33, at 98, § 100, at 392 (1963).

claratory judgment to be sought would protect the rights of those suffering financial and physical injuries in an unconstitutional war. It would thus protect them from losing value exceeding the amount of 10,000 dollars. Many citizens may lose their lives in the currently unconstitutional war. Surely, each human life intrinsically exceeds the value of 10,000 dollars. Moreover, men who will be killed or rendered unable to work in this war would have earned 10,000 dollars many times over in their lifetimes. Furthermore, some Americans will individually lose more than 10,000 dollars in taxes paid to support the war, purchasing power lost because of the unconstitutional war, and earnings lost while in military service because of the war. In addition, a citizen could bring what was formerly known as a true class action, since the citizen's success or failure would depend upon a right which all citizens possess in common:[197] the right to be free of financial and physical injuries imposed because of a large and sustained war not declared by Congress. Where a true class action exists because of the existence of a common right, the amount in controversy is the aggregate amount of the individual claims,[198] which would here run into millions or even billions of dollars.

In conclusion, the courts plainly have jurisdiction of the war issue under section 1331. Indeed, when the jurisdictional statutes were revised by Congress in 1958, the Senate Report said the jurisdictional amount of 10,000 dollars should have very little effect on federal question cases, stating that it was designed only to bar petty suits and that "the only significant category of 'Federal question' cases subject to the jurisdictional amount are suits under the Jones Act and suits contesting the constitutionality of State statutes."[199] This statement is a clear indication that there is no jurisdictional problem over a case challenging the war, which would be a non-petty action, and that the 10,000 dollar limitation should not prevent suit under section 1331 in such a case because life itself is at stake—the most non-petty situation imaginable. Any other conclusion would not only be erroneous, but should be strenuously avoided, since it would raise a serious constitutional question: namely, whether the Congress, consistently with the concept of equal protection contained in the due process clause of the fifth amendment, can grant citizens access to the federal courts when a mere 10,001 dollars is at stake, yet deny them access to the courts when billions of dollars and life itself are at stake.[200]

---

[197] 1 J. Moore, Federal Practice § 0.97[5], at 894 (2d ed. 1964).

[198] Koster v. Lumbermens Mut. Cas. Co., 330 U.S. 518 (1947); Gibbs v. Buck, 307 U.S. 66 (1939); Buck v. Gallagher, 307 U.S. 95 (1939); 1 J. Moore, Federal Practice § 0.97[5], at 894 (2d ed. 1964); C. Wright, Federal Courts § 72, at 271 (1963).

[199] S. Rep. No. 1830, 85th Cong., 2d Sess., 2 U.S. Code Cong. & Admin. News 3099, 3103 (1958).

[200] Venue in a suit challenging the constitutionality of the war would be properly laid in the district where plaintiffs reside. 28 U.S.C. § 1391(e), a venue statute, provides that "[a] civil action in which each defendant is an officer or employee of the United States or any agency thereof acting in his official capacity or under color of legal authority, . . . may, except as otherwise provided by law, be brought in any judicial district in which: . . . (4) the plaintiff resides if no real property is involved in the action." In a case against the war, each defendant could be an officer of the United States acting in his official capacity and under color of law, and no real property would be involved. It is worth noting that the purpose of 28 U.S.C. § 1361, the jurisdiction statute discussed in the text, and § 1391(e), the venue statute, was to permit citizens to sue government officials outside of Washington, D.C. The statutes accomplished this

C. *The Doctrine of Sovereign Immunity*

In a case which raised the constitutionality of the current war, the Government claimed that an action was barred because of the doctrine of sovereign immunity.[201] Such a claim is frivolous. Even if the doctrine of sovereign immunity might otherwise apply, the issue involved here would bring a case squarely under the well-established exceptions to that doctrine. Even the government admits[202] that sovereign immunity does not apply to "(1) action by officers beyond their statutory powers, and (2) even though within the scope of their authority, the powers themselves or the manner in which they are exercised are unconstitutionally void."[203] In the present instance, the executive is acting outside its statutory and constitutional authority. Thus a suit challenging the war's constitutionality falls under the exceptions to the doctrine of sovereign immunity.

The foregoing is a dispositive answer to a possible sovereign immunity argument. However, it is not even necessary to bring the problem under the *exceptions* to the sovereign immunity doctrine, since that doctrine is totally inapplicable in the first place. (1) The government has urged that sovereign immunity applies because a suit against the war might interfere with the executive's ability to administer the governmental apparatus as it sees fit.[204] But it is obvious that Congress contemplated that individuals could sue to prevent officials from administering the government in any manner they might choose. Such intent is implicitly one reason why the Senate Report of 1958 accompanying the revision of the jurisdictional statutes indicated that the federal courts have jurisdiction over most cases involving significant federal questions;[205] it is the reason that Congress provided in section 1361 that actions in the nature of mandamus can be brought against government officers; and it is the reason that the Senate Report on this statute specifically said that the statute permits plaintiffs to bring "actions which are in essence against the United States."[206] (2) Why should the doctrine of sovereign immunity block a suit on the issue

---

purpose by placing jurisdiction and venue, among other places, in the district where plaintiffs reside.

If a court should decide that it does not have jurisdiction under 28 U.S.C. § 1361 and that it also lacks jurisdiction under 28 U.S.C. § 1331 because the amount in controversy is less than $10,000—a decision on §§ 1361 and 1331 which the author would find inconceivable— then the plaintiffs could move to make the United States the defendant. Such a motion should be approved under Federal Rules 15(2), 19(a) and 21. Jurisdiction would then lie under 28 U.S.C. § 1346(a), which says "[t]he district courts shall have original jurisdiction . . . of: (2) Any other civil action or claim [*i.e.,* other than recovery of internal revenue taxes or penalties illegally assessed or paid] against the United States, not exceeding $10,000 in amount, founded . . . upon the Constitution." The jurisdictional requirements of this statute would be met because the case would be a civil action against the United States founded upon the Constitution, and the amount in controversy would not exceed $10,000. Venue would be where plaintiff resides under 28 U.S.C. § 1402(a)(1), which provides that venue lies in the home districts of non corporate plaintiffs who sue the United States under § 1346(a).

[201] Brief for Appellees at 5-13, Luftig v. McNamara, 373 F.2d 664 (D.C. Cir.), *cert. denied,* 88 S. Ct. 282 (1967).

[202] *Id.* at 9.

[203] Dugan v. Rank, 372 U.S. 609, 621-22 (1963).

[204] Brief for Appellees at 6-7, Luftig v. McNamara, 373 F.2d 664 (D.C. Cir.), *cert. denied,* 88 S. Ct. 282 (1967).

[205] S. REP. No. 1830, 85th Cong., 2d Sess., 2 U.S. CODE CONG. & ADMIN. NEWS 3101, 3103 (1958).

[206] S. REP. No. 1992, 87th Cong., 2d Sess., 2 U.S. CODE CONG. & ADMIN. NEWS 2784, 2786 (1962).

at hand when it did not block suit in *Youngstown,* which, like a challenge to the war, was a suit to restrain a cabinet member and the President from usurping the powers of Congress?[207] Why should it block suit here when it did not block suit in *Hammer v. Dagenhart,*[208] which was a suit to prevent a government official from administering a child labor act; when it did not block suit in *Waite v. Macy,*[209] which was a suit to restrain officials from preventing the importation of tea; when it did not block suit in *Hill v. Wallace,*[210] which was a suit to restrain the Secretary of Agriculture from administering sections of the Grain Futures Act; when it did not block suit in *Helvering v. Davis,*[211] which was an attempt to block the collector of Internal Revenue from administering a Social Security Act; when it did not block suit in *Joint Anti-Fascist Refugee Committee v. McGrath,*[212] which was a suit to block the Attorney General from administering an executive order in a particular way; and, in general, when it has not blocked suit in scores of other actions that prevented government officials from administering the government in any way they saw fit? (3) As the Supreme Court has said, the doctrine of sovereign immunity is looked on with "disfavor."[213] In point of fact, it is a judge-made limitation upon jurisdiction which should be eliminated. "Courts of justice are established," the Supreme Court has said, "not only to decide upon the controverted rights of the citizens as against each other, but also upon rights in controversy between them and the government."[214] The latter function of courts is negated by the doctrine of sovereign immunity, however. Under this doctrine, the government, which was established for the protection and welfare of its citizens, can instead bring harm upon them without being subjected to judicial scrutiny. Moreover, when courts invoke this doctrine, they place themselves in the position of saying that, even though it is commonplace for them to overturn unconstitutional decisions made by the 535 federal legislators, they will not overturn unconstitutional decisions made by a single executive official or a small group of such officials. The doctrine of sovereign immunity, then, is a pernicious one which should be abrogated by its creators, the judges.[215]

VII. The Remedy

A particularly apt remedy would be to require the executive to either (1) obtain a congressional declaration of limited or general war, or (2) discontinue fighting in Viet Nam, such discontinuance to be carried out with all deliberate speed. Alternatively, if there are hopes for peace when a court makes its de-

---

[207] See text accompanying notes 37, 38, and 41 *supra.*
[208] 247 U.S. 251 (1918).
[209] 246 U.S. 606 (1918).
[210] 259 U.S. 44 (1922).
[211] 301 U.S. 619 (1937).
[212] 341 U.S. 123 (1951).
[213] Federal Housing Adm'n v. Burr, 309 U.S. 242, 245 (1940).
[214] United States v. Lee, 106 U.S. 196, 220 (1882).
[215] Sovereign immunity is obviously irrelevant under 28 U.S.C. § 1361 which in terms provides for suits against the United States. See note 195 *supra.*

cision, it should merely issue a declaratory judgment that the war is unconstitutional. If, subsequent to the granting of an order that the executive either obtain a declaration of war or discontinue fighting, the executive were in fact to go to Congress for a declaration of war, the Congress would then decide whether to continue fighting. If it wished, it might also decide what objectives should be authorized, what amounts of force should be authorized, and for how long a period the use of force should be authorized. While the Congress is making its decision—and doubtlessly the decision would be made relatively expeditiously—the executive would have the authority to take the military actions necessary to repel attacks upon American forces in Viet Nam.[216] Thus, were the executive to seek a declaration of war subsequent to the judicial order suggested here, the order of the court would achieve the double objective of (1) enabling the proper constitutional authority to make the decision as to whether and to what extent to fight, while (2) permitting the executive to repel attacks during the doubtlessly short period during which Congress is making its decision.

On the other hand, the executive could decide not to seek a declaration of war, but to begin discontinuing the war with all deliberate speed. In this event, the executive could be allowed some latitude as to the best means of disengaging and as to what speed of disengagement is best suited to the safety of the armed forces. The allowance of some latitude provides a good practical solution and is supported by precedent from two other areas which have involved crucial national events, the civil rights cases and the reapportionment cases. In *Brown v. Board of Education,* the school segregation case, the Supreme Court recognized that lower courts should give school boards some latitude in working out the details of plans of desegregation.[217] Also, in *Reynolds v. Sims,* the Court recognized that lower courts should initially give state legislatures an opportunity to work out suitable plans of reapportionment.[218] Thus, were the executive to begin discontinuance of the war subsequent to the granting of the judicial order suggested here, the court's action would accomplish the objective of permitting the political branch to do its duty in a practical and flexible way.

Finally, if peace negotiations were under way or in the offing when a court

---

[216] Whether the President, in taking the actions necessary to repel attacks, could take offensive actions or must limit himself to defensive actions is only a theoretical point. It has little practical significance, first, because Congress will doubtlessly act quickly. Second, some actions which might ordinarily be considered offensive cannot in actuality be restricted to this category. For example, if the executive were to bomb enemy troops traveling down the Ho Chi Minh trail, this action could be considered an offensive one. On the other hand, the action can also be considered defensive because the troops might ultimately attack Americans in South Viet Nam.

Not only does the offensive-defensive action dichotomy have little practical significance in regard to the actions which the President might take in repelling attacks while Congress deliberates, but in today's world it has little meaning in most important contexts. For example, suppose that nation X launches a preemptive war against nation Y. X's action can be considered offensive because X's tanks, planes, etc., crossed the border and struck first, or it can be considered defensive because X merely sought to prevent Y from obtaining favorable circumstances under which to launch an attack upon X at a later time. To take another illustration, the Cuban blockade could be considered to have been an offensive action because the American navy intercepted foreign ships at sea, or it could be considered to have been defensive because America sought only to prevent the landing of missiles which could later have been used against the United States. Examples could be multiplied indefinitely.

[217] 349 U.S. 294, 300-01 (1955). (This is the second *Brown* case.)

[218] 377 U.S. 533, 586-87 (1964).

decision is made, the court would merely issue a declaratory judgment that the war is unconstitutional; and even this judgment could be postponed if necessary in the interests of peace. By issuing a declaratory judgment the court would accomplish the objective of not endangering the hopes for peace in any way, while at the same time establishing an institutional restraint on the power of future executives to conduct large and sustained wars without congressional authorization.

It should be stressed that the issue of the war's constitutionality would not be moot if there are hopes for peace when a court renders its decision in a case challenging the war. Indeed, the issue should be resolved even if the war were to be over when a decision is rendered. The case would not be moot if there are merely hopes for peace because many of the injuries accruing from the executive's actions will continue to be imposed upon people at least until peace is actually achieved and even beyond. For example, deaths and wounds, inflation, taxes, and the cutting off of funds for research and social welfare are all likely to continue at least until the war is over. And, even if the war were to be over tomorrow, the case should be decided in order to place institutional restraints upon future executive action. Many times in the past executives have used force without congressional approval, and one cannot confidently predict that this will not happen again in the future. People, after all, have short memories, as evidenced by the facts that, less than two years after the agonies of Korea were over, the United States almost became embroiled in Indo-China in order to help the French; and, only twelve years after the agonies of Korea, this nation did become massively involved in Viet Nam without a congressional declaration of war. The shortness of memories means that, even if the war should be over when a court decision is made, the case should still be decided so that future executives will not be tempted to follow the unconstitutional path trod by previous ones. Further, if courts do not decide that the present war is unconstitutional, future executives will have not one but two precedents, Korea and Viet Nam, for saying that they can carry on large and sustained wars without proper congressional declarations.

Some might suggest that the executive might not heed a court's decision, but might simply flout judicial authority. This is not a realistic possibility. If it is first assumed that there are no hopes for peace when a decision is made, and that a court will therefore order the executive either to seek a declaration of limited or general war or to discontinue fighting in Viet Nam with all deliberate speed, it is difficult to presume that the executive would ignore this order. An analogous possibility seemed to be suggested by Justice Frankfurter in the reapportionment area, when the Justice, in his dissent in *Baker v. Carr,* apparently indicated that legislatures might ignore judicial orders, which would consequently prove unenforceable.[219] However, the legislatures did not ignore the judicial authority, and neither will the executive. Like the legislators, the

---

[219] 369 U.S. 186, 267-68, 269-70 (1962).

executive is sworn to uphold the Constitution of the United States. As the Supreme Court emphasized in the Little Rock case, *Cooper v. Aaron*:[220]

> In 1803, Chief Justice Marshall, speaking for a unanimous Court, referring to the Constitution as "the fundamental and paramount law of the nation," declared in the notable case of *Marbury v. Madison,* 1 Cranch 137, 177, that "It is emphatically the province and duty of the judicial department to say what the law is." This decision declared the basic principle that the federal judiciary is supreme in the exposition of the law of the Constitution, and that principle has ever since been respected by this Court and the Country as a permanent and indispensable feature of our constitutional system.

It cannot really be assumed that the executive, sworn as it is to uphold the Constitution, would flout the basic principle that the federal judiciary is supreme in the exposition of the law of the Constitution by ignoring the lawful orders of a court. That this cannot be assumed is amply demonstrated by the case of *Youngstown Sheet & Tube Co. v. Sawyer,* in which the executive claimed that the seizure of the steel mills was essential to avert a national catastrophe.[221] Despite this claim, when the Supreme Court ruled on June 2, 1952, that the seizure was unconstitutional, the executive, on the very same day as the Court's ruling, turned the mills back to their owners.[222] Lest it be thought that the executive did so because the labor dispute which engendered the seizure was settled by the date of the Court's decision, the facts are that the dispute was not settled at that date, and, indeed, a renewed stoppage of steel production subsequently occurred because of an industry-wide strike arising out of the dispute.[223]

Moreover, aside from constitutional matters, it is politically unrealistic to assume that the executive will flout the lawful orders of the federal judiciary. Assume that the court's order to either obtain a declaration of war or discontinue fighting were to be delivered to the present administration. If the present President changes his mind about not running for reelection, he would no doubt face severe electoral opposition, both from members of his own party and of the opposition party. In such circumstances it would seem that the President would not wish to give further political ammunition to his opponents by flouting the lawful orders of the judiciary. If, on the other hand, the present President were to remain a non-candidate, it would still not be politically wise for him to ignore the orders of the federal judiciary. Such an action would create further breaches in an already divided nation, breaches which the Presi-

---

[220] 358 U.S. 1, 18 (1958).

[221] Note 148 *supra* and accompanying text.

[222] J. BLACKMAN, PRESIDENTIAL SEIZURE IN LABOR DISPUTES 281 (1967). As a practical matter, of course, if a lower court should decide that the war is unconstitutional, any order it hands down will be stayed pending appeals all the way to the Supreme Court. Thus, any final order requiring the executive to obtain a declaration of war or else cease fighting will, as did the order in *Youngstown,* come from the Supreme Court.

Incidentally, the President, in *Youngstown,* could have invoked proper injunctive remedies after relinquishing possession of the mills. (In fact, however, he simply allowed the dispute to be settled through collective bargaining.) *Id.* at 73. Similarly, subsequent to a successful challenge to the war, the President would have a lawful procedure which he could use if necessary; he could obtain a declaration of war.

[223] J. BLACKMAN, *supra* note 222, at 62, 151, 314 n.g.

dent has sought to heal; it would increase the criticism directed at the executive; it might harm the President's party in the November elections; and it would likely cause the President to receive historical asperity as a man who deliberately ignored judicial orders.

If the court's order were to be delivered to a new President, it would not be politically wise for him to ignore a judicial order either. If a future President should decide to resume large and sustained warfare, he would likely face many of the same problems of criticism and divisiveness that have been faced by the present executive. Thus, no more than the present executive could a future one afford to ignore judicial orders. From the political standpoint, it is obvious that a future executive who wishes to resume large-scale warfare would be far better off if he first went to Congress to make sure of the support of that branch—especially if he had run as a "dovish" candidate and later tried to reverse his position; and going to Congress is exactly what the court would be ordering.

The above constitutional and political discussion has been predicated on the idea that the court would order the defendants to either obtain a declaration of war or cease fighting. If there were hopes for peace when the court delivers its decision, it would merely issue a declaratory judgment that the war is unconstitutional. There is no danger here either that the executive would flout lawful judicial orders. Since a declaratory judgment orders nothing, there is no order for the executive to flout; and, if the hopes for peace were to ripen and bear fruit, there never would be any order to flout. Suppose, however, that instead of flowering, the peace negotiations were to drag on indefinitely or were to break off subsequent to the declaratory judgment and that the war were then to resume in unabated fury without a congressional declaration of limited or general war. In this event, it is likely that one of the plaintiffs or a member of the class for whom the declaratory judgment was issued might properly bring a suit (1) asserting that the previous judgment established the executive's lack of constitutional power to carry on a long and sustained war without a congressional declaration of war, and (2) requesting that the court order the executive either to obtain a congressional declaration of war or to discontinue fighting, such discontinuance to be carried out with all deliberate speed. In other words, if hopes for peace were to be dashed and the war were to resume in unabated fury without a suitable congressional declaration of war subsequent to the declaratory judgment, it is likely that suit would be properly brought asking for the same relief that the court would have given if, at the conclusion of the original case, there had been no hopes for peace. In a case subsequent to the original case, it is again unlikely that the executive would ignore lawful judicial orders to obtain a declaration of war or else discontinue fighting. Exactly the same reasons which have been set forth above in regard to why the executive will not ignore lawful judicial orders in the original case would similarly control in a second action subsequent to and based upon a declaratory judgment.

VIII. Conclusion

The framers of the Constitution deliberately lodged the power to declare war in the Congress rather than the executive. The framers did so because of their fear of executive power and because war inevitably causes economic burdens and great personal sufferings. The framers' reasons for giving the Congress the power to decide if America is to engage in war are still valid today. Indeed, perhaps they are more valid than ever in a world where even small wars can conceivably lead to holocausts. Thus, the principle that only Congress has the power to declare war should be maintained in its full vitality.

In fighting the Vietnamese war without a congressional declaration of limited or general war, the executive has in effect usurped Congress' power to decide if America is to fight a war. The Vietnamese war thus raises the question of whether Congress' power to declare war does in fact retain vitality. This is a question which has arisen in the past and which, in a revolutionary world, could arise again many times in the future. It is therefore a highly important question; it is, indeed, a critical question. It is a question which courts should decide in the exercise of their traditional function of assessing where the divisions of power lie in the federal government.

IX. Addendum

A. *Introduction*

On June 10, 1968, subsequent to the printing of the page proofs of this article, the Supreme Court handed down its decision in *Flast v. Cohen.*[224] (This case was entitled *Flast v. Gardner* until Wilbur Cohen became Secretary of HEW.) In this case, the Court overturned the *Frothingham* rule[225] under which a plaintiff, to have standing, must suffer a direct injury which is neither indefinite nor shared in common with people generally. In a prior section of this article, the author has attempted to show that the Vietnamese war is causing citizens to suffer direct and definite tax and non-tax injuries, some of which are in no way shared in common with people generally and others of which are not shared to the same degree by people generally.[226] In other words, the author has attempted to show that, particularly if a case were brought as a class action, citizens would have standing to challenge the war under the *Frothingham* doctrine. After *Flast*, however, it is no longer necessary for citizens to show direct injuries which are neither indefinite nor shared by people generally in order to have standing. As indicated above, *Flast* has laid down new rules of standing to replace the *Frothingham* rule. Therefore, this addendum shall, first, briefly summarize the principles of the *Flast* case, and

---

[224] Citations to the *Flast* case will be in two forms. The first form will be references to the page numbers of the U.S. Supreme Court Bulletin printed by Commerce Clearing House; and, illustratively, will read as follows: B2592. The second form will be references to the page numbers of the advance sheets printed by the Supreme Court; *e.g.* p. 5.

[225] 262 U.S. 447, 488 (1923).

[226] See pp. 485-88, 489-90 *supra*.

second, show how the principles of the *Flast* case would affect the standing of citizens who challenge the constitutionality of the war.

B. *The Principles Set Forth In Flast*

Flast v. Cohen gives a general explanation of the reason which lies behind the doctrine of standing. The reason is that standing implements the require-ment that disputes must be presented in an adversary context and in a form capable of resolution through the judicial process.[227] In other words, standing is a way of insuring that cases will present truly adversary disputes rather than friendly or collusive suits;[228] that cases will present questions which are framed with specificity[229] rather than ill-defined questions,[230] or abstract questions,[231] or hypothetical questions[232] or questions which are merely generalized griev-ances about the conduct of government or the allocation of powers in the fed-eral system;[233] and that cases will be argued with the necessary vigor.[234]

In addition to giving an explanation of the reason which underlies the doc-trine of standing, *Flast*, quoting *Baker v. Carr*, set forth a verbal rule for deter-mining when, in general, a party has standing. In general, a party has stand-ing if he has " 'alleged such a personal stake in the outcome of the controversy as to assure that concrete adverseness upon which the Court so largely depends for illumination of difficult constitutional questions.' "[235] To paraphrase this verbal rule, in general a party has standing if he has a personal stake which in-sures that he is truly adverse to his opponent.

Finally, *Flast* not only lays down the "personal stake" rule for determining when, in general, a party has standing, but it also states when, in particular, a taxpayer *qua* taxpayer will be deemed to meet the "personal stake" rule. A taxpayer *qua* taxpayer will be deemed to have a sufficient personal stake in the controversy[236] when he meets two requirements.[237] First, he must be challeng-ing the exercise "of Congressional power under the taxing and spending clause of Article I, Section 8 of the Constitution. It will not be sufficient to allege an incidental expenditure of tax funds in the administration of an essentially regulatory statute."[238] Second, the taxpayer "must show that the challenged enactment exceeds specific constitutional limitations imposed upon the exer-cise of the congressional taxing and spending power and not simply that the enactment is generally beyond the powers delegated to Congress by Article I, Section 8."[239]

---

[227] B2599; *cf.* B2592-93; p. 17; *cf.* pp. 10-11.
[228] B2598; B2604; p. 16; p. 22.
[229] B2604; p. 22.
[230] B2598; p. 16.
[231] *Id.*
[232] *Id.*
[233] B2604; p. 22.
[234] *Id.*
[235] B2598; p. 16. The personal stake rule is also set forth at B2599; p. 17.
[236] B2599; B2600; B2601; B2604; pp. 17, 18, 19, 22.
[237] B2600-01; B2604; pp. 18-19; p. 22.
[238] B2600-01; pp. 18-19.
[239] B2601; p. 19.

C. *The Application of Flast to a Case Challenging the War*

Under the doctrines of *Flast v. Cohen,* citizens have standing to challenge the constitutionality of the war in Viet Nam. They have standing both under the rule for determining when, in general, a party has standing and under the rules for determining when, in particular, a taxpayer *qua* taxpayer has standing. That citizens have standing under the general rule—the rule that a party must have a sufficient personal stake in the controversy as to assure the concrete adverseness which sharpens the presentation of issues—can be made clear in several ways.

First, it is a familiar idea in the law that, when a party satisfies the reasons which have led to a particular rule, the party ought to be held to satisfy the rule as well. In a case challenging the war, citizens could satisfy the reason which underlies the general "personal stake" rule, and therefore they should be held to satisfy the rule as well. As said above, the reason for the "personal stake" rule is that disputes should be presented in an adversary context and in a form capable of judicial resolution:[240] disputes need be adversary[241] rather than friendly[242] or collusive;[243] questions need be framed with specificity[244] and should not be abstract[245] or hypothetical;[246] questions need present more than mere generalized grievances;[247] and cases should be pressed with vigor.[248] In the case under discussion, the parties would be completely adverse. There must not be the slightest possibility that they are collusive or friendly. Citizens could assert in the strongest possible way that the executive's actions in carrying on the war are grossly unconstitutional. The executive, on the other hand, has often stated its belief that the current war is constitutional. The adverseness of the parties could also be shown by the fact that there is a severe clash of interests, a clash which arises because the executive's actions are unconstitutionally causing citizens and those whom they might represent in a class action to suffer extensive financial and physical injuries.[249] Furthermore, the question in the case would be in a form which is proper for judicial resolution. The question would be whether, despite the fact that the Constitution explicitly gives the Congress the power to declare war, the executive has the constitutional authority to carry on the current long-sustained and large-scale war in Viet Nam without a congressional declaration of limited or general war. This is a specific and well-defined constitutional question, not a generalized grievance. It is surely a concrete question, not a hypothetical or abstract question. Finally, citizens could and undoubtedly would press a case with the necessary vigor.

---

[240] B2599; *cf.* B2592-93; p. 17; *cf.* pp. 10-11.
[241] B2598; B2599; B2604; p. 16; p. 17; p. 22.
[242] B2598; p. 16.
[243] *Id.*
[244] B2604; p. 22.
[245] B2598; p. 16.
[246] *Id.*
[247] B2604; p. 22.
[248] *Id.*
[249] See pp. 486-87, 489-90 *supra.*

A second reason why citizens could satisfy the general "personal stake" rule is that they and those whom they might represent have a deep interest in maintaining the integrity of Article I, Section 8, Clause 11, the fundamental constitutional provision which states that the *Congress* shall have the power to declare war. As pointed out above,[250] this provision was placed in the Constitution because of the framers' fears of executive power and because the framers did not want the executive, in its own discretion, to be able to bring down upon Americans the taxes and burdens and personal sufferings which accompany war. And the framers' reasons for giving Congress the power to declare war are still valid today; indeed, perhaps they are more valid than ever, since today even small wars carry the risk of an ultimate holocaust. Thus, citizens and those whom they might represent have a great personal stake in the upholding of the fundamental constitutional provision which is designed to insure that the most critical decision a nation can make—whether to go to war—remains in the hands of the entire Congress and is not arrogated unto themselves by a small group of men in the executive.

A third reason why citizens have standing under the general "personal stake" rule is that the executive, by unconstitutionally carrying on the current large-scale and long-sustained war in Viet Nam, has illegally caused dire injuries to be visited upon citizens and those whom they would represent. As pointed out above,[251] the unconstitutional war has materially contributed to a severe inflation which has caused great financial injury to citizens and which threatens them with future financial injury. It has materially contributed to a balance of payments problem which has led to a gold crisis, which in turn could lead to severe economic dislocations or even a devaluation of the dollar. Severe economic dislocations or devaluation would work great hardship on citizens. The war has led to serious curtailments in the funds spent for research and social welfare projects, thus causing harm to many citizens. Over twenty-five thousand Americans have died, and over one hundred thousand have been wounded in the current unconstitutional war. The existence of these injuries demonstrates the depth of the personal stake of citizens in the controversy involved here. Additionally, the depth of the personal stake involved is shown by the fact that the war has cost scores of billions of dollars in tax money, has led to the continuation of excise taxes and has led to a significant income tax surcharge. Under *Flast* these tax ramifications do not of themselves establish that citizens have standing to sue under the rules which govern when, in particular, a taxpayer has standing *qua* taxpayer; however, they do provide yet another illustration of why citizens and those whom they would represent have such a deep personal stake in the question of the war's constitutionality that the citizens have standing under the general "personal stake" rule, the rule which governs when, in general, a party has standing.[252]

---

[250] See pp. 451-53 *supra.*

[251] See pp. 486-87 *supra.*

[252] At page 489 *supra*, it has been pointed out that, in Baker v. Carr, 369 U.S. 186, 207-08 (1962), plaintiffs living in underapportioned counties had had a sufficient personal stake in the controversy because

As indicated before, the Court in *Flast* said that a taxpayer *qua* taxpayer will be deemed to have the requisite personal stake when he meets two requirements: he must challenge an exercise of congressional power under the taxing and spending clause, and he must invoke a specific constitutional limitation upon the taxing and spending power.[253] As to the first of these requirements, it is obviously true that this article has been cast in the form of an attack upon the executive's usurpation of Congress' power to declare war rather than in the form of an attack upon Congress' power to tax and spend in order to support that unconstitutional usurpation. However, since these two ways of casting the case are in reality only the two sides of the same coin, essentially the same arguments apply regardless of which way the case is cast. Therefore, regardless of the form in which he casts his case, a citizen should be held to have met the requirement that he must attack an exercise of Congress' power to tax and spend. The truth of these observations can be exemplified as follows. It has been shown that Congress was given the power to declare war in order to guard against excessive executive power and in order to prevent the executive, in its own discretion, from being able to bring down upon citizens the taxes, economic sufferings, and personal injuries which inevitably accompany war.[254] Clearly, then, the Congress cannot use its Article I, Section 8 power to tax and spend for the national defense in a way which enables the executive to usurp the power to declare war and to thereby bring down upon citizens, in its sole discretion, the taxes, economic injuries, and personal sufferings which accompany war.[255] Since Congress cannot use its power to tax and spend in a way which enables the executive to usurp the power to declare war, the only question really involved here is whether the executive has in fact usurped the power to declare war; and regardless of whether citizens attack the executive's actions in carrying on the war directly or attack them indirectly by alleging that Congress is illegally using its power to tax and spend in a way which supports an unconstitutional war, the citizens are in reality attacking the same problem.

As to the second requirement which must be met by a taxpayer *qua* taxpayer, the Congress, by providing funds to support the executive's unconstitutional actions in Viet Nam, has violated a specific limitation upon its power to tax and spend, and not simply gone beyond its general powers under Article I, Section 8. As said before, one of the specific reasons why *Congress* was given the power to declare war in Article I, Section 8, Clause 11 is that war is inevitably accompanied by burdensome taxes, and the framers therefore did not

---

they alleged that malapportionment impaired their right to vote. It was further pointed out that the right to vote is also seriously impaired if, without any constitutional authority, the executive can fight a large and sustained war which visits dire consequences upon citizens. The latter impairment of the right to vote provides yet another illustration of why citizens have a deep personal stake in the instant controversy.

[253] B2600-01; B2604; pp. 18-19; p. 22.

[254] See pp. 451-52 *supra*.

[255] This is particularly true because, as discussed at page 466 *supra*, Greene v. McElroy, 360 U.S. 474 (1959), makes plain that the congressional appropriation of money will not serve to ratify executive actions of dubious constitutionality, let alone the kinds of clearly unconstitutional executive actions that are at issue in the present situation.

want the executive to have the power to declare war.[256] In view of the framers' purpose of forestalling taxes stemming from wars declared by the executive, Article I, Section 8, Clause 11 is clearly a specific limitation on Congress' power to tax and spend in support of the current war, which has in effect been declared by the executive. In this respect, Article I, Section 8, Clause 11 is analogous to the Establishment Clause, which was discussed in *Flast* and which was held to be a specific limitation on Congress' power to tax and spend to aid one religion or all religions.[257]

In concluding this section on why citizens have standing under the doctrines laid down in *Flast,* it should again be pointed out, as it has been pointed out above[258] and as Justice Douglas pointed out in his concurring opinion in *Flast,*[259] that it is a function of the federal judiciary to protect citizens against the unconstitutional actions of government. What is involved in the present situation is a massive breach of the Constitution by the executive branch of the government, a breach which has unlawfully visited the most dire consequences upon large numbers of Americans.[260] With the possible exception of the actions of the Confederate States of America in leaving the Union and the actions of certain states in denying Constitutional rights to Negroes for nearly one hundred years, this breach is probably the most serious constitutional violation ever undertaken by any organized government in the United States; and it is probably the most serious breach ever undertaken by the federal government. In circumstances such as these, when the excutive is engaged in a massive constitutional violation which has visited dire consequences upon so many citizens, it must be eminently clear that citizens have a vital "personal stake" in having the Constitution upheld, and that citizens should therefore have standing to invoke the Constitution. Similarly, in the circumstances outlined above, it must also be eminently clear that the federal judiciary ought to protect citizens against the executive's violation of the Constitution. For the need to obey the law is not applicable to citizens alone, but to the government as well. The Constitution is a law not just for the ruled, but also for the rulers.

---

[256] In regard to this point, see pp. 451-52 *supra.*

[257] B2601-B2603; pp. 19-21.

It should be carefully noted that not only does *Flast* overturn the rules of *Frothingham v. Mellon* upon which the government so heavily relies, but it also gives support to two of the standing arguments which were set forth in a prior section of this article, and which were not directly related to the *Frothingham* case. First, at pages 489-90 *supra,* it was pointed out that in certain situations individuals have standing to raise the rights of third parties, and it was argued that the current war presents such a situation. In footnote 20 of the *Flast* opinion, the Court reaffirmed that upon occasion parties have standing to raise the rights of third parties. B2597 n.20; p. 15, n.20. Second, at footnote 189 *supra* are set forth several arguments showing that citizens would have standing to challenge the unconstitutionality of the war even if such a challenge might also be raised by others, such as soldiers who refuse to go to Viet Nam or citizens who refuse induction. At footnote 17 of *Flast,* the Court gave support to such arguments by asserting that, in "circumstances under which a taxpayer will be a proper and appropriate party to seek judicial review of federal statutes, the taxpayer's access to federal courts should not be barred because there might be at large in society a hypothetical plaintiff who might possibly bring such a suit [*e.g.* a suit challenging unconstitutional appropriations]." B2596-97 n.17; pp. 14-15 n.17.

[258] See p. 498 *supra* (quoting United States v. Lee, 106 U.S. 196 (1882)).

[259] B2609-B2612; pp. 4-7.

[260] See pp. 452, 485-87, 489-90 *supra.*

The Vietnam War: The President
versus the Constitution

FRANCIS D. WORMUTH

I. The Text of the Constitution

DEFYING the critics of his Vietnamese adventure in a speech in Omaha on June 30, 1966, President Lyndon B. Johnson said: "The American people have chosen only one man to decide." Walter Lippmann very properly protested that this was "a claim to arbitrary power" which offends "the prevailing principle in the whole constitutional system."[1]

Nevertheless, the State Department has officially asserted that the President has the power to initiate war on his sole authority. In a memorandum submitted to the Senate Committee on Foreign Relations on March 8, 1966, it argued that President Johnson was under no obligation to consult Congress before attacking North Vietnam on February 7, 1965; but as an act of supererogation he had obtained the permission of Congress in the Tonkin Gulf Resolution of August 10, 1964.[2]

This is a matter of the greatest moment. Does the Constitution authorize a single man to commit the whole nation to the hazards and the hecatombs of modern war? Or, if the Constitution assigns this power to the Congress, has Congress the right to abdicate decision, transferring its authority and its responsibility to a single man? Behind the legal question lies a political question—the question of the nature

---

[1] *Newsweek*, July 18, 1966, p. 17. At a press conference on August 18, 1967, President Johnson said that he had asked for the Tonkin Gulf Resolution because it was "thought desirable": "We stated then, and we repeat now, we did not think the resolution was necessary to do what we did and what we are doing. . . . We think we are well within the grounds of our constitutional responsibility." *U.S. Commitments to Foreign Powers*, Hearings before Senate Committee on Foreign Relations, 90th Cong., 1st Sess. (1967), p. 126. Before the Senate Committee on Foreign Relations, in response to a question by the chairman, Senator Fulbright—"Would the President, if there were no resolution, be with or without constitutional authority to send U.S. soldiers to South Vietnam in the numbers they are there today?"—Under Secretary of State Katzenbach said: "It would be my view, . . . Mr. Chairman, that he does have that authority." *Ibid.*, p. 141.

[2] The text is to be found in *Congressional Record*, Vol. 112, No. 43 (March 11, 1966), pp. 5274-5279, and in *Vietnam and International Law* by the Consultative Council of the Lawyers Committee on American Policy towards Vietnam (Flanders, N.J.: O'Hare Books, 1967), pp. 113-130. It will be cited as *Memorandum* from the latter source.

of the political order established by the framers of the Constitution, and the subsequent evolution of that political order.

"An elective despotism was not what we fought for," said Thomas Jefferson.[3] In arguing that the President should not have the power to make treaties on his sole authority, Alexander Hamilton used words of broader application: "The history of human conduct does not warrant that exalted opinion of human virtue which would make it wise in a nation to commit interests of so delicate and momentous a kind, as those which concern its intercourse with the rest of the world, to the sole disposal of a magistrate created and circumstanced as would be a President of the United States."[4]

Without design, but as a natural consequence of their experience with institutions and their stock of political ideas, the members of the Constitutional Convention produced a governmental structure which paralleled the British. Best known accounts of the British structure were those of Locke and Montesquieu.

In his *Two Treatises of Government*, John Locke had said that there were three powers of government, the legislative, the executive, and the federative. Federative power was the power over foreign relations —"the power of war and peace, leagues and alliances, and all the transactions with all persons and communities without the commonwealth."[5] At English law these topics were royal prerogatives, and Locke, following English practice on this question, attributed both the executive power and the federative power to the King.

The Baron de Montesquieu, in his account of the English constitution in *The Spirit of the Laws*,[6] recognized three powers of government: "the legislative; the executive in respect to things dependent on the law of nations; and the executive in regard to matters that depend on the civil law." The third he then subdivided into executive power proper and the power of judging. He too followed English constitutional theory by assigning the executive power in foreign affairs as well as that in domestic matters to the King.

The framers of the United States Constitution were persuaded of the need for unity and energy in the execution of the laws, and after some debate agreed to entrust this function to a President. But they departed sharply from the British model by denying to the President almost all features of the federative power. He might make treaties only with

3 *Notes on Virginia* (1784), Query 13, par. 4.   4 *Federalist*, No. 75.
5 *Second Treatise* (1690), ch. 12-13, § 145.
6 Nugent trans. (1748), Book XI, ch. 6.

the consent of two-thirds of the Senate; he might appoint ambassadors with the consent of the Senate. It was for Congress to regulate commerce with foreign nations; to raise and support armies (but, in order to prevent the President from establishing a military dictatorship, "no appropriation of money to that use shall be for a longer term than two years"); to provide and maintain a navy; to make rules for the government and regulation of the land and naval forces; to provide for calling the militia of the states into the service of the United States; to provide for organizing, arming, and disciplining the militia; and to exercise exclusive legislative authority over "forts, magazines, arsenals, dry docks, and other needful buildings."

Only one of the powers in foreign affairs mentioned in the Constitution was vested by the framers in the President alone. The President was to be "commander-in-chief of the army and navy of the United States, and of the militia of the several states when called into the actual service of the United States." Does this give him the power to initiate war?

The draft proposals introduced in the Constitutional Convention on August 6, 1787 contained the provision that the legislature of the United States should have the power "to make war." In the debate on August 17,[7] Charles Pinckney objected that the two houses could not act with expedition and proposed that the power be given to the Senate. Pierce Butler suggested that the power be given to the President; this drew from Elbridge Gerry the rejoinder that he "never expected to hear in a republic a motion to empower the executive alone to declare war." James Madison and Gerry moved "to insert '*declare*,' striking out '*make*' war; leaving to the Executive the power to repel sudden attacks." Roger Sherman agreed that the executive "should be able to repel and not to commence war"; he thought " 'make' better than 'declare' the latter narrowing the power too much." George Mason "was against giving the power of war to the Executive, because not safely to be trusted with it; or to the Senate, because not so constructed as to be entitled to it. He was for clogging, rather than facilitating war; but for facilitating peace. He preferred '*declare*' to 'make.' " The change of language was adopted by a vote of eight states to one. On September 5 the Convention unanimously agreed to add to the clause the words "grant letters of marque and reprisal."[8] The assignment to

---

[7] Charles C. Tansill, ed., *Documents Illustrative of the Union of the American States* (Washington: Government Printing Office, 1927), pp. 561-2.

[8] *Ibid.*, p. 665.

Congress of the power to "make rules concerning captures on land and water," which rounds out the war clause, had been agreed to unanimously on August 17.[9]

The framers merely replaced the verb "make" in the list of powers of Congress in Article I of the Constitution with the verb "declare." They did not insert in the list of powers of the President in Article II: "He shall have the power to make war." Yet the State Department has attempted thus to revise the Constitution. In its memorandum of March 8, 1966, it said:

At the Federal Constitutional Convention in 1787, it was originally proposed that Congress have the power "to make war." There were objections that legislative proceedings were too slow for this power to be vested in Congress; it was suggested that the Senate might be a better repository. Madison and Gerry then moved to substitute "to declare war" for "to make war," "leaving to the Executive the power to repel sudden attacks." It was objected that this might make it too easy for the Executive to involve the nation in war,* but the motion carried with but one dissenting vote.

In 1787 the world was a far larger place, and the framers probably had in mind attacks upon the United States. In the 20th century, the world has grown much smaller. An attack on a country far from our shores can impinge directly on the nation's security. In the SEATO treaty, for example, it is formally declared that an armed attack against Vietnam would endanger the peace and safety of the United States.

Since the Constitution was adopted there have been at least 125 instances in which the President has ordered the armed forces to take action or maintain positions abroad without obtaining prior Congressional authorization, starting with the "undeclared war" with France (1798–1800). . . .

The Constitution leaves to the President the judgment to determine whether the circumstances of a particular armed attack are so urgent and the potential consequences so threatening to the security of the United States that he should act without formally consulting the Congress.[10]

It would be difficult to find a bolder or more childish attempt at deception. It is not probable but certain that the attack Madison and Gerry had in mind was an attack upon the United States. When they

---

[9] *Ibid.*, p. 558.

* There was no such objection and no such discussion.—F.D.W.

[10] *Memorandum*, pp. 123-4.

attributed to the President a power to repel a sudden attack upon the United States, they did not impute to him a discretionary right to choose between war and peace, or the right to make a judgment concerning the security of the United States. Their motion was not intended to recognize any power in the President to institute a state of war; it recognized that foreign countries are able to institute a state of war. When a foreign country attacks the United States, war exists, and the President as commander-in-chief may and must make—that is, wage—the war. Alexander Hamilton thus explained the clause:

"The Congress shall have the power to declare war"; the plain meaning of which is, that it is the peculiar and exclusive duty of Congress, *when the nation is at peace*, to change that state into a state of war; whether from calculations of policy, or from provocations or injuries received; in other words, it belongs to Congress only *to go to war*. But when a foreign nation declares or openly and avowedly makes war upon the United States, they are then by the very fact *already at war*, and any declaration on the part of Congress is nugatory; it is at least unnecessary.[11]

Apparently Madison and Gerry, when they used the expression "sudden attack," contemplated that the President would refer the problem to Congress at an early date. This is in keeping with the division of functions between the President and Congress; of the two, Congress is the policy-making organ. On the other hand, in war the enemy may be the effective policy-making organ: he can introduce a state of war, regardless of what the President or Congress desires. It is then for the President to wage the war. As we shall see, the scope of his powers and the role of Congress in the case of sudden attack were an issue between Jefferson and Hamilton in 1801[12] and again in the *Prize Cases* in 1863.[13]

The Constitution recognizes that the power to initiate war is lodged in two places: in Congress, and in a foreign enemy. It recognizes no such power in the President. The power of decision must be given to some single authority. There may arise circumstances under which the commander of a Polaris submarine believes that the peace and safety of the United States require him to launch atomic missiles at the Soviet Union without pausing to consult his commander-in-chief or the

[11] No. 1 of "Lucius Crassus" (Dec. 17, 1801), in Richard B. Morris, ed., *Alexander and the Founding of the Nation* (New York: Dial Press, 1957), p. 526.
[12] Below, Section 2.   [13] Below, Section 2.

Congress. Whether he is right or wrong—if these words have any meaning in such a setting—he is not legally authorized to take such a decision. There may arise circumstances in which the commander-in-chief judges that the peace and safety of the United States require him to initiate hostilities without consulting Congress. These need not be limited to attacks by one foreign state upon another foreign state; indeed, this is one of the less probable occasions. But our legal order does not commit the question of the measures appropriate to protect the peace and safety of the United States to the judgment of the commander-in-chief any more than it commits it to the judgment of the commander of a Polaris submarine; it commits it to Congress. Until Congress takes action the United States cannot legally initiate hostilities.

Of course this may mean a missed opportunity, just as denying the power to make war to a submarine commander, or to a seaman on the submarine, may mean a missed opportunity. Those who desire a government which affords such opportunities to a single man are free to seek an amendment to the Constitution which transfers the war power to the President. But if in 1787 it was the wiser course to entrust the decision as to war and peace to a broadly representative body rather than to the judgment of a single man, the greater hazards of the modern world seem to make it all the more important to retain this check on an impetuous executive.

The State Department's argument about a sudden attack is offered as a justification for President Johnson's action in making an undeclared war in Vietnam. It appears, then, according to the State Department, that on an altogether unspecified date North Vietnam made a sudden attack upon South Vietnam which directly imperiled the security of the United States, and that this unidentified attack occurred in unnamed circumstances of such urgency that the President had no opportunity to ask Congress to declare war. This does not agree with President Johnson's own version of the facts. In his annual message to Congress in 1966 he said that the "sudden attack" of North Vietnam upon South Vietnam to which he responded in 1965 had begun in 1959: "Then little more than six years ago North Vietnam decided upon conquest, and from that day to this soldiers and supplies have moved from north to south in a swelling stream that is swallowing up the remnants of revolution in aggression."[14] To be sure, he asserted that the tempo of the sudden attack had increased in 1965. "Swiftly

---

[14] Fred L. Israel, ed., *The State of the Union Messages of the Presidents, 1790-1966* (New York: Chelsea House, Robert Hector, 1966), Vol. 3, p. 3178.

increasing numbers of armed men from the North crossed the borders to join forces that were already in the South. Attack and terror increased, spurred and encouraged by the belief that the United States lacked the will to continue and that their victory was near."[15] But Johnson cited no circumstance of extreme urgency that made it impossible for him to consult Congress before he attacked North Vietnam on February 7, 1965. His war upon North Vietnam was not provoked by a military emergency threatening the security of the United States which could not wait for Congressional action. Even by the standard of the State Department's generous definition of the powers of the President, Johnson usurped the war power of Congress.

But the State Department does not rest solely on its novel interpretation of the Constitution. It ekes this argument out with four other arguments, equally unsubstantial. It asserts that historic practice supplies 125 precedents for the President's action; that the Southeast Asia Collective Defense Treaty authorizes it; that the Tonkin Gulf Resolution authorizes it; and that Congress has ratified it by passing appropriation acts.[16] First we will review the precedents on hostile military action and the relevant judicial and legislative decisions; then we will examine the legal consequences of the Treaty and the Resolution and the law on ratification by appropriation.

II. Wars Authorized or Ratified

The original understanding and subsequent views as to the significance of the constitutional assignment of the power to make war to Congress are best shown by a review of the cases in which Congress has authorized or ratified military action by the President, and the court decisions associated therewith; of the cases in which the President has referred the question of using force in external affairs to the Congress and Congress has refused to act; of the cases in which the executive has refused to employ armed force without Congressional authorization; and of the cases in which Presidents have used the armed forces abroad without Congressional authorization. The first three classes of cases will supply a standard to judge the fourth.

Even before the adoption of the Constitution, American law recognized that it was possible to wage war at different levels. In 1782 the Federal Court of Appeals, the prize court established under the Articles of Confederation, observed: "The writers upon the law of nations, speaking of the different kinds of war, distinguish them into perfect

[15] Ibid., p. 3179.   [16] Memorandum, pp. 124-7.

and imperfect: A perfect war is that which destroys the national peace and tranquillity, and lays the foundation of every possible act of hostility. The imperfect war is that which does not entirely destroy the public tranquillity, but interrupts it only in some particulars, as in the case of reprisals."[1]

The framers of the Constitution accepted this conception and assigned the power to initiate both perfect and imperfect war to Congress, which was "To declare war, grant letters of marque and reprisal, and make rules concerning captures on land and water."

Our first war was a naval war with France, 1798-1801. The State Department memorandum of 1966, in its attempt to supply precedents for executive initiation of war, calls this an "undeclared war" undertaken "without obtaining prior Congressional authorization."[2] This is altogether false. The fact is that President Adams took absolutely no independent action. Congress passed a series of acts which amounted, so the Supreme Court said, to a declaration of imperfect war; and Adams complied with these statutes.

As a result of French interference with American shipping, Congress suspended commercial intercourse with France,[3] denounced the treaties with France,[4] established a Department of the Navy[5] and a Marine Corps,[6] augmented the navy,[7] and provided for raising an army in case of need.[8]

The Congress enacted a number of statutes that provided for belligerency. An act of May 28, 1798 recited that French vessels had recently captured vessels and property of the United States citizens on and near the coast, and authorized the President to instruct the commanders of United States naval vessels to seize as a prize "any such armed vessel which shall have committed or which shall be found

[1] Miller v. The Ship Resolution, 2 Dall. 19.

[2] *Memorandum*, in *Vietnam and International Law* by the Consultative Council of the Lawyers Committee on American Policy towards Vietnam (Flanders, N.J.: O'Hare Books, 1967), p. 124.

[3] 1 Stat. 565 (June 13, 1798); 1 Stat. 613 (Feb. 9, 1799).

[4] 1 Stat. 578 (July 7, 1798).

[5] 1 Stat. 553 (Apr. 27, 1798); 1 Stat. 709 (Mar. 2, 1799).

[6] 1 Stat. 594 (July 11, 1798); 1 Stat. 729 (Mar. 2, 1799).

[7] 1 Stat. 547 (Mar. 27, 1798); 1 Stat. 552 (Apr. 27, 1798); 1 Stat. 595 (July 11, 1798); 1 Stat. 556 (May 4, 1798); 1 Stat. 569 (June 22, 1798); 1 Stat. 576 (July 6, 1798); 1 Stat. 556 (May 4, 1798); 1 Stat. 621 (Feb. 25, 1799).

[8] 1 Stat. 558 (May 28, 1798); 1 Stat. 569 (June 22, 1798); 1 Stat. 604 (July 16, 1798); 1 Stat. 725 (Mar. 2, 1799). See also 1 Stat. 549 (Apr. 7, 1798); 1 Stat. 552 (Apr. 27, 1798); 1 Stat. 554 (May 3, 1798); 1 Stat. 555 (May 4, 1798); 1 Stat. 604 (July 16, 1798).

hovering on the coasts of the United States, for the purpose of committing depredations on the vessels belonging to citizens thereof," and also to recapture American vessels taken by the French.[9] An act of June 25, 1798 authorized any American-owned merchant vessel to resist search, restraint, or seizure by a French vessel, to capture any French ship making such an attempt as a prize, and to retake any American-owned vessel captured by the French.[10] On June 28, 1798, Congress passed further prize legislation for "public armed vessels."[11] On July 9, 1798, Congress enacted that the President might instruct public armed vessels to make prizes of armed French vessels on the high seas, and that he might grant commissions to owners of private armed ships to capture armed French vessels and to recapture American vessels.[12] An act of March 3, 1799 provided that if the President should find that American seamen impressed on the ships of the enemies of France and captured by the French were maltreated, he must cause "the most rigorous retaliation" to be inflicted on French prisoners.[13] The naval war founded on these acts was ended by treaty in 1801.

This episode raised the questions whether Congress might declare an "imperfect" war, or only "perfect" war, and whether the determination of the scope of imperfect war lay with Congress.

The first case was *Bas v. Tingey*,[14] decided in 1800. The commander of the *Ganges*, a vessel of the United States Navy, filed a libel for salvage against the *Eliza*, which he had rescued from the French. The claim was founded on an act of 1799. The owners of the *Eliza* defended on the ground that the United States was not at war, France was not an enemy, and the act was inapplicable.

The Supreme Court unanimously held for the libellant. Justice Washington wrote the most extended opinion:

> It may, I believe, be safely laid down, that every contention by force between two nations, in external matters, under the authority of their respective governments, is not only war, but public war. If it be declared in form, it is called solemn, and is of the perfect kind; because one whole nation is at war with another whole nation; and all the members of the nation declaring war, are authorized to commit hostilities against all the members of the other, in every place, and under every circumstance. In such a war all the members act

9 1 Stat. 561.
10 1 Stat. 572, extended 2 Stat. 39 (Apr. 22, 1800).
11 1 Stat. 574.   12 1 Stat. 578.
13 1 Stat. 743.   14 4 Dall. 37.

under a general authority, and all the rights and consequences of war attach to their condition.

But hostilities may subsist between two nations, more confined in its nature and extent; being limited as to places, persons, and things; and this is more properly termed imperfect war; because not solemn, and because those who are authorized to commit hostilities, act under special authority, and can go [no] further than to the extent of their commission. Still, however, it is a public war, because it is an external contention by force between some members of the two nations, authorized by the legitimate powers. It is a war between two nations, though all the members are not authorized to commit hostilities such as in a solemn war, where the government restrains the general power.

Now, if this be the true definition of war let us see what was the situation of the United States in relation to France. In March, 1799, Congress had raised an army, stopped all intercourse with France; dissolved our treaty, built and equipped ships of war; and commissioned private armed ships; enjoining the former, and authorizing the latter, to defend themselves against the armed ships of France, to attack them on the high seas, to subdue and take them as prize, and to re-capture armed vessels found in their possession. Here, then, let me ask, what were the technical characters of an American and French armed vessel, combating on the high seas, with a view the one to subdue the other, and to make prize of his property? They certainly were not friends, because there was a contention by force; nor were they private enemies, because the contention was external, and was authorized by the legitimate authority of the two governments. If they were not our enemies, I know not what constitutes an enemy. . . .

What then is the evidence of legislative will? In fact and law we are at war: an American vessel fighting with a French vessel, to subdue and make her prize, is fighting with an enemy, accurately and technically speaking: and if this be not sufficient evidence of the legislative mind, it is explained in the same law.[15]

Congress had established a state of imperfect war.

Justice Chase said:

Congress is empowered to declare a general war, or Congress may wage a limited war; limited in place, in object, in time. If a general

[15] Id. at 40-42.

war is declared, its extent and operations are only restricted and regulated by the *jus belli*, forming a part of the law of nations; but if a partial war is waged, its extent and operation depend on our municipal laws.

What then is the nature of the contest subsisting between America and France? In my judgment it is a limited, partial war. Congress has not declared war in general terms; but Congress has authorized hostilities on the high seas by certain persons in certain cases.[16]

Justice Paterson agreed:

The United States and the French republic are in a qualified state of hostility. An imperfect war, or a war, as to certain objects, and to a certain extent, exists between the two nations; and this modified warfare is authorized by the constitutional authority of our country. It is a war *quoad hoc.* As far as Congress tolerated and authorized the war on our part, so far may we proceed in hostile operations. It is a maritime war, a war at sea for certain purposes. . . . It is therefore a public war between the two nations qualified, on our part, in the manner prescribed by the constitutional organ of our country.[17]

Chief Justice John Marshall was not yet on the bench when *Bas v. Tingey* was decided, but he had an opportunity to discuss the war in *Talbot v. Seeman*[18] in 1801. Upholding the right of a United States ship of war to take a prize, he said:

The whole powers of war being, by the Constitution of the United States, vested in Congress, the acts of that body can alone be resorted to as our guides in this inquiry. It is not denied, nor in the course of the argument has it been denied, that Congress may authorize general hostilities, in which case the general laws of war apply to our situation; or partial war, in which case the laws of war, so far as they actually apply to our situation, must be noticed.[19]

The third case is *Little v. Barreme*,[20] decided in 1804. The non-intercourse act of February 9, 1799 authorized the seizure within American waters of vessels owned or hired by residents of the United States which after March 1 should trade with any French territory, and also authorized the President to instruct the commanders of public armed ships to seize on the high seas any American vessel "bound to or sail-

16 Id. at 43.   17 Id. at 45-46.   18 1 Cranch, 1.
19 Id. at 28.   20 2 Cranch, 170.

ing to any port or place within the territory of the French republic, or her dependencies." President Adams instructed naval commanders to seize American vessels "bound to or from French ports." Captain Little captured a Danish brigantine, the *Flying Fish*, which was bound from the French port of Jeremie to the Danish island of St. Thomas. In the course of the chase the captain of the *Flying Fish*, apparently in the erroneous belief that he was exposed to capture under American law, threw overboard the ship's log and other papers. He had prepared a false document to the effect that he had been forced into Jeremie by French ships. In the belief that the vessel was American, Captain Little took it into Boston as a prize.

In the district court for Massachusetts Judge Lowell ordered the vessel and cargo to be restored to the owner, but refused to award damages for the unlawful seizure. The actions of the captain of the *Flying Fish* in destroying his papers and in preparing a written excuse were suspicious and constituted reasonable cause for the seizure. "If a war of a common nature had existed between the United States and France, no question would be made but the false papers found on board, the destruction of the logbook and other paper, would be a sufficient excuse for the capture, detention and consequent damages." In a state of war, neutrals owe certain duties; they "shall destroy none of their papers, nor shall carry false papers, under the hazard of being exposed to every inconvenience resulting from capture, examination, and detention; except the eventual condemnation of the property." "It does not appear to me to be material what is the nature of the war, general, or limited. Nothing can be required of neutrals but to avoid duplicity."[21]

On appeal the circuit court awarded $8,504 damages against Captain Little, and the Supreme Court affirmed. Chief Justice Marshall wrote the opinion of the Court:

> It is by no means clear that the President of the United States, whose high duty it is to "take care that the laws be faithfully executed," and who is commander in chief of the armies and navies of the United States, might not, without any special authority for that purpose, in the then existing state of things, have empowered the officers commanding the armed vessels of the United States, to seize and send into port for adjudication, American vessels which were forfeited by being engaged in this illicit commerce. But when

[21] Id. at 173-4.

it is observed that the general clause of the first section of the act, which declares that such vessels may be seized, and may be prosecuted in any district where the seizure shall be made, obviously contemplates a seizure within the United States, and that the 5th section gives a special authority to seize on the high seas, and limits that authority to the seizure of vessels bound, or sailing to, a French port, the legislature seems to have prescribed that the manner in which this law shall be carried into execution, was to exclude a seizure of any vessel not bound to a French port. Of consequence, however strong the circumstances may be, which induced Captain Little to suspect the *Flying Fish* to be an American vessel, they could not excuse the detention of her, since he would not have been authorized to detain her had she been really American.[22]

Since the President's instructions collided with the act of Congress, they were illegal, and could neither justify the seizure nor excuse Captain Little from damages.

The Supreme Court has from the beginning held that contemporaneous legislative interpretations of the Constitution are highly persuasive as to its meaning.[23] Here we have not only legislative but judicial judgments that Congress may initiate action short of general war, that the initiation both of general war and of action short of general war belongs to Congress, and that it is for Congress to prescribe the dimensions of the war.

The war with France was ended in 1801; in the same year began a limited war with Tripoli. The Bashaw of Tripoli was dissatisfied with the size of the annual tribute from the United States and after various acts of harassment he declared war on the United States on May 14, 1801. On May 21, 1801, before he learned of this, President Jefferson wrote the Bashaw that he was sending a "squadron of observation" to the Mediterranean "to superintendent the safety of our commerce, and to exercise our seamen in martial duties"; "we mean to rest the safety of our commerce on the resources of our own strength and bravery in every sea."[24] The ships were instructed not to initiate hostilities, but two Tripolitan ships were blockaded in Gibraltar. Being attacked by the *Tripoli*, Captain Sterrett of the *Enterprise* reduced that ship to a

[22] Id. at 177-8.

[23] Stuart v. Laird, 1 Cranch, 299, 308 (1803); Burrow-Giles Lithographic Co. v. Sarony, 111 U.S. 53, 57 (1884); The Laura, 114 U.S. 411, 416 (1885).

[24] Glenn Tucker, *Dawn Like Thunder* (Indianapolis: Bobbs-Merrill, 1963), p. 135.

shambles; then he disarmed and released it. In his first annual message to Congress on December 8, 1801, Jefferson observed:

To this state of general peace with which we have been blessed, one only exception exists. Tripoli, the least considerable of the Barbary States, had come forward with demands unfounded either in right or in compact, and had permitted itself to denounce war on our failure to comply before a given day. The style of the demand admitted but one answer. I sent a small squadron of frigates into the Mediterranean, with assurances to that power of our sincere desire to remain in peace, but with orders to protect our commerce against the threatened attack. The measure was seasonable and salutary. The Bey had already declared war. His cruisers were out. Two had arrived at Gibraltar. Our commerce in the Mediterranean was blockaded and that of the Atlantic in peril. The arrival of our squadron dispelled the danger. One of the Tripolitan cruisers having fallen in with and engaged the small schooner *Enterprise* . . . was captured, after a heavy slaughter of her men, without the loss of a single one on our part. . . . Unauthorized by the Constitution, without the sanction of Congress, to go beyond the line of defense, the vessel, being disabled from committing further hostilities, was liberated with its crew. The Legislature will doubtless consider whether, by authorizing measures of offense also, they will place our force on an equal footing with that of its adversaries. I communicate all material information on this subject, that in the exercise of this important function confided by the Constitution to the Legislature exclusively their judgment may form itself on a knowledge and consideration of every circumstance of weight.[25]

The Congress responded by passing on February 6, 1802 an act[26] which authorized the President "fully to equip, officer, man and employ such of the armed vessels of the United States as may be judged requisite by the President of the United States, for protecting effectually the commerce and seamen thereof on the Atlantic Ocean, the Mediterranean and adjoining seas"; to instruct the commanders of these vessels to "subdue, seize, and make prize of all vessels, goods and effects, belonging to the Bey of Tripoli, or to his subjects . . . ; and also to cause to be done all such other acts of precaution or hostility as the state of war will justify, and may, in his opinion, require." He might also commission privateers.

[25] James D. Richardson, ed., *Messages and Papers of the Presidents, 1789-1908* (Washington: Bureau of National Literature and Art, 1908), Vol. 1, pp. 326-7.
[26] 2 Stat. 129.

Alexander Hamilton made a violent attack on Jefferson's legal theory. He focused his argument on the release of the *Tripoli*:

"The Congress shall have power to declare war"; the plain meaning of which is, that it is the peculiar and exclusive province of Congress, *when the nation is at peace*, to change that state into a state of war; whether from calculations of policy, or from provocations or injuries received; in other words, it belongs to Congress only *to go to war*. But when a foreign nation declares or openly and avowedly makes war upon the United States, they are then by the very fact *already at war*, and any declaration on the part of Congress is nugatory; it is at least unnecessary. . . .

Till the Congress should assemble and declare war, which would require time, our ships might, according to the hypothesis of the message, be sent by the President to fight those of the enemy as often as they should be attacked, but not to capture and detain them; if beaten, both vessels and crews would be lost to the United States; if successful, they could only disarm those they had overcome, and must suffer them to return to the place of common rendezvous, there to equip anew, for the purpose of resuming their depredations on our towns and our trade.[27]

The war with Tripoli was ended by treaty in 1805. The War of 1812 was our first general war and was initiated by a formal declaration by Congress.

From the time of the Louisiana purchase there had been friction with the Spanish authorities in Florida; and pirates and smugglers based in Florida were a vexation. In 1811 President Madison obtained a secret act of Congress authorizing him to take possession of Florida if local consent could be obtained or if another foreign power attempted to occupy it.[28] In 1812 General George Matthews seized Amelia Island, but the President repudiated this action on the ground that neither of the contingencies specified in the statute had occurred. However, he did not withdraw the troops from Florida until 1813. In that year Madison obtained another secret act under which General Wilkinson seized disputed territory, Mobile and the portion of Florida west of the Perdido river.[29]

[27] No. 1 of "Lucius Crassus" (Dec. 17, 1801), in Richard B. Morris, ed., *Alexander Hamilton and the Founding of the Nation* (New York: Dial Press, 1957), p. 526.
[28] 3 Stat. 471 (Jan. 15, 1811).   [29] 3 Stat. 472 (Feb. 12, 1813).

In 1815 Algiers attacked American shipping in the Mediterranean and President Madison obtained a declaration of limited war.[30] This was copied almost verbatim from the declaration against Tripoli. Commodore Decatur quickly won the war and a treaty of peace was concluded.

By an act of March 3, 1839,[31] Congress resolved: "That the President of the United States be, and he hereby is, authorized to resist any attempt on the part of Great Britain to enforce, by arms, her claim to exclusive jurisdiction over that part of Maine which is in dispute between the United States and Great Britain; and for that purpose, to employ the naval and military forces of the United States and such portions of the militia as he may deem it advisable to call into service."

The act further provided that if actual invasion of the United States should occur, or if in the opinion of the President there was imminent danger of invasion "before Congress can be convened to act upon the subject, the President be, and he is hereby, authorized if he deem the same expedient, to accept the services of volunteers not exceeding fifty thousand." And, in the event of war with Great Britain or invasion or imminent danger of invasion, the President was authorized to employ the naval force of the United States and to build or procure vessels on the Great Lakes "as he shall deem necessary to protect the United States from invasion from that quarter."

The war with Mexico, which lasted from 1846 to 1848, is particularly interesting. After the annexation of Texas the territory between the Nueces and the Rio Grande was in dispute with Mexico. It was held by Mexico, and President Polk sent in an army which in two battles destroyed the Mexican forces. On May 13, 1846, Congress instituted a general war by a declaration which recited that Mexico had initiated the war. But in 1847 both houses began to inquire into the circumstances that had produced the war.[32] On January 3, 1848, the House by a vote of 85 to 81 resolved that the war had been "unnecessarily and unconstitutionally begun by the President of the United States."[33] The war was concluded by a treaty a few months later.

President Polk produced the war and Congress recognized the *fait accompli* by declaring war. Nevertheless, the vote of reproof demonstrates the understanding of the House—a perfectly correct under-

[30] 3 Stat. 230 (Mar. 3, 1815).   [31] 5 Stat. 355.
[32] Richardson, *op.cit.*, Vol. 4, pp. 519, 565, 568-9.
[33] *Congressional Globe*, 30th Cong., 1st Sess. (Jan. 3, 1848), p. 95.

standing—that the President has no right to initiate war. And it makes it clear that when the President obliges the Congress to declare war this ratification does not exculpate him for his illegal action.

In a letter to his friend Herndon, Representative Abraham Lincoln defended his vote for the resolution:

> Let me first state what I understand to be your position. It is that if it shall become necessary to repel invasion, the President may, without violation of the Constitution, cross the line and invade the territory of another country, and that whether such necessity exists in any given case the President is the sole judge. . . .
>
> . . . Allow the President to invade a neighboring nation whenever he shall deem it necessary to repel an invasion, and you allow him to do so whenever he may choose to say he deems it necessary for such a purpose, and you allow him to make war at his pleasure. Study to see if you can fix any limit to his power in this respect, after having given him so much power as you propose. . . .
>
> The provision of the Constitution giving the war-making power to Congress was dictated, as I understand it, by the following reasons: Kings had always been involving and impoverishing their people in wars, pretending generally, if not always, that the good of the people was the object. This our convention understood to be the most oppressive of all kingly oppressions, and they resolved to so frame the Constitution that no one man should hold the power of bringing oppression upon us. But your view destroys the whole matter, and places our President where kings have always stood.[34]

In 1853 an American naval vessel, the *Water Witch*, was navigating a tributary of the Rio de la Plata under license from Argentina. It was in waters allegedly common to Paraguay and Argentina but was on the Paraguayan side of the river. Paraguay had closed its waters to foreign ships of war, and a Paraguayan fort shelled the *Water Witch*, which returned the fire. In his annual message to Congress of December 8, 1857, President Buchanan revived this grievance, and also reported that Paraguay had seized the property of citizens of the United States. He announced his intention to demand redress for these two wrongs, and asked Congress to authorize him to use "other means in the event of a refusal."[35] By joint resolution of June 2, 1858, he was authorized to

---

[34] Arthur B. Lapsley, ed., *The Writings of Abraham Lincoln* (New York: Putnam's, 1905), Vol. 2, pp. 51-2.

[35] Richardson, *op.cit.*, Vol. 5, p. 449.

"adopt such measures and use such force as, in his judgment, may be necessary and advisable, in the event of a refusal of just satisfaction by the government of Paraguay."[36] Several ships of war were sent and the difficulties with Paraguay were, as Buchanan said in his annual message of December 19, 1859, "satisfactorily adjusted" by commissioners without resorting to violence.[37]

In a message to Congress on January 28, 1861, President Buchanan reported a series of resolutions passed by the legislature of Virginia with a view to resolving the issue between North and South.[38] Virginia proposed that a conference of states be held in Washington, and that in the meantime the states which had seceded and the President should agree to abstain from all acts of violence. Buchanan applauded the plan, but said he could not make the agreement proposed:

> However strong may be my desire to enter into such an agreement, I am convinced that I do not possess the power. Congress, and Congress alone, under the war-making power, can exercise the discretion of agreeing to abstain "from any and all acts calculated to produce a collision of arms" between this and any other government. It would therefore be a usurpation for the Executive to attempt to restrain their hands by an agreement in regard to matters over which he has no constitutional control. If he were thus to act, they might pass laws which he should be bound to obey, though in conflict with his agreement.
>
> Under existing circumstances, my present actual power is confined within narrow limits. It is my duty at all times to defend and protect the public property within the seceding States so far as this may be practicable, and especially to employ all constitutional means to protect the property of the United States and to preserve the public peace at this seat of the Federal Government. If the seceding States abstain "from any and all acts calculated to produce a collision of arms," then the danger so much to be deprecated will no longer exist. Defense, and not aggression, has been the policy of the Administration from the beginning.

Thus Buchanan clearly adopted the position Jefferson had taken at the inception of the war with Tripoli. The war power belongs entirely to Congress, and the President is its servant. Until Congress acts, the President must confine himself to repelling attacks.

[36] 11 Stat. 370.
[38] *Ibid.*, pp. 661-2.

[37] Richardson, *op.cit.*, p. 560.

President Lincoln took the Hamiltonian view. He had statutory power to call up the militia, but he had no statutory authority to issue his two proclamations of April 19 and April 27, 1861 for the blockade of Southern ports. These were issued on the theory that a state of general war already existed by virtue of the Southern attacks on federal property; in a general war, the commander-in-chief may use any means of belligerency permitted by the international law of war. On July 4, 1861, he asked the special session of Congress to ratify his actions, "whether strictly legal or not,"[39] and on August 6 Congress declared that his orders to the army and navy and his calling up militia and volunteers "are hereby approved and in all respects legalized and made valid . . . as if they had been issued and done under the previous express authority and direction of the Congress."[40]

The question of the legality of the seizure of prizes under the Presidential proclamations before Congress acted came before the Supreme Court in the *Prize Cases*[41] in 1863. Five Justices upheld the blockade. Justice Grier for the majority asserted that war could exist without declaration: "war is that state in which a nation prosecutes its right by force."

By the Constitution, Congress alone has the power to declare a national or foreign war. . . . The Constitution confers on the President the whole executive power. He is bound to take care that the laws be faithfully executed. He is commander in chief of the armed services and the militia of the several States when called into actual service. He has no power to initiate or declare a war against a foreign nation or domestic State. . . .

If war be made by invasion from a foreign nation, the President is not only authorized but bound to resist force by force. He does not initiate the war, but is bound to accept the challenge without waiting for any special legislative authority. Whether the hostile party be a foreign invader, or States organized in rebellion, it is nonetheless an act of war, even if the declaration be "unilateral."[42]

The need for a blockade was a question for the judgment of the President:

Whether the President in fulfilling his duties, as commander in chief, in suppressing an insurrection, has met with such armed hos-

39 *Ibid.*, p. 662.   40 12 Stat. 326.
41 2 Black, 635.   42 Id. at 668.

tile resistance, and a civil war of such alarming proportions as will compel him to accord to them the character of belligerents, is a question to be decided by *him,* and this Court must be governed by the decisions and acts of the political department of the Government to which this power was entrusted. "He must determine what degree of force the crisis demands." The proclamation of blockade is itself official and conclusive evidence to the Court that a state of war existed which demanded and authorized a recourse to such a measure, under the circumstances peculiar to the case.[43]

Then Justice Grier pointed to the Congressional ratification: "Without admitting that such an act was necessary, it is plain that if the president had in any manner assumed powers which it was necessary should have the authority or sanction of Congress, . . . the ratification has operated to perfectly cure the defect."[44] The law of due process was not at that time well developed, or the Court might have noticed that a retroactive validation of a confiscation of ships for action legal when undertaken was a taking of property without due process of law.

Justice Nelson wrote the opinion for the four dissenters. A blockade was possible only when a state of public war existed at the law of nations, and "a war cannot lawfully be commenced on the part of the United States without an act of Congress."[45] The President had had statutory authority to call out the militia to suppress the insurrection, but "the president had no authority or power to set on foot a blockade under the law of nations or the Constitution until Congress acted."[46]

So angry were the four dissenting Justices that Justice Catron took the unusual step of writing to counsel for the libellees, the day after his argument, asking for a copy to be included in the official report of the decision, and expressing his own opinion informally:

It is idle to disguise the fact that the claim set up to forfeit these ships and cargoes, *by the force of a proclimation* [*sic*], is not founded on constitutional power, but on a power assumed to be *created* by Military necessity. *Necessity* is an old plea—old as the reign of Tibereas [*sic*]; its limits should be looked for in Tacitus. It is the commander's will. The End, we are told is to crush the Rebellion; that the whole means are at the Presd'ts discretion and that he

[43] Id. at 670.   [44] Id. at 671.
[45] Id. at 693.   [46] Id. at 698.

is the sole Judge in the Selection of the means to accomplish the End. This is a rejection of the Constitution with its limitations.[47]

Surely this is an overstatement. The majority claimed nothing more than Hamilton had maintained against Jefferson—that when the United States is attacked the President is a commander-in-chief in a state of general war at international law until Congress acts.

In 1871 three American steamships were seized by one of two belligerent factions which were contending for control of the government of Venezuela. One was voluntarily surrendered; the other two were yielded up on demand of the commander of the U.S.S. *Shawmut*. On June 17, 1890, Congress passed a resolution which became law without the President's signature.[48] It authorized the President to take "such measures as in his judgment may be necessary to promptly obtain indemnity . . . and to secure this end he is authorized to employ such means or exercise such power as may be necessary." The matter was arbitrated and an indemnity of $150,000 was awarded to the United States.

In 1886 Spain acknowledged a debt to the heirs of a naturalized American citizen, Antonio Maximo Mora, for property losses during the Ten Years War in Cuba; but no payment was made. On March 2, 1895, Congress passed a "Joint Resolution Calling on the President to take such measures as he may deem necessary to consummate the agreement";[49] the text recited "That the President be, and he is hereby, requested to insist upon the payment of the sum agreed upon." It is not clear that the use of force was contemplated. The State Department collected the sum, according to the *New York Sun*, "by a process closely suggesting blackmail": there was a threat of American interference in Cuba.[50]

The Spanish-American War was initiated by a joint resolution signed by the President on April 20, 1898.[51] The resolution was an ultimatum to Spain to withdraw from Cuba and relinquish its authority over the island; the President was directed to use the land and naval forces to carry the resolution into effect. Spain replied by severing diplomatic relations and initiating hostilities, and on April 25 Congress passed an

[47] *The Legal Historian*, Vol. 1 (1958), pp. 51-2.
[48] 26 Stat. 674.   [49] 28 Stat. 975.
[50] Joseph E. Wisan, *The Cuban Crisis as Reflected in the New York Press* (New York: Octagon Books, 1965), p. 87.
[51] 30 Stat. 738.

act declaring that a state of war with Spain had existed since April 21, 1898.[52]

Woodrow Wilson refused to recognize the government of President Huerta of Mexico and raised the embargo on the export of arms and munitions to Mexico. On April 9, 1914, a squad of the Mexican Army arrested eight men from the American whaling ship *Dolphin* and paraded them through the streets of Tampico. They were released as soon as the Mexicans encountered a superior officer. But Wilson seized upon this episode as a pretext for striking a blow at Huerta. Wilson demanded that Huerta order a salute of honor to United States naval vessels; Huerta refused to do this unless the United States simultaneously paid tribute to Mexico. On April 20 the President asked Congress for permission to "use the armed forces of the United States in such ways and to such an extent as may be necessary to obtain from General Huerta and his adherents the fullest recognition of the right and dignity of the United States, even amidst the distressing conditions now unhappily prevailing in Mexico."[53] On April 21 American forces occupied Vera Cruz. On April 22 the two houses passed a resolution which disavowed any purpose "to make war on Mexico" but asserted that the President "is justified in the employment of the armed forces to enforce his demands for unequivocal amends for affronts and indignities committed against the United States."[54] This amounted to a ratification, and Wilson continued to occupy Vera Cruz for seven months.

Both the First and Second World Wars were declared by Congress at the request of the respective Presidents.

III. Presidential References to Congress

In establishing the early and general understanding as to where the authority resides to use armed force abroad, it is instructive to examine the cases in which Presidents have referred the question as to whether such action should be taken to Congress, or have asked Congress for authority, and Congress has failed to authorize hostile actions. Most of these have not been proposals for general war; several of them have not even been proposals for limited war. It is not even the case that they all involved what was known at international law as acts of war,

[52] 30 Stat. 364.
[53] *Congressional Record*, Vol. 51, Pt. 7, 63d Cong., 2d Sess., p. 6988.
[54] 38 Stat. 770.

for classical international law recognized types of forceful redress by an injured state which a wrongdoer had no legal right to resent. Nevertheless, in all the following cases the President conceded that the monopoly of Congress over the declaring of war gave Congress the exclusive right to decide on the adoption of lesser military measures as well.

The first occasion was a proposal of President Jefferson. In a special message to Congress on December 6, 1805, he described the dispute with Spain over the boundary between Louisiana and Florida, and the course of conduct adopted by Spain:

> That which they have chosen to pursue will appear from the documents now communicated. They authorize the inference that it is their intention to advance on our possessions until they shall be repressed by an opposing force. Considering that Congress alone is constitutionally invested with the power of changing our condition from peace to war, I have thought it my duty to await their authority for using force in any degree which could be avoided. I have barely instructed the officers stationed in the neighborhood of the aggressions to protect our citizens from violence, to patrol within the borders actually delivered to us, and not to go out of them but when necessary to repel an inroad or to rescue a citizen, or his property; and the Spanish officers remaining at New Orleans are to depart without further delay. . . .
>
> The present crisis in Europe is favorable for pressing such a settlement, and not a moment should be lost in availing ourselves of it. Should it pass unimproved, our situation would become much more difficult. Formal war is not necessary—it is not probable it will follow; but the protection of our citizens, the spirit and honor of our country require that force should be interposed to a certain degree. It will probably contribute to advance the object of peace.
>
> But the course to be pursued will require the command of means which it belongs to Congress exclusively to yield or to deny. To them I communicate every fact material for their information and the documents necessary to enable them to judge for themselves. To their wisdom, then, I look for the course I am to pursue, and will pursue with sincere zeal that which they shall approve.[1]

In his annual message to Congress on December 7, 1824, President

---

[1] James D. Richardson, ed., *Messages and Papers of the Presidents, 1789-1908* (Washington: Bureau of National Literature and Art, 1908), Vol. 1, pp. 389-90.

James Monroe described the activities of pirates who put out from the Cuban shore, plundered American shipping, and fled again to the safety of Spanish territory:

> It is presumed that it must be attributed to the relaxed and feeble state of the local governments, since it is not doubted, from the high character of the governor of Cuba, who is well known and much respected here, that if he had the power he would promptly suppress it. Whether those robbers should be pursued on the land, the local authorities be made responsible for these atrocities, or any other measure be resorted to to suppress them, is submitted to the consideration of Congress.[2]

The Senate asked for further information, and Monroe sent a special message on January 13, 1825. He proposed three expedients: "one by pursuit of offenders to the settled as well as the unsettled parts of the island from whence they issue, another by reprisal on the property of the inhabitants, and a third by the blockade of the ports of those islands." Probably neither Spain nor the local government of Cuba would resent such action. "It is therefore suggested that a power commensurate with either resource be granted to the Executive, to be exercised according to his discretion and as circumstances may imperiously require."[3] Congress took no action. The problem was resolved by United States naval commanders who on their own initiative pursued the pirates ashore and destroyed their bases.

By treaty in 1831 the French government agreed to satisfy American claims dating back to the Napoleonic wars, but in 1834 this still had not been done. In his annual message on December 9 of that year, President Jackson asked for the power to exact reprisals from French shipping and property if the French Chambers failed to vote the money at their next session.[4] The Senate by resolution unanimously rejected this request. Since this proposal was one for the delegation of the war power to the President, it will be considered at greater length in Section VIII.

On April 29, 1848, President James K. Polk reported to Congress an offer from the Governor of Yucatan to transfer the "dominion and sovereignty of the peninsula" to the United States in return for assistance against the Indians, who were "waging a war of extermination against the white race." Similar offers had been made to Spain and Great

---

[2] *Ibid.*, Vol. 2, p. 258. [3] *Ibid.*, p. 279. [4] *Ibid.*, Vol. 3, p. 106.

Britain. Polk said that he did not intend to propose the acquisition of sovereignty over the territory, but the United States could not afford to allow Spain or Great Britain to acquire it either:

I have considered it proper to communicate the information contained in the accompanying correspondence, and I submit it to the wisdom of Congress to adopt such measures as in their judgment may be expedient to prevent Yucatan from becoming a colony of any European power, which in no event could be permitted by the United States, and at the same time to rescue the white race from extermination or expulsion from their country.[5]

It appears that President Polk may have already employed the United States Navy in Yucatan.[6] Congress took no action.

On February 28, 1854, the American ship *Black Warrior* was seized in Havana, allegedly for violation of harbor regulations. On March 10 the House of Representatives asked for information. On March 15 President Franklin Pierce sent a special message, together with a report from the Secretary of State. Pierce said that he had demanded indemnity from Spain:

In case the measures taken for amicable adjustment of our difficulties with Spain should, unfortunately, fail, I shall not hesitate to use the authority and means which Congress may grant to insure the observance of our just rights, to obtain redress for injuries received, and to vindicate the honor of our flag.

In anticipation of that contingency, which I earnestly hope may not arise, I suggest to Congress the propriety of adopting such provisional measures as the exigency may seem to demand.[7]

On August 1 Pierce replied to a resolution of inquiry from the Senate that "nothing has arisen since the date of my former message to 'dispense with the suggestions therein contained touching the propriety of provisional measures by Congress.' "[8] But on December 4 he held out hope of an amicable settlement as a result of a change of ministers in Spain,[9] and on December 31, 1855, he reported to Congress: "Spain has not only disavowed and disapproved the conduct of the officers who illegally seized and detained the steamer *Black Hawk* at Havana, but has also paid the sum claimed as indemnity for the loss thereby inflicted on citizens of the United States."[10]

[5] *Ibid.*, Vol. 4, p. 583. [6] *Ibid.*, p. 584. [7] *Ibid.*, Vol. 5, p. 235.
[8] *Ibid.*, p. 246. [9] *Ibid.*, p. 278. [10] *Ibid.*, p. 336.

President James Buchanan must have been the most frustrated President in our history. On December 8, 1857,[11] December 6, 1858,[12] February 18, 1859,[13] and December 19, 1859,[14] he requested authority to use the land and naval forces to protect transit over the Isthmus of Panama if need should arise. On February 18, 1859[15] and December 19, 1859,[16] he asked for the power to enforce redress in case American ships were confiscated in Latin-American harbors. These requests were refused on the ground that compliance would involve the delegation of the war power of Congress, and they will therefore be treated at greater length in Section VIII.

On December 6, 1858, Buchanan reported that hostile Indians in northern Mexico raided over the border, committing depredations on settlers and arresting the settlement of Arizona:

> I can imagine no possible remedy for these evils and no mode of restoring law and order on that remote and unsettled frontier but for the Government of the United States to assume a temporary protectorate over the northern portions of Chihuahua and Sonora, and to establish military posts within the same; and this I earnestly recommend to Congress.[17]

He repeated the proposal in his message of December 19, 1859.[18] In the same message he recommended sending an expeditionary force into Mexico to obtain redress from a rebel government which had killed several American citizens.[19]

These requests, too, were rejected by Congress.

Aside from Jefferson, no President has been so explicit on the war power as Buchanan:

> The executive government of this country in its intercourse with foreign nations is limited to the employment of diplomacy alone. When this fails it can proceed no further. It cannot legitimately resort to force without the direct authority of Congress, except in resisting and repelling hostile attacks. It would have no authority to enter the territories of Nicaragua even to prevent the destruction of the transit and to protect the lives and property of our own citizens on their passage. It is true that on a sudden emergency of this character the President would direct any armed force in the vicinity to

---

[11] *Ibid.*, p. 447.   [12] *Ibid.*, pp. 516-17.   [13] *Ibid.*, p. 539.
[14] *Ibid.*, p. 569.   [15] *Ibid.*, p. 539.   [16] *Ibid.*, p. 569.
[17] *Ibid.*, p. 514.   [18] *Ibid.*, p. 568.   [19] *Ibid.*, pp. 567-68.

march to their relief, but in doing this he would act upon his own responsibility.[20]

Since Buchanan no presidential request for authorization to use force has been rejected. This is in part because in the last hundred years Presidents adopted the policy of executive usurpation.

IV. Presidential Refusals to Act

On a number of occasions the executive authority has refused to employ armed force abroad because Congress had not authorized it, and a certain evidentiary value attaches to the statements made in these cases.

In view of the current contention, which we shall examine in Section VII, that the President may make an executive commitment and thereby invest himself with the war power, it is interesting to see what legal effect the authors of our first and most famous commitment, the Monroe Doctrine, attributed to that declaration. In his seventh annual message, on December 2, 1823, President James Monroe told the Congress and the world:

> With the existing colonies or dependencies of any European power we have not interfered and shall not interfere. But with the Governments who have declared their independence and maintained it, and whose independence we have, on great consideration and on just principles, acknowledged, we could not view any interposition for the purpose of oppressing them, or controlling in any other manner their destiny, by any European power in any other light than as the manifestation of an unfriendly disposition toward the United States.[1]

On July 1, 1824, José Maria Salazar, the minister of Colombia to the United States, told Secretary of State John Quincy Adams that he had authentic information that the French plenipotentiary to Colombia was instructed to inform the Colombian government that France would recognize the independence of Colombia only if it instituted a king, Bolívar or another; the threat of French aggression was implicit. Adams asked Salazar to present his views in writing, and on July 2 the minister addressed to him a communication which expressed the satis-

---

[20] Ibid., p. 516.

---

[1] James D. Richardson, ed., *Messages and Papers of the Presidents, 1789-1908* (Washington: Bureau of National Literature and Art, 1908). Vol. 2, p. 218.

faction of his government with the announcement of the Monroe Doctrine and inquired "In what manner the Government of the United States intends to resist on its part any interference of the Holy Alliance for the purpose of subjugating the new Republics or interfering in their political forms?"[2]

Adams took the matter to the President, and on July 7 summarized in his diary the cabinet discussion on Salazar's note: "The Colombian republic to maintain its own independence. Hope that France and the Holy Allies will not resort to force against it. If they should, the power to determine our resistance is in Congress. The movements of the Executive will be as heretofore expressed. I am to draft an answer."[3] But apparently this was a tentative disposition of the question, for on August 2 President Monroe wrote to James Madison describing the problem and commenting: "The subject will of course be weighed thoroughly in giving the answer. The Executive has no right to compromit the nation in any question of war, nor ought we to presume that the people of Columbia [sic] will hesitate as to the answer to be given to any proposition which touches so vitally their liberties."[4] On August 6 Adams replied to Salazar: "You understand that by the Constitution of the United States, the ultimate decision of this question belongs to the Legislative Department of the Government."[5] Apparently the French threat was empty, for nothing more transpired.

In 1848 Secretary of State Buchanan wrote to the Commissioner to Hawaii of a proposal to collect claims by force:

> But if the claim were never so just, if it had been a case in which this Government were bound officially to interfere and if the amount due the claimant had been acknowledged by the Hawaiian Government, the President could not employ the naval force of the United States to enforce its payment without the authority of an act of Congress. The war-making power alone can authorize such a measure.[6]

In 1851 Secretary of State Daniel Webster rejected a proposal that the United States participate in a dispute between France and Hawaii:

> In the first place, I have to say that the war-making power in this Government rests entirely with Congress; and that the President can

---

[2] W. S. Robertson, "South America and the Monroe Doctrine, 1824-1828," *Political Science Quarterly*, Vol. 30 (1915), p. 89.

[3] *Ibid.*, p. 90.

[4] John Bassett Moore, *Digest of International Law* (Washington: Government Printing Office, 1906), Vol. 6, p. 446.

[5] Robertson, *op.cit.*, p. 91.   [6] Moore, *op.cit.*, Vol. 7, p. 163.

authorize belligerent operations only in the cases expressly provided for by the Constitution and the laws. By these no power is given to the Executive to oppose an attack by one independent nation on the possessions of another. We are bound to regard both France and Hawaii as independent states, and equally independent, and though the general policy of the Government might lead it to take part with either in a controversy with the other, still, if this interference be an act of hostile force, it is not within the constitutional power of the President; and still less is it within the power of any subordinate agent of government, civil or military.[7]

This statement is particularly interesting in view of the current claim of the State Department that a "sudden attack" by one foreign nation upon another confers upon the President the right to intervene if he feels that the security of the United States is threatened.

In 1857 Secretary of State Cass wrote to the British Foreign Secretary, Lord Napier, explaining the American refusal to join in the Anglo-French expedition against Peking:

This proposition, looking to a participation by the United States in the existing hostilities against China, makes it proper to remind your lordship that, under the Constitution of the United States, the executive branch of this Government is not the war-making power. The exercise of that great attribute of sovereignty is vested in Congress, and the President has no authority to order aggressive hostilities to be undertaken.

Our naval officers have the right—it is their duty, indeed—to employ the forces under their command, not only in self-defense, but for the protection of the persons and property of our citizens when exposed to acts of lawless outrage, and this they have done both in China and elsewhere, and will do again when necessary. But military expeditions into the Chinese territory cannot be undertaken without the authority of the National Legislature.[8]

Congress, as previously noted, rejected President Buchanan's four requests for power to police the Panama Isthmus. In 1860 the American Atlantic & Pacific Steamship Canal Company asked for executive action to enforce certain claims against Nicaragua. On March 3 Secretary of State Cass wrote to the Secretary of the Company:

[7] *Loc.cit.*   [8] *Ibid.*, p. 164.

You seem to suppose that the defence of the rights of our country or its citizens, and the avowal that their violation will justify the employment of force, commits the Executive in your case to resort to it, and you accordingly call for the application of "the armed force" of the United States for the protection of your rights in Nicaragua.

The employment of the national force, under such circumstances, for the invasion of Nicaragua is an act of war, and however just it may be, it is a measure which Congress alone possesses the constitutional power to adopt. The President has in three [*sic*] separate messages brought to the attention of that body this subject of the employment of force for the protection of our citizens. . . . But these appeals to Congress have produced no result. . . .

Cases may occur where the circumstances may justify the employment of our naval or military forces, without special legislative provision, for the protection of our citizens from outrage, but it is not necessary to examine the extent or limit of this right, because the principle is inapplicable in your case, where you demand a forcible interposition with the Nicaraguan Government, in order to give effect to the contract to which you refer.[9]

When in 1876 a United States naval officer asked permission to seize a quantity of silver belonging to a United States citizen, which had been taken by a Mexican official, Acting Secretary of State Hunter wrote: "The President is not authorized to order or approve an act of war in a country with which we are at peace, except in self-defense. This is a peculiarity of our form of government, which at times may be inconvenient, but which is believed to have proved and will in future be found in the long run to be wise and essential to the public welfare."[10]

Julio R. Santo, a naturalized citizen of the United States of Ecuadorean origin, was imprisoned in Ecuador on account of alleged participation in a political uprising. The U.S.S. *Wachusett* was despatched to Ecuador on May 1, 1881, but Secretary of State Bayard wrote to the consul-general at Guayaquil that its mission was one of peace and good-will, to achieve a mutually honorable solution: "The purpose of her presence is not to be deemed minatory; and resort to force is not competently within the scope of her commander's agency. If all form of redress, thus temperately but earnestly solicited, be unhappily

---

[9] *Ibid.*, pp. 165-6.   [10] *Ibid.*, p. 167.

denied, it is the constitutional prerogative of Congress to decide and declare what further action should be taken."[11]

In 1911 the Ambassador to Mexico informed President Taft that "President Diaz was on a volcano of popular uprising," "in which case he feared that the 40,000 or more American residents in Mexico might be assailed, and that the very large American investments might be injured or destroyed." Accordingly, President Taft assembled troops in Texas and California, and ships at Galveston and San Diego and instructed the Chief of Staff:

> It seems my duty as Commander in Chief to place troops in suffi-cient number where, if Congress shall direct that they enter Mexico to save American lives and property, an effective movement may be promptly made. . . .
>
> The assumption by the press that I contemplate intervention on Mexican soil to protect American lives or property is of course gra-tuitous, because I seriously doubt whether I have such authority under any circumstances, and if I had I would not exercise it without express congressional approval. Indeed, as you know, I have already declined, without Mexican consent, to order a troop of Cavalry to protect the breakwater we are constructing just across the border in Mexico at the mouth of the Colorado River to save the Imperial Valley, although the insurrectos had scattered the Mexican troops and were taking our horses and supplies and frightening our work-men away. My determined purpose, however, is to be in a position so that when danger to American lives and property in Mexico threatens and the existing Government is rendered helpless by the insurrection, I can promptly execute congressional orders to protect them, with effect.[12]

V. Unauthorized Presidential Actions

The 1966 State Department memorandum attaches importance to the fact that "Since the Constitution was adopted there have been at least 125 instances in which the President has ordered the armed forces to take action or maintain positions abroad without obtaining prior congressional authorization, starting with the 'undeclared war' with France (1798–1800)." These precedents are supposed to justify President

[11] *Ibid.*, p. 109.

[12] Third Annual Message, in Fred L. Israel, ed., *The State of the Union Messages of the Presidents, 1790-1966* (New York: Chelsea House, Robert Hector, 1966), Vol. 3, pp. 2447-8.

Johnson's action in committing more than a half million troops in South Vietnam and attacking North Vietnam.

Three collections of precedents have been published. In 1912 the Solicitor for the State Department, J. Reuben Clark, published a memorandum entitled *Right to Protect Citizens in Foreign Countries by Landing Forces*. An appendix listed forty-one episodes. The study was republished in 1934; a Supplemental Appendix added a considerable number of later cases under the headings of China, Cuba, Dominican Republic, Guatemala, Haiti, Honduras, Mexico, Nicaragua, Panama, France (in 1914 six men from the U.S.S. *Tennessee* were stationed as guards at the Embassy in Paris for one week), and Smyrna.[1] In 1928 Milton Offutt's *The Protection of Citizens Abroad by the Armed Forces of the United States*[2] was published. Offutt estimated that "The armed forces of the United States have been landed on foreign soil for the protection of the lives and property of American citizens living abroad on more than one hundred occasions during the past hundred and fifteen years."[3] In 1945 a former Assistant Secretary of State, James Grafton Rogers, published *World Policing and the Constitution*.[4] In an appendix he listed 149 cases or clusters of cases. In not more than a dozen or two of these, he said, had Congress authorized "the employment of guns or men." "In all the other affairs listed, running to well over a hundred, the Executive alone has assumed responsibility."[5] It may be added that in the great majority of these cases there was no collision of hostile forces and no bloodshed.

In a number of the cases compiled by these authors the President reported the action to Congress; sometimes he offered a justification. In other cases he did not report. In still other cases the action was taken by naval officers on their own initiative; only very infrequently were these actions ever reported to Congress.

It is possible to classify the cases of executive action into several types. They are presented here in what is more or less an order of increasing gravity.[6]

In several cases the executive authority has apparently felt justified in taking unauthorized action because the foe was politically unor-

---

[1] *Right to Protect Citizens in Foreign Countries by Landing Forces*. Memorandum of the Solicitor for the Department of State, October 5, 1912, Third Revised Edition with Supplemental Appendix up to 1933 (Washington: Government Printing Office, 1934).

[2] Baltimore: Johns Hopkins Press, 1928.   [3] *Ibid.*, p. 1.

[4] Boston: World Peace Foundation, 1945.   [5] *Ibid.*, p. 79.

[6] Most of the cases are to be found in one or more of the three books cited. Usually Offutt's account is the fullest.

ganized. The assumption has been that war can exist only between states. The first such case President Jackson reported in his fourth annual message on December 4, 1832:

> An act of piracy having been committed on one of our trading ships by the inhabitants of a settlement on the west coast of Sumatra, a frigate was dispatched with orders to demand satisfaction for the injury if those who committed it should be found to be members of a regular government, capable of maintaining the usual relations with foreign nations; but if, as was supposed and as they proved to be, they were a band of lawless pirates, to inflict such a chastisement as would deter them and others from like aggressions. This last was done, and the effect has been an increased respect for our flag in those distant seas and additional security for our commerce.[7]

There were other punitive attacks on Sumatra in 1838 and 1839. In 1840, 1855, and 1858 retaliatory attacks were made in the Fiji Islands. In 1841 there was a raid on Drummond Island in the Pacific and on Samoa. In 1843 there were raids on the West African coast. In 1867, in Formosa, there was an unsuccessful pursuit of natives who were in effect independent of the official government of the island.

The most important case in this category was the bombardment of Greytown, Nicaragua, in 1854. The mouth of the San Juan River was the eastern terminus of one of the routes across the Isthmus. Great Britain claimed a protectorate over the "Mosquito Coast," and under a charter from the Mosquito King a company of American and European adventurers set up a transit company to conduct travelers over the Isthmus. In 1852, with the consent of the Mosquito King and under the patronage of the British consul, this group established the sovereign state of Greytown. A rival enterprise, the Accessory Transit Company, held a charter from the Nicaraguan government and enjoyed the patronage of the United States government; it had its seat directly across the river in Punta Arenas. Inevitably friction arose. During a visit in May of 1853 Captain Hollins of the U.S.S. *Cyane* temporarily placed a marine guard on property of the Accessory Transit Company which had been ordered to be cleared by the Greytown authorities. After his departure there occurred various incidents; in the course of one of them the American Minister to Central America suffered a slight

---

[7] James D. Richardson, ed., *Messages and Papers of the Presidents, 1789-1908* (Washington: Bureau of National Literature and Art, 1908), Vol. 2, p. 596.

cut from a bottle thrown by a member of a Greytown mob. The Secretary of the Navy ordered Hollins to return and obtain redress for the damages suffered by the Accessory Transit Company and an apology for the attack upon the Minister. His instructions were ambiguous. The people of Greytown "should be taught that the United States will not tolerate these outrages, and that they have the power and the determination to check them. It is, however, very much to be hoped that you can effect the purposes of your visit without a resort to violence and destruction of property and loss of life. The presence of your vessel will, no doubt, work much good. The Department reposes much in your prudence and good sense."[8]

Upon his arrival on July 12, 1854, Captain Hollins demanded an indemnity of $24,000 for the Accessory Transit Company, an apology for the attack on the Minister, and assurances of good behavior. Greytown did not comply, and on July 13 Hollins shelled the town intermittently throughout the day, and at four o'clock he sent a party ashore to burn what remained of the town. He reported: "The execution done by our shot and shell amounted to the almost total destruction of the buildings; but it was thought best to make the punishment of such a character as to inculcate a lesson never to be forgotten by those who have for so long a time set at defiance all warnings, and satisfy the whole world that the United States have the power and determination to enforce that reparation and respect due to them as a Government in whatever quarter the outrages may be committed."[9]

This episode is frequently paraded today as an illustration of the constitutional powers of the President. It was not so regarded at the time. The leading study of the affair reports:

Hollins's action met with strong condemnation from the American press and people. The New York *Times* was particularly bitter, and, assuming that the action was directed or approved by the government, intimated that the terms of the Clayton-Bulwer treaty had been broken, and denounced President Pierce for a violation of the Constitution of the United States, on the ground that Congress alone could declare war. The *Times* was an opposition paper, but the best elements of the Democrats themselves felt that they could not honestly defend the deed. The fact that resolutions from both houses of

[8] John Bassett Moore, *Digest of International Law* (Washington: Government Printing Office, 1906), Vol. 7, pp. 113-14.
[9] *Ibid.*, p. 181.

Congress, asking for the correspondence upon the subject, with a copy of Hollins's instructions, were carried by a large majority and in spite of administrative opposition was indicative of the general disapprobation of the country.[10]

The Minister to Great Britain, James Buchanan, assured the British government that Hollins' action was unauthorized and would be disavowed by the United States.[11] Secretary of State Marcy, however, saw no way of repudiating Hollins' act; at the same time, he dared not indorse it, and so when the British Ambassador approached him he said that he could not express an opinion because the matter was under the consideration of the government.[12] Both the Senate and the House demanded information on the bombardment. In the meantime, France, the German Confederation, and Nicaragua demanded indemnification for the destruction of the property of their nationals.

On August 8 Marcy wrote to Buchanan: "The occurrence at Greytown is an embarrassing affair. The place merited chastisement, but the severity of the one inflicted exceeded our expectations. The government will, however, I think, stand by Capt. Hollins."[13] The government had no choice. To admit the impropriety of Hollins' action, which was more or less warranted by his instructions, would put the administration in a hopeless position in domestic politics and would oblige it to satisfy the foreign claims.

President Pierce finally broke the official silence in his annual message to Congress on December 4, 1854. He brazened the matter out. After a tendentious and highly colored report of the events which were alleged to justify the destruction of Greytown, he undertook to remove the action from the category of war by denying the status of an organized society to Greytown and representing the community as a band of outlaws or pirates:

> Justice required that reparation should be made for so many and such gross wrongs, and that a course of insolence and plunder, tending directly to the insecurity of the lives of numerous travelers and of the rich treasure belonging to our citizens passing over this transit way, should be peremptorily arrested. Whatever it might be in other respects, the community in question, in power to do mischief, was not despicable. It was well provided with ordnance, small

[10] Mary W. Williams, *Anglo-American Isthmian Diplomacy* (New York: Russell & Russell, 1965) , pp. 179-80.
[11] *Ibid.*, p. 181.   [12] *Loc.cit.*   [13] *Loc.cit.*

arms, and ammunition, and might easily seize on the unarmed small boats, freighted with millions of property, which passed almost daily within its reach. It did not profess to belong to any regular government, and had, in fact, no recognized dependence on or connection with anyone to which the United States or their injured citizens might apply for redress or which could be held responsible in any way for the outrages committed. Not standing before the world in the attitude of an organized political society, being neither competent to exercise the rights nor to discharge the obligations of a government, it was, in fact, a marauding establishment too dangerous to be disregarded and too guilty to pass unpunished, and yet incapable of being treated in any other way than as a piratical resort of outlaws or a camp of savages depredating on emigrant trains or caravans and the frontier settlements of civilized states.[14]

This riot of language bore no relation to fact. There had been no complaint whatever that Greytown plundered or abused travelers. Neither the $24,000 at stake between Greytown and the Accessory Transit Company nor the insult to the American Minister involved any act of piracy or depredation. Pierce therefore supplemented his analogy to piracy with an analogy to acts of reprisal by European states: "If comparisons were to be instituted, it would not be difficult to present repeated instances in the history of states standing in the very front of modern civilization where communities far less offending and more defenseless than Greytown have been chastized with much greater severity, and where not cities only have been laid in ruins, but human life has been recklessly sacrificed and the blood of the innocent made profusely to mingle with that of the guilty."[15]

But Pierce was not able to offer any precedent in which the United States had inflicted injury on such a scale without an act of Congress.

This is the most famous case of unauthorized war-making by the executive in the nineteenth century. It is a precedent not to be imitated but to be avoided.

In cases of this class, the executive assumed that the use of force was not an exercise of the war power because the victim was not a formally organized state. The next stage of gravity is reached by limited incursions into the territory of an organized state which were not directed against the government of that state but against pirates or bandits who had taken shelter there. The undeclared Seminole War lasted from

---

[14] Richardson, *op.cit.*, Vol. 5, p. 282.   [15] *Ibid.*, p. 284.

1816 to 1818; General Jackson pursued the Seminoles into Florida and while there engaged the Spanish as well and hanged two British subjects: this last action touched off much criticism of the whole enterprise.

In 1817, on the orders of President Monroe, American forces attacked pirates and smugglers on Amelia Island in Spanish Florida. In 1822, 1823, 1824, and 1825, American commanders pursued pirates ashore in Cuba and destroyed their ships and bases. In 1827 naval vessels policing the waters about the Greek Islands not only destroyed piratical vessels at sea but twice landed in search of pirates. In 1857 Commodore Paulding arrested the filibusterer William Walker on Nicaraguan soil and returned him to Washington, where he was immediately released. President Buchanan confessed to Congress that Paulding's action had been improper, but insisted that he had acted with good intentions.[16] This extenuation provoked bitter criticism in Congress of Buchanan himself. In 1859 Captain Ford with fifty men pursued the bandit Cortino into Mexico. A large number of such pursuits occurred in the next fifty years; the latest occurred in 1916 when President Wilson sent a punitive force in pursuit of Pancho Villa. This force penetrated four hundred miles into Mexico and remained in that country several months; it engaged in hostilities with troops of the Mexican government. President Carranza protested against this invasion as a hostile act.

In a number of cases naval action has been taken against subordinate local authorities of a foreign state who had committed acts of hostility without the authorization of their national government. In 1863 occurred a naval engagement with ships of the Prince of Nagato of Japan in the straits of Shimonoseki; in 1864 an American ship participated in a successful allied attack on the Prince's forts on the shore. Conceivably the landing to protect citizens in Yokohama in 1868 could be brought under this heading. In 1871 forts in Korea which had shelled American ships were stormed and destroyed.

In still another class of cases, marines or sailors have been landed in order to protect United States citizens from a temporary threat of mob violence. In August of 1859 marines were landed in Woosung and Shanghai to protect citizens during a riot against foreigners. When the British shelled Alexandria, Egypt in 1882, causing fires and a breakdown of government, a force of 126 men was landed, primarily to

16 Richardson, op.cit., Vol. 5, p. 466.

protect the United States consulate; they were withdrawn the next day. There were a large number of such landings in China between 1911 and 1933, and considerable bodies of marines were stationed in various ports for long periods of time.

Mob violence usually has no political aspect; it is not an effort to overthrow the local government. The landing of American troops in time of revolution is another matter, for even undesignedly it may favor one side or the other. There have been a number of such landings. Sometimes they have been invited by the de jure government; sometimes they have been tolerated or indorsed; sometimes they have occurred over the objection of the de jure government; sometimes they have been welcomed by both parties. In 1852-1853, during a civil war in Argentina, there were several landings in Buenos Aires to protect citizens. In 1855 and 1858 there were landings in Uruguay in time of revolution, on the second occasion at the request of the de jure government. There have been a large number of landings to protect American citizens and interests in the Caribbean. These began with concern to keep the Isthmus routes open, so that Nicaragua and Colombia were the scenes; after the Spanish-American War the protection of citizens and their investments during a revolution became a cause for intervention in all the Central American and Caribbean states.

A broadening pattern of intervention can be discerned. The first cases are landings to protect the consulate or a railroad station. Next we find marines garrisoning trains to insure their movement across the Isthmus. We find American forces policing towns during a revolution, receiving the custody of a town from a retreating force and turning it over to the other faction when it arrives. When Panama rebelled and seceded from Colombia in 1903 President Theodore Roosevelt interposed American forces to prevent the Colombian government from attacking the rebels and thus aided the revolution.

The device of the "neutral zone" appears to have been invented in 1904. During a rebellion in the Dominican Republic against the Morales government, which enjoyed the favor of Washington, Commander Dillingham landed American forces and announced that there could be no fighting in the city of Puerto Plata. The rebels, who held the city, marched out to fight, were defeated, and were required to throw down their arms when they re-entered the city. The Morales government triumphed.

The same device worked to the disadvantage of the legitimate government in Nicaragua in 1910. Commander Gilmer of the *Paducah* issued a proclamation to both sides that there should be no bombardment of or fighting in Bluefields; he would permit no more than one hundred armed men in the city to serve as police. President Madriz complained to President Taft that this action enabled the rebels to neglect their base in Bluefields and to concentrate their forces and defeat him. Secretary of State Knox replied: "The United States took only the customary step of prohibiting bombardment or fighting by either faction within the unfortified and ungarrisoned city of Bluefields, thus protecting the preponderating American and other foreign interests."[17] On a later occasion, when General Rivas of the Madriz forces threatened to shell ships which were supplying the rebels, Commander Hines warned him that if he did so he would attack him. Madriz was defeated and fled.

Sometimes intervention for the ostensible purpose of protecting citizens in time of revolution is quite naked military intervention on one side or the other. In 1874 there was a dispute over the succession to the throne of Hawaii. At the request of the Hawaiian Minister of Foreign Affairs, relayed by the United States Minister to Hawaii, Commander Belknap landed 150 men and a Gatling gun, took possession of the courthouse, and insured the installation of King David Kalakaua. This action for the protection of the rights of American citizens was undertaken against an American citizen, the dowager Queen Emma, who was the other claimant of the throne.

In 1893, desiring to overthrow Queen Liliuokalana, American residents in Hawaii asked the Minister for forces to protect their lives and property. A party was landed from the U.S.S. *Boston,* and on the next day the Queen was deposed. Sanford B. Dole was made president and the Minister agreed to institute a kind of protectorate; the American flag was run up over public buildings. President Cleveland repudiated the whole proceeding and the flag came down. Dole, however, continued as the president of a republic until the annexation of Hawaii by the United States in 1898.

In 1899 there was a dispute over the succession to the throne of Samoa. One claimant was favored by the United States and Great Britain, the other by Germany. Rear Admiral Kautz occupied the town of Apia and insured the installation of King Malietoa. There was snip-

---

[17] Offutt, *op.cit.,* pp. 106-107.

ing from the other faction; with British help Kautz suppressed the rebels.

Dr. Juan Bosch was elected President of the Dominican Republic in 1963 by 58 percent of the vote in that country's first free election. He was not favored by Washington, and was overthrown by a military coup within a few months. On April 24, 1965 a portion of the army rebelled against the ruling military junta and called upon President Bosch to return. By April 28 the junta was hard-pressed, and Colonel Benoit asked for American assistance on the ground that their defeat would be a victory for communism. He was told that "the United States would not intervene *unless he said that he could not protect American citizens present in the Dominican Republic.*"[18] He amended his plea and on the same day President Johnson announced:

> The United States government has been informed that American lives are in danger. These authorities are no longer able to guarantee their safety and they have reported that the assistance of military personnel is now needed for that purpose. I have ordered the Secretary of Defense to put the necessary American troops ashore in order to give protection to hundreds of Americans who are still in the Dominican Republic and to escort them safely back to this country.[19]

To rescue these hundreds of Americans, 21,000 troops were landed and 9,000 more deployed on naval vessels off the shore. The troops were not withdrawn when the citizens were evacuated; they remained to insure that Bosch did not return and that his faction capitulated. This occurred.

Before intervening, President Johnson informed Congressional leaders "that United States Marines would be landed in Santo Domingo that night for the sole purpose of protecting the lives of Americans and other foreigners."[20] Senator Fulbright has written:

> Four months later, after an exhaustive review of the Dominican crisis by the Senate Foreign Relations Committee in closed sessions, it was clear beyond reasonable doubt that although saving American lives may have been a factor in the decision to intervene on

[18] J. William Fulbright, *The Arrogance of Power* (New York: Random House, 1966), p. 89. (Italics in original.)

[19] Richard P. Stebbins, ed., *Documents on American Foreign Relations, 1965* (New York: Harper & Row, 1966), p. 234.

[20] Fulbright, *op.cit.*, p. 49.

April 28, the major reason was a determination on the part of the United States government to defeat the rebel, or constitutionalist, forces whose victory at that time was imminent.[21]

One step further than intervening in a revolutionary situation is to attack the legitimate government of a foreign country in such a manner that the United States and that government are the only antagonists. In 1824 Commodore Porter of the *John Adams*, in reprisal for maltreatment of an American naval lieutenant, attacked the town of Foxardo in Puerto Rico and extorted apologies. He was recalled, court-martialed, and suspended for six months, whereupon he resigned. In 1831, on orders of President Jackson, the U.S.S. *Lexington* rescued the crews of three sealing schooners who had been imprisoned by the military governor of the Falkland Islands.

In 1853 Martin Koszta, a native of Hungary who had declared his intention of acquiring American citizenship but had not yet taken out his "second papers," was seized in Smyrna and carried aboard the Austrian vessel *Hussar*. Captain Ingraham of the American sloop of war *St. Louis* learned of this, trained his guns on the *Hussar*, and demanded the release of Koszta. The two commanders agreed to consult with the French consul and the outcome was that Koszta was awarded to Ingraham. Subsequently the Austrian government complained of Ingraham's conduct and demanded the return of Koszta, but President Pierce rejected the complaint and Congress voted the Captain a gold medal.

In 1851 Captain Pearson of the sloop of war *Dale* extorted from the king of Johanna Island $1,000 as indemnity for the imprisonment of an American whaling captain by threatening to bombard the town. In 1854, during the Taiping rebellion, the Imperial forces in Shanghai conducted themselves badly toward foreigners, and American and British forces landed and routed the Chinese. In 1856 a force of sailors and marines stormed and razed the "barrier forts" at Canton.

For some reason Clark, Offutt, and Rogers have omitted one of the most famous of these episodes. In 1904 Ion Perdicaris, an American citizen, was kidnapped by a Moroccan bandit, Ahmed ibn-Muhammed Raisuli, and was held for ransom. President Roosevelt sent ships of war to Tangier, and Secretary of State John Hay sent to Sultan Abd-al-Aziz IV a terse telegram, "Perdicaris alive or Raisuli dead." The Sultan, threatened with war, paid the ransom.

[21] *Loc.cit.*

Even before the establishment of the United Nations, the "pacific blockade" had dubious standing at international law. The United States was one of the states that recognized the validity under some circumstances of the pacific blockade, but it approved only of the interdiction of vessels belonging to the blockaded state. But in 1962 President Kennedy, without a recourse to Congress, announced what he called a pacific blockade of Soviet shipping bound for Cuba. This was a threat to commit an act of war against the Soviet Union without consulting Congress.

An intervention for the protection of citizens against a mob is sometimes converted into a war with the government of the state which is invaded. At the time of the Boxer Rebellion in China in 1900, President McKinley sent forces, eventually 5,000 men, in what began as an allied effort to rescue citizens in Peking and ended as a war with the Imperial Government of China. China was obliged to sign a protocol, which was never submitted to the Senate, promising to pay an indemnity of $330,000,000, of which $24,000,000 was to be paid to the United States.

In the twentieth century a still more spectacular level of intervention in the affairs of foreign states was reached. This consisted in actually taking over and administering the governments of foreign states by unauthorized executive action. Haiti was occupied from 1915 to 1934; after the initial conquest the marines conducted an election and this yielded a government which legitimized the occupation by treaty. In 1916 President Wilson occupied the Dominican Republic, and this state was under direct military government until 1922, when a Dominican government was installed; the marines were withdrawn in 1924. From 1912 to 1925, and from 1928 to 1933, the United States maintained a dominating military presence in Nicaragua. In 1906 the government of Cuba was paralyzed by insurrection. Thereupon President Theodore Roosevelt appointed Secretary of War Taft provisional governor; soon he replaced him with the governor of the Canal Zone. Troops were sent in; the occupation lasted three years. Roosevelt relied upon the so-called Platt amendment, which had been incorporated in the Cuban constitution in 1902 and in a treaty between the United States and Cuba ratified in 1904:

> The Government of Cuba consents that the United States may exercise the right to intervene for the preservation of Cuban inde-

pendence, the maintenance of a government adequate for the protection of life, property, and individual liberty, and for discharging the obligations with respect to Cuba imposed by the Treaty of Paris on the United States, now to be assumed and undertaken by the Government of Cuba.[22]

This brings up our last category of involvement, which might be called war by invitation. The Platt amendment did not authorize the President to intervene, but the United States; and in any case Cuba could not transfer the power of Congress to initiate military action to the President either by amending its constitution or by signing a treaty. But when an intervention is sanctioned by the law or government of the state invaded, the action looks less like war. And in some cases, of course, it is not war. In 1941 President Franklin D. Roosevelt occupied Greenland and Iceland by agreement with the local authorities, and in the same year he occupied Dutch Guiana by agreement with the Netherlands government-in-exile. Clearly he usurped the treaty power, but he did not usurp the war power, for there was no question of hostilities within these territories. In 1958 President Eisenhower landed troops in Lebanon "to protect American lives and by their presence there to encourage the Lebanese in defense of Lebanese sovereignty and integrity."[23] There was no military action and apparently no threat either to American citizens or to the Lebanese government; the fact seems to be that the government of Lebanon consented to the use of its territory as a staging area for possible action in Jordan.

The case is quite different with President Truman's intervention in the Korean war in 1950. He committed air and naval forces at the request of the South Korean government. Then he procured a vote of the Security Council of the United Nations appealing for action by members and he thereafter purported to act by authority of the United Nations. But Congress in enacting the United Nations Participation Act[24] in 1945 had stipulated that any agreement by which the United States supplied troops to the United Nations must be approved by Con-

---

[22] *Papers Relating to the Foreign Relations of the United States*, 85th Cong., 3d Sess., Doc. No. 1 (1905), p. 244.

[23] Message to Congress, *Congressional Record*, Vol. 104, Pt. 11 (July 15, 1958), pp. 1376-78. In his Ninth Annual Message, Jan. 12, 1961, President Eisenhower said: "Our Government responded to the request of the friendly Lebanese Government for military help, and promptly withdrew American forces as soon as the situation was stabilized." Fred L. Israel, ed., *The State of the Union Messages of the Presidents, 1790-1966* (New York: Chelsea House, Robert Hector, 1966), Vol. 3, p. 3109.

[24] 27 U.S.C. 287d; 59 Stat. 621 as amended 63 Stat. 735 (1949).

gress. Truman neither sought nor received any Congressional authorization for a war which lasted three years and cost more than 140,000
casualties.

Similarly President Johnson has engaged in two wars in Vietnam.
Presumably he is fighting the war in South Vietnam, which by October
of 1968 has cost well over 200,000 casualties, at the invitation of the
South Vietnamese government. The war against North Vietnam is
justified by the various other arguments we are examining.

If war by invitation is constitutional, there is a new and easy formula
for usurpation of the war power. It is only necessary for the executive
to lodge a puppet government on foreign territory, recognize it, and
then accept its invitation to send troops to suppress all opposition to
the puppet government. This has been the history of the American
intervention in South Vietnam. Apparently it was the plan that lay
behind the invasion of Cuba in 1961. The Bay of Pigs was chosen as a
landing point because it was relatively inaccessible from the rest of the
island. An informed study reports that "Dulles and Bissell did not
suggest that the Castro regime would topple the moment Artime's men
hit the beach, but they did predict that there would be enough uprisings around the country so that the beachhead could be held and consolidated and so that the rebels could establish a government on Cuban
soil which the United States then could recognize and support."[25] One
supposes that the support would have taken the form of landings of
marines and attacks from the air.

These are by no means all the cases in which the executive has committed American forces abroad or committed or threatened to commit acts of violence without Congressional authorization; but they
illustrate all the types of cases and include the more important ones.

VI. The Unaided Power of the President

It is clear that the President has the power to repel a sudden attack
upon the United States without waiting for authorization by Congress.
In Sections II, III, and IV we have reviewed official opinions concerning a great variety of proposals for hostilities; they add up to the
proposition that when the United States takes the initiative in the
use of military force, although for a limited objective, this is war and
requires the approval of Congress. But to this general proposition it
is sometimes said that there are two exceptions. These alleged excep-

---

[25] Andrew Tully, *CIA: The Inside Story* (New York: Morrow, 1962), p. 249.

tions embrace most of the cases of unauthorized action reviewed in Section V.

When the international law of war was taking form, there was a body of opinion which argued that neither intervention for the protection of citizens nor acts of reprisal were acts of war. International law is, to a degree, incorporated in American law. Therefore it has been argued that the President, under his power to execute the laws, may execute international law; that is, he may afford protection to citizens or may perpetrate acts of reprisal without Congressional authorization.[1]

J. Reuben Clark, the Solicitor of the State Department, who prepared the fullest study on the subject, distinguished between what he called "political intervention"—"an intervention by one power in the local affairs of another power"—and "interposition which is exercised solely for the protection of the citizens of the intervening state resident or domiciled within the non-protecting state." Apparently he assimilated acts of reprisal for injuries inflicted upon citizens to non-political interposition. Intervention was an act of war, and belonged to Congress; interposition was merely an execution of the laws and might be undertaken by the President.[2]

In fact, it is well settled that citizens have a constitutional right to protection at the municipal law of the United States. President Washington recognized this in his Neutrality Proclamation of 1793;[3] the Supreme Court recognized it as one of the rights of national citizenship in the *Slaughter-House Cases*[4] in 1873 and in *In re Neagle*[5] in 1890. The right to such protection is inherent in the idea of citizenship.

In the execution of the laws, the President may and should protect citizens from oppression in foreign countries. But in doing so he must observe constitutional limits. He may employ only those means which the Constitution places at his command. He could not, for example, impose a tax in order to rescue citizens, or make a treaty without the approval of the Senate in order to enlist foreign support in an effort to rescue citizens. Has he the right to employ force to rescue citizens without authorization by Congress?

[1] *Right to Protect Citizens in Foreign Countries by Landing Forces* (1912; Washington: Government Printing Office, 1934), pp. 44-48; Milton Offutt, *The Protection of Citizens Abroad by the Armed Forces of the United States* (Baltimore: Johns Hopkins Press, 1928), p. 5.

[2] *Op.cit.*, pp. 38-40.

[3] James D. Richardson, ed., *Messages and Papers of the Presidents 1789-1908* (Washington: Bureau of National Literature and Art, 1908), Vol. 1, p. 156.

[4] 16 Wall. 36.   [5] 135 U.S. 1.

As Secretary of State, Henry Clay advised in 1827 that the navy might not use force to liberate American seamen unjustly imprisoned in a foreign port: "The employment of force is justifiable in resisting aggressions before they are complete. But when they are consummated, the intervention of the authority of government becomes necessary if redress is refused by the aggressor."[6]

This seems reasonable. The right to resist aggression is analogous to the President's power to repel a sudden attack. It does not involve the initiation of hostilities. But to launch a rescue operation is to assume the initiative. We need not debate whether this is war at international law. It is clear that under the Constitution the power of Congress to declare war embraces limited war and very limited war—all recourse to force in international relations. It makes no difference that the President's purpose is to redress a wrong, and that redressing the wrong is permitted by international law. War is a sanction for redressing wrongs, but by the Constitution this sanction is entrusted only to Congress.

There is some authority to the contrary. In the last chapter we noted the rescue of Martin Koszta from an Austrian ship of war by Captain Ingraham of the *St. Louis*. President Pierce approved Ingraham's action in his annual message on December 5, 1853:

> After a careful consideration of the case I came to the conclusion that Koszta was seized without legal authority at Smyrna; that he was wrongfully detained on board of the Austrian brig of war; that at the time of his seizure he was clothed with the nationality of the United States, and that the acts of our officers, under the circumstances of the case, were justifiable, and their conduct has been fully approved by me, and a compliance with the several demands of the Emperor of Austria has been denied.[7]

In 1890, in *In re Neagle*,[8] the Supreme Court held that it was lawful for the President to assign a bodyguard for Justice Field, even though no act of Congress authorized it. Justice Miller said that it was the President's duty to take care that the laws be faithfully executed, and asked: "Is this duty limited to the enforcement of acts of Congress or of treaties of the United States according to their express terms, or does it include the rights, duties and obligations growing out of the Constitution

---

[6] John Bassett Moore, *Digest of International Law* (Washington: Government Printing Office, 1906), Vol. 7, p. 163.

[7] Richardson, *op.cit.*, Vol. 5, p. 210.   [8] 135 U.S. 1.

itself, our international relations and all the protection implied by the nature of the government under the Constitution?" In order to show that there are non-statutory rights which the President may and should protect, Justice Miller adverted to the case of Koszta, and asked: "upon what act of Congress then existing can any one lay his finger in support of the action of our government in this matter?"

The proposition that dicta are unreliable because they raise problems which the court may not have thought through is vindicated here. Miller wished to show that there were rights which the executive might enforce without statutory authorization, and adduced the right of citizens to protection abroad. But he seemed also to approve of the means employed to protect this right, although that means involved an unauthorized threat of force. This issue was not germane to his argument.

Justice Miller pointed out that Congress had voted Captain Ingraham a gold medal. This does not seem to indicate a Congressional recognition that the field belongs to the executive so much as to constitute a legislative ratification of the action.

In one class of cases, the Constitution explicitly forbids the executive to use force for the protection of citizens without the authorization of Congress. Article I, Section 8 authorizes Congress "to define and punish piracies and felonies on the high seas, and offenses against the law of nations." On April 30, 1790, Congress passed the first act against piracy.[9] On March 3, 1819, the President was authorized and requested "to employ so many of the public armed vessels as, in his judgment, the services may require, with suitable instructions to the commanders thereof, in protecting the merchant vessels of the United States and their crews from piratical aggressions and depredations."[10] And on December 20, 1822, Congress appropriated $160,000 for the suppression of piracy and to afford "effectual protection to the citizens and commerce of the United States."[11]

On at least two other occasions Congress has asserted its jurisdiction over the topic of the protection of citizens abroad. In 1856 Congress enacted that when a citizen of the United States should discover a deposit of guano on an island "not within the lawful jurisdiction of any other government" he might, with the approval of the President, occupy the island in the name of the United States. The act provided "That the President of the United States is hereby authorized, at his discre-

[9] 1 Stat. 112.   [10] 3 Stat. 510.
[11] 3 Stat. 720.

tion, to employ the land and naval forces of the United States to protect the rights of the said discoverer or discoverers or their assigns."[12]

In the nineteenth century, European states which did not recognize the right of expatriation dealt with naturalized American citizens who returned to their birthplace as though they still owed the obligations of their original citizenship. In 1868 Congress affirmed the right of expatriation and enacted that naturalized citizens should receive the same protection abroad as native-born citizens, and

> That whenever it shall be made known to the President that any citizen of the United States has been unjustly deprived of his liberty by or under the authority of any foreign government, it shall be the duty of the President forthwith to demand of that government the reasons for such imprisonment, and if it appears to be wrongful and in violation of the rights of American citizenship, the President shall forthwith demand the release of such citizen, and if the release so demanded is unreasonably delayed or refused, it shall be the duty of the President to use such means, *not amounting to acts of war,* as he may think necessary and proper to obtain or effectuate such release, and all the facts and proceedings relative thereto shall as soon as practicable be communicated by the President to Congress.[13]

Whatever one may think of the legality of unauthorized landings in foreign territory to protect citizens, the case for unauthorized executive reprisals is much weaker. Here it is not a question of averting injury, or of rescuing beleaguered citizens. A reprisal is a military act performed for the purpose of inflicting harm. The decision to perform such acts belongs to Congress.

In 1793 Secretary of State Thomas Jefferson wrote:

> The making of a reprisal on a nation is a very serious thing. Remonstrance and refusal of satisfaction ought to precede; and when reprisal follows, it is considered an act of war, and never failed to produce it in the case of a nation able to make war; besides, if the case were important and ripe for that step, Congress must be called upon to take it; the right of reprisal being expressly lodged with them by the Constitution, and not with the executive.[14]

As we have seen, Presidents have several times asked Congress for authority to make reprisals, and sometimes Congress has authorized

---

[12] 11 Stat. 119.
[14] Moore, *op.cit.,* Vol. 7, p. 123.
[13] 15 Stat. 223. (Italics supplied.)

them—against Paraguay in 1857 and against Colombia in 1890. Wilson requested authority to make reprisal against Mexico in 1914 and then anticipated the Congressional action, which must be regarded as a ratification. Presidents Monroe, Jackson, and Buchanan requested the power to make reprisals and were denied it. In the committee report refusing Jackson's request, Henry Clay pointed out that "The framers of our Constitution have manifested their sense of the nature of this power, by associating it in the same clause with grants to Congress of the power to declare war, and to make rules concerning captures on land and water."[15]

Nevertheless, the bombardment of Greytown in 1854 is very frequently cited as evidence that the President possesses a native power of reprisal. We have seen that President Pierce defended Captain Hollins' action out of desperation rather than out of conviction. But the legality of the action was upheld by Justice Nelson of the Supreme Court while sitting on circuit in *Durand v. Hollins*[16] in 1860.

In vindicating the property rights of American citizens, Captain Hollins destroyed the property of Durand, an American citizen in Greytown, and Durand sued him for damages. Justice Nelson took an expansive view of the President's powers:

> As the executive head of the nation, the president is made the only legitimate organ of the general government, to open and carry on correspondence or negotiations with foreign nations, in matters concerning the interests of the country or its citizens. It is to him, also, the citizens abroad must look for protection of person and of property and for the faithful execution of laws existing and intended for their protection. For this purpose, the whole executive power of the country is placed in his hands, under the Constitution, and the laws passed in pursuance thereof; and different departments of government have been organized, through which this power may be most conveniently executed, whether by negotiation or by force —a department of state and a department of the navy.
>
> Now, as it respects the interposition of the executive abroad, for the protection of the lives or property of the citizen, the duty must, of necessity, rest in the discretion of the president. Acts of lawless violence, or of threatened violence to the citizen or his property, cannot be anticipated and provided for; and the protection, to be effectual or of any avail, may, not infrequently, require the most

---

[15] *Ibid.*, p. 127.   [16] 8 Fed. Cas. 111.

prompt and decided action. Under our system of government, the citizen abroad is as much entitled to protection as the citizen at home. The great object and duty of government is the protection of the lives, liberty, and property of the people composing it, whether abroad or at home; and any government failing in the accomplishment of the object, or the performance of the duty, is not worth preserving.

I have said, that the interposition of the president abroad, for the protection of the citizen, must necessarily rest in his discretion; and it is quite clear that, in all cases where a public act or order rests in executive discretion neither he nor his authorized agent is personally civilly responsible for the consequences.[17]

This opinion has nothing to do with the case. It is an argument that the President must have power to act speedily to prevent harm to citizens abroad; he cannot wait to consult Congress. But what was involved in the bombardment of Greytown was not the protection of citizens but reprisal. There was no feature of urgency. The Secretary of the Navy gave Hollins his instructions. Congress could have done so as well.

We may suspect that Justice Nelson, as a partisan Democrat, was concerned to vindicate the action of a Democratic President. When he wrote the bitter dissenting opinion in the *Prize Cases*[18] in 1863, Justice Nelson expressed a very different opinion of the powers of a Republican President.

There was available a more plausible justification. President Pierce himself had asserted that the action was not war because Greytown was not a political community: it was "a piratical resort of outlaws." John Bassett Moore thought this a satisfactory argument. Denouncing Wilson's occupation of Vera Cruz as an act of war, he said: "The Greytown incident, which has often been cited to prove that such a

---

[17] Id. at 112. In 1868 a French subject who had suffered loss in the destruction of Greytown brought an action against the United States in the Court of Claims. That Court ruled that it lacked jurisdiction. "The claimant's case must necessarily rest upon the assumption that the bombardment and destruction of Greytown was illegal and not justified by the law of nations. And hinging upon that, it will be readily seen that the questions raised are such as can only be determined between the United States and the governments whose citizens it is alleged have been injured by the injurious acts of this government. They are international political questions, which no court of this country in a case of this kind is authorized or empowered to decide." Perrin v. United States 4 Ct. Cl. 543 (1868).

[18] 2 Black, 635, 682 (1863).

proceeding would not be war or an act of war, can not properly be invoked as a precedent, since Greytown was a community claiming to exist outside the bounds of any recognized state or political entity, and the legality of the action taken against it was defended by President Pierce and Secretary Marcy on that express ground."[19]

Most of the State Department's 125 purported precedents for the Vietnamese War were interventions for the protection of citizens; a few were acts of reprisal and there were a few others. The mere fact that they occurred does not establish their legality. If this were true, the frequency with which banks are robbed would establish the legality of bank robbery. The analogy is worth pursuing. Just as a bank robber acts only when he thinks he can escape apprehension, so on most occasions when Presidents have usurped the war power there has been little likelihood of complaint or political retribution. Landings on the soil of states that had no navies, and acts of violence against defenseless distant ports, disturbed no domestic interest. They were more likely to produce applause than censure. "Perdicaris alive or Raisuli dead" evokes in Congressmen and citizenry that thrill of aggressive national pride which they seem to value more highly than they value constitutional government.

This is not to suggest that it is always morally discreditable to prefer other values to legal values. The tradition that prefers religious to legal values is very old. And, as Aristotle pointed out, because of the generality of legal rules their literal application may produce in marginal cases results which are inconsistent with the values of the legal order itself. In these circumstances he recommended the abandonment of law for equity, to do what the lawgiver would have done "if he had known."[20] American law has no such formal alternative. Very often the solution in what are called hardship cases is to abandon the general rule and introduce a local rule which gives legal status to a value which was originally exterior to the formal legal order. This practice is commemorated in the maxim, "Hard cases make bad law."

In some cases the forcible intrusion of non-legal values into the legal order produces only a local asymmetry, unaesthetic but otherwise insignificant. But in other cases the incorporation of alien values may entail the surrender of basic values of the legal order. We are given to understand that this is the case with the protection of citizens abroad.

[19] "The Control of the Foreign Relations of the United States," in *The Collected Papers of John Bassett Moore* (New Haven: Yale University Press, 1944), Vol. 5, p. 196.

[20] *Nicomachean Ethics*, v. 10.

Apparently the State Department believes that the only way to justify the landing of six sailors in a longboat to rescue a citizen is to concede that the President has a constitutional right to commit 525,000 men in a foreign war without the consent of Congress. Surely the State Department has made the wrong choice. If this is necessary in order to restrain the President, it is better to restrain the longboat. As Abraham Lincoln said, the possession of the war power by a single man was understood by the Constitutional Convention to be "the most oppressive of all kingly oppressions"; but the view of the State Department "destroys the whole matter, and places our President where kings have always stood."[21] The assignment of the war power to Congress is an essential feature of the political philosophy of the Constitution. The framers had learned from the history of Rome that the concentration of uncontrolled military power in the hands of a single man means the end of republican government.

In the past, the official apology for landings to protect citizens and for acts of reprisal has always been that they were not acts of war at international law and that the President in performing them was merely executing international or municipal law. On this theory, these cases are not precedents for President Johnson's engaging in what is undeniably war at international law in South Vietnam and North Vietnam. He is not making landings to protect citizens; nor is he engaging in measured acts of reprisal for injury to citizens.

But despite J. Reuben Clark, there is not even a persuasive legal case for unauthorized landings or acts of reprisal. The Constitution reserves to Congress the exclusive right to initiate hostilities. It is possible to account for the precedents without legalizing them. On various occasions, for reasons more or less appealing, executive officers have overstepped their authority. President Buchanan acknowledged that he had no inherent authority to make landings to protect citizens, but said that any President would in case of need do so "on his own responsibility."[22] Undoubtedly many naval commanders likewise acted on their own responsibility. Nor does our legal system necessarily leave them in the lurch. If the circumstances appear compelling, if the officer has acted in good faith and with good judgment, there is every likelihood that Congress will ratify his action.

J. Reuben Clark, who asserted that interposition for the protection of citizens was proper, believed that intervention, or interference with the internal political affairs of another state, was improper. On these principles, it seems that when an interposition grows to such magnitude as to involve collision with an army of the state which is invaded, interposition has passed into intervention, and even on Clark's principles the approval of Congress is needed. The American intervention in China at the time of the Boxer Rebellion, the Pershing expedition in pursuit of Pancho Villa, were war. And indeed a United States Circuit Court held that the Boxer invasion was war for the purposes of the Articles of War;[23] a Texas court held that the hostilities with Mexico were war for purposes of state criminal law;[24] a Pennsylvania court held that the Korean war was war in the meaning of the language of an insurance policy.[25] These are not decisions that the President has a right to make war. Clearly he has no such right. They are decisions that the President, when he represented himself as taking action less than war—as in the protection of American citizens or in reprisal—had in fact intruded on the authority of Congress and had made war.

In the twentieth century, as we have seen, there emerged a third occasion for participation in war abroad, war by invitation. The fact that the President is invited to send troops by what he recognizes as the legitimate government of a foreign state insures that we are not at war with that foreign state when he sends troops. But if the purpose of sending troops is to engage in combat with another government or local faction, we are at war with that government or that faction. The Korean War and the intervention in South Vietnam are the best examples of war by invitation.

The United States originally put troops in Vietnam at the invitation of the Emperor Bao Dai. In 1955 Diem, with American assistance,[26] ousted Bao Dai; Diem renewed the invitation. As a result of an American decision,[27] Diem was overthrown and murdered in 1963; the new government was presumed to have extended the invitation; and all the succeeding military dictatorships have been equally hospitable to their

[23] Hamilton v. McClaughry, 136 Fed. 445 (C.C.D. Kan. 1905).

[24] Arce v. State, 83 Tex. Crim. R. 292, 202 S.W. 951 (1918).

[25] Beley v. Pennsylvania Mutual Life Ins. Co., 373 Pa. 231, 95 A.2d 202 (1953).

[26] Joseph Buttinger, *Vietnam: A Dragon Embattled* (New York: Praeger, 1967), Vol. 2, pp. 880-81 and accompanying notes.

[27] For an incomplete but adequate documentation of American responsibility for the coup, see Anthony T. Bouscaren, *The Last of the Mandarins: Diem of Vietnam* (Pittsburgh: Duquesne University Press, 1965), chap. 9. See also Jean Lacouture, *Le Vietnam entre deux paix* (Paris: Editions du Seuil, 1965), pp. 95-101.

dangerous guest. Active participation of United States military forces in the fighting in South Vietnam appears to date from 1961. This too has been on the invitation of the successive Saigon regimes.

Very clearly an invitation to engage in combat from Premier Ky or President Thieu is no substitute for an act of Congress. No Vietnamese government can authorize President Johnson to engage in war in South Vietnam. But he has no other authority. He cannot pretend to be protecting citizens or vindicating their rights by reprisal.

In the case of the war with North Vietnam, there is not even an invitation. When on February 7, 1965, President Johnson launched air raids against North Vietnam, he relied on the theory of reprisal. The White House announcement of that date said that these were "retaliatory attacks" in response to specified injuries:

> Commencing at 2 a.m. on February 7th, Saigon time (1 p.m. yesterday, eastern standard time), two South Vietnamese airfields, two U.S. barracks areas, several villages, and one town in South Viet-Nam were subjected to deliberate surprise attacks. Substantial casualties resulted.
>
> Our intelligence has indicated, and this action confirms, that Hanoi has ordered a more aggressive course of action against both South Vietnamese and American installations.[28]

If the President's power to execute the laws of the United States includes a power of reprisal, it cannot include a power of reprisal for injuries done to the South Vietnamese. But the mention of reprisal was merely a pretext to prepare the way for escalation. Reprisal is a measured response to a specified injury. Johnson embarked upon a program of bombing which exceeds in intensity the bombing of Germany in the Second World War. The announced purposes of the bombing were to destroy the routes by which assistance passed to those fighting the Americans in South Vietnam, and goods in passage or likely to pass to South Vietnam; to destroy domestic facilities, so as to divert materials and labor to repair in North Vietnam and thus reduce the volume of assistance to South Vietnamese who were fighting Ameri-

---

[28] The announcement is reproduced in *Vietnam and International Law* by the Consultative Council of the Lawyers Committee on American Policy towards Vietnam (Flanders, N.J.: O'Hare Books, 1967), p. 151.

cans;[29] and to break the will of the North Vietnamese.[30] This is not reprisal; it is general war. Whatever one thinks of lesser actions, an enterprise on this scale can be authorized only by Congress.

There is another way of approaching the problem of the war power of the executive. If it can be shown that the President lacks the legal power to take action in foreign affairs which falls short of the use of armed force, it seems to follow that he has no power to engage in actual hostilities.

In 1793 President Washington issued a proclamation of neutrality in the current European war, and adjured all citizens to observe neutrality under penalty of prosecution.[31] On the theory that the law of nations required the neutrality of citizens of a neutral state, and that the President could by proclamation invoke the law of nations, Gideon Henfield was indicted for serving on a French privateer. Henfield was acquitted by the jury, and the legal theory was abandoned.[32] Much the same problem arose in *Gelston v. Hoyt*[33] in 1818. The President directed the collector and the surveyor of customs of New York to seize a vessel for violations of the Neutrality Act of 1794. But the statute permitted him to act only through the land or naval forces; the Supreme Court held that executive seizure by civil authority was therefore illegal.

Retortion is the practice of peaceful retaliation, whereas reprisal is retaliation by force. A series of non-intercourse acts was passed during the Napoleonic wars, and in 1817,[34] 1818,[35] and 1820[36] Congress passed acts closing our ports to British ships because the British naviga-

[29] Among other statements, consider that of General Harold Johnson, Army Chief of Staff, on the CBS News television program on August 12, 1967 in defense of the bombing that it slows up supplies to the South but "More importantly, it creates a disruption" so that the enemy is obliged to spend more effort in supplying the people of North Vietnam.

[30] This is called "bringing the enemy to the conference table." The conference contemplated is one which will eventuate in the capitulation of North Vietnam, a state with which, purportedly, we are not at war. This means there can be no conference until the enemy is ready to accept Johnson's terms. The long record of evasion of discussions and of outright lies to the American public about North Vietnamese proposals to negotiate on the part of the Johnson administration is documented in Edward S. Herman and Richard B. DuBoff, *America's Vietnam Policy: The Strategy of Deception* (Washington: Public Affairs Press, 1966) and Franz Schurman, Peter Dale Scott, and Reginald Zelnik, *The Politics of Escalation in Vietnam* (Boston: Beacon Press, 1966).

[31] *Supra*, note 3.

[32] See the discussion in Bernard Schwartz, *Commentary on the Constitution of the United States* (New York: Macmillan, 1963), Vol. 2, p. 174.

[33] 3 Wheat, 246.

[34] 3 Stat. 351.

[35] 3 Stat. 432.

[36] 3 Stat. 612.

tion acts restricted the carrying trade to British colonies in the western hemisphere to British vessels. The passage of these acts is clear evidence that non-amicable peaceful retaliation through the interruption of commerce belongs to Congress, and indeed there is a decision to that effect. In 1810 President Madison undertook by proclamation to revive the Non-Intercourse Act of 1809. Justice Story of the Supreme Court, sitting as circuit judge, held that this was an attempt to accomplish by executive action what could only be done by act of Congress; the President had no power to impose an embargo on trade.[37] Chief Justice Marshall indorsed this opinion.[38]

In 1870 President Grant asked Congress for authority to respond to Canadian maltreatment of American fishermen by suspending the laws authorizing the transit of goods in bond across the United States to Canada and, if necessary, excluding Canadian vessels from American waters.[39]

The fact that retortion is legal at international law does not authorize the President to practice it. If the power invoked for this purpose belongs to Congress, only Congress may undertake retortion. On the other hand, the President may use his own constitutional powers for the purpose of retortion. After an initial period of uncertainty, it became settled that the President may on his own authority interrupt diplomatic relations with a foreign state; and this has been done by way of retortion.[40]

It would be odd if the President were unable to take peaceful action authorized by international law, such as the invocation of neutrality and embargo, because these topics are assigned to Congress, and were empowered to take the greater step of initiating hostilities in reliance on international law. The initiation of hostilities belongs only to Congress.

On the whole question, it is impossible to improve on the words of the distinguished international lawyer John Bassett Moore, the author of *Moore's Digest*:

> There can hardly be room for doubt that the framers of the constitution, when they vested in Congress the power to declare war,

---

37 The Orinoco, 18 Fed. Cas. 830 (C.C. Mass. 1812).

38 Schwartz, *op.cit.*, p. 182.   39 Richardson, *op.cit.*, Vol. 7, p. 104.

40 A rather more doubtful case occurred in 1855. The Chinese government admitted a claim for injuries to a citizen of the United States but refused to pay. The United States minister to China was instructed to withhold customs duties in his hands to the amount of the claim, and this was done. John Bassett Moore, *Digest of International Law*, Vol. 7, p. 106.

never imagined they were leaving it to the executive to use the military and naval forces of the United States all over the world for the purpose of actually coercing other nations, occupying their territory, and killing their soldiers and citizens, all according to his own notions of the fitness of things, so long as he refrained from calling his action war or persisted in calling it peace.[41]

VII. SEATO and Other Commitments

The Southeast Asia Collective Defense Treaty[1] was ratified by the Senate in 1955. The other parties were Australia, France, New Zealand, Pakistan, the Philippines, Thailand, and Great Britain. It was to apply in "the general area of Southeast Asia, including also the entire territory of the Asian Parties, and the general area of the Southwest Pacific not including the Pacific area north of 21 degrees 30 minutes north latitude." By protocol the parties specified that the treaty should apply to Cambodia, Laos, "and the free territory under the jurisdiction of the State of Vietnam."

The purpose of a treaty is to raise an obligation at international law between the signatories. It need hardly be said that the obligations which we incurred in the SEATO treaty run only to the other signatories of the treaty. South Vietnam was not a party: indeed, the treaty does not recognize the existence of a state of South Vietnam, but only of a state of Vietnam, of which, at the Geneva Conference of 1954, the Hanoi government of Ho Chi Minh was accepted as the international spokesman.[2] The treaty therefore imposes no duty upon

---

[41] "The Control of the Foreign Relations of the United States," p. 196.

---

[1] *United States Treaties and Other International Agreements* (Washington: Government Printing Office, 1955), Vol. 6, Pt. 1, pp. 82-88. The treaty is reproduced in *Vietnam and International Law* by the Consultative Council of the Lawyers Committee on American Policy towards Vietnam (Flanders, N.J.: O'Hare Books, 1967), pp. 152-4.

[2] Both the Saigon government of Bao Dai and the Hanoi government were represented at the Geneva Conference. Between 1949 and 1954 the French had made seventeen ambiguous statements to the effect that Vietnam was an independent state; on June 4, 1954, a treaty with Saigon to this effect was initialed, but it was never signed, ratified, or implemented. Bernard B. Fall, *Viet-Nam Witness, 1953-66* (New York: Praeger, 1966), p. 56; Fall, *The Two Viet-Nams* (2d ed.; New York: Praeger, 1967), pp. 222-3. Bao Dai had been appointed by the French and had no other support; realistically viewed, he was a colonial representative of the French, and so they continued to treat him. On July 20, 1954, the French and the Hanoi government, as the two interested parties—the French did not even consult Saigon—signed the "Agreement on the Cessation of Hostilities in Vietnam." This agreement provided for a cease-fire and the withdrawal of the forces of "the People's Army of Vietnam" to a northern zone and of those of the French Union to a

us toward the so-called state of South Vietnam. Three of the signatories to whom we are obligated under the treaty disapprove of or have refused to support the war in either South or North Vietnam. Four have made token commitment of troops for the war in South Vietnam: Australia and New Zealand, because they believe they are buying American protection in the event of a future war with mainland Asia; and the Philippines and Thailand, which are pensionary states of the United States. But none of these has joined in the attack on North Vietnam. It is not only the case that the war against North Vietnam does not discharge any legal obligation to any party to the SEATO Treaty: it is conducted completely outside the framework of the Southeast Asia Collective Defense Organization and without the support of any member of the Organization.

But the State Department has invented a dazzling new theory of the treaty power. Article VI of the Constitution provides that treaties, like the Constitution and acts of Congress, shall be "the supreme law of the land." The purpose of including this provision was to give assurance to foreign states that international obligations would be observed. But the State Department now contends that a treaty can work conse-

---

southern zone in order to prevent the resumption of hostilities; it provided for enforcement of the cease-fire by the French commander-in-chief and the commander-in-chief of the People's Army of Vietnam. But the regrouping zones were to endure only until "the general elections which will bring about the unification of Vietnam." On July 21, Anthony Eden, who presided, presented to the Geneva Conference a "Final Declaration." Among other things, this Declaration indorsed the Franco-Vietnamese armistice agreement and recognized "that the military demarcation line is provisional and should not in any way be interpreted as constituting a political or territorial boundary." It provided for general elections in July, 1956 for the unification of Vietnam; these were to be supervised by the International Supervisory Commission which was to be created under the armistice agreement. France, Great Britain, the People's Republic of China, the Soviet Union, Cambodia, Laos, and the Hanoi government orally announced their acceptance of the Declaration. Under Secretary Bedell Smith said that the United States was not prepared to join in the Declaration but said that the United States would not disturb the agreements by force or the threat of force, and that it favored the unification of countries divided against their will by free elections supervised by the United Nations. On August 23, 1965, Secretary Rusk said that this statement "in effect embraced those agreements on behalf of the United States." Edward S. Herman and Richard B. DuBoff, *America's Vietnam Policy: The Strategy of Deception* (Washington: Public Affairs Press, 1966), p. 16n. Only Tran Van Don of Saigon denounced the settlement as "catastrophic and immoral." The documents are reproduced in *Vietnam and International Law*, pp. 137-50. The history is reviewed in Joseph Buttinger, *Vietnam: A Dragon Embattled* (New York: Praeger, 1967), Vol. 2, pp. 824-44. It was not until October 26, 1955 that Diem officially ousted Bao Dai, ending the French tie and making South Vietnam (or all of Vietnam, as he claimed) "independent." The SEATO treaty, which was signed September 8, 1954, could involve no obligation to a state which came into existence more than a year later.

quences in municipal law where no international obligation is involved. Thus a treaty becomes a piece of domestic legislation like an act of Congress, and the other parties to the treaty merely decorative supernumeraries.

Article IV, Section I of the SEATO Treaty provides that "each Party recognizes that aggression by means of armed attack in the treaty area against any of the Parties or against any state or territory which the Parties by unanimous agreement may hereafter designate, would endanger its own peace and safety, and agrees that it will in that event act to meet the common danger in accordance with its constitutional processes." There was no consultation with the Southeast Asia Treaty Organization before President Johnson attacked North Vietnam on February 7, 1965. The position of the State Department is that the treaty authorizes independent decision and independent action by any signatory. Consequently it would be open to France to regard Johnson's activities as an "armed attack in the treaty area" and to "act to meet the common danger" under the aegis of the treaty. An interpretation of the treaty which makes it possible for the American action to be simultaneously legal and illegal is an odd interpretation.

Not only did President Johnson not consult SEATO; although the treaty requires that each signatory act "in accordance with its constitutional processes," he did not consult Congress either. The claim that the treaty relieves the President of the need to consult Congress was first advanced in 1966 in the State Department memorandum:

> Under Article VI of the United States Constitution, "all treaties made, or which shall be made, under the Authority of the United States, shall be the supreme Law of the Land." Article IV, paragraph 1, of the SEATO treaty establishes as a matter of law that a Communist armed attack against South Vietnam endangers the peace and safety of the United States. In this same provision the United States has undertaken a commitment in the SEATO Treaty to "act to meet the common danger in accordance with its constitutional processes" in the event of such an attack.

> Under our Constitution it is the President who must decide when an armed attack has occurred. He has also the constitutional responsibility for determining what measures of defense are required when the peace and safety of the United States are endangered. If he considers that deployment of U.S. forces to South Vietnam is required, and that military measures against the source of Communist

aggression in North Vietnam are necessary, he is constitutionally empowered to take those measures.[3]

The first difficulty with this argument is the assumption that the President and the Senate may use the instrumentality of a treaty to make war, depriving the House of Representatives of its voice. If this is true, the President and the Senate might make a treaty with Liberia, let us say, and then embark upon a war with any country in the world. This is to substitute Liberia for our House of Representatives.

Although a treaty made within the scope of the treaty-making power is equally with an act of Congress the supreme law of the land, it is clear that some powers are vested exclusively in Congress. The framers intended this to be true of the war power. Alexander Hamilton submitted a draft proposal to the Constitutional Convention which would have vested the power to make war in the Senate,[4] but the report of the committee of detail gave it to the Congress. When this clause came up for debate, Charles Pinckney suggested that the power should be given to the Senate—"It would be singular for one authority to make war, and another peace"—but he found no second.[5] As we have seen, the report of the committee was adopted with a change of the word "make" to "declare."

The question of the scope of the treaty power arose in the first decade of our constitutional history. The Jay Treaty with Great Britain was ratified by the Senate in 1795, but it was very unpopular. In 1796 it was argued in the House that the House of Representatives was legally bound to appropriate money to pay the British claims recognized as valid by the treaty. James Madison replied that on such a theory the President and the Senate might by treaty deprive the House of its voice in making war, which appeared to him unthinkable: "Under a constitutional obligation with such sanctions to it, Congress, in case the President and Senate should enter into an alliance for war, would be nothing more than the heralds for proclaiming it."[6]

The House adopted a resolution drafted by Madison declaring that it was entitled to an independent judgment on all appropriations, and then voted money to satisfy the British claims.

[3] *Memorandum*, in *Vietnam and International Law*, p. 124.

[4] Charles C. Tansill, ed., *Documents Illustrative of the Union of the American States* (Washington: Government Printing Office, 1927), pp. 979-88.

[5] *Ibid.*, pp. 561-2.

[6] Quoted by Edward S. Corwin, *The President: Office and Powers* (New York: New York University Press, 1940), p. 401.

In his argument Madison contended that a treaty could not establish binding law on any topic on which Congress possessed legislative power. This is unquestionably too broad. Congress has the power to regulate commerce with foreign states, but treaties concerning commerce have been familiar since the beginning of our history, and appear to have been challenged only when they altered import duties.

But the right of the House of Representatives to participate in the making of appropriations is universally admitted. Sitting on circuit in 1852, Justice McLean of the Supreme Court said:

> A treaty under the federal constitution is said to be the supreme law of the land. This, unquestionably, applies to all treaties, where the treaty-making power, without the aid of Congress, can carry it into effect. It is not, however, and cannot be the supreme law of the land, where the concurrence of Congress is necessary to give it effect. Until this power is exercised, as where the appropriation of money is required, the treaty is not perfect. It is not operative, in the sense of the constitution, as money cannot be appropriated by the treaty-making power. This results from the limitations of our government. The action of no department of our government can be regarded as a law until it shall have all the sanctions required by the constitution to make it such. As well might be contended that an ordinary act of Congress, without the signature of the President, was a law, as that the treaty which engages to pay a sum of money is in itself a law.

> And in such a case the representatives of the people and the States exercise their own judgments in granting or withholding the money. They act upon their own responsibility and not upon the responsibility of the treaty-making power. It cannot bind or control the legislative action in this respect, and every foreign government may be presumed to know, that so far as the treaty stipulates to pay money, the legislative sanction is required.[7]

The House of Representatives again asserted its right when it appropriated money to complete the Alaska purchase in 1867. It was argued in the House that because action by the House was necessary the ratification of the treaty should have been made expressly conditional upon the consent of the House; and the admonition that some treaty provisions "cannot be carried into full force and effect except

---

[7] Turner v. American Baptist Missionary Union, 2 McLean, 344 (1952).

by legislation to which the consent of both Houses of Congress is necessary" was incorporated in the appropriation bill.[8]

Since the Constitution says that "All bills for raising revenue shall originate in the House of Representatives," it might appear to be even more clear that a tax cannot be imposed by treaty. And surely no one would suppose this possible in the case of internal revenue. But the issue has been debated with regard to treaties altering import duties.

The treaty of Ghent, which was negotiated with Great Britain in 1815, contained provisions for reduction of import duties. In the House of Representatives Cyrus King revived Madison's position, that "whenever a treaty or convention does, by any of its provisions, encroach upon any of the enumerated powers vested by the Constitution in the Congress of the United States, such treaty or convention, after being ratified, must be laid before Congress, and such provisions cannot be carried into effect without an act of Congress." King received support in the House, and the two houses created a conference committee to discuss differences. The committee members reported that

> They are persuaded that the House of Representatives does not assert the pretension that no treaty can be made without their assent; nor do they contend that in all cases legislative aid is indispensably necessary, either to give validity to a treaty, or to carry it into execution. On the contrary, they are believed to admit, that to some, nay many treaties, no legislative sanction is required.
>
> On the other hand the committee are no less satisfied that it is by no means the intention of the Senate to assert the treaty-making power to be in all cases independent of the legislative authority. So far from it, that they are believed to acknowledge the necessity of legislative enactment to carry into execution all treaties which contain stipulations requiring appropriations, or which might bind the nation to lay taxes, raise armies, to support navies, to grant subsidies, to create states, or to cede territory; if indeed this power exists in the government at all.[9]

On December 23, 1815 President Madison sent a message to Congress requesting that such legislative provisions as were necessary should be

[8] Chandler P. Anderson, "The Extent and Limitations of the Treaty-Making Power under the Constitution," *American Journal of International Law*, Vol. 1 (1907), p. 650.

[9] *Ibid.*, p. 649.

passed.[10] Debating the bill in the House on January 9, 1816, John Calhoun said: "The treaty making power has many and powerful limits; and it will be found, when I come to discuss what those limits are, that it cannot destroy the Constitution, or our personal liberty, or involve us, without the assent of this House, in war, or grant away our money."[11] An act putting the treaty into effect was passed on March 1, 1816.[12]

On June 4, 1844, Rufus Choate, chairman of the Committee on Foreign Relations of the Senate, reported against ratification of a reciprocity treaty with the German Zollverein: "The convention which has been submitted to the Senate changes duties which have been laid by law. . . . In the judgment of the Committee, the Legislature is the department of government by which commerce should be regulated and laws for revenue passed."[13] In his annual message on December 3, 1844, President Tyler repeated his request for ratification of the treaty.[14] In February of 1845 the Committee again reported adversely and the treaty was never ratified.[15]

It is a little surprising to find the Senate taking this position. A treaty with Brazil which went into effect in 1829 contained a most-favored-nation clause, and other such treaties had been negotiated thereafter.[16]

In 1875 a treaty with Hawaii by which each country agreed to admit certain articles from the other free of duty was ratified. Article V recited that it should not come into effect "until a law to carry it into operation shall have been passed by the Congress of the United States of America."[17] An act putting the treaty into effect was passed on August 15, 1876. The treaty expired by its own terms at the end of seven years. In 1884 a seven-year extension was negotiated. This was approved by the Senate on January 20, 1887.[18] On January 22 Representative Wallace introduced in the House a resolution complaining that the treaty of renewal contained no provision requiring Congressional action and charging the Committee on the Judiciary with inquiring "how far

[10] James D. Richardson, ed., *Messages and Papers of the Presidents* (Washington: Bureau of National Literature and Art, 1908), Vol. 1, p. 570.

[11] Quoted in Henry St. George Tucker, *Limitations on the Treaty-Making Power* (Boston: Little, Brown, 1915), p. 215.

[12] 3 Stat. 255.   [13] Quoted in Tucker, *op.cit.*, p. 221.

[14] Richardson, *op.cit.*, Vol. 4, pp. 339-40.   [15] Tucker, *loc.cit.*

[16] William N. Malloy, compiler, *International Acts, Protocols and Agreements between the United States and Other Powers* (Washington: Government Printing Office, 1910), Vol. 1, p. 134.

[17] Malloy, *op.cit.*, pp. 915-19.   [18] *Ibid.*, pp. 919-20.

the power conferred on the House by the Constitution of the United States to originate measures to lay and collect duties can be controlled by the treaty-making power under the said Constitution."[19] On March 3 J. Randolph Tucker submitted a lengthy report by the Committee. It proposed two resolutions. One declared that import duties could not be regulated by the treaty power; the other requested the President to withhold final action until Congress sanctioned the treaty.[20] Nevertheless, on November 7 the President announced ratification.

In 1902 Senator Cullom, Chairman of the Senate Committee on Foreign Relations, discussing proposed reciprocal trade treaties, pointed out that the House, despite its protests, had always made appropriations to carry out the stipulations of a treaty, "and I contend that it was bound to do this, at least as much as Congress can be bound to do anything when the faith of the nation has been pledged. And this appears to me to be the only case in which any action by the House is necessary, unless the treaty itself stipulates, expressly or by implication, for such Congressional action." The House then instructed the Committee on Ways and Means to investigate the question whether the President and the Senate, "independent of any action on the part of the House of Representatives, can negotiate treaties with foreign governments by which duties levied under an act of Congress for the purpose of raising revenue are modified or repealed, and report the result of such investigation to the House." It does not appear that a report was made.[21]

The question of the treaty power and import duties must remain for the time in the realm of unsettled questions.

In 1854 a treaty was negotiated with Venezuela which provided that if a citizen of either country should accept a commission in the service of a state at war with the other he should be treated as a pirate. But President Pierce did not submit the treaty to the Senate because the definition and punishment of piracy belonged to Congress.[22] And indeed one would suppose that no action can be made criminal by the treaty power without the assistance of an act of Congress. Certainly such a thing has never been attempted.

The question of the scope of the treaty power has also been raised concerning other topics: the acquisition and the cession of territory, and the alienation of the public domain, for example. But those un-

[19] Tucker, op.cit., pp. 342-3.
[20] Tucker, op.cit., pp. 342-79.
[21] Anderson, op.cit., pp. 650-51.
[22] Ibid., p. 654.

resolved problems need not concern us. There emerges very clearly the proposition that the treaty power and the legislative powers of Congress are only in part concurrent. It is well known that treaties may deal with topics on which Congress has no delegated power to legislate. It is equally clear that Congress has exclusive legislative power on certain topics, and a treaty on such a topic does not have legal standing at municipal law; it cannot be put into effect without an act of Congress.

The general principle is that the treaty power cannot be used in such a way as to alter the constitutional distribution of powers. So the United States objected to the proposal for the creation of an international Prize Court because the Constitution does not permit appeals from decisions of the United States Supreme Court.[23] In *Reid v. Covert*[24] in 1957 the Supreme Court had before it an act of Congress which provided for the trial of civilian dependents of military personnel abroad, thus ousting the constitutional courts of their jurisdiction under Article III and depriving the dependents of their right to jury trial. The government justified the act as one necessary to carry out executive agreements with Great Britain and Japan which were treated as having the force of treaties. Justice Black said: "The obvious and decisive answer to this, of course, is that no agreement with a foreign nation can confer power on the Congress, or on any other branch of Government, which is free from the restraints of the Constitution."[25]

Does the Constitution vest the war power exclusively in Congress? As we have seen, the Constitutional Convention expressly rejected the proposal that it be given to the President and the Senate. The German jurist Ernst Meier observed: "The Constitution gives Congress the right of declaring war; this right would be illusory if the President and the Senate could by treaty launch the country into a foreign war."[26] Apparently Francis Wharton and John Bassett Moore, two of our leading international lawyers, agreed with him.[27]

After reviewing the evidence, a former Assistant Secretary of State, James Grafton Rogers, concluded: "The Constitution says, therefore, in effect, 'Our country shall not be committed formally to a trial of force with another nation, our people generally summoned to the effort

[23] Bernard Schwartz, *Commentary on the Constitution of the United States* (New York: Macmillan, 1963), Vol. 2, p. 137.

[24] 354 U.S. 1.   [25] Id. at 16.

[26] John Bassett Moore, *Digest of International Law* (Washington: Government Printing Office, 1906), Vol. 5, §737.

[27] *Loc.cit.*

and all the legal consequences to people, rights and property incurred until the House, Senate and the President agree.' "[28]

This does not mean that it is impossible for the President and the Senate to enter into a treaty of alliance. It does mean that when it is alleged that circumstances have arisen which under the treaty require the United States to go to war it is necessary for the two houses of Congress and the President, not for the President alone, or for that matter for the President and the Senate, to judge of those circumstances and to make the decision to go to war.

But suppose the law were otherwise: suppose the Senate might by treaty authorize the President to make war. The fact is that no word of the SEATO Treaty purports to do so. Nor was it in any way intimated to the Senate when it ratified the treaty that it involved a delegation of the power to make war in Southeast Asia. The treaty provides that in the event of an armed attack in the future each member is to act in accordance with its "constitutional processes." This clearly contemplates that when it is alleged that an armed attack has occurred the facts are to be laid before the two houses of Congress, and Congress, if it finds this proper, is to pass a joint resolution to be submitted to the President.

Nevertheless the State Department, completely without textual support, contends that the SEATO treaty, which was negotiated in 1954, delegates to any incumbent of the Presidency, in all perpetuity, the power to engage in war in Southeast Asia whenever he makes the appropriate findings. It gives him exclusive power to make these findings, and they are unchallengeable. He may take whatever action seems to him appropriate at that time. The State Department memorandum concedes that at the time the treaty was ratified it was not supposed that the United States would engage in land warfare in Southeast Asia, and indeed Secretary of State Dulles gave assurances that this was not contemplated.[29] But things change in eleven years, and a new President is free to arrive at a new judgment.

If the Senate had really done this extraordinary thing, the SEATO treaty would clearly be unconstitutional. As we shall see in the discussion of the Tonkin Gulf Resolution, the two houses of Congress cannot delegate the power to make war to the President. Whether or not

[28] James Grafton Rogers, *World Policing and the Constitution* (Boston: World Peace Foundation, 1945) , p. 35.

[29] *Memorandum*, p. 124.

the Senate has the power to make war by treaty, it cannot delegate this power by treaty.

But the Johnson administration has advanced another argument, even more novel than that founded on the SEATO treaty. President Johnson has asserted that he has the right to make war in South Vietnam and on North Vietnam because three Presidents have made "commitments" to South Vietnam.

The State Department memorandum recites several commitments.[30] At the conclusion of the Geneva Conference of 1954, Under-Secretary Bedell Smith said that the United States would not use force to disturb the accords, and that it "would view any renewal of the aggression in violation of the aforesaid agreements with grave concern and as seriously threatening international peace and security." President Eisenhower promised that the United States would "not use force to disturb the settlement," but said that "any renewal of Communist aggression would be viewed by us as a matter of grave concern." In October, 1954, President Eisenhower offered economic assistance to help make South Vietnam "capable of resisting attempted subversion or aggression through military means." On May 11, 1957, President Eisenhower and President Ngo Dinh Diem issued a joint statement in which they spoke of "the large build-up of Vietnamese Communist military forces in North Vietnam" and "agreed that aggression or subversion threatening the political independence of the Republic of Vietnam would be considered as endangering peace and stability." On August 2, 1961, President Kennedy declared that "the United States is determined that the Republic of Vietnam shall not be lost to the Communists for lack of any support which the United States Government can render." On December 14, 1961, President Kennedy assured Diem that the United States was "prepared to help the Republic of Vietnam to protect its people and to preserve its independence."

These assurances fall short of a promise to engage in war. They could not have misled Diem or the Vietnamese, for the same Presidents stated that our assistance would not take the form of troops. It was deceptive of the State Department to omit these clarifying statements. On October 26, 1960, President Eisenhower congratulated Diem on "the fifth anniversary of the Republic of Viet-Nam" and concluded his message: "Although the main responsibility for guarding that independence will always, as it has in the past, belong to the Vietnamese people and

30 *Ibid.*, pp. 119, 121.

their government, I want to assure you that for so long as our strength can be useful, the United States will continue to assist Viet-Nam in the difficult yet hopeful struggle ahead."[31] The promise to "continue to assist" with economic aid and military instruction could not be construed as a promise to take over the principal military burden in a struggle in which the "main responsibility" lay with "the Vietnamese people and their government."

When President Johnson asserted that in making war he was fulfilling a commitment of President Eisenhower's, the former President felt obliged to make a public denial: "We said we would help that country. We were not talking about military programs but foreign aid."[32]

President Kennedy, on September 2, 1963, said: "In the final analysis it is their war, they are the ones who have to win it. We can help them, we can give them equipment, we can send our men out there as advisors, but they have to win it."[33]

On February 21, 1964, President Lyndon B. Johnson said: "The contest in which South Vietnam is now engaged is first and foremost a contest to be won by the government and people of that country."[34] On September 25, 1964, he said: "There are those that say you ought to go north and drop bombs to try to wipe out the supply lines. . . . We don't want our American boys to do the fighting for Asian boys."[35] On September 28, 1964, he said: "What I have been trying to do with the situation that I found, was to get the boys in Vietnam to do their own fighting with our advice and with our equipment. That is the course we are following. So we are not going north and drop bombs at this stage of the game."[36] On October 21: "We are not about to send American boys 9 or 10,000 miles away from home to do what Asian boys ought to do for themselves."[37]

The commitment of three Presidents to the Vietnamese people was identical with their commitment to the American people. It was to give aid short of war.

But the word commitment has more than one meaning. In the hearing of the Senate Foreign Relations Committee on February 17, 1966, Senator Hickenlooper asked: "When was the commitment made

[31] *Public Papers of the Presidents of the United States: Dwight D. Eisenhower, 1960-61* (Washington: Office of the Federal Register, 1961), p. 808.

[32] *The New York Times*, August 18, 1965.   [33] *The New York Times*, Sept. 3, 1963.

[34] *Public Papers of the Presidents: Lyndon B. Johnson, 1963-64* (Washington: Government Printing Office, 1965), Vol. 1, p. 304.

[35] *Ibid.*, Vol. 2, p. 1126.   [36] *Ibid.*, p. 1164.

[37] *Ibid.*, p. 1391.

for us to actively participate in the military operations of the war as American personnel?" And General Maxwell Taylor replied: "Well, insofar as the use of our combat ground forces are [*sic*] concerned, that took place, of course, only in the spring of 1965. In the air, we had been participating more actively over 2 or 3 years."[38] Taylor did not misunderstand the question. He knew that Hickenlooper by "commitment" meant "pledge"; but Taylor knew of no pledge, although he had been personal military representative of President Kennedy, 1961-62, Chairman of the Joint Chiefs of Staff, 1962-64, and Ambassador to South Vietnam, 1964-65, and was currently Special Consultant to President Johnson on Vietnam. So he identified the only commitment he knew, the commitment of troops. On September 29, 1967, President Johnson enlarged his claim; his war was now to redeem "the commitment that three Presidents and a half a million of our young men have made."[39] The commitment of the half million young men was objective rather than subjective; they made no commitment, but they were committed by Johnson. In the President's Thanksgiving Day proclamation on November 9, 1967, the commitment became "a sacred promise";[40] on December 12, before the AFL-CIO Convention, President Johnson promised to "honor and respect our sworn commitments to protect the security of Southeast Asia."[41]

We have already established that the President has no right to commit, or to make a commitment to commit, a half million men to war. He has a limited power to make executive agreements with foreign states; this is in the area of administrative relationships which carry no general legal consequences—where the latter are involved, the treaty procedure must be used. But even a treaty cannot commit our nation to war.

In his annual message to Congress on January 11, 1944, President Franklin D. Roosevelt undertook to reassure "some suspicious souls who are fearful that Mr. Hull or I have made 'commitments' for the future": "I wish to say that Mr. Churchill, and Marshal Stalin, and Generalissimo Chiang Kai-shek are all thoroughly conversant with the provisions of our Constitution. And so is Mr. Hull. And so am I."[42]

---

[38] *Supplemental Foreign Assistance Fiscal Year 1966—Vietnam*, Hearings before the Senate Committee on Foreign Relations, Pt. 1 (1966), p. 450.

[39] *Weekly Compilation of Presidential Documents*, Vol. 3, No. 40 (Oct. 9, 1967), p. 1372.

[40] *Ibid.*, No. 45 (Nov. 13, 1967), p. 1540.   [41] *Ibid.*, No. 50 (Dec. 18, 1967), p. 1740.

[42] Fred L. Israel, ed., *The State of the Union Messages of the Presidents, 1790-1966* (New York: Chelsea House, Robert Hector, 1966), Vol. 3, p. 2876.

When the President pleads that he is fulfilling a Presidential military commitment, he is confessing that he is guilty of usurping power.

VIII. The Tonkin Gulf Resolution

On several occasions during the spring and summer of 1964, South Vietnamese vessels attacked islands and coastal areas of North Vietnam. On August 2 and August 4, according to the Johnson administration, North Vietnamese patrol boats attacked two American destroyers in the Gulf of Tonkin. The administration asserted that the presence of these vessels at the time of a South Vietnamese attack on North Vietnam was pure coincidence. They were not convoying the attacking vessels but were quite independently carrying out their duty of patrolling the high seas.[1] The American destroyers suffered no hits and were reported to have sunk at least three North Vietnamese patrol boats.

On August 4 President Johnson ordered air attacks on North Vietnamese naval installations by way of reprisal for these two attacks by patrol boats and on August 5 he sent a message to the Senate. The message recited that "Our purpose is peace"; "the United States intends no rashness, and seeks no wider war." But he requested the passage of a resolution like the Formosa Resolution "to give convincing evidence to the aggressive Communist nations, and to the world as a whole, that our policy in Southeast Asia will be carried forward—and that the peace and security of the area will be preserved."[2] Senator Fulbright promptly introduced the Tonkin Gulf Resolution. The process of Congressional enactment was completed on August 10.[3]

After reciting that, as a part of a campaign of aggression that the Communist regime in North Vietnam was waging against its neighbors and the nations joined with them in defense of their freedom, North Vietnamese vessels had deliberately and repeatedly attacked United States naval vessels in international waters, and that the United States desired only that the peoples of southeast Asia "should be left in peace to work out their own destinies in their own way," the resolution said "That the Congress approves and supports the determination of the President, as Commander in Chief, to take all measures necessary to repel any armed attack against the forces of the United States and to prevent further aggression," and that "the United States is, therefore,

[1] *Congressional Record*, Vol. 110, Part 14, 88th Cong., 2d Sess. (Aug. 5, 1964), p. 18402-403.

[2] *Ibid.*, p. 18132.   [3] 78 Stat. 384 (1964).

prepared, as the President determines, to take all necessary steps, including the use of armed force" to assist Cambodia, Laos, South Vietnam, Australia, New Zealand, Pakistan, the Philippines, Thailand, and the Asian possessions of Great Britain and France to maintain their freedom if requested to do so. The language is vague, but it is very broad. The resolution did not initiate a war, but it authorized the President to initiate war "as the President determines"—that is, in his uncontrolled discretion. Senator Cooper asked Senator Fulbright, the sponsor of the resolution: "looking ahead, if the President decided that it was necessary to use such force as could lead into war, we will give that authority by this resolution?" And Fulbright replied: "That is the way I would interpret it."[4]

Two years later Fulbright had reason to complain: "I feel that I was led into the Tonkin Gulf Resolution. I should have been more intelligent, more far-seeing, more suspicious."[5] "Each time Senators have raised questions about successive escalations of the war, we have had the blank check of August 7, 1964 waved in our faces as supposed evidence of the overwhelming support of the Congress for a policy in Southeast Asia which in fact has been radically changed since the summer of 1964."[6]

The Tonkin Gulf Resolution is indeed a blank check. But our Constitution does not permit Congress to issue blank checks to determine policy; Congress must make the determination itself. In an early decision Chief Justice Marshall wrote:

> It will not be contended, that Congress can delegate to the courts, or to any other tribunals, powers which are strictly and exclusively legislative. . . . The line has not been sharply drawn which separates those important subjects which must be entirely regulated by the legislature itself, from those of less interest, in which a general provision may be made and power given to those who are to act under such general provisions to fill up the details.[7]

Clearly the war power is legislative. As we mentioned in Section III, Congress refused one request of President Jackson, and six requests of President Buchanan, for discretionary power to use force on the ground that the war power cannot be delegated.

[4] *Congressional Record*, p. 18409.   [5] *The New York Times*, Nov. 24, 1966.

[6] *The Arrogance of Power* (New York: Random House, 1966), p. 51.

[7] Wayman v. Southard, 10 Wheat. 1 (1825).

In 1831 the payment by France of outstanding claims for injuries to American shipping during the Napoleonic wars was agreed upon by treaty, but Louis Philippe was unable to persuade his legislature to vote the money. In his annual message to Congress on December 9, 1834, President Andrew Jackson said: "I recommend that a law be passed, authorizing reprisals upon French property, in case provision shall not be made for the payment of the debt at the approaching session of the French Chambers."[8] On the same day Representative Claiborne complained in the House: "If this power be conferred upon him, it will be virtually conferring upon the President unconstitutional power—a power to declare war. . . . Gentlemen have read history to little effect, if they are ready to clothe a single individual with the power of making war."[9]

On January 5, 1835, Albert Gallatin wrote to Edward Everett:

> In every case, particularly when hostilities are contemplated, or appear probable, no government should commit itself as to what it will do under certain future contingencies. It should prepare itself for every contingency—launch ships, raise men and money, and reserve its final decision for the time when it becomes necessary to decide and simultaneously to act. The proposed transfer by Congress of its constitutional powers to the Executive, in a case which necessarily embraces the question of war or no war, appears to me a most extraordinary proposal, and entirely inconsistent with the letter and spirit of our Constitution, which vests in Congress the power to declare war and grant letters of marque and reprisal.[10]

On January 6, 1835, Henry Clay presented a report for the Senate Committee on Foreign Relations, and on the basis of this report the Senate unanimously rejected Jackson's request:

> Reprisals do not of themselves produce a state of public war; but they are not infrequently the immediate precursor of it. When they are accompanied with an authority, from the Government which admits them, to employ force, they are believed invariably to have led to war in all cases where the nation against which they are directed is able to make resistance. . . .

[8] James D. Richardson, ed., *Messages and Papers of the Presidents, 1789-1908* (Washington: Bureau of National Literature and Art), Vol. 3, p. 106.

[9] *Congressional Globe*, 23d Cong., 2d Sess. (Dec. 9, 1834), p. 23.

[10] John Bassett Moore, *Digest of International Law* (Washington: Government Printing Office, 1906), Vol. 7, pp. 127-8.

Reprisals so far partake of the character of war, that they are an appeal from reason to force; from negotiation, devising a remedy to be applied by the common consent of both parties, to self-redress, carved out and regulated by the will of one of them; and, if resistance be made, they convey an authority to subdue it, by the sacrifice of life, if necessary.

The framers of our Constitution have manifested their sense of the nature of this power, by associating it in the same clause with grants to Congress of the power to declare war, and to make rules concerning captures on land and water. . . .

In the first place the authority to grant letters of marque and reprisal being specially delegated to Congress, Congress ought to retain to itself the right of judging of the expediency of granting them under all the circumstances existing at the time when they are proposed to be actually issued. The committee are not satisfied that Congress can, constitutionally, delegate this right. It is true that the President proposes to limit the exercise of it to one specified contingency. But if the law be passed as recommended, the President might, and probably would, feel himself bound to execute it in the event, no matter from what cause, of provision not being made for the fulfillment of the treaty by the French Chambers, now understood to be in session. . . . Congress ought to reserve to itself the constitutional right, which it possesses, of judging of all the circumstances by which such refusal might be attended; of hearing France, and of deciding whether, in the actual posture of things as they may then exist, and looking to the condition of the United States, of France, and of Europe, the issuing of letters of marque and reprisal ought to be authorized, or any other measure adopted.[11]

Jackson was very unhappy with this action, and blamed the Senate for his failure to obtain immediate satisfaction; but the matter was adjusted by negotiation in 1836. Perhaps this was better than war.

In his first annual message on December 8, 1857,[12] President James Buchanan described the interest of the United States in "the freedom and security of all the communications across the isthmus" of Panama, and the danger that these communications might be interrupted either by invasions of American filibusterers—these were the days of William Walker—"or by wars between the independent States of Central America." He also recited the irrelevant circumstance of the American

---

[11] *Ibid.*, pp. 126-7.   [12] Richardson, *op.cit.*, Vol. 5, p. 447.

guarantee of the neutrality and sovereignty of New Granada or Colombia. "Under these circumstances I recommend to Congress the passage of an act authorizing the President, in case of necessity, to employ the land and naval forces to carry into effect this guaranty of neutrality and protection. I also recommend similar legislation for the security of any other route across the Isthmus in which we may acquire an interest by treaty." No action was taken, and Buchanan renewed his request in his message of December 6, 1858. The routes over the Isthmus were "of incalculable importance" to the United States; they were a highway in which Nicaragua and Costa Rica had "little interest when compared with the vast interests of the rest of the world. Whilst their rights of sovereignty ought to be respected, it is the duty of other nations to require that this important passage shall not be interrupted by the civil wars and revolutionary outbreaks which have so frequently occurred in that region."

> Under these circumstances I earnestly recommend to Congress the passage of an act authorizing the President, under such restrictions as they shall deem proper, to employ the land and naval forces of the United States in preventing the transit from being obstructed or closed by lawless violence, and in protecting the lives and property of American citizens traveling thereupon, requiring at the same time that these forces shall be withdrawn the moment the danger shall have passed away. Without such a provision our citizens will be constantly exposed to interruption in their progress to lawless violence.
>
> A similar necessity exists for the passage of such an act for the protection of the Panama and Tehuantepec routes.[13]

The Senate Committee on Foreign Relations reported a bill but no action was taken. On February 18, 1859 President Buchanan sent a special message repeating his request. Not only was there interruption of peaceful transit over the Isthmus; the continual revolutions produced successive confiscations of American property in Central American harbors:

> As one or the other party has prevailed and obtained possession of the ports open to foreign commerce, they have seized and confiscated American vessels and their cargoes in an arbitrary and lawless manner and exacted money from American citizens by forced loans and

13 *Ibid.*, pp. 516-17.

other violent proceedings to enable them to carry on hostilities. The executive governments of Great Britain, France, and other countries, possessing the war-making power, can promptly employ the necessary means to enforce immediate redress for similar outrages upon their subjects. Not so the executive government of the United States.

If the President orders a vessel of war to any of those ports to demand prompt redress for outrages committed, the offending parties are well aware that in case of refusal the commander can do no more than remonstrate. He can resort to no hostile act. . . . The remedy for this state of affairs can only be supplied by Congress, since the Constitution has confided to that body alone the power to make war. Without the authority of Congress the Executive cannot lawfully direct any force, however near it may be to the scene of the difficulty, to enter the territory of Mexico, Nicaragua, or New Granada for the purpose of defending the persons and property of American citizens, even though they may be violently assailed whilst passing in peaceful transit over the Tehuantepec, Nicaragua, or Panama routes. He cannot, without transcending his constitutional power, direct a gun to be fired into a port or land a seaman or marine to protect the lives of our countrymen on shore or to obtain redress for a recent outrage on their property. . . .

In reference to countries where the local authorities are strong enough to enforce the laws, the difficulty here indicated can seldom happen; but where this is the case and the local authorities do not possess the physical power, even if they possess the will, to protect our citizens within their limits recent experience has shown that the American Executive should itself be authorized to render this protection. Such a grant of authority, thus limited in its extent, would in no just sense be regarded as a transfer of the war-making power to the Executive, but only as an appropriate exercise of that power by the body to whom it belongs. . . .

I therefore earnestly recommend to Congress, on whom the responsibility exclusively rests, to pass a law before their adjournment conferring on the President the power to protect the lives and property of American citizens in the cases which I have indicated, under such restrictions and conditions as they may deem advisable.[14]

14 *Ibid.*, pp. 539-40.

Senator Seward made a speech directly challenging the message; his argument on the delegation of the war power is today fully applicable to the Tonkin Gulf Resolution:

It was thought, seventy years ago, that it was a great improvement, conducive to peace, essential to the permanent stability of republican institutions, that the Executive should be destitute of the power to make war, and that this last final remedy for national grievance should never be resorted to in any case without the deliberate consent and determination of the nation itself. . . . The President of the United States now regrets that those nations living under arbitrary forms of government are safer than we are who live under this, as we thought, improved system.

But, sir, I am unable to understand the logic which brings the President of the United States to the conclusion that this application to us will not be a surrender of the war-making power. He tells us that it would not be a surrender of the war-making power; but that we should be making war ourselves. Could anything be more strange and preposterous than the idea of the President of the United States making hypothetical wars, conditional wars, without any designation of the nation against which war is to be declared; or the time, or place, or manner, or circumstance of the duration of it, the beginning or the end; and without limiting the number of nations with which war may be waged? No, sir. When we pass this bill we do surrender the power of making war or preserving peace, in each of the States named, into the hands of the President of the United States.[15]

Neither house acted on the President's proposal.

In his third annual message, on December 19, 1859, Buchanan made a last futile request. He asked for a law to permit him to police the Isthmus and also "to employ the naval force to protect American merchant vessels, their crews and cargoes, against violent and lawless seizure and confiscation in the ports of Mexico and the Spanish American States when these countries may be in a revolutionary condition." He argued that such a law would not involve an unconstitutional delegation of the war power:[16]

The chief objection urged against the grant of this authority is that Congress by conferring it would violate the Constitution;

---

[15] *Congressional Globe*, 35 Cong., 2d Sess. (Feb. 18, 1859), p. 1120.
[16] Richardson, *op.cit.*, pp. 569-70.

that it would be a transfer of the war-making, or strictly speaking, the war-declaring, power to the Executive. If this were well founded, it would, of course, be conclusive. A very brief examination, however, will place this objection at rest.

Congress possesses the sole and exclusive power under the Constitution "to declare war." They alone can "raise and support armies" and "provide and maintain a navy." But after Congress shall have declared war and provided the force necessary to carry it on the President, as Commander-in-Chief of the Army and Navy, can alone employ this force in making war against the enemy. This is the plain language, and history proves that it was the well-known intention of the framers, of the Constitution.

It will not be denied that the general "power to declare war" is without limitation and embraces within itself not only what writers on the law of nations term a public or perfect war, but also an imperfect war, and, in short, every species of hostility, however confined or limited. Without the authority of Congress the President cannot fire a hostile gun in any case except to repel the attacks of an enemy. It will not be doubted that under this power Congress could, if they thought proper, authorize the President to employ the force at his command to seize a vessel belonging to an American citizen which had been illegally and unjustly captured in a foreign port and restore it to its owner. But can Congress only act after the fact, after the mischief has been done? Have they no power to confer upon the President the authority in advance to furnish instant redress should such a case afterwards occur? Must they wait until the mischief has been done, and can they apply the remedy only when it is too late? To confer this authority to meet future cases under circumstances strictly specified is as clearly within the war-declaring power as such an authority conferred upon the President by act of Congress after the deed had been done. In the progress of a great nation many exigencies must arise imperatively requiring that Congress should authorize the President to act promptly on certain conditions which may or may not afterwards arise.

And Buchanan appealed to the precedent of the *Water Witch*. To obtain redress for the shelling of the *Water Witch* and the satisfaction of certain outstanding claims of American citizens against Paraguay, Congress had on June 2, 1858 by joint resolution authorized the President "to adopt such measures and use such force as in his judgment may be necessary and advisable in the event of a refusal of just satisfaction by the Government of Paraguay."

"Just satisfaction" for what? For "the attack on the United States steamer *Water Witch*" and "other matters referred to in the annual message of the President." Here the power is expressly granted upon the condition that the Government of Paraguay shall refuse to render this "just satisfaction." In this and other similar cases Congress have conferred upon the President power in advance to employ the Army and Navy upon the happening of contingent future events; and this most certainly is embraced within the power to declare war.

Now, if this conditional and contingent power could be constitutionally conferred upon the President in the case of Paraguay, why may it not be conferred for the purpose of protecting the lives and property of American citizens in the event that they may be violently and unlawfully attacked in passing over the transit routes to and from California or assailed by the seizure of their vessels in a foreign port? To deny this power is to render the Navy in a great degree useless for the protection of the lives and property of American citizens in countries where neither protection nor redress can be otherwise obtained.

The case of the *Water Witch* was contingent legislation of a sort. Congress had authorized the President to make war unless Paraguay averted the war by submission—for that was what "just satisfaction" meant. But it was not a precedent for Buchanan's request. In the case of the *Water Witch*, the occasion for war was in the past. Congress had determined that the shelling of the *Water Witch* was a *casus belli*, and that the use of force against Paraguay was feasible and in accord with the national interest under existing circumstances. But in his request for power to police the Isthmus routes and foreign harbors Buchanan was asking that the President be authorized to determine on future occasions whether circumstances as yet unknown constituted a *casus belli*, and whether under these circumstances it was desirable or prudent to use force. He was asking Congress to grant him the power of decision for war or peace.

Suppose, on the other hand, that Congress should pass genuine contingent legislation requiring rather than permitting the President to go to war when specified events occurred in the future. Henry Clay had considered it a peculiarly unfortunate feature of Jackson's proposal for reprisal on French shipping that the President might interpret the legislation as mandatory. He might feel obliged to go to war when stated events occurred, regardless of the circumstances. According to Clay, the Constitution requires that Congress itself appraise the immediate circumstances before the nation voluntarily enters into a state of war. Therefore Congress could not authorize war with France without hearing what France had to say as to the reasons for the failure to pay the claims, and without deciding that "in the actual posture of things as they may then exist," including the contemporary state of international politics, and in particular the attitude of Great Britain, a limited war was the wisest course of action.

Clay's argument went beyond the rule against the delegation of legislative power. He argued, in effect, that Congress itself cannot make a declaration of war which is to come into effect upon the occurrence of stipulated facts in the future, because war is an enterprise in which all the contemporary circumstances must be weighed.

Almost from the beginning of our history, in the exercise of other powers than the war power, Congress has passed laws that are to come into effect when a given state of affairs exists, and has authorized the President to determine the existence of the relevant facts and to invoke the law by proclamation. But there is a world of difference between contingent legislation in the exercise of the power over interstate and foreign commerce and a contingent declaration of war. In the first case, a rule of conduct for citizens is established by Congress and is called into play by the President. This takes place within a legal order shaped and controlled by Congress itself. Under these circumstances, Congress can foretell the consequences of the delegation and is genuinely determining the policy to be applied. In the second case, the invocation of a conditional declaration of war changes the legal status of the nation itself. It changes the status and relations of the nation in an international order whose significant details, perhaps even its major outlines, change from month to month or day to day. The posture of international affairs in the future cannot be known to Congress at the time the resolution is passed. If Congress makes a contingent declaration of war, it is not determining policy for the future; it is casting dice. Henry Clay's ultimate position was that Congress is authorized to declare only present and not future wars. Surely this is what the framers intended.

Unless one considers the secret resolution of 1811 to fall in that category,[17] Congress has never passed a declaration of war contingent

---

[17] 3 Stat. 471 (Jan. 15, 1811).

upon the occurrence of specified future events. In recent years, however, it has passed no less than four laws purporting to give the President the option of making war on future occasions. These are clearly uncontrolled delegations of the war power.

Article 43 of the United Nations Charter provides for agreements between the Security Council and member states by which the latter are to promise to supply armed forces for military action ordered by the Security Council to maintain or restore international peace and security. The United Nations Participation Act, passed by Congress in 1945, authorized the President to negotiate such an agreement with the Security Council. If it should be confirmed by Congress by act or joint resolution, "The President shall not be deemed to require the authorization of the Congress to make available to the Security Council on its call in order to take action under Article 42 of said Charter and pursuant to such special agreement or agreements the armed forces, facilities, or assistance provided for therein."[18] The act does not say that the President must make the force available. It seems to assume that he may do so or fail to do so as he thinks best. If he chooses to do so, he need not seek the approval of Congress. This is indisputably a delegation of the power to make war.

Champions of the United Nations are likely to resent this criticism. But the Constitution does not forbid support for the United Nations. It merely says that it is for Congress rather than for the President to afford that support, and that Congress may not transfer to the President the duty of determining when support should be afforded.

Secretary of State John Foster Dulles was responsible for two other delegations. In 1955 President Eisenhower requested what has come to be known as the Formosa Resolution. After cursory hearings and limited debate, Congress resolved "That the President of the United States be and he hereby is authorized to employ the Armed Forces of the United States as he deems necessary for the specific purpose of securing and protecting Formosa and the Pescadores against armed attack, this authority to include the securing and protecting of such related positions and territories of that area now in friendly hands and the taking of such other measures as he judges to be required or appropriate in assuring the defense of Formosa and the Pescadores."[19] Dulles was also responsible for the passage of the Middle East Resolution of March 9, 1957. The resolution recited the determination of

18 22 U.S.C. 287d; 59 Stat. 621 (1945) as amended 63 Stat. 735 (1949).
19 69 Stat. 5.

the United States to preserve "the independence and integrity of the nations of the Middle East" and provided: "To this end, if the President determines the necessity thereof, the United States is prepared to use armed forces to assist any nation or group of nations requesting assistance against armed aggression from any country controlled by international communism. . . ."[20]

The Tonkin Gulf Resolution is the fourth attempt of Congress to transfer its constitutional responsibility to the President.

Let us assume that Henry Clay was wrong, and that Congress has the power to declare future wars which are contingent upon the President's finding of appropriate facts recited in the resolution. These delegations do not meet the tests which courts apply to legislative delegations in other areas.

Problems of two sorts have arisen in connection with domestic legislation. In the case of contingent legislation, the Congress itself enacts the provisions of a law which is to come into effect upon the occurrence of recited circumstances, and the President invokes the law when those circumstances occur. In the case of delegation of the rule-making power, Congress recites a general policy to be pursued, and authorizes the President to make detailed rules putting that policy into effect.

A good deal of discretion can be allowed to the President in finding the facts. In *Field v. Clark*, in 1892,[21] the Court upheld a grant of power to the President to remove certain foods and hides from the free list in the case of an exporting nation levying duties on our goods which "he may deem to be reciprocally unequal and unreasonable"; upon such a finding, duties recited in the statute were to attach:

That Congress cannot delegate legislative power to the President is a principle universally recognized as vital to the integrity and maintenance of the system of government ordained by the constitution. The act of October 1, 1890, in the particulars under consideration, is not inconsistent with that principle. It does not, in any real sense, invest the President with the power of legislation. . . . Nothing involving the expediency or the just operation of such legislation was left to the determination of the President. . . . As the suspension was absolutely required when the President ascertained the existence of a particular fact, it cannot be said that in ascertaining that fact, and in issuing his proclamation, in obedience to the legisla-

[20] 71 Stat. 5. [21] 143 U.S. 649.

tive will, he exercised the function of making laws. . . . He was the mere agent of the law-making department to ascertain and declare the event upon which its expressed will was to take effect.

Delegation of the rule-making power was upheld in *United States v. Grimaud* in 1911.[22] The Supreme Court upheld an act authorizing the Secretary of Agriculture to make rules concerning public forests and forest reservations "to regulate their occupancy and use, and to preserve the forests thereon from destruction." The Court stated the controlling considerations:

> In the nature of things it was impracticable for Congress to provide general regulations for these various and varying details of management. Each reservation had its peculiar and special features; and in authorizing the Secretary of Agriculture to meet these local conditions, Congress was merely conferring administrative functions upon an agent, and not delegating to him legislative power.

These cases make the relationship unmistakable. Congress is the principal, the President is the agent. If Congress determines the general policy to be pursued, it may authorize the President to determine the facts which call the Congressional policy into play, or to make detailed rules which apply the policy established by Congress to particular sets of facts.

But Congress may not pass contingent legislation without specifying the circumstances in which it is to be invoked, nor may it authorize the President to make rules on a topic without supplying standards to guide him. To do either of these things would be to attempt to delegate legislative power.

The first situation was presented in 1935 in *Panama Refining Company v. Ryan*.[23] The National Recovery Act of 1933 authorized the President to forbid the interstate transportation of petroleum produced in excess of the amount permitted to be produced by state law in the state of production, and the Panama Refining Company brought an action to enjoin the enforcement of a Presidential order. The Court said:

> Section 9 (c) is brief and unambiguous. It does not attempt to control the production of petroleum and petroleum products within a state. It does not seek to lay down rules for the guidance of state legislators or state offices. It leaves to the states and to their consti-

22 220 U.S. 506.   23 293 U.S. 388.

tuted authorities the determination of what production shall be permitted. It does not qualify the President's authority by reference to the basis or extent of the state's limitation of production. Section 9 (c) does not state whether or in what circumstances or under what conditions the President is to prohibit the transportation of the amount of petroleum or petroleum products produced in areas of the state's permission. It establishes no criterion to govern the President's course. It does not require any finding by the President as a condition of his action. The Congress in section 9 (c) thus declares no policy as to the transportation of the excess production. So far as this section is concerned, it gives the President an unlimited authority to determine the policy and to lay down the prohibition, or not to lay it down, as he may see fit.[24]

Justice Cardozo dissented on the theory that the recitation of the purposes of the act supplied a standard to govern the President. But he joined in the unanimous decision in *Schechter Poultry Company v. United States*[25] in the same year that the delegation of code-making authority to the President in the National Recovery Act was unconstitutional. The only standard to guide the President was that the codes "tend to effectuate the policy of this title." The policy itself was stated as a number of happy outcomes, including industrial recovery, increased consumption, improvement of the condition of labor, and the conservation of natural resources. Surely Chief Justice Hughes was right in saying that Congress had authorized the President to approve as law whatever codes appeared to him to be "wise and beneficent measures for the government of trades and industries in order to bring about their rehabilitation, correction, and development, according to the general declaration of policy in section 1."[26] Surely Justice Cardozo was right in calling this a delegated power "unconfined and vagrant."[27]

Three cases decided during the Second World War upheld acts of Congress which authorized administrative rule-making. For our purposes it is decisive that the Court applied to these statutes, which were passed under the war power, the orthodox tests which govern the delegation of legislative power in domestic affairs.

On March 21, 1941, Congress authorized the President or a designated agent to establish military zones and to prescribe the terms on which any person should "enter, remain in, leave, or commit any act

24 Id. at 415. 25 295 U.S. 495.
26 Id. at 535. 27 Id. at 551.

in such a zone"; violation of such an order was made criminal. Hira-bayashi ignored a curfew for persons of Japanese origin established by the commanding general of the Pacific Coast zone. The language of the delegation seems to be excessively broad, but in a troubled and confused opinion Chief Justice Stone reduced it to constitutional dimensions.[28] All that was involved was a curfew order, and Congress had been "advised that curfew orders were among those intended, and was advised also that regulation of citizen and alien Japanese alike was contemplated."[29] Since Congress had contemplated the issuance of a curfew order when it passed the statute, Stone apparently felt that it had discharged its duty of fixing policy.[30]

The Emergency Price Control Act of 1942, which was also adopted under the war power, was challenged twice on the theory that it unlawfully delegated legislative power. Each time the Court applied the traditional formula and found it to be satisfied.

The first case, *Yakus v. United States*,[31] was a prosecution for selling at a price in excess of that fixed by the Administrator of the Office of Price Administration under authority granted in the act. Chief Justice Stone held that Congress had discharged the legislative function, as it must do, and had left to the Administrator only the task of applying its policy:

> Congress enacted the Emergency Price Control Act in pursuance of a defined policy and required that the prices fixed by the Administrator should further that policy and conform to standards prescribed by the Act. . . .
> The Act is thus an exercise by Congress of its legislative power. In it Congress has stated the legislative objective, has prescribed the method of achieving that objective—maximum price-fixing—and has laid down standards to guide the administrative determination of

[28] Hirabayashi v. United States, 320 U.S. 81 (1943).

[29] Id. at 91.

[30] On the other hand, there is perplexing language which seems to echo the Curtiss-Wright case, which is discussed below, note 36: "The question then is not one of Congressional power to delegate to the President the promulgation of the Executive Order, but whether, acting in cooperation, Congress and the Executive have constitutional authority to impose the curfew restriction here complained of." Id. at 91-2. And Stone silently alters the law of separability in the field of delegation of legislative power. The earlier cases had implicitly held that one could not give effect to an overbroad statute within the range of Congressional intention; it was void on its face. But here Stone enforces a rule made under a confessedly excessive delegation because the promulgation of the rule was contemplated by Congress at the time the act was passed.

[31] 321 U.S. 414 (1944).

both the occasions for the exercise of the price-fixing power, and the particular prices to be established. Compare Marshall Field and Co. v. Clark. . . .

The Act is unlike the National Industrial Recovery Act of June 16, 1933, . . . considered in A.L.A. Schechter Poultry Company v. United States. . . .[32]

The act also authorized the Administrator to fix maximum rents under certain circumstances. In *Bowles v. Willingham*[33] Justice Douglas wrote the opinion upholding this feature of the act:

The considerations which support the delegation of authority under this Act over commodity prices (Yakus v. United States) are equally applicable here. The power to legislate which the Constitution says shall be vested in Congress (Art. 1 §1) has not been granted to the Administrator. Congress in §1 (a) of the Act has made clear its policy of waging war on inflation. In §2 (b) it has defined the circumstances when its announced policy is to be declared operative and the method by which it is to be effectuated. Those steps constitute the performance of the legislative function in the constitutional sense. . . .

There is no grant of unbridled administrative discretion as appellee argues. . . .[34]

The test acknowledged and applied in all these cases is not satisfied by the Formosa Resolution, the Middle East Resolution, or the Tonkin Gulf Resolution. These resolutions do not say: If the President finds that aggression has occurred, he shall make war. The Formosa Resolution says: If Formosa and the Pescadores are attacked, the President is "authorized to employ the Armed Forces"—that is, he is to go to war or not—"as he deems necessary." The Middle East Resolution says: If the President shall find that aggression has occurred, there is to be war "if the President determines the necessity thereof." The Tonkin Gulf Resolution says: Aggression has occurred, and there is likely to be future aggression; there shall or shall not be war, "as the President determines," of such character and in such parts of Southeast Asia as the President shall determine. In none of the three cases could it be said of the President, in the language of *Field v. Clark*, above, that "He was the mere agent of the law-making department to ascertain and declare the event upon which its expressed will was to take

[32] Id. at 423. [33] 321 U.S. 503 (1944). [34] Id. at 514.

effect." Congress did not express a will as to war or peace. Not only the language of the resolutions but the debates show beyond doubt that Congress intended to transfer the power of decision to the President. This was an illegitimate purpose, and the resolutions are void.

Almost no one would wish to revise these resolutions by eliminating Presidential discretion and making war perfectly automatic upon the occurrence of a future event. This could appeal only to the admirers of Herman Kahn's Doomsday Machine, which is to be set irrevocably to blow up the earth when the Soviet Union violates one or another ultimatum.[35] Henry Clay was perfectly right when he said that the decision for war must be taken contemporaneously with the declaration of war, in the light of current circumstances. But he was right also in saying that the decision for war must be taken by Congress, to whom alone the Constitution gives the responsibility for evaluating the occasion and the circumstances and for making the fateful choice.

All this seems pellucidly clear, but it is necessary to consider one eccentric Supreme Court opinion, *United States v. Curtiss-Wright Export Corporation*,[36] decided in 1936, for there the Court did in fact say that the rule against the delegation of legislative power does not apply in foreign affairs. The case did not involve the war power, but the power over foreign commerce; and the cases decided under the war power reviewed above, which held that the rule against delegation applies in this area, were subsequent to the *Curtiss-Wright* case. But since *Curtiss-Wright* dealt with the problem of delegation, and in a startling manner, it should be considered.

In 1934 Congress passed a joint resolution authorizing the President, if he should find that the prohibition of the sale of arms in the United States to the belligerents in the Gran Chaco war would contribute to the restoration of peace, to prohibit such sale by proclamation. Violation of the prohibition was made a crime. Curtiss-Wright was indicted for conspiring to sell arms to Bolivia; it demurred to the indictment, arguing that the resolution unconstitutionally delegated legislative power to the President.

The resolution might have been sustained as contingent legislation: Congress had specified both the purpose of Presidential action and the means. But Justice Sutherland, who wrote the majority opinion, wished to introduce a cherished theory into constitutional law. Whether or

---

[35] *On Thermonuclear War* (Princeton: Princeton University Press, 1960), pp. 145-9.
[36] 299 U.S. 304.

not the joint resolution would have been invalid if its operation were internal, he said, it was not "vulnerable to attack under the rule that forbids a delegation of the lawmaking power" because its purpose was "to affect a situation entirely external to the United States, and falling within the category of foreign affairs."

This was because sovereignty was of two sorts, external and internal. At the Revolution the external sovereignty of the British crown passed to the United States; internal sovereignty passed to the several states. By adopting the Constitution, the several states transferred a portion of their internal sovereignty to the Union, but the Constitution had no effect upon the external sovereignty which the Union already possessed; therefore the constitutional rule against the delegation of legislative power could not apply to exercises of external sovereignty.

The notion that "the states severally never possessed international powers" would have surprised the signers of the Declaration of Independence, for that document reads:

> We therefore, the representatives of the United States of America, in General Congress, assembled, . . . do . . . solemnly publish and declare, that these united colonies are, and of right ought to be free and independent states; . . . and that as free and independent states, they have full power to levy war, conclude peace, contract alliances, establish commerce, and to do all other acts and things which independent states may of right do.

Sutherland's theory is not only historically but theoretically unsound. The notion that sovereignty can come in two parts is absurd, for the reason Sutherland himself gives: "A political society cannot endure without a supreme will somewhere." As Hans Kelsen puts it, a coherent legal order must derive from a single *Grundnorm*;[37] to use another figure, it must rise pyramidally to a single apex. For us, the *Grundnorm* is the Constitution, and even for Justice Sutherland, for he says that external sovereignty remained in the Union "save in so far as the Constitution in express terms qualified its exercise." The Constitution entirely qualified its exercise. It created the several organs of national government and assigned powers to each. It apportioned the powers of "external sovereignty"—treaties and war and foreign commerce. War and foreign commerce it assigned to Congress in Article

---

[37] See Hans Kelsen, *General Theory of Law and State* (Cambridge: Harvard University Press, 1945).

I of the Constitution, which begins with the words which forbid the delegation of Congressional power: "The legislative power herein granted shall be vested in a Congress."

But even if Sutherland's reasoning would hold water the *Curtiss-Wright* case would not be a precedent for the Tonkin Gulf Resolution. The joint resolution involved in the *Curtiss-Wright* case did not give the President a choice. If he found that a prohibition on the sale of arms would help restore peace, he was required to proclaim the prohibition. The Tonkin Gulf Resolution, after stating the objective, provides for action only at the President's option. Nothing in Sutherland's opinion in the *Curtiss-Wright* case suggests that when the Congress has specified the goal the President is free to pursue it or not as he chooses.

Quite aside from this, the foundation has been cut from under the *Curtiss-Wright* case, as well as the few other cases which look in the same direction. The notion of extra-constitutional legal power was always nonsense, and it was decisively rejected by the Supreme Court in *Reid v. Covert*[38] in 1957. Holding that the allocations of power in the Constitution—in this case, Article III, assigning judicial power to the constitutional courts—and the prohibitions of the Constitution —in this case, the Sixth Amendment, guaranteeing jury trial in criminal cases—invalidated an act of Congress which provided for trial by court martial of civilian dependents of military personnel abroad, Justice Black said: "The United States is entirely a creature of the Constitution. Its power and authority have no other source. It can only act in accordance with all the limitations imposed by the Constitution."[39]

As we have said, the joint resolution in the *Curtiss-Wright* case was passed under the commerce power. In *Kent v. Dulles*,[40] decided in 1958, another delegation of rule-making power in the field of foreign commerce was held to be an impermissible delegation on the principle of *Panama Refining Company v. Ryan.*

In 1926 Congress had provided that "The Secretary of State may grant and issue passports . . . under such rules as the President shall designate and prescribe." In 1952 the Secretary of State, acting under Presidential authorization, made the issuance of a passport conditional upon the satisfaction of tests as to political belief and affiliation. Rockwell Kent refused on principle to take an oath as to present or past

---

[38] 354 U.S. 1.   [39] Id. at 5-6.   [40] 357 U.S. 116.

membership in the Communist party and was denied a passport. The majority of the Supreme Court held that the Secretary's rules were not authorized by Congress. If Congress delegates power, "the standards must be adequate to pass scrutiny by accepted tests. *Panama Refining Co. v. Ryan.*" Where a constitutional right, such as that to travel, is involved, delegations will be construed narrowly. So construed, the statute can be taken to authorize rules only on the two topics with which Congress was familiar in 1926: citizenship and criminality. To save the statute, the delegation must be interpreted to be confined to these topics. Therefore Acheson's rules were invalid. It does not disturb our argument that in 1965, in *Zemel v. Rusk,*[41] the Court discovered that Congress in 1926, or at any rate at the reenactment of the passport legislation of 1952, had contemplated executive rule-making on three subjects rather than two. The third was the prohibition of travel to designated areas. The delegation was therefore held to be valid as to this third topic. The majority did not disagree with the principles, but only disputed the relevance, of Justice Black's dissent: "For Congress to attempt to delegate such an undefined law-making power to the Secretary, the President, or both, makes applicable to this 1926 Act what Mr. Justice Cardozo said about the National Industrial Recovery Act: 'This is delegation running riot. No such plenitude of power is susceptible of transfer.' "

The attempt of Congress to transfer its power and responsibility to make war to the President is constitutionally unauthorized and destroys the political system envisaged by the framers.

IX. Ratification and Delegation by Appropriation

On February 7, 1965, President Johnson began his air attacks on North Vietnam. Then he began to move substantial bodies of troops into South Vietnam, a commitment which has not reached its end with 525,000 men. It would have been politically imprudent to take these momentous actions without making some gesture toward Congress. On May 4, he asked Congress to appropriate another $700,000,000 "to meet mounting military requirements in Vietnam. This is not a routine appropriation. For every Member of Congress who supports this request is also voting to persist in our effort to halt Communist aggression in South Vietnam. Each is saying that the Congress and the

41 381 U.S. 1.

President stand united before the world in joint determination that the independence of South Vietnam shall be preserved and Communist attack will not succeed."[1]

If President Johnson had sought Congressional support in any other way, it would have been necessary to draft a bill which stated what he was authorized to do. The bill would have gone to the Foreign Relations and Armed Services Committees, and these would have been obliged to review the policy proposed in the bill. They would have canvassed alternatives. The two houses would have debated the concrete recommendations of the President. Congress would have played its constitutional role in the exercise of the war power.

But as it was, Congress left the determination of policy, the question of war and peace, the scope of limited war, the choice between limited war and general war—even the choice of adversary—entirely in the hands of the President, where it had already undertaken to place all these decisions by the Tonkin Gulf Resolution. The only change was that it enlarged his choice by giving him $700,000,000 to spend in doing whatever he should decide to do.

Nevertheless, an act of Congress was passed. This enabled the State Department in its justificatory memorandum to boast: "The appropriation act constitutes a clear endorsement and approval of the actions taken by the President."[2]

This suggests that the act was viewed as a ratification of past actions of the President. Where there is doubt as to the validity of executive action already completed Congress may, unless there is some constitutional obstacle to retroactive legislation, lend the necessary legislative authority to such action by ratification. An illustration is afforded by the act of August 6, 1861, in which Congress provided "That all the acts, proclamations and orders of the President of the United States after the fourth of March, eighteen hundred and sixty-one, respecting the army and navy of the United States, and calling out or relating to the militia or volunteers from the States, are hereby approved and in all respects legalized and made valid, to the same intent and with the same effect as if they had been issued and done under the previous express authority and direction of the Congress of the United States."[3]

---

[1] *Congressional Record*, Vol. 111, Pt. 7, 89th Congress, 1st Sess. (May 4, 1965), p. 9282.

[2] *Memorandum*, in *Vietnam and International Law* by the Consultative Council of the Lawyers Committee on American Policy towards Vietnam (Flanders, N.J.: O'Hare Books, 1967), p. 127.

[3] 12 Stat. 326.

William Howard Taft considered Wilson's occupation of Vera Cruz an act of war, and illegitimate in that it occurred before Congress had given the necessary authority, but said that the resolution which passed on the following day was "full and immediate ratification."[4]

It is possible to ratify executive actions of dubious validity by means of an appropriation act, but the standards of ratification are rather exacting.

The most generous decision is that in *Brooks v. Dewar*[5] in 1941. Instead of issuing term permits for the use of public grazing lands at reasonable fees based on the individual values of the permits, as the law required, the Secretary of the Interior had made a practice of issuing temporary licenses at a uniform fee. Congress, with full knowledge of this practice, had acted on the disposal of the revenue from the licenses. The Court held that this was ratification.

In *Isbrandtsen-Moller Co. v. United States*,[6] in 1937, the Court held that an executive order by which the President abolished the Shipping Board and transferred its functions to the Department of Commerce had been ratified by three successive appropriations acts "all of which make appropriations to the Department of Commerce for salaries and expenses to carry out the provisions of the shipping act as amended and refer to the executive order."

In *Fleming v. Mohawk Co.*,[7] in 1947, the Court held that when the President had consolidated agencies and Congress had appropriated funds for the use of the consolidated agencies this was "confirmation and ratification of the action of the Chief Executive."

In *Ex parte Endo*,[8] in 1944, Justice Douglas, writing the opinion of the Court, denied that an appropriation act ratified all the activities it supported. Without statutory authority, the Relocation Authority had adopted the policy of detaining citizens of Japanese origin whose loyalty had been satisfactorily established in relocation centers if they would not agree to go to an approved place of residence upon release. In a habeas corpus action the Authority contended that Congress had ratified this policy by appropriating funds for the continued operation of the relocation centers. Justice Douglas said:

It is argued . . . that there has been Congressional ratification of the detention of loyal evacuees . . . through the appropriation of

---

[4] *Our Chief Magistrate and His Powers* (New York: Columbia University Press, 1925), p. 96.

[5] 313 U.S. 354, 361.   [6] 300 U.S. 139, 147.

[7] 331 U.S. 111, 116.   [8] 323 U.S. 283.

sums for the expenses of the Authority. . . . It is pointed out that the regulations and procedures of the Authority were disclosed in reports to the Congress and in Congressional hearings. . . . Congress may of course do by ratification what it might have authorized. . . . And ratification may be effected through appropriation acts. . . . But the appropriation must plainly show a purpose to bestow the precise authority which is claimed. We can hardly deduce such a purpose here where a lump sum appropriation was made for the overall program of the Authority and no sums were earmarked for the single phase of the total program which is here involved. Congress may support the effort to take care of these evacuees without ratifying every phase of the program.[9]

Justice Roberts concurred in the result, but he asserted that Congress had actually ratified the practice of detaining loyal citizens. He complained of the test applied by Douglas: "The decision now adds an element never before thought essential to congressional ratification, namely, that if Congress is to ratify by appropriation any part of the programme of an executive agency the bill must include a specific item referring to that portion of the programme."[10]

Quite possibly Justice Roberts was indignant that the Court relied on a proposition about ratification because he wished to press on to what he considered the central issue, the detention of citizens in violation of the due process clause. In any case, Douglas seems to have the better of it. There can be no ratification without an identification of what is being ratified. In the *Isbrandtsen-Moller* case, the executive order that was being ratified was identified in the act. In the *Fleming* case, Congress identified the consolidated agencies by name. It is true that in *Brooks v. Dewar* Congress made no explicit reference to the administrative practice that was being ratified. But in disposing of the revenue from that practice it did single out the practice and authorize its continuance.

In his message of May 4, 1965 asking for a supplementary appropriation, President Johnson described several things he had done in recent months. He had increased the armed forces in South Vietnam to 35,000; he had sent marines and airborne troops to two important areas; he had enormously increased the helicopter activity in South Vietnam; he had increased the number of sorties against North Vietnam from 160 in February to more than 1,500 in April; he had begun

---

[9] Id. at 303n.   [10] Id. at 309.

strike sorties in South Vietnam, and in March and April there were more than 3,200 of these. And, no doubt as a balancing measure to the strike sorties, he had sent the Deputy Surgeon General of the Army to assist in formulating "an expanded program of medical assistance for the people of South Vietnam."

But he did not ask for ratification of these concrete actions:

> I do not ask complete approval for every phase and action of your Government. I do ask for prompt support of our basic course: resistance to aggression, moderation in the use of power, and a constant search for peace. Nothing will do more to strengthen your country in the world than the proof of national unity which an overwhelming vote for this appropriation will clearly show. To deny and delay this means to deny and delay the fullest support of the American people and the American Congress to those brave men who are risking their lives for freedom in Vietnam.[11]

In short, he asked for two things. The first was $700,000,000: "The additional funds I am requesting are needed to continue to provide our forces with the best and most modern supplies and equipment. They are needed to keep an abundant inventory of ammunition and other expendables. They are needed to build facilities to house and protect our men and supplies."[12] The second request was for a vote of confidence.

On May 7, President Johnson signed into law a joint resolution of less than a hundred words which authorized the Secretary of Defense, "upon determination by the President that such action is necessary in connection with military activities in southeast Asia," to transfer $700,000,000 from unappropriated funds to any existing military account.[13]

It was said in *Ex parte Endo* that to constitute a ratification "the appropriation must plainly show a purpose to bestow the precise authority which is claimed." The joint resolution of May 7 contained no other language than that authorizing the transfer of funds. It did not purport to alter the legal status of any past event. In view of this fact, and of President Johnson's denial that he asked "complete approval for every phase and action of your Government," it is hard to see how the appropriation can be read as a ratification of any particular

---

[11] *Congressional Record*, p. 9284.   [12] *Ibid.*, p. 9283.
[13] 79 Stat. 109.

action. The joint resolution had legal effect as an appropriation measure. It had no other legal effect.

Of course it had extralegal significance. President Johnson said that a vote for the appropriation was also a vote "to persist in our effort to halt Communist aggression in South Vietnam." This latter vote would not grant authority but would strike a posture. It would announce that "the Congress and the President stand united before the world"; it would be "proof of national unity." The striking of postures is not an exercise of the legislative power of Congress; it cannot take the place of the words "Be it enacted."

Suppose, however, that we supply the words "Be it enacted," and that we further interpret into the resolution the entire statement of purpose in the President's message. Suppose we assume that the resolution authorizes the President to accomplish these purposes: halting Communist aggression, preserving the independence of South Vietnam, "resistance to aggression, moderation in the use of power, and a constant search for peace." Do these words prescribe a definite course of action? Do they supply standards to guide the President? Do they specify the means which he is to employ? Clearly a resolution cast in these terms would be another attempt at the delegation of legislative power, which is forbidden by the Constitution.

When a supplementary defense appropriation bill came before the Senate in 1967, certain Senators attempted to forbid further escalation of the war by amendment to the bill. From a legal point of view, the administration was ill-advised to oppose the amendment, for by accepting limits to Presidential action it could easily have obtained a Congressional mandate for action within those limits. But the administration preferred to retain the whole war power in the President's hands. Accordingly, in the amendment which emerged from debate in the two houses and from conference committee and which passed both houses on March 8 Congress declared neither for war nor for peace. As before, it left the conduct of affairs entirely in the hands of the President, who might either abandon the war or further escalate it into a war with China without violating the amendment:

The Congress hereby declares:

(1) Its firm intentions to provide all necessary support for members of the armed forces of the United States fighting in Viet Nam;

(2) its support of efforts being made by the President of the United States and other men of good will throughout the world to prevent

an expansion of the war in Viet Nam and to bring that conflict to an end through a negotiated settlement which will preserve the honor of the United States, protect the vital interests of this country, and allow the people of South Viet Nam to determine the affairs of that nation in their own way; and

(3) its support for the convening of the nations that participated in the Geneva Conferences or any other meeting of nations similarly involved and interested as soon as possible for the purpose of pursuing the general principles of the Geneva accords of 1954 and 1962 and for formulating plans for bringing the conflict to an honorable conclusion.[14]

The first paragraph is not an exercise of the war power of Congress. It does not instruct the President to prosecute the war; it is merely a statement of the intention of Congress, which of course is not legally binding, to pass other appropriation acts if he does. Nor does it appear that the second and third paragraphs have any legal effect. The most general principle of the Geneva accords of 1954 was the agreement upon the unification of the north and south zones of Vietnam by nationwide elections.[15] The announced purpose of the Johnson administration in waging war is the establishment of an independent South Vietnam. But even if the implied indorsement of unification in the third paragraph did not conflict with the second paragraph, it could

[14] *Congressional Quarterly Weekly Report*, Vol. 25, No. 10 (Mar. 10, 1967) , p. 337.

[15] "Agreement on the Cessation of Hostilities in Vietnam, July 20, 1954," Article 14 (a) : "Pending the general elections which will bring about the unification of Vietnam, the conduct of civil administration in each regrouping zone shall be in the hands of the party whose forces are to be regrouped there [*i.e.*, the Vietminh and the French] by virtue of the present Agreement." *Vietnam and International Law* by the Consultative Council of the Lawyers Committee on American Policy towards Vietnam (Flanders, N.J.: O'Hare Books, 1967) , p. 140.

"Final Declaration of the Geneva Conference, July 21, 1954," para. 5: "The Conference recognizes that the essential purpose of the agreement relating to Vietnam is to settle military questions with a view to ending hostilities and that the military demarcation line is provisional and should not in any way be interpreted as constituting a political or territorial boundary." Para. 6: "The Conference declares that, so far as Vietnam is concerned, the settlement of political problems, effected on the basis of respect for the principles of independence, unity and territorial integrity, shall permit Vietnamese people to enjoy the fundamental freedoms, guaranteed by democratic institutions established as a result of free general elections by secret ballot. In order to ensure that sufficient progress in the restoration of peace has been made, and that all the necessary conditions obtain for free expression of the national will, general elections shall be held in July, 1956, under the supervision of an international commission composed of representatives of the Member States of the International Supervisory Commission, referred to in the agreement on the cessation of hostilities." *Ibid.*, pp. 148, 149.

not be argued that Congress by approving the Geneva accords—which, incidentally, forbade the introduction of foreign troops into Vietnam[16] —had forbidden the President to prosecute the war. The words are merely precatory. In the amendment Congress resolutely maintained its position of interested bystander. It refused to discharge its constitutional duty of determining whether there should be war or peace. Representative Bates was quite right when he said of the amendment: "It is almost innocuous. It is barely a pious preachment."[17]

Clearly a majority of the Congressmen are happy to leave matters in this posture. They prefer that the President take the decisions; this spares them a responsibility to which they feel unequal. But in a republican form of government they must bear that responsibility. And there is every likelihood that the task will be better discharged by the collective judgment of the two houses after full debate than by the private resolution of a single man.

The President has no inherent constitutional power to engage in war. Whatever one thinks of the scope of his right to protect citizens or to practice reprisal for injuries to citizens, neither of these is involved in Vietnam. The Senate has no power to authorize war by treaty, nor does the SEATO treaty purport to do so. Congress cannot delegate the war power. The Tonkin Gulf Resolution is unconstitutional because it affronts the most fundamental principle of the division of powers in our constitutional system. Nor can this fundamental principle be avoided by passing appropriations.

[16] "Agreement on the Cessation of Hostilities in Vietnam, July 20, 1954," Article 16: "With effect from the date of entry into force of the present Agreement, the introduction into Vietnam of any troop reinforcements and additional military personnel is prohibited." Article 17 (a): "With effect from the date of entry into force of the present Agreement, the introduction into Vietnam of any reinforcements in the form of all types of arms . . . is prohibited." Article 18: "With effect from the date of entry into force of the present Agreement, the establishment of new military bases is prohibited throughout Vietnam territory." Article 19: "With effect from the date of entry into force of the present Agreement, no military base under the control of a foreign State may be established in the regrouping zone of either party; the two parties shall ensure that the zones assigned to them do not adhere to any military alliance and are not used for the resumption of hostilities or to further an aggressive policy." *Ibid.*, pp. 141-3.

"Final Declaration of the Geneva Conference, July 21, 1954," para. 4: "The Conference takes note of the clauses in the agreement on the cessation of hostilities in Vietnam prohibiting the introduction into Vietnam of foreign troops and military personnel as well as all kinds of arms and munitions." Para. 5: "The Conference takes note of the clauses in the agreement on the cessation of hostilities in Vietnam to the effect that no military base under the control of a foreign power may be established in the regrouping zones of the two parties. . . ." *Ibid.*, p. 148.

[17] *Congressional Quarterly Weekly Report* (Mar. 10, 1967), p. 373.

Although executive war-making is illegal, it is practiced; and ultimately practice makes the law. And the transfer of the war power to the executive will draw other powers with it. If we continue to follow the easy downward course of executive aggrandizement, our republican institutions will become as unsubstantial as those of imperial Rome. But perhaps this was our destiny. When the United States embarked upon a course of imperialism with the Spanish-American War, the distinguished political scientist John W. Burgess warned that this meant the end of constitutional government:

> There is nothing now to prevent the Government of the United States from entering upon a course of conquest and empire. . . . We are by no means a peaceably inclined people. . . . In fact, besides being belligerent and boastful, we are restless, nervous, and at times hysterical. We have just the qualities to answer the call of a Napoleon in the Presidency.[18]

[18] *The Reconciliation of Government With Liberty* (New York: Scribner's, 1915), p. 373.

The National Executive and the Use
of the Armed Forces Abroad*

JOHN NORTON MOORE

THE BREADTH of my assigned topic "The National Executive and International Law" suggests that my mission this morning is about like that of the fan dancer; to call attention to the subject without really covering it. But rather than attempt a superficial survey of the range of problems in allocating the foreign affairs power between Congress, the President, and the Court, it may be more rewarding to instead concentrate on the currently most important of those problems, the power of the president to use the armed forces abroad.

Historically, the controversy over the war power and the controversy over the treaty power seem to have been the most important constitutional issues in the scope of the president's foreign affairs power. Of these, the treaty power controversy has been in at least a state of temporary quiescence since the heated controversy in 1954 over the Bricker amendment. With the defeat by a narrow margin of the Bricker amendment, which had been aimed at restricting the president's power to make international agreements, this controversy was resolved in favor of a continuing broad view of executive authority. In contrast, the debate on Vietnam has heated white hot the controversy over the extent of presidential power to use the armed forces abroad, and has generated a concern with presidential power as insistent as any in our century.[1]

Basically the controversy concerns the authority of the president to order the armed forces into combat abroad and the question of when and how Congress must authorize the use of the armed forces abroad.

---

* Delivered as an address on October 11, 1968 in the International Law Study series at the Naval War College.

---

[1] See generally on the national executive and the use of the armed forces abroad E. Corwin, *The President: Office and Powers* (4th edn., 1964); Wormuth, *The President v. The Constitution* (an Occasional Paper of the Center for the Study of Democratic Institutions, 1968); P. Kurland, *The Impotence of Reticence,* 1968 *Duke Law Journal* 619; Moore and Underwood, *The Lawfulness of United States Assistance to the Republic of Viet Nam,* 112 *Congressional Record* 14943, 14960-67, 14983-89 (daily edn., July 14, 1966); Velvel, *The War in Viet Nam: Unconstitutional, Justiciable, and Jurisdictionally Attackable,* 16 *Kansas Law Review* 449 (1968); *U.S. Commitments to Foreign Powers, Hearings Before the Committee on Foreign Relations of the United States Senate,* 90th Cong., 1st Sess. (1967); *National Commitments Report,* S. Rep. No. 797, 90th Cong., 1st Sess. (1967).

Although this problem is presented more dramatically today than ever before, it is not new. Much of the current debate borrows argument from the clashes of Jefferson and Hamilton over the power of the president in the 1801 naval war against the Bashaw of Tripoli and from the rhetoric of President Polk and Representative Abraham Lincoln in the 1846 Mexican war.

The starting point of the debate is the constitution, which gives Congress the power to declare war and to raise and support armies and which makes the president the commander-in-chief and in practical effect the chief representative of the nation in foreign affairs. It seems reasonably clear from the debates at the federal constitutional convention that most of the framers sought to place the major war power in Congress and to leave the president only the right to repel sudden attacks. The framers sought this restriction on presidential power because of their fear of concentrated power in the president. But the convention debates are not very useful in telling us who has power in situations which may be short of war or in resolving controversy about how Congress might authorize the president to use the army and navy. Moreover, the constitution is a living document and its meaning is shaped by the experience of successive congresses and presidents in filling in its broad outlines and in adapting it to changing circumstances. As Mr. Justice Frankfurter pointed out: "It is an inadmissibly narrow conception of American constitutional law to confine it to the words of the Constitution and to disregard the gloss which life has written upon them."[2] Nowhere is this statement or that of Mr. Justice Holmes that "the life of the law has not been logic: it has been experience"[3] been more apt than in the interpretation of the war power.

In the one hundred and eighty years since the adoption of the constitution our nation has moved from a position of comparative isolation epitomized by Washington's warning to stay clear of entangling alliances to one of intense international involvement evidenced in 1968 by agreements for collective defense with forty-two countries. In the same period the international system has shifted from a balance of power system to a loose bipolar system marked by intense global competition among competing public order systems and a nuclear balance of terror. And international law has moved from the notion of a just war to the prohibition of all force as a means of major change under

---

[2] Mr. Justice Frankfurter, concurring in *Youngstown Sheet and Tube Co. v. Sawyer*, 343 U.S. 579, 593 at 610 (1952).

[3] O. W. Holmes, *The Common Law*, 1 (1881).

the U.N. Charter. The increasing involvement of the United States in world affairs, the shift to an intensely competitive bipolar system, and the limitation of the lawful use of force to defense have greatly strengthened the hand of the executive in the contest with Congress over the war power. Hamilton and Jefferson fought over whether in the absence of congressional authorization to use force a Tripolitan cruiser must be released after capture by an American naval vessel. Jefferson took the position that in the absence of congressional authorization for U.S. naval forces to go on the offense, the cruiser must be released after being disabled from committing further hostilities. But the contemporary debate is about the power to commit from a quarter to a half million troops in major wars such as Korea and Vietnam. As the contrast in subjects debated shows, there has been a gradual increase in presidential power to use the military abroad over this period, an increase which has accelerated during the twentieth century.

Some commentators such as Professor Wormuth and Senator Fulbright tell us that the increase in presidential power vis-à-vis Congress has gone too far. They paint a picture of executive usurpation of authority. But though they have a great deal to show us, the trouble is that the frame they use may be too small. We cannot just look to the language of the Constitution or the experience of 150 years ago for the answer to problems and conditions not wholly anticipated. If we are to display a proper instinct for the jugular instead of an instinct for the capillaries, we must apply the policy of the framers to the diverse problems and conditions of today.

The policy of requiring congressional authority for the major use of force abroad as a check on presidential power remains as valid today, if not more so, than in 1789. But problems of collective defense pursuant to treaty obligations, the need for implementation of sanctions under article 42 of the United Nations Charter, an increasingly global defense interdependence, the wide range of responses to situations of intrastate conflict, and the swiftness of modern attack militate against absolute answers based on that policy.

The nature of our problem is such that we are unlikely to find many of what Mr. Justice Frankfurter termed bright-line distinctions. It will help immeasurably, however, if we first briefly indulge in the luxury of a minimum of clarification about the nature of the major questions we must deal with. Although there are really many more, as a first-stage complexity it is convenient to take four questions. With each we are concerned with authorization to use the armed forces abroad in conflict situations.

First, what may the president do on his own authority without congressional authorization? Second, if congressional authorization is necessary what form must it take? Must there be a formal declaration of war? Third, what terms of congressional authorization are valid? Can Congress delegate the authority to use troops abroad to the president and if so how broad a delegation is permissible? Lastly, to what extent can the answers to the first three questions be resolved by the courts? Are they "political questions" or issues which it is unwise for a court to adjudicate? Failure to separate these questions has carried more than its share of confusion. I will deal with these one at a time and then apply them all to the Vietnam situation.

First, what may the president do on his own authority without congressional authorization?

There is no doubt that the president, acting on his own authority, may order the military to repel sudden attacks on the United States or American forces. The draft proposals of the constitution initially contained language authorizing Congress to "make war," but at the instance of James Madison the language was changed from "to make war" to "to declare war." The reason given for the change was to leave to the president "the power to repel sudden attack." Beyond that, there is greater controversy. On the one hand, there are those who take a broad view of presidential power such as Craig Mathews who writes:

> Constitutional history has shown that the President can take military action under his independent powers whenever the interests of the United States so require. In the modern world the scope of America's interest can be determined only by reference to the state of affairs in the international arena as a whole and to the overall purposes of our foreign policy. Any rigid test of protectable interest would leave the nation dangerously unequipped for survival.[4]

Similarly, Under-Secretary Katzenbach in testifying recently before the Senate Foreign Relations Committee said that he doubts that any

---

[4] Mathews, *The Constitutional Power of the President to Conclude International Agreements*, 64 *Yale Law Journal* 345, 365 (1955).

president has ever acted to the full limits of his presidential authority.[5] There is substantial precedent in history for this broad interpretation of presidential authority. Former Assistant Secretary of State James Grafton Rogers tells us that in the over 100 uses of United States forces abroad from 1789-1945 that the executive ordered the use on his own authority in at least 80.[6] And a 1951 study for the Committee on Foreign Relations says that: "Since the Constitution was adopted there have been at least 125 incidents in which the President, without congressional authorization, . . . has ordered the Armed Forces to take action or maintain positions abroad."[7]

Since these studies were completed we could add President Truman's use of a quarter of a million American troops in Korea, President Eisenhower's landing of the marines in Lebanon, President Kennedy's limited use of American forces in the Bay of Pigs invasion and as "advisors" in Vietnam, and President Johnson's landing of troops in the Dominican Republic. All of this certainly represents a substantial gloss which experience has placed on the constitution.

On the other hand, those who take a narrow view of presidential power, such as Professor Ruhl Bartlett in testimony before the Senate Foreign Relations Committee during the National Commitment hearings, point out that most of these actions, with the greatest exception being Korea, did not involve sustained hostilities or more than minor casualties.[8] Typically they involved protection of United States citizens abroad, pursuit of pirates, alleged humanitarian intervention, reprisals, or consensual assistance to a recognized government. And protracted and sustained use of troops abroad resulting in substantial casualties have usually been highly controversial; the Korean War and President Polk's initiation of the Mexican War of 1846 being prime examples.

Given this degree of disagreement by sincere and informed scholars, what guideposts are there for delimiting presidential authority in those situations in which the president acts without congressional authorization? Although they can easily be overstated, there are some policy

[5] U.S. Commitments to Foreign Powers, Hearings Before the Senate Committee on Foreign Relations on S. Res. 151, 90th Cong., 1st Sess., 76 (Comm. Print, 1967).

[6] Rogers, World Policing and the Constitution in 11 America Looks Ahead 78 (World Peace Foundation 1945).

[7] Study prepared for the use of the joint committee made up of the Committee on Foreign Relations and the Committee on Armed Services of the Senate, 82d Cong., 1st Sess., Powers of the President to Send the Armed Forces Outside the United States 2 (Comm. Print, Feb. 28, 1951).

[8] See U.S. Commitments to Foreign Powers, note 5 supra, at 9-21.

considerations which in my opinion suggest a need for substantial presidential authority. First, there is a need for the president to be able to quickly react to sudden armed attacks threatening United States defense interests. The sudden attack in Korea and the rapid response of President Truman in initiating a process of troop commitment to Korea is, I believe, a real example of this need. Though subject to abuse, possibly some actions to protect American citizens abroad fall into an analogous category. The joint U.S.-Belgian rescue operation in the Congo and the first stage of the Dominican operation are examples. There is also sometimes a need for secrecy, decisiveness, and negotiating responsiveness which can best be met by presidential action. In this category I would cite the actions of President Kennedy in the Cuban missile crisis. It seems to me that the wisdom of congressional debate about whether the response to the Soviet emplacement of medium range ballistic missiles in Cuba should be quarantine, air strikes on the missile sites, invasion of Cuba, or no response at all, which is the debate which went on within the administration, is open to serious doubt. Robert Kennedy tells us in his account of the missile crisis that he doubts as satisfactory an outcome could have been achieved if the debate over alternatives had taken place in the full glare of publicity. And lest we succumb to the myth that the president is always hawkish and Congress is always dovish, we should remember Kennedy's account of the hawkish pressures from leading congressman during the missile crisis. There is also a category of what might be called "ongoing command decisions," which are day-to-day decisions about the operation of existing military assistance programs within the network of United States defense interests or about defensive deployment of our armed forces. By their recurrent nature, many of these decisions inevitably will be left, in the first instance at least, to presidential authority. Examples would be the conduct of established military advisory missions, military assistance programs, and intelligence missions necessary for national security. Moreover, I believe that some of the arguments for strictly limiting presidential authority misconceive the nature of presidential power and elevate form over substance. Presidential power, even in the exercise of the commander-in-chief power, is not autonomous and as Richard Neustadt compellingly argues is in large measure the power to persuade.[9] It is difficult for a president to pursue sustained military actions without the active support of a

---

[9] See R. Neustadt, *Presidential Power* (1964).

substantial segment of Congress and the American people. And although Congress would usually be reluctant to do so, if things got too bad Congress could refuse to appropriate funds or could even institute impeachment proceedings against the president. And short of these measures, the Congress can bring great pressure to bear on the president through the power of critical public hearings, as the Fulbright hearings on Vietnam perhaps more than adequately demonstrate.

Despite these reasons for some presidential authority in the use of troops abroad it neither seems wise nor necessary to encourage too great an expansion of presidential power. Within the limit of survival in the world we live in we should require the more broadly based authorization which only Congress can give and should strive to revitalize the role of Congress in the making of foreign policy.

As a dividing line for presidential authority in the use of the military abroad, one test might be to require congressional authorization in all cases where regular combat units are committed to sustained hostilities. This test would be likely to include most situations resulting in substantial casualties and substantial commitment of resources. Under this test, the Mexican War, the Korean War and the Vietnam War would all require congressional authorization. The test has the virtue of responsiveness to precisely those situations historically creating the greatest concern over presidential authority but like all tests is somewhat frayed at the edges. In conflicts which gradually escalate, the dividing line for requiring congressional authorization might be initial commitment to combat of regular United States combat units as such. As to the suddenness of Korea, and conflicts like Korea, I would argue that the president should have the authority to meet the attack as necessary but should immediately seek congressional authorization. In retrospect the decision not to obtain congressional authorization in the Korean War, in which the United States sustained more than 140,000 casualties seems a poor precedent. And in those situations in which presidential authority is based on the need for secrecy or immediacy of response the need should be a real one.

To say that the president should have authority to act in some circumstances without congressional authorization is not to advise that he should not consult Congress or key congressional leaders. The president should involve Congress as much as practicable in every case. In fact, failure to pursue congressional involvement meaningfully when it could have been done has been the cause of a great deal of unnecessary presidential grief. As Under-Secretary Katzenbach points out "there can be no question that . . . [the President] acts most effectively when he acts with the support and authority of the Congress."[10]

The second question is: When congressional authorization is necessary what form should it take? Is a formal declaration of war required?

Much of the popular discussion about the war power seems to assume that a formal declaration of war is the only means of constitutionally obtaining congressional authorization for the use of the military. But this one is largely a red herring. As a matter of logic, the syntax of the constitution that "Congress should have power . . . to declare war" does not mean that Congress may not authorize hostilities without a formal declaration of war. And as a matter of intent of the framers the requirement is congressional control of hostilities, not a particular mode of authorization. This was so clear that within twelve years of the adoption of the constitution no less an authority than Chief Justice John Marshall recognized in the case of *Talbot v. Seeman*[11] that congressional action not amounting to a formal declaration of war could be a valid congressional authorization of hostilities. The case arose out of the 1789 naval war with France, the first war of a fledgling United States. As a result of French raiding of American shipping, Congress had passed a series of acts suspending commercial relations with France, denouncing the treaties with France, and establishing a Department of the Navy and a Marine Corps. The Court treated these acts as congressional authorization for limited hostilities with France. Practice since then shows that Congress has declared war only five times, despite the much larger number of occasions on which the United States has been at war. There is little reason, then, to believe that a formal declaration of war is the only means of congressional authorization of hostilities. A joint congressional resolution, which must be approved by both houses of Congress, authorizing the president to use the military abroad is certainly as Under-Secretary Katzenbach puts it "a functional equivalent of the declaration of war."

There are also numerous policy arguments why the formal declaration of war is undesirable under present circumstances. Arguments made include increased danger of misunderstanding of limited objectives, diplomatic embarrassment in recognition of nonrecognized guerrilla opponents, inhibition of settlement possibilities, the danger of widening the war, and unnecessarily increasing a president's domestic authority. Although each of these arguments has some merit, probably the

[10] *U.S. Commitments to Foreign Powers*, note 5 supra, at 76.
[11] (The Amelia) 5 U.S. (1 Cr.) 1, 25 (1801).

most compelling reason for not using the formal declaration of war is that there is no reason to do so. As former Secretary of Defense McNamara has pointed out "There has not been a formal declaration of war—anywhere in the world—since World War II."[12]

More serious questions as to form of congressional authorization include to what extent can Congress authorize the president to engage in hostilities by prior approval of an international agreement? And to what extent can congressional acquiescence in appropriation measures constitute congressional authorization to engage in hostilities? One obvious problem with treaty authorization is that although the House of Representatives would participate in a declaration of war it would not participate in treaty-making. This objection would be alleviated if the international agreement took the form of a congressional-executive agreement sanctioned by a joint-resolution. Problems in recognizing appropriation measures as authorization include confronting Congress with a *fait accompli,* and ascertaining the scope of congressional intent in a vote to approve an appropriation measure.

The third question is what terms of congressional authorization are valid? Can Congress delegate the authority to use troops abroad to the president and if so, how broad a delegation is permissible?

The permissibility of congressional delegation of the war power to the president and exactly what constitutes a delegation have been disputed throughout United States history. In 1834 President Jackson sought congressional authorization to undertake reprisals upon French property unless France paid her outstanding debts for damages to American shipping during the Napoleonic wars. There were objections in Congress on the grounds that it would amount to an unconstitutional transfer of Congress's war power to the president and Jackson did not get his resolution. Similarly, in 1857 President Buchanan sought congressional authorization to use the military in his discretion, if necessary to preserve freedom of communication across the Isthmus of Panama. Despite three requests, Congress refused to grant Buchanan the authority he requested. A principal argument against granting his request was that to do so would be a surrender to the president of Congress's war power. The objection was again raised by Senators opposed to President Wilson's request for congressional authority to take defensive measures in protection of American shipping. Corwin tells

---

[12] The statement is from an address by former Secretary of Defense McNamara to the American Society of Newspaper Editors on May 18, 1966. *New York Times,* May 19, 1966, p. c 11, col. 1 (city edn.) , at col. 2.

us that Wilson went ahead and armed American merchant vessels despite congressional inaction.

More recent experience has seen Congress take a broader view on the delegation issue. In the 1945 United Nations Participation Act, Congress provided for delegation of authority to the president to engage in hostilities if acting pursuant to an Article 43 U.N. collective peace force agreement approved by Congress. Apparently, however, no such agreement has yet been approved by Congress. And in the 1955 Formosa Resolution, the 1957 Middle East Resolution, and the 1964 Tonkin Gulf Resolution Congress authorized the president to use force to assist certain areas if subjected to armed attack. In the case of the Formosa Resolution, the Middle East Resolution, and the Tonkin Gulf Resolution, all were passed over the objection of at least one congressman, Senator Wayne Morse, that the resolution amounted to an "unconstitutional predeclaration of war." In none of these situations does the delegation issue seem to have been considered very adequately and the practice is probably inconclusive.

Professor Wormuth, arguing largely on the basis of now defunct precedents of domestic delegation law, urges a strict antidelegation rule.[13] But the domestic delegation analogy concerned with the limits of congressional delegation of legislative power is not only nebulous today, but is also of only limited usefulness in the war power context. The president has in his own right both substantial authority to use the military abroad and authority as commander-in-chief, none of which are present in comparable degree in the domestic delegation cases.

And in view of the great power of the president to pursue a diplomatic course leaving Congress little choice but war, and his great discretion as commander-in-chief after formal congressional authorization is given, it seems somewhat quixotic to take a rigid antidelegation stance. Moreover, there are substantial problems in any antidelegation stance as to when Congress is granting authorization with full knowledge of the circumstances. And what is the standard for too broad a delegation? Certainly the test would be unrealistic if simply one of whether discretion is left to the president, as the president probably always has the right as commander-in-chief to refuse to order American troops into combat. And unless Congress speaks to the issue he certainly has very crucial discretion as to theater of operations, weapons systems employed, and settlement terms, any of which can be as decisive for conflict limitation as the original decision to use force.

13 See Wormuth, *The President v. The Constitution*, note 1, supra.

It is hard to get away from the fact that the war power is in reality a joint executive-congressional power and that the president is always going to have a substantial discretionary role. The delegation problem is more likely to be resolved by a pattern of practice responding to felt needs than by overly neat *a priori* constitutional hypotheses. If there is to be a delegation test I would suggest that it be one asking whether there has been meaningful participation by a congress reasonably informed of the circumstances giving rise to the need for the use of U.S. forces.

The fourth question is to what extent can the answers to the first three questions be resolved by the courts? Are they "political questions" or otherwise issues which it is unwise for a court to adjudicate?

The tradition of judicial review runs deep in the American system. But it is not every question that is suitable for judicial review. Considerations of lack of manageable standards and interference with another coordinate branch of government are reasons which the Supreme Court has given for declining to decide a question. These considerations frequently arise in the separation-of-powers context and are all present to some degree in judicial determination of the scope of presidential authority to use the armed forces abroad. For example, what could the Court do which would not have a major adverse impact on the course of a war if it wanted to declare the war unconstitutional? This dilemma has led one ingenious advocate to argue that the Court should give a declaratory judgment in such circumstances. According to him, "a declaratory judgment would give little comfort to the other side in the negotiations since the executive can always go to the Congress for a declaration of war if the negotiations break down."[14]

If that is the case, one wonders why the need for a declaratory judgment. And in any event, the suggestion shows a most unprofessional naivete in understating the possible impact of such a ruling.

For these and other reasons, a United States District Court in Kansas last July dismissed a class action instituted against the President, the Secretary of State, and the Secretary of Defense seeking a declaratory judgment that they had acted unconstitutionally in the Vietnamese War.[15] Though the scope of the President's authority to use the armed forces abroad is a constitutional question, it is a question in separation of powers with few manageable standards, often running great

[14] The context was that of the Vietnam conflict. Velvel, *The War In Viet Nam*, note 1, supra, at 449, 484.

[15] *Velvel v. Johnson*, 287 F. Supp. 846 (1968).

risk of serious interference with legitimate defense requirements, and which is probably subject to more lasting solution from the continuing interplay between the checks and powers of Congress and the president. Though I believe that a decision on the merits would uphold the constitutionality of executive action in the Vietnam War, the refusal to adjudicate the issue is certainly the wisest course during the continuation of the conflict. There are, after all, other checks in our system than judicial review, the chief among them being the election of a president.

Let me briefly apply these tests to the constitutional issues in the Vietnam conflict. First, the present magnitude of the Vietnam War in terms of troop levels, casualties, and impact on the nation strongly militates for requiring congressional authorization. I would say that the point at which congressional authorization should be required in Vietnam was the initiation in February, 1965 of the regular interdictive air attacks against the North and the first sustained use of regular United States combat units in the summer and fall of 1965.

And though I believe that at the current level of hostilities congressional authorization should be required, given the Korean experience and the breadth of executive authority acquiesced in by both Congress and the president for the last fifty years, argument to the contrary can certainly be made in good faith.

Second, congressional authorization need not and should not take the form of a formal declaration of war. A joint resolution authorizing the use of combat forces in hostilities in Vietnam, such as the Tonkin Gulf Resolution of August 1964, is preferable and adequate. Preferable since there is no good reason to declare war, since a formal declaration of war might connote an objective of subjugating North Vietnam and thus widening the war, and since avoidance of NLF recognition at too early a stage in the negotiating process or prior to reciprocal concessions may be an important diplomatic goal. And adequate since Congress authorized President Johnson to use the armed forces "to assist any member or protocol state of SEATO requesting assistance in defense," and the president's use of United States forces in Vietnam pursuant to this Resolution is constitutionally authorized executive-congressional action. Some argue that Congress was not aware of the magnitude of the war which it was authorizing, that the Tonkin Gulf Resolution was hurried through Congress with a sense of urgency precluding adequate consideration, that Congress was poorly informed as to the extent of attacks on American ships, and that therefore the

Resolution cannot be taken as sufficient congressional authorization. But the language of the Resolution is certainly broad enough to include the present hostilities. It is that "Congress approves and supports the determination of the President, as Commander-in-Chief, to take all necessary measures to repel any armed attack against the forces of the United States and to prevent further aggression." And I believe that a fair reading of the congressional debates in their entirety shows that although there was confusion and disagreement about the scope of the authorization, the Congress and the Senate floor leader of the Resolution, Senator Fulbright, were aware that Congress was giving the president the authority, within his discretion, to take whatever action he deemed necessary with respect to the defense of South Vietnam. In fact, that is the wording of an exchange on the floor of the Senate between Senators Fulbright and Cooper. The same exchange indicated an understanding that the Resolution was intended to ratify the constitutional process requirement of Article IV of the SEATO Treaty.[16]

Although consideration of the Tonkin Gulf Resolution was hasty, President Johnson clearly went to Congress because of his awareness of doubts raised during the Korean War as a result of President Truman's failure to request formal congressional authorization. The attacks on American ships in the Gulf of Tonkin were the opportunity but not the object of the Resolution.

The Tonkin Gulf Resolution has also been attacked as an invalid

---

[16] The relevant exchange was:

MR. COOPER. . . . Does the Senator consider that in enacting this resolution we are satisfying that requirement [the constitutional processes requirement] of Article IV of the Southeast Asia Collective Defense treaty? In other words, are we now giving the President advance authority to take whatever action he may deem necessary respecting South Vietnam and its defense, or with respect to the defense of any other country included in the treaty?

MR. FULBRIGHT. I think that is correct.

MR. COOPER. Then, looking ahead, if the President decided that it was necessary to use such force as could lead into war, we will give that authority by this resolution?

MR. FULBRIGHT. That is the way I would interpret it. If a situation later developed in which we thought the approval should be withdrawn, it could be withdrawn by concurrent resolution.

110 *Congressional Record* 18409-410 (1964).

For a compilation of excerpts from the congressional debates supporting a broad interpretation of presidential authority under the Tonkin Gulf Resolution see Moore and Underwood, *The Lawfulness of United States Assistance* note 1, supra. For a highly selective compilation of excerpts suggesting a narrower interpretation, see Velvel, note 14, supra, at 473-77. To resolve the controversy a reading of the debates in their entirety is suggested.

delegation of the congressional war power. But even if there is a constitutional requirement as to the breadth of congressional delegation of the war power to the president, a proposition open to considerable doubt, the Congress which passed the Tonkin Gulf Resolution was, I believe, reasonably informed of the circumstances giving rise to the need for the use of U.S. forces. It was aware that there was an ongoing guerrilla war in Vietnam which had been escalating since 1959, that the United States had had over 12,000 advisory troops there since 1962, a figure dramatically on the increase since then, and that recently the president had ordered retaliatory air strikes on facilities in the North. As such Congress was validly exercising its war power no matter how desirable or illuminating additional debate might have been.

Although there are, as indicated, difficulties in reading too much into appropriation measures or other indices of congressional authorization, the subsequent refusal to repeal the Tonkin Gulf Resolution and passage of military appropriation measures also lend some congressional authority to President Johnson's actions. This is particularly true of the $700 million special Vietnam appropriation measure of May 1965. This measure, requested shortly after President Johnson's major step-up of the U.S. response, was billed as an opportunity for expression of congressional opinion on the build-up.

Lastly, although there are those who argue for judicial review of the constitutionality of the authorization of the use of American forces in Vietnam, the lack of standards, the availability of other checks in the system, and the possibly grave impact on the course of negotiations strongly suggest the lack of wisdom of judicial review of such questions while the war continues. Without passing judgment on all future questions which may arise, the constitutional questions involved in the use of the armed forces in Vietnam should best be left to resolution between Congress and the president and almost certainly will be.

If in grappling with these questions there is a complexity that tends to overwhelm, or if we vacillate from time to time in our thinking as to precisely where the line should be drawn, we can take comfort in Arthur Schlesinger, Jr.'s point that sometimes the genuine intellectual difficulty of a question makes a degree of vacillation and mind changing eminently reasonable.

Congressional Inquiry into Military Affairs
Staff Report of the Committee on Foreign Relations, U.S. Senate, March 1968

Introduction

[I]s it not possible to argue that Congress, especially now that the appropriations for the Armed Forces are the largest items of the budget, should be allowed to inquire in as much detail as it wishes, not only how past appropriations have in fact been spent, but in general about the conduct of the national defense? (Hand, "The Bill of Rights," pp. 17–18 (1958).)

The logic of the argument Judge Learned Hand suggests, that Congress should be allowed to inquire in as much detail as it wishes about the conduct of the national defense, would seem quite compelling. The argument becomes even stronger, if one takes into account the additional power of Congress "To make Rules for the Government and Regulation of the land and naval Forces" (U.S. Constitution, art. I, sec. 8). Judge Hand guesses, however, that the Court would refuse to pass on such a controversy.

A Department of Justice study reached the conclusion that:

Congress cannot, under the Constitution, compel heads of departments by law to give up papers and information; regardless of the public interest involved; and the President is the judge of that interest. ("The Power of the President To Withhold Information From the Congress—Memorandum of the Attorney General," compiled by the Subcommittee on Constitutional Rights of the Committee on the Judiciary, U.S. Senate, 85th Cong., second sess., pp. 3–4 (committee print, 1958) (hereafter cited as committee print).)

The study also indicated that the reason for the rule "that the President and heads of departments are not bound to produce papers or disclose information communicated to them, where, in their own judgment, the disclosure would, on public considerations, be inexpedient," had been succinctly stated in *Marbury* v. *Madison* (1 Cranch 137, 143–144) and reaffirmed in *Cunningham* v. *Neagle* (135 U.S. 1, 63) and *Meyer* v. *United States* (272 U.S. 132–135). According to the Justice study, the reason is that:

By the Constitution, the President is invested with certain political powers. He may use his own discretion in executing those powers. He is accountable only to his country in his political character, and to his own conscience. To aid the President in performing his duties, he is authorized by law to appoint heads of the executive departments. They act by his authority; their acts are his acts. Questions which the Constitution and laws leave to the Executive, or which are in their nature political, are not for the courts to decide, and there is no power in the courts to control the President's discretion or decision, with respect to such questions. Because of the intimate relation between the President and the heads of departments, the same rule applies to them (committee print, p. 3).

Whatever value such paraphrase of court opinions might have as a partial delineation of the doctrine of separation of powers, it has little value as support for the conclusion that the Constitution gives the President, and through him the department heads, absolute discretion to determine when they will refuse information demanded by Congress.

Nor does it support the conclusion that the validity of such determination to withhold information is a political question which is not for the courts to decide.

There is a very real difference between an Executive decision to act pursuant to a constitutional power and an Executive decision to refuse to furnish Congress the information which led the Executive to decide to act. Although Congress may have no power to prevent the act of the Executive, it may have a duty to respond to it, e.g., to appropriate or to refuse to appropriate moneys necessary to give full effect to the action of the Executive. The response of Congress is less likely to be a reasonable one if it is refused access to the information, the facts, which prompted the Executive to act in the first place.

Neither logic, nor the law, would seem to support so broad a claim as this for an unreviewable right in department heads, at their own discretion, to refuse information demanded by Congress. Nor would either logic, or law, support an absolute right of Congress to demand and receive information about the operations of the departments and agencies. Both logic and the law, however, would seem to support the thesis that, in an appropriate case, the courts would decide whether a claim of executive privilege was a valid response to a congressional demand for information.

If there is to be a judicial test, the initiative will probably have to come from the Congress. Because of its broad claims, the Executive would have more to lose than gain by such a test. There is reason to suppose, from statements in cases in which private parties have sought information from the Government, that not even the President's constitutional role as "Commander in Chief of the Army and Navy" would give him or his department heads absolute discretion to refuse a proper demand from Congress for information needed in the exercise of its own powers to "declare War," "raise and support Armies," "provide and maintain a Navy", and "make Rules for the Government and Regulation of the land and naval Forces". In any case, because there has been no decision, there is no certainty that these are questions "which the Constitution and laws leave to the Executive" and which are "not for the courts to decide" as claimed in the Department of Justice study. As we shall see, Congress has at its disposal the means to initiate, or precipitate, depending upon the method it chooses, a judicial action of which the courts must make some disposition.

The Literature and Precedents

The literature dealing with the conflict between the power of Congress to demand information and the privilege of the Executive to withhold it is voluminous and its conclusions varied. Both its volume and variety stem from the paucity of judicial precedents and the ability of writers to drape the language of such judicial dicta as there are over the framework of their own arguments. This addition to the literature is subject to the same limitations. Nevertheless, however persuasive, for either side, may be the arguments drawn from the cases, there is no case holding that the Executive has the absolute discretion to determine that a department head or other officer may refuse to furnish information demanded by Congress.

To be sure, as the Department of Justice study stated:

American history abounds in countless illustrations of the refusal, on occasion, by the President and heads of departments to furnish papers to Congress, or its committees for reasons of public policy (committee print, p. 1).

The writers disagree, however, about the purport of many of the refusals. For example, in 1796, a resolution of the House asked the President for a copy of the instructions given the U.S. Minister who negotiated a treaty with the King of Great Britain. Apparently the House desired this information before it appropriated the money necessary to carry out the treaty. Washington's refusal to furnish the information was based in part upon his "understanding that the assent of the House of Representatives is not necessary to the validity of a treaty" and a conviction that "the boundaries fixed by the Constitution between the different departments should be preserved." Of this example, one writer says:

Washington's message respecting the Jay Treaty, after stressing the occasional need for secrecy in "foreign negotiations," concluded that this was the reason for confining such information "to a small number of members" (i.e., to the Senate) through the medium of the advice and consent clause. Here was a treaty clamorously assailed by the public, and yet Washington felt constrained to put the "secret" information before the Senate, disclaiming any "disposition" (claim of privilege) to withhold any information that either House had a "right" to require. His turnover to the Senate, while denying to the House the "right" to treaty information, constitutes recognition of the Senate's *right* to it. Vice President Adams was of the opinion that the House too had a right to the information. This is scarcely stuff from which to fashion a wholesale claim of executive privilege (Berger, "Executive Privilege Versus Congressional Inquiry," pt. II, 12 UCLA L. Rev. 1287, 1291 (1965), footnotes omitted).

There is equally strong disagreement among the partisans of congressional power and executive privilege about the conclusions to be drawn from some of the other instances of executive refusal to furnish information. Whatever conclusions may be drawn from such historical precedents, however, it cannot be said that, by its acquiescence in refusals, Congress has been estopped from denying the existence of an absolute privilege in the Executive to withhold information from Congress at its discretion. If the Constitution gives Congress the power to demand information, that power cannot be abandoned, even by a continued failure to exercise it. No more can the Executive be said to have abandoned its privilege, if the Constitution give it one, by the frequency with which it has acceded to the demands of Congress, even after an initial refusal based on grounds of public policy.

The Ultimate Problem

Individual Members or committees of Congress have, at one time or another, acknowledged the existence of circumstances in which it might be completely appropriate for the President, or even a department head, to refuse to furnish information or documents which Congress has requested. See Kramer and Marcuse, "Executive Privilege—A Study of the Period 1953–1960, Part II" (29 Geo. Wash. L. Rev. 827, 900–902 (1961)). Most of the congressional complaint, however, is directed either to the exercise of the privilege by subordinate officers rather than by the President or his department heads, or to the validity of particular determinations, even if made by the President, that giving this or that piece of information to Congress would be contrary to the public interest.

To be sure, delegation is a problem; but it is not the ultimate problem. Moreover, the problem exists for both branches. It must be just as disturbing to the Executive when an individual Member of Congress makes unreasonable demands for information as it is to the House or Senate or a committee of either pursuing its duly authorized legislative duties when a departmental subordinate makes an unreasonable refusal.

In *Reynolds* v. *United States* (345 U.S. 1, 7–8 (1953)), the Court stated that the claim of privilege "is not to be lightly invoked * * * [and must be] lodged by the head of the department * * * after actual personal consideration by that officer." From a practical point of view, however, even if not from the legal, the identity of the person claiming the privilege is not likely to be decisive. Even if it be assumed that the privilege can be claimed only by the President and that a court would compel disclosure if it were exercised by a subordinate officer, no test involving a subordinate officer's refusal seems likely to reach the courts. If a military officer, for example, should claim the privilege while testifying before a Senate committee and the Senate gave evidence that it intended to press its demand, it seems likely that the President would either adopt the claim as his own or order the officer to accede to the Senate's demand.

The President's response, in any particular case, would probably be influenced by the degree of congressional determination. A committee resolution would be less impressive than a Senate resolution which would in turn be less impressive than a concurrent resolution. A Congress determined enough to pass a concurrent resolution asking for information would seem to be a Congress determined enough to resort to one or another of the responses which even the most extreme advocates of executive privilege admit are available to a thwarted Congress: failure to appropriate, abolishment of an agency, impeachment of the offending officer.

Though admittedly available, such responses would rarely, if ever, be wise, and should never be resorted to if another remedy is available. The ultimate, and unresolved, constitutional question is whether another remedy is available; the ultimate question is whether the President's decisions to withhold information from the Congress are, as has been claimed, unreviewable by the courts.

Judicial Review of Claims of Executive Privilege

The keystone of the argument for executive privilege, exemplified by the statements in the Department of Justice study, supra, at page 1, is that determinations to exercise it, whether made by the President or his department heads, are not reviewable by the courts. Among the text writers cited by the Attorney General as "confirming the soundness" of the conclusion that there is lodged in the executive branch "the power to to determine what information to divulge and what to keep secret" was Professor Corwin who, at pages 281–282 of "The President, Office and Powers," states:

* * * Thus neither the President nor the Secretary of State is ever "directed" by the house to furnish desired information or papers, but only "requested" to do so, and then only if it is "in the public interest" that they should comply—a question left to be determined by the President. More than that, however, Presidents have sometimes intervened to exonerate other heads of departments than the Secretary of State, and even lesser administrative officials, from re-

sponding to congressional demands for information, either on the ground that the powers sought were "private," "unofficial," or "confidential," or that the demand amounted to an unconstitutional invasion of presidential discretion.

Thus far at least, Corwin does not contradict the Attorney General's conclusion, though what he says does not really "confirm the soundness" of it either. But the Corwin statement continues:

> Nevertheless, should a congressional investigating committee issue a subpena duces tecum to a Cabinet officer ordering him to appear with certain adequately specified documents and should he fail to do so, I see no reason why he might not be proceeded against for contempt of the house which sponsored the inquiry. And the President's power of pardon, if measured by that of the King of England, does not extend to contempts of the houses of Congress (pp. 281–282; committee print, 43).

Instead of supporting an absolute discretion in the Executive, Corwin states that Congress can hold a Cabinet officer in contempt for refusing information. It should be mentioned, of course, that the Attorney General's study attempts to show—

> that Mr. Corwin is probably in error in stating that a Cabinet officer can be held in contempt by reason of a failure to produce papers or give testimony which he or the President considers confidential in the public interest (ibid).

Whatever arguments may be made for unreviewability of claims of executive privilege when interposed against the Congress, a problem the courts have not yet considered, the courts have left no doubt that they will review such claims when interposed against private parties who seek governmental information through court process. In *United States* v. *Reynolds*, the Supreme Court stated that "judicial control over the evidence in a case cannot be abdicated to the caprice of executive officers" (345 U.S. 1, 9–10 (1953)). Is it any more logical or necessary for Congress to abdicate to "executive caprice" control over the evidence it needs to make an appropriation or enact other legislation?

Berger examines exhaustively, and rejects, the arguments against justiciability of the conflict between the Congress and the executive branch (12 UCLA L. Rev. at 1333–1360). He observes that:

> The power finally to decide whether Congress has an absolute right to demand information or whether the executive has an absolute right to refuse it plainly was not lodged in either of those branches. Essentially this is a dispute about the scope of intersecting powers; if one branch has the claimed power the other branch necessarily has not. It seems axiomatic that one branch cannot finally decide the reach of its own power when the result is to curtail a power claimed by another. Madison said in the Federalist that neither of the departments "can pretend to an exclusive or superior right of settling the boundaries between their respective powers. * * *" Unless the two branches are to be remitted to the "trial of physical strength" which *United States* v. *Texas* decried, the power to decide such disputes must reside in the courts (id. at 1354 (footnotes omitted)).

If, as Berger concludes, claims of executive privilege are reviewable by the courts, two questions remain:

    1. How might the courts deal with a claim based on the need for secrecy of military matters?
    2. How can Congress get into court?

JUDICIAL DISPOSITION OF CLAIMS OF PRIVILEGE BASED ON THE NEED FOR MILITARY SECRECY

The cases involving executive resistance to disclosure of military secrets have arisen out of attempts by private parties, rather than Congress, to obtain evidence they thought necessary to proper disposition of their claims. Perhaps two observations might be made about demands for information made by Congress. It seems likely that the courts would consider the right of Congress to information superior to that of any private litigant. Perhaps more important is the fact that disclosure to the Congress need not be the equivalent of disclosure to the public. In 1843, a House committee observed that:

Information * * * may be referred to a committee under a charge of secrecy until an examination of it can be made, when, if the committee concur in opinion with the Executive, its publication will be dispensed with. This is the true parliamentary course. It furnishes at once a security against secret abuses and the irresponsibility of public officers and agents which would follow the denial of the right of the House to demand information, and at the same time protects the State against the discovery of facts so important for the time to be concealed. (H. Rept. 271 (27th Cong., third sess.), p. 7 (1843)).

The Senate also recognizes certain needs for secrecy and provides measures for its enforcement. Rule 35, section 5, provides that:

Whenever, by the request of the Senate or any committee thereof, any documents or papers shall be communicated to the Senate by the President or the head of any department relating to any matter pending in the Senate, the proceedings in regard to which are secret or confidential under the rules, said documents and papers shall be considered as confidential, and shall not be disclosed without leave of the Senate.

Rule 35, section 3, provides, in part, that:

All confidential communications made by the President of the United States to the Senate shall be by the Senators and officers of the Senate kept secret.

And rule 35, section 4, provides that:

Any Senator or officer of the Senate who shall disclose the secret or confidential business or proceedings of the Senate shall be liable, if a Senator, to suffer expulsion from the body; and if an officer, to dismissal from the service of the Senate, and to punishment for contempt.

Presumably, congressional assurances of secrecy would not be given lightly, lest the Executive use such assurances to hide administrative ineptitudes rather than military secrets.

A further observation about the cases is that, even when the courts have denied the privilege they have not ordered executive disclosure. This is not necessarily because such an order would be beyond the power of the courts or because there would be no "coercive means to compel" performance of the duty to disclose but because an acceptable alternative was available—the Government would lose its case. The courts had no hesitation about enjoining the seizure of the steel companies ordered by the President (*Youngstown Co.* v. *Sawyer*, 343 U.S. 579 (1952)). To avoid the appearances of an infringement by the judicial branch on the coequal executive branch such orders may be rationalized on the ground that when an executive officer acts in excess of his constitutional power he ceases to be an executive officer and an order to rescind the act or to do something to repair it is not an order to an executive officer but to an individual.

The privilege against revealing military secrets is well established in the law of evidence, although "judicial experience with the privilege which protects military and state secrets has been limited in this country" (*United States* v. *Reynolds*, 343 U.S. 1, 6, 7 (1953)). *Reynolds*, however, would seem to dispel any inference which might be drawn from earlier cases that the privilege is an absolute one which the courts will not review. Although the Court, in *Reynolds*, sustained the claim of privilege, one factor in its holding was the failure on the part of the moving party to accept a Government offer which resulted in posing the question "with the formal claim of privilege set against a dubious showing of necessity" (id. at 11). The Court's further comments on the claim of privilege would seem to indicate how the Court will deal with such claims:

> The privilege belongs to the Government and must be asserted by it; it can neither be claimed nor waived by a private party. It is not to be lightly invoked. There must be a formal claim of privilege, lodged by the head of the department which has control over the matter. *The court itself must determine whether the circumstances are appropriate for the claim of privilege, and yet do so without forcing a disclosure of the very thing the privilege is designed to protect* (id., at 7–8). [Emphasis added, footnotes omitted.]

>   *   *   *   *   *   *   *

> Judicial control over the evidence in a case cannot be abdicated to the caprice of executive officers. Yet we will not go so far as to say the court may automatically require a complete disclosure to the judge before the claim of privilege will be accepted in any case. It may be possible to satisfy the court, from all the circumstances of the case, that there is a reasonable danger that compulsion of the evidence will expose military matters which, in the interest of national security, should not be divulged. When this is the case, the occasion for the privilege is appropriate, and the court should not jeopardize the security which the privilege is meant to protect by insisting upon an examination of the evidence, even by the judge alone, in chambers (id., at 9–10).

In a subsequent case, *Halpern* v. *United States* (258 F. 2d 36, 44 (2 Cir., 1958)) the court stated that "the privilege relating to state secrets is inapplicable when disclosure to court personnel in an in camera proceeding will not make the information public or endanger the national security." Can the rights of Congress be inferior to those of a private litigant and can Congress be considered any less a guardian of the national security than the officers of either the executive or judicial branches?

CONGRESSIONAL INITIATION OF A JUDICIAL TEST

Contempt of Congress by reason of failure of a witness, summoned by authority of either House, to testify or produce papers, is punishable as a misdemeanor (R.S., sec. 102, as amended; 2 U.S.C. 192 (1964)). Another provision (R.S., sec. 104, as amended, 2 U.S.C. 194 (1964)), sets forth a procedure for certification of such failure "to the appropriate U.S. attorney, whose duty it shall be to bring the matter before the grand jury for its action." Congress seems never to have reported to a U.S. attorney any failure of an executive officer to testify by reason of a claim of executive privilege. Bishop observes that such a certification seems improbable and goes on to say that:

> Even if Congress should certify such a case to a U.S. attorney, it seems intrinsically likely that the Attorney General would take the position that Congress could not constitutionally command its prosecution (*The Executive's Right of Privacy: An Unresolved Constitutional Question*, 66 Yale L. J. 477, 484 (1957)).

There is no necessity, however, if Congress is determined to test a claim of executive privilege, to certify a case to the Attorney General and await his decision to prosecute, or not, under the provisions of 2 U.S.C. 192. There can be no doubt that either House of Congress has the power to seize a recalcitrant witness, try him before the bar of the House, and punish him for contempt by imprisoning him in the Capitol (*Jurney* v. *McCracken*, 294 U.S. 125 (1935), *McGrain* v.

Daugherty, 273 U.S. 135 (1927)). Should this be done, the judicial test would come when the prisoner seeks his release by way of a writ of habeas corpus (Bishop, supra, 66 Yale L. J. 477, 484–85 (1957)).

There can be no doubt that a less dramatic method for testing a claim of privilege would be more desirable if one were available. Berger suggests that one might be: 28 U.S.C. 1345 gives the U.S. district courts "original jurisdiction of all civil actions, suits, or proceedings commenced by the United States, or by any agency or officer thereof expressly authorized to sue by act of Congress"; 28 U.S.C. 2201 provides that:

> In a case of actual controversy within its jurisdiction, except with respect to Federal taxes, any court of the United States * * * may declare the rights and other legal relations of any interested party seeking such declaration, whether or not further relief is or could be sought * * *

Further relief may be granted on the basis of a declaratory judgment under the provisions of 28 U.S.C. 2202. Berger suggests that any doubts about the existing availability of this route could be eliminated by relatively simple clarifying legislation (12 UCLA L. Rev. at 1333–34).

CONCLUSION

An unreviewable discretion on the part of the Executive to withhold information could operate to deprive Congress of the tools it needs to fulfill its own constitutional role.

An unlimited power on the part of Congress to demand and receive information from the Executive could operate to infringe upon the constitutional role of the Executive.

When a claim of privilege is interposed against a committee, the House or Senate is more likely to get the information, without initiating a judicial action, if it demands it by way of House or Senate resolution than if the committee acts alone. A Congress determined enough to demand information would seem to be a Congress determined enough to refuse to appropriate if the demand was not met.

If a controversy between the Executive and the Legislature were to reach the courts in a proper case, it seems a good possibility that the courts would decide the issue in much the same manner as they have reviewed claims of executive privilege when interposed against private parties seeking information and convictions of private parties for contempt of Congress.

It seems probable that the courts would find the executive privilege of withholding information to be less broad than the Executive has sometimes claimed, yet not so narrow as some Members or committees of Congress would like it to be.

VINCENT A. DOYLE,
Legislative Attorney.

O

United States v. Mora 389 US 934 (1967) : Decision of the United States Supreme Court

November 6, 1967.

No. 401. MORA ET AL. *v.* McNAMARA, SECRETARY OF DEFENSE, ET AL. C. A. D. C. Cir. Certiorari denied. MR. JUSTICE MARSHALL took no part in the consideration or decision of this petition. *Stanley Faulkner* and *Selma W. Samols* for petitioners. *Solicitor General Marshall* for respondents. Reported below: See—, U. S. App. D. C.—, 373 F. 2d 664.

MR. JUSTICE STEWART, with whom MR. JUSTICE DOUGLAS joins, dissenting.

The petitioners were drafted into the United States Army in late 1965, and six months later were ordered to a West Coast replacement station for shipment to Vietnam. They brought this suit to prevent the Secretary of Defense and the Secretary of the Army from carrying out those orders, and requested a declaratory judgment that the present United States military activity in Vietnam is "illegal." The District Court dismissed the suit, and the Court of Appeals affirmed.

There exist in this case questions of great magnitude. Some are akin to those referred to by MR. JUSTICE DOUGLAS in *Mitchell* v. *United States,* 386 U. S. 972. But there are others:

I. Is the present United States military activity in Vietnam a "war" within the meaning of Article I, Section 8, Clause 11, of the Constitution?

II. If so, may the Executive constitutionally order the petitioners to participate in that military activity, when no war has been declared by the Congress?

III. Of what relevance to Question II are the present treaty obligations of the United States?

IV. Of what relevance to Question II is the Joint Congressional ("Tonkin Gulf") Resolution of August 10, 1964?

DOUGLAS, J., dissenting.

(a) Do present United States military operations fall within the terms of the Joint Resolution?

(b) If the Joint Resolution purports to give the Chief Executive authority to commit United States forces to armed conflict limited in scope only by his own absolute discretion, is the Resolution a constitutionally impermissible delegation of all or part of Congress' power to declare war?

These are large and deeply troubling questions. Whether the Court would ultimately reach them depends, of course, upon the resolution of serious preliminary issues of justiciability. We cannot make these problems go away simply by refusing to hear the case of three obscure Army privates. I intimate not even tentative views upon any of these matters, but I think the Court should squarely face them by granting certiorari and setting this case for oral argument.

Mr. Justice Douglas, with whom Mr. Justice Stewart concurs, dissenting.

The questions posed by Mr. Justice Stewart cover the wide range of problems which the Senate Committee on Foreign Relations recently explored,[1] in connection with the SEATO Treaty of February 19, 1955,[2] and the Tonkin Gulf Resolution.[3]

Mr. Katzenbach, representing the Administration, testified that he did not regard the Tonkin Gulf Resolution to be "a declaration of war"[4] and that while the Resolution was not "constitutionally necessary" it was "politically, from an international viewpoint and from a domestic viewpoint, extremely important."[5] He added:

"The use of the phrase 'to declare war' as it was used in the Constitution of the United States had a particular meaning in terms of the events and the practices which existed at the time it was adopted. . . .

"[I]t was recognized by the Founding Fathers that the President might have to take emergency action to protect the security of the United States, but that if there was going to be another use of the armed forces of the United States, that was a decision which Congress should check the Executive on, which Congress should support. It was for that reason that the phrase was inserted in the Constitution.

"Now, over a long period of time, . . . there have been many uses of the military forces of the United States for a variety of purposes

---

[1] Hearings on S. Res. No. 151, 90th Cong., 1st Sess. (1967).
[2] [1955] 6 U. S. T. 81, T. I. A. S. No. 3170. [3] 78 Stat. 384.
[4] Hearings on S. Res. No. 151, *supra*, n. 1, at 87. [5] *Id.*, at 145.

without a congressional declaration of war. But it would be fair to say that most of these were relatively minor uses of force. . . .

   .   .   .   .   .

"A declaration of war would not, I think, correctly reflect the very limited objectives of the United States with respect to Vietnam. It would not correctly reflect our efforts there, what we are trying to do, the reasons why we are there, to use an outmoded phraseology, to declare war."[6]

The view that Congress was intended to play a more active role in the initiation and conduct of war than the above statements might suggest has been espoused by Senator Fulbright (Cong. Rec., Oct. 11, 1967, pp. 14683-14690), quoting Thomas Jefferson who said:

"We have already given in example one effectual check to the Dog of war by transferring the power of letting him loose from the Executive to the Legislative body, from those who are to spend to those who are to pay."[7]

These opposed views are reflected in the *Prize Cases*, 2 Black 635, a five-to-four decision rendered in 1863. Mr. Justice Grier, writing for the majority, emphasized the arguments for strong presidential powers. Mr. Justice Nelson, writing for the minority of four, read the Constitution more strictly, emphasizing that what is war in actuality may not constitute war in the constitutional sense. During all subsequent periods in our history—through the Spanish-American War, the Boxer Rebellion, two World Wars, Korea, and now Vietnam—the two points of view urged in the *Prize Cases* have continued to be voiced.

A host of problems is raised. Does the President's authority to repel invasions and quiet insurrections, do his powers in foreign relations and his duty to execute faithfully the laws of the United States, includ-

[6] *Id.*, at 80-81.

[7] 15 Papers of Jefferson 397 (Boyd ed., Princeton 1958). In The Federalist No. 69, at 465 (Cooke ed. 1961), Hamilton stated:

"[T]he President is to be Commander in Chief of the army and navy of the United States. In this respect his authority would be nominally the same with that of the King of Great-Britain, but in substance much inferior to it. It would amount to nothing more than the supreme command and direction of the military and naval forces, as first General and Admiral of the confederacy; while that of the British King extends to the *declaring* of war and to the *raising* and *regulating* of fleets and armies; all which by the Constitution under consideration would appertain to the Legislature."

ing its treaties, justify what has been threatened of petitioners? What is the relevancy of the Gulf of Tonkin Resolution and the yearly appropriations in support of the Vietnam effort?

The London Treaty (59 Stat. 1546), the SEATO Treaty (6 U. S. T. 81, 1955), the Kellogg-Briand Pact (46 Stat. 2343), and Article 39 of Chapter VII of the UN Charter deals with various aspects of wars of "aggression."

Do any of them embrace hostilities in Vietnam, or give rights to individuals affected to complain, or in other respects give rise to justiciable controversies?

There are other treaties or declarations that could be cited. Perhaps all of them are wide of the mark. There are sentences in our opinions which, detached from their context, indicate that what is happening is none of our business:

> "Certainly it is not the function of the Judiciary to entertain private litigation—even by a citizen—which challenges the legality, the wisdom, or the propriety of the Commander-in-Chief in sending our armed forces abroad or to any particular region." *Johnson* v. *Eisentrager*, 339, U. S. 763, 789.

We do not, of course, sit as a committee of oversight or supervision. What resolutions the President asks, and what the Congress provides are not our concern. With respect to the Federal Government, we sit only to decide actual cases or controversies within judicial cognizance that arise as a result of what the Congress or the President or a judge does or attempts to do to a person or his property.

In *Ex parte Milligan*, 4 Wall. 2, the Court relieved a person of the death penalty imposed by a military tribunal, holding that only a civilian court had power to try him for the offense charged. Speaking of the purpose of the Founders in providing constitutional guarantees, the Court said:

> "They knew . . . the nation they were founding, be its existence short or long, would be involved in war; how often or how long continued, human foresight could not tell; and that unlimited power, wherever lodged at such a time, was especially hazardous to freemen. For this, and other equally weighty reasons, they secured the inheritance they had fought to maintain, by incorporating in a written constitution the safeguards which *time* had proved were essential to its preservation. Not one of these safeguards can the President,

or Congress, or the Judiciary disturb, except the one concerning the writ of *habeas corpus*." *Id.*, 125.

The fact that the political branches are responsible for the threat to petitioners' liberty is not decisive. As Mr. Justice Holmes said in *Nixon v. Herndon*, 273 U. S. 536, 540:

> "The objection that the subject matter of the suit is political is little more than a play upon words. Of course the petition concerns political action but it alleges and seeks to recover for private damage. That private damage may be caused by such political action and may be recovered for in a suit at law hardly has been doubted for over two hundred years, since *Ashby* v. *White*, 2 Ld. Raym. 938, 3 *id.* 320, and has been recognized by this Court."

These petitioners should be told whether their case is beyond judicial cognizance. If it is not, we should then reach the merits of their claims, on which I intimate no views whatsoever.

VI. THOUGHTS ON SETTLEMENT

Revolution in Viet Nam: The Political Dimension of War and Peace*

JOHN T. MC ALISTER, JR.

STANDING before our new behemoth transport airplane, the C-5A, President Johnson, at an Air Force base in Georgia a few weeks ago, characterized our options in Viet Nam as being either to stand and fight or to cut and run. In his view, the alternatives in the war are clear-cut: either we choose the path of honor and fight or that of dishonor and withdraw. Because the other side has failed to negotiate on our terms, he feels that it is imperative that we take our stand and go on fighting as we have for the past three years. But will a continuation of our military policies bring us any results which are worthwhile fighting for? Can there really be any honor from continuing to seek a military victory in Viet Nam?

As the war drags on, a policy of more of the same merely causes Americans to ask why our military strength there has thus far been so powerless to bring the conflict to an end. And is there any prospect that our military force, even if expanded massively, can—by itself— end the war any time soon?

The gravity of the current military situation, especially at Khe Sanh and around Saigon, and the possibility of a full-scale mobilization here at home call into question our earlier rationalizations about the utility of force in Viet Nam and the level of strength required there. Now, before events overtake us completely, is there any possibility of finding some more dependable basis, other than existing ones, on which to assess the present dangers and future prospects of our military operations in Viet Nam?

In searching for answers to these questions it may be useful to note that as late as 1938, only 11,000 French troops aided by a 16,000 man local militia were able to maintain France's colonial control throughout the whole of Indochina—an area nearly half again as large as France itself—which included Viet Nam along with the states of Laos and Cambodia. Even after the war broke out in Viet Nam in 1947, a French-led force consisting of only 70,000 French regulars, 68,000

* In a slightly different form this article was presented in testimony before a public hearing of the Committee on Foreign Relations of the U.S. Senate on March 7, 1968. The author wishes to thank the Chairman, Senator J. William Fulbright, for this opportunity to present his views.

Legionnaires and Africans, and 300,000 Vietnamese, or a total of less than 450,000 men, was able to hold out for seven years against the Communists and ultimately—by using its military strength as a bargaining instrument—to contain them to a territory north of the 17th parallel.

Why is it that more than 500,000 American troops cannot now quell the armed opposition in a small portion of the territory in 1968, that only 11,000 French troops were able to control with hardly firing a shot just thirty years ago? Certainly this is not because American troops have not fought bravely and fiercely. On the contrary, as the events of recent weeks have shown again, our men have fought with rare courage and uncommon tenacity.

The reason a force nearly fifty times larger than the one in 1938 cannot now be more effective in two-thirds less territory is that during the past three decades Viet Nam has undergone far-reaching and fundamental political changes—changes which have not resulted in political stability or agreement about the kind of political order the Vietnamese might desire or accept, but changes which have led to a pattern of conflict involving increasingly larger numbers of Vietnamese in military operations.

Our own difficulties have arisen because when we went into Viet Nam our policies did not take into account that the country was in the midst of an unresolved political conflict, nor did they reflect an understanding of what the underlying nature of this conflict really was. We are not fighting against an external invader who is attempting to gain control over a culturally distinct foreign country by force, nor are we fighting in a civil war that is a purely internal matter among southern Vietnamese, but, instead, we have become engaged in a revolutionary war involving all of the Vietnamese people.

Saying that Viet Nam is in the midst of a revolution has usually been interpreted as a polemical attack or as a purely ideological assertion. But when I identify the political conflict in Viet Nam as a revolution it is not because I wish to engage in polemics but because I wish to lay the basis for an assessment of the utility of American military force in that country.

The war now raging in Viet Nam is a continuation of the pattern of conflict launched by the Communist-led independence movement, the Viet Minh, against France and the non-Communist Vietnamese during the First Indochina War of 1947-1954; it is not a war being fought between two separate nations but it is a revolutionary struggle involving two competitor governments within one nation. More conspicuously than in wars between nations, revolutionary war is a "continuation of politics by other means." It is a competition between two or more governments, each of which wants to become the sole legitimate government of a people.

Since it was founded on September 2, 1945, by Ho Chi Minh, the Democratic Republic of Viet Nam has claimed to be the legitimate government for all the Vietnamese people, and in fighting to eliminate French rule it carried out military operations and enjoyed political support in all sections of Viet Nam. By accepting a military cease-fire and the partitioning of the country in 1954, the Hanoi government did not, in the process, relinquish its claims to legitimacy throughout the country.

Despite United States assumptions to the contrary, the Republic of Viet Nam founded in Saigon in 1956 by Ngo Dinh Diem has also seen itself as the sole government for all the Vietnamese. For example, the constitution of the Republic of Viet Nam, written in Saigon in March 1967, states that the purpose of the government is to unite the nation and unite the territory. The constitution's first article says that "Viet-Nam is a territorially indivisible, unified, and independent republic," and article 107 says that "Article 1 of the constitution and this article may not be amended or deleted."

While the United States regards the Saigon government as sovereign over only the territory south of the 17th parallel and, therefore, believes it to be a separate Vietnamese state known as South Viet Nam, this has not been the way that the Vietnamese have looked at it. Though the Saigon regime has been hard pressed to maintain its claims to sovereignty even in the cities of southern Viet Nam, it has never given up its goal—as the new constitution again indicates—to be the sole legitimate government for the whole country. Thus there has been a recognition by both Saigon and Hanoi that, as long as the country remains divided, a revolutionary conflict will go on until some form of agreement is reached on the nature of the political order for all Vietnamese.

Revolutionary wars not only have unique political objectives, but these objectives are the immediate goal of the conflict, and their pursuit directly governs the conduct of military operations. In wars between nations, political objectives are, by contrast, usually sought indirectly by destroying the military power of an adversary and then using a position of military supremacy to dictate political terms. The object of revolutionary warfare, however, is to eliminate the political structure of an opponent government and replace it with a political structure of one's own.

In this process the elimination of an opponent's political effectiveness by assassinating village chiefs and terrorizing provincial officials is much less important than the task of filling the vacuum which such terror creates. The primary goal of a revolutionary competitor in Viet Nam must be to forge peasant villagers into a totally new political community—one which can command loyalties because it rewards performance in support of the revolutionary cause by offering increasing amounts of political power and personal authority. Through this strategy, military force is used not just to decimate the institutions and armed forces of an adversary such as the Saigon government, but also, and more importantly, to provide means for popular participation in revolutionary politics.

The Communists have been able to develop more and more power in Viet Nam because as they have forged a new political community they have been effecting a revolution in Vietnamese politics. In Viet Nam, revolution has been characterized not only by the effort to eliminate French colonial rule and create a single legitimate government for all the Vietnamese people, but also by fundamental changes in participation in politics and in the access to political power. Through new institutions—such as revolutionary committees and assemblies which have been established throughout southern Viet Nam, as well as military units and popular associations—Vietnamese peasants are having a chance to achieve a greater share of power as their participation contributes to an increase in the overall power of the revolutionary movement.

Only when such institutional links reach out into the society and create political opportunities which are qualitatively different from those of the past can a modern political elite in Viet Nam identify itself with those still living traditional lives of relative isolation in the countryside. As these new opportunities have enlisted the participation of rural people in new forms of politics and won their commitment to a new and much broader political identity it has been possible to mobilize ever larger amounts of popular strength.

Through the opportunities which the Communist system provides, the Vietnamese villager has been able to find a more predictable access to the attributes of modern life (i.e., literacy, technical skills, organizational ability, etc.), and the rewards of political influence than through any other governmental structure in Viet Nam. And by this mobilization of the potential strength of the peasants and the sharing of governmental authority with them, the Communists have been acquiring greater legitimacy and gaining increasing compliance with their will as they have conducted their military campaign.

Without a political structure linking it to the people, a government in a revolutionary war like the one in Viet Nam may exist in name but not in fact. It will be unable to rally a people behind it since it will have no dependable means of sharing power and influence with those called up to participate in its behalf. But with such a structure of political commitment a government can lose much of its regular military strength and even much of its territory, yet still continue to be a serious revolutionary competitor.

Because it will not have to hold on to territory in order to insure the political loyalty of the inhabitants, a revolutionary movement with an effective political structure like that which the Communists have in Viet Nam can achieve a greater freedom to maneuver its armed forces against an adversary. Moreover, its adversary may more likely be required to keep his troops in static positions in order to provide security for a population whose loyalty he has not otherwise been able to win.

As one revolutionary competitor develops the strength of its political structure so that it can—despite heavy casualties—mobilize progressively larger armed forces and also free itself of local security responsibilities, then it will be able, by its greater maneuverability, to force its opponent into more and more fixed positions of defense. With his forces spread out and tied down, such an adversary will be vulnerable to the piecemeal decimation of his paralyzed and helpless troops by the highly maneuverable forces of his revolutionary competitor.

United States forces were pinned down to vulnerable fixed positions at Khe Sanh and numerous other similar locations in Viet Nam because we have not understood that the conflict there is a revolutionary war and that in such a war the lack of an effective governmental structure is not just an annoying drawback but a decisive military liability. Communist-led forces were for a time able to achieve the third and final stage of their revolutionary war strategy, that of positional warfare, because we had for political reasons lost both the initiative in combat and operational mobility in our strategy.

Most of our military problems have arisen because we have been attempting to compensate with ever larger amounts of our military force for the political weaknesses of the Saigon government. Since the Republic of Viet Nam has not been able to mobilize increasingly larger portions of its own population for revolutionary war by putting their young men into the field as troops, United States troops have had to take over the major role of fighting for them. And since Saigon has not had the political structure to consolidate its hold on territory in the countryside once it is cleared of the adversary, the military strength of the United States has had to offset this political weakness by using our troops to try to hold on to the ground by force.

Because no better way has been devised to win the political support of the people in the countryside than by trying to provide them with security, the result has been that larger and larger numbers of Vietnamese and American troops have been tied down to static positions. And when these forces have been moved to other locations in response to more pressing problems elsewhere, the political support, which had been won by temporary security, is lost. Despite its rhetorical commitment to revolution as, for example, in the Revolutionary Development Cadre program, the Saigon government has not been able to carry out fundamental change—revolutionary change— in the means of access to political power and the sharing of governmental authority. Consequently, it has not been able to win the far-reaching political commitment of the peasants in the countryside or mobilize them into revolutionary war programs.

Saigon's only hope has been that through a program of pacification it could win the temporary commitment of the peasants not to join the Communist-led National Liberation Front. But pacification has meant, in effect if not in design, a military occupation of the countryside. Any more positive commitment has been out of the question because the Saigon government has had no program in which it might share power with the peasants or provide a pattern of predictable rewards in return for performance in support of the Republic of Viet Nam. For instance, the village militiaman in the so-called Popular Forces does not have the opportunity to progress upwards into the regional forces and then into the regular army, as does his village counterpart who joins with the National Liberation Front. Through the NLF a peasant villager might become an officer, but up until very recently no one could become an officer in the ARVN unless he were a graduate of a lycée and had a baccalaureate degree; and even now there is little likelihood that a non-degree holder can become an officer.

So long as our ally, the Saigon government, does not have any effective political structure with which to gain popular support and bring order to the countryside, it can only try to achieve these goals by the use of force. But the lack of such a political structure also means that the Saigon government cannot mobilize the recruits for an army large enough to hold on to the countryside by force alone. Since the Saigon government cannot survive except by the use of force, and since it cannot mobilize the force to provide for its own survival, the United States is faced with an anguishing dilemma.

Just as President Johnson's speech in Georgia makes clear, the current focus of our policies leaves us with only two alternatives. Either we go on fighting with the realization that the conflict will intensify and demand greater numbers of American troops as the political strength of the Saigon government deteriorates further and that of the Communists increases, or we acknowledge that our ally does not have the political capacity for victory and that our policies have been wrong. In the days ahead these harsh alternatives will have to be confronted as they have not been before.

Whatever approach adopted in the immediate future, it seems apparent from the official interpretations of the recent Tet offensive that our estimates of the utility of force in Viet Nam and the level of strength our strategy requires still do not take into account the revolutionary character of the war. Yet even official statements make clear that no matter what the purpose of the Tet attacks on the cities, their principal effect has been to weaken further the political structure of the Saigon government and shift even more of the burden of fighting the Communsits on to the shoulders of the United States.

Such a pattern of attacks seems certain to continue because the Communists, by destroying the last remaining shreds of political strength and effectiveness that Saigon still enjoys, could leave the United States with no indigenous political ally to carry on the war. A political collapse of the Saigon regime might then permit the Communists to achieve a revolutionary war victory without ever having to defeat United States forces in the field. But whether or not a sudden governmental cave-in occurs, the past performance and the existing resiliency of the Saigon regime—as was demonstrated by the political collapse of the government at Hué—suggests that we be fully prepared for its role in the war to diminish substantially, probably to the vanishing point.

Even without a governmental collapse, however, the military situation in Viet Nam is a critical one. By trying to compensate for the political weaknesses of the Saigon regime and at the same time trying to stop a revolutionary movement by force, we have positioned many of our troops in dangerously exposed locations. Because there are not now enough Americans in Viet Nam to defend the cities, keep open the roads, carry out pacification, fight infiltration, and launch attacks against enemy main force units, they have been spread thin, and therefore have been exposed to attack. While all eyes were on Khe Sanh, it was not the only such exposed position and, following the pattern of previous surprise attacks, the Communists might well choose to hit some other location. They will have many options to select from since troops have had to be drawn around the cities to provide them protection, and others have been shifted north around Hué and the DMZ.

As the Saigon government declines in its political strength, it becomes more and more clear that we are primarily fighting against a revolutionary movement and are trying primarily by force to prevent it from forming a Communist-led government in southern Viet Nam. Since we cannot sponsor an effective political alternative to this revolutionary movement we must, if we are to force it to give up its goals, achieve a clear-cut position of military supremacy which will allow us to dictate political terms of our own choosing.

A basis for calculating the strength required to achieve such supremacy in a revolutionary war is either the 10-to-1 ratio of military strength which the French amassed in Algeria or the 50-to-1 ratio which the British mounted in Malaya. If these ratios are applied to Viet Nam where the Communists have approximately 300,000 men in all their forces, then the United States would have to send either 3 million men to achieve the same kind of supremacy France had in Algeria where the war was won militarily but lost politically, or 15 million men to repeat the British success in Malaya.

Many military specialists will dispute the efficacy of these ratios but whatever the ratio required to achieve pure military supremacy in Viet Nam, it must be calculated with the realization that so long as the Communist political system is not affected, they can be expected to mobilize greater and greater amounts of force. And if we expect to prevail militarily, then we had better plan on matching the Communists' increase in military strength with increases of 100 to 500 of our own troops for every 10 more of theirs. Thus there is no net gain in military supremacy from such troop increases.

If our fighting men in their exposed positions are to avoid a humiliating military setback, then more massive reinforcements are required to assist them. But if there is a full-scale mobilization here at home then our people should realize just how high the price will be for an illusive military supremacy.

If we want to avoid both military humiliation in Viet Nam and years of full-scale mobilization here at home, then it seems necessary for our military power to be used to achieve some more feasible political objective in Viet Nam. This must be done in a manner which will focus the political energies of both the combatants and the relevant members of the international community such as France, China, and the Soviet Union.

Obviously, the path toward a political accommodation in Viet Nam will be an unhappy and protracted one, but it is the path that offers the least danger to our national prestige and international credibility.

In searching for an effective political accommodation, the United States cannot withdraw its forces from Viet Nam without guarantees concerning the future international actions of the resulting government in southern Viet Nam. If the war were to end without any certainty that the Vietnamese would be restrained from extending their political sway over Cambodia and the lowlands of Laos, then there is a risk of a larger war—just as the administration has warned—between the Thai and the Vietnamese for control over these smaller buffer states, particularly Laos.

But instead of minimizing the risks of a larger war, a continuation of our present military policies in Viet Nam actually makes this larger scale conflict a greater possibility. Such a larger war would result not because of the dangers of Chinese intervention but because, as the political strength of the Vietnamese increases, it becomes less possible to get guarantees of their future action.

Although it will be a difficult task to achieve, the United States must reach a political accommodation with those groups who have the comparative advantage among the Vietnamese in political organization and political mobilization. We must no longer try to prevent them from using their political power in forming a government in southern Viet Nam, but instead we should try to get a maximum number of guarantees about the future actions of that government.

Because of the strategy and power of our present adversaries, as well as our own entrenched position, a political accommodation with them cannot be achieved through a conventional international conference in which diplomats bargain with each other across a green, cloth-covered table in an ornate building in some European capital. Instead, we will have to be prepared to compete with our adversary through the process of "fighting while negotiating." In this competition we must be able to use the threat of our military force to bargain for political goals that are more feasible objectives than the ones we are presently trying to achieve.

While there will surely be much disagreement over which specific path might most effectively lead to a political accommodation in Viet Nam, there has thus far been little public discussion concerning various feasible alternatives. Accommodation in Viet Nam—when it has been discussed at all—has usually been advocated by those who have opposed further escalation rather than by those who have had detailed plans on resolving the conflict. In what follows, one path toward an accommodation is presented in bare outline form with the hope that it can become a focus for further discussion rather than being regarded as a call for a specific course of action.

The political objectives which are achievable and which it is in our interest to achieve might best be sought on three different levels which—though they are distinctive in their own right—are closely related to each other. These three levels include political accommodation: (1) within southern Viet Nam, (2) between southern and northern Viet Nam, and (3) between the regional and international powers concerned with peace in Southeast Asia.

The goal of political accommodation at all three of these levels ought to be a recognition of the legitimacy of the political power which our present adversaries have achieved in southern Viet Nam, the establishment of means by which they can share in governmental authority on the basis of their power, and the creation of ways through which all parties can compete for power on nonviolent terms.

A beginning toward a political accommodation can best be initiated at the provincial and district level within southern Viet Nam where, in certain areas, a *de facto* accommodation between the representatives of Saigon and the NLF has already occurred. For example, Saigon's provincial officials have in many instances tacitly agreed not to enter certain areas of their provinces to contest NLF strength in return for roads being left free of NLF attempts to halt traffic; NLF prisoners have "escaped" from detention as a result of pay-offs to some provincial officials; installations such as bridges, oil depots, water storage facilities, etc. have been left untouched by the NLF in various areas in return for the privilege of collecting taxes in certain rural locations; and in a variety of other ways there have been trade-offs between the local representatives of the two sides and a tacit determination not to "rock the boat" in a slowly evolving process of revolutionary politics. Generally, these areas of existing accommodation are ones where the Communists have been unopposed for the longest period of time and have had the greatest success in creating a social and political community with attitudes and values unique to itself.

Since Saigon's provincial officials are believed to know their NLF counterparts extremely well and often have conferences with them, it appears that without United States forces to compensate for our ally's political weaknesses in the countryside, this process of accommodation would be accelerated. And since our troops are spread dangerously thin, it would seem prudent militarily on our part to regroup our forces not only with an eye to providing for their security but also with the hope of facilitating and stimulating further provincial level accommodation between the NLF and Saigon.

Such a recommendation differs from the enclave concept put forward by General Gavin in that there would not necessarily be a wholesale withdrawal to coastal positions but rather that in certain provinces there might be an almost complete reduction of the American military presence, while in others defensible positions would be held. But the real leverage would result not from withdrawal but from an American decision not to launch in selected provinces military operations by our own troops or to support those of the Vietnamese with air, artillery, or logistics back-up.

The purpose of this strategy would be to achieve a *de facto* cease-fire in certain areas of Viet Nam and thus confirm or legitimize the power of the political community created there by the NLF. However, we would not give up our military positions in these areas without a corresponding cessation of NLF activity in provinces which are clearly loyal to Saigon. In these provinces, especially those inhabited by such coherent social groups as the Catholics, the Cao Dai, Hoa Hao, and the Montagnard organization known as FULRO, an extensive effort would be made to provide protection militarily and accelerate the political accommodation between these groups and the

Saigon government which dates from at least the Presidential elections of September-October 1967.

While a *de facto* cease-fire would be relatively easy to achieve in areas of NLF strength, as well as in places where its rival political and religious groups are strong, it will be the presently contested areas which will challenge attempts to bring the fighting to a stop through a political accommodation. In an effort to stabilize these areas, United States and Vietnamese troops should create defensive perimeters around only as much of the contested areas as they can protect without needlessly exposing themselves.

This does not mean that United States and Vietnamese forces should adopt a totally passive role with respect to protecting certain areas against NLF incursions. But retaliatory military thrusts should be measured in response to the NLF violation of the *de facto* cease-fire which our forces would be trying to achieve at the local level. In addition, search and destroy missions which have already been curtailed because of the lack of available troops should not be started again. Overall, our military power in Viet Nam should be used to achieve a *de facto* cease-fire by (1) withdrawing from certain areas of NLF political strength and leaving them uncontested militarily, provided the NLF does not contest areas inhabited by rival social and religious groups, (2) protecting these areas where non-NLF groups have maintained a relatively effective pattern of social and political authority, and (3) using punitive retaliation against NLF forces in an effort to stimulate the spread of the cease-fire and to demonstrate that American military power is committed to achieving as orderly and equitable an accommodation as possible.

Ultimately, our goal should be to encourage the incorporation of NLF-controlled areas into a national governmental framework in the south so that for the indefinite future the NLF will find it in their interest to participate in a distinctly southern government. This suggestion carries with it the assumption that while the NLF is an intimate part of the Communist-led revolutionary movement in Viet Nam, it also has autonomous, distinctly southern goals of its own to which we can appeal in trying to achieve a political settlement. Such an assumption will be hard to validate, but based on the writings of the governmental expert Douglas Pike, the author of *Vietcong*, it seems worth testing by using it as a basis for action.

Our capacity to see a broadly based southern government formed will obviously be quite limited but there are several steps we can take to facilitate this outcome. Initially, we should call for a mixed Saigon-NLF committee for administering reconstruction funds to be provided by the United States and as many other countries as we could interest. Each side would, of course, carry out reconstruction projects in its own areas but we should use the bargaining power which relief funds might afford to create some sort of mixed ad hoc consultative body.

Perhaps such a consultative body can never be made to function, and in that case other long-range efforts should be made to incorporate the NLF into a southern government or else we should accept the fact that no greater accommodation is possible beyond a *de facto* cease-fire. But through a combination of initiatives including the threat of a permanent positioning of troops in Viet Nam against the NLF and the discontinuance of certain programs of support toward the Saigon regime, we should work for a consultative arrangement between these adversaries.

The goal of their consultation would be the establishment of means by which all parties in southern Viet Nam could share in governmental authority on the basis of their power—or as President Johnson expressed it on December 19, 1967, share power on a "one man, one vote basis." Also included in this goal should be the creation of ways in which all parties can compete for power on nonviolent terms. One way to achieve these objectives would be through a series of elections organized by the mixed Saigon-NLF ad hoc consultative committee and, although it is unlikely to be acceptable to the parties, impartial international inspection and supervision should be urged. Elections could be held first at the village level to choose representatives for district assemblies which would in turn choose representatives for provincial assemblies where representatives for a national assembly would be chosen. Through such a process a political link with the countryside would be forged by all parties and the institutions for sharing national governmental authority might be established.

The resulting government would not be a "coalition" regime in the sense of its being the fruition of an effort to juggle cabinet posts in order to try to accommodate the NLF within the existing governmental structure in southern Viet Nam.

It will be virtually impossible for the United States to guarantee that any electoral process of this kind will be forthcoming from consultations between the contending Vietnamese political groups or that this process will be effective in achieving a shared basis of governmental power. But what we can do is to try to create the environment for some form of institutionalized accommodation by using our military power to achieve a *de facto* cease-fire and to assure that warfare is not started again if the process of accommodation breaks down.

Since our military power has up to now been used to compensate for the political weakness of the Saigon regime, the Thieu-Ky government cannot be expected to embrace with enthusiasm any move toward a *de facto* cease-fire. They might even try to sabotage such an effort by launching attacks against the NLF areas where we are trying to achieve a cease-fire, or by publicly accusing us of handing the country over to the Communists or by demanding that the United States get out of Viet Nam. If we have any leverage over the Saigon regime at all, it seems unlikely that Thieu and Ky would carry out these potential threats, but if they do, this would give us an opening to repudiate them for their corruption and unwillingness to make the sacrifices necessary to fighting the Communists. A repudiation of this kind might actually strengthen our hand in dealing with the Vietnamese and especially with other oligarchical anti-Communist regimes in underdeveloped countries.

Clearly, a *de facto* cease-fire in southern Viet Nam cannot be spread beyond certain restricted local areas until some form of accommodation is reached with the Hanoi government which causes them to withdraw their regular units from the south. However, a beginning toward a north-south accommodation probably cannot come until the United States has demonstrated to itself that it can achieve local *de facto* cease-fires through the use of its military power as a bargaining instrument. To facilitate these local accommodations, the United States should inform Hanoi through secret diplomatic channels of its intention to seek these cease-fires and ask the northern government to use its influence in furthering this goal. At the same time, the United States should announce publicly that it will indefinitely restrict its air attacks against the north to the region south of the 18th parallel, with the hope that this act will signal the strength of its intention to move toward an accommodation.

Once local cease-fires have been achieved, and hopefully they can be achieved rather quickly, the United States should then announce that it will observe a general cease-fire throughout the 1st Corps, and that it is immediately withdrawing 10 percent of its troops from Viet Nam. Moreover, it should also announce that at the end of ninety days another 10 percent of America's military contingent will be withdrawn, providing the cease-fire in the 1st Corps has been observed and there has been a net decrease of 25 percent in manpower within the ranks of Hanoi's regular units by their being withdrawn into the north. In effect we would be withdrawing 5 men for every 1 of theirs.

If these conditions are fulfilled, then the United States should announce its observance of a general cease-fire throughout the 2nd Corps as well as the 1st. It should also announce that at the end of a second ninety-day interval, an additional 20 percent of American forces will be withdrawn from the country, providing the cease-fire is being respected and there has been a net decrease of an additional 25 percent of Hanoi's regulars by their withdrawal to the north. And if these conditions are fulfilled, then a similar procedure should be followed with respect to the 4th Corps, the region comprising the Mekong Delta south of Saigon.

Under such a schedule there would be at the end of nine months less than half of the original contingent of American troops, and there would be recognized cease-fires in effect in all areas of the country except the 3rd Corps, the region immediately surrounding Saigon. As the United States announces its intention of observing a cease-fire in the 3rd Corps and the withdrawal of another 20 percent of its men at the end of ninety days provided the cease-fire is observed and an additional 20 percent of the northern regulars are withdrawn, then the mixed NLF-Saigon consultative committee, if it exists, should be urged to begin elections at the village level.

Simultaneously with this final stage of the cease-fire, the United States ought to cease all of its air attacks against the north, and perhaps even sooner these air operations could be phased as punitive retaliations for violations of the cease-fire rather than being governed by other considerations. In this manner, the northern government could be given more clear-cut incentives to respect the cease-fire.

Perhaps by the end of a year after achieving a total cease-fire and the beginning of elections, a national assembly will have been elected and national executive officers chosen. With this level of political accommodation achieved, negotiations could then begin for the complete withdrawal of the remaining 20 percent of American troops who would have been kept on in the country as a guarantee of the cease-fire during the election period and who would have provided some of the manpower required for reconstruction projects.

These negotiations would be closely linked with the third level of political accommodation, that between regional and international powers concerned with the creation of a durable peace in Southeast Asia. At the same time that the United States announces the withdrawal of its first contingent of men, it should also call upon the United Nations Secretary-General, the Soviet Union, France, and China, as well as other concerned parties, to use their influence in support of the process of political accommodation in southern Viet Nam. Not only would this include efforts to persuade Hanoi to observe the cease-fire and begin withdrawing portions of its regulars, but it would also consist of immediate consultations on the international status of Cambodia and Laos.

The ultimate goal of these consultations would be guarantees that the Vietnamese would not take advantage of the cessation of conflict in their own country by turning their martial energies toward Cambodia and the lowlands of Laos. Any such Vietnamese initiative would undoubtedly be met by a vehement reaction by the Thai. Thus far, however, the Thai have been relatively restrained in pursuing their historic goals of recapturing that territory which the French took from them to incorporate into Cambodia and Laos when they were formed as colonial dependencies within Indochina.

But it is not simply the recapturing of territory that the Thai would be seeking in any future conflict. In the aftermath of a political settlement in Viet Nam, they will probably be prepared to take far-reaching action to prevent the Vietnamese from extending their political control over Cambodia and the lowlands of Laos. Because of the deep-seatedness of these rival political positions there arises the possibility of an even larger scale conflict than the war we are now trying to end.

The matter is further complicated by China's effort to assert its political predominance in Cambodia through the indigenous Chinese community there, alliances with various Cambodian groups as well as by diplomatic efforts. This Chinese gambit in Cambodia may be part of a larger Chinese strategy to restrain the Vietnamese from becoming the political masters of the territory of the former French Indochina. China may have concluded that the best means of preserving a political buffer between the Thai and the Vietnamese is to interpose its own strength. But such an intervention necessarily depends on China's ability to form some effective political coalition to hold power in Cambodia or to influence profoundly the present power holder, Prince Norodom Sihanouk. And it is the combination of internal political instability and the ease with which external, primarily Asian, powers can intervene in the country's politics that makes guarantees for Cambodia's political autonomy so vitally important to a durable accommodation in Southeast Asia.

A similar situation exists in Laos where the Vietnamese, through their long sponsorship of the Pathet Lao movement, exercise substantial influence over Laotian politics and where the Chinese have been much less successful in interposing themselves than in Cambodia. Most Americans believe that the Geneva Agreements of 1961-62 on Laotian neutrality are positive proof that no form of diplomatic accord can be reached which will have any practical effect in restraining the Vietnamese from intruding with impunity into Laos. But this popular belief overlooks the fact that the Pathet Lao movement consists almost exclusively of upland minorities who have been proselytized and organized by the Vietnamese and does not include any substantial number of lowland ethnic Laotians.

While it is relatively easy for the Vietnamese to enjoy nearly complete freedom of movement in the mountains of Laos, they cannot move into the lowlands with impunity either politically or militarily. Since the Pathet Lao does not have an extensive lowland political base among the ethnically Lao people, any thrust into the lowlands along the Mekong River would require them to hold power primarily by force. And due to the Pathet Lao dependency on the Vietnamese, such a move into the lowlands would more certainly invite Thai military intervention than almost any other event. But because the lowland Laotians have been unable to integrate the upland minority people into any national political community there is in effect a *de facto* partition of the country along both ethnic and political lines.

Guarantees that this *de facto* partition will be maintained and stabilized should be a prime means of assuring that a political accommodation in Viet Nam will not lead to an upsetting of the delicate process of politics in Laos. Similar guarantees should be sought for Cambodia but they will be more difficult to specify since there are no *de facto* arrangements and the lines of competition there are much less clear-cut. But whatever the specificity achieved in these guarantees, the United States should not deceive itself concerning the texts of formal diplomatic documents—a deception that has led us to conclude that negotiations are useless because formal agreements are never kept.

Instead, the United States should use its position in both Viet Nam and Thailand to bargain for as many reciprocal guarantees of a political accommodation in Southeast Asia as can possibly be achieved. For example, the Soviet Union should be persuaded that its interests will not be served by a larger war since it would make their influence more difficult to exercise in Southeast Asia. In bringing the present conflict under control the Russians should be involved in both restraining the Vietnamese and in sustaining the political autonomy of Cambodia and the lowlands of Laos. Their aircraft support for Hanoi should be an effective lever in the former task while their more active participation in the development of the Mekong River might provide a cover for the latter.

The Chinese will be more difficult to persuade but if they really are concerned with maintaining a political buffer between the Vietnamese and the Thai then an international guarantee of the autonomy of Cambodia and the lowlands of Laos would seem a more certain means of achieving their goal. But if the Chinese really want to make these two buffer states into dependencies of their own, then perhaps the threat of Vietnamese pressure on them would also induce the Chinese to seek a settlement.

Furthermore, the southern Vietnamese government ought to relinquish its control of islands in the Gulf of Thailand, claimed by the Cambodians, and the Thai should resolve the lingering animosities with the Cambodians over the temple of Preah Viharn.

Most of these acts, including the possible reestablishment of diplomatic relations between Cambodia and Thailand and Cambodia and the United States, would largely be symbolic gestures requiring sacrifices of national prestige rather than strategic position. But in symbolic sacrifices the United States and other powers might acquire more certain guarantees of political accommodation in Southeast Asia than through any other kind of formal diplomatic agreement.

The path toward a political accommodation which has been sketched out here in bare outline form will require more thought and refinement to be used as a guide for action. Moreover, its general thrust does not promise a quick panacea for our anguishing difficulties in Viet Nam: on the contrary, it traces out a prolonged process of accommodation to be achieved through the application of power to carefully phased political objectives. Its goal is the attainment of a

pattern of politics among Southeast Asians in which violence is reduced to manageable proportions and reduced altogether by international powers.

The achievement of this protracted process will require enormous
patience, sophistication, and sacrifice on the part of the United States
military and other organizational instruments of our national policy
in Southeast Asia. The use of force in achieving feasible goals of political accommodation and the reduction of conflict seems, however, a
wiser course than the strength-sapping and illusive military objectives
we now pursue. When all factors are considered, would it not be a
more honorable, prestigious, and durable achievement of our fighting
men to have won a peace rather than suffered a stalemate.

The Bases of Accommodation

SAMUEL P. HUNTINGTON

A VIABLE political settlement in South Viet Nam will reflect and give some legitimacy to the balance of political, military and social forces produced by a decade of internal conflict and five years of large-scale warfare. A successful settlement can also inaugurate a process of political accommodation through which the various elements of Vietnamese society may eventually be brought together into a functioning polity. American objectives and American expectations of what can be achieved at the conference table and on the battlefield should, correspondingly, be based on the realities of power and the opportunities for accommodation.

Much of the discussion of Viet Nam in the United States, however, has been couched in terms of stereotypes and slogans which have little relation to the political forces and social trends in Vietnamese society. Critics of the Administration often tend to glorify the Viet Cong and the National Liberation Front and to magnify the extent of their support. They see the war as a popular uprising against a military-landlord oligarchy dependent upon foreign military support. Hence they see little need for, or basis for, accommodation: if the United States withdrew, it is held, the Saigon régime would quickly collapse, and a new, broadly representative government would come to power under the leadership of the NLF but drawing support from Buddhists, workers, students and other groups.

Spokesmen for the Administration, on the other hand, have in the past underrated the strength of the Viet Cong and have ascribed to the Saigon Government a popularity which had as little basis in fact as that which the critics attributed to the NLF. They have bolstered their case with statistics on kill rates, infiltration rates, *chieu hoi* (defection) rates, hamlet pacification categories and voting turnouts. These figures may be reasonably accurate but they are also often irrelevant to the conclusions which they are adduced to support. At times key figures in the Administration have made statements which at least *seemed* to predict the imminent collapse of the Viet Cong. The misplaced moralism of the critics has thus confronted the unwarranted optimism of the advocates.

The realities of the situation in Viet Nam will not please the extremists on either side. If properly perceived and accepted, however, they may provide some basis for accommodation and an eventual compromise settlement. The military strengths and weaknesses of each side are manifest in each day's news reports and will no doubt shape the outcome of the negotiations. The success of that outcome, however, may well depend on the extent to which it reflects the political and social strengths and weaknesses of both sides. These are less obvious but more fundamental than the military factors.

II

The overall proportion of the population that is more under Government than Viet Cong control has risen rather strikingly in three years from a little over 40 percent of the total to 60 percent or more. This change, however, has been largely, if not exclusively, the result of the movement of the population into the cities rather than the extension of the Government's control into the countryside. The two most important facts which an accommodation will have to reflect are, first, the continuing role of the Viet Cong in the countryside and, second, the declining role of the countryside in South Viet Nam as a whole.

Viet Nam is a plural society, whose regional, ethnic and religious differences are now widely recognized. But there is another sense in which there are at least four South Viet Nams, each of them present in every geographical region and in almost every province. The first consists of the urban population, which is now perhaps 40 percent of the total and which lives under more or less continuing control by the Government. The other three South Viet Nams divide the rural population in approximately equal shares: the rural communal population, roughly 20 percent of the total, who belong to a religious or ethnic minority and who at present are aligned with the Saigon Government against the Viet Cong; the hard-core Viet Cong, again perhaps 20 percent of the total, who in some rural areas have lived under Viet Cong control for many years; and the remaining 20 percent, which constitutes the population of the most heavily and continuously contested rural areas.

These proportions are very rough and, moreover, they refer to population control, not political support. Discussion of Viet Nam often revolves about the question: "Whom do the majority of the people really support?" This is a reasonable and practical question to ask in a stable Western constitutional democracy. For Viet Nam, however, it is unanswerable and, in large part, irrelevant simply because it is quite clear that no government or political grouping has been able to win widespread popular support— or seems likely to do so. The most one can realistically speak of is the relative ability of the Government and the VC-NLF to exercise authority and to control population. And even here, as the allied sweeps through hard-core Viet Cong areas and the Tet offensive amply demonstrate, each side's authority is nowhere beyond at least temporary challenge by the other side. In addition, an underground Viet Cong organization presumably exists in many areas where Government authority is normally exercised.

The crucial characteristic of the heavily contested rural areas is the absence of effective social and political organization above the village level, if even there. The strength of the Viet Cong is its ability to fill this vacuum of authority; the weakness of the Government has been the failure of its pacification programs to generate self-sustaining local organizations.

It is often said that the war in Viet Nam is a "political" war, and that consequently winning the war requires the Government to appeal to "the hearts and minds of the people" by promoting rural development, land reform, education, official honesty and other specific and usually material benefits. In fact, however, there is little evidence to suggest that the appeal of the Viet Cong derives from material poverty or that it can be countered by material benefits. The one systematic study of this question, focusing on land tenure, indeed came to precisely the opposite conclusion. Government control was found to be greatest in those provinces in which "few peasants farm their own land, the distribution of landholdings is unequal, no land redistribution has taken place, large French landholdings existed in the past, population density is high, and the terrain is such that accessibility is poor."[1] This seemingly perverse product of statistical analysis is bolstered by other substantial if less systematic evidence for Viet Nam as well as by much experience elsewhere. The appeal of revolutionaries depends not on economic deprivation but on political deprivation, that is, on the absence of an effective structure of authority. Where the latter exists, even though it be quite

[1] Edward J. Mitchell, "Inequality and Insurgency: A Statistical Study of South Vietnam," *World Politics*, April 1968, p. 438.

hierarchical and undemocratic, the Viet Cong make little progress.

Since the late 1950s successive Saigon governments have attempted to meet this need by a variety of pacification programs. None of these has been successful, with the partial exception of the current program of "Revolutionary Development," which was interrupted by the Tet offensive. Governmental control can be produced either by a massive military and administrative presence or by effective local political organization. In the past, forces have been inadequate to provide a substantial presence in a significant portion of the countryside for a significant length of time. The current pacification effort was mounted on a scale which dwarfs the earlier ones, but like them it has attempted to achieve security by the extension into the countryside of the military and administrative apparatus of the Central Government. In some cases, the successes of pacification can be seen in quite striking fashion. Voter turnout in the 1967 presidential election as compared with the 1966 constituent assembly election increased by 50 percent in Binh Dinh province, 23 percent in Phu Yen, 22 percent in Hau Nghia and 20 percent in Binh Duong. These changes were undoubtedly the result of the strong pacification efforts made in those provinces.

Yet these same provinces also illustrate the limits of pacification. When military forces were withdrawn from Binh Dinh and Hau Nghia, security rapidly began to deteriorate. The fragility of the whole pacification effort was reflected by the extent of its at least temporary collapse during the Tet offensive, despite the fact that the offensive was directed at the cities rather than the pacification cadres. The acid test of pacification is whether a locality develops the will and the means to defend itself against Viet Cong attack or infiltration. With a few exceptions, mostly among the communal groups, the current pacification effort has not as yet met this test. In some cases, the intrusion of national governmental authority from the outside may undermine the authority of the local village leaders; when the agents of the national Government move on, they may leave the situation worse than it was before they arrived. In those instances, the Government prepares the way for the Viet Cong.

It thus seems unlikely that the current pacification program will significantly change the pattern of political control—or lack of control—in the contested areas in the immediate future. If a cease-fire led to reductions in either the Government's military-administrative presence or U.S. forces in these areas, the way would be opened for the Viet Cong to move in and extend its control through political means. The only practical alternative, available in some instances, would be for the authority vacuum to be filled by some other social-political group with roots in the locality.

The security of that one-third of the rural population which is under a relatively high degree of Government control is in large part the product of communal—ethnic or religious—organizations. It is commonly assumed that rural security is the product of identification with and loyalty to the Government, which, in turn, is the product of the extension of governmental presence into the villages. In much of South Viet Nam, however, the sequence has not been: governmental control, national loyalty, internal security. It has been, instead: communal organization, internal security, governmental control. The exercise of governmental authority has resulted from internal security produced by other factors. Governmental authority is, in fact, most effectively exercised in those rural areas where the Government has come to terms with the local power structure and with ethnic or religious groups.

The relationships between these communal groups and the Central Government have typically evolved through four phases. First, the group develops social and political consciousness. In due course, the evolution of the group produces a challenge to central authority and a confrontation between the group and the Central Government, as with the Cao Dai and Hoa Hao during the 1950s or the Montagnard uprisings against more recent governments. Defeat by the Central Government leads to the group's withdrawal from the national political scene. Finally, however, there is a renewal of ties and an accommodation is worked out. At present, all of the rural communal groups—Hoa Hao, Cao Dai, Catholic, Khmer and Montagnard—have reached such accommodations with the existing system, stimulated no doubt by shared hostility toward the Viet Cong.

The relationship between communalism and governmental authority in South Viet Nam today is thus almost precisely the opposite of what it is in most other Southeast Asian countries. In Thailand, Burma, Malaysia and elsewhere the ethnic and religious minorities are the principal sources of opposition to the political system. In South Viet Nam, in contrast, the religious and ethnic minorities are centers of support for the system, and the relatively unorganized rural majority—the ethnic Vietnamese with Confucian, Buddhist and animist religious beliefs—is the principal source of alienation and disaffection.

Rural areas which have been continuously secure are those organized by religious or ethnic communities. The most secure province in South Viet Nam is An Giang, in which there have been no major U.S. or Government combat units. The security of An Giang results from the political control of the Hoa Hao. The Hoa Hao in the surrounding provinces have achieved similar areas of security, as have the Cambodians elsewhere in the Delta. Catholic and Cao Dai villages tend to be more scattered geographically and hence more vulnerable to attack. None the less, many isolated villages belonging to one of those faiths remain relatively secure in otherwise highly insecure areas, simply because the Viet Cong know that they will be tough nuts to crack.

The ethnic and religious communities have thus played a crucial role in extending Government control into rural areas. They have done this despite the suspicion and hostility of at least some elements in the Government. After a cease-fire, these are the principal groups which will be able to compete with the Viet Cong in the political organization of the peasantry.

The remaining third of the rural population lives in "hard-core" Viet Cong areas, some of which have been almost continuously under Viet Minh and Viet Cong control since the 1940s. They include the Camau peninsula, much of the Delta coast, the Plain of Reeds, War Zones "C" and "D" north and west of Saigon, and portions of Binh Dinh and Quang Ngai in the central part of the country. In some villages an entire generation has grown up under communist rule. In some of these areas the VC-NLF has been able to develop a well-organized structure of government at the village and even district level.

To eliminate Viet Cong control in these areas would be an expensive, time-consuming and frustrating task. It would require a much larger and more intense military and pacification effort than is currently contemplated by Saigon and Washington. Consequently, effective Viet Cong control of these areas is a political fact which does not seem likely to change for some while, if indeed it ever does. In a politically reintegrated South Viet Nam, there would probably be a fairly steady population drain from them into more prosperous rural and urban localities. The achievement of such political reintegration clearly will depend, however, upon the recognition and acceptance of Viet Cong control of local government in these areas. It is here that accommodation in the most specific sense of the word is a political necessity.

The most striking feature of these varied patterns of rural political control—contested, communal and Viet Cong—has been their resistance to change. The French, Diem, the post-Diem régimes, the Viet Minh and Viet Cong have all tried, without significant success, to produce permanent changes in them. The huge current pacification program has been another effort to bring about a *political* revolution in the relations between the Government and the countryside. It may succeed where the others have failed, but as yet there is no conclusive evidence of this. On the other hand, the massive American effort is producing a *social* revolution in the Vietnamese way of life which will be of far greater consequence to the future of the country.

III

The most dramatic and far-reaching impact of the war in South Viet Nam has been the tremendous shift in population from the countryside to the cities. In the early 1960s it was still accurate to speak of South Viet Nam as 80 to 85 percent rural. Today, no one knows for certain the size of the urban population, but it is undoubtedly more than double and perhaps triple what it was a few years ago. A reasonable current estimate of people in cities of 20,000 or more would be about 40 percent of the total, or 6,800,000 of a total of 17,200,000. By this standard South Viet Nam is now more urban than Sweden, Canada, the Soviet Union, Poland, Austria, Switzerland and Italy (according to early 1960s data). Apart from Singapore, it is easily the most urban country in Southeast Asia. The image of South Viet Nam as a country composed largely of landlords and peasants—an image still prevalent among many Vietnamese intellectuals who continue to quote the 85 percent rural figure—has little relationship to reality.

The movement of people into the cities during the past four years is a nationwide phenomenon. In 1962 Saigon's population was estimated at 1,400,000. Today it is at least twice that, and the population of the Saigon metropolitan area is probably about 4,000,000, more than 20 percent of the entire country. The increases in population of cities like Danang, Nha Trang, Qui Nhon,

Pleiku, Kontum and Ban Me Thuot have been even more spectacular. Smaller cities and towns have also had extraordinary growth rates, with many provincial capitals doubling or tripling their population in two or three years.

The principal reason for this massive influx of population into the urban areas is, of course, the intensification of the war following the commitment of American combat troops in 1965. About 1,500,000 of the total increase in urban population is accounted for by refugees, half still in refugee camps and others settled in new areas. At least an equal number of people have moved into the cities without passing through refugee camps. The social costs of this change have been dramatic and often heart-rending. The conditions in the refugee camps, particularly in I Corps, have at times been horrendous, although some significant improvements are now taking place. Urban welfare and developmental programs require increasing priority from the United States and Vietnamese Governments.

The immediate economic effects of urbanization are somewhat more mixed. Those who were well-off in the countryside often suffer serious losses in the move to the city. The rural poor, on the other hand, may well find life in the city more attractive and comfortable than their previous existence in the countryside. The urban slum, which seems so horrible to middle-class Americans, often becomes for the poor peasant a gateway to a new and better way of life. For some poor migrants, the wartime urban boom has made possible incomes five times those which they had in the countryside. In one Saigon slum, Xom Chua, in early 1965 before the American build-up, the people lived at a depressed level, with 33 percent of the adult males unemployed. Eighteen months later, as a result of the military escalation, the total population of the slum had increased by 30 percent, but the unemployment rate had dropped to 5 percent and average incomes had doubled.[2] In several cases urban refugees from the war refused to return to their villages once security was restored because of the higher level of economic well-being which they could attain in the city. The pull of urban prosperity has been a secondary but not insignificant factor in attracting people into the city.

In the long run urbanization will create major political prob-

[2] Marilyn W. Hoskins and Eleanor M. Shepherd, "Life in a Vietnamese Urban Quarter," Carbondale, Ill.: The Graduate School, Southern Illinois University, 1965, (updated in 1966 as a U.S. AID memorandum).

lems. Typically, the second generation—the children of the slums, not the migrants to the slums—provides participants for urban riots and insurrections. After the war, massive government programs will be required either to resettle migrants in rural areas or to rebuild the cities and promote peacetime urban employment. In the meantime, while the war continues, urbanization is significantly altering the balance of power between the Saigon Government and the Viet Cong.

More than anything else urbanization has been responsible for the striking increase in the proportion of the population living under Government control between 1964 and 1968. The depopulation of the countryside struck directly at the strength and potential appeal of the Viet Cong. For ten years the Viet Cong had waged a rural revolution against the Central Government, with the good Maoist expectation that by winning the support of the rural population it could eventually isolate and overwhelm the cities. The "first outstanding feature . . . of People's Revolutionary War, as developed by Mao Tse-tung and refined by the North Vietnamese in the two Indochina wars," Sir Robert Thompson argued in a recent issue of this journal, "is its immunity to the direct application of mechanical and conventional power."[3] In the light of recent events, this statement needs to be seriously qualified. For if the "direct application of mechanical and conventional power" takes place on such a massive scale as to produce a massive migration from countryside to city, the basic assumptions underlying the Maoist doctrine of revolutionary war no longer operate. The Maoist-inspired rural revolution is undercut by the American-sponsored urban revolution.

The full significance of the Tet offensive becomes clear against this background. This attack on the cities, like the subsequent attacks in May, was less of an offensive than it was a counter-offensive against the fundamental social change taking place in Vietnamese society. The war in Viet Nam is a war for the control of the population. If the Viet Cong are to compete effectively with the Government, they must be able to assert their power in the cities. If they can assert their control over the newly urbanized population in the cities as easily as they were able to assert their control over the rural population and win their support in the countryside, the movement of population will have been only a Trojan horse.

[3] Sir Robert Thompson, "Squaring the Error," *Foreign Affairs*, April 1968, p. 447.

The Tet offensive produced several clear gains for the Viet Cong in Viet Nam, apart from the impact abroad. For the first time they significantly disrupted, albeit very temporarily in all cities but Hue, the security of the urban population, thus diminishing the principal attraction of the city to the country dwellers. With a decline in the differences in the sense of security provided by city and countryside, there may well be a decline in the rate of movement from one to the other. Secondly, before Tet relatively few military forces were committed primarily to urban defense. Most Vietnamese cities were virtually open cities with traffic moving in and out of them freely. The Viet Cong have now compelled the redeployment of U.S. and South Vietnamese forces from other tasks, such as rural pacification, to city protection. Thirdly, the Viet Cong cut many of the transportation and communication routes into the cities in an apparent effort to isolate urban areas from each other and from the surrounding countryside. The most notable action here concerned road and water communication routes between the relatively secure areas of the Delta and Saigon. The weeks following the offensive saw a sharp drop in the previous level of supplies moving over these routes. This caused some economic dislocation in both the farm areas and the cities, but not of either a prolonged or highly threatening character.

These were significant achievements for the Viet Cong, and their impact was notably heightened by their surprise. The real test of their urban offensive, however, is whether they can mobilize and organize sufficient popular support in the cities to substitute their authority for that of the Government. To invade the cities by stealth or by frontal assault is a relatively easy task. To seize and hold urban areas is something else again. It is reasonably clear that this was an objective of the Tet offensive. Viet Cong units moving in from the countryside appealed for a "general uprising" of the urban populace and brought with them the political cadres to set up block committees and a political structure in urban areas. In several cities such as Pleiku and Nha Trang the Viet Cong infrastructure within the city surfaced and was substantially destroyed.

No general uprising took place, however, and the invaders were quickly driven out of all cities except Hue. In several cities the people, in spontaneous and unprecedented fashion, organized themselves to defend their neighborhoods against the Viet Cong.

In Hoi An (capital of Quang Nam province) the overwhelming majority of the students in the local high school rallied to the Government, requested arms to fight the enemy and helped to capture most of the Viet Cong cadre which had entered the city expecting to set up its own administration. Similar responses by students, labor-union members and civil servants elsewhere produced a rallying of support for the Government which had not been equalled since the early days of the Diem régime. The weak spot was not in the people's lack of hostility toward the Viet Cong but in the suspicion of many Government officials toward the people.

In the past the Viet Cong could expect to win the war simply by preventing Saigon from extending its control in the rural areas. This the Viet Cong can still do but it is no longer sufficient to achieve victory. Increasingly the Viet Cong must also demonstrate their ability to win support and to exercise authority in the cities. So far, they have been even less successful in these efforts than the Government has been in winning support in the countryside. In this sense, history—drastically and brutally speeded up by the American impact—may pass the Viet Cong by. Societies are susceptible to revolution only at particular stages in their development. At the moment the rates of urbanization and of modernization in the secure rural areas exceed the rate of increase in Viet Cong strength. At a time when the South Vietnamese Army is beginning to show signs of being able to operate on its own, the Viet Cong are becoming increasingly dependent on North Viet Nam for manpower as well as supplies. A movement which once had the potential for developing into a truly comprehensive revolutionary force with an appeal to both rural and urban groups could now degenerate into the protest of a declining rural minority increasingly dependent upon outside support.

In an absent-minded way the United States in Viet Nam may well have stumbled upon the answer to "wars of national liberation." The effective response lies neither in the quest for conventional military victory nor in the esoteric doctrines and gimmicks of counter-insurgency warfare. It is instead forced-draft urbanization and modernization which rapidly brings the country in question out of the phase in which a rural revolutionary movement can hope to generate sufficient strength to come to power.

Time in South Viet Nam is increasingly on the side of the Government. But in the short run, with half the population still in the countryside, the Viet Cong will remain a powerful force which cannot be dislodged from its constituency so long as the constituency continues to exist. Peace in the immediate future must hence be based on accommodation.

IV

During the past three years the pattern of the military conflict has been largely determined in Hanoi and Washington, which are also playing the dominant role in negotiations. The stability of the political settlement which eventually results in South Viet Nam, however, will depend primarily upon the extent to which it reflects the social and political forces within that country rather than on external influences, either military or diplomatic. Hence, there is good reason to encourage the early inauguration of a political process within South Viet Nam in which all significant political groups can participate and to allow that process rather than a diplomatic conference to have the lion's share in determining the future of the country.

It is often argued that this process should begin with the creation of a coalition government. There are, however, many disadvantages to such an approach. Neither the NLF nor Saigon wants a coalition with the other, and it is difficult to envision how the existing leaderships could work together. From the viewpoint of the Government such an arrangement would, as one moderate Vietnamese leader put it, simply allow "the wolves into the chicken pen." More specifically it would surrender to the Viet Cong a major share in the exercise of authority in urban areas, which is precisely what they have been unable to win through military means.

Conversely, it would be difficult for the NLF to enter into association with a group of men whom it has repeatedly denounced as puppets and traitors. Even if external pressure from the United States, Hanoi and the Soviet Union produced something in Saigon which could be labeled a "coalition government," it clearly would not be a coalition government in fact. A "coalition" implies sustained coöperation between autonomous groups. If there was a reasonable balance of power within the Government, however, it would be a government divided against itself, a temporary expedient which neither side would expect to endure; each side would be busily organizing its military and political forces for the final showdown. Alternatively, pressure from Moscow and Hanoi plus impatience in Washington might lead to a coalition weighted on the side of the communists. In this case, the "coalition" would not only be temporary, it would be a sham, with the political outcome a foreordained conclusion.

The rural-urban division of the country and the mixed pattern of political control in rural areas suggests that the process of political accommodation should start at the bottom and work up rather than the reverse. Some forms of local accommodation have, of course, existed for some time in parts of the country, particularly in the Delta. Most frequently they have involved "live-and-let-live" arrangements among local military commanders. To some extent they have also involved mutual tolerance of each other's revenue-raising activities. On the Government side, the weakness of its forces and the natural desire to remain in the towns and avoid the efforts and dangers of combat have provided incentives to accept these arrangements, while for the Viet Cong it has been a general war-weariness among local cadres, especially in the Delta. To expand these local accommodations substantively and geographically will entail many difficulties. None the less, this is the way to start a political process which will reflect the actual balance of forces within the society.

In some respects this pattern of accommodation would not be very different from that worked out between Saigon and the Hoa Hao. It would mean that the Viet Cong would as effectively dominate its hard-core areas as the Hoa Hao and Catholic organizations do in their villages and districts. To be sure, the indigenous Viet Cong clearly differs in important respects from the religious sects and the nationalist parties, but it also shares many characteristics with them. Up to a point, the evolution of relations between the Viet Cong and the established political system paralleled that of the sects and other parties. Like them, the Viet Minh developed organizational and political consciousness in the 1930s; it then came into conflict with the French and their puppet authorities; after 1954 it in effect withdrew and, like the other sects and parties, went underground during the period when Diem was attempting to centralize authority and eliminate local centers of power.

Unlike the other parties and sects, however, the Viet Cong began in the late 1950s to receive significant reinforcements in the form of returnees and supplies from North Viet Nam. Consequently, at that point the Viet Cong broke the pattern of evolution which it had shared with the other groups—consciousness, confrontation, withdrawal—and instead instituted a renewed period of confrontation. After 1963 the other groups reached varying degrees of accommodation with the Government while the confrontation between the Government and the Viet Cong intensified. Yet it is not unreasonable to assume that when it becomes clear that this confrontation cannot succeed, the indigenous Viet Cong will again move into a phase of withdrawal, which conceivably could then be followed by accommodation and incorporation into a restructured and expanded political system.

Initially, the practical needs for and benefits from accommodation are likely to be greater at the local than at the national level. Differing patterns of control will be possible in different areas, and concessions in one area can be traded for comparable concessions in other areas. If the cease-fire arrangements divide the country into military zones of control, political control in a village will in most cases be determined by the zone in which it is located. A large number of districts and the majority of provinces, however, will undoubtedly be divided between zones. At these levels, consequently, the functioning of government will require some coöperation between, and eventual integration of, local NLF and Saigon governmental structures. One means of accomplishing this would be to elect province chiefs and/or enlarged and strengthened provincial councils. Elections at the provincial level are likely to encourage political candidates and groups to appeal to both rural and urban voters and to promote coöperation among non-communist groups. They would give the VC-NLF the legitimate opportunity to enter the political process and to demonstrate their ability to win power at the grass-roots level. Provincial elections could also be suitably staggered so as to permit more effective supervision by outside observers and international bodies.

If accommodation worked in a majority of provinces, the way would be opened for its extension to the national Government. The next step would be the election of a new constituent assembly, perhaps in part by universal suffrage and in part by the provincial councils, to devise new basic laws and choose a new Central Government. If as a result of this process the VC-NLF secured control of the Central Government, the United States would obviously regret the outcome but could also accept it and feel under little compulsion to re-intervene.

In the interests of promoting widespread access to the Government and accommodation among groups, it would be wise for the constituent assembly to shift some authority from the Central Government to provincial and local governments. Centralization of authority in the national Government simply complicates the problem of accommodating Viet Cong and noncommunist forces. If all power resides in the Central Government, the struggle for control is all the more intense; coöperation becomes nearly impossible. Political integration from the bottom up will facilitate the loosening up of the political structure, and the loosening of the political structure will at the same time promote political accommodation, particularly at the national level.

Any suggestion for greater decentralization of authority in Viet Nam is always met with the charge that it will encourage "wardlordism," to which a strong Central Government is the only antidote. In actuality, however, as the earlier history of China, Viet Nam and even Western Europe amply demonstrates, warlordism is the product not of efforts to provide a structured decentralized authority, but rather of efforts to maintain a narrowly based, centralized authority where it is inappropriate to the situation. Warlordism is the illegal, disruptive and violent way in which a centralized system is adapted to the realities of dispersed power. Warlordism is the alternative to the formal decentralization of authority, not a product of it.

In the recent past, the French, Bao Dai, Diem, each in different ways, attempted to perpetuate centralized authority, and in every case they weakened it. To strengthen political authority, it is instead necessary to decentralize it, to extend the scope of the political system and to incorporate more effectively into it the large number of groups which have become politically organized and politically conscious in recent years. Such a system might be labeled federal, confederal, pluralistic, decentralized—but, whatever the label, it would reflect the varied sources of political power. In the recognition of and acceptance of that diversity lies the hope for political stability in Viet Nam.

A Political Settlement for Vietnam: The 1954 Geneva Conference and Its Current Implications

JOHN S. HANNON, JR.

With a Preface by John Norton Moore

Historical truth is at best elusive. But conditions for research about a major war are rarely at best while the conflict is raging. It is not surprising, then, that there are continuing disagreements about historical truth in the Viet Nam war which go far deeper than any alleged credibility gap. Though one can easily overemphasize this fact ambiguity in assigning reasons for the disagreement about United States Viet Nam policy, contradictory fact assumptions undoubtedly play a significant part in this disagreement. Chief among the disputed facts have been the origins of the insurgency within South Viet Nam and the nature of the 1954 Geneva Agreements. Yet despite the unprecedented outpouring of writing from the scholarly community, there have been relatively few studies of these important issues. The Geneva Accords particularly have suffered from this lack of basic research. To date there have been only three major studies of the agreements: Lacouture and Devillers' *La Fin D'Une Guerre,* published in 1960, and still largely not translated into English, Ngo Ton Dat's "The Geneva Partition of Vietnam and the Question of Reunification During the First Two Years," an unpublished 1963 Cornell doctoral dissertation, and Franklin Weinstein's *Vietnam's Unheld Elections,* a pamphlet published in 1966 by the Cornell Southeast Asia Program. John Hannon's major article in this issue of the Journal is the first systematic study of the content of the settlement reached at Geneva and in my judgment is the most balanced, most complete and best documented study available with respect to the total context of the Geneva Accords. One should bear in mind, however, that the full truth about the Agreements reached at Geneva remains locked in the diplomatic archives of the Conference participants. Conclusions about those Agreements on the basis of secondary sources are of necessity approximations.

A principal danger in seeking to record historical truth about the Viet Nam war is not so much reliance on inaccurate facts as it is unconscious selection and emphasis of facts which support the model of the conflict most favorable to the world view of the writer. Particularly in the case of the ambiguous and complex guerrilla war in Viet Nam some facts can always be found which support almost any major view of the issues, and as a result facts can sometimes be the enemy of truth. In seeking to unravel this kind of tangle it is particularly helpful to utilize a methodology which will provide an overview of the competing facts and which will minimize the danger of one-sided fact selection. In meeting this danger John Hannon has been influenced by the method of analysis developed by Yale scholars McDougal, Lasswell and Miller for the systematic interpretation of agreements.[1] This approach rejects both the nihilism of the extreme realists, who say that interpretation is so difficult that nothing useful can be said about it, and the ostrich-like approach of the traditionalists who blindly exclude all but textuality from the focus of the decision maker. In their place, McDougal, Lasswell and Miller provide a systematic framework for analysis of the total context of the process of agreement, giving appropriate weight to the text of the agreement.

Perhaps it bears emphasis that though the McDougal, Lasswell, Miller method provides a very sophisticated tool for interpretation, its use does not guarantee "correct results" or indicate that all scholars using the system would arrive at identical conclusions. Differences in human perception belie such unanimity. John Hannon's use of the system, however, has aided in the depth of insight which is evident throughout his study.

If there has been any one error running through the popular discussion of the Geneva Accords, it has been an overemphasis on textuality at the expense of other features of the process of agreement. Though the text of an agreement provides a focal point for interpretation, the use of the text alone may badly distort the actual shared expectations of the parties. Nowhere has this been more evident than in some critics' uncritical reliance on the language of sections six and seven of the Final Declaration of the Conference to prove that the Viet Nam war is a "civil war" between the North and the South precipitated by United States sabotage of the Accords. As Hannon's exploration of the broadest context of the Agreements indicates, real-world Viet Nam has never been this simple. The Agreements, with their incompleteness, ambiguity and contradictions, largely contained their own seeds of destruction. Moreover, there are important lessons to be learned from study of these weaknesses. The Accords were fatally incomplete in failing to clearly bind all interested parties, in failing to spell out the crucial details of any political settlement and in failing to provide a workable policing agency to ensure continued compliance with the agreements. Any future Geneva Conference would do well to ponder these shortcomings.

Though beyond the scope of John Hannon's study, it is essential when passing judgment on the Viet Nam war to relate discussion of the Geneva Accords to the overriding problem of control of coercion. The 1954 Accords share the difficulties and ambiguities characteristic

---

1. *See* M. McDougal, H. Lasswell & J. Miller, The Interpretation of Agreements and World Public Order (1967).

of many major political compromises between powerful international rivals. As such, if it is accepted that states may resort to force to remedy non-forceful breach of treaty, there will be little left of the United Nations Charter principle that major force may only be used in response to an armed attack. It is imperative that this judgment about resort to force be recognized as an issue qualitatively different from judgment about breach of agreement. And in the Viet Nam context, focus on the Geneva Agreements, as important as they are, must not obscure the critical importance of Hanoi's decision to use the military instrument to enforce its view of those agreements.

JOHN NORTON MOORE
Associate Professor of Law
The University of Virginia

JOHN S. HANNON, JR.

I. Introduction

Open warfare has ravaged the land of Vietnam for the better part of the last quarter century. While the cast of characters has changed somewhat, and the military developments appear more prominent, the underlying political issues remain basic to the search for a viable settlement of the tragic conflict.

The majority of the present combatants partipicated in at least one previous attempt to settle the problems of Vietnam: the Geneva Conference of 1954. Paradoxically enough, major combatants on both sides of the conflict have stated that a return to the essentials of these Agreements would bring peace to Vietnam. On the Communist side, both the Democratic Republic of Vietnam[1] and the National Liberation Front[2] have called for strict implementation of the Geneva Agreements. Anthony Eden, one of the Co-Chairmen of the 1954 Conference, has suggested that the Geneva precedents be followed in any future peace negotiations, since the Communist powers show a "firm will" to do so.[3] The United States has similarly expressed repeated interest in a return to the Agreements of 1954.[4] And a reconvening of the 1954 Geneva Conference lies at the very heart of U.N. Secretary-General U Thant's peace proposals of March 14, 1967, which the United States has openly accepted.[5]

Where both contending sides can point to these agreements as sup-

---

1. During Soviet Premier Kosygin's visit to Hanoi, the two governments issued a joint communique on February 11, 1965, calling on all participants of the 1954 Geneva Conference to respect and correctly implement them. RECENT EXCHANGES CONCERNING ATTEMPTS TO PROMOTE A NEGOTIATED SETTLEMENT OF THE CONFLICT IN VIET-NAM, CMND. NO. 2756, at 18 (1965).
2. Liberation Radio, Mar. 23, 1965, *National Liberation Front on U.S. Escalation of War*, in THE VIET-NAM READER 235 (M. Raskin & B. Fall eds. 1965).
3. A. EDEN, TOWARD PEACE IN INDOCHINA 4 (1966).
4. The United States summary of the elements necessary for an honorable peace, the Fourteen Points, begin with the statement "The Geneva agreements of 1954 and 1962 are an adequate basis for peace in southeast Asia." *Hearings on S. 2793 Before the Senate Committee on Foreign Relations*, 89th Cong., 2d Sess., pt. 1, at 573 [hereinafter cited as *Vietnam Hearings*].
5. Washington Post, Mar. 29, 1967, at A-1, col. 7.

porting their own policy goals, a great deal of confusion necessarily exists as to their content. This confusion is particularly evident in reference to the provisions in the 1954 Agreements for a political settlement, namely, general elections throughout Vietnam, to be held in July 1956.[6] The Democratic Republic of Vietnam (hereinafter "DRV") has steadfastly maintained that the elections were an integral part of the Geneva settlement, and that it was prepared to carry out these political provisions faithfully. The Communist world has accused the United States of being "saboteurs of the Geneva Accords"[7] by furnishing substantial political and economic support to the Diem government in the South from 1954 to 1956 and supporting Diem's refusal to proceed with consultations on the elections. While there still appears to be some confusion as to the reasons behind the U.S. policy at Geneva in 1954,[8] in the years since Geneva the United States has argued that it did not sign the Geneva Convention, that it expressed definite reservations to the basic agreements at the time, and that it therefore is not bound by them.

While such a debate may appear to be only of academic interest, it may unfortunately have very important consequences. Most of the analysts writing as of the end of the 1954 Conference felt that Ho Chi Minh had sufficient nationalist backing to win any such election. If the DRV sincerely believes it was cheated by the West of its just gains in the period following the Geneva Agreements, and is not merely advancing these arguments as a shield against its own military operations in the South, it may be reluctant to attempt another session of deliberations with the West short of total military victory or defeat. Certainly the expectations of the participants in the 1954 Geneva Conference regarding the political future of Vietnam form a major starting-point in the search for the origins of the present tragic conflict. Finally, analysis of the 1954 Geneva Conference might reveal defects either in the negotiating procedures or in the substantive content of the Agreements, and at least produce a warning against such pitfalls in any further negotiations on Vietnam.

Surprisingly little scholarly attention has been focused on the political aspects of the 1954 Geneva Agreements,[9] possibly because of the

---

6. Final Declaration of the Geneva Conference, July 21, 1954, § 7, in SENATE COMM. ON FOREIGN RELATIONS, 89th Cong., 2d Sess., BACKGROUND INFORMATION RELATING TO SOUTHEAST ASIA AND VIETNAM 67 (2d rev. ed. Comm. Print 1966) [hereinafter cited as BACKGROUND INFORMATION].

7. Liberation Radio, Mar. 23, 1965, *National Liberation Front on U.S. Escalation of War*, in THE VIET-NAM READER 233 (M. Raskin & B. Fall eds. 1965).

8. During the Senate Foreign Relations Committee hearings in 1966, Secretary of State Rusk openly admitted he could not even find in the record a full discussion of why the United States refused to associate itself with the Geneva Agreements. *Vietnam Hearings* at 48.

9. The only extensive study in English is a doctoral dissertation by Ngo Ton Dat, a member of the State of Vietnam delegation at Geneva for the first

extreme difficulty of obtaining reliable primary source material.[10] This article will explore these questions, attempting to determine whether a political settlement was an integral part of the Geneva Agreements. "Political settlement," as used here, refers to the explicit provisions of the Final Declaration of the Conference: general elections, to be held in July 1956, to determine the future leadership of a unified Vietnam.

In the tangled maze of literature on Vietnam, subjective considerations have become so predominant as to resemble Anthony Eden's 1954 description of a U.S. diplomat's approach to Vietnam: ". . . so emotional as to be impervious to argument or indeed to facts . . . ." [11] In an attempt to counteract such influences, this article marshals to its aid the more disciplined approach of International Law. The following survey of the 1954 Geneva Agreements employs an analytical framework which has been influenced to some degree by a recent text on treaty interpretation by Professors McDougal, Lasswell & Miller.[12]

---

half of the 1954 Conference. Ngo Ton Dat, The Geneva Partition of Vietnam and the Question of Reunification, 1963 (unpublished Ph.D. dissertation, Cornell University). The dissertation generally supports the activities of the State of Vietnam (later the Republic of Vietnam) and the United States, but has enjoyed an extremely limited circulation due to its unpublished nature. The most complete study of the Geneva negotiations is J. LACOUTURE & P. DEVILLERS, LA FIN D'UNE GUERRE (1960). Bernard B. Fall, a noted authority on Vietnam until his untimely death in 1967, said that the Lacouture-Devillers work was ". . . beyond a doubt one of the finest pieces of diplomatic history recently written anywhere." B. FALL, THE TWO VIET-NAMS; A POLITICAL & MILITARY ANALYSIS 465 (1963). Despite such high praise, LA FIN D'UNE GUERRE has never been translated into English. The only published work of any length in English, F. WEINSTEIN, VIETNAM'S UNHELD ELECTIONS (Data Paper #60, Southeast Asia Program, Cornell University, 1966), supports the DRV position that elections were a crucial part of the Geneva bargain. The study unfortunately consists of a relatively unsystematic selection and presentation of material and omits key data on the other side: the degree of independence of the State of Vietnam from France, the nature and degree of United States involvement and particularly the domestic political climate in the United States. Most other books and law review articles relegate the problem of a political settlement at Geneva to a few paragraphs.

10. The discussion of Indo-China at Geneva began in open session on May 8, 1954. The nine groups represented then went into restricted session on May 17, and, except for a brief flurry of open sessions from June 8 to June 10, the diplomats remained in restricted session from May 17 until the end of the Conference on July 21, 1954. The British Papers by Command cover only the open sessions of the Conference and even then are not all-inclusive. For instance, the remarks of the United States representative, Walter Bedell Smith, are cut to several insignificant passages. Thus, little in the way of official *travaux preparatoires* are available to the analyst. Of the key diplomats who took part in the Conference, only Anthony Eden, then Foreign Minister of Great Britain and a Co-Chairman of the Geneva Conference, has written of his participation. This necessitates resort to secondary material for the greater part of the survey.

11. A. EDEN, FULL CIRCLE 126 (1960).

12. M. McDOUGAL, H. LASSWELL & J. MILLER, THE INTERPRETATION OF AGREEMENTS AND WORLD PUBLIC ORDER (1967).

This new treatise challenges the principle of textuality, *i.e.*, that the *text* of an agreement must be taken as the only authentic expression of the intentions of the parties. In its place the authors recommend the "contextuality principle": "Interpret the focal agreement according to the expectations shared by the parties during the course of their interaction, including both the making and performance of the agreement, as indicated by the context considered as a whole." [13] Since the Geneva Agreements were based on a military and political situation where the strengths and weaknesses of the participants could be roughly assessed and where the Agreements would necessarily reflect something of this evaluation, a full contextual survey may make possible the drawing of something of a balance-sheet as to the bargaining positions of the two major sides, and thereby highlight the major agreements and undertakings involved.

The following analysis attempts to assemble and to appraise objectively all the relevant evidence on both sides of the Geneva Agreements dispute. It also draws certain conclusions. These conclusions are necessarily limited by the ambiguity of many basic facts in the Vietnam equation, each of which may well be susceptible to several widely varying interpretations. Even in a total contextual survey these difficulties cannot be fully overcome, and argument over the 1954 Geneva Agreements will doubtless continue until the diplomatic archives are opened at some uncertain date in the distant future. This does not absolve the student of current events from the responsibility of at least attempting an analysis based on the evidence currently available.

II. HISTORICAL SKETCH

By early 1954, the French were extremely weary of the war in Indo-China.[14] At the conclusion of the Four-Power Foreign Ministers Conference in Berlin, the foreign ministers agreed on a conference to begin April 26 in Geneva; at French insistence, the conference would discuss both Korea and Indo-China.[15] In early 1954, the French had moved 20,000 of their best troops to an isolated fortress named Dien Bien Phu in hopes of drawing the Vietminh [16] military forces out of the jungle into an open engagement. On March 20, 1954, General Paul Ely, Chief of Staff of the French Army, was

---

13. *Id.* at 50.
14. N.Y. Times, Jan. 3, 1954, § 4, at 6E, col. 3. French Indo-China in 1954 included the territories now known as Laos, Cambodia, and the two Vietnams.
15. N.Y. Times, Feb. 19, 1954, at 1, col. 8.
16. The Vietminh comprised the military forces of the Democratic Republic of Vietnam, which had been proclaimed by Ho Chi Minh after the Second World War. The DRV had begun military operations against the French in late 1946, after the Fontainebleau Agreements had failed to establish a peaceful *modus vivendi* between France and the DRV.

sent to Washington to inform the startled U.S. leaders that events at Dien Bien Phu were going very poorly and to inquire about the possibility of an American guarantee of immediate air intervention against any enemy air action.[17] For the next two months the Eisenhower Administration debated a military involvement in Indo-China,[18] eventually deciding in the negative.

The talks on Indo-China began on May 8, with the western delegations extremely gloomy over the fall of Dien Bien Phu the day before. French Foreign Minister Georges Bidault spent a considerable portion of his speech lauding the fallen heroes and confined his initial proposals solely to military affairs; he made no proposals concerning a political settlement.[19] The Vietminh's initial proposals, presented on May 10, called for free general elections throughout Vietnam, supervised by an Advisory Conference composed of representatives of both sides.[20] The State of Vietnam, formed by the French in 1949 under former emperor Bao Dai to present a Vietnamese alternative to the Vietminh,[21] proposed on May 12 that free general elections be held throughout Vietnam under U.N. supervision as soon as the Security Council determined that the authority of the State was established and the conditions of freedom were fulfilled.[22] While the underlying realities may possibly have suggested otherwise, at the Conference the principle of Vietnamese unity remain unquestioned; partition was ". . . officially rejected with indignation by both sides." [23]

After this initial flurry of debate on the political question, ap-

17. J. LACOUTURE & P. DEVILLERS, LA FIN D'UNE GUERRE 65 (1960).
18. The possibility of U.S. military involvement in Indo-China in 1954 has been reasonably well chronicled. The most detailed analysis is contained in V. BATOR, VIETNAM: A DIPLOMATIC TRAGEDY 1-122 (1965). *See generally* A. EDEN, *supra* note 11, at 102-27 (1960); B. FALL, *supra* note 9, at 224-29; B. Fall, Political Development of Viet-Nam, VJ-Day to the Geneva Cease-Fire, 1954 (unpublished Ph.D. dissertation, Syracuse University) at 927-36; Roberts, *The Day We Didn't Go to War*, in THE VIET-NAM READER 56 (M. Raskin & B. Fall eds. 1965).
19. DOCUMENTS RELATING TO THE DISCUSSION OF KOREA AND INDO-CHINA AT THE GENEVA CONFERENCE, CMD. NO. 9186, at 109 (1954) [hereinafter cited as CMD. NO. 9186].
20. *Id.* at 118.
21. By the Elysee Agreement of March 8, 1949, France established former emperor Bao Dai as leader of an Associate State within the French Union. France retained control of the State of Vietnam's defense and foreign relations. DOCUMENTS RELATING TO BRITISH INVOLVEMENT IN THE INDO-CHINA CONFLICT 1945-1965, CMND. NO. 2834, at 10 (1954) [hereinafter cited as CMND. NO. 2834]. The degree of independence achieved by the State of Vietnam by the start of the Conference remains questionable, and the quality of its leadership to that point was low.
22. *Id.* at 124.
23. Devillers, *Ngo Dinh Diem and the Struggle for Reunification in Vietnam*, VIETNAM: HISTORY, DOCUMENTS AND OPINIONS ON A MAJOR WORLD CRISIS 210 (M. Gettleman ed. 1965).

parently the military issue alone engaged the delegates' attention at Geneva until June 8.[24] There was, however, one report that if an armistice could be reached, the United States would propose that a permanent political settlement be determined by the U.N. General Assembly. According to the report, the United States desired the Geneva Conference merely to lay down general principles to guide the General Assembly.[25]

On June 8, Soviet Foreign Minister Molotov unleashed a tirade in open session, accusing both the United States and France of showing little interest in restoring peace as soon as possible.[26] The speech produced the desired result, for the French government of Joseph Laniel, which had stood fast at Geneva, received such a shaky vote of confidence that Laniel soon resigned.[27] On June 13, Pierre Mendes-France, an outspoken critic of the Laniel government's Indo-China policy, was invited to form a government [28] and was voted into office under a promise to reach an honorable peace in Indo-China by July 20 or resign.[29] Possibly in reaction to this turn of events, Prince Buu Loc, Prime Minister of the State of Vietnam, resigned from office on June 16,[30] and Bao Dai replaced him with Ngo Dinh Diem, little known even in his own country but with a strong record of incorruptibility and nationalism.[31]

Mendes-France immediately began consultations on Indo-China, and on June 23 a meeting with Chou En-lai, Foreign Minister of Communist China, reportedly ended in agreement on a political settlement.[32] Minor officials conducted the diplomatic efforts at Geneva between June 20 and July 15, the major officials returning to Geneva only near the end of the Conference. The last week before Mendes-France's deadline saw intense diplomatic activity, with Mendes-France and Chou En-lai conducting the discussions, and Eden and Molotov performing merely as intermediaries.[33] Final agreement was reached on July 20. Military representatives of the French and the Vietminh officially signed an "Agreement on the Cessation of Hostilities",[34] dated July 20, which was concerned with the military details of the armistice and mentioned a political solution only rather obliquely in Article 14 (a) : "Pending the general elections which will bring about the unification of Viet-Nam, the conduct of civil administration in each regrouping zone shall be in the hands of the

24. CMD. No. 9186 at 143.
25. N.Y. Times, May 24, 1954, at 1, col. 6.
26. CMD. No. 9186 at 143.
27. N.Y. Times, June 13, 1954, at 1, col. 8.
28. N.Y. Times, June 14, 1954, at 1, col. 8.
29. N.Y. Times, June 18, 1954, at 2, col. 4.
30. N.Y. Times, June 16, 1954, at 4, col. 2.
31. N.Y. Herald Tribune, June 16, 1954, at 2, col. 2.
32. N.Y. Times, June 27, 1954, § 4, at 5, col. 1.
33. B. FALL, VIET-NAM WITNESS 61 (1966).
34. BACKGROUND INFORMATION at 36.

party whose forces are to be regrouped there in virtue of the present agreement. . . ." [35] Provision for successors to the agreement is made in Article 27: "The signatories of the present Agreement and their successors in their functions shall be responsible for ensuring the observance and enforcement of the terms and provisions thereof." [36] The provisions for a political settlement are contained in the "Final Declaration of the Geneva Conference",[37] dated July 21, which was signed by no one but which was verbally approved by seven of the nine participants: Cambodia, the Democratic Republic of Viet-Nam (Vietminh), France, Laos, Communist China, USSR, and the United Kingdom. Both the United States and the State of Viet-Nam issued reservations. The text of the Final Declaration contains two highly significant sections dealing with a possible political settlement:

> 6. The Conference recognizes that the essential purpose of the agreement relating to Viet-Nam is to settle military questions with a view to ending hostilities and that the military demarcation line is provisional and should not in any way be interpreted as constituting a political or territorial boundary. The Conference expresses its conviction that the execution of the provisions set out in the present declaration and in the agreement on the cessation of hostilities creates the necessary basis for the achievement in the near future of a political settlement in Viet-Nam.
>
> 7. The Conference declares that, so far as Viet-Nam is concerned, the settlement of political problems, effected on the basis of respect for the principles of independence, unity and territorial integrity, shall permit the Viet-Namese people to enjoy the fundamental freedoms, guaranteed by democratic institutions established as a result of free general elections by secret ballot. In order to ensure that sufficient progress in the restoration of peace has been made, and that all the necessary conditions obtain for free expression of the national will, general elections shall be held in July 1956, under the supervision of an international commission composed of representatives of the Member States of the International Supervisory Commission, referred to in the agreement on the cessation of hostilities. Consultations will be held on this subject between the competent representative authorities of the two zones from 20 July 1955 onwards.[38]

III. The Focal Agreement

The texts cited above may readily be taken as at least an initial version of whatever agreement as to a political settlement the par-

---

35. *Id.* at 39.
36. *Id.* at 45.
37. *Id.* at 66.
38. *Id.* at 67.

ticipants at Geneva actually reached; in other words, these texts serve as an initial focal agreement.

A. *A Viable Political Settlement.*

At first examination, these texts clearly provide for a political settlement. The Final Declaration sets a definite date for the elections, thereby differentiating Vietnam from such other divided lands as Korea and Germany, where no date has yet been set for any political settlement. Provision is made for free general elections by secret ballot, thus laying down the mode of expressing a choice. A supervisory body is specifically charged with the task of overseeing the elections—the International Supervisory Commission, the composition of which was long a major issue at the Conference. A deadline is also named for consultations between representatives of both zones, a year in advance, ensuring sufficient "lead time" to iron out difficulties and agree on procedures.

The only signed document, the Agreement on the Cessation of Hostilities, does not include any firm political provisions; however, the Final Declaration clearly states that the signed document was designed to settle military questions. It provides in plain language that the demarcation line is merely provisional and is not a political boundary, speaking in terms of the achievement of a political settlement "in the near future."

When compared to the treatment of political questions in the agreements on Laos [39] and Cambodia,[40] those in the Final Declaration deal-

---

39. Although Vietminh forces were operating in Laos, and although the indigenous "Pathet Lao" Communist forces were to be assembled in two provinces of northeastern Laos in accordance with Article 14 of the signed "Agreement on the Cessation of Hostilities in Laos," the same provision contains only the words "Pending a political settlement . . . ." Agreement on the Cessation of Hostilities in Laos, July 20, 1954, art. 14, in BACKGROUND INFORMATION at 61. Article 14 fails to mention the method of achieving a political settlement, in contrast to Article 14 of the signed "Agreement on the Cessation of Hostilities in Viet-Nam," which also speaks of "general elections" and eventual "unification." Agreement on the Cessation of Hostilities in Viet-Nam, July 20, 1954, art. 14, in BACKGROUND INFORMATION at 39. Only in the Final Declaration does the plan for a political settlement for Laos become clear; the Conference in Section 3 takes note of a unilateral declaration by Laos which promises general elections by secret ballot sometime in 1955. Final Declaration of the Geneva Conference, July 21, 1954, § 3, in BACKGROUND INFORMATION at 66. There are no provisions in the Final Declaration for international supervision of these elections, despite the presence of three major contending factions in Laos (Communist, neutralist, rightist). Nor is there any language stressing that the assembly of Pathet Lao forces in the two northeastern provinces is merely temporary and is not intended to herald a permanent division.

40. The signed "Agreement of [sic] the Cessation of Hostilities in Cambodia" merely acknowledges the existence of a unilateral declaration by the Royal Government of Cambodia to allow all Cambodian citizens to participate freely in general elections by secret ballot. Agreement of the Cessation of

ing with Vietnam are considerably more detailed. By laying down a definite time-table for the elections, a body to supervise them, as well as spelling out in express language their desires that the territorial boundary not become permanent, the seven delegations which approved the Final Declaration catalogued their expectations in reasonably specific terms.

B. No Political Settlement Intended.

However, over the years since Geneva, a strong dissent has arisen, claiming that there was no definite political settlement, that the provisions in the Final Declaration were merely a face-saving sop thrown to the Vietminh at the last minute. Proponents of this view advance substantial arguments. The provisions for carrying out the armistice are considerably detailed, amounting with annexes to over thirteen pages of text; those dealing with political matters involve less than a half-page of text. These political provisions are contained in an unsigned document from which two of the Geneva participants —the United States and the State of Vietnam—specifically dissociated themselves by making reservations. Even Jean Lacouture, whose book on the Conference [41] endorses the view that a viable political settlement was envisioned at Geneva, has stated that the reservations made by these two participants meant that the Final Declaration ". . . carried only the force of suggestion." [42] Ngo Ton Dat argues that the Final Declaration is not a valid international agreement, since it lacks the most essential ingredient: agreement of the "principal parties" concerned, the United States and the State of Vietnam.[43]

Certainly the documents issued at the end of the Conference were notable due to the absence of any sort of international guarantee. The Final Declaration was unsigned; it was verbally approved by only seven of the nine participants at Geneva, and contained only an extremely weak formula for dealing with possible conflicts in the execution of the Agreements:

> 13. The members of the Conference agree to consult one another on any question which may be referred to them by the International Supervisory Commission in order to study such measures as may prove necessary to ensure that the agreements

---

Hostilities in Cambodia, July 20, 1954, art. 6, in BACKGROUND INFORMATION at 52. No date is specified for these elections, nor is there provision for international supervision. This may, however, reflect the general situation in Cambodia: with only small numbers of resistance forces then operating in the country, and almost no Vietminh forces there, the problem of arranging a viable political settlement was considerably less acute than in Laos or Vietnam.

41. J. LACOUTURE & P. DEVILLERS, *supra* note 17.
42. Lacouture, *Vietnam: The Lessons of War*, in *Vietnam Hearings* at 657.
43. Ngo Ton Dat, *supra* note 9, at 316-17.

on the cessation of hostilities in Cambodia, Laos and Viet-Nam are respected.[44]

This provision only commits the seven to discuss possible measures; it does not compel them to act, nor does it provide a formula for possible action, be it unanimity or simple majority vote.

Article 13 is particularly striking in view of the fact that both Western [45] and Communist [46] delegations at Geneva had earlier called for very strong guarantees by the participants. Anthony Eden later explained the absence of such guarantees [47] by stating that the Communist representatives at Geneva wanted a collective guarantee which would then require unanimous agreement before being put into force.[48] Eden felt such a veto arrangement was not acceptable to western delegations,[49] and therefore the Final Declaration contained only individual pledges from the participants. More significant, however, is the fact that the United States refused to participate in any sort of guarantee, despite strong demands from both sides that it do so.[50] Anthony Eden and Molotov eventually worked out a compromise solution whereby the Final Declaration was headed by a list of all the participating countries,[51] an empty formalism which did little to disguise the fact that the Conference ended without agreement on any sort of future guarantee by all the participating states.

Another major issue concerns the powers and duties of the International Supervisory Commission in overseeing the elections. While the signed "Agreement on the Cessation of Hostilities in Viet-Nam" contains eighteen well-detailed provisions on the activities of the Commission with regard to the military situation,[52] the Final Decla-

---

44. BACKGROUND INFORMATION at 68.
45. *See, e.g.*, Cmd. No. 9186 at 111 (Georges Bidault, May 8); *id.* at 141 (Bidault, June 8).
46. *Id.* at 144-46 (Molotov, June 8); *id.* at 158 (Chou En-lai, June 9).
47. 532 PARL. DEB., H.C. (5th ser.) 930 (1954).
48. Chou En-lai had demanded on June 9 that the countries which provide the guarantee should carry on consultations and ". . . adopt collective measures on violations." CMD. No. 9186 at 163.
49. Eden stated on June 8 that the guarantee must be so designed as to ensure no veto power over action considered necessary to secure observance of the agreements. *Id.* at 153.
50. On June 30, the newspapers reported that France was convinced that the United States must join the guarantee. N.Y. Times, June 30, 1954, at 3, col. 6. On July 19, the eve of the Mendes-France deadline for reaching an agreement, Communist China demanded that the United States join in guaranteeing the proposed settlement. When Mendes-France replied that the United States had consistently refused to do so, the Chinese even suggested that Mendes-France prolong his deadline by a day or so to permit further consideration of both the guarantee and other problems. N.Y. Times, July 20, 1954, at 1, col. 8; Ngo Ton Dat, *supra* note 9, at 257-58. Mendes-France rejected this suggestion, and the Conference terminated without United States participation in the settlement.
51. A. EDEN, *supra* note 11, at 160.
52. *See* Articles 29 through 46, in BACKGROUND INFORMATION at 45-48.

ration merely designates it to supervise the elections, without laying down any guidelines for its operations. No provision was made in the Agreements for the non-military specialists needed to observe that election.[53] Even in its specified powers, the Commission was extremely limited; in contrast to other international peace-keeping forces, it had no police powers and could only inform the members of the Geneva Conference if a party to the Agreements refused to implement one of the Commission's recommendations.[54]

A basic lack of agreement on a political settlement might also be indicated by the extremely haphazard machinery instituted by the assenting participants to settle future disputes over the implementation of the Agreements. Article 13 of the Final Declaration merely contained their agreement to "consult" and "study" necessary measures. Thus, there was no standing machinery through which the seven member states could discharge their responsibilities. By default, the Co-Chairmanship, consisting of the Foreign Ministers of Great Britain and the Soviet Union, who had rotated as Chairmen of the daily sessions at Geneva, became the only residual machinery of the Conference.[55] Although the Co-Chairmanship was not even mentioned in the Final Declaration, the Co-Chairmen had agreed to consult each other in settling the financial problems generated by the Conference, and, through this seemingly insignificant agreement, the Co-Chairmen soon found themselves acting as intermediaries between the International Supervisory Commission and the seven assenting participants.[56] The British attempted to explain this by stating that no one foresaw a long-term need for an International Supervisory Commission,[57] but it is difficult to perceive how the Vietnam solution could ever have been implemented without at least some central authority empowered to make binding decisions once the inevitable disputes began to arise.

The signed armistice agreement also provided for free transfer of population between the two zones until the movement of troops was completed.[58] In the ensuing months hundreds of thousands of "refugees" were transported to the south. Although these refugees may only have feared short-term recriminations, and may have been resigned to unification in 1956, it is entirely possible they were

---

53. The first President of the Commission, M. Desai of India, felt that radically different types of personnel would be required in performing the Commission's two major functions. The armistice supervision was of a military character and called for large numbers of armed forces, while elections were of a political and administrative nature and called for jurists and civil officials. Ngo Ton Dat, *supra* note 9, at 319.

54. Agreement on the Cessation of Hostilities in Viet-Nam, July 20, 1954, art. 43, in BACKGROUND INFORMATION at 47.

55. CMND. No. 2834 at 19.

56. *Id.* at 19-20.

57. *Id.* at 20.

58. Agreement on the Cessation of Hostilities in Viet-Nam, July 20, 1954, art. 14(d), in BACKGROUND INFORMATION at 40.

genuinely concerned about a lasting partition and were fleeing the control of the DRV permanently.

Even the physical positioning of the provisions which concern the elections has raised questions. The Final Declaration is basically concerned with taking note of numerous unilateral declarations by participants and of key provisions in various of the other documents. The only provisions which discuss new material are Articles 6 & 7, both of which deal with a political settlement for Viet-Nam. The remainder of the Final Declaration is designed merely to tie together the loose threads remaining from a whole host of other documents now being promulgated. The provisions for a political settlement look very much like an afterthought, included at the last minute to placate one side which would otherwise return home in disgrace.

The final argument concerns the parties bound by the Agreements. Representatives of the French High Command and the Vietminh were the only signatories. While the Agreement included a clause (Article 27) stating that the successors of the signatories would also be responsible for observance of the terms, the State of Vietnam refused to approve the Final Declaration and even made reservations to these very terms. A treaty of independence had been promulgated in Paris on April 29, nearly three months before, purporting to grant the State of Vietnam full independence. Thus, the question whether France could legally bind the State of Vietnam to carry out these agreements over its own objections must have been very much in the minds of the delegates at Geneva on July 20 and 21, 1954.

C. Summary

These, then, are the arguments on both sides as to the nature of the provisions in the Geneva Agreements dealing with a political settlement. The substantial evidence advanced by both sides shows how insufficient the "textuality principle", restricting the analyst to the four corners of the text involved, can be in such an involved situation. For this reason, the study will now consider the entire context surrounding these Agreements.

The early phase of the McDougal-Lasswell-Miller framework calls for appraisal of various limited aspects of the "participants" in the negotiations and the "general situation" under which the negotiations proceeded. Analysis of the 1954 Geneva Conference fails to uncover significant trends and indicia in those considerations which might be of use in weighing all the available evidence at the end of the contextual survey. Therefore the analysis of the "participants" (the various delegations,[59] the characteristics of the entities repre-

---

59. *Delegations.* The nine delegations included Cambodia, the Democratic Republic of Vietnam, France, Laos, Communist China, the State of Viet-Nam, the Soviet Union, the United Kingdom, and the United States. Cambodia and Laos played no significant role in the negotiations concerning the future of Vietnam. All delegations were headed by the Foreign Ministers of

sented by the delegations,[60] and the degree of involvement of each delegation in the actual negotiations [61]) and also of the "general situation" at Geneva (the "spatial position" maintained during negotiations,[62] time features,[63] and crisis levels [64]) has been relegated to footnotes.

IV. OBJECTIVES

An important step in any process of treaty interpretation involves analysis of the objectives of the various participants,[65] for these may

the various entities except for the United States, which was represented by Undersecretary of State Bedell Smith. Presumably no concessions need be made because of the inexperience of any delegation's major representative.

60. *Characteristics.* This principle makes allowance for any differences in perspective where the parties to the negotiations include a mixture of nation-states, international organizations, private associations, etc. M. MCDOUGAL, H. LASSWELL & J. MILLER, *supra* note 12, at 54. The entities at Geneva either had already attained the status of nation-states or claimed such status and operated as if it had already been attained; thus no allowance need be made.

61. *Involvement.* The principle of involvement defers to the expectations of those participants most actively engaged in the negotiation process. M. MC-DOUGAL, H. LASSWELL & J. MILLER, *supra* note 12, at 386. Only five delegations played major roles in the final round of negotiations on Vietnam: France, the United Kingdom, Communist China, the Soviet Union, and the Vietminh; primary deference is accordingly paid to the expectations of these five. The United States withdrew from major participation once it had decided not to pursue military intervention and once it was clear that its allies would not support development of a regional defense organization prior to the end of the Conference. The State of Vietnam desired to play an active part in the negotiations, but was simply by-passed by French Premier Mendes-France, who dealt directly with the Communists in the last crucial days before his deadline. The expectations of the United States and the State of Vietnam are accordingly given less weight.

62. *Spatial Position.* Preference is given to ". . . inferences drawn from situations in which the parties have achieved the fullest psychophysical confrontation." M. MCDOUGAL, H. LASSWELL & J. MILLER, *supra* note 12, at 54. All major negotiations were conducted in person at Geneva, and were on an equal level of "psychophysical confrontation."

63. *Time Features.* Under this principle, preference is given to inferences drawn from enduring and repeated interactions between the delegations. M. MC-DOUGAL, H. LASSWELL & J. MILLER, *supra* note 12, at 54. The major negotiations were conducted between time of the selection of Mendes-France as Premier of France in mid-June and the close of the Conference on July 21, a highly compact time-frame characterized by constant interaction between the five most active delegations. Since there was never any question of sporadic, long-term interactions, no preferences need be drawn here.

64. *Crisis Level.* The crisis level under which each of the major delegates was forced to operate may have had significant influence on their shared subjectivities. The French military situation continued to worsen during the negotiations, placing a severe burden on Mendes-France. The Vietminh, while clearly the victors on the military level, face the possibility of substantial United States military involvement should the Geneva Conference end in failure. The crisis levels of the two sides thus came close to balancing each other out.

65. M. MCDOUGAL, H. LASSWELL & J. MILLER, *supra* note 12, at 51-52.

provide insights into the final expectations of those involved in the agreement process. In the case of the 1954 Geneva Conference, the analysis of objectives is necessarily quite involved. The delegations included members of both major power blocs, Communist (the USSR, Communist China, the Vietminh) and Western (France, Great Britain, the United States, the State of Vietnam). The bargaining position of any one participant, rather than being evaluated solely on its own merits, must be assessed in conjunction with the objectives of the other participants from its power bloc. To the extent that these objectives meshed, the "bloc position" gained in strength; where separate and divergent objectives were pursued, the "bloc position" was weakened. At Geneva the allies of both the French and the Vietminh pursued certain separate and divergent objectives, and to that extent weakened the bargaining position of each. The amount of decline in their positions was roughly comparable, however, and resulted in a near standoff.

A. *Objectives Shared By Both Blocs*

The policy of peaceful coexistence found supporters in both blocs, Communist (the USSR and Communist China) and Western (the United Kingdom). In mid-1952, the Soviet Union had changed its method of seeking further Communist expansion by the use or threat of force in favor of the more subtle tactic of courting the awakening nations under the banner of peace, aid, and support for their anti-colonial, anti-western tendencies.[66] The desire to demonstrate a peace-loving nature was a primary factor in the Soviet Union's decision to come to Geneva.[67] Anthony Eden reported that Soviet Foreign Minister Molotov remained genuinely anxious throughout the Conference to reach a settlement at the bargaining table, and often produced a helpful suggestion or concession at crucial times.[68] In promoting the strategy of peaceful coexistence, both the Soviet Union and Communist China launched repeated attacks during the Conference on the policy of the United States, claiming it was designed to widen the war and foster the development of an aggressive military bloc in Southeast Asia. While such statements were also designed to prevent United States military intervention, which might have upset a military situation then turning in favor of the Vietminh, it also allowed both Communist powers to present themselves as champions of negotiations and peaceful coexistence. This was particularly evident in the statements issued by both Molotov and Chou En-lai at the close of the Conference that the "forces of peace are irresistible" and that the Communist desire to negotiate and to bring peace to the world had triumphed over the obstructionist efforts of the United

---

66. J. BRIMMELL, COMMUNISM IN SOUTH EAST ASIA 279-83 (1959).
67. J. LACOUTURE, VIETNAM: BETWEEN TWO TRUCES 34 (1965).
68. A. EDEN, *supra* note 11, at 136.

States.[69] Subsequent activities by both the Soviet Union and Communist China confirmed the belief they had been laying the groundwork at Geneva for an attempt to win the support of the newly independent states with the policy of peaceful coexistence.[70]

The policy of peaceful coexistence, which could be pursued best through negotiations, placed a severe strain on the Vietminh, whose forces were in position militarily to sweep through the entire Indo-China peninsula with relative ease. Molotov and Chou En-lai probably put strong pressure on Ho Chi Minh to subordinate his objective of Vietminh domination of all of Indo-China,[71] which could be attained only by military measures, in favor of the over-all peace strategy of the Communist bloc.[72] But joint Sino-Soviet pressure alone could not have forced Ho to forego all hope of converting his military gains into concrete victories at the conference table, since there were also strong pressures from the western side at Geneva to come to a peaceful settlement. The United Kingdom placed especial faith in the power of international diplomacy and rejected all attempts by the United States to consider military alternatives. British Prime Minister Winston Churchill summed up the British attitude on June 26 during his visit to the United States by stating, "to jaw-jaw is always better than to war-war." [73] Presumably these pressures from participants on both sides to reach a settlement at Geneva, rather than to revert to the field of battle, came close to balancing each other. The loss to Ho Chi Minh's bargaining position, while still severe, would not approach disastrous proportions.

There was one other factor impelling both sides at Geneva to accept a negotiated settlement, whatever the terms: fear of the consequences of a failure at Geneva, with the possibility of the conflict spreading from Indo-China to other areas. This was the first major international conference which operated under the shadow of the hydrogen bomb. The pressures were especially severe in the United Kingdom, where the recent Pacific test series had caused widespread demands for a lessening of world tension *via* the conference table.[74] These pressures were also strongly felt by France.[75] Such attitudes

---

69. N.Y. Times, July 25, 1954, § 4, at 1, col. 6.
70. J. BRIMMELL, *supra* note 66, at 287-93, 381-83.
71. D. PIKE, VIET CONG 319 (1966).
72. Deutscher, *How the Russians Bet a Little in Asia to Win a Lot in Europe*, THE REPORTER, Sept. 23, 1954, at 19.
73. N.Y. Times, June 27, 1954, at 1, col. 8. Churchill soon added that "I am of the opinion that we ought to have a try for peaceful coexistence, a real good try for it." N.Y. Times, June 29, 1954, at 1, col. 6.
74. Ngo Ton Dat, *supra* note 14, at 97. Anthony Eden firmly believed that the deterrent power of the bomb played a crucial role in coming to terms at Geneva: "I do not believe that we should have got through the Geneva Conference and avoided a major war without it." A. EDEN, *supra* note 11, at 139.
75. French Premier Mendes-France, in his investiture speech on June 17, showed great concern: "And today there appears a new and fearful threat:

placed limits on the Vietminh, for whom the military alternative to continued negotiations at Geneva must have been more appealing.

B. Other Communist Bloc Objectives

The other joint Sino-Soviet objective at Geneva, the attainment of great-power status for Communist China by virtue of its participation in the negotiations, came to light as early as mid-1953.[76] Molotov and Chou En-lai arrived in Geneva in the same aircraft, and Molotov remarked that this would be the first conference in recent years attended by representatives of all the great powers.[77] Chou En-lai became a major participant, and by the end of the conference could report this objective fully accomplished.[78] But the desire to attain big-power status for Communist China inevitably detracted somewhat from the stature of the Vietminh delegation.

Both Communist China and the Soviet Union had other purely individual policy considerations that may have detracted from the Vietminh's bargaining position. Communist China possibly desired a period of peace to push ahead with its domestic reforms and economic development after a lengthy participation in the Korean War.[79] The Soviet Union, for its part, sought means of further splitting the western coalition and may have found its vehicle in the long-delayed French ratification of participation in the European Defense Com-

if the conflict in Indochina is not settled and settled very quickly, it is a risk of war, of international war and perhaps atomic war, that must be envisaged." N.Y. Times, June 18, 1954, at 2, col. 4.

76. Ellen Hammer has written that France sent a secret mission to the Vietminh in early 1953 to seek negotiations on the basis of independence and neutrality for Vietnam. This offer was eventually rejected, she states, because the Vietminh were committed to a tight alliance with the Communist Chinese, who ". . . intended the war to go on until they could use it as a means of winning a seat at an international conference table." E. HAMMER, VIETNAM—YESTERDAY AND TODAY 141-42 (1966).

77. N.Y. Times, April 25, 1954, at 1, col. 5.

78. "The international position of the Peoples Republic of China as one of the big world powers has been recognized universally. Its international prestige has been greatly enhanced. The Chinese people take the greatest joy and pride in the efforts and achievements of the Chinese delegation." New China News Agency, July 22, 1954, in Foreign Broadcast Information Service, July 23, 1954, at AAA6 [hereinafter cited as FBIS].

79. Anthony Eden felt that the Chinese Communists had been diverted from domestic problems by the Korean War, and thought they might show some interest in reaching a settlement at Geneva, in order to gain a breathing spell for land reform and the nationalization of the economy. A. EDEN, *supra* note 11, at 138. Ngo Ton Dat reports a speech by Chen Yuh, the fifth ranking member of the Chinese Communist Politburo, in March 1954, which specifically stated that China needed time to consolidate itself. Chen Yuh dwelt on the twenty years of peace enjoyed by the Soviet Union between 1921 and 1941 in which the USSR built itself into a great power, and concluded by saying such considerations ". . . could lead Communism in other countries to make temporary but necessary retreats." Ngo Ton Dat, *supra* note 9, at 38.

munity. French Foreign Minister Georges Bidault had stated publicly in early 1954 that the USSR might call off the Communists in Indo-China in exchange for French rejection of the EDC.[80] He was quickly forced to retract the suggestion,[81] but rumors of a French-Soviet "deal" on the EDC persisted in the American press,[82] and found some support in the Soviet press toward the end of the Conference.[83] Mendes-France was well known for his reservations about the EDC, and the USSR may well have made concessions in the last days to bring about a settlement within his time-limit and so keep him in power.[84] Obviously any such concessions would be at the expense of the Vietminh. Within ten days of the close of the Conference, Mendes-France was proposing changes in the EDC treaty, and on August 30 the French National Assembly killed any hope of French participation,[85] a bitter blow for the United States.[86]

C. Other Western Objectives

While these objectives placed certain limitations on the Vietminh's bargaining position, that of France was also weakened by its allies' non-conforming objectives. Due to its central significance, the general position of the United States will be discussed in detail in a sub-

---

80. N.Y. Times, Jan. 11, 1954, at 3, col. 4.
81. N.Y. Times, Jan. 21, 1954, at 1, col. 2.
82. *See, e.g.,* N.Y. Times, Feb. 7, 1954, § 4, at 8, col. 2 (editorial: the USSR will bring pressure to bear on France over the ratification of the EDC); N.Y. Times, Mar. 4, 1954, at 24, col. 2 (possibility that the Geneva Conference might be used by both the USSR and France as a lever to cause further delay in ratifying the EDC "begins to assume concrete form"); N.Y. Times, Mar. 15, 1954, at 7, col. 4 (fears persist in Washington that France will trade a settlement in Indo-China for rejection of the EDC).
83. B. Fall, Political Development of Viet-Nam, VJ-Day to the Geneva Cease-Fire, 1954 (unpublished Ph.D. dissertation, Syracuse University) at 854.
84. "What is quite certain is that Russia is taking for granted that M. Mendes-France will remain a staunch opponent of the European army scheme and that, so long as he is at the helm, there will be further delays and confusion over western German rearmament. Therefore she is not anxious to see him thrown overboard." The Times (London), July 21, 1954, at 7, col. 2.
85. *See* A. EDEN, *supra* note 11, at 164-67.
86. Robert Shaplen attributes American failure to persuade France to take a stronger position on independence for Vietnam to the earnest desire to obtain a firm French commitment to EDC. R. SHAPLEN, THE LOST REVOLUTION 84 (1965). EDC was indirectly responsible for United States participation of any sort in the Geneva Conference. At the Berlin Conference, Bidault felt the Laniel government could not survive without at least a tentative pledge to discuss Indochina at Geneva. President Eisenhower was convinced that no French Government would take a stronger stand on the EDC than the Laniel government, and so eventually gave in to French entreaties. D. EISENHOWER, MANDATE FOR CHANGE 415 (1963). Secretary of State Dulles defended the American commitment to go to Geneva by claiming that the Geneva plans have so improved American-French relations that we can now look "with confidence" for French ratification of EDC. N.Y. Times, Feb. 23, 1954, at 2, col. 2.

sequent section.[87] Briefly, the United States came to the Conference with an extremely negative attitude, viewing the Conference as a necessity occasioned solely by French internal politics.[88] This was the McCarthy era in the United States (the Senate debate on a motion to censure McCarthy was to begin only nine days after the Conference ended), and the daily press and President Eisenhower's memoirs continued to assess the Indo-China situation in vibrantly anti-Communist terms. The conflict in Indo-China was being fought to contain Communism, as part and parcel of the overall world strategy pursued by the United States and its allies since the start of the cold war.[89] According to Vice-President Nixon, the U.S. objective at Geneva was to oppose any settlement which would mean surrender and to hold Indo-China while avoiding a war involving the United States.[90] Nixon's position showed little recognition of the military realities in Indo-China, where the Vietminh were very much in the ascendancy.[91] After the United States rejected any military intervention, its policy was unclear and uncertain for the remainder of the Conference. The Communists could fear U.S. military intervention only in the event they imposed severely humiliating terms on the French. Such a position provided only the most limited support for France.

According to one treatise, the British had already made a key decision to withdraw gradually from Southeast Asia and concentrate on areas of greater importance.[92] The British definitely rebuffed all United States overtures for a military plan of "united action" in Indo-China to shore up the French position, and refused to discuss plans for a defensive alliance while there was still hope for meaningful negotiations at Geneva. The British view of the situation in Indo-China was considerably more realistic than that of the United States; as Anthony Eden stated,

> It was clear to me that any negotiated settlement was bound to produce either a Communist share in the government of most of Indo-China, or complete Communist control of part of the country, and I thought that the latter alternative was preferable. Although I had every sympathy with the American view that both these solutions were disagreeable, I thought it unrealistic to expect that a victor's terms could be imposed upon an undefeated enemy.[93]

---

87. See § V (c), *infra*.
88. Ngo Ton Dat, *supra* note 9, at 115.
89. Morgenthau, *The 1954 Geneva Conference: An Assessment*, A Symposium on America's Stake in Vietnam 65 (1956).
90. N.Y. Times, Apr. 21, 1954, at 4, cols. 5-8.
91. B. Fall, *supra* note 83, at 934.
92. J. Brimmell, *supra* note 66, at 284.
93. A. Eden, *supra* note 11, at 101.

The British had considered a partition of Vietnam since early 1954,[94] and Anthony Eden spoke of erecting a barrier of states, a "protective pad," halting communism outside of Cambodia and Laos and as far north as possible in Vietnam.[95] British objectives were directed not so much at a doctrinaire containment policy as they were at protecting their own interests in Malaya, far to the south.[96] The British could well afford to concede territory in Vietnam to the Communists in exchange for a firm and lasting settlement at Geneva which would bring peace to Indo-China and draw the line well clear of Malaya.

Great Britain paid great deference throughout the Conference to the views of the Asian members of the British Commonwealth on a possible settlement. These nations, led by Prime Minister Nehru of India, were strongly in favor of a negotiated settlement and just as strongly opposed to any extension of the war and in particular to a British-United States military involvement. Eden's memoirs show a constant concern for the opinions of the Asian members of the Commonwealth, and he told the House of Commons on June 23 that there would never be any real security in Southeast Asia without the good will of the free Asian countries.[97] Krishna Menon of India spent some time at the Conference, presenting India's views unofficially to the delegations concerned with the Indo-China deliberations. The necessity of paying some respect to Asian viewpoints also influenced Great Britain to remain at the bargaining table as long as any hope of a peaceful settlement continued, and thus further weakened the French bargaining position by diminishing the possibilities of allied military aid for the embattled French Union forces.

The French objectives at Geneva can be stated very simply: to save the French Expeditionary Corps and to preserve French commercial interests in Indo-China as much as possible.[98] As the military

---

94. *Id.* at 97.
95. *Id.* at 138.
96. Anthony Eden, when first considering a partition of Vietnam in early 1954, revealed that: "My chief concern was for Malaya. I wanted to ensure an effective barrier as far to the north of that country as possible." A. EDEN, *supra* note 11, at 97. On May 17, press reports stated that a French General of the highest professional qualifications had informed the British government that Hanoi would fall within four months. The analysis concluded that if Hanoi fell, the military position in Malaya, in which the British had an important stake, would become "a matter of great urgency." N.Y. Times, May 18, 1954, at 4, col. 4. A New York Times dispatch at the very height of last-minute diplomatic activity in Geneva, carried without comment by both the London Times and the Manchester Guardian, stated that joint British-United States military talks of the past few weeks, dealing with a possible defense alliance, had indicated the British would not commit themselves to defend any line north of the Isthmus of Kra, the narrow peninsula well south of the Vietnam-Cambodia area which separates Malaya from Thailand. The report stated that the British even doubted the feasibility of a military guarantee of the defense of Thailand and Burma. N.Y. Times, July 18, 1954, at 2, col. 4.
97. 529 PARL. DEB., H.C. (5th ser.) 434 (1954).
98. J. LACOUTURE & P. DEVILLERS, *supra* note 17, at 283.

situation worsened and finally reached crisis proportions, the need for saving the Expeditionary Corps through a settlement at Geneva became extremely vital. There were other domestic considerations which influenced the French to settle the problem at Geneva rather than to continue military operations. Mendes-France had been voted into office partly because of his promise to present a plan of economic recovery and expansion to "unlock" the static cartel-ridden French national economy.[99] Mendes-France's particular skills and interests lay more in this line, and certainly he was anxious to turn to this problem. Also, the French were beginning to feel the first shock waves of nationalism in their North African colonies, and their attention was just beginning to turn to this more vital area. Only ten days after the end of the Geneva Conference, Mendes-France flew to Tunisia to begin consultations with the Bey over home rule,[100] which France had been promising for some time. Morocco was clamoring for independence, and Algeria was about to become a problem of great moment to France.[101] The attitudes of the United States and Great Britain, the military situation in Indo-China, and the other pressing problems of the Mendes-France government prompted France to push for a settlement at Geneva.

V. Bargaining Strengths and Weaknesses

A. *The Vietminh (DRV)*

The Vietminh came to Geneva very much in control of the situation in Indo-China. Two-thirds or even more of Vietnam was under Vietminh domination, and neither Hanoi nor Saigon were secure from attack.[102] The Vietminh troops were well-trained and ably commanded by the brilliant General Giap; their political cadres had already acquired considerable expertise; the Vietminh had a definite and simply stated objective for the Vietnamese: to free the country from the colonialists; and they enjoyed a considerable support from the non-Communist Vietnamese, whose "passionate desire for independence" led them to join forces with the Vietminh.[103] And their greatest asset was perhaps the leadership of Ho Chi Minh,[104] who

---

99. The Times (London), July 22, 1954, at 6, col. 1.

100. D. SCHOENBRUN, AS FRANCE GOES 254 (1957).

101. *Id.* at 259-71.

102. Jean Lacouture estimated the Vietminh-controlled area at two-thirds of Vietnam, and asserted that both Hanoi and Saigon were in danger of attack. Lacouture, *supra* note 42, at 656. George Kahin and John Lewis fixed the area of Vietminh domination at three-fourths of Vietnam, at the start of the Geneva Conference, and stated that the Vietminh was ". . . poised to overrun considerably more." G. KAHIN & J. LEWIS, THE UNITED STATES IN VIETNAM 47 (1967).

103. R. SHAPLEN, *supra* note 86, at 45.

104. For excellent sketches of Ho Chi Minh's background, see B. FALL, LAST REFLECTIONS ON A WAR 59-90 (1967); R. SHAPLEN, *supra* note 86, at 35-40.

employed his great organizational skills to excellent advantage in the long war against the French.

The Vietminh had suffered extremely heavy casualties during their seige of Dien Bien Phu, and it is possible the Vietminh now desired a period of consolidation. They had also to contend with the desires of their Communist allies, who were pursuing other goals which might well detract from the Vietminh bargaining strength. In the total context, however, the Vietminh bargaining position was very strong; according to Douglas Pike, "The Democratic Republic of Vietnam [Vietminh] was monolithic, powerful and a winner. . . ." [105]

B. France

At the beginning of the Conference France was extremely discouraged about her situation in Indo-China and her bargaining position at Geneva. Reports of French war-weariness had been circulated at the very start of 1954,[106] and many Frenchmen were arguing it was senseless to fight on since many other nations had won their independence since World War Two and it was clear independence should be granted to Indo-China regardless of who won.[107] Many western statesmen now reported a mood of hopelessness in France.[108] A severe political crisis occupied France's attention during the first month of the Conference, and the key French delegates at Geneva were so preoccupied with the possible fall of the Laniel government that their showing at the Conference suffered measurably.[109] The emergence of Mendes-France as Premier solved the domestic political problem for the remainder of the Conference, of course, but by then France's military situation in Indo-China had already begun to deteriorate rapidly.

While the loss of Dien Bien Phu the day before the Conference began actually involved only 4 per cent of the available military man-

---

105. D. PIKE, *supra* note 71, at 52. Anthony Eden, one of the two Co-Chairmen, estimated that the Vietminh ". . . were in a position to demand a high price" at the Conference. A. EDEN, *supra* note 11, at 147.
106. N.Y. Times, Jan. 3, 1954, § 4, at 6E, col. 3.
107. Ngo Ton Dat, *supra* note 9, at 18.
108. In early Spring of 1954, Senator Stuart Symington discussed Indo-China with the French Minister of War, who had just returned from that area: "There was nothing we proposed to him as a possible solution but what he said it could not be done. Everything could not be done. Finally, we said, 'Well, then, you see no hope of any kind whatever, is that it?' and he said, 'That is right.'" VIETNAM HEARINGS at 531. In mid-April President Eisenhower reported a "defeatist attitude" in France. D. EISENHOWER, *supra* note 86, at 423.
    On April 25 the New York Times noted a "spirit almost of desperation" in France. N.Y. Times, Apr. 25, 1954, § 4, at 5, col. 5. Finally, French Foreign Minister Bidault told Anthony Eden on April 30 that, as far as negotiations were concerned, ". . . he had hardly a card in his hand, perhaps just a two of clubs and a three of diamonds." A. EDEN, *supra* note 11, at 124.
109. *Id.* at 129.

power in Indo-China, it proved a crippling blow. French morale was shattered and the Vietminh were jubilant. With these victorious units plus other elements already in place, the Vietminh could now begin a final push to capture the entire Red River Delta, employing a favorable manpower ratio of 2½ to 1 over the demoralized French forces. Certain Vietnamese units among the French Union Forces, sensing the change of the tide, began to disintegrate.[110] The New York Times reported on May 18 that a French General of the highest professional qualifications estimated Hanoi would fall within four months.[111] Five days later, France warned her allies she would have to pull out of the Delta unless an armistice were called swiftly or greater allied aid were dispatched.[112]

The military crisis reached disastrous proportions in late June, when France was forced to abandon An Khe, its largest base in central Vietnam, and also ordered the evacuation of the entire southern portion of the Red River Delta in an attempt to reduce the defense perimeter and further strengthen the vital railroad link between Haiphong and Hanoi.[113] The evacuation gave the Vietminh 1600 square miles of rice-producing territory, one-third of the people in the Delta, as well as control of the largest towns. It also showed the contrast between the desperate military situation and France's political objectives at Geneva, which would normally dictate holding as much ground as possible as a negotiating strength.[114] The very day the evacuations were announced, the New York Times reported the French now felt the Vietminh could win all of Indo-China in a few months in battle.[115] France was now talking of the need to "save the furniture from the burning house;" [116] indeed it was reported that Premier Mendes-France described the Geneva Conference as a "stock clearance sale." [117]

By early July 1954 the Vietminh could send 120 well-armed battalions against the 80 battalions of the French Union, of which one-third were Vietnamese units now becoming panicky. The French seemed obsessed with keeping open the Hanoi-Haiphong evacuation route, and on July 6, after considering the deterioration in the French defensive perimeter, Marshal Juin suggested Hanoi be evacuated.[118] In central Vietnam, the failure of Operation Atlante had proved an important strategical and psychological success for the

110. B. FALL, *supra* note 33, at 38-39.
111. N.Y. Times, May 18, 1954, at 4, col. 4.
112. N.Y. Times, May 23, 1954, at 1, col. 6.
113. N.Y. Times, June 30, 1954, at 1, col. 6.
114. N.Y. Times, July 2, 1954, at 1, col. 3.
115. N.Y. Times, June 30, 1954, at 3, col. 6.
116. B. FALL, *supra* note 33, at 59.
117. Lancaster, *Power Politics at the Geneva Conference 1954*, VIETNAM: HISTORY, DOCUMENTS AND OPINIONS ON A MAJOR WORLD CRISIS 133-34 (M. Gettleman ed. 1965).
118. J. LACOUTURE & P. DEVILLERS, *supra* note 17, at 275-76.

Vietminh and reduced the French command to impotence.[119] The military situation led one French military authority to declare on July 16 that ". . . any agreement, even a mediocre one, is preferable to no agreement at all." [120] Just after the Conference ended, Mendes-France told the French National Assembly he had set a 30-day deadline on negotiations, to terminate on July 20, because French forces in the Red River Delta would then be in "grave danger." [121] He also told the Assembly the impact of the Geneva Agreements on France was ". . . cruel because they sanction cruel facts" and reflected ". . . losses already suffered or made inevitable by the military situation." [122]

C. The United States

While the French bargaining position was weakened measurably by its military reversals, France's allies might have counterbalanced this by offering strong political or military support. The French believed that Communist China greatly feared American military intervention,[123] and many reports were circulated that France urgently needed support from the United States if she were to avoid too damaging a settlement.[124]

While the United States rejected any military intervention in 1954, the political position it took in lieu of such intervention forms the single most vital issue in any attempt to project the expectations of the Conference participants. If the United States, prior to the end of the Conference, clearly had drawn a line which included what is now known as South Vietnam within its sphere of protection, it would have been most unrealistic for the other participants at Geneva to assume that provisions for general elections and reunification of Vietnam could be readily implemented. But analysis of United States policy in these crucial months fails to indicate the drawing of any such line. In fact, United States conduct in the last days of the Conference may even have led the other participants to assume tacit

---

119. *Id.*
120. *Id.* at 276.
121. N.Y. Times, July 23, 1954, at 1, col. 3.
122. *Id.* at 2, col. 3. Bernard B. Fall estimates that the war in Indo-China cost the French about nine billion dollars and 172,000 dead or missing. B. FALL, *supra* note 33, at 39.
123. N.Y. Times, Mar. 31, 1954, at 8, col. 6.
124. *See, e.g.,* N.Y. Times, May 1, 1954, at 1, col. 1 (without any pledge of U.S. intervention, the French find their bargaining position considerably weakened); N.Y. Times, May 23, 1954, § 4, at 10, col. 5 (little chance of obtaining an honorable peace unless the Communists are confronted with the probability or even certainty of United States and British intervention); N.Y. Times, June 30, 1954, at 3, col. 6 (France feels a firm promise of American "support" is essential to prevent too damaging a settlement); N.Y. Times, July 9, 1954, at 3, col. 1 (France can no longer defend the Red River Delta alone; in absence of a United States guarantee of the area, France can only negotiate and prepare to abandon the Delta).

American approval of the major provisions of the Geneva Agreements, including a provision to hold general elections and unify the country. Given the vital nature of this issue, a more extended analysis will be presented, in keeping with the principle of "adjusting effort to importance." [125]

Although the United States had declined previous opportunities to participate in a solution of the problem of Indo-China,[126] in early 1950 it took the first steps toward what was to become substantial involvement. The Soviet Union, Communist China and others had formally recognized the Vietminh regime in January, 1950,[127] causing Secretary of State Dean Acheson to state that all illusions as to the supposedly nationalist orientation of the Vietminh had been dispelled.[128] The United States thereupon recognized the State of Vietnam, the French-sponsored government of former emperor Bao Dai, on February 7, 1950,[129] and followed this up with pledges of economic and military aid (channeled through France) three months later.[130] While the underlying reasons for United States involvement have been

---

125. M. McDougal, H. Lasswell & J. Miller, *supra* note 12, at 386.
126. The first opportunity occurred in 1874, when the Vietnamese Emperor appealed to the Chinese, British and Americans for help against an oppressive treaty forced upon Vietnam by France, which was then consolidating its colonialist position in Indo-China. There is no indication of any response by the United States. E. Hammer, *supra* note 76, at 109. The second opportunity centered around President Franklin D. Roosevelt's 1943 plan for a joint American-Chinese-British trusteeship for Indo-China. The President was unenthusiastic about French return to Indo-China after the war, and secured approval for a trusteeship from both Stalin and Chiang Kai-Shek. Churchill unfortunately declined, and the idea died with the President in 1945. R. Shaplen, *supra* note 86, at 31. A detailed account of the trusteeship plan may be found in B. Fall, *supra* note 83, at 878-87. *See also* E. Hammer, *supra* note 101, at 135; A. Schlesinger, Jr., The Bitter Heritage 2-3 (1967); N.Y. Times, May 2, 1954, § 4, at 8, col. 5. The third opportunity consisted in working out some sort of *detente* with Ho Chi Minh immediately after World War II. Ho had proclaimed the Democratic Republic of Vietnam and established himself in Hanoi, securing Emperor Bao Dai's abdication in his favor. The American OSS was in close contact with him at this time, and French requests evidently had to be channeled through the Americans. *See* B. Fall, *supra* note 83, at 901-09. When the French began to turn away from working with Ho Chi Minh, he appealed to the United States for support. D. Schoenbrun, *supra* note 100, at 233. Several commentators have argued that with United States support Ho Chi Minh might well have established an independent Communist state and governed, in effect, as an "Asian Tito." *See, e.g.,* B. Fall, *supra* note 33, at 7-8; D. Schoenbrun, *supra* note 100, at 242.
127. Communist China recognized the Democratic Republic of Vietnam on January 18, 1950, and the Soviet Union followed suit on January 31, 1950. Cmnd. No. 2834 at 11.
128. N.Y. Times, Feb. 2, 1950, at 6, col. 5.
129. The full text of the United States recognition of the State of Vietnam as an independent state within the French Union is contained in Background Information at 29.
130. For the full statement of the Secretary of State, see Background Information at 30.

roundly attacked,[131] financial involvement increased measurably as the war continued,[132] and by fiscal year 1955 the United States was prepared to pay 78 per cent of the cost of prosecuting the war effort.[133]

The United States took a fairly optimistic view of the progress of the war in early 1954, and President Eisenhower echoed a prominent American feeling when he stated on February 10 that he could see "no greater tragedy" than for the United States to get involved in an all-out war in Indo-China.[134] The United States had committed only 200 Air Force technicians to help the French in Vietnam, but the Chief of Staff of the French Army in late March convinced administration leaders that, unless the U.S. intervened militarily, the situation could soon alter drastically against the French.[135] The ensuing debate, during the period from March to June 1954, within the administration and with allies over shoring up the French position has been extensively described.[136] Beginning with the President's statement that the freedom of Southeast Asia was of "transcendent importance" (March 24),[137] Secretary of State Dulles' urging of "united action" by the free world (March 29),[138] and the President's application of the "falling dominoes" theory to Southeast Asia (April 7),[139] many types of corrective action were proposed by Administration officials.[140]

---

131. "From a warm relationship with Ho Chi Minh's Democratic Republic of Viet-Nam in Hanoi in 1945-46 and a rather well-documented refusal to let France use American-donated military equipment in Indochina, there is an almost incomprehensible transition to full-fledged support for France as of early 1950, even before the outbreak of the Korean War would have given it at least the semblance of a *Realpolitik* explanation." B. FALL, *supra* note 33, at 5.

132. Miriam S. Farley has estimated American military aid to Indo-China as follows: 1950 & 1951: $120 million per year; 1952: $300 million; 1953: $500 million; 1954: over a billion dollars; the Eisenhower Administration had requested 1.3 billion dollars for fiscal 1955. M. FARLEY, UNITED STATES RELATIONS WITH SOUTHEAST ASIA, WITH SPECIAL REFERENCE TO INDOCHINA, 1950-55, at 4 (1955). Bernard B. Fall has estimated the worth of military equipment actually delivered to Indo-China from 1950-54 at $1.877 billion, not far from the Farley estimate. B. Fall, *supra* note 83, at 921.

133. N.Y. Times, Mar. 28, 1954, § 4, at 5, col. 1.

134. N.Y. Times, Feb. 11, 1954, at 1, col. 6.

135. Roberts, *supra* note 18, at 60.

136. *See* the authorities cited in note 18, *supra.*

137. N.Y. Times, Mar. 25, 1954, at 1, col. 5.

138. N.Y. Times, Mar. 30, 1954, at 1, col. 8.

139. R. DONOVAN, EISENHOWER: THE INSIDE STORY 261 (1956); N.Y. Times, Apr. 8, 1954, at 18, col. 1.

140. The proposals included: a joint warning by several Western allies of naval/air action against the China coast (early April), then active intervention in Indo-China itself and a collective defense organization for Southeast Asia (a week later) (A. EDEN, *supra* note 11, at 103); unilateral intervention by American ground troops if all else failed (proposed by Vice-President Nixon on April 16, seemingly without the backing of the President) (N.Y. Times, Apr. 18, 1954, at 1, col. 8, and § 4 at 1, col. 2); an

All these proposals failed to gain approval, because of the anti-intervention standpoints of three key elements: the people of the United States, Congress, and the major ally, Great Britain. The majority of American voters had little understanding of the situation in Indo-China and were strongly opposed to any military intervention.[141] The United States had finally gained a peace settlement in Korea less than a year before (July, 1953), and a promise to end the Korean War had formed an important part of the 1952 Eisenhower campaign platform. With the first Congressional elections during the Eisenhower administration scheduled for late 1954, it was clearly felt that the Panmunjon truce agreement would be a major argument in the Republican Party's favor.[142] And the American people saw great differences between the war in Indo-China and that in Korea, where the United States had acted as a representative of the United Nations to stop a clear-cut case of invasion across national frontiers.[143] One newspaper report said that even the thought of limited naval and air intervention, without committing any ground forces, ". . . gives the political members of the Eisenhower administration a bad case of the jitters." [144]

President Eisenhower clearly did not intend to repeat the mistake he felt President Truman had made in 1950 in sending air and naval forces to South Korea without consulting Congress.[145] On March 10 he had stated with unusual emphasis his intention not to by-pass Congress on Indo-China at his news conference.[146] Congress remained strongly opposed to intervention throughout this period;

American air strike against Vietminh positions encircling Dien Bien Phu (from late March until the fall of the fortress) (A. EDEN, *supra* note 11, at 112, 119; Roberts, *supra* note 18, at 58-59); and the training of Vietnamese forces by the United States, and the holding of some sort of beachhead in Vietnam until these troops were ready to recapture their country from the Vietminh (May 1) (A. EDEN, *supra* note 11, at 167). After Great Britain categorically refused to participate in any of these programs (*Id.* at 118-19, 127), the United States considered military intervention with Australia, New Zealand, and other friendly Asian nations (late April—early May) (V. BATOR, *supra* note 18, at 81-82); a special military agreement with France alone (mid-May) (*Id.* at 85-86); a collective defense organization for Southeast Asia even without British participation (May 19) (merely hinted at by President Eisenhower in a news conference; N.Y. Times, May 20, 1954, at 1, col. 1); and, as a mark of final desperation, the use of atomic weapons and an all-out strategy in Southeast Asia *if* the United States intervened (by Admiral Radford, Chairman of the Joint Chiefs, May 26) (N.Y. Times, June 2, 1954, at 2, col. 5).

141. N.Y. Times, May 5, 1954, at 30, col. 5.
142. N.Y. Times, Feb. 4, 1954, at 6, col. 6.
143. A. SCHLESINGER, JR., *supra* note 126, at 52.
144. N.Y. Times, Feb. 4, 1954, at 6, col. 6.
145. S. ADAMS, FIRST HAND REPORT 130 (1961).
146. "There is going to be no involvement of America in war unless it is a result of the constitutional process that is placed upon Congress to declare it. Now, let us have that clear. And that is the answer." N.Y. Times, Mar. 11, 1954, at 1, col. 1.

—2

Senator John F. Kennedy echoed the opinion of the majority when he stated that a unilateral intervention, with widespread popular support in Vietnam for the Vietminh and the extremely difficult terrain, would be ". . . a hopeless situation."[147] On April 3, Secretary of State Dulles, the Chairman of the Joint Chiefs of Staff, and other administration officials met secretly with eight key Congressional leaders. Dulles evidently wanted a joint Congressional resolution authorizing the President to use air and naval forces in Indo-China; in fact, it has been hinted that Dulles was even carrying a copy of the joint resolution at the time. The Congressional leaders crossed party lines to present a united front: no Congressional resolution would be passed unless the United States could convince some allies to go along with a joint intervention.[148]

The Eisenhower administration thereupon turned to the only major ally then capable of committing forces to Southeast Asia, Great Britain. During conferences in London from April 11-13, British leaders told Dulles that, in line with Britain's objectives (peaceful coexistence, avoiding nuclear war), they favored negotiations and not military involvement.[149] Anthony Eden twice complained that the United States had no clear idea of what form such military involvement should take,[150] and responded: ". . . we must at least see what proposals, if any, the Communists had to make at Geneva."[151] An emergency Cabinet meeting on April 25 laid down a firm British policy: no military undertakings now, nothing more than discussions over a collective defense pact for Southeast Asia until after the Geneva Conference, full support for negotiations at Geneva.[152] This British policy remained reasonably consistent throughout the Conference; it added little to the French bargaining position, but played a major role in forestalling United States intervention in the war.

About this time President Eisenhower received the results of a study of the military aspects of intervention, arranged by General Matthew Ridgway, Army Chief of Staff. The report was extremely negative; in General Ridgway's own words:

---

147. A. SCHLESINGER, JR., *supra* note 126, at 8. Bernard B. Fall states that the overwhelming majority of senators of both parties were against American military intervention as early as mid-April. B. FALL, THE TWO VIET-NAMS 228 (1963). Joseph C. Harsh reported an informal survey of Congressional opinion which showed "overwhelming opposition" to any bold act of initiative by the United States alone; only five members of Congress at most favored quick and decisive action. Christian Science Monitor, Apr. 29, 1954, at 1, col. 5.

148. Roberts, *supra* note 18, at 57, 59-60.

149. A. EDEN, *supra* note 11, at 106. Very early in April, Great Britain had informed the United States that ". . . it would be unrealistic not to face the possibility that the conditions for a favourable solution in Indo-China may no longer exist." *Id.* at 102.

150. *Id.* at 105, 127.

151. *Id.* at 107.

152. *Id.* at 118-19.

I felt that it was essential therefore that all who had any influence in making the decision on this grave matter should be fully aware of all the factors involved. To provide these facts, I sent out to Indo-China an Army team of experts in every field: engineers, signal and communications specialists, medical officers, and experienced combat leaders who knew how to evaluate terrain in terms of battle tactics . . . The area, they found, was practically devoid of those facilities which modern forces such as ours find essential to the waging of war. Its telecommunications, highways, railways—all the things that make possible the operation of a modern combat force on land—were almost non-existent. Its port facilities and airfields were totally inadequate, and to provide the facilities we would need would require a tremendous engineering and logistical effort.[153]

Ridgway further stated the United States was once again on the verge of making the same bitter error it made in Korea: air and naval power alone cannot win a war, and inadequate ground forces cannot win one either. To Ridgway any intervention using only air and naval forces would have to be followed up immediately with ground forces in support.[154] The President followed the unusual procedure of having Ridgway state these views before the National Security Council, and his presentation was believed the turning point in persuading the President to reject the Radford approach and adopt a more cautious line on Indo-China.[155] On April 26, the day after the British Cabinet meeting, the President spoke of trying to agree on a *modus vivendi* at Geneva, and his statement was interpreted as implying a more moderate position on intervention.[156]

United States policy on Indo-China vacillated incessantly from this point to at least the end of the Geneva Conference; both domestic forces [157] and allies [158] criticized the lack of clarity. Secretary of

153. M. RIDGWAY, SOLDIER 276 (1956).
154. *Id.* at 276-77.
155. M. CHILDS, THE RAGGED EDGE: DIARY OF A CRISIS 153-59 (1955).
156. N.Y. Times, Apr. 27, 1954, at 1, col. 3. The press release also stated that Washington now felt that Indo-China was extremely important but that the United States could not be a "gladiator" for the whole world. *Id.* at 6, col. 5.
157. A prominent Herblock cartoon of the day depicted one State Department official asking another, "What's our unswerving Asia policy this week?"

158. On May 13, France finally asked the United States point-blank if it would fight if an honorable truce could not be obtained. N.Y. Times, May 14, 1954, at 1, col. 6. A week later Drew Middleton reported that uncertainty at the highest levels persisted, thereby complicating policy-making for both France and Great Britain. N.Y. Times, May 22, 1954, at 2, col. 6. On June 26, Cambodian officials were reportedly trying to get the United States to define its intentions in Indo-China. N.Y. Times, June 27, 1954, at 4, col. 1. And on June 30 France was still holding up a decision on how much the Communists would get at Geneva until the United States indicated what its intentions were. N.Y. Times, June 30, 1954, at 1, col. 5.

State Dulles, evidently blaming the British refusal to join an allied intervention as the source of all troubles,[159] abandoned Geneva prior to the start of discussions on Indo-China, offering only unsatisfactory explanations.[160] Within a week he made his famous statement that Indo-China was extremely important but not essential to the preservation of the rest of Southeast Asia from Communist control,[161] which brought immediate French demands for clarification. From mid-May until the end of the Conference many reports, talking in terms of "salvage" or "limited loss," stated that the United States was beginning to distinguish between the ideal solution for Indo-China and the settlement it would accept.[162]

Bernard B. Fall accused the State Department of being "bewildered." B. Fall, *supra* note 83, at 934. Fall also reports Dulles was using a "hard line" for foreign consumption, while the President was being more conciliatory for domestic consumption, both without contradicting each other; Fall felt they succeeded, ". . . but at the expense of hopelessly confusing everyone concerned." *Id.* at 928. Professor Hans Morgenthau stated that "It is certainly amazing to see how confused our position was." Morgenthau, *The 1954 Geneva Conference: An Assessment*, A SYMPOSIUM ON AMERICA'S STAKE IN VIETNAM 67 (1956). Morgenthau paid the administration a compliment by listing its confusion as an advantage, saying it kept the other side as confused as we were! *Id.* Victor Bator summed up the debacle: "On the policy level, also, it was impossible to disentangle true United States policy from the confused, conflicting and ever-changing statements claiming official status. It was intransigently indecisive." V. BATOR, *supra* note 18, at 103.

159. *See, e.g.,* N.Y. Times, May 1, 1954, at 3, col. 1.
160. Secretary Dulles stated that his early return to the United States was arranged in February, when he gave notice he would only attend the opening sessions, with Walter Bedell Smith taking his place thereafter. N.Y. Times, May 8, 1954, at 4, col. 2. In February, far from giving any such notice of taking early leave of the Conference, Dulles had stressed the utility of the conference method in seeking solutions to international tensions, and stated that he was "determined to carry on the efforts" started at the Berlin Conference. N.Y. Times, Feb. 19, 1954, at 3, col. 1. Bedell Smith, on leaving for Geneva, stated that the plans for him to replace Dulles had been made more than a week before (making no mention of any plans laid in February). N.Y. Times, May 1, 1954, at 3, col. 3. Dulles' return was rightly analyzed as a "tactical withdrawal." N.Y. Times, May 5, 1954, at 30, col. 5.
161. N.Y. Times, May 12, 1954, at 1, col. 1. The situation was further confused by Dulles' aides, who deleted the suspect material from the official text of the news conference. N.Y. Times, May 13, 1954, at 3, col. 3. The statement in its context was not damning, and was accurately paraphrased by the President as indicating American determination not to give up the rest of Southeast Asia if Indo-China fell. *Id.* But Dulles' statement, coupled with his report to the Senate Foreign Relations Committee the next day, was interpreted as an attempt to prepare Congress and the American people for the possible loss of Indo-China. *Id.* at 3, col. 1.
162. *See, e.g.,* N.Y. Times, May 26, 1954, at 2, col. 2 (United States now more willing to tolerate important concessions to the Communists in Indo-China); N.Y. Times, June 24, 1954, at 1, col. 5 (the administration is thinking largely in terms of salvage or limited loss); N.Y. Times, June 26, 1954, at 3, col. 7 (Dulles now prepared to accept far less in Indo-China); N.Y. Times, July 18, 1954, § 4, at 3, col. 4 (current Dulles policy is an attempt to salvage something from a situation that, from the American point of view, is "extremely unpleasant at best").

Just how much of a loss the United States was willing to accept remains unclear. The sole constant in policy on Indo-China until after the end of the Conference was extremely strong anti-Communism. Reports of Communist "conquest" in Indo-China had begun even prior to the debate on military intervention,[163] as had the description of the United States as the "guardian of free-world interests." [164] The basis of Dulles' March 28 speech urging "united action" was supposedly his belief that even a partition of Vietnam would be ". . . tantamount to handing over the whole country to the Communists." [165] During the Churchill-Eden visit to Washington (June 25-29), rumors began that the United States had refused to associate itself with any agreement that seemed to sanctify the placing of millions of persons under Communist rule.[166] President Eisenhower's memoirs are almost moralistic in tone concerning the Vietminh; he condemns Communist enslavement [167] and presses the policy of containment.[168] The President stated his position in a news conference at the end of June in similar terms: "I will not be a party to any agreement that makes anybody a slave; now that's all there is to it." [169]

Rather than drawing a line across Indo-China or supplying firm support to the French, the United States temporized. Asked at the same late-June press conference whether the administration's "enslavement" stand on Communism meant the United States would refuse to acknowledge a settlement based on partition, the President merely suggested that the settlement provide for a transfer of that segment of the population which wished to reside in the other zone.[170] And the month of July saw American policy-makers resurrecting the old policy that the French had the "primary responsibility" for Indo-China. Such statements had characterized the very early arrangements to provide economic aid,[171] but had not been prominent during the debate on intervention. On July 9, Washington informed the French that the training of Vietnamese troops by American technicians would no longer continue, a measure interpreted as a "declaration of complete disinterest," marking the end of American in-

---

163. N.Y. Times, Feb. 4, 1954, at 1, col. 3, and at 6, col. 5 (official view in Washington now states that any deal with the Vietminh "probably" would result in a Communist conquest of the whole peninsula).
164. N.Y. Times, Feb. 28, 1954, at 1, col. 5 (State Department officials believe a political settlement would foredoom Vietnam to Communist subversion in the manner of Czechoslavakia), and at 3, col. 2 (the same officials cannot conceive of a solution acceptable to the United States as guardian of free-world interests in Southeast Asia).
165. N.Y. Times, Apr. 4, 1954, § 4, at 8, col. 5.
166. N.Y. Times, June 29, 1954, at 3, col. 4.
167. D. EISENHOWER, *supra* note 86, at 404, 432.
168. *Id.* at 404, 419.
169. N.Y. Times, July 1, 1954, at 1, col. 8.
170. *Id.*
171. BACKGROUND INFORMATION at 30 (May 8, 1950), 32 (June 18, 1952).

fluence on French policy in the last days of the Geneva Conference.[172] On July 10 the State Department was reportedly convinced that the responsibility for the Indo-China phase of the Conference ought to rest with the French.[173] Two days later, the London Times stated that Washington wished to dissociate itself from Geneva since any settlement on Indo-China is "purely a French matter." [174] On July 18, with the Conference on the verge of making its vital decisions, Bedell Smith summed up the United States stand: it is not a belligerent, it had not sought and would not seek ". . . to impose its views in any way on the belligerents, who are the parties primarily interested." [175]

There was perhaps one attempt by the United States to draw a line in Indo-China. After veering away from a military intervention, it had been trying to interest its allies in establishing a collective defense organization for Southeast Asia while the Conference was in progress, a proposal which Great Britain had effectively nullified. Prime Minister Churchill and Foreign Secretary Eden flew to Washington on June 25 for several days of meetings with President Eisenhower and other administration leaders. The major British objective for the visit was the bridging of the gulf which now divided the two allies on Indo-China, by persuading the United States at least to give the French a chance of reaching a settlement at Geneva.[176] In this they were particularly successful and the final communique promised little immediate action by the United States, merely stating: "In the case of nations now divided against their will, we shall continue to seek to achieve unity through free elections supervised by the United Nations to insure they are conducted fairly." [177] No specific reference was made to Germany or Korea, which were already divided, nor to Vietnam, whose future was now in doubt. While a joint study group was to be set up to work out details for a collective defense organization, no formal steps to proclaim such an organization would be taken until after Geneva; the British again avoided any chance of united action; the United States agreed to partition of Vietnam; and the British gave ground only on the Eisenhower/ Dulles determination not to sign any agreement which would imply its consent to the surrender of North Vietnam.[178] Not made public until July 14 [179] was a joint British-American seven-point memorandum which set up certain "minimums" on a settlement at Geneva. The memorandum stated that both countries would be willing to respect an armistice agreement which: ". . . (2) preserves at least the southern half of Vietnam, and if possible an enclave in the delta;

---

172. V. BATOR, *supra* note 18, at 91.
173. N.Y. Times, July 11, 1954, at 2, col. 3.
174. The Times (London), July 12, 1954, at 8, col. 2.
175. N.Y. Times, July 19, 1954, at 1, col. 8.
176. A. EDEN, *supra* note 11, at 148.
177. N.Y. Times, June 30, 1954, at 3, col. 3.
178. V. BATOR, *supra* note 18, at 117.
179. N.Y. Times, July 14, 1954, at 1, col. 6.

... (4) does not contain political provisions which would risk loss of the retained area to Communist control; (5) does not exclude the possibility of the ultimate reunification of Vietnam by peaceful means...." [180]

This seven-point memorandum, which might well appear to draw a line in Vietnam, unfortunately contains ambiguities. Any attempt at reunification under point (5) by peaceful means, including general elections, might well involve risks of a Vietminh victory.[181] It is possible that point (4) deals only with the possibility of a coalition government, composed of Vietminh and State of Vietnam ministers. The example of coalition governments in Eastern Europe, with subsequent Communist takeovers, was certainly fresh in the minds of the Eisenhower administration. Indeed, State Department officials had expressed concern in late February that a political settlement would doom Vietnam to Communist subversion in the manner of Czechoslovakia.[182] Other hypotheses as to point (4) are equally possible; the U.S. position was simply left unclear. If point (4) was meant to register opposition to any election provisions for Vietnam, that opposition was extremely well-veiled.

As the date neared for the last crucial discussions at Geneva prior to Mendes-France's deadline on July 20, it appeared doubtful that the United States would even send a major representative (Smith or Dulles) for fear of appearing to sanction "appeasement." [183] According to President Eisenhower, Dulles met with Eden and Mendes-France in Paris from July 13-15, and reported that the French attitude "seemed to be firm enough;" Bedell Smith then returned to Geneva, saving the French from the spectacle of desertion by a major ally at the crucial moment.[184] Bernard Fall, however, reports that many observers in Paris saw a ". . . not uncertain haste in Dulles' entourage in wanting to 'bury' the whole Indo-China problem. . . ." after U.S. military intervention was impossible, and states that, during the tripartite discussions, Dulles at first was in favor of early elections in Vietnam.[185] Dulles did at least take great pains in the final communique to emphasize the limitations which the United States desired to observe in its Geneva participation ". . . as not itself having a primary responsibility in the Indo-China war." [186]

180. A. EDEN, *supra* note 11, at 149.
181. Ngo Ton Dat, *supra* note 9, at 239.
182. N.Y. Times, Feb. 28, 1954, at 1, col. 5.
183. Assistant Secretary of State Thruston B. Morton stated on July 11 that the United States would not be a party to any Indo-China settlement "which smacks of appeasement." The United States, he emphasized, would not acknowledge the legitimacy of Communist control of any segment of Southeast Asia. N.Y. Times, July 12, 1954, at 2, col. 5.
184. D. EISENHOWER, *supra* note 86, at 447.
185. B. Fall, *supra* note 83, at 851.
186. The U.S. statement pointed out with "unusual emphasis" that the United States was not directly interested in the war, "which remains a French concern." Manchester Guardian, July 15, 1954, at 1, cols. 4-5.

The United States assumed no concrete position on Southeast Asia during the few short days remaining of the Conference. On July 14, at his last press conference prior to Mendes-France's July 20 deadline, President Eisenhower was extremely evasive concerning Indo-China.[187] Bedell Smith told Conference delegates on July 18 that the United States would make a unilateral declaration at the end of the Conference if it found it could "respect" the settlement; otherwise the United States would ". . . dissociate itself entirely from a settlement that will leave the Communist-led Vietminh rebels in control of about half the people of Indochina." [188] The same day the New York Times reported the terms which the United States could "respect." According to this report, State Department officials saw some misunderstanding in Paris and Geneva over the U.S. intentions. If the Conference should fail to reach agreement, there had been suggestions that the United States and its allies consider some form of immediate action to check Communist expansion, but there had been no agreement as to what it might involve. It was believed in some quarters that the United States, Great Britain and others might issue a "thus far and no farther" declaration, but neither the United States nor Great Britain had any intention of putting forces into Indo-China to back up such a declaration. The key sentence openly and boldly stated: "The line whose defense might eventually be guaranteed by a Southeast Asian defense set-up remains to be defined." [189] This report was also carried without comment by the London Times and the Manchester Guardian.[190] Such an analysis can be confirmed elsewhere. Jean Lacouture reports that Washington's answer to French requests for military intervention was: "Indochina does not fall within the perimeter of the area vital to the defense of the United States." At Geneva, according to Lacouture, "Washington seemed prepared to accept the conequences of its failure to intervene." [191]

At the close of the Conference the United States did issue a unilateral declaration,[192] indicating the terms were such as it could "respect." The United States took note of the various armistice agreements signed by the two opponents, along with articles 1 through 12 of the unsigned Final Declaration (by failing to take note of article 13, it absolved itself of any continuing responsibility to assist the

---

187. N.Y. Times, July 15, 1954, at 16, col. 7.
188. N.Y. Times, July 22, 1954, at 2, col. 2.
189. N.Y. Times, July 18, 1954, at 1, col. 6, and at 2, col. 4.
190. The Times (London), July 19, 1954, at 8, col. 2; Manchester Guardian, July 19, 1954, at 7, col. 6. All three newspapers also carried the story that the British had refused to draw a defense line north of the Isthmus of Kra, which separates Malaya and Thailand at a point far south of Vietnam. See note 96 *supra*.
191. Lacouture, *supra* note 42, at 656.
192. Statement by the Undersecretary of State at the Concluding Plenary Session of the Geneva Conference, July 21, 1954, in BACKGROUND INFORMATION at 69.

other participants in implementing the various measures), and promised to "refrain from the threat or the use of force to disturb them. . . ." The United States would also ". . . view any renewal of the aggression in violation of the aforesaid agreements with grave concern and as seriously threatening international peace and security." Finally, it supported free elections under United Nations supervision (in contrast to International Supervisory Commission supervision as contemplated by the Agreements).

United States support for elections under United Nations supervision might appear to indicate total dissatisfaction with the political provisions of the Geneva Agreements. But statements of administration leaders on the Agreements were generally resigned and conciliatory. President Eisenhower issued a statement on July 21,[193] once again disclaiming "primary responsibility" for Indo-China, stating that the United States "accordingly" was neither a party to the Agreements nor bound by them, but hoped that they would lead to the "establishment of peace consistent with the rights and the needs of the countries concerned." In his news conference the same day, the President indicated the basic policy-making dilemma during this period: "When one is up against it to find an alternative and cannot find one, he is not going to criticize what others did."[194] Bedell Smith, the chief American delegate at Geneva, was coldly realistic upon his return on July 23, stating the results were ". . . the best we could have possibly obtained under the circumstances. . . .", and wryly commented that ". . . diplomacy has rarely been able to gain at the conference table what cannot be gained or held on the battlefield."[195] The New York Times reported that U.S. "respect" for the agreement centered around the existence of a clause allowing for free transfer of populations.[196] The administration's primary concern over the Geneva Agreements, then, was to rebut congressional accusations of subjecting millions of people to "Communist enslavement", of "appeasement" and of "selling out" on Vietnam. President Eisenhower had earlier suggested a clause in the agreements providing for free transfer of population between the two zones, and, possibly to placate the United States, provisions for such a clause in the armistice agreement were specifically taken note of in a separate provision in the final declaration.[197] According to Jean Lacouture, while the United States refused to confirm the basic texts of the Agreement, it still found itself able to "applaud the solution."[198]

193. BACKGROUND INFORMATION at 68.
194. N.Y. Times, July 22, 1954, at 1, col. 8.
195. N.Y. Times, July 24, 1954, at 4, cols. 6-7.
196. N.Y. Times, July 21, 1954, at 1, col. 4.
197. Section 8 of the Final Declaration reads: "The provisions of the agreements on the cessation of hostilities intended to ensure the protection of individuals and of property must be most strictly applied and must, in particular, allow everyone in Viet-Nam to decide freely in which zone he wishes to live." BACKGROUND INFORMATION at 67.
198. J. LACOUTURE, supra note 67, at 62.

Mendes-France, perhaps a bit carried away by reaching agreement at all, interpreted this declaration "as amounting virtually to a guarantee." [199]

In only one particular did the United States now appear to propose a forward-looking program for Southeast Asia, that of a collective defense organization. Considerable opposition, notably from Great Britain, had arisen over the establishment of such a body while the Conference was still in session, and the United States had been forced to postpone major efforts in this direction until after the Conference. Both President Eisenhower [200] and Secretary of State Dulles,[201] in their news conferences at the end of the Conference, showed determination to "press forward" with plans for collective security in Southeast Asia, and the State Department promptly announced plans for a conference of western and Asian nations to consider the formation of such a defense alliance.[202] Two points, however, limit the effect such an organization would have on the expectations at Geneva. First, in Secretary Dulles' own words, the defense alliance would protect Southeast Asia against Communist aggression and subversion; [203] the plans said nothing about support for the State of Vietnam in its determination to resist a political settlement by peaceful means, through general elections. When the Southeast Asia Treaty Organization (SEATO) was eventually established at Manila on September 8, 1954, the special protocol granting protection also to Vietnam was interpreted as a joint guarantee against external aggression and subversion of Indochina; in effect, SEATO offset any threat of a military invasion of the south by the Vietminh.[204] The philosophy embodied in the concepts which led to the establishment of SEATO contained no position whatever on the broader issue of holding elections in 1956. Indeed, Bernard B. Fall, in his doctoral thesis published in October, 1954, the very month of the now-famous Eisenhower letter promising support to Diem, stated very bluntly the United States had not yet taken a firm stand on Vietnam: ". . . it may already be considered as certain that a strong American policy—all claims about the 'Manila Charter' of September 1954 notwithstanding—in the Associated States [of Indo-China] will be most

199. N.Y. Times, July 24, 1954, at 3, col. 6.
200. N.Y. Times, July 22, 1954, at 3, col. 5.
201. N.Y. Times, July 22, 1954, at 3, col. 4.
202. N.Y. Times, July 23, 1954, at 1, col. 1.
203. ". . . the problem is not merely one of deterring open armed aggression, but of preventing Communist subversion which, taking advantage of economic dislocations and social injustice, might weaken and finally overthrow the non-Communist governments." N.Y. Times, July 24, 1954, at 3, col. 6.
204. Devillers, *supra* note 23, at 213. *See also* E. HAMMER, *supra* note 76, at 250; Editorial, *Vietnam in the Hazard*, THE ECONOMIST, July 21, 1956, at 202.

unlikely." [205] Since Ho Chi Minh could expect strong nationwide support in the elections, as all sides admit, and had little reason to resort to aggression or subversion, SEATO did little to offset Communist expectations of consolidating their victory in Vietnam through general elections in 1956.

Second, the Communist delegations evidently expected the provisions of the Geneva Agreements to forestall any attempt by the United States to influence events in Vietnam or elsewhere in Indo-China. Anthony Eden depicts the chief Chinese opposition during the negotiations as directed against any American presence, however innocuous, in any part of Indochina; the Chinese felt very strongly that American activities were directed against them and not in defense of these territories, and harbored a very deep conviction that the United States intended a day of reckoning for them.[206] The Communist statements at Geneva are replete with charges that the United States was planning to widen the war and form an aggressive military bloc.[207] Once the possibility of military intervention diminished, the Communists began to fear the United States would attempt to bring the states in Indo-China inside the military alliance, and establish bases there.[208] The signed armistice

---

205. B. FALL, *supra* note 83, at 939. Anthony Eden fixes the time of the first firm United States commitment to South Vietnam of any kind of assistance, military or political, at October 23, 1954, the date of the Eisenhower letter to Diem. A. EDEN, *supra* note 3, at 7.

206. A. EDEN, *supra* note 3, at 4-5. A Pravda editorial, issued at the conclusion of joint preparatory meetings between Molotov and Chou En-lai on the eve of the Conference, stressed one of the "major Soviet pre-Geneva theses": the basis of American foreign policy in the Far East is an attempt to carry out aggression against Communist China. N.Y. Times, Apr. 24, 1954, at 3, col. 2.

207. These charges are catalogued by "intervention" (charges that the United States planned to widen the war) and "military bloc" (charges that the United States was planning an aggressive military bloc): N.Y. Times, Apr. 22, 1954, at 4, col. 2 (Communist China, intervention); CMD. No. 9186 at 120 (May 10, Pham Van Dong of the Vietminh, intervention); N.Y. Times, May 12, 1954, at 1, col. 2 (May 11, Molotov, military block); CMD. No. 9186 at 125 (May 12, Chou En-lai, military bloc); *Id.* at 143 (June 8, Molotov, military bloc); *Id.* at 164 (June 9, Chou En-lai, intervention, military bloc); *Id.* at 168 (June 10, Molotov, intervention); N.Y. Times, July 1, 1954, at 3, col. 1 (Pravda, intervention, military bloc); A. EDEN, *supra* note 11, at 158 (July 17, Chou En-lai, military bloc); New China News Agency, July 18, 1954, in FBIS, July 19, 1954, at AAA3 (military bloc, attempt to keep Vietnam permanently divided).

208. As early as June 9, Chou En-lai had demanded that the agreement include a ban on introduction of United States military personnel or equipment into any part of Indo-China. CMD. No. 9186 at 159. On July 18, the Communist Chinese cited an AP dispatch which reported Bedell Smith was returning to Geneva to work out a way to extend aid and protection to the states of Indochina. The Chinese interpreted "protection" to mean that the United States wanted to place them inside the military alliance as members, and bitterly attacked such a position. New China News Agency, July 18, 1954, in FBIS, July 19, 1954, at AAA6. The New York Times reported on July 18 that Chou En-lai wanted the settlement to incorporate assur-

agreement on Vietnam did provide that no military base under the control of a foreign state could be established in either zone, and neither zone could adhere to any military alliance.[209] This was stressed in the unsigned Final Declaration by all assenting participants.[210] The statements of the Communist delegations at the end of the Conference show that they placed great emphasis on these provisions, which they expected to forestall any American military presence in Indo-China.[211] The defense alliance which was eventually arranged lacked the participation of the Colombo powers [India, Ceylon, Pakistan, Indonesia and Burma] and included no provisions for American bases on the soil of Southeast Asia. It was far less imposing than the United States military commitments which the Communists originally feared.

The United States failed to give the French substantial support during the Geneva Conference by deciding against intervention, failing to draw a line militarily before the end of the Conference, and failing to protest strongly and clearly the provisions for a political settlement which the Communists strongly advocated. It was many months before the United States finally decided to back the Diem government's opposition to those elections. At the Conference, France could gain strength in her bargaining position only from the widespread fears that the United States might yet intervene militarily if the Communists demanded such severe terms at Geneva that the French were virtually humiliated.[212] While this gave the French a certain minimum bargaining position, it did not provide nearly the support the French would have required, given their demoralized state, to resist a political settlement.

---

ances that the United States would establish no bases nor engage in other military activity anywhere in Indochina. N.Y. Times, July 18, 1954, at 1, col. 6. Chou reportedly stated that China would be "fearful" of any defense alliance that might result in American utilization of bases on the mainland, whereupon Eden and Mendes-France assured him that if agreement were reached at Geneva, none of the three states would be allowed to join the alliance. *Id.* at 3, col. 5.

209. Agreement on the Cessation of Hostilities in Viet-Nam, July 20, 1954, art. 19, in BACKGROUND INFORMATION at 43.

210. Final Declaration of the Geneva Conference, July 21, 1954, § 5, in BACKGROUND INFORMATION at 66.

211. Chou En-lai placed heavy emphasis on the provisions which forbade Vietnam, Laos, and Cambodia from joining any military alliance and permitting any foreign bases on their territory. N.Y. Times, July 22, 1954, at 2, col. 2. Pravda's key editorial on the results of the Conference took note of Chou's emphasis, and continued:

These undertakings inflict a blow on the plans of American aggressive circles who reckoned on including the southern part of Vietnam, Laos, and Cambodia in an aggressive pact and on setting up on their territory military bases directed against the countries of the democratic camp. Pravda editorial, *Serious Victory of the Forces of Peace*, July 22, 1954, in FBIS, July 22, 1954, at BB 18.

212. Ngo Ton Dat, *supra* note 9, at 159.

D. *The State of Vietnam*

1. Physical Control in Vietnam. Created by the French in 1949 as a nationalist alternative to the Vietminh, the State of Vietnam came to Geneva extremely weak and divided,[213] fully incapable of resisting the power of the Vietminh without the military presence of the French. In the middle of the negotiations, however, Prime Minister Buu Loc resigned unexpectedly, claiming that the conclusion of independence treaties with France had fulfilled his mission.[214] Ngo Dinh Diem, who had previously refused the position because of the lack of strong powers, was now granted full powers by the French, and succeeded to the post with Bao Dai's approval. Diem had been in exile for several years, and had spent some time in the United States, becoming known by many government officials.[215] Ellen Hammer has written that Diem was appointed with the encouragement of the United States,[216] but no evidence is currently available of any such support for Diem during this period,[217] and his appointment was ignored by most of the influential newspapers in both the United States and Great Britain.[218] With Diem's strong anti-Communist background,[219] the French may have been attempting to inspire a

---

213. Jean Lacouture ascribes the ineptitude of the government of the State of Vietnam to France's method of selecting its Vietnamese ministers:

    The French . . . were unwilling to alter their patronizing colonialist attitudes and deal with Asians with some sense of mutual respect or cooperation. For the most part they preferred instead to appoint and then control the manageable, the incompetent, and the operators, many of whom made fortunes out of the corrupt French aid program.

    Lacouture, *supra* note 42, at 657.
214. The Times (London), June 17, 1954, at 5, col. 5.
215. Scheer & Hinckle, *The Viet-Nam Lobby*, THE VIET-NAM READER 66 (M. Raskin & B. Fall eds. 1965).
216. E. HAMMER, *supra* note 76, at 160-61.
217. The absence of any significant evidence that the United States endorsed the appointment of Diem and rendered strong support for the State of Vietnam position in the secret negotiations at the Geneva Conference necessarily plays an important role in the analysis presented. Either or both may in fact have occurred, and it is at least possible that evidence to that effect may be released at some future time. Since the United States Government has itself played a role in the debate on intervention, however, it is difficult to believe such information would be intentionally withheld.
218. The New York Times covered Buu Loc's resignation, but carried no report of Diem's appointment at all. The London Times merely reported Diem's appointment, as a "nationalist Catholic leader," offering no analysis. The Times (London), June 17, 1954, at 5, col. 5. The Manchester Guardian said very little more about Diem, and most of it was inaccurate. Manchester Guardian, June 17, 1954, at 7, col. 3. Only the New York Herald Tribune gave the event any coverage; Marguerite Higgins filed a story entitled "Strong New Leader for Vietnam." It praised Diem's "incorruptible personality," and quoted one American diplomat as saying, "If Bao Dai wants to establish in this country a clean strong government, Diem is a good man to do it." N.Y. Herald Tribune, June 16, 1954, at 2, col. 2.
219. There are excellent sketches of Diem's background in B. FALL, *supra* note 147, at 234-44, and R. SHAPLEN, *supra* note 86, at 104-13.

stronger United States commitment to Vietnam, but the survey of its policy *supra* shows little indication of any move in this direction prior to the end of the Conference. In his inaugural speech, Diem expressed hope he could yet save Vietnam as an independent and unified state.[220] Both the French and the Vietminh had many previous encounters with Diem, and each must have carefully calculated his chances of fulfilling this inaugural promise.

Any possibility that the Diem government might present a strong front at Geneva soon fell before the totally chaotic situation of the State of Vietnam. Some Vietnamese claim that when Diem began his duties in 1954, he controlled little more than a dozen square blocks of downtown Saigon.[221] The French bureaucrats who had held most of the key positions in the government had panicked after Dien Bien Phu and fled. Much of the south was controlled by the religious sects (Cao Dai, Hoa Hao), who maintained only loose relations with Saigon. There was little government in the countryside beyond the traditional village structure. Diem had no political party, no loyal political followers; he had no means of enforcing an order unless the army sided with him.[222] But the Vietnamese Army had few native officers and was totally dependent on the French, who were themselves demoralized by the military situation. There were also difficulties with Diem himself, for he had spent much of his life in spiritual and physical isolation, had a background as a mandarin, and had little understanding of or sympathy for the people of Vietnam.[223] Diem returned to Vietnam with a strong background of personal integrity and anti-communism, but for the time and place that was simply not enough.

In this context, it is fully understandable that the Vietminh chose to deal solely with the French. France still controlled all the military forces opposed to the Vietminh, including those of Vietnamese origin. The Armistice Agreement placed responsibility for administration in the south with the French,[224] and the Vietminh could reasonably expect the French to proceed with consultations and elections on schedule without the need for going through the State of Vietnam.[225] France did make a unilateral declaration at the end of the Conference that it was ready to withdraw its troops from Cambodia, Laos, and Vietnam at the request of the governments concerned,[226] but at this time there was no indication that the State of Vietnam could obtain in-country military backing elsewhere sufficient to offset Vietminh military power should the French forces be withdrawn prior to elec-

---

220. B. Fall, *supra* note 33, at 58.
221. D. PIKE, *supra* note 71, at 80.
222. *Id.* at 57-58.
223. R. SHAPLEN, *supra* note 86, at 104-05.
224. Agreement on the Cessation of Hostilities in Viet-Nam, July 20, 1954, arts. 1 & 14, in BACKGROUND INFORMATION at 36, 39.
225. G. KAHIN & J. LEWIS, *supra* note 102, at 53.
226. CMND. No. 2834 at 83.

tions. There were even reports that the State of Vietnam was expected to collapse prior to the scheduled elections despite a continued French military presence in the south.[227] Diem's demands for French withdrawal, made possible by United States backing at a later date, came as a surprise to everyone, for such an eventuality had not been foreseen at Geneva in 1954.

2. Legal Authority to Govern. Since 1954, it has frequently been argued that the State of Vietnam had already attained effective independence prior to the end of the Geneva Conference, and France therefore had no legal capacity to bind it as a "successor" under Article 27 of the Agreement on the Cessation of Hostilities in Vietnam.[228] The movement toward independence supposedly began with the Elysée Agreement of March 8, 1949, under which Bao Dai was to become the head of an Associated State within the French Union.[229] In 1954, the United States took this agreement as the mark of independence for Vietnam, officially at least, for President Eisenhower sent a congratulatory telegram to the State of Vietnam on March 8, 1954, the "anniversary of its independence." [230] But under the standard definition of a state in International Law (people, territory, a government, and capacity to enter into relations with other states),[231] the Elysée Agreement failed to grant independence, for the French retained full control over foreign relations.[232] Due to this major retention of power by France, the British government years later was able to rationalize its recognition of the State of Vietnam on February 7, 1950 as "conditional". Since it was by no means clear that Vietnam was truly independent under international law, British recognition was phrased in "cautious" terms, as an "Associated State within the French Union",[233] in contrast to United States recognition of the State of Vietnam, Laos and Cambodia as "independent states within the French Union." [234] Under the Oppenheim view that recognition marks the beginning of international rights and duties for the recognized community, it is arguable that full recognition, as granted by the United States and some 35 other states prior to mid-1954, marked the beginning of statehood for the State of Vietnam.[235] Oppenheim was the first to admit, however, that political considerations may occasionally influence the granting of recognition.[236] The Communist bloc had recognized the DRV in January

227. Fall, *How the French Got Out of Viet-Nam*, THE VIET-NAM READER 88 (M. Raskin & M. Fall eds. 1965).
228. For the wording of Article 27, see the text *supra* at note 36.
229. CMND. No. 2834 at 10.
230. N.Y. Times, Mar. 9, 1954, at 12, col. 6.
231. Jessup, *On the Conditions of Statehood*, in H. BRIGGS, THE LAW OF NATIONS 70 (2d ed. 1952).
232. CMND. No. 2834 at 10.
233. *Id.* at 10-11.
234. BACKGROUND INFORMATION at 29.
235. 1 L. OPPENHEIM, INTERNATIONAL LAW 128 (8th ed., Lauterpacht, 1955).
236. *Id.* at 127.

1950, a short time before the United States recognized the State of Vietnam. Such action and counteraction provides a classic example of how diplomatic recognition is employed as a political tool in the cold war, irrespective of the merits of the individual situation.

A second argument revolves about the French proposal in 1952 that the State of Vietnam be admitted to the United Nations, since the United Nations Charter allows membership only to states.[237] By 1952 the State of Vietnam was a member of several United Nations specialized agencies,[238] and was able to enter into at least some treaties in its own name.[239] On September 19, 1952, the Security Council voted 10-1 in favor of admitting the State of Vietnam, but a veto by the Soviet Union prevented such action.[240] On December 21, 1952, the General Assembly adopted a resolution (40 to 5, with 12 abstentions) that the State of Vietnam was a state qualified for membership in the United Nations, calling on the Security Council to take note.[241] While the Soviet Union's veto power made further action impossible, the General Assembly's resolution is a strong argument in support of the proposition that the State of Vietnam at least by 1952 had attained statehood in the full meaning of the term under International Law.

The State of Vietnam did acquire considerable autonomy over domestic affairs in the years immediately preceding the Geneva Conference. But in foreign affairs and even in some domestic areas the State of Vietnam failed to gain any considerable measure of authority prior to the start of the Conference. Jean Lacouture was later to write of the government of the State of Vietnam that " . . . their power and prestige and autonomy were always limited." [242] And Senator John Kennedy severely criticized strong French control in the State of Vietnam on June 30, 1953, many months after the Security Council resolution: ". . . the degree of military, civil, political, and economic control maintained by the French in the State of Vietnam goes well beyond what is necessary to fight a war. . . ."; he then demanded that the United States insist on genuine independence,[243] a demand which was continued by the Eisenhower Administration at least into 1954.

As the military situation in Vietnam began to deteriorate for the French, the Laniel government began showing increased interest in

---

237. U.N. CHARTER art. 4.
238. 7 U.N. SCOR, 603rd meeting 1-2 (1952).
239. On June 18, 1952, the State of Vietnam ratified the Treaty of Peace with Japan. 136 U.N.T.S. 46 (1952). On November 5, 1952, the State of Vietnam accepted the jurisdiction of the International Court of Justice with respect to disputes arising under the Treaty of Peace with Japan. 150 U.N.T.S. 147-49 (1952).
240. 7 U.N. SCOR, 603rd meeting 11 (1952).
241. 7 U.N. GAOR 410 (1952).
242. Lacouture, *supra* note 42, at 656.
243. R. SHAPLEN, *supra* note 86, at 94.

legitimatizing the State of Vietnam in a last-ditch attempt to gain nationalist support for it. French Foreign Minister Bidault stated as early as February 23, 1954, that no position on Indo-China would be adopted by the Laniel government without the formal agreement of the Associated States.[244] Consultations began in March on a treaty of independence for the State of Vietnam, culminating in a joint declaration by France and the State of Vietnam, on April 28, 1954, of total independence.[245] The delegate of the State of Vietnam, in his first speech to the Conference at Geneva on May 12, read aloud the texts of two treaties, one on independence,[246] the other on association; under these treaties, France recognized the State of Vietnam as a "fully independent and sovereign state invested with full rights and obligations recognized by International Law" and the State of Vietnam indicated its desire to associate freely in the French Union. The treaty on independence also contained a devolution clause, under which the State of Vietnam agreed to assume responsibility for all pre-independence treaties signed by France on her behalf. The treaties, however, were not to be signed until supplementary accords were worked out on military, economic, and cultural affairs.[247] The State of Vietnam's delegate indirectly acknowledged this in his speech at Geneva by prefacing his reading of the texts of the treaties by saying, "in a few days this independence will be achieved in a total and absolute fashion. . . ." [248]

After the joint declaration of intent on April 29, the Laniel government, now beginning to feel severe pressure from the Vietminh in Indochina and from its political opposition in France, immediately began speaking of the State of Vietnam as a fully independent state. Foreign Minister Bidault, in his speeches to the Conference

244. Ngo Ton Dat, *supra* note 9, at 120.
245. N.Y. Times, Apr. 29, 1954, at 1, col. 3.
246. Treaty of Independence:
    (1) France recognizes Vietnam as a fully independent and sovereign state invested with full rights and obligations recognized by International Law.
    (2) Vietnam takes over from France all rights and obligations resulting from international treaties or conventions contracted by France in the name of the state of Vietnam or all other treaties or conventions concluded by France in the name of French Indo-China, in so far as these affect Vietnam.
    (3) France undertakes to transfer to the Government of Vietnam all rights and obligations and public services assured by her on Vietnam territory.
    (4) The present treaty, which enters into force on the date of signature, abrogates all earlier and contrary acts and dispositions. The instruments of ratification of the present treaty will be exchanged immediately following approval by the qualified institutions of Vietnam and France.
    N.Y. Times, May 13, 1954, at 6, col. 4.
247. N.Y. Times, Apr. 29, 1954, at 2, col. 5.
248. N.Y. Times, May 13, 1954, at 4, col. 2.

on May 8 [249] and May 12 [250] asserted in unequivocal terms that the independence treaty had already taken effect, and France had thereby removed all reasons for the conflict in Indo-China to continue. Premier Laniel and State of Vietnam Prime Minister Buu Loc initialled the treaties on June 4.[251] Some observers have taken this ceremony as the consummation of independence for Vietnam. Bernard B. Fall thought Buu Loc had signed the treaties, not just initialled them, and felt the activity on June 4 ". . . consecrated the political independence . . ." of Vietnam.[252] The International Law Association's Committee on State Succession to Treaties and Other Governmental Obligations lists June 4, 1954 as the date of effective independence for Vietnam,[253] quoting the full text of the devolution clause (article 2 of the treaty of independence), and pronouncing it fully effective.[254]

The public record, however, shows that the initialling of the treaties on June 4 was not intended to be the final step in the process. The treaties were yet to be signed by Bao Dai and French President Coty. Premier Laniel stated that by initialling the treaties even before the supplementary accords had been completed, France had given public proof of its will to grant independence.[255] The London Times therefore concluded:

> In the strictly legal sense to-day's ceremony appears to have changed nothing, for the treaties cannot be signed until the conventions governing the economic and juridical questions involved in the transfer of powers have been completed; and after that they must be ratified in the ordinary way.[256]

The New York Times reported hope that the accords would be finished by June 9, but that even then there was doubt that French President Coty, as guarantor of the French Constitution, would be able to sign the treaties, since many observers claimed the text would conflict with the definition of "French Union" in the French Constitution.[257] The Communist delegates at Geneva clearly did not regard the treaties as effective as of June 4, for Molotov, on June 8,

---

249. ". . . France has been able to keep its promises and full independence has been recognised and has become effective." CMD. NO. 9186 at 109. "The French Government is thus confident that it has done everything in its power to put an end to the conflict. [It has] removed all reason for this conflict to exist by recognising fully and unreservedly the independence of Viet Nam, Laos and Cambodia . . . ." *Id.*
250. CMD. No. 9186 at 132-34.
251. N.Y. Times, June 5, 1954, at 2, col. 3.
252. B. FALL, *supra* note 147, at 244.
253. Committee on State Succession to Treaties and Other Governmental Obligations, The International Law Association, THE EFFECT OF INDEPENDENCE ON TREATIES 7 (1965).
254. *Id.* at 199.
255. The Times (London), June 5, 1954, at 6, col. 5.
256. *Id.*
257. N.Y. Times, June 5, 1954, at 2, col. 3.

remarked that the treaty on independence ". . . still remains unsigned . . .";[258] it was not signed by the close of the Geneva Conference,[259] and had not been ratified the next year.[260]

The reasons for the failure to implement these treaties are quite simple. The Laniel government resigned on June 12, prior to completion of the supplementary accords of the treaties, after considerable opposition in France to its Indo-China policies. Prince Buu Loc stepped down four days later as Prime Minister of the State of Vietnam, claiming the job of gaining independence to be complete; privately it was rumored that he feared Mendes-France, the new French Premier, would be a "peace at any price" negotiator.[261] Thus, less than ten days after the treaties were initialled, neither of the two governments which proposed and drafted them was any longer in existence. Mendes-France had strongly criticized Laniel's policies, had placed himself under a rigid one-month time limit to gain a settlement, and had little time for esoteric considerations such as treaties of independence for Vietnam. The military situation was falling apart, all of Vietnam was in immediate danger of being taken by the Vietminh, and Mendes-France, attuned to the realities of the situation, immediately began discussions with the other world power which could actually influence events in Indo-China, Communist China. The delegates of the State of Vietnam protested bitterly against being completely cut out of any meaningful negotiations, but themselves admitted, on July 4, that the State of Vietnam was ". . . militarily and politically too weak to oppose Paris alone."[262] United States policy remained unclear throughout the last negotiations at Geneva, and the State of Vietnam looked for no help from this quarter, believing the United States was ready to accept the best settlement Paris could get.[263] One reliable source reports the head of the State of Vietnam, during the last days at Geneva, informed the American Ambassador in Saigon that he was prepared to take a position against the contemplated agreement at Geneva and denounce all Vietnamese agreements towards France if he received the slightest support from the United States; the United States Ambassador, however, dissuaded the Saigon government from such a move.[264] As Bernard B. Fall saw it, "Ngo Dinh Diem and the State of Vietnam were quite alone in the last days before the signature of the cease-fire."[265] At the end of the Conference, when the delegate of the State of Vietnam charged France with taking vital decisions

258. CMD. No. 9186 at 147.
259. M. FARLEY, *supra* note 132, at 22.
260. Crozier, *The Diem Regime in Southern Vietnam*, FAR EASTERN SURVEY, April, 1955, at 50 n. 3.
261. NGO TON DAT, *supra* note 9, at 207 n.12.
262. N.Y. Times, July 5, 1954, at 2, col. 1.
263. *Id.*
264. J. LACOUTURE & P. DEVILLERS, *supra* note 17, at 264.
265. B. Fall, *supra* note 83, at 748.

without the consent of the State of Vietnam, Mendes-France coolly replied: "The French delegation has the assurance that the French High Command [which signed the armistice agreement] has acted in the framework of its competence and attributions with regard to its own decisions and responsibilities." [266]

VI. The Political Settlement

As stated in the short historical sketch, *supra* Section II, both the Vietminh and the State of Vietnam included in their initial proposals to the Conference explicit provisions for a political settlement. The Vietminh (May 10) called for free general elections, supervised by an Advisory Conference of representatives from both sides.[267] The State of Vietnam (May 12) similarly called for free general elections, but under United Nations supervision and not until the Security Council had determined that the authority of the state was established and conditions of freedom were fulfilled.[268] The French (May 8) concentrated on military provisions, and ignored political issues entirely.[269] After an initial flurry of comments by the allies on both sides, Molotov demanded (May 14) that a political settlement be discussed simultaneously with a military armistice,[270] but Bidault (May 14) replied that military settlement should precede a political one.[271] The Conference evidently discussed only military provisions from mid-May until at least June 8, when Molotov angrily demanded that the Conference discuss both military and political terms together.[272] The one exception during this period came from the United States, whose representative, Bedell Smith, had urged France on May 10 to accompany her proposals on military matters with a program for the resolution of political problems as well.[273] On May 24, the New York Times reported that, if an armistice were to be reached, the United States would then propose a permanent political settlement for Vietnam be determined by the United Nations General Assembly. The United States hoped that negotiations at Geneva would result only in general principles to guide the General Assembly, and predicted that elections under United Nations auspices would emerge as one of the principal issues at Geneva.[274] This appears to be the first and last major statement by the United States on a political settlement, and its negotiators, in keeping with shifts in policy, soon faded into the background at Geneva.

---

266. Ngo Ton Dat, *supra* note 9, at 467.
267. CMD. No. 9186 at 118.
268. *Id.* at 124.
269. *Id.* at 109.
270. N.Y. Times, May 15, 1954, at 1, col. 1.
271. CMD. No. 9186 at 134.
272. *Id.* at 143.
273. N.Y. Times, May 11, 1954, at 4, col. 6.
274. N.Y. Times, May 24, 1954, at 1, col. 6.

On June 8, Molotov demanded that the elections be preceded by the withdrawal of all foreign troops from Indochina, and recommended that the Vietnamese people ensure freedom of activity in preparing for elections by taking the matter into their own hands.[275] Chou En-lai on June 9 also recommended discussion of political issues by the Conference together with the military issues,[276] and the great debate was fully underway. Jean Lacouture and Philippe Devillers report a secret meeting that day between the military representatives of France and the Vietminh, at which the Vietminh demanded a capital (Hanoi) and a port for that capital (Haiphong). Asked if the concessions necessary for the Vietminh to obtain these areas would not imply partition, the Vietminh representative replied it would only be a temporary partition, as elections were provided for the whole of Vietnam, under which the reunification of Vietnam would be legally achieved, and ". . . the Vietminh would insist essentially on these elections." [277]

Once the Mendes-France government came to power in France, faced with a self-proclaimed one-month deadline for reaching a settlement, negotiations on a political settlement began in earnest. Mendes-France soon went to Bern to meet Chou En-lai, and on June 24 the press reported that they had agreed on the basic terms of a political settlement, which would then be applied if an armistice could be arranged at Geneva. The settlement envisioned a unified government for Vietnam, to be selected in all-Vietnam elections, to be held "eventually." These were reportedly the same terms which had been passed to Anthony Eden on June 16.[278] The New York Times expressed concern, in view of the positions previously taken by United States delegates, that elections might be dangerous, according to the timing: if held immediately, Ho Chi Minh would certainly win.[279] President Eisenhower later verified this estimate in his memoirs:

> I have never talked or corresponded with a person knowledgeable in Indo-Chinese affairs who did not agree that had elections been held as of the time of the fighting, possibly 80 per cent of the population would have voted for the Communist Ho Chi Minh as their leader rather than Chief of State Bao Dai.[280]

A follow up story on the Mendes-France/Chou En-lai meetings in Bern stated that free elections became a losing card when the Communists, relying partly on clippings from American newspaper-

---

275. CMD. No. 9186 at 150.
276. *Id.* at 164-65.
277. J. LACOUTURE & P. DEVILLERS, *supra* note 17, at 211-12.
278. N.Y. Times, June 24, 1954, at 1, col. 8.
279. *Id.* at 5, col. 1.
280. D. EISENHOWER, *supra* note 86, at 449.

men,[281] accused the West of being afraid of elections since it antici-pated victory by Ho Chi Minh.[282]

The first negative report occurred on June 28, when the New York Times stated that, although the main outlines of a settlement were developing and did include elections in Vietnam to form a unified government, both sides were fearful that a political settlement would never be realized, and that the occupation zones would become perma-nent lines of division as in Korea.[283] The next day, however, the same paper returned to reporting concrete measures being taken to fashion a political settlement, stating that the French desired only general principles for an "eventual" election in Vietnam to be pre-scribed by the Conference, while the Communists would probably in-sist on completing political arrangements at Geneva.[284]

The major delegates at Geneva were in recess from June 20 until mid-July while discussions continued at a lower level. Chou En-lai journeyed to India to exchange views with Prime Minister Nehru, who had been keeping close tabs on the Conference through his representative at Geneva, Krishna Menon. Their joint communique at the end of the visit expressed hope that the Conference would end with a political settlement creating unified and independent states in Indochina.[285] This was interpreted as implying India's support for Communist determination to win all of Vietnam,[286] and upset Ameri-can officials, who had long assumed that the long-range objective for Vietnam would be a fully Communist state, even if settlement were reached on the basis of divided territory.[287]

As the delegates began to reassemble in Geneva, Mendes-France (July 11) reportedly hoped to establish in the southern zone a state that could function "pending elections, held with ample guarantees", and recommended partition at the 18th parallel and no fixed date for these elections, or none until mid-1955 at the earliest. Presum-ably his object was to give the State of Vietnam time to reconstitute itself and to provide effective opposition to the Vietminh.[288] But the same day Hanson Baldwin reported that the Geneva terms would in-clude elections in the near future.[289] On July 13, reports circulated that France and Great Britain had already gone far in agreeing to a

281. *See, e.g.*, N.Y. Times, May 17, 1954, at 2, col. 3 (most Western delegates say the Communists would win *free* elections); N.Y. Times, May 18, 1954, at 2, col. 2 (the Western powers are apprehensive that if elections are held now, even under United Nations supervision, the Communists would win; thus they want to avoid a political settlement, or at least delay it for 18 months or more).
282. N.Y. Times, June 27, 1954, § 4, at 5, cols. 1-2.
283. N.Y. Times, June 28, 1954, at 2, col. 8.
284. N.Y. Times, June 29, 1954, at 4, col. 1.
285. *Id.* at 4, cols. 4-6.
286. *Id.* at 4, col. 4.
287. N.Y. Times, June 30, 1954, at 4, col. 7.
288. N.Y. Times, July 11, 1954, at 2, col. 4, and at 3, cols. 1-2.
289. N.Y. Times, July 11, 1954, § 4, at 5, col. 2.

political settlement,[290] and on July 14, that the French were resigned to some provisions for ultimate elections in Vietnam.[291]

The next day, with less than a week remaining until Mendes-France's deadline (July 20), the Communists began a final push to define concrete provisions for these elections. Molotov argued on July 15 for a specific election date, pointing out that the Vietminh had already switched their demands from the 13th parallel to the 16th, even though France held fast at the 18th, and that ". . . after all it would only be a transitory partition preceding the reunification of Vietnam." [292] On July 16, the French were reportedly determined not to fix a date for elections, a position which had United States support, but the British were not sure France would be able to induce the Communists to sign an agreement without fixing a date for the elections.[293] On July 17 Mendes-France summed up the difficulty in a letter to the acting French Prime Minister: ". . . I strive to delay to the maximum the date of the elections. It is useless to say that on this point our opponents are particularly tough and they find rather a lot of help and support, even among the neutrals." [294] The same day, the Manchester Guardian termed the fixing of a date for elections the "central issue" at Geneva, and claimed that the French arguments might justify a delay of eighteen months or two years but failed to demonstrate the impossibility of fixing any date whatsoever.[295] The New York Times on July 17, also saw the question of whether a specific date should be set for elections as a "main issue", sharing the limelight with the location of the temporary partition line.[296]

The Communists now began to suspect that the West wished to make the dividing line a permanent boundary, and protested bitterly. The London Times stated, on July 17, that the Communists believed the French really wanted to make the 18th parallel a permanent frontier, and were therefore all the more insistent on fixing a date for elections.[297] It was later reported that Molotov had expressed his suspicions on July 15 that Mendes-France and other Western delegates were beginning to regard the line of military demarcation as a frontier, and were again insisting on early elections.[298]

The first reports that Mendes-France was prepared to compromise on the French resistance to setting a date for elections appeared on July 19; the Communists had previously offered 18 months and the French now believed they could get two years, a span of time which

---

290. N.Y. Times, July 13, 1954, at 22, col. 1.
291. N.Y. Times, July 14, 1954, at 1, col. 8.
292. J. LACOUTURE & P. DEVILLERS, *supra* note 17, at 262.
293. N.Y. Times, July 16, 1954, at 1, col. 7.
294. J. LACOUTURE & P. DEVILLERS, *supra* note 17, at 263.
295. Manchester Guardian, July 17, 1954, at 1, col. 1.
296. N.Y. Times, July 17, 1954, at 2, col. 2.
297. The Times (London), July 17, 1954, at 6, col. 1.
298. The Times (London), July 19, 1954, at 7, col. 5.

the French thought would offer at least a "good chance" of preventing a Communist victory through a vigorous rebuilding of the stature of the State of Vietnam's government.[299] Mendes-France's estimate that the Communists might go beyond 18 months found some confirmation the next day, when the London Times reported that Molotov was not particularly insistent on the length of time before the elections, ". . . provided that the election date is fixed." The Times article also stated that France still wanted to leave the fixing of the election date to the International Supervisory Commission, but it estimated a date "in practice about the beginning of 1956" would be agreed upon at Geneva.[300]

The Conference drew near to its climax with the bargaining sessions on July 19. The London Times reported that these sessions resulted in at least near agreement on a dividing line for the armistice and on a date for elections, and cited a French spokesman as saying that these two issues—dividing line and date for elections—were linked in the negotiations and could be settled in a matter of minutes. The spokesman said there was already agreement on the dividing line, provided the election date was satisfactorily settled.[301] The Manchester Guardian subsequently reported that agreement on both the 17th parallel as the dividing line and elections in two years was reached the night of July 19.[302] If the report is accurate (the New York Times stated the negotiators were still deadlocked on these issues as of thirty minutes past midnight on July 20),[303] it supports the statement that the two issues were linked together, each being a vital issue, with concessions granted on one point necessarily being rewarded by gains on the other.

The statements of the chief Communist negotiators at Geneva at the end of the Conference indicate their expectations that elections were an integral part of the bargain and would be held as scheduled.[304] Major representatives and publications on both Communist [305] and

299. N.Y. Times, July 19, 1954, at 1, col. 8.
300. The Times (London), July 20, 1954, at 8, col. 2.
301. The Times (London), July 20, 1954, at 8, col. 1.
302. Manchester Guardian, July 21, 1954, at 1, col. 1.
303. N.Y. Times, July 20, 1954, at 1, col. 8, and at 2, col. 3.
304. Pham Van Dong, the Vietminh's delegate, stated that "We shall have to construct a stable and sound peace in Indo-China by settling the political problems especially the achievement of our national unity by way of elections . . . ." FACTS AND DATES ON THE PROBLEM OF REUNIFICATION OF VIET-NAM 9 (Hanoi, Foreign Languages Publishing House, 1956) [hereinafter cited as FACTS AND DATES]. According to the Soviet Union's Molotov, "That agreement which fixes the provisional demarcation line between the North and South of Vietnam, raises a new and urgent task: the rapid achievement of national reunification in peaceful conditions." Id. at 9-10. Communist China's Chou En-lai emphasized the provision that "The three Indochinese states will hold nation-wide free elections within respective specified periods of time to achieve democracy and unity of their respective countries." Id. at 6.
305. Chou En-lai's statement of July 21 was quite specific:
    It is my firm belief that the agreements we have reached will not only

Western [306] sides of the conference table emphasized the amount of time and energy dedicated to finding an acceptable political settlement. The Communists placed great emphasis on setting a specific date for the Vietnam elections, a provision which elevated the Vietnam unification issue above the class of Germany and Korea.[307] There were also many indications throughout the course of the Conference that the Western delegations understood the implications of elections in Vietnam, were calculating the future prospects of the possible candidates, and were considering means of shoring up the Western candidates.[308] It seems reasonable to conclude that a political settle-

end the eight year Indochina war and bring peace to the peoples of Indochina and France, but will also result in further relaxation in the tensions in Asia and all over the world. Undoubtedly the success of our conference is tremendous. In order to enable the peace in Indo-China to become firm and lasting, this conference has made repeated efforts so that both the armistice question and the political question in Indo-China may be settled. The agreements that we have achieved carry concrete provisions for ending the Indo-China war and lay down the principles for the settlement of the political questions in Indo-China.

N.Y. Times, July 22, 1954, at 2, col. 7. Pravda editorialized on July 22 that:

It is known that this decision on an 'accurately defined time for elections' was adopted as a result of the protracted and determined struggle of the representatives of the USSR, the Chinese People's Republic, and the DRV. The American aggressive circles, striving [for a final] split of Vietnam, have suffered a defeat.

Pravda Editorial, *Serious Victory of the Forces of Peace*, July 22, 1954, in FBIS, July 22, 1954, at BB 18. The same day Tass stated that the decision on elections was ". . . adopted as the result of persistent efforts by the democratic States . . . ." Tass, July 22, 1954, in FBIS, July 23, 1954, at BB 2.

306. Premier Mendes-France told the French National Assembly on July 22 that "The date of these elections . . . was the subject of a long and difficult debate." Ngo Ton Dat, *supra* note 9, at 271 n.5. Anthony Eden, in reviewing the weaknesses of the Geneva Agreements years later, stated that the provision for elections in two years was altogether too short: "Some of us thought so at the time, but the pressure from the North was strong and even the French, with their intimate knowledge of the country, had once been willing to accept eighteen months." A. EDEN, *supra* note 3, at 36.

307. The major Pravda editorial on the results of the Geneva Conference asserted that "The provision for an accurately defined time for the general election in Vietnam is of enormous political importance." Pravda Editorial, *Serious Victory of the Forces of Peace*, July 22, 1954, in FBIS, July 22, 1954, at BB 18.

308. As early as May 17, Western delegations had estimated that the Vietnamese people could be won back to a democratic (western-backed) government if the Vietnamese government received sufficient help from outside and could take hold. N.Y. Times, May 17, 1954, at 2, col. 3. On June 17, one of the chief French military negotiators wrote that even a partition at the 18th parallel, the point initially demanded by France, would place a very important part of the total population under the Vietminh. If there were to be an election, there would be a risk of seeing the Vietminh win easily. Ngo Ton Dat, *supra* note 9, at 460. In a most revealing statement, the delegate of the State of Vietnam, on July 16, with the Conference in its last days, argued for the 18th parallel as the dividing line, plus retention of Hanoi

ment was indeed reached at Geneva in 1954. John W. Holmes, Canada's observer at the Geneva Conference in 1954 and the individual responsible for Canadian policy in the International Supervisory Commission throughout the next several years, lent this conclusion strong support in mid-1967:

> The Geneva settlement does . . . make it possible to argue almost any legal position. I don't think any of us who watched the Geneva negotiations up close, however, had any doubt at the time that the whole settlement was a package deal. The Communists, who were winning the war, were persuaded to stop fighting in exchange for certain things most important of which was the promise of elections in two years.[309]

VII. THE OUTCOME PHASE

The outcome phase spans the period where negotiations produce some sort of agreement. The expectations of the participants are set forth in documents or in some other manner, and the participants disperse to begin implementation of the agreements according to their shared understandings, at whatever levels these exist. A great deal of the material concerning the outcome phase of the Geneva Conference has been necessarily included in the discussion of the political settlement above. Equally significant indices of the participants' expectations can be found in the many other statements and analyses which appeared during the days immediately following the conclusion of the Conference. The following section discusses the reactions of the participants most vitally affected by the Geneva Agreements (France, the Vietminh, the State of Vietnam) and also the positions taken by non-participants (third parties).

A. *France and the Vietminh*

The French expectations were aptly depicted by Premier Mendes-France in his appearance before the French National Assembly the

---

by the French and the creation of a neutralized zone in the Catholic provinces of the southern part of the Red River Delta. These measures would be necessary, for "Only by these means could the Saigon Government retain sufficient influence and control in the country as a whole to balance Vietminh power and have a chance in national elections." N.Y. Times, July 17, 1954, at 2, col. 1. On July 18, Mendes-France was prepared to abandon his resistance to fixing a date for elections because he believed he could get the date set back to two years, long enough to prepare to offset Communist attractiveness. The French emphasized, however, that "considerable United States economic help" plus a "more vigorous Vietnamese Government" would be necessary if the Vietminh were to be defeated at the polls. N.Y. Times, July 19, 1954, at 1, col. 8. Philippe Devillers later described the French strategy at Geneva as avoiding quick elections, giving Vietminh prestige a chance to decline, and allowing the people some time to think it over and give an opportunity for non-Marxist parties to step in if they could. Devillers, *supra* note 23, at 211.

309. Holmes, *Geneva: 1954*, 12 INT. J. 476-77 (1967).

day after the Conference ended. The keynote was realism: the impact of the Agreements on France was ". . . cruel because they sanction cruel facts;"[310] considering the unfavorable military situation in Indo-China and the consequent weakness of the French bargaining position, however, Mendes-France was convinced that the Agreements were "undoubtedly the best which were attainable in the present state of affairs."[311] Replying to charges from several deputies that the Geneva Agreements implied the handing over of all of Vietnam to the Communists either through the elections or through the South's disintegration beforehand,[312] Mendes-France reminded the Assembly that France had successfully delayed the elections for two full years (to mid-1956), during which the South could attempt to improve its standing and show it had a system preferable to that of the North. To that end, Mendes-France promised that France would protect and aid southern Vietnam.[313]

Mendes-France's speech to the Assembly also brought to light evidence that the Geneva Agreements may have been predicated on a French-Vietminh *detente* on economic matters. The Premier reminded the Assembly that the Viet-Minh in the last days of Geneva had affirmed their wish to maintain cultural and economic contact with France, and had promised that French property would be respected and French interests in every way considered. The Geneva Agreement thus left intact the chance for France to continue her role in the Far East.[314] Soon, the text of a letter to Mendes-France from Pham Van Dong was released; the letter, dated July 21, the last day of the Conference, expressed the Vietminh's readiness to discuss with France any problems connected with the continuance of French business and cultural activities in the North. It proposed that property rights be respected in both zones, that businesses be permitted to continue their activity "without hindrance or discrimination", and that French cultural activities be continued in the North.[315] Bernard B. Fall sketched out several reasons why the Vietminh would benefit from a continued French economic presence. In the years after Geneva, the DRV would require large amounts of consumer goods, drugs, and machinery, items which the Soviet Union and Communist China simply could not furnish, as they had already demonstrated in North Korea. The DRV also had only an interior currency, and Fall, writing in October 1954, saw a strong likelihood that it would attempt to remain within the French franc area.[316]

The DRV's economic problems were soon to achieve massive proportions. The resources of Vietnam were definitely complementary,

310. N.Y. Times, July 23, 1954, at 2, col. 3.
311. Ngo Ton Dat, *supra* note 9, at 271.
312. *Id.* at 276-78.
313. The Times (London), July 24, 1954, at 6, col. 2.
314. The Times (London), July 23, 1954, at 6, col. 1.
315. The Times (London), July 26, 1954, at 8, col. 3.
316. B. FALL, *supra* note 83, at 858.

with the raw materials and skilled artisans of the North matched against the agricultural riches of the South.[317] The South was able to maintain relative self-sufficiency: it was far less damaged by the war, possessed some underdeveloped rice lands, plus some capacity to produce rubber, spices, and corn, and had an ample supply of labor. The North, on the other hand, was badly battered by the war, had little surplus rice land, and had to find ways of offsetting the 250,000 ton yearly deficit in rice.[318] This had been filled in the past by shipments from the South, but Diem's government soon refused to agree to a restoration of normal relations between the two zones, and the DRV was forced to turn to its allies.[319] The economic situation made reunification an urgent necessity for the North; in its publications urging the implementation of the political settlement through elections, the North stressed the "complementary character" of the resources for the two zones.[320] Jean Lacouture wrote that reunification was pressed more for economic reasons than for national pride, communism, or any other reasons.[321] Surely, if a lasting partition were the settlement at Geneva, the immense economic consequences would have been readily apparent to DRV negotiators, who would, of necessity, have fought strongly and openly against such a measure.

Vietminh leader Ho Chi Minh presented his expectations in a major speech the same day as did Mendes-France (July 22), stating that the Vietminh were determined to "faithfully implement" the agreements and calling on the Vietnamese to ". . . fight for the holding of free general elections throughout the country to achieve national unity." [322] He saw the Geneva Agreements as a "great victory" for the Vietminh, and emphasized:

> During the cease-fire we must adjust the military zones as the first step toward our final goal. The demarcation of the military zones, however, is just a provisional measure to be taken to restore the peace and realize the unification of the nation by means of general elections.

> The demarcation line does not mean the political and territorial border line. Northern, Central and Southern Vietnam are inseparable parts of our nation's territory.[323]

---

317. E. HAMMER, *supra* note 76, at 1, 20, 22.
318. B. FALL, *supra* note 33, at 64.
319. E. HAMMER, *supra* note 76, at 186.
320. The official DRV argument for reunification listed the North's resources as coal, iron, copper, tin, lead, gold, silver, manganese, chromium, mercury, cement, and consumer goods, while the South was credited with coconut fibre, rubber, cotton, copra oil, and rice; the author specified the last product, southern rice, as "an important tonnage." NGUYEN-VIEN, VIET-NAM IS ONE 9-10 (Hanoi, Foreign Languages Publishing House, 1956).
321. J. LACOUTURE, *supra* note 67, at 36. This argument is strongly supported by Bernard Fall; *see* B. FALL, *supra* note 104, at 49-59, 92-96.
322. FACTS AND DATES at 10.
323. N.Y. Times, July 26, 1954, at 1, col. 3.

Doubt immediately appeared, however, that the Agreements represented a "great victory" for the Vietminh. The New York Times correspondent at Geneva broke a story on July 25 that the Vietminh negotiators at Geneva were "not entirely happy" with the agreements, claiming that the Vietminh military successes had given them a dominating position in Indo-China, and that pressure from Molotov and Chou En-lai forced the Vietminh to accept less than they rightfully should have obtained.[324] The commentators are virtually unanimous in asserting that the Vietminh got less than they deserved,[325] and most ascribe this failure to some form of joint Sino-Soviet pressure.[326] In light of the objectives of the Soviet Union (peaceful coexistence, prestige for Communist China) and Communist China (the same, plus a breathing spell for domestic reconstruction) in 1954, all of which pointed toward a negotiated settlement at Geneva, it is quite likely that strong pressure was applied to the Vietminh to subordinate their own objectives to the overall advance of international Communism. The memoirs of Anthony Eden strongly support the position that both Molotov and Chou En-lai wanted a settlement at Geneva.[327]

The same article stated that the Vietminh were upset over the provisions requiring withdrawal of Vietminh forces from Laos [328] and Cambodia,[329] since they had made headway in both areas and believed they could eventually have gained control.[330] Vietminh penetration into Cambodia had been minimal at best and received scarcely more than token support from the Soviet or Chinese spokesman at any time at Geneva.[331] Vietminh operations in Laos were quite a different

---

324. N.Y. Times, July 25, 1954, at 1, col. 6.
325. *See, e.g.*, P. HONEY, COMMUNISM IN NORTH VIETNAM 5 (1963) (the Agreements gave the Vietminh far less than even their most pessimistic supporters could have expected).
326. J. BRIMMELL, *supra* note 66, at 284; D. PIKE, *supra* note 71, at 52; Devillers, *supra* note 23, at 212. *But see* P. HONEY, *supra* note 325, at 5. Honey, an acknowledged authority on the affairs of North Vietnam, claims that they were pressured into agreement only by the Soviet Union. Honey says the Vietminh showed no public signs of resentment at the Soviet Union's tactics, but notes the possibility that the Vietminh were compensated by promises of economic aid. *Id.* at 43. Other commentators, while positing joint Sino-Soviet pressure, feel that Communist China was the primary restraining influence. H. HINTON, CHINA'S RELATIONS WITH BURMA AND VIETNAM—A BRIEF SURVEY 21 (1958); Ngo Ton Dat, *supra* note 9, at 415.
327. According to Eden, Molotov was genuinely anxious to reach a settlement throughout the Conference and often came forward with a helpful suggestion or concession at vital moments. A. EDEN, *supra* note 11, at 136. Chou En-lai offered to persuade the Vietminh to withdraw from Laos and Cambodia, and Eden reported a strong impression that Chou wanted a settlement. *Id.* at 145.
328. Agreement on the Cessation of Hostilities in Laos, July 20, 1954, art. 4, in BACKGROUND INFORMATION at 59.
329. Agreement on the Cessation of Hostilities in Cambodia, July 20, 1954, art. 4, in BACKGROUND INFORMATION at 51.
330. N.Y. Times, July 25, 1954, at 1, col. 6.
331. A. EDEN, *supra* note 3, at 56.

matter, for the Vietminh had a "substantial" number of troops there, and at one time had nearly broken through to the Mekong River, which would have split Laos in two. On June 27, the New York Times reported that Communist China had called for withdrawal of Vietminh and French forces from Laos and Cambodia, followed by neutralization, and that the Vietminh were going along with the Chinese proposals, but without enthusiasm.

In the last days at Geneva, the Communists altered these proposals somewhat by demanding two provinces in northeastern Laos as "regroupment areas" for indigenous Pathet Lao guerrillas.[332] This proposal was made part of the armistice agreement, "pending a political settlement," [333] but the Pathet Lao later failed to yield control of these provinces.[334] To the extent, however, that Vietminh forces were withdrawn into Vietnam, leaving the Laotian area to Laotian Communist guerrillas, it represented a major concession by the Vietminh. In return for such a concession, the Vietminh must have been compensated at least to a considerable extent, either by their Communist allies in the form of promises of future support, or by the French, who undoubtedly were delighted to gain relative safety for Laos and Cambodia.

Once the Geneva Agreements were reached, the DRV's official policy followed the pattern set forth in Ho Chi Minh's speech of July 22. The hallmarks of this approach, as stated frequently in the national press, included both faithful implementation of the agreements and preparation for national elections. Typical of the approach were these words from the Vietnam News Agency on July 25:

> Henceforward the main task of our struggle is to consolidate the peace we have won, faithfully and rapidly implement the provisions of the armistice agreement, and go forward to the settlement of the Indochinese political issues, so as to fully regain our national rights, that is—complete unity, independence, and democracy.[335]

If deference is paid to the McDougal-Lasswell-Miller principle of giving highest priority to the expectations of those delegations which participated most fully in the negotiations,[336] in the case of the Geneva Conference deference would be given to expectations that the political settlement was intended to be implemented. Both France and the Vietminh, who played major roles in the negotiations and who were the only participants to sign any document concerning Vietnam, indicated such expectations during the Outcome Phase of the Conference.

---

332. N.Y. Times, July 20, 1954, at 1, col. 6.
333. Agreement on the Cessation of Hostilities in Laos, July 20, 1954, art. 14, in BACKGROUND INFORMATION at 61.
334. Editorial, *Vietnam in the Hazard*, THE ECONOMIST, July 21, 1956, at 202.
335. Vietnam News Agency, July 25, 1954, in FBIS, July 28, 1954, at CCC 7.
336. *See supra* note 61.

B. *Third Parties*

While not nearly as significant as the statements of the participants themselves, the reaction of the press and public figures not connected with the negotiations are still important secondary sources of information on the expectations of conference participants. The great majority of such sources in the months after the Conference clearly believed that a political settlement was concluded there. Typical of these reports were remarks by two United States public officials. Since the war in Indo-China had now ended, the question immediately arose whether the United States would discontinue aid to Indo-China; there were reports that some Congressmen favored a switch of these already-appropriated funds to South Korea. Harold Stassen, the coordinator for foreign aid in the administration, immediately squelched such rumors (July 24), and expressed support for a reconstruction program in South Vietnam, saying it must now compete with the Communists politically and economically, instead of militarily, and it must prepare for elections.[337] Representative Franklin D. Roosevelt, Jr., on the same day, called for social and military aid to win the promised election.[338]

While Great Britain was much less concerned over the future of Indo-China, and the British press failed to take a stand on building up the South before the future elections, the major newspapers at least implied that all of Vietnam would soon go Communist. The Manchester Guardian published an editorial on July 17, at the peak of Conference activity, in which it complained that what China had failed to gain in Korea, it was gaining in Vietnam, and cited a recent foreign affairs debate in the House of Commons in which it was taken for granted that Peking had won Indo-China.[339] The London Times sympathized with Vietnamese misgivings over the settlement, for, with the examples of Korea and Germany before them, ". . . they are bound to look with disfavour on any agreement which might lead to a permanent division of their country." [340] But the same day the paper editorialized that for the West to refuse fair elections in Vietnam would cut the moral basis from under western demands that Korea and Germany be unified by free elections or not at all; it felt free elections in Vietnam could not be blocked simply because the wrong side might win; and it claimed that, "given the state of feeling in Viet Nam, the terms were by far the best attainable." [341] The same editorial in effect wrote off Vietnam to the Communists: "There emerges a probability . . . that Cambodia and most of Laos can be neutralized to serve as buffer states between Viet Nam and Siam. Few people could hope for that when the conference be-

---

337. N.Y. Times, July 25, 1954, at 2, col. 4.
338. *Id.* at 2, col. 6.
339. Manchester Guardian, July 17, 1954, at 4, col. 1.
340. The Times (London), July 21, 1954, at 6, col. 2.
341. *Id.* at 7, col. 2.

gan." [342] The Spectator on July 23 stated that the partitioning of Vietnam would be valuable only ". . . to the extent that the West can use the time between now and the Vietnamese elections to build a strong anti-Communist front behind Indo-China." [343] A year later, in mid-July of 1955, *The Economist* took a hard look at the Conference results:

> The Geneva Agreements followed a catastrophic military defeat; it was regarded by the Chinese and Vietnamese Communists as an unavoidable device to save French face, and they took it for granted that it merely entailed a delay of two years before the Viet Minh would take over the other half of the country, thus gathering the full harvest of their military victory. [344]

Philippe Devillers presents a similar analysis, stating that the basic hypothesis at Geneva was that the agreements would be implemented and that in 1954 "almost no one" thought the two-year delay was anything but a French respite in which to salvage as much as possible from the wreck. [345]

In America, the reports were similar. The New York Times, in the first days after the Agreements were reached, stated that a political settlement had been reached which gave a strong advantage to the Communists, since the northern zone would contain a majority of the population of Vietnam and the Communists could also count on "millions of Communist sympathizers in the south." [346] The first Times editorial, on July 22, mentions the provisional nature of the demarcation line, the provisions for elections, stated that such provisions were under the circumstances perhaps the best that could be obtained, and then leaped to the attack:

> [T]hose who now cry 'appeasement' and 'Munich' have a right to do so only if they were ready to plunge America's youth into what would have been, even more than an expanded Korean conflict, the wrong war, at the wrong time, in the worst possible place. [347]

Subsequent stories began to express considerable doubt about a political settlement; on July 24, the Times reported ". . . the Vietnamese and many other observers have little confidence that it actually will prove possible to hold such elections any more than it has proven possible in divided Korea or Germany." [348] The next day it reported that the agreements are ". . . shot through with ambiguities" and that "there is no great expectation that all-Vietnam elections will

342. *Id.*
343. Editorial, *Peace at a High Price*, THE SPECTATOR, July 23, 1954, at 101.
344. Editorial, *Deadline in Viet Nam*, THE ECONOMIST, July 16, 1955, at 203.
345. Devillers, *supra* note 23, at 211.
346. N.Y. Times, July 21, 1954, at 4, cols. 7-8.
347. N.Y. Times, July 22, 1954, at 22, col. 1.
348. N.Y. Times, July 24, 1954, at 5, col. 1.

ever take place." [349] But these negative reports do not appear to have had a significant impact even on the key personnel of the Times itself, for the main Sunday editorial on July 25 demanded extensive and more effective economic aid for the South and the selection of a free Vietnamese patriot of splendid ability, who must then have strong support from France and the United States, all to one end: defeating the Communists in the national elections in 1956. The editorial stressed the urgency of the situation: "We are obliged to put the hard fact of performance up against the rosy promises of a Communist utopia if the Vietnamese can be expected to vote for freedom." And the reason for this was clear: "If the Communists live up to the Agreements reached there will be a free and supervised election in Vietnam two years hence." [350]

The months after Geneva showed a continuing concern over the 1956 elections and the relative strengths and weaknesses of the two sides. In September, 1954, an article in *America* highlighted the urgent task in the southern zone: to raise living standards, develop political consciousness and to build up a truly independent government through French political backing and United States economic and technical aid within the allotted two-year timespan before elections.[351] In October 1954, Bernard B. Fall urged political reforms and the necessity for the leadership to develop courage enough to stand the test of popular scrutiny; otherwise it was likely that all of Vietnam would become ". . . a very secondary pawn on the USSR's diplomatic checkerboard" in the elections in the offing for 1956.[352] In December, 1954, *The New Republic* predicted only a last faint chance to save the southern zone, requiring radical changes in the internal political line-up and a drastic measure of controlled economic aid prior to the elections, ". . . otherwise 100,000 men will have died in vain, and Communism will be able to record another tremendous victory in Asia." [353] Of those who were to take unequivocal positions on these elections in later years, the majority felt that a political settlement was indeed concluded at Geneva in 1954: Professors Brimmell, Kahin-Lewis, Scigliano, and Young, Senators Fulbright and Morse, and Ambassador Reischauer.[354]

Commentators of more recent vintage have of course not reached unanimity on the possibility of a political settlement being part of

---

349. N.Y. Times, July 25, 1954, § 4, at 1, col. 3.
350. *Id.* at 8, cols. 1-2.
351. Kearney, *Viet Nam After Geneva*, AMERICA, Sept. 11, 1954, at 565-66.
352. B. Fall, *supra* note 83, at 974-75.
353. Jackson, *Viet-Nam: A House Divided*, THE NEW REPUBLIC, Dec. 6, 1954, at 16.
354. J. BRIMMELL, *supra* note 66, at 285; G. KAHIN & J. LEWIS, *supra* note 102, at 47-48, 57; R. SCIGLIANO, SOUTH VIETNAM: NATION UNDER STRESS 13 (1963); K. YOUNG, JR., THE SOUTHEAST ASIA CRISIS 109 (1966); *Vietnam Hearings* at 667 (Fulbright); *Id.* at 457, 502 (Morse); Reischauer, *What Choices Do We Have in Viet-Nam*, LOOK, Sept. 19, 1967, at 24.

—3

the terms at Geneva in 1954. For example, P. Honey felt that the unsigned Final Declaration of the Conference, the only document with any specific provisions on national elections, was a face-saving concession to the North Vietnamese which would prove worthless.[355] Honey quotes Pham Van Dong, the chief Vietminh negotiator at Geneva, as telling "one of my Vietnamese friends", when asked about elections, "You know as well as I do there won't be any elections." [356] Due to the nature of the source, the quote is not confirmed elsewhere; it may have merely reflected substantial Vietminh confidence that the regime in the south would crumble of its own ineffectiveness long before the scheduled elections in 1956.[357]

Professor Hans Morgenthau depicted the Geneva Conference as illustrative of the usual cold-war deadlock; Morgenthau felt the line of military demarcation was also intended as a political boundary as well, and the provision for elections was ". . . a device to hide the incompatibility of the Communist and Western positions, neither of which can admit the domination of all of Vietnam by the other side." [358] Ellen Hammer stated that the foreign powers had no means nor intention of imposing their will on the Vietnamese people,[359] and laid great emphasis on the reservations of the United States and the State of Vietnam.[360]

C. The State of Vietnam

The reservation issued by the State of Vietnam at the end of the Conference was an angry tirade against the other participants at Geneva for ignoring the views of the State of Vietnam and proceeding to a settlement despite her continued protests. The Geneva solution thus had an "Achilles heel" from the very beginning, but the protests of the State of Vietnam had little effect on the expectations created at Geneva, for at that time these protests found no backing from any of the other participants at Geneva, including the United States. The State of Vietnam's conduct at Geneva thus stood only as a warning to the other participants that, if she were able to rally the support of other nations around her prior to mid-1956, she might well seek to avoid the elections. And her conduct throughout the Geneva Conference shows consistency in opposing the activities of the Conference, thus laying out that warning in the clearest terms.

The first stage of the State of Vietnam's warning came on April

---

355. P. HONEY, *supra* note 325, at 5-6.
356. *Id.* at 6.
357. Bernard B. Fall estimated the State of Vietnam's governmental chances of surviving even until the 1956 elections as "poor" and backed the argument that the two-year provision on elections was a face-saver for the West, not for the Vietminh as Honey argues. B. FALL, *supra* note 33, at 76.
358. Morgenthau, *The 1954 Geneva Conference: An Assessment,* A SYMPOSIUM ON AMERICA'S STAKE IN VIETNAM 69 (1956).
359. E. HAMMER, *supra* note 76, at 246.
360. *Id.* at 144, 246-47.

25, before the Conference had even begun to discuss Indo-China. Rumors of partition had already begun to flow around Geneva, and Bao Dai's government moved to squelch any notion of a settlement being negotiated behind its back by the French:

> Viet-Nam would never be prepared to consider the possibility of negotiations in which France, violating the basic principles of the French Union from which her authority is derived, were to negotiate with those who are in rebellion against the Viet-Namese nation or with hostile Powers, thereby disregarding or sacrificing her partner. Whatever may happen, neither the Head of the State nor the Viet-Namese Government will consider themselves bound by decisions which by running counter to national independence and unity would violate the rights of peoples and reward aggression, contrary to the principles of the United Nations Charter and to democratic ideals.[361]

Partition was indignantly rejected by both the State of Vietnam and the Vietminh in their initial proposals to the Conference in early May, and Ngo Dinh Diem took office as Prime Minister in late June with the express hope of saving Vietnam as an independent and unified state. As it became evident in July that Mendes-France was ignoring the views of the State of Vietnam in his desire to reach agreement at Geneva prior to July 20, the State of Vietnam delegation began a series of protests.

On July 17, Tran Van Do, the chief delegate of the State of Vietnam, handed Mendes-France a note officially protesting France's failure to inform the State of Vietnam of the details of the Eden-Mendes-France-Dulles meetings in Paris from July 13-15; the note reiterated the State of Vietnam's objections to partition, and its desire to see the all-Vietnam elections supervised by the United Nations.[362] On July 18, Tran told the Conference in restricted session that the State of Vietnam must reject both the French and Soviet drafts of the final Conference resolution since both were based on partition, a provision totally unacceptable to the State of Vietnam.[363] Even at this late date he announced the intention of his government to present its own peace plan, and reserved the right to ask for a special plenary session at which to do so.[364] The press analyzed these statements as designed solely to increase the State of Vietnam's popularity at home, and doubted that it would refuse to accede to the final Conference agreements. There were several reports that Tran had even told Eden shortly after making the above speech that his government would "consider" any solution reached by the Conference.[365] Yet, in view of the actual power solution in Indo-China,

361. CMND. No. 2834 at 87.
362. N.Y. Times, July 18, 1954, at 3, col. 5.
363. CMND. No. 2834 at 87.
364. N.Y. Times, July 19, 1954, at 1, col. 7.
365. Id. at 3, col. 2.

there was precious little opportunity for the State of Vietnam to act otherwise. Fears were expressed that the State of Vietnam would simply walk out of the Conference, following the example of South Korea;[366] Tran may have concluded, however, that since Mendes-France was determined to reach a solution at Geneva despite the views of the State of Vietnam, there would be greater value in remaining at the Conference and protesting as vigorously as possible in that international forum.

Perhaps indicating the desperateness of its situation, the State of Vietnam actually did circulate its own peace plan to the Conference on July 19. The plan completely rejected the partition concept, calling instead for the regroupment of forces in two small zones, the disarmament of the Vietminh simultaneous with the withdrawal of French troops, and control of all of Vietnam by the United Nations until it deemed order and security sufficiently restored to conduct general elections.[367] It also predicted that the temporary partition being considered would have "disastrous" consequences for the people of Vietnam and for world peace.[368] While the prediction was ignored at Geneva, where conditions appeared favorable for a lasting settlement, it became most prophetic many months later, when the United States came out firmly in support of the Diem government and its refusal to submit to elections. The State of Vietnam proposals of July 19 were "rejected without examination," [369] since the other delegations were within hours of achieving a settlement.

Tran Van Do played out his lonely part at the last session of the Conference on July 21. The Chairman for the day, Anthony Eden, called the roll to obtain the approvals of those seven delegations which had agreed on a settlement. The State of Vietnam had mimeographed a rather lengthy declaration of protest, and Tran rose to declare that the State of Vietnam would support every effort to establish a lasting peace in Vietnam and would not use force to resist the implementing procedures of the Geneva Agreements, ". . . in spite of the objections and reservations that the State of Viet Nam has expressed, especially in its final statement," [370] which he wished to have incorporated in the Final Declaration of the Conference. Eden summarily brushed this request aside, saying the best the Conference could do was to take note of this declaration by the State of Vietnam.[371] Eden asked if there were any objections to such a procedure, and no delegation responded.[372] After this refusal to

366. *Id.* at 2, col. 3.
367. N.Y. Times, July 20, 1954, at 1, col. 6.
368. *Id.*
369. This at least was the situation as announced by Tran Van Do on July 21. Ngo Ton Dat, *supra* note 9, at 466.
370. FURTHER DOCUMENTS RELATING TO THE DISCUSSION OF INDO-CHINA AT THE GENEVA CONFERENCE, CMD. No. 9239, at 7 (1954) [hereinafter cited as CMD. No. 9239].
371. *Id.*
372. *Id.* at 8.

deal with the State of Vietnam's declaration, several delegates made the necessary complimentary remarks about the efforts of the Conference co-chairmen (Eden and Molotov). Eden, in closing, then went through the formality of asking whether anyone had something more to say. Tran rose once again to restate his previous demand that the Conference include the reservations of the State of Vietnam in its Final Declaration. Eden once again brushed this aside, and the Geneva Conference was officially closed.[373] But the very act of closing the last session was thereby tinged with the dissatisfaction registered by the State of Vietnam, especially in light of the content of its reservation: [374] the State of Vietnam protested against the "hasty conclusion" of the agreement by the French and Vietminh alone, and against the fixing of a date of future elections without the agreement of the State of Vietnam; and it reserved "full freedom of action" in looking to the future.[375] On July 22, Diem made a speech in which he described the Geneva Agreements as an "iniquity" against which his government "raised a most solemn protest"; faced with a *fait accompli*, Diem felt that to attempt forcible resistance would only have precipitated a catastrophe and destroyed all chance of one day recreating a free, united Vietnam. He called on his listeners to engage in the difficult struggle which should finally deliver Vietnam from all foreign interference and from all oppression.[376] The statements of Tran Van Do during the last days of Geneva, and the speech of Diem on July 22, provide clear indication that the State of Vietnam would absolutely refuse to implement the Geneva Agreements if it could elicit strong backing for its position before the scheduled elections. Unknown to the delegates at Geneva, for whom the reservation of the weak and divided State of Vietnam had little more than sentimental value, the Geneva Conference had sown the seeds of destruction of the political settlement before the homeward-bound delegates even reached the Geneva airport.

VIII. Post-Outcome Effects

The conduct of the various participants subsequent to the conclusion of an international agreement furnishes an "exceptionally reliable source" of evidence concerning the parties' shared expectations, for such subsequent conduct often demonstrates the parties' continuing consensus as to the content of those agreements, or highlight the lack of any genuine expectations as evidenced by diverging patterns of conduct.[377] The two-year period between the publi-

---

373. *Id.* at 9.
374. The full text of the State of Vietnam reservation appears in Ngo Ton Dat, *supra* note 9, at 466.
375. CMND. No. 2834 at 125.
376. The Times (London), July 23, 1954, at 6, col. 2.
377. M. McDougal, H. Lasswell & J. Miller, *supra* note 12, at 134. For a thorough discussion of the importance of subsequent conduct in treaty interpretation, see *id.* at 132-44.

cation of the Geneva Agreements on July 21, 1954, and the elections then scheduled for July 1956 provides an excellent opportunity to observe the subsequent activities of the various participants at Geneva as they reflect on each participant's expectations as to the holding of those elections. Analysis shows that both the Vietminh and France expected the elections to be held on schedule. France, contrary to her promises to help strengthen the State of Vietnam in preparation for those elections, attempted to establish a subsequent regime in the South and thereby "build a bridge" to the DRV. The State of Vietnam continued its vociferous objection to the Agreements, claiming it was not bound by them and refusing to cooperate on preparations for elections. The United States turned from its period of indecision on Indo-China to economic and technical support of the Diem government, and then, much later, it also began to support Diem's refusal to proceed with elections. Great Britain, the Soviet Union, and Communist China all spoke out in favor of the holding of elections, but failed to enforce these preferences by concrete action; all three had long since turned to other problem areas and all three now denied any effective support to the Vietminh demands that elections be conducted on schedule.

A. The DRV (Vietminh)

The actions of the DRV in the two years after the Agreements were concluded fully establish the truth of Robert Scigliano's remark that "The Vietminh had set heavy store by these elections. . . ." [378] The DRV issued many statements stating its intentions to abide by the terms of the Geneva Agreements and to work hard for the realization of those elections. [379] In due time (January 1, 1955), the DRV suggested the re-establishment of normal relations between the two zones—communications, trade, transportation, postal service, etc.— so that the economic and cultural relations might benefit both sides. [380]

---

378. Scigliano, *South Vietnam: Nation Under Stress*, in *Vietnam Hearings* at 83.
379. Typical of these was a major policy statement on November 5, 1954, by Foreign Minister Pham Van Dong, the chief Vietminh negotiator at Geneva:
    The Government of the Vietnamese Democratic Republic and the Vietnamese people undertake broadly to unite all the patriotic forces with a view scrupulously to implement the armistice agreements, and realize the unification of Vietnam through free and democratic general elections. Vietnam News Agency, Nov. 5, 1954, in FBIS, Nov. 9, 1954, at CCC 10.
380. The proposal was first made by Ho Chi Minh on January 1, 1955. FACTS AND DATES at 17. The DRV underscored its good will in this regard on February 4, 1955, promising to do its best to encourage and support exchanges between the two zones in the economic, cultural, and social fields. FACTS AND DATES at 18. The Diem government rebuffed these overtures, claiming the North would abuse the reestablishment of normal relations by efforts at subversion in the South. E. HAMMER, *supra* note 76, at 165. But as long as elections remained in the offing, the North had no need to resort to subversion, since it expected victory at the polls in 1956, and was attempting to show good faith in 1955-56 in order to facilitate the holding of those elections.

The DRV also reorganized its administrative and political structure to make it more popular at the polls and thus to prepare all of Vietnam for reunification under Communist control. To appeal to nationalist opinion in the south and further enhance the respectability of Communism throughout Asia, Ho Chi Minh at least formally relinquished his tight hold on the DRV policy machine; in September 1955 the offices of President and Premier were separated, with Ho retaining the Presidency and Pham Van Dong assuming the Premiership; two vice-Premierships were also established, thus completing a hierarchical governing structure. At the same time, an extremely broad front organization was established, the Fatherland Front, whose program was based on unifying the country by peaceful means through mutual agreement between the two zones. The DRV proposed the establishment of a single National Assembly through free general elections; the Assembly would then appoint a central coalition government, and an administrative organ invested with broad powers would be set up in both zones. In an attempt to mollify suspicions that the North would dictate policy all the way to the local level, the proposals stressed the fact that each zone would be allowed to issue local laws consistent with the characteristics of that particular region, if not inconsistent with the common laws of the unified state. And the proposals played down any concept of a North-South struggle: it was not a matter of the North or the South "winning" the elections, it was merely a matter of reaching agreement on the unification of Vietnam. Finally, the DRV concluded an important pact with Communist China on July 7, 1955; China would provide substantial economic aid and would also make full technical cooperation available, with Vietnamese students being trained in China and China sending its own technical personnel to Vietnam. These three measures were intended to be ". . . the lures which . . . would bring the whole of Vietnam under Communist control." [381] Throughout the period the DRV avoided any moves which might antagonize public opinion in the South, making reunification more difficult. [382]

The Agreements had called for consultations "between the competent representative authorities of the two zones from July 20, 1955, onwards" to settle the arrangements for the elections. [383] On June 7, 1955, the DRV issued a statement demonstrating its readiness to hold consultations; [384] the tone of the statement was quite argumentative, with the DRV clearly fighting hard to see these political provisions of the Agreements fully implemented. When no positive response resulted, Ho Chi Minh journeyed to Peking and Moscow to seek a public endorsement of the DRV's demands; joint communiques

---

381. J. BRIMMELL, *supra* note 66, at 297-98.
382. P. HONEY, *supra* note 325, at 17.
383. Final Declaration of the Geneva Conference, July 21, 1954, art. 7, in BACKGROUND INFORMATION at 67.
384. CMND. No. 2834 at 101.

in Peking on July 7, 1955, and in Moscow on July 18, 1955, stressed the necessity for strict implementation of the Agreements, and demanded that consultations begin as scheduled on July 20.[385] On July 19, 1955, the DRV by-passed the normal chain of communications and addressed a letter directly to the Prime Minister of the State of Vietnam (Diem), proposing that the South appoint representatives to the consultative conference, to begin the next day.[386]

When all these requests failed to bring about the scheduled consultations, the DRV's Premier, Pham Van Dong, turned to the Co-Chairmen of the Geneva Conference on August 17, 1955, asking them to take all necessary measures to guarantee observance.[387] In response to a request from the Co-Chairmen for comments and suggestions about the political settlement for Vietnam from the Conference members, Pham Van Dong, on February 14, 1956, bitterly assailed the referendum held in the State of Vietnam on October 23, 1955, in which Diem was "elected" over Bao Dai as the new President. Pham Van Dong argued that this election and Diem's subsequent establishment of the "Republic of Vietnam" (RVN) completely contradicted the spirit of the Geneva Agreements, which had laid down a military demarcation line of only temporary nature and provided for general elections to reunify Vietnam.[388] He also urged the summoning of a new Geneva Conference on Indo-China, to include the original participants as well as the three member countries of the International Supervisory Commission; this proposal was also advanced by Communist China (January 25, 1956) and the Soviet Union (February 18, 1956).[389] Eventually, these suggestions produced only a weak response from the Geneva Co-Chairmen, and elections became a dead issue for Vietnam. But the DRV left little doubt of its disappointment; as Ho Chi Minh stated on July 12, 1956, eight days before the elections were to have been held, "Viet Nam is a whole from the north to the south. It must be reunified. It cannot be cut into two separate nations any more than the United States can be cut into two separate nations." [390] And for several years thereafter the DRV continued to suggest periodically that the two zones begin the consultations which would culminate in elections.[391]

B. The Soviet Union and Communist China

During the 1955-56 period, both the Soviet Union and Communist China failed to render any substantial assistance to the DRV in its

---

385. FACTS AND DATES at 24-25.
386. CMND. NO. 2834 at 109.
387. *Id.* at 112-13.
388. *Id.* at 115-16.
389. *Id.* at 117-19.
390. Vietnam News Agency, July 12, 1956, in FBIS, July 13, 1956, at CCC 1.
391. The suggestions were advanced in July of 1957, 1959, and 1960, and in March of 1958; all of these were rebuffed by the South. Devillers, *supra* note 23, at 219.

attempts to reunify Vietnam by general elections; as Philippe Devillers stated it, their support was limited to ". . . kind words, warm gestures of solidarity, and propaganda campaigns." [392] Both states had issued demands for a new Geneva Conference once the political provisions of the 1954 Conference had been jeopardized. Yet the Soviet Union joined with the other Co-Chairman, Great Britain, in issuing an astonishingly weak declaration on May 8, 1956, which ignored all recommendations for a new Conference; instead, the Co-Chairmen strongly urged both sides to make every effort to implement the Geneva Agreements, "invited" both sides to forward their views on the timing of a consultative conference, and registered their belief that the "continued good offices" of France could be valuable.[393] This reply weakened any chance of the elections ever taking place, and the DRV's Communist ally took full part. Douglas Pike has written that the DRV was "sold out" later by its allies, who persuaded the DRV to accept the Geneva Agreements under promises that elections would be held in 1956, then "betrayed" the DRV by refusing to give any substantial backing to their claims.[394] Whether it was indeed a "sell-out" in 1956, or whether the DRV's allies had refused further backing during the conference itself, is one of the greatest unanswered (and currently unanswerable) questions dealing with Geneva in 1954.

The extension of the date for elections to a two-year waiting period came back to haunt the DRV, for the majority of its allies' objectives at Geneva were short-range goals which had long since been attained prior to the 1955-56 period. The Geneva Conference had perhaps avoided a major world conflict in 1954, had brought substantial prestige to Communist China, split the western allies for a considerable period of time, given the Chinese Communists a period of internal peace and consolidation after the Korean War, and had perhaps proven instrumental in the French rejection of EDC. Thus, there was little to gain in furnishing strong support to the DRV in 1955-56. The only long-range Sino-Soviet goal at Geneva, peaceful coexistence, had achieved considerable recognition in the wake of a successful conclusion at the conference table. Strong backing for the DRV on elections might force a resumption of hostilities, and thus work against this objective.

But looking ahead from Geneva in 1954, prosecution of the peaceful coexistence program might not have been expected to interfere with a political settlement of the Vietnam problem. France and the

392. *Id.*
393. CMND. No. 2834 at 97-99.
394. D. PIKE, *supra* note 71, at 52. Bernard Fall supports this assertion, describing the USSR's failure to press more vigorously for elections in 1956 as the greatest DRV disappointment with the USSR. According to Fall, the DRV has been repeatedly "sold out" by the USSR for small tactical reasons of no ultimate benefit even to the USSR. B. FALL, *supra* note 104, at 114-16.

Vietminh controlled the only military forces of any significance in Vietnam, and France clearly sought an end to the conflict. The participants at Geneva might have concluded that France and the Vietminh would be in a position to hold the elections on schedule, thereby avoiding another East-West confrontation over Vietnam in 1956. But by mid-1955, the United States had placed its considerable weight behind the Diem government's refusal to proceed with the elections. By 1956, the Soviet Union and Communist China were deeply engaged in an over-all endeavor to woo the underdeveloped nations under the banner of peaceful coexistence, and this major effort clearly took precedence over the DRV's desires to consolidate its 1954 military victory through elections.[395] The Soviet Union and Communist China may have then shelved their Geneva expectations rather than risk a confrontation with the United States over Vietnam. Other interpretations of the Sino-Soviet actions are also possible—the diplomatic files are obviously unavailable, and the other evidence is speculative at best. But in the last analysis, every participant in the 1954 Geneva Conference secured major benefits under the Agreements except the military winners in Indo-China, the Vietminh.[396]

Anthony Eden mentions another reason why the Communist powers, notably the Soviet Union, were unwilling to furnish strong support for elections in 1956: the DRV might lose.[397] While Ho Chi Minh enjoyed a very substantial popularity throughout Vietnam in 1954, the argument states, the agrarian reforms introduced in the North after 1954 proved extremely unpopular. Revolts sprang up after the July 20, 1956, election deadline, and had to be suppressed. Several newspapers, given the opportunity to speak freely during the "Hundred Flowers" campaign in late fall 1956, criticized the regime severely and had to be suppressed.[398] While most of these events occurred after the election deadline, their origins and growth were clearly distinguishable in advance of that dealine. Thus, as Eden saw it, for the Soviet Union, ". . . whose Government is ever chary of even the slightest electoral risk", there was reason to backpeddle on the election question in mid-1956.[399] Jean Lacouture states that United States Ambassador Reinhardt had at least considered the risks involved in urging the South to proceed with elections, since the North was at lowest ebb and the South's position had clearly improved since the Geneva Conference.[400] For the DRV's allies, the risk of losing the election might well have provided a suitable excuse for refusing strong support to the DRV; with the degree of popularity Ho Chi Minh enjoyed in Vietnam at the time of the Conference in 1954, however, no one foresaw this excuse at the Conference.

395. J. BRIMMELL, *supra* note 66, at 299-300.
396. D. PIKE, *supra* note 71, at 52.
397. A. EDEN, *supra* note 3, at 11.
398. P. HONEY, *supra* note 325, at 13; B. FALL, *supra* note 33, at 97-103.
399. A. EDEN, *supra* note 3, at 11.
400. J. LACOUTURE, *supra* note 67, at 244.

C. France, Great Britain and the United States

The DRV's hopes of reunification were based in considerable part on their faith that the French would implement the political provisions of the Geneva Agreements as well.[401] This became increasingly clearer as the political provisions came more and more into jeopardy; Pham Van Dong told the French on January 1, 1955, that "It was with you, France, that we signed the Geneva Agreements, and it is up to you to see that they are respected." [402] Several days after the Geneva Conference ended, the New York Times correspondent in Vietnam wrote that it remained unclear how much support the Diem government in the South would obtain from the French and Americans. In the next few months, a clear split developed between France and the United States over this question. The French became interested in "building a bridge to the North," in cooperating with the DRV in an attempt to salvage something of French economic interests in both parts of Vietnam after the elections then anticipated for 1956.[403] As part of their "bridge building" plans, the French desired to replace Diem with a more pliable man in the South. To a very definite extent this plan ran counter to the French promises at Geneva to assist in building up the South in preparation for elections. The United States, in contrast to the French plan of playing up to the North, soon came around to the belief that the South could indeed be strengthened and transformed to serve as an anti-Communist bastion.[404] The bitter struggle between these two concepts of Vietnam's future was to last nearly a year, until the Americans won the day and the French elected to withdraw from Vietnam.

Although he felt the United States had expressed no clear policy regarding Vietnam by the end of the Geneva Conference, Bernard B. Fall saw the settlement as a definite advantage, for thereafter the United States might be able to dissociate itself from French interests and policies in Indo-China and develop a strictly American policy: anti-colonialism, national independence, open door trade policies.[405] The first American move of any kind along these lines was probably President Eisenhower's news conference of August 11, 1954, in which he expressed hope for the United States to do something constructive in both Korea and Vietnam: build up economic alliances, raise standards of living, and build a structure that could resist Communist subversion or armed force.[406] The SEATO Treaty was promulgated on September 8, 1954, thus drawing a line against Communist subversion or military force directed against the South.

401. D. PIKE, *supra* note 71, at 74.
402. Introduction to Part Five, VIETNAM: HISTORY, DOCUMENTS AND OPINIONS ON A MAJOR WORLD CRISIS (M. Gettleman ed. 1965), at 160-61.
403. R. SHAPLEN, *supra* note 86, at 118.
404. E. HAMMER, *supra* note 76, at 163.
405. B. FALL, *supra* note 83, at 936-37.
406. N.Y. Times, Aug. 12, 1954, at 2, cols. 4-5.

And American support for the Diem government may have fore-stalled a coup d'etat in mid-September, 1954, by General Hinh, Commander in Chief of Bao Dai's army; it was reported that Hinh was in a strong position with the military and could have pulled off the coup with little difficulty, but that American officials warned him that the United States would then cut off all economic aid.[407] This strong stand discouraged Hinh from proceeding.

The first France-United States confrontation over Vietnam policy occurred in September, 1954, when France sent a special mission to the United States. Although Mendes-France in July had promised support in building up the South, now France sought a secret agree-ment to replace Diem, and thereby improve relations with the North so as to protect French economic and cultural interests in both zones before and after the elections. The United States, on the other hand, wanted to use Diem as a nationalist spearhead of reform, build-ing up an American-trained army to serve as an instrument of pacification in the countryside, followed by a land redistribution pro-gram and other social-economic reforms. These plans stunned the French, who had had little advance warning of any such plans dur-ing the months at Geneva and afterward; nonetheless, they signed a communique promising continued support to Diem.[408]

From this point, however, the roads began to diverge. The French, consistent with their expectations that the North would easily win the elections in 1956, strove to make the best deal they could with the North. Jean Sainteny, the French envoy who had dealt with Ho Chi Minh after the Second World War and who favored a French move to support only the North, returned to Hanoi in the fall of 1954, prepared to sign an agreement for the protection of French interests in the North.[409] The DRV had suggested a continuing eco-nomic partnership with France during the closing days at Geneva, and on November 5, 1954, Pham Van Dong left no doubt that the door remained open:

> The Government of the Vietnamese Democratic Republic has undertaken to establish with France economic and cultural re-lations—upon the principle of equality and mutual benefit—and is ready to settle the question of French interests in Vietnam on the principles mentioned in the letters exchanged at Geneva be-tween the delegation of the Vietnamese Democratic Republic and that of France.[410]

In early December 1954 there was talk of arranging credits and trade representatives between France and the DRV, and the State of Viet-

407. Schmid, *Free Indo-China Fights Against Time*, COMMENTARY, Jan., 1955, at 28.
408. R. SHAPLEN, *supra* note 86, at 118.
409. *Id.* at 97-98.
410. Vietnam News Agency, Nov. 5, 1954, in FBIS, Nov. 9, 1954, at CCC 10.

nam was reported fearful that the French would make a deal with the Vietminh in order to protect their own economic interests.[411] On January 22, 1955, the New York Times reported that the French were actively courting the North, because "They are convinced South Vietnam will be taken over by the Communists next year." The French reasoned that the DRV could not rely on sufficient economic aid from the USSR or Communist China, and would like to build ties with France.[412] This would confirm both Bernard B. Fall's estimate in October 1954 that the DRV would be unable to obtain sufficient goods and materials from the Sino-Soviet bloc, necessitating continued economic relations with France, as well as the French expectations that a political settlement was part of the Geneva bargain.

The United States, on the other hand, now took its first halting steps towards bolstering the Diem regime in the South. On September 29, 1954, the administration announced that both economic and military aid would be extended directly to the three states of Indo-China; there would be no more channeling aid through the French.[413] On October 23, 1954, President Eisenhower wrote his now-famous letter to Diem, voicing grave concern over the future of a country "temporarily divided" and pledging American aid in order to develop a "strong, viable state, capable of resisting attempted subversion or aggression through military means." The letter was phrased in cautious tones, possibly as an indication of the precariousness of Diem's position as Prime Minister and of some uncertainty as to future policy: the United States demanded assurances as to standards of performance by Diem's government, and announced it would "expect" the aid to be met with "needed reforms" in the South.[414] Although both the September 29 announcement and the October 23 letter from the President spoke in terms of "independence", their primary task was simply to consolidate Diem's position in the South and allow his government to survive. The United States took no position at this time on the elections. Presumably, the aid flowing to the Diem government would strengthen its internal position and make it a more worthy opponent at the polls in 1956, a factor which undoubtedly influenced United States planning.

On November 3, 1954, President Eisenhower appointed General Lawton Collins as his personal envoy to the South, to establish security, initiate military training programs, and prepare the way for agrarian reforms.[415] In late November, the United States moved

---

411. Jackson, *Viet-Nam: A House Divided*, THE NEW REPUBLIC, Dec. 6, 1954, at 16.
412. N.Y. Times, Jan. 22, 1955, at 10, col. 5.
413. BACKGROUND INFORMATION at 74-75.
414. *Id.* at 75-76.
415. R. SHAPLEN, *supra* note 86, at 118-19. The text of the Eisenhower appointment is contained in BACKGROUND INFORMATION at 76.

strongly in support of the Diem government. Collins announced in Saigon in mid-November that the United States would give ". . . every possible aid to the Government of Diem and to his Government only;"[416] the statement was clearly aimed at General Hinh, and was followed by American representations made to Bao Dai, who then dismissed Hinh on November 29.[417] By the end of 1954, the United States was firmly committed to assisting Diem in consolidating his government. Assistance in aiding Diem's struggle to avoid the political provisions laid down at Geneva was yet to come, however.

The American-French confrontation over Vietnam policy reached its climax in the early months of 1955. While Diem had established his control over the army, there remained a substantial amount of military power controlled by the sects in the South, all of which were opposed to strong central control from Saigon. The Cao Dai and Hoa Hao were religious sects which promulgated their own local policies and maintained large standing armies; another potent force belonged to the Binh Xuyen, who controlled vice and gambling in the Saigon area (under contract from Bao Dai). In January 1955 Diem closed the Binh Xuyen gambling casinos in Cholon, the Chinese city adjacent to Saigon. While France publicly joined the United States in supporting Diem's attempts to broaden his political base and remove these other sources of power, and announced formal withdrawal of financial support to the sects, there was reason to believe that the French continued to support the sects privately in attempts to remove Diem. The French now envisioned a new coalition for the South, composed of the sect leaders and a number of pro-French politicians. The French still expected elections to be held in 1956 and to be won by the North and estimated that their best chance of maintaining some economic and cultural position in both areas lay in promoting a more malleable administration in the South than the Diem Government had proved to be. The French thus saw a way of using their responsibility for implementing the Agreements in the South to help them "appease" the powers in the North. The entire American program for the South—aid, security, reform—was "obviously antipathetic" to France's plans.[418]

By February 1955 the covert French campaign against Diem had borne abundant fruit, for they were able to convince General Collins, the President's personal envoy, and other United States Embassy personnel that Diem was a "hopeless proposition"; Diem was not an especially likeable or persuasive person, and was in constant conflict with Collins on major policy decisions. Collins went to see President Eisenhower in mid-April, and the President promised to

416. N.Y. Times, Nov. 18, 1954, at 3, col. 4.
417. Crozier, *The Diem Regime in Southern Vietnam*, FAR EASTERN SURVEY, April, 1955, at 51.
418. R. SHAPLEN, *supra* note 86, at 120.

support him in whatever he recommended; this resulted in Collins' demand that Diem be replaced. Only the Dulles brothers, Assistant Secretary of State for the Far East Robertson, and the head of the special Vietnam task force, Kenneth Young, were strongly in favor of Diem, and Young reports that a Presidential decision was probably made that Diem must go. A compromise was worked out, under which Diem would become President of the State of Vietnam, a symbolic nationalist leader with few powers, and Dr. Phan Huy Quat would take over actual political control, probably as Premier. A cable to that effect was actually dispatched on April 28 to the American Embassy in Saigon, according to Robert Shaplen, but arrived after fighting had broken out in Saigon between the Binh Xuyen and Diem's forces. In the midst of the fighting, Bao Dai sent a cable to Diem dressing him down for the bloodletting and ordering him to return to France, most likely to be dismissed in person by Bao Dai. But Diem's forces saved the day, defeating the Binh Xuyen; with this show of strength, the Eisenhower administration made a hasty reassessment of the situation, and ordered its cable sacking Diem to be burned.[419] Diem soon established his control over the other sects, and United States support was thereafter unflagging. This was made very clear on May 6, shortly after the Binh Xuyen defeat, when Washington "strongly reaffirmed" its support of Diem, and disavowed any intention of trying to save Bao Dai as head of the government, for Bao Dai had now ". . . outlived whatever theoretical value he once had."[420]

The American-French confrontation was finally settled at a Conference May 7-11, of the Foreign Ministers of Great Britain, France, and the United States. At first the French and American foreign ministers each suggested that his government abandon its interests in Indo-China so the other could carry out its own policies "as best it could:"[421] the French called Diem an "American puppet," and threatened to withdraw their troops and cancel what other types of assistance they were still providing to the South unless Diem were removed; Secretary Dulles responded by telling the French to go ahead, and at one point he threatened that if the French left the Americans would leave too. At this point, a cable arrived from the chief British representative in Southeast Asia, Malcolm Macdonald, urging that nothing more be done in Vietnam to further confuse the situation.[422] Faced with the growing strength of the Diem government, a strong new American commitment to Diem, and a British plea for a return to normality, the French gave way and agreed to the United States insistence that Diem be supported in the South

---

419. *Id.* at 121-24.
420. N.Y. Times, May 7, 1955, at 1, col. 5. The "theoretical value" undoubtedly refers to Bao Dai's position as recipient of authority to govern from the French, and thus to the legitimacy of his regime.
421. N.Y. Times, May 11, 1955, at 1, col. 4.
422. R. SHAPLEN, *supra* note 86, at 127.

"pending elections." The United States stated its desire that the 1956 all-Vietnam elections under the Geneva Agreements ". . . should be held under genuine freedom," and in turn agreed to get Diem to stop his anti-French propaganda. One New York paper stated that the best way to achieve this would be for Diem to be convinced ". . . that the French are backing him instead of trying to overthrow him."[423] This conference effectively marked the end of any French attempts to replace Diem with a more pliable minister and thereby "build its bridge to the North." The French had already yielded to joint Vietnamese-American pressure on military affairs in February 1955, agreeing to transfer operational command of the military forces in the South to the State of Vietnam and to allow the United States to assume responsibility for the reorganization and training of those forces.[424] Now the French had given way on the political aspects as well, with a pledge to back Diem for at least another year. From this point on, the French showed increased resignation to an American presence in Vietnam, coupled with increasing bitterness over this unexpected change in its future prospects in Southeast Asia. Consequently, the French had far less influence over policy in the South; while they continued to press for elections in 1956, the French military, at Diem's insistence, had fully evacuated the country by April 1956, several months before the elections for which the French, as a "signatory", bore primary responsibility. Foreign Minister Edgar Faure highlighted all these trends in his remarks near the end of this conference, saying that the French decision to back Diem was both difficult for him personally and also unsound politically.[425]

D. The United States and the State of Vietnam

While the question of French versus American involvement in the South was thereby settled in favor of the United States, there remained the question of consultations scheduled to begin July 20, 1955, and the more basic issue of elections scheduled for July, 1956. As proof of their expectations that elections were part of the Geneva bargain, Great Britain and France both maintained throughout the spring and summer of 1955 that Diem should both agree to begin the consultations and also to prepare for all-Vietnam elections.[426] The United States position was both more ambiguous and more flexible; as one writer summed up the situation in April, 1955, the British government desired to observe the Geneva Agreements to the letter regarding the election provisions, and would refuse to extend any aid to the South if it boycotted elections; the same posi-

---

423. N.Y. Times, May 12, 1955, at 1, col. 8.
424. Ngo Ton Dat, *supra* note 9, at 360-61.
425. N.Y. Times, May 11, 1955, at 1, col. 4.
426. For evidence of British and French insistence on elections, see, e.g., G. KAHIN & J. LEWIS, *supra* note 102, at 82; B. S. N. MURTI, VIETNAM DIVIDED 181-85 (1964) ; F. WEINSTEIN, *supra* note 9, at 29-33.

tion was maintained even more staunchly by France, and "the responsibility for the fatal decision would thus rest squarely upon the Americans. . . ."[427]

In March 1955 Homer Bigart reported the United States had as yet taken no position on elections, but that "obviously, the United States is not pouring money into South Viet Nam simply to build up the place for the Communists."[428] However, newspaper reports stated that France's agreement at the foreign ministers' conference to back Diem "pending elections" was purchased at the price of a United States promise not to delay those elections.[429] On June 8, C. L. Sulzberger reported that France, Great Britain, and the United States were of one mind ". . . that the Geneva pledge for all-Vietnam elections must be carried out;" Sulzberger listed this as a concession made by Dulles in exchange for French and British support for Diem.[430] This unanimity began to crack as early as June 28, when Secretary Dulles stated that the United States would favor elections only if "conditions of genuine freedom" were possible.[431]

On June 7, 1955, the DRV had communicated its readiness to hold consultations on the elections. Two days later, the New York Times cited "competent South Vietnamese sources" as stating that the State of Vietnam did not sign the Geneva Agreements and was not legally bound by the accords, that any comment on the election provisions should come from the signatories (France and the Vietminh), and that free elections could hardly be expected in the North.[432] On July 16, Diem replied officially to the DRV request, repeating in essence what had been said the week before.[433] At this time, the Western foreign ministers were in session in Paris in preparation for the 1955 Geneva Summit Conference, and, fearing bitter recriminations from the Soviet Union over Diem's attitude toward the elections, reportedly did their "utmost" to get Diem to change his mind.[434] At the Summit Conference, M. Faure reportedly asked Anthony Eden and President Eisenhower to urge Diem to respect the Geneva Agreement's provisions on elections; both supposedly pledged to do their best, stressing that the State of Vietnam was an independent state and that they could only "point out this matter" to Diem.[435] A Western note was sent to Diem on July 26, provoking considerable confusion as to its content: the newspapers generally stated that the note urged Diem to agree to consultations with the DRV;[436] the State of Vietnam, however, claimed that all

427. Crozier, *supra* note 417, at 55.
428. N.Y. Herald Tribune, Mar. 2, 1955, at 6, col. 6.
429. N.Y. Times, May 14, 1955, at 1, col. 4.
430. N.Y. Times, June 8, 1955, at 28, col. 5.
431. 33 DEP'T STATE BULL. 50 (1955).
432. N.Y. Times, June 9, 1955, at 7, col. 2.
433. CMND. No. 2834 at 107.
434. B. S. N. MURTI, *supra* note 426, at 184.
435. *Id.* at 184-85.
436. *Id.* at 185.

three Western powers sent identical notes expressing "sympathy" for Diem's position.[437] The contents of the note have never been revealed; more important, however, were the next American actions. "A diplomat of one of the nations involved" (probably Great Britain) denied that the notes supported Diem's position, and stated that it wanted the South to go through with elections.[438] The State Department retorted that the United States was in sympathy with Diem's position, but it had pointed out to Diem the wisdom of some sort of consultations with the DRV so that he could not be accused of breaking the accords.[439] And the next day, August 10, Secretary Dulles furnished strong support for the Diem position, stating that Diem was "correct" in denying that the State of Vietnam was bound by the Geneva Agreements, since it had indeed not signed them.[440] Strengthened by at least some United States support for his refusal to hold consultations and proceed to elections, Diem issued a statement on August 12, 1955, in answer to Pham Van Dong's direct request to the State of Vietnam on July 19, that the consultations begin on time; the statement reiterated that the State of Vietnam was not in any way bound by the Geneva Agreements, and continued:

> Serving the cause of true democracy the Viet-Nam Government considers the principle of really free elections to be a peaceful and democratic institution, but the conditions of freedom, of life and of the vote must first be satisfied. Nothing constructive from this point of view will be achieved so long as the Communist regime in the North does not allow each Viet-Namese citizen to exercise democratic liberties and the fundamental rights of man.[441]

Professors Kahin and Lewis feel this statement echoes the remarks Dulles made on June 28, that elections could not be held unless "appropriate conditions" (freedom of choice, etc.) could be assured.[442]

---

437. N.Y. Times, Aug. 9, 1955, at 6, col. 3.
438. *Id.*
439. *Id.*
440. *Id.* at 186; Ngo Ton Dat, *supra* note 9, at 390.
441. CMND. No. 2834 at 109-110. There may be some controversy over the date of this statement. Professors Kahin and Lewis also use 12 August (G. KAHIN & J. LEWIS, *supra* note 102, at 81), yet several other sources use the exact same quote as occurring on August 9: B. S. N. MURTI, *supra* note 426, at 185-86; F. WEINSTEIN, *supra* note 9, at 32; Ngo Ton Dat, *supra* note 9, at 389-90. If August 9 is taken as the date of the Diem government's reply, it would of course not have had the benefit of the Dulles remarks on August 10 that Diem was "correct" in refusing to consider elections since his government had not signed the Geneva Agreements. But Diem had already received the State Department's announcement it was in "sympathy" with his position, and the request that Diem go ahead with the consultations "for form's sake" would not obscure the underlying premise that the United States was no longer demanding that Diem go through with elections as well.
442. G. KAHIN & J. LEWIS, *supra* note 102, at 81.

On August 30, 1955, the Secretary of State again emphasized support for the Diem position, stating, "We certainly agree that conditions are not ripe for free elections." [443] With such backing from the United States, Diem ended all debate about the South agreeing to elections with his statement on September 21, 1955 that ". . . there can be no question of a conference, even less of negotiations" with the DRV.[444] The Diem government continued its opposition to elections or even consultations throughout the months prior to the scheduled date of elections, July, 1956. The United States furnished increasingly stronger support for this position, culminating in a speech on June 1, 1956, by Assistant Secretary of State for the Far East, Walter Robertson, which left no doubt in anyone's mind as to the degree of U.S. support:

> We hope and pray that the partition of Viet-Nam, imposed against the will of the Vietnamese people, will speedily come to an end. For our part we believe in free elections, and we support President Diem fully in his position that if elections are to be held, there must first be conditions which preclude intimidation or coercion of the electorate. Unless such conditions exist there can be no free choice.[445]

Elections for Vietnam in 1956 had truly become a dead letter.

The major weakness of the Geneva Agreements was thus made known to the world. While the State of Vietnam's protests went for naught at Geneva in 1954, and the other states harbored expectations of a political settlement for Vietnam, the Diem government found strong and ample support from the United States prior to the expiration of the waiting period in July, 1956. This had not been foreseen at Geneva, where the United States appeared to make its peace with the Agreements as promulgated. The expectations at Geneva were that the Diem government might well not even survive the two-year period, and that, even if it did, it would be in no position to resist French pressure to go through with the elections. In leaving

---

443. Ngo Ton Dat, *supra* note 9, at 391. It must be acknowledged that the U.S. statements from July through August 1955 on which this U.S. change of position is based each received little attention and comment from the U.S. press. For instance, the New York Times failed to carry a transcript of Secretary Dulles' press conference on August 30, from which the above quote was taken; instead it merely stated that:

> On Viet Nam, Mr. Dulles was pessimistic as to the possibility of free elections. He supported the general position of South Viet Nam's Premier Ngo Dinh Diem. The United States, Mr. Dulles said, does not oppose free elections but doubts whether free electoral conditions can be established in Communist North Viet Nam.

N.Y. Times, Aug. 31, 1955, at 4, col. 3. Thus it is only by taking all of the U.S. statements of this period as a group that the policy change can be detected.

444. The Times (London), Sept. 22, 1955, at 6, col. 5.

445. BACKGROUND INFORMATION at 80.

two of the Geneva participants (the State of Vietnam and the United States) outside the bounds of the agreements, the delegates at Geneva failed to foresee that these two non-assenting participants might bind themselves together in opposition at a much later date. A British editorial on July 21, 1956, the day after the Vietnam elections were to have been held, could find only two assets possessed by the Diem government: Diem's extraordinary obstinacy and single-mindedness, and ". . . staunch political support and bountiful material aid from the Americans. . . ." [446] Under the circumstances, this proved more than enough to block the elections, for, as B. S. N. Murti summarized the dilemma presented to the other participants in the Geneva Conference, ". . . Britain and France were not in a position to press for the fulfilment of the Geneva Agreement, which might mean the overthrow of Diem, in the face of full American support to him." [447]

E. United States-State of Vietnam Legal Position on Elections

1. Free Elections. The argument that the North would never permit really free elections has been advanced by many sides, and plays a central role in the State Department's White Papers.[448] This argument obviously proceeds from the standard western hypothesis that the Communist bloc could never allow "free" elections in its zones, and from the available evidence it does enjoy a certain validity. Unfortunately, the United States and the State of Vietnam, while positing as dogma the assertion that the North would not allow free elections, failed to take advantage of the explicit machinery laid down by the Geneva participants to ensure the elections met the specifications of both sides. Article 7 of the Final Declaration at Geneva provided that consultations "between the competent representative authorities of the two zones" would be held from July 20, 1955, onwards. These consultations, to begin a year before the scheduled elections, would have given the two sides ample opportunity to specify the guarantees necessary to ensure freedom of choice and freedom from recriminations. To this end provision was made in Article 7 for supervision of the elections by an International Supervisory Commission, which had already proved reasonably effective in administering the armistice agreement throughout Vietnam. By refusing to participate even in the consultations, the Diem government demon-

---

446. Editorial, *Vietnam in the Hazard,* THE ECONOMIST, July 21, 1956, at 202.

447. B. S. N. MURTI, *supra* note 426, at 188.

448. Thus the 1966 White Paper asserts "The conditions in North Viet Nam during that period were such as to make impossible any free and meaningful expression of popular will." It claims that executions, terror and torture were commonplace in the North, and finally that "A nationwide election in these circumstances would have been a travesty." Department of State, *The Legality of United States Participation in the Defense of Viet Nam,* 75 YALE L.J. 1085, 1099-1100 (1966).

strated not only its contempt for the Geneva Agreements and the DRV, and its concern for free elections, but also its considerable fear of losing the elections even under ideal conditions.[449]

The readiness of the North to allow truly free elections has received little attention; Arthur Schlesinger, Jr., has claimed that ". . . Ho himself never displayed any interest in permitting free elections on his side of the 17th parallel." [450] The full context is not that simple. The DRV's official statements throughout the 1954-56 period emphasized its readiness to participate in "free elections." Ho Chi Minh himself dispelled any doubt as to the interpretation the DRV placed on the word "free" with two letters published in the official DRV publication Nhan Dan under his well-known pseudonym "C.B.":

> FREE ELECTIONS: All the Vietnamese citizens, male or female above 18 years old, regardless of class, nationality, religion, political affiliation, have the right to participate in the elections, to vote freely for the persons in whom they have confidence.
> FREE CANDIDATURE: All Vietnamese citizens, male or female above 21 years old, also with the above-mentioned non-restriction clauses, have the right to stand for elections.
> FREE CANVASS: All Vietnamese citizens, whether from the North or the South, have the right to canvass freely throughout the country through conference, leaflets, press etc. The Government of the North and the authorities of the South should ensure the liberty and the security for all citizens during their activities for elections.
> METHOD OF VOTING: Totally equal, secret and direct. In short, the Vietnamese people and the Government of the Democratic Republic of Vietnam shall ensure complete freedom and democracy to the nation-wide elections (as provided in the Geneva Agreement).[451]

Even after the deadline for elections had passed, and it was clear the West would not agree to elections at any time in the future on the basis of the Geneva Agreements, the North in its many requests for the beginning of consultations concerning elections continued its offer to negotiate on the basis of "free general elections by secret ballot." [452]

It is difficult to determine whether free elections would have been possible in the North in 1956. There is evidence of repression in the North during 1955-56, and the Nghe An uprisings of late 1956 required the use of troops. A diplomat who was responsible for the formulation of Canadian policy in the International Control Com-

449. *See* G. KAHIN & J. LEWIS, *supra* note 102, at 81-83.
450. A. SCHLESINGER, JR., *supra* note 126, at 15.
451. B. S. N. MURTI, *supra* note 426, at 187-88.
452. Devillers, *supra* note 23, at 219.

mission felt that the North in 1956 represented a "Communist state in its iron phase," and dispels any thought of free elections:

> During my visit to Vietnam in 1955 the question of the elections was one of my major concerns. In Hanoi with the barbed wire still in the boulevards, the curfew and the iron discipline, free elections seemed about the last thing one could contemplate.[453]

But by failing to prod Diem into entering consultations with the North in 1955, the United States lost a considerable opportunity to test the sincerity of Ho Chi Minh's statements on the North's readiness to hold elections. And the same Canadian diplomat argues persuasively that the failure of the West to begin consultations in 1955, as had been specified in the Geneva Agreements, also had a costly effect on world public opinion.[454]

2. Not Bound by Geneva Agreements.

The second argument advanced by the Diem government and the United States in opposing elections was that the State of Vietnam had not signed the Geneva Agreements, and was therefore not bound by them.[455] The DRV countered with the assertion that the State of Vietnam was nevertheless bound by the "successor" clause, Article 27 of the signed Agreement on the Cessation of Hostilities in Viet-Nam, and found considerable support for its position among the neutrals, most notably Prime Minister Nehru of India.[456] While the State of Vietnam was probably not independent of France as of the end of the Geneva Conference,[457] it can nevertheless present several arguments against its being bound by any successor clause.

First, since the Treaty of Independence with France was never

---

453. Holmes, *supra* note 301, at 478.
454. *Id.*
455. The 1966 State Department White Paper claims there is "considerable question" as to whether the State of Vietnam was bound by the Geneva Agreements, since it did not sign them. Department of State, *supra* note 448, at 1099.
456. An aide-memoire from the Government of India to the Co-Chairmen of the Geneva Conference on June 14, 1955, stressed the fact that the French Union had transferred their sovereign authority in the southern zone to the State of Vietnam, and therefore the representative authorities in each zone were now the DRV in the north and, by virtue of article 27, the State of Vietnam in the south. CMND. No. 2834 at 104. On July 19, 1955, Prime Minister Nehru himself spoke forth: "Being a successor of France which signed the pact, the South Viet-Nam Government is bound by the Geneva Agreements. At Geneva in 1954, France represented South Viet-Nam. It would be impossible if all successor governments deny the agreement signed by their predecessors." FACTS AND DATES at 26. And on February 29, 1956, Nehru invoked a principle familiar in the law of contracts: "The major difficulty for the holding of elections is that Mr. Diem does not accept the Geneva Agreements and he does not consider himself bound by them, although he accepts the benefits afforded by those agreements." *Id.* at 53.
457. See the discussion *infra* at § V (D) (2).

signed nor ratified, the devolution clause binding the State of Vietnam to carry out prior agreements contracted by France in its name is invalid and of no effect. France seemingly regarded the devolution clauses as necessary parts of the turnover of responsibility to its former colonies during the mid-1950s, for during this same period it included them in independence treaties with Tunisia (June 3, 1955) and Morocco (May 28, 1956).[458] The necessity for such a devolution clause in ensuring continuity of obligation between the former colonial power and its newly independent colonies remains an unsettled and highly fluid concept in the law of succession at this time. Where there is a valid devolution clause, the United Nations Secretary General, as depositary for multilateral conventions, has a set policy of presuming continuity.[459] There is no set policy where a devolution clause is lacking, but the policy of the United States Department of State argues against continuity of obligation in such cases: where there is a valid devolution agreement, the Department of State's publication "U.S. Treaties in Force" lists all pre-independence treaties next to the name of the newly-independent state; where there is no such agreement, the pre-independence treaties are not listed.[460]

The second line of argument stems from the degree of attention paid by France, in concluding treaties in the name of the "Associated States of Indo-China," to the needs and desires of these entities. The Legal Committee of the French Union filed an Information on April 13, 1950, dealing with the validity, with respect to the Associated States, of international treaties concluded by France before recognizing the independence of these states. The information stressed the continuity of obligation: "Treaties regularly concluded under the previous regime and which were hitherto applicable to these States continued to bind them as a matter of law despite subsequent changes." But, to alleviate any hardship imposed on these states by treaties concluded by France, the Legal Committee emphasized two means of disengaging from these obligations. First was the freedom of the Associated States to ". . . utilize on their own account the faculties of denunciation which have been inserted in previous treaties."[461] The Geneva Agreements contained no such denunciation provision; rather, they attempted to chain the three Associated States, Laos, Cambodia and the State of Vietnam, in-

---

458. Lauterpacht, *The Contemporary Practice of the United Kingdom in the Field of International Law—Survey and Comment*, VI, 7 INT'L & COMP. L. Q. 525 (1958). It is readily admitted, however, that French practice in later years does not follow this pattern: the French independence agreements with Algeria and the other French territories in Africa do not contain devolution agreements. Committee on State Succession, *supra* note 253, at 191.

459. Committee on State Succession, *supra* note 253, at 192.

460. *Id.*

461. *Id.* at 168-69.

flexibly to the will of France. Second was their right to invoke the principle of *rebus sic stantibus,* based upon changes in their constitution and in their relations with foreign powers, as a defense in "certain cases" to demands for performance.[462] The operation of this principle would be limited to the customary conditions which international law imposes on its exercise.

Assuming neither of these legal means are available for disengagement, the conclusions of the Legal Committee in favor of continuity of obligation would nevertheless be supportable, according to R. De Muralt, ". . . since Indochina's position was taken into consideration before a treaty was made applicable to her. . . ."[463] In the Geneva Agreements, however, France took no consideration of the desires of the State of Vietnam, and signed the armistice agreement containing a "successor" clause over the State of Vietnam's extremely strong protest. Mention has already been made of French characterization of the Geneva Conference as a "stock clearance sale"; obviously France was trying to save whatever she could for herself, and had little regard to the wishes of her very junior partner, the State of Vietnam.

The third argument focuses on the delegation of military powers from the State of Vietnam to the Commander-in-Chief of the French Union under the Elysée Agreement of March 8, 1949, and the military Conventions of Application of December 30, 1949 and December 8, 1950.[464] These agreements placed the indigenous Vietnamese armed forces under the control of the Commander-in-Chief of the French Union forces. The Vietnamese units then became functioning parts of the French Expeditionary Corps, and were thereafter commanded by the Commander-in-Chief of the French Union forces under the delegation of military powers from Chief of State Bao Dai. This delegation of power was never revoked by the State of Vietnam, and a representative of the Commander-in-Chief of the French Union forces in Indo-China signed the armistice agreements at Geneva, including the phrase "pending the general elections which will bring about the unification of Viet-Nam. . . ." It is highly questionable whether a military representative could bind the State of Vietnam to implement political provisions under authority derived from a purely military delegation of powers. While the delegation of powers would suffice in the case of military provisions such as the armistice agreements, most of which were indeed implemented by the State of Vietnam, the political provisions may well have exceeded traditional lines of military competence. The specific provisions on elections were actually contained in the Final Declaration, which was unsigned. Since the military representative had nothing to do with that Final Declaration, it would be difficult for France

---

462. *Id.*
463. R. DE MURALT, THE PROBLEM OF STATE SUCCESSION 130 (1954).
464. *See* Ngo Ton Dat, *supra* note 9, at 306-07.

to argue that the delegation of military powers stretched to cover France's verbal assent to the Final Declaration. Some have argued that the delegation of military powers bound the State of Vietnam because it was never revoked;[465] in view of the extensive efforts made by the State of Vietnam at Geneva to indicate dissatisfaction with the Agreements, the military representatives of the French Union Command clearly understood that the State of Vietnam was extremely unwilling to comply with any such political arrangements. To hinge the obligations of the State of Vietnam on the French military representative's signature in the absence of any formal revocation of military powers by the State of Vietnam, in view of the virulent protests of that government, seems to ignore the actual expectations of those who participated in the ceremony of signing the documents.

Finally, the mere presence of the State of Vietnam's delegation at Geneva, as one of the nine participants, argues in favor of its having the final say as to its destiny. During the final session of the Conference, when Anthony Eden was polling the delegations on their willingness to accede to the Final Declaration, he called on "France" and the "State of Vietnam" separately. France answered only in response to her name, and gave no indication of her intent to bind the State of Vietnam as well. Indications were that Eden, who had been a close observer of the last days' negotiations, regarded the State of Vietnam and France as separate entities, at least for the purpose of acceding to the Final Declaration of the Conference. This, of course, the State of Vietnam failed to do.

The simple answer to all these arguments, from a *realpolitik* standpoint, is that none of them influenced the expectations of the participants at Geneva. There is no indication that any of these problems on succession were actively discussed at Geneva. Since both its legal authority to act and also its physical control were very limited, the State of Vietnam was summarily ignored in the last days of the Conference. To the other delegates at Geneva, the State of Vietnam was an anomaly: created by the French to provide a nationalist alternative to the Vietminh, operating under severe French restrictions and through ministers chosen with French approval, it had totally failed to win popular support in Vietnam away from Ho Chi Minh. Few of the delegates at Geneva could envision any sort of strong United States commitment to that government, and even fewer expected Diem to remain in power long enough to resist the political settlement set forth at Geneva.

IX. POLICING

In this nuclear age, where even slight miscalculations in policy may involve extreme consequences, it is vital that the international community restrict itself to peaceful methods of change. This prin-

---

465. *Id.* at 307-08.

ciple of a "minimum world order" has been enshrined in Article 2(4) of the United Nations Charter, which calls on its members to refrain from force or the threat of force as an instrument of change. The operation of "policing" involves analysis of international agreements for their compatibility with the use of peaceful methods of change. To the extent that such agreements sanction the use of coercion, such provisions should be rejected as incompatible with the standards of a minimum world order.

The one area of the Geneva Agreements which might contradict the fundamental principle of minimum world order is Article 7 of the Final Declaration:

> The Conference declares that, so far as Viet-Nam is concerned, the settlement of political problems, effected on the basis of respect for the principles of independence, unity, and territorial integrity, shall permit the Viet-Namese people to enjoy the fundamental freedoms, guaranteed by democratic institutions established as a result of free general elections by secret ballot. In order to ensure that sufficient progress in the restoration of peace has been made, and that all the necessary conditions obtain for free expression of the national will, general elections shall be held in July 1956, under the supervision of an international commission composed of representatives of the Member States of the International Supervisory Commission. . . .[466]

There have been two major interpretations of these provisions. The State of Vietnam and the United States have steadfastly maintained that there could be no elections until conditions exist in Vietnam which preclude coercion of the voters. On the other hand, the American left argues that the elections were themselves designed to ensure the existence of necessary conditions for free expression of the national will, and there is therefore no basis for assuming these conditions had to precede the election.[467] Under this analysis the fundamental freedoms and democratic institutions were to be established only through a unified Vietnam emerging from the general elections.[468] If the pattern of negotiations at Geneva in the month of July 1954 is analyzed, both these hypotheses give way to a third, namely that the first part of the sentence specifying elections for July 1956 merely explains why it was necessary to delay the elections for such a lengthy period.

At Geneva, the Vietminh originally insisted on general elections within six months of the armistice date, whereas the French attempted to delay the fixing of a date for elections to an indefinite future. The French argued strongly that conditions within Vietnam would still be chaotic six months after the armistice went into effect,

---

466. BACKGROUND INFORMATION at 67.
467. See, e.g., F. WEINSTEIN, supra note 9, at 11.
468. See, e.g., G. KAHIN & J. LEWIS, supra note 102, at 52.

precluding any assurance of freedom of choice for the voters. The principal French objections to early elections were thereby framed in terms of absence of conditions for a free and fair election. As a result of intense bargaining the election date was pushed back to one year, then 18 months, and finally two years, which the French stated would be sufficient time to bring order to the country and ensure sufficient time for consultations between the two sides to hammer out specific provisions to cover the elections. The date for elections was fixed most firmly at July 1956, with an explanation inserted as to why two years must first pass: to ensure sufficient progress in restoring the peace, and prepare all necessary conditions for a free election. There is no indication whatever in the Agreements that the election date could slide further into the future. By providing for consultations between the representatives of the two zones, and for supervision of the elections by an international commission, the two sides expected to provide the type of elections specified: free general elections by secret ballot.

To the extent that the necessity for proceeding with elections on that fixed and firm election date might fail to account for the absence of some or all conditions for ensuring freedom of choice (deadlock during the consultations, hindrance of the supervisory commission by one zone or both, etc.), the Geneva Agreements failed to measure up to the standards of minimum world order. This principle would demand that, consistent with the fundamental policy of rejecting coercive methods, each individual should be free to register his own choice of a government and make it count; this individual might be courted by persuasion during an electoral campaign, but not forced to abandon the dictates of his own beliefs and preferences by external force. The principle of minimum world order would therefore demand that elections be held under full freedom of choice, regardless of the timing.

Fortunately, the debate over elections followed these lines. The provisions of the Agreements notwithstanding, the DRV consistently spoke in terms of free elections, as seen above, and elaborated these statements in specifications which truly appeared to envision a free election under western democratic procedures. Thus, the conduct of the parties would itself appear to have patched up any deficiencies in the Agreements, as related to minimum world order, and makes it all the more regrettable that the West failed to at least proceed with the consultations as scheduled in July 1955 to further sound out the DRV intentions on elections. Their failure to do so contradicts the expectations of the participants at Geneva in 1954.

X. SUMMARY

The political settlement for Vietnam, envisioned at Geneva in 1954, has failed completely. Many factors must share the responsibility for this failure. The Soviet Union and Communist China failed to back up the promises they must have made to the DRV in 1954 with strong support in 1955-56, when the political provisions became jeopardized. Although the French had indicated a desire to build up the South prior to elections, they soon began trying to undercut the South and to "build a bridge" to the North. The French failed to provide strong opposition to United States backing of Diem's refusal to proceed with consultations and elections, and the French themselves withdrew from Vietnam at Diem's insistence prior to the scheduled date of the elections for which the French bore primary responsibility under the Agreements. But the major share of the responsibility for the failure of the political settlement must be shouldered by the United States, which swung around from an equivocal position at Geneva, or possibly a tacit approval of the Agreements, to strong economic support of the Diem government by October-November, 1954, and finally to strong political support during the summer of 1955 for Diem's refusal to proceed with consultations and elections.

While the military and political conditions of the DRV and NLF will ultimately determine their willingness to accept a negotiated solution, the effects of the failure of the 1954 Geneva Conference will at least cut in the opposite direction. For the DRV, the 1954 negotiations, joined with the failure of similar negotiations with the French alone in 1946,[469] provided a double-dose of negative experience at the bargaining table. In the words of Arthur Schlesinger, Jr., Ho Chi Minh has had a trying time:

> He has twice in the past entered into negotiations with the west —in 1946-47 and again in 1954. Each time, in his view, he was cheated at the negotiating table of the gains he thought he had

---

469. The French negotiations with the Vietminh in early 1946 go far beyond the scope of this review and can only be briefly summarized. An agreement between the French and Vietminh of March 6, 1946, had recognized the independence of Vietnam under Ho Chi Minh. While supplementary accords were being worked out in France, the French High Commissioner for Vietnam took various steps in Vietnam to circumvent Ho Chi Minh's government and establish a separate Indo-China federation. Due to the weakness of the French government at this time, the High Commissioner proceeded without opposition from Paris to convene a conference of the Indo-Chinese states, excluding the Vietminh. Faced with the inability of the French government to control its man in Vietnam, the Vietminh walked out of the discussions in France. The situation deteriorated to open warfare between France and the Vietminh prior to the end of 1946. D. PIKE, *supra* note 71, at 29-30. At Geneva in 1954 the initial speech by the Vietminh delegate, Pham Van Dong, on May 10 accused France of violating the treaty of 1946 because it wanted to ". . . wage war for the reconquest of our country . . . ." CMD. No. 9186 at 120. For the text of the 1946 treaty, see VIETNAM: HISTORY, DOCUMENTS AND OPINIONS ON A MAJOR WORLD CRISIS (M. Gettleman ed. 1965) at 61.

made in the battlefield. He no doubt feels, like Will Rogers, that he has won every war and lost every conference.[470]

The activity of the West in avoiding the political provisions of the 1954 Agreements may have run contrary to the expectations of the participants in the negotiations at Geneva, but the issues of responsibility for the resumption of hostilities several years later and intervention by the United States are beyond the scope of this review. However, the debate on intervention and permissible use of force, conducted in great detail elsewhere,[471] cannot be disregarded by anyone attempting to reach a full understanding of the origins and legality of the conflict in Vietnam. The remainder of this review concerns itself with questions more suited to the scope of the evidence already presented, discussing the lessons learned from the 1954 negotiations and their possible application to any future negotiations on Vietnam.

XI. CURRENT IMPLICATIONS

The timing of any negotiations on Vietnam might be of critical importance, in view of previous Communist success in fashioning a deadlock at the conference table and attempting thereby to influence the political situation of their opponents.[472] If negotiations should, however, become the accepted mode of settlement for Vietnam, strong

---

470. A SCHLESINGER, JR., *supra* note 126, at 105. Douglas Pike reports a bias against a negotiated settlement in 1965-66 among cadres of the NLF. These cadres regarded the 1954 Agreements and the subsequent failure of the DRV's Communist allies to vigorously support its demands for elections in 1956 with "undiminished bitterness," and feared a "second sellout" if a negotiated settlement were again attempted. D. PIKE, *supra* note 71, at 52.

471. The United States Government's position on the use of force in Vietnam is contained in the 1966 State Department White Paper. Department of State, *supra* note 448. For the law review debates on the legality of United States intervention, see Alford, *The Legality of American Military Involvement in Viet Nam: A Broader Perspective*, 75 YALE L.J. 1109 (1966); Falk, *International Law and the United States Role in the Viet Nam War*, 75 YALE L.J. 1122 (1966); Falk, *International Law and the United States Role in Viet Nam: A Response to Professor Moore*, 76 YALE L.J. 1095 (1967); Moore, *Lawfulness of Military Assistance to the Republic of Viet-Nam*, 61 AM. J. INT'L L. 1 (1967); Moore, *International Law and the United States Role in Viet Nam: A Reply*, 76 YALE L.J. 1051 (1967); Moore & Underwood, *The Lawfulness of United States Assistance to the Republic of Viet Nam*, 5 DUQUESNE L. REV. 235 (1967); Wright, *Legal Aspects of the Viet-Nam Situation*, 60 AM. J. INT'L L. 750 (1966). Many of these articles will be contained in an anthology entitled the "Princeton Reader," to be published in early 1968 under the auspices of the Committee on Civil War and Intervention of the American Society of International Law.

472. At the 1954 Geneva Conference, initial policy discussions soon produced a Communist deadlock with the delegation of the Laniel Government of France. The USSR's Molotov used the Conference as a platform for a public denouncement of the Laniel Government for its "lack of interest" in a peaceful settlement in Indo-China. The French National Assembly immediately produced such a shaky vote of confidence that Laniel resigned.

elements on both sides of the conflict have expressed a preference for the Geneva Conference's machinery as a procedural framework.[473] Use of this machinery would offer the added advantage of utilizing a considerable amount of experience concerning the strengths and weaknesses of the 1954 Conference and its Agreements, in both procedural format and substantive content.

A. Procedural Format

1. *Representation.* The participants in any new Conference on Vietnam should include those with major forces in the field as well as those in a position to subsequently destroy an unacceptable political solution. Participants in the 1954 Conference included all the potential entries in both categories; the Conference failed for other reasons. Representation in any new Conference should include not only several of the participants in the 1954 Geneva Conference (the USSR, Communist China, the DRV [the North], the RVN [the South], and the United States), but should also include some sort of participation by the NLF.[474] The control and political orientation of the NLF is highly disputed, but both the Secretary General of the United Nations [475] and Communist China [476] desire full NLF participation, and the United States in early November 1967 abandoned its total opposition to all forms of NLF participation.[477] Full representation for the NLF at the Conference would increase its prestige considerably, as in the case of Communist China at Geneva in 1954. Since there is a considerable issue as to the orientation of the NLF, full NLF participation should be looked on as a major concession, calling for major concessions by the other side; in the alternative, lesser forms of participation by the NLF might be ex-

---

473. In early September, 1967, the United States sounded out the United Nations delegates to determine whether there was any new interest in a "Geneva-type conference" on Vietnam. Washington Post, Sept. 8, 1967, at A-1, col. 5. The Soviet Union rejected any United Nations approach and emphasized the problem of Vietnam ". . . can only be considered within the framework of the Geneva Agreement which provides the appropriate machinery." *Id.* at A-13, cols. 3-4.

474. The National Liberation Front was established in South Vietnam toward the end of 1960. Its mission was to lead the total campaign against the established government of the South: political, economic, military, etc. The NLF's military forces are popularly known as the Viet Cong.

475. The Secretary General's early 1967 peace proposals included representation for both RVN and NLF in any negotiations. Washington Post, Mar. 29, 1967, at A-14, col. 4.

476. D. PIKE, *supra* note 71, at 338.

477. Both United Nations Ambassador Goldberg's testimony before the Senate Foreign Relations Committee on November 2, 1967, and a subsequent State Department release, indicated considerable openness to NLF participation in any deliberations on Vietnam. If a Geneva-type Conference were called, the United States would ". . . accept the judgment of the members of the conference" as to NLF participation. Washington Post, Nov. 4, 1967, at A-14, col. 4.

plored. But since the NLF might be able to negate a solution unacceptable to it, it is of paramount importance that its view be ascertained in some way at the conference table. Despite the Soviet Union's readiness to exclude Communist China from any negotiations on Vietnam,[478] similar reasoning demands Communist China's participation as well, if at all feasible.

2. Participation. The delegation of the State of Vietnam was ignored at the 1954 Conference, and a considerable amount of ill will arose in this group even before the Agreements had been signed. A similar situation could arise in any future negotiations with respect to either the NLF, with the other delegations assuming that Hanoi possessed effective control of the NLF's policy machinery, or the RVN, with the other delegations assuming it would collapse without American aid (a situation analogous to that of the State of Vietnam *vis-à-vis* France in 1954). Since either NLF or RVN might be able to circumvent a settlement imposed without its consent, all points of view must be fully considered in the negotiations. No delegation should be left adrift at the end of the Conference.

3. Truce Arrangements. There was no standstill truce during the 1954 negotiations, and the Vietminh skillfully employed its military forces to influence those negotiations. The Conference opened the day after the French military disaster at Dien Bien Phu, and Vietminh military activity during the negotiations made the French military position increasingly more untenable. Ultimately the French were forced to make extensive troop withdrawals to a smaller defensive perimeter, thereby diminishing their bargaining position. Secretary General U Thant's early 1967 peace proposals make provision for a general standstill truce in Vietnam during negotiations.[479] This has been endorsed by the United States, but in view of past experience, Communist approval seems doubtful.

B. *Substantive Content*

1. Enforcement Machinery. The 1954 Conference established no residual machinery among the delegations to the Conference to settle the inevitable disputes during the implementation phase. The delegates evidently relied on the good will of the French and Vietminh, and their power positions in Southeast Asia, as a means of enforcement. The International Supervisory Commission had no police powers, and could only report violations to the original Conference members, who were in turn obliged only to "study such measures as may prove necessary" [480] to carry out the agreements. By default,

---

478. Soviet Premier Kosygin told industrialist Cyrus Eaton on June 30, 1967, that Communist China could be bypassed in any agreement to settle the Vietnam problem. Eaton states that Kosygin was "very positive" about this. Washington Post, July 14, 1967, at A-8, col. 1.

479. Washington Post, Mar. 29, 1967, at A-1, col. 7.

480. Final Declaration of the Geneva Conference, July 21, 1954, § 13, in BACKGROUND INFORMATION at 68.

the Conference Co-Chairmen (Britain and the Soviet Union) became the clearing house for reports, suggestions and entreaties.

The enforcement machinery of any future settlement must be more clearly defined and involve greatly strengthened powers. Various possibilities for such enforcement machinery deserve exhaustive study by scholar and statesman alike. Anthony Eden, a Co-Chairman of the 1954 negotiations, is one of very few who have written on the subject to date. Eden feels that all Conference delegations should guarantee the final settlement, in the form of a joint and several guarantee which would allow the guarantors to act "in certain conditions" without waiting for unanimity. Eden also recommends an international supervisory force, but feels its powers must be considerably expanded.[481] Other methods and proposals must also be developed and considered, with the objective of elaborating that type of enforcement machinery which might offer promise of successfully implementing a firm and lasting settlement.

2. Humanitarian Concerns. After the 1954 Armistice went into effect, there were many reports of reprisals by both sides against opponents who fell into the other sides's hands. Since Vietnamese have been fighting Vietnamese in increasingly greater numbers since then, and since even the NLF policy statement of late 1967 repeatedly asserts a desire to "severely punish" those ultimately categorized as "agents" of the United States,[482] future armistice provisions simply must contain very strong measures for preventing reprisals. This will undoubtedly require a greater number of supervisory commission personnel, improved methods of reporting, and a capability for the commission to act immediately to prevent further incidents. Provision should also be made for immediate repatriation of all prisners of war; if some desire to remain behind, all effort must be made to ensure that the choice was made willingly.

Finally, the many years of conflict in Vietnam have ravaged the land from end to end. Much of the industrial potential has been destroyed, communications have been severely affected, and both zones are economically unstable at this time. As a gesture of good will, the participants in negotiations should discuss and hopefully implement measures to restore Vietnam. This could include both direct financial

---

481. A. EDEN, *supra* note 3, at 32. John W. Holmes, who was responsible for Canadian policy in the International Supervisory Commission from 1954-60 in his position as Assistant Under Secretary of State for External Affairs, feels that any new agreement on Vietnam would necessarily provide for some sort of supervisory body. Based on his prior experience, Holmes felt it might well be much larger, and similar to a "peace force" on the order of Cyprus or the Middle East. Holmes, *supra* note 301, at 473-74.

482. The NLF policy statement, circulated to United Nations delegates on December 14, 1967, mentions a desire to punish the "die-hard agents" of the United States (presumably to include large numbers of Vietnamese) in no less than three of its fourteen points. See N.Y. Times, Dec. 15, 1967, at 16, cols. 2, 5, and 8.

grant to both sides, and, as recommended by President Johnson in his Johns Hopkins speech of April 1965,[483] joint cooperation in finally undertaking the much-heralded but little-implemented Lower Mekong Basin development project.[484]

483. BACKGROUND INFORMATION at 208-09.
484. For a general discussion of the proposed Lower Mekong project and its great potential, see White, *Viet-Nam—The Fourth Course*, THE VIET-NAM READER 351 (M. Raskin & B. Fall eds. 1965).

—4

Address at DePauw University
October 12, 1968

MC GEORGE BUNDY

JOHN MCNAUGHTON and I lived next door in Cambridge for many years, and we worked together for five years more in Washington. He was a good man to have beside you in a tight spot. He proved it once to a small boy of ours who caught his head between the rungs of a chair—John eased him out—and he proved it many times to all of us in Washington. He was cool under pressure; clear in thought and firm in decision. He loved law; he loved the service of his country; he cared effectively for what was good and right. In a short life he did many good things, and since we have lost him and Sally and their son Ted we must take the comfort we can in what they were. No reminder could be more fitting than this memorial convocation. The McNaughtons were unusually direct and easy with friends of all ages; they were a living denial of any generation gap. So a meeting of this sort fits the way they lived themselves, and it is an honor to have a part in it.

The topic assigned to me today is a big one—"how to build a greater America." I think John McNaughton would have smiled at it. He had the lawyer's taste for careful statement both of ends and means, and I think he might have said to me that I had let myself be mousetrapped in accepting such a large assignment. So I have asked myself what he would have done if he had been caught this way. And my guess is that his mind would have turned at once to the hardest immediate problem before anyone who confronts the question of building a better society here at home—the question of the war in Vietnam. He might or might not have decided to speak about it, and I do not intend in any way to hold him accountable for the views I myself intend to present, but I do think he would have agreed that there is a certain lack of realism in the fall of 1968 in describing any vision of the next years in this country without beginning from the hardest single present question of our public affairs. Until the present burden of Vietnam is at least partly lifted from our society, it will not be easy—it may not even be possible—to move forward effectively with other great national tasks. This has not always been my view, but it seems to me wholly clear now that at its current level of effort and cost the war cannot be allowed to continue for long. Its penalties upon us all are much too great.

But it is not enough to say that the burden must be lifted. The real question—the McNaughton question if you will—is how to go about it.

Decisive change in the war can come in only three ways—by imposing a military solution, by reaching agreement with our adversaries, or by a self-imposed decision to change our own level of effort. My own view is first, that we cannot expect a military solution, second, that we should seek agreement but be prepared for the strong chance that we may not get it, and third, that with or without such agreement we should plan and execute a gradual but substantial reduction in the level of our own military effort there. I also believe that to plan and to execute such a policy will place upon our government heavier requirements of control and self-discipline than any it has faced for many years—with a single two-week exception of the Cuban missile crisis. Because the subject is so difficult and its analysis so demanding, I want to frame my own remarks in terms of the problem of policy-making as it may present itself in 1969. As a private citizen, I have no desire to play the role of second-guesser on the present efforts of the President and his negotiators in Paris. All of us must hope that there will be progress in these efforts between now and January, just as we should also hope for progress on the ground in South Vietnam. If important corners can be turned in either place within the next three months, then certainly the prospects for a greater America will be brightened. But it is reasonable, in dealing with a problem so very large and painful, not to assume it away. It is prudent for all of us to face the probability that in its main outlines this problem will still be with us in 1969. At the very least, we cannot assume the opposite.

I also wish to separate this discussion from partisan politics. A memorial meeting is no place for a partisan speech. Vietnam is a necessary and proper part of the political campaign, and all of us as voters must ask ourselves about each candidate as a man who will have to place this problem first on his agenda if he wins. But my purpose today is not to shed either light or heat on that problem of choice, but rather to take the problem as one of policy-making for any administration next year.

So it is in the context of the decisions of government in 1969 that I would offer the argument that follows. The first premise of this argument is simple and strong: this war cannot continue at its present level of cost and sacrifice, not only because of what it means in Southeast Asia, but still more because of what it means in the United States. It is not right for Asia that it should go on as it is going, and the people of our own country simply will not support the current level of cost and sacrifice for another period of years.

Just as we have been divided and confused about its causes and its purposes, so now we are divided and confused about the ways and means of stopping it. And it is just this hard question of ways and means that needs more thought than it has had. But the first and essential point is that such thought should be addressed to the right goal, and the right goal now is to lift the burden of this war as we now know it. On this necessity we are not divided. It is now plainly unacceptable that we should continue with annual costs of $30 billion and an annual rate of sacrifice of more than 10,000 American lives. It is equally wrong to accept the increasing bitterness and polarization of our people. There is a special pain in the growing alienation of a generation which is the best we have had. So we must not go on as we are going.

I am addressing myself to the future and not to the past. But it may be proper here to insert one word about that past. To say that the burden of this war must now be lifted is not at all to say that it should never have been fought. It is not even to say that it has been fought the wrong way, although that is a somewhat different question. My own view has been and remains that the avoidance of defeat in Southeast Asia was an object of such importance to us and to the people of the area that the basic decision of 1965, to stand and fight in South Vietnam, was right. I also believe that in this fundamental sense the decisions of 1965 have already been validated by events in the area. Furthermore, I do not believe that we are required now, by our new necessities, to lose what has been gained in this strategic sense. But I do believe we have to change our course. Whatever the rights and wrongs of past decisions, the imperative of the future is to begin to lift this burden from our national life.

We Must Not Escalate

There is no solution to the war in Vietnam through U.S. military escalation. There is no prospect of military victory against North Vietnam by any level of U.S. military force which is acceptable or desirable, either in our own interest or in the interest of world peace. I take it as self-evident that it would be the worst kind of folly to use nuclear weapons of any sort at any time in this contest. What is somewhat less evident is that it would be equally fruitless to seek military victory by an escalation of conventional force—by renewed and intensified bombing of the North, or by air and naval blockade, or by enlargement of the American commitment in the South. The last three years have demonstrated plainly that American forces can prevent defeat, and it was for this purpose that they were initially introduced in large numbers. But they have also shown us that they cannot produce victory. In the last twelve months President Johnson has wisely resisted military pressure for continuing escalation. The advocates of bombing not only opposed his major cutback of March 31, but both before and after they have wanted a wider and deeper air campaign against the North. They have been wrong. Similarly, the predictable military reaction to the events of Tet last spring was to urge a major U.S. military reinforcement in the South—the requests appear to have totaled more than 200,000 men. These requests too were wisely rejected, with marginal exceptions, and the record of the last six months—a time in which the course of the battle has been better for us than for the opposition—demonstrates the wisdom of this decision. For what they can do, there are more than enough Americans in South Vietnam today. And what they cannot do could not be done by twice as many men.

The importance of the case against escalation lies in the danger that some may draw false analogies from the last months of the war in Korea fifteen years ago. General Eisenhower has suggested in his memoirs that the threat of nuclear escalation by the United States was effective in bringing Communist acceptance of the Armistice Agreement of July 1953. No one outside the Communist world can prove or disprove this suggestion, but what seems very clear about Vietnam is that no similar threats will succeed there. The Government of North Vietnam has demonstrated plainly that it is prepared to accept a level of physical damage, and of battle casualties too, which is very much higher than any of us in the West would think "reasonable" in our own terms. Neither the framework of the primitive but tightly controlled North Vietnamese society nor the level of the Communist military effort has been broken by the levels of force we have so far employed. Short of nuclear weapons, no higher use of force can be expected to produce such a change, and since the American people would rightly reject by an overwhelming majority any actual use of nuclear weapons, no nuclear threat would be remotely credible.

So there is no solution in escalation. Its only consequence would be a higher level of sacrifice and cost without an early ending of the war.

We Can Seek Agreement, But We May Not Get It Soon

Most Americans—and notably all political candidates—favor negotiations for peace in Vietnam. I strongly agree. It is a real step forward that we now have a diplomatic process going in Paris, and I believe that in 1969 we can do more than we have done so far to test the possibilities of peace by agreement. At the same time I do not think we can be sure that this path is really open. It is not clear at all that Hanoi will accept any settlement that will be remotely acceptable to the people of this country. That may be the fault of Hanoi or the fault of our public opinion or both—but it is important to recognize that it is one thing to seek a negotiated peace and quite another to get it. This distinction may appear more clearly if we look hard at a few of the particular issues which must be negotiated. For convenience in argument let me take the recommendations of the Vietnam plank which was proposed by opponents of Administration policy in the Democratic Convention in Chicago. This remains the most "dovish" document with demonstrated support from a major political group.

The first recommendation of this plank was an unconditional halt in the bombing. I agree with this recommendation. The bombing was begun at a time when it appeared that a prompt and resolute demonstration of American will and purpose was essential to the prevention of Communist military victory in South Vietnam. That purpose is now far out of date, and the particular values which the bombing of the North still has, for the limitation of infiltration and resupply, are far outweighed by its political costs. If it has not stopped before, it would seem to me both prudent and practical to stop it early in 1969. The risk to our own troops can be minimized by alternative means of defense and if necessary by alternative deployments.

The diplomatic advantages of stopping the bombing are obvious: It would shift the burden of response from Washington to Hanoi. It would test the estimates and offers which have come from the United Nations and from Moscow. It would underline the reality of our purpose of peace.

But stopping the bombing in itself will not bring peace. It will simply remove one obstacle to further negotiations. So let us continue with the agenda of the minority plank. "Second," it says, "We will then negotiate a mutual withdrawal of all U.S. forces and all North

Vietnamese troops from South Vietnam. This should be a phased withdrawal over a relatively short period of time." This point—which incidentally is parallel to a similar point in the majority plank—is quite different from the first in that it calls for action by Hanoi. It therefore depends not upon our will alone but also upon theirs. And can any American assume with assurance today that this point is in fact negotiable? I think not. I do not say that it cannot be done, but I do say that we do not know it can be done. For myself, I believe that it would be a good bargain for us and for South Vietnam, but I do not know that it is a bargain we can get. The United States Government, as I understand its policy, has been ready for this bargain for years. Surely the government of 1969 must be ready for it. But what of Hanoi? What is the likelihood that given the current state of affairs in the South, the men in the North would in fact agree to remove all of their forces in return for the departure of ours? There have been hints, at least, in recent months of a developing insistence by Hanoi that no such trade is justified or possible. Whereas for years the government of North Vietnam refused to admit the presence of its forces in the South, now there is a shift in the line and we begin to hear that it is right and proper for the forces for the DRV to go wherever they are needed throughout Vietnam, without regard for the armistice lines of 1954. If we can negotiate mutual withdrawal we should, but what if we cannot? The minority plank opposes unilateral withdrawal, so its assumption must be that without such agreement we would fight on. I submit that a proposal which depends on the agreement of the enemy is a proposal which may not of itself produce the changes we must have.

The third point in the minority plank is more complex—and it reflects an evident effort to reconcile significantly different views among those concerned. It says, "Third, we will encourage our South Vietnamese allies to negotiate a political reconciliation with the National Liberation Front looking toward a Government which is broadly representative of these and all elements in South Vietnamese society. The specific shape of this reconciliation will be a matter for decision by the South Vietnamese, spurred to action by the certain knowledge that the prop of American military support will soon be gone."

Here again we have a requirement which it is not within our power to enforce. As the document itself proclaims, the decisive choices in this matter must be made by South Vietnamese and not by

Americans. To me it has always seemed far from likely that there is in fact a possibility of a government broadly representative of the National Liberation Front and "all elements in South Vietnamese society." The two main parties to the conflict have always defined their concept of representative government in ways that exclude their main enemy. I know of no close observer of the Communists who supposes that they intend to accept any settlement in which they do not have de facto control of the future of South Vietnam, and I know of no prospect that the present government of South Vietnam would accept the concept of "political reconciliation" with Communists in the sense that we use these words at home. I do not quarrel with the objective of reconciliation, but I do wonder whether it is possible. I do not believe any policy for reducing the cost of the war can be solidly based on the assumption that such a reconciliation will come soon.

You will see that in my judgment the minority plank goes through some murky waters in its second and its third points. Yet I repeat that it is not the objective that is in question, but rather the likelihood of its achievement. I believe there would be no harm and much good in maintaining the general purpose of these two points as American purposes, whatever the response of others. It is a sound part of our own negotiating position that we should be ready to withdraw as the North Vietnamese withdraw. Similarly, while I do not myself believe that we should try to force a coalition—and especially not as a cover for intended capitulation—I do believe that we should emphasize the broad objective of reconciliation and also the requirement that peaceful participation in the political life of South Vietnam must in the end be open to all, in any final settlement we would support.

Now I turn from the minority plank to another frequently heard proposal—that we should negotiate a prompt cease-fire. This too is nice work if we can get it. But can we? A genuine cease-fire, in any war so largely civil as this one, is bound to work strongly in favor of the official government—since the end of violence, almost by definition, would give that government new authority and strength. So we can ask for a cease-fire every day, but we must not count on getting it soon. I do not mean for a minute that it is wrong to seek a cease-fire. To emphasize our own readiness to stop the slaughter is as reasonable as it is helpful in showing just who wants more war. But it is something else to expect the Communists to agree in a hurry.

There may be more hope here in more moderate results—the majority plank speaks of "an immediate end *or limitation* of hostilities" (italics added)—and the notion of such limitation does not seem out of bounds at all. But even that will take time.

Let me sum up my own view of negotiation. It is that we should be ready for a compromise well short of victory in which the eventual outcome would remain to be settled by the people of South Vietnam. But I do not think that we can be sure of any such readiness for compromise on the other side, and my personal bet is against it, at least for 1969. I would test the hypothesis by relentless diplomatic process, and I would begin by stopping the bombing. But I do not think I could be sure that these steps alone would begin to lift our burden. I believe that they would not, and that more will be needed.

We Ourselves Must Choose to Cut Back

If there is no solution in escalation, and if the promise of diplomacy is uncertain, then let us return to our initial premise: that we must begin to lift this burden from our lives. The one course that remains is to lift it by our own choice and decision—and this is the course, it seems to me, that is the fundamental first necessity for the next administration. It must decide that it will steadily, systematically, and substantially reduce the number of American casualties, the number of Americans in Vietnam, and the dollar cost of the war. It must make this decision without bargaining or negotiation and establish it as a fact of American policy which must be understood, observed, and recognized by friend and foe alike, and shared in, as they decide, by the other allies of Saigon. This will not be an easy decision. What will make it especially hard is that it will not at first have widespread support among the men who must carry it into effect. Many of us are familiar with the difficulties which come in reducing the cost of so simple a private civil undertaking as building a house: if you add a room it will cost $5,000 more, but if you take one off you seem to save only a few hundreds. There will be a parallel difficulty here. Yet what is difficult and what is impossible are two entirely different things. We have already learned in the last six months that 500,000 men do not need 200,000 reinforcements to keep our end up in the fighting. If the decision is firmly made and effectively executed, we can come to the end of 1969 with as many as 100,000 or 150,000 fewer allied troops on the scene and with an overall cost to the United States that is cheaper by $5 billion to $8 billion a year. A reduction of similar magnitude should be planned for 1970. After that the course of our withdrawal would have to depend on the progress of the search for peace—but at the levels of 1971 we could and should have a volunteer war, if we have a war at all. And even before 1971 we can do some other things to help hold ourselves together—though most of them, unlike steps that I have so far recommended, would require help from Congress. We can and should make drastic increases in our rewards for extended service in Vietnam—a force which rotates every twelve months is no force for this kind of war. We can and should increase substantially our after-service benefits for veterans of truly combat service. We can and should reform both the legislation and the management of our Selective Service system. We cannot end danger or dissent—but we can do a lot about uncertainty, about unfairness, and about administrative insensitivity.

I do not at all say that these are the figures to which a careful review would lead a responsible decision-maker. I do say that such changes are possible. This rate of de-escalation would be slower, indeed, than our rate of escalation—and what goes up can come down if men decide it so. And I will say something more. This reduced level of effort is more than enough still to sustain and execute the basic purpose of our forces in Vietnam—the purpose of preventing defeat. My own belief is that a force of this size could in fact do much more—that it could continue to maintain the standard of tactical success which has been set so high by General Abrams in recent months. Certainly it is large enough to permit the intensification of our more sophisticated and sensitive methods of action—such as the improvement of intelligence and the strengthening of military advice to our allies. It would also be wholly consistent with the important decision to strengthen limitations upon the use of force in civilian areas which has been put in effect under the leadership of Secretary Clifford. It would underline our own limited purpose and strengthen our hand in the process of diplomacy. But most of all, it would begin to lift the burden of the war upon our life at home. And it would do this by our own decision in a way that is quite independent of the will of others. In that sense it is a decision that is genuinely and plainly open for us to make.

I am well aware that a policy of this sort will be open to attack both from those who think it goes too far and those who think it does not go far enough. That has been the character of our involvement from the beginning, and unless we go to the extremes of escalation or of abandonment, there is no way to escape it. I remind you that if a compromise peace by negotiation can be had, I am for it. My concern is with the choice that we must make if that hope fails. I remind you also, if you stand on the other side, that my argument against escalation and against an indefinite continuation of our present course has been based not on moral outrage or political hostility to the objective, but rather on the simple and practical ground that escalation will not work and that continuation on our present course is unacceptable.

There is a real question, which I recognize, whether the sort of reduction I have suggested is too large or too small. My own instinct would be to move to my larger targets of reduction, but my sense of the realities of government and of the requirement of reasonable mutual confidence between civilian and military leaders makes me believe that even a lesser level of changes will not be easily reached. But in any case I do not think the argument stands or falls on specific quantities. It is the decision itself and the direction it points which are central to my case. For the burden of Vietnam upon our lives at home is a burden whose heaviest weight comes from the fact that no end is in sight. Once the American government has made it plain to the American people that the burden will in fact be lifted—even though only gradually, and even though no final promise of perfect peace is possible—then I believe that we shall see a beginning of the necessary healing process among us. Certainly at the edges there will be those who speak of betrayal and those who press for much more drastic movement. But the administration which proves it knows the way down—if not surely the way out—in Vietnam, will be able to reknit the essential relation of confidence between itself and the nation.

And I repeat again that this is the only sure way. It takes two to make peace but only one to move troops. There is support for the course I am suggesting in the words of all the platforms this year. The Republicans would "de-Americanize" the war, the Democrats would "carry out cutbacks of U.S. military involvement as the South Vietnamese forces are able to take over their larger responsibilities"; the minority plank would amend our tactics to enable "an early withdrawal of a significant number of our troops." So it is reasonable to suppose that there could be general support at home for a clear decision candidly explained. We can also expect that the decision will be understood—and even applauded after its fashion—in Hanoi.

But what of Saigon? What happens there as we cut down? The honest answer to this question is that no one knows. Hostile critics of the Saigon government may believe that it will collapse of its own weakness at the first sign of reduction in American commitment.

Optimists and friends may believe rather that the necessary prospect of reduced American effort can stimulate increased self-reliance among those who are determined to survive against all Communist pressure. So far as it is within our means, we should act within this policy of cutback to confound the pessimists and reinforce the determined. In particular we can and should continue the emphasis which we have placed since Tet upon the modernization and reinforcement of South Vietnamese forces. We can sustain and even intensify our efforts at political and economic cooperation. We can emphasize that no one who means to keep at least 100,000 troops in place for years (always assuming there is no decent settlement) can be accused of precipitate or faithless withdrawal. We can emphasize what is the simple brutal fact—that this policy is the only policy which will allow us to stay on the scene at all. We can remind ourselves and our friends that almost no one in Saigon or Washington ever supposed only four years ago that half a million Americans would be needed in South Vietnam and that it is in part a measure of strength and not weakness on the scene that we can now prevent defeat with much smaller forces. But above all, what we can emphasize—and not only in Saigon—is that while the armed forces of the United States can and do stand in the path of defeat, they cannot be the instrument of victory. The contest in Vietnam is a contest for the allegiance of the South Vietnamese. No foreign force can win that battle. This is why the root of the struggle has always been in the South. This is why the bombing has always been marginal in its final meaning; this is why the necessities of American politics now coincide with the necessities of the South Vietnamese future. In a policy of cut-back there is still ample room for steadfast support of our friends, and ample guarantee against defeat imposed by the external aggressor. There is also ample demonstration for all who live in the area not only that we keep our commitments but also that we know how to change our course with care and clarity.

The recommendations I offer are not really new. Not only do we hear closely parallel proposals from among the campaigners, but in the larger sense what I am urging is no more than a continuation of the course we have set since Tet. That sudden assault made three things plain at once: that we were not about to "win," that Saigon was not about to lose, and that the Communists could do more to our public opinion, and less on the ground, than they had hoped. Now we should cut back—but we need not and should not give up.

If John McNaughton were with us I think he might still be smiling a little. He knew the complexities of the contest in Vietnam and he knew at close hand the problems of command and control in Washington. He would know that while I have kept you a long time I have only sketched the outlines of a policy. He would know how much hard work and how much imperfection—both in formulation and in execution—must attend any course of action like the one I have described. He would also know, I think, that there can be no easy assurance that lightening the burden of Vietnam will—in and of itself—push open the doors to liberty and progress in a greater America. He would also surely have changes and improvements to suggest in specific parts of my argument, and he might well come out in a wholly different place. I cannot claim his name for what I urge. But I think perhaps I can claim his spirit for the spirit in which I have tried to speak. He was a man unafraid to confront reality and yet unwilling to abandon the test of right when he accepted the test of possibility. He did not suppose that war could be left to the soldiers alone or that peace could be made without them. He cared for Southeast Asia, but he cared also for the fabric of our free society. Above all, he believed that we must not kid ourselves, and he was right.

VII. APPROACHES TO THE RELATIONSHIP BETWEEN LAW AND FOREIGN POLICY

Intervention as a Scientific Concept,[1] and a Postscript

JAMES N. ROSENAU

THE DEEPER one delves into the literature on intervention, the more incredulous one becomes. The discrepancy between the importance attached to the problem of intervention and the bases on which solutions to it are founded is so striking that at first one wonders whether an adequate sample of the literature has been examined. Enlargement of the sample, however, only makes the discrepancy more glaring, and after pursuing every footnote that suggests a different approach and ruminating in a wide variety of documents, one is compelled to conclude that the literature is indeed incredible. The spirit of scientific explanation appears to have had no impact on it whatsoever. In an age when it is second nature to assume that the solution of problems requires comprehension of their sources, scholarly writings on the problem of intervention are singularly devoid of efforts to develop systematic knowledge on the conditions under which interventionary behavior is initiated, sustained, and abandoned. Rather than treating intervention as a challenge to empirical explanation as well as to moral principles, legal precedents, and strategic doctrines, the literature consists wholly of inquiries into these three dimensions of the problem. The empirical bases are either taken for granted or varied to suit the normative, juridical, or policy-oriented thrust of the analysis.

This is not to imply that a moral, legal, or strategic concern with intervention is misguided. Intervention is the international form of the most pressing moral issues to be found in any community. It involves the human spirit, the liberty of individuals, the structure of groups, the existence of order. It can undermine or enhance the dignity of people and it can facilitate or inhibit their capacity to realize their aspirations and work out their own destinies. Thus one needs only a modicum of humanity to be concerned about the question of when and how it is appropriate for one international actor to intervene in the affairs of another. And, given a moral concern about intervention, it is only logical that attention should turn to the legal question of when

[1] The preparation of this paper was facilitated by the Center of International Studies of Princeton University and its support is gratefully acknowledged. I am also indebted to my wife Norah for her many helpful suggestions. Prepared for the Conference on Intervention and the Developing States, Princeton, N.J., November 10-11, 1967.

it is legitimate for one actor to intervene in another's affairs and the strategic question of how to intervene successfully when the legitimacy of such behavior is either accepted or ignored. Far from being misguided, in short, the predominance of moral, legal, and strategic emphases in the literature is both understandable and desirable. The incredulity pertains rather to the absence of a fourth emphasis upon scientific explanation.

This is not to say that the literature is lacking in empirical data and propositions about the sources of interventionary behavior. Meaningful analysis of the legality and strategy of intervention cannot proceed without some consideration of the conditions under which legitimacy attaches to its use and success to its results. Indeed, since interventionary behavior is of such crucial importance to the course of international affairs and the prospects for world order, inquiries into the subject are especially rich in descriptions and interpretations of actual situations. Many of the legal studies, for example, focus on the question of how a more widespread acceptance of the norm of nonintervention can be achieved and most of their authors are thus led to examine historical cases for clues as to the limits to which international behavior may be governed by such a norm. Likewise, those who approach the subject from a strategic viewpoint are usually concerned with the question of how foreign policy goals can be efficiently and effectively realized through intervention and this focus leads them to investigate the attitudes, institutions, and other conditions abroad that must be altered for intervention to succeed. Hence there is no dearth of empiricism in the literature. Data and insights in themselves, however, do not necessarily lead to an ever-cumulating body of reliable knowledge about the conditions under which intervention does and does not occur. This requires a process in which interrelated propositions are constantly being formulated, tested, and revised, and it is on the total absence of such scientific procedures that incredulity concentrates. All the data to be found in the literature were gathered and analyzed for the instrumental purposes of either establishing the legitimacy of interventionary norms or improving the quality of interventionary behavior and, consequently, they lack the empirical comparability and theoretical explicitness that is necessary for a scientific explanation of the dynamics of intervention.[2]

[2] The comparability and theoretical explicitness necessary for scientific explanation need not involve quantitative data, complex formulae, and involved statistical analyses. To call for the scientific study of intervention is not to ask students of the subject to re-

For all the vast literature on the subject, in other words, not much is known about intervention. There is an abundance of specific detail, but no general knowledge; a profusion of elaborate impressions, but no verified findings. The role of intervention in the Spanish Civil War of 1936-39, in the Hungarian uprisings of 1956, in the Middle Eastern crises of 1956, 1958, and 1967, and in a host of other historical situations has been amply documented, but no attempt has been made to use the case materials as data with which to frame or test hypotheses that might apply to any intervention or even to specific types of interventionary behavior. The factors that foster, precipitate, sustain, channel, constrain, and/or curb intervention simply have not been scientifically explored, with the result that the literature is barren of any established generalizations. All that exists is an enormous amount of conventional and legal wisdom in which conclusions are asserted on the basis of a jumble of ringing affirmations, impressive insights, clear-cut preferences, and supportive historical examples. It is as if the literature on lung cancer consisted of treatises written by either thoughtful smokers or their concerned spouses.

Nor need the characterization of the literature be so mild. After all, conventional and legal wisdom has its place and in any realm of inquiry—there is always room for creative insights and clear-cut values. Indeed, if all the literature was of this order, it would not be difficult to interject scientific procedures and move quickly to the accumulation of a reliable body of knowledge about intervention. Unfortunately, however, a large preponderance of the conventional and legal wisdom does not lend itself to scientific processing and is more obtuse than insightful and more confounding than clarifying. Quite apart from a persistent naivete in which moral aspirations are allowed to shape and guide empirical assessments, the normative, legal, and strategic studies all seem to be plagued by analytic problems that inhibit wisdom and leave major questions unanswered. Stated more specifically, the moral dimension of the literature is plagued by a double-standard problem, the legal dimension suffers from a definitional problem, and

---

train themselves in new methods of research. Rather it involves processing their case materials in such a way that findings derived from one case can be applied to and tested by other cases. For an elaboration of this point, see my "Moral Fervor, Systematic Analysis, and Scientific Consciousness in Foreign Policy Research," a paper presented at the Conference on Political Science and the Study of Public Policy, sponsored by the Committee on Governmental and Legal Processes of the Social Science Research Council, Cape Newagen, Maine, August 30, 1967.

the strategic dimension is beset by the problem of operationalizing the national interest. To the extent that the three dimensions are interdependent, moreover, so are the problems, thus further compounding the confusion. In addition, to the extent that the three dimensions are concerned with empirical phenomena, they are all harassed by the problem of measuring influence.

I. The Double Standard

Like many problems of morality, those that involve the use of intervention as a technique of international action are not simple and clearcut. However it may be defined, intervention is not in and of itself either good or bad. A double standard prevails: most interventions may be undesirable for a variety of reasons, but some are eminently desirable for equally compelling reasons. Most interventions probably invade the privacy of people and undermine the stability of the international system, but some interventions uphold human rights and preserve international order. Intervention, in other words, is normally an instrument of action, a means and not an end, and the morality or immorality of interventionary behavior thus depends on the end toward which it is directed. To intervene in the affairs of a peaceful Latin American country may be unwarranted, but to intervene in the stormy and horrendous activities of a Hitler's Germany seems entirely justifiable, even mandatory. The moral problem, then, is that of developing a view of intervention in which it is generally condemned but which also allows for specifiable types of exceptions. This problem plagues the literature and doubtless it is also disturbing to those in high policy-making positions. For while acceptance of a double standard is not in itself morally difficult, consistency with respect to the legitimate exceptions is anything but easy. While consistency may be the mark of small minds, men everywhere like to think that their occasional tolerance or advocacy of intervention stems not from sheer whim or capricious interpretations of prevailing circumstances, but from some larger principle that is applicable across a variety of situations. And, once one admits that one's own morality must be the ultimate arbiter of when exceptions are to be tolerated as legitimate, one must acknowledge that the morality of others is entitled to the same discretion, an admission that opens up the possibility, even the probability, that interventionary behavior will come to enjoy a greater legitimacy than it deserves. If every actor makes his own determination of what violations of the doctrine of nonintervention are acceptable and legitimate, the system becomes one of men, not laws, and what is despicable intervention for one actor is welcome liberation for another.

Further complications set in, moreover, when it is recognized that even if the problem of specifiable exceptions is solved, intervention may still not be warranted. An exceptional situation in which intervention is a moral imperative may nevertheless require a noninterventionary stance. If, for example, intervention greatly heightens the probability of global war even as it also serves humanitarian values— a choice that faced the West with respect to the Hungarian uprising of 1956—then presumably the rule pertaining to exceptional cases would not obtain. In other words, intervention is only a means to an end, but sometimes there are more highly valued ends than the one for which it is a means. Clearly, as one astute observer put it, "There is no obvious synthesis between morality and intervention."[3]

In sum, essentially the moral problem seems to stem from the fact that whereas an actor must—to use a colleague's favored phrase—often "rise above his principles," in the area of intervention this necessity has yet to be acknowledged. Most observers and actors prefer to seek justifications for rising above their principles that are just as compelling as the principles themselves, an effort which results in a never-ending "clarification" of the moral issues involved.

A number of solutions to the moral problem are available, most of them in the international law literature. Perhaps the best is to treat the doctrine of nonintervention as an absolute insofar as national actors are concerned and to allow for exceptions to it only on the part of international actors whose interventionary behavior stems from a collective rather than an individual morality.[4] Such a procedure amounts, in effect, to a government of laws and not of men, but it suffers from the fact that social and political factors or changes may produce an international morality from which the individual actor dissents, thus facing him again with a double standard.

Which resolution of the double standard is adopted—and there are many approaches to the problem besides the one noted in the previous paragraph—depends on the priorities one attaches to man's needs

[3] Manfred Halpern, "The Morality and Politics of Intervention," in James N. Rosenau (ed.), *International Aspects of Civil Strife* (Princeton: Princeton University Press, 1964), p. 255.

[4] For a persuasive case along these lines, see Richard A. Falk, "The Legitimacy of Legislative Intervention by the United Nations," in Roland J. Stanger (ed.), *Essays on Intervention* (Columbus: Ohio State University Press, 1964), pp. 31-61.

and wants. A scientific analysis of intervention would thus not solve the moral problem. Science can explain empirical phenomena, but it can never provide the basis for choosing among value alternatives. Yet, it seems reasonable to assert that the moral problem would not be confounded by the availability of a scientific literature on intervention; that, on the contrary, it might be greatly clarified if the sources, processes, and consequences of interventionary behavior were more fully comprehended. If, for example, more reliable knowledge was available on the conditions under which international actors would be likely to undertake interventions, the utility of the collective solution to the moral problem noted above would be clearer and thus possibly its selection or rejection among a variety of alternatives would be more easily determined.

II. The Problem of Definition

Notwithstanding the voluminous literature on intervention, there appears to be no agreement whatsoever on the phenomena designated by the term. Even in international law, where the definitional problem is an especially recurrent preoccupation, uniformity of usage has yet to develop.[5] On the contrary, both in law and in general "intervention has a perplexing vagueness of meaning."[6] Some observers posit it as certain forms of behavior; others conceive it to involve certain intentions underlying behavior; still others think of it in terms of certain consequences stemming from behavior; and a fourth approach is to equate it with certain standards to which behavior ought to conform.[7] A major result of so many definitional options is that a

[5] Indeed, the absence of definitional uniformity has recently been the source of heated controversy among students of international law. See Eberhard P. Deutsch, "The Legality of the United States Position in Vietnam," *American Bar Association Journal*, Vol. 52 (May, 1966), pp. 436-42, and William L. Standard, "United States Intervention in Vietnam is Not Legal," *American Bar Association Journal*, Vol. 52 (July, 1966), pp. 627-34. See also John Norton Moore, "International Law and the United States Role in Viet Nam: A Reply," and Richard A. Falk, "International Law and the United States Role in Viet Nam: A Response to Professor Moore," *Yale Law Journal*, Vol. 76 (May, 1967), pp. 1051-1158.

[6] Percy H. Winfield, "Intervention," *Encyclopedia of the Social Sciences*, Vol. 8 (New York: The Macmillan Co., 1932), p. 236.

[7] For a more detailed discussion of some of the definitional problems encountered in the field of international law, see William T. Burke, "The Legal Regulation of Minor International Coercion: A Framework of Inquiry," in Stanger, *op.cit.*, pp. 88-90; Ann Van Wynen Thomas and A. J. Thomas, Jr., *Non-Intervention: The Law and Its Import in the Americas* (Dallas: Southern Methodist University Press, 1956), pp. 66-74; and Martin Wight, "Western Values in International Relations," in Herbert Butterfield and

number of observers merge two or more of them and, in effect, end up by defining intervention as any action whereby one state has an impact upon the affairs of another. Thus the literature is pervaded with discussions of military interventions,[8] propaganda interventions,[9] economic interventions,[10] diplomatic interventions,[11] and ideological interventions,[12] not to mention customs interventions and other highly specific actions through which one state experiences the impact of another.[13] Indeed, often intervention is defined in such a general way that it appears to be synonymous with imperialism, aggression, colonialism, neocolonialism, war, and other such gross terms that are used to designate the noncooperative interactions of nations. One observer, for example, finds it useful to define imperialism in terms of "actions that . . . are intrusions into the affairs of another people,"[14] a definition which is hardly differentiable from the view that " 'intervention' refers to conduct with an external animus that intends to achieve a fundamental alteration of the state of affairs in the target nation."[15] Nor is noncooperative animus necessarily considered to be a characteristic of interventionary behavior. Foreign aid programs have been classified as intervention[16] and so, to the distress of some inter-

---

Martin Wight (eds.), *Diplomatic Investigations: Essays in the Theory of International Politics* (Cambridge: Harvard University Press, 1966), pp. 111-20.

[8] Cf. Quincy Wright, "Intervention, 1956," *American Journal of International Law*, Vol. 51 (April 1957), pp. 257-76.

[9] Cf. C. G. Fenwick, "Intervention By Way of Propaganda," *American Journal of International Law*, Vol. 35 (October 1941), pp. 626-31.

[10] See, for example, W. B. Dickinson, Jr., "Challenged Monroe Doctrine," *Editorial Research Reports*, Vol. II (August 10, 1960), pp. 585-602.

[11] Cf. Quincy Wright, "The Munich Settlement and International Law," *American Journal of International Law*, Vol. 33 (January 1939), pp. 12-32.

[12] See Hans J. Morgenthau, "To Intervene or Not to Intervene," *Foreign Affairs*, Vol. 45 (April 1967), pp. 425-36.

[13] Cf. L. Morley, "Invasion and Intervention in the Caribbean Area," *Editorial Research Reports*, Vol. II (July 22, 1959), pp. 535-52.

[14] Paul A. Varg, "Imperialism and the American Orientation Toward World Affairs," *Antioch Review*, Vol. 26 (Spring 1966), p. 45. For a similar conception with a different label, see Kenneth J. Twitchett, "Colonialism: An Attempt at Understanding Imperial, Colonial and Neo-Colonial Relationships," *Political Studies*, Vol. 13 (October 1965), pp. 300-23.

[15] Falk, in Stanger, *op.cit.*, p. 42.

[16] For example, see Michael H. Cardozo, "Intervention: Benefaction as Justification," in Stanger, *op.cit.*, pp. 63-85; and Doris A. Graber, "The Truman and Eisenhower Doctrines in the Light of the Doctrine of Non-Intervntion," *Political Science Quarterly*, Vol. LXXIII (September 1958), pp. 321-34.

national law specialists,[17] have collective security measures taken by several nations to protect their common interests. Finally, the height of definitional vagueness is occasionally reached when inaction is regarded as intervention. Having defined intervention as the impact that one state has on the affairs of another, logic leads some observers to classify inaction as intervention whenever consequences follow within a state from the failure of another to intrude upon its affairs.[18] Such a conception, for example, leads to the absurd conclusion that the United States avoidance of the conflict in Indochina in 1954 and its extensive involvement in that part of the world a decade later both constitute intervention.

Concerned about the problem of vagueness inherent in general definitions, some analysts have sought to conceptualize intervention in more precise terms. Most notably, precision is sought through a formulation in which interventionary behavior is limited to dictatorial interference by one state in the affairs of another. That is, intervention occurs when the affairs of one state are altered against its will by the actions of another. So conceived, intervention is associated with the use or threat of force. Coercion must be the indicator of intervention, the reasoning seems to be, because states are sovereign and thus would not undergo unwanted alteration if force were not threatened or applied.[19] Most students of international law, however, reject such a precise formulation because it omits so much behavior that seems relevant to the subject. Even worse, the military or coercive definition

> excuses various types of interference that have often occurred, particularly in modern times. The totalitarian nations have reduced intervention to a science, and to them it has become a duty and a legitimate method of political warfare. Economic pressures on other states; diplomatic demands backed up with political threats to force a state to curb freedom of speech, press, and radio; fifth column activities; the inciting of another state's people to rise against its government; and a multitude of other refined techniques of interference must in many instances come under the heading of intervention.[20]

17 James Oliver Murdock, "Collective Security Distinguished From Intervention," *American Journal of International Law*, Vol. 56 (April 1962), pp. 500-503.

18 For a summary of the literature that adheres to this logic, see Thomas and Thomas, *op.cit.*, pp. 67-68.

19 For a further discussion of this reasoning, see *ibid.*, pp. 68-69.

20 *Ibid.*, p. 69.

Accordingly, it is argued that compulsion or constraint, which may or may not be based on the coercive use of force, is the key to both a precise and useful definition of intervention, that whether an act of interference is undertaken through physical force, economic pressure, or some other form of compulsion, it is the compulsion and not its form that constitutes intervention.[21] More accurately, "the essence of intervention is the attempt to compel."[22] The trouble with this broader formulation, of course, is that it reintroduces a vagueness about the line that divides interventionary behavior from other types of international action. How are acts of compulsion or constraint to be differentiated from those that allow for voluntary compliance or outright rejection? Is not the nature of international transactions such that a price is attached to every offer (i.e., attempt to compel) and therefore cannot acceptance of the offer be interpreted as an unwillingness to suffer the penalty attached to its rejection (i.e., as an acquiescence to constraint)? It would seem, in other words, that once definitions move beyond observable behavior to the motivation or intent underlying it, precision suffers and ambiguity prevails.

However loosely or precisely intervention may be defined, its use as an analytic concept is further complicated by a variety of distinctions that are sometimes drawn in terms of the identity of the intervening actor or the nature of the affairs into which the intervening actor intrudes. Falk, for example, distinguishes five types of intervention (unilateral, counter-, collective, regional, and universal) and argues that the differences among them are sufficient to generate different normative and legal structures for evaluating their application.[23] Other writers make a similar argument with respect to the distinction between "internal" and "external" intervention, the former involving "interference by one state between disputant sections of the community in another state" and the latter pertaining to "interference by one state in the relations . . . of other states without the consent of the latter."[24]

But there is no need to pile distinction upon distinction. Plainly the concept of intervention suffers from a lack of definitional clarity. Notwithstanding all the ways in which it has been defined—and many more could be cited—the line that differentiates the presence of intervention from its absence remains elusive. So many diverse activities, motives, and consequences are considered to constitute intervention that the key terms of most definitions are ambiguous and fail to dis-

---

21 *Ibid.*, p. 72.
22 *Ibid.*
23 In Stanger, *op.cit.*, pp. 40-41.
24 Winfield, *op.cit.*, pp. 236-37.

criminate empirical phenomena. Animus, intrusion, interference, impact, compulsion, and other such terms convey meaning, but they do not enable one to recognize an interventionary act when it occurs. The meaning they convey is thus of little use when the concept of intervention is applied to a specific moral, legal, or strategic situation. What is animus for one observer is responsibility for another. What some call compulsion, others regard as acquiescence. Little wonder, then, that uniformity in usage does not characterize the concept of intervention.

The vagueness and inapplicability of the concept is further compounded by a tendency to presume that intervention has an objective existence apart from those who define it. The literature is full of efforts to determine what constitutes the "essence" of intervention. The belief seems to be that if the proper definition is formulated, and if the evidence to which it points is carefully examined, intervention will unmistakably reveal itself. Of course, since different observers prefer different definitions and interpret their evidence differently, the essence of intervention reveals itself to be highly variable, with what is essential for one observer being peripheral for another.

A scientific approach to intervention would go a long way toward resolving these definitional problems. In contrast to its marginal usefulness in solving the moral problems posed by intervention, scientific analysis does offer a means for precisely discriminating among empirical phenomena and avoiding a fruitless search for their essence. Science deals exclusively with observables—with phenomena that can be measured, either presently or theoretically—and thus those who engage in scientific inquiry must operationalize their definitions before they proceed to make empirical observations. Scientists may construct models with conventional concepts, but ultimately—i.e., when they move to test their models—they must either employ operational definitions or abandon the models. To operationalize a concept is to specify the operations that one performs in order to observe the phenomena that it encompasses. Bridgeman's original formulation of operationalism still makes this point most succinctly: "In general, we mean by any concept nothing more than a set of operations; *the concept is synonymous with the corresponding set of operations.*"[25] Intervention, then, becomes the operations that one uses in order to identify its existence. If "conduct

[25] P. W. Bridgeman, *The Logic of Modern Physics* (New York: The Macmillan Co., 1928), excerpted in Herbert Feigl and May Brodbeck (eds.), *Readings in the Philosophy of Science* (New York: Appleton-Century-Crofts, Inc., 1953), p. 36. Italics in the original.

with an external animus that intends to achieve a fundamental alteration of the state of affairs in the target nation" is operationalized in terms of certain types of hostile and motivational statements made by the leaders of the intervening nation, then intervention exists when these statements are observed and not otherwise. If intervention is equated with interference and interference is operationalized in terms of protests voiced by specific segments of the target nation, then intervention is neither more nor less than the observed occurrence of these protests. Operational definitions, in short, avoid ambiguity. The resulting concepts may or may not be incisive and relevant, but they will not be vague. Operational definitions cannot be either right or wrong, but only more or less useful. If they are not useful—if they involve operations that do not adequately identify all the phenomena in which one is interested—then they will not be widely employed. Eventually agreement forms around those operational definitions that prove most incisive for most observers. The scientific literature on a subject, therefore, perpetuates precision rather than vagueness.

Such precision may not be concentrated in a single operational formulation. Several definitions of the same concept may be widely accepted, either because different schools of thought approach the phenomena to which it refers differently or because the purposes for which it is used are variable. One does not operationalize the concept of an inch with a ten-cent store ruler if one is building a space vehicle. Contrariwise, one does not go to a precision-instrument store for an instrument to measure whether a newly purchased grand piano can be moved through one's front door. Similarly, agreement may form around several operational definitions of intervention that variously reflect the different uses to which the concept may be put. If one is interested in military intervention, operationalization may be accomplished in terms of the movement of a specified number of troops into or near the target society. Such a definition does not emcompass other forms of intervention, but the omission of these does not mean that other forms do not occur. It simply means that the user of this definition has a particular interest in the military dimension of interventionary phenomena, and the question to be asked about the definition is not whether it encompasses all interventionary phenomena, but whether counting the movement of troops is an appropriate operation to perform for the purposes that the concept is designed to serve.

All of this is not to say that intervention is an easy concept to operationalize or that agreement will quickly form around a few useful definitions. As noted below, intervention presents difficulties hardly less formidable than those that attach to the concept of influence. It is to say, however, that an inclination to operationalize the concept of intervention would surely reduce the vagueness and confusion that presently marks its use.

III. Strategic Analysis and the Problem of the National Interest

The lack of a scientific approach to interventionary phenomena is also conspicuous with respect to their strategic dimension. For here the central concerns are empirical rather than evaluative. Under what conditions can intervention successfully achieve its goals? What risks have to be run and what unintended consequences have to be endured if success is to be realized? What will be the consequences of nonintervention? When is intervention likely to result in outright failure? Such questions, of course, cannot be answered by moral principles and juridical standards. They are queries about behavior—about how individuals, small groups, and large aggregates are likely to react to new stimuli. Normative and juridical evaluations may be made of the uses that are subsequently made of these strategic estimates, but the estimates themselves are neutral predictions of behavior and, as such, can be developed accurately only through theoretical and empirical inquiry. Indeed, it is not an exaggeration to note that strategic estimates of this kind probe the very core of political behavior and are thus concerned with central problems of empirical political inquiry. Politics is about the way in which actors seek to modify each other's behavior across wide functional distances[26] and in this sense, given the extent of the modification attempted and the functional distances spanned through intervention, no situation is more purely political than the attempt of one nation to intervene in the affairs of another.

The vast literature on the strategic dimension of intervention is not lacking in sensitivity to the empirical character of the queries to which it is addressed. On the contrary, there is a pervasive recognition, sharpened by the significance of such postwar interventions as have occurred in Hungary, the Suez Canal, Cuba, the Dominican Republic, and Vietnam, that the strategic problems of intervention as an instrument of foreign policy must be approached through assessments of behavioral

---

[26] For an elaboration of this conception, see my *Calculated Control as a Unifying Concept in the Study of International Politics and Foreign Policy* (Princeton: Center of International Studies, Research Monograph No. 15, 1963).

probabilities rather than through adherence to moral or legal imperatives. In the words of one distinguished observer, "It is futile to search for an abstract principle which would allow us to distinguish in a concrete case between legitimate and illegitimate intervention."[27] The strategic literature is thus pervaded with both empirical propositions and data pertaining to the conditions under which success or failure can be expected to follow intervention. Citing, for example, the postwar failures of the United States, China, the Soviet Union, and Cuba to achieve interventionary goals in, respectively, Vietnam, Africa, Europe, and Latin America, many authors stress the obstacles to successful intervention and conclude with the general proposition that normally the prevailing conditions do not conduce to success. "Intervention is a better-late-than-never proposition at best," observes one analyst.[28] "When in doubt, don't intervene," echoes another.[29] On the other hand, it is also recognized that some interventions do achieve their goals, that, say, the Soviet Union did achieve success in Hungary in 1956[30] and the United States "did intervene to good advantage in Lebanon in 1958,"[31] and that therefore the risks of failure are sometimes less than the gains of success. In other words, "the nature of the opportunity [for successful intervention] differs from country to country,"[32] with the result that "Intervention, like surgery, is not an evil in itself, but it must be applied sparingly and with consummate skill. Just as intervention cannot be a guiding principle of diplomacy, so nonintervention cannot be observed irrespective of time or place. All situations are not equally important."[33]

However, notwithstanding its empirical orientation and its clear-cut recognition that different conditions conduce to different interventionary results, the strategically oriented literature is conspicuously lacking in a scientific approach. For instead of formulating and testing empirical hypotheses in order to comprehend the range of situations in which interventionary behavior is likely to occur and the conditions

[27] Morgenthau, op.cit., p. 430.

[28] David W. Tarr, "The American Military Presence Abroad," Orbis, Vol. 9 (Fall 1965), p. 649.

[29] Adam Yarmolinsky, United States Military Power and Foreign Policy (Chicago: University of Chicago Center for Policy Study, 1967), p. 17.

[30] Morgenthau, op.cit., p. 431.

[31] Leonard Binder, The Middle East Crisis: Background and Issues (Chicago: University of Chicago Center for Policy Study, 1967), p. 16.

[32] John N. Plank, "The Caribbean: Intervention, When and How," Foreign Affairs, Vol. 44 (October 1965), p. 42.

[33] Ronald Steel, Pax Americana (New York: The Viking Press, 1967), p. 334.

under which it is likely to succeed or fail, students of intervention strategy invariably fall back on a standard that is just as misleading and unempirical a means of explanation as any moral principle or legal precept, namely, the national interest. To examine a sample of interventions and conclude that such behavior occurs because nations are "guided in their decisions to intervene and their choice of the means of intervention by what they regard as their respective national interests"[34] is not to offer a meaningful explanation. The national interest is merely a label that may denote the entire spectrum of human wants and needs and thus it in no way differentiates the circumstances that are likely to lead a nation to define its wants and needs as requiring interventionary behavior.[35] To advise policy-makers that they ought to base their strategy on the national interest rather than on abstract principles and then intervene only when situations are "vital" to their "own security,"[36] when "vital interests are unmistakably and imminently threatened,"[37] is to give unusable advice. The criteria for vital, unmistakable, or imminent remain unexplicated. All situations —or none—can be viewed as inescapable and pending threats to security, depending on how the world is viewed and what is meant by security. These are not self-evident phenomena. What is vital for one observer is peripheral for another and what is unmistakable for the former may be obscure to the latter.

In other words, the concepts of interest and security are infinitely variable. They can be used to interpret the advent and avoidance of intervention, to recommend both the necessity of intervention and the wisdom of nonintervention, to justify both rejection of abstract principles and adherence to legal norms. A good example of this infinite variability can be found in the contrast between Morgenthau's unqualified warning against making interventionary decisions on the basis of national interests derived from abstract conceptions of legitimacy[38] (such as the tenets of international law) and Falk's vigorous argument that in such decisions "real interests" are best served by "a fair-minded attention to the restraints and procedures of the international legal

[34] Morgenthau, *op.cit.*, p. 430.

[35] For a lengthy discussion of the limitations of the national interest, see my article on the concept in the *International Encyclopedia of the Social Sciences* (New York: Crowell-Collier, forthcoming) .

[36] Steel, *op.cit.*, p. 331.

[37] Herbert S. Dinerstein, *Intervention Against Communism* (Baltimore: Johns Hopkins Press, 1967) , p. 53.

[38] *Op.cit.*, pp. 430-36.

order."[39] In effect, the national interest becomes a substitute for understanding. Since any behavior can be classified as serving or undermining national interests, the concept cannot provide comprehension of when, how, and why interventionary behavior unfolds as it does and, instead, can only offer the comfort that an attempt at explanation has been made.

It is not difficult to discern some of the reasons why discussions of the strategy of intervention are so dependent on the national interest concept rather than on scientific explanation. One reason, perhaps the most important one, is that values and value conflicts—conflicts over what are moral or immoral goals and legitimate or illegitimate means—are so central to the phenomena of intervention that the utility of building upon scientific answers to strategic questions is neglected in the search for clarity on the value questions. Scientific procedure seems too slow and value questions too urgent to postpone finding solutions to the latter until the time when they can be considered in the context of empirical probabilities. The national interest, on the other hand, appears to offer a means of solving the normative and juridical problems while at the same time taking advantage of the lessons that can be learned from an examination of a sample of past interventions. To have an explicit interest, be it personal or national, is to have a guide to moral choice. Why, then, devote energy to the development of scientific theory and findings? These have to be assessed in the light of value preferences anyway. So is it not wiser to rely on the dictates of the national interest, which does not ignore realities but which also builds in the necessary evaluative considerations? The question appears to compel an affirmative response, with the result that for all its empirical propositions and data, the strategic literature is void of any systematic theory and tested findings.

The second reason for the reliance on national interest follows. In the absence of any empirical theory and systematic data—as opposed to a selected sample of cases—that differentiate the sources and outcomes of intervention under varying conditions, the very variability of the national interest as an analytic concept gives the impression of advancing understanding to the point of distinguishing between those interventions that succeed and those that fail. This is especially so for the preponderant majority of analysts who interpret postwar American interventions as based exclusively on the general principle of contesting and containing Communism. Since it ignores situational differences

[39] *Yale Law Journal, op.cit.*, p. 1153.

and treats all Communist threats as uniform in their nature and degree, this principle is seen to underlie many occasions when an intervention policy has not proved successful. Hence a more adequate concept, one that allows for the empirical fact that the Communist world has split into several camps and that thus takes account of situational differences, seems needed and it is at this point that further support for the idea of founding interventionary strategy on considerations of the national interest arises. Given the variability of the concept, it seems logical to assert that intervention succeeds when it is consistent with the national interest and fails when it is not. Why? Because consistency with national interests means that the attempt to intervene is pursued unqualifiedly and without vacillation, whereas in situations of failure other interests intrude to reduce the commitment to—and thus the effectiveness of—the intervention. Morgenthau, for example, explains that this is why the 1956 Soviet intervention in Hungary succeeded, whereas the opposite outcome followed the 1961 U.S. intervention in Cuba. The Soviet Union, heeding its national interest, "put the success of the intervention above all other considerations, and succeeded." Soviet prestige subsequently suffered, to be sure, but only temporarily. Today its prestige has been recovered and Hungary remains in the Communist world. The United States, on the other hand, did not approach "the problem of intervening in Cuba in a rational fashion." It allowed its national interest to become obfuscated by trying to topple the Castro government without a temporary loss of prestige. Consequently, Castro remained in power even as U.S. prestige suffered a serious setback.[40]

To repeat, however, such an explanation is profoundly deceptive. It cannot be wrong. If an intervention succeeds, it is rational and consistent with the national interest. If it fails, it is irrational and inconsistent. To apply national interest criteria, therefore, is not to identify either the conditions under which an unqualified commitment to interventionary policy will be made or the situations in which such a commitment can bring about modifications in the target nation. Systematic knowledge about these crucial matters can be obtained only through the procedure of formulating and testing empirical theory.

IV. The Problem of Measuring Influence

Perhaps another reason why strategic analyses have been guided by the concept of the national interest rather than by scientific explana-

---

[40] *Op.cit.*, p. 431.

tion is that the central process of intervention—influence—is so diffi-cult to measure. However it may be defined, intervention involves modifications of the behavior of persons and groups in the target na-tion that would not have occurred if the interventionary nation had not engaged in interventionary activities. Intervention succeeds when the intended modifications occur and it fails when they do not. The production of intended effects—i.e., influence—is thus both the cen-tral purpose and process of intervention. As has been amply docu-mented elsewhere, however, observing and measuring the unfolding of influence processes presents enormous analytical and methodolog-ical problems.[41] Indeed, the measurement of influence is easily the most troublesome problem of political analysis. For it not only involves the tracing of changes in political behavior, but it also requires link-ing the changes to a specific set of actors who sought to evoke them, and this is an awesome task because there is always the possibility that the behavior deemed to represent intended effects would have occurred even in the absence of efforts to produce it. A multiplicity of factors underlies any modification of behavior and identifying the particular factors that result from influence attempts is thus a task that staggers the imagination and taxes the patience of even the most so-phisticated political analyst. Since intervention subsumes influence processes that span national boundaries and that weave their way through extraordinarily complex social networks, it is little wonder that analyses of the subject have shied away from scientific procedures. For these procedures require the formulation of theory in which in-fluence processes are key variables and the perfection of techniques for observing and measuring their operation.

V. A Basis for an Operational Definition

It could well be argued that if a concept is as laden with normative dimensions, legal precedents, and strategic orientations as is interven-tion, it ought not be the subject of scientific inquiry. Overtones of morality, vague definitional habits, and reliance on ambiguous terms seem bound to intrude and render the development of empirical theory and systematic data on interventionary phenomena virtually impossi-ble. It would be better to formulate new concepts or break interven-tion down into its component parts, the argument might conclude,

[41] For example, see James G. March, "An Introduction to the Theory and Measure-ment of Influence," *American Political Science Review*, Vol. XLIX (June 1955), pp. 431-51.

than to try to work with the concept at the emotionally charged level at which it has been customarily used.

Although similar reasoning has led this author to urge abandonment of the national interest as an analytic concept,[42] such a conclusion cannot be accepted in the case of intervention.[43] For interventions have an empirical existence as well as an evaluative one. They embrace moral questions and legal standards, but they also find expression in the activities of identifiable human beings. Policy-makers plan interventions, nations sustain them, international organizations debate them, citizens ponder them. The Soviets have a doctrine of intervention; so do the Chinese; so do the Cubans; and the three argue vigorously over the behavior through which their doctrines are implemented.[44] Nor are Americans incapable of wrangling over interventionary doctrines and governing their behavior accordingly. Not only are recent activities in the Dominican Republic and Vietnam widely considered to be interventions in the affairs of nations, but the policy reflected in these activities is now the central issue of American foreign policy.[45] In short, intervention may be differently and vaguely conceptualized, but it does refer to empirical phenomena and these do constitute a central problem of world politics. Indeed, as technology shrinks the world and makes nations ever more dependent, interventionary phenomena may grow increasingly important behaviorally as well as morally. Hence the scientifically oriented analyst cannot turn aside. If he dismisses interventionary phenomena as too illusory or too difficult for the procedures he employs, he prevents himself from confronting the theoretical challenge of explaining primary international processes. For analytic purposes he may find it useful to break intervention down into its component parts, but in the end he will have to piece them together again—not only because the resulting knowl-

[42] See my article in the *International Encyclopedia of the Social Sciences, op.cit.*

[43] It should be noted, however, that apparently others have found so little analytic utility in the concept as to justify its abandonment. Such, at least, would seem to be a logical conclusion to be drawn from the fact that the forthcoming *International Encyclopedia of the Social Sciences* does not follow the lead of its illustrious predecessor (see footnote 6). According to the former's *Preliminary Table of Contents* (New York: Crowell-Collier, 1964), an article on intervention is not to be included in its ten volumes.

[44] For an interesting and succinct discussion of these arguments and the behavior to which they refer, see Georgie Anne Geyer, "The Threat of 'Vietnams' in Latin America," *The Progressive,* Vol. 31 (August 1967), pp. 22-25.

[45] See, for example, Don Oberdorfer, "Noninterventionism, 1967 Style," *The New York Times Magazine,* September 17, 1967, pp. 28-31, 102-12.

edge can serve moral, legal, and strategic purposes, but also because it will significantly advance comprehension of world politics.

This is not the occasion to develop a scientific theory of intervention. Time and space limitations permit only a brief identification of the basic elements that would enter into such a theory. More specifically, the ensuing analysis suggests the basis for an operational definition of interventionary phenomena and then indicates how theoretical propositions about them might be constructed.

The first of these tasks is the easiest. The criteria for an operational definition seem plain. It must be broad enough to identify those phenomena that are generally associated with the term and yet not be so broad that it fails to discriminate them from other aspects of international politics. As previously implied, a scientific approach to intervention requires a formulation that is more precise than the common sense usage of the term which, in effect, allows for any action directed toward another nation to be regarded as intervention. As it is commonly used, the word "intervene" suggests an event that occurs between two other events. Viewed in this way, the term becomes applicable to any international action: for example, a request for negotiations or an offer of aid to earthquake victims is an intervention in the sense that the request or the offer comes between the condition that preceded it and the response to it. Indeed, as noted, this common sense usage permits even the absence of action to be regarded as intervention, since the choice of inaction in a situation necessarily intervenes between the conditions that prevailed before and after the choice. Clearly, intervention would lose its utility as an analytic concept if its operationalization allowed for such broad interpretations. Lest interventionary phenomena be equated with all of international politics, therefore, a more restricted definition must be developed.

However intervention may be defined in the literature, and irrespective of whether it is approached from a moral, legal, or strategic perspective, two characteristics are usually associated with the behavior that is classified as interventionary. Indeed, although the association is often left implicit, it is so pervasive in the literature that the two characteristics would appear to be necessary attributes of interventionary phenomena and, as such, to provide a basis for an operational definition. One is what might be called the *convention-breaking* character of interventions. The other is their *authority-oriented* nature. Stated briefly, all kinds of observers from a wide variety of perspectives seem inclined to describe the behavior of one international actor toward another as interventionary whenever the form of the behavior constitutes a sharp break with then-existing forms *and* whenever it is directed at changing or preserving the structure of political authority in the target society. The first of these characteristics highlights widespread agreement on the finite and transitory nature of interventions. Virtually all the historical cases cited in the literature are conceived to have a beginning (when conventional modes of conduct are abandoned) and an end (when the conventional modes are restored or the convention-breaking mode becomes conventional through persistent use). Their consequences for the target society may be profound and enduring, but once the consequences become accepted and established, the behavior is no longer regarded as interventionary even if the presence of the intervening actor in the target society remains undiminished. Throughout the period between 1945 and 1956, for example, the Soviet Union expended considerable energies and resources through diplomatic, economic, propaganda, and other channels to preserve the prevailing authority structure of Hungary, but at no point during these eleven years did actors or observers characterize these activities as interventionary. They were the accepted mode of behavior even though they had significant preservative consequences for the Hungarian authority structure (i.e., even though the Russians had, in the common sense use of the term, long been intervening in Hungarian affairs). However, when in October 1956, Russian behavior with respect to this structure was drastically altered, the changed behavior was widely regarded as an intervention. The preservative goal remained the same, but the adoption of a fundamentally new means of achieving it altered the conventional pattern of behavior so sharply as to evoke interventionary norms and perceptions on the part of both actors in and observers of the international system. Once the new means achieved the preservative goal and the conventional pattern was restored with the withdrawal of Soviet troops from Hungary, the intervention was considered to have come to an end. Not since 1956 has Russian behavior with respect to Hungary been viewed as interventionary even though it has continued to be directed toward the authority structure of that country. Much the same can be said about the U.S. intervention in Vietnam. Such a characterization was not widely used prior to February 7, 1965, although American efforts to affect the authority structure of South Vietnam had been conducted through conventional diplomatic, economic, and military channels for several years.

When the United States resorted to bombing on that date, however, the conventional pattern was abruptly changed and the world came to view it as interventionary and to assess it accordingly. When the bombing is halted, moreover, the intervention is likely to be regarded as having ended even though a massive U.S. presence in that country may continue for years.

Persistent patterns of behavior, in other words, have a way of establishing their own legitimacy, irrespective of their illegitimacy when they originate. Although it does not involve behavior directed at authority structures, an especially clear-cut example of this point is provided by the argument during the Cuban missile crisis that U.S. missile sites in Turkey were no different from Soviet sites in Cuba. Such an argument may be compelling in terms of moral logic, but it did not prove to be compelling in terms of the logic of politics because during the previous fifteen years the sites in Turkey had come to be accepted as part of the conventional mode. Similarly, although acceptance of U.S. bombing in Vietnam would take much longer because different norms and attitudes are evoked by the use of devastating weapons than by their emplacement for use, if it persists for, say, a decade, the inclination to view it as interventionary will probably dissipate slowly and at some point the "American intervention" will have ceased and have been replaced by the "Vietnam situation."

In short, the study of intervention is the study of the unconventional in international politics and, since unconventionality becomes conventional as it persists over time, it is also the study of finite and temporary phenomena. For this reason, interventions may be more easily operationalized and measured than is the case with other types of influence. Inasmuch as they occur only when sharp breaks with prevailing patterns also occur, interventions are readily recognizable and thus do not seem to present such great obstacles to observation as those that, as noted above, usually obtain in the analysis of influence processes.

It must be emphasized that the convention-breaking characteristic of interventionary phenomena need not take the form of a sudden shift to armed force. Although all the examples used above to illustrate this characteristic are of a military nature, obviously there are a variety of other ways in which the prevailing mode of conduct can be abruptly altered. Military interventions are perhaps the most dramatic and clearcut departures from existing patterns and, for reasons having to do with the resistance of authority structures to external manipulation, they may also be the most frequent form of intervention.[46] Yet, as illustrated by the recent episode in which General de Gaulle spoke out about self-determination and federalism in Canada during a tour of that country, other kinds of intervention do occur. The definitional stress, in other words, is on the sharpness of the break with existing patterns and not on the type of pattern that is broken. De Gaulle's comments about Quebec constituted an intervention because such a theme had not previously marked French diplomatic behavior toward Canada. Similarly, a propaganda program that abruptly gave up a stress on cultural themes and turned to emphasizing desired changes in the authority structure of the target society would be widely regarded as interventionary. The introduction of political "strings" into a previously unpolitical foreign aid program is another obvious example of a nonmilitary type of intervention.

Not all sharp breaks with conventional patterns, however, are considered to be interventions. The second characteristic of such phenomena is no less important than the first. A close reading of the literature reveals that the inclination to classify international or foreign policy behavior as interventionary does not arise when the goal of the behavior is other than political. A nation might suddenly decide on a trade program designed to obtain a larger portion of a particular market in the target society, and its officials might pursue the program aggressively, but such behavior would not be deemed as interventionary. Likewise, to cite a more concrete example, the newly adopted American program to get more foreign tourists to vacation in the United States rather than elsewhere was not condemned as an intervention by actors in the international systems nor classified as such by students of the subject. Reactions of this sort by actors and scholars occur only when the convention-breaking behavior is addressed to the authority structure of the target society—that is, to the identity of those who make the decisions that are binding for the entire society and/or to the processes through which such decisions are made. New foreign policy initiatives designed to modify the behavior of voters

---

[46] The closeness of the link between military action and interventionary phenomena that is suggested by the examples used here can also be seen in the fact that some analysts are inclined to use the word "intervention" to describe certain kinds of situations in domestic politics, namely, those in which military officers seek to capture the governance of their own society. Cf. Robert D. Putnam, "Toward Explaining Military Intervention in Latin American Politics," *World Politics*, Vol. XX (October 1967), pp. 83-110; and Martin C. Needler, "Political Development and Military Intervention in Latin America," *American Political Science Review*, Vol. LX (September 1966), pp. 616-26.

abroad are thus likely to be regarded as interventionary even though equally extensive efforts to modify the behavior of tourists in the same country are not. In a like manner a convention-breaking attempt to get more representation for large groups of disenfranchised people (such as the blacks in Angola) would be viewed as an intervention, but a new program aimed at encouraging large groups to look more favorably upon the motives and achievements of the propagandizing society would not.

In short, neither of the two characteristics of intervention that seem appropriate as a basis for an operational definition is in itself sufficient to allow for the delineation of empirical materials. Both must be present. Either alone may sustain important types of foreign policy behavior, but both are necessary to sustain interventionary behavior. Moreover, as implied above, the two are often interdependent. The dearness of an authority structure to those encompassed by it makes it extraordinarily difficult to change or preserve from abroad even if its nature is the subject of controversy at home. Hence the inclination to resort to convention-breaking behavior is often reinforced whenever a desire to affect a foreign authority structure arises.

The advantages of using these two prime characteristics of interventions as a basis for operationalizing the concept are numerous. In the first place, such a formulation narrows the subject to manageable proportions and prevents all foreign policy actions (or inactions) from being treated as interventionary. By restricting intervention to convention-breaking behavior, the danger of analysis being confounded by the common-sense usage of "intervene" is greatly reduced and perhaps even eliminated. Secondly, the fact that the convention-breaking behavior must be directed at external authority structures serves as a further preventative against equating the study of intervention with the analysis of foreign policy. A large proportion of the foreign policy undertakings that interest the student of the subject are convention-breaking (or they would not catch his eye), but relatively few are directed at the structure of authority in other nations. A severance of diplomatic relations, a Marshall Plan, an alliance, or a Cuban missile crisis, for example, involves behavior that breaks sharply with the past and is central to foreign policy analysis, but such actions are directed at the policies or capabilities of other nations and not at their authority structures. Hence they would not fall within the analytic scope of the study of intervention. To be sure, authority structures might be indirectly affected by such actions, but by the time long-run consequences of this sort became manifest the original policies that brought them about would no longer be convention-breaking. Thirdly, the foregoing approach also narrows the concept of intervention in such a way that it is not equivalent to colonialism or imperialism. These latter phenomena involve the continued presence of the intervening actor in the target society, whereas interventions are considered to come to an end as time elapses and the presence of the intervening actor becomes conventional.

Another important advantage of the basis for operationalizing intervention outlined above is that it obviates the enormously difficult task of tracing motivation. In this formulation, neither the underlying goals of the intervening actor nor the attitudes of those in the intervened society need to be probed in order to determine the existence of interventionary phenomena. Under the best of circumstances goals and attitudes can be inferred from observed behavior only crudely, and interventions hardly constitute the best conditions for deriving motivational inferences. To be faced—as many students of international law consider they are—with the task of inferring whether the intervening actor really meant to behave coercively and whether the targets of the action actually felt coerced is to take on a staggering, if not impossible assignment. As developed above, however, such problems do not arise at the definitional level. Whatever the purposes of the intervenor and whatever the feelings of the intervened, an intervention exists when the former makes a sharp break with the prevailing manner of relating to the latter and directs behavior at the latter's structure of authority. The analyst may want to probe the motives and attitudes of the parties to an intervention in order to evaluate its success, but the foregoing formulation has the advantage of not requiring him to do so merely in order to identify the phenomena of interest.

This is not to say, of course, that operationalizing this formulation will be easy. When a conventional mode of behavior has been broken, or when the unconventional behavior has persisted long enough to have established a new convention, is not necessarily self-evident. Nor is it always plain whether authority structures are the target of the unconventional behavior. Difficulties will thus doubtless arise when the analyst turns to specifying the operations that will be performed to differentiate between conventional and unconventional behavior on the part of the intervening actor and between the authority structure and other aspects of the target society. However, generally speaking—or at least in comparison to most definitions of an intervention—these difficulties do not appear insurmountable and the definition suggested here does seem to be particularly conducive to operationalization.

VI. Toward a Theory of Intervention

Assuming that it can be used operationally, moreover, this formulation facilitates theory building. It does so by clarifying the key questions around which scientific inquiry can usefully be organized. In turn these questions provoke a line of reasoning that can be transformed into hypotheses subject to empirical testing. Hence let us conclude by outlining some of the theoretical implications of the foregoing formulation. More specifically, let us pursue the questions suggested by the conception of intervention as convention-breaking behavior directed at foreign authority structures. Under what conditions is a nation or an international organization likely to be ready to break with the prevailing mode of conduct and attempt to alter or preserve the structure of authority in another society? To what extent are developments within nations or international organizations likely to heighten their propensities to engage in such behavior? To what extent are differences among individual leaders, role-generated perceptions of bureaucracies, and the nature of constitutional restraints likely to contribute to interventionary propensities? To what extent are developments within the authority structure of a nation likely to attract convention-breaking behavior on the part of actors external to it? To what extent are the dynamics of intervention to be found in neither the actor that undertakes such behavior nor the one toward which it is directed, but elsewhere in the international system? In short, what is the relative potency of individual, role, governmental, societal, and systemic variables insofar as intervention as a form of foreign or international policy is concerned?[47]

Several lines of reasoning are precipitated by casting the task of theory building in this form. The clearest concerns the potency of the societal variable. Insofar as this involves the demands made upon officials by individuals and groups in the society, the likelihood of so-

[47] For a lengthy discussion of how an assessment of the relative potencies of these variables can facilitate scientific explanation of behavior in the international system, see my "Pre-Theories and Theories of Foreign Policy," in R. Barry Farrell (ed.), *Approaches to Comparative and International Politics* (Evanston: Northwestern University Press, 1966), pp. 27-92. For an empirical attempt to compare the potencies of two of the variables, see my "Private Preferences and Political Responsibilities: The Relative Potency of Individual and Role Variables in the Behavior of U.S. Senators," in J. David Singer (ed.), *Quantitative International Politics* (New York: Free Press, 1967), pp. 17-50.

cietal variables heightening interventionary propensities seems extremely small. Public opinion can constrain the behavior of foreign policy officials,[48] but rarely is it so aroused and organized as to press for new initiatives that break with conventional modes. Passivity tends to be the dominant posture of publics toward foreign affairs. Moreover, on the few occasions when developments abroad do arouse major segments of the public to clamor for convention-breaking behavior, the focus is usually the actions of foreign governments and not their authority structures. Publics do get preoccupied with enemies or potential enemies, for example, and they may thus press for severance of diplomatic relations, for retaliatory economic measures, for reversals of votes in U.N. debates, or for new departures in alliance policy. Such preoccupations, however, are rooted in a desire for protection against the threats posed by the enemy and, perhaps for a variety of reasons, the threats never seem so great as to generate public pressure for efforts to alter the personnel or procedures by which the enemy governs itself. The principles of sovereignty and self-determination relieve publics of worrying about how and by whom others are governed and, in any event, foreign authority structures are too far removed from the daily concerns of citizens to warrant their sustained advocacy of convention-breaking behavior.[49] In addition, given the nature of their target, interventions normally rely on an element of surprise and are launched suddenly, with the result that the processes of opinion formation and submission do not ordinarily get precipitated in the pre-decisional stage. Subsequently they may well be provoked by officials anxious to insure the success of the intervention by demonstrating the depth and breadth of public support for it, but we are concerned at this point with the variables that give rise to interventions and not those that account for their success or failure.

The relatively low potency that thus seems to attach to societal variables serves to emphasize the high potency of individual and bureaucratic role variables as sources of intervention. In the absence of public pressure for or against convention-breaking behavior of this kind, and in view of the advantages that stem from surprise and secrecy, interventions are very much the product of the perceptions, calcula-

[48] For an analysis of this relationship, see my *Public Opinion and Foreign Policy: An Operational Formulation* (New York: Random House, 1961), esp. Chap. 3.

[49] The reasoning underlying this conclusion is spelled out in greater detail in my "Foreign Policy as an Issue-Area," in James N. Rosenau (ed.), *Domestic Sources of Foreign Policy* (New York: The Free Press, 1967), pp. 11-50. For a possible empirical exception to this reasoning, India's 1961 intervention in Goa might be cited.

tions, and decisions that occur within decision-making organizations and their leaderships. Indeed, since conventions in international politics are not easily broken if support for such behavior is sought from other governments prior to its initiation, the planning of interventions also tends to be cut off from the international system and the flow of encouraging and restraining messages from it that any proposed policy normally evokes. Hence it could well be argued that interventions are more exclusively a consequence of decision-making activity than any other type of foreign policy, that assessments of the need for and probable outcome of interventionary behavior are more subject to the whims of individual leaders and the dynamics of bureaucratic structures than the diplomatic, economic, military, and political policies through which nations conventionally relate themselves to the international system. It is not mere coincidence, therefore, that unlike other innovations in foreign policy, interventions are normally followed by intense debates over the responsibility of individual leaders for their initiation and conduct. Eden's role in the Suez intervention of 1956, Eisenhower's in the Lebanon intervention of 1958, Kennedy's in the Bay of Pigs intervention of 1961, and Johnson's in the Dominican Republic intervention of 1965 were controversial highlights of their respective careers not only because of the moral issues that attach to interventions, but also and perhaps primarily because their authority in these instances—and thus their range of choice —was greater than at most other points during their tenures in office.[50]

Further evidence of the strength of individual and bureaucratic role variables is provided by the apparent irrelevance of basic governmental structure as a source of interventions. If the more outstanding postwar interventions are any indication, the hierarchical arrangements among the various branches of government and the degree to which they are accessible to each other and to nongovernmental organs of public sentiment would seem to bear little relationship to the level of a nation's interventionary propensities. A strong cabinet system with two highly disciplined parties, a weak cabinet system with many parties, a presidential government with two loosely knit parties, and a totali-

---

[50] The autobiographies of top leaders offer ample support for this point. Or at least chapters recounting interventionary decisions always seem to cite fewer external restraints and greater personal anguish over the decisional alternatives than do any other chapters. See, for example, Dwight D. Eisenhower, *Waging Peace 1956-1961* (Garden City: Doubleday, 1965), esp. 266-82.

tarian system with only a single party have all spawned interventions within the same six-year period,[51] and the only feature common to all of them is that the authority of the top leadership in all four cases could be challenged only after the convention-breaking undertaking had been launched.

Yet top policy-makers and their staffs do not act in a vacuum. Whatever their unique attitudes and characteristics, they do operate in an international context and they do have some view of what is a desirable state of affairs abroad and what events foster or inhibit its realization. Consequently, irrespective of whether they are rational or irrational, paranoic or confident, rigid or flexible, arrogant or accommodative, strong or weak—to mention but a few of the many individual variables to which high potency can attach—leaders and bureaucracies accord salience to some aspects of the international environment and ignore others. Pressure for or against interventions may not arise in the domestic environment, but developments in the foreign environment can be perceived to alter (or threaten to alter) the structure and/or functioning of the international system to such a degree that decision-makers and their organizations feel compelled to consider whether interventionary behavior is in order. In sum, as filtered through the screen of individual variables, systemic variables can be highly potent as sources of the perceptions, calculations, and decisions that result in interventionary behavior.

While the potency of individual variables is such that different leaders and bureaucracies will respond differently to the same developments in the international system, certain systemic variables seem likely to be especially potent as sources of interventions for those leaders and bureaucracies that, perhaps for a variety of individual reasons, are predisposed to undertake such behavior. In particular, three systemic variables appear likely to have a high potency in this regard, namely, the basic structure of the international system, the degree to which ideological rivalry sustains the structure, and the stability of the nations that comprise the system. By the basic structure of the international system is meant the degree to which the capability for affecting the conduct of international life is dispersed or concentrated within the system. A balance of power structure, for example, involves a greater dispersion of capabilities than a bipolar structure. The more dispersed

[51] The reference is, respectively, to England's 1956 Suez intervention, India's 1961 Goa intervention, the U.S.'s 1961 Cuba intervention, and the U.S.S.R.'s 1956 Hungarian intervention.

the structure of the international system, of course, the less the likelihood that it can be rapidly and radically altered by a single development. Hence decision-makers are less likely to succumb to the temptation to engage in convention-breaking behavior toward an unfolding situation in the international system the less capabilities are concentrated in the system. Contrariwise, interventionary behavior seems more likely to occur the more tightly the system is structured.[52] In a tight system a potential shift in the allegiances and ties of a nation will seem more threatening to other nations that stand to suffer if the shift occurs than would be the case in a loosely structured era of world politics.

The potency of these variables is closely related to the second type of systemic variable noted above. The kind and degree of ideological conflict that marks the international system both shapes its structure and is in turn channeled by the distribution of capabilities. When ideological rivalry is intense, decision-makers are more likely to attach greater import to possible governmental changes abroad than is the case when blueprints of the future are less salient features of international life. For the more such blueprints are seen to be at stake in international politics, the more are top officials and their staffs likely to allow their personal inclinations to become involved in their perceptions and calculations, and thus the more will they be ready to undertake convention-breaking behavior. Indeed, under the circumstance of a highly ideological politics, the desirability of governmental changes abroad may generate interventionary behavior even if the possibility of such changes is extremely remote. United Nations interventions in South Africa and externally sponsored guerrilla movements in Latin America are illustrative in this regard.

Apart from the interventionary behavior that arises out of dynamic ideological sources, however, the more precarious authority structures are abroad the greater is the likelihood that convention-breaking attempts to preserve or alter them will be launched. This is perhaps the most potent of all the systemic variables. While publics may be unconcerned about authority structures abroad, plainly those responsible for the maintenance of a favorable international environment

---

[52] These hypotheses were stimulated by Morton A. Kaplan, "Intervention in Internal War: Some Systemic Sources," in Rosenau (ed.), *International Aspects of Civil Strife*, pp. 92-121. Indeed, this is one of the few works in the literature on intervention that is rooted in a scientific mode of analysis. Kaplan's conclusions about intervention are derived not from moral, legal, or strategic considerations, but from a theoretical model of the international system.

will be constantly alert to any sudden changes that may alter the personnel and orientations of foreign governments. Aside from the consequences of war, the major turning points in world politics occur when old regimes collapse and are replaced by new ones with substantially different policies.[53] A nationalist regime in China succumbs to a Communist one, a Sukarno is ousted, a military revolt in France brings a de Gaulle to power, a Stalin dies—changes in authority structures such as these lie at the root of radical transformations in the international system and thus top officials everywhere are, whatever their individual differences, likely to be particularly sensitive to the stability of foreign governments. The less the stability, the greater their readiness to break with tradition and to undertake unconventional efforts to avert the dangers of—or to seize upon the advantages in—the unstable situations.

THE FOREGOING is, of course, only the beginning of a theoretical inquiry into intervention. It only suggests some lines of reasoning that might be pursued and leaves undone the task of deriving operational hypotheses through which the relative potency of the key variables can be assessed. Certain implications for the problem of intervention in the developing states posed by this symposium, however, can be discerned even in this highly general formulation. Most notably, it follows directly from these tentative assessments that interventionary behavior in the coming decades is likely to be a recurrent feature of the world scene. The developing nations are by definition—that is, by virtue of the fact that they are undergoing rapid economic, social, and political change—burdened with unstable and delicate authority structures. The legitimacy of the developmental process is in itself a political issue and so, therefore, is the authority structure committed to its continuance and the identity of the persons and groups who at any moment in time occupy the key positions in the structure. Hence the international system appears likely to be characterized by a preponderance of unstable subsystems in the foreseeable future. Since this condition will doubtless be accompanied by a continuance of the pattern whereby the distribution of capabilities in the system is concentrated in but a few of the subsystems, and inasmuch as the Soviet-Chinese split has heightened the ideological content of world politics, incidences of intervention seem likely to occur at a greater rather than a lesser rate

[53] Cf. Richard N. Rosecrance, *Action and Reaction in World Politics* (Boston: Little, Brown & Co., 1963), pp. 280-85.

in the years ahead and the developing nations appear destined to be the primary focus of this form of international behavior. The one factor that seems capable of negating this hypothesis is that the nature and potency of individual and role variables will change as leaders and bureaucracies are exposed to and learn from a succession of interventionary experiences.

Here, it might be added, is where scientific inquiry can serve moral, legal, and strategic concerns. The very fact that individual variables appear to be so potent as sources of interventions gives those who aspire to the creation of new moral, legal, and strategic norms a basis for action. By developing a more profound comprehension of the dynamics of interventionary behavior, the lessons of experience can be fed back into the roles occupied by top leaders and their staffs, thereby altering the individual variables that determine the inclination to break with convention and intervene in authority structures abroad.

A Postscript

PERFORCE this chapter must begin on a personal note. It was solicited because of a vigorous reaction to a paper on the concept of intervention (printed immediately preceding this section of this chapter) that I presented to the opening session of a two-day conference on the subject.[1] The central theme of that paper appeared to be rejected by a large majority of the specialists in political science, economics, and international law who participated in the conference, and while it might be best to leave well enough alone, it nevertheless seems useful to sustain the dialogue and attempt to establish communication, something that did not occur during those days of discussion. Perhaps the five weeks between the conference and this writing is not sufficient time for sober reflection on the merits of and reasons for the extended criticism of the original paper, but its widespread rejection contains a lesson that might be lost with the passage of more time. As memory fades, the fact that absence of communication marked the deliberations is likely to be obscured, and there is a lesson in this fact which it seems important to try to understand. In addition, the experience of the Princeton conference is now an inescapable part of my thinking on the problems posed by the concept of intervention and it would be unfair not to alert the reader to the possibly biased nature of what follows.

[1] "Intervention as a Scientific Concept."

I. An Operational Definition

The earlier paper stressed that the concept of intervention is used in a very precise way in the literature; that operational definitions are conspicuously lacking; that instead ambiguous and contradictory formulations characterize the voluminous moral, legal, and strategic writings on the subject; that as a result intervention has come to be treated as synonymous with influence; and that it is thus necessary to approach interventionary phenomena scientifically, as well as morally, legally, and strategically, if comprehension of this crucial aspect of world politics is to advance. In order to demonstrate that a scientific approach is not unmanageable and that it could be of great assistance to those with moral, legal, and strategic concerns, an operational definition of the concept was developed and some theoretical propositions suggested by the formulation were outlined. This operational definition of intervention and the case that was made for it were at the heart of the criticism occasioned by the paper. Hence it seems appropriate to refer the reader to key passages in the preceding section of this chapter in which the definition was developed and justified: see pages 997-1003.

II. The Rejection of the Definition

At the conference the main grounds expressed for rejecting this formulation was that it is too narrow. In the words of one critic, "The definition sacrifices relevance for precision." A number of conferees reiterated this idea by citing examples of significant historical episodes that endured for years—thus losing their convention-breaking character—and that they had always classified as interventions, but that fell outside the scope of the definition. Others criticized the narrowness of the formulation by noting that it omitted foreign aid programs, which they had always regarded as interventionary because the aid-givers can profoundly alter economic and social structures even though alteration may not also occur in the authority structures of the recipient societies. Still others misconstrued the definition as being limited to situations in the West and failing to encompass the subtler forms of intervention that occur in underdeveloped countries.

Offered an opportunity to comment on these reactions, my response seemed obvious. While relevance ought not to be abandoned for the sake of precision, relevance without precision cannot serve the goals of comprehension and communication. No claim is made, the response emphasized, that my formulation can or should be the last word on the subject. All that is claimed for it is that it encompasses important phenomena and does so in a way that allows for clear distinctions between interventionary and noninterventionary behavior. Other formulations may be preferable, and possibly several are needed to encompass all the phenomena that the word "intervention" generally connotes, but the one offered here at least has the virtue of achieving some degree of *both* relevance and precision. If, the response concluded, we do not agree on the need for precision and proceed instead in terms that equate intervention with any consequence that transpires across national boundaries, the two days of deliberation will be marked by the absence not only of clarity and communication but also of direction. Unrestrained by a commitment to precision, our discussion might well extend across a vast array of unrelated matters. In effect, it was warned, we might spend two days analyzing the problems of world politics rather than the problems of intervention.

It is fair to say that this is exactly what happened. The discussion knew no bounds. The dilemmas of American foreign policy, the dynamics of African politics, the future of international law, the fiscal policies of the United Nations, the stability and transformation of international systems, the grants vs. loans problem of foreign aid, the challenge of colonial and neocolonial relationships—these are but a few of the topics that came up and received extended consideration. The bearing of the deliberations on intervention was taken for granted throughout. Occasionally a participant expressed doubt about the utility of dealing with so many and such diverse problems, but acquiescence to the impulse to avoid a narrow conception of interventionary phenomena was the predominant mood. When aid and trade problems were being analyzed, reference was made to economic intervention. When the role of force entered the discussion, the rubric of military intervention was used. When the activities of the United Nations were mentioned, the focus was seen as having shifted to multilateral intervention. When the dynamics of colonial and neocolonial relations were examined, attention was viewed as having moved on to political intervention. Each topic was treated as constituting a different form of intervention and the question of whether one person's conception of interventionary phenomena was similar to anyone else's was ignored. In effect, ideas were presented, but not exchanged. The topic of intervention served as license for undisciplined thought, special concern, ambiguous expression, and unrestrained impression at least as much as for disciplined insight, systematic proposition, and clear-cut elaboration.

Perhaps it is self-righteous to depict these proceedings so critically. It could well be argued that conferences never stick to a narrowly defined subject and it is erroneous to expect otherwise—that the foregoing describes the fate of any conference in which discussion is limited to two days. Long experience confirms that this is hardly enough time for specialists in a single field to establish the basis of communication, much less those in fields with such diverse approaches and concerns as political science, economics, and international law. Viewed in this way, it could be further argued that at least the various specialists were brought together and exposed to each other's mode of analyzing the same problem, that some intriguing ideas were advanced, and that hopefully the basis for communication in the future may have thus been established.

This line of reasoning, however, does not go far enough. While it is valid and provides a rationale for the proceedings and for participation in them, the explicitness of the rejection of the idea that relevance must be accompanied by precision cannot be ignored. It is difficult to dismiss the insensitivity to conceptual boundaries and the uncritical readiness to equate intervention with influence as merely an example of "conference behavior." The unwillingness to adhere to a narrow and tentative formulation developed by someone else is quite understandable, but the widespread and unreserved avoidance of definitional and conceptual considerations for the sake of relevance gives pause. One cannot help wondering what it is about interventionary phenomena that lead to a preference for ambiguity and to the abandonment of any criteria of methodological rigor. In retrospect, the root of the problem seems to be that two basic and interrelated distinctions were overlooked—namely, the distinction between the common-sense and operational meanings of intervention on the one hand and between intervention as empirical phenomenon and analytic concept on the other.

III. The Distinction between the Common-Sense and Technical Meanings of Intervention

The analysis of political phenomena is plagued by the fact that they are also the subject of everyday conversation. In the latter kind of discourse precise terminology and exact meaning is neither an aspiration nor a ground rule. One relies on common sense, general understanding, and metaphoric suggestion to convey the essentials of an idea and whether nuance has been grasped and complexity delineated is not a major concern. In systematic analysis, however, nuance and complexity are aspirations and strict ground rules have evolved to insure their realization. Most notably, one must specify the operations one performs to identify the phenomena about which ideas are being communicated in order that different analysts may know how and when to observe the same phenomena. In fields of inquiry where operationalization has become accepted procedure, a special terminology has developed for the delineation of the various operations that analysts perform. Perhaps for a variety of reasons, a comparable technical language for the systematic study of political phenomena has not developed. In this field the same terminology serves both the popular and professional concern and thus both casual conversation and causal analysis make use of the same conceptual equipment. Illustrating with an analogy from another field, it is as if medical experts used, for example, broken bones, aching muscles, and tired blood as their conceptual tools for understanding pathological phenomena.

Burdened with a common-sense terminology, the political analyst must be especially conscious of the technical meanings he ascribes to it. Otherwise he can easily slip into popular rhetoric without knowing it, thus greatly reducing his chances of successfully probing the complex processes in which he is interested.

Viewed retrospectively, it seems clear that the concept of intervention is particularly susceptible to confusion in this regard and that the proceedings at Princeton succumbed to it. There is, as noted, the common-sense notion that intervention occurs whenever one nation becomes involved in the affairs of another and, in the absence of additional technical concepts to deal with the aspects excluded from the operational definition outlined above, the limitations imposed by the definition seemed excessive and the temptation to fall back on common usage prevailed. Confronted with an attempt to infuse the concept with a narrow and precise technical meaning, the conferees preferred the breadth of the common sense meaning of the word "intervene." In rejecting a particular operational definition, they thus rejected operationalization as a whole and affirmed the legitimacy of using the concept in a variety of ambiguous ways.

INTERVENTION AS A SCIENTIFIC CONCEPT

IV. The Distinction between Intervention as
Empirical Phenomenon and Analytic Concept

The tendency to resist the distinction between a common-sense and a technical meaning of intervention is reinforced by the fact that actors in the political arena use the term. The Russians have a doctrine of "intervention" and so do the Chinese and Cubans, with the result that controversy over the strategy and tactics of "intervention" is a persistent feature of the Communist world. Similarly, Latin Americans have long complained about the "interventions" launched by the colossus to the North and in the United States itself recent months have witnessed the mushrooming of debate over the propriety of "intervention." As a symbol for ideas and actions to which politicians and public pay lip service, in other words, intervention is pervasive and inescapable. Obviously, however, its meaning in such usage is not necessarily the same as that of the analytic concept to which the intervention label is also given. The empirical data observed by an analyst and the conceptual equipment he employs need to be distinguished if the latter is to give coherence to the former. What officials and citizens call "intervention" may be the complex resultant of multiple processes for the analyst, and he will never comprehend these processes if he allows the subject of his investigation to define his terms for him.

Again taking advantage of hindsight, it seems clear that the Princeton proceedings suffered from a clouding of the distinction between the empirical and analytic uses of intervention. The existence of identifiable individuals and groups in the political arena who contest the merits of "intervention" as an instrument of foreign policy made the operational definition seem insufficient and made the common-sense use of the term seem justifiable. After all, the reasoning seems to have been, if military intervention can be condemned by Latin Americans, economic intervention protested by Africans, and cultural intervention derided by Europeans, the phenomenon is in fact diverse and it is thus a distortion to limit one's horizons only to those interventionary activities directed at authority structures. Moreover, if people in the underdeveloped areas of the world complain that the colonial interventions of earlier centuries have never really ended, it is absurd to adhere to a definition in which the phenomenon is conceived to be transitory.

V.   Conclusion

The lesson seems clear. If comprehension of international political phenomena is ever to move beyond simple impressions and moral assertions, students of the subject must be able to communicate with each other and thereby build upon each other's ideas and findings. Communication that leads to an ever more profound comprehension is not necessarily accomplished through verbal and written exchange. Discipline is also required, so that words have the same meanings and ideas the same referents. For this to occur one must be ready to forego the luxury of common-sense analysis and accept the rigors of a technical language and the boundaries of a specialized set of concepts. Definitional consistency may appear to curb creativity and limit relevance, but without it creativity can never be more than speculation and relevance can never extend beyond a particular moment in time.

To be sure, there is nothing magical about disciplined communication. Men will doubtless wrangle over the use of the more rigorous concepts and many of the operational definitions may well prove inadequate. Yet, without this type of communication, findings cannot cumulate and comprehension cannot deepen. If impression is not tempered by discipline and if common sense is not refined by technical competence, the dynamics of interventionary phenomena will remain obscure and the many important problems subsumed therein will continue to resist understanding.

Intervention and International Systems

ORAN R. YOUNG

The term "intervention" is employed widely in analyses of international politics. There is no consensus, however, on the content of this term, and disparate phenomena are commonly lumped together in a large grab-bag under the heading of intervention. Little attention is devoted to the formulation of criteria of inclusion and exclusion in dealing with the topic, and to make matters worse, the term is frequently imbued with strong normative or ideological connotations that make it difficult to treat intervention analytically without being propelled willy-nilly into prescriptive debates on the subject.[1]

Under the circumstances, generalizations about intervention in international politics cannot be developed without first considering the problems of definition. In order to avoid a fruitless prolongation of debate over incompatible "essential" definitions of intervention, it seems crucial to adopt a "nominal" definition at the outset.[2] In the present essay, there-

[1] For a useful discussion of the normative ambiguity associated with the term "intervention" consult William T. Burke, "The Legal Regulation of Minor International Coercion: A Framework of Inquiry," in Roland J. Stanger, ed. *Essays on Intervention*, (Columbus, Ohio: Ohio State University Press, 1964), pp. 87-96.

[2] For a definitive discussion of the differences between "essential" and "nominal" definitions see Karl R. Popper, *The Poverty of Historicism* (New York: Harper and Row, 1964), pp. 26-34.

fore, intervention refers to organized and systematic activities across recognized boundaries aimed at affecting the political authority structures of the target.[3]

Several features of this definition should be emphasized. Intervention refers to organized and systematic activities; haphazard and inadvertent activities are not included in the definition. Next, the term is used to refer to activities across recognized boundaries. Border conflicts and clashes over disputed territory, therefore, are not taken as cases of intervention. In addition, the term intervention is associated with activities aimed at changing or preventing change in political authority structures. Straightforward efforts to induce changes in particular policies on the part of another government without attempting to alter the government itself in any important way are not included under the heading of intervention.

Intervention in History

Intervention has been a recurrent feature of the history of international politics. It has not, however, been a constant or unchanging phenomenon.

During the fifth century B.C., as relations among the Greek states began to polarize around the affairs of Athens and Sparta, intervention by the major powers in the affairs of the lesser Greek states grew to substantial proportions. What began as alliance relationships linking the lesser states to Athens and Sparta quickly developed into coercive patterns of intervention on the part of the great powers.[4] Imperial Rome at the height of its power occupied a position of such dominance in the international system that it could intervene in the affairs of most of the lesser actors in the system with virtual impunity. In the European system of the sixteenth and seventeenth centuries, which included several distinctive types of actors, intervention also reached substantial proportions.[5] During this period, the combination of religious conflicts and the widespread upheavals associated with the transition to a states system made intervention a major feature of international politics. Similarly, the Na-

[3] Activities of this kind may, of course, be designed either to replace existing structures or to shore up structures thought to be in danger of collapse.

[4] For a useful discussion consult Peter J. Fliess, *Thucydides and the Politics of Bipolarity* (Baton Rouge: Louisiana State University Press, 1966), Chapter 4.

[5] With regard to types of actors, international systems can vary from homogeneity to extreme heterogeneity. The international system of the sixteenth and seventeenth centuries was relatively heterogeneous since it encompassed states, nation-states, city-states, empires, and the Church.

poleonic and post-Napoleonic periods in Europe were characterized by high levels of intervention. The continuing ideological appeal of the French Revolution combined with the power of Napoleonic France to produce a state of ferment in Europe in which intervention and counter-intervention became the order of the day. The reaction to this ferment in the post-Napoleonic period produced a situation in which "conserva-tive" interventions became prominent.[6] Interestingly, one of the classic debates concerning the circumstances under which intervention is legit-imate and the forms which it should take occurred during the post-Na-poleonic period. This debate was symbolized by the growing divergence between Metternich and Castlereagh after the Congress of Vienna.[7]

Finally, the contemporary international system is also one in which intervention across recognized boundaries is common.[8] Intervention is not of equal importance in every region of the world; in comparison with various earlier periods, for example, intervention among the states of Europe is currently quite limited. Nevertheless, considering the con-temporary international system, intervention remains a major feature of international politics.

At the same time, the importance of intervention in international pol-itics clearly has not remained constant over time. Though intervention has seldom been an insignificant feature of international politics, there have been periods in which intervention has been far less pervasive than during those mentioned in the preceding paragraphs. From the Peace of Utrecht in 1713 to the French Revolution and from approximately 1850 to the First World War, for example, intervention was less prevalent in the European states system than it was during the sixteenth and seventeenth centuries or the Napolenoic era.[9] And in many periods of history hege-monial and colonial patterns of rule have served to minimize the relevance of interventionary activities across recognized boundaries.[10]

[6] French intervention in Spain in 1823 is a good example. In this case, France acted under a mandate from the Congress of Verona.

[7] This debate is discussed at length in Henry A. Kissinger, *A World Restored* (New York: Grosset and Dunlap, 1964).

[8] In this system interventionary activities are stimulated both by ideological com-petition (the so-called East-West problem) and by the asymmetrical distribution of values among actors (the so-called North-South problem).

[9] It should be noted, however, that interventions by European powers in non-European areas played a significant role during these periods in permitting a low level of intervention among the European states themselves.

[10] British colonial rule in India, for example, served to minimize external inter-ventions in the area even though it accorded hegemonial control to Great Britain.

Opportunities for Intervention

This essay will explore the relevance of systemic factors in determining the frequency of intervention in international politics and the variations in that frequency, both over time and from one region to another. In analyzing intervention from this perspective, it is important to focus on systems characterized by horizontal rather than hierarchical patterns of order and by relatively high degrees of autonomy among their actors. Empirically, international systems are members of this general class of systems.

Several systemic factors determine the *opportunities* for intervention in international politics. Intervention is apt to be conditioned by disparities in effective power among the actors in an international system. In general, the more extensive the disparities in power, the greater the opportunities for intervention among the actors in the system. Though systems in which the distribution of power is relatively equal may be characterized by extensive conflict, the resultant clashes are apt to take the form of direct confrontation *between* actors rather than interventions by some actors in the internal affairs of others. This is the result of the ability of individual actors to fend off interventionary activities by other actors.[11] Where disparities in power are extensive, on the other hand, the ability of the weaker actors to fend off outside intervention is likely to be sharply limited. This relationship is important, for example, in explaining the prevalence of intervention in ancient Greece, the period of Roman Imperium, Napoleonic Europe, and the contemporary international system.

A second systemic determinant of the opportunities for intervention is the *structure* of an international system in contrast to the distribution of effective power within it. The relevance of structure can be illustrated easily by contrasting unipolar and multipolar systems. In a system clearly dominated by a single actor there is little lesser powers can do to prevent intervention by that actor.[12] For example, peripheral actors had limited ability to fend off intervention by imperial Rome.[13] When there are several major powers, on the other hand, lesser powers may acquire some ability to resist intervention by playing the major

[11] In such situations there is little prospect of avoiding conflict through the development of dominance-submission relationships. Under the circumstances, a competition for status is apt to be a characteristic feature of international politics.

[12] Some analysts argue that the contemporary international system is evolving toward unipolarity based on American predominance. For an example consult George Liska, *Imperial America* (Baltimore: Johns Hopkins University Press, 1967).

[13] *Ibid.*, especially Chapters II and III.

powers off against each other. Moreover, the major powers may be inhibited in their actions by the dangers of becoming seriously entangled
with each other through processes of competitive intervention in the affairs
of a lesser actor.[14]

The precise impact of these structural restraints on intervention, however, is apt to be sharply conditioned by several additional factors. If
the relevant major powers engage in *de facto* collusion, the ability of
a lesser power to resist intervention will decline precipitously. This is
what happened, for example, in the case of Poland during the second
half of the eighteenth century as well as in the case of Poland and the
Baltic states in the aftermath of the Molotov-Ribbentrop Pact of 1939.[15]
Furthermore, the willingness of major powers to intervene in the affairs
of others is shaped by the nature of the prevailing military technology
and by the presence or absence of third powers that would benefit from
confrontations between the major powers of the system. For example,
the existence of nuclear weapons is a major restraint on the interventionary activities of the United States and the Soviet Union in the contemporary system. Similarly, the presence of China is an important
determinant of Soviet and American proclivities to intervene in
Asian politics in the current period.[16]

A third determinant of the opportunities for intervention in international politics is the relative *internal* viability of the actors in an
international system. The less viable an actor is, the more susceptible
it will be to intervention by outside powers. During periods of extended
civil strife, the ability of an actor to resist external incursions tends to
decline. In fact, various local factions are apt to find it expedient, at

[14] For a case study illustrating the relevance of this factor see Oran R. Young,
Intermediaries and Interventionists: Third Parties in the Middle East Crisis," *International Journal*, Vol. XXIII, No. 1, Winter, 1967-1968, pp. 52-73. At the same
time, fears of entanglement can have the reverse effect when there is reason to
believe that a lesser power could deliberately precipitate a great-power clash. The
United States has periodically intervened in the affairs of Nationalist China for this
reason. And Soviet activities with regard to Egypt appear to be moving in this
direction at the present time.

[15] The drastic nature of the consequences in such cases is no doubt one important reason why Chinese charges concerning Soviet-American collusion sometimes
find receptive audiences in the current period.

[16] The Chinese factor, however, cuts both ways for the United States and the
Soviet Union. The presence of China gives these powers strong incentives to avoid
competitive interventions in Asia. At the same time, however, it increases the incentives of each superpower to intervene in unstable situations in Asia to offset
the potential influence of China. Under the circumstances, the dividing line between competitive and cooperative interventions tends to become a very fine one.

least in proximate terms, to encourage intervention.[17] Moreover, the presence of upheaval or ferment in local politics often makes it possible for outside powers to exercise considerable influence through quite limited and indirect activities. Internal weakness was an influential catalyst of the "conservative" interventions of the post-Napoleonic period. And the internal problems of the Ottoman Empire and of China were major determinants of the opportunities for intervention in these areas during the nineteenth century. Moreover, this factor is an important source of pressures for both "conservative" and "revolutionary" interventions in the contemporary international system.

Finally, the opportunities for intervention tend to vary with the *level of interdependence* (as opposed to autonomy) among the actors in an international system. The higher the level of interdependence, the greater the opportunities for intervention in international politics. The growth of interdependence among actors increases both the volume and the functional significance of interactions among them. While this may produce opportunities and incentives for the expansion of political community, it also enlarges the scope for interventions on the part of any given actor in the affairs of other actors.[18] By definition, the actors in an international system are not totally autonomous. Intervention, therefore, is possible in any international system. Nevertheless, opportunities for intervention are particularly marked in the contemporary international system since the level of interdependence among the actors in the system is both high and rising.

Motivations for Intervention

In addition to systemic determinants of *opportunities* for intervention, there are also systemic determinants of *motivations* for intervention. Incentives for intervention are linked to the political revisionism concerning the existing distribution of values in an international system. As revision toward values increases and intensifies, incentives become more powerful. This applies both to "revolutionary" and to "conservative" interventions. The more intolerable the existing distribution of values is thought to be, the more decision-makers with revisionist attitudes are likely to adopt policies involving interventionary activities as a means of altering them.

---

[17] The Vietnam situation is a case in point.

[18] This view is often discussed in very optimistic terms. It generally stems from some version of the fundamental tenets of functionalism. For the classic presentation of the functionalist thesis see David Mitrany, *A Working Peace System* (Chicago: Quadrangle Books, 1966), pp. 25-99.

Interventionary practices are apt to be especially important during periods when the distribution of effective power is changing more rapidly than the distribution of other values.[19] The resultant prospect of "revolutionary" intervention, however, will increase incentives among decision-makers in "satisfied" states to use interventionary activities to stem the tide of revolution. These patterns are quite evident in Napoleonic and post-Napoleonic Europe. Moreover, these relationships between revisionism and intervention appear to be particularly marked in the contemporary international system, which is characterized by a highly asymmetrical distribution of values among the actors.[20] The political structures and processes of the system are rapidly changing, and the level of human sensitivity to inequalities in the distribution of values between actors (as well as within the actors) is extremely high in the contemporary period.[21]

Political ideologies and normative conceptions of appropriate forms of political order in international systems also affect incentives for intervention. This includes both conceptions concerning the internal politics of individual actors and conceptions oriented toward the political order of the international system as a whole. In general, the prevalence of intervention will tend to increase as these politically dynamic ideologies become more pervasive and influential. The existence of one or more actors with strong predispositions concerning appropriate forms of political order will raise pressures both for intervention and for counterintervention in international politics. This is quite similar to what has been described as the crusading or proselytizing syndrome.[22]

Beyond this, the coexistence of *competing* conceptions of appropriate forms of political order will tend to heighten incentives for intervention. As this competition becomes more pronounced, the incentives for interventionary activities involving a crusading spirit are apt to

[19] The role of Germany in the interwar period constitutes an illustration of this phenomenon. Even if Hitler had not come to power, it seems likely that Germany's evolving position in the international system would have propelled the country toward at least some interventionary activities during this period.

[20] Moreover, the pattern taken by these asymmetries is such as to exacerbate other potentially disruptive issues such as racism.

[21] Until quite recently, human sensitivities along these lines appear to have been directed overwhelmingly toward the distribution of values within individual states. The contemporary "revolution of rising expectations," however, focuses explicitly on inequalities *between* states with regard to the distribution of values.

[22] Actors involved in crusading activities are apt to intervene in the affairs· of others either to win converts or to stamp out perceived heresies.

increase.[23] In extreme cases, decision-makers of the major competing actors are likely to dichotomize the world ideologically and favor intervention wherever it helps extend the sway of their conceptions or preserves their influence over other actors.[24]

Historically, these factors are important in explaining the prevalence of intervention in the international politics of the sixteenth and seventeenth centuries as well as of the Napoleonic and post-Napoleonic periods. And they are major determinants of patterns of intervention characteristic of contemporary international politics.

The Regulation of Intervention

What are the implications of these systemic determinants for contemporary international politics? Above all they indicate that intervention will continue to be an important feature of the international system for the foreseeable future. The present system rates high in the determinants of intervention outlined earlier. Especially striking in the present system is the strength of interdependence among actors and the degree of political revisionism toward the distribution of values in the system. Other factors of intervention notable in the system are the disparities in power, differences in internal viability, and variance of normative conceptions of the various actors.

Under the circumstances, it seems clear that existing "norms" of nonintervention in international politics will be ineffective and unacceptable in the foreseeable future.[25] Norms of nonintervention are particularly characteristic of states systems in which the boundaries between actors are clear and the ability of individual actors to operate autonomously is great. In this sense, norms of nonintervention are corollaries

[23] The terms "immoderate" and "revolutionary international politics" are commonly applied to situations of this kind. This usage is employed by writers such as Arnold Toynbee and Stanley Hoffmann. See, for example, Stanley Hoffmann, "International Systems and International Law," in Klaus Knorr and Sidney Verba, eds., *The International System* (Princeton: Princeton University Press, 1961), pp. 205-235.

[24] Both Soviet and American attitudes toward intervention during the early years of the Cold War appeared to approximate this image from time to time.

[25] The notion of nonintervention is still generally regarded as an integral part of international law. For useful discussions of the problems involved in applying this notion to contemporary conditions see Wolfgang Friedmann, *The Changing Structure of International Law* (New York: Columbia University Press, 1964), pp. 262-272, and Richard A. Falk, "Janus Tormented: The International Law of Internal War," in James N. Rosenau, ed., *International Aspects of Civil Strife* (Princeton: Princeton University Press, 1964), pp. 185-248.

of norms concerning state sovereignty.[26] Historically, norms of non-intervention attained˙ considerable influence during the latter half of the nineteenth century in the European states system along with the modern version of the doctrine of state sovereignty. And in this setting such norms were reasonably congruent with the nature of political reality. These norms continue to be an integral component of the underlying conceptual framework of international politics. The nature of political reality in the international system, however, has moved increasingly away from these enshrined concepts, and the resulting incongruities are an important barrier to the development of norms that are more appropriate to contemporary international politics.

Given the fact that intervention is likely to remain a major feature of international politics for the foreseeable future, several new sets of questions arise in place of discussions of nonintervention. One set focuses on the purposes or objectives for which intervention is to be considered legitimate. The problem here is fundamentally one of making normative distinctions among political values. The distinction between "conservative" and "revolutionary" intervention, which was introduced in a preceding section, is relevant. Other normative factors are also relevant in the contemporary international system. Is intervention legitimate, for example, in the interests of encouraging democracy, free enterprise, or Communism? What would be the status of interventionary activities designed to break the hold of racism in countries such as Rhodesia and South Africa?[27] And is intervention an acceptable means of altering the highly asymmetrical distribution of welfare values in the contemporary system? Despite the prevalence of intervention, there appears to be a notable lack of consensus on these normative problems in the present international system.[28] Moreover, it is virtually impossible, at this time, to reach any confident conclusions concerning trends in this area.[29]

[26] For an interesting short discussion of the evolution of the doctrine of state sovereignty see F. H. Hinsley, "The Concept of Sovereignty and the Relations Between States," *Journal of International Affairs*, Vol. XX, No. 2, 1967, pp. 242-252.

[27] Potential United Nations actions along these lines have been widely debated in recent years. Interestingly, this may lead more and more to discussions of the extent to which the United Nations can engage in "peacebreaking" activities in the interests of specified goals.

[28] Internationally, the competition of divergent ideologies constitutes a major source of this lack of consensus. At present, however, the absence of consensus is quite evident within individual states as well as internationally.

[29] The confusion associated with the American involvement in Vietnam illustrates this problem clearly. At this time, it is impossible to judge whether the predominant American reaction to the Vietnam involvement will be against all forms of intervention in the future or only against certain specified forms of intervention.

A second set of questions deals with the forms of intervention in international politics. It is possible, for example, to distinguish between collective intervention by a regional organization or a general international organization, and intervention by individual states. Similarly, there are important differences between unilateral and competitive intervention in the affairs of a particular actor. There are also many gradations between the most indirect and covert forms of intervention and the most direct and overt types of intervention.

Several sets of criteria are relevant in evaluating the various forms of intervention. Normative criteria can be applied here just as they can be employed in evaluating the purposes or objectives of intervention. It is often argued, for example, that collective intervention is normatively preferable to intervention by individual actors. However, there appears to be widespread normative confusion about the choice between regional and general international organizations in the area of intervention at the present time.[30] Various instrumental criteria can also be employed in evaluating cases of intervention in international politics. For example, it is possible to differentiate forms of intervention in terms of their capacity to generate serious challenges to the stability of the overall international system.[31] In the contemporary international system it is clear that competitive intervention involving the great powers poses a real problem for international stability. Unilateral intervention, whatever its normative values, is hardly likely to generate serious challenges to international stability.[32]

A final set of questions concerns the development of "rules of the game" in order to regulate or manage the consequences of intervention.[33] Rules of the game in international politics are frequently ambiguous, loosely applied, or poorly enforced. But they are, nonetheless, influential determinants of decision-making within national elites. In the case of intervention, rules of the game would deal with problems such

[30] For a discussion of the relevant problems see Linda B. Miller, "Regional Organization and the Regulation of Internal Conflict," *World Politics*, Vol. XIX, No. 4, July 1967, pp. 582-600.
[31] Similarly, forms of intervention could be differentiated in terms of the destruction of human life and property they are apt to produce.
[32] From this perspective, compare the unilateral interventions in Hungary in 1956 and the Dominican Republic in 1965 with the competitive interventions in Korea and South Vietnam.
[33] The concept "rules of the game" is *not* used here as a synonym for international law. Some rules of the game may be incorporated in legal prescriptions, but many effective standards of action have no legal standing.

as what actors can intervene, under what circumstances, in what places, and for what purposes. In various historical periods, these questions have been widely debated in both normative and expediential terms. The Metternich-Castlereagh debate, mentioned above, is a classic example. At present, however, the continuing influence of norms of nonintervention at the conceptual level, as well as the impact of ideology on international politics, make it difficult to debate questions of this kind systematically, despite the obvious importance of intervention in empirical terms. As a result, the barriers to the development of effective rules of the game concerning intervention are substantial. Since some forms of intervention could seriously threaten stability or have destructive consequences in the contemporary international system, the dangers associated with this situation are by no means trivial.

Conclusion

Intervention is a major feature of international politics in the contemporary international system. Moreover, there is good reason to suppose that this will continue to be the case for the foreseeable future. As a result, there is a clear need to come to grips with the problems of regulating intervention in international politics.

This conclusion does not, however, imply that extensive intervention must inevitably continue to characterize international politics indefinitely. The international system is presently undergoing rapid and far-reaching change. Under the circumstances, there is considerable room for efforts to alter the characteristics of the system which tend to generate interventionary activities. From a long-term perspective, therefore, there is reason to think in terms of reducing the prevalence of intervention in international politics should this seem desirable in normative or instrumental terms.[34] The existence of this long-term prospect, nevertheless, in no way reduces the importance of coming to grips with the problems of regulating intervention in the immediate future.

---

[34] It seems reasonable to suppose that widespread support could be found for the desirability of minimizing the prevalence of certain types of intervention. It should not, however, be assumed that this is the case with regard to all types of intervention. Although the point is rarely articulated in explicit terms, many individuals hold views of international politics which are incompatible with undifferentiated concepts of nonintervention.

United States Intervention: Doctrine and Practice

WILLIAM D. ROGERS

With Commentaries by
Wolfgang Friedmann and David Morris

I

ALL CRISES POLARIZE. But the Vietnam trauma has divided the United States more deeply than any other international issue, with the possible exception of the great debate over the League of Nations after World War I. As the conflict has become more brutal, as General Westmoreland's winter optimism has given way to dismay with the Tet spring offensive, public debate has intensified and the divisions of opinion have become wider. The nation is divided not only between hawks and doves over immediate tactics in Vietnam itself, but over the longer-term lessons of this phenomenon for our future foreign policy throughout the world as well.

Many of those who defend our present Vietnam effort have justified it on a "showdown" theory. They argue that we must be willing to use our armed might whenever and wherever necessary until the Communists learn that wars of national liberation do not pay. This I call the neo-interventionist school of U.S. foreign policy. On the other side are those who have drawn from Vietnam the lesson that the United States is over-committed in this world—perhaps because of some latent but basic yearning for the discarded mantle of European imperialism—and must strictly limit and husband its worldwide strengths, its engagements, and its commitments in the future. These, I think, are the neo-isolationists.

Both groups, I fear, have misread history and are drawing the wrong lessons for the future. The neo-interventionists are preoccupied with the impression that the world is divided into Communist and non-Communist nations, that the line of Communist hegemony must be stabilized, and that the United States has the final responsibility to itself and to the world to ensure this kind of world stability. As Under Secretary Eugene V. Rostow made the point earlier this year:

[W]e have a vital national interest in world peace. And we cannot delegate the protection of that interest to anyone else. There is no one to pick up the torch if we let it fall . . . .

. . . .

. . . What we sought [since World War II] was Communist acceptance of the idea that force could not be used to change the boundaries of the two systems . . . .[1]

"Right" is the camp follower of "interest." So, from the view that the United States must intervene in other nations to resist Communist aggression has emerged the doctrine that it may in law do so whenever a particular outburst of civil strife seems to represent another forward thrust of Communism. Secretary of State Dean Rusk, in his address to the American Society of International Law on April 23, 1965,[2] put the point this way:

[In the view of the Communists,] a "war of national liberation" . . . is, in essence, any war which furthers the Communist world revolution . . . .

. . . .

. . . I would agree with General Giap and other Communists that [Vietnam] is a test case for "wars of national liberation." We intend to meet that test.

Thus, he said, in resisting that "aggression," South Vietnam was exercising its right of self-defense. And, by the same token, in using its land forces in South Vietnam and its air power against North Vietnam, the United States was exercising its legal right of collective self-defense against the danger posed to its national interest by wars of national liberation. "[O]ur own security," Mr. Rusk pointed out, "is threatened by those who would embark upon a course of aggression whose announced ultimate purpose is our own destruction." If I read this correctly, the Secretary is saying that the United States has both the duty and the right to use its own armed force in foreign civil strife in which the issue is Communists against non-Communists. This neo-interventionist doctrine in its most ambitious form goes rather far beyond the record of U.S. policy since World War II. Yet, it is not a very promising guideline for the future.

The neo-isolationists from their posts on the other side of the chasm dividing Vietnam debaters have also misread the past and could mislead

---

[1] National Security or a Retreat to Isolation? The Choice in Foreign Policy, address made before the Women's Forum on National Security at Washington, D.C., on Feb. 20, 1968 (as-delivered text), 58 DEP'T STATE BULL. No. 1501, at 431, 433 (April 1, 1968).

[2] AM. SOC'Y INT'L L., PROCEEDINGS 247, 250–53 (April 22–24, 1965).

us in the years to come. Many of them, including Senator Fulbright[3] but not Senator Robert Kennedy,[4] have been so horrified by Vietnam that they seem to suggest that the United States has taken on the role of world policeman: The only way to save the United States—and the world—from the misuse of vast mechanical and conventional war power is to severely restrict the future role of the United States in world events. In my view, however, the full record of American interventions since World War II does not support the conclusion that the United States has latent international gendarme ambitions. I further feel that if the United States lapses back into isolationism in recoiling from Vietnam, it would be an international catastrophe.

II

Let me first turn to the 20 years since World War II to illustrate why I believe that both the neo-interventionists and the neo-isolationists are wrong in their reading of history. World War II, of course, is an apt beginning point. It was then that the United States frankly and radically altered its posture in the world from isolationism to direct and major engagement in the affairs of others. (And it is also fair to point out, as have Edmund Stillman and William Pfaff, that there was a continuum of attitude from isolationism to engagement; "*Mutatis mutandis*, America's modern global interventionism, is only the old moral separateness, the belief in the special goodness of America, projected outward into the world."[5]) Of course, before World War II, the United States had no little experience with the use of its military power in civil strife situations in Latin America. In my view, however, the special record of intervention in Latin America was the result not of ideology or economic interest, but rather of turn-of-the-century military and naval strategy; in this sense it is not a direct precedent for our experience since World War II.

III

Of course, the postwar use of armed force in civil strife situations does not exhaust the spectrum of U.S. intervention if, by intervention, one means the variety of ways in which one nation affects and qualifies domestic events in another nation. In this sense, any analysis of U.S. intervention in the modern era could quite justifiably touch on cultural, economic, and political as well as military matters. The immenseness of

---

3 *See* J. W. FULBRIGHT, THE ARROGANCE OF POWER (1967).

4 *See* R. F. KENNEDY, TO SEEK A NEWER WORLD (1967).

5 E. O. STILLMAN AND W. PFAFF, POWER AND IMPOTENCE: THE FAILURE OF AMERICA'S FOREIGN POLICY 18 (1967).

United States power and the smallness of the world community today mean that virtually all dimensions of American presence in the world are a form of intervention. When Talleyrand said that "intervention" was a curious word meaning approximately the same thing as "nonintervention," he must have had in mind something like the phenomenon of the United States today.

Our music, our art, and our literature—from *Playboy* to Hemingway—have all invaded the cultural consciousness of peoples around the globe; U.S. corporations have established their presence in industry, finance, and markets throughout the world. Our official trade and aid policies since World War II have had a profound and direct impact on the hopes and aspirations of others—in some instances, as in the case of restrictive trade practices, for ill; in most cases, for good.

But just as war is the ultimate recourse of any foreign policy, so American military intervention is the ultimate test of its interventionist record in the postwar era. As I have said, I do not think that this record supports the hyperbolic views of either the new interventionist or the new isolationist schools.

There are at least five categories or clusters of U.S. responses to civil strife situations since World War II. Each is different. Whatever one may say of doctrine, intervention practice presents no coherent pattern.

In the first category are the instances where the United States openly has projected its military power into the domestic civil strife of another nation, where the issue was the continuation or disruption of the existing government. The United States has openly intervened with military force, however, in astonishingly few cases since World War II: Lebanon in 1956, the Dominican Republic in 1961, the Dominican Republic again in 1965—and Vietnam today.

A second category might include those situations in which the United States engaged in covert intervention either by arming and staging local dissidents for the scrap or by providing assistance, usually air cover in mufti. The instances where this sort of international "messing around" has had any real impact are somewhat broader than those in the overt intervention category: Guatemala in 1954 and the Cuban Bay of Pigs effort in 1961 as well as occasional incidents elsewhere, such as Iran in 1953 and the Congo in 1960–62. Interestingly enough, most of these interventions were on the side of the dissidents and potential guerrillas. Thus, they demonstrate that U.S. intervention since World War II is not universally in favor of the status quo. For this reason, they have provided some rather awkward moments for official U.S. spokesmen, such as Ambassador Stevenson's explanation to the United Nations Security Council that the United States was not involved in the Bay of Pigs invasion.

These first two categories exhaust the civil strife situations in which the United States has actually sought to exercise its military force. The record is not very impressive. On the other hand, there have been a number of instances in which the United States has stood aside. In some, which might be grouped into a third category, are those crises with distinctly cold war implications but where the United Nations provided the intervening military force which affected the final outcome. The best examples are, of course, the Congo from 1960 to 1964 and Cyprus in 1964.

There have also been a significant number of instances of civil strife which posed no Communist/anti-Communist issues but which could have proved tempting to any power with real pretensions to the world policeman role. Nigeria from 1967 to the present and Rhodesia in 1965 are examples. These conflicts, however, have been allowed to burn themselves out, isolated from both great power dispute and any outside military involvement.

My fifth and final category is perhaps the most troublesome. It includes the truly major turning points where violence altered, or threatened to alter, the postwar balance of power relationship in a fundamental way. In each instance American interest was supreme. But for the scale of international importance of the local strife, they are in fact otherwise indistinguishable from the first two categories, where the United States did intervene. These include China after the Second World War through 1949, Malaysia in the 1950's, Hungary in 1956, and Indonesia in the 1960's up to the decisive events of late 1965.

Consider postwar China, for example, in the light of the two contending theories about U.S. intervention policy. Senator Joseph McCarthy built an historic reputation on the proposition that the failure of the United States to support Chiang Kai-shek after 1947 was so frightfully against U.S. national interests that it could only have been the fruit of treason. Many Americans believed that charge, yet the United States did not intervene. Indonesia is another example worth pondering. By 1965, so the evidence reads, the United States was resigned to potential domination of Indonesia by a Communist Party affiliated with Peking, yet did not seriously consider intervening although this would have altered the Rusk–Rostow demarcation line and changed the government of over 100 million people.[6] In short, *vice* both Rusk and his critics, there have been major civil strife situations quite clearly involving extensions of Communist will where the United States has not intervened.

What, then, can be said of this pattern? First and most significant, all American and United Nations interventions—all of the first three cate-

6 R. N. GOODWIN, TRIUMPH OR TRAGEDY: REFLECTIONS ON VIETNAM 15 (1966); T. DRAPER, ABUSE OF POWER 121–24 (1966).

gories—have been in the underdeveloped world. Strife, conflict, and violence of the kind which commands outside involvement have arisen not in Europe, but in Asia, Africa, and Latin America. It is also apparent that Cuba, the Dominican Republic, and Lebanon—the nations where the United States has resorted to armed force—have been small in the world scale of values in comparison with China, Poland, or Indonesia, where the United States has not intervened.

Finally, in each case, with the major exception of Vietnam, the intervention has occurred because the equation of power seemed to suggest not only that there was a low risk of Russian counterintervention, but also that the probable time required to accomplish the objective would be short and the cost would be low. The Bay of Pigs is the classic example of the importance of the time-cost evaluation; when it became apparent that success would require a greater U.S. involvement than the original calculations had suggested, we desisted. Vietnam, on the other hand, is a history of miscalculation. This, in my view, is why it stands out so markedly in the record of U.S. intervention policy since World War II and why it represents not only a faulty guide to the past, but a misleading and dangerous precedent for the future.

IV

What of the future? Will we witness a series of U.S. military involvements in civil strife in Asia, Africa, and Latin America in the name of collective self-defense against "wars of national liberation"? Or will the United States lapse into a nervous and frustrated isolationism, appalled by the domestic and international costs of its Vietnam experience? I hope both scenarios are wrong. In my view, we have other lessons to draw from Vietnam.

Vietnam should teach, first, that the underdeveloped world—Asia, Africa, and Latin America—is basically unpredictable and fundamentally complex. To attempt to reduce the bewildering domestic politics of the 75-odd nations of these regions to "Communist" and "non-Communist" terms is to search for a pattern which does not exist and to pose the question in a way which almost invites a military or paramilitary interventionist answer. Civil strife, turbulence, and political violence in these regions are not primarily the fruit of Communist imperialism. I believe that even a clear, quick victory in the "test case for 'wars of national liberation' "[7] would not by itself produce "a world of independent nations, each with their own institutions, settling their disputes by peaceful

---

[7] See note 2 *supra*.

means, banding together to resist aggression, striving to establish a rule of law."[8]

In the effort to get an intellectual grip on Vietnam, both schools of thought have oversimplified and underestimated the future problem of civil strife in the underdeveloped world. I see instability for the rest of the century in Asia, Africa, and Latin America. This instability, like the civil strife which has triggered our interventions in the past two decades, will be born of the combination of racial unrest, poverty, and national frustration.

The Arbenz–Arévalo conflict in Guatemala, which gave rise to our covert intervention there, was only the surface outcropping of a much deeper resentment against the frozen social structure and skewed system of privilege in Guatemala; that resentment and the violence which is its handmaiden continue to this day in Guatemala. By the same token, our open intervention in the Dominican Republic was not a matter of policy but a failure of policy; the explosion of April 1965 was merely the climax of the failure of the Dominicans—and of the United States—to build between 1961 and 1965 a viable, self-respecting nation on the ruins of the Trujillo dictatorship.[9] That effort, too, is still in doubt. I am certain that we will see other nations break apart under the growing pressures for change and development and that the United States similarly will be challenged to use its power as a last resort measure in those nations as well.

But if instability, racial tension, and political division are the hallmarks of most of the poor nations of the world and if, therefore, the incidence of civil war is rising, the capacity of the United States to work its will by conventional military power in foreign conflict is, paradoxically enough, declining. We have force far beyond the fondest dreams of any general of the past; we can drop more tons of explosives on North Vietnam than we did on Germany in all of World War II. Yet, in a relative sense, our ultimate power is severely limited. This is fundamentally so because the causes of violence in the poor nations of the world are poverty, ignorance, frustration, and the monopolization of power by an intransi-

---

[8] Building a Decent World Order, address by Secretary of State Dean Rusk made before the International Congress of Publishers at Washington, D.C., on June 5, 53 DEP'T STATE BULL. No. 1358, at 27, 29 (July 5, 1965). [Secretary of State Rusk had stated: "I would call your attention to the preamble and articles 1 and 2 of the United Nations Charter. In all sincerity, I would propose those as a succinct summary of the foreign policy attitudes of the American people. . . . We and others sat down to draft that charter when we were thinking long and hard and deeply and soberly about the kind of a world it was in which we wished to live. And so, in a few paragraphs we sketched out such a world—a world of independent nations, each with their own institutions, settling their disputes by peaceful means, banding together to resist aggression, striving to establish a rule of law."—Ed.]

[9] For a more extended analysis see W. D. ROGERS, THE TWILIGHT STRUGGLE: THE ALLIANCE FOR PROGRESS AND THE POLITICS OF DEVELOPMENT IN LATIN AMERICA 136–40 (1967).

gent elite. Communists or no, military power is an inadequate, perhaps even a counterproductive, response to those problems.

This does not, however, dictate that we withdraw from the world, proclaiming that foreign controversies are no business of ours. The United States has a vital and constructive role to play in the world in helping to meet the frustration, hopelessness, and injustice which are the lot of so many of the world's millions and which seem for many to justify —indeed, to command—a resort to violence.

In my view, the answer is neither withdrawal nor a constant policy of counterviolence, but effective development to dampen the sparks of civil conflict in the developing nations before they reach the point of explosion. We must learn this lesson from Vietnam not only because of our own humanitarian concern with the fate of the billions of the world's poor, but because it is in our own national interest to do so.[10]

The point may be simply stated: What would have been the history of Vietnam if Diem had instituted a thorough program of civil reform in the late 1950's to heal the deep divisions within that tragic land? And how many other interventions have we avoided because of our modest but tangible successes in cooperative economic, social, and political development in countries such as Chile, Venezuela, or Iran?

[10] *Id.* at 288.

A Summary of the
Commentary on "United States Intervention:
Doctrine and Practice"

WOLFGANG FRIEDMANN

THE GUIDING MOTIVE OF UNITED STATES INTERVENTION

PROFESSOR FRIEDMANN first addressed himself to the nature of the guiding motive, if any, of United States foreign policy and alluded to the basic division in the most commonly expressed views. Some see the primary concern of U.S. foreign policy as the pursuit of national interests. Others find that the foremost objective lies in the "disinterested" quest of social progress or ideological goals.

Eschewing any neat separation of national interests from disinterested motives, Friedmann noted that throughout the postwar period and particularly in recent policy pronouncements the same governmental action has often been said to promote both sets of interests. Thus, the United States is said to be fighting in Vietnam to defend freedom and international law while at the same time preventing the further advance of Communism in its national interests.

Nevertheless, there is an ultimate contradiction between these motives; they may, but do not necessarily, converge. If the South Vietnamese should be so "perverse" as to desire peace even at the price of a coalition with the Communists, the United States would have to choose between the two objectives. Friedmann feared, however, that national interests would overshadow humanitarian goals on the basis of a political "realism" which concentrates on promoting national policy. Dean Acheson, when he frankly admitted that international law and morality played very little part in the Cuban missile crisis, revealed such an attitude.

Conceding to Mr. Rogers that there is, in fact, a strong concern for the destinies of other people despite the *Realpolitik* of U.S. foreign policy, Friedmann suggested that the desire to find moral justification for

America's actions cannot be ignored when assessing this concern. In his opinion, a lack of candor can be more harmful than an acknowledgment that purely national interests prompted an action.

This dichotomy between the realism of national interest and the desire to further humanitarian progress exists in the United States approach to economic aid. Professor Friedmann observed that aid administrators seeking budgetary appropriations from Congress cannot appeal to humanitarian purposes but find it necessary to argue that the aid is in the nation's interest; *i.e.*, foreign aid will keep the peoples concerned from falling victim to Communism. (It has recently been suggested that in order to obtain congressional support for proposals of the Presidential Riot Commisssion, it should be argued that aid will keep the ghetto populations from being seduced by Communists.) Contrary to Mr. Rogers' theory, Professor Friedmann believes that economic aid has usually been given where it would serve the interests of the United States. But the national interests promoted by U.S. foreign aid policy seem to be short-range rather than long-range ones. For example, the Marshall Plan was justifiable in short-range terms since the rebuilding of the European infrastructure aided American economic progress. Professor Friedmann agreed with Mr. Rogers that the United States was guided at that time by statesmen who wisely recognized that the world could not be remade in the American image; therefore, on the whole, they achieved productive results. He even conceded that a desire to promote social progress has been a prevalent factor in the field of economic aid.

However, the national interest-disinterest dichotomy of motives becomes apparent when economic aid is viewed as a form of intervention by the recipient country. Today nationalism is stronger than ever; consequently, any conditions attached to the aid extended may be regarded as an intervention in national autonomy. Friedmann mentioned the case of Peru, which recently declined an offer of aid to meet its budget since the offer was coupled with the demand that the budget adopted encompass an austerity program. Not long ago a recipient country would have acquiesced in such a demand.

Alternatives to Unilateral Intervention

Since aid programs are now being identified with national interests and perceived as interventional devices, the Professor suggested that multilateral rather than unilateral aid programs should shoulder the aid-giving responsibilities. Not only would the stigma attached to national aid programs be muted, but multinational institutions like the International Monetary Fund and the World Bank could more professionally and efficiently investigate national economies before arranging loans.

The International Monetary Fund, for example, has a duty to couple its grants or standby credits with demands for budgetary reform. These institutions, therefore, present one means to couple economic intervention with very sensitive reform measures in a manner unoffensive to national pride.

Professor Friedmann then turned to the question of military intervention in civil strife. The counterpart to multilateral aid agencies in this area would be intervention by the United Nations. There is, however, a major difference between these two functions. Economic aid involves technical expertise and specialized competence which, to some extent, insulate the process from political pressures. On the other hand, the United Nations is increasingly a highly political organ making military intervention much more precarious since it is subject to the exigencies of compromise and debate by the Security Council or the General Assembly.

He agreed with Richard Falk that U.N. intervention should be viewed as different from unilateral intervention.[1] Nevertheless, the theoretical justification for such action as a function of the overall task of maintaining world peace and security cannot entirely eliminate the general problems encountered in unilateral intervention. Intervention by the United Nations in the Congo to prevent secession was as vulnerable to criticism as unilateral intervention. Furthermore, the United Nations has not been ideologically consistent. Although conditions similar to those in the Congo exist today in Nigeria, intervention has not been considered, perhaps because of the Congo experience or simply because of practical considerations. Yet there is no difference in principle. Inaction in the case of Nigeria was due to considerations of power, opportunism, and sheer lassitude.

He contrasted the Congo experience to the generally beneficial but limited interventions by U.N. forces in which the big powers, such as the United States, have not been involved. Without seeking to alter the internal structure of a strife-torn country or to interpose themselves between parties of different states, these U.N. forces serve as fire brigades, containing and cooling down a conflict as in Cyprus. But the success of such limited peacekeeping missions does not necessarily mean that the United Nations can function effectively in situations that have resulted in unilateral intervention by the great powers. Friedmann indicated that such a function cannot be exercised by the United Nations as it is presently constituted, a conclusion that becomes increasingly obvious as U.N. ranks are swollen by small nations of differing political persuasions. Since

[1] *United States Foreign Policy and the Vietnam War: A Second American Dilemma, supra* [hereinafter cited as *Vietnam*].

these political variances obviate any unanimity on what interventional measures should be taken, if any, the conception of U.N. intervention as a substitute for unilateral intervention is but a hoped-for surrogate, one not likely to materialize in the foreseeable future.

THE NATURE OF U.S. INTERVENTION

Indicating that Rogers had characterized U.S. foreign policy as some-times confused and pragmatic, Friedmann concurred. With regard to the nature of any foreign policy, he recalled that Great Britain and, in the postwar period, Stalinist Russia had been viewed by Europeans as the originators of cunning, skillful, and well-planned strategies in the foreign policy sphere when in fact they often stumbled from one decision to another with more or less common sense. Analogizing these cases to the United States at present, he noted that any great power will be presumed to have a long-range, consistent policy even when it merely reacts to un-expected situations. It should be asked whether there is ultimately a degree of common sense or just righteousness. If the confusion is adorned with a moral purpose or long-term policy which in fact does not exist, the matter is certainly made worse.

He found it difficult to accept conclusions that the major motivation of U.S. intervention policy has been the awareness of social and economic tension and the desire to bridge the gap between rich and poor. As an illustration, intervention in Guatemala was neither prompted by, nor did it lead to, progressive social change. Nor did a desire to achieve social change underlie the Vietnam intervention; rather, the United States un-doubtedly thought it necessary to secure another bastion to contain Communism. In Vietnam as in the overwhelming majority of cases, the United States has intervened more by accident than design in favor of the incumbent right wing regimes. He recalled that only our intervention in support of the Shah of Iran furthered social progress. Yet, even there social progress was an indirect consequence of a desire to restore Western oil interests. It would require a very benevolent interpretation to regard this case as conscious intervention for social progress. The near-interven-tion in the Dominican Republic in 1961, however, did support the theory. The show of U.S. naval strength off the Dominican coast, it is widely believed, forestalled an attempt by Trujillo forces to wrest control from President Joaquin Balaquez. On the other hand, the massive mili-tary interventions in the Dominican Republic in 1965 and in Vietnam have been clearly against forces that promised social change. Our history of intervention was very disturbing to Professor Friedmann, who found a method (perhaps half-conscious) in the madness which is not in favor of the forces of change.

In answer to Rogers' inquiry as to why the United States did not intervene in China, Indonesia, or Hungary,[2] Friedmann noted that anti-Communist sentiment in those cases did not prevail over countervailing considerations, such as the danger of a world war or the predictable inability of the United States to overcome the established regime. (He confessed his puzzlement, however, at our intervention in Vietnam even on the basis of the containment of Communism in light of the fact that Ho Chi Minh was once a widely acknowledged national leader and an ardent anti-Communist who looked to the United States in 1947 as his only friend.)

INTERVENTION AND INTERNATIONAL LAW

Moving to another plane in his discussion, Professor Friedmann inquired whether there were any available guidelines other than ideology or pseudo-moralistic purposes for American policies with respect to intervention in civil strife. Although he agreed with Falk[3] and Rogers that "neo-Kennanism" was not an acceptable alternative, he felt that any viable options must be analyzed from the perspective of both international law and national policy.

Under international law, the answer was relatively simple. Intervention in civil wars is totally incompatible with elementary principles of international law, which are based on the coexistence of states regardless of the form of the regime. Therefore, under no guise can such interventions be justified except as a response to what is in effect an aggression by a third power. Under this rule, U.S. intervention in the 1965 Dominican Republic crisis was clearly without any shred of legal justification. He rejected, along with Falk,[4] the vindication of our Vietnam intervention as a response to aggression, since the object of that aggression was but the deliberate creation of the United States itself, the sovereign state of South Vietnam. On the other hand, the Cuban missile crisis did, in his opinion, approximate a legitimate response to aggression by a third power. The legal justification may be doubtful, but it was generally acceptable in a moral sense.

---

2 Mr. Rogers was referring to the cases in Category V. During his oral speech he had said, "If one analyzes these cases in Category I terms, where we have intervened, one might well ask, 'Why no intervention?' These are the cases, of course, of . . . China after the War, Hungary in 1956, and Indonesia in the 1960's." In his final paper, Mr. Rogers said, "[O]n the scale of international importance of the local strife, [these cases] are in fact indistinguishable from Categories I and II, where the United States did intervene. These include China after the Second World War through 1949, Malaysia in the 1950's, Hungary in 1956, and Indonesia in the 1960's up to the decisive events of late 1965."—Ed.

3 *Vietnam, supra.*

4 *Id.*

The legal injunction against intervention in civil strife applies to the United Nations as fully as it does to nation states. Intervention on behalf of the United Nations as a collective measure authorized by the proper organs may be legitimate to repel aggression, but such intervention is not a legitimate use of force in a civil strife situation. There is no difference in character between unilateral and U.N. action under these circumstances. The functions of the United Nations do not include, for example, deciding whether Katanga should be part of the Congo or whether Biafra should be part of Nigeria. The support of the new African states for U.N. intervention on their behalf stems from their willingness to defend to the last drop of blood the colonial frontiers they have taken over, however artificial these frontiers may have been. Colonialism may lose its stigma and become sacrosanct when a loss of territory is threatened, but it does not inevitably follow that rebels against the resulting "national unity" are aggressors. Even though blood may be shed during this process of social change, neither a nation nor an international organization may properly interfere, especially since the status of both the incumbents and the rebels is tenuous.

Friedmann concluded that nonintervention in truly civil war situations is the best legal norm available although far from an ideal solution. The nonintervention norm, of course, can be supplemented by the nonviolent means implemented at times by the United Nations whereby the civil tension is mitigated in order to facilitate a peaceful resolution of conflict.

From the perspective of national policy, the disadvantages of a policy designed to contain Communism by encouraging intervention in civil strife are now evident. Since world Communism is visibly dissolving into numerous national movements, some of them antagonistic to each other, the objective of stopping the spread of Communism is (a) illusory in fact, (b) impossible to apply, as Rogers pointed out, and (c) immensely disproportionate in cost to any possible gain. In fact, our anti-Communist policy in many cases has forced the United States to oppose the strongest and most viable national forces, which is part of the tragedy in Vietnam. Moreover, postwar interventions have tended to oppose forces of change and progress (today, often forces of liberal nationalism) in favor of incumbent regimes.

Professor Friedmann, in discussing at the outset the motivation for United States foreign policy, had seen national interests as being more predominant than disinterested desires to ensure the progressive development of other nations. An analysis of U.S. policy in actual practice, however, led him to conclude that our interventions have neither furthered our national interests nor aided the forces of progress.

Intervention or Nonintervention: A Dilemma

Professor Friedmann capped his commentary with the observation that we are faced with a dilemma regarding the legitimacy and appropriateness of intervention as a means to achieve certain objectives. This dilemma confronts government policymakers dedicated to the use of American power to contain Communism or to maintain world order. But it is also a dilemma for the liberals and humanitarians, whose goals from 1919 until quite recently paralleled those of the collective interventionists and elicited liberal support for the League of Nations and the United Nations as instruments of social progress. The postwar experience with intervention, particularly United States intervention, has made it clear that intervention, the lauded vehicle for securing human rights, may be incapable of attaining that objective. Those who are skeptical of the present U.S. intervention policy, however, must to some extent accept the less palatable consequence of cruel oppression of human rights unchecked by foreign intervention. Friedmann confessed that it is much easier to agree on negatives—to cite cases where there should be no intervention on either legal or policy grounds—than to reach a consensus on a positive program. If the only recognized alternatives are intervention and nonintervention, the dilemma will continue, for the price of either alternative is the partial sacrifice of national interests and humanitarian goals.

A Summary of the
Commentary on "United States Intervention: Doctrine and Practice"

DAVID MORRIS

THE NATURE OF U.S. FOREIGN POLICY

Does It Exist?

BELIEVING it was distorting and unrealistic to discuss only military intervention in civil strife, Mr. Morris took the broadest view of the term "intervention," concentrating on U.S. intervention in Latin America as the best illustration of American foreign policy.

Morris first raised three issues: (1) Whether an identifiable "Establishment" that directs U.S. foreign policy exists; (2) whether the decisions of this Establishment form a pattern or policy; and (3) whether such a policy can be characterized as benevolent.

Mr. Rogers, according to Morris, did not acknowledge the existence of an Establishment, which Morris defined as a group of persons or institutions that molds U.S. decisions in the foreign relations field. Morris himself was more compatible with the New Left thinking, which recognizes a discernible Establishment and condemns its actions as detrimental to the welfare of the peasants in underdeveloped nations, the "Third World."

In response to Rogers' suggestion that United States actions cannot be discussed in policy terms,[1] Morris noted that "the essential oneness of the economic, political, and strategic interests" of the United States described by Bernard Baruch forty years ago is still apparent. The United States does have a defined policy at least with respect to the Third World. The suggestion in Rogers' presentation that the United States

---

[1] During his oral speech, Mr. Rogers had stated, "With respect to [U.S. military intervention] policy, I rather regret that I cannot bring you a very broad and helpful generalization covering all cases. Abe Fortas used to say that he never trusted a man who used the word 'policy' because in most human affairs there was no such thing as policy. There are only specific responses to specific problems. . . . I think there is [no policy] in a broad general sense. There is, of course, a doctrine which is being hammered out, discussed, and argued about in the context of the Vietnam crisis at the present time." In his final paper, *supra*, Mr. Rogers did not discuss the policy question but, rather, concentrated on the emerging doctrines of neo-isolationism and neo-interventionism.—Ed.

has only specific responses to specific actions elicited Morris' retort that those responses have been extraordinarily consistent during the past two decades. The means, the tactics, the rhetoric have changed, but the goals of the policy and, therefore, its effects remained unaltered.

Morris pointed out that America's status as the richest nation in the world has made it one of the most insecure. We are constantly fearful that someone will take this wealth away. As Lyndon Johnson has been reported as saying, "There are two billion of them and only three hundred million of us. They want what we got, we got what they want, and we ain't going to give it to them." Dean Rusk also carries this paranoia around in his mental set, as is evidenced by his statement, "Every time I go to sleep, two-thirds of the world is awake and making trouble for us."[2]

A fear of losing this preeminent economic position, coupled with a desire to maintain military superiority and to retain access to strategic resources and raw materials, has led to a coherent American foreign policy with respect to the Third World. This policy is not based on whimsy but reflects an overriding desire to maintain stability in the world, since the unpredictability that accompanies instability may occasion the loss of American possessions or, at least, American control.

Stability Above All

The Government, the military, the corporation, and the university are all bureaucracies and instill certain bureaucratic values in their members. These values include love of law, order, hierarchy, and specific role function. Instability, as the antithesis of these values, is treated accordingly. For the military, stability both proves the success of its function as a crisis bureaucracy and assures the security of strategic resources. Corporations exporting capital and corporations exporting goods, although split on the direction of U.S. foreign policy, both agree that stability helps business and permits further corporate intrusion into foreign economies. Even American universities are becoming more and more involved in the stability consensus. Social scientists are fascinated by counterinsurgency work (or, as they call it, "resolution of conflict" studies) because of an alleged correlation between economic development and democracy, stability being a precondition for the former. Although this analysis of the stability consensus was acknowledged as oversimplified, the important point was that the interests of various powerful groups in the United States do coincide to present a formidable domestic front in support of U.S. foreign policy.

---

[2] These statements have been repeatedly attributed to President Johnson and Secretary of State Dean Rusk in various newspapers and magazines. The quotations represent an approximation of the original statements.

ECONOMIC INTERVENTION: PROMOTING AMERICAN INTERESTS

Government Aid to Private Investors

During his presentation, Rogers had stated that "economic intervention goes on willy-nilly without even the pretense of a government policy."[3] In support of his own theory that the Government actively works
to permit intervention of private economic interests, Morris declared
that the international financial institutions controlled by the voting
power of the United States have always subsidized or been bargaining
agents for American economic interests. As a result, Latin American
governments are coerced to discriminate against domestic or other foreign investors in favor of American sources. For example, President
Eisenhower stated in 1953 that he would commit his Administration to
"[d]oing whatever our Government can properly do to encourage the
flow of private American investment abroad. This involves, as a serious
and explicit purpose of our foreign policy, the encouragement of a hospitable climate for such investment in foreign nations."[4]

The Export-Import Bank, set up in the 1930's, has been used over the
past 30 years expressly to enable American capital to penetrate foreign
lands. The World Bank, when first created, potentially could have lent
money for native development projects in the Third World. For that
reason, according to Morris, the business community was against the
Bank. The United States, however, has a controlling interest in that
bank, and the appointment of conservative officers essentially destroyed
the Bank's potential for benevolent works. The Bank made it clear from
the beginning that if, in its judgment, the policies of a government were
tending to favor the public sector of the economy too much, no loans
would be made regardless of the ability to pay or the willingness to pay.
The most effective thing, the Bank felt, that the underdeveloped nations
with poor credit standing could do to improve their position would be
to "clear up their external debt records."[5] Another step would be to
eliminate the "inequitable and restrictive legislation"[6] which encumbered U.S. corporations abroad.

Other agencies were set up in the late 1950's and early 1960's to aid

---

*   [3] Mr. Rogers made this statement during his oral speech with reference to private corporate intervention. His final paper, *supra*, does not deal extensively with this aspect of U.S.
intervention.—Ed.

[4] The State of the Union, Message by President Eisenhower to the Congress, 28 DEP'T
STATE BULL. 207, 208 (1953).

[5] INT'L BANK FOR RECONSTRUCTION AND DEVELOPMENT, SECOND ANNUAL REPORT 13 (1946–
47).

[6] *Id.* at 14.

development projects, but they proceeded with much the same outlook. The International Finance Corporation, created in 1956, was to be more flexible in its policies than the World Bank, but it was affiliated with, and controlled by, the World Bank. Some of its major policies were: (1) To invest only in enterprises which are essentially private in character, (2) to invest only in association with private investors, and (3) not to invest if sufficient private capital is available on reasonable terms.[7]

The A.I.D. loan program was not much better. John Kennedy initiated the policy whereby the Latin American countries would have to pay back loans in American dollars. The only way for a country to get American dollars is by increasing its export of raw materials, thus decreasing the possibility of diversification and industrialization. United States A.I.D. loans to Guatemala for industrial development, for instance, have few but noteworthy requirements. The industries which are eligible are (1) those whose products are not in competition with products from the United States companies and (2) those which will increase the sales of products imported from the United States.[8] If a Guatemalan industry can be developed which will stop the import of a foreign product other than from the United States, however, that industry can receive a loan.[9]

Morris then asked whether it was undesirable for the American Government to actively support private investment in the Third World. Economists argue that foreign capital is needed to bring a nation to the takeoff stage of economic development. Foreign business introduces entrepreneurial skills and modern business techniques into the country as well as creating an internal market for native business. Morris then listed the disadvantages of this form of economic intervention. Using Latin America as his example, he pointed out that U.S. corporations traditionally export more capital than they import, although this trend is changing. Second, a lack of corporate control by the host country can lead to situations where an underdeveloped nation is economically harmed rather than aided by the presence of foreign investments. For example, while crude oil is being exported by a foreign enterprise, the domestic cost of refined oil may be very high. More important, the ability of a corporate manager in the United States to make a decision that significantly affects a foreign country is fundamentally wrong and may be harmful to the country. It has already led to the political impotence of several Latin American reformist governments.

[7] D. A. BALDWIN, ECONOMIC DEVELOPMENT AND AMERICAN FOREIGN POLICY, 1943–62, at 126 (1966).

[8] Taken from *La Empresa Privada y La Alianza para el Progreso, USAID*, cited in D. Tobis, *Foreign Aid: The Case of Guatemala*, 19 MONTHLY REVIEW, Jan. 1968, at 40, 41.

[9] Interview with the manager of a large United States company in Guatemala, cited in *Foreign Aid: The Case of Guatemala, id.*

Protecting Strategic Areas and Supplies

Morris found a strong motivation among American policymakers to protect accesses to certain strategic resources. The massive Paly Commission Report of 1952 concluded that ores such as manganese, nickel, and tin are vitally important for the United States but obtainable mainly from sources external to its territory. The Paly study has not been ignored. Access to these strategic materials often has been a condition of U.S. military and economic assistance. Nelson Rockefeller, important in policy planning at the early stage of postwar Latin American policy, declared,

> North American industries every day depend more and more on the raw materials of the Western hemisphere. These sources are indispensable for the U.S. to maintain industrial production that amounts to more than half of the total goods manufactured in the free world.[10]

Morris perceived such a motivation as extremely important for an understanding of present and future trends in U.S. foreign policy. If expanding the trade of underdeveloped areas and fulfilling their pent-up aspirations is but a means to maintain access to strategic regions and materials, U.S. foreign policy will continue to be adjusted in terms of the ultimate goal rather than the means.

Protecting Domestic Trade

Trade policies are yet another aspect of U.S. foreign policy that Morris found harmful to underdeveloped countries. For support, he pointed to our import quota list, where three of the seven items—coffee, oil, and sugar—are the most important exports for the Third World, accounting for as much as 94 percent of their foreign exchange at times. In addition, the United States Government's subsidization of domestic agricultural exports tends to keep foreign prices down.

Morris disagreed with Rogers' assertion that American participation in the first United Nations Conference on Trade and Development (UNCTAD) indicated a trend toward liberalization of U.S. trade policies.[11] When the conference began in 1964, the United States was extremely reluctant to participate. After being coerced into ceremoniously signing an agreement to create no new import quotas after 1965, the United States promptly broke its promise.

Will this nonbenevolent aspect of U.S. foreign policy continue? Morris saw U.S. participation in trade conferences more as a symbolic

---

10 J. J. Arévalo, The Shark and the Sardines 150 (Cobb and Osegueda transl. 1961).
11 Mr. Rogers' statement was contained in his original position paper.—Ed.

gesture to placate the Third World than as a major change in American trade policy. As evidence of the hypocritical attitude of the United States, he recalled the retention by the United States of its trade preferences in the Philippines while attempting to persuade France to give up its preferences with former North African colonies.

MILITARY AID AND INTERVENTION: MISGUIDED PROGRESSIVE MEASURES

Leaving the economic areas of U.S. intervention, Morris mentioned counterinsurgency programs as a mode of intervention short of military force. Whereas the United States once provided military assistance to Latin America to protect the hemisphere from Soviet aggression, such assistance is now given to combat civil uprisings. Most of the Latin American military purchases under U.S. sales assistance programs, for instance, are related to internal security requirements. Instead of supporting certain insurgents as a way to attack basic social and economic problems, the United States concentrates on strengthening the national police force. Underlining America's commitment to this approach is the increased emphasis in American military schools since 1961 on "riot control, counterguerrilla operations and tactics, intelligence procedures, public information, [and] psychological warfare" training for "selected Latin American military personnel."[12]

Morris then attacked Rogers' dismissal of U.S. military interventions as unimportant since the invaded countries were small and insignificant for major American policies. The list, Morris declared, is not admirable: Greece (1947), Iran (1954), Guatemala (1954), Lebanon (1957), Indonesia (1958), Cuba (1961), Dominican Republic (1965), and Vietnam (1961 to the present). Referring back to his stability consensus theory, he acknowledged that the United States does attempt to avoid intervention by maintaining stability and that these nonmilitary means usually are successful. Nevertheless, America certainly does not hesitate to resort to planes and troops to achieve stability. One tragic element of such action is the contribution of support, advice, weapons, and money to terrorist government campaigns, such as in Guatemala and in the Dominican Republic. Although there undoubtedly would be turmoil should the United States withdraw its aid from such countries, is the alternative of supporting governments that brutally repress the protests of sensitive, intelligent students preferable?

[12] Statement by Assistant Secretary of State for Inter-American Affairs, Hon. Edwin M. Martin, *Hearings on Castro-Communist Subversion in the Western Hemisphere Before the Subcomm. on Inter-American Affairs of the House Comm. on Foreign Affairs,* 88th Cong., 1st Sess. 19 (1963).

THE METHOD AND GOAL OF U.S. INTERVENTION:
A CONTRADICTION IN FACT

Arthur M. Schlesinger, Jr., in his book *A Thousand Days* described the aims of U.S. foreign policy as enunciated by President Kennedy after the assassination of Trujillo in the Dominican Republic:

> The assassination took Washington by surprise. . . .Kennedy examined the situation realistically. "There are three possibilities," he said, "in descending order of preference: a decent democratic regime, a continuation of the Trujillo regime or a Castro regime. We ought to aim at the first, but we really can't renounce the second until we are sure that we can avoid the third."
>
> The problem was whether a country where potential political leadership had been suppressed, murdered or exiled for more than a generation could easily acquire the instincts and skills of self-government.[13]

In the view of Morris, the practice has not been geared to the theory. The policies of the United States on the whole are not designed to establish democratic political processes in the Third World, although they do attempt to avoid another Castro-type regime.

Blame for this paradox lies partially with the inability of U.S. policy-makers to identify with rural guerrillas, just as white middle-class Americans still cannot identify with the plight of the Indians, the poor whites, and the blacks. Since the national security managers cannot understand the aspirations and frustrations of a guerrilla in Guatemala or Vietnam, they attempt to foster understandable aspirations by molding the indigenous culture in the American image. Morris found this craving for security and this desire for less ambiguity to be natural human reactions but ones with unjustifiable results. First, the unfortunate correlate of security is control. The United States has discovered that predictability and security in foreign affairs require infinite knowledge and infinite power. A combination of this desire for security, the values of a bureaucratic system, and the tremendous power capability of the United States constitutes the root of American imperialism.

Second, the manner in which this control is exercised will be guided by American values. To Morris, these values include a condemnation of inefficiency and shoddiness but not a condemnation of immorality. This leads to the ironic situation where America attempts to achieve progressive reforms by aiding a foreign government in the suppression and elimination of the progressive elements in that society. Morris viewed

---

[13] A. SCHLESINGER, JR., A THOUSAND DAYS 769 (1965).

this as a consequence of America's faith in stability as a means to achieve progress: Inculcate in the Third World the same apolitical detachment which has characterized the United States and in fact resulted in a measure of stability. When this tactic fails and guerrilla activity makes it evident that a significant restructuring of society is needed, America underwrites immoral methods to eliminate the instability by arming the government to kill the guerrilla, all to the end theoretically of creating a stable climate wherein peaceful reforms can be accomplished. Although people like Walt Rostow believe that this present sacrifice is only the prelude to future benefits, that economic development and its correlate, democracy, will occur without radically changing a feudal political system, Morris concluded that the goals and the means are too contradictory. Yet America has supported this inconsistent policy and is paying the price in Vietnam while the underdeveloped nations pay the price all of the time.

The Measuring Line of Occasion

THOMAS EHRLICH

I will set a sober limit to all defending of faith and exacting of justice by force. I will bound God's righteousness by the measuring line of occasion.
—From a Psalm in the Dead Sea Scrolls

I

M Y AIM in this brief paper is to suggest some ways in which international law may draw "the measuring line of occasion" for foreign intervention in civil strife.

The United Nations Charter puts primary emphasis on precluding forceful action, reflecting humanity's primary fear at the end of World War II. That emphasis has understandably led to lessened concern with the role of law in structuring decisions on how to use force and on the role of lawyers in developing legal bases for that use. My thesis is that those roles are more, rather than less, important than before and that more time and attention, rather than less, should be devoted to them.

This development must take place, however, within a framework quite unlike the international legal order that produced the Declarations of Paris and London. In that era, war was generally viewed in legal literature as a legitimate, if not necessarily beneficial, instrument of national policy. The two declarations were efforts to establish codes of conduct for belligerents to follow in their foreign relations—not with each other, but rather with neutrals. Today, however, the existence of "a state of war" without more no longer legitimizes the use of force. At the same time, a declaration of war requires a total commitment to armed conflict that all sides may find unacceptable; for this reason, war has not been declared in Vietnam. Predictably, however, force will continue to be used in international affairs. More specifically, nations will continue to intervene militarily in strife occurring beyond their borders.

If these predictions are valid, procedures are needed that are both conducive to restrained decisions on intervention and not so utopian as to be disregarded. Those procedures should provide safeguards against unlimited force—safeguards built into the very process of legitimizing force. In contrast to a highly normative approach emphasizing detailed rules of conduct, an analysis along those lines would stress the structure of decisionmaking within the broad but indefinite norm of article 2(4) of the United Nations Charter. It would "take due regard for the limitations of law as an instrument of social order . . . [and] avoid the temptation to deal with very difficult political and moral issues as though they could be resolved by rather simple and very general legal imperatives."[1]

I am not suggesting that the search for acceptable norms is not important. Process is not possible without some normative structure. But norms are no longer received from Mount Sinai. In international affairs, the United Nations Charter provides at least a normative framework, but the meaning of Charter rules in specific situations is often unclear. Parties to a conflict may agree on the importance of such general concepts as "self-determination" and "fundamental human rights" but disagree on the application of those concepts in the particular case that causes their controversy. In such situations, procedures are needed to develop precepts that are neither so broad as to be useless nor so specific as to be unacceptable to the parties. More important, while the search for principles continues, actual conflicts must be resolved or at least contained. Arrangements must be developed to bring the parties together to work out their differences—and meanwhile to restrain their military actions. In that very process, norms for regulating their future conduct may emerge—if the nations have not blown each other up in the interim.

This approach no doubt reveals the bias of one familiar with the United States Constitution; its broad standards are given substance through specific controversies. One flaw in the constitutional analogy is that the international scene provides neither a comparable quantity of cases nor comparable judicial forums. Each new crisis presents new problems, particularly in the peacekeeping area, and there are dangers that distinctions will be blurred. Given those dangers, there is value, I think, in the approach I have suggested for analyzing the relevance of international law to foreign intervention in civil strife.

Such an approach assumes, of course, that international law and its practitioners can have substantial impact on a nation's essentially political decision to use force and on the willingness of other countries to accept the decision as legitimate. It is not possible here to develop full empirical underpinnings for that premise. At the same time, the impli-

---

[1] A. Chayes, *Remarks*, PROCEEDINGS, AM. SOC'Y INT'L L. 12 (1963).

cations of my thesis may be clarified by a brief comparative analysis of two recent examples of foreign intervention in civil strife: The 1964 Turkish intervention in Cyprus and the 1965 United States intervention in the Dominican Republic. In the first, lawyers were engaged in their professional capacity from the outset. There was a continuous interplay between law and action and between law and an appeal for world support. In the second, lawyers were very much on the sidelines. Law was involved only after the fact and as a rather insignificant form of rhetoric.

In turn, the legal issues involved in the Cypriot and Dominican affairs may be sharpened by comparison to the United States legal case during the Cuban missile crisis. Such an examination may serve to develop the notion that law can and should draw "the measuring line of occasion."

II

Violence exploded throughout Cyprus on Christmas Eve 1963 and throughout the Dominican Republic 16 months later. The Turkish Prime Minister responded to the Cyprus crisis by announcing that Turkey would intervene unilaterally under article IV of the Treaty of Guarantee between Cyprus, Greece, Turkey, and the United Kingdom.[2] By that treaty—one of the package of accords concluded in 1960 when Cyprus became independent—Cyprus undertook to ensure "respect for its Constitution"; and Greece, Turkey, and the United Kingdom "recognized and guaranteed" not only "the independence, territorial integrity and security of the Republic of Cyprus," but also the "state of affairs established by the basic Articles of the [Cypriot] Constitution." Intervention in the wake of the Turkish Prime Minister's announcement was confined to a single warning flight of jet fighters. On March 12, 1964, Turkey again threatened to invade Cyprus under article IV unless "all . . . assaults . . . against the Turkish community in Cyprus . . . [are] stopped . . . [and] an immediate cease-fire . . . [is] established. . . ."[3] Turkey backed away from that threat under strong Security Council pressure. But she refused to be restrained five months later when Cypriot Government forces attacked several Turkish Cypriot villages in the northwest corner of the Island. On August 7 and 8, 1964, the Turkish Air Force bombed the attackers, causing substantial loss of life to many unarmed civilians as well as to Greek Cypriot forces.

Shifting some 6,500 miles, it appeared for a time that the 1965 Dominican revolt would be put down without foreign involvement. On the

---

[2] Conference on Cyprus, CMND. 1253 (T.S. No. 5 of 1961), 382 U.N.T.S. No. 5475.

[3] *See* Letter from the Permanent Representative of Turkey to the Secretary-General, Mar. 13, 1964, in U.N. DOC. S/5996, Annex 2 (1964).

afternoon of April 28, 1965, however, the tide quickly turned and the junta requested "unlimited and immediate military assistance" from the United States to crush the revolt.[4] Ambassador Bennet at first recommended that troops be landed to protect United States citizens. A few hours later, however, he made another proposal: "[A]rmed intervention which goes beyond the mere protection of Americans" to prevent "another Cuba."[5] United States Marines began landing almost immediately.

President Johnson initially stated that the purpose of United States forceful intervention was "to give protection to hundreds of Americans who were still in the Dominican Republic. . . ." He added, "This same assistance will be available to the nationals of other countries, some of whom have already asked for our help."[6] On May 2, however, the President added a new element: "Communist leaders, many of them trained in Cuba . . . took increasing control" of the revolt.[7] No persuasive evidence ever was released to substantiate this charge, but by May 2 some 14,000 Marines were in the Dominican Republic.

Meanwhile, on April 30 the O.A.S. Council called a Meeting of Consultation under the Organization's Charter. That meeting quickly produced calls for a cease-fire, an international zone of refuge, and an investigating commission to be sent to the scene. It was not until May 6, however, after several days of intense debate and strenuous lobbying by the United States, that the meeting established an Inter-American Peace Force in the Republic. United States troops were then made a part of the Force.

III

From the outset, the Turkish legal case for intervention in Cyprus was based on a key sentence in article IV of the Treaty of Guarantee: "In so far as common or concerted action may not prove possible, each of the three guaranteeing Powers reserves the right to take action with the sole aim of re-establishing the state of affairs created by the present Treaty."

First, argued the Turkish Government, the conditions precedent to action under article IV were properly met because there had been both a "breach of the provisions of the present Treaty" and a failure of "common or concerted action."

Second, "action" must be read to include the use of force. The bloody history of the Island made it unlikely that anyone in 1960 supposed the

[4] J. B. MARTIN, OVERTAKEN BY EVENTS 656 (1966).
[5] *Id.* at 656–57.
[6] Statement by the President, Press Release, Apr. 28, 1965.
[7] Statement by the President, Press Release, May 2, 1965.

responsibilities of Guarantor Powers could be met forever through peaceful persuasion.

Third, the use of force under article IV was consistent with the United Nations Charter. Such use did not contravene the article 2(1) guarantee of Cypriot "sovereign equality," for that provision neither conferred rights nor imposed obligations in addition to those created elsewhere in the Charter. Further, the use of force was in accord with article 2(4). It was not "against the territorial integrity or political independence" of Cyprus since that was what the Treaty of Guarantee was designed to protect. Finally, it was consistent with the Purposes of the United Nations since the very aim of the treaty was to promote peace on the Island. Its guarantees were drafted to prevent an internal breakdown of the constitutional machinery from becoming a threat to international peace. If such a threat did occur, the Charter authorized the Security Council to act. Until then, a group of nations by prior agreement might determine the means to settle or to contain the violence.

The formal opinion of the State Department Legal Adviser on the United States intervention in the Dominican crisis stated three grounds for that action.[8] First, intervention was "essential to preserve the lives of foreign nationals—nationals of the United States and of many other countries." Delay in landing the Marines would have caused a "needless sacrifice of many more lives . . . entailing serious danger to the peace and security of the Hemisphere." Second, the Legal Adviser contended that United States forces remained after the threat to foreign nationals had passed "so that the organs of the Inter-American system could carry out their intended responsibilities under Inter-American treaties and assist the people of the Dominican Republic in reestablishing democratic government under conditions of public order." Finally, the opinion referred to a "further consideration." "Available information has suggested that what began as a democratic revolution fell into the hands of a band of communist conspirators."

IV

Turkey's legal case was not, of course, the sole determinant of its forceful action. The United States reportedly dissuaded Turkey from invading the Island on two previous occasions, and diplomatic pressure no doubt had an impact throughout the crisis. Nor were all elements of the Turkish legal case fully developed on Christmas Day 1963. Yet the perceived need for a legal analysis that would persuade other United

8 Legal Basis for United States Actions in the Dominican Republic, opinion of the Legal Adviser, Department of State, May 7, 1965, in THE INTERNATIONAL LEGAL PROCESS, Vol. III, Problem XII, at 32.

Nations Members was a major element both in shaping the Turkish use of force and in narrowing its precedential implications. The remarkable extent to which Turkey was able to withstand the pressure of Archbishop Makarios's call for self-determination and then to shift the burden of international persuasion onto Greece and Cyprus was due in no small measure to that legal case.

The essential choice for Turkish legal advisers in defending their country's use of force was to rest on article IV of the Treaty of Guarantee or on article 51 of the United Nations Charter.[9] At one point in the Council debates on the crisis, the Turkish representative did allege that the August 1964 bombings were a limited police action taken in legitimate self-defense.[10] But this occurred months after the Council had established a peacekeeping force on the Island and was thus fully seized of the crisis. Until that time and after, with the one exception, Turkey relied solely on article IV. That article is, in my view, a much narrower ground for the use of force, much less liable to use as a future precedent than article 51.

The analogy to the Cuban missile crisis is striking. The legal basis of the quarantine, as argued by the United States Government, was rooted in the collective action of a regional arrangement, the Organization of American States (O.A.S.), acting under the Rio treaty.[11] A major stumbling block in that analysis was whether the requirement of Security Council "authorization" in Charter article 53 means prior and express authorization. The United States contended that subsequent and implied approval was sufficient.[12]

I do not suggest that without a legal case under chapter VIII, force would not have been used—quite the contrary. If regional arrangements could not engage in "enforcement action" absent prior and express Security Council approval, the Soviet Union's veto power would have made the O.A.S. impotent in the Cuban crisis, and no other Council measures could have been taken. But all this would not have restrained the United States. As much, and perhaps more, force would have been used in response to Soviet missiles in Cuba. In such a situation, the United States would have almost certainly framed its argument in terms of article 51 and the right of self-defense. In fact, a substantial group of

---

[9] U.N. CHARTER art. 51 reads: "Nothing in the present Charter shall impair the inherent right of individual or collective self-defense if an armed attack occurs against a Member of the United Nations, until the Security Council has taken the measures necessary to maintain international peace and security. . . . "

[10] 19 U.N. SCOR, 1142d meeting 12 (1964).

[11] Inter-American Treaty of Reciprocal Assistance, Sept. 2, 1947, T.I.A.S. No. 1838, 21 U.N.T.S. 77.

[12] Legal Basis for the Quarantine in Cuba, opinion of the Legal Adviser, Department of State, Oct. 22, 1962, in THE INTERNATIONAL LEGAL PROCESS, Vol. III, Problem XI, at 55.

advocates, both in and out of government, claimed that aricle 51 provided the only sound legal basis for the quarantine. But action in self-defense is founded on the unilateral judgment of one country that it has been subject to an "armed attack." If the United States had adopted that position, it would not have been implausible for many nations throughout the world to claim a similar right. Certainly the Soviet Union, ringed by missile sites in Europe, Greece, and Turkey, could have made that case.

Were the consequences less serious because the United States claimed that article 53 permits Security Council "authorization" that is both subsequent and implied? Arguably under that view any permanent Council Member may, by its veto, ensure Council authorization of a regional arrangement's enforcement action, although the position need not be carried that far. But at least the considered judgment of the regional arrangement is brought to bear on the problem. The approach provides some check on the unilateral use of force. National actions based on the authority of a regional arrangement must be submitted to the collective decisionmaking processes of that arrangement. Further, the precedential implications of the quarantine were sharply narrowed by adoption of the article 53 rationale. It is unlikely that many cases will arise that both involve a threat from within the territory of a regional arrangement and emanate from a member of that arrangement.

In the Cyprus crisis, when the issue was foreign intervention in civil strife, was not the situation much the same as in the Cuban missile crisis? And for much the same reason, was not Turkey's judgment to base its case on article IV of the Treaty of Guarantee a sound one? The decision meant that Turkish armed action was limited to "re-establishing the state of affairs created by the Treaty" and ensured prior consultation with the other Guarantor Powers. The process of validating the use of force thus both restrained that use and reduced the risk that it would justify future military efforts. The set of circumstances that produced the Treaty of Guarantee may be repeated elsewhere in the future, but this appears unlikely. If anything, reliance on article IV would seem to involve a narrower exception to the Charter prohibition on the use of force than reliance on chapter VIII in the Cuban case—to be a less dangerous expansion of permissible armed actions than enforcement action by regional arrangements.

Turkey's decision to base its legal case on article IV of the Treaty of Guarantee rather than on Charter article 51 was sound, therefore, in terms of limiting the use of force outside the United Nations and restricting the scope of unilateral action. Article IV provides a legal basis that is both more persuasive and less subject to use as a future precedent.

There were, of course, significant differences between the legal cases made by Turkey in the Cyprus crisis and by the United States in the Cuban crisis. Perhaps most obvious, the legal basis for the quarantine, as argued by the United States, depended on the prior assent of O.A.S. members to the Organization's powers and procedures and on the checks and balances inherent in its political processes. One may question whether Cuba really "consented" to any O.A.S. action after its Government had been excluded from participation in the Organization and whether the Soviet Union was not at least an equal object of the enforcement action. However one resolves those issues, neither prior agreement to an organization's decisions nor collective decisionmaking are as clearly discernible in the Cyprus situation. No representatives of Cyprus participated in negotiating the 1960 Accords. The Cypriot choice, in essence, was to take the settlement or leave it. Further, unilateral decisions under article IV of the Treaty of Guarantee obviously have no basis in collective judgment. On the contrary, those decisions may not be made unless the Guarantor Powers are unable to agree on joint action.

On the other hand, the treaty requirement of prior consultation does provide at least a cooling-off period and an opportunity to consider the views of all Guarantor Powers before unilateral action. Perhaps more important, the treaty itself was the product of multilateral negotiations, though Cyprus cannot fairly be said to have been a party to them. Article IV does not ensure collective decisionmaking; but are not its procedures preferable to sole reliance on one nation's judgment?

The United States and Turkish cases may also differ in the persuasiveness of article 51 as an alternative legal basis for the use of force. In the Cuban case, the question was whether there had been an "armed attack" at all; if so, it was clearly directed against the United States. In the Cyprus crisis, however, an "armed attack" by Greek Cypriot forces had unquestionably occurred prior to the August bombing. The question rather was whether the Turkish Cypriots subject to that "attack" were part of Turkey's "self" for purposes of article 51.

Finally, the crises differed in the likelihood of a Security Council judgment restraining the use of force. Even article 51 limits such uses to an interim period until the Council has taken effective measures. Council action was not a realistic possibility in the Cuban case. It was much more likely in the Cyprus crisis.

But given those differences, the essential point is that the United States and Turkey both sought to develop cases in law that were structured to fit particular and limited uses of force. Those cases were persuasive to nations that heard them in forums throughout the world, and their persuasiveness was attributable in major measure to reliance on legal analysis that could not be easily manipulated to justify any and all armed action. Law and lawyers acted as the "measuring line of occasion." They not only provided reasoned support for their countries' military efforts, they also created barriers to both the expansion and the precedential impact of such efforts.

In contrast to the Cypriot and Cuban cases, consider the legal basis for the United States intervention in the Dominican Republic from the perspectives of maximum persuasiveness and minimum precedent. In my judgment, the United States made a series of wrong decisions during the Dominican crisis. Those decisions significantly altered the position and prestige of the United States throughout the world, particularly in Latin America. But I choose the Dominican case precisely for that reason—to determine whether, even in an extreme case, lawyers may make more of a contribution than to declare simply and solely, "Any use of force is illegal." Once the basic decision to land troops in the Dominican Republic had been made, what more could have been done?

Initially, at least, the United States legal argument might have been framed exclusively in terms of protecting United States citizens and, perhaps, foreign nationals, much as was done in the Congo rescue operation. One can question whether the United States should ever intervene militarily to save even its own citizens on foreign shores, but there is substantial support for such action in traditional international law. No less important, might not such a publicly announced argument have put some brake on United States involvement in succeeding days?

That option was closed on May 7, 1965, however, when the opinion of the State Department Legal Adviser on the Dominican case was issued. If United States citizens and other non-Dominicans had been in danger, they were then safe. Apart from the wisdom of the United States military involvement, did the opinion make the strongest case that could have been made and the one with the least danger of creating a precedent for future intervention?

First, anyone who has seen the opinion recalls that it does not look or read like a legal opinion. It appears to have come straight from the Department's Dominican desk officer. Not only is it devoid of a single citation of authority, but it does not even mention the United Nations or give any sense of the structure of the O.A.S. and its institutional problems. Consider this example: "The United States refused to observe merely the form of legalistic procedures to the detriment of fundamental rights of a nation under the O.A.S. Charter."[13] That is the worst possible phrasing. Far more important than bad phrasing, it is bad substance—it

---

[13] Legal Basis for United States Actions in the Dominican Republic, *supra* note 8.

implies that "to observe merely the form of legalistic procedures," whatever that means, was an open option. What could be worse, particularly in the context of an argument that smacks of manipulating the law?

Would it not have been preferable to base the United States action solely on the ground of preserving the jurisdiction of the O.A.S.? Could not a more persuasive argument have been made, in light of past O.A.S. history, that the Organization's members would probably seek to bring some order out of the Dominican chaos? In this context, the alleged Communist threat was relevant not as an independent legal basis for United States intervention—the degree of proof required to make that argument persuasive is certainly more than the evidence then or now reveals —but rather as support for the judgment that the O.A.S. was likely to take jurisdiction of the problem, as witness recent Organization resolutions opposing Communist involvement in the hemisphere.

Would not such an argument, made in support of a United States "holding operation" until the O.A.S. had time to act with its own peace force, have been not only more persuasive than the opinion actually issued—and that's not saying much—but also have created a much narrower precedent? The Legal Adviser's opinion seems to suggest that unilateral intervention is an appropriate solution when any one of the three circumstances is present—whenever any nationals of any nation are in danger, whenever it is possible that the O.A.S. might act, and whenever Communists are involved.

One of the final ironies of the whole Dominican tragedy is that, despite all of the United States blustering, blundering, and quite incredible inarticulateness, it was forced to trade a large measure of control over the situation for the aura of O.A.S. legitimacy and the transformation of a United States force into an Inter-American one. True, the United States tried to position the O.A.S., but in the end the United States had less than complete command over affairs and events in the Dominican Republic once the machinery of the O.A.S. became involved.

The distinction between the legal cases in the Cyprus and Cuban crises, on the one hand, and in the Dominican situation on the other, is one of degree, not of kind, no less than the distinction between the relative unilateralism involved. As one White House adviser put it on October 22, 1962: "We don't want just the United States and 13 one-armed bananas." But the shift in the missile crisis away from a wholly normative analysis—is it "legal" or "illegal"?—and toward a more procedural focus is largely absent in the Legal Adviser's Dominican opinion. Had the United States lawyers been more successful during the Dominican crisis both in involving the O.A.S. in the decisionmaking processes and in placing their legal case on the need to preserve O.A.S. jurisdiction, they might have performed a much more useful role.

V

At the height of the Dominican affair, according to the *New York Times*, President Johnson quoted a line he had learned at the age of eight or nine for a recitation contest: "But the fairest vision on which these eyes ever looked was the flag of my country in a foreign land."[14] The lawyer's task is not easy in the face of such philosophizing. Yet with deference to Professor Friedmann of Columbia, I find his 1966 statement at the Hammarskjöld Forum on the Dominican crisis only a little less troublesome: "We all know that many legal situations are open and subject to different interpretations but law *is* ultimately a matter of black and white, or we should have no business to sit here and profess to be lawyers. . . . I submit we must find an answer in terms of right and wrong."[15]

No one at this symposium would suggest that the lawyer's proper perspective in analyzing the issues of the meeting is "my country, right or wrong." But I hope some will agree that the relevance of international law to intervention in civil strife is not confined to the question: "My country, is it right or is it wrong?" Rather, as I have tried to suggest, law and lawyers can and do have a role in drawing "the measuring line of occasion" and thus, when force is used, limiting both the expansion of that use and its precedential repercussions.

[14] N.Y. Times, May 4, 1965, at 15, col. 1.
[15] The Dominican Republic Crisis 1965 (Background Paper and Proceedings of the Ninth Hammarskjöld Forum) 112 (1967).

Intervention: A Monochromatic Term
for a Polychromatic Reality

JOHN NORTON MOORE

IT HAS become increasingly evident over the last few years that the control of international involvement in real or pretended domestic upheaval is one of the central problems of peace in our time. Since World War II the world has witnessed major international involvement in conflicts within Greece, Korea, and now Vietnam and numerous lesser involvements in such conflicts as Laos, Malaysia, Cyprus, Guatemala, Hungary, Yemen, Cuba, Lebanon, Venezuela, Bolivia, the Dominican Republic, Thailand, Czechoslovakia, and the Congo. This development, while never wholly absent from the international scene, seems to have been stimulated after World War II by the parameters of a nuclear confrontation, a shift from a balance of power toward a loose bipolar system, an accelerating rate of social change in the developing countries with a concomitant decrease in stability, and a militancy of some new leaders who advocate use of force for the expansion of ideology.

International law has been slow to respond to the challenge of these new developments and in doing so has been hampered by an antiquated set of intellectual tools which has threatened to make international law scholars amateurs of the irrelevant. In this vacuum legal scholars have tended either to take a super legalistic approach by the deification of simplistic all-encompassing norms or have capitulated to the not so real reality of the *realpolitik* school.[1]

[1] Happily in recent years there has been a growing list of thoughtful treatments of intervention. For a general introduction to the problems of intervention see: *International Aspects of Civil Strife* (Rosenau ed., 1964); *Essays on Intervention* (Stanger ed., 1964); Thomas & Thomas, *Non-Intervention: The Law and Its Import in the Americas* (1956); *The Dominican Republic Crisis 1965* (The Ninth Hammarskjold Forum, 1967); Cabranes, "Human Rights and Non-Intervention in the Inter-American System," 65 *Mich. L.R.* 1147 (1967); Falk, "The United States and the Doctrine of Nonintervention in the Internal Affairs of Independent States," 5 *How. L.J.* 163 (1959); Falk, "International Law and the United States Role in the Viet Nam War," 75 *Yale L.J.* 1122 (1966); Moore, "International Law and the United States Role in Viet Nam: A Reply," 76 *Yale L.J.* 1051 (1967); Falk "International Law and the United States Role in Viet Nam: A Response to Professor Moore," 76 *Yale L.J.* 1095 (1967); Farer, "Intervention in Civil Wars: A Modest Proposal," 67 *Col. L.R.* 266 (1967); Fenwick, "Intervention and the Inter-American Rule of Law," 53 *Am. J. Int'l L.* 873 (1959; Friedmann, "Intervention, Civil War and the Role of International Law," 59 *Am. Soc'y Int'l L. Proc.* 67 (1965); Henkin,

One of the principal roadblocks to clarity has been the failure to define the rainbow of events obscured by the intervention—nonintervention proscription. As Professor Burke has observed the term intervention is used ambiguously to refer both to operative facts and to purported legal consequences.[2] Moreover, it is used indiscriminately to refer to a range of practices as diverse as student exchange programs and the dispatch of Soviet tanks to the streets of Budapest. Used in this fashion the term intervention obscures the fact that the critical nexus between the operative facts of transnational interaction and the normative force of nonintervention lies in the coerciveness of the interaction. This does not mean that use of armed forces is the only intervention problem. If the principal community concern is with the degree of coercion in transnational interactions, we should recognize that undesirable levels can be reached through a range of strategies. This recognition is implicit in Article 15 of the OAS Charter, which gives the doctrine of nonintervention one of its broadest formulations. Article 15 provides that:

> No State or group of States has the right to intervene, directly or indirectly, for any reason whatever, in the internal or external affairs of any other States. The foregoing principle prohibits not only armed force but also any other form of interference or attempted threat against the personality of the State or against its political, economic and cultural elements.

One task facing the international law scholar is to pour content into the community aspirations reflected by this and similar provisions. That means the explicit recognition that undesirable levels of coercion can be achieved by use of the economic, diplomatic, or ideological instruments as well as by the more dramatic use of "volunteers" or marines. It also means the exploration of limiting norms with respect to these strategies. Such exploration would have as one guideline, ascertainment of the coerciveness of a particular transnational interaction, whatever its modality. Such exploration should also clarify that coercive economic or ideological strategies may sometime be in conformance with community policy, for example as seems to have been true of OAS economic sanctions against Trujillo, and as may be true

"Force, Intervention and Neutrality in Contemporary International Law," 57 *Am. Soc'y Int'l L. Proc.* 145 (1963).

[2] Burke, "The Legal Regulation of Minor International Coercion: A Framework of Inquiry," in *Essays on Intervention* (Stanger ed., 1964), 87, at 88.

of some restrictions on foreign aid designed to induce needed social reforms. Professor Friedmann's sensitive discussion of some of the forms of "economic intervention"[3] (a term which fails to distinguish objectives from modalities) indicates both the complexities of drawing these lines in a world filled with transnational interactions and the relatively primitive state of normative and procedural control in this area. The future legal order, however, probably will and should have a great deal to say about the coercive limits on employment of the economic and ideological instruments. For example, in a world increasingly polarized between have and have not nations, to what extent should economic sanctions such as trade or travel restrictions be available to the have nations to secure political objectives? To what extent do political restrictions on foreign aid result in unacceptable levels of economic coercion? For the moment, however, the focus remains on control of armed forces, a modality of interaction which characteristically involves high order coercion, and which for that reason is the most pressing concern.

Here again, however, talk of intervention has obscured the great diversity of situations characterized by transnational uses of armed force and as a result existing norms have tended to place all such uses into a single undifferentiated category.

A use of armed forces which was perhaps central to the notion of intervention during much of the nineteenth and the early part of the twentieth centuries was the use of troops or naval bombardment to collect debts or to enforce asserted breach of agreement or violation of international law. In United States foreign policy this took the form of the Roosevelt Corollary to the Monroe Doctrine, an assertion of the right of outright military occupation throughout Latin America to forestall European intervention. This period witnessed the military occupation of Haiti, Cuba, Nicaragua, and the Dominican Republic, and the Latin American reaction in the form of the Drago doctrine and the principal of absolute nonintervention.

At the Seventh International Conference of American States in 1933, however, the United States accepted in principle the nonintervention doctrine and in effect repudiated the right to enforce nonforceful breach of international obligations by force.[4] This principle, that

---

[3] Friedmann, "Intervention and the Developing Countries," 16-32 (Paper delivered at the Princeton Conference on Intervention and the Developing Countries Nov. 10-11, 1967).

[4] See Thomas & Thomas, *Non-Intervention: The Law and Its Import in the Americas*

force not be used as a modality of major change or to provide a remedy for nonforceful breach of agreement has subsequently become one of the cornerstones of the United Nations Charter.[5]

The use of armed forces which is perhaps central to the largest contemporary invocation of intervention centers around external participation in real or pretended domestic upheaval. Some of the instances are cold-war conflicts in the sense that they are fought between Communist and non-Communist factions over form of government or ideology.[6] Frequently the battleground is the developing nations with the competing factions more or less proxies of a particular system or subsystem. In their ideological orientation and structural objectives such conflicts are closer to the ideological conflict of the Spanish Civil War than to the armed intervention for the collection of debts characteristics of an earlier era.[7] Though the distinction is one of degree, and earlier military interventions were never free of political overtones, there does seem to have been a significant shift in the pattern of intervention over the last fifty years. Not all civil strife since World War II, however, neatly fits this pattern. In recent years civil strife has included a wide range of different types of conflicts: "wars of national liberation" or proxy wars represented by the conflicts in Vietnam, Greece, Thailand, Malaysia, Laos, and Bolivia, anticolonial wars as in Algeria and Angola, wars of secession as in Nigeria and the Congo, and conflicts primarily involving a breakdown of law and order as in Cyprus, the Dominican Republic, and the Congo. This great range of conflicts is also matched by the great range of modalities of external participation or nonparticipation. Such external reactions may range from premature recognition, through propaganda support, to commitment of military advisory units or tactical troops. Other fea-

---

61-64 (1956); Cabranes, "Human Rights and Non-Intervention in the Inter-American System," 65 *Mich. L. Rev.* 1147, 1153 (1967).

[5] See generally, McDougal & Feliciano, *Law and Minimum World Public Order* (1961).

[6] It is peripheral but perhaps useful to point out that the recognition of a "cold war" or of contending public order systems does not depend on acceptance of dogma about "monolithic Communism." Similarly, one can applaud the attempted shift from cold war and containment to a policy of "peaceful engagement" in United States trade relations with the Soviet Union and its Eastern European allies.

[7] The Spanish Civil War was particularly significant for the development of norms of intervention in that it served as one of the major triggering events for writing in this area. See Borchard, " 'Neutrality' and Civil Wars," 31 *Am. J. Int'l L.* 304 (1937); Garner, "Questions of International Law in the Spanish Civil War," 31 *Am. J. Int'l L.* 66 (1937); O'Rourke, "Recognition of Belligerency and the Spanish War," 31 *Am. J. Int'l L.* 398 (1937).

tures of the process of intervention reflect this same diversity. As a result, though the varieties of cold-war intervention are probably the primary concern today, a fundamental reality of the process of intervention is the great diversity of situations in which the issue is raised.

Given this diversity it is not surprising that the norms of intervention have been controversial. For traditional legal theory has sought one rule applicable to all forms of intervention in all forms of civil strife.

The traditional view has been that it is lawful to aid a widely recognized government but not insurgents.[8] More recently, some scholars have urged a "neutral nonintervention rule" to the effect that a foreign power may not aid either side engaged in purely civil strife once some threshold of indigenous conflict is exceeded.[9]

The principal dangers of the traditional rule are that it may serve as a Maginot line for vested privileges, deterring necessary reforms in feudal or totalitarian societies, and that it may be invoked by recognizing a puppet government as in the Soviet-Finnish war or the Soviet intervention in the 1956 Hungarian uprising. A principal danger of the newer "neutral rule" is that by focusing its normative weight on the more visible overt response it may provide a shield for aggressive takeover through covert attack. The fate of the 1936 Non-Intervention Pact in the Spanish Civil War illustrates in a somewhat different context the danger of an unrealistic "neutral" rule. The effectiveness of the "neutral" norm is also substantially impaired by the almost unanimous acceptance of authorization of counterintervention and by the difficulty of limiting pre-insurgency assistance. Both rules are largely unresponsive to the range of significant variables involved in external participation in intrastate conflict in the present world, although both may intuitively reflect valid policies in particular contexts.

The basic principle of the United Nations Charter that force not be used across international boundaries as an instrument to remedy nonforceful international violations or to compel political change is of

[8] See Farer, *supra* note 1, at 271-72. Professor Friedmann states: "What is probably still the prevailing view is that the incumbent government, but not the insurgents, has the right to ask for assistance from foreign governments, at least as long as insurgents are not recognized as 'belligerents' or 'insurgents.'" Friedmann, "Intervention, Civil War and the Role of International Law," 1965 *Proc., Am. Soc. Int'l L.* 67. Professor Friedmann also criticizes this rule.

[9] See Friedmann, *The Changing Structure of International Law* 265-66, 1964) ; Wright, "United States Intervention in the Lebanon," 53 *Am. J. Int'l L.* 112 (1959) .

overwhelming relevance to many nonconsensual interventions. But in many other situations of external participation in intrastate conflict the armed attack—defense abstractions of Articles 2(4) and 51 offer little guidance. A principal reason is the ambiguity in determining whether a genuine request has been made for external assistance and the ambiguity in appraising the legitimacy of the requesting faction. Interestingly, the OAS Charter and associated agreements, purportedly dealing more explicitly with intervention, also reflect this complimentarity of the armed attack-defense abstractions of the Charter. On the one hand, Articles 15 and 17 of the OAS Charter reflect a purportedly absolute nonintervention doctrine and on the other hand Articles 19 and 25 of the Charter, Article 6 of the Rio Pact and the 1962 Punta del Este Resolution reflect the need for mutual security and declare Communism incompatible with the principles of the Inter-American system. Sadly, but perhaps understandably, the OAS Charter and the Rio Pact offer only minimal guidance to the resolution of value conflicts when mutual security may be threatened by events which are otherwise primarily internal.

As an alternative to the traditional search for a single norm to regulate intervention, and in the absence of complete guidance in the charters of existing international institutions, it may be useful to first attempt greater clarification of the community policies at stake. That is, to explore as explicitly as possible the reasons why the international community regards certain practices labeled intervention as undesirable. And secondly, in the light of these policies, to try to clarify the features of the process of intervention which are critical for normative and procedural control.

As is characteristic of many legal norms, whether international or domestic, "intervention" suffers from a definitional problem. The answer to the problem of defining "intervention," though, lies not in a quixotic search for a new verbal test but in careful analysis of the functions to be served by the norms of intervention. As any systems analyst would agree, a starting point for clarification is goal definition. Goal definition alone, however, is only part of the job of operationalizing the concept of intervention. A second necessary step is the anchoring of policies in context by isolation of features crucial to policy realization. Since the traditional norms of intervention tend to be single factor oriented it would seem particularly useful to attempt this anchoring by a systematic method of inquiry. The next two sections of this paper are a preliminary attempt to adopt this method to the problem of intervention, first by attempting a preliminary clarification of community policies to be served by the norms of intervention and second by systematic analysis of the critical features of the process of intervention. In suggesting this method my purpose is to demonstrate the diversity of intervention problems and to attempt preliminary clarification and is not to formulate a definitive normative framework.

Similarly, though strategic questions in achieving national objectives are an important concern, this analysis is not directed primarily at clarifying the problem of intervention and the national interest, though some features suggested as critical may also be critical for evaluating the chances of "success" by intervention. The identification sought instead, is that of the scholar concerned with the broadest question of long-run global common interest.

External Participation in Intrastate Conflict: A Clarification of Community Policies

One of the strengths of an approach to international relations which inquires of international law is the almost unique opportunity for focus on long-run community common interest. Moreover, to the extent that clarified community policies are actually reflected in community perspectives about authority, these community subjectivities represent an important reality in predicting and altering events. The principal policies relevant to decision about the permissibility of external participation in intrastate conflict seem to be self-determination and the maximization of human rights, the maintenance of peace and avoidance of destructive coercion, a preference for centralized community decision making in situations involving transnational use of force, the desirability of mutual assistance in an interdependent world, and perhaps also a preference for a culturally pluralistic world community.

Self-determination, the right of peoples within an entity to choose their own institutions and form of government, is a basic community policy reflected in the principle of equality of states and community condemnation of colonialism. This policy is set out in Article 1, section 2 of the Charter as one of the fundamental purposes of the United Nations.

Somewhat greater difficulty is encountered in defining self-determination at a lower level of abstraction when it is asked what is meant by the right of peoples within an entity to choose their own institutions and form of government. A simplistic answer espoused by Hall[10] identifies self-determination with anything that happens in an entity. According to this view, if aid to the recognized government were legitimate then it would impair the right to revolution and if aid to the insurgents were legitimate it would violate independence by interfering with the regular organ of the state. This judgment that self-determination requires that neither the recognized government nor insurgents can ever be aided conceals the erroneous assumption that whatever takes place within the confines of a territorial entity is pursuant to genuine self-determination of peoples. Such simplistic deductive notions that territorial entities should in all circumstances be left alone ignores the reality that minorities can through terror, sabotage, and the control of the military establishment capture or maintain control of governmental machinery. The Hall view seems to adopt a kind of Darwinian definition of self-determination as survival of the fittest within the national boundaries, even if fittest means most adept in the use of force. To be meaningful, the right to revolution must be limited to the right to overthrow an unrepresentative government when avenues of peaceful change are foreclosed. It is not a right to minority military takeover whenever another political system is preferred. And similarly, in the converse situation, self-determination does not mean the right of minority maintenance of power by imposition of totalitarian controls.[11]

In place of the Hall rigidity, and despite the formidable obstacles in empirical translation of self-determination, it seems preferable to treat the policy of self-determination as one which turns on the genuine identifications and demands of a populace rather than on territorial isolation. The results of free elections provide probably the best criterion for ascertaining these subjectivities, but there are others as well. Thus, the amount of popular support received by an insurgency, the number of prominent leaders of a society attracted to its cause, responses to calls for general strikes (such as provided substantial indication of popular feeling for independence in Algeria), opinion polls, demonstrations, the commentary of a more or less free press, and the willingness of the participants—including interven-

[10] See W. Hall, *International Law* 287 (6th edn., 1909); W. Hall, *International Law* 347 (8th edn., 1924).

[11] See the Resolution by the Eighth Meeting of Consultations of the Ministers of Foreign Affairs held at Punta del Este January 22-31, 1962, Art. IV (adopted by a vote of 20 to 1).

ing parties—to agree to free elections, all provide a useful indication of the genuine identifications and demands of the people.

Perhaps the point of the self-determination policy in evaluating external assistance is simply that we do not want external coercive imposition of a particular political ideology against the genuine demands of the people of an entity. But in evaluating what kinds of external interactions produce this effect it is neither realistic nor philosophically sound simply to draw a line around the boundaries of a state and say that within these boundaries anything goes.

With respect to the policy of maximization of human rights—even apart from its self-determination aspects—the recent events in Rhodesia and the more dramatic events in Indonesia, Biafra, and the Sudan suggest a role for community intervention to preserve a minimum level of human rights or at least to prevent mass starvation.

A second policy relevant to decision about the permissibility of external participation in intrastate conflict is the maintenance of peace and avoidance of destructive coercion. This might be broadly termed the requirements of minimum world public order, after a phrase made familiar by Harold Lasswell and Myres McDougal. In relation to the permissibility of intervention this requirement of minimum world public order embodies a series of relevant policies.

In its broadest sense, it reflects the need in a nuclear world for maintenance of a certain stability and balance of power in what Morton Kaplan hypothesizes as a loose bipolar system.[12] If the danger of prolonged conflict or nuclear disaster is greater when external coercive change is sought in nations committed to an opposing bloc, or in nations located in the primary security zone of an opposing power, or in the "unfriendly" half of a cold-war divided nation, then resulting norms of intervention should enable clearer focus on the peculiar danger of such strategies. As both Korea and Vietnam demonstrate, one of the greatest threats to world order today is external intervention seeking coercive change across a boundary separating the *de facto* halves of a cold-war divided country. This is a major reason why it is crucial that international legal scholars clearly condemn the strategy of Hanoi in seeking coercive change across such a cold-war dividing line.[13]

[12] See Kaplan, "Intervention in Internal War: Some Systemic Sources," in *International Aspects of Civil Strife* 92 (Rosenau ed., 1964).

[13] For development of this point see Moore, "The Lawfulness of Military Assistance to the Republic of Viet-Nam," 61 *Am. J. Int'l L.* 1 (1967); Moore, "International Law and the United States Role in Viet Nam: A Reply," 76 *Yale L.J.* 1051 (1967); Moore, "Law

Although not decisive of legitimacy, the need for minimum bloc security and the dangers perceived by national decision makers in sudden and unpredictable shifts within "committed" areas (particularly within primary security zones, perhaps as given empirical content by reference to such factors as the need to prevent an opposing power from achieving a nuclear first strike capability) provide a strong motivating force for intervention within these zones to prevent sudden shifts to an opposing bloc or sub-bloc. United States actions with respect to Guatemala, Cuba, and the Dominican Republic and Soviet reactions when faced with insurgencies in East Germany and Hungary, although differing in other crucial aspects, were in part similarly motivated by this perceived need for stability. In fact, the failure of the United States to prevent the sudden shift in its primary security zone in Cuba, a "failure" caused largely by a perception (initially accurate) of the Cuban civil strife as a personnel rather than a structural conflict, did result in direct confrontation between the major powers in the later Cuban missile crisis. When the Soviets secretly and unexpectedly pressed advantage from the sudden shift by emplacement of offensive nuclear missiles in Cuba, the resulting perceived shift in deterrence capabilities precipitated an unusually dangerous inter-bloc confrontation. An unanswered question is to what extent it is legitimate, if at all, to reflect this kind of danger from sudden shifts in "committed" areas in the norms of intervention. Obvious dangers of overemphasis of such a policy include legitimation of intervention against the genuine demands of self-determination, as for example Soviet intervention in Hungary and Czechoslovakia, uncertainty as to Chinese claims to a "sphere of influence," and a return to a Roosevelt Corollary for Latin America. But though, standing alone, this policy is a doubtful one for legitimation of intervention, its converse is crucial in condemning intervention for the purpose of maintaining or achieving change in areas long "committed" to an opposing system or subsystem.

Minimum public order also reflects the Charter principle that use of force as a modality of major change or for dispute settlement is outlawed. The danger and disruptiveness of coercive change in today's world strongly militates for strict adherence to the Charter proscription that force may not be used except in defense against an armed attack. Clearly it is impermissible for either Communist or non-Com-

---

and Politics in the Vietnamese War: A Response to Professor Friedmann," 61 *Am. J. Int'l L.* 1039 (1967).

munist nations to use major force as a means of expanding ideology or remedying asserted nonforceful breach of international obligations. In a nuclear world the international system cannot tolerate major use of force as a modality of major change, whether by the United States in Cuba, North Vietnam in South Vietnam, or either Israel or the Arab states in the Middle East. This is perhaps the principal attractiveness of outlawing all assistance to insurgents as under the traditional approach.

Lastly, minimum public order reflects the range of policies for minimization of destruction to all values with respect to ongoing coercion. For example, in evaluating the Dominican Republic operation it is relevant to consider the extent, if any, which United States and later OAS actions contributed to damping down destructiveness and avoiding a prolonged bloodbath in the Dominican Republic. Similarly, a major policy concern with regard to the Vietnam conflict is the major destruction to Vietnamese society involved in the decision to wage a protracted defense within Vietnam. Policies involved in minimizing the destructiveness of ongoing coercion also include those of proportionality in tailoring the amount of force employed to that necessary to achieve lawful objectives with the least cost to all participants.

A third policy concerning external participation in intrastate conflict is the preference for inclusive community decision making in situations involving transnational use of force. The problem of auto-interpretation of events and the dangers of major power involvement on opposite sides of intrastate conflict are such that there is a strong community preference for centralized decision making with respect to transnational use of force. This policy is reflected in the United Nations Charter which makes unilateral use of force subject to later community review, and in the provisions of the OAS Charter and the Rio Pact which call for collective regional determination in situations endangering the peace of the Americas.

Presumably the more inclusive the participation in the decision to intervene the greater the likelihood that the intervention will reflect fundamental community policies. This premise is felt to be so decisive when the level of decision making becomes global that Article 39 of the Charter gives the Security Council great discretion to determine the existence of a "threat to the peace, breach of the peace, or act of aggression," and Articles 40-42 provide the Security Council with equal discretion in choosing the modality of response. At the intermediate regional level of decision making, for example OAS decisions, there is greater controversy as to the permissible discretion to intervene. Doctrinally the controversy centers on the meaning of "enforcement action" in Article 53 of the U.N. Charter, but functionally the problem is one of allocation of competence to initially employ transnational coercion in situations not involving an armed attack within the meaning of Article 51.

Insofar as this policy favoring institutional decision making is based on greater likelihood that a particular decision will reflect fundamental community policies, it is also applicable to interventions other than by the use of armed force. For example, political restrictions on foreign aid to the developing states designed to promote needed social reforms might be better imposed by a global or regional organization more representative of inclusive interests.

A fourth policy evident in external participation in intrastate conflict, and in fact in any kind of transnational interaction, is the desirability of mutual assistance in an interdependent world. Like the policy for inclusive community decision making in situations involving use of force, the policy of mutual assistance is not entirely separate from the demands of self-determination and minimum world public order. But it is perhaps useful to state it as an additional policy in order to focus on the felt interdependence in the world today, both in matters of defense and otherwise. The many regional defense treaties such as NATO, CENTO, the Rio Pact, SEATO, the Warsaw Pact, and the Arab League, to name a few, demonstrate the real defense interdependency felt in a world which though not composed of monolithic blocs, East or West, is divided between fundamentally different and actively competing public order systems and subsystems. Given this evidence of interdependency it may be relevant to ask to what extent focus on self-determination of a single entity is realistic or desirable in situations in which the impact of intrastate conflict is substantial in third states. A tentative answer is that it is still fundamentally necessary to emphasize the genuine demands of the peoples of the entity undergoing the intrastate strife but that the decision maker may also be legitimately concerned with the genuine demands of the people of a wider area which may be affected by the outcome.

With respect to interests other than defense there is a great interdependency also, and it is certainly a widely shared community policy that the developed nations should assist the developing nations in attaining higher economic outputs and a wider distribution of goods and services. It is the tension with these real interdependencies, defense and otherwise, which makes it impossible and undesirable to adopt easy line-drawing solutions to shut out external interactions, and which makes modern day isolation unthinkable.

Lastly, perhaps the norms of intervention reflect a preference for a culturally pluralistic world community. The sociologists tell us that it is frequently the surface superficiality and more undesirable cultural traits that are the first to be transmitted from one culture to another. And the cultural anthropologist has provided greater insights into the values of other cultures that are all too frequently characterized on superficial knowledge as backward. These findings suggest the desirability of restraining missionary zeal in attempts to foster transnational cultural or political change. The excesses of the early missionaries provide ample proof of the dangers of cultural imperialism even for the most beneficient of motives. Perhaps Article 13 of the OAS Charter reflects this preference for cultural pluralism when it provides that: "Each State has the right to develop its cultural, political and economic life freely and naturally."[14]

Necessarily, however, this policy preference for cultural pluralism is difficult to implement in an era when the level of transnational interactions is such that we may accurately speak of a world community. And necessarily, the focus of policies against intervention will remain the more coercive strategies of change.

This preliminary analysis of the policies involved in decision about the permissibility of external participation in intrastate conflict is not intended to be exhaustive. Rather, it is an attempt to isolate the more fundamental reasons why we regard intervention as right or wrong so that resulting norms will be more responsive to the functions they are intended to serve and to encourage a dialogue on the community values at stake. Even an analysis of all operative policies is not a clear chart to wisdom. For in a concrete instance policies may be conflicting. But without such clarification, sound decision becomes little more than chance.

Elsewhere I have attempted to analyze the principal existing norms of intervention with respect to the major policies of self-determination

[14] Similarly, § 2 (e) of the draft recommendation adopted on April 22, 1966 by the Special Committee on Principles of International Law Concerning Friendly Relations and Co-operation Among States provides that: "Each State has the right freely to choose and develop its political, social, economic and cultural systems." U.N. Doc. A/6230 at 176, 183 (1966).

and minimum public order and have concluded that existing norms are too oversimplified to be meaningfully policy responsive in the wide range of situations in which they are applied.[15] Nevertheless, existing norms such as the traditional view that assistance could be rendered to widely recognized governments only, may intuitively reach sound results in particular contexts. For example, the traditional view that a widely recognized government may be lawfully aided and that insurgents may not, seem on analysis to have some merit in the cold-war divided nation context. Considerations which suggest this conclusion are the desirability of focusing on the great threat to peace in providing sustained assistance to insurgents across cold-war boundaries, the difficulty of appraising covert assistance in externally sponsored "wars of national liberation," the perceived threat to the balance of power from sudden shifts in committed areas, and realism about constraints felt by opposing bloc powers to support existing friendly regimes, as evidenced by the events in Hungary, East Germany, Malaysia, Korea, Greece, and now Vietnam.

But since this paper is a preliminary inquiry into method, rather than repeat a policy analysis of the existing norms or formulate a new set of nonintervention norms, it seems most useful in light of the great diversity of situations subsumed under intervention to attempt to clarify the critical features of the process of intervention. The features selected as "critical," of course, are "critical" from the standpoint of one or more of the community policies just explored. Focusing on these critical features of the process is a way of operationalizing the community policies served by the nonintervention proscription. Hopefully this exposition of a systematic method for anchoring nonintervention policies in context might aid in eventual formulation of a more responsive normative framework for controlling intervention. And in the short run, it seems a substantial improvement to at least move from certainty for the wrong reasons to uncertainty for the right reasons.

The Critical Features of the Process of Intervention: Some Unanswered Questions

The critical features of the process of intervention can be most conveniently explored by systematic analysis of the process with regard

---

[15] See Moore, *supra* note 13, 61 *Am. J. Int'l L.* at 28-32, 76; *Yale L.J.* at 1080-88. See also my brief recommendation of a framework for inquiry about nonintervention norms in the 1967 *Proc. Am. Soc'y Int'l L.* 75.

to the participants involved, the objectives sought by the participants, the situations spatially and temporally of the intervention, the resources or base values available to the participants, the strategies pursued by the participants, the immediate outcomes of the process, the longer range effects of the intervention on the international system and the conditions of the system shaping the process. This method of analysis is intended to focus attention on the range of variables in the process which may be useful for normative judgment and to suggest the disutility of attempting the formulation of norms for all contexts by reference to a single feature of the process of intervention.

PARTICIPANTS

One important feature of the process of intervention is the degree of collectivization of the action. Because of the community policy favoring inclusive decision making in situations involving transnational coercion it is highly relevant to judgment about such transnational interactions whether the principal decision was made at a global level by the United Nations, or at a regional level by perhaps the OAS, or unilaterally.

The Charter provides wide competence to the United Nations Security Council to take action, including the use of force to take measures to deal with "any threat to the peace, breach of the peace, or act of aggression." Moreover, this competence is specifically excluded from the Article 2 prohibition against intervention "in matters which are essentially within the domestic jurisdiction of any state." The community policies militating for a broad United Nations competence to intervene "whenever civil strife threatens world peace or whenever gross abuses of fundamental human rights take place," have been eloquently stated by Professor Falk at an earlier regional meeting of the Society, which was also attempting to grapple with the question of intervention.[16] Since then, the substance of Professor Falk's thesis "that the United Nations should be authorized on a selective basis to coerce domestic social changes," has been adopted in the limited form of United Nations sanctions against Rhodesia.[17]

[16] Falk, "The Legitimacy of Legislative Intervention by the United Nations," in *Essays on Intervention* 31 (Stanger ed., 1964).

[17] See McDougal & Reisman, "Rhodesia and the United Nations: The Lawfulness of International Concern," 62 *A.J.I.L.* 1 (1968); Rabinowitz, "U.N. Application of Selective, Mandatory Sanctions Against Rhodesia: A Brief Legal and Political Analysis," 7 *Va. J. Int'l L.* 147 (1967).

An unanswered question which must also be met even by those applauding the Rhodesian sanctions, however, is whether Security Council competence to intervene under Chapter VII of the Charter is to be absolute, limited only by the necessity of permanent member assent and the requisite vote of seven members, or whether it is to be limited by other substantive community policies. The answer, it would seem, should lie in the further exploration and application of the broad community policies explored in the preceding section. Since one of those policies is a preference for inclusive decision making in situations involving transnational use of force or threatening the stability of world order, it seems desirable that the United Nations have a broad competence along the lines suggested by Professor Falk whenever an otherwise "domestic" question is a threat to the stability of the international system. The Rhodesian situation is such a case. Effective exercise of this competence in conformance with inclusive community concern presupposes the maintenance within the United Nations of effective representation of inclusive interests.

When the decision to intervene is made at a regional level, for example by the OAS, the institutionalization and collectivization of the actions do increase the legitimacy of those actions. One reason for this increase is the greater assurance that such actions represent legitimate inclusive interests. But since by definition regional actors do not share the global representation of the United Nations, they should not have the degree of discretion available to the global organization. Moreover, a factor militating against wide regional discretion to use major force is the danger that regional action poses for major power confrontation, since regional action does not need the concurrent vote of all major powers voting as is true of Security Council authorization. Again, however, the answer to the degree of competence of regional actors is suggested not so much by an analysis of the "enforcement action" language of the U.N. Charter as by careful analysis of the community values at stake in any particular type of action, particularly the effect on self-determination and the danger to minimum public order.

Though individual or collective action which falls short of regional or global authority does not share the greater assurance offered by the wider collectivization and institutionalization of regional and U.N. action, the imperfections of existing global and regional peace keeping machinery make it inevitable that a substantial area of individual discretion be retained, subject to later community review. This is particularly true of the need for an effective right of individual and collective defense but may also extend to other actions in conformance with basic community policies. The effect of timing of institutional consent, whether prior approval or later ratification of unilateral action, may also reflect important policy consequences worth further contextual exploration.

Other features which might be explored with respect to intervening participants include the resources available for the intervention, geographic distance from the intervention, and degree of participation in a regional bloc or movement.

OBJECTIVES

A particularly relevant feature of the process of intervention, though often one of the most difficult to appraise, is the objectives with which the participants initiate and sustain an intervention.

Anticolonial wars such as the Algerian War may evidence objectives which are basically in conformance with widely shared community notions about self-determination. The totalitarian pattern of "wars of national liberation," on the other hand, if carried on by a minority using terrorist tactics, may be the antithesis of genuine self-determination, despite rhetoric about democracy and anticolonialism.

In the Vietnam conflict, Hanoi's sustained assistance to the insurgents in the South seems to be given with the more or less long-run objective of territorial and political unification of a *de facto* divided country. This at times self-proclaimed objective of Hanoi in intervening in South Vietnam is a highly relevant feature in assessing the legitimacy of third party assistance to the government of South Vietnam.

A somewhat different objective evidenced in the American Civil War, the Congo strife, and currently the Nigerian Civil War is the desire for secession. Analysis of the requirements of self-determination here raise such imponderables as how to define an "entity" as a starting point for appraisal of self-determination. This question, which is crucial to many situations of civil strife, is conspicuously neglected by the nonintervention literature. Presumably inquiry aimed at this question might consider the desirability of existing boundaries in terms of geographic, historic, economic, political, and ethnic factors.

Major intervention by military force which evidences as an objective the collection of asserted debts or which seeks to impose sanctions for asserted breach of international law not amounting to an "armed attack" offers no justification either in terms of the requirements of self-determination or minimum public order and as such should be condemned. The joint British-French-Israeli invasion of Suez would seem a recent example of intervention in which such objectives played a substantial role.

On the other hand, limited use of force for the protection of the lives of nationals or for "humanitarian intervention" may serve community policies and should be accepted if narrowly confined to these objectives. For example, even those critical of later stages of the Dominican Republic operation seem to have conceded the propriety of landing limited American forces for the protection of the lives of nationals in a situation of near anarchy, though they dispute to what extent the lives of American nationals were threatened. Although perhaps more controversial, I would place the November 1964 joint U.S.-Belgian Congo intervention for the protection of civilian hostages, nationals of at least eighteen foreign countries, in the same category. The much needed Biafran relief, if aimed at avoiding mass starvation rather than establishing a second state, would also fall in this category.

The point is that the objectives evidenced by intervening powers and by national participants in civil strife vary widely, and as objectively appraised by both conduct and statement, such objectives provide a highly relevant feature in assessing permissibility of intervention. It is inaccurate to take the absolutist position that all intervention is alike and should be impermissible. The truth is that some interventions promote community policies while others do not and a quest for a "neutral" rule which ignores these policies may be self-defeating.

Of course, just because a particular action is consistent with self-determination does not mean that it should be legitimate. Other community policies, particularly the maintenance of minimum public order may also be threatened. Where the risk of major conflict is slight, grave and continuing denial of self-determination may outweigh dangers of the use of coercive strategies of change. But where such risk is grave, minimum public order may be the most important consideration.[18]

18 James N. Rosenau's classification of internal wars as personnel wars, authority wars, and structural wars is a useful characterization based principally on the objectives of the participants. Of these, the structural war, which he defines as "those which are perceived as being not only contests over personnel and the structure of political authority, but also as struggles over other substructures of the society . . . or its major domestic and foreign policies," could be expected to be the most disruptive of the international system and the most likely to invite external participation. See Rosenau, "Internal War

SITUATIONS

One feature of the process of intervention which has been almost entirely overlooked in traditional treatments but which seems highly relevant in evaluating the consequences of intervention with respect to minimum public order is the location of the intervention in relation to major power security.

The risk that intervention will trigger major or prolonged conflict is much higher for interventions aimed at altering the status quo in the primary security areas or among the committed nations of a competing bloc. And the risk is much less for interventions aimed at maintaining the status quo within the corresponding areas of the intervening power. For example, regardless of their substantial dissimilarities, the Soviet interventions in Hungary and Czechoslovakia, and the United States interventions in Guatemala and the Dominican Republic ran substantially low risks of major power conflict or prolonged war. And each was at least partially a reaction to a perceived threat (erroneously perceived or not) to the stability of the defensive posture of the intervening power. If intervention does not threaten to alter the primary security interests of opposing major powers, there is even less threat to the global implications of minimum public order. Indian intervention in Goa and a hypothetical British intervention in Rhodesia would seem to offer examples of this. On the other hand, the Egyptian and Saudi Arabian intervention on opposing sides in the Yemen illustrate that minimum public order in its other senses may still be a major value at stake even if the global threat is minor.

Perhaps the clearest example of this geographic principle is provided by the Korean and Vietnam conflicts where North Korea and North Vietnam sought change by in the one case overt and in the other covert use of the military instrument across lines clearly separating the major contending public order systems. Probably few interventions possess the potential for major and escalating conflict as such interventions across the cold-war demarcation lines in these divided countries. Both Korea and Vietnam amply demonstrate this danger. And though it would seem desirable in many ways for the contending cold-war camps to recognize the real-world division of these divided countries in Germany, Korea, China and Vietnam, it is *imperative* that rhetoric about "one nation" used by both sides not conceal the great community inter-

as an International Event, in *International Aspects of Civil Strife* 45, at 63 (Rosenau ed., 1964).

est in at least clearly recognizing the separateness of such entities for the purpose of assessing the legitimacy of the use of force across the boundaries and cease-fire lines separating them.

Similarly, though the problem in how to define an "entity" may be considerably more complex with reference to the requirements of self-determination, when the principal policy at stake becomes minimum public order the criterion is essentially *de facto* separateness.

Again, this geographic feature of the process of intervention is not necessarily decisive, primarily because other important community values may be at stake. But intervention clearly within the "committed" area of another major power presents a grave threat to world public order which should usually be enough *ipso facto* to render such intervention impermissible. Even within one's own bloc, however, intervention which blatantly denies self-determination should be impermissible. Thus, in analyzing the Hungarian uprising it would seem that the requirements of self-determination made it impermissible for the Soviets to intervene to crush the revolt (and *a fortiori* impermissible in Czechoslovakia) and that the requirements of minimum public order made it impermissible for the United States to intervene to assist the revolt against the Soviet imposed regime. In circumstances like the Hungarian uprising, intervention by either party would threaten fundamental community policies, though for different reasons, and should not be undertaken.

BASE VALUES

The single feature emphasized in the traditional nonintervention norm is whether external assistance was requested by a recognized government. This feature of the process of intervention—whether assistance was rendered to insurgents or at the request of a widely recognized government—conceals a number of important questions which may be relevant to normative clarification. In fact, because the traditional norm largely conceals the real importance of the recognized government-insurgent distinction with respect to policies both of self-determination and minimum public order, it has obscured its own real relevance, an obfuscation which has made it unnecessarily vulnerable to the seeming attractiveness of the "neutral" nonintervention norm. It is not suggested, however, that this traditional norm is policy responsive in a broad range of contexts.

More explicitly, the question is whether there are any real differences between insurgents and a widely recognized government which make a difference in impact on community policies whether assistance is rendered to one or the other.

On analysis, the distinction between widely recognized governments and insurgents does seem to reflect important differences, but these differences may be more precisely stated by reference to degree of authority and control exercised by each faction, by reference to which faction controls the organized military apparatus, and by reference to which faction may have the greater communicated expectation of international support.

A government whose credentials are undisputed is usually characterized both by widespread expectations, internal and external, of its authority, and by effective control of its territory and population. To the extent that either authority or control, or both, is lacking, a government's legitimacy to request external assistance is reduced. The degree to which insurgents or the widely recognized government possess authority, both internal and external, in the sense of expectations as to their "rightness" to govern, is relevant from the standpoint of self-determination in determining which faction may be assisted. And the degree to which insurgents or the widely recognized government exercise effective control over territory and population is relevant from the standpoint of minimum public order in determining which faction may be assisted. In fact, the traditional law of civil strife contains the label "belligerent" for insurgents who exercise greater effective control, and when so labeled accords them greater international status. Thus, one relevant aspect of the recognized government-insurgent distinction is really a question of where each faction falls on a continuum of authority and control. Assistance to a faction which exercises little authority and control is essentially nothing but an external attack (which may or may not rise to the level of an "armed attack" within the meaning of Article 51 of the Charter), if provided against a faction which exercises substantial authority and control. Real nakedness of authority and control cannot be cured by puppet governments or instant recognition. For example, the Soviet creation of an instant government which invited them in to the Russo-Finnish War, and the same Soviet ruse in the 1956 Hungarian uprising, did not in any but a propaganda sense render Soviet actions more permissible. The 1968 invasion of Czechoslovakia was even more blatant. And on the other hand, assistance at the request of a widely recognized government which exercises substantial authority and control is not "intervention" in any primary sense.

On the whole, it can be expected that a government which is widely recognized over a significant period of time can be expected to exercise substantial authority and control and as such, the traditional rule may often reflect an important feature, albeit intuitively.

A second important feature underlying the recognized government-insurgency dichotomy is the question of control of the organized military apparatus. It seems to be particularly important in predicting the consequences for minimum public order if sustained military assistance is rendered to a faction which does not control the organized military. A comparison of such diverse situations as Hungary and Lebanon with Algeria and Vietnam indicates that sustained assistance to an insurgency which is opposed by the organized military is likely to lead to a prolonged costly struggle. One of the reasons for the "success" of the United States Guatemalan intervention was that the low-level assistance to the insurgents was premised on the organized military switching to the insurgent cause of Castillo Armas. When the organized military did switch from Arbenz to Armas the brief fight was over.[19] And conversely, one of the principal reasons for the failure of the Bay of Pigs venture was its effective opposition by the organized military which seemed to have little inclination toward a shift in loyalties. The failure of the attempted Maoist coup in Indonesia may be partly attributable to this same factor. Similarly, one of the principal reasons for the prolonged war in Vietnam is that the organized military is perhaps the principal opposition to the insurgent cause. The decision by North Vietnam to provide sustained assistance to an insurgency opposed by the organized military is another factor making such decision extremely dangerous for world order, and which one suspects may have resulted from a persistent miscalculation about political collapse in the South or the degree of United States support to be expected.

To the extent that widely recognized governments more often command the loyalties of the organized military apparatus, sustained assistance to insurgents is likely to be an intervention which is particularly dangerous to world peace.

A third factor underlying the recognized government-insurgency dichotomy, and there may be others, is the degree to which a faction has, and communicates expectations of having, access to external support. One manifestation of such support might be a preexisting treaty of guarantee against external attack or internal subversion. The

19 See Westerfield, *The Instruments of America's Foreign Policy* 422-42 (1966).

SEATO Treaty is a common example of a loose agreement of this type.[20] To the extent that assistance is rendered to a faction opposed by an elite which is party to such an agreement, or which otherwise has expectations of external assistance, the conflict stands a substantial likelihood of being internationalized in a dangerous fashion. To the extent, then, that widely recognized governments are more likely to have access to such external support, sustained assistance to insurgents runs a greater risk of dangerous international escalation of the conflict. To some extent, these expectations of access to external support may also be said to be a function of the external authority position of a particular faction. Thus, degree of external authority may be important with respect to the minimum public order policy as well as with respect to the self-determination policy.

STRATEGIES

The strategies or modalities of intervention may range from propaganda support of one faction or another, through diplomatic recognition, economic assistance, supply of military hardware, shows of force, commitment of advisory and training forces, and commitment of troops in tactical operations. Moreover, failure to provide assistance or withdrawal of assistance previously begun with respect to each of these modalities may also have internal effects which are sometimes characterized as intervention.

Though this feature of the process of intervention seems highly relevant to the permissibility of intervention, traditional theory has accorded it little weight. Recently, however, Tom Farer has suggested, in a provocative reevaluation of the norms of intervention, that there should be "a flat prohibition of participation in tactical operations, either openly or through the medium of advisors or volunteers."[21] This proposal has considerable merit. It is particularly sensitive to the

[20] There has been considerable controversy surrounding the weight to be given the SEATO "obligation" to defend South Vietnam. On balance it would seem that SEATO has been neither all-important nor inconsequential.

One of the ways in which SEATO is relevant is simply its function as a manifestation of expectations of international assistance for the Saigon government. The existence of such a communication is a relevant feature in predicting the danger to minimum world public order of a decision to provide sustained assistance to insurgents aimed at the structural overthrow of established elites.

[21] Farer, "Intervention in Civil Wars: A Modest Proposal," 67 *Col. L. Rev.* 266, 275 (1967).

need for reducing the danger of great power confrontation on opposing sides of civil strife and also has the substantial merit of ruling out one of the most coercive forms of interaction.

Like the norms which preceded it, however, this proposal is keyed to only one feature of the process of intervention and as such is incomplete. It is highly questionable, for example, whether in light of the applicable community policies it is desirable to legitimate all external assistance by any participant for any objective in any situation and to any faction which falls short of the threshold of participation in tactical operations. For example, continuing supply of military hardware by the United States to insurgents in Hungary or such continuing supply from Taiwan to insurgents in mainland China or from North Korea to South Korea would also seem to carry substantial risk of escalation.

Presumably also the rule breaks down unless reciprocity is accorded when one side resorts to tactical operations. And as Vietnam demonstrates this transition may provide a difficult line to draw when the operations of one side are largely covert. Like the "neutral" nonintervention rule, there is some danger that this tactical operations rule will be largely focused on the overt response rather than the precipitating covert assistance.

Despite my reservations about this proposal as a panacea, however, it is probably the single most useful normative suggestion which has been made for dealing with the intervention problem and provides a long overdue focus on the possibility of using the modality of intervention as a normative base. Perhaps its major shortcoming is that there are simply too broad a range of intervention situations to be adequately dealt with by one rule.

OUTCOMES

Another significant feature of the process of intervention which might be usefully employed as a normative base and which has been largely ignored in formulating the traditional rules, is the question of whether an external participation is followed by genuine elections or some other means of ascertaining the requirements of self-determination. Since this feature of the process of intervention may more directly reflect the requirements of genuine self-determination than any other feature of the process, it would certainly be worthwhile to explore to what extent the permissibility of particular types of intervention might be conditioned on holding supervised elections.

EFFECTS

The relatively long-run consequences for world order of a particular intervention or type of intervention may also be a relevant factor in formulating normative restraints on intervention. One such feature might be that the state in which intervention takes place has itself been widely intervening by fostering and supporting insurgencies, as for example is true of the activities of Castro's Cuba in a number of Latin American countries, though as Che Guevara's death indicates, probably with a generally unfavorable prognosis. A related question at an earlier stage of the process would be whether the dominant myth espoused by a particular faction engaged in civil strife includes revolutionary assistance to insurgencies elsewhere.

One relatively long-run effect of insurgency is particularly interesting and may suggest some questions relevant to the norms of intervention. That is, the degree to which successful insurgencies foster more insurgencies. George Modelski has described what he terms a "diffusion effect" in the international system by which the prevailing subjectivities and myths of the time are translated into such movements as a wave of colonial wars or a movement toward democratic regimes, as occurred immediately after the Second World War, or a noticeable trend toward fascist governments as was true throughout the world in 1938-1941.[22]

It is conceivable in some cases that the subjectivities, demands, and identifications fostered by a decision to intervene or not to intervene may even be the most important single feature of the process of intervention in terms of effects on world order. The underestimation of this kind of psychological factor, the subjectivities involved in the process, is a consistent error of the *realpolitik* school. If this factor is an important feature of the process of intervention it may be useful to inquire to what extent the principal revolutionary myths today are anticolonial wars and "wars of national liberation" and what the consequences of this should be, if any, for the norms of intervention.

CONDITIONS

The broader context of conditions in which the process of intervention takes place is also of importance for the formulation of norms of intervention.

---

[22] Modelski, "The International Relations of Internal War," in *International Aspects of Civil Strife*, 14, 32 (Rosenau ed., 1964).

Conditions of particular relevance to this process have been implicit in much of the discussion thus far. Perhaps the overriding condition is the presence in the world of competing but loosely coordinated public order systems maintaining a precarious nuclear balance of terror.

This condition renders minimum world public order of crucial dimension. In this context norms which reduce the possibility of direct inter-bloc conflict and which place a premium on the stability of the international system may well be more important than norms which evince great sensitivity to other community policies but which perform poorly in terms of minimum public order.

Another general condition affecting the process of intervention is the great interdependency of nations today and the high level of interaction achieved on a global level. The rapid transformation of communications and transportation technology in the last fifty years has shrunk the world as never before. This interdependency and high level of interaction intensifies the effect of internal war on the international system and the effect of system change on internal war. At the same time the knowledge and technology explosions tend themselves to promote rapid social change which lacking other outlets may take the form of revolution. The combination of factors produces an unusually high number of intrastate conflicts with resulting intensified instability to the international system and tends to make the developing countries a battleground for competing public order systems. These conditions suggest the need for international legislative competence to ease explosive change and for institutions and practices which protect the developing countries from cold-war tensions.

It is also of great concern that the international system currently offers only a low level of institutionalization for the control of intrastate conflict. What has been termed by Abram Chayes as "the process side" of the control of external participation in such conflict is extremely primitive.[23]

Lacking to a greater or lesser degree are readily available and reliable fact-finding institutions for ascertaining the level and occurrence of covert external participation, effective mediating agencies, agencies for conducting elections, and other forms of desirable process controls.

Internal war is most tractable to settlement and least dangerous in early stages, and it is in these early stages that an effective international

[23] This is a term which caught my fancy during the panel discussion of the "Norms of Intervention" at the 1967 Annual Meeting of the American Society of International Law.

process should intervene to secure settlement. The existing process controls, however, show little sign of functioning before a high order of chaos is reached. And though regional organization such as SEATO and the OAS have performed some fact-finding functions, SEATO to a lesser extent in Vietnam and the OAS more forcefully in Venezuela, the potentiality even of these "committed" organizations to secure and publish facts has largely gone untapped. It would be particularly helpful if reasonably reliable permanent fact-finding agencies were available at a global level. The willingness of one faction or another to resort to the agency could be a relevant factor in evaluating assistance to that faction.

It is particularly important that the role of the U.N. in damping down dangerous intrastate conflict, already begun in the Congo and Cyprus, and the existing potentiality of the U.N. to provide some of the suggested process tools, be strengthened. In fact it is probable that development of this "process side" offers greater hope for control than does normative clarification. Certainly attention should be directed at creating and strengthening the kinds of institutions needed. But as perhaps the controversy surrounding the Congo operation demonstrates, "process" is a means to a goal, not a substitute for goal definition. Normative clarification remains necessary for direction and for evaluation.

This preliminary analysis of the critical features of the process of intervention is intended to call attention to the broad range of contextual features which may be important in formulating a normative framework for the control of external participation in intrastate conflict and to suggest the importance of several critical features of the process of intervention. It is not intended as a definitive formulation of a normative framework or as a complete analysis of all the relevant features. Undoubtedly there are other important factors which might also be profitably analyzed in a thorough systematic analysis of the process of intervention.

An Appraisal

The traditional approach to the norms of intervention has sought one rule applicable to all forms of civil strife. Characteristically that rule has focused on only a single feature of the process of intervention. The great diversity of situations in which intervention is invoked, however, and the variety of critical features of the process of intervention have rendered such rules hopelessly oversimplified. It is not surprising that they have not been widely observed. Furthermore, since the traditional rules usually lacked policy clarification, what function they have performed has been largely intuitive. The traditional controversy between the legitimacy theory and the so-called neutral nonintervention norm, for example, has distracted attention from a meaningful search for other normative bases, such as limitations on types of assistance, area limitations, international procedural processes, or conditioning external assistance on willingness to hold free elections. The mechanical application of these rules has also obscured focus on the community policies at stake in situations of intervention. The traditional dialogue must move beyond controversy about these rigid rules and give way to more flexible and thoroughgoing inquiry.

As an alternative method for clarifying policy choices with respect to the control of intervention it is recommended that we first seek greater clarification of the function to be served by the norms of intervention. Such clarification offers standards which may then be used for the isolation of critical features for each major type of civil strife which in turn may provide a base for more effective normative refinement.

Empirical research may not support some of these contextual features as crucial for policy realization and thorough analysis may reveal other critical features. But the important point is that the method of inquiry should serve as a way of operationalizing the nonintervention proscription for a badly needed more responsive and realistic normative structure.

Harnessing Rogue Elephants:
A Short Discourse on
Intervention in Civil Strife

TOM J. FARER

*Introduction**

I HAVE three primary objectives in this chapter: First, to review the difficulties associated with efforts to define "intervention" and to suggest rather hesitantly one possible solution to this controversy; second, to identify the criteria for evaluating proposed international legal rules; third, to measure against those criteria two alternative prescriptions for regulating the participation of foreign states in third world civil strife.

1. INTERVENTION: IN PURSUIT OF A DEFINITION

The pursuit must move across rough terrain where conflict is a way of life. Late last year James Rosenau, one of the more astute members of the fraternity of foreign policy analysts, made the trip in broad daylight. He urged limitation of the normally opprobrious term "intervention" to conduct that is convention-breaking and is "addressed to the authority structure of the target society—that is, to the identity of those who make the decisions that are binding for the entire society and/or to the processes through which such decisions are made."[1]

On the basis of this definition he would distinguish the exercise of Soviet influence in Hungary prior to the revolution from the suppression of the revolution, because the latter was in its form a perceptible departure from the behavior of the prior decade although at all times the Soviet Government was influencing the structure of authority in Hungary. Similarly, he would distinguish U.S. behavior in Vietnam before and after the escalation of 1965.

Rosenau's purpose appears to be academic rather than polemic. He recognizes the immense difficulties associated with theorizing about the general thrust of a state's foreign policy. He undoubtedly appreci-

---

* This chapter is based on a paper presented at the March 1968 Symposium on Intervention in Civil Strife, sponsored by the International Society of the Stanford School of Law, and published in the *Stanford Journal of International Legal Studies*.

---

[1] Rosenau, "The Concept of Intervention" (paper prepared for the Conference on Intervention and the Developing States, held at Princeton, N.J., November 10-11, 1967).

ates that much foreign policy behavior is the product of myriad, individually insignificant decisions made by men with little, if any, sense of the broad consequences of their choices. Convention-breaking activities designed to affect the authority structure of another state are almost invariably initiated at the highest level of government, after substantial deliberation. If conscious, idiosyncratic preferences are significant in foreign policy formation, this is the occasion when their impact is most likely to be experienced. It is, in other words, the moment when the decision-making process obtains maximum self-consciousness and the time when the operation of that process is most susceptible to scholarly analysis.

The distinctive nature of convention-breaking, authority-oriented behavior and the desirability of directing attention to this phenomenon are hardly reasons for endowing it with an exclusive title to the emotive term "intervention." But such a restriction of the term's applicability might be justified on grounds quite unrelated to the exigencies of scholarship, on grounds summarized in the homely truism that in defining a form of behavior which is to be legally prohibited, the relevant conduct should be described with sufficient precision so that violations of the prohibition can be detected with reasonable consistency. Failure to heed this canon in domestic law creation produces whimsical enforcement and consequent injustice. On the international scene with its fragile and rudimentary fact-finding and law-applying machinery, the likely product of such failure is covert disregard of the announced prohibition and diminution of the binding power of all international legal restrictions.

Rosenau has succeeded in his objective of operationalizing the concept, that is, of defining it in terms of perceivable behavior. In the process, he has shrunk it to the point where it no longer fits activities which do have a powerful and designed impact on the target society. Such a contraction of the term's potential scope is normatively jarring, because the normative conceptions of international society are peculiarly bound up with definite verbal formulae. If a legally operative term is withdrawn from a given behavioral phenomenon, the associated constraints also tend to be torn away.

The only semblance of a consensus centers on the notion that the behavior must be *consciously* directed toward producing an effect in the target state. Some scholars would limit the term's applicability to activities designed to affect the authority structure of the target society.[2] Others prefer a more expansive definition which would include efforts to affect any policy choice as well as the modalities through which such choices are made. A third alternative would reserve the opprobrium of "intervention" for conduct designed to affect a society's choice of *domestic values*. This last distinction has considerable merit, since it prevents the term from becoming little more than the equivalent of "political interaction" and thus helps to preserve its affective quality as something special and presumptively undesirable.

States with genuine respect for each other's sovereign independence have always consciously sought by threat, bounty, or other means to influence each other's foreign policies, and frequently the effort has been successful. Until recently, no one appeared to regard this unflagging effort to influence foreign policy choices as interventionary activity. Today, the distinction continues to be accepted by the developed states in their mutual relations, but the less-developed states seem inclined to regard any effort to influence their internal and external policies as intervention. Their effort to withdraw the mantle of legitimacy from every exercise in influence projection is in the grand tradition of King Canute. It may be admirable, but it is a blunder. The concept of intervention should not be stretched to the point where it loses its efficacy.

Once the focus of concern shifts from intervention in all its conceivable manifestations to intervention in *civil strife* certain features of the definitional controversy should subside, because any activity designed to affect the outcome of serious civil strife is by definition directed toward the society's authority structure and hence, under what appears to be the majority's criteria, is "intervention."

The contemporary dependence of many regimes in the least developed states on the largesse of the great powers must seriously impede any effort to operationalize the concept of intervention in civil strife. Suppose, for example, that on January 1, 1965, country X becomes independent. Country Y immediately offers massive economic and military assistance which is accepted. In 1967, armed civil strife breaks out in X and quickly reaches dimensions which threaten the survival of the incumbent government. Will country Y be perceived as an interventionary power if it fails to terminate its aid program? Of course, the sudden withdrawal of aid will not place the incumbent regime in the position in which it would have been if aid had never been given. For

2 See, e.g., *id.*

it has doubtlessly organized its economic efforts, its administration, and its armed forces on the assumption that aid programs would be sustained. At a minimum, it has probably failed to explore and develop alternative sources of supply, which it surely would have done if it had not been able to rely on country Y. More critically, the interface between its own operations in the economic and military fields and Y's foreign assistance bureaucracy may be so elaborate that the withdrawal of the latter effectively paralyzes the former. Furthermore, since country Y has always used the limited resources it had available for foreign assistance in a manifestly discriminating manner, its program in country X has been universally regarded as compelling evidence of enthusiastic support for the incumbent regime. Therefore, unless Y had already, by word and deed, convincingly conveyed its intention of implementing the norm of neutrality in every case of civil strife, the termination of assistance might be regarded as a vote of no confidence, despite assertions to the contrary by spokesmen of country Y. Moreover, even if Y's withdrawal is not *perceived* as an effort to affect the outcome of internal strife, for the reasons described above it probably does place the incumbent regime in a more vulnerable position than it would have occupied had aid never been extended. As an objective matter, then, the interaction of X and Y may well determine the configuration of X's authority structure. If country Y's concern was not merely to avoid legal characterization as an "intervening" power, but primarily to avoid any actual interference in the political processes of X, it would seem to be confronted with something of a dilemma.

Formally the dilemma may not seem novel. A minority of scholars have contended for some time that international law compels other states to assume a completely neutral posture once serious civil strife has erupted.[3] With respect to relations among states which possess the attributes of genuine political and economic independence, this injunction is relatively easy to obey. But where the relationship among states is essentially one of dependence, as it is in most cases where regimes in the less developed countries are interacting with developed states, neutrality floats out of reach; and at least initially a proclaimed dedication to the ideal of neutrality is certain to evoke mocking disbelief.

For those who, with respect to civil strife, see some advantage in preserving the pejorative connotations of the term "intervention," per-

[3] W. Hall, *International Law*, 287 (6th edn. 1909); Wright, *United States Intervention in the Lebanon*, 53 *American Journal of International Law*, 112, 121-22 (1959).

haps the most plausible means is to equate intervention with *illegitimate* participation by one state in the internal processes of another; in other words, state action would become intervention at the point it came into conflict with normative restraints. This definitional route leads directly to the enterprise of identifying the norms which do or should limit foreign state behavior.

2. A STRUCTURE FOR NORMATIVE INQUIRY

An apparent majority of scholars agree that under the traditional prescriptions of international law, foreign governments had the option of assisting a regime attempting to suppress civil strife or of remaining aloof from the struggle, but were precluded from assisting the rebels in any way.[4] If the rebellion persisted and the rebels succeeded in establishing effective political administration in some appreciable territory, the insurgency was deemed to have ripened into a state of belligerency. At that point, foreign states that did not wish to be treated as active participants in the war were obliged to assume the legal posture of "neutrality": to treat the two competitive authority structures as equals, each sovereign within a given geographic area.

Reference to this norm as the mere *perceptions* of a majority of scholars is not so much intended to imply that it was honored in the breach by decision-makers—although this certainly occurred, the Spanish Civil War being the final example before World War II—as that there were an insufficient number of cases of sustained civil strife to provide a fully convincing test to these restrictions or sufficient opportunity for their elaboration under the stress of real events. Reference to this norm as "traditional" is calculated to underline its present flaccidity induced by casual violation and scholarly flagellation. The two are, of course, related. Academicians are the accountants of the international decision-making process. They tell us when the play of the diplomatic-military market has generated normative bankruptcy; they tell us, in other words, when a customary rule of international law has ceased to be customary and hence to be law.

---

[4] See, e.g., L. Oppenheim, *International Law*, 2, §298, at 660 (7th edn. 1952). Whether this preclusion included the affirmative duty to restrain the activities of individual citizens who wished to aid the rebels (for example, by supplying them with arms) is somewhat obscure. See American Society of International Law, Study Group on the Role of International Law in Civil Wars, A. V. Thomas and A. J. Thomas, Jr., "International Legal Aspects of the Civil War in Spain 1936-1939," 87, 90-91, January 1967 (limited distribution).

One might conclude that mutilation of the traditional prescription has turned civil strife into a legal no-man's land where the quickest gun is entitled to free exercise inhibited only by trepidation at the prospect of an opponent who might prove quicker. One who did so conclude, however, would be exposing a rather straitened perception of the process of law formation in international society. The process is analogous to the life-cycle of Anglo-American common law rules. In both cases concrete prescriptions are drawn from general principles which reflect basic social values. Prescriptions have assumed form and been vitalized as these principles have been applied in specific contexts. The emergent elaborations of principle are hardly immutable; as international society undergoes perpetual change, they grow or modify their form or are pushed out by new applications which more effectively express essential societal values. International society unfortunately lacks institutional machinery specially designed for the continuing evaluation and revision of particular expressions of its essential or primary values, although the rudiments of such machinery can be found in the political organs of the United Nations which perform this task episodically and in some degree incidentally. Outside the United Nations, the burden falls primarily on scholars and national decision-makers.

Concrete international law might be seen as the survivor of a simple Darwinian strugg'e among initially inconsistent national assertions concerning the appropriate application of international base values to a specific behavioral phenomenon.[5] But since in the absence of one state's universal hegemony, no prescription can enjoy general acceptance unless it serves the perceived interests of the vast majority, it is futile for national decision-makers and their kept publicists to espouse restraints which are calculated to legitimate asymmetrically their power-acquisitive activities, *if* they equate their national society's fundamental interests with a more developed international order. For those who accept this equation the exigent task is clarification of the primary values of international society as a pre-condition to fashioning detailed rules governing third-party participation in civil strife, because these values are our guides for predicting the ultimate acceptability of alternative prescriptive proposals.

[5] See M. Kaplan and N. Katzenbach, *The Political Foundations of International Law,* 3-29 (1961).

The Primary Values of International Society

The means for identifying the primary values of international society seem to have changed far less than the values themselves. Today, as in the eighteenth century, these values can be induced from treaties and the practice of states (i.e., tacit agreements about appropriate behavior under defined circumstances), from the ubiquity of certain norms in domestic law, the writings of scholars and propagandists, and the public declarations of foreign policy decision-makers when they are not performing as propagandists, which is most frequently the case when they are attempting to communicate with adversaries. Since the nineteenth century, but particularly in the twentieth, the press and popular journals have provided revealing evidence of normative preferences. Resolutions of the various organs of the United Nations are the principal contemporary additions to our evidence of base values. My own examination of the evidence contained in these varied sources compels the conclusion that our immense polyglot society, though rent by fierce political and ideological conflict and gross economic inequality, recognizes the following primary values: self-determination, minimum human rights, minimum public order, and modernization.

Self-Determination. One of the great rallying cries of our century, it has fallen from the lips of men of every color and, ironically, almost every political posture. An intellectual construction of moralists who were themselves a handsome expression of the high culture of the West, it has served as the ideological glue of the assault in this century on Western hegemony. In our epoch it has had a remarkable, universal appeal, evoking a fiercely sympathetic response in minds which stretched from the cerebral altitude of German philosophy to huts on the seared bushland of East Africa. Protean in form, it has lent itself to many movements. This has been one of its great strengths. But increasingly it has also been a cause of prescriptive impotence.

Self-determination has moved into the van of universal values encumbered by a too intimate identification with racial conflict. The identification seems inevitable, because self-determination's contemporary triumphs are more or less indistinguishable from the process of decolonization. Many of the most difficult cases of self-determination are the residue of that process, the colonial era's final contribution to the delirium of international society.

As Rupert Emerson has pointed out, for the native elites who assumed power following the departure of the colonialists, the frontiers of self-determination are coterminous with decolonization.[6] Self-determination, in other words, is a one-shot affair. This position has a plausibly moral basis. Independence, the new elites argue, had positive objectives, not merely the negative one of ejecting the white sovereign. During the independence struggle, colonialism had been condemned as the source of the indigenous people's economic deprivation. Moreover, in the twentieth century, it has become the moral duty of all governments to promote rising standards of living and a more equitable distribution of wealth. Hence, the lode-star of every new regime is economic development. And development, the elites have been informed by Western experts, requires a large internal market.

In addition, decolonization has frequently meant nothing more than the severing of overt political ties. The resultant societies remain highly permeable; their policies continue to be affected vitally by conscious, external forces. Despite the contrary lesson of the Congo, many African and Asian leaders seem committed to the belief that greater size always promotes greater independence. Preservation of the precise geographic entity deeded by the departing colonial power is seen, therefore, as a necessary condition for *completing* at least this first great stage of the self-determination process.

Another justification for denying self-determination to the various tribal groupings which cluster together uneasily beneath the umbrella of the postcolonial states is that these states are implementing the operational values of self-determination. The heart of the argument is that the impulse for self-determination arose from the concrete reality of coerced inequality. Those who died in the name of this luminous abstraction were actually martyred in the pursuit of a decent but thoroughly mundane objective—equal access to the political, economic, and social perquisites of society.

Have the new states actually achieved this objective? Other than in extremely simple and homogeneous societies, no political system, however democratic, can offer access to political office which is perceived as being equal, because the constant of political process in any heterogeneous society is group participation. Members of the majority group or coalition will inevitably have disproportionate opportunities to exercise power in majoritarian democracies. Where only two or three groups occupy one territorial state, electoral arrangements based on communal representation and revolving offices may offer a means of assuring

6 See R. Emerson, *Self-Determination Revisited in the Era of Decolonization*, December 1964 (Harvard University Center for International Affairs).

equal access. The example, of course, is Lebanon; but its stability is premised on the irrefutable and initially credible presumption of numerical equivalence between the Muslim and Christian populations. In societies populated by a substantial number of self-conscious groups, the Lebanese solution may be available theoretically—with each group being denied a return to any major office until representatives of every other group have held it—but would almost undoubtedly prove to be politically unacceptable. In subordinating the criteria of ability and efficiency to the interest of inter-group harmony, the Lebanese solution is inconsistent with one of the dominating conceptions of our time: the affirmative obligation of government to assist in private goal realization. The Lebanese solution in a multi-group society is appropriate to the laissez-faire, not the welfare, state. Frustration generated by the difficulty of governing effectively appears to have been an important factor behind the collapse of power-sharing arrangements in Cyprus.

The Lebanese solution is also inconsistent with the almost metaphysical majoritarianism of our time; it practically denies the validity of that evocative slogan—"One man, one vote." Finally, by enhancing every group's sense of identity, it permanently hampers the growth of the national loyalty which, among other things, helps to insulate the state from foreign penetration and to encourage transient sacrifice in the name of potential national gain.

The unavoidable conclusion is that the consensus supporting the evaluation of state behavior in terms of its impact on processes of self-determination collapses long before one reaches the conception's logical limits. The consensus is clearest where colored people living within recognized political boundaries demand independence from the government of another political entity inhabited primarily by whites. While there seems little doubt that the colored-white dichotomy is the central feature of the present consensus, it might extend to any racial juxtaposition. Probably its second most significant aspect is a challenged relationship between geographically separate territories which possess a single authority structure dominated by persons indigenous to one of the territories. The refusal of the United Nations General Assembly to accept Portuguese efforts to cover Angola and Mozambique in the legal cloak of "a matter of domestic jurisdiction" illustrates the consensus in action.[7]

[7] See, e.g., G.A. Res. 2107, 20 U.N. GAOR, Agenda Item No. 23, at 62, U.N. Doc. A/6209 (1965); G.A. Res. 2148, 21 U.N. GAOR, U.N. Doc. A/6554 (1966).

When applied in the context of civil strife, the idea of self-determination generates sharp normative discord. Some observers are inclined to treat civil strife in less developed states as a "legitimate" self-determination process, if foreign participation is minimal or is neutralized because both sides received support. A critic of this position characterizes it as "a kind of Darwinian definition of self-determination as survival of the fittest within the national boundaries, even if fittest means most adept in the use of force."[8] As an alternative he finds it preferable,

> . . . to treat the policy of self-determination as one which turns on the genuine identifications and demands of a populace rather than on territorial isolation. The results of free elections provide probably the best criterion for ascertaining these subjectivities, but there are others as well. Thus, the amount of popular support received by an insurgency, the number of prominent leaders of a society attracted to its cause, responses to calls for general strikes (as provided substantial indication of popular feeling for independence in Algeria), opinion polls, demonstrations, the commentary of a more or less free press, and the willingness of the participants—including intervening parties—to agree to free elections all provide a useful indication of the genuine identification and demands of the people.[9]

Only troglodytes, of course, could object to this impeccably liberal definition, but the stated criteria "for ascertaining these subjectivities" are rather more vulnerable. Overall they evidence a depressing naivete about the real gritty world in which they must be applied.

This suggestion that intervenors might resort to opinion polls should charitably be ascribed to a covert facetiousness. One can envision a host of Joe Smiths plodding dutifully through the rice paddies of the Mekong Delta—Viet Cong to the right of them, South Vietnamese rangers to the left—courteously asking each passing peasant for a few moments of his time to fill out a little questionnaire prepared by Mr. Gallup. At least this criterion is sufficiently ludicrous not to be pernicious. Most of the others are dangerously susceptible to manipulation.

Free elections are abnormal in most of the world even during periods of domestic tranquillity. In times of strife, they are a luxury which few

---

[8] J. Moore, "The Norms of Intervention: A Method of Inquiry" (paper prepared for the Princeton Conference on Intervention and the Developing States, November 10-11, 1967) , 14.

[9] Id., at 15-16.

governments seem able or willing to afford. But in desperately poor countries, and some wealthy ones as well, the techniques of political prestidigitation designed to make elections *appear* free are really quite varied. They are unlikely to fool anyone in the country where the elections are held, but the citizens of liberal states located thousands of miles from the scene may prove a good deal more gullible. How many Americans, for example, when they were informed by a number of straight-faced governors that the 1967 election in South Viet Nam was "free"[10] recalled that persons suspected of an indecent desire for peace were excluded from the list of candidates, that the popular general, Big Minh, was not even allowed to enter the country, and that all the facilities of the South Vietnamese Government, including the means of transportation, were at the disposal of Generals Thieu and Ky. Careful readers of the *New York Times* might have recalled these phenomena but did many of them grasp the critical factor of the average individual's overwhelming dependence on the beneficence of a government party which did little to allay the fear that a result which appeared antagonistic to its interests would, in one way or another, be avoided? How many recalled that not long before their departure from Algeria, but before it was clear that they would shortly consent to leave, the French were able to extract a vote of support from the Algerian people for association with France?[11] Given the malleability of the election process in most places, can the announced willingness to submit to the arbitrament of free elections normally be taken very seriously?

Enthusiastic demonstrations are even easier to manufacture than complaisant electoral majorities. In poor countries an ambulatory body is one of the cheapest local commodities.

The announced commitments of "permanent leaders" is a curious criterion. One wonders precisely what is thought to constitute a *permanent* leader. In a society ripped by revolutionary conflict, the leaders best known to the foreign press and the diplomatic community are almost invariably the incumbents, the traditional holders of power. The very existence of civil strife is some measure of their failure as a governing elite and is evidence that a new group of leaders is moving toward the capital to become prominent. And if some contemporane-

[10] See *New York Times*, September 7, 1967, at 3, col. 2; *id.*, September 4, 1967, at 1, col. 6.

[11] See *id.*, January 10, 1961, at 1, col. 8.

ously prominent figure does support the rebels, he frequently may find it more prudent and more useful to his cause to conceal his sympathies.

In evaluating the efficacy of this criterion, it may be useful to recall that right up to the moment of their virtual expulsion from Aden, the British were unable to discover the identity of a single member of the FLN leadership.[12] Moreover, even when the FLN elite emerged to assume formal power, few if any were figures who would have been called prominent had their identities been discovered during the revolution.

The implied dichotomy between pure Darwinians on the one hand and liberals on the other is a gross oversimplification, a swelling of the academic imagination. Many of the so-called Darwinians are prepared to accept any outcome of a predominantly indigenous process (except where there is a community determination of illegitimacy as, for example, in the case of Rhodesia), not because they harbor any illusions about the necessary triumph of the forces of human dignity but because they are profoundly disillusioned about the motives which actually move foreign states to participate in civil strife and the ease with which allegedly democratic procedures are manipulated. This disillusionment is coupled with the empirically based assumption that in cases of protracted internal strife in less developed states, the rebels will succeed only when they enjoy broadly based popular support; without such support the natural advantages of incumbents— including control of the mass media, foreign exchange reserves, and in most cases ports and airfields, plus the normal dependence of most of the middle class on government employment—should prove overwhelming. In view of their numerous handicaps, defeat of the guerrillas is not necessarily compelling evidence that the government enjoys great popular support. But being unable to believe that the great powers will intervene for the purpose of ascertaining and enforcing the "genuine identifications and demands of a populace" and recognizing the tendency of great powers to intervene massively in precisely those cases where incumbents seem unable to survive unaided, the liberals among Professor Moore's Darwinians pursue a modest aspiration. They link hands with those who are genuinely indifferent to the travail of alien peoples in order to neutralize that rhetorical liberalism which in our age has too often cloaked the instinct for domination.

12 DeCarvalho, "A Case History of Terror, *Life*, 63, No. 23 (December 8, 1967), at 94A, 95, 99.

Minimum Human Rights. Long before Nuremberg, international society experienced tremors of concern for human rights, a concern which
was, however, both parochial and restrained. Normally it was limited
to the abuse of aliens;[13] no one seriously questioned the natural right
of each equal Christian sovereign to be monstrous to his own people.
The European powers admitted transnational responsibilities only
where Europeans were abused by states regarded as beyond the pale
of civilization.[14] The insulation afforded by the concept of "domestic
jurisdiction" was deemed unavailable to "barbarian rulers."

Despite the formal opening of the international order to embrace
most of the free states of Asia and Africa, the Western nations are still
capable of indulging, from time to time, in that casually discriminatory
concern which characterized international society prior to the middle of the twentieth century. The Stanleyville rescue operation was a
recent manifestation of this well-conditioned reflex. Having created
the occasion for the seizure of hostages by providing the feeble Leopold-
ville government with airpower, logistical support, and the means for
assembling a mercenary strike force, the Western governments saved
most of the incidental victims of their foreign policy, flattened the
slight fighting capacity of the rebels, and, having completed their
"mercy mission," left the city's black inhabitants to the exotic mercies
of the mercenaries and central government troops.

Yet one must be quick to add that the prevailing confusion and
ambivalence about human rights is hardly the peculiar responsibility
of the West. How many African states condemned the massacre of
30,000 Ibos in Northern Nigeria? How many Asian states expressed
horror, much more any desire to act, over the staggering death toll in
Indonesia?

Where amid all the shifting, selective concern for the slaughter of
human beings can one find a solid base of agreement? Perhaps the only
clear case is one in which a whole people are consciously consigned to
a permanent menial role or, of course, to physical extinction. In other
words, a society cannot, at least on ethnic grounds, deny a group of
people fair access to political, economic, and social opportunities. Although the less developed states have generally cast the condemnation
of the Union of South Africa in terms of frustrated self-determination,
the hostility of people in the West seems grounded in moral revul-

[13] L. Oppenheim, *International Law*, 1 §292 (8th edn. 1958).

[14] *See id.,* §§26-29, §318; R. Phillimore, *International Law*, 1 460-73, 618-638 (3rd edn.
1879).

sion over the planned permanent poverty of the Union's black population.

Less clear but, I believe, increasingly affective are strictures concerning conflict-related conduct. The Vietnamese War has accelerated the growth of broad and articulate support for enforcement and, indeed, expansion of the pathetically minimal inhibitions imposed by the Geneva and Hague Conventions. Highly impressionistic data suggests that the growing fury of antiwar dissent in the United States is in significant measure a reaction to the tactics which the United States and its allies have employed, particularly within South Vietnam.[15] I suspect that the pollsters' findings of growing anti-American feeling in Europe also is associated with war tactics.[16]

Optimists might conclude that neither nuclear weapons, nor the reality of the nation as war machine, nor even the experience of World War Two has obliterated the distinction between military and civilian casualties. But this appears true only with respect to civil strife. The failure of efforts to prohibit use of nuclear weapons testifies to the continuing rejection of restraint on military operations in a general war. Nevertheless, phenomena such as the strong movement at the Vatican Council to condemn all resort to nuclear weapons[17] evidences powerful and widespread sentiment for refurbishing the civil-military distinction even in a general war among great powers.

Minimum Public Order. By minimum public order[18] I refer primarily to the consensus that conflict *between* states must be contained below the level of violence. This is, in fact, the central principle of contemporary international law, as respect for the equal dignity of sovereign, "civilized" states was the keystone of international law for the preceding three centuries. I by no means intend to imply that in the last two decades all states have in fact acted in ways which relatively detached or at least retrospective observers would deem consistent with this

---

15 For a description of those tactics, see, e.g., S. Melman and R. Falk, *In the Name of America* (1968).

16 *New York Times*, May 14, 1967, §4, at 3, col. 6; *id.*, November 27, 1967, at 14, col. 1; *id.*, May 27, 1967, at 3, col. 1.

17 See, e.g., *id.*, October 7, 1965, at 1, col. 7; *id.*, April 28, 1968, at 11, col. 1.

18 While I have borrowed the phrase from Harold Lasswell and Myers McDougal, connoisseurs of their work will note that the signification I attribute to it is somewhat distinct. See, e.g., McDougal and Lasswell, *The Identification and Appraisal of Diverse Systems of Public Order*, 53 *American Journal of International Law*, 1 (1959); M. McDougal, H. Lasswell, and I. Vlasio, *Law and Public Order in Space* (1963); M. McDougal and F. Feliciano, *Law and Minimum World Public Order* (1961).

value, only that both decision-makers and polities will evaluate state activity in terms of its relation to general-war risks and are very likely to treat general-war avoidance as the international system's preeminent criteria for judging state action, as well as for evaluating the merits of particular prescriptions. The Chinese Communists may be dissenters from this view. They say they are, but their prudent policies are thoroughly consistent with the belief that high-risk-of-general-war behavior should be that restricted to instances where the behavior of foreign states is perceived as a critical threat to a regime's existence.

The United Nations Charter is the great divide of international legal history because it attempts to outlaw force as a modality of conflict resolution.[19] It does not, of course, purport to inhibit intrastate violence except, by implication, when such violence poses a threat to international peace.[20] In addition to the evidence of the Charter, less inclusive international treaties[21] and bilateral agreements,[22] a not unimpressive body of international practice supports the view that the avoidance of inter-state violence is the dominating concern of international society even where potential violence does not threaten international peace. Among the more notable cases are the Algerian-Moroccan and Kenyan-Ethiopian-Somali disputes. In both instances the antagonist, concededly after initial experiments with violence, have accepted mediation and conciliation from fellow African states despite the seemingly irreconcilable nature of the disputes. Inter-state conflict in Central and Latin America also has been contained by pressure for the avoidance of violence. The Security Council's consistent condemnation of reprisals in the Arab-Israeli conflict further evidences the rooted conviction that conflicts of interest should not be resolved through the arbitrament of force.[23]

[19] Art. 2 (4) of the Charter reads: "All Members shall refrain in their international relations from the threat or use of force against the territorial integrity or political independence of any state, or in any other manner inconsistent with the Purposes of the United Nations."

[20] U.N. Charter arts. 2 (7), 39-51. The Charter does not specify what would constitute a "threat to the peace." See L. Goodrich and E. Hambro, *Charter of the United Nations*, 263-64 (2d edn. 1949).

[21] North Atlantic Treaty with Other Governments, April 4, 1949, art. 1, 63 Stat. 2241 (1949), T.I.A.S. No. 1964; Charter of the Organization of American States, April 30, 1948, art. 5 (g), 2 U.S.T. 2394, T.I.A.S. No. 2361.

[22] Arbitration Treaty with Greece, June 19, 1930, Preamble, Art. 1, 47 Stat. 2161 (1930), T.S. No. 853; Treaty with Denmark on the Advancement of Peace, April 17, 1914, art. 1, 38 Stat. 1883 (1915), T.S. No. 608.

[23] See 21 U.N. SCOR, 1328th meeting (1966) (res. 228).

Modernization. Modernization describes the effort to replace traditional, generally decentralized, static societies with centralized, innovative, production-oriented societies patterned on the model of developed states, both capitalist and socialist.[24] It is important to emphasize that modernization is not a purely economic conception. Its objectives seem twofold: to reach a point of self-sustaining economic growth; to create a society in which the strength of an individual's psychological ties to the central political authority exceeds his local or transnational affections. In recognizing the legitimacy of these broad objectives, international society inevitably restricts the scope of other values. For instance, as I suggested above, international society has been determinedly indifferent to the independence claims of cohesive groups within the new states even where they have been effectively autonomous for centuries. The Somalis of Kenya and Ethiopia are only one of the better known examples. Claims for the merit of peaceful settlement also seem impotent when faced with the putative requirements of modernization, as the Ibos are now discovering.

The present active hostility of the United States toward radical modernizers has generated doubt about the short-run compatibility of modernization and minimum public order. In the long run, the two base values seem destined to develop a symbiotic relationship, since a general war would at least destroy the main sources of capital, if not the fragile new states themselves, while the failure of these states to achieve steady growth in their standards of living could ultimately prove to be the most serious threat to international peace.

3. NORMATIVE ALTERNATIVES

There are two polar approaches to the task of elaborating norms to govern foreign participation in civil strife:

1. The legitimacy of foreign participation in any instance of civil strife should be determined by an elaborate contextual analysis with the objective of achieving optimal world order characterization and outcome.

2. The legitimacy of foreign participation in any instance of civil strife should be determined by one or a few categorical rules the applicability of which will be dependent on the existence or nonexistence of a very limited number of easily identifiable phenomena. The objec-

---

[24] See generally, D. Apter, *The Politics of Modernization* (1965); J. Finkle and R. Gable, *Political Development and Social Change* (1966); G. Almond and J. Coleman, *The Politics of Developing Areas* (1960).

tive is not optimal outcome in each case but minimization of primary threats to international order.

Today, in the absence of established categorical rules, the first approach offers the only means for evaluating the legality of foreign participation. Thus sophisticated legal critics and supporters of U.S. involvement in Vietnam have evaluated it in terms of a host of factors which are implied by the international system's primary values.[25] These include at a fairly high level of generalization the objectives and policies of the participants, the systemic position of the target society (e.g., geographic location, resources, bloc-identity), and the quantity and nature of foreign participation. Within this analytic structure, the legal scholar pursues detailed factual enquiries. He will, for example, explore rival claims to the expression of self-determination sentiment. He will study opinion polls, election results, the allegiance of important representative figures and every other kind of data which might reveal the thrust of popular preference.[26] And, one suspects, he will find whatever it was he wanted to find.

The apparent assumption that in the chaotic and emotionally charged context of civil strife persuasive data can be secured within any time span relevant to legal characterization for purposes of inhibiting state conduct is so manifestly false that one wonders whether it is entertained seriously by legal scholars. Even if this were not a grotesque illusion, the possibilities for generating normative restraints through ad hoc characterization would still seem negligible. To this point I have been speaking only of first-order data: Who advocates X or supports Y or has done Z. For want of a better word we might call this sort of data "objective," in the sense that it conceivably might be perceived in identical fashion by men with vastly different political values.

In this form, unfortunately, data is frequently useless; without the introduction of value preferences, it cannot be translated into propositions which would in turn permit conclusions about normatively optimal outcomes. Suppose, for example, that 15 percent of the population supports the rebels, 25 percent supports the government and 60

[25] See, e.g., Friedmann, *Law and Politics in the Vietnamese War: A Comment*, 61 *American Journal of International Law*, 776 (1967); Falk, *International Law and the United States Role in the Viet Nam War*, 75 *Yale Law Journal*, 1122 (1966); Moore, *The Lawfulness of Military Assistance to the Republic of Viet-Nam*, 61 *American Journal of International Law*, 1 (1967).

[26] Cf. J. Moore, supra note 8, at 16.

percent dislike both but are incapable of establishing a political alternative. The rebels say nothing about elections; the government has held several and has always manipulated the results. Given these "facts," how does one evaluate the relative merits of rebels and incumbents as instruments of self-determination?

Or from the standpoint of minimum human rights how can one evaluate this data: the rebels propose to eliminate the merchant-landlord class by confiscating its wealth and banning its members from participation in public life. The incumbents will not extract sufficient revenue from the merchant-landlord class to permit the creation of free institutions of secondary and higher learning; consequently, the children of peasants and artisans are rarely able to enter the civil service or the officer corps.

The ad hoc, multiple-factor approach is little more than an invitation to unilateral national judgment. Its impact on world order is more deleterious than a frank disavowal of legal restraints, since it encourages every participant to increase the psychological stakes by stigmatizing other parties as law breakers or aggressors. I find it difficult to disagree with Stanley Hoffman's observation that proponents of this normative scheme are the contemporary counterparts of the old Hobbesian cynics.[27]

At best, a multiple-factor evaluation provides domestic critics in states which are peculiarly rule oriented (and which do not impose effective censorship) with a twig to wave censoriously at the national decision-makers. Even when conducted on the battleground chosen by legal critics, rhetorical combat with the government is pathetically unequal. The government's ability to manipulate data reaching the general public, the complexity of the data, and the powerful material and psychological ties between government and public all impede widespread acceptance of allegations of illegal governmental behavior, even in cases where the rules are simple and factual nuance is irrelevant. Where neither condition is present, there can be no hope of influencing governmental conduct through its desire to avoid categorization as a lawbreaker.

The cardinal virtue of relatively simple rules probably is not their potential use in the hands of domestic critics but rather their prophylactic effect on the decision-making process, an effect which is considerably heightened by the mortal dangers inherent in contemporary

[27] Hoffman, *International Systems and International Law*, 14 *World Politics* (1961-62), 205, 232.

international politics. Decision-makers in both super powers probably perceive international law as a useful feature of international society, however repugnant the impact of particular prescriptions on specific occasions. It provides a highly necessary medium for communication. Demands and objections can be transmitted in terms which have some agreed content. Moreover, by standardizing responses to certain phenomena, international law reduces the increasingly heavy burden on each society's foreign policy decision-making processes with respect to matters thought to have limited political significance. Law also facilitates consolidation and elaboration of areas of accommodation. Both super powers then have a vested interest in avoiding behavior which will seriously erode the effectiveness of international law. It would be naive or profoundly cynical to recommend normative developments which fail to exploit the interest in preserving international law as a means for facilitating nonviolent national interactions.

For the reasons suggested above, I find a pure version of the first approach objectionable at a time when the international community does not possess effective fact-findings and law-applying institutions.

Incumbents as the Only Legitimate Recipients of Assistance. This traditional majority view expresses the values of a vanished international system, the world of European mastery. Possible efforts to resuscitate the old majority rule cannot, however, be aborted merely by demonstrating a shift in basic values. Whatever interests it may have been designed to serve, inadvertently it might still be the optimal prescription for regulating foreign participation in civil strife.

This does not on its face seem very likely. After all, in denying the initial legitimacy of any rebellion, even if occasioned by the most grotesque invasions of human dignity or the most cavalier disregard of the claims of self-determination, the traditional rule might well appear wholly inconsistent with two basic systemic values. Yet there are possibly plausible contrary arguments. With respect to basic human rights, for example, sophisticated advocates of the no-aid-to-rebels prescription would allege that contemporary civil strife wholly involves the society's civilian population in all the agonies of armed conflict, because it normally assumes the form of relatively covert violence, which confronts the incumbents with the often insuperable problem of distinguishing rebel activists from the remainder of the civilian population. This special contemporary feature merely intensifies the normal virulence of civil strife which always has tended to generate peculiarly intense emotional antagonism leading to the indiscriminate and disproportionate application of violence. The explanation for this is not in all cases pathological. Rebellion is a challenge to the society's whole authority structure. Defeat means change not only in policy or influence, but in personnel as well. The least the incumbent can anticipate if defeated is deprivation of all power and influence. The most and more likely outcome for defeated elites is death or exile. Where the rebellion has social as well as political objectives, whole functional groups or classes may be threatened. With these stakes, violence denies restraint. Even if some restraints are accepted at first, they tend to erode if conflict is prolonged. And regardless of restraint, prolonged conflict in the territory of a single state is bound to cause grave physical and psychological damage to the entire society. Prolongation of conflict also increases the probability of foreign intervention. *In extremis*, if not before, either side will proclaim ideological identifications which will generate pressure on the United States, the Soviet Union, or Red China to intervene. Great power involvement will vastly augment the destructive capacities of the assisted party.

In light of these considerations, if the mere assertion by scholars of the existence of a "legal" rule sufficed to coerce affected parties into obedience, the old, majority rule might advance the international system's interest in human rights. Foreign states would refuse to aid rebels and, the argument presumes, rebels anticipating such refusal would be far less inclined to resort to violence. And where they did, the rebellion would be quickly suppressed, often with external support. The status quo would be preserved, there would be no reason for the murder and torture of civilians. Stripped of all embellishments, this sounds like a highly sophisticated version of the old argument that the evils attendant on violent, revolutionary change will generally be worse than the evils experienced under barbarous rulers, unless they are engaged in genocide.

In the extraordinarily unlikely event of a community determination that rebellion is illegitimate, would most rebellions be deterred? The sheer existence of such a rule is unlikely to influence revolutionary elites. Men outside a state's authority structure are naturally indifferent to the ordering and limiting efficacy of the system of international law. Nor, if they are sufficiently aroused to contemplate armed rebellion, are they likely to be rule-oriented.

It is psychologically implausible, then, to believe that a community determination of illegitimacy will of its own weight affect the decision to rebel. That decision might, however, be influenced by the inability to secure foreign support. But the historical evidence is inconsistent with the proposition that the prospect of foreign support is always or even frequently a critical consideration. External assistance to the Greek rebels of the mid-forties was virtually nonexistent at the outset of the struggle, and little and sporadic afterwards.[28] Indeed, at one point Stalin expressed flat hostility toward the rebel cause.[29] The initial guerilla activity in South Vietnam was an act of sheer self-defense against Diem's policy of harassing veterans of the Viet Minh anti-French campaign; requests for assistance from the North were initially resisted but as rebellion grew (and prospects for unification through elections diminished) the compulsion to aid and seek to control quickly overwhelmed tactical doubts.[30] The now-deceased organizers of Indonesia's antiarmy coup certainly had no basis to anticipate foreign assistance. One might distinguish Indonesia on the grounds that the rebels did not anticipate protracted guerilla conflict. The leaders of future coups in various countries will undoubtedly entertain similar sanguine expectations. Sometimes they too will fail; then chance or calculation may enable them to retreat to the forest. Surely they cannot be expected to submit docilely to the often extreme sanctions associated with failure.

The simple truth is that under a variety of circumstances men will fight and die without any high confidence of success. After last summer, Americans should be acutely conscious of this phenomenon. And in many less developed countries with their fragile administrative apparatus and authority structures that do not command widespread respect, rebels can generally find reasons for an optimistic prognosis.

If civil strife will occur despite a recognized legal proscription of foreign assistance, defense of the old rule in terms of its relevance to the protection of minimum human rights is considerably more difficult. Even if augmented foreign assistance enables the incumbents to reduce the duration of armed conflict by facilitating suppression of the rebels, the society not only will experience in some measure those transgressions of minimum human rights occasioned by civil strife, but will have done so in vain if the status quo was marked by human rights vio-

---

[28] R. Barnet, *Intervention and Revolution: The United States in the Third World* VI: 13-14, 16-17 (1967), (to be published by New American Library) ; M. Djilas, *Conversations with Stalin*, 181-83 (1962).

[29] R. Barnet, supra note 28, at VI: 29; M. Djilas, supra note 28, at 181-83.

[30] Cf. J. Lacouture, *Vietnam: Between Two Truces* 35, 53-56, passim; G. Kahin and J. Lewis, *The United States in Vietnam*, 110-16 (1967).

lations or was an impediment to modernization. If rebel success will facilitate modernization, there is at least a value trade-off.

Furthermore, there is no reason to presume that external assistance will reduce the duration of conflict. A weak regime might quickly disintegrate without external support. In such a case, Vietnam is one vivid example: foreign intervention prolongs conflict. Foreign intervention may also prolong conflict by inflaming nationalist sentiment and thus driving additional groups into opposition.

Does the traditional rule support community conceptions of minimum public order? While opposing any single rule to govern intervention, John Norton Moore, an able student of Myres McDougal, finds substantial merit in the traditional prescription because of

> ... the desirability of focusing on the great threat to peace in providing sustained assistance to insurgents across cold-war boundaries, the difficulty of appraising covert assistance in externally sponsored "wars of national liberation," the perceived threat to the balance of power from sudden shifts in committed areas, and realism about constraints felt by opposing bloc powers to support existing friendly regimes, as evidenced by the events in Hungary, East Germany, Malaysia, Korea, Greece and now Viet Nam.[31]

In other words, the independent prestige of international law should be lent to the advocates of prudential policies, of policies which accept the present distribution of political and ideological allegiance. This analysis is curiously foreshortened; it fails to contemplate the rule's post-violation impact which, it seems to me, is dangerously detrimental to world order. If one may be forgiven the indulgence of quoting oneself,

> In states whose governments identify with the fortunes of the incumbent, it becomes relatively easy to convince the public that the issue is not the relative merits and capacities of the internal antagonists, but the sanctity of international law. Moreover, as public attention focuses on the external aid rendered to the rebels, it becomes far easier to cultivate the idea that they are mere instruments of the foreign power. When the struggle is cast in these terms, acceptance of insurgent victory seems a pusillanimous withdrawal at High Noon.

[31] J. Moore, supra note 8, at 25.

In other words, the traditional approach generates or facilitates generation of moral pressure to escalate.[32]

Of course, supporters of the incumbent regime might simply allege breach of this rule, characterize the breach as an "armed attack," and escalate across the relevant national boundary. But the alleged aggressor probably could abort this stratagem by consenting to fact finding by an impartial body. It would, I suspect, be extremely difficult to reject such an offer.

Aid Short of Tactical Support. Last year in a *Columbia Law Review* article[33] I attempted to confirm and justify the death of the old rule. For its replacement I proposed the legitimation of assistance short of tactical military support both to incumbents and rebels. This alternative's alleged cardinal virtue was the converse of the traditional rule's vice: it precluded transformation of civil strife into a defense of international law. The foreign supporters of rebels could no longer be characterized as aggressors merely on the grounds that they were providing material and training facilities. Moreover, given the enormous contextual variations in the less developed parts of the world—the central stage for civil strife—it did not seem to bestow clearly asymmetric benefit on any one of the super powers, and therefore had some chance of being accepted as an optimal accommodation of international society's prime values. At first it had seemed to me indisputable that the old rule suffered severely on this account in that it heavily advantaged the United States. On further reflection, my initial conclusion seems excessively confident. Today most governments in Latin America and Asia obviously are not antagonistic to substantial American participation in their societies. The principal threat to the survival of such governments may not, in fact, be insurgency. Crescending population pressures, intensified racial antagonism, a widening gap between developed and underdeveloped states, and the in part related spread of national-socialist ideology may radicalize large elements of the very functional groups, such as the officer corps, we have helped to train and whose allegiance we have carefully cultivated. This tendency may be intensified by the political liberalization of the Catholic Church and the moderating tactics and increasing national coloration of at least some Communist parties. Consequently, even if the prohibi-

---

[32] Farer, *Intervention in Civil Wars: A Modest Proposal,* 67 *Columbia Law Review,* 266, 272 (1967).

[33] *Id.*

tion of aid to rebels had survived, in another decade it might have ceased to appear as the buttress of a conservative status quo.

The no-tactical-support rule would also help to limit the potential level of damage to the "host" country: "Educational limitations will prevent either side from disposing of fire-power on a scale comparable to the capability of major military powers. The grave cultural damage which is the inevitable concomitant of the presence of large numbers of foreign troops will also be avoided."[34]

Since the rule favors neither rebel nor incumbent, it may at first seem unresponsive to the equal opportunity aspect of minimum human rights. In application, however, it should prove eminently superior to the traditional rule in advancing this primary value. Governmental restrictions on the right of distinct racial, religious, or cultural groups to compete freely for economic and social status necessarily generate a collective will to resist which may require only some external assistance to find effective expression.

Since under the proposed test for determining the legality of foreign participation in civil strife United States "intervention" in South Vietnam could be identified as early as 1961, I was not surprised when in certain quarters it encountered a critical response. One critic charged that the rule "may undersell the *efficiency* of major covert assistance which falls short of tactical support."[35] (my emphasis) At the risk of seeming obtuse, I must concede some difficulty in grasping this point. What possibly could be intended by use of the word *efficiency*? If Professor Moore means that covert assistance might enable rebels to defeat incumbents overtly and covertly supported by great power patrons, he may well be right. So what? Is Professor Moore covertly announcing that the only good rule is one that will facilitate the efficient suppression of all rebellions? If so, his elaborate scheme for a multifactor analysis seems either a waste of cerebral effort or an exercise in cynicism. Furthermore, the Holy Alliance syndrome would be incongruous in a scholar who believes that the "principal dangers of the traditional rule are that it may serve as a Maginot line for vested privileges, deterring necessary reforms in feudal or totalitarian societies."[36] I am reminded of Mark Twain's comment: The more you explain it, the more I don't understand it.[37]

---

[34] *Id.*, at 278.   [35] Moore, supra note 8, at 43.

[36] *Id.*, at 8-9.

[37] As quoted in dissenting opinion of Justice Jackson, in SEC v. Chenery Corp., 332 U.S. 194, 214 (1947).

A second criticism is that it will be difficult to identify violations of the rule, ". . . when the operations of one side are largely covert. For example, how much field leadership and direction need a nation supply before it is participating in tactical operations? Yet this leadership factor may be the most crucial need of an insurgency, as seems to have been true in Vietnam."[38]

Here again there is some difficulty in comprehending Professor Moore's precise concern. He offers no evidence, and would I suspect be hard put to find any, that participation in tactical operations by foreign officers as unit commanders could long escape detection. Being participants in sustained conflict, they endure proportional risks of death or capture. In addition, news of their arrival can be obtained from captured members of their units and defectors. It might be more difficult to identify foreigners infiltrated for purposes of political organization. But their use would be contrary to first principles of guerilla warfare. As the Cubans recently discovered in Bolivia, it is extremely difficult for foreigners to blend into the population or to win its trust and confidence.

Professor Moore's reference to Vietnam is a peculiarly infelicitous choice for purposes of sustaining his position. I have never seen any suggestion that the villages of South Vietnam were organized by ethnic Northerners. Unless Professor Moore is prepared to defend the proposition that mere training in a foreign state (assuming, only for purposes of avoiding an argument extraneous to the instant question, that North Vietnam is a "foreign state") requires characterization of the trainee as an agent of that state, I am perplexed about the relationship between his argument and his example and am therefore still a bit uncertain about the real thrust of his concern for rule evasion. I might add in passing that one does wonder why the academic janissaries of administration foreign policy simultaneously attribute almost superhuman finesse to radical revolutionaries while implicitly disparaging their cardinal operational principle—namely, that the primary instruments of successful revolutionary warfare are indigenous human beings.[39]

A recent article by Professor Edwin Firmage of the University of Utah adopts a somewhat different tack.[40] The first weakness he detects

---

[38] Moore, supra note 8, at 43.

[39] See Lin Piao, *Long Live the Victory of People's War!*, Peking Review (September 3, 1965), at 19, 22; Vo Nguyen Giap, *People's War, People's Army* 43, 48, 77, 103 (1962).

[40] E. Firmage, *International Law and the Response of the United States to "Internal War,"* 1967 Utah Law Review, 517 (1967).

in the no-tactical-support test "is that it is as necessary to define civil war under Professor Farer's norm as under the traditional one."[41] Under the traditional norm it was necessary to define and identify the moment when an insurrection ripened into belligerency. Now that distinction did create prickly operational problems because the legitimacy of foreign state behavior was determined by the problematic course of domestic strife. My proposal obviates that problem; the legitimacy of foreign state activities is in no way affected by the unpredictable achievements of other parties concerning which it may in any event be extremely difficult to secure adequate information. The rebels' patron may pour material into its neighbor as long as it likes. If there are no rebels left to use the arms, incumbents might, I suppose, complain on aesthetic grounds about the litter.[42]

The second edge of Professor Firmage's "critique" is constructed along the following lines:

In addition, the events concerning Cuba, the United States, and the Soviet Union from the Bay of Pigs to the missile crisis present especial difficulty for this norm. There was an internal conflict with significant third power intervention—the Soviet Union actively supported the Castro government and the United States extended erratic support to various insurgent groups. The transportation of Cuban exiles by the United States to the Bay of Pigs would represent a violation of Professor Farer's norm. Yet the potentially far more dangerous placement of offensive missiles in Cuba by the Soviet Union would not represent a violation since no tactical "zone of combat" existed there, and, according to the proposed norm, any type of supplies could be extended by third powers. That under Farer's norm, the Soviets could supply the Castro government with missiles but no Soviet troops would be permitted to man them, would further unstabilize the situation and make international war more probable. The suggested rule would in this case violate almost all of the criteria suggested by Farer as prerequisite tests for the norm. The likelihood of great power confrontation would be encouraged by the allowance of a supply of weapons which could be used against the territory of the United States; if the weapons were used, geographic containment would be virtually impossible; and the degree of ambiguity

[41] *Id.*, at 530.

[42] On the other hand, if the incumbents use the seized weapons, perhaps the rebels' patron could seek compensation on some *quantum meruit* theory.

in the suggested norm which permits such a disparate treatment of *two types of intervention in Cuba* by the Soviet Union and the United States is obvious. Farer's focus upon a "war zone" as the critical area in which outside intervention would not be permitted is unrealistic in an age of intercontinental missiles.[43] (emphasis added)

Far more easily than in the case of Professor Moore, one detects a curious incongruity between thesis and example. It probably was imprudent for the United States to place soft jupiter missiles in Turkey. And it certainly was imprudent for the Soviet Union to place medium-range missiles in Cuba. But prior to Professor Firmage, it never seems to have occurred to anyone that the use of foreign bases, air or missile, was an intervention in civil strife or illegal for any other reason. At the Bay of Pigs, the Castro government utterly destroyed the only serious rebel movement it has faced. When the missiles began to arrive, there was no civil strife in Cuba; there was only the hanging threat of invasion by American forces. I suppose I should be astounded that Professor Firmage apparently does not suspect any possible connection between American threats against the government of Cuba and the willingness of that hypersensitively nationalist government to accept Soviet missiles *under Soviet control* on its soil.

If any significant group of people are really prepared to associate themselves with Firmage's view that the Cuban missile crisis can be characterized as a civil-strife phenomenon, I will have to concede that the term may in fact require definition. For the moment, however, I will rest on the assumption that such a characterization will strike most people as "strained."

Conclusion

No one, I trust, will confuse the proposed norm with a panacea for the epidemic phenomenon of intervention. As I have already suggested, a norm which would legitimate foreign participation short of tactical support is not designed to and cannot achieve in each case an outcome which when measured against the international community's primary values will seem optimal. It is frankly meliorative. My modest objective was to construct a norm which would respond to the most dangerous and morally disturbing characteristics of contemporary civil strife in less-developed countries: The use of grossly destructive fire power within target states, the tendency toward geographic escalation,

[43] E. Firmage, supra note 40, at 530-31.

and the blank-check support of rigid autocracies. A sacrifice of normative flexibility seemed required in order to facilitate the always onerous task of effective legal characterization of state behavior.

This sacrifice is avoided in cases where the international community, acting through the United Nations, either intervenes collectively or authorizes unilateral intervention. Unfortunately, the consensus required for a particularized articulation of community values continues to be a frustratingly elusive phenomenon. Some people are inclined to believe that regional associations of states provide an alternative means for applying community values in specific cases. I am thus far unable to share their enthusiasm. Most of these associations are far too implicated in bloc conflict; their actions tend to reflect the felt exigencies of that conflict rather than a genuine concern for the full range of community values. And those few associations, most notably the Organization for African Unity, which are not essentially holding operations for the East-West status quo, seem hardly more successful than the United Nations in generating consensus.

So during this feverish moment in the life of international society, we remain without consistently effective institutions for implementing its primary values. When found outside supporting institutions, norms may appear pathetically fragile; but who today is in a position to belittle even humble allies?

United States Military Power and Foreign Policy

ADAM YARMOLINSKY

The military power of the United States of America is by any standards enormous. Its current defense budget is almost four times that of its nearest rival, the Soviet Union. When the comparison is made in terms of current purchasing power rather than at the official exchange rate, the U.S. defense budget is still almost twice the Soviet figure—and we spend more than twice the total defense spending of our NATO allies. Even as a percentage of our huge Gross National Product, our defense spending is exceeded only by that of war-torn South Vietnam—I have found no figures for North Vietnam—the tiny fortresses of Taiwan and Israel, the UAR, and, although the figure is largely guesswork, Communist China. And so strong is our national economy, that our defense expenditure represents a declining percentage of GNP, down from ten per cent in the early sixties to eight per cent for fiscal 1967, and not likely to exceed its former level even with a large supplemental this winter.

For our dollars we get good value. They have provided us a force of over three million men on active duty in the Army, Navy, Air Force, and Marine Corps, with a supporting civilian personnel structure of more than one million. We have a strategic retaliatory force totaling well over 1,300 nuclear-tipped missiles, including the land-based MINUTEMAN and the submarine-launched POLARIS. We have more than 600 long-range bombers. We have 21 divisions on the ground, including 17 Army and 4 Marine divisions. Our Navy consists of almost 1,000 commissioned ships, including 16 attack carriers, one of them nuclear-powered, and another nuclear-powered carrier under construction. And there are some 1,200 combat and support aircraft in the three separate Marine air wings.

In addition to these great expenditures for our military establishment, we spend the better part of a billion dollars every year to help strengthen the military forces of our friends around the world, primarily the forces on the periphery of Chinese and Soviet power.

Not only is this military strength measured in quantities that stretch the imagination; it has increased vastly in the last six years.

Today, our strategic force provides some 2,600 nuclear warheads on alert, more than three times the number we had in 1961.

Before the build-up in Southeast Asia, there was a 45 per cent increase in the number of combat-ready Army divisions.

Airlift capability of U.S. forces is up about three times from that of 1961, and by 1971 it should be more than ten times greater than the 1961 figure.

There has been a 100 per cent increase in general ship construction and conversion to modernize the Fleet.

—Over a 50 per cent increase in the number of Air Force tactical fighter squadrons.

—Over a 1,000 per cent increase in the Special Forces trained to deal with counterinsurgency threats.

As the Secretary of Defense has pointed out, no single threat, no combination of threats; no single conflict, no combination of conflicts; no single adversary, no combination of adversaries, can attack us and remain out of reach of our retaliatory power.

The existence of this large and expensive arsenal provokes a number of automatic reactions: concern that so significant an amount of our national resources, measured both absolutely and relatively, goes to purposes of destruction; fear that the existence of this arsenal makes its eventual use more likely; and, conversely, fear that in so large and complex an enterprise, we are overlooking some element essential to our protection.

I prefer to pass these questions, not because I think they are unimportant, but rather because I believe that before we can have intelligent public discussion of the size and character of our military establishment, we have to have better public understanding of its purposes as they relate to the foreign policy objectives that it must necessarily serve. The ultimate test of our military establishment, as has been pointed out by the Secretary of Defense, is how well it serves U.S. foreign policy. And I believe that the best description of the efforts of the Kennedy-Johnson Administration in this area is that these efforts have made our military establishment a better servant of our foreign policy.

It is customary to begin any account of U.S. foreign policy objectives by a catalogue of self-abnegation: We seek no territories, no new military bases, no spheres of influence, nor do we hold to the nineteenth-century doctrine that trade follows the flag. I believe this is quite true. But I believe also that it is more useful to begin by cataloguing the limitations on the foreign policy objectives of any nation, and particularly of any great power in the nuclear age.

These limitations were perhaps most strikingly described by Nikita Khrushchev in his famous observations to a meeting of the Soviet Communist Party Organizations, which he delivered in the same month that John F. Kennedy pronounced his Inaugural Address. In that speech, Mr. Khrushchev described three kinds of wars: nuclear wars, conventional wars, and what he called wars of national liberation, which we might classify anywhere between legitimate revolution and wars of subversive aggression. Nuclear wars, he said, could have no victor, because they would only end in mutual destruction; and even conventional wars were too dangerous, because they might escalate into nuclear war. Only wars of national liberation were safe to pursue—a conclusion that Khrushchev may have lived to regret, as he views the situation in Viet Nam from the Soviet side lines.

The opportunity for any nation to affect the conduct of its neighbors' affairs, at least through the use of force or the threat of force, is indeed more restricted than it has probably ever been before. Every nation lives in the shadow of thermonuclear holocaust. And paradoxically, that shadow lies more heavily on the great powers than on the small ones, because action by any great power creates a stronger likelihood that another great power will feel its national interests vitally affected so that its nuclear deterrent might be invoked. Indeed, the scope of nuclear deterrence is limited by mutual estimates of what are vital national interests—and the penumbra of deterrence is measured by the range of mutual uncertainty about those interests.

Smaller powers can afford to lose their tempers at each other, and even to strike out in the anger of the moment. A border dispute between two Latin American countries is not felt to threaten seriously the peace of the world—at least where both parties to the dispute are thought to be acting independently, and neither one on behalf of a great power. Even where a small power dispute takes place in a great power danger zone relatively close to the Iron or Bamboo Curtain, like the UAR–Saudi Arabian dispute over the Yemen, for example, it is more threatening, but still less worrisome than a disagreement over the locus of the curtain itself. We shall return to the significance of outbreaks of violence anywhere in the world, but here I merely want to note that great powers are a good deal less free to use force to achieve their foreign policy objectives than small powers are.

Any examination of U.S. foreign policy objectives, therefore, begins with the proposition that those objectives are extremely limited, not only by choice, but by necessity. The relative powerlessness of a great power is perhaps best demonstrated within our own federal system, in which the federal power of the United States must stand by while law and order are flouted, and even human life is taken, with the acquiescence of sovereign states of the Union. Beyond the geographical limits of its sovereignty, every sovereign, no matter how powerful, can only bargain; it cannot rule.

All these things being so, what objectives of U.S. foreign policy can be served by our military power, and how do the actual uses of U.S. military power over the last 20 years jibe with these purposes? To begin with, it seems clear that the most important use of U.S. military power is to put an absolute ceiling—albeit a fairly stratospheric one—on the willingness of other nations to risk a nuclear attack against us or our allies, or a non-nuclear confrontation of equal seriousness. Khrushchev's gamble with the missiles in Cuba may have been the last great confrontation at the nuclear level. In other words, our nuclear power deters other nations from taking actions that would so affect our own freedom that we would risk our survival to prevent them. So long as nuclear weapons remain in the hands of only a few, each of whom is comparatively responsible and would fear retaliation, our nuclear weapons should deter a major attack by creating a large risk that despite the destruction they could impose upon us, we would have the ability—and the desire—to inflict enormous damage on the land and people we thought responsible for the attack. By the same token, we know that we have sufficient force to react to any other unacceptable action, for example, a nuclear attack on one of our allies, provided we recognize, as we do, that such an attack would be so great an invasion of our vital interests that we would be prepared to risk massive destruction of our own society in the process.

The class of cases in which our nuclear deterrent is effective is thus necessarily limited to the cases in which our survival as a nation is involved, and the potential aggressor knows it. We cannot enlarge this class of cases by fiat—although we can certainly shrink it by evidence of indecision or cowardice. This leaves an enormous variety of situations in which aggressive action might disturb the peace of the world, but would fall short of creating the conditions that could be counted on to deter a potential aggressor, because he would know that the potential action did not so affect our survival as a nation that if he acted we would be forced to a nuclear response. Our nuclear power was not relevant to the situation in Korea, in Lebanon, in the Caribbean off Cuba, and it is not relevant to the situation in Viet Nam.

These are the situations where the only relevant ability is the ability to respond with less than nuclear force. If the Soviets for any reason were to contemplate launching a probe into West German territory, they could not reasonably anticipate a nuclear response to such a probe—at least at first—and therefore they would not be deterred by the U.S. capability to launch such a response. The United States and its allies would like to be able to mount the kind of non-nuclear defense that could meet and physically contain any aggression at any level so that the burden would be on the aggressor to make the terrible decision whether to withdraw, or to escalate, moving that much closer to a nuclear confrontation.

Another way to describe the objective is to refer to Tom Schelling's distinction between force and violence: force physically prevents action; violence influences action by inflicting great pain. The use of force is inherently a good deal less destabilizing than the use of violence. If we can prevent aggression by force (or even by the threat of the use of force), we leave to the aggressor the more difficult task of invoking violence or the threat of violence. We shall have occasion to refer to this distinction again in another connection.

Our principal quarrel with our NATO allies during the last six years has been over the need for a common capacity to maintain a non-nuclear force in Europe that would shift the burden of decision to the aggressor. Our allies have learned all too well the lessons about the claimed universal efficacy of massive retaliation that the Eisenhower Administration offered to teach them. Some still believe it, while some only believe that any aggression in Europe is too unlikely to bother deterring. But too many European politicians are still inclined to look at their armed forces today as American politicians looked at our armed forces until the present decade—as repositories for an arbitrary (and shrinking) share of the government budget, to be spent as the generals and admirals thought best, without any particular relationship to foreign policy commitments. And, by the same token, the greatest value of the new Select Committee of NATO Defense Ministers, generally known as the McNamara Committee, is that the political leadership of each of our European allies must now take a hard look at its military establishment, and relate its resources more directly to its obligations.

Thus far we have been concerned with the ability of the United States to deter, to prevent, to discourage clear-cut aggression across national frontiers, particularly where that aggression threatens the delicate balance among the major powers in the world today. This ability is quite consistent with the limited goals of U.S. foreign policy in a nuclear world, where we seek to protect our friends in their exercise of their own free choice, and to give our antagonists time to resolve their internal difficulties without taking them out on their neighbors.

It nevertheless requires that we maintain a strategic nuclear retaliatory force clearly adequate to deter major aggression, because it is, in the jargon of the military analysts, survivable, and is subject to a survivable command and control system. That ability also requires a continental air defense system adequate to make an effective strategic nuclear force terribly expensive both to acquire and to keep up, so that potential aggressors who have already acquired nuclear weapons and vehicles to deliver them on a distant target, are discouraged from raising the ante, and those who have not yet acquired their own nuclear weapons are discouraged from getting into the game. This ability also requires that we have the kind of non-nuclear forces that are presently deployed in Europe, in Asia (apart from the forces fighting in Viet Nam), and in our strategic reserve at home. The existence of these forces and our ability to move them rapidly wherever they may be needed serve to deter aggression just below the nuclear threshold.

The policy conditions that prescribe the need for these forces do not determine in any precise way how large the forces should be. The question, "How much is enough?," is still a troublesome one. But an awareness of the absolute limitations on military force in a thermonuclear world at least provides a framework for answering the question of what is useful and necessary by way of military power to deal with overt aggression across national boundaries.

The fact is, however, that we live in a rapidly shrinking world where violence is not confined to clear-cut aggression across national frontiers. We need to have a foreign policy that addresses these limited situations of violence, and that gives us some guidance on the proper character of our own involvement. I say involvement because a decision not to become involved is as much a decision about our own involvement as a decision to send in X divisions of American troops. And the pattern of these decisions determines the kind of military establishment that we need to maintain, apart from our strategic retaliatory and continental air defense forces, which themselves represent a steadily declining fraction of our defense budget.

As Robert McNamara pointed out last summer, there have been 164 "internationally significant outbreaks of violence" in the last eight years, and the number of prolonged conflicts in progress today is almost twice as many as the number eight years ago. McNamara noted three significant facts about these conflicts:

First, none of them has involved a formally declared war—and indeed there has been no formal declaration of war in any conflict since World War II;

Second, less than half of these conflicts has been a product of Communist aggression, even counting as products of Communist aggression the seven instances of uprisings against entrenched Communist regimes; and

Third, there is a direct correlation between the number of instances of violence and the poverty and economic backwardness of the countries in which violence occurs.

McNamara concluded that in the long run we could best help to reduce the incidence of violence in the world by encouraging and assisting in economic development. "Security," he said, "is development." But meanwhile the speed and continuity of economic development depend on a minimal degree of security within the developing nations. We can and do help other nations to maintain that security by making available military assistance, providing them with military hardware, training and advice; by committing ourselves to alliances that discourage dissident elements within these countries from seeking outside intervention to overthrow established governments; and, on occasion, by direct intervention with military force.

Our role in helping to maintain short-term security in the developing world involves us in a number of difficult policy choices. Our commitments must be limited by our resources, if we are not to be a paper tiger. And we simply do not have the resources to provide a global constabulary; in fact, a number of Administration officials have already pointed out that a global policeman's life is not only unhappy, but impossible.

It is especially difficult to mobilize enough military power so that we can deal with a particular crisis by the use of force, in Tom Schelling's sense, rather than by the use of violence. Whenever a policeman has to use violence in arresting or subduing a citizen, he creates waves of trouble that spread well beyond the original point of impact of the public force.

Even a nation as rich and powerful as the United States could not afford to maintain a military establishment large enough and flexible enough to deal with more than a limited number of military crises simultaneously, assuming that we wished to do so.

A decision to intervene with military force in a particular situation amounts to a decision to deny the availability of that quantum of military power for other contingencies in the foreseeable future. A reasonable decision to intervene, therefore, involves consideration of what other situations may require even more urgently the forces that are about to be committed. One of the principal achievements of the first two years of the Kennedy Administration was to provide the kind of force that could deal with more than one major crisis in the world at the same time. The availability of this force made a major difference at the time of the Cuba missile crisis, but the ability to deal with more than one crisis does not imply the ability to deal with an infinite number. This is indeed the limiting case on the ability of the military power of any single nation to serve its foreign policy.

And military intervention is costly in indirect ways as well. The United States has discovered, to its sorrow, that it cannot walk into a foreign military adventure, defeat the forces of darkness, and then walk out again. There seems always to be a moral and indeed a practical political commitment to stay behind to help pick up the pieces. We were still picking up the pieces in Europe a decade after World War II; and our commitment of two United States divisions to Korea, plus substantial military assistance, remains essentially an open-ended one almost 15 years after the termination of overt hostilities. We are committed to withdrawing our troops from Viet Nam within six months after the aggression has been ended here—and I am confident we will meet that commitment—but I am equally confident that our involvement in the economic rehabilitation and development of Viet Nam, and Southeast Asia generally, will be at least the work of a generation; as will the economic effort now under way in the Dominican Republic.

There are other policy dilemmas for the United States in contemplating military assistance and intervention, dilemmas quite unrelated to the availability of our resources. How does one judge whether an outbreak of internal violence is likely in fact to be a check to positive progress, or a necessary convulsion in the often spasmodic process of positive social change? How does one judge whether an indigenous revolutionary movement has the internal vitality to maintain itself, or will settle down to giving orders hot off the teletype from Peking or Moscow? And how can one make a reasonable guess as to whether a country's internal resources to defeat subversive aggression would, on balance, be strengthened or weakened by assistance from outside?

There are no handy rules for locating the answers to these questions. Whatever the United States chooses to do, there is no lack of critics to point out why the choice was the wrong one. On the Right, it is argued that the developing world is helpless before the spreading tide of world Communism, and, with no great internal consistency, that the United States can and must intervene on the side of whatever force appears at the moment to be struggling to push back that tide. From the Left, we are accused of a paranoid fear of social change which, it is said, leads us to oppose change simply because it may be infected with a Communist-tinged ideology.

Nevertheless, a few general principles, none of them decisive of particular cases, may be tentatively offered for consideration.

A reasonable first principle in foreign affairs seems to me, "When in doubt, don't intervene." Sovereignty is still the normal condition for the effective use of power. Many, if not most, of the political difficulties of states are self-limiting. And scatteration is perhaps the worst enemy of the effective use of one's energies. There is even a practical political as well as a moral question: How do we know what is best for other people, when those other people do not have the opportunity to administer to us the admirable corrective of an occasional resounding defeat at the polls? I assume, although others may differ, that we have no substantial selfish motives for intervention abroad; but we are still liable to errors of judgment.

My second general proposition is that we should be even more reluctant to intervene militarily where military intervention requires the use of violence than where it can be accomplished simply by the use of force. Even apart from the moral considerations involved in a decision to inflict pain and death on other human beings (rather than to restrain them directly from accomplishing their objectives), it is just a good deal more difficult and chancy to have to rely on violence as a means to persuade people to stop, rather than simply stopping them by main force. This is true whether the people we are concerned with are North Vietnamese Communists or Rhodesian neo-Colonials.

It is perhaps worth noting that the function of U.S. military power in the Dominican Republic was not to engage in violent action, but rather, by interposing itself between contending forces, to prevent by force what would otherwise have been a major blood bath. Our troops spent most of their time in the corridor between the two warring camps, absorbing bursts of hostile fire which they did not return. It is also worth noting to what extent we have applied a self-denying ordinance in our conduct of specific military operations—and the adverse consequences we have suffered when, as in Korea, we temporarily abandoned those limitations.

My third general proposition is that we cannot help those who are unable or unwilling to help themselves. The job of governing any nation is so difficult that it is a miracle it is accomplished at all. We may be able to help remove some impediments to the process, but we cannot provide a substitute for the imagination and dedication and immensely hard work that has to go into it on the ground. This seems to me our principal problem in Viet Nam today. The fact of outside aggression in South Viet Nam has been amply demonstrated, and any illusions about the general popularity of the Viet Cong or its Communist front, the NFL, should by now have been pretty well dissipated. But the problem remains that the Saigon Government is a weak reed indeed on which to rest our hopes for effective and humane administration of the countryside.

Similarly, the great significance of the argument apparently going on in Washington today over the nature and extent of our military assistance to Thailand in coping with its growing insurgency problem in the northeastern part of that country goes to the question of the present Thai Government's ability to develop the kind of program that can win and hold the allegiance of its own peasantry.

My fourth principle is that any effort to intervene in the affairs of another sovereign nation must sooner or later, and preferably from the outset, be a multilateral effort. This is the lesson we learned in Korea, and we have tried to apply it, albeit with varying degrees of urgency and of success, in Viet Nam and the Dominican Republic.

A fifth principle, or perhaps a special case of the fourth one, is that, in the last analysis, responsibility for the security of any country depends on its neighbors. The United States cannot contain the export of subversion from Cuba unless the other nations of Latin America are also committed to that containment. Nor can the United States help to protect the smaller nations of Asia against the potential of Chinese expansionism unless the major Asian powers—Japan, India, Australia, and even eventually Indonesia—undertake primary responsibility on their side of the globe.

All of these principles, it seems to me, apply with equal force to our Military Assistance Program as to direct military intervention. They apply particularly to that part of the present program—comprising less than half the dollars, but more than half the countries—which is designed to help our allies in dealing with their own internal security problems. The other function of military assistance, to provide equipment to countries that share with us the immediate burden of patrolling the Iron and Bamboo Curtains, when their own economies are too weak to provide adequate military budgets, has a different and more easily supportable rationale. There is a third aspect to the Military Assistance Program—nation building, or civic action—as to which I would only observe there is no reason not to use indigenous military for economic development, but not as a rationalization to continue an old program under a new label.

But these are all limiting principles, and one may well ask why the United States should be prepared to intervene at all, whether through the Military Assistance Program or with direct military force, in her neighbors' troubles, particularly when some of her neighbors are halfway around the world. We insist that we have no motives of economic or political aggrandizement. Our political goal is a world made safe for diversity—including presumably diversity with which we do not agree.

But we do have a stubbornly ineradicable interest in frustrating aggression, because aggression, like other appetites, grows on what it feeds on. This is not to suggest that one can draw direct analogies between Hitler and Ho Chi Minh. But it is to point out that in every significant episode of violence there is likely to be some element of aggression. Where that element is itself more than minimal, and where the aggression cannot be checked by the victim himself, the fitful progress toward a world rule of law is checked or thrown back.

That progress is the ultimate guarantee of our national security, and it affects the eventual goals of our international relations—detente, arms control, even eventual programs of cooperation with those who make themselves our antagonists. But achievement of all of these objectives is deferred when aggression succeeds anywhere in the world.

Intervention is necessarily a painful process. It can be costly in treasure and in blood. And it can injure us in other ways: A democratic nation is a community of individuals supported by mutual respect and undermined by shared violence, even when we can agree on its necessity.

Yet if we look at the record of the last ten years, there is some ground for hope. The verdict of history is not yet in on our intervention in Southeast Asia. But South Korea is a rapidly modernizing nation with a viable economy and a political system moving toward democratic goals. And in the Dominican Republic a new government, installed through free elections, has successfully met its first and perhaps severest challenge to the principle of civilian supremacy, a principle that had never before found stable or lasting expression in that long-unhappy country.

It may be argued that this kind of peace-keeping function is best performed by smaller powers than the United States under the pacific aegis of the United Nations. But whatever our eventual hopes for a United Nations as a peace-keeping agency, its present scale of peace-keeping operations and the narrow limits necessarily set for them suggest that there is a power vacuum here that United States military power can and must help to fill for some time to come.

Another way of saying this is to say that military power at most buys time to pursue non-military solutions to foreign policy problems. The durable solutions to foreign policy problems generally turn out to be non-military, even where an immediate military solution seems feasible. Suppressing a guerrilla outbreak doesn't remove the conditions that led to the outbreak. A man who can make a decent living on a Latin American hacienda is unlikely to turn to banditry, just as a student who can find a real intellectual challenge in a Latin American university is unlikely to turn to kidnapping government officials. A guerrilla, an insurgent, is a man with a grievance. His theories about the causes may be imaginary, but the grievance itself is real enough to keep him out in the rain and the dark while less aggrieved citizens sit quietly by their hearthsides—or their TV sets.

We recognize the need for more effective law enforcement to curb juvenile delinquents. But we don't suppose that even the most efficient— or Draconic—law enforcement would eliminate juvenile delinquency. And insurgents are even more strongly motivated to engage in insurgency than delinquents are to engage in delinquency.

What does this excursion into foreign policy tell us about the kind of non-nuclear military power the United States ought to maintain? I submit that we can identify at least three priority areas of concern for the managers of the United States military establishment.

The first is readiness, the ability to move quickly with decisive force, because the availability of that force is itself both the best deterrent to aggression and the most effective weapon to block it in its initial stages of development. If military force buys time, the best values are to be had when the time has just begun to run. The ability to mount a decisive force at a specific time and place is much more important than the existence of massive numbers in reserve. When we moved into the Dominican Republic, I believe we were right to move in with clear numerical superiority—we could afford to be less violent because we were able to exert more force. And we could not have moved decisively in a matter of days and hours without the readiness that took years to develop.

A corollary of the concern for readiness is the concern for flexibility. Without flexibility we cannot be prepared to deal with the enormous range of contingencies that confronts us. If the odds are heavily against the desirability or utility of military force in any given crisis, specialization becomes a luxury that only a garrison state can afford.

The last, and perhaps the most crucial concern is responsiveness. The

Cuba missile crisis is of course the classic example both of the need and of the United State military capacity for precise responsiveness to political control. But even in less intensely dangerous situations, military power is a relatively blunt instrument for what are becoming more and more precise and delicate operations. It needs to be handled with extraordinary attention to what is happening at the other end of the Line of Communications.

Military operators have, I believe, become better servants of U.S. foreign policy at least over the period in which I had the opportunity to observe them from the E Ring of the Pentagon. But there is one major aspect of foreign policy making in which I believe the masters may have something to learn from the servants. Defense policies nowadays are articulated in the language of plans and programs. Foreign policy is still too often expressed in terms of attitudes. Our policy toward X is one of friendship, toward Y one of containment, toward Z one of non-recognition. This is all very well if the statement is only shorthand for a program to carry it out. But I note that doctors do not say that their policy toward high blood pressure is one of hostility, economists do not say that their policy toward unemployment is one of containment, and even practicing domestic politicians are beginning to form the habit of telling us how they propose to reach the goals they embrace.

In the military sphere, policy is inseparable from program. In the political sphere, policy too often becomes a substitute for program. One consequence of this separation is that wherever a military problem exists in the world—in Viet Nam, in Berlin, in Thailand—the necessarily defensive, short-range, time-buying military program tends to obscure the need for a detailed, long-range non-military program.

Even when our foreign policy problems cannot be characterized as military, our foreign policy makers do not habitually think about the relationships between resources and objectives. They are inclined to be more concerned about reacting to cables than about in-depth analysis.

Their consideration of alternative means tends to be less searching than their consideration of alternative ends.

It is relatively easy to get agreement on what our goals and hopes should be for the troubled areas of the world. It is more difficult to focus attention on how to get there from here. In this connection, the Department of Defense may be able to provide one model for the organized application of knowledge to the marshalling and selection of resources.

But that is at least the raw material for another lecture.

Vietnam and American Foreign Policy

STANLEY HOFFMANN

THE POSTWAR record of American foreign policy is, on the whole, a record of success—so much so that one of the senior advisers, and chief ideologue, of the President, has been able to forecast a future almost entirely in accordance with America's vision of a moderate, "pragmatic" world.[1] But he also presented Vietnam as the last battle, the last obstacle before Erewhon; and Vietnam, to put it candidly, has been the most spectacular failure in postwar American policy.

The question which the Vietnam fiasco raises is both crucial and difficult to answer. Has Vietnam been an accident, an aberration, an exception, or—as Walt Rostow's preaching would have us believe, and as so many "revisionists" assert—has it been a logical and necessary development in American foreign policy? If they are right, then our failure there should oblige us to revise drastically our whole policy, to follow a totally new course in the future and also to reexamine more critically our past successes so as to find in them the germs of our later failure. If they are wrong, then the only lesson of Vietnam is that we applied valid concepts clumsily, and that in future interventions we ought to be more careful about the means and strategy we use to reach our goals.

My own contention is somewhere in between. On the one hand, Vietnam is an extreme case: the most inappropriate terrain for the application of concepts that have proved fertile and adequate elsewhere. On the other hand, the very attempt, indeed the massive and often frenzied effort, at pursuing goals, applying notions, and devising strategies that turned out to be irrelevant, self-defeating, and dangerous, in so unrewarding an area, with such persistence in wishful thinking and self-delusion, tells us a great deal about what ought to be discarded in the future. It reveals flaws that come from the depths of our political style and machinery, but had never been so clearly brought to light in any previous operation. An extreme case that is an aberration teaches little; an extreme case which is at the margin, in the sense of disclosing either a logic or a set of contradictions that are not apparent in run-of-the-mill cases, and of forcing one to make explicitly choices that are normally made without much thought or pain, can perform

[1] Cf. Walt W. Rostow's speech at the University of Leeds, Feb. 23, 1967.

the same functions as an ideal-type: it is an intensification, an enlargement of normally blurred features. Vietnam is like a blow-up of many of our flaws.

I will not examine here those aspects of our Vietnam policy that illuminate the weaknesses of our decision-making process; this has been done elsewhere.[2] I will focus on the substance of the policy itself.

I

1. The central problem does not lie in the *nature* of America's objectives. The idea that a majority of the South Vietnamese people does not want to live under Communist rule and ought to be allowed to choose its form of government, the goal of a united and stable regime in South Vietnam, the objective of proving that an armed minority using the ideology and techniques of "national liberation wars" and supplied from outside the limits of the country it tries to seize can be defeated—so as both to protect the majority in the country and to prevent the diffusion of the movement, the goal of assuring other Asian governments of America's concern for their security, the idea of preserving a balance of power in Asia, of "buying time" for the countries situated around China: these were all worthy ends. The central problem of American policy—of any policy—is the relevance of its ends to specific areas: the more ambitious or ideological a policy, the more indispensable it is to analyze the realities of each area with critical rigor before applying to it one's concepts or preconceptions, for otherwise the statesman will trip into the pitfalls of irrelevance, "adventurism," or unreality. Our own policy was, of necessity, ambitious due to our very role as a superpower; and it has, if not an ideology, at least a set of principles and dogmas such as resistance to aggression, attachment to self-determination, opposition to forceful Communist takeovers, etc. *The tragedy of our course in Vietnam lies in our refusal to come to grips with those realities in South Vietnam that happened to be decisive from the viewpoint of politics.*

What was determining, or operational, was not the inchoate and unorganized opposition of a majority of its people to a Communist takeover. It was, and remains, the inability of this majority to pull itself together sufficiently to resist a determined attempt by the Vietcong to seize power, in a conflict whose stakes are both a social revolution (in a society whose traditional order is crumbling and whose leaders have

---

[2] Cf. James Thomson's searching essay in the Atlantic, April 1968. See also my *Gulliver's Troubles, or the Setting of American Foreign Policy* (N.Y., 1968), Part 3.

been unable to replace that order with a new, effective, and legitimate one) and the completion of a movement of national unification undertaken over twenty years ago against the French and interrupted in 1954. It is the failure of the leadership in South Vietnam to establish a legitimate and authoritative government capable of rallying and mobilizing the energies of the people, of appealing to the villagers' desire for security, of providing the citizens with the incentives and means of self-defense, of establishing procedures for the redress of grievances. The root of the tragedy is the demonstrated absence in the South of the capacity for sustained self-government, for which there is no substitute. In its absence, the controlling factor is not the fact that the Vietcong constitutes only a minority, but the fact that it constitutes the only national movement that cuts across religious and social lines. We have refused to recognize both the *uniqueness* of this situation by comparison with the other guerrilla or revolutionary wars that we have known intimately, and the *similarity* of the predicament of the outside power in a situation such as this with that of the French both in Indochina and in Algeria. If we want, in the future, to avoid new Vietnams, we must find out *why* we have refused to recognize what, to this writer, has been, ever since the beginning of our involvement, the decisive and blindingly obvious facts.

Part of the answer lies in our fear of the consequences of recognizing reality. To acknowledge South Vietnam's inability to provide for its own, non-Communist "political development" would have meant resigning oneself to a Communist take-over by force, or after a face-saving negotiation. In the eyes of our policy-makers, this would have meant a betrayal of the non-Communist majority, a victory for the most militant part of the world Communist movement, a demoralization of the other non-Communist governments of Asia, an encouragement to armed minorities, etc. Two points should be stressed. One, our fears of the unpleasant or disastrous consequences of reality have led us to try to deny and reverse it so as to avoid those effects, instead of trying to attenuate them; this, in turn, will have to be explained. Two, our own vision of those results revealed an overestimation of the "domino effect," an underestimation of the purely domestic reasons for the potential triumph of a Communist movement in South Vietnam— reasons that did not exist to any comparable degree elsewhere and that made of this case a perfectly unsuitable model for other "national liberation movements," in Asia or (as Regis Debray has recognized) in Latin America. In other words, our fear of the consequences was magnified by our very tendency to misinterpret reality; had we understood it correctly, then the effects would have appeared to us less catastrophic. Thus, we must look beyond and behind that fear.

Another, deeper part of the answer lies in a certain form of ignorance that I would call the shock of nonrecognition. Our understanding of South Vietnamese society was poor, the expertise at our disposal limited. In such circumstances, we tended to distort our analysis by reducing South Vietnamese uniqueness to elements that seemed familiar and reassuring—to features that we had met *and managed* elsewhere. All those traits were indeed present in the picture, and we have been clinging to them mentally; yet in the total picture, they have turned out to be far less important than all the other, disturbing traits whose ominous meaning we have tried to deny by repeated rhetorical exorcisms. We have exaggerated the possibility of reaching our final objectives by invoking two analogies. One has been the Korean analogy; to be sure, in both cases we have a mixture of civil war (one was a war among Koreans, the other a war among Vietnamese) and aggression (the crossing of the 38th parallel by the North Koreans, infiltrations into Laos and the South despite the 1954 Geneva Agreements, first by returning Southerners who had gone North after Geneva, later by North Vietnamese supplies and units). But these similarities were quite superficial. The war in Korea was a conventional war; the way in which Pyong Yang tried to dominate Seoul was invasion. The fragmentation of South Korean politics, the backwardness of the South Korean economy, the authoritarianism of Syngman Rhee might have eventually provided the Communists with opportunities for insurgency in the South; but their very resort to invasion threw those chances away and consolidated a regime and a society that showed at once their aptitude to rally under attack, and have shown later a remarkable capacity for self-government, change, and growth. One reason why the Korean Communists resorted to invasion and found no help in the South was that the cause of nationalism, the appeal of self-determination had been clearly captured by the South Korean regime; it was Pyong Yang, in those days, that looked like a puppet. In Vietnam, Diem had a claim on nationalism and did a superficially effective job of governing in the early years, when it was Hanoi's efforts at total control in the North that were producing revolts and refugees; but his social policies, his police, his methods, his entourage, and his aloofness paved the road to insurgency; after him, the whirlwind of shaky governments and the growing involvement of the United States gave a kind of monopoly of the nationalist image to Ho-Chi-Minh, who could hardly be called anyone's puppet.

The other analogy was that of countries in which Communist insurrections had been defeated: Greece, the Philippines, Malaysia—all of which had shown that a determined and well-organized minority can be brought under control by a divided society, riddled with hates, corruption, and factional strife. However, the analogy was misleading in one decisive respect: in none of these cases had the insurgency reached such levels, and the threatened regime fallen to such depths, that the minority appeared defeatable only by a colossal foreign intervention. Our superficial emphasis on similarities made us neglect a quantitative difference that amounts to a qualitative one: the difference between a society and polity that manage—with limited foreign help and with domestic means that may be rough but are effective—to pull itself together and to meet the challenge, and a society and polity that literally have to entrust their survival to a foreign trustee. We have forgotten that in the cases to which we have pointed for hope, the threatened regime finally won because it was able to appeal to the population's national consciousness, to provide it with security, and to present the Communists as agents of outside powers; Magsaysay also stole much of the Communists' appeal as social reformers.

We have blundered through failure to analyze rigorously enough the conditions for large-scale insurrection. We were used to seeing in Communist movements mere branches of a central trunk. We refused to believe that large masses of people could willingly embrace Communism for essentially local reasons—i.e., we had refused to learn from the Chinese precedent. We did not want to admit that the fusion of Communism and nationalism achieved by Ho-Chi-Minh had survived the phase of the fight against the French. We mistook the presence in the South of distinguished, but unorganized non-Communist nationalists for evidence of the good nationalist standing, and therefore of the representative character, of the Saigon regimes. We have been incapable of distinguishing a sect from a party, a clique from an organization, a group of intellectuals or politicians with tiny clienteles from a political movement, a police force, officer corps, and set of rich merchants from a political class. We have tended to attribute South Vietnamese chaos to a combination of Communist disruptiveness and reversible South Vietnamese mistakes (such as Diem's way of applying the strategic hamlet idea). We failed to realize that those "mistakes" were, so to speak, doubly of the essence: they were the inevitable product of a narrowly based, unrepresentative, insecure and artificial regime deeply suspicious of or removed from its own people, and they provided the Communists with a cause and opportunities for disruption that allowed them to reach proportions unknown in all the other cases. The proper analogy ought to have been Chiang's China—but Chiang's China was too huge for us to have had any illusions about our capacity to "save" it from Mao; and yet the very precedent of China must have somehow led our officials to want to do for Saigon, what we could not do for Chiang—something that turned out not to be feasible here either; for what has defeated us is not the physical size of the area (our consolation in the case of China) but the very nature of the issue. Our "loss of Cuba" made us move into the Dominican revolution; there, we prevailed, because that revolution turned out not to have reached in any way the proportions of Castro's insurgency in, say, the last months of Batista. Our "loss of China" made us step into South Vietnam, and we have not prevailed.

At the time when we were faced with the choice between letting South Vietnam fall to Communist subversion, and massive intervention to "save" the Saigon regime, the very terms in which we saw the alternatives indicate that the chances the South Vietnamese regime had had of defeating the insurgents on its own (or with minimal help) according to those rules of counterinsurgency laid down by Sir Robert Thompson were gone:[3] the "clear political aim," the respect for the law, the good administration, the priority to the defeat of political subversion (rather than the guerrillas), the close contact with the people, the effort to destroy the enemy's infrastructure, the ability to protect the population and look after its needs, the avoidance of a large conventional army whose operations would be self-defeating, all of this had been neglected or played down. We failed to recognize how all these errors differentiated the case of Saigon from those we had invoked, and resulted from that very inability to provide South Vietnam with the rudiments of nationhood which the various regimes in Saigon had demonstrated (in sharp contrast with Hanoi). The long-term interest of the Saigon leadership may have been reform for survival. But its nature was such that drastic reform would have eliminated it as surely as a Communist sweep: this, too, had not been the case in Athens or in Manila, although it was Batista's and Chiang's. In the short run, Saigon's interest was *not* to reform, and to let us

[3] See his book, *Defeating Communist Insurgency*, and his article in *Foreign Affairs*, April 1968.

fight for its survival. We were led by our misreading of reality to believe that our intervention could somehow bring to South Vietnam all that had failed to grow there in the years of our mere "advice."

2. Thus we come to the other great failing of our policy. An optimistic and simplified reading of reality served as the basis for our *hybris*: if the situation in South Vietnam was serious mainly for the very reason that triggered our intervention (i.e., Communist mischief), it was easier to believe in our capacity to save South Vietnam: for we saw, hopefully, our task as saving it from its enemies, instead of seeing our task, hopelessly, as saving it from itself.

Our misreading of reality and our self-confidence have fed one another in a vicious circle of ever-increasing delusions. What the South Vietnamese could not do for themselves, we could not do for them; but our self-confidence has misled us into thinking both that we could and that they would do it with us; and our need to cling to our illusions has led us, for years, to analyze the evolution of the war with an optimism that it took the Tet offensive to begin to shatter, but which sprang from our initial misreading: the Korean analogy helped us misjudge the Vietcong's strategy (and to call enemy defeats his failure to reach objectives that he did not have), the Greek or Filipino analogy helped us misjudge the "progress" of South Vietnamese political and economic development.

Our *hybris* is that old "illusion of omnipotence" denounced by Brogan, which I have analyzed elsewhere in some detail.[4] In South Vietnam, our faith in our talent for *fixing* has taken several forms. One has been our belief in the possibility of bringing insurgency under control, and its North Vietnamese directors to their knees, by the massive exertion of mechanical power, without realizing either that, short of invasion and occupation, airpower alone was not likely to defeat North Vietnam, or that the degree of guerrilla "immunity to the direct application" of our military power was high, and that we were indeed up against the "Asian birthrate," in a Sisyphean contest with the manifestations of insurgency (search-and-destroy) that left its roots intact. This has been pointed out so often, and so frequently cited as an example of our fondness for military or hardware solutions to complex problems—our "engineering" approach to politics—that one would feel almost ashamed of mentioning it again, were it not both the most blatant demonstration of our misreading of reality, and a symptom of another, deeper form of our *hybris*.

---

[4] *Gulliver's Troubles*, Part 2; *The State of War* (N.Y., 1965), Chapter 6.

On the one hand, not only were we encouraged in our double escalation of the war (in the South and in the North) by the Korean analogy, but we have also acted as if our massive despatch of troops and our air war were going to be able to turn what was essentially a colossal insurgency into something more manageable by us—a conventional war that we would win through what Herman Kahn has called an "attrition-pressure-ouch" strategy,[5] aimed at breaking Hanoi's will and at forcing the enemy in the South into increasingly costly battles. This can be read only as an attempt at changing reality by acting as if it did not exist: as if we could both impose our rules of the game on our enemy on the ground, and turn into a predominantly "Northern" war what was still at heart an insurrection in the South (helped, to be sure, by the North, but neither so decisively as to collapse even if the "will of Hanoi" had snapped, nor, most importantly, by means easily susceptible to our kinds of pressure).

On the other hand, we had been warned by all kinds of experts about the irrelevance of conventional war machinery to insurgency situations. We thought that we would overcome its tactical disadvantages by ingenious innovations in technological gadgetry which would increase mobility and our firepower. But mobility, while capable of thwarting enemy moves and making enemy bases insecure, is no substitute for pacification (seize-and-hold). Moreover, both mobility and firepower increase destructiveness and disruption. In letting ourselves be swayed by the advantages rather than by the disadvantages of our kind of might, we have shown again the combination of a wishful reading of reality (i.e., a permanent underestimation of the damage we do, a refusal to see the fundamentally political character of the struggle) with a conviction that the people would, so to speak, forgive us our destructiveness—by contrast with, say, that of the French in Indochina and Algeria—because they would realize that it was a necessary evil inflicted upon them for the sake of their protection—as in the case of our bombings of France in 1943-44. This is the *hybris* of believing that others will interpret our deeds in the light in which we see them, and that our intentions cancel out our acts; it matches our illusion that the South Vietnamese intention of remaining non-Communist amounts both to the willingness and capacity to organize, and to the acceptance of any act of war against Communism. Whether we could ever have made the South Vietnamese people look at us as their defenders against insurgents who are—after all—their kin is a big ques-

---

[5] *Can We Win in Vietnam?*, Chapter 6.

tion, although one *could* argue that different tactics and a less obtrusive presence might have helped us put all the blame for disruption on the Vietcong and Hanoi. But the very scale of our operations has made this a moot point—and a smaller scale might have proved ineffective sooner.

Another form of *hybris* shows in our belief that we could do what no other nation has done—build someone else's nation, create a stable society and polity elsewhere in the midst of a large-scale war. "Pacification" is, of course, not only compatible with counterinsurgency operations but an indispensable complement to them, and their ultimate target. But pacification is, in any case, very difficult to achieve once the military operations reach a certain level: the clash between search-and-destroy and hold-and-protect becomes unbearable when, say, relocation for greater security gives way to the mass production of refugees. Moreover (as one well-qualified expert, Moshe Dayan, has written), pacification must be undertaken by the native country; indeed, it must be an undertaking of the villagers themselves, under the protection of the military and with the help of the government. *Pace* Herman Kahn, there is more to pacification than good administration, and to begin with it must be self-administration. Out of *hybris*, we failed to understand that, as Americans, we simply could not play this role—being, to quote Dayan again,[6] not mere foreigners but strangers, whose very presence undermines the standing of the people they came to defend, and, indeed, that the more we tried to be the "pacifiers," the more we undermined any capacity the South Vietnamese people and government might have had in this connection, as well as their self-respect. Yet we paid lip service to the notion that pacification was their affair. But out of our misunderstanding of reality, we failed to see that the South Vietnamese regime and military both could not and would not be the right agent for this: they *could* not, because of the lack of confidence of the people in a regime that had too often proved ineffective or repressive or corrupt, and they *would* not, because they never showed enough confidence in their own people to entrust the villagers with the authority and the means (military and financial) to provide for their self-defense. The villagers were thus left in a kind of physical, administrative, and emotional no man's land, torn between identification with the Vietcong which they respect but fear and identification with a regime for which they have no respect. And whatever normalization of local life could be achieved in this no

[6] Unpublished article.

man's land—in the absence of any self-identification with the regime—
is regularly disrupted by the Americans, whether they come as temporary administrators or as warriors.

Our faith in omnipotence has expressed itself in our conviction that
we could "win" this war, not merely *with* but to an increasing extent
for the South Vietnamese—without a true understanding of what "winning" means in such a context. Our first instinct, or reflex, has been
to look for victory in military terms—with the help of body counts and
victories won ever closer to, and recently in, Saigon. We have, over the
years, learned that this is not the only or the most significant index, and
we have spoken of "winning the hearts and minds" of the people, but
our power to raid has always been greater than our power to hold and
our lack of experience in this sort of a war has deprived us of handles,
tools, techniques, organizations, which would in any case have been
effective only if they had been used by the South Vietnamese. We
have been too easily satisfied with the fragile *appearances* of pacification, without asking ourselves whether the schools built would stay
open, or whether the population under control was truly loyal. Our
hybris has consisted of not taking seriously, or not applying to us, Ray-
mond Aron's warning: in a revolutionary war, the insurgents win if
they do not lose, the defenders lose if they fail to win; we have interpreted our failure to lose as a victory, and their failure to win as a defeat. We have, in the process, misread not only the realities of South
Vietnam but our own.

If there was ever any chance of success after our decision to intervene more massively than up to 1963, it depended on two factors. One
was our capacity to incite the South Vietnamese regime to broaden
its base, to include all those anti-Communist leaders with a respectable
nationalist past who served as our alibis (in our belief that their
country really wanted to be saved from Communism), and to reform
ARVIN so as to make it truly a national army. But here, we have been
inhibited both by that merciless reality we had tried to ignore, and by
ourselves. On the one hand, we always wondered whether any reform
and re-equipment of ARVIN would not ultimately benefit our enemies
rather than improve its will and ability to fight, and whether any significant broadening of the Saigon regime would not weaken its own
determination—i.e., whether the anti-Communist *majority* was truly
resolved to do battle with the Communist minority, and would not
prefer to deal with it in negotiations that we feared would ultimately
lead to a Communist take-over because of superior Communist co-

hesion and resolve. We wondered whether there was really more than a militant but unpopular and narrow (hence necessarily unstable *or* dependent) minority that wanted to do battle. On the other hand, we were also deterred by one of our qualities which both tempers our *hybris* and makes it even less justified: our reluctance, when we intervene, to act as if we had the right to push our protégés around and do more than advise them. Somehow, we realize our limitations and become humble, when faced with the stark need to take extensive measures of political and social reform in friendly territory; although it is more accurate and fair to say that we are stopped less by our ignorance (*vide* our extensive interventions in defeated Germany and Japan) than by our credo and principles: respect for self-determination, in the country that we came to defend, even when there are only shallow, indeed self-defeating *forms* of self-determination. Thus, our pride of omnipotence stops, so to speak, at our client's doorstep; which makes our conviction that we could clean house for him even more extravagant. For we end up having all the disadvantages of colonialism, and none of the advantages.

Another condition for improbable success was time—time to convince (if one would not coerce) the South Vietnamese establishment to change its course, time to relegate the insurgency to certain areas while the rest of the country convalesces out of the war and of its awful side effects, time to instil in the villagers a sense of confidence and identification with Saigon, in the city dwellers a sense of being the citizens of a genuine nation. But, once more, our lack of experience in these realms buttressed our somewhat hectic approach to world affairs: however often the frustrations of the years brought to our leaders' lips the litany of calls to patience and fortitude, the frenzied need for quick results (to reassure a nation that reacts badly to defeats and uneasily to protracted, inconclusive conflicts) brought on our officials in South Vietnam a constant pressure for quick results, and to our briefings and communiqués a constant flow of comforting statistics thoroughly devoid of meaning in the context of a long-term operation. Our impatience both fed our *hybris* and defeated it.

There was another manifestation of our sense of omnipotence: our whole policy, and the terms in which it has been presented, made sense *only* if we achieved that final victory (on the battlefield or in a negotiation to save our enemies' faces). Everything was predicated on success. We failed, in so tricky an operation, to protect ourselves against possible failure; we left ourselves no room for maneuver, or for the sort of elegant retreat that does not look like an admission of failure. We have repeatedly burned, or let the South Vietnamese regime, burn bridges behind us: by destroying or jailing political opponents to it who could have been of help to us had we wanted to change our course, by discarding possibilities of negotiation at a time when the military balance was more favorable to us. We have encouraged other Asian regimes to stake their safety on our presence in Vietnam, without realizing that this way of buying time for them could easily become an alibi for their neglect of those domestic factors that could kindle an insurgency on their soil far more surely than a victory of Ho-Chi-Minh on his. We failed to realize that their taking seriously our conviction that we were their main shield could lead them to revulsion against us if we did not succeed. But, in the meantime, it serves as an excuse for us to persist in trying to do the impossible—"other Asians want us to stay on." We made thereby the consequences of eventual failure far more critical than they might have been, had we understated the general significance of Vietnam instead of trumpeting its cosmic importance. But the more we have needed success to justify our investment, the more we have exaggerated the effects of failure, and the resort to false analogies: oversell was not a salesman's trick but a trapped man's need.

Above all, we have constantly rationalized the damage and disruption we inflicted on the country, and explained away the corruption and mismanagement of the Saigon regime with the argument that our final victory would prove the ruins worthwhile, allow the scars to heal, and cure the traditional diseases of Vietnamese society. It is indeed true (alas) that in many other cases, as in Korea, success retroactively vindicated horrors and inequities. But in Vietnam, the more atrocious the evils, the more we have had to put all our hopes on success, which became the only justification for an intolerable process; and the more success became the only tolerable outcome, the higher the price one has had to pay (or inflict) in order to try to succeed. The two great extenuating circumstances of war's moral outrages: final success, and a certain proportionality of means to ends, have both been war casualties here. The worst aspect of our *hybris* has been our assumption of the right to "destroy in order to save" in conditions where "salvation" was never likely to begin with, and has been made even less likely by our presence and methods.

II

1. It is becoming fashionable, among men who at one time or another supported the American effort in Vietnam, to assert that a different strategy could have produced better results. It is my contention that this is not the case: this was never a "winnable" contest. As long as our presence was small, conditions in South Vietnam—first, Diem's neglect and distortion of the requirements of counterinsurgency, later the chaos that followed his assassination—brought the insurgents very close to victory. Our intervention on the ground made sense in the perspective of thwarting an impending *forcible* Communist take-over and negotiating rapidly a *political* solution that would have given to the non-Communist South Vietnamese a last chance and framework to prove their worth, and to the Communists a chance to win by means of the ballot.[7] But this "scenario"—which has finally become our last resort, except that officially we continue to beat around the bush and look for ways so to sweeten the pill as to change its nature—would have required a deliberate effort at reforming the Saigon regime; and it would have been far more credible if it had come *before* instead of *after* America's failure to achieve a military victory, the failure to "pacify" the countryside, the demonstration of domestic disunity and the systematic attempt at strengthening and legitimizing the Thieu-Ky regime. In any event, such a political solution could never have been more than a framework within which the non-Communist South Vietnamese, with their backs to the wall, might have *tried* to save their country from Communist rule.

There was a great difference between intervention-for-extrication and the kind of intervention-for-victory that we chose. One, its failure makes the costs of extrication higher, and, in my opinion, the chances of survival of a non-Communist South Vietnam far worse, due to the disruption which the war has inflicted and which, far from providing the non-Communist with belated opportunities for organization, must have laid the groundwork for the totalitarian *encadrement* of sullen and destitute masses, ready for revolution but alienated from anything Saigon stood for. Also, the possibility of organizing a coherent coalition of non-Communist leaders after the lacerations of jail or exile and the lassitude of war is pretty slim.

[7] To argue now that a peaceful Communist victory through elections was always an acceptable solution to us makes one wonder why we did not try to negotiate on such a basis sooner—and why we remain so ambivalent about any Communist participation in a post cease-fire, interim government.

Two, intervention-for-victory ensnared us in a network of traps and dilemmas we were foolish first not to see and later to court. To send a small army (say, up to 100,000 men) seemed too little for victory. To send an army capable of holding once and for all the liberated country-side (and given the fundamental need for pacification, holding was far more important to us than to our foe) would have required an effort we never really contemplated. To send a large army, yet one smaller than this was to create insuperable strategic problems. To keep our men in enclaves sacrificed what we deemed our main assets (mobility and firepower), as well as the countryside. To send them to fight guerrillas in the countryside would have meant far worse attrition for us than for them and given great opportunities to North Vietnam's main forces. To concentrate on fighting the latter meant focusing most attention on the conventional aspects of the war, and neglecting the villages and pacification. In trying a melange of the second and third strategies, we have ended with the worst of all worlds: the North Vietnamese forces have not been broken, the countryside has been lost, and while our mobility has kept us stabbing in the dark, the enemy has succeeded both in preserving most of his sanctuaries and in depriving us of security in ours.

Other sets of dilemmas have affected our policy toward Hanoi. In order to "break Hanoi's will," we would have had to bomb much closer to China, to close Haiphong, perhaps to invade the North; but effectiveness *on the spot* (in addition to being of debatable relevance to the final stake: control of the South) collided with the needs of prudence *at large*: our purpose, allegedly, was to avoid World War Three, to contain China, to convince Russia of its interest in such containment —not to destroy the regime in Hanoi, to promote a larger war, to provoke China's entry into it, and to oblige Russia to demonstrate more militantly its solidarity with a small Communist state. Thus, we chose prudence, at the cost of effectiveness. In our choice, however, we again produced the worst of all worlds: we put enough pressure on Hanoi to make impossible the reintroduction of external restraints on North Vietnam (comparable to Soviet and Chinese pressure in Geneva in 1954), and to reenforce the North Vietnamese national resolve and regime. But a combination of calculations of prudence and miscalculations of strategy (due to the misapplication of concepts derived from mixed-interest conflicts to one that was far closer to a zero-sum game) led us to apply our pressure so gradually as to allow the other side to adjust.

We also got the worst of all worlds in our relations with the South Vietnamese. Too reticent to take over those functions which they were mismanaging but which we know how to manage (be it garbage collection, or health services), reluctant or incompetent to reform areas of blatant corruption or brutality, unwilling to appear in control of the political process, we have nevertheless been saddled in the eyes of many—in South Vietnam and elsewhere—with responsibility for a client who would be swept away without us. At the same time, the Americanization of the war has worsened the client's condition: by providing the insurgents with a cause that is now both national and social, i.e., by reducing the difference between the second and the first Indochina wars, and making this one appear as the mere prolongation of the earlier one; by discouraging many non-Communists (in the villages or in the cities) from actively opposing the Communists on the side of the Americans; by introducing into an old, fragile and backward society a technological Frankenstein that completed the Communists' job of fostering insecurity and disruption (but *they* hope to be the beneficiaries, and are playing their game, whereas ours ought to have been the opposite) ; by thus bringing not merely physical but social destruction to the people we came to protect—and it is no solace to say that this is true in any war, given the special political nature and stakes of *this* one.

Caught in a lasso from which we could not escape, we could only tighten the noose through our twisting and squirming. If the anti-Communist majority failed to organize and unite because of Vietcong and North Vietnamese mischief, the situation was hopeless because the elimination of this mischief required both the demolition of South Vietnam's society and the political and social success of pacification which our acts of war precluded. If this lack of organization was inherent in South Vietnamese society, our task was hopeless because either the reform of that society would fail to take place as long as it was entrusted to its present leadership, product and beneficiary of its corruption, or else reform would have to be undertaken by us, and we neither knew how nor wanted to take over. We were in a vicious circle: in such a war, there can be no genuine pacification without security, but the search for security against so obstinate and omnipresent a foe could not but interfere with pacification, and one ended up with neither pacification nor security.

The verdict is somber: we have fought a war for objectives that were unreachable (the exemplary defeat of a large "national liberation movement," the restoration of our version of the Geneva Agreements, a stable South Vietnam with a non-Communist regime, the preservation of international stability by sticking to the partition line agreed upon between the great powers). The more those objectives eluded us, the more we have escalated our means, without realizing that the means we used made our goals even more unreachable and destroyed any chance there might have been of getting near them. As in previous total wars, the escalation of the means has led to an emotional and ideological escalation: for the greater the war machine, the losses, the wreckage, the more one had to justify them in terms of the vital importance of the stakes—thus making retreat so much more painful, since military deescalation will have to be accompanied by a kind of deescalation of the stakes: an operation that may well leave deep traces both in a public whose consent to future involvements may be affected by the leaders having cried wolf too often and too loud, and among Asian leaders whose earlier admiration for our stamina may lead to a mixture of horror for our excesses and distress at our failure to deliver goods we had proclaimed so essential to us and to them. The more we escalated the stakes, the higher (and more erroneous) were the expectations we created at home and abroad.

2. In this predicament, our original mistakes and the need to succeed made us grasp every illusion in the wind, and delude ourselves instead of facing the stark realities of South Vietnamese disaster and American *hybris*. Thus, we have pointed to facts that were true yet irrelevant as a way of comforting ourselves about our mission. We have demonstrated Hanoi's grip over the NLF in order to confirm our views about aggression, but we failed to see that the controlling facts were not Hanoi's control but the Vietcong's achievements and the connection between the civil war and the struggle for national unification. We have stressed the totalitarian character of North Vietnam, the post-1954 flow of refugees to the South, and thus justified our commitment to a free government for the South; but we failed to note that in an area where Western democracy is unknown, the efficiency of Hanoi's regime, its sense of purpose, and the remarkable discipline and commitment of its population were the decisive features: in the battle of symbols, we were fighting the steely image of a united and dedicated North with the misty mirage of a future model South. We have taken solace from the Southerners' failure to rally around the Vietcong, yet the decisive features here were, one, that

the Southern politicians who refused to go over to the NLF also refused to lead, or were prevented from leading, the South, and two, that the urban population that did not rise when the Vietcong came to the cities nevertheless provided the Vietcong with at least some help in organizing infiltration, and with the negative protection of secrecy; even *passive* support for us would not be enough to insure final victory in this kind of a war.

Sometimes, we have grasped at myths. One of them has been the great success of the elections in September 1967. Whatever progress they have represented on the long and tricky road to self-government, we should not conceal from ourselves either the fact that they were marked by irregularities that go far beyond tolerable, Western-type corruption, or the fact that the dominant branch of the Saigon regime is not the Assembly but an Executive whose representative character is small, or the fact that both the Assembly and Executive display South Vietnam's actual fragmentation far more than its potential unity. Another myth is that we may now turn many of our responsibilities back to the South Vietnamese—it is a myth in the sense that if we turn them over to the present Saigon regime, we are in all likelihood going to accelerate the decomposition of our protégés, and find that all the reasons that led us to rush in in 1965 operate even more strongly half a million men, God knows how many ruins and casualties, and three years later; whereas if we turn over those responsibilities to an enlarged and improved regime in the South, that regime may negotiate with the Vietcong terms of settlement that, at worst, could be far removed from those we still seem to hope to achieve in Paris, and at best, could have been obtained less bloodily some years ago. It would be a myth to believe that because of the military "stalemate" our foes might accept a kind of piece-meal solution (of local accommodations and cease-fire zones), as if the significance of a stalemate in this sort of asymmetrical war were the same as in Korea, as if there were truly organized political forces on both sides of the "stalemate," as if Communists were interested in a partition of South Vietnam, and as if one could avoid the crucial issue of ultimate control. It would anyhow be another myth to believe that we can achieve by negotiations with Hanoi what we have failed to win on the battlefield—the guarantee of a united, non-Communist independent South Vietnam, in which Communists would be disarmed and reduced to the position of a minority political party as in Greece.

And it was (or should I write *is*) a myth to believe that what we were engaged in was nation-building. This was both an illusion fed by a social science imbued with engineering pretensions, and an ideological justification for the less savory aspects of our role. In the first place, no state can do more than create or restore the conditions in which another nation's citizens can take the political, economic, and social measures that will provide the nation with a sense of community, adequate institutions and essential services. In the second place, whereas a war is often the crucible of national consciousness, internal peace is the requisite for nation-building. The disruptions of civil war may create the conditions for future nation-building: by sending to the cities large numbers of peasants in search either of a refuge or of a better income, by weakening the hold of the traditional family, of village notables, of regional, religious, or ethnic separatisms, by enriching certain "modern" classes and impoverishing other groups, etc. But out of such upheavals can come either final chaos, or nation-building; and the chances of the latter depend on the success of pacification, or on the advent of a negotiated peace. The destruction of an old building, the scattering of bricks and stones, the delivery to the construction site of cement, mortar, and sand, are not to be confused with the construction of a new edifice: on some sites, nothing ever gets built. We have too often confused the side effects of war with the labors of peace.

Finally, we have grasped at another, familiar kind of reassurance, which could hardly be suspected of being an illusion or a myth, since it is (or so it seems to us) the short-hand translation of hard facts: statistics. As long as the quest for certainty in the realms of essential uncertainty remains within the bounds of social science, one can marvel without indignation. But when the same fallacies become props of policy, irony is not enough. We have copulated with figures, and discovered at the end that it was incest, for the figures were all too often not the offspring of external achievements but the creations of our own phantasies. We have forgotten, first, that many of the statistics that comforted us were false, partial, or suspect in their origins; secondly, that even the believable figures had to be interpreted, and were meaningless out of context: thus, figures about the percentage of the population controlled by us, or about the miles of roads returned to safety, or the number of incidents, could either mean progress toward pacification and victory, or indicate a temporary shift in enemy strategy—such as his regrouping for the Tet offensive. One always comes back to our original sins—ignorance of the context and excessive self-confidence.

III

If we want to draw some lessons from this story, let us distinguish those that apply primarily to Vietnam, and the broader ones.

1. In Vietnam, all the reasons that we gave for fighting the war now ring hollow. Some of them were never really relevant. We have exaggerated the role of China in this conflict, and the degree to which a victory for Hanoi would mean an expansion of China's power and prestige: "it is hard to see how any likely outcome in Vietnam will ... speed up China's long and difficult effort to become a great power. ... China's power in Asia is dependent much more on factors other than what happens in Vietnam."[8] We have also exaggerated the domino effect of "national liberation" movements: they break out only where there are objective and subjective conditions of serious discontent, administrative and social neglect, ethnic or religious grievances, class inequities, and they do not reach the proportions of a civil war unless the degree of decomposition or inadequacy of the polity is very high. The chances for a Communist domination of such movements depend very largely on the Communists' aptitude at capturing the nationalist symbols. Thus, the two main deterrents are—positively—domestic attention to and reform of legitimate grievances, and—negatively—careful American abstention from too close an identification with threatened regimes, which could deprive them of their claim to represent their nations.

Many of the reasons we have given, while impressive, either have become irrelevant or cannot anymore be used as arguments for the war. The notion that our failure to save South Vietnam from a Communist take-over would, by itself, have a domino effect in Southeast Asia, weaken other governments and make them eager to appease their Communist neighbors is not false. But the force of the argument has never been sufficient to allow us to prevail in Vietnam, and indeed the argument required that we prevail at a reasonable cost: the higher the costs of our involvement, the more disquiet in Asian countries, not only because of the spectacle of the ruins accumulated by our protection, but also because of the likelihood that so massive

---

[8] Donald Zagoria, "Who's Afraid of the Domino Theory?," NY Times Magazine, April 21, 1968.

(and frustrating) an effort would never be tried again. When a German politician praised the American undertaking because of his conviction that "what the Americans do for South Vietnam they would do for us," the only likely reactions are a mixture of shudder *and* disbelief. The lesson learned by other Asians from our policy may well be that, rather than leaning too closely on us, they ought to placate our foes, instead of relinquishing to them the causes of nationalism, anti-imperialism, and anti-White racism.

The argument that our effort in Vietnam was necessary to weaken China's position and improve Russia's within world Communism also had some strength. Once again, however, the policy followed failed to serve the goal. China's weakening, while obvious, can hardly be attributed to us: a combination of domestic turmoil and diplomatic clumsiness explains it. But insofar as we are concerned with China's view of the way in which national liberation movements can effectively tie down the world's greatest power, neutralize its nuclear arsenal, and carry forward the struggle against imperialism, the spectacle of our entrapment in Vietnam—"the fly that captured the fly-paper"— can hardly be said to have disproved Marshal Lin Piao: as Professor Reischauer has written, if our goal was to demonstrate that such movements do not work, we have lost. As for the Soviets, whose enthusiasm for such movements has indeed been limited, our behavior has obliged them to display their solidarity with and support to North Vietnam, and it is only with the reversal of America's policy—not through its pursuit—that a chance for their playing a moderating role reemerges.

Finally, the argument about the need to establish a balance of power in Asia has evolved favorably for reasons largely independent of our stand in Vietnam, and connected with the fact that (besides China) only in Vietnam have Communism and nationalism been fused. Thus, the upheaval in Indonesia had to do with a nationalist revulsion against the Chinese and a China-inspired Communist party—and with the desperate instinct of survival of the Indonesian military, whom it is hard to imagine willing to let themselves be slaughtered but for America's stand in the jungles of Vietnam. Secondly, America's policy can hardly be said to have contributed to a balance of power in Asia. I have said earlier what I thought of our "buying-time" argument: if the main threat to "free Asia" is internal disruption (supported, to be sure, from outside but triggered and sustained by domestic factors), our military enterprise only diverted attention and (as in Thailand) resources from the "nation-building" tasks in Asian countries. In Europe, a balance could be established largely by military means, both because the threat was primarily military, and because the polities, economies, and societies could absorb, and provide a largely stable basis for, those military means. In Asia, neither the nature of the threat nor the nature of the societies justifies a transposition. There, the imbalance between America's might and the local friendly powers is such that a massive American military presence could only lead to a disastrous mixture of domination and disruption. Even if there were a serious threat of Chinese (or Communist Vietnamese) invasion of neighboring countries, the answer could not simply be the stationing of large quantities of American troops: for the political, economic, and social implications would be such as to open the way for internal wars while we were trying to plug holes at the borders.

2. We have thus reached the broader implications of our Vietnam experience. They can all be summarized in one formula: *from incorrect premises about a local situation and about our abilities, only a bad policy can follow.* Our policy in Vietnam has been exemplary in the sense of providing a complete catalogue of all the mistakes that can result from false premises. Let us proceed to three imperatives, and two final lessons.

A first imperative is to examine with greater rigor and depth each of the situations of trouble in which our intervention is at issue. This means that

a. we must shift from a vision of the world which gave at least implicitly priority to the notion of an external threat (spread *across* borders either by blatant means of outside intervention or invasion, or else by devious techniques of subversion) to an understanding of the *domestic priority,* i.e., of the fact that the opportunities open to our foes as well as to us depend on the internal realities of the various areas. This is why, for instance, there is no universal, standardized model of "national liberation": it was not the Maoist model that worked in Cuba, and the Cuban one failed in Bolivia. It was China's neglect of these domestic realities that has led to various setbacks; yet both in China's and in Russia's ideological pronouncements (for reasons that have to do with the focus and message of Marxism-Leninism) there is much more awareness of those domestic priorities than we have shown. Whatever reservations one may have on specific proposals he made throughout the years, one must pay tribute to George Kennan for his constant understanding of this point. The "internalization" of conflict results from the excessively high costs of conventional war, from the fact that the stakes of world politics are, more and more, the shaping of domestic societies, and from the phenomena of social mobilization which make the waging of foreign policy increasingly dependent on internal support, images, and institutions. Consequently, the policy-maker needs to find in the works of theoretically oriented social scientists not merely broad generalizations about the international system or about political development, but more particular and differentiated theories that attempt "to account for the policy-relevant variation among"[9] cases.

b. We must learn to distinguish much more carefully between types of interventions. We are primarily used to contests in which "winning" means imposing our strategy on an adversary in open battle. We also have some experience of waging successful, swift, and superficial coups. We have much less of the kind of intervention we found ourselves ensnared in on behalf of the Saigon regimes: an asymmetrical fight against a foe who obstinately refused to play our game, while being inventive and flexible enough to adapt his tactics to our presence; who succeeded in keeping the initiative even while we thought that our forays—on the ground and in the air—meant that it was ours; in a territory and over stakes that made of "winning" merely the gradual by-product of military control, social change, administrative and political reform, institutional creation and organization. We must learn in particular to distinguish between two kinds of interventions: *marginal* ones (which does not mean unimportant: they can be decisive) that allow a threatened society to deal with its problems in a way that strengthens its cohesion but does not jeopardize its autonomy and self-respect, and interventions that are so *massive* that they are counter-productive, either because they weaken the assisted partner (by spreading corruption, disrupting his administration or his economy), or because that partner lacks the institutional ability and social cohesion without which our intervention will be in vain. There is no substitute for area expertise, historical knowledge—

---

9 Alexander L. George, "Bridging the gap between scholarly research and policy-makers: the problem of theory and action," Rand Document, May 8, 1968. The implications of Vietnam for social science and for its relation to policy deserve a separate study.

and the kind of informed judgment that allows one to separate a hopeless case from a merely difficult one. There is, in this respect, at least one clear message from Vietnam: when a regime that is oppressive, or ineffective, or both is faced, not with an ordinary insurgency, but with a movement that is both superbly organized and capable of mounting an effective government and a social revolution in the areas that it holds, the chances of reversing the trend are very poor. It would be as foolish to mistake every rebellion for a genuine social movement, as it is to mistake every political leader for an authentic force. The key issues are those of the roots, the organization, the appeals; we must learn to distinguish movements that are broad, effective and legitimate from pseudo movements. Once again, the ability to discriminate is a prerequisite of policy, and requires in turn a social science more interested in asking the key questions of historical sociology than in collecting swamps of data.

A second imperative is to reexamine critically the limits of our power. This does not mean indulging either in an orgy of self-doubt or in a repudiation of an ungrateful outside world that resists our good intentions. It means assessing more realistically:

(1) The limits in the present international system of the kind of power that we have in greatest amounts: military and economic. Having written abundantly on this topic elsewhere,[10] I will merely sum up my point here: the new conditions of the use of force, the rise and strength of the nation-state, the heterogeneity of the system that reduces considerably the *direct* ability of any major power to shape the world according to its wishes. There is an excess of the power to *deny* over the power to *achieve* gains. In other words, our greatest impact comes through creating conditions in which the forces on which we count—the defenders of the status quo or the champions of moderate reform—can work: through military deterrence and various kinds of assistance. But these forms of help cannot succeed in denying all enemy gains, for they are not capable either of preventing him from exploiting at our expense (and through similar techniques of assistance, ranging from military and diplomatic) regional interstate disputes (as in the Middle East), nor are they capable of transforming an internal situation as hopeless as Vietnam. Moreover, when our deterrence and assistance succeed in consolidating non-Commu-

10 *Gulliver's Troubles*, Part 1.

nist regimes, there is no guarantee that these regimes will use their own power in ways that will please us, as we have found out in various parts of the world.

(2) The specific limitations that our history, our style and our institutions impose on our effectiveness. It is imperative that we know ourselves better. To be sure, one could argue that our massive resort to technological power in Vietnam results precisely from our exploitation of what we know to be our greatest asset. But this has to be weighed, not only against our ignorance of local realities that vitiated this asset, but also against our neglect of some serious psychological weaknesses: an overbearingly self-confident approach to complex problems; a tendency to reduce them to mere issues of management, without questioning the realism of the ends and therefore the adequacy of the means; an activism that conflicts with the needs for prudence and patience, and often reduces our associates to the position of subordinates and makes them resentful of our protection and of their dependence; an underestimation of the way in which other people's history and customs condition their reactions to present issues; a lack of understanding of social revolutions, of the kinds of violent movements that develop when there are no procedures of peaceful change and that are often not led by the kinds of elites with whom Americans are comfortable (a lack that results from our own experience of no such revolution, and makes us reserve our sympathies to non-Communist, purely nationalist ones);[11] also—last but not least —a tendency, when challenged, to be far more concerned with proving ourselves than with finding out whether our objectives are worthwhile or reachable, and whether our involvement serves them adequately. For what has been most striking in Vietnam is our way of turning that intricate contest (in which, by our own admission, we are not fully in control even of our side) into a test of our resolve, competence, and moral and material superiority. This is an old, and not a disgraceful feature. But precisely because of its importance in our make-up, it should make us careful about getting involved, if not only in confrontations we can win so as to avoid the self-lacerations of defeat (this would not be a very realistic imperative), at least only in confrontations that are so essential as to justify this heavy investment of our pride.

A third imperative, following from the first two, is precisely to redefine more carefully our national interest in the international com-

11 Cf. U.S. reticence toward the French resistance, in World War Two.

petition. Again, I will refer the reader to another piece of writing,[12] and make only a few remarks here:

a. For several reasons, we must learn to distinguish between two kinds of threats to "stability" (a much abused notion). On the one hand, there will arise in scores of countries risks of internal disruption that may be helped from abroad yet correspond to domestic realities. We must learn to live with such perils and to accept violent social and political change—even if private American interests happen to be the targets—even if Communists should occasionally be the local beneficiaries, and Communist powers the likely allies of the local winners. For there will never be any manageable international system if our statesmen pretend to play the role of cosmic Metternichs; and unless the consequence of those upheavals would be to put into power regimes hostile to us in important countries, such changes would not seriously endanger our position in the international competition. As for a revolutionary Communist takeover in countries that are of great importance in the world balance of power (by which I mean, not the nuclear balance, which seems safely in the hands of the two super powers, but the conventional military balance and even more the far less tangible diplomatic one), while it would undoubtedly be a blow to American interests and a source of international instability, it is hard to see how the United States could prevent it (would we have tried to overthrow a Communist regime in Indonesia?). We can only provide such countries with assistance to help them consolidate their internal cohesion, and avoid providing Communist or pro-Communist forces there with a cause through our excessive involvement. On the other hand, we should be concerned with the *external* implications of *internal* changes; we should be especially interested in preventing domestic disruptions from engulfing the major powers, and domestic revolutionary regimes from exporting their recipes by force. Our national interest in the moderate management of conflict ought therefore sometimes (as in inter-African conflicts) lead us to promote formulas for international or regional localization and neutralization, and in other places (as in Southeast Asia, where the threat comes from Communist regimes) encourage us to promote regional efforts at self-defense against risks either of invasion or of military interference with communications, under an American

12 *Gulliver's Troubles,* Chapter 10.

guarantee or with as unobtrusive a military assistance on our part as possible. Similarly, in Vietnam, our effort now ought to bear on the distinction between the settlement of the internal issues (which should be left as much as possible to the various factions of South Vietnamese) and the solution of the external implications of South Vietnam's self-determination (such as the withdrawal of foreign troops, neutralization of the country, the conditions of eventual unification of Vietnam, the guarantee of the borders in the area, and the immersion into this process of as broad a section of the international community as possible).

b. We must learn to establish a hierarchy of interests, of which the separation described in the previous paragraph is but one example. We must be guided by the following considerations. One, not every part of the world is of the same importance to us: it depends largely on two sets of factors—the intrinsic importance of the country or area, in resources, population, political influence, and (as in the case of Israel) abundance and intimacy of ties with us, and also its importance to our main adversaries (i.e., whether or not it constitutes a major stake for them). Two, even in countries or areas that are important to us, we may have a hierarchy of concerns. Whereas one could argue that in all such instances we have an interest in preserving them from outside aggression, the scope of our interests beyond this one must vary from case to case; in particular, a prudent foreign policy must beware of turning into a major stake the internal control of a highly unstable polity that we are badly equipped to preserve and reform.

In Vietnam, although a Vietcong victory was important to Peking as a test of its doctrine, such a victory was never tantamount to Peking control; therefore, the area itself should not have been deemed essential to us, to begin with. Moreover, the nature of the threat there was such as to justify a deliberate effort on our part to *minimize* the importance of domestic control, and to concentrate our efforts on the external aspects. For here lies one important lesson: in present day confrontations, when the super powers for obvious reasons engage only a small part of their military resources, tests of will are resolved less on the basis of the ratios of military might, than on that of the "balance of interests as manifested in the relative capacity of the opponents to convince each other that they will support their positions with war if necessary."[13] Let us apply this to Vietnam; our escalation in the South and in the North was an attempt to convince Hanoi and the NLF of our determination to support our position massively. But we failed to convince them that what was at stake—the control of South Vietnam—was of such overriding importance to us that we would pay for it the price of sacrificing more important American interests, such as our interest in avoiding heightened tension with Russia, and war with China; in avoiding a depletion of our military forces in Europe; in avoiding a domestic crisis over escalation: interests that would have been threatened, had we decided that denying the enemy control of Saigon was worth either even greater efforts at trying to "win," or a perpetuation of an indecisive war. We failed to convince them because, as we discovered the depth of our earlier illusions, we failed to convince ourselves: after the long and bloody detour of an escalation that was an escape from unsavory realities, they prevailed when we understood that the only way out of the lasso was an end to the war. On his side, the enemy succeeded in convincing us of his determination: for we came to realize that within the limits of escalation which were tolerable to us, he could continue to fight for stakes that were infinitely more central to his existence and *raison d'être*, than our stakes were to ours. So we gave up the fiction, backed by an impressive display of force, that Vietnam was like the wilderness of the international civil war; and the enemy imposed on us the reality of his resolve and of the difference between our power to destroy and our power to create.

There is one final lesson from Vietnam that ought to be remembered when the issue of intervention arises again. In international affairs, the normative requirements of political order and the normative requirements of ethics do not always coincide: not all moderate international systems, not all world empires have been based on or have dispensed justice. But it is both the moral duty and the political interest of statesmen to avoid policies that compound political and moral error, political inefficiency, and ethical ugliness. In Vietnam, our political and our moral roads, paved with good intentions, have led to hell. That same inadequacy of our means to unreachable objectives, that same tendency of the means to make the goals even more illusory, which have marked the political course of the war, also justify moral condemnation. For the ethics of foreign policy behavior

---

[13] Robert E. Osgood and Robert C. Tucker, *Force, Order and Justice* (Baltimore, 1967), p. 152.

is an ethics of consequences; no policy is ethical, however generous its ends, if success is ruled out; and no policy is ethical if the means corrupt or destroy the ends, if they are materially out of proportion with the ends, if they entail costs of value greater than the costs of not resorting to them—three precepts violated by our conduct in Vietnam. The ethics of foreign policy must be an ethics of self-restraint: our moral duty coincides with our political interest. From neither point of view can one support any policy of universal intervention; here again, prudence on the one hand, the ethical judgment on the ends and on the relation of means to ends on the other converge.

By definition, political interest and moral duty in political affairs can be defined only case by case, and general guidelines are of little help. But the extreme case of Vietnam gives one a good, if tragic idea, of the kinds of things that cannot be brought off and should not be undertaken; of the bad effect of letting general principles and familiar techniques of action be sloppily applied without sufficient consideration of the special circumstances of the case and of the special disabilities of the actors. The saddest aspect of the Vietnam tragedy is that it combines moral aberration and intellectual scandal—and yet perhaps we should be impressed by the rather rare fact that in a world where these two sets of values—those of moral action and of political effectiveness—are often far apart, they have been reunited in so exemplary an instance.

Patterns of Intervention

RICHARD J. BARNET

THE UNITED STATES has become increasingly outspoken in claiming the unilateral right to make the determination whether a conflict anywhere in the world constitutes a threat to its national security or international order, and what should be done about it. Only those states "with enough will and enough resources to see to it that others do not violate" the rules of international law, Secretary of State Rusk has declared, are the ones to be entrusted with enforcing the peace. When he was Under Secretary of State, George Ball suggested that such responsibility "may in today's world be possible . . . only for nations such as the United States which command resources on a scale adequate to the requirements of leadership in the twentieth century." In other words, power is the basis of legitimacy. Conceding that the "world community" has not granted the United States the warrant to police the world in any legal sense—the United Nations Charter gives the Security Council the primary responsibility for dealing with threats to the peace—those in charge of U.S. national security policy nonetheless assert that because of the deep divisions in the United Nations which render that organization immobile, the United States must act alone. John Foster Dulles recognized that "most of the countries of the world" did not share his ideological view of international politics—"the view that Communist control of any government anywhere is in itself a danger and a threat." Pointing out that it was not difficult "to marshal world opinion against aggression," he noted in the midst of the 1954 Indo-China crisis that "it is quite another matter to fight against internal changes in one country. If we take a position against a Communist faction within a foreign country we have to act alone." His brother, Allen, formerly director of the Central Intelligence Agency, candidly stated the unilateral criteria by which the United States decides whether or not to intervene in a civil war:

> . . . we cannot safely limit our response to the Communist strategy of take-over solely to those cases where we are invited in by a government still in power, or even to instances where a threatened country has first exhausted its own, possibly meager, resources in the "good fight" against Communism. We ourselves must determine when and

how to act, hopefully with the support of other leading Free World countries who may be in a position to help, keeping in mind the requirements of our own national security.

There is nothing exceptional about powerful countries asserting the imperial prerogative of using force and coercion on the territory of another without its consent. The Athenian empire minced no words about this; "The strong do what they can and the weak do what they must," Pericles reminded his fellow citizens. Empire is its own justification, the fifteenth century Italian humanist, Lorenzo Valla advised his prince. The expansion of a nation's power comes through "mere violence," but this should not dismay a conscientious leader, his contemporary Poggio Bracciolini observed, for has it not always been "the most powerful empires such as Athens, which promoted letters and learning?" Most empires have claimed the right to control the politics of other peoples in the name of a great idea. Athens offered protection and civilization; Rome, the blessings of the law; Britain, enlightenment of savages; and so on. Once having assumed "responsibility" for other countries, imperial bureaucracies feel as Pericles did, that "it is not safe to let it go."

The United Nations Charter rests on the principle that the preservation of peace and the protection of national security is a matter for multilateral decision. The community of nations is supposed to decide what action to take to meet threats to the peace. In a bow to realism the framers of the Charter vested the primary "community" responsibility in the hands of the big powers who were given permanent seats on the Security Council. Adlai Stevenson remarked shortly before his death that it was time "to decide whether we're going to be international and multilateral or not." He was alluding to the fact that despite the rhetorical commitment to multilateralism the U.S. was more and more making the great decisions alone. No other country or international organization was consulted over the Kennedy administration decision to force a nuclear confrontation over the Cuban missile crisis or the Johnson administration decision to send a huge expeditionary force to Vietnam and to subject that country to daily aerial bombardment. The State Department has been sensitive to the charges of unilateralism and has tried to deal with it in two ways. One is by asserting that since the criminal elements in world politics make the operation of a true multilateral structure impossible, the United States, by vigorously opposing them, is actually working to build a true "world of diversity." As Secretary of State Rusk put it, "Once we remove this kind of aggression, as we are trying to do in Viet Nam, the human race can perhaps look forward to peace, to the solution of lesser problems, and to the benefits deriving from the conquest of science." This is the image of a surgeon removing a cancer. The operation, President Johnson has hinted in his more optimistic moments, can be completed "in this generation." Once the enemies of freedom are defeated, then the U.S. can perhaps share some of its police responsibilities with others.

The second way the U.S. has tried to deal with charges of unilateralism has been increased reliance on nominal or subservient multilateral organizations such as the Inter-American Force for the Dominican Republic which was called into being at the initiative of the United States and was always under its operational direction. Where the U.S. is a member of a regional organization which excludes another great power, that organization, simply because of the overwhelming might of the United States, inevitably becomes its instrument. The essential difference between the Organization of American States and the United Nations is that the latter organization contains some nations that are economically and politically independent of the United States.

Behind the speeches and diplomatic maneuverings to soothe "world opinion," the architects of U.S. foreign policy have developed a rationale to justify global intervention which frankly recognizes that the American responsibility to police the world is inconsistent with the multilateralism of the U.N. Charter and the dictates of traditional international law. Anthony Eden recalls that when John Foster Dulles warned the British Foreign Secretary in 1954 that he would stop British vessels on the high seas to prevent any arms shipments to Guatemala, he observed that the U.S. was prepared to take "whatever action was necessary, whatever the law might be" and went on to remark that "in the cold war conditions of today, the rules applicable in the past no longer seemed to him to meet the situation and required to be revised or flexibly applied." The Johnson Doctrine which denies the validity of the distinction between civil wars and international wars and the State Department's "modern" view of the doctrine of nonintervention are more recent additions to official legal revisionism.

There are two principal arguments advanced in support of the policy which purport to rest on broad world community interests rather than narrow nationalistic considerations. They simply do not stand up to examination. One is that the U.S. is defending "freedom" against "totalitarianism." The free governments that have received either generous U.S. military aid, friendly nods from the U.S. embassy, or direct military intervention in their behalf, constitute a group that on the whole is rather careless about civil liberties—Formosa, Korea, South Vietnam, Iran, Brazil, Paraguay, etc. Indeed, the overwhelming majority of U.S. aid has gone to a series of military dictatorships located at the periphery of Russia and China.

Nor has the test of U.S. concern been the violent character of a government's accession to power. Military coups which seize power from constitutional regimes are consistently recognized and supported, and, on occasion (Brazil in 1964, for example) encouraged. Here are a few examples of military takeovers which the United States did not oppose (and in most cases welcomed): Argentina (1955); Turkey (1960); South Korea (1961); Peru (1962); Burma (1962); Indonesia (1966) ; Ghana (1966).

The defense of freedom has not even resulted in a consistent anti-Communist policy. In the area under the direct control of the Soviet Union and China, U.S. involvement has been circumspect. After the State Department lost the diplomatic battle at the close of the Second World War to retain some Western influence in Eastern Europe, the United States did not take military measures to oppose the Communist coup in Czechoslovakia in 1948 or to aid anti-Soviet insurgent movements including the Berlin uprising of 1953, the Poznan riots, and the Hungarian revolution. Low-level covert operations were conducted against the Eastern European regimes from 1947 into the 1960's, including espionage, and U-2 overflights, as well as subversive propaganda over Radio Free Europe and Radio Liberation. But the rhetorical goal of "liberation" was proclaimed by Dulles only after the actual attempt to roll back Soviet power in Eastern Europe had been abandoned. With respect to China, the United States has given the Taiwan government $2,000,000,000 with which to equip its 600,000 man army and has put U-2 aircraft at its disposal for overflights of the mainland, but for many years it has made it reasonably clear that it will not sponsor the invasion Chiang still says he will mount.

While most U.S. support has gone to right-wing dictatorships, in the late 1950's, and particularly in the Kennedy administration, the U.S. attempted to modernize its strategy of intervention. The Truman administration and the Eisenhower administration in its first term had given wholehearted support to "legitimate" governments if they were non-Communist and friendly to the United States, no matter how oppressive or reactionary they might be. President Eisenhower symbolized this policy by inviting Pedro Jimenez, the brutal dictator of Venezuela to Washington and awarding him the Medal of Merit. But a few years later American intelligence agencies and private groups acting in their behalf began to support more liberal and even leftist elements in Latin America and Africa. The Central Intelligence Agency gave funds for the support of institutions like the Inter-American Center of Economic and Social Studies and the Institute for International Labor Research in the Dominican Republic and the Institute of Political Education in Costa Rica. These institutions train, finance, and encourage political groups which often oppose their own governments for being too conservative and are also critical of official U.S. policy in Latin America, but are anti-Communist. It appears that resistance leaders from Mozambique and South Africa have been offered covert assistance by the C.I.A. and in certain cases have received it. In Algeria the A.F.L-C.I.O., acting for the C.I.A., gave direct financial assistance to the National Liberation Front from 1957 until the successful end of the War of Independence. The American labor organization sponsored the Algerian rebels in international labor circles and arranged for membership of the F.L.N. union in the I.C.F.T.U., the U.S. dominated world federation of trade unions. The National Student association, an ostensibly private organization, distributed C.I.A. funds to Algerian resistance leaders in the form of scholarships. The operation in Algeria in support of the rebels was designed to discourage them from turning to Communist countries for help. At the same time the State Department, still officially supporting France, continued to sanction military aid for use against the F.L.N.

The worldwide pattern of U.S. military involvement which emerges is thus impossible to reconcile with a global campaign to preserve freedom. For the most part U.S. interventions have had a strong ideological thrust, either to support anti-Communist regimes threatened with subversion or to subvert Communist, Communist-leaning, or potentially Communist-leaning regimes, many of which have been at least as "free" as Stroessner's Paraguay or Ky's Vietnam. In some cases, such as Laos, the Dominican Republic, and Algeria, different U.S. agencies have intervened on both sides. The almost automatic reaction has been to commit U.S. military power where it appears necessary to prevent a Communist takeover, except where the Soviets or the Chinese are likely to respond with a major war. The Chinese invasion of Tibet, for example, a much less ambiguous case of violent seizure of power by an external Communist regime than either Greece or Vietnam, was ignored because it was so clearly beyond the power of the U.S. to do much about it short of a war with China. But it appears that the only areas where U.S. leaders consider it too risky to sponsor a major military intervention are the immediate rimland of China and Eastern Europe. Elsewhere, while the dangers of escalation are always present, the experience of twenty years suggests that the Communist powers will support the Communist side but will not seek to deter or oppose U.S. intervention through a direct confrontation with American military power. Naturally, however, the U.S. prefers to rely on intelligence operations, aid officials, and military missions to influence the political direction of third-world governments rather than to order its counter-insurgency forces into action.

U.S. national security managers have tried in some countries to promote reforms, but they have continually shown, as in Guatemala, Vietnam, and in other places, that they are prepared to sacrifice reform to the goal of anti-Communism. And by covertly supporting leftist revolutionaries in Latin America and Africa they have shown themselves to be willing to compromise ideological purity for the sake of maintaining a degree of U.S. influence and control, which often becomes the principal end in itself.

U.S. officials make a second claim that America is somehow acting in the interest of the international community by undertaking a worldwide campaign against revolution. The argument is that by stamping out insurgent movements the U.S. is preventing World War III. With his eyes firmly fixed on the shore he has left, to quote Tocqueville's phrase, the national security manager is trying to squeeze the baffling chaos of postwar revolution into the familiar mold of great-power politics as practiced in the 1930's. Ho Chi Minh becomes Hitler. Vietnam is the Rhineland. Negotiation is Munich. If the insurgents are not stopped in Vietnam, they will have to be stopped eventually in San Francisco.

President Kennedy's speech to the American people after his encounter with Khrushchev in Vienna is a good example of this official thought process:

He was certain that the tide was moving his way, that the revolution of rising people would eventually be a Communist revolution, and that the so-called wars of national liberation supported by the Kremlin would replace the old methods of direct aggression and invasion.

In the 1940's and early 50's the great danger was from Communist armies marching across free borders, which we saw in Korea . . . now we face a new and different threat. We no longer have a nuclear monopoly. Their missiles, they believe, will hold off our missiles, and their troops can match our troops should we intervene in the so-called wars of liberation. Thus, the local conflicts they support can turn in their favor through guerrillas, or insurgents, or subversion.

The essence of the argument is that guerrillas in Vietnam, Thailand, Peru, Guatemala, and Angola are all part of the same army. If the army can be defeated in Vietnam, it will not be necessary to fight it in Thailand or the Philippines. If the insurgencies are not opposed, that will demonstrate a lack of resolve, just as Munich did, and eventually the guerrillas will challenge the U.S. directly and then we will have to fight World War III to defend our homes and honor. The assumption that insurgencies are inspired by outside powers or that they are orchestrated by some central authority is false. The defeat of the Vietcong will not mean that the insurgents in Thailand will surrender. Nor will a guerrilla victory in Vietnam insure a guerrilla victory in Thailand. True, revolutionary successes will encourage insurgents elsewhere. More important, it will demonstrate to governments whose survival depend upon U.S. military aid to rule their discontented populations that since the U.S. cannot keep its commitments to them, their days are numbered.

Why, however, the overthrow of corrupt feudal regimes by local insurgents should pose a danger of World War or a direct military threat to the United States is hard to see. The danger of World War arises only if the United States is committed to resisting revolution by force and is prepared to "pay any price" to do it, and then only if another major power is prepared to stand in the way. Even if we assume a wave of successful revolutions throughout Asia, Africa, and Latin America, the notion that the Castros of the future will muster an army of millions, transport them by sampan and burro, and loose them on our cities is nothing less than a psychotic phantasy, so absurd in fact that it is never explicitly stated, only hinted at in vague anxiety producing historical analogies. (What is so sad about being ruled by such phantasies is that the diversion of money and energy to the fight which is supposed to keep Asian Communists from landing on our shores helps perpetuate the conditions which have created native insurgents and guerrilla warfare in American cities.)

Thus the means which the U.S. has chosen to deal with the phenomenon of revolution make war more likely rather than less. The idea of preventive war—you fight a little one now to avoid a great one later—has some validity if you are facing a single adversary such as Hitler. Where there are many adversaries, each with its own local reasons for fighting, the idea can be understood only as an exercise in mysticism, not logic. In short, the arrogation by a single power of the policeman's warrant is not a solution to the problem of war.

The ideology of the American responsibility rests on a fundamental assumption concerning American self-interest. The only alternative to a Pax Americana is a Pax Sovietica or the Peace of Peking. The most powerful nation in the world has always dominated the rest. The only question is which one will emerge on top. Comforted by Talleyrand's fashionable aphorism about nonintervention—"a metaphysical term which means about the same as intervention"—the national security manager concludes that the fate of the powerful is to dominate whether they wish to do so or not. There is much to this observation. If the United States never sent a soldier or an aid dollar beyond her shores, it would still wield enormous power over other nations, particularly in the third world, by virtue of the fact that it is the world's biggest customer. The power to cut off imports from a one-crop country is as effective an instrument of control as occupying its capital. The United States has the dominant voice in the World Bank and the International Monetary Fund and private U.S. financial interests control much of the world money market. Countries struggling to industrialize are heavily dependent upon U.S. machinery. Most of the state-owned airlines of the world, to take one example, fly American equipment and are dependent upon U.S. corporations for servicing and replacement.

But beyond the operation of what is still termed the "private market," despite the considerable involvement of the government in these activities, is the panoply of techniques available to the national security bureaucracy to influence the political behavior of other countries. In many countries of the world the United States is the sole supplier of the army, the primary source of training for its officers, and the educator and supplier of its police force. In addition, through its aid program the United States is likely to have conceived and staffed the educational system, to be the dominant voice in its agricultural development, the organizer of its labor movement, and the decisive influence in setting the national priorities for economic development. U.S. views, private and official, predominate as a consequence of Voice of America, of the Armed Forces Radio and T.V. stations which are widely distributed, and of the increasingly wide circulation of U.S. newspapers and periodicals. Many of the individuals who provide these services do so with generous intentions but the effect of their efforts is to give the United States a powerful voice in the internal affairs of other countries. And that, as a succession of secretaries of state have promised Congress, is their primary purpose. Desmond Fitzgerald, formerly a high official of the International Cooperation Administration (predecessor to A.I.D.) who later directed covert operations for the C.I.A. put it this way: "A lot of criticism of foreign aid is because the critic thought the objective was to get economic growth, and this wasn't the objective at all. . . . The objective may have been to let a lease or to get a favorable vote in the U.N., or to keep a nation from falling apart, or to keep some country from giving the Russians airbase rights or any one of many other reasons." In a small country like the Dominican Republic, or even a larger one with a fairly primitive political structure and a large contingent of American officials, like Ethiopia, the U.S. embassy is inevitably the center of power in the country, if only because its capacity to control communications and intelligence is so far superior to that of the native government. In Ethiopia, the U.S. dramatized this fact by returning the Emperor to his kingdom (he had been deposed in a military coup while on a foreign visit) in a U.S. Air Force plane.

These facts of international life are cited by the proponents of an interventionary foreign policy as proving the inevitability of the unilateral use of force for "peace-keeping," i.e., police purposes. The United States is so deeply involved anyway in the use of coercive techniques to influence political behavior that the overt use of force, regrettable as it is, is merely a difference in degree, not in kind. If the U.S. were not prepared to use violence to deal with internal political problems in other countries when it conceives that its own national interests warrant it, its chief rivals would sponsor violence to their own advantage. In short, the prevailing official view is that there is no way for a great country to relate to a small one other than as manipulator or exploiter.

History appears to support this view. All the pressures of contemporary politics seem to push great nations into familiar imperial patterns. Indeed, when the United States adopted the policy embodied in the Truman Doctrine, State Department officials quite consciously saw themselves as inheritors of Britain's imperial responsibilities, which, they assumed, they would exercise more wisely and more humanely.

As a State Department publicity release would put it years later, "Strict adherence to our ideals requires us to face the challenge of reshaping the world in the image of human dignity, political freedom, and authority by consent, not decree." Like their models in Whitehall, the national security manager too assumed that if America could bring order to the world as a consequence of amassing an empire, that was not a bad bargain for the rest of mankind.

Thus, despite the rhetorical hopes for collective security and community responsibility which U.S. officials voice in speeches before the United Nations, back in their own offices they see no better alternative model for world order than the imperial model, to be constructed, hopefully, with as light a touch as possible. It is not surprising that they should come to this conclusion. The very nature of the nation-state, their oath of office, and their primary allegiance as well as the pressures of Congress and their superiors, all require the national security manager to serve the national interest, as the military, the corporations, the farmers, and the labor unions see it, rather than an abstract "world community" or such altruistic a goal as removing the grossest inequalities among the developed and undeveloped nations. He is quite free to think about a world security system as long as he does not compromise the power of the Joint Chiefs of Staff to decide where the forces should be deployed, what weapons should be used, and when. He is encouraged to develop an aid program provided U.S. business benefits adequately and he can convince Congress that the U.S. has received sound value in influence, business concessions, or political support. Above all, he must not be so indiscreet as to sponsor a "give away." The pressures of various interest groups within the United States for an imperialist relationship are enormous, but one should not ignore the role of the bureaucracy itself. It is an exhilarating experience for a GS-14 to run the police force, lecture the Minister of Interior, or reform the agriculture of a little country. Many Americans have found an outlet for social and political experimentation on new frontiers abroad that is denied them at home. Since the overseas bureaucracy totals some five million individuals it constitutes, in itself, an impressive interest group with a vested interest in keeping the mechanics of foreign relations much as they are. This means retaining control of vital decisions concerning a country's policies on defense and economic development in American hands.

Unilateralism is a politer and perhaps less image-rich term than imperialism, which not only evokes memories of Lord Clive, Cecil

Rhodes, and the French Foreign Legion, but also has become saddled with Lenin's particular theories of economic causation. But they mean essentially the same thing—"the extension of control" by a single nation. Unilateralism is so much taken for granted within the national security bureaucracy that when critics point out the discrepancy between our professed political and legal ideals as embodied in the U.N. Charter and our actual behavior as a nation, it makes very little impression. What's wrong with imperialism or unilateralism? Is there anything better?

There are two ways of trying to answer the first question. One is to look at unilateralism from the point of view of U.S. national interests. The second is to consider it from what might be called a "world order" perspective, looking specifically toward the development of a strong legal and constitutional structure for dealing with war, hunger, disease, and other overriding global problems. I recognize that the two categories are not wholly distinct, that there are few objective criteria for determining national interests, and that a sensible government in the nuclear age would have as a primary "national interest" the development of a good system for "world order." But the categories are useful for distinguishing the most short-range and parochial considerations from longer range perspectives. I will however limit myself here to a consideration of aspects of U.S. national interest.

From the standpoint of a U.S. president, thinking about reelection, concerned with solving domestic problems, and assuring himself a decent place in history, unilateralism is proving to be a disastrous policy. C. E. Black in *The Dynamics of Modernization* estimates that we must anticipate "ten to fifteen revolutions a year for the foreseeable future in the less developed societies." The suppression of a single revolutionary movement in Vietnam, admittedly a long developing and powerful one, costs the U.S. Treasury almost $60 billion a year, at least 10,000 battle deaths annually, and has stirred up political dissension unprecedented in our history. The attempt of one nation to deal simultaneously with insurgent movements in a dozen other places and to forestall still others in a variety of backward countries on three continents would tax the intellectual and political energies of the government to the breaking point.

One of the problems with imperialism is that as decision-making authority becomes centralized, the burdens on the imperialist leaders become intolerable, for along with the trappings of added power come political headaches. The Founding Fathers wisely spared the president of the United States the burden of appointing state and local officials. I suspect that they would be appalled to discover that he must now regularly pass on the qualifications of provincial governors in South Vietnam and ministers of agriculture in the Dominican Republic. There is literally no country in which the foreign policy bureaucracy cannot discover a "U.S. interest," and since the president has at his disposal an almost infinite variety of techniques for furthering those interests, he is constantly called upon to exercise his judgment. Having no first-hand knowledge of the politics of the countries he is asked to set on one course or another, this imposes something of a strain on him. As Telford Taylor puts it, "the road to everywhere leads nowhere." The President faces a familiar problem of empire. Having asserted an interest in a far-away land, he is expected to be able to control events there. In fact, the events begin to control him. Once military forces are committed, for example, it is usually impossible to limit the objectives to those which originally impelled the intervention. The commitment of national power unleashes political forces both in the country concerned and in the United States which then severely limit future choices.

The essence of unilateralism is that you recognize no limits except those of your own making. Such enlargement of the area of political discretion invites miscalculation and error. One of the functions of legal limits in a society is to provide external standards to relieve men of the responsibility to decide every issue anew. Sharing responsibility for decision with others who are also affected by it, the essence of democratic theory, is another old political device for rescuing human leaders from the dangers of distorted vision, a disability that always afflicts those who exercise power despotically. The possession of great power is not, as Secretary of State Rusk and others have suggested, a justification for using it unilaterally. It is rather a condition, as the framers of the U.S. Constitution recognized, which cries out for legal restraints to protect the community from tyranny and the possessor from his own *hubris*.

The assertion of a police responsibility to prevent violent revolution and insurgency inevitably requires a militarization of a nation's foreign policy. *Webster's International Dictionary* uses the terms "militarism" and "imperialism" interchangeably, and this makes good political as well as linguistic sense since no nation, no matter how great its economic and political resources, can hope to maintain control of events in distant lands without eventually relying chiefly on force. We have seen how, in Greece, for example, and later in Vietnam non-military strategies of "counterinsurgency" were swallowed up in the military effort. If the United States sets as a goal the prevention of regimes in the third world which call themselves Communist or which seem to lean to Communism, it must be prepared to fight for that goal with its military power.

The result of such a decision, and it is one that was made a long time ago, is to make the United States the Number One Enemy of a great number of people. State Department officials are privately scornful about foreign policy criticism based on the argument that "world opinion" is turning against us. They point out, rightly, that no one knows what that means or how to measure it if they did. The U.S., however, is very much interested in those leaders of the third world who are convinced that only radical change can rescue their societies from political tyranny and economic stagnation. Such leaders, who are coming increasingly to see violence as the only avenue of change, are being drawn together only by their common fear and hatred of the United States. American foreign policy is providing what Marxism-Leninism has failed to offer revolutionary movements: An ideological bond to tie together nationalist revolutionary movements spread across three continents. These movements originate in the local political soil. They are primarily concerned with local issues and local enemies. But the leaders of insurgent movements are establishing international links and are attempting to help one another, despite their limited resources. They do this not because of shared ideological goals so much as because of the belief that they are partisans in the same war. What gives unity to the struggle in their analysis is "imperialism," which means chiefly the United States. To be able to characterize the enemy in an insurgent struggle as a giant White Imperialist Power brings nationalists of all classes into the revolutionary coalition. Juan Bosch exaggerated only slightly when he declared that where there were 53 Communists in the Dominican Republic before the intervention, there were now 53,000.

Nationalism and anti-imperialism are such strong forces that only those politicians, businessmen, and generals, who benefit directly and personally from the American presence in their country, can be counted on to oppose nationalist movements. Such movements may start, as we have seen, with the efforts of a few energetic individuals. A small minority always takes the lead. But the nationalist impulse runs through the societies of the third world. If the United States continues to make it a policy to oppose nationalism wherever it is entwined with a radical political and economic program or with Communist rhetoric, it must count on being hated and feared by political leaders who will increasingly come to speak for a majority of the world population. It must be prepared to pay heavily to keep the loyalty of its clients. Pericles warned the people of Athens that the fate of greatness was to be hated and feared and some of the same philosophy prevails today in the corridors of the State Department. Yet even the most powerful country in the world takes a reckless view of national security if it ignores repeated historical patterns. As Walter Lippmann has pointed out, where one nation arrogates to itself the responsibility to shape a world order, it invites others to combine against it. In a world where nuclear weapons will, in all likelihood, be widely distributed before the end of the century, this is not a reassuring road to national security for the American people.

VIII. DOCUMENTARY APPENDICES

The April 1968 Manifesto and Political Program of the Alliance of Nationalist, Democratic, and Peace Forces

[Text] The conference of delegates of the Vietnam Alliance of Nationalist, Democratic, and Peace Forces was held 20-21 April near Saigon-Cholon to elect its central committee and issue a declaration asserting its stand and program of action. The objective of the conference is to unite the line and organization of the alliance movement, which has come into existence and made rapid developments in many urban cities, to fully develop its influence and role and worthily contribute to the national salvation task of our entire people. Attending the conference were many members of the alliance's Saigon steering committee and representatives of various patriotic and democratic forces, including many notables, intellectuals, students, writers, newsmen, businessmen, officers, civil servants, and many others, representing different political and religious organizations. Many organizations of the Vietnam Alliance of Nationalist, Democratic, and Peace Forces in various areas sent messages expressing full support for and confidence in the conference, their readiness to implement all its decisions, and their trust in the central committee elected by the conference.

1—In his opening speech on behalf of the steering committee, Lawyer Trinh Dinh Thao related the South Vietnamese people's 10-year struggle for national salvation, especially the struggle movement of urban people, and the progressive changes among the above-mentioned strata, including civil servants and officers under U.S. imperialist neocolonialism, particularly from the time when U.S. expeditionary troops were flown in to directly invade the south. Lawyer Trinh Dinh Thao also reviewed the evolution and composition of the Vietnam Alliance of Nationalist, Democratic, and Peaceful Forces, pointing out the objectives and requirements of the conference.

2—Based on the above consideration of the situation and requirements of the revolution, the conference warmly debated and passed a statement clearly defining the enemy, asserting the alliance's stand, and setting forth a short-range and long-range action program for liberating and rebuilding South Vietnam and advancing toward national unification peacefully.

Mr. Lam Van Tot, by appointment of the conference, read this national salvation statement. The conference unanimously noted that during the past 10 years, the U.S. imperialists have intervened increasingly deeper in South Vietnam, have brazenly encroached upon the 1954 Geneva accords on Vietnam, have set up a series of puppet governments—from Ngo Dinh Diem to Nguyen Van Thieu and Nguyen Cao Ky—have waged an aggressive war against the Vietnamese people, and have plotted to partition Vietnam forever and turn South Vietnam into a new-type U.S. colony. To save their lackeys in South Vietnam from complete collapse, since 1965 the U.S. Government has massively introduced hundreds of thousands of U.S. expeditionary and satellite troops to directly wage the aggressive war against South Vietnam while waging the war of destruction against the Democratic Republic of Vietnam.

The South Vietnamese people have fought very gallantly, achieved increasingly big victories—especially during spring 1968—dealt decisive blows to the Americans, and driven them and their lackeys into serious defeat and stalemate in both north and south. The U.S. imperialists' unjust war has been strongly condemned by world people, including Americans.

Although they have sustained heavy defeats, the obdurate and cunning U.S. imperialists have set forth deceitful peace arguments while escalating the war. Their unprecedentedly violent, protracted, and increasingly fierce aggressive war has caused numerous deaths, suffering, and savage destruction, (?seriously damaging) the material and intellectual life of our urban and rural compatriots. National sovereignty and democratic freedoms have been trampled. The South Vietnamese economy faces deadlock and decline. Cultural and social activities are depraved daily. The aggressive face of the U.S. Government and the country-selling face of the Saigon authorities—from Ngo Dinh Diem to Nguyen Van Thieu and Nguyen Cao Ky—have been bared to city dwellers.

Aspirations for independence and peace have become increasingly pressing. The struggle movement of city people's strata has mounted higher and higher in harmony with the repeated victories of rural compatriots. Intellectuals, students, writers, journalists, teachers, civil servants, private enterprise employees, businessmen, and others of various political parties and tendencies and increasingly large numbers of political and cultural organizations have joined the anti-U.S. movement, and those movements struggling for peace, independence, sovereignty, and democracy. From these struggle movements has gradually emerged a political front called the Vietnam Alliance of Nationalist, Democratic, and Peace Forces, founded to unite all patriotic forces and individuals that are determined to struggle against foreign aggression, overthrow the Nguyen Van Thieu-Nguyen Cao Ky puppet regime, set up a national coalition government, and gain independence, democracy, and peace.

The alliance's action program composes the following main points: To put an end to the war, restore peace, achieve national independence and sovereignty, build South Vietnam into an independent, free, peaceful, neutral, and prosperous nation, and advance toward unifying the country peacefully on the basis of equal discussions between north and south.

3—After many consultations and exchanges of views, the conference has elected the Vietnam Alliance of Nationalist, Democratic, and Peace Forces Central Committee which consists of lawyer Trinh Dinh Thao, chairman; engineer and proprietor Lam Van Tot and Venerable Thich Don Hau, vice chairmen; Prof. (Phan Vuong Tri), secretary general; woman doctor Duong Quynh Hoa, Thanh Nghi, writer; and Le Hieu Bang, student, deputy secretary generals; and Prof. Nguyen Van Kiet, specialist Huynh Van Nghi, and Prof. Tran Tu Luc, standing committee members; not to mention the names of other members and representatives of people from all walks of life and various political and religious trends which have not been announced yet.

4—The conference highly welcomed the heroic and courageous combat spirit of our people in North and South Vietnam, in rural areas and in the cities, who have overcome tremendous hardships and have made innumerable sacrifices, to bring national liberation near to complete success. The conference particularly praised the 1968 early spring successes which will certainly be fostered more strongly.

The conference sent greetings of sincere unity to the South Vietnam National Liberation Front, a patriotic force which has contributed substantially to the national liberation. It advocated associating its activities with that Front to regain independence for our people and restore peace in our country. The conference sent greetings and thanks to the government and people of various countries, including progressive Americans, who have unanimously supported the Vietnamese people's just cause; and it fervently hopes that such support will become stronger and more intense. The conference appealed to all our people in the country and abroad, especially the urban people, to close their ranks, develop their forces, and double their efforts to defeat the foreign aggressors to regain independence, freedom, democracy, and true peace for our people. The conference also appealed to patriotic forces among the Saigon puppet government's officers, enlisted men and civil servants to cooperate with the people to defeat the U.S. war of aggression, overthrow their lackey puppets, to regain independence for our people, and to achieve true peace in our country.

5—After many exchanges of views, the conference adopted the official flag and anthem for the Vietnam Alliance of Nationalist, Democratic, and Peaceful Forces.

The conference ended in an encouraging atmosphere of unity and confidence in certain victory for the just cause of our people and the glorious role of the Vietnam Alliance of Nationalist, Democratic, and Peaceful Forces in stopping the war, restoring peace, and achieving independence for our people.

21 April 1968

Working Paper of U.S. State Department on the North Vietnamese Role in the War in South Vietnam

THIS WORKING paper discusses the role of North Viet-Nam in the origin, direction and support of the war in South Viet-Nam. It is based on the appended compilation of more than 100 verbatim captured documents, intelligence briefs and the whole or part of interrogations edited for security. The information in this compilation goes as far as is now justifiable in the public interest. Obviously such a compilation cannot include information from sensitive sources who could be easily compromised under present wartime conditions. If such information were releasable, the paper would be considerably more conclusive. Nonetheless, even with these limitations, it is believed that the paper and accompanying compilation are both useful and informative.

The footnotes to this paper are based largely on the material in the compilation. The nature of the material is, however, fully described in the footnotes so that the reader can get a fairly good idea of the kind of information involved even if he does not have the compilation fully before him.

Among the documents in the compilation, perhaps the three most important ones, captured within the past two years and of great interest to any student of this subject, are as follows:

(a) *CRIMP Document*: A 23,000-word review of the "Experience of the South Viet-Nam Revolutionary Movement during the Past Several Years" which was written about 1963 by an unidentified Communist cadre and was captured by Allied Forces in early January 1966 during Operation CRIMP.

(b) *Le Duan Letter*: A letter dated March 1966, presumably written by Le Duan, First Secretary of the Lao Dong [Communist Party of Viet-Nam] Central Committee and member of the Politburo; captured by units of the 173rd Airborne Brigade, January 21, 1967 during Operation Cedar Falls.

(c) *Talk of General Vinh*: A talk by General Nguyen Van Vinh, Chief of Staff of the North Vietnamese High Command and Chairman of the Lao Dong's Reunification Department, made before the Viet Cong Fourth Central Office (COSVN) Congress in April 1966. It was captured by U.S. Forces in Ninh Thuan Province in early 1967. The reader may find that the style of these and other documents is heavy and frequently hard to follow. These characteristics make close scrutiny of the texts and a knowledge of the historical context essential to their interpretation.

The following discussion of North Viet-Nam's role in the current war is in two parts. The first deals briefly with certain aspects of the setting in which the war started. The second outlines what can be said, on the basis of this documentary material, about the origins and evolution of the war.

1. *The Setting of the War*

This paper does not attempt to provide an account of the complex series of events that led up to the current war. However, there are two features of the Vietnamese political landscape in the period following the French decision to end the fighting in 1954 that require mention.

A. THE GENEVA ACCORDS, 1954

The Geneva Accords constitute the first of these features. Although much has already been written about them, their most important practical effect was to create two separate international entities in Vietnam. That a separate national entity—South Viet-Nam—existed against which aggression could be committed is evident from the following facts:

1. Anyone reading the Accords will recognize that the establishment of the 17th parallel as a dividing line between North and South Viet-Nam, the provision for the movement of the Vietnamese people north or south of the parallel according to their political preferences, the postponement of general elections for two years, and the ambiguity as to how such election could be organized—all point to the conclusion that the country was being divided. Arthur Schlesinger, Jr. makes this point in his book, *The Bitter Heritage*, when he says that the negotiations in Geneva "resulted in the *de facto* partition of Viet-Nam at the 17th parallel and the independence of Laos and Cambodia."[1] As far back as 1955, South Viet-Nam was recognized, *de jure*, by 36 countries, and North Viet-Nam had full relations with 12 countries. Today the Republic of Viet-Nam has *de jure* diplomatic relations with 52 nations. North Viet-Nam has diplomatic relations with 24 countries, 12 of whom belong to the Communist bloc.

2. The situation had ample precedent in what had happened in Korea. There, the country had been divided at the 38th parallel, and

[1] Arthur M. Schlesinger, Jr., *The Bitter Heritage* (Boston: Houghton Mifflin Co., 1967), p. 10.

remained so even though a resolution of the United Nations General Assembly in 1947 recommended elections not later than the end of March 1948, to be followed by the convening of a Korean national assembly, and the formation of a national government.[2]

3. The Soviet Union, in 1957, proposed to admit North Viet-Nam, South Viet-Nam, and the two Koreas to the United Nations as four separate states. In fact, Soviet spokesmen have specifically said: "The realistic approach was to admit that there were two States with conflicting political systems in both Korea and Viet-Nam."[3] They later reversed their position regarding South Viet-Nam; the United States was opposed to the admission of both North Viet-Nam and North Korea.

4. The United States, for its part, indicated in 1954 that it would "refrain from the threat or the use of force to disturb" the Geneva Accords. But it also stated that "it would view any renewal of the aggression in violation of the aforesaid Agreements with grave concern and as seriously threatening international peace and security."[4]

5. When President Kennedy wrote to President Ngo Dinh Diem on December 14, 1961, announcing a major increase in U.S. assistance to South Viet-Nam, he noted that "the campaign of force and terror now being waged against your people and your Government is supported and directed from the outside by the authorities in Hanoi." He further referred to the U.S. declaration of 1954: "At that time, the United States, although not a party to the Accords, declared that it 'would view any renewal of the aggression in violation of the agreements with grave concern and as seriously threatening international peace and security.' We continue to maintain that view."[5]

B. THE COMMUNIST APPARATUS IN SOUTH VIETNAM

A second feature of the Vietnamese landscape both before and since 1954 has been the existence of a Communist political and military apparatus in South Viet-Nam. Party documents captured by French

[2] William Reitzel, Morton A. Kaplan, and Constance G. Goblenz, United States Foreign Policy, 1945-1955 (Washington: Brookings Institution, 1956), pp. 176-177.

[3] John Norton Moore, "The Lawfulness of Military Assistance to the Republic of Viet-Nam," in American Journal of International Law, Vol. 61, No. 1 (January, 1967), pp. 1-34.

[4] Statement by the Under Secretary of State, Walter Bedell Smith, at the concluding Plenary Session of the Geneva Conference, July 21, 1954; Department of State Bulletin, August 2, 1954, pp. 162-163.

[5] Letter from President Kennedy to President Diem, December 14, 1961; Department of State Bulletin, January 1, 1962, pp. 13-14.

forces during their war against the Viet Minh described the Communist organization of the period.

1. In the South, the apparatus was broadly divided between two regions, or "interzones," and a special zone in the area of Saigon. Each of these zones originally reported directly to Communist Party headquarters in Hanoi. Interzone 5 (Trung Bo) encompassed the northern and central part of South Viet-Nam. Interzone Nam Bo consisted of the south and southwest, including the Delta. Province, district, town, and village cells reported to these "interzones."[6]

2. In 1951, when the Communist Party in the North was reconstituted as the *Lao Dong* Party, its apparatus in the South was reorganized under a six-man *Trung Uong Cuc Mien Nam*, or Central Office for South Viet-Nam (COSVN).[7]

3. The head of COSVN and senior Party representative in the South was Le Duan, an Annamite, who is now First Secretary of the *Lao Dong* Party in Hanoi. His deputy was Le Duc Tho, a northerner, who today is also a member of the Politburo of the *Lao Dong* Party. Le Duan and Tho appear to have had considerable independence of action in directing day-to-day military and political operations in the South, but remained answerable on broad policy questions to the heads of the *Lao Dong* Party in the North.[8]

4. The end of the war against France in 1954, and the establishment of North and South Viet-Nam, brought no significant change in the centralized control of the Party by Hanoi. Although COSVN was phased out, its functions in the southern and southwestern provinces were assumed by the Regional Committee for Nam Bo. Hanoi took direct charge of party activities in Interzone 5, the northern part of South Viet-Nam.[9]

[6] A report of "The Expansion of the Party" and other matters by the Party Central Committee in 1948; "Remarks on the Official Appearance of the Vietnamese Workers' Party," dated November 1951; "Report on the Work of Edification of the Party During the July/September Quarter of 1949." "Principles and Organizational Structure of the Committee for Zones Occupied by the Enemy"; March 12, 1949; "Resume of Decisions Taken by the Permanent Central Committee of the Party Regarding the Organization of the Party in the Army"; Instructions dated August 13, 1949 to the Nambo Regional Committee. (Items 1-6).

[7] "Decision to Create the Central Office for South Viet-Nam"; a *Lao Dong* Party document dated June 7, 1951. (Item 211)

[8] See a 1961 intelligence summary, compiled during the Indo-China War, describing Le Duan's and Tho's positions. (Item 11)

[9] Report of the interrogation of Tran Ha Buu after his capture in 1956. (Item 12) Intelligence summary from ralliers, cadres, infiltrated agents and captured documents; deals particularly with Nambo Region (southwestern provinces). (Item 210)

II. *Origins and Evolution of the Current War*

It was in this setting that the current war in South Viet-Nam started and evolved. Five major phases in this development can be readily identified. The evidence for each of the five phases and the inferences that can be drawn about the role played by North Viet-Nam are summarized below.

A. THE POLITICAL PHASE, 1954-56

This was the period in which both Hanoi and Saigon were working to secure control over their respective parts of Viet-Nam. At the same time, although one cannot be certain about the precise numbers, approximately 900,000 people fled the North to the South; about 90,000 people chose to go North under the terms of the Geneva Accords.[10] During these years, Ngo Dinh Diem—first as Premier, then as President of South Viet-Nam—undertook his campaigns to bring various dissident factions and sects under the authority of the Government of South Viet-Nam. Ho Chi Minh consolidated his power in the North, and North Viet-Nam, for its part, took the following steps with respect to South Viet-Nam:

1. Deputy Premier Pham Van Dong, at the closing session of the Geneva Conference on July 12, 1954, expressly stated that "We shall achieve unity. We shall achieve it just as we have won the war. No force in the world, internal or external, can make us deviate from our path . . ." Ho Chi Minh emphasized this determination the next day by calling publicly for a "long and arduous struggle" to win the southern areas, which he characterized as "territories of ours."[11]

---

[10] *Fourth Interim Report of the International Commission for Supervision and Control in Viet-Nam* (April 11, 1955 to August 10, 1955) (London: HMSO, 1955, 30, Appendix IV) C.f., B.N.S. Murti, *Viet-Nam Divided* (New York: Asia Publishing House, 1964), pp. 88-91; Bernard B. Fall, *The Two Viet-Nams* (New York: Praeger, Revised Edition, 1964), pp. 153-154, 358, uses the figure 860,000 from North to South; Fall *Viet-Nam Witness* (New York: Praeger, 1966), p. 76. For estimates on movements from South to North, see Murti, *op.cit.*, p. 224; R. P. Stebbins and the Research Staff of the Council on Foreign Relations, *The United States in World Affairs*, 1954 (New York: Harper and Bros., 1956), p. 285, quoted in Kahin and Lewis, *United States in Viet-Nam* (New York: Dial Press, 1967), p. 75; both the latter cite figures in excess of 100,000. The Viet Minh claim 140,000; e.g., Wilfred G. Burchett, *Viet-Nam, Inside Story of the Guerrilla War* (New York: International Publishers, 1965), p. 128. The 1965 White Paper gives the figure 90,000; U.S. Department of State, *Aggression from the North* (Department of State publication 7839, February, 1965), p. 11.

[11] Ho Chi Minh, "Appeal made after the successful conclusion of the Geneva Agreements," (July 22, 1954). *Ho Chi Minh on Revolution*, Bernard B. Fall, ed., (New York: Praeger, 1967) p. 272: "North, Central and South Viet-Nam are territories of ours. Our

2. Hanoi did withdraw the bulk of its fighting men from the South. However, most of these "regroupees" were placed in special units. They formed into the 305th, 324th, 325th, 330th, and 338th Divisions of the North Vietnamese Army. At least until 1959, these divisions were reportedly composed entirely of South Vietnamese.[12]

3. Hanoi also left a small but experienced military force in South Viet-Nam. Although its exact size is unknown, in 1956 the U.S. military attache estimated it at about 5,000 men.[13]

4. In addition, and perhaps more decisive to long term Communist strategy, North Viet-Nam continued to maintain its political network in the South.[14] Even in the first year after Geneva, it sent a small number of cadres across or around the 17th parallel.[15] A notable arrival was General Van Tien Dung, then and since chief of staff of the North Vietnamese Army, who dropped abruptly from public view in the North for a period in 1955-56. Intelligence reports placed him in South Viet-Nam, where he was working to organize additional units of former Viet Minh cadres who had not gone North, and to prepare for future infiltration and expansion of the apparatus in the South.[16]

5. Most important of all, Hanoi ordered its apparatus in the South to go underground. As the *CRIMP Document* puts it: "The party apparatus in South Viet-Nam . . . became covert. The organization and methods of operation of the party were changed in order to guarantee the leadership and focus forces of the Party under the new struggle condition." A Party policy paper of the time defines as part of "the immediate mission of Nambo . . . the consolidation and reformation of

---

country will certainly be unified. Our entire people will surely be liberated." Also, Department of State, Intelligence Brief, August 5, 1954. (Item A)

[12] Interrogation of Le Van Thanh, Viet Cong signal platoon leader, in which five divisions were described that were composed of South Vietnamese were regrouped in the North following the 1954 Geneva Accords. (Item 84)

[13] U.S. Army Attache situation report, Saigon, July 1956. (Item 25)

[14] Interrogation of a man who handled Viet Cong agents at the time of his capture in 1964; 1958 South Vietnamese counter-espionage report; Memorandum to All Provincial Committees from Eastern Interzone Committee, Lao Dong Party, obtained November 29, 1964; Intelligence report of November 1955. (Items 27, 28, 29, 205)

[15] South Vietnamese counter-espionage report of 1958 giving details of DRV intelligence activities; and Intelligence report of November 1955, noting the arrival of 50 experienced regroupees in South Viet-Nam in October 1965. (Items 28 and 205)

[16] Interrogation of Viet Minh cadre who deserted in 1956; document taken from a political officer with Communist forces in South Viet-Nam on November 27, 1956; description by a North Vietnamese of the Van Tien Dung/Pham Van Bach missions; summary of intelligence reports concerning Van Tien Dung and the Hoa Hao. (Items 16, 19, 21, 22)

Party organisms and popular groups on a clandestine basis, based upon vigilance and revolutionary procedures designed to safeguard our forces..."[17]

6. These orders were apparently obeyed. There are reports of Party meetings in 1956-57 to discuss a change of tactics, and Le Duan is represented as urging increased military action. "Our political struggle in the South will sometimes have to be backed up with military action to show the strength of [our] forces," he told a Party conference in the South on March 18, 1956. "Therefore we should increase our forces in the South and develop military action."[18] Nonetheless, despite these outbursts, the apparatus seems to have followed the line of the *Lao Dong* Party through 1956, and to have worked for unification by political means; i.e. by subversion and all means short of resorting to open armed conflict.

It is clear from this evidence that:

1. Hanoi was indeed both committed and determined to bring the South under its control.

2. Hanoi was also willing to accept unification by way of the Geneva Accords, provided that it could manipulate these Accords so as to ensure victory for the *Lao Dong* Party and control of the South by the North.

3. Even so, the North Vietnamese leaders hedged their bets. They were willing to rely upon political means according to their own interpretation of the Geneva Accords. They left enough of their political and military apparatus in South Viet-Nam so as to weaken it from within and be able to take advantage of any elections should these come about. But they also were prepared to expand the apparatus in order to return to "armed struggle" or an all-out military effort if the political gambit failed. And, of course, the political gambit did fail.

Indeed, the period from 1954 through 1956 saw the consolidation of the Diem government in South Viet-Nam, and what has sometimes been described as a "miracle" of settling down and accomplishment,

[17] *The CRIMP Document;* also a Viet Minh policy paper on strategy issued by the Central Committee on the Lao Dong Party to the Nam Bo Interzone, obtained in November 1954. (Item 200)

[18] Interrogation of Viet Minh cadre who surrendered in March 1966, in which Le Duan's disgust with DRV policy toward the ICC and his eagerness to invade South Viet-Nam are described; see also a document taken from a political officer of communist forces in South Viet-Nam on November 27, 1956, in which Le Duan is reported to feel the time for a military struggle has come; see also a document issued by the Lao Dong Party Central Committee for guidance of cadres, probably dated late Spring 1956. (Items 18, 19, 204)

at least in relation to what may well have been North Viet-Nam's expectations of early collapse.

Moreover, the elections scheduled for July 1956 under the Geneva Accords never did take place. On this much-debated issue, the key points to recall are the fact that the Geneva Accords called for "free" elections and that, as all responsible observers at the time agreed, North Viet-Nam would not conceivably have permitted any supervision or any determination that could remotely have been called free. Hence, Diem refused to go through with the elections, and we supported him in that refusal.[19]

B. THE OUTBREAK OF THE WAR, 1956-59

The period from 1956 to 1959 is a particularly difficult one to characterize in a few words. In South Viet-Nam, despite earlier political and economic gains, President Diem was becoming increasingly repressive in his efforts to maintain his authority; in the process he undoubtedly contributed to growing, if relatively disorganized, opposition. In the countryside, peasant discontent was aroused particularly by his brother's excessive measures to ferret out Communist cadres; and urban discontent was aroused by his efforts to discredit and neutralize any opposition that went beyond mere dissent.

This dissatisfaction was exploited by the Communist underground apparatus which now became less reluctant to use overt means, and, in areas where its strength was relatively unchallenged by the Government, to resort to selective terrorism. Although statistics for the period are neither complete nor entirely reliable, a sharp rise in terrorism seems to have begun as early as 1957. It appears that by 1958 the Government was losing about 40 civilian officials and 40 military personnel per month, and it is widely conceded that an organized uprising against Diem got underway sometime between then and 1960.[20]

What about the role of North Viet-Nam in this uprising? The evidence indicates the following:

1. There was considerable debate within the Communist apparatus

---

[19] A somewhat more detailed discussion of the election problem, including the contemporary comments of Senator John F. Kennedy and Professor Hans Morgenthau, will be found in "The Path to Vietnam," by William P. Bundy, published by the Department of State in the Fall of 1967. (Item L)

[20] Robert Seigliano, *South Viet-Nam: Nation Under Stress* (Boston: Houghton Mifflin, 1964), p. 138; Bernard B. Fall, *Viet-Nam Witness* (New York: Praeger, 1966), pp. 185-188. Denis Warner, *The Last Confucian* (New York: Macmillan, 1963), p. 154ff.

in the South as to what strategy they should follow, given the failure to achieve unification by political means.

2. By 1958, according to the CRIMP document, "the majority of the party members and cadres felt that it was necessary to launch immediately an armed struggle in order to preserve the movement and protect the forces. In several areas the party members on their own initiative had organized armed struggle against the enemy." Yet at the same time, there were others who were hesitant to push the armed struggle. "These people did not fully appreciate the capabilities of the masses, of the Party and of the movement and therefore did not dare mobilize the masses in order to seek every means to oppose the enemy." The Nam Bo Regional Committee leadership hesitated, "but the principal reason was the fear of violating the party line."[21]

3. During this period, the *CRIMP Document* reports that "the political struggle movement of the masses, although not defeated, was encountering increasing difficulty and increasing weakness; the Party bases although not completely destroyed were significantly weakened, and in some areas quite seriously; the prestige of the masses and of the revolution suffered."[22]

4. Meanwhile, Le Duan left South Viet-Nam sometime in 1957, emerged in Hanoi, and became First Secretary of the *Lao Dong* Party —an indication that those favoring the armed struggle had prevailed.[23]

5. In 1958, there is evidence that Hanoi took the first steps to organize the movement of men and supplies both through Laos and across the Demilitarized Zone (DMZ).[24]

6. Then, in May 1959, the Politburo of the *Lao Dong* Party announced the decision for war against South Viet-Nam. Although the decision itself may have been taken earlier, the directive of the Politburo, again according to the *CRIMP Document*, "stated that the time had come to push the armed struggle against the enemy. Thanks to this . . . in October 1959 the armed struggle was launched." As described by the *CRIMP Document*, "it immediately took the form in

---

[21] The CRIMP Document.   [22] *Ibid.*

[23] Intelligence report, March 1, 1956; intelligence report, June 15, 1956; Radio Hanoi broadcasts of September 3, 1957 and October 19 and 30, 1957, describing Le Duan's activities. (Items B-F)

[24] Interrogation of a Montagnard in Quang Tri Province, who turned out to be a Viet Cong agent, and infiltrated into South Viet-Nam in October, 1961. (Item 70)

South Viet-Nam of revolutionary warfare, a long-range revolutionary warfare."[25]

7. By the end of 1959, more than 400 civilians had been murdered and another 579 kidnapped in South Viet-Nam.[26] Armed attacks had increased significantly in size, with company-strength Viet Cong units appearing in assaults on army outposts and patrols. In January 1960, a Viet Cong battalion some 500 strong successfully attacked an ARVN regiment.

The history that seems to emerge from these data is as follows:

1. Hanoi had committed itself publicly and irrevocably to a return to armed struggle in the South.

2. The southern part of the Communist apparatus had become restive with the political approach by 1956, and Le Duan in particular was persuaded that force would be required to bring about unification.

3. The Diem regime's trend toward repression made the "objective" conditions seem ripe for launching the struggle.

4. The Party apparatus was gradually reactivated into militant actions where local conditions permitted.

5. By May 1959, at the latest, Hanoi in effect declared war on South Viet-Nam and committed its political and military apparatus in the South to the struggle.

It is at least conceivable that Diem strengthened Hanoi's hand by virtue of the measures he was taking against both the dissident sects and the Communist apparatus in the South. It may even be that the sense of weakness felt by the leaders of Nam Bo, and Hanoi's fear that it would lose control over the apparatus, triggered the decision. But the fact is that Hanoi decided to reunify the country by force. Moreover, it appears to have had the only apparatus in the South capable of organizing and controlling an outbreak of violence of the magnitude that then occurred.

C. THE SPECIAL WAR, 1959-63

For the next four years, from the end of 1959 to the end of 1963, the Viet Cong engaged in what the *CRIMP Document* called a long-range revolutionary warfare against the Diem regime and its immediate successor. During those four years, the strength of the Viet Cong

---

[25] *The CRIMP Document;* see also Party Communique, May 13, 1959 and Comments on Party Communique, May 14. (Items J and K)

[26] See Table IV.

increased substantially, and a revolutionary apparatus emerged in South Viet-Nam that was ostensibly independent of North Viet-Nam.

What role did North Viet-Nam play in these developments? On the military side, there is the following evidence of Hanoi's activities:

1. The North Vietnamese authorities formed border-crossing teams in early 1959 to transport medicines, ammunition, food, and documents across the DMZ.[27]

2. The Central Committee of the *Lao Dong* Party ordered the formation of the 559th Transportation Group to provide for the support of Viet Cong bases in the South. Founded in May, 1959, the 559th was placed directly under the Central Committee and in close liaison with the Ministry of Security, the Army General Staff, and the Logistics Bureau.[28]

3. The 70th Battalion of the 559th, also formed in May 1959, was sent to the panhandle of Laos. Its responsibilities were to transport weapons, ammunition, mail, and supplies by way of 20 stations along the Laotian trails into South Viet-Nam. The Battalion was also charged with guiding infiltrating groups, and with bringing the sick and wounded back to North Viet-Nam.[29]

4. In June 1959, the 603rd Battalion was formed with a strength of 250 men. It was placed under the command of the Army General Staff and located near Quang Khe, a naval base in North Viet-Nam. It had the responsibility for clandestine maritime operations into South Viet-Nam.[30]

5. In January 1960, a special training base for infiltrators became operational at a North Vietnamese Army base in Son Tay, northwest of Hanoi.[31]

6. The 324th Division, the Nghe Au Province, was ordered to begin training infiltrators early in 1960.[32]

7. During this same period, the Xuan Mai Infiltration Training Center was set up southwest of Hanoi in the former barracks of the

[27] Interrogation of member of North Vietnamese border-crossing supply team. (Item 71)

[28] Interrogation of two members of 603rd Battalion. (Item 72)

[29] Interrogation of a Senior Sergeant, Viet Cong, 5th Military Region, captured in Quang Ngai. (Item 73)

[30] Interrogation reports of Viet Cong agents dispatched by maritime infiltration unit of Hanoi's Directorage, captured in July, 1961; intelligence summary based on interrogation of numerous Viet Cong agents, captured in June and July, 1961. (Items 75 and 76)

[31] Interrogation of a Viet Cong communications cadre. (Item 78)

[32] Interrogation of Viet Cong infiltrated into South Viet-Nam in 1962. (Item 79)

228th Brigade. Once in operation, it apparently was capable of handling several 1000-man classes at one time.[33]

8. Infiltration on a substantial scale began in 1959. At the end of 1960, Viet Cong Main Force strength was estimated at 10 battalions and 5,500 men. Regional and local guerrillas probably had a strength of about 30,000. By the end of 1963, Viet Cong Main Force strength had risen to 30 battalions and around 35,000 men. It is important to note that this figure represents only a fraction of the total Viet Cong political/military apparatus operating in the South. During this same period, infiltration is estimated to have proceeded at the following rates:[34]

Year	Comfirmed	Probable	Total
1959-60	4,556	26	4,582
1961	4,118	2,177	6,295
1962	5,362	7,495	12,857
1963	4,762	3,180	7,906
Total	18,798	12,878	31,676

9. Until late 1963, most of these infiltrators were ethnic Southerners, veterans of the Viet Minh with years of military experience and training, who had regrouped to the North. They were preponderantly officers or senior noncommissioned officers; through 1961, a high proportion of them were members of the *Lao Dong* Party. They assumed command positions in the Viet Cong forces and also carried out a wide range of political assignments. They provided, in sum, the core of the Viet Cong military and political apparatus.[35]

10. Prior to 1961, the Viet Cong had equipped themselves from Viet Minh caches of old French and American weapons, by the local manufacture of crude hand guns and rifles, and by capturing weapons from South Vietnamese units. Hanoi became an active supplier of weapons in 1961. At that point, modified versions of the French Mat-49 rifle began to appear on the battlefield. Their chambers had been reworked

---

[33] Interrogation of former North Vietnamese Army officers who surrendered in 1963; interrogation of former North Vietnamese Army officer who surrendered in 1963; interrogation of an officer of 1st Viet Cong Regiment, who turned himself in in April 1963. (Items 80, 81, 83)

[34] See Table I for infiltration data since 1959; Table II for growth of Main Force strength.

[35] Summary of 19 interrogations of Vietnamese officers and senior noncommissioned officers who infiltrated into South Viet-Nam during the period 1959-1963; also interrogation of former North Vietnamese Army officers who surrendered in 1963. (Items G and 80)

to use the standard Communist 7.62 mm. cartridge, a technique which required factory tooling.[36]

On the political side, the evidence about North Viet-Nam's activities is as follows:

1. On September 10, 1960, a resolution was adopted at the Third National Congress of the *Lao Dong* Party which highlighted the dominant role the North would play and stated guidelines for what was to become the National Front for the Liberation of South Viet-Nam (NLF). The resolution stated: "In the present state, the Vietnamese revolution has two strategic tasks: first, to carry out the socialist revolution in North Viet-Nam; second, to liberate South Viet-Nam from the ruling yoke of the U.S. imperialists and their henchmen in order to achieve national unity and complete independence and freedom throughout the country. . . . To insure the complete success of the revolutionary struggle in South Viet-Nam, our people there must strive to establish a united bloc of workers, peasants, and soldiers and to bring into being a broad national united front directed against the U.S.-Diem clique and based on the worker-peasant alliance."[37]

2. On January 29, 1961, Hanoi announced that the National Front for Liberation had been formed the previous month, on December 20. The principal function of the Front was to conduct overt propaganda campaigns. Even so, the Front committee leadership has included *Lao Dong* Party agents who directed the work.[38] One high-ranking member of the Front is apparently Major General Tran Van Tra of the North Vietnamese Army, a top Viet Cong commander and an alternate member of the *Lao Dong* Party Central Committee in Hanoi. He seems to use the alias of Tran Nam Trung.[39]

[36] Based on a technical analysis done at the John F. Kennedy Special Warfare Center, Fort Bragg, North Carolina, in November, 1965.

[37] Resolution of the Third National Congress of the *Lao Dong* Party, September 10, 1960. (Item H) It is sometimes alleged that the NFL had already been formed as early as March of 1960, in the southern tip of South Viet-Nam. However, if this had been so, it would surely have been enormously to the advantage of Hanoi to endorse the existence of a truly southern organization. Instead, the Resolution of September 1960 clearly speaks of *future* creation of an NLF, and the January 1961 announcement in Hanoi clearly states that such an organization was established, *in Hanoi*, in December of 1960. The allegation that there was any pre-existing NLF, formed in the South, has no evidence other than obviously self-serving later statements of NLF spokesmen abroad, and must, on any fair reading of the evidence, be dismissed as a myth.

[38] Interrogation of cadre from Western Region Committee, captured in 1962; document turned in by a Viet Cong deserter who subsequently lead GVN forces to a buried cache of Communist documents on training and propaganda. (Items 40 and 41)

[39] Interrogation of Le Xuan Chuyen, former operations officer of the Viet Cong 5th

3. Shortly after the foundation of the NLF, Hanoi announced that the insurgent forces in the South had been joined together in a "Liberation Army of South Viet-Nam" under the NLF. However, captured documents of 1962 state explicitly that "the present Liberation Army has been organized by the [*Lao Dong*] Party."[40] Other documents state that "the Liberation Army is . . . an instrument for the Party . . . for the Liberation of South Viet-Nam and the reunification of the Fatherland."[41]

4. In January, 1962, Hanoi Radio announced that a conference of "Marxist-Leninist" delegates in South Viet-Nam had organized a "People's Revolutionary Party" (PRP), which had immediately "volunteered" to join the NLF. However, documentation shows that in Hanoi's own words, "The People's Revolutionary Party has only the appearance of an independent existence; actually, our party is nothing but the Lao Dong Party of Viet-Nam, unified from North to South, under the direction of the Central Executive Committee of the Party, the chief of which is President Ho."[42] The PRP's Central Committee was later stated to comprise of 30 to 40 high-ranking Communists, with the size and composition of the committee varying from time to time as members rotated to and from the North and between regions of South Viet-Nam.[43]

5. Within this Committee, the real decision-making power lies in a select group of its highest ranking members, a standing committee known like its forerunner of the 1950's as the *Trung Uong Cuc Mien Nam* or Central Office for South Viet-Nam (COSVN). The new COSVN was apparently formed in Hanoi after the *Lao Dong* Party Congress of 1960.[44] At that time, several Southern and Central Vietnamese were chosen to organize the COSVN, and were elevated to

---

Division, deserted in August, 1966; background information on Le Xuan Chuyen. (Items 56 and 110)

[40] Training bulletin, written in 1962 and captured in November, 1963. (Item 38)

[41] "Regulations for the Party Committee System in the South Viet-Nam Liberation Army", a party document captured by the U.S. 173rd Airborne Brigade in March 1966. (Item 54)

[42] Instructions from the Provincial Committee of the *Lao Dong* Party in Ba Xuyen to the Party's district committees concerning the formation of the new People's Revolutionary Party; dated December 7, 1961. (Item M)

[43] Interrogation of North Vietnamese Army Lt. Col. Le Xuan Chuyen, who defected in August 1966; states that the PRP is the same thing as the LDP and that the PRP directly controls the NLF. (Item 46)

[44] Intelligence summary on *Lao Dong* Central Committee membership in COSVN, from interrogation of a party cadre arrested in 1967. (Item 208)

membership in the *Lao Dong* Central Committee. Since 1965 and perhaps earlier, COSVN and its military committee have been heavily weighted with North Vietnamese general officers. Political and military directives for the conduct of the war, captured by allied forces in South Viet-Nam, have consistently issued from Party and military organs and not from the NLF.[45]

6. Hanoi has tried to conceal its role in the political military campaigns in the South. A Southern party unit was reprimanded for copying and distributing a message from the North Vietnamese Ministry of Public Health to the party medical section in South Viet-Nam; this was considered a violation of party "secrecy regulations."[46] A party letter states: "The Central Party Committee directs that propaganda should rather praise nationalism, patriotism, revolutionary heroism and the role of the National Liberation Front. Indoctrination and propaganda referring to Uncle Ho, Party, class struggle, etc., should be conducted orally within internal organizations and among the people only."[47] Further, a recently captured cadre notebook for late 1967 indicates that: "The Central Headquarters of the [*Lao Dong*] Party and Uncle [Ho Chi Minh] have ordered the [*Lao Dong*] Party Committee in South Viet-Nam and the entire army and people of South Viet-Nam to implement a general offensive and general uprising in order to achieve a decisive victory for the Revolution within the [1967] Winter and 1968 Spring and Summer. . . . The above subject should be fully understood by cadre and troops; however, our brothers should not say that this order comes from the Party and Uncle [Ho Chi Minh], but to say it comes from the [Liberation] Front."[48]

The evidence on both the military and political side leads to the following conclusions:

1. From 1959 onward, Hanoi established an extensive organization

---

[45] Interrogation of a Viet Cong officer who defected in the Spring of 1967; interrogation of Le Xuan Chuyen, document captured by U.S. 173rd Airborne in March 1966, entitled "Regulations for the Party Committee System in the South Viet-Nam Liberation Army", cited under Note No. 41; intelligence summary in *Lao Dong* Central Committee membership in COSVN, cited under Note No. 44. (Items 47, 48, 54, 208)

[46] Instructions to cadres, March 23, 1965, captured by the U.S. 503rd Infantry in September 1965. (Item 44)

[47] Directive to Propaganda and Training Section, April, 1966, captured by U.S. 1st Infantry Division in April 1966. (Item 45)

[48] Party document instructing subordinate level party activists that the final phase of the revolutionary war is near, captured by the U.S. 101st Airborne Division in Quang Tin on November 13, 1968. (Item 1)

for the training and infiltration of personnel, and at a later point major equipment, into the South.

2. The personnel infiltrated from the North between 1959 and 1963 provided the core and cutting edge of the Viet Cong military and political apparatus.

3. Hanoi established, from the outset, firm control over the direction and policy-making structure of the whole campaign against South Viet-Nam.

4. The National Liberation Front was established, in Hanoi, in December of 1960 in order to give the appearance of local leadership. In fact, the NLF has never been in charge of the political and military conduct of the war. The covert nature of the total apparatus, and the desire for outward appearances that it was totally indigenous to the South, did contribute to its ability to attract and hold local support in South Viet-Nam.

5. The evidence suggests that Hanoi hoped to avoid overt intervention in this period and was seeking to overthrow the Saigon Government and set the stage for unification through the Viet Cong, with only leadership and control from the North.

D. EXPANSION OF THE WAR, 1963-65

The period from late 1963 to the end of 1965 is in some ways the most intriguing period of the current war. During those two years, which witnessed the downfall of the Diem regime, great political instability in South Viet-Nam, and an expansion of the war toward its current dimensions, both the United States and North Viet-Nam committed regular military units to the conflict. That Hanoi became overtly involved in the South during this period is generally recognized; exactly why and how is not so widely understood.

On this score, there is evidence to the following effect:

1. Hanoi probably took the decision to commit units of the North Vietnamese Army (NVA) to the South as early as December, 1963. This was shortly after the overthrow of Diem (November 1, 1963); when it became clear that the overthrow of Diem had not produced any significant defections to the Communist cause whatever, Hanoi simply changed its anti-Diem propaganda line and intensified the struggle. The 9th Session of the *Lao Dong* Party's Third Central Committee held a meeting in December and, according to a captured docu-

ment, "assessed the balance of forces between us and the enemy and set forth plans and guidelines to win special war."[49]

2. Starting in early 1964, Hanoi began to develop its infiltration trails through Laos into an army-scale supply route, capable of handling continuous truck traffic to South Viet-Nam. A large group of North Vietnamese army construction battalions in at least three "Combined Forces" (Binh Tram 3, 4, and 5) was deployed in the area by 1964 to oversee the development of this roadnet.[50]

3. Some regular NVA units are known to have begun preparing for infiltration as early as April, 1964. Several prisoners from the 95th Regiment of the 325th Division have reported that their unit was recalled in that month from duty in Laos. Back in North Viet-Nam, the 95th underwent special military and political training for operations in the South.[51]

4. Hanoi also began to form new regimental-sized units for dispatch to the South. One of these, the 32nd Regiment, was activated sometime in the Spring of 1964, with personnel drawn from a number of established units. Trained draftees were added from the Son Tay and Xuan Mai infiltration centers which were in operation by 1961.[52]

5. In October, 1964, the first complete tactical unit of the North Vietnamese Army, the 95th Regiment, left the North. This was a new unit, with cadre drawn mainly from the 325th Division. It reached South Viet-Nam in December.[53] The 32nd Regiment left the North in September or October, 1964, arriving between January and March, and a second regiment of the 325th Division, the 101st, had left North Viet-Nam by December 1964. All of these dates of departure were prior to the beginning of U.S. bombing of North Viet-Nam in February, 1965. In short, the evidence does not support the claim, sometimes made, that the sending of regular North Vietnamese units was only in response to the U.S. bombing.

6. Between November, 1964, and the end of 1965, a buildup of 33 NVA battalions (about 10 regiments) took place in South Viet-Nam.

[49] The Talk of General Vinh.

[50] Interrogation of a North Vietnamese officer of a support regiment who was responsible for the transportation of supplies from Cambodia, through Laos, to Route 96. (Items 100 and 101)

[51] Interrogation in 1965 of four North Vietnamese Army soldiers of the 325th NVA Division. (Item 86)

[52] Interrogation of a member of the 32nd Regiment, North Vietnamese Army, captured by South Vietnamese forces in November, 1965 in Pleiku. (Item 91)

[53] See Table III.

Of these, about 3 NVA battalions (2,000 men) had arrived by the end of 1964. By the end of 1965, the NVA already constituted about 30 per cent of the total Main Force operating in South Viet-Nam.[54]

The following inferences can be drawn from this evidence:

1. Hanoi probably became dissatisfied with the failure of the Viet Cong, by itself, to capture South Viet-Nam.

2. It therefore decided to provide the increment of strength necessary to ensure seizure and control of the South. NVA regular units were to be the means to this end.

3. The relatively slow pace of the buildup is probably explainable in terms of poor transport and logistics, and the belief that time was on Hanoi's side.

4. Far from triggering the regular North Vietnamese buildup, U.S. actions were in response to it: the bombing of the North and the introduction of U.S. troops all followed not only the earlier movement of men and supplies from the North, but specifically came after regular North Vietnamese units had begun to be sent in quantity.

E. THE CURRENT PHASE, 1965-67

The past two years, from 1965 to the end of 1967, have been marked particularly by major clashes between U.S. and NVA units, by the heavy bombing of North Viet-Nam, and by continuing efforts, thus far abortive, to negotiate a settlement of the conflict.

Here again, there is considerable evidence regarding North Viet-Nam's role in this phase of the war:

1. By early 1966, NVA units were described by Hanoi as "the organic mobile forces of South Viet-Nam."[55]

2. By the end of 1967, NVA strength in South Viet-Nam had risen to the point where its units constituted at least 45 per cent of the enemy Main Force. If one includes the NVA personnel who are in Viet Cong Main Force units, North Vietnamese troops now account for more than 50 per cent of the Main Force total.[56]

3. Dependence on logistic support from North Viet-Nam has increased commensurately. From aerial photography and pilot sightings, it is estimated that more than 300 trucks are operating on the infiltration routes in Laos alone during the dry season.

[54] See Table II for growth of Main Force strength.

[55] Letter of Division Party Committee to Youth Members", captured by USMC in Quang Tri in July, 1966. (Item 66)

[56] See Table II for growth of Main Force strength.

4. Since 1964, the Viet Cong Main Forces have been extensively re-equipped with the latest Communist Chinese and Soviet automatic weapons. In addition to small arms, the Viet Cong Main Forces and the NVA units are now supplied with Soviet and Chinese heavy machine-guns, mortars, and rocket launchers. Modern Communist fire-arms have also been supplied to some of the local forces, although French, American, and homemade weapons still figure in the guerrilla arsenals.[57]

5. As a result of the large NVA presence in the South, it has become necessary to explain their role to the rural populace of South Viet-Nam. Communist political cadre are told to say that "we are backed up by a large war area which is the heroic socialist North Viet-Nam. It con-stitutes a major factor for success . . . North Viet-Nam is a large and stable rear area for South Viet-Nam and is providing us everything we need, including soldiers." Recruits from North Viet-Nam are described as having been "assigned to South Viet-Nam to liberate this part of the country. . . ."[58]

6. Although the COSVN Military Affairs Committee supervises both Viet Cong and North Vietnamese Army military activity, the North Vietnamese Army command in Hanoi has increasing assumed direct control over military operations in the northernmost provinces of South Viet-Nam.[59]

7. There is close consultation between Hanoi and COSVN before policy is decided, and the recommendations of the latter are influential. COSVN also has much leeway in applying the policy thus decided. But all basic matters are firmly reserved for direct decision by the *Lao Dong* Politburo-specifically including the nature and continuation of the war, the diplomatic program of the NLF, and the peace terms de-scribed in the public statements of the Front.[60] This can be vividly seen in the *Le Duan letter* and the talk of General Vinh, both of which lay down strategic and negotiating policies extensively with

[57] See Table V.

[58] Document to serve as a guide for the cadre, Party members and others in answering questions likely to be asked of them, captured by the U.S. 199th Infantry Brigade in February, 1967; also, document on "Guidance for Handling of Recruits", captured by U.S. 25th Division in February, 1967. (Items 111 and 112)

[59] Interrogation of Viet Cong officer who defected in Spring of 1967 in which Viet Cong command organization in northern province of South Viet-Nam is discussed. (Item 47)

[60] Intelligence report on command relationships between *Lao Dong* Party and COSVN from an intellectual proslyting cadre arrested in Spring 1967. (Item 207)

hardly a reference to the NLF. No one who reads these documents can have any doubt of Hanoi's control.

8. Thus, Resolution 12 of the Twelfth Conference of the Third Central Committee of the *Lao Dong* Party, passed in secret in December, 1965, required that the "buildup of all types of forces was to be accelerated and the pace of battle increased."[61]

9. Thus, Resolution 12 also laid down the line about the relationship between fighting and negotiating. According to Le Duan's report of it: "At present the U.S. imperialists . . . are trying to force us to the negotiation table for some concessions . . . [but] our strategy on negotiations must serve in a practical manner our concrete political aims. For this reason, the Party Central Committee has unanimously entrusted the Politburo with the task of carrying out the above strategy in conformity with the policy of our Party and on the basis of the situation between us and the enemy whenever necessary."[62] *The Talk of General Vinh*, discussing the same Resolution, reports the view of the *Lao Dong* Central Committee that "The future situation may lead to negotiations . . . while negotiating, we will continue fighting the enemy more vigorously. (It is possible that the North conducts negotiations while the South continues fighting, and that the South also participates in the negotiations while continuing to fight.) . . . We must fight to win great victories with which to compel the enemy to accept our conditions . . . we will take advantage of the opportunity offered by the negotiations to step up further our military attacks, political struggle and military proselyting."

The evidence for this phase of the war speaks for itself. It leaves no question but that Hanoi not only directs and controls the war in South Viet-Nam, but also plays the dominant role in the Main Force war.

Conclusion

The foregoing is intended as a meticulous summary of the releasable evidence of the North Vietnamese role in the conflict. While improved intelligence in the past two years makes it possible to document North Viet-Nam's role most completely for this period, the evidence appears conclusive that the North was the driving force in bringing about the conflict from 1959 onward and in raising it to its successive dimensions at all stages. Likewise, the evidence seems conclusive that Hanoi had every intention of taking control over South Viet-Nam by one means or another from 1954 onward.

[61] Le Duan letter.   [62] *Ibid.*

Yet, this being said, it is important to add one final note. Although the evidence is substantial that native North Vietnamese and North Vietnamese-trained personnel, coming from the North, dominate the Communist apparatus in South Viet-Nam, one cannot preclude the possibility that individuals within the apparatus now question and may come to reject the line imposed by Hanoi and the *Lao Dong* party. Reconciliation of all elements within South Viet-Nam is the declared policy of the South Vietnamese Government, which seeks also a determination of the political future of the South under Constitutional processes. Even as the United States must remain committed to assisting in resisting and bringing to an end the aggression from the North, its ultimate objective must be that the people of South Viet-Nam be free to work out their own system without external interference.

TABLE I. INFILTRATION OF PERSONNEL FROM
NORTH VIETNAM, 1959-67 (1ST HALF)

Year	Confirmed[1]	Probable[2]	Possible[3]	Total[4]
1959-60	4,556	26		4,582
1961	4,118	2,177		6,295
1962	5,362	7,495		12,857
1963	4,726	3,180		7,906
1964	9,316	3,108		12,424
1965	23,770	1,910	8,050	33,730
1966	44,300	10,500	30,000	84,800
1967 (1st half)	20,700	5,100	14,100	39,900
Total	116,848	33,496	52,150	202,494

[1] A confirmed unit/group is one which is determined to exist on the basis of accepted direct information from a minimum of 2 prisoners, returnees or captured documents (any combination), in addition to indirect evidence.

[2] A probable infiltration unit/group is one believed to exist on the basis of accepted direct information from 1 captive, returnee or captured document, in addition to indirect evidence.

[3] A possible infiltration unit/group is one which is believed to exist on the basis of indirect evidence, even though no captive, returnee or document is available to verify the report or reports directly. This category was not listed separately before 1965.

[4] The total does not represent all infiltration data on hand. Other information is held which, based upon the application of consistent criteria and the professional judgment of analysts, has been evaluated as insufficient to warrant inclusion in one of the above categories.

Note.—There is normally a long leadtime between the infiltration of a given unit or group and the collection of sufficient intelligence to confirm the fact and time of the infiltration. In 1967, the infiltration has continued at a very substantial rate, but it will be some months before comparable figures for the year can be compiled.

TABLE II. EXPANSION OF COMMUNIST MAIN FORCE
UNITS IN SOUTH VIETNAM
[End of year]

	1960	1961	1962	1963	1964	1965	1966	[1]1967
Vietcong battalions[2]	10	20	26	30	60	91	83	83
Vietcong main force, local force strength[2]	5,500	26,700	33,800	35,000	51,300	64,300	68,000	64,000
North Vietnamese battalions					6	33	63	69
Strength of North Vietnamese Army units					2,000	26,600	46,400	54,000

[1] End of 3d quarter.

[2] These units do not include a substantial number of native North Vietnamese. Guerrilla forces are not included in these figures. It is important to note that these figures for main force units represent only a fraction of the total strength.

TABLE III. INFILTRATION OF NORTH VIETNAMESE ARMY REGIMENTS INTO SOUTH VIETNAM, SEPTEMBER 1964 TO JUNE 1967

Unit	Infiltration data			Number of prisoners on which confirmation based	Number of captured documents on which confirmation based	Total number of prisoners taken from each unit
	Dep NVN	Arr SVN	Strength			
95th Regiment	October 1964	December 1964	2,000	7	1	35
32d Regiment	September to October 1964	January to March 1965	1,800	4	4	53
101st Regiment	December 1964	February 1965	2,000	3	2	13
18th Regiment	February 1965	April 1965	2,000	5	2	43
22d Regiment	July 1965	September 1965	2,000	5	1	42
33d Regiment	do	October 1965	2,000	2	0	53
250th Regiment	do	do	1,000	2	2	13
6th Regiment	Unknown	do	1,500	7	1	18
21st Regiment	August 1965	do	2,000	7	3	37
66th Regiment	do	November 1965	1,500	6	1	34
18B Regiment	December 1965	February 1966	2,000	4	1	62
24th Regiment	January 1966	do	2,000	3	0	19
95B Regiment	December 1965	March 1966	2,000	2	1	17
141st Regiment	January 1966	do	1,500	6	1	10
88th Regiment	do	do	2,000	5	0	22
3d Regiment	February 1966	do	1,500	2	1	34
812th Regiment	June 1966	June 1966	1,500	2	0	15
90th Regiment	do	do	1,500	3	0	12
803d Regiment	do	do	1,500	2	0	7
165th Regiment	February 1966	July 1966	2,000	1	3	1
52d Regiment	March 1966	do	1,600	3	1	3
84th Artillery Regiment	do	August 1966	1,200	1	3	1
5th Regiment	Activated in SVN	February 1967	1,800	0	2	0
95C Regiment	August 1966	March 1967	1,550	1	2	1
29th Regiment	Unknown	April 1967	2,200	3	1	6
368B Artillery Regiment	do	May 1967	1,400	2	2	2
174th Regiment	January 1967	June 1967	2,000	2	2	10

TABLE IV. Assassinations and Kidnapings in South Vietnam

	1958		1959		1960	
	Assassi-nations	Kid-napings	Assassi-nations	Kid-napings	Assassi-nations	Kid-napings
January	10	25	10	17	96	37
February	36	5	11	6	122	72
March	26	43	31	21		
April	17	12	13	16		
May	13	5	16	22		
June	21	15	5	15		
July	11	24	16	22		
August	7	18	12	11		
September	8	24	22	34		
October	15	26	29	42		
November	8	19	35	189		
December	21	20	33	148		
Total	193	236	233	343		

1 Incomplete

Source: Saigon Situation Report; January, 1960

TABLE V. Composition of Vietcong Weapons

	Chinese	Soviet	United States	French	Home-made and other
Vietcong main force:					
1963	13	2	40	39	6
1964	28	4	38	25	5
1965	38	5	35	17	5
1966	51	7	24	13	5
Irregular forces:					
1963	0	0	14	63	23
1964	0	0	24	49	27
1965	1	0	35	37	27
1966	3	0	38	32	27
Total (main force and irregular):					
1963	7	1	28	50	14
1964	15	2	32	36	15
1965	21	3	35	26	15
1966	29	4	30	22	15
1967 (mid)	35	6	26	18	15
North Vietnamese Army:					
1963	0	0	0	0	0
1964	0	0	0	0	0
1965	90	8	0	0	2
1966	80	18	0	0	2
1967 (mid)	80	18	0	0	2

Source: Defense Intelligence Agency report, July 1967.

1967 Programme of the National Front for Liberation

In 1960, the South Viet Nam National Front for Liberation came into being with a 10-point Programme aimed at uniting the entire people against the U.S. imperialists and their lackeys.

Since then, the Front has achieved broad union *of the various sections of the people, the political parties, organizations, nationalities, religious communities, and patriotic personalities with a view to jointly fighting against U.S. aggression, for national salvation. It has successfully consolidated its base among the broad masses of the people; at the same time, it has engaged in joint action with many political and religious forces, and won over large numbers of manufacturers and traders, officials and functionaries of the puppet administration, and officers and soldiers of the puppet army.*

The Front has constantly enjoyed wholehearted encouragement and assistance from our compatriots in the North *and* abroad. *It has also enjoyed ever stronger approval and support from the peoples of neighbouring* Cambodia *and* Laos, *from the peoples of the* socialist, nationalist *and* other countries *in the world,* including progressive people *in the United States.*

Under the leadership of the N.F.L., our people in the South have gone from victory to victory. The prestige of the Front has been unceasingly enhanced at home and abroad. The South Viet Nam National Front for Liberation has become the sole genuine representative of the heroic South Vietnamese people.

These great achievements prove that the line and policy of the Front are correct, and that the strength of our people's unity and struggle is invincible.

At present, despite heavy defeats, the U.S. imperialists are still unwilling to give up their aggressive designs against Viet Nam. They are stepping up the war, trampling the South, and intensifying the bombing of the North of our country. The monstrous crimes of the U.S. imperialists, however, have only deepened our people's hatred and strengthened their indomitable will. The people of all walks of life in South Viet Nam, even a number of persons in the puppet army and administration, have clearly seen the true features of the U.S. imperialists and their lackeys, hate them, and want to contribute to the struggle against U.S. aggression, for national salvation.

Never before in our nation's history has the mettle of our entire people, united for the fight to wipe out the enemy and save the coun-

try, been so strong as now. Our people are in a victorious position, they firmly hold the initiative and are acting on the offensive. The U.S. imperialists and their lackeys have been driven into a state of increasing passivity and perplexity; they are in an impasse and are sustaining defeats.

At this juncture, in a spirit of developing its former Programme, the South Viet Nam National Front for Liberation has worked out this Political Programme with a view to further broadening the bloc of great national union, encouraging and urging the entire people to rush forward, resolved to fight and defeat the U.S. aggressors, and to build an independent, democratic, peaceful, neutral and prosperous South Viet Nam.

I. Unite the Entire People, Fight the U.S. Aggressors, Save the Country

1. During the four thousand years of their history, the Vietnamese people have united and fought against foreign invasions to preserve their independence and freedom.

Ever since our country was conquered by the French colonialists, our people have fought unremittingly for their liberation. In 1945, our people from North to South rose up, successfully carried out the August Revolution, seized political power from the Japanese militarists and their lackeys, and founded the Democratic Republic of Viet Nam.

When the French colonialists came back to invade our country once again, our entire people heroically fought for nearly nine years, brought our sacred resistance to the great victory of Dien Bien Phu, smashing the aggressive schemes of the French colonialist and the interventionist policy of the U.S. imperialists.

The independence, sovereignty, unity and territorial integrity of Viet Nam were formally recognized by the 1954 Geneva Conference. Since then, our compatriots in South Viet Nam, together with the people all over the country, should have been living in peace and building a free and happy life. However, the U.S. imperialists have sabotaged the Geneva Agreements, ousted the French colonialists, set up in South Viet Nam an extremely cruel puppet regime, and tried to turn the southern part of Viet Nam into a neo-colony and a military base in an attempt to prolong the partition of our country, conquer the whole of Viet Nam and impose their domination throughout Indo-China and South East Asia.

The U.S. imperialists have shrunk from no cruel method to carry out their dark designs. Defeated in their "special war" they have switched to a "local war," using over half a million U.S. and satellite troops, along with more than half a million puppet soldiers, for aggression against South Viet Nam; at the same time, they have undertaken a war of destruction against the northern part of our country. They have also stepped up their "special war" in Laos and carried out continual provocations aimed at wrecking the independence and neutrality of Cambodia.

The U.S. imperialists are daily causing untold sufferings and mourning to our compatriots throughout the country. They have resorted to all kinds of modern war means and weapons, including strategic aircraft, napalm bombs, toxic chemicals and poison gas, to massacre our fellow-countrymen. They have launched repeated operations, "sweeping" again and again many areas, carrying out the "kill all, burn all, destroy all" policy to raze villages and hamlets to the ground. They have herded the population, grabbed land, and set up "no man's land" and fascist-type concentration camps dubbed "strategic hamlets" "prosperity zones," "resettlement areas," etc. In the North, they have wantonly bombed and strafed streets, villages, industrial centres, heavily populated areas; they have even struck at dikes, dams, schools, hospitals, churches, pagodas.

The U.S. imperialists are clearly the most ruthless aggressors in history, the saboteurs of the 1954 Geneva Agreements, the wreckers of the peace and security of the peoples of Indo-China, South East Asia and the world, the enemy number one of our people and of mankind.

Over the past few years, the U.S. imperialists have continually escalated the war, yet they have unceasingly clamoured about "peace negotiations" in an attempt to deceive the American and world people.

The Saigon puppet administration has sold out South Viet Nam to the U.S. imperialists. It has oppressed and exploited our Southern compatriots in an extremely ruthless way. It has forced South Viet Nam youths into the army to serve the U.S. in the massacre of our fellow-countrymen. In a demagogic bid, it has also staged the farce of "working out a constitution" and "holding elections." It is only a clique of traitors, a *tool for the U.S. imperialists* to enslave the South Vietnamese people, prolong the partition of our country and serve the U.S. war of aggression.

2. The U.S. aggressors and their lackeys think they can intimidate our people by the use of force and deceive them by means of tricks. But they are grossly mistaken. Our people definitely will never submit to force, never let themselves be deceived!

Developing our nation's tradition of dauntlessness, our 31 million compatriots from South to North have resolutely stood up, united as one man, to fight the U.S. aggressors and save the country.

In the frontline of the Fatherland, our Southern fellow-countrymen have over the past 13 years shown splendid heroism. Irrespective of age, sex, political tendency, religious belief, and no matter whether they live in the plains or in mountain areas, our people of all strata and all nationalities have resolutely fought shoulder to shoulder to liberate the South, defend the North, and advance toward the reunification of the Fatherland.

As early as 1959-1960, our compatriots in the South Viet Nam countryside carried out "simultaneous uprisings," destroyed whole series of concentration camps and "prosperity zones" of the U.S. imperialists and the puppet administration, and liberated vast rural areas.

Our armed forces and people then rushed forward, destroyed thousands of "strategic hamlets," liberated millions of people, and defeated the U.S. "special war."

Since 1965, although the U.S. aggressors have brought in hundreds of thousands of U.S. expeditionary troops for direct aggression against South Viet Nam, our armed forces and people have repeatedly won big victories, smashed two successive U.S. dry-season strategic counter-offensives, defeated over one million enemy troops (U.S., puppet and satellite). *The liberated areas have continuously expanded and now already make up four-fifths of the South Viet Nam territory with two-thirds of its population. In these liberated areas, a national and democratic power is taking shape and a new life is blossoming. In addition to big military victories, we have also recorded important successes in the political, economic, cultural and diplomatic fields.*

In the beloved Northern part of the Fatherland, our 17 million compatriots are heroically defeating the U.S. imperialists' war of destruction, maintaining and boosting production, wholeheartedly encouraging and helping the cause of liberating the South, thus fulfilling the obligations of the great rear toward the great front.

In the world, the peoples of the socialist, nationalist and other countries, including progressive people in the United States, are sternly condemning the U.S. imperialists' war of aggression, and are giving their approval, support and assistance to our people's struggle against U.S. aggression, for national salvation.

Facts have clearly shown that the more the U.S. imperialists obdurately intensify and expand their war of aggression against our country, the more bitter defeats they sustain and the more they are isolated; on the other hand, our people win ever greater victories and get ever more friends.

3. The most dangerous enemies of our people at present are the U.S. imperialist aggressors and their lackeys—the traitorous puppet administration.

The present tasks and objectives of the South Vietnamese people in their struggle for national salvation are: *to unite the entire people, resolutely defeat the U.S. imperialists' war of aggression, overthrow their lackeys, the puppet administration, establish a broad democratic national union administration, build an independent, democratic, peaceful, neutral and prosperous South Viet Nam, and advance toward the peaceful reunification of the Fatherland.*

The force that guarantees the fulfilment of the above task of fighting against U.S. aggression to save the country is our *great national union.* The South Viet Nam National Front for Liberation constantly stands for uniting *all social strata and classes, all nationalities, all political parties, all organizations, all religious communities,* all patriotic personalities, all patriotic and progressive individuals and forces irrespective of political tendency, in order to struggle together against the U.S. imperialists and their lackeys, wrest back our sacred national rights, and build up the country.

The South Viet Nam National Front for Liberation is ready to welcome into its ranks all patriotic forces and individuals who oppose the U.S. aggressors, to shoulder together the common duties. It proposes that any force which, for one reason or another, does not join its ranks, take joint actions with it against the common enemy, the U.S. aggressors and their lackeys.

The South Viet Nam National Front for Liberation pledges itself to strive, shoulder to shoulder with the Viet Nam Fatherland Front, to fulfil gloriously the common task of *fighting against U.S. aggression to liberate the South, defend the North and advance toward the peaceful reunification of the Fatherland.*

While fighting for their sacred national rights, the people of South Viet Nam actively accomplish their internationalist duty. Their resistance war against U.S. aggression is an integral part of the revolutionary struggle of the people all over the world.

The South Viet Nam National Front for Liberation undertakes to stand within the united bloc of the Indo-Chinese peoples to fight against the U.S. imperialists and their lackeys, to defend the independence, sovereignty, unity and territorial integrity of Viet Nam, Cambodia and Laos.

The South Viet Nam National Front for Liberation pledges itself to take an active part in the common struggle of the world's peoples against the bellicose and aggressive imperialists headed by U.S. imperialism, for peace, national independence, democracy and social progress.

4. The cruel U.S. aggressors are trampling our homeland. We, the people of South Viet Nam, must stand up to make revolution and wage a people's war with a view to annihilating them, driving them out of our borders, and wresting back national independence and sovereignty.

Having experienced over 20 years of war, our Southern compatriots eagerly want to live in peace and rebuild our war-devastated country. But the U.S. imperialists have trampled upon this legitimate aspiration. That is why our people have to fight against them to win peace in independence. Nothing is more precious than independence and freedom. *Only when real independence is secured can we have genuine peace!*

The enemy of our nation is ruthless and obdurate. But our entire people are determined to fight and to defeat the U.S. aggressors and their lackeys. So long as the U.S. imperialists do not end their war of aggression, withdraw all U.S. and satellite troops from our country, and let the South Vietnamese people settle themselves the internal affairs of South Viet Nam without foreign interference, our people will resolutely fight on until total victory. The South Vietnamese people's liberation war is a long and hard one, but it is sure to end in victory.

Our people rely mainly on their own forces; at the same time, they strive to win the sympathy, support and assistance of the world's peoples.

To defeat the U.S. aggressors and their lackeys, our people shrink from no sacrifice, they enthusiastically contribute manpower, material resources and talent to the national liberation war, in the spirit of doing everything for the front, everything for victory.

The South Viet Nam National Front for Liberation undertakes to develop the liberation armed forces comprising the main-force units, the regional troops and the militia and guerilla units, with the aim of promoting the people's war, combining guerilla with regular warfare, wiping out as much vital force of the enemy as possible, crushing the enemy's will for aggression, and winning final victory.

The Front undertakes to *build and develop the political forces of the masses*, promote political struggle, combine armed struggle with political struggle and agitation among enemy troops, thus forming three converging prongs to defeat the enemy.

The South Viet Nam National Front for Liberation undertakes to *encourage all strata of the population in the towns and rural areas still under enemy control* to unite and struggle in every possible form to break the grip of the U.S. aggressors and their lackeys, destroy the "phuong" (guilds) and "strategic hamlets," demand democratic freedoms, national sovereignty, and a better life, oppose pressganging and forced labour, struggle against enslaving and depraved culture, and march forward, together with the entire people, to overthrow the enemy's rule and seize political power.

At the same time, the Front undertakes *to encourage all strata of the people in the liberated areas* to unite closely, build the people's self-management system, set up step by step a local national democratic administration, build base areas; strive to produce and fight against U.S. aggression, for national salvation; continue solving the agrarian problem satisfactorily; build a new economy and culture for the liberated areas, foster the people's forces with a view to ensuring supplies for the frontline and carrying the resistance war through to complete victory.

II. Build an Independent, Democratic, Peaceful, Neutral and Prosperous South Viet Nam

The people of South Viet Nam are determined to defeat the U.S. aggressors and their lackeys, and to devote themselves body and soul to building a political system that guarantees the independence and sovereignty of the nation and the freedom and happiness of the people, to heal the wounds of war, to liquidate the social evils left by the U.S.-puppet regime, to restore normal life and build an independent, democratic, peaceful, neutral and prosperous South Viet Nam. To achieve these objectives, the South Viet Nam National Front for Liberation lays down the following concrete policies:

1. TO SET UP A PROGRESSIVE REGIME
OF BROAD DEMOCRACY

—To abolish the disguised colonial regime established by the U.S. imperialists in South Viet Nam, to overthrow the puppet administration, hireling of the United States; not to recognize the puppet "national assembly" rigged up by the U.S. imperialists and their lackeys; to abolish the "constitution" and all anti-national and anti-democratic laws enacted by the U.S. imperialists and the puppet administration.

—To hold free general elections to elect a National Assembly in a really democratic way in accordance with the principle of universal, equal, direct suffrage and secret ballot. This National Assembly will be the State body with the highest authority in South Viet Nam; it will work out a democratic constitution which fully embodies the most fundamental and most eager aspirations of all social strata in South Viet Nam and guarantee the establishment of a progressive State structure of broad democracy. To guarantee the immunity of the deputies to the National Assembly.

—To set up a democratic national union government including the most representative persons among the various social strata, nationalities, religious communities, patriotic and democratic parties, patriotic personalities, and forces which have contributed to the cause of national liberation.

—To proclaim and ensure broad democratic freedoms: freedom of speech, freedom of the press and publication, freedom of assembly, trade-union freedom, freedom of association, freedom to form political parties, freedom of creed, freedom of demonstration.

—To guarantee to all citizens inviolability of the body, freedom of residence, secrecy of correspondence, freedom of movement, the right to work and rest, and to study.

—To enforce equality between man and woman and equality among the various nationalities.

—To set free all persons detained by the U.S. imperialists and the puppet administration on account of their patriotic activities.

—To dissolve the concentration camps set up in all forms by the U.S. imperialists and their lackeys.

—To give all people who have had to seek asylum abroad because of the U.S.-puppet regime, the right to return home to serve the country.

—To severely punish the die-hard cruel agents of the U.S. imperialists.

2. TO BUILD AN INDEPENDENT AND SELF-SUPPORTING ECONOMY;
TO IMPROVE THE PEOPLE'S LIVING CONDITIONS

—To abolish the policy of economic enslavement and monopoly of the U.S. imperialists.

—To confiscate the property of the U.S. imperialists and their die-hard cruel agents and turn it into State property.

—To build an independent and self-supporting economy. To rapidly heal the wounds of war, to restore and develop the economy so as to make the country prosperous.

—To protect the citizens' right to ownership of means of production and other property in keeping with the laws of the State.

—To restore and develop agricultural production. To improve cultivation, animal husbandry, fish-rearing and forestry.

The State will encourage the peasants to unite and help one another boost production; grant them loans at low interest rates for the purchase of buffaloes, oxen, farm implements, agricultural machines, seeds, fertilizers, etc.; help them develop irrigation works and apply advanced agricultural techniques.

—To guarantee outlets for agricultural products.

—To restore and develop industry, small industries and handicrafts.

—To guarantee to the workers and employees the right to take part in the management of enterprises.

The State will encourage businessmen to participate in the development of industry, small industries and handicrafts.

—To ensure freedom of enterprise beneficial to national construction and the people's welfare; to apply a customs policy designed to promote and protect home-production.

—To restore and develop communications and transport.

—To encourage and step up economic exchanges between town and country, between the plains and the mountain areas.

—To give due consideration to the interests of small traders and small manufacturers.

—To set up a State bank.

—To create an independent currency.

—To apply an equitable and rational tax policy.

The State will adopt a policy of granting loans at low interest rates to encourage production, and will prohibit usury.

—To develop economic relations with the North; the two zones will help each other so that Viet Nam's economy may prosper rapidly.

—In accordance with the Front's policy of neutrality and the principles of equality, mutual benefit and respect for the independence and sovereignty of the Vietnamese nation, foreign trade will be expanded, and economic and technical assistance from foreign countries will be accepted, regardless of political and social systems.

3. TO IMPLEMENT THE LAND POLICY, TO CARRY OUT THE SLOGAN: "LAND TO THE TILLERS"

—To confiscate the lands of the U.S. imperialists and the die-hard cruel landlords, their lackeys; to allot those lands to landless or land-poor peasants.

—To confirm and protect the peasants' ownership of the lands allotted to them by the revolution.

—The State will negotiate the purchase of land from landlords who possess land upward of a certain amount varying with the situation in each locality; it will allot these lands to landless or land-poor peasants. The recipients will receive the lands free of charge, and will not be bound by any condition whatsoever. In areas where the required conditions for land reform do not yet obtain, land-rent will be reduced.

—To entrust the lands belonging to absentee landlords to peasants for cultivation and enjoyment of the produce. Adequate steps will be taken on this subject at a later stage upon consideration of the political attitude of each landlord.

—To allow landlords to offer land to the Liberation Peasants' Association or to the State. The Liberation Peasants' Association and the State will allot those lands to landless or land-poor peasants.

—To encourage the owners of industrial crop or fruit tree plantations to keep production going.

—To respect the legitimate right to land ownership of churches, pagodas and holy sees of religious sects.

—To carry out a fair and rational re-distribution of communal lands.

—To guarantee the legitimate right to ownership of reclaimed lands to those who have reclaimed them.

—Those who have been herded into "strategic hamlets" or concentration camps of any form are free to return to their former villages.

—Those who have been compelled to "evacuate" or to "move away" and who wish to stay where they are, will enjoy ownership of the lands and other property resulting from their labour, and will be helped so that they can continue earning their living in those places; those who wish to return to their native places will also receive help.

4. TO BUILD A NATIONAL DEMOCRATIC CULTURE
AND EDUCATION, TO DEVELOP SCIENCE AND TECHNOLOGY;
TO PROMOTE PUBLIC HEALTH

—To eliminate the American-type enslaving and depraved culture and education now adversely affecting our people's fine, long-standing cultural traditions.

—To build a national democratic culture and education; to develop science and technology to serve national construction and defence.

—To educate the people in the Vietnamese nation's tradition of struggle against foreign invasion and its heroic history. To preserve and develop the fine culture and good customs and habits of our nation.

—To raise the people's cultural standard: to liquidate illiteracy, to promote complementary education; to open new general education schools, higher education establishments and vocational schools. To make all-out efforts to train and foster scientific workers, technicians and skilled workers.

—To use the Vietnamese language as teaching medium in higher education establishments. To reduce school and college fees;

—To exempt poor pupils and students from school fees, and grant them scholarships.

—To reform the system of examinations.

—To give every possible help to the youth and children who have rendered services in the fight against U.S. aggression, for national salvation, the children of families who have rendered services to the revolution, and other outstanding youth so as to enable them to study and develop their capabilities.

—To enable all citizens to carry out freely scientific and technological researches, to devote themselves to literary and artistic creation, and to participate in other cultural activities. To encourage intellectuals, writers, artists and scientists and afford them favourable conditions for research work, creation and invention in the service of the Fatherland and the people.

—To give help to cultural workers, writers and artists who have been persecuted by the U.S. imperialists and their lackeys owing to their patriotic activities.

—To develop health services, hygiene and prophylaxis. To attend to the people's health. To prevent and eliminate epidemics, to do away with dangerous diseases left by the U.S.-puppet regime.

—To develop physical culture and sports.

—To develop cultural relations with the North; the two zones will help each other raise the people's educational level and foster talent.

—To promote cultural relations with foreign countries on the basis of equality and mutual benefit.

5. TO SAFEGUARD THE INTERESTS OF FACTORY AND OFFICE WORKERS AND OTHER LABOURING PEOPLE AND SEE TO THEIR LIVELIHOOD

—To promulgate labour legislation, to put into practice the 8-hour working day; to provide for a regime of rest and recreation; to set up a rational system of wages and bonuses for increased productivity.

—To improve the living and working conditions of workers, labourers and civil servants.

—To apply a policy of adequate remuneration for apprentices.

—To see to the employment of workers and poor urban people; actively to do away with unemployment.

—To put into practice a social security policy in order to care for and assist workers, labourers and civil servants in case of disease, incapacitation, old age or retirement.

—To improve living conditions in working people's residential quarters.

—To settle disputes between employers and employees through negotiations between the two sides and mediation by the national democratic administration.

—To strictly prohibit ill-treatment of workers and labourers; to strictly prohibit wage dockings, fines and unjustified sacking of workers.

6. TO BUILD POWERFUL SOUTH VIET NAM LIBERATION ARMED FORCES WITH A VIEW TO LIBERATING THE PEOPLE AND DEFENDING THE FATHERLAND

—The South Viet Nam Liberation Armed Forces (comprising the main-force units, the regional troops, and the militia and guerilla units) are sprung from the people; they are boundlessly loyal to the interests of the Fatherland and the people, and duty-bound to fight shoulder to shoulder with the entire people to liberate the South, defend the Fatherland and make an active contribution to the defence of peace in Asia and in the world.

—To pay due attention to the building of the Liberation Armed Forces. To strive to raise their quality and increase their fighting capacity with a view to stepping up the people's war, defeating the U.S., satellite and puppet troops, and bringing the fight against U.S. aggression, for national salvation, to total victory.

—To strengthen political work with a view to enhancing the patriotism and determination to fight and win of the Liberation Armed Forces; to raise their sense of discipline; to continuously tighten the "fish-and-water" relations between the Army and the people.

—Officers and men of the Liberation Armed Forces enjoy the right to vote and to stand for election, and enjoy land rights and all other citizen rights.

7. TO SHOW GRATITUDE TO WAR MARTYRS, TO CARE FOR DISABLED ARMYMEN, TO REWARD ARMYMEN AND CIVILIANS WHO HAVE DISTINGUISHED THEMSELVES IN THE FIGHT AGAINST U.S. AGGRESSION, FOR NATIONAL SALVATION

The entire people are grateful to, and constantly honour the memory of war martyrs of the Liberation Armed Forces and of all other revolutionary services and organizations, and those who laid down their lives in political struggles. Their families are cared for and assisted by the State and the people.

—To give care and assistance to armymen and civilians disabled in the course of armed and political struggle.

—To reward in a worthy manner all armymen and civilians who have distinguished themselves in the struggle against U.S. aggression, for national salvation.

Families who have rendered services to the revolution will be remembered and will receive help.

8. TO ORGANIZE SOCIAL RELIEF

—To give relief to compatriots victims of the war of aggression unleashed by the U.S. imperialists and the puppet regime.

—To care for orphans, old folk and invalid people. To organize relief work in areas affected by natural calamities or bad crops.

—To give consideration also to disabled puppet soldiers and to needy and helpless families of puppet soldiers killed in action.

—To help those driven to depravation by the U.S. imperialists and their lackeys to rebuild their lives to serve the Fatherland and the people.

9. TO CARRY OUT EQUALITY BETWEEN MAN AND WOMAN;
TO PROTECT MOTHERS AND CHILDREN

—To pay the utmost attention to raising the political, cultural and vocational standard of the women, in view of their merits in the struggle against U.S. aggression, for national salvation. To develop the Vietnamese women's traditions of heroism, dauntlessness, fidelity and ability to shoulder responsibilities.

—Women are equal to men in the political, economic, cultural and social fields.

—Women who do the same job receive the same salary and allowances and enjoy the same rights as men.

—Women workers and civil servants enjoy two months' maternity leave with full pay, before and after childbirth.

—To apply a policy of actively favouring, fostering and training women cadres.

—To promulgate progressive marriage and family regulations.

—To protect the rights of mothers and children. To develop the network of maternity homes, creches and infant classes.

—To eliminate all social evils brought about by the U.S. imperialists and their lackeys, which are harmful to women's health and dignity.

10. TO STRENGTHEN UNITY AND PRACTICE EQUALITY
AND MUTUAL ASSISTANCE AMONG NATIONALITIES

—To abolish all systems and policies applied by the imperialists and their lackeys with a view to dividing, oppressing and exploiting the various nationalities. To oppose discrimination against and forcible assimilation of national minorities.

—To develop the long-standing tradition of unity and mutual assistance among the various fraternal nationalities in our country with a view to defending and building the country. All nationalities are equal in rights and obligations.

—To implement the agrarian policy with regard to peasants of national minorities. To encourage and help them settle down to sedentary life, improve their lands, develop economy and culture, and raise their living standard so as to catch up with the general standard of the people.

—The national minorities have the right to use their own spoken and written languages to develop their own culture and art; they have the right to maintain or change their customs and habits.

—To strive to train minority cadres so as to enable the minorities within a short time to manage local affairs by themselves.

—In the areas where national minorities live concentrated and where the required conditions prevail, autonomous zones will be established within independent and free Viet Nam.

11. TO RESPECT FREEDOM OF CREED, TO ACHIEVE UNITY AND EQUALITY AMONG THE DIFFERENT RELIGIOUS COMMUNITIES

—To fight against all manoeuvres and tricks of the imperialists and their lackeys, who use a number of persons putting on the cloak of religion to oppose our people's struggle against U.S. aggression, for national salvation, sow dissension between believers and non-believers and among different religious communities, and harm the country, the people, and religion.

—To respect freedom of creed and worship. To preserve pagodas, churches, sanctuaries, temples.

—All religions are equal and are not subject to any discrimination.

—To achieve unity among believers of various religions, and between believers and the entire nation, for the sake of the struggle against the U.S. aggressors and their lackeys to defend and build the country.

12. TO WELCOME PUPPET OFFICERS AND SOLDIERS AND PUPPET OFFICIALS BACK TO THE JUST CAUSE; SHOW LENIENCY AND GIVE HUMANE TREATMENT TO RALLIED ARMYMEN AND PRISONERS-OF-WAR

—To oppose the U.S. imperialists' and the puppet administration's attempts to pressgang mercenaries to serve the U.S. aggressors against the country and massacre the people.

—To severely punish the die-hard thugs acting as obedient agents of the U.S. imperialists.

—To afford conditions for puppet officers and soldiers and puppet officials to come back to the just cause and join the people's fight against U.S. aggression to save and build the country.

—Individuals, groups or units of the puppet army and administration who have fought against U.S. aggression, for national salvation will be rewarded and promoted to adequate positions. Those who sympathize with and support the struggle against U.S. aggression, for national salvation, or those who refuse to carry out orders of the U.S. and puppets to harm the people, will have their merits recorded.

—Individuals, groups or units who have broken away from the puppet army and voluntarily apply to join the liberation armed forces for fighting against the U.S. to save the country are welcomed and enjoy equal treatment.

Regarding those individuals or units who have broken away from the puppet army and administration and risen against the U.S. aggressors to save the country, the Front stands ready for joint action with them against the U.S. aggressors, on a basis of equality, mutual respect and assistance so as to protect the people and liberate the Fatherland.

—Functionaries of the puppet administration who volunteer to serve the country and the people in State services after the liberation of South Viet Nam will enjoy equal treatment.

—Those in the puppet army and puppet administration at any level who have committed crimes against the people but are now sincerely repentant will be pardoned. Those who redeem their crimes by meritorious deeds will be rewarded accordingly.

Captured officers and soldiers of the puppet army will enjoy humane treatment and leniency.

—Men in the U.S. army and its satellite armies who cross over to the people's side will be given kind treatment and helped to return to their families when conditions permit.

—Captured U.S. and satellite troops will receive the same treatment as captured puppet troops.

13. TO PROTECT THE RIGHTS AND INTERESTS
OF OVERSEAS VIETNAMESE

—To hail the patriotism of overseas Vietnamese and highly value all their contributions to the people's resistance to U.S. aggression, for national salvation.

—To protect the rights and interests of overseas Vietnamese.

—To help all overseas Vietnamese who wish to return to the country to take part in national construction.

14. TO PROTECT THE LEGITIMATE RIGHTS AND INTERESTS
OF FOREIGN RESIDENTS IN SOUTH VIET NAM

—To hail those foreign residents who have contributed to the Vietnamese people's resistance to U.S. aggression, for national salvation.

—All foreign residents living in South Viet Nam must respect the independence and sovereignty of Viet Nam and obey the law of the national democratic administration.

—To protect the legitimate rights and interests of all foreign residents who have not cooperated with the U.S. imperialists and their henchmen in opposing the Vietnamese people, and who have not harmed the independence and sovereignty of Viet Nam. To give adequate consideration to the rights and interests of those foreign residents who have directly or indirectly supported the Vietnamese people's resistance to U.S. aggression, for national salvation.

—To resolutely oppose and abolish all policies of the U.S. imperialists and their henchmen aimed at sowing dissension between the Vietnamese people and Chinese residents in South Viet Nam, exploiting and repressing Chinese residents, and forcing them to adopt Vietnamese citizenship.

—To punish the die-hard agents and secret agents of the imperialists and the South Viet Nam puppet administration.

III. To Restore Normal Relations Between North and South Viet Nam; Advance Toward Peaceful Reunification of the Fatherland

Viet Nam is one, the Vietnamese people are one. No force can divide our Fatherland. Reunification of the country is the sacred aspiration of our entire people. Viet Nam must be reunified.

The policy of the South Viet Nam National Front for Liberation is as follows:

1. The reunification of Viet Nam will be realized step by step and through peaceful means on the principle of negotiation between the two zones without either side using pressure against the other and without foreign interference.

2. Pending the reunification of the country, the people in both zones will make joint efforts to oppose foreign invasion and defend the Fatherland, and at the same time endeavour to expand economic and cultural exchanges. The people in both zones are free to exchange letters, to go from one zone to the other and to choose their place of residence.

IV. To Carry Out a Foreign Policy of Peace and Neutrality

The South Viet Nam National Front for Liberation carries out a foreign policy of peace and neutrality, which guarantees the independence, sovereignty, unity and territorial integrity of the country and helps safeguard world peace. This policy consists of the following concrete points:

1. To establish diplomatic relations with all countries regardless of their social and political system, on the principles of mutual respect for each other's independence, sovereignty and territorial integrity; non-infringement upon each other's territory; non-interference in each other's internal affairs; equality, mutual benefit and peaceful co-existence.

To abolish all unequal treaties which the puppet administration has signed with the United States or any other country.

To respect the economic and cultural interests of those countries which sympathize with, support or assist the Vietnamese people's struggle against U.S. aggression, for national salvation.

To accept from all countries technical and economic assistance without political conditions attached.

To join no military alliance; to accept no military personnel or military base of foreign countries on South Viet Nam territory.

2. To strengthen friendly relations with all countries which sympathize with, support or assist the Vietnamese people's struggle against U.S. aggression, for national salvation.

To strengthen good neighbourly relations with Cambodia and Laos. To unceasingly strengthen the solidarity and mutual assistance between the peoples of the Indo-Chinese countries, with a view to defending their respective independence, sovereignty and territorial integrity against the aggressive and warlike policy of the U.S. imperialists and their henchmen.

3. To actively support the national liberation movement of the peoples of Asia, Africa and Latin America against imperialism and old and new colonialism.

To actively support the struggle of the American people against the U.S. imperialists' war of aggression in Viet Nam.

To actively support the just struggle of American Negroes for their fundamental national rights.

To actively support the struggle for peace, democracy and social progress in all countries of the world.

4. To actively struggle to contribute to the safeguarding of world peace, oppose the bellicose and aggressive imperialists headed by U.S. imperialism. To demand the dissolution of all aggressive military blocs and foreign military bases of imperialism.

To unceasingly consolidate and develop relations with international democratic organizations and the peoples of all countries, including the American people.

To actively contribute to the consolidation and development of the world peoples' front in support of Viet Nam against the U.S. imperialist aggressors, for national independence and peace.

Our people's struggle against U.S. aggression, for national salvation, is extremely hard but very glorious.

It concerns not only the destiny of our people at present and in future, but also the interests of the peoples in the world who are struggling for peace, national independence, democracy and social progress. In order to accomplish that glorious task, our people, already united, must achieve still closer and broader unity.

The South Viet Nam National Front for Liberation warmly hails all political parties, mass organizations, patriotic and progressive personalities who broadly rally within and without the Front and pool their efforts to defeat the U.S. aggressors and their henchmen.

Our people's struggle against U.S. aggression, for national salvation, is a just one. Our people throughout the country are of one mind in their determination to fight and defeat the U.S. aggressors and their henchmen. The sympathy, support and assistance of the peoples of the socialist countries, the Asian, African and Latin American countries, and peace- and justice-loving people all over the world, including progressive people in the United States, is becoming deeper and stronger day by day. We are winning, and will surely win complete victory.

No matter how frenzied, brutal, obdurate and perfidious the U.S. imperialists may be, they will inevitably meet with bitter failure in their criminal schemes.

In the supreme interest of the Fatherland, let the entire people of South Viet Nam strengthen solidarity, millions as one, and rush forward shoulder to shoulder in the impetus of our victories to completely defeat the U.S. aggressors and their lackeys, the puppet administration, and together with our northern compatriots fulfil the great and glorious cause of liberating the South, defending the North and advancing toward the peaceful reunification of the Fatherland.

The South Viet Nam National Front for Liberation pledges itself to remain always worthy of the confidence of our compatriots and our friends on the five continents.

THE VIETNAMESE PEOPLE WILL SURELY BE VICTORIOUS!

THE U.S. AGGRESSORS AND THEIR HENCHMEN WILL CERTAINLY BE DEFEATED!

The Programme of the South Viet Nam National Front for Liberation is sure to be carried into effect.

Fighters and compatriots throughout South Viet Nam, under the glorious banner of the South Viet Nam National Front for Liberation, march forward heroically!

July 20, 1968 Honolulu Communiqué after Meeting of Presidents Johnson and Thieu

PRESIDENT Nguyen Van Thieu of the Republic of Vietnam and President Lyndon B. Johnson of the United States of America met in Honolulu, Hawaii, U.S.A., on July 19 and 20.

The meeting was held at President Thieu's suggestion, in light of the fact that the pressing military situation did not permit him to be absent from South Vietnam for the longer time required for a state visit and made it necessary for him to request the postponement of the state visit to a later time this year.

The primary purpose of the meeting was to allow the two leaders to discuss current military and diplomatic developments in South Vietnam and Paris. Their discussions were chiefly private, though they drew on the assistance of senior members of their respective Governments.

Basic Policy

The two Presidents once again declared that their common objectives, both in Vietnam and in East Asia and the Pacific, were those stated in the Manila Declaration of 1966:

To be free from aggression.
To conquer hunger, illiteracy and disease.
To build a region of security, order and progress.
To seek reconciliation and peace throughout Asia and the Pacific.

They reaffirmed their deep belief that the struggle to defeat aggression and to restore an honorable and secure peace in Vietnam was vitally related to these broader objectives, and had already contributed to confidence and constructive efforts by other nations in Asia.

THIEU VOICES GRATITUDE

President Thieu expressed to President Johnson the abiding gratitude of the South Vietnamese people for the sacrifice of the American people in the cause of freedom in South Vietnam and peace in Southeast Asia. President Thieu further expressed his gratitude for the significant military contributions of the five other Asian and Pacific nations with military forces in the Republic of Vietnam.

President Thieu stated his Government's determination to continue to assume all the responsibility that the scale of the forces of South

Vietnam and their equipment will permit, while preparing the Vietnamese nation and armed forces for the important and decisive role that will be theirs in the coming stages of the struggle.

Review of the Situation

The Presidents reviewed the course of events since their December meeting in Canberra: the treacherous Communist attack at Tet; President Johnson's speech of March 31, and the resulting Paris talks, being conducted on the United States side by Ambassadors Harriman and Vance.

They noted that the last six months have revealed a major and continuing change in North Vietnamese strategy. With greatly stepped-up infiltration of men and modern equipment from the North, Hanoi has sought and continues to seek military and psychological successes that would shift the balance of the conflict in its favor in a relatively short period. In spite of its failure in February and May this year, this strategy continues.

The two Presidents noted the tremendous losses suffered by the other side during 1968. These losses are being increasingly replaced by North Vietnamese infiltration, rather than by local recruitment. As a result, it now appears that North Vietnamese comprise over 70 per cent of the main force battalions on the other side, as compared to 26 per cent in late 1965.

Reviewing the current situation in the light of these significant basic changes, the two presidents noted that the rate of infiltration from the North—evidenced by massive movement in North Vietnam and Laos—continues at a high level. They agreed that the pattern of military activity on the other side continues to indicate renewed offensive action at some time in the next two months. Military factors—enemy regrouping and effective allied spoiling actions—appear to account for the drop in the level of fighting over the last two to three weeks, including the lull in indiscriminate attacks on the civilian population in Saigon.

The two Presidents noted the negative position of North Vietnamese negotiators at Paris. They also reviewed the evidence together and concluded there had been no response to the major limitation of bombing put into effect on March 31, which freed 90 per cent of the people of North Vietnam and 78 per cent of its territory from attack.

Hanoi appeared to be continuing to follow the policy of "fighting while negotiating," long foreshadowed in North Vietnamese strategic documents. The two Presidents called on the authorities in Hanoi to respond to the substantial de-escalation initiated on March 31 and open the door to serious peace negotiations.

The two Presidents agreed that in the face of this North Vietnamese strategy the fundamental aims of the Government of the Republic of Vietnam and its allies must be:

A. To meet and defeat whatever military and terrorist actions might be initiated by the other side, under direction from Hanoi.

B. To strengthen the South Vietnamese armed forces.

C. To continue to seek a reduction in the level of hostilities and an honorable and secure peace that would assure the right of the South Vietnamese people to decide their own affairs without external interference, be in accord with the essential principles of the Geneva accords of 1954 and provide for full compliance with the Geneva accords of 1962 respecting Laos.

Strengthening South Vietnam

The two Presidents reviewed the basic military dispositions and strategy of South Vietnamese and allied forces, on which President Johnson had just received a full report from Secretary Clifford. It was agreed that the measures being taken provided a solid basis for confidence that further major attacks by the Communist side would be repelled.

The two Presidents then devoted major attention to the steps under way to increase the numbers and improve the fighting power of the South Vietnamese armed forces. President Thieu reported that the increase in volunteers, the extension of the draft to 18 and 19-year-olds, and the calling back to service of veterans and reserve officers, have brought the armed forces of South Vietnam to a level of 765,000 men in June—some 48,000 more than the original goal for this date. With the mobilization law enacted at the end of May, it is expected that the total will exceed 800,000 men by the end of 1968—the equivalent in population ratio of some 15 million men in the United States.

It is also anticipated that an additional 200,000 men will be made available at the end of 1968 in auxiliary and paramilitary forces, such as the police and self-defense forces.

President Johnson expressed himself as encouraged by these efforts and reviewed the joint program under way to equip South Vietnamese armed forces with improved weapons, accelerated technical training programs and financial assistance. M-16 automatic rifles have already been provided to all regular Vietnamese infantry, airborne, marine and ranger battalions. The supplying of these weapons to paramilitary troops, down to the hamlet level, is proceeding on a high priority basis. Increased production of the M-16 should make it possible to get the weapon into the hands of all South Vietnamese forces during 1969.

Military authorities would consult further on a program to work in this direction, and that additional items would be programmed in the near future toward this end. President Thieu then reviewed significant developments in the strengthening of the South Vietnamese Government and in key areas essential both for war and peace.

He specifically noted:

¶The formation of a new Cabinet in May under Prime Minister Tran Van Huong, with a broader political base,

¶The actions of the National Assembly in passing a series of important measures—including tax increases, war-risk insurance, and the mobilization law—and in developing the necessary spirit of cooperation between legislative and executive,

¶The progress being made in dealing with corruption and ineffective administration,

¶The resiliency shown by the economy in recovering from the damage caused by enemy action, and the high percentage of refugees and evacuees now rehoused,

¶The dramatic success achieved in spreading new and improved rice seed, the measures being taken to assure an adequate return to the farmer even under wartime conditions, and the progress of the program directed toward a more equitable distribution of land,

¶The substantial recovery of the pacification and security program in the countryside, after the setbacks incurred at Tet.

President Thieu expressed the policy of his Government to support fully the program of revolutionary development, and to improve security in a lasting way through the use of both revolutionary development cadre and, to an increasing degree, regional and apular forces —with the continued support of regular forces wherever required.

Paris Talks

The two Presidents considered the current status of the Paris talks— already fully reported to South Vietnamese and allied governments— and weighed at length contingencies that might arise.

The two Presidents deplored the use of the discussions for propaganda purposes on the North Vietnamese side, and such unrealistic position as Hanoi's refusal to admit the presence of North Vietnamese forces in the South. They agreed that the basic objective in the Paris talks is to open the way to a stable and honorable peace. In the face of continued high infiltration and other military actions directed from Hanoi, however, they saw no alternative but to continue to press for realistic discussions on the appropriate actions by both sides.

The two Presidents again affirmed that the Republic of Vietnam should be a full participant playing a leading role in discussions concerning the substance of a final settlement, and that their two Governments would act in full consultation with each other, and with their allies, both in the present phase and throughout.

The Restoration of Peace

The two Presidents further reviewed and reaffirmed the Manila Communiqué of October, 1966, and the additional matters covered in the Canberra communiqué of 1967.

President Thieu summarized the views of his Government as to the essential conditions of peace in South Vietnam in the following terms:

¶The re-establishment of the 17th Parallel as the demarcation line between South and North Vietnam, pending a determination, by the free choice of all Vietnamese, on reunification.

¶Respect for the territorial integrity of the Republic of Vietnam.

¶Full compliance with the principle of noninterference between South and North Vietnam.

¶The withdrawal from South Vietnam of military and subversive forces from the North.

¶An end to aggression and a complete cessation of hostilities throughout Vietnam.

¶Effective international supervision and guarantees for the carrying out and preservation of the above measures.

President Thieu reaffirmed the policy of his Government to resolve the internal problems of all the South Vietnamese people in an amicable, just, and peaceful way in accordance with the principle of one man, one vote.

He noted his Government had rejected the principles of retaliation and revenge in favor of national reconciliation. He offered full participation in political activities to all individuals and members of groups who agree to renounce force and to abide by the Constitution of Vietnam.

President Thieu further stated that, when peace was restored, it would be the policy of his Government to explore all the avenues which may lead to the reunification of Vietnam by peaceful means, through the free and democratic choice of all Vietnamese in the North and in the South. To that end he would consider favorably the gradual development of relations beneficial to both South Vietnam and North Vietnam, subject only to essential safeguards against renewed subversion.

ENDORSED BY JOHNSON

President Johnson endorsed these principles and policies as essential elements of an honorable and secure peace. He described American policy in the following way:

U.S. forces are fighting to repel external aggression. The United States has no other ambitions in Vietnam. It desires no bases, no continued military presence, and no political role in Vietnamese affairs.

As North Vietnam takes its men home and ends its aggression against South Vietnam, U.S. forces will be withdrawn, in accordance with the Manila Communiqué.

The United States will not support the imposition of a "Coalition Government" or any other form of Government, on the people of South Vietnam. The people of South Vietnam—and only the people of South Vietnam—have the right to choose the form of their Government.

The United States wants to help the people of Southeast Asia— including the people of North Vietnam—develop their rich region in conditions of peace.

SETTLEMENT PREFERRED

Though the United States is prepared to fight if necessary, it much prefers to reach a just settlement at the conference table. In search of such a settlement, U.S. negotiators are meeting with those of North Vietnam in Paris now. The American people are deeply hopeful of their success.

Conclusion

The two Presidents stated that a complete cessation of hostilities must be part of a final peaceful settlement. U.S. negotiators are attempting to discover in Paris important elements of mutual de-escalation. They then reviewed the arrangements necessary for a general cessation of hostilities in South and North Vietnam. They concluded that such a cessation would be possible whenever the Government of North Vietnam is prepared earnestly to examine the arrangements required. Effective controls and guarantees would be necessary.

The two Presidents thus solemnly called on the authorities of North Vietnam to forsake the path of violence and to take the road toward peace now open to them through the Paris talks, which should lead to negotiations involving directly North Vietnam and South Vietnam.

Until these hopes are realized, the two Presidents confirmed their determination to halt aggression and to defend the Republic of Vietnam. Toward that end, the President of the Republic of Vietnam affirmed the unrelenting efforts of his Government and people, and President Johnson pledged the continued support and assistance of the United States to the people and Government of the Republic of Vietnam as long as such aid is needed and desired.

Preliminary Convention of March 6, 1946
between France and Vietnam

Entre les hautes parties ci-après désignées, le Gouvernement de la République Française représenté par M. SAINTENY, Délégué du Haut Commissaire de France, régulièrement mandaté par le Vice-Amiral d'Escadre Georges Thierry d'ARGENLIEU, Haut Commissaire de France, Dépositaire des Pouvoirs de la République Française d'une part, et le Gouvernement de la République du Viet Nam représenté par son Président, M. HO CHI MINH et le Délégué spécial du Conseil des Ministres M. VU HONG KHANH d'autre part, il est convenu ce qui suit:

1) Le Gouvernement Français reconnait la République du Viet Nam comme un Etat libre ayant son Gouvernement, son Parlement, son Armée et ses Finances, faisant partie de la Fédération Indo-Chinoise et de l'Union Française. En ce qui concerne la réunion des trois "KY," le Gouvernement Français s'engage à entériner les décisions prises par les populations consultées par réferendum.

2) Le Gouvernement du Viet Nam se déclare prêt à accueillir amicalement l'Armée Française, lorque conformément aux accords internationaux, elle relèvera les troupes chinoises. Un accord annexe joint à la présente Convention Préliminaire fixera les modalités selon lesquelles s'effectueront les opérations de relève.

3) Les stipulations ci-dessus formulées entreront immédiatement en vigueur, aussitot apres l'échange des signatures. Chacune des Hautes Parties contractantes prendra toutes les mesures nécessaires pour faire cesser sur-le-champ les hostilités, maintenir les troupes sur leurs positions respectives et créer le climat favorable nécessaire à l'ouverture immédiate des négociations amicales et franches. Les négociations porteront notamment sur:

a) les relations diplomatiques du Viet Nam avec les Etats Etrangers;
b) le statut futur de l'Indochine;
c) les intérêts économiques et culturels français au Viet Nam.

Hanoi, Saigon ou Paris pourront être choisis comme siège de la Conférence.

Fait à Hanoi, le 6 mars 1946

Ho Chi Minh
Vu Hong Khanh

Sainteny

Fontainebleau Agreement, September 14, 1946— "Modus-Vivendi"

Article 1 - Les ressortissants Vietnamiens en France, les ressortissants Français au Viet Nam jouiront de la même liberté d'établissement que les Nationaux ainsi que des libertés d'opinion, d'enseignement, de commerce, de circulation et plus généralement, de toutes les libertés démocratiques.

Article 2 - Les biens et entreprises/au Viet Nam ne pourront être soumis à un régime plus rigou- /français/ reux que celui réservé aux biens et entreprises des ressortissants vietnamiens notamment en ce qui concerne la fiscalité et la législation du travail Cette égalité de statut sera reconnue à titre de réciprocité aux biens et entreprises des ressortissants vietnamiens dans les territoires de l'Union Française.

Le statut des biens et entreprises français qui sont au Viet Nam ne pourra être modifié que d'un commun accord entre la République Française et la République Démocratique du Viet Nam.

Tous les biens français réquisitionnés par le Gouvernement du Viet Nam, ou dont les personnes ou entreprises auront été privés par les autorités vietnamiennes seront rendus à leurs propriétaires et ayant-droit. Un Comité mixte sera désigné pour fixer les modalités de cette restitution.

Article 3 - En vue de reprendre dès maintenant les relations culturelles que la France et le Viet Nam sont également désireux de développer, des Etablissements français d'enseignement des divers degrés pourront fonctionner librement au Viet Nam. Ils appliqueront les programmes officiels français. Il sera, par accord spécial, dévolu à ces établissements les bâtiments nécessaires à leur fonctionnement. Ils seront ouverts aux élèves vietnamiens.

La recherche scientifique, l'établissement et le fonctionnement d'Instituts Scientifiques sont libres sur tout le territoire du Viet Nam pour les ressortissants français. Les ressortissants vietnamiens jouissent du même privilège en France.

L'Intitut Pasteur sera rétabli dans ses droits et biens. Une Commission mixte réglera les conditions dans lesquelles l'Ecole Française d'Extrême-Orient reprendra son activité.

Article 4 - Le Gouvernement de la République Démocratique du Viet Nam fera appel par priorité aux ressortissants français chaque fois qu'il aura besoin de conseillers, de techniciens ou d'experts. La priorité accordée aux ressortissants français ne cessera de jouer qu'en cas d'impossibilité pour la France de fournir le personnel demandé.

Article 5 - Aussitot résolu le problème d'harmonisation monétaire actuel, une seule et même monnaie aura cours dans les territoires qui sont placés sous l'autorité du Gouvernement de la République Démocratique du Viet Nam et dans les autres territoires de l'Indochine.

Cette monnaie est la piastre Indochinoise émise actuellement par la Banque de l'Indochine en attendant la création d'un Institut d'émission.

Le Statut de l'Institut d'émission sera étudié dans une Commission mixte où tous les membres de la Fédération seront représentés. Cette Commission aura aussi pour fonction de coordonner la monnaie et les changes. La piastre indochinoise fait partie de la zone franc.

Article 6 - Le Viet Nam forme avec les autres pays de la Fédération Indochinoise une Union douanière. En conséquence, il n'existera aucune barrière douanière intérieure et les mêmes tarifs seront partout appliqués à l'entrée et à la sortie du territoire indochinois.

Un comité de coordination des douanes et du commerce extérieur qui pourra d'ailleurs être le même que celui de la monnaie et des changes étudiera les mesures d'application nécessaires et préparera l'organisation des douanes de l'Indochine.

Article 7 - Un Comité mixte de coordination des communications étudiera les mesures propres à rétablir et à améliorer les communications entre le Viet Nam et les autres pays de la Fédération Indochinoise et de l'Union Française: transports terrestres, maritimes, aériens, communications postales, téléphoniques, télégraphiques et radio-electriques.

Article 8 - En attendant la conclusion par le Gouvernement Français et le Gouvernement de la République Démocratique du Viet Nam d'un accord définitif réglant la question des relations diplomatiques du Viet Nam avec les pays étrangers, une Commission mixte franco-vietnamienne fixera les arrangements à prendre pour assurer la représentation consulaire du Viet Nam dans les pays voisins et les relations de celui-ci avec les Consuls étrangers.

Article 9 - Soucieux d'assurer au plus tôt en Cochinchine et dans le Sud Annam la restauration d'un ordre public aussi indispensable au libre épanouissement des libertés démocratiques qu'à la reprise des transactions commerciales et conscients des répercussions heureuses que pourrait avoir sur ce point la cessation de part et d'autre de tous actes d'hostilité ou de violence, Le Gouvernement Français et le Gouvernement de la République Démocratique du Viet Nam arrêtent en commun les mesures suivantes:

a) il sera mis fin de part et d'autre à tous actes d'hostilité et de violence;

b) des accords des Etats-Majors français et vietnamiens régleront les conditions d'application et de controle des mesures décidés en commun;

c) il est précisé que les prisonniers actuellement détenus pour des motifs politiques seront libérés à l'exception de ceux poursuivis pour crimes et délits de droit commun.

Il en sera de même pour les prisonniers faits au cours d'opérations.

Le Viet Nam garantit qu'aucune poursuite ne sera engagée et qu'aucun acte de violence ne sera toléré contre toute personne en raison de son attachement ou de sa fidélité à la France. Réciproquement, le Gouvernement Français garantit que nulle poursuite ne sera engagée et qu'aucun acte de violence ne sera toléré entre toute personne en raison de son attachement au Viet Nam.

d) la jouissance des libertés démocratiques définies à l'article Ier sera réciproquement garantie.

e) il sera mis fin aux propagandes inamicales de part et d'autre.

f) le Gouvernement Français et le Gouvernement de la République Démocratique du Viet Nam collaboreront pour la mise hors d'état de nuire des ressortissants des puissances ex-ennemies.

g) une personnalité désignée par le Gouvernement de la République Démocratique du Viet Nam et agrée par le Gouvernement Français sera accéditée auprès du Haut-Commissaire pour établir la coopération indispensable en vue de l'éxécution des présents accords.

Article 10 - Le Gouvernement de la République Française et le Gouvernement de la République Démocratique du Viet Nam conviennent de rechercher en commun les conclusions d'accords particuliers sur toutes les questions qui pourront y donner lieu, en vue de resserrer leurs relations d'amitié et de préparer la voie à un traité général définitif. Les négociations seront reprises dans ce but aussitôt que possible et au plus tard au mois de Janvier 1947.

Article 11 - L'ensemble des dispositions du présent modus-vivendi établi en double exemplaire entrera en vigueur le trente Octobre 1946.

Fait à Paris le quatorze septembre 1946

| Pour le Gouvernement Provisoire de La République Française Le Ministre de la France-d'Outre Mer, (*signé*) MARIUS MOUTET | Pour le Gouvernement de la République Démocratique du Viet Nam Le Président du Gouvernement (*signé*) HO CHI MINH |

Declaration of Independence of the
Democratic Republic of Viet Nam, September 1945*

(Excerpts)

All men are created equal. They are endowed by their Creator with certain inalienable rights, among these are Life, Liberty and the pursuit of Happiness.

This immortal statement was made in the Declaration of Independence of the United States of America in 1776. In a broader sense, this means: All the peoples on the earth are equal from birth, all the peoples have a right to live, to be happy and free.

The Declaration of the French Revolution made in 1791 on the Rights of Man and the Citizen also states: "All men are born free and with equal rights, and must always remain free and have equal rights."

Those are undeniable truths.

Nevertheless, for more than eighty years, the French imperialists, abusing the standard of Liberty, Equality and Fraternity, have violated our Fatherland and oppressed our fellow-citizens. They have acted contrary to the ideals of humanity and justice.

In the field of politics, they have deprived our people of every democratic liberty.

They have enforced inhuman laws; they have set up three distinct political regimes in the North, the Centre and the South of Viet Nam in order to wreck our national unity and prevent our people from being united.

They have built more prisons than schools. They have mercilessly slain our patriots; they have drowned our uprisings in rivers of blood.

They have fettered public opinion; they have practised obscurantism against our people.

To weaken our race they have forced us to use opium and alcohol.

In the field of economics, they have fleeced us to the backbone, impoverished our people and devastated our land.

They have robbed us of our ricefields, our mines, our forests and our raw materials. They have monopolized the issuing of banknotes and the export trade.

---

* SOURCE: Ho Chi Minh, *Selected Works* (Hanoi: Foreign Languages Publishing House, 1961), Vol. III.

They have invented numerous unjustifiable taxes and reduced our people, especially our peasantry, to a state of extreme poverty.

They have hampered the prospering of our national bourgeoisie; they have mercilessly exploited our workers. . . .

The truth is that we have wrested our independence from the Japanese and not from the French.

The French have fled, the Japanese have capitulated, Emperor Bao Dai has abdicated. Our people have broken the chains which for nearly a century have fettered them and have won independence for the Fatherland. Our people at the same time have overthrown the monarchic regime that has reigned supreme for dozens of centuries. In its place has been established the present Democratic Republic.

For these reasons, we, members of the Provisional Government, representing the whole Vietnamese people, declare that from now on we break off all relations of a colonial character with France; we repeal all the international obligation[s] that France has so far subscribed to on behalf of Viet Nam and we abolish all the special rights the French have unlawfully acquired in our Fatherland.

The whole Vietnamese people, animated by a common purpose, are determined to fight to the bitter end against any attempt by the French colonialists to reconquer their country.

We are convinced that the Allied nations which at Teheran and San Francisco have acknowledged the principles of self-determination and equality of nations, will not refuse to acknowledge the independence of Viet Nam.

A people who have courageously opposed French domination for more than eighty years, a people who have fought side by side with the Allies against the fascists during these last years, such a people must be free and independent.

For these reasons, we, members of the Provisional Government of the Democratic Republic of Viet Nam, solemnly declare to the world that Viet Nam has the right to be a free and independent country—and in fact it is so already. The entire Vietnamese people are determined to mobilize all their physical and mental strength, to sacrifice their lives and property in order to safeguard their independence and liberty.

September 2, 1945

Civil War Panel

Richard J. Barnet, Director, Institute for Policy Studies; author of *Who Wants Disarmament?*

Thomas Ehrlich, Associate Professor of Law, Stanford Law School

Richard A. Falk, *Chairman*, Civil War Panel; Milbank Professor of International Law and Practice, Princeton University

Tom J. Farer, Assistant Professor of Law, Columbia University

Wolfgang Friedmann, Professor of Law, Columbia University; author of *The Changing Structure of International Law*

G. W. Haight, Member of New York Bar

Eliot D. Hawkins, Member of New York Bar

Brunson MacChesney, Professor of Law, Northwestern University; former President of the American Society of International Law

Myres S. McDougal, Sterling Professor of Law, Yale University; former President of the American Society of International Law; co-author of *Law and Minimum World Public Order*

John Norton Moore, Associate Professor of Law, University of Virginia

Stephen Schwebel, Executive Director of the American Society of International Law and Professor of International Law at the School of Advanced International Studies, The Johns Hopkins University; former Assistant Legal Adviser of the Department of State

John R. Stevenson, Member of New York Bar and President of the American Society of International Law

Howard J. Taubenfeld, Professor of Law, Southern Methodist University; co-author of *Controls for Outer Space*

Burns H. Weston, Associate Professor of Law, University of Iowa

Contributors

THURMAN ARNOLD, member of the bar of the District of Columbia.

RICHARD J. BARNET, Director, Institute for Policy Studies.

LINCOLN P. BLOOMFIELD, Professor of Political Science, Massachusetts Institute of Technology.

ALASTAIR BUCHAN, Director, Institute of Strategic Studies, London.

MCGEORGE BUNDY, President, The Ford Foundation.

WILLIAM BUNDY, Assistant Secretary of State for East Asian and Pacific Affairs, United States Department of State.

CHARLES CHAUMONT, Professor of Law, University of Nancy and Brussels Free University.

HARDY C. DILLARD, Professor of Law, University of Virginia.

THOMAS EHRLICH, Associate Professor of Law, Stanford University.

RICHARD A. FALK, Professor of International Law, Princeton University.

TOM J. FARER, Assistant Professor of Law, Columbia University.

EDWIN BROWN FIRMAGE, Associate Professor of Law, University of Utah.

WOLFGANG FRIEDMANN, Professor of Law, Columbia University.

MAX GORDON, author.

GIDON GOTTLIEB, Associate Professor of Law, New York University.

JOHN S. HANNON, JR., law student, University of Virginia.

STANLEY HOFFMANN, Professor of Government, Harvard University.

SAMUEL P. HUNTINGTON, Professor of Government, Harvard University.

D.H.N. JOHNSON, Professor of International and Air Law, London University.

HOWARD S. LEVIE, Professor of Law, St. Louis University.

JARO MAYDA, Professor of Law, University of Puerto Rico.

JOHN T. McALISTER, JR., Assistant Professor of Public Affairs, Woodrow Wilson School, Princeton University.

HENRI MEYROWITZ, attorney to the Court of Paris.

JOHN NORTON MOORE, Associate Professor of Law, University of Virginia.

DAVID J. MORRIS, Fellow, Institute for Policy Studies.

CORNELIUS F. MURPHY, JR., Professor of Law, Duquesne University.

LAWRENCE C. PETROWSKI, law student, Columbia University.

WILLIAM D. ROGERS, member of the bar of the District of Columbia.

JAMES N. ROSENAU, Professor of Political Science, Rutgers University.

OSCAR SCHACHTER, Associate Director of United Nations Institute of Training and Research and President, American Society of International Law.

F. B. SCHICK, Professor of Political Science, University of Utah.

LAWRENCE R. VELVEL, Assistant Professor of Law, University of Kansas.

FRANCIS D. WORMUTH, Professor of Political Science, University of Utah.

ADAM YARMOLINSKY, former Special Assistant to the Secretary of Defense, Professor of Law, Harvard University.

ORAN R. YOUNG, Associate Professor of Politics, Princeton University.

Permissions*

WILLIAM P. BUNDY, "The Path to Vietnam: A Lesson in Involvement," reprinted with the permission of the author and publisher from *Department of State Bulletin*, Sept. 4, 1967, pp. 275-87.

ALASTAIR BUCHAN, "Questions About Viet Nam," reprinted with the permission of the author and publisher, from *Encounter*, Vol. 30, 1968, pp. 3-12.

THURMAN ARNOLD, "The Growth of Awareness: Our Nation's Law and Law Among Nations," reprinted with the permission of the author and publisher from *The International Lawyer*, Vol. 1, 1967, pp. 534-47.

HARDY C. DILLARD, "Law and Conflict: Some Current Dilemmas," reprinted with the permission of the author and publisher from *Washington and Lee Law Review*, Vol. 24, 1967, pp. 177-204.

EDWIN BROWN FIRMAGE, "International Law and the Response of the United States to 'Internal War,'" reprinted with the permission of the author and publisher from *Utah Law Review*, Vol. 1, 1967, pp. 517-46.

CORNELIUS F. MURPHY, JR., "Vietnam: A Study of Law and Politics," reprinted with the permission of the author and publisher from *Fordham Law Review*, Vol. 36, 1968, pp. 453-60.

CHARLES CHAUMONT, "A Critical Study of American Intervention in Vietnam," reprinted with the permission of the author and publisher from *Revue Belge de Droit International*, No. 1, 1968, pp. 5-35.

F. B. SCHICK, "Some Reflections on the Legal Controversies Concerning America's Involvement in Vietnam," reprinted with the permission of the author and publisher from *International and Comparative Law Quarterly*, Vol. 17, 1968, pp. 953-95.

D.N.H. JOHNSON, "Aquinas, Grotius, and the Vietnam War," reprinted with the permission of the author and publisher from *Quis Custodiet?*, No. 16, 1967, pp. 60-71.

RICHARD A. FALK, "Six Legal Dimensions of the United States Involvement in the Vietnam War," reprinted with the permission of the author and publisher from Research Monograph #34, Princeton University, Center of International Studies, 1968, pp. 1-53.

* Permissions are listed to correspond to the sequence of the material included in this volume.

OSCAR SCHACHTER, "Intervention and the United Nations," reprinted with the permission of the author and publisher from *Stanford Journal of International Studies*, Vol. 3, 1968, pp. 5-12.

LINCOLN P. BLOOMFIELD, "The U.N. and Vietnam," reprinted with the permission of the author and publisher from the Carnegie Endowment for International Peace, 1968, pp. 3-44.

HOWARD S. LEVIE, "Maltreatment of Prisoners of War in Vietnam," reprinted with the permission of the author and publisher from *Boston University Law Review*, Vol. 48, 1968, pp. 323-59.

Note, "The Geneva Convention and the Treatment of Prisoners of War in Vietnam," reprinted with the permission of the publisher from *Harvard Law Review*, Vol. 80, 1967, pp. 851-68.

Note, "The Geneva Convention of 1949: Application in the Vietnamese Conflict," reprinted with the permission of the publisher from *Virginia Journal of International Law*, Vol. 5, 1965, pp. 243-65.

HENRI MEYROWITZ, "Le droit de la guerre dans le conflit Vietnamien," translated and reprinted with the permission of the author and publisher from *Annuaire Français de Droit International*, Vol. 13, 1967, pp. 143-201.

Note, "International Law and Military Operations Against Insurgents in Neutral Territory," reprinted with the permission of the publisher from *Columbia Law Review*, Vol. 68, 1968, pp. 1127-48.

GIDON GOTTLIEB, "Vietnam and Civil Disobedience," reprinted with the permission of the author and publisher from *1967 Annual Survey of American Law*, pp. 699-716.

Note, "Congress, the President, and the Power to Commit Forces to Combat," reprinted with the permission of the publisher from *Harvard Law Review*, Vol. 81, 1968, pp. 1771-1805.

LAWRENCE R. VELVEL, "The War in Viet Nam: Unconstitutional, Justiciable, and Jurisdictionally Attackable," reprinted with the permission of the author and publisher from *Kansas Law Review*, Vol. 16, 1968, pp. 449-503 (e).

FRANCIS D. WORMUTH, "The Vietnam War: The President Versus the Constitution," reprinted with the permission of the author and publisher from an occasional paper for the Center for the Study of Democratic Institutions, Vol. 1, 1968, pp. 2-63.

JOHN NORTON MOORE, "The National Executive and the Use of the Armed Forces Abroad," reprinted with the permission of the author and publisher from *Naval War College Review*, Jan. 1969, pp. 28-38.

JOHN T. MCALISTER, JR., "Revolution in Viet Nam: The Political Dimension of War and Peace," reprinted with the permission of the author on the basis of his testimony before the Senate Foreign Relations Committee of the United States.

SAMUEL P. HUNTINGTON, "The Bases of Accommodation," reprinted with the permission of the author and publisher from *Foreign Affairs*, Vol. 46, 1968, pp. 642-56.

JOHN S. HANNON, JR., "A Political Settlement for Vietnam: The 1954 Geneva Conference and Its Current Implications," reprinted with the permission of the author and publisher from *Virginia Journal of International Law*, Vol. 8, 1967, pp. 4-93, with Preface by John Norton Moore, pp. 1-3.

MCGEORGE BUNDY, Address at DePauw, October 12, 1968, printed with the permission of the author.

JAMES N. ROSENAU, "Intervention as a Scientific Concept," reprinted with the permission of the author and publisher from *The Journal of Conflict Resolution*, Vol. 13, 1969; and "Postscript," reprinted with the permission of the author and publisher from *Journal of International Affairs*, Vol. 22, 1968, pp. 165-76.

ORAN R. YOUNG, "Interventions and International Systems," reprinted with permission of the author and publisher from *Journal of International Affairs*, Vol. 22, 1968, pp. 177-87.

WILLIAM D. ROGERS, "United States Intervention: Doctrine and Practice," reprinted with permission of the author and publisher from *Stanford Journal of International Studies*, Vol. 3, 1968, pp. 99-106, with Commentary by Wolfgang Friedmann, pp. 107-113 and David J. Morris, pp. 114-21.

THOMAS EHRLICH, "The Measuring Line of Occasion," reprinted with permission of the author and publisher from *Stanford Journal of International Studies*, Vol. 3, 1968, pp. 27-37.

Tom J. Farer, "Harnessing Rogue Elephants: A Short Discourse on Intervention in Civil Strife," reprinted with permission of the author and publisher from *Harvard Law Review*, Vol. 82, 1969, pp. 511-41.

Adam Yarmolinsky, "United States Military Power and Foreign Policy," reprinted with permission of the author and publisher from the Center for Policy Study, University of Chicago, 1967.

Stanley Hoffmann, "Vietnam and American Foreign Policy," printed with the permission of the author.

Richard J. Barnet, "Patterns of Intervention," printed with the permission of the author.

Index

Nuremberg Principles and Draft Code, 471-74
Nuremberg trials, 50, 52, 250-55, 260, 373, 394, 444, 450, 462-70, 511, 514, 555, 575; and international law, 470-76; procedural criticisms of, 463-64; substantive criticisms of, 464-66

OAS, see Organization of American States
O'Brien, Conor Cruise, 356-57
occupation, law of, 547-49
Office of Strategic Services, 323
Office of War Information, U.S., 323
Offut, Milton, 742
One Man, One Vote principle, 48
operationalism, defined, 988-99; rejection of, 1010-13, 1090
operational supremacy claims, UN Charter, 195
Oppenheim, L., 180, 556n, 913
order, vs. arbitrary action, 62
Organization of American States, 74, 1053, 1055, 1057-62, 1066, 1071-72, 1076, 1087, 1164

pacification, ideology of, 454; program of, 143n, 859
"pacific blockade," 752
Pacific Islands, UN trusteeship for, 327
pacifism, just war and, 207
Paly Commission Report, 1046
Panama, intervention in, 634, 748, 816; "policing" of, 784-87; seizure of, 603-04
Panama Refining Co. v. Ryan, 792, 798-99
"paper war," 626
Paraguay, reprisal against, 759
Paris Treaty of 1856, 197
Parthasarathy, Gopalaswami, 100
Pascal, Blaise, 149n
past events, "shackles" of, 210
Pathet Lao, 853, 881n, 928
Paul VI, Pope, 281
PAVN (Peoples Army of Viet-Nam), 91, 101, 108, 166, 786n
Pax Americana, 326, 1169
peaceful coexistence, 888, 927
peace initiatives, U.S., 28
peacekeeping, by UN, 277, 308-10
Peace of Westphalia, 75, 235-39
peace program, U.S., 287, 319-20
Pearl Harbor attack, 52, 56
Pell, Claiborne, 676
Pentagon, use of bombing sanctioned by, 39-40
Percy, Charles H., 678
Pericaris, Ion, 751
Pershing, Gen. John J., 763
personnel wars, 1078n
peasants, massacre of by DRVN, 113

Petrowski, Lawrence C., 439-515
Pfaff, William, 1029
Pham Van Dong, see Dong, Pham Van
Philippines, Communist defeat in, 1138
Phouma, Souvanna, 20
Piao, see Lin Piao
Pierce, Franklin, 745, 751, 756, 760-61, 774
Pierce v. Society of Sisters, 691
Pike, Douglas, 100, 894
pilots, as war criminals, 388-89, 406-07
Pinckney, Charles, 713, 770
pineapple bomb, 553n
Pinto, Roger, 332, 532
piracy, suppression of, 633, 734, 743, 747, 760
Plato, 441n
Platt amendment, 752-53
Pleiku, attacks on, 101, 188-89, 235
poison gas, see gas warfare
Polaris submarine, 715-16, 1117
policy framework, of U.S. Vietnam role, 219-32
Polish Insurrection of 1830, 577
political question doctrine, 606-11
politics, dichotomy with law, 121. See also international politics
"politics of inadvertence," 38
Polk, James K., 625-26, 666, 726, 734-35, 809, 812
Popular Forces, 842
popular resistance, total war and, 547
population, influx of to cities, 862-63; war for control of, 864
"Population Classification Decree," 113
Potsdam Conference, 324
Pound, Roscoe, 268
poverty, civil war and, 275
power, arrogance of, 147; intervention and, 1006; limits of, 1156; proper allocation of in U.S., 639-48. See also great powers
President, area of conflict with Congress, 622-23; armed attack and, 714-15; armed forces used abroad by, 808-21; as Chief Executive, 620-22, 658-59; as Commander-in-Chief of armed forces, 616, 620-22, 659-60; and Congressional inquiry into military affairs, 822-29; vs. Constitution, 711-807; defense preparations by, 630-32; diminished power of, 635-39; fait accompli problem and, 641; foreign policy powers of, 660; and Gulf of Tonkin Resolution, 780-800; historical record of power, 670-73; "major conflict" and, 640; military zone established by, 793-94; as people's representative, 662; power to protect American rights abroad, 632; power to repel attack, 655-57, 715-17, 809, 813; references to Congress, 732-37; refusal to act, 737-41; restraint of, 762,